THE OXFORD HISTORY OF THE BRITISH EMPIRE

THE OXFORD HISTORY OF THE BRITISH EMPIRE

Volume I. *The Origins of Empire*
EDITED BY Nicholas Canny

Volume II. *The Eighteenth Century*
EDITED BY P. J. Marshall

Volume III. *The Nineteenth Century*
EDITED BY Andrew Porter

Volume IV. *The Twentieth Century*
EDITED BY Judith M. Brown and Wm. Roger Louis

Volume V. *Historiography*
EDITED BY Robin W. Winks

THE OXFORD HISTORY OF THE BRITISH EMPIRE

Wm. Roger Louis, CBE, D.Litt., FBA

Kerr Professor of English History and Culture, University of Texas, Austin and Honorary Fellow of St Antony's College, Oxford

EDITOR-IN-CHIEF

VOLUME IV

The Twentieth Century

Judith M. Brown, Ph.D

Beit Professor of Commonwealth History, University of Oxford and Fellow of Balliol College

and

Wm. Roger Louis, CBE, D.Litt., FBA

EDITORS

Alaine Low, D.Phil.

ASSOCIATE EDITOR

Oxford New York

OXFORD UNIVERSITY PRESS

OXFORD
UNIVERSITY PRESS

Great Clarendon Street, Oxford OX2 6DP

Oxford University Press is a department of the University of Oxford.
It furthers the University's objective of excellence in research, scholarship,
and education by publishing worldwide in

Oxford New York

Auckland Cape Town Dar es Salaam Hong Kong Karachi Kuala Lumpur
Madrid Melbourne Mexico City Nairobi New Delhi Shanghai Taipei Toronto

With offices in

Argentina Austria Brazil Chile Czech Republic France Greece
Guatemala Hungary Italy Japan Poland Portugal Singapore
South Korea Switzerland Thailand Turkey Ukraine Vietnam

Published in the United States
by Oxford University Press Inc., New York

First published 1999
First published in Paperback 2001

British Library Cataloguing in Publication Data

Data available

Library of Congress Cataloging in Publication Data

Data available

ISBN 978-0-19-820564-7 (V.4) Hbk
ISBN 978-0-19-924679-3 (V.4) Pbk

Typeset by Kolam Information Services Pvt Ltd, Pondicherry, India
Printed in Great Britain
on acid-free paper by the
MPG Books Group, Bodmin and King's Lynn

The Editor-in-Chief and Editors of *The Oxford History of the British Empire* acknowledge with gratitude support from

The Rhodes Trust

The National Endowment for Humanities, Washington, DC

St Antony's College, Oxford

The University of Texas at Austin

FOREWORD

From the founding of the colonies in North America and the West Indies in the seventeenth century to the reversion of Hong Kong to China at the end of the twentieth, British imperialism was a catalyst for far-reaching change. British domination of indigenous peoples in North America, Asia, and Africa can now be seen more clearly as part of the larger and dynamic interaction of European and non-Western societies. Though the subject remains ideologically charged, the passions aroused by British imperialism have so lessened that we are now better placed than ever before to see the course of the Empire steadily and to see it whole. At this distance in time the Empire's legacy from earlier centuries can be assessed, in ethics and economics as well as politics, with greater discrimination. At the close of the twentieth century, the interpretation of the dissolution of the Empire can benefit from evolving perspectives on, for example, the end of the cold war. In still larger sweep, the *Oxford History of the British Empire* as a comprehensive study helps to understand the end of the Empire in relation to its beginning, the meaning of British imperialism for the ruled as well as the rulers, and the significance of the British Empire as a theme in world history.

It is nearly half a century since the last volume in the large-scale *Cambridge History of the British Empire* was completed. In the meantime the British Empire has been dismantled and only fragments such as Gibraltar and the Falklands, Bermuda and Pitcairn, remain of an Empire that once stretched over a quarter of the earth's surface. The general understanding of the British imperial experience has been substantially widened in recent decades by the work of historians of Asia and Africa as well as Britain. Earlier histories, though by no means all, tended to trace the Empire's evolution and to concentrate on how it was governed. To many late-Victorian historians the story of the Empire meant the rise of worldwide dominion and Imperial rule, above all in India. Historians in the first half of the twentieth century tended to emphasize constitutional developments and the culmination of the Empire in the free association of the Commonwealth. The *Oxford History of the British Empire* takes a wider approach. It does not depict the history of the Empire as one of purposeful progress through four hundred years, nor does it concentrate narrowly on metropolitan authority and rule. It does attempt to explain how varying conditions in Britain interacted with those in many other parts of the world to create both a constantly changing territorial Empire and ever-shifting patterns of social and economic relations. The *Oxford History of the British Empire* thus deals with the impact of

British imperialism on dependent peoples in a broader sense than was usually attempted in earlier historical writings while it also takes into account the significance of the Empire for the Irish, the Scots, and the Welsh as well as the English.

Volume IV, *The Twentieth Century*, relates the history of Britain's Empire in the era of unprecedented violence of the two world wars and the two tumultuous decades after 1945 that marked the rising ascendancy of Asian and African nationalism. In contrast to conventional historical interpretation, the volume does not present the view that the Empire underwent a steady decline and fall on the model of Gibbon's Roman Empire. On the contrary, the British Empire experienced a renewal of the colonial mission after both world wars, ultimately transforming itself into a Commonwealth of freely associated states. In the twentieth century the Empire thus revived and adjusted to changing circumstances of nationalist challenge and economic crisis.

There are certain themes that *The Twentieth Century* shares with previous volumes. One of these is the response of the British government to criticism of the Empire. The Colonial Office at mid-century found itself forced on the defensive against anti-colonial sentiment in the United States and in the United Nations. International condemnation of the Empire, however, merely added a dimension of dissent to a long British tradition. In the attack against imperialism, British radicals and other critics did not, on the whole, want to liquidate the Empire but to reform it and make it more accountable. As in the nineteenth century, the debates on the Empire in Parliament and in the press demonstrated a sense of ethical responsibility that remains, in retrospect, one of the principal characteristics of the British colonial era.

'Informal empire' is a theme common to the nineteenth- and twentieth-century volumes that raises a controversial question: to what extent was there an empire of trade and commerce which carried with it degrees of indirect political control in such places as China and Latin America? The idea of informal empire involves historical judgement and argument. It is revisionist in the sense that it is an issue of interpretation which changes in nuance and focus from one generation of historians to the next. The essential questions however remain the same. Should a country such as Iran, or for that matter other Middle Eastern states, be included in an analysis of the British imperial system because of the exploitation of oil resources and gradations of British political control? Does 'informal empire' help in understanding the complexity of the Empire as a world system? In this volume as in the nineteenth-century volume, authors accept or qualify the concept of informal empire in varying degrees, but in any event it enriches understanding of the formal empire.

A general economic theme connects with those of the preceding volumes. The aim of those who shaped the Empire's destinies in the twentieth century was the same as their Victorian predecessors. Despite the rationale that the British had a responsibility to protect the indigenous inhabitants and to develop the colonies for the benefit of the world's economy, colonies were expected to be self-sufficient. The goal was not that the British should sustain the Empire but that the Empire should continue to sustain Britain. The First World War revived the notion popular at the turn of the century that the Empire might fuel the British economy by the exploitation of tropical dependencies. This hope waned, but after 1929 and again after 1945, in circumstances of depression and war, the future of Britain as well as the Empire seemed to lie in colonial development, which would buoy up the British economy within the closed economic system known as the sterling area. Faith in the Empire as a source of British economic strength began to weaken only in the late 1950s. The dismantling of the sterling area marched hand in hand with decolonization.

The volume possesses a specific British cultural and social theme in common with others in the series. The Empire provided the opportunity to pursue a better life and to advance one's career: in the army and civil service, in business and industry, in agriculture and mining, in missionary work and education, in banking and shipping, and in such professions as medicine, law, and engineering. The Irish and Scots as well as the English took advantage of the Empire, but, in proportion to the population of the United Kingdom, the Scots seized the initiative to a remarkable degree. Migration moved in many directions: from Britain to all corners of the world, but also within the dependent Empire and the Dominions, and, towards the latter part of the century, increasingly from the colonies to Britain. Migration to Britain and the opportunities there for employment, business, and education brought about an historic change. As a result of the Empire, Britain became an evermore complex, multicultural, multi-religious, post-colonial society.

A special feature of the series is the Select Bibliography of key works at the end of each chapter. These are not intended to be a comprehensive bibliographical or historiographical guide (which will be found in Volume V) but rather they list useful and informative works on the themes of each chapter.

The Editor-in-Chief and Editors acknowledge, with immense gratitude, support from the Rhodes Trust, the National Endowment for the Humanities in Washington, DC, St Antony's College, Oxford, and the University of Texas at Austin. We have received further specific support from Lord Dahrendorf, former Warden of St Antony's College, Oxford; Sheldon Ekland-Olson, formerly Dean of Liberal

Arts, now Provost, at the University of Texas; and, for the preparation of maps, the University Cooperative Society. Mr Iain Sproat helped to inspire the project and provided financial assistance for the initial organizational conference. It is also a true pleasure to thank our patrons Mr and Mrs Alan Spencer of Hatfield Regis Grange, Mr and Mrs Sam Jamot Brown of Durango, Colorado, and Mr and Mrs Baine Kerr of Houston, Texas. We have benefited from the cartographic expertise of Jane Pugh and Mina Moshkeri at the London School of Economics. We are indebted to Dr Peter Austin for assistance in preparing the index. Our last word of gratitude is to Dr Alaine Low, the Associate Editor, whose dedication to the project has been characterized by indefatigable efficiency and meticulous care.

Wm. Roger Louis

PREFACE

Volume IV of the *Oxford History of the British Empire* not only relates the history of the Empire in the twentieth century in a British context but also assesses the significance of colonial rule for peoples under British sway. The rise of nationalism and the coming of colonial independence are two of the volume's principal concerns.

The themes of the Empire's economy, the White Dominions in relation to migration and security, India's special position in the Empire, and the administration of the colonies, all build on the foundation of Volume III, *The Nineteenth Century.* As in the previous volumes, some chapters in *The Twentieth Century* choose an earlier point of departure than might be suggested by the sharp hundred-year breaks. The twentieth-century Empire cannot be understood without taking into account the expansion of the Empire into Africa and the Pacific in the latter part of the nineteenth century and the consolidation of colonial rule in the decades before the First World War. Some chapters commence by examining the Victorian legacy. Others respect the view that the reach of the nineteenth century extended to 1914. There is a similar ambiguity on the point of termination. The Empire came to an end mainly in the 1960s in the era of African independence. Yet certain important but quite different issues remained unresolved until the closing decades of the century: the conclusion of the Rhodesian crisis with Zimbabwean independence in 1980, the end of the apartheid regime in South Africa in 1991, and the return of Hong Kong to China in 1997. The volume thus explicitly embraces different views on the periodization of the Empire's history in the twentieth century.

At the turn of the century few anticipated the rapid changes in the Empire and fewer still its dissolution. By 1910 Canada, Australia, New Zealand, and South Africa had all become self-governing Dominions, but the issue of self-rule in Ireland, and later in India, divided the British public. Ireland was a member of the Commonwealth from 1922 until 1949; but as late as 1947 it was still uncertain whether an independent India would remain associated with Britain by joining the Commonwealth. India's decision not to break away is fundamental to the volume as a whole. India set the precedent for other non-European nations to join the Commonwealth, thus enabling over fifty states to be Commonwealth members at the end of the twentieth century. This long-range development has affected the way the history of the Empire and Commonwealth has been often written. India's decision strengthened the Whiggish view of the Empire's progress and purpose including the belief that British rule had been designed originally to allow dependent peoples to advance towards self-government and to reach fulfilment in the Commonwealth. Some of the chapters in this volume challenge that assumption. The Commonwealth, according to this counter interpretation, was not intended to end the Empire but to continue it by other means.

At least until the Second World War, the prevailing assumption among those involved in the affairs of the Empire was the long-term nature of British rule. The Empire might or might not last for a thousand years, in Churchill's phrase, but few, nationalists and British alike, dreamed that it would come clattering down so quickly. In analysing the reasons for the rapid dissolution of the Empire, and its aftermath, the book makes clear that the Empire was the casualty of war, of shifts in international opinion and the world economy, and of the rising tide of Asian, African, and Caribbean nationalism. The consequences of the Empire's dissolution, and the legacy of British rule, remain perhaps the most controversial issues in the volume. Can the lasting impact of British rule ultimately be judged as beneficial or harmful? The book as a whole adopts a pluralistic approach, implicitly at least, in answering that question and, as different chapters face the issue in different ways, they reflect the uneven and complex nature of the colonial experience itself.

The book is divided into thematic chapters that deal with Britain and the Empire throughout the world, and regional chapters on specific areas and countries. A preliminary chapter places the Empire in the spirit of the times of the Edwardian era. The chapter on the Dominions focuses on the critical question of Dominion loyalty and the place of the Dominions within the British Imperial system. Individual chapters are devoted to Canada and South Africa, with a chapter covering Australia, New Zealand, and the Pacific islands coming late in the volume because the independence of the Pacific islands took place mainly from the 1970s. The chapter on Ireland is placed fairly early to connect with themes in the previous volume and to demonstrate the continuing centrality of Ireland in the Empire into the twentieth century. Two chapters deal with the economic structure of the Empire, one on the British economy and the sterling area, the other on regional economies, with the latter chapter covering the post-colonial as well as the colonial era.

Chronologically the book reaches its half-way point with the Second World War. The second half of the book, though concerned mainly with regions such as South-East Asia, Africa, the Caribbean, and the Pacific contains certain thematic chapters including one on the Empire and Islam and another on gender. The chapters on the whole, however, focus mainly on the impact of British imperialism on specific countries such as India. The chapters in this latter part of the book give point to the overall unifying theme of nationalism and independence. The concept of 'informal empire' is especially evident in the chapters on the Middle East, Latin America, and China. One chapter deals with the Commonwealth legacy. An epilogue draws together the main themes of the volume by reflecting on the meaning of the history of the British Empire at the close of the twentieth century.

W.R.L.

CONTENTS

LIST OF MAPS

LIST OF FIGURES

LIST OF TABLES

ABBREVIATIONS AND LOCATION OF MANUSCRIPT SOURCES

The following abbreviations are used for records at the Public Record Office, London:

ADM	Admiralty
CAB	Cabinet Office
CO	Colonial Office
CRO	Commonwealth Relations Office
DO	Dominions Office
FO	Foreign Office
PREM	Prime Minister's Office
T	Treasury

All other abbreviations and manuscript sources will be found in the first reference in each chapter.

LIST OF CONTRIBUTORS

S. R. Ashton (Ph.D., London) is a Research Fellow at the Institute of Commonwealth Studies, University of London. He is author of *British Policy Towards the Indian States, 1905–1939*, and General Editor of the British Documents on the End of Empire Project, and co-editor of *Imperial Policy and Colonial Practice, 1925–1945*.

Glen Balfour-Paul (MA, Oxford) served in the Middle East during the Second World War and then for a decade in the Sudan Political Service. He has been Ambassador in Iraq, Jordan, and Tunisia. He is a Research Fellow at Exeter University and the author of *The End of Empire in the Middle East*.

Peter John Brobst (Ph.D., Texas) prepared the draft maps for this volume. He is author of *The Official Mind of the Great Game: Sir Olaf Caroe, Indian Independence, and World Power, 1939–1945* (forthcoming), as well as articles in the *Journal of Commonwealth and Comparative Studies* and *Middle Eastern Studies*.

Judith M. Brown (Ph.D., Cambridge) is Beit Professor of the History of the British Commonwealth, and Fellow of Balliol College, Oxford. She is author of *Gandhi's Rise to Power: Indian Politics, 1915–1922*; *Gandhi and Civil Disobedience: The Mahatma in Indian Politics*; *Modern India: The Origins of Asian Democracy*; *Gandhi: Prisoner of Hope*; and co-editor of *Migration: The Asian Experience*.

John W. Cell (Ph.D., Duke) is Professor of History at Duke University. His books include *British Colonial Administration in the Mid-Nineteenth Century*; *By Kenya Possessed*; *The Highest State of White Supremacy: The Origins of Segregation in South Africa and the American South*; and *Hailey: A Study in British Imperialism, 1872–1969*.

Anthony Clayton (Ph.D., St. Andrews) Chevalier dans l'Ordre de Palmes Académiques, is a Senior Research Fellow at De Montfort University, and former Senior Lecturer in Modern History at the Royal Military Academy, Sandhurst. He is author of *The British Empire as Superpower, 1919–1939*; *The Zanzibar Revolution and its Aftermath*; and *Counter-Insurgency in Kenya, 1952–1956*.

STEPHEN CONSTANTINE (D.Phil., Oxford) is Senior Lecturer in History at the University of Lancaster. His publications include *The Making of British Colonial Development Policy, 1914–1940*; and *Buy and Build: The Advertising Posters of the Empire Marketing Board.* He has edited *Emigrants and Empire: British Settlement in the Dominions between the Wars.*

JOHN DARWIN (D.Phil., Oxford) is Beit Lecturer in the History of the British Commonwealth, University of Oxford, and Fellow of Nuffield College. His books include *Britain, Egypt, and the Middle East: Imperial Policy in the Aftermath of War, 1918–1922*; and *Britain and Decolonisation: The Retreat from Empire in the Post-War World.*

TOYIN FALOLA (Ph.D., Ife) is Professor of African History at the University of Texas. He is the author of *Yoruba Historiography* and *Decolonization and Development Planning in Nigeria*, and articles in the *Journal of African History.* He has served as Editor of the *Journal of West African Studies* and is Joint Editor of *African Economic History* and the Rochester series in African History and the Diaspora.

D. K. FIELDHOUSE (D. Litt., Oxford) FBA is former Vere Harmsworth Professor of Imperial and Naval History, University of Cambridge, and Fellow of Jesus College. His books include *The Colonial Empires*; *The Theory of Capitalist Imperialism*; *Economics and Empire*; *Unilever Overseas: The Anatomy of a Multinational, 1895–1965*; *Black Africa, 1945–1980*; and *Merchant Capital and Economic Decolonization.*

W. TRAVIS HANES III (Ph.D., Texas), author of the Chronology of this volume, is a Research Associate at the Center for Middle Eastern Studies, University of Texas at Austin. His publications include *Imperial Diplomacy in the Era of Decolonization: The Sudan and Anglo–Egyptian Relations, 1945–56*; and *World History: Continuity and Change.*

ROBERT HOLLAND (D.Phil., Oxford) is Reader in Imperial and Commonwealth History at the Institute of Commonwealth Studies, University of London. He has published widely on the British Empire in the twentieth century, especially on decolonization. His most recent book is *Britain and the Revolt in Cyprus, 1954–1959.*

RONALD HYAM (Litt.D., Cambridge) is President of Magdalene College, Cambridge, and University Reader in British Imperial History. His books include *Elgin and Churchill at the Colonial Office, 1905–1908*; *Britain's Imperial Century, 1815–1914*

(2nd edn., 1993); and, as Editor, *The Labour Government and the End of Empire, 1945–1951* (4 vols.).

KEITH JEFFERY (Ph.D., Cambridge) is Professor of History at the University of Ulster at Jordanstown. His publications include *The British Army and the Crisis of Empire, 1918–1922*; and as editor, *An Irish Empire? Aspects of Ireland and the British Empire*; and *The Military Correspondence of Field Marshal Sir Henry Wilson.*

HOWARD JOHNSON (D.Phil., Oxford) is Professor in Black American Studies and History at the University of Delaware. He is the author of *The Bahamas in Slavery and Freedom; The Bahamas from Slavery to Servitude, 1783–1933*; and Editor of *After the Crossing: Immigrants and Minorities in Caribbean Creole Society.*

ALAN KNIGHT (D.Phil., Oxford) FBA is Professor of the History of Latin America, University of Oxford, and Fellow of St Antony's College. He was formerly professor of Latin American History at the University of Texas at Austin. His publications include *The Mexican Revolution* (2 vols.); and *US–Mexican Relations, 1910–1940.*

JOHN LONSDALE (Ph.D., Cambridge) is University Reader in African History and Fellow of Trinity College, University of Cambridge. He is co-author (with Bruce Berman) of *Unhappy Valley: Conflict in Kenya and Africa.* He has edited *South Africa in Question* and is General Editor of the Cambridge University Press series in African Studies.

WM. ROGER LOUIS (D. Litt., Oxford) FBA is Kerr Professor of English History and Culture, and Distinguished Teaching Professor at the University of Texas, Austin, and Fellow of St Antony's College, Oxford. His books include *Imperialism at Bay*; and *The British Empire in the Middle East.* His study *Leo Amery and the British Empire* is based on the Chichele Lectures, All Souls College, in 1990.

W. DAVID MCINTYRE (Ph.D., London) OBE is Emeritus Professor of History at the University of Canterbury, Christchurch, New Zealand. His books include *Colonies into Commonwealth; The Imperial Frontier in the Tropics; The Rise and Fall of the Singapore Naval Base; The Significance of the Commonwealth*; and *Background to the Anzus Pact.*

DAVID MACKENZIE (Ph.D., Toronto) is the author of *Inside the Atlantic Triangle: Canada and the Entrance of Newfoundland into Confederation,*

1939–1949; *Canada and International Civil Aviation, 1932–1948*; and *Arthur Irwin: A Biography.*

JOHN M. MACKENZIE (Ph.D., British Columbia) is Professor of Imperial History at Lancaster University and Editor of *Studies in Imperialism.* He is author of *Propaganda and Empire*; *The Empire of Nature*; and *Orientalism: History, Theory and the Arts.* He has edited *Imperialism and Popular Culture*; *Imperialism and the Natural World*; and *Popular Imperialism and the Military.*

DEIRDRE MCMAHON (Ph.D., Cambridge) teaches at the University of Limerick. She is the author of *Republicans and Imperialists: Anglo-Irish Relations in the 1930s* and of a forthcoming two-volume biography of Eamon de Valera.

SHULA MARKS (Ph.D., London) OBE, FBA is Professor of Southern African History at the School of Oriental and African Studies, University of London. Her publications include *Reluctant Rebellion: The 1906–8 Disturbances in Natal*; *The Ambiguities of Dependence*; and *The Separate Worlds of Three South African Women*; and *Divided Sisterhood.*

ROSALIND O'HANLON (Ph.D., London) is Lecturer in History at Clare College, Cambridge. Her publications include *Caste, Conflict and Ideology: Jotirao Phule and Low Caste Protest in Nineteenth-Century Western India*; and *A Comparison between Women and Men: Tarabai Shinde and the Critique of Gender Relations in Colonial India.*

JÜRGEN OSTERHAMMEL (Dr.phil. habil., Freiburg) is a former Research Fellow at the German Historical Institute in London and now Professor of Modern History at the University of Konstanz. His books include *Britischer Imperialismus in Fernen Osten*; *China und die Weltgesellschaft*; and *Colonialism: A Theoretical Overview.*

NICHOLAS OWEN (D.Phil., Oxford) is University Lecturer in Politics at the University of Oxford, and a Fellow and Praelector of The Queen's College. He is author of several chapters and articles on British party politics and decolonization. He is writing a book on the British Labour Party and the Indian independence movement.

A. D. ROBERTS (Ph.D., Wisconsin) is Emeritus Professor of the History of Africa, School of Oriental and African Studies, University of London. He edited the

Cambridge History of Africa, Vol. VII (1905–40). His books include *A History of Zambia*. He was an Editor of the *Journal of African History* from 1974 to 1990.

FRANCIS ROBINSON (Ph.D., Cambridge), is Professor of the History of South Asia, Royal Holloway College, University of London. His books include *Separatism Among Indian Muslims*; and *The Atlas of the Islamic World Since 1500*. He has edited *The Cambridge Encyclopedia of India*; and *The Cambridge Illustrated History of the Islamic World*.

A. J. STOCKWELL (Ph.D., London) is Professor of Imperial and Commonwealth History at Royal Holloway College, University of London. His publications include *British Policy and Malay Politics*; *British Imperial Policy and Decolonization, 1938–1964* (edited with A. N. Porter); and British Documents on End of Empire: *Malaya* (editor). He is Joint Editor of the *Journal of Imperial and Commonwealth History*.

B. R. TOMLINSON (Ph.D., Cambridge) is Professor of Economic History at the University of Strathclyde. He is the author of *The Indian National Congress and the Raj*; *The Political Economy of the Raj, 1914–1947*; and *The Economy of Modern India, 1870–1960*, as well as numerous articles on the economic, political, and business history of the British Empire.

1

Introduction

WM. ROGER LOUIS

Queen Victoria's death in 1901 and the end of the South African War in the following year mark the beginning, in a convenient but nevertheless arbitrary fashion, of the British Empire in the twentieth century. Nearly a century later, the handover of Hong Kong to China in 1997 represents the termination of the Empire save for scattered remnants. To emphasize the continuity in the British Imperial experience, the chronological starting-point might be extended to the acquisition of many of the African and Pacific domains in the last two decades of the nineteenth century. This expanded view of a 'long' twentieth century holds that the forces of British imperialism remained constant from the nineteenth century, and flowed or were channelled into a more informal empire of influence by means of the Commonwealth in the latter part of the twentieth.

There is an alternative way of viewing the great events in the expansion and contraction of the Empire in the last one hundred years. In this scheme the critical epoch falls within the framework of a 'short' twentieth century. The nineteenth-century Empire comes to a close only with the outbreak of war in 1914, and the twentieth-century Empire comes clattering down in the 1960s. To use a symbolic date, the death of Churchill in 1965 signifies the beginning of post-colonial Britain or the dividing-line between Imperial and contemporary Britain. Many of the chapters in this volume focus on the years of the short twentieth century. The overall view reflects both the 'long' and the 'short' perspectives. Some chapters connect with themes that go back at least to the occupation of Egypt in 1882, the 'Scramble for Africa', and the 'Great Game' or struggle for supremacy between Britain and Russia across Central Asia. Indeed, the twentieth-century British Empire cannot be understood without taking into account its Victorian origins. Thus, the volume begins with a chapter on the Empire before 1914, but the thematic design emphasizes the period from the outbreak of the First World War to the principal era of decolonization in the 1960s.

For the British Empire no less than for Britain, the twentieth century was dominated in the first four decades by two world wars, and in much of the remaining part of the century by the cold war. The volume finds its chronological halfway point with the chapter on the Second World War. For the period up to 1914, the Introduction emphasizes the contemporary view that the British Empire rested on sea power, that India was far and away its single most important component, and that the 'Colonial Empire' still included the Dominions as well as the colonies. In the first half of the volume there are certain overarching themes that march more or less in line with the progression of the chapters and clarify the complexity of the topics. In the second half the chapters are arranged mainly by regions. The Introduction draws out of the regional chapters the dominating themes of nationalism and the granting of independence by the British.

'The British Empire is pre-eminently a great Naval, Indian and Colonial power,' declared the Committee of Imperial Defence in 1904 in a description that had held true throughout most of the previous century.[1] Yet at the turn of the century the public mood became more defensive and anxious. The Royal Navy had traditionally attempted to maintain a fleet that could predominate over all others combined, but by 1897 Britain had lost absolute naval supremacy. The battleships of other nations had now overtaken Britain's by ninety-six to sixty-two.[2] In a development of paramount strategic significance, the conclusion of the Anglo-Japanese Alliance in 1902 eventually allowed the British fleet to concentrate in European waters. Britain continued to hold, and would hold throughout much of the twentieth century, the five strategic keys that locked up the British world: Dover, Gibraltar, Suez, the Cape of Good Hope, and Singapore.[3] But the loss of naval hegemony, and especially the challenge by Germany, created a sense of insecurity that intensified the debate on how India as well as the colonies might help to sustain British power.

In the thirty years or so before 1914 there was a sea-change in public attitude towards colonial expansion. In the 1880s and 1890s there had been a scramble for remaining territory in Africa and the Pacific as well as a frenzied activity in naval construction and the modernization of the Royal Navy. Sailors and soldiers, explorers and adventurers, missionaries and traders all tangibly extended British influence and affected, for better or worse, the lives of non-Europeans throughout the world. Docks, roads, railways, plantations, and mines spread in Asia and Africa at the same time that British goods and money penetrated indigenous societies. In a Darwinian atmosphere of survival of the fittest, the British competed against their European rivals in the world beyond Europe. There developed a spirit of

[1] Quoted in Elizabeth Monroe, *Britain's Moment in the Middle East, 1914–1956* (London, 1963), p. 11.

[2] Paul M. Kennedy, *The Rise and Fall of British Naval Mastery* (London, 1983 edn.), p. 209.

[3] Arthur J. Marder, *The Anatomy of British Sea Power* (London, 1940), p. 473. For sea power in relation to the Empire, Gerald Graham, *The Politics of Naval Supremacy* (Cambridge, 1965). For the theme of defence, see chap. by Anthony Clayton.

fierce Britannic nationalism—'Britannic' in the sense of a vibrant identity associated with the Empire as a whole.[4] The historian W. K. Hancock later expressed the essential idea: 'Imperial patriotism became an extension of Australian nationalism . . . it is not impossible for Australians . . . to be in love with two soils.'[5] At the turn of the century the awakening idea of a strong and united Empire brought with it the notion of 'national efficiency' demanding the co-ordination of financial and strategic efforts throughout the world to meet the challenges to British power.[6]

The colonies of white settlement were essential in the drive towards national efficiency, but Australia, New Zealand, South Africa, and Canada represented only part of a vast Empire (Map 1.1). In the Indian Ocean and Mediterranean, Britain ruled over India, Ceylon, Aden, Mauritius, the Seychelles, Gibraltar, Malta, and Cyprus. The African territories included Nigeria, the Gold Coast, the Gambia, Sierra Leone, the Anglo-Egyptian Sudan, British Somaliland, the East Africa Protectorate (Kenya), Uganda, Nyasaland, Rhodesia, Bechuanaland, Basutoland, and Swaziland. In East and South-East Asia, British possessions encompassed Hong Kong, Malaya, Burma, Singapore, and parts of Borneo. In the Pacific, Britain administered Fiji, the Gilbert and Ellice Islands, the Solomons, and lesser groups. In the Caribbean, British colonies included Jamaica, Trinidad, British Guiana, British Honduras, the Leewards and Windwards, and the Bahamas, and in the Atlantic, Bermuda. The list is by no means complete. The informal empire of trade and commerce and of concomitant political influence, which sometimes amounted in all but name to colonial control, stretched from the valley of the Nile to the Yangtze to the River Plate in Argentina. In its formal representation—the parts of the world coloured red on the map—the British Empire was a complex, worldwide system stretching over 12.1 million square miles, roughly one-quarter of the Earth's surface, that included territories acquired during every stage of expansion since the seventeenth century.

In the Edwardian era most people in Britain, pro-imperialist as well as anti-imperialist, accepted that territorial expansion had come to a halt. 'The present generation', according to a perceptive writer in 1909, 'is the first of a new order, and looks forward upon a prospect in which the idea of conquest and expansion find no place.'[7] The problem was now one of consolidating British power, of making the

[4] 'Britannic Nationalism' is a theme of the chap. by John Darwin. See also chap. by David MacKenzie and chap. 29 by W. David McIntyre; and John Eddy and Deryck Schreuder, *The Rise of Colonial Nationalism: Australia, New Zealand, Canada and South Africa First Assert Their Nationalities, 1880–1914* (Sydney, 1988), chap. 1.

[5] W. K. Hancock, *Australia* (London, 1930), p. 68.

[6] See G. R. Searle, *The Quest for National Efficiency* (Oxford, 1971).

[7] F. S. Oliver, quoted by Bernard Porter, 'The Edwardians and their Empire', in Donald Reid, ed., *Edwardian England* (London, 1982), p. 128. For the intellectual currents of this period, see chap. 2 by Ronald Hyam, and chap. by Nicholas Owen.

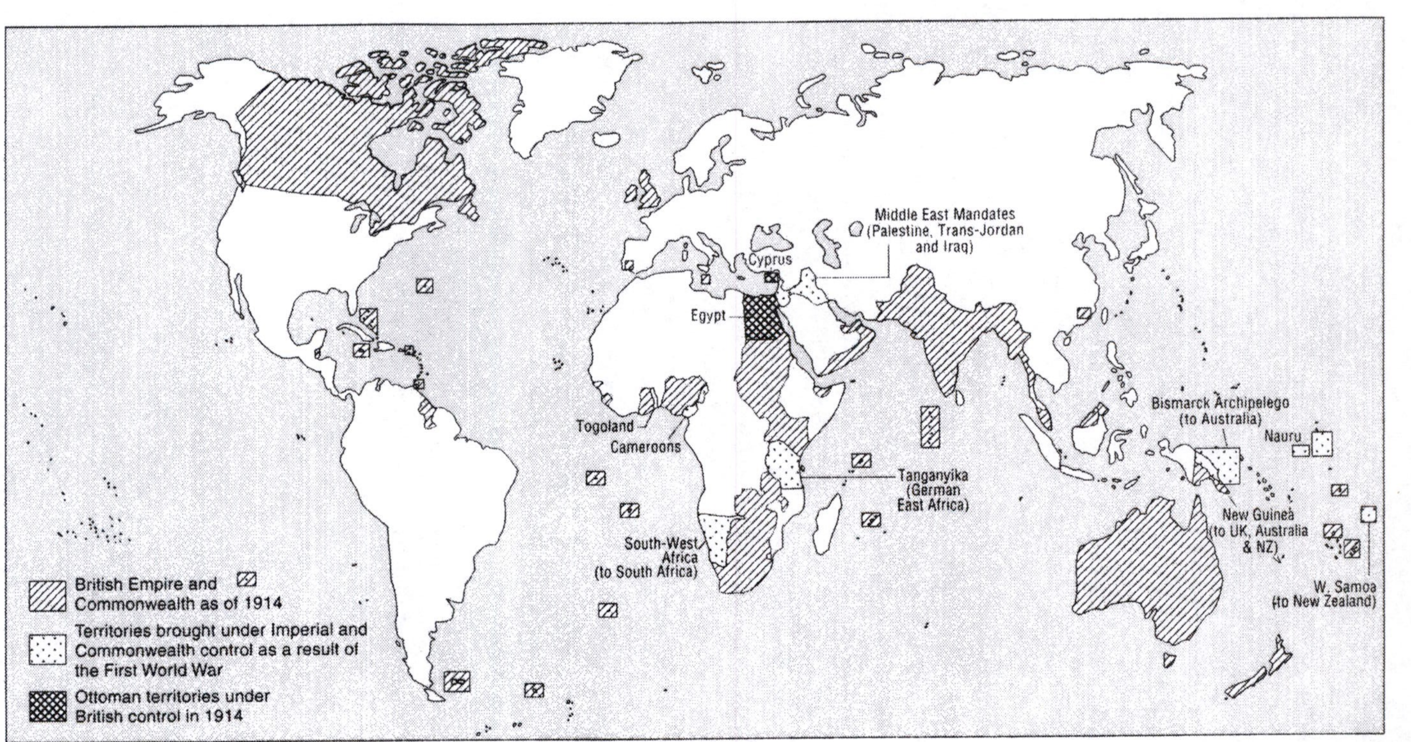

MAP 1.1 Expansion of the British Empire in the First World War

Empire more united as well as more efficient. Trains and telegraphs, steamships and cables increasingly formed an intricate system. Before 1914 Britain possessed 40 per cent of the world's shipping, with Germany as her nearest rival with 10 per cent. Shipping lines such as the P&O carried mail bearing penny postage to all points in the Empire. 'All-red routes' of ships, railways, telegraphs, cables, and wireless stations linked all the areas coloured red on the map. In one of the century's early breakthroughs in technology, the completion of the trans-Pacific cable took place in 1902. The cable extended from Vancouver to Fanning Island, Suva (Fiji), and Norfolk Island, where it divided into two branches running to Queensland and New Zealand. The achievement had almost metaphysical significance. It complemented the earlier work of laying deep-sea cables in the late nineteenth century, when London had been linked westwards with Newfoundland and eastwards with Bombay, Melbourne, and Wellington. The worldwide system was now complete (Map 1.2). Cables put merchants in direct touch with sources of supply. Tea and sugar, raw wool and cotton could now be purchased before shipment and dates of arrival could be accurately estimated. Transactions on the commodity exchanges in London, Liverpool, and Manchester assumed their twentieth-century form.[8] Rudyard Kipling, perhaps the greatest poet of the age, certainly the greatest of the Imperial poets, wrote of 'Deep-Sea Cables':

> Hush! Men talk today o'er the waste of the ultimate slime,
> And a new World runs between: whispering, 'Let us be one!'[9]

By 1911 Imperial wireless stations supplemented the cables and connected Britain with Cyprus, Aden, Bombay, the Straits Settlements, Hong Kong, and Australia.

India was the most important element in British strength. 'As long as we rule in India,' the Viceroy, Lord Curzon, stated in 1901, 'we are the greatest power in the world. If we lose it we shall drop straight away to a third rate power.'[10] The Empire in India, or the British Raj, was a domain in its own right, represented in the Cabinet by a Secretary of State for India and in India itself by the Viceroy, who was the Sovereign's representative as well as the head of the Government of India. At the turn of the century India had a territorial scope 'Greater than the Roman Empire' of 1,802,629 square miles (a subcontinent equal in size to Europe minus Russia), and a population, according to official statistics, of 294,361,056 (India alone in 1900 had a population nearly five times that of the entire French colonial empire). India was administered by fewer than 1,000 covenanted members of the

[8] C. E. Carrington, *The British Overseas: Exploits of a Nation of Shopkeepers* (Cambridge, 1950), pp. 466–71.

[9] Quoted in James Morris, *Pax Britannica* (London, 1968), p. 61.

[10] David Dilks, *Curzon in India*, 2 vols. (London, 1969), I, p. 170.

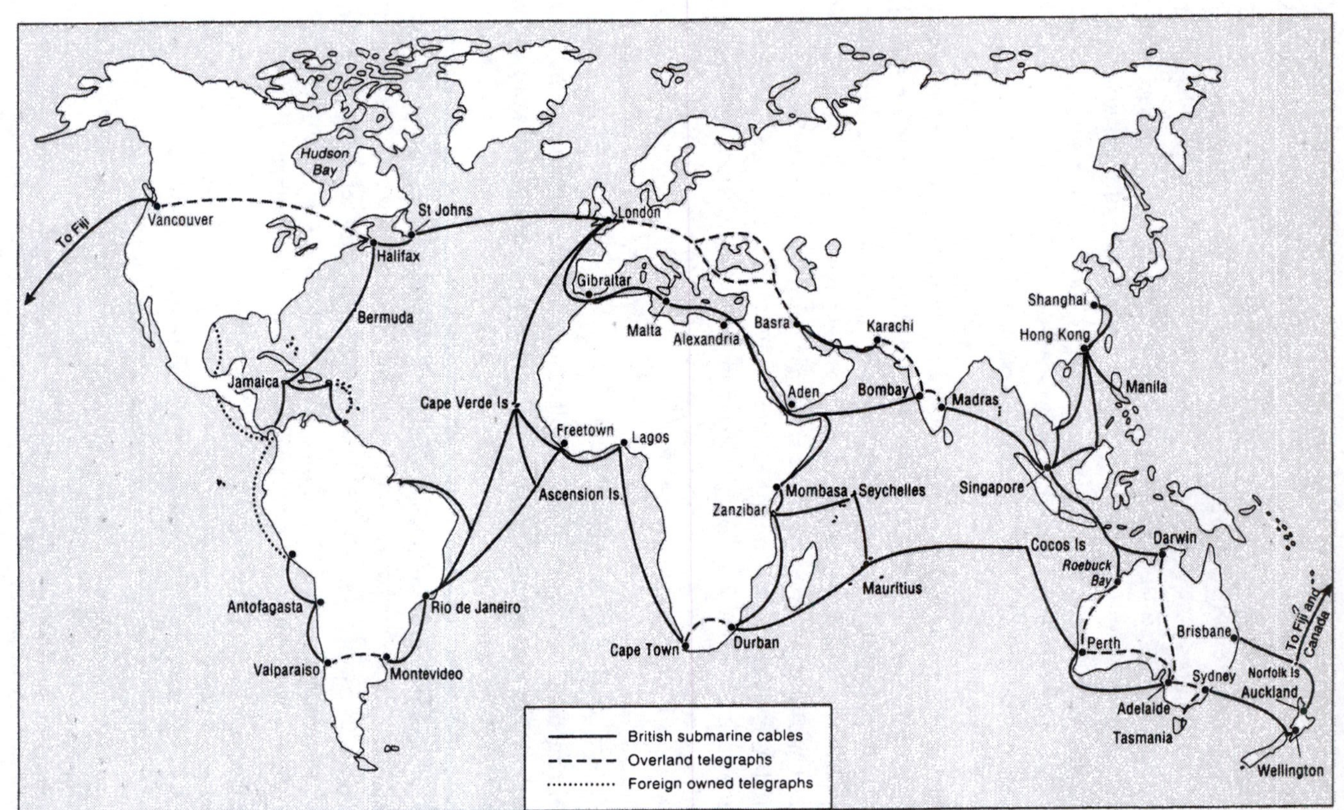

Map 1.2. Cables and Telegraphs, *c.*1920

Indian Civil Service, almost exclusively British.[11] Never, perhaps, had so few governed so many for the benefit of the British state. The Indian Army, with a core of 150,000 troops, made Britain the great military power in the East in the early years of the century. India bore the cost of an additional British garrison comprising 75,000 men, one-third of the British army.[12] The Indian Army itself, supported by British sea power, could deploy troops throughout maritime Asia. Since the British state refused to subsidize either the civilian or military arms of the Raj, India was compelled to be self-financing.[13] Indian revenues served as a guarantee for British investments in the subcontinent, especially in the immense Indian rail network, already the largest rail system in Asia.[14]

British rule in India was authoritarian, 'an unabashed autocracy, tempered by the rule of law'.[15] In the late nineteenth century the historian J. R. Seeley had observed that Britain could be despotic in Asia and democratic in Australia, standing in the East 'as a great military Imperialism' and in the West as 'the foremost champion of free thought and spiritual religion'.[16] There were thus two sides to the British Empire, as there had been since the eighteenth century, one of 'enlightened' despotism, the other of evolving representative government. Lord Milner, the leader of the movement to strengthen the Empire and the champion of British 'race patriotism', observed in 1906 that there were 'two empires', one non-white and dependent, the other white and self-governing.[17] The contrast continued to provoke comment, not least by Indian nationalists. Indians as well as French Canadians and Afrikaners quoted John Locke, Lord Durham, and John Stuart Mill.[18] In 1909 the Morley–Minto Reforms conceded Indian nationalist demands by considerably extending the range of Indian participation in the

[11] By the First World War the percentage of Indians in the ICS had risen to about 5%. By 1929 there were 894 Europeans and 367 Indians in the ICS. See David C. Potter, *India's Political Administrators, 1919–1983* (Oxford, 1986).

[12] See chap. by Anthony Clayton.

[13] For the economy of India and the impact of the British, see chap. 18 by Judith M. Brown; and chap. by B. R. Tomlinson.

[14] Indian railways open in 1912, 33,484 miles; Britain and Ireland, 23,441 miles; Russia, 46,573 miles; Germany, 39,065 miles; China, 5,960 miles; United States 360,714 miles.

[15] Anil Seal, *The Emergence of Indian Nationalism* (Cambridge, 1968), p. 3.

[16] J. R. Seeley, *The Expansion of England* (London, 1883); quotation from the 1971 Chicago edition edited by John Gross, p. 141. For the development of this theme, see chap. by Nicholas Owen.

[17] For Milner and the South African war, see chap. by Shula Marks. See also esp. L. M. Thompson, *The Unification of South Africa, 1902–1910* (Oxford, 1960); and G. H. L. Le May, *British Supremacy in South Africa, 1899–1907* (Oxford, 1965).

[18] A. F. Madden, 'Changing Attitudes and Widening Responsibilities, 1895–1914', in E. A. Benians and others, eds., *Cambridge History of the British Empire*, Vol. III, *The Empire-Commonwealth, 1870–1919* (Cambridge, 1959).

governance of their country.[19] But even British radicals such as John Morley, the Secretary of State for India, or a relatively forward-looking Viceroy such as Lord Minto, did not believe Indians capable of self-government, still less of democracy. Despite constitutional adjustments designed to win the loyalty of the literate intelligentsia and the politically conscious, India before 1914 had little prospect of evolving on the model of self-government enjoyed by the 'White Dominions'.

By 1910 Canada, Australia, New Zealand, and South Africa had all become self-governing, but two critical questions about their relationship to the Empire continued to be asked for the next half-century. Could the Dominions be kept within the Imperial system? And should Britain and the Dominions adhere to a system of 'free trade', the nineteenth-century legacy, or form a protectionist bloc known as 'Imperial Preference', which would enhance the military as well as the economic capacity of the Empire?[20] Britain had to accommodate Dominion nationalist sentiment, which held economic control to be an essential component in self-government.[21] The British overseas were ambivalent towards 'Britannic nationalism'. They were divided in their own minds, not merely on the prospect of strengthening or eventually severing links with Britain, but also—as were later nationalists in Asia and Africa—on the possibility of distinct and separate political identities, perhaps not in one but in several states or nations.[22] From the metropolitan vantage-point there were further fundamental perplexities. Could the Dominions be persuaded to form an economic union? Would a failure to create a closer political as well as economic union lead to a breakup of the colonial system?[23] There were no clear answers to those questions in 1914.

The First World War tested to the ultimate degree the Empire's capacity to mobilize resources of manpower and strategic commodities.[24] Lord Curzon later paid tribute to the technical achievement in the exploitation of Middle Eastern oil, the critical ingredient without which the Empire would have ground to a halt, by stating that Britain and her allies 'floated to victory on a wave of oil'. The mobilization of manpower was no less significant, but it strained political loyal-

[19] See Thomas R. Metcalf, *Ideologies of the Raj* (Cambridge, 1994), pp. 223–24; see also esp. Ronald Hyam, *Britain's Imperial Century, 1815–1914* (London, 1976), pp. 237–42.

[20] See chap. by D. K. Fieldhouse.

[21] This is a major theme in W. K. Hancock, *Survey of British Commonwealth Affairs*, 2 vols. (London, 1937–42), II, Part 1.

[22] Nicholas Mansergh, *The Commonwealth Experience* (London, 1969), analyses the complexity of the problem, p. 127 and elsewhere.

[23] The exponent of the theory of 'unite or bust' was Lionel Curtis, a Fellow of All Souls College, Oxford. See Deborah Lavin, *From Empire to International Commonwealth: A Biography of Lionel Curtis* (Oxford, 1995).

[24] See chap. by Robert Holland.

ties. All of the Dominions and India rallied to the cause, but in December 1914 a rebellion broke out in South Africa. Half the Afrikaner population opposed the war. South Africa threatened to explode into civil strife. As the European war progressed, old resentments of French Canadians came again to the surface, though Canada alone sent some 400,000 troops to the European theatre. Australian and New Zealand troops in the Middle East and in Europe were also an indispensable addition to British and Indian military power, but the long casualty list at the defeat at Gallipoli in 1915 provoked Australians and others to question the quality of British military leadership. Even those Irish sympathetic to the British cause believed that Irish units at Gallipoli and elsewhere bore the brunt of casualties. Strong pro-Empire sentiment did exist in Ireland, but the Easter rebellion in 1916 occurred at a critical point of the war. The executions that followed it transformed a fiasco into a heroic myth, so delivering a shattering blow to the assumption of a harmonious evolution of political unity within the Empire.[25] In the same year the British in India faced the choice of conciliation or repression. Fear of civil unrest in India contributed to the decision to press for a declaration of British intent in favour of eventual self-government.[26] The crisis that swept David Lloyd George into power in December 1916 thus represented not merely a juncture in British politics but an emergency that extended to many parts of the Empire. Representatives from the Dominions met, on the basis of tacit equality, with members of the British government in an Imperial War Cabinet. The principle of 'no fighting without representation' transformed the constitutional relationship, while the war itself sharpened the sense of national identity.[27]

In the context of this volume, the two most significant results of the First World War were the emergence of a British Middle Eastern Empire and the intervention in colonial affairs by the United States. Egypt, which had been under British occupation since 1882, was declared a Protectorate in December 1914 as a consequence of war between Britain and the Ottoman empire. The Middle Eastern campaigns led eventually to British control over Palestine, Transjordan, and Iraq.[28] In a decision taken for complex reasons in 1917, Britain declared support for a Jewish national home in Palestine, provided there would be no damage to the rights of the Arab inhabitants.[29] British, Dominion, and Allied forces had already

[25] See chap. by Deirdre McMahon.

[26] For the significance of the First World War reforms in India, see chap. 18 by Judith M. Brown.

[27] See below, pp. 129–30; and 670–71; and chap. by David MacKenzie in which the theme of Canadian identity is discussed in relation to 'Americanization', pp. 582–83.

[28] See chap. by Glen Balfour-Paul.

[29] The literature on the Balfour Declaration is vast but see esp. Mayir Vereté, 'The Balfour Declaration and its Makers', in Norman Rose, ed., *From Palmerston to Balfour: Collected Essays of Mayir Vereté* (London, 1992).

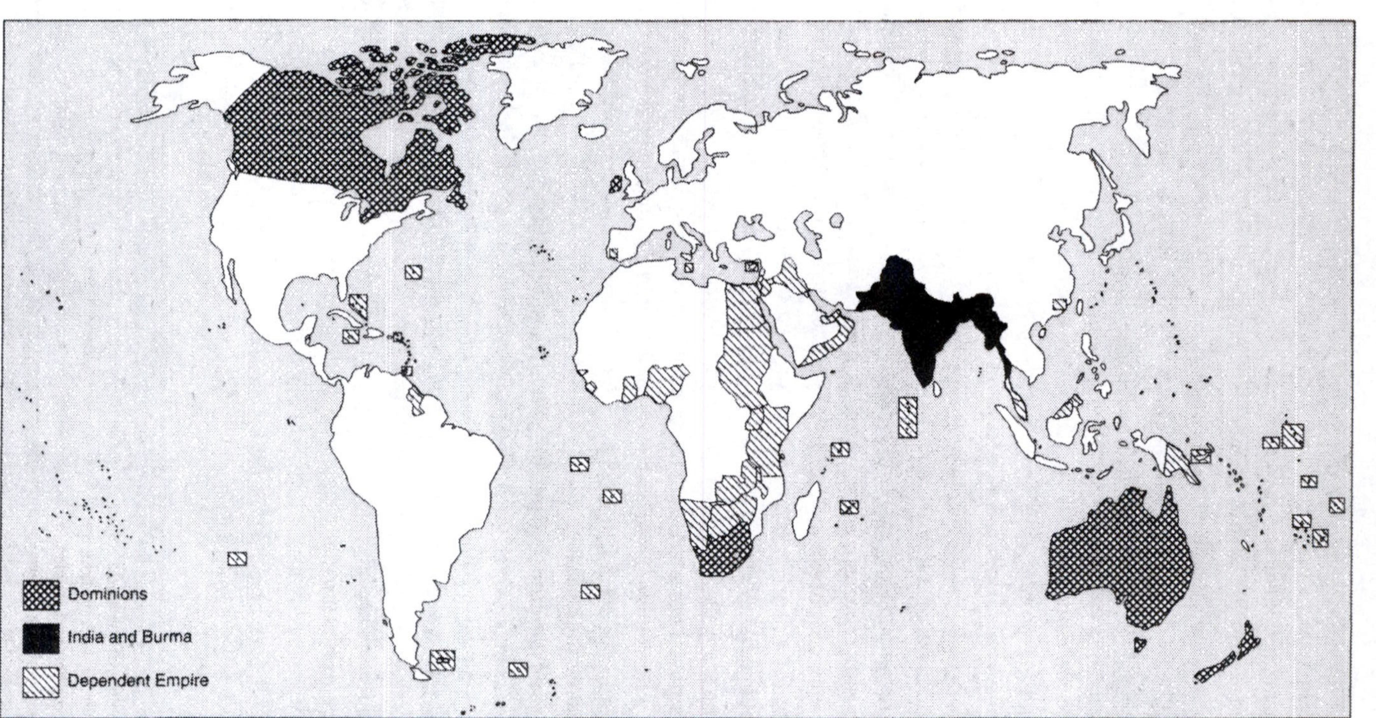

Map 1.3. The British Empire in 1930

captured the German colonies in Africa and the Pacific. The British Empire now extended, in Milner's words, up the entire backbone of the African continent into an arc through the Middle East to the Persian Gulf (Map 1.3).[30] None of these conquered territories was annexed. At the insistence of the United States, they were held as 'a sacred trust of civilization' as Mandates under the League of Nations. President Woodrow Wilson hoped to check the imperialistic impulses of at least the British and French, though he seems to have been reconciled to the idea that South-West Africa would eventually be incorporated into South Africa and that the inhabitants of New Guinea would be ruled permanently by Australia. The mandatory powers submitted reports to the League of Nations, but 'international control' amounted to little else. Most of the African and Pacific Mandates eventually became Trust Territories under the United Nations, and 'international interference', as the Colonial Office called it, probably accelerated, if only slightly, the pace towards decolonization. In 1950, for example, the United Nations conferred on Italy the trusteeship of former Italian Somaliland for only ten years, a period well in advance of timetables envisaged elsewhere in tropical Africa.

Did the First World War mark the point of irretrievable dependence on the United States? It did not seem so to contemporaries. But in 1921–22, when confronted with a choice between Japan and the United States, the British took into account the growing antagonism between the two countries and decided to remain on friendly terms with the United States. They did not renew the Anglo-Japanese Alliance.[31] The striking feature of the discussions on Japan is the concern not merely with British sea power but also with race, not merely the 'Yellow Peril', especially as it appeared to Australia and New Zealand, but also the racial make-up of America. According to the Prime Minister of New Zealand, William F. Massey, the Americans were a 'mongrel race' who could be trusted only as long as 'men of our stock' continued to rule in Washington, and sometimes not even then.[32] The fickleness of the Americans continued to be a theme in British discussions throughout the inter-war period. Some 'old Far East hands' believed the termination of the Anglo-Japanese Alliance had been a false turn in the road, that Japan

[30] This is a theme in John Darwin, *Britain, Egypt and the Middle East: Imperial Policy in the Aftermath of War, 1918–1922* (London, 1981); see also Wm. Roger Louis, *Great Britain and Germany's Lost Colonies, 1914–1919* (Oxford, 1967).

[31] See below, p. 466; and chap. 29 by W. David McIntyre on Australia, p. 672.

[32] Massey continued: 'As for America's future, I consider that the future of America itself is the biggest problem of the world to-day. No one can look at all those mixed races in the United States; 13 million Negroes and millions of people from Southern Europe, Northern Europe, all sorts and conditions of men and women, without wondering what the population will be like in another forty or fifty years from now or even a much shorter period, and I say it is quite impossible for anybody to predict the result.' Quoted in Wm. Roger Louis, *British Strategy in the Far East, 1919–1939* (Oxford, 1971), p. 72.

with British tutelage might not have taken an expansionist and militarist course in the 1930s, that the Japanese with British friendship might have continued to play cricket rather than baseball.[33] When Neville Chamberlain became Prime Minister in 1937, he made it clear that he regarded the decision to terminate the alliance to have been a mistake and he explored ways of resurrecting it. Had he succeeded, Britain conceivably might not have lost Hong Kong, Malaya, and Burma during the Second World War. In the event Britain emerged from the 1939–45 war virtually bankrupt and more dependent than ever on the United States. But hopes of Britain acting independently from the United States ended only in the Suez crisis in 1956. What Suez demonstrated was what many had feared from the beginning of the century: Britain was no longer a 'world power' or, in post-Second World War phrase, a 'superpower', even though much of the Colonial Empire as late as 1956 remained intact.

Seven organizing themes can be identified in the first half of the volume that help in understanding its overall design and purpose. The themes connect directly with those of the nineteenth-century volume and generally with the five volumes in the series. They are: (1) the importance of Ireland in the unfolding history of the Empire and Commonwealth; (2) emigration patterns and the consequences for the British economy; (3) the Empire as a field of opportunity for women, and for the Scots, Welsh, and Irish as well as English; (4) missionary activity; (5) champions and critics of British imperialism; (6) British rule in India and Africa, and the idea of trusteeship; and (7) the defence of the Empire. In chapters 1–15 it is useful also to bear in mind a dominant economic argument sustained in the second half of the volume as well: the First World War resurrected the idea prevalent at the turn of the century that Empire might be the salvation of Britain through protectionism and exploitation of tropical territories. Such ideas faded after 1919, but after 1929 and again after 1945, in the crises of depression and war, the fate of Britain once more seemed to lie in the hope of developing the colonies to sustain the British economy. Only in the late 1950s did faith in the Imperial economy generally begin to wane.[34]

The chapter on Ireland finds a place at the beginning of the volume because of the central importance of the Irish question in the twentieth century no less than in previous centuries. The significance of Ireland in the colonial context should not be exaggerated, for Ireland was always first and foremost a problem in British politics, but no other issue so divided the British among themselves, and it thus

[33] See Malcolm D. Kennedy, *The Estrangement of Great Britain and Japan, 1917–35* (Manchester, 1969).

[34] See chaps. by D. K. Fieldhouse and B. R. Tomlinson.

had a pervasive influence on the Empire and Commonwealth. Ireland provided the example to British politicians and Governors as the model *not* to follow.[35] But to fellow nationalists the Irish provided inspiration. Just as the struggle by the Afrikaners against the British at the turn of the century stimulated the Irish, so the Irish provided an example to Indians and Egyptians. In a wider perspective Ireland was Britain's Algeria.[36] But in 1914 and as late as 1921 the status of Ireland as a Dominion still seemed possible. Chapter 6 discusses the developing crisis and the consequences of the Easter Rising of April 1916, when Irish nationalists rebelled in Dublin to secure Irish independence. In all parts of the Empire anti-Irish sentiment rose. The British generally regarded the Irish as disloyal and seditious. At the same time, however, the British government muted the extent of the uprising because of possible adverse reaction in the United States.

In the post-war period in Ireland, the military-police force known as the Black and Tans acquired the reputation of a crude instrument of repression.[37] Yet the Black and Tans became a model for similar forces in other Imperial trouble-spots, and provided recruits for the new Palestine Gendarmerie and for the Royal Air Force's armoured companies in Iraq. Ireland thus helped to shape the later counter-insurgency forces used to combat anti-British nationalism. In India the partition of Ireland cast a long shadow.[38] Had British policies encouraged Muslim as well as Unionist resistance? Might India become 'a larger and noisier Southern Ireland'? The lessons learned from Ireland's secession from the Commonwealth steeled the Labour government in 1949 to avert a similar disaster. India remained in the Commonwealth as a Republic. Ireland severed its ties, but at a price. Nationalists in the predominantly Catholic south regarded Northern Ireland as a colony in the grip of Protestant settlers backed by British military power. It would now remain a part of the United Kingdom. Ulster thus became a beacon for white settler communities in Africa, as the pace towards independence quickened. Could Ulster provide inspiration for a solution in Southern Rhodesia, if not by integration into the United Kingdom then perhaps by Dominion Status on the South African model? 'Rhodesia was Ulster writ large.'[39]

Emigration within the Empire, the second theme, had a critical bearing on the British economy. Those at the turn of the century who were optimistic about the destiny of the British Empire assumed that free labour mobility could exist within

[35] See Ronald Hyam, *Elgin and Churchill at the Colonial Office, 1905–1908: The Watershed of the Empire-Commonwealth* (London, 1968), pp. 55, 183, 533.

[36] Kenneth Robinson, *The Dilemmas of Trusteeship* (London, 1965), p. 4. This is a seminal work.

[37] In the context of the Empire, see Charles Townshend, *Britain's Civil Wars: Counterinsurgency in the Twentieth Century* (London, 1986), pp. 57–59, 91–92.

[38] See esp. T. G. Fraser, 'Ireland and India', in Keith Jeffery, ed., *'An Irish Empire'? Aspects of Ireland and the British Empire* (Manchester, 1996), pp. 77–93.

[39] See chap. by Deirdre McMahon.

an Imperial economy controlled by London.[40] The British Nationality Act in 1914 defined British subjects as anyone born 'within His Majesty's dominions and allegiances', and by implication confirmed the right of entry into Britain. The political as well as economic flaws in the assumption about free mobility became apparent as the century progressed. To preserve Imperial unity, the government in London acquiesced in restrictive immigration legislation designed to keep Australia, New Zealand, and Canada white, and to achieve white supremacy in South Africa.[41] At the time of the Ottawa economic agreements in the Depression era of the early 1930s, the British government had increasingly to accept tariffs and other economic controls by the Dominions. The ideal remained free trade within the Empire, but free trade did not always appear advantageous to the constituent parts. The economic development of the Dominions became increasingly competitive and not necessarily harmonious with attempts to centralize the economy on London. Nevertheless, for the first five or six decades in the century the Empire and Commonwealth did become increasingly 'British' in the sense that emigrants from the British Isles tended to settle or work in the Dominions or colonies. The total of inter-war migration dropped from that of the pre-First World War level. But four-fifths of those emigrating from the British Isles migrated to British destinations between the world wars, as compared with one-third before 1914. In 1922 the Empire Settlement Act facilitated passage and settlement on the basis of sharing expenses. Between 1922 and 1936 some 3 per cent of those emigrating received some form of assistance. Overall in that period 186,524 people emigrated to Canada, 172,735 to Australia, 44,745 to New Zealand, but only 1,226 to South Africa and Southern Rhodesia. To give one of the most extreme examples at the other end of the spectrum, at the close of the period there were fifty-six Britons in Somaliland.[42]

Changes in demography and in the political economy marched hand in hand. As late as the 1960s assisted passage schemes such as the £10 fares to Australia were still available. But instead of an Imperial economy controlling economic and immigration policies on the periphery, the Dominions increasingly went their own ways. The Dominions abolished or modified ethnic discrimination: Canada in 1962, Australia in 1973, New Zealand in 1987, and South Africa with the collapse of apartheid in 1990. British legislation had progressed in the other direction, becoming more discriminatory. The 1948 Nationality Act guaranteed the right of free entry of all Empire subjects into Britain, but the Commonwealth Immigrants Act of 1962 reduced the inflow of 'New Commonwealth' immigrants who did not hold British passports. The Act of 1968 imposed further restrictions. The

[40] See chap. by Stephen Constantine.

[41] See chap. 11 by Ronald Hyam, p. 58.

[42] See chap. by Constantine.

Immigration Act of 1971 removed with finality the distinction between Commonwealth and foreign immigrants, thus repudiating the Imperial mobility and the integrity of the Empire upheld since the beginning of the century.[43] Following Britain's entry into the European Economic Community in 1973, people of 'British stock' from such places as Australia found themselves waiting along with US and other aliens to pass through UK immigration while Europeans swept past.

The third theme is the opportunity in the Empire at large for a better life offered to women as well as men, to Scots as well as Irish.[44] The Empire, specifically India but later South-East Asia and Africa, gave many women the opportunity to advance their careers, especially as missionaries. Did the arrival of British women in increasing numbers in India and the tropical colonies, and the subsequent official attempt to prohibit native mistresses, widen the gulf between the British and the peoples under British rule and foster social exclusiveness?[45] British women were generally seen as guardians of 'civilized standards' of morality and family life. They were mothers and custodians of the home, and they stood for 'racial strength and fitness for the responsibilities of Empire'.[46] They were a compelling icon. But the period also witnessed the challenge by the suffragettes for the vote, and the peak of the feminist movement in early twentieth-century Britain. Would the 'female howling dervishes'—Curzon's phrase—precipitate revolt in the Empire? In fact, most British women accepted the underlying assumptions of the Empire.[47] Some hoped to reform it as well as to acquire the vote. Admiring the courage of the suffragettes, Gandhi once commented: 'It is no wonder that a people which produces such daughters and mothers holds the sceptre.' The suffragettes were a 'British' phenomenon encompassing Irish, Scottish, and Welsh as well as English women. But English feminists sometimes assumed the pre-eminence of England within Britain—an assumption 'that at times brought them into conflict with their Scotch and Irish sisters'.[48]

Englishmen as well as Englishwomen tended to assume 'the hegemony of England within the United Kingdom' and continued to disparage 'the thievish

[43] Ibid.

[44] See chap. by Rosalind O'Hanlon, pp. 395–96, for the links with British feminism. See also chaps. by John M. MacKenzie, p. 217; Shula Marks, pp. 555, 559; in Vol. III, see chap. by Afaf Lutfi al-Sayyid-Marsot; and in Vol. V, chap. by Diana Wylie.

[45] On this theme, see Ronald Hyam chap. 11, pp. 60–61; Rosalind O'Hanlon pp. 395–96; see also esp. Claudia Knapman, *White Women in Fiji, 1835–1930* (London, 1986), pp. 6–10. American oilmen in Burma have a prominent place in the mythology of resistance to official attempts to regulate sexual activity in the tropics because of a passage in George Orwell's *Burmese Days*. In an open telegram, they declared 'No cunt, no oil'. Bernard Crick, *George Orwell: A Life* (London, 1980), p. 89.

[46] See below, p. 391.

[47] See Vol. V, chap. by Diana Wylie.

[48] Antoinette Burton, *Burdens of History: British Feminists, Indian Women, and Imperial Culture, 1868–1915* (Chapel Hill, NC, 1994), pp. 6 and 207.

Welsh, the beggarly Scots, the drunken, impractical Irish'.[49] But the Scots had as good a claim as the English to the construction and dynamism of the nineteenth- and twentieth-century Empire.[50] The Empire generally provided opportunities for a better life, to the Irish as well as the English and the Scots, but in proportion to population the Scots seized the opportunity to a remarkable degree. At the turn of the century, 75 per cent of Britain's population lived in England, 10 per cent in Scotland, 10 per cent in Ireland, and 5 per cent in Wales. But overseas the English ratio dropped to about 50 per cent. Scots constituted 23 per cent of the British-born in New Zealand, 21 per cent in Canada, and 15 per cent in Australia. The Irish held comparable figures: 21 per cent in Canada and New Zealand, 27 per cent in Australia. By contrast, the Welsh formed less than 1 per cent of the British-born in Australia and New Zealand and probably less in Canada.[51] Apart from South Africa, the Scots and Irish thus made as great a contribution as did the English, and the Scots figured prominently in shipping, banking, and industry as well as medicine and engineering. Glasgow was the Empire's second city. Dundee produced fine carpets as well as rough sacking by importing Indian jute. In the Antipodes and in North America, Scots were prominent in business, farming, education, and religion. Toronto and Dunedin (named after the Gaelic word for Edinburgh) were predominantly Scottish cities. In India and Ceylon, tea plantations were owned and managed by Scots. In Malayan production of tin and rubber, and later in Rhodesian copper, Scots often held critical positions in management. Scottish publishing houses such as Blackwood's, Chambers', and Murray's published works of literature available at cheap prices throughout the world.[52] In the Indian Civil Service, as in the Colonial Service, Scots again played a significant role.[53] There were social, indeed mystical, ramifications to the Scottish diaspora. By 1914 virtually half of the Scottish Masonic lodges were overseas.[54] The Scots tenaciously retained their identity as a people. One could be Scottish, Irish, Welsh, or English, and at the same time 'British' and benefit from the opportunities offered by the worldwide British Empire.[55]

[49] Graham Dawson, 'The Blond Bedouin', in John Roper and Michael Tosh, eds., *Manful Assertions* (London, 1991), p. 139; G. C. Bolton, *Britain's Legacy Overseas* (Oxford, 1973), p. 46.

[50] For this theme see chap. by John M. MacKenzie, pp. 215–16.

[51] See P. J. Marshall, ed., *The Cambridge Illustrated History of the British Empire* (Cambridge, 1996), p. 265.

[52] On the cultural dimension of Scotland and the British Empire, George Shepperson, 'Scotland: The World Perspective', in *The Diaspora of the British* (University of London, Institute of Commonwealth Studies: Collected Seminar Papers, No. 31, 1982), pp. 44–54.

[53] In 1939 in the Indian Civil Service there were 564 English and Welsh, 84 Scots, and 37 Irish. Potter, *India's Political Administrators*, p. 57.

[54] Hyam, *Britain's Imperial Century*, p. 155.

[55] On the theme of identity, see Judith M. Brown, Epilogue, pp. 707–09.

The fourth theme concerns missionaries.[56] Christian missions represented the religious composition of the United Kingdom.[57] Irish Catholic and Scottish Presbyterians as well as the Church of England and English Methodists carved out distinct fields. In Asia, India and China competed for missionary attention, with British missionary societies predominating in the former and American in the latter. China remained mainly beyond British colonial control, but in other parts of Asia and in Africa there were often tensions between missionaries and the servants of the colonial state. To put the argument in its most extreme form, missionaries sometimes brought with them revolutionary influences.[58] As hundreds of thousands of children took their first steps towards literacy by reading Bible stories, one lesson to be learned was the virtue of equality as well as humility. Africans in Nyasaland, to use one celebrated example, discovered in missionary teaching a means of expressing social and political aspirations based on biblical concepts of history as progress, revolt, and millenarian expectation. In the early stage of the First World War, John Chilembwe, an African who had received American Negro Baptist support to found his own mission, became the leader of Africans who had suffered from the settler economy in the Shire Highlands. Leading a violent but brief apocalyptic rising, he was killed in February 1915.[59] Chilembwe's was an exceptional case, but the consequences of African response to Christian millenarianism could not but alarm those in colonial administrations. Faith in the millennium might lead to the hope for the departure of the Europeans. Religious education might inspire anti-European societies. African churches could serve as the basis for resistance against the colonial regimes. Missionary teaching could thus produce unintended results.[60]

Sympathizing with their converts, some missionaries did moderately criticize colonial policies, above all in taxation and labour. On the other hand, there existed a bond between missionaries and local colonial officials, the latter respecting the former for work in difficult circumstances and often in remote areas. In the colonies as well as in Britain there was widespread admiration for the missionaries. When they returned to Britain on leave, missionaries spoke in churches and Sunday schools, showing magic-lantern slides and soliciting contributions to medical and educational work.[61] Missionary activity became one of the main ways by which the British public learned about the colonies in Africa and Asia,

[56] See Vol. II, chap. by Boyd Stanley Schlenther; Vol. III, chap. 11 by Andrew Porter; and chaps. by T. C. McCaskie and Susan Bayly.

[57] See Vol. V, chap. by Norman Etherington.

[58] See e.g. Vol. III, chap. by Gad Heuman on Baptist activity in Jamaica.

[59] George Shepperson and Thomas Price, *Independent African: John Chilembwe and the Nyasaland Rising of 1915* (Edinburgh, 1958).

[60] See below, p. 560; see also Vol. III, chaps. by Susan Bayly and T. C. McCaskie.

[61] See below, p. 212.

sometimes with a transcendent message: 'The British Empire is itself an expression of the Christianity which the Church has to guard...'[62] Many British officials would have disagreed. The British Empire was a great Muslim as well as Christian power and must also be seen in a Hindu and Buddhist context.[63] Missionaries and government officials thus had an ambivalent relationship, but they often worked together in common cause. Missionaries required protection by Britain, but in turn they provided vital services, especially in education and medicine. The Colonial Office appointed missionary representatives to advisory committees on education and attempted to make sure that educational goals would complement official aims. In 1925 J. H. Oldham, the Secretary to the International Missionary Council, took a prominent part in a Colonial Office committee which reported that education should not only promote 'true ideals of citizenship' but should also concentrate on such things as 'the improvement of agriculture'. By promoting expertise in such areas as cultivation and water purification, and by dispensing quinine and remedies for dysentery, missionaries helped to modernize rural economies, raise standards of public health, and extend life expectancy.[64] The religious results were mixed. In India by 1947 less than 2 per cent of the population had converted to Christianity, but in Africa by the end of the colonial era Christianity rivalled Islam as the major religion of the continent.

The fifth theme is concerned with the champions of the Imperial idea and the development of anti-colonial sentiment.[65] The twentieth century eventually became profoundly anti-imperial. J. A. Hobson led the attack on imperialism against the background of the South African War, but at the same time Joseph Chamberlain inspired a romantic, patriotic vision of imperialism that embodied a coherent economic programme. In a sense Chamberlain and Hobson stood for two great rival traditions. Chamberlain was Secretary of State for the Colonies from 1895 to 1903. At the Colonial Office he replaced candles with electricity. He helped found Schools of Tropical Medicine in London and Liverpool. He encouraged the investment of British capital in colonial development. He believed in improved communications as a means of opening up vast regions. And he held that the aboriginal must not impede civilization.[66] Chamberlain stood above all

[62] The Warden of Keble College, Oxford, quoted in Richard Symonds, *Oxford and Empire: The Last Lost Cause?* (London, 1986), p. 227.

[63] See chap. by Francis Robinson. For Hindu and Buddhist themes see Vol. II, chap. by Rajat Kanta Ray; Vol. III, chaps. by Susan Bayly and A. J. Stockwell.

[64] For example, Edmund M. Hogan, *The Irish Missionary Movement: A Historical Survey, 1830–1980* (Dublin, 1990), chap. 10 and esp. pp. 129–30.

[65] For the critics of British imperialism, see chap. by Nicholas Owen.

[66] Madden, 'Changing Attitudes and Widening Responsibilities', esp. pp. 383–84, which catches the complexity of Chamberlain's personality and political ideas. See also esp. Peter T. Marsh, *Joseph Chamberlain: Entrepreneur in Politics* (New Haven, 1994).

for Imperial Preference or Tariff Reform as means by which the Empire would be unified politically as well as economically. In one of his most momentous decisions, he appointed as High Commissioner in South Africa Sir Alfred Milner, 'who, more than any other single individual, shaped its early twentieth-century destiny'.[67] Whatever might be the assessment of Milner's attempt to transform South Africa from the weakest into the strongest link in the British Imperial chain, he was, along with Curzon and Cromer, one of the great Proconsuls of his age.[68] Milner attracted a band of young men known as the 'Kindergarten', who gave him total allegiance and carried on his work far into the century. His disciples in the *religio Milneriana* founded the *Round Table*, the journal dedicated to Imperial unity.[69] Milner's most devoted lieutenant was Leopold Amery, Secretary of State for the Colonies, 1924–29.[70] Amery was, in A. J. P. Taylor's phrase, 'the Empire's theoretician' as well as its indefatigable champion. Through the period of the Second World War he upheld the principles of the Empire. He, perhaps more than anyone else, managed to reconcile 'Britannic' and Dominion nationalism. In a straight line of descent from Chamberlain to Milner to Amery, the defence of the Imperial idea found vigorous expression as late as the 1950s.

In the anti-imperial tradition, Hobson exerted the greatest influence.[71] Analysing the question of motive and profit during the South African War, he speculated in his book *Imperialism* that Europe's expansion in tropical Africa was motivated by profit. His interpretation gave rise to the widespread misinterpretation of the South African or Boer War as a capitalist plot. But all twentieth-century theories of imperialism, including those of Rosa Luxemburg and Lenin, can be traced to his work. Hobson expressed the moral outrage of scores of other writers. Heirs to the free-trade tradition of John Bright and Richard Cobden and to the humanitarian and radical movements of the late nineteenth century, critics as diverse as Mary Kingsley and E. D. Morel helped to shape the humanitarian conscience of twentieth-century British imperialism.[72] There was a strong evangelical component in anti-imperial thought, for example, in the activities of the former missionary and Secretary of the Anti-Slavery and Aborigines Protection Society, John H. Harris.

[67] See below, p. 548.

[68] Milner is best portrayed in A. M Gollin, *Proconsul in Politics: A Study of Lord Milner in Opposition and in Power* (London, 1963). For Cromer see Afaf Lutfi al-Sayyid-Marsot, *Egypt and Cromer* (London, 1968); and her chap. in Vol. III.

[69] *Religio Milneriana* was the sardonic phrase used by Sir Henry Campbell-Bannerman. J. A. Spender, *The Life of the Right Hon. Sir Henry Campbell-Bannerman, G.C.B.*, 2 vols. (London, 1923), I, p. 264.

[70] See Wm. Roger Louis, *In the Name of God Go! Leopold Amery and the British Empire in the Age of Churchill* (New York, 1992).

[71] See chap. by Nicholas Owen.

[72] For the antecedents including the anti-slavery movement in the nineteenth century, see Vol. III, chap. 10, by Andrew Porter.

By the time of the First World War writers such as Hobson, H. N. Brailsford, and Norman Angell believed that the colonies should be placed under international administration. These ideas linked the Wilson–Lenin concept of 'self-determination' with post-war League of Nations idealism. In the thought of Leonard Woolf and others on the political left can be found the connection between the creation of the Mandates System of the League of Nations and the Trusteeship System of the United Nations. There is one outstanding characteristic of most of these writers. They were not anti-imperial in the sense of wanting to liquidate the Empire, at least not immediately. They wanted to reform it and to make it more accountable. Their criticism infused into the debate a deep sense of ethical responsibility that remains one of the distinguishing characteristics of the colonial age.

Colonial experts seldom attracted attention in the daily newspapers or indeed in the House of Commons. But the writers and intellectuals known as the Bloomsbury Group had a profound influence on public perceptions of the Empire. In 1918 Lytton Strachey published *Eminent Victorians*, which was, among other things, a polemic against Victorian Christianity and Imperialism. Virginia Woolf attacked Kipling, who nevertheless remained popular despite the intellectual disparagement of Bloomsbury and academic disapproval of him as an 'Imperialist' poet.[73] In *Empire and Commerce in Africa* (1920), Leonard Woolf supported Hobson and others in the proposal for international control over the colonial system.[74] E. M. Forster's *A Passage to India* (1924) was especially significant in causing people to reflect on the arrogance of the British Raj, though the book itself is filled with racial smugness and reinforces stereotypes of Hindus and Muslims. *A Passage to India* continued as late as the 1980s to exert a powerful influence, in David Lean's film version. The iconoclasm and anti-imperial outlook of Bloomsbury thus cast a long shadow, offset only in part by such works as the film *Sanders of the River* (1935), which idealized the District Officer, and, much later and ambiguously, in Paul Scott's *Raj Quartet*, described by Max Beloff as one of the great historical novels of our age.[75] Bloomsbury, of course, merely helped to set the intellectual climate of the times. The two world wars, the rise of the nationalist movements, and the development of anti-colonial sentiment in the United States as well as in the United Nations created a general international climate hostile to British assumptions. One can detect a note of sadness in the last major apologia for the British

[73] For Kipling's intellectual rehabilitation, see esp. Noel Annan, 'Kipling's Place in the History of Ideas', *Victorian Studies*, III, 4 (June 1960), pp. 323–48; for an assessment of Kipling as a poet of the same rank as T. S. Eliot, see Thomas Pinney, in Wm. Roger Louis, ed., *More Adventures with Britannia* (Austin, Tex., 1998).

[74] See chap. by Nicholas Owen.

[75] Max Beloff, 'The End of the Raj: Paul Scott's Novels as History', *Encounter*, XLVI, 5 (May 1976), pp. 65–70. See also esp. R. J. Moore, *Paul Scott's Raj* (London, 1990). For the literature and films inspired by the Empire see chap. by John M. MacKenzie.

Empire, Margery Perham's *Colonial Reckoning*, published in 1961, that the colonial mission had been misunderstood as well as maligned.

The sixth theme is colonial rule and its underlying philosophy as summed up in the words 'Indirect Rule', a phrase indelibly associated with Sir Frederick Lugard,[76] the founder of British Nigeria. With a small staff and scarce resources, he had of necessity to accommodate the large Islamic societies in the northern regions. He faced the problem, as did other Proconsuls throughout the world, of how best to administer vast territories and peoples with minimal expense and military commitment. Indirect Rule had its roots in expediency. When Lugard wrote the *Dual Mandate* after his retirement and published the book in 1921, he put forward essentially the same idea that Joseph Chamberlain had popularized two decades earlier on the economic potential of vast tropical estates. Britain, according to Lugard, should develop the colonies for the benefit of the world economy and, at the same time, administer them for the well-being of the Africans. Here were two closely related ideas: 'development', making explicit the mutual advantage to both Britain and Africa, and 'trusteeship', expressing the humanitarian mission. Africans would be protected against baleful economic or social influences and against such rapacious commercial exploitation as had existed in the Congo before 1908. They would be allowed to evolve along their own lines, managing their own affairs, but under the benevolent guardianship of the British, who would slowly and cautiously modify indigenous customs and institutions. The British would 'rule through chiefs', who would dispense traditional law and collect taxes, thereby making the districts legally and financially self-sufficient.[77] Gradually the colonies would be developed economically and integrated into the world economy, thus upholding the dual principle of trusteeship and development.

The administrative methods of Indirect Rule had deep roots in India. The system later developed in parallel fashion in Malaya, Fiji, and Africa, but in Africa Lugard and his disciples elevated Indirect Rule to a doctrine. Margery Perham, then the foremost authority on Africa, contributed greatly to the theory's academic respectability.[78] It was attuned to the temper of the time, coming after the turbulent acquisition of the African colonies but before the reforms demanded by such critics as W. M. Macmillan and, implicitly at least, by W. K. Hancock.[79] The ideology of Indirect Rule inhibited ideas on the long-term political future of the

[76] See chaps. by John W. Cell; and by Toyin Falola and A. D. Roberts, pp. 518–19.

[77] A. D. Roberts, 'The Imperial Mind', in Roberts, ed., *The Colonial Moment in Africa: Essays on the Movement of Minds and Materials, 1900–1940* (Cambridge, 1990) p. 49.

[78] Margery Perham, *Native Administration in Nigeria* (London, 1937).

[79] W. M. Macmillan, *Africa Emergent* (London, 1938); Hancock, *British Survey*, but see also his *Argument of Empire* (London, 1943), which distills the more polemical element in *British Survey*. See also John D. Fage, 'British and German Colonial Rule', in Prosser Gifford and Wm. Roger Louis, eds., *Britain and Germany in Africa* (New Haven, 1967), pp. 699–704.

colonial system, while the system itself limited education and political opportunities. Though the British in its name sometimes restructured African societies, creating new 'tribes', on the whole it retarded rather than accelerated the forces of social change and thereby tended to perpetuate British overrule. Its principal significance was that of a rationale for British administration. Its pre-eminent assumption was the long-term character of British rule.[80]

After the Second World War the Colonial Office played the key part in the dismantling of Indirect Rule and in the attempt to 'democratize the Empire', or at least to shift to a system of local government based on principles more in line with British democracy. Local government would gradually lead to national self-government. The British would align themselves on the side of rising nationalism.[81] Pursuing such inspired goals, the Colonial Office entered the most original era in its history. In the words of one official, it was a time 'of unprecedented vigour and imagination', as men such as Andrew Cohen, the head of the African Department, attempted to reconcile, at least in theory, African nationalism with the aspirations of the white settlers in eastern and central Africa. The static concept of 'trusteeship' now acquired a new dynamic as 'partnership' in which different ethnic groups would co-operate in building harmonious and stable societies. The Colonial Office, however, brought to bear a historic predilection. From early on in the century, Colonial Office officials had been pro-African as well as anti-settler and anti-Indian in Africa. On the other hand, the Government of India defended the rights of Indian emigrants. The conflicting strains in British policy had the overall effect of containing white settler aspirations for self-government. In 1923 the Secretary of State for the Colonies, the Duke of Devonshire, had stated that in Kenya the interests of the Africans must be paramount.[82] The retreat from a settler state had begun, but in Kenya, as in central Africa, according to a Colonial Office official, it seemed 'unthinkable' that any British government 'would bring military force to bear upon a community of our own blood'. The stage was thus set for the conflict that continued between Africans and settlers in Rhodesia until 1980.

In most parts of the world, except the Pacific, the main outcome of British decolonization was clear by the mid-1960s. Africa remained the principal location of the drama despite the existence of other trouble-spots. From 1945 South-East Asia had also been a key area that preoccupied Colonial Office officials, but they

[80] See Roberts, 'The Imperial Mind', pp. 49–52. See also esp. S. R. Ashton and S. E. Stockwell, eds., *Imperial Policy and Colonial Practice, 1925–1945*, British Documents on the End of Empire Project (BDEEP), 2 vols. (London, 1996), I, chap. 3.

[81] See below, p. 524; and R. E. Robinson, 'Why "Indirect Rule" Has Been Replaced by "Local Government" in the Nomenclature of British Native Administration', *Journal of African Administration*, II, 3 (July 1950), pp. 12–15.

[82] 'One of the most famous and powerfully worded declarations of Imperial policy ever made.' See Ronald Hyam, chap. 11, p. 269; see also chap. by John Lonsdale, pp. 535–36.

saw Africa as 'the core of our colonial position'.[83] Modern states would replace colonies. The Commonwealth would replace the Empire. The Colonial Office anticipated that preparation for self-rule would take at least twenty or thirty years in the Gold Coast and Nigeria, and considerably longer in the east and central African territories. But the preparation for independence proved to be much shorter than expected. The Colonial Office believed it necessary to move at a fast pace to keep one step ahead of the demands by radical nationalists. By going faster rather than slower, and at the same time attempting to reduce the rate of nationalist acceleration, the Colonial Office hoped that nationalism could be constructively controlled. The tempo in Africa proved to be so rapid, however, that extremists had to be refurbished as respectable moderates. The era of independence in the 1960s came so suddenly that the flimsy infrastructure posing as 'modernity' generally collapsed into social and political units, with loyalties to leaders who were backed by militias.

The seventh and last theme deals with the defence of the Empire before the Second World War and the revolution in technology that occurred during and after the war.[84] 'We are a very rich and a very vulnerable Empire,' Neville Chamberlain wrote in early 1938, 'and there are plenty of poor adventurers not very far away who look upon us with hungry eyes.'[85] The strategic vulnerability can be summed up by stating that Britain could not fight a war simultaneously in the Far East, in the Mediterranean, and in Europe without disastrous consequences.[86] These large strategic issues are discussed in Chapter 12. In the inter-war years the Royal Navy remained the foundation of British power. The British army served in large part to secure the Empire internally and had a strength of 180,000, one-third of which continued to be stationed in India. The pre-eminent technological development was the growth of air power. In 1920 the Royal Air Force played a critical part in the defeat of Mohammed Abdallah Hasan, known universally in British circles as the 'Mad Mullah of Somaliland'.[87] The British maintained peace in the Middle East by a combination of aircraft, armoured-cars, and locally recruited troops: in words caricaturing Churchill's phrase, 'hot air, aeroplanes and Arabs'. On India's North-West Frontier, the RAF conducted 'Imperial policing' operations in remote mountainous areas. By 1930 there were RAF squadrons in Malta, Aden, and Singapore, as well as India, Iraq, and Palestine. In 1937 the RAF

[83] Ronald Hyam, ed., *The Labour Government and the End of Empire, 1945–1951*, BDEEP, 4 vols. (London, 1922), I, p. xxx.

[84] See chap. by Anthony Clayton.

[85] Keith Feiling, *The Life of Neville Chamberlain* (London, 1946), p. 336.

[86] See esp. Michael Howard, *The Continental Commitment: The Dilemma of British Defence Policy in the Era of the Two World Wars* (London, 1972).

[87] See chap. by Francis Robinson.

led the last campaign of colonial conquest in the hinterland of Aden.[88] Hilaire Belloc's line that

> Whatever happens we have got
> The Maxim gun and they have not

could now be extended to include the deadly firepower of aircraft. Yet civilian control over the military checked arbitrary or excessive reprisals. The doctrine of 'minimum force', as formulated by Churchill at the War Office in the early 1920s, exerted a profound influence on British military actions. There was usually strict control over orders to shoot, but the British military and police presence was effective.[89] On the eve of the Second World War British security forces still effectively kept the peace in the Empire. Only in 1938 did the army begin seriously to prepare for war in Europe. In the same year the great dry dock was formally opened at Singapore (though without vital workshops and other essentials). Overall, the British military structure was very much an Imperial force designed to defend the Empire, with a fleet that could be deployed to points of trouble, but without adequate air defence against Japanese bombers, and with light tanks more suitable for internal security than for combat against heavier German panzers.

During the Second World War the rapid development of technology had a virtually revolutionary effect on political as well as military communications within the Empire. By 1949 the Minister of Defence could travel to Hong Kong by a marathon three-day flight (Map 1.4). After a two-day flight from London, a businessman could arrive in Iran at the Anglo-Iranian Oil Company's Abadan refinery, the largest oil refinery in the world, and enjoy a full English breakfast of eggs and even bacon with copies of *The Times*. He could listen to the overseas programme of the British Broadcasting Corporation.[90] A Reuters correspondent staying in the same Gymkhana Club could report over the Company's wireless system how the community of 4,500 in the British enclave at Abadan responded to Egyptian guerrilla warfare against the military base at Suez, where some 80,000 troops were stationed. The Suez base in 1949 provides the principal example of British post-war military strength and sophisticated technology. It was the largest military complex of its kind, with radar and wireless communications centres, a network of roads, railways, harbours, and port installations, and hospitals, bakeries, sewage plants, ammunition dumps, airfields, and a flying-boat station.

The problem at Suez, as elsewhere, was how to secure the base against a hostile population. In the short term the British could usually cope with local

[88] See chap. by Francis Robinson.

[89] See chap. by Anthony Clayton.

[90] See chap. by John M. MacKenzie, pp. 218–19. For the beginnings of BBC broadcasting to India and the Dominions, see Asa Briggs, *The Birth of Broadcasting* (London, 1961), pp. 323–24.

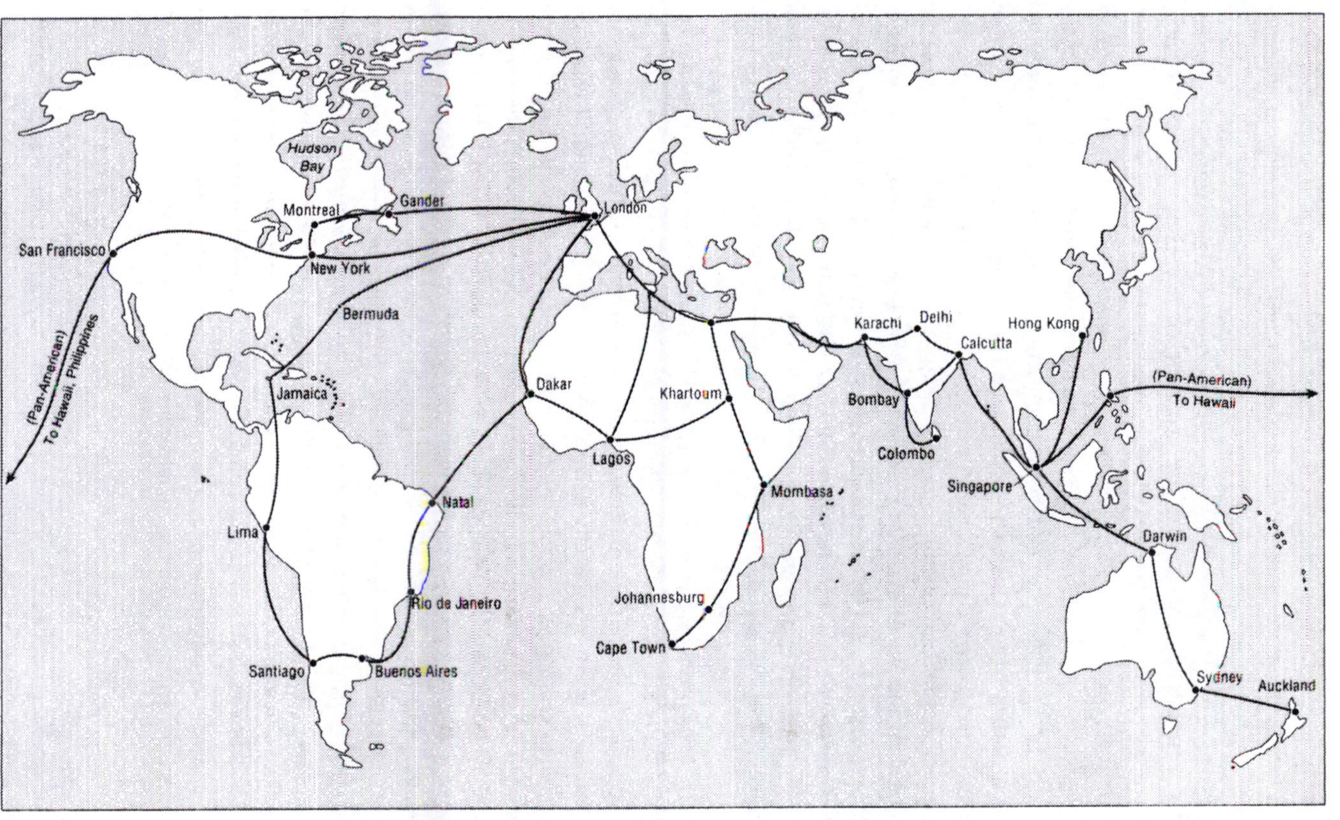

Map 1.4. Imperial Air Routes, 1920–50

insurgencies, as they did in Malaya, Cyprus, and Kenya, though they did not do so well in Palestine. By the 1950s and 1960s further advances in technology allowed the British to conduct counter-insurgency operations not only with land-based aircraft but also from the sea, with 'commando carriers' lifting Marines in helicopters. The Intelligence Corps of the army worked with the Special Branches or political surveillance arms of the colonial administration to provide an integrated civil, military, and police strategy to counter political subversion and guerrilla warfare.[91] But in the long term the British economy could not bear the cost. By the early 1960s the expense of air and naval equipment, of campaigns such as the fiasco in Aden, of the garrisons in South-East Asia and the Army on the Rhine—and not least the maintenance of a nuclear arsenal—had become intolerable for the economy. The political dissolution of the Empire, the economic breakup of the sterling area, and the military liquidation of bases came as a climax—to many as an anti-climax—in the late 1960s. The 1968 decision to withdraw forces East of Suez effectively marked the end of Britain as a global military and Imperial power. Within a period of three decades the Empire had been through the ordeal of emergency, renewal, and collapse.

With the conclusion of the seven themes, the book finds its half-way point with the chapter on the Second World War. The revival of Britain's Imperial mission began paradoxically with the fall of Singapore on 15 February 1942. At the beginning of the war, when there was scarcely strength to defend the home islands, the British were able to crack down on nationalists in India and Egypt and to mobilize the Empire to fight against Japan, Italy, and Germany. Cairo became the military capital of the British Empire.[92] In the Far East, however, the British met with disaster. The catastrophe occurred with the surrender of 16,000 British, 14,000 Australian, and 32,000 Indian troops at Singapore.[93] In Churchill's words, it was 'the worst disaster and largest capitulation in British history'. Soul-searching comment occurred in the British press. Margery Perham wrote in *The Times* in March 1942: 'The Malayan disaster has shocked us into sudden attention to the structure of our colonial empire. Events such as we have known in the last few weeks are rough teachers, but our survival as a great power may depend upon our being able to learn their lesson.'[94] Japan had brought about a revolution in 'race relationships' by destroying the myth of the white man's supremacy.

[91] See chap. by Anthony Clayton.

[92] See below, p. 318.

[93] See below, p. 474. The literature is extensive, but see esp. W. David McIntyre, *The Rise and Fall of the Singapore Naval Base* (London, 1979).

[94] Quoted in Wm. Roger Louis, *Imperialism at Bay 1941–1945: The United States and the Decolonization of the British Empire* (Oxford, 1977), p. 136.

Unless the British could bring about their own revolution in race relations and treat Asians and Africans as equals, according to contemporary critics, the Empire would be doomed. The ethos of the post-war Labour government between 1945 and 1951 embodied the premise of equality. The goals of post-war British governments could be achieved only by dealing with the peoples of Asia and the Middle East, and eventually those of Africa, on an equal footing. The colonial system could not be maintained by bayonets. The necessity to transform the Empire into a multirracial Commonwealth became an article of faith. In the post-war period the history of the Empire may be read as the attempt to convert formal rule into an informal basis of equal partnership and influence by means of the Commonwealth. The purpose of this transformation was the perpetuation of Britain as a great 'world power'. The British in the wartime period and the post-war decade saw that British power had declined in relation to that of the United States and the Soviet Union, but they did not generally believe that decline was irreversible.[95]

The depletion of British economic resources in the Second World War is a further theme of fundamental importance in the resurgence of the Imperial mission. The story hinges on the wartime Alliance with the United States. Britain emerged from the war virtually bankrupt and dependent on American financial support. In financing the war, Britain liquidated over £1bn of overseas investments and at the same time brought the general foreign debt to more than £3bn. There was a huge deficit in balance of payments. In Asia and the Middle East the principal creditors eventually holding favourable sterling balances were India (£1,100m), Egypt (£400m), and Iraq (£70m). In sum, the adverse sterling balances were equivalent to seven times the value of Britain's gold and dollar reserves.[96] After the war the United States extended a loan to Britain for $3.75bn, to which Canada added $1.25bn.[97] British economic survival seemed bound up increasingly with the hope that the colonies might now save the British economy through a protectionist system, and specifically through the exploitation of tropical territories.[98]

If the colonies were to be developed, not merely for the reciprocal advantage of the British and their subjects but also to sustain British power, then more money would be needed than was provided for under the terms of the Colonial

[95] On the issue of decline, see esp. Peter Clarke and Clive Trebilcock, eds., *Understanding Decline: Perceptions and Realities of British Economic Performance* (Cambridge, 1997).

[96] P. J. Cain and A. G. Hopkins, *Imperialism: Crisis and Deconstruction*, (London, 1996), hereafter *Crisis and Deconstruction*, p. 270.

[97] The Canadian loan was much greater in relation to the size of the economy, amounting to more than 10% of Canada's GNP in 1946. See chap. by David MacKenzie, p. 591.

[98] See chaps. by D. K. Fieldhouse as well as B. R. Tomlinson.

Development and Welfare Act of 1945.[99] The Act of 1945 provided £120m for the development of tropical agriculture, education, forestry, fisheries, water supplies, irrigation, and transport. Larger projects beyond 'colonial' development, such as the Egyptian High Dam at Aswan, for example, alone would cost, in the preliminary estimate, $1.3bn. Only the American economy, or perhaps the Russian, could bear such financing. The United States had long since become 'the single most important influence on world stability, growth, and development'.[100] British economic assistance paled in comparison but was effective within its compass, especially in the smaller colonial territories. In view of the convertibility crisis in 1947, the devaluation of the pound sterling from $4.03 to $2.80 in 1949, and the balance-of-payments crisis in 1951, the British demonstrated remarkable ability not merely to fund overseas projects but to manage the 'sterling balances', in other words, the money owed by Britain in the sterling area, in strict accordance with the needs of the British economy.[101] In the late 1940s the sterling area still accounted for one-half of all international monetary transactions.[102] People identified themselves as 'British' in part because of sterling.

The post-war period was one of severe austerity for the British people. The year 1947 was critical. The meat ration in England was cut by one-sixth. Bread was placed on ration for the first time. The private use of petrol was restricted. A ban was imposed on holidays abroad. Dairy products, fats, tea, sugar, and sweets were still under wartime ration. The Groundnuts Scheme, for the growing of peanuts in Tanganyika, was designed in part to ensure that 'the harassed housewives of Great Britain get more margarine, cooking fats and soap in the reasonably near future'.[103] Africa and the Middle East would replace India as new fields for development. It was not merely a question of India achieving independence. The economic relationship had eroded.[104] During the same year the British public had the impression that endless amounts of money were going down the drain in Palestine in military expenditures, not development. Palestine had become a major source of controversy between Britain and the United States. At specialized levels of government, however, British officials argued the case in Washington for large

[99] See D. J. Morgan, *The Official History of Colonial Development: The Origins of British Aid Policy, 1925–1945*, 5 vols. (London, 1980), II; also esp. Robinson, *Trusteeship*, and Ashton and Stockwell, *Imperial Policy*, II, chap. 4. For CD&W as a theme in this volume, see esp. the chap. by Howard Johnson.

[100] See below, p. 361, n. 9.

[101] See below, p. 613.

[102] Cain and Hopkins, *Crisis and Deconstruction*, p. 280.

[103] John Strachey, Minister of Food, quoted in David Fieldhouse, 'Decolonization, Development, and Dependence', in Prosser Gifford and Wm. Roger Louis, ed., *The Transfer of Power in Africa: Decolonization, 1940–1960* (New Haven, 1982), p. 488. See chap. by John Lonsdale, p. 450.

[104] See below, p. 439; See also B. R. Tomlinson, *The Political Economy of the Raj, 1914–1947* (London, 1979), chap. 3; and Michael Lipton and John Firn, *The Erosion of a Relationship* (London, 1975), chap. 2.

development schemes, sometimes affecting entire continents. The argument did not fall on deaf ears, but not simply for reasons concerning Africa or Asia. This was the era of the cold war, which profoundly affected the destinies of peoples throughout the world, economically no less than politically, from the mid-1950s when the dollar and the rouble began to compete in development projects.

The cold war worked generally to the advantage of the British Empire.[105] Despite its tradition of anti-colonialism, the United States buoyed up the British colonial system for cold war purposes until the mid-1960s. American dollars helped to sustain British power overseas by underwriting the balance-of-payments costs of British forces in NATO (the North Atlantic Treaty Organization) and, indirectly, the expense of British garrisons in the colonies. The United States eased the pressure for decolonization in return for assurances that the British would modernize as well as democratize the Empire. The cold war thus gave the British Empire an extended lease on life. American containment aims ran broadly parallel with British Imperial purposes. American attitudes reflected more than power politics. Apart from Irish and Jewish parts of the population, Americans knowledgeable of colonial affairs, including some historians,[106] were, on the whole, favourably disposed towards the colonial mission or at least to the work of the idealized, incorruptible British District Officer keeping an even-handed peace and helping Asians and Africans to improve standards of life.

Throughout the post-war era, despite the rift over Suez, the United States shored up the Empire as a defence against the Soviet Union and the possibility of Communist revolution from within. By the late 1950s, however, the colonies began to lose their economic attraction as the British economy revived and the false lure of quick development faded. The cost of maintaining the Empire against nationalist opposition now threatened to spin out of control. In the early 1960s the Prime Minister, Harold Macmillan, began to use the word 'Algeria' in comparison with Central Africa. The atmosphere of the cold war raised nationalist expectations. At the same time Britain's trading links with the Dominions weakened.[107] In 1961 the British made a first bid for membership in the European Economic Community. It took another twelve years before the application was accepted, but the British had already begun 'to abandon that ship [of Empire] and attempt to climb aboard another'.[108] The end of the colonial era saw not only the British entry into Europe as well as the withdrawal of troops East of Suez and the collapse

[105] See Wm. Roger Louis and Ronald Robinson, 'The Imperialism of Decolonization', *Journal of Imperial and Commonwealth History*, XXII, 3 (Sept. 1994), pp. 462–511.

[106] Notably Robert Heussler in *Yesterday's Rulers* (Syracuse, NY, 1963) and other works.

[107] Cain and Hopkins, *Crisis and Deconstruction*, p. 282.

[108] See below, p. 112.

of the sterling area, but also, it will be recalled, the Immigration Act of 1971, which removed the distinction between Commonwealth and foreign immigrants.[109]

In a complex subject such as the dissolution of the Empire, it is sometimes easy to lose sight of the individual, or to err on the other extreme by exaggerating the part played in the historical process by human agency. There were certain individuals in the last stage of the Empire who played as important a part as had Chamberlain and Milner in the early decades of the century. During the Second World War, Leopold Amery, who has already been mentioned, served as Churchill's Secretary of State for India. Amery's reputation has suffered because many have assumed that he shared Churchill's reactionary views on India. In fact Amery and Wavell, the Viceroy (1943–47), prepared the way for India's independence.[110] One of the great achievements of the Labour government of 1945–51, and specifically of C. R. Attlee, the Prime Minister, and Lord Mountbatten, the last Viceroy in 1947, was the granting of independence to India, but they built on the work for Amery and Wavell. India and Pakistan remained in the Commonwealth, thus setting the standard for the last two great practitioners of decolonization, Harold Macmillan, Prime Minister (1957–63), and Iain Macleod, the Secretary of State for the Colonies (1959–61). Macmillan at first kept an open mind whether or not the colonial system was an asset or a liability. He became convinced in 1959 that the Empire increasingly was becoming an albatross. In an age of superpower rivalry and colonial insurgency, the British economy could not sustain prolonged anti-nationalist campaigns, nor would the British public tolerate suppression. The specific job of decolonization was done mainly by Macleod, who moved at a pace in Africa almost comparable to the speed with which Mountbatten had wound up the Raj in India. Macmillan and Macleod together achieved a work of historic magnitude.[111]

The meaning of the cold war for the peoples of the British Empire is a theme that emerges in the second half of the volume. In a sense, the losers of the cold war included many countries in Asia and Africa as well as the former Soviet Union because the end of superpower rivalry saw a decline in economic assistance. Chapter 15 explores the nature of the post-colonial economy as well as the economic principles of the colonial system itself.[112] Two further chapters pursue topics on gender and on Islam that are essential in understanding the general

[109] See below, p. 57.

[110] For Wavell's part, see esp. the introduction by Penderel Moon in Penderel Moon, ed., *Wavell: The Viceroy's Journal* (London, 1973).

[111] See chap. 14 by Wm. Roger Louis.

[112] See chap. by B. R. Tomlinson.

context in several of the regional chapters.[113] Most of the chapters in the latter part of the book are organized by regions, covering the history of individual colonies from the beginning of the century, and most share a common theme on the rise of nationalism and the granting of independence by the British. These concluding introductory comments focus on that theme in each of the principal British parts of the world. Like the British in the Seven Seas, the chapters progress through seven regions: South and South-East Asia, the Middle East, Africa, the West Indies, Latin America, China, and the Pacific.

In this part of the book there are controversies as well as implicit judgements, notably on three subjects: the interaction of periphery and centre in understanding political and social change; the question of the origins of nationalism, and how men and women previously not involved in politics became nationalists; and the way in which the fate of the post-colonial states influences interpretation of the colonial period. These themes have a bearing on the ultimate question with which a book on the twentieth-century Empire must be concerned. How can the moral worth of the British Empire be assessed, taking for granted that some will regard empire itself as wrong or immoral? What of the structures in British colonies for keeping a measure of social and political order—the Pax Britannica in a large sense—that allowed social mobility, outside contacts, open markets, and a reasonably free press? These questions on the ethical justification of the Empire are predicated on the assumption of the desirability of orderly and efficient government as well as rule under law, the establishment of the courts, and the development of constitutions, which need to be mentioned if only to emphasize their later demise in Africa and elsewhere. Whether morally justified or not—for perspectives will vary—these things mattered.

The need for judgement is all the more necessary to counter two quite different interpretations of British rule, both at variance with the main themes of the volume. One is the belief that British decolonization was a planned and orderly process, as if from the beginning the British had intended to advance the colonies towards independence. As many of these chapters demonstrate, pressures in the colonies and at the international level have to be taken into account along with British policy and its critics. The British were by no means fully in control of events. The general conclusion is that the framework of law and government held long enough, with notable exceptions such as Palestine, Aden, and perhaps Ireland, for the British themselves to retreat in good order regardless of the consequences, for example, of the partition of India. The other view is held by those who wish to diminish the significance of the British Empire and maintain that British influence was merely ephemeral. Whatever the fate of British political

[113] See chaps. by Rosalind O'Hanlon and Francis Robinson.

institutions, the nation-state system is part of the European colonial legacy, and standards of British law and democracy at least continue to provide the measure by which governments are judged. In many ways, as these chapters make clear, the British legacy is lasting and substantial. Democracy in India is but one conspicuous example.

The chapters on the Dominions establish the perspective on nationalism, 'Britannic' as well as colonial.[114] That on Canada deals with a specific theme: 'The North Atlantic Triangle' of Britain, Canada, and the United States. The chapters on Canada, Australia, New Zealand, and South Africa all share the theme of the quest for equality within the British system. Embodied in the Statute of Westminster of 1931, the definition of Dominion Status set the context for the debate on the future of the British Empire both before and after the Second World War: the Dominions 'are autonomous Communities within the British Empire, equal in status, in no way subordinate one to another in any aspect of their domestic or external affairs...' One chapter deals specifically with the Commonwealth.[115] For the 'New Commonwealth' nations of Asia and Africa, Dominionhood eventually proved to be 'a distinctive blend of national status and Imperial identity'.[116]

Gender is important in this part of the volume no less than in the first part. In the sense that gender deals with the wider social relationship between men and women, it is a relatively new and useful field of research in the history of the Empire and helps to set other themes in relief. The lives and opportunities of generations of indigenous women in the colonies were profoundly affected by colonial rule.[117] Female labour was often critical in the profitability of colonial enterprise.[118] Colonial law substantially altered property rights and marriage.[119] Notably in India, but also in Asia generally and later in Africa and the Caribbean, women played an important part in the nationalist movements. As mentioned previously, the Empire offered employment and other opportunities for British women, who were, however, relatively few in number. They were in a sense an élite, of which there was a corresponding indigenous élite, often educated in mission schools and sometimes, in Egypt for example, more fluent in English or French than Arabic.[120]

The era of the British Empire in the nineteenth and twentieth centuries coincided with a period of Islamic revival and creativity.[121] Muslim attitudes towards

[114] See chaps. by David MacKenzie and chap. 30 by W. David McIntyre.

[115] See chap. 30 by McIntyre.

[116] See chaps. by John Darwin, David MacKenzie, Shula Marks, and chap. 30.

[117] See chap. by Rosalind O'Hanlon.

[118] See chap. by John Lonsdale.

[119] See Vol. III, see chap. by Susan Bayly.

[120] See Vol. III, chap. by Afaf Lutfi al-Sayyid-Marsot.

[121] See chap. by Francis Robinson.

the British varied from place to place according to Islamic circumstances and the variations of British rule.[122] By the turn of the century, educated Hindus and Buddhists as well as Muslims had reacted to Christian evangelism.[123] The British witnessed a resurgence not merely of Islam but also Hindu and Buddhist reform or revival movements. Religious reformers became dedicated anti-imperialists. From the First World War to the 1930s, Pan-Islamic movements challenged Western hegemony. In the Middle East the British cautiously helped to promote pan-Arabism, believing that Arab nationalism and British imperialism might be compatible. 'Dreams of Arab unity foundered on the nation-state system in the Middle East which the British Empire had done so much to create.'[124]

The critical period for Indian nationalism embraced the inter-war years, when the British were forced to reconsider many of their assumptions, not merely on the emergence of a modern Indian nation but also on the time-scale for political advance.[125] Ideas of racial superiority died hard. The British continued to regard Indians as divided by religion, caste, and language, and hence incapable of national unity. After the return of M. K. Gandhi from South Africa during the First World War, however, the British began to perceive that the nationalist movement had acquired high moral ground from which the British themselves were viewed as violent and repressive. The Indian National Congress appealed to a sympathetic international audience by demonstrating that it was a peaceful nationalist movement. By the end of the 1930s it was evident to many contemporaries that the Raj was becoming a thing of the past. The Indian economy was far less complementary to Britain's than even a decade previously. But despite weakened economic circumstances, the British held firm against Indian nationalism. There was no failure of British will, no excessive scruple about using force to crush the Quit India movement in 1942. The precipitate end of the Raj was caused by shifts in world politics and power, not by nationalist demands or liberal British intent. The termination of British rule in August 1947 came more quickly than most believed possible.

After 1945 the urgent question became: who would inherit the Raj? Before the war the slogan of 'Pakistan', a Muslim homeland, was scarcely heard, but the movement for a separate Muslim state thereafter gained increasing momentum. Although the British have often been blamed for the partition of the Subcontinent,

[122] See Ronald Robinson, 'Non-European Foundations of European Imperialism: Sketch for a Theory of Collaboration', in Roger Owen and Bob Sutcliffe, eds. *Studies in the Theory of Imperialism*, (London, 1972).

[123] See Vol. III, chap. by Susan Bayly.

[124] See below, p. 418.

[125] See chap. 18 by Judith M. Brown.

ultimately 'India was divided because the Indian nationalists wished it.'[126] The British had intended to leave India as a strong and united country locked into the Empire's defence and trading structures. In the end they reluctantly divided the continent and gave Muslims a truncated, two-winged Pakistan. Who were the beneficiaries? In Pakistan, Islam proved to be an ambiguous foundation for nationhood. In Britain, there was a sense of great relief. In return for a quick and decisive 'transfer of power', India and Pakistan would remain in the Commonwealth. In India, 'Congress inherited a secular state where the centre could become extremely powerful'.[127]

The phrase 'transfer of power' implies an orderly and planned progress of events in which the British presided over independence. It served British purpose to give the impression to the world at large that they remained in control of the process of decolonization in South-East Asia as in other parts of the world. But in Burma, Ceylon, and Malaya, as elsewhere, the British lurched from one crisis to the next, improvising rather than adhering to fixed ideas.[128] In all three countries the inter-war years, as in India, were the formative period, but the era of the Second World War was critical. In Ceylon the demand for independence did not emerge as the principal political aim until 1942. Ceylon co-operated with Britain during the war and, after the fall of Malaya, produced 60 per cent of the allies' natural rubber supplies. Would loyalty be rewarded by independence? Ceylon later developed the reputation of having been a 'model colony' in the years preceding independence, but the campaign against the British was acrimonious and substantial. It was accompanied by a rise in communal tension between the majority Sinhalese and the minority Tamils, both indigenous and Indian. The Colonial Office consequently viewed Ceylon as 'the most difficult problem' of the post-war era, and one complicated by India's impending independence.[129] The Colonial Office officials, nevertheless, did not feel bound by the precedents set by India and Burma, and Ceylon thus had paramount significance as the first transfer of power permitted by the Colonial Office.

Burma and Malaya were both conquered by the Japanese. In 1942 the leading nationalist in Burma, Aung San, returned with the invading Japanese army, convinced that Japan would further the cause of Burma's independence.[130] The Japanese in effect adopted the institutions of the British system and introduced a puppet regime in Burma, just as in Malaya the traditional rulers, the sultans, retained their positions and many of the Malay administrators kept their jobs. The Japanese interlude was probably less revolutionary than has been commonly supposed, but it dealt a blow to the reputation of the British and created

[126] See below, p. 411. [127] See below, p. 437. [128] See chap. 14 by Wm. Roger Louis.
[129] See chap. by S. R. Ashton, p. 460. [130] See below, p. 479.

complex allegiances. Local Communists began a struggle for supremacy. In circumstances of impending civil war, the assassination of Aung San in July 1947 doomed any chance of Burma remaining in the Commonwealth. '[T]he British never established a grip on developments in Burma after the reconquest but simply ran before the wind...'[131] Burma achieved independence as a republic in January 1948. The events in India and Burma stiffened nationalist resolve in Ceylon and inspired Communists as well as other nationalists in Malaya. Some ministers in the Labour government wanted to delay Ceylon's independence as long as possible, fearing that it would stimulate nationalist demands in Malaya, but in June 1947 the Cabinet calculated that it was better to guard against a drift to the left in Ceylon and consolidate the relationship with the conservative nationalists in return for a defence agreement guaranteeing access to the naval base at Trincomalee.[132] Ceylon thus became independent in early 1948. Malaya remained in a state of emergency, in effect a state of war against the Communists, from 1948. Here the British held on tenaciously, not merely to contain Communism but to earn dollars for the sterling area from rubber and tin production. Along with the Middle East and Africa, Malaya was part of the triple engine of British economic development in the post-war colonial world. Through intelligence operations, police measures, and psychological warfare the British defeated the Communists, one of the remarkable episodes in the cold war. A decade later than in India, Malaya received independence in August 1957, the same year that the Gold Coast achieved independence as Ghana.

The critical problems in the Middle East stretched back to the opening of the Suez Canal in 1869, the discovery of oil in Iran at the turn of the century, and the Balfour Declaration in 1917. As in South and South-East Asia, the inter-war years were crucial for the British in the Middle East, especially in Palestine. Had it not been for Hitler's persecution of the Jews and the Holocaust there would not have been the creation of the Jewish state of Israel in 1948. In 1945 the British still hoped to establish a bi-national state with a fixed proportion of about two-thirds Arabs and one-third Jews, with the guarantee of religious and political rights. Canada was often mentioned as a model for the bi-national state. But whatever the analogy, no solution could be found that was acceptable to the Arabs on the one hand, and the Zionists and the United States on the other.[133] In July 1946 Jewish extremists blew up the British military headquarters at the King David Hotel in Jerusalem. Palestine had become a British military and economic liability. In

[131] See below, p. 488.

[132] See below, p. 462.

[133] See below, pp. 410, 507.

February 1947 the Labour government referred the problem to the United Nations, and in the following September, in the wake of the severe economic crisis caused by the convertibility of sterling, decided to withdraw the British administration and military forces. In November 1947, against all British expectations, the United Nations voted in favour of partition. The British withdrew in May 1948 without designating a successor power, but the United States quickly recognized the new state of Israel and became its guardian. In a representative comment in the British press, the *New Statesman* lamented that President Harry Truman was 'a weak but very honest man' and had 'the typical American sympathy for the Jewish colonists struggling to achieve independence against the modern George III, and the typical American ignorance of Middle East realities'.[134] The American era in the Middle East had begun.

Two further seminal events in the modern Middle East were the nationalization of the Anglo-Iranian Oil Company in 1951, and that of the Suez Canal Company in 1956. In the case of Iran, British and American intelligence agencies in 1953 overthrew Mohammed Musaddiq, the Prime Minister of Iran. The involvement of the Central Intelligence Agency had lasting consequences. The United States gradually replaced Britain as the 'Great Satan' in the demonology of Iranian nationalism. In the shaping of Arab nationalism at about the same time, the ascendancy of Gamal Abdel Nasser after 1952 was critical. As a young military officer two events had a formative influence on Nasser: the humiliation inflicted on Egypt in 1942 by the British installing a collaborative government, and the defeat of the Egyptian army in the war against Israel in 1948. A charismatic orator, Nasser became the champion of the Arabs against Zionism and British imperialism. Nationalization of the Suez Canal Company in July 1956 was an act of defiance against Britain. In response the British government planned to use force if necessary to dislodge Nasser. The Prime Minister, Anthony Eden, in collusion with the French and Israelis, aimed to restore European hegemony in the Middle East. The invasion of Egypt in late 1956 was brought to an abrupt halt by the United States.[135] No other single event so divided post-war Britain as did 'Eden's war', which cut across party lines, disrupted common rooms, and even divided families. Had the British Parliament and public been betrayed by the government? Had Britain abandoned the United Nations? Had the 'imperial will' snapped just as victory was within Britain's grasp? The Suez crisis left an indelible mark on the collective consciousness of the British people. Nevertheless, the crisis quickly passed. In the Middle East tensions continued to increase. In 1958 the Iraqi revolution overthrew the

[134] Quoted in Wm. Roger Louis, *The British Empire in the Middle East: Arab Nationalism, the United States, and Postwar Imperialism, 1945–1951* (Oxford, 1984), pp. 530–31.

[135] See chap. by Glen Balfour-Paul.

pro-British regime and virtually ended, in Elizabeth Monroe's memorable phrase, 'Britain's moment in the Middle East'.

British rule in tropical Africa lasted scarcely longer, little over six decades. In West and East Africa the colonial state or the 'Leviathan Africanus' from early in the century had, with varying degrees of success, combated endemic diseases, built railways, roads, and wharves, kept the peace, and above all imposed customs revenues and collected taxes.[136] The underlying principle, as elsewhere, was that colonies should benefit Britain or at least pay their own way. Before the First World War medical advances had halved the death-rate among white officials in West Africa, but climate precluded white settlement. By contrast, in East Africa there were by 1914 over 1,200 British settlers in Kenya, already on its way to becoming known as a 'white man's country'. By the inter-war years inchoate modern states had come into existence in the four West African territories of the Gold Coast, Nigeria, Sierra Leone, and the Gambia, and in the East African territories of Kenya, Uganda, Tanganyika, and Zanzibar. In Uganda, for example, cotton earned two-thirds of the export income, Africans cycled to work, and in the Kingdom of Buganda alone there were 80,000 Baganda at school. In the West African territories literate Africans rose to high rank in government service and some prospered as businessmen, journalists, and lawyers. By 1945 African leaders such as Kwame Nkrumah, who had studied in the United States and was soon to return to the Gold Coast, demanded 'autonomy and independence'.

The British responded to nationalist pressure by introducing the same constitutional process as in the White Dominions, but they did so in a greatly compressed time-frame. When the Gold Coast became independent as Ghana in 1957, Nkrumah soon ruled in a manner even more authoritarian than the British Governors who had preceded him.[137] In both West and East Africa, nationalism did not merely or necessarily develop in an ethnic context but in the shared experience of separate colonial regimes that did not introduce democracy until late in the day. In Tanganyika the first elections were not held until 1958–59, only three years before independence. 'It was a late start in democracy.'[138] Could the British have done more to have prevented the later erosion of the rule of law? Certainly, though in view of the short period of colonial rule and the accelerated pace of independence, expectations for the post-colonial era were probably unrealistic. The overall judgment must be that 'the colonial past must bear some

[136] See chaps. by Toyin Falola and A. D. Roberts and by John Lonsdale. For the 'Leviathan Africanus', see Ronald Hyam, chap. 2, pp. 58–60.

[137] Nkrumah's authoritarian tendencies had been long apparent before independence. See Richard Rathbone, ed., *Ghana*, BDEEP, 2 vols. (London, 1992), II.

[138] See below, p. 541.

responsibility for failure'.[139] British expertise did continue for a time to be crucial in the armed forces, the police, the judiciary, and the professions.[140]

The case of South Africa demonstrates the advantages of viewing the colonial era in the framework of a 'long' twentieth century. In southern Africa, from the late-nineteenth century, South Africa dominated British attention because of the region's mineral resources. The discovery of gold established South Africa as a centre of wealth in the Empire at large. South Africa's influence in Africa extended far beyond its frontiers. There are two questions that connect with those of other chapters. Who would control the colonial state? Most whites thought that the main conflict was between Afrikaners and English-speakers. In the First World War, however, men of both groups fought in East Africa and in Europe, while in South Africa itself Afrikaner commandos helped to quell an Afrikaner rebellion. But a shared belief in white supremacy did not preclude sharp differences over the economy, language, and the relationship to the British Empire. The watershed came in 1948, when militant Afrikaner nationalists captured the state. They now found themselves confronted with a more dangerous contender in the form of African nationalism.[141] Black resistance to the pass laws spiralled into violence at Sharpeville in 1960 when South African security forces fired on demonstrators, leaving 69 dead and 180 injured. Sharpeville marked the beginning of a thirty-year international campaign against apartheid. The second question concerns British opposition to South African influence and resistance to the dominance of the white settlers in Southern Rhodesia. In the early 1950s the Central African Federation was created out of Nyasaland, Northern Rhodesia, and Southern Rhodesia to prevent South African regional domination and to counter African demands for majority rule with an alternative formula: 'power-sharing' or 'partnership' between blacks and whites. Economically a plausible case was made for federation. Africans in Northern Rhodesia and Nyasaland suspected, however, that the Federation would lead to the supremacy of white settler-dominated Southern Rhodesia. In 1963 the Federation was dissolved, and two years later Southern Rhodesia declared independence unilaterally. The prediction that the British government would not use military force against 'a community of our own blood' proved to be true. The Rhodesian conflict was not brought to a close until 1980. The apartheid regime in South Africa collapsed ten years later.

[139] See below, p. 528.

[140] See below, Falola and Roberts, p. 528. This is a theme that emerges also in chap. by Balfour-Paul: 'One thing... [the British] certainly failed to bequeath to the Middle East was the practice of western democracy.' But the British left a mark in many fields, 'administrative, developmental, education, judicial, agricultural, medical, in the transfer of technology, in frontier delimitation and over slave-trading', p. 513.

[141] See below, p. 555; chap. by Ronald Hyam, pp. 272–74.

The wave of nationalism and anti-colonialism that swept over Asia and Africa in the 1940s crested slightly later in the Caribbean. But a sense of 'black racial pride and identity' and of British colonial consciousness had existed there since the late nineteenth century. The First World War had heightened the racial awareness of soldiers who were subjected to humiliating discrimination while serving in the West Indies Regiment in Europe. A sergeant commented: 'We are treated neither as Christians nor British Citizens, but as West Indian "Niggers".'[142] In 1919 riots and strikes occurred in Jamaica, British Honduras, and Trinidad. By the end of the inter-war period labour disturbances were common and increasingly severe. Racial tension reflected underlying economic causes of distress. The British West Indian economy depended on a narrow range of agricultural exports. The price of sugar, the mainstay of the economy, plummeted sharply when world supplies exceeded demand. In the depression years of the 1930s the consequences were catastrophic. The historian W. M. Macmillan visited the region in 1935. In *Warning from the West Indies* (1936) he described the colonies as the 'slums' of the British Empire, characterized by poverty, disease, malnutrition, ignorance, and Colonial Office neglect.[143] He advocated the abandonment of the doctrine of minimal government, or 'trusteeship' that merely guarded but did not guide. He believed that the Caribbean colonies should be treated as if they were depressed areas of Britain. He urged not merely agricultural assistance but the creation of health services and education even at the university level. He insisted that the Imperial government face up to the financial responsibility. In 1938 outbursts of violent working-class militancy occurred in Jamaica.[144] The riots had a galvanizing effect in the Colonial Office, which feared not only Parliamentary criticism but also the unwelcome scrutiny of the United States.[145]

In the inter-war years New York City had become a centre for Caribbean political activists, the most famous of whom was Marcus Garvey, the Jamaican who founded the Universal Negro Improvement Association and proclaimed 'the beauty and dignity of being black'. Many of these writers and intellectuals came from Trinidad, Barbados, and British Guiana as well as Jamaica. Their influence extended not only to the Caribbean but to Africa. To them the United States represented a source of new and invigorating ideas and a means of exerting influence on the British colonial system.[146] By the time of outbreak of war in

[142] See below, p. 599.

[143] See below, p. 195.

[144] See John E. Flint, 'Macmillan as a Critic of Empire: The Impact of an Historian on Colonial Policy', in Hugh Macmillan and Shula Marks, eds., *Africa and Empire: W. M. Macmillan, Historian and Social Critic* (London, 1989), pp. 168–91.

[145] See chap. by Howard Johnson, p. 608.

[146] See Cary Fraser, *Ambivalent Anti-Colonialism: The United States and the Genesis of West Indian Independence, 1940–1964* (Westport, Conn., 1994), chap. 2.

1939 little progress had been made to implement plans for economic and social reform. But the establishment of American bases in the West Indies in 1940 brought in its wake the Anglo-American Caribbean Commission, which increased public awareness of the acute problems of the West Indies. The British now began seriously to plan for a regional federation that would hold together Jamaica, Trinidad, and Barbados as well as the smaller islands of the Leewards and Windwards. The aim was to promote a viable regional economy that would avert the danger of the islands becoming perpetual wards and would stop the drain on the British economy. The project had substantial popular support in the smaller islands, but especially in Jamaica public sentiment was sceptical and even hostile. The Federation came precariously into existence in 1958. The principal problem was that of finance. Jamaica and Trinidad contributed in about equal measure 85 per cent of the budget. Britain's financial responsibility for the smaller and less-developed islands would be gradually shifted to the larger islands. The refusal of Jamaica and Trinidad to bear the cost precipitated the breakdown of the Federation in 1962. As in the case of the Central African Federation, a federated territory would have made sense economically but could not be sustained without the willing participation of the component parts. From the 1940s onwards the hope had been that smaller units would merge into more economically viable federations. The crack-up of the West Indies Federation ominously indicated that the trend would be towards fragmentation and the birth of micro-states in the Commonwealth as well as in the United Nations.

The theme in Latin America, as in China, is Britain's 'informal empire', an empire of trade and commerce and various degrees of indirect political control. The concept of informal empire is the subject of historical revision and argument, in Latin America as in other parts of the world. Just as in the nineteenth century Britain had been the predominant free-trading nation, so in the twentieth the hegemonic power in Latin America was the United States, with US-style dollar diplomacy. It would not be an exaggeration to say that Latin America became to the US State Department what Africa was to the British Colonial Office. As in the novels of Evelyn Waugh and Graham Greene, the subject is not without a note of comic relief, though it provides serious scope for the study of Britain's dwindling economic and political influence. The Americans accused the British of 'blimpish complacency' and regarded Britain as a power 'in complete decline'.[147] Before 1914 British investment in Latin America had been more than in Australia, New Zealand, and South Africa combined.[148] Yet the United States had become commercially dominant in Mexico, took more of Brazil's exports than Britain, and had a growing stake in Peruvian and Chilean copper mining. Even in Argentina, the

[147] See chap. by Alan Knight, p. 637. [148] See Fig. 27.2.

bastion of British economic and political strength, American business was becoming a serious competitor by 1929 with a major participation in foreign debt, purchase of formerly British-owned utilities, and the entry of large US manufacturing multinationals.[149]

The First World War accelerated American economic penetration.[150] For Americans the opening of the Panama Canal in 1914 was an event comparable to the earlier opening of the Suez Canal. The establishment of direct American cable lines to Brazil and Argentina broke the British monopoly. In Mexico the British, along with others, suffered from the expropriation of foreign oil, railways, and real estate. By the mid-1930s, as the Nazi shadow fell across Europe, German ships with swastikas entered Latin American harbours. The British now stood behind the shield of the US Navy, but during the Second World War they also believed that the United States aimed not merely to defeat Germany and Japan but to supplant British interests.[151] In most of Latin America political leaders looked ambivalently to the United States, just as their grandfathers had looked to Victorian Britain. In Argentina and elsewhere, nationalists worked towards industrialization, economic protectionism, and social reform. The British complained of 'drivelling rhetoric' and 'chauvinistic foolishness', but they accommodated Latin American nationalism to maintain trade relations. In Argentina, as in Brazil and Uruguay, Britain after the war sold off assets of railways and utilities. 'In its small way, British "decolonization" of its South American "informal empire" appears to have been quite self-servingly adroit.' The 'imperialism of free trade' had come to the end of the line.[152] Yet there was one British relic of the nineteenth century that was not liquidated. In 1982 Britain went to war to defend the Falkland Islands against an Argentine invasion—'a throwback to an older era of violent confrontation'.[153]

Hong Kong also provides a connection with the late twentieth century, and one infinitely more significant than the Falklands. Yet Hong Kong was a backwater until 1945 if compared with the cosmopolitan centre of British trade and commerce, Shanghai. Before 1941 British investment in Shanghai was ten times greater than in Hong Kong. There was a basic distinction. Hong Kong was a British

[149] See Mira Wilkins, *The Emergence of Multinational Enterprises: American Business Abroad from the Colonial Era to 1914* (Cambridge, Mass., 1970) chap. 9; and also *The Maturing of Multinational Enterprise* (Cambridge, Mass., 1974), esp. chap. 7; and Rory Miller, *Britain and Latin America in the Nineteenth and Twentieth Centuries* (Harlow, 1993).

[150] See Vol. III, chap. by Alan Knight, p. 142.

[151] See chap. by Alan Knight, p. 639.

[152] The chap. by Alan Knight in Vol. IV as in Vol. III tests the thesis of Robinson and Gallagher, 'The Imperialism of Free Trade', but note the assumption: '"The Imperialism of Free Trade"... [is] an *ex post facto* historical induction, not an explicit guiding principle of British policy.' Vol. III, p. 129.

[153] See Knight, p. 623. Britain also had long-drawn-out border disputes with Guatemala over British Honduras and Venezuela over British Guiana.

colony; Shanghai was an international settlement and part of the larger network of Britain's informal empire. The British justified their presence in Shanghai and other ports on the basis of treaties that they had exacted from the Chinese. The treaty-port system sometimes represented the equivalent of colonial control because the concessions or enclaves in some cases gave Britain and other foreign powers absolute rights of extraterritoriality and local self-government. The British businesses in China, such as Jardine Matheson and Butterfield & Swire, had operations that extended far up the Yangtze and into other interior areas of China. British missionaries as well as British businessmen required protection. The problem for the Foreign Office in the inter-war years was not merely the disorder caused by bandits and warlords but the larger problem of how to accommodate growing Chinese nationalism.[154] In December 1926 the British turned from adamantly opposing nationalist demands to sympathizing with 'the legitimate aspirations of the Chinese people', including the abolition of extraterritoriality. The message of conciliation was the same as to the Indian National Congress, to the Egyptian nationalists, and later, with ever-increasing desperation, to African nationalists. The British would yield to the moderates before the initiative passed to the extremists, in this case the Chinese Communists. The outbreak of war between Japan and China in July 1937, and the loss of Britain's Far Eastern Empire during the Second World War doomed any chance of the revival of British businesses in most of China. Shanghai fell to the Communists in 1949. The last of the great British firms, Jardine Matheson, was squeezed out in 1954.[155] Hong Kong, which had been retaken by the British in 1945, survived as a British colony. In the post-war era a basic decision confronted the Colonial Office. Should Hong Kong be encouraged to acquire a separate identity and eventually become an independent city-state in the Commonwealth on the model of Singapore? Or should the British acknowledge that Hong Kong was essentially a Chinese port in which British rights would expire in 1997?[156] The decision to respect Hong Kong as part of China probably explains the success in Hong Kong becoming Britain's last major, and certainly most commercially valuable, colony.

The era of decolonization in the Pacific came later than in Asia and Africa, and the year 1975 may be used as a symbolic date. In 1975 Papua New Guinea became independent and joined the Commonwealth. Three decades earlier Franklin D. Roosevelt had remarked on 'head-hunters' in New Guinea still living in the 'stone age'.[157] His characteristically flippant comment reveals much about contemporary

[154] See chap. by Jürgen Osterhammel.

[155] See below, p. 665.

[156] See Wm. Roger Louis, 'Hong Kong: The Critical Phase, 1945–1949', *American Historical Review*, XIV, 4 (October 1997), pp. 1052–84.

[157] See Louis, *Imperialism at Bay*.

attitudes. Though he upheld the principle of self-determination, as had his predecessor Woodrow Wilson, Roosevelt was sceptical about its universal application. Neither Roosevelt nor virtually anyone else would have dreamed that New Guinea would achieve independence in so short a time. In 1961 the Australian Department of Territories continued to believe that New Guinea would remain a dependency at least until the turn of the century, perhaps forever. The idea of Commonwealth membership would have been inconceivable. How can the change in the temper of the times be explained? Part of the answer in regard to New Guinea is that in 1962 a UN Visiting Mission urged Australia to take steps towards representative government.

At the end of the Second World War there were two principal conflicting views in the Pacific on the region's future, one American and one Australian, with one point in common: 'Mother Britannia . . . was far away and in decline.'[158] The American view held that the wave of the future was with the United States, and many islanders seemed to agree, in part because during the war American troops had brought with them massive amounts of Coca-Cola and Spam as well as baseball. The camaraderie of American troops, which included black soldiers, left lasting impressions on the islanders. The Australian view, expressed most articulately by H. V. Evatt, the Australian Minister for External Affairs, held that Australia would inherit the British Empire in the Pacific but in a way that would be compatible with the idealism of the United Nations. New Zealanders shared neither the American nor the Australian outlook, though the Prime Minister of New Zealand, Peter Fraser, did believe along with Evatt that the United Nations would play an increasing role in the Pacific. In 1945 Fraser and Evatt became champions of the trusteeship system of the United Nations. The UN Trusteeship Council took over the functions of the League of Nations Mandates Commission, but had the additional power to despatch missions to trusteeship territories. The UN Visiting Missions played a significant part in the process of decolonization, especially in the Pacific, by accelerating the pace towards independence. Western Samoa is an outstanding example. The UN Visiting Missions, the first as early as 1950, helped to call international attention to Samoa's bid for nationhood, which had roots stretching back to the nineteenth century. The Samoans had a strong sense of historical consciousness. The nationalist movement, the Mau, which included Europeans, had become increasingly united in the 1920s and 1930s against the New Zealand administration.[159] As in other island groups, Christian churches helped to shape nationalist aims, which included the protection of land rights and village autonomy as well as independence. The New Zealand

[158] See below, p. 676.

[159] See J. W. Davidson, *Samoa mo Samoa: The Emergence of the Independent State of Western Samoa* (Melbourne, 1967).

government, committed to the principle of international trusteeship and sympathetic in any event to the proposition that the Samoans should be allowed to stand on their own, granted Samoa independence in 1962. The case of Samoa was critical, coming at the same time as the full flood of nationalism swept the African colonies into independence. In the 1960s the United Nations underwent a transformation of membership. Afro-Asian anti-colonialism now dominated the General Assembly. The Pacific in the 1970s became the last bastion of colonialism, with the United States and Australia along with Britain and France in the dock at the United Nations.[160]

The colonial revolution transformed the character of the Commonwealth, the Empire's institutional successor in which former British colonies freely associate as equal sovereign states.[161] Until 1947 the Commonwealth had resembled a white man's club consisting of Britain and the old Dominions of Australia, New Zealand, Canada, South Africa, and Ireland. The year 1947, when the question of India's membership arose, was the first of three critical years. There was substantial opposition within the British government to Indian membership. C. R. Attlee, the Prime Minister, overrode those attempting to block Indian entrance into the Commonwealth, and the Indians themselves decided in self-interest to remain within the British system. 'India's decision to stay proved the salvation of the Commonwealth', by breaking the dead hand of the white man's grip.[162] The next crisis came a decade later when Ghana became independent in 1957. Again there was resistance within the British government and officials gave considerable thought to granting 'mezzanine' or 'associate' status. The Governor in the Gold Coast, Sir Charles Arden-Clarke, informed the Colonial Office that Nkrumah would not accept anything short of full status. Ghana was admitted as a full member, thus paving the way for Nigeria and the other larger African states. The question now became one of 'smaller territories'. Until the late 1950s the Colonial Office, and the British generally, resisted the idea of independence for small colonies. The Commonwealth Relations Office quivered with anguish on the problem of how to prevent small countries from swamping the Commonwealth. The turning-point came in the third critical year, 1960, when Cyprus, with a population of only 500,000, became independent and achieved Commonwealth status. Thereafter the door was open to any colony, no matter how small, becoming independent and a member of the Commonwealth.[163] Malta became independent in 1965, the Maldive Islands in the same year, Mauritius in 1968, and

160 See below, p. 680.

161 See chap. 30 by W. David McIntyre.

162 See below, p. 696. See esp. R. J. Moore, *Escape from Empire: The Attlee Government and the Indian Problem* (Oxford, 1983).

163 See below, p. 680.

the Seychelles in 1976. The principle of self-determination reached its *reductio ad absurdum*—or, depending on one's point of view, its ultimate justification—in the Pacific. Fiji became independent in 1970, the Ellice Islands in 1978, the Gilbert Islands in 1979, and the New Hebrides (Vanuatu) in 1980. Not all immediately became members of the Commonwealth, but most eventually did.

The Commonwealth, like the Empire, has been through phases of decline and revival. It demonstrated its utility, especially to smaller members, through economic assistance, educational programmes, and professional associations, and as a pressure group at the United Nations resembling a club within a club. Perhaps its greatest significance is cultural, in the realm of football, cricket, and rugby, and in the domain of literature, where post-colonial novelists such as Salman Rushdie and other winners of the Booker Prize, and poets, such as the Nobel Laureate Derek Walcott, have invigorated the English language and added to the richness of its literature. When the post-apartheid state of South Africa rejoined in 1994, morale rose throughout the Commonwealth. The Commonwealth seemed to be recovering from a post-colonial slump, when its main value had been assessed, at least in Britain, as a psychological cushion for the loss of Empire.

We now live in a post-Britannic age, but there are remnants of Empire (Map 30.2). Two dependencies, Gibraltar and the Falklands, pose political problems with Spain and Argentina. Like the Falklands, the rest are islands, some with strategic significance. In the West Indies there are Montserrat, Anguilla, and the British Virgins, among others. In the Atlantic there are Ascension, Bermuda, St Helena, and Tristan da Cunha. In the Indian Ocean there are the Chagos or the Indian Ocean Territory with the military base at Diego Garcia. In the Pacific there is Pitcairn. All are reminders of a grand theme in world history.

Select Bibiliography

S. R. Ashton and S. E. Stockwell, *Imperial Policy and Colonial Practice, 1925–1945*, British Documents on the End of Empire Project (BDEEP), 2 vols. (London, 1996).

Max Beloff, *Imperial Sunset*, 2 vols. (London, 1969; 1989).

Judith M. Brown, *Gandhi: Prisoner of Hope* (New Haven, 1989).

P. J. Cain and A. G. Hopkins, *British Imperialism: Crisis and Deconstruction, 1914–1990* (London, 1993).

John W. Cell, *Hailey: A Study in British Imperialism, 1872–1969* (Cambridge, 1992).

D. K. Fieldhouse, *Economics and Empire* (London, 1973).

John Gallagher, *The Decline, Revival and Fall of the British Empire* (Cambridge, 1982).

Sarvepalli Gopal, *Jawaharlal Nehru: A Biography*, Vol. I (London, 1975).

W. K. Hancock, *Survey of British Commonwealth Affairs*, 2 vols. (London, 1937–42).

—— *Smuts*, 2 vols. (Cambridge, 1962 and 1968).

Michael Howard, *The Continental Commitment: The Dilemma of British Defence Policy in the Era of the Two World Wars* (London, 1972).

Denis Judd, *Empire: The British Imperial Experience, from 1765 to the Present* (London, 1996).

Anthony Kirk-Greene, *On Crown Service: A History of H. M. Colonial and Overseas Civil Services, 1837–1997* (London, 1999).

Wm. Roger Louis, *Imperialism at Bay, 1941–1945: The United States and the Decolonization of the British Empire* (Oxford, 1977).

D. A. Low, *The Eclipse of Empire* (Cambridge, 1991).

A. F. Madden, 'Changing Attitudes and Widening Responsibilities, 1895–1914', in E. A. Benians and others, eds., *Cambridge History of the British Empire*, Vol. III, *The Empire-Commonwealth, 1870–1919* (Cambridge, 1959).

Nicholas Mansergh, *The Commonwealth Experience* (London, 1969).

A. D. Roberts, 'The Imperial Mind', in A. D. Roberts, ed., *The Colonial Moment in Africa: Essays on the Movement of Minds and Materials, 1900–1940* (Cambridge, 1990), pp. 24–76.

Kenneth Robinson, *The Dilemmas of Trusteeship* (London, 1965).

Ronald Robinson, 'Non-European Foundations of European Imperialism: Sketch for a Theory of Collaboration', in Roger Owen and Bob Sutcliffe, eds., *Studies in the Theory of Imperialism* (London, 1972).

2

The British Empire in the Edwardian Era

RONALD HYAM

> Land of Hope and Glory, Mother of the Free,
> How shall we extol thee, who are born of thee?
> Wider still and wider, shall thy bounds be set;
> God who made thee mighty, make thee mightier yet.

These words—written as an ode for the coronation of King Edward VII in 1902 to accompany Elgar's brilliantly rousing music—became the transcendent anthem of Empire. In the popular imagination they may seem to symbolize Edwardian sentiment about the British Empire. In fact it is doubtful whether they did. Certainly to the man who wrote them they were purely 'occasional' and represented no sort of personal credo: A. C. Benson was a disenchanted Eton schoolmaster about to move to Cambridge, where he began the editing of Queen Victoria's letters and became a charismatic don. In later years, when Empire Day was becoming established, Benson was much in demand to make speeches for schools on 24 May. He always refused, confiding to his diary:

> The 'Empire', thus treated, leaves me cold. I think that most people have quite enough to do with thinking about their neighbour. How can little limited minds think about the colonies, & India, & the world at large, and all that it means?... The world at large, outside of the people I can actually touch & know, seems to me a great dim abstraction. I am not in the least interested in the human race, nor can I back our race against all races. I believe in our race, but I don't disbelieve in theirs.[1]

This confession may provide us with important clues as to how educated Edwardians, other than politicians and administrators, thought about the Empire. And there is a direct line of intellectual descent from Benson to Noel Annan, who recalled in 1990 that although the word Empire was officially coupled with 'duty' and 'heritage' in the years before and after 1914, 'These sentiments were not in fact shared by the country... which had always been bored with the Empire: on this

[1] Benson Diary, 1917, pp. 36–37, F/ACB/165, Magdalene College Archives, Cambridge.

matter a gulf yawned between the mass of the population and the ruling class. There were few imperialists among Our Age.'[2]

Of what did this Empire consist? It was made up of about 400 million people, of whom only 41.5 million lived in the UK, and 294 million in the Indian Empire. There were about 6 million elsewhere in Asia, 43 million in Africa, 7.5 million in the Americas, and 5.25 million in Australasia. There were 94 million Muslims (Map 17.1). The British ruled approximately one-quarter of the globe: 12 million square miles out of a habitable total of 60 million (Map 1.1). Or, to put it in terms of the enumerative lists beloved of contemporary authors of school geography textbooks, the British held sway over 'one continent, a hundred peninsulas, five hundred promontories, a thousand lakes, two thousand rivers, ten thousand islands'.[3] Represented as large swathes or myriad dots of pink-red on maps of the world, these extraordinary territorial facts gave the British people a sense of pride, all too often coupled with a notion of racial superiority. To some, the Empire really seemed to be ordained by God, an Imperial mission which was nothing less than a divine vocation. To others, the Empire was actually useful. It gave employment to officials, soldiers, traders, and missionaries. Large sums were invested overseas: somewhere between £3,100m and £3,700m by 1913, though not all of it was in the formal Empire. But attitudes towards Imperial problems have to be seen in perspective. And the qualified nature of interest in the Empire started at the top, for Edward VII was not as interested in Imperial as in European affairs. For most of the ruling élite, Ireland remained a more deep-rooted anxiety even than post-war South Africa. Again, 'it proved easier to bring peace to South Africa than to remove the grievances of the Free Churchmen under the Education Act of 1902'.[4] Educational issues, the House of Lords, temperance reform, and the suffragette movement excited and divided Edwardians more fundamentally than did the problems of the colonies. It was eccentric for an MP to argue against female suffrage on the grounds that it would shake the Empire as a great Muslim power.[5] In 1907 the second international Peace Conference at The Hague evoked more interest than the Colonial Conference held in London. Few Edwardians would have agreed with J. A. Hobson that the question of how one nation could properly help another to develop its resources was 'quite the most important of all practical questions for this generation'.[6] Though women had genuine Imperial roles as

[2] Noel Annan, *Our Age: Portrait of a Generation* (London, 1990), p. 32. For popular attitudes to Empire, see chaps. by John M. MacKenzie in this Volume and in Vol. III.

[3] William W. S. Adams, *Edwardian Heritage: A Study in British History, 1901–06* (London, 1949), p. 18, quoting *St James's Gazette*, 1901; *Census of the British Empire, 1901, P[arliamentary] P[apers]*, CII (1905).

[4] G. P. Gooch, *Under Six Reigns* (London, 1958), p. 123.

[5] Peter Clarke, *Lancashire and the New Liberalism* (Cambridge, 1971), p. 119.

[6] J. A. Hobson, *Imperialism: A Study* (London, 1902), p. 229.

memsahibs, missionaries, and teachers, not many of them entered into the debate about the Empire. Mary Kingsley's travels in and reflections upon West Africa, or Flora Shaw's articles on the Empire for *The Times*, were hardly typical examples of involvement, although there were as many as thirty-nine women out of the total 433 subscribing membership of the African Society (later the Royal African Society) in 1906.[7] However, out of fifty contributors to a major survey of the Empire in 1905, only one was female, the aforementioned Flora Shaw, by then Lady Lugard.

This 894-page compilation, entitled *The Empire and the Century*, was brought out as an assessment to celebrate, 'in the light of a national sacrament', the centenary of the naval victory at Trafalgar.[8] It was not a particularly triumphalist or polemical volume, but naturally enough the contributors found plenty to be proud of. W. F. Monypenny (a journalist with *The Times* and Disraeli's biographer) described the Empire as 'the truly representative State of the modern world, a very microcosm of the world at large', giving 'a certain catholicity, a truly cosmopolitan ideal' to the otherwise insular British people. India, he believed, was governed 'with an amplitude and, on the whole, an excellence such as the world has hardly seen before', and provided 'a shelter from anarchy for hundreds of millions of human beings'. The true relationship between Britain and India, wrote the explorer Francis Younghusband, should be one of 'manly comradeship'. A central essay in the volume dealt with the Imperial cable networks, 'the nerves of Empire'. Written by George Peel, it celebrated the fact that in not much more than a generation the British had girdled the world with 121,000 miles of cable, thus transforming the conduct of trade and diplomacy, and bringing together 'an imperial commonwealth' (Map 1.3). There were only seven maps in *The Empire and the Century*, six of them devoted to the cable networks by region (the seventh was a map of the River Nile). There was satisfaction too in the introduction of the Imperial penny postage. By 1903–04 12.5 million pounds weight of letters, newspapers, and circulars was despatched from the United Kingdom to the colonies, and 3.25 million pounds-worth was received in return. There was pride in the achievements of Anglo-Saxon settlements overseas. There was relief that South Africa had been 'retained for the Empire'. There was conviction that the challenge of ruling new tropical dependencies would be met.

Nevertheless, several contributors posed the question: 'will the Empire last the century?' J. L. Garvin, a leading journalist, doubted it: 'Despite the narcotic

[7] J. D. Fage, 'When the African Society was Founded, Who Were the Africanists?' *African Affairs*, XCIV (1995), p. 370.

[8] Charles Sydney Goldman, ed., *The Empire and the Century: A Series of Essays on Imperial Problems and Possibilities by Various Writers* (London, 1905).

optimism which is the fashion of the hour, national instinct recognizes that the answer is no foregone affirmative.' The concerns of contributors about this were reflected in a broad spectrum of British opinion. Chamberlain's striking phrase of 1902, 'the weary Titan staggers under the too vast orb of its fate', would not quickly be forgotten. Even within the sober corridors of the Colonial Office itself, the legal expert, H. B. Cox, wrote in 1906, 'The British Empire won't last another hundred years, if so long . . .' (earning himself a Churchillian rebuke from the Parliamentary Under-Secretary: 'such pessimism is unworthy of the C.O.').[9] From a rather different perspective, Rajah Charles Brooke, ruler of Sarawak, predicted in 1907 with almost uncanny accuracy: 'before we reach the middle of the century all nations now holding large Colonial possessions will have met with severe reverses . . . India to a certainty will be lost to us.'[10]

Pessimism was in fact an all-pervasive and quintessential characteristic of Edwardian thinking about the Empire. Their periodicals and journals were surprisingly full of defeatist talk.[11] The reason is not hard to find. The South African War (which used to be known as the Anglo-Boer War, 1899–1902) cast a sulphurously long and exceedingly sober shadow. The complacency of the pre-war years, the mindless jingoism of Mafeking night (17 May 1900), had comprehensively faded in the cold light of day, in the aftermath of the most important and divisive war of Empire since the loss of the American colonies, a difficult and humiliating conflict in which an Imperial army of a quarter of a million men had taken three years, at a cost of £270m (exclusive of post-war reconstruction), to subdue an amateur backwoods army from two archaic states whose combined (white) population did not exceed that of Flintshire and Denbighshire, as Lloyd George scornfully put it. The war had indisputably been conducted by 'methods of barbarism'. As L. T. Hobhouse wrote, the war in South Africa was the death-blow to the optimistic idea that the Englishman was the born ruler of the world: 'within a few years fear had definitely taken the place of ambition as the mainspring of the movement to national and imperial consolidation.'[12] The recruitment and performance of soldiers had revealed shocking physical deficiencies in working-class health. Three thousand young men had to be invalided back home on account of acutely bad teeth. Military blunders sparked off logistical investigations into the organization of the army. A drive for 'national efficiency' was given an irresistible momentum within the context of the need to re-engine the Empire. The formation of the Boy Scout movement was part of the fall-out; eugenics,

[9] Minutes, 1 and 3 April 1906, C[olonial] O[ffice] 225/71, no. 27566.

[10] Steven Runciman, *The White Rajahs: A History of Sarawak, 1841–1946* (Cambridge, 1960), p. 277.

[11] Bernard Porter, 'The Edwardians and Their Empire', in Donald Read, ed., *Edwardian England* (London, 1982), pp. 128–44.

[12] L. T. Hobhouse, *Liberalism* (London, 1911), pp. 216–17.

conscription, circumcision, county schools, 'imperial motherhood', the beginnings of the welfare state, naval reforms, and the proliferation of rifle clubs were also symptomatic of the largest reappraisal of national strength, health, and organization, Imperial strategy, and maritime power undertaken in Britain before 1945. For, as C. F. G. Masterman had declared in a resonating sentence, 'no amount of hectic, feverish activity on the confines of the Empire will be able to arrest the inevitable decline' if the metropolitan 'heart' did not put its house in order.[13] The days of an expanding Empire were over. For the moment, at any rate, there would be no 'wider still and wider': even Younghusband's Tibetan initiative in 1904 was repudiated.

On the Conservative and Unionist side of politics, pessimism arose largely from fears that they would be thwarted in their constructionist, consolidationist programmes for an 'imperial spirit', for Imperial federation and a supra-parliamentary council, which together might enable the Empire in the twentieth century to hold its own against the great, rising, land-based empires of Russia and the United States. Lord Selborne (First Lord of the Admiralty and then Lord Milner's successor as High Commissioner in South Africa) was convinced that an overly sentimental House of Commons must be bypassed: '*the* problem we have to solve is how to substitute some really Imperial Authority for the House of Commons as ruler of the Empire . . . the alternative is the end of the Empire.'[14] However, the ten years of Unionist government from 1895 to 1905, the heyday of the so-called 'New Imperialism', had produced a massive ideological reaction, a fierce and fundamental debate about the nature of the Empire and the 'best' form of what contemporaries called 'Imperialism', which thus became in Edwardian times a sharply contested category. It focused a division of opinion which went back to the Irish Home Rule Crisis of 1885–86. The Liberals argued that they would never have gone to war against Boer farmers in South Africa, let alone fought for the reconquest of the Sudan or control of the remoter North-West Frontier of India. These were 'unjust and uncalled for wars, the product of crude, boyish ambitions and unworthy policy' (F. W. Hirst). Concession-hunting in China was, said J. A. Hobson, 'the crowning instance of irrational government'. Sir Charles Dilke (the Liberals' so-called 'lost leader') reaffirmed the need to recall 'the true as against the bastard imperialism', the doctrine of self-government on which British rule should be based, 'remembered in Canada, forgotten in South Africa'.[15] The future Liberal

[13] C. F. G. Masterman, ed., *The Heart of Empire: Essays* (London, 1901), p. 24.

[14] D. George Boyce, ed., *The Crisis of British Power: The Imperial and Naval Papers of the Second Earl of Selborne, 1895–1910* (London, 1990), pp. 318, 349.

[15] S. Gwynn and G. M. Tuckwell, *The Life of the Rt. Hon. Sir Charles Dilke*, 2 vols. (London, 1918) I, p. 68. Compare Augustine Birrell, 'False imperialism is a new kind of religion of a most bastard order', quoted in R. Spence Watson, *National Liberal Federation* (London, 1907), p. 289.

Prime Minister (1905–08), Sir Henry Campbell-Bannerman, also articulated the notion of 'bastard imperialism' in 1899: 'We do not shrink from adding to [the Empire] if duty or honour compels us; but we abjure the vulgar and bastard Imperialism of... provocation and aggression... of grabbing everything even if we have no use for it ourselves.'[16]

Throughout the left wing there was a chorus of denunciation of the Unionist government's jingoistic policy as the form of imperialism most likely to damage the Empire.[17] It was 'insane and irrational' (J. A. Hobson), 'rash, costly, deadly' (John Burns), 'sham and harum-scarum' (F. W. Hirst), 'braggart' and 'jubilee' (Mary Kingsley), 'bombastic' (J. R. MacDonald), 'almost Prussian' (Lord Crewe), and 'hooligan' (Robert Buchanan). Lord Cromer called it 'commercial', in contradistinction to his own brand of supposedly 'philanthropic' imperialism. The humanitarian concerns of a wider public fed into this rhetorical barrage. The campaign against Chinese Labour in the Rand mines in 1905–06 and E. D. Morel's Congo Reform Movement powerfully focused attention on what was moral and acceptable and what was not.[18] Few critics actually rejected imperialism as such, like Wilfrid Scawen Blunt.[19] Most preferred to assert the need for a 'true' alternative, which would be more sympathetic, more humane, more democratic, a great moral force on the side of world peace, and perhaps a model for international progress.

The Unionists continued to propound 'a grand imperialism' as against what they saw as 'an insular socialism'. They remained committed to their programme as George Wyndham (a former Chief Secretary of Ireland) had defined it: 'The Empire must be defended; the Empire must be united; the manhood of the Empire must be safeguarded.' But in virtue of their convincing electoral victory in January 1906, the Liberals could prevail, and the ideological debate was in effect won by them. Inspired by Campbell-Bannerman's watchwords—encourage confidence, freedom, and responsibility, promote justice, liberty, and humanity, avoid privilege and monopoly—the Liberal view gradually pulled the administration of the Empire away from the more aggressive and centralizing methods. In 1913 Wyndham

[16] Sir Henry Campbell-Bannerman, *Speeches, 1899–1908, Reprinted from 'The Times'* (London, 1908), p. 10.

[17] In addition to those of Hobson and Masterman, the principal contemporary works include: F. W. Hirst, G. Murray, and J. L. Hammond, *Liberalism and the Empire: Three Essays* (London, 1900); Herbert Samuel, *Liberalism: Its Principles and Proposals* (London, 1902); J. R. MacDonald, *Labour and the Empire* (London, 1907); J. A. Hobson, *The Crisis of Liberalism: New Issues of Democracy* (London, 1909); for assessments by historians see Bernard Porter, *Critics of Empire: British Radical Attitudes to Colonialism in Africa, 1895–1914* (London, 1968), and H. J. Field, *Toward a Programme of Imperial Life: The British Empire at the Turn of the Century* (Oxford, 1982).

[18] On humanitarians, see Vol. III, chap. 10 by Andrew Porter.

[19] Wilfrid Scawen Blunt, *My Diaries: Being a Personal Narrative of Events, 1888–1914: Part II, 1900–1914* (London, 1920).

lamented, 'I think my Child—an Imperial spirit in England—is dead.'[20] And so it proved to be. Most Conservatives, except a diehard, imperial-federationist group, conceded defeat. The future would lie with the Liberals' loosely structured 'Commonwealth of free nations'. Consequently the Radical critique of Empire was mollified, and the Labour Party became more Imperial-minded. Policy towards the Empire became increasingly bipartisan as the century progressed, until for about twenty-five years after 1940 there was almost no serious difference between the British political parties.

The three principal achievements of the Liberal government in Imperial policy from December 1905 were the post-war settlement in South Africa, the Morley–Minto reforms in India, and the underwriting of the conference system as the focus of the emerging Commonwealth.[21] Of these, incomparably the most important was South Africa. Responsible government for the Transvaal (1906), the Orange Free State (1907), and the Union of South Africa (1910) were Imperial issues in which all ministers took an interest.

Posterity has tended to judge the Liberal government's South African policy harshly because it endorsed a system which precluded any enlargement of African political participation and restricted the Union Parliament to white MPs. Secretary of State Lord Crewe had not actually believed a uniform franchise was necessary, and in a way this may have preserved a Cape 'native' franchise which might easily have been swept aside. It certainly is not true that the British government was unconcerned about protecting African interests. Moreover, it is difficult to see what course ministers could have taken other than accepting the South African plan, granted that their predecessors had accepted a fatally compromising clause in the Treaty of Vereeniging (1902) which prevented the native franchise from being dealt with until after the introduction of self-government for the Boer republics. Crewe would have preferred to have 'a new charter for Zululand', but if they were not to wreck unification altogether there was no hope of pressing white South Africans to do more than they were prepared to do. In any case, he believed that the submerging of Natal in a wider entity must provide relief for the hard-pressed Zulu. What the Liberal government did achieve for African rights, against not only the ardent demands of the white South Africans but also against the strong recommendation of the High Commissioner, was the retention of control over the three High Commission Territories of Basutoland,

[20] J. W. Mackail and Guy Wyndham, *The Life and Letters of George Wyndham*, 2 vols. (London n.d.), I, p. 115, and II, pp. 540, 734.

[21] Ronald Hyam, *Elgin and Churchill at the Colonial Office, 1905–1908: The Watershed of the Empire-Commonwealth* (London, 1968); J. E. Kendle, *Colonial and Imperial Conferences, 1887–1911* (London, 1967); S. R. Mehrotra, *India and the Commonwealth, 1885–1929* (London, 1965), chap. 1; for the Morley–Minto reforms, see also Vol. III, chap. by Robin J. Moore.

Bechuanaland, and Swaziland. Crewe stuck firmly to the line that their unconditional transfer to the Union was 'absolutely out of the question'.[22] They even managed to rescue for the Swazi one-third of their land, which had been entirely swallowed up in concessions. The Liberals thus set the pattern of British relations with southern Africa for the next seventy years or so: a determination to try to maintain good relations with the Union government despite deepening disgust with its native policy; together with careful concern that the High Commission Territories should not fall victim to South African expansion; and maintenance of British strategic as well as economic interests.

In India, the reforms of John Morley (Secretary of State) and Lord Minto (Viceroy) offered a programme of 'order plus reforms', which might prepare for eventual self-government, but 'not in their own day'. Definite but limited concessions were made, establishing the principle of representative government in the provinces. Morley saw a clear difference from Unionist and Curzonian policy, which he regarded as basically one of mere order without reform, and he wanted to get away from two ideas he regarded as equally stupid: that they should merely keep the sword sharp, or merely concede straightaway the principle of 'one man one vote'. Liberal reforms should be cautious but genuine. They would try to allow Indian political expression. They would try to be friendly and to train 'moderate' Indians such as G. K. Gokhale in habits of political responsibility. Such, at any rate, was the theory. Yet Morley remained 'cool and sceptical about *political* change, whether in India or other places'.

In fact the Liberal Cabinet and many pundits shared this scepticism. There was distinct uncertainty in the Edwardian era about what the best policies for non-European peoples might be. Perhaps the best thing was not to aim to do too much but to concentrate on protecting them from violence and expropriation, gin and brandy (L. T. Hobhouse). Although Lord Elgin, an underrated Secretary of State (1905–08), was keen to inaugurate a sympathetic and comprehensive study of native policy, he was removed from office only a few weeks after launching his initiative, which was in consequence never properly followed through. Such theorizing as there was merely confirmed policies of 'developing native institutions on native lines' and what became known as Indirect Rule.[23] Not even the sharpest commentators (Hobson, Morel, MacDonald) had any alternative to propose. The pervading pessimism simply precluded anything more dynamic.

Scepticism about the value of constructive political action also largely explains why the government rejected elaborate schemes presented to the Colonial Con-

[22] Lord Crewe to H. W. Massingham, 25 Sept. 1908, Crewe Papers, C/38, University Library, Cambridge.

[23] See chap. by John W. Cell.

ference of 1907, held amid the full panoply of Edwardian entertainment. After a surfeit of gargantuan luncheons and dinners (one of them upon a vast Union flag carpet in the Albert Hall), a waggish colonial Premier said he did not know if the Empire needed a new constitution, but its leaders certainly did. Plans for an Imperial Council and a permanent secretariat to service it were thrown out. Instead, what emerged was an institutionalization of the system of periodical conferences of Prime Ministers from the Dominions (a new term). The future shape of the Commonwealth was not finally decided in 1907, but it was clear what that future form was going to be. All-in-all, 1907 can be regarded as a decisive turning-point.

Of course none of these specific policies for the Empire was evolved in a vacuum. The international context was all-important, not least in South African unification, for it was believed that in a general war Germany would exploit South African divisions from her springboard in South-West Africa. At least as early as 1906 (and 1904 in the Admiralty), it was accepted in Whitehall that a German war seemed to be inevitable. France and Russia were by 1907 incorporated into a surprising new alliance structure, although worries about the security of India remained. Foreign Secretary Sir Edward Grey had 'an overwhelming sense of an impending storm in India' (1908). Containment of a freshly arising Japanese threat was elegantly solved by the conclusion of an alliance in 1902, even if some regarded it as a Faustian pact. The unexpected defeat of Russia by Japan in 1905 was an electrifying event, which the historian A. F. Pollard thought surpassed in significance even the South African War. The 'slumbering East' had awakened, and how long would it be before the 'yellow hordes of Asia' would turn against the West?[24] A cleverly written anonymous booklet entitled *The Decline and Fall of the British Empire*, purportedly issued in Tokyo in 2005 and translated, but actually published in Oxford in 1905,[25] forecast the scenario: 'India has fallen to Russia, South Africa to Germany, Egypt to the Sultan, while Canada has taken shelter beneath the wings of the American Eagle, and Australia has become a protectorate of the Mikado.' Although arguing that it was international competition which had made the collapse of the British Empire a messier business than the end of the Roman Empire, the writer echoed Gibbon in emphasizing British decadence. The country had become 'too effete and nerve-ridden' as a result of the 'false system of education prevailing', in which public schools 'presented the nation with thousands of genial athletes, but did very little to provide study of present-day problems'.

[24] M. V. Brett, ed., *Journals and Letters of Viscount Esher*, 3 vols (London, 1934), II, pp. 350–51; A. F. Pollard, *The History of England: A Study in Political Evolution, 55 BC–AD 1911* (London, 1912), pp. 224–25.

[25] Author unknown: the pamphlet is not listed in Halkett and Laing, *Dictionary of Anonymous and Pseudonymous English Literature*.

Behind all these apprehensions loomed the United States, now also manifestly an expanding power, and the new economic giant. By 1914 American exports to the Empire had reached £160m, and the proportion was increasing by leaps and bounds. Of all the changes in the world, the international role and status of the United States probably carried the biggest implications for the British global position. The First World War would only be won with American aid, but American intentions were widely distrusted.

Other perceived long-term threats included Islam, especially in Africa. Its 'fanaticism', which later generations learned to call fundamentalism, and the propensity of its radical leaders to proclaim jihad (holy war), were bogeys to informed experts, which they sought to head off by encouraging more conservative religious élites. Nor was there any confidence that non-Muslim Africans might not mount massive rebellions, though in fact the Natal uprising of 1906–08 proved to be the last of its kind.

To meet the German naval threat in home waters the entire disposition of Imperial naval resources throughout the globe was revised, with major ramifications for the Empire. The withdrawal of five battleships from the Far East (as part of the closure of the Pacific station) in 1905 has been seen by Northcote Parkinson as 'the turning point', the effective beginning of the road to the disastrous fall of Singapore in 1942.[26] West Indian and North American naval squadrons were also withdrawn, leaving only the Channel, Atlantic, Mediterranean, and Eastern commands.

In this tense international situation, the Dominions seemed unlikely to give as much help as Britain would have wished. Not merely were they reluctant to contribute to the escalating costs of Imperial defence; they had no real grasp of the effect of pursuing their own local objectives, such as a separate Australian navy. H. B. Cox complained witheringly at the time of the negotiation of the New Hebrides Condominium with France: 'The Australians, who have never had to face any diplomatic difficulty, seem to think we can treat France as if she were Tonga or Samoa.'[27] The Prime Minister of Newfoundland, Robert Bond, was thought to have behaved with wilful disregard for diplomatic courtesies and American susceptibilities in the dispute over the access of the United States to fishing rights in Newfoundland. Natal was disapproved of in 1906 for treating her Zulu population in a dangerously unacceptable manner: 'the hooligan of the British Empire', in Churchill's famous phrase. Colonial leaders, such as Australia's Alfred Deakin and Canada's Wilfrid Laurier, were disliked as touchy, brash, swaggering, and socially boring. Others were thought to be mere practitioners of

[26] C. Northcote Parkinson, *East and West* (London, 1963), pp. 230–34.

[27] Minute, 19 March 1906, CO 418/44, no. 8653.

'vestry politics'. Lewis Harcourt (as Secretary of State) in 1911 was disdainfully prepared to consider establishing a separate permanent under-secretaryship for Dominion affairs: 'these social vanities of the new rich must be reckoned with and pandered to unless and until they can be convinced of the folly of their foibles.' Ogden Nash, it seems, was right: the British attitude was distinguished by 'their affection for their colonies and their contempt for the colonials' (see his poem, 'England Expects'). Colonial attempts to restrict Indian and Japanese immigration were a particular worry. Several observers across a spectrum of opinion, from W. S. Blunt to Sir Charles Lucas of the Colonial Office, believed that colonials could not be trusted and brought opprobrium upon Britain: that the British would soon be forced to choose between the Colonial Empire and the Indian Empire, between the self-governing Dominions and the Japanese alliance, and, worst of all, between the Empire and the emerging supposed 'special relationship' with the United States. Thus it was not, they thought, Afro-Asian nationalists who would one day destroy the Empire, but the white colonials, who would bring this about by their sheer stupidity, brutal insensitivity to non-European races, and parochial inability to view any problem either in its essential wider Imperial perspective or within the overriding realities of international relations, seen as becoming increasingly ominous.[28]

Nevertheless, it was equally the case that Whitehall was more insensitive than it should have been to the valid aspirations of young new nations. It was not easy to appreciate the dynamics of Dominion political development when they could not treat with perfect seriousness the cultural pretensions of Melbourne, Vancouver, or Auckland, let alone understand why Afrikaners might want to speak Afrikaans, or Greek Cypriots join in union with Greece (*enosis*). As one civil servant wrote to Richard Jebb in 1899: 'there is a sort of conspiracy of silence about our colonies . . . really, all the colonies are extremely one-horse affairs, with one foot in the grave and the other in the sands of fraudulent speculation, and quite unable to run for a day without British help. That is my view of them.'[29] Jebb, then engaged on a comprehensive tour of the white colonies, came to know better, but his perceptions revealed a man before his time. He could understand that Canada and Australia, New Zealand and white South Africa were 'new nations bursting the colonial chrysalis', that they 'possessed the potentiality of a separate national career'. The phenomenon of white colonial nationalism helped to focus and

[28] Memorandum, 'Suggested Reconstruction of the Colonial Office', April 1911, Bodleian Library, MSS Harcourt Lewis Papers, Box 7; minute by C. P. Lucas, 4 Jan. 1907, CO 194/271, no. 197.

[29] Quoted in John Eddy and Deryck Schreuder, eds., *The Rise of Colonial Nationalism: Australia, New Zealand, Canada and South Africa First Assert Their Nationalities, 1880–1914* (Sydney, 1988); this book, which has a brilliant introductory chap. on the Edwardian Empire, revolves around discussions of Richard Jebb, *Studies in Colonial Nationalism* (London, 1905).

legitimize processes of state-evolution in the maturing Dominions. But it was a qualified and ambiguous force, a local patriotism seeking self-rule and self-respect, but unwilling to break its links with 'the Mother Country' or the chain of 'Anglo-Saxon power and progress encircling the globe'. This was a form of nationalism lacking confrontational attitudes to the metropole. It was also predicated on ethnic exclusiveness. All colonial societies around the Pacific Rim, fearing the 'yellow peril', were determined to be 'white man's countries'. The maintenance of 'White Australia' was even identified in 1919 by her Prime Minister, W. M. Hughes, as a primary war aim: Australia had gone to war 'to maintain those ideals, which we have nailed to the very topmost of our flag-pole'.[30]

If relations between the metropolitan power and the white colonies were ambivalent, a much purer field for Imperial endeavour seemed to exist in those other sectors of the periphery inhabited by Asians and Africans, many of whose countries had only recently come under the flag as a result of international partitions. In describing the establishment of Imperial rule, modern historiography is dominated by the concept of 'the colonial state'. Notable Governors, such as Sir Frank Swettenham in Malaya or Sir Hesketh Bell in Uganda, could be important in its formation ('lighting the dark places', as they saw it), but the colonial state was an entity compounded of elements other than a government supervised by the metropole; it also had to establish its own legitimacy with the populations it coerced and ruled. The terminology is perhaps unfortunate, as 'colonial' is here employed with a deliberately pejorative overtone, and divorced from the older meaning which restricted it to places of white settlement. It might have been better to follow J. S. Furnivall's appropriation of Hobbes's term 'Leviathan' (as the personification of a masterful modern state), and conceptualize a new 'Leviathan Asiaticus'[31] or 'Leviathan Africanus' as appropriate.[32]

[30] Quoted by Avner Offer in Eddy and Schreuder, *Rise of Colonial Nationalism*, pp. 240–41.

[31] J. S. Furnivall, *The Fashioning of Leviathan: The Beginnings of British Rule in Burma* (Canberra, 1991), repr. from *Journal of Burma Research Society*, XXIX (1939), pp. 3–137. For the colonial state in Asia, see Nicholas Tarling, ed., *Cambridge History of Southeast Asia*, Vol. II, *The Nineteenth and Twentieth Centuries* (Kuala Lumpur, 1992), chaps 2 and 3; F. A. Swettenham, *British Malaya: An Account of the Origin and Progress of British Influence*, revised edn. (London, 1948); R. H. Taylor, *The State in Burma* (London, 1987), chap. 2; Michael Adas, *The Burma Delta: Economic Development and Social Change in an Asian Rice Frontier, 1852–1941* (Madison, 1974); Lim Teck Ghee, *Peasants and Their Agricultural Economy in Colonial Malaya, 1874–1941* (Kuala Lumpur, 1977), chaps 2 and 3; P. J. Drake, 'The Economic Development of British Malaya to 1914: An Essay in Historiography', *Journal of South-East Asian Studies*, X (1979), esp. pp. 272–76; P. H. Kratoska, 'The Peripatetic Peasant and Land Tenure in British Malaya', ibid., XVI (1985), pp. 16–45; and esp. T. N. Harper, *The End of Empire and the Making of Malaya* (Cambridge, forthcoming), chap. 1 and 'The Politics of the Forest in Colonial Malaya', *Modern Asian Studies*, XXXI (1997), pp. 1–29.

[32] For the colonial state in British Africa, see Bruce Berman and John Lonsdale, *Unhappy Valley: Conflict in Kenya and Africa*, 2 vols. (London, 1992), Book 1, *State and Class*; Crawford Young, *The*

This new Leviathan, although far from omnipotent, brought profound changes to indigenous peoples. At its most basic level it represented a shift from society to state, from local linkages of regulatory social integration to networks of rationalizing bureaucracy and intrusive policing, ever-widening and ever-tightening in their grip. This Leviathan was more interventionist in economic life than Western states were in their own home-bases. Priority was given to increasing productivity, often with strict control and direction of labour. This Leviathan was an obsessive cartographer. New state boundaries were invented, sometimes with disconcertingly straight lines; within them, too, new rural boundaries were drawn to pin down pastoralists (such as the Masai in Kenya) or control peripatetic forest cultivators (like the Orang Asli in Malaya). This Leviathan, backed by technological superiority in weapons, by accumulating knowledge,[33] self-confidence, and reams of paperwork, penetrated more intensively into the lives of individual peasants than traditional governments had ever been able to do. This was principally felt as a hugely increased burden of taxation, either imposed for the first time or collected with a much greater efficiency. A famous passage in James Scott's *The Moral Economy of the Peasant* makes the point well:

> To follow the development of the colonial regime is to follow the inexorable progress of cadastral surveys, settlement reports for land revenue, censuses, the issuance of land title and licences, identity cards, tax rolls and receipts, and a growing body of regulations and procedures. The collection of revenue was the end of much of this activity... Although it may be possible to exaggerate the official reach of established colonial regimes, there is little doubt that, compared to the kingdoms they replaced, they left few places to hide.[34]

The introduction of ideas of equality before the law and Western systems of justice were crucial. 'The rule of Leviathan is the rule of law' (Furnivall). Those who did not conform were put into jails or lunatic asylums. In India, 'criminal castes and tribes' were categorized. Leviathan's policemen seemed omnipresent, leaving 'no place to hide' indeed. Rival jurisdictions were destroyed and the state asserted a sole prerogative to take life. Leviathan also aimed to impose uniformity of land law, from Nigeria to Fiji. There were benefits here: the protection of land rights and

African Colonial State in Comparative Perspective (New Haven, 1994); J. Forbes Munro, *Africa and the International Economy, 1800–1960* (London, 1976), chap. 4; John Iliffe, *Africans: The History of a Continent* (Cambridge, 1995), chap. 10; R. E. Robinson, 'Non- European Foundations of European Imperialism', in Roger Owen and Bob Sutcliffe, eds., *Studies in the Theory of Imperialism* (London, 1972), pp. 117–42; Joan Vincent, *Teso in Transformation: The Political Economy of Peasant and Class in East Africa* (Berkeley, 1982), and 'Prolegomena to the Study of the Colonial State', in Ronald Cohen and J. D. Toland, eds., *State Formation and Political Legitimacy* (New Brunswick, NJ, 1988).

[33] Thomas Richards, *The Imperial Archive: Knowledge and the Fantasy of Empire* (London, 1993).

[34] James C. Scott, *The Moral Economy of the Peasant: Rebellion and Subsistence in South-East Asia* (New Haven, 1976), p. 94.

insistence on leasehold tenures rather than freeholds in West Africa and Uganda were valuable paternalist measures on behalf of indigenous interests, although they did not always reflect the position land had previously occupied in traditional society.

The transforming impact of Leviathan often came in the form of cash-cropping, which again was far from being merely exploitative. Huge areas of the Burma Delta were given over to rice, of forest Malaya to rubber, of the Gold Coast to cocoa, of Uganda to cotton. Large irrigation projects were established at Krian in Malaya and Gezira in the Sudan. For many of these areas, somewhere between 1901 and 1917 was their 'first development decade'. Leviathan was a keen provider of a transport infrastructure: a thousand miles of railway in British Africa between 1906 and 1911 alone, a trunk network for Malaya by 1910, and 1,599 miles of rail for Burma by 1914, all built and run by the state. India had 32,000 miles of railway by 1910, and 1,500 under construction. Swettenham's aim was 'great works: roads, railways, telegraphs, wharfs'. The state began in this period also to establish forestry departments (for conservation and management), public health departments, and the first government schools. Tropical diseases were tackled energetically, though as John Iliffe has noted, government had more success against epidemic diseases (smallpox, sleeping sickness) than endemic diseases (leprosy, bilharzia), which affected the workforce less.

Underpinning all this activity was a self-conscious professionalization of bureaucracies. In post-conquest or post-pacification societies, the European civil services had been hastily created mainly out of whatever materials were to hand locally. These were frequently of a low character: ill-educated, incompetent, and eccentric at best, unsavoury and megalomaniac at worst. In Malaya, for example, there was C. F. Bozzolo, a promiscuous Italian who had worked at digging the Suez Canal; Hubert Berkeley, who seduced the girls from a nearby orphanage; Tristram Speedy, who dressed up in Ethiopian robes and played the bagpipes to astonished Chinese tin-miners; and Hugh Low, who lived with a gibbon and a Malay girl. In Africa, there was 'Chirupula' Stephenson, who took more than one African wife and had eight children by them. All this began to change as Whitehall imposed its own iron rules of discipline, hard work, and more efficient tax-collection. Following the model of the Indian Civil Service, examinations were introduced for recruits, and the ensuing takeover of colonial civil services by Oxbridge and public school men produced a profound change. They were not just more professional, but more conformist, more socially distanced from indigenous populations.[35] Tough new rules were introduced, first in Burma

[35] J. de Vere Allen, 'The Malayan Civil Service, 1874–1941: Colonial Bureaucracy-Malayan Élite', *Comparative Studies in Society and History* (hereafter *CSSH*), XII (1970), pp. 149–78.

(1903), then throughout the Empire, to disconnect officials sexually from local populations. The redefinition and rewriting of the sexual protocols were fundamental in the construction of the colonial state. Leviathan was a tremendous prude, deeply agitated about the dangers of mixed race unions (*métissage*). In fact all European regimes clamped down on these, the French and Portuguese famously excepted. In the British Empire this came definitively in the shape of the Crewe Circular on Concubinage (1909), which warned officials that taking local concubines would jeopardize careers. The background to this lay in a number of unpleasant scandals in Kenya and Rhodesia.[36] So overheated did the prurient atmosphere and puritanical backlash become that even the Chief Justice of Grenada, J. B. Walker, was suspended on charges of 'moral delinquency', which were not in fact upheld by the Judicial Committee of the Privy Council.[37] Social distancing also expressed itself in Indian hill stations and new types of planned town. Leviathan promoted urbanization and then agonized over segregation. He was rather attracted to it, largely on grounds of hygiene (the 'sanitation syndrome'), but was never entirely convinced by it. However, separate urban locations were certainly not confined to southern Africa, but were also being set up in Nairobi and Kampala, Nigeria and Hong Kong.[38]

In the long term, the fashioning of these new Leviathans provided the framework within which Afro-Asian nationalist protest was effectively articulated, and within which alternative 'post-colonial' states could be constructed. African and Asian headmen, lawyers, soldiers, policemen, clerks, teachers, and traders, operating within the new colonial states, and initially colluding with them, began to use Western languages, methods, and opportunities to further their own interests and redefine their own ideologies and ethnicities: a process which John Lonsdale has called 'the vulgarization of state power'.[39]

Responses to emergent African and Asian nationalism went through a critical phase in the Edwardian era. It was difficult for many of the British élite to come to terms with. Like so much else in the Empire, initial responses were forged in the

[36] Ronald Hyam, 'Concubinage and the Colonial Service: The Crewe Circular (1909)', *Journal of Imperial and Commonwealth History*, XIV (1986), pp. 170–86. See also J. G. Butcher, *The British in Malaya: 1880–1941: The Social History of a European Community in Colonial South-East Asia* (Kuala Lumpur, 1979); Ann L. Stoler, 'Making Empire Respectable: The Politics of Race and Sexual Morality in Twentieth-Century Colonial Cultures', *American Ethnologist*, XVI (1989), pp. 634–60, and 'Sexual Affronts and Racial Frontiers: European Identities and Cultural Politics of Exclusion in Colonial South-East Asia', *CSSH*, XXXIV (1992). pp. 514–51; John D. Kelly, *A Politics of Virtue: Hinduism, Sexuality and Countercolonial Discourse in Fiji* (Chicago, 1991).

[37] Memorandum, 'The Case of J. B. Walker', Crewe Papers, C/52, 3 March 1908; see also I/2, no. 10 (1911) for prostitution in the Indian Army.

[38] M. W. Swanson, 'Sanitation Syndrome: Bubonic Plague and Urban Native Policy in the Cape, 1900–09', *Journal of African History*, XVIII (1977), pp. 387–410.

[39] Berman and Lonsdale, *Unhappy Valley*, pp. 36, 192.

crucible of Irish experience. Viscount Goschen (a Chancellor of the Exchequer) had dismissed the Home Rule agitation as a fraud, a 'bastard nationalism', thus setting the precedent for tackling nationalist movements simply by denying their validity.[40] In this way India could be dismissed as 'a geographical expression', 'no more a united nation than the Equator' (Churchill); Egypt was just a 'fortuitous concourse of international atoms'; the 'voiceless millions' of each were allegedly content with the Pax Britannica. To Curzon, the Indian National Congress was 'an unclean thing', absurdly unrepresentative of the people, led by a 'microscopic minority', and 'tottering to its fall'. Non-Europeans in general, and Egyptians in particular, were held to be incompetent and lacking in character: every experiment in transferring administrative departments to their control only seemed to prove it. What was good as a system of government for Britain or its White Dominions was said not to be necessarily suitable for universal export. Morley expressly ruled out Canadian and South African constitutional analogies as irrelevant to India. The British might be able to do business with 'moderates', but most nationalists appeared to be 'extremists', and these, whether in Dublin, Cairo, Delhi, or Lagos, it was simply not possible to conciliate, 'save on terms which in India and Ireland spell political suicide, and in Egypt would involve a relapse into all the misgovernment and disorder of the past' (Cromer). All this psychological blockage was cemented together by a personal dislike, a derogatory rhetoric against nationalist leaders. Again, this went back to Unionist vilification of the Irish leader C. S. Parnell. Curzon denounced Surendranath Banerjea as 'that vitriolic windbag'. Cromer blamed all protest in Egypt on the Khedive personally. Sheikh Muhammad Abdille Hassan of Somaliland was referred to by everybody as 'the mad Mullah'.[41]

Congress, however, did not totter to its fall. Nationalists eroded the legitimacy of the colonial state, and the Empire did not last the century. The Empire came to an end, not from any failure of metropolitan will or from white colonial machinations, still less any physical degeneration of the British race. International pressures contributed to eventual decolonization, but these were not quite those of Edwardian apprehension. The devastating imperatives came not from the successful competition of other expanding powers, but from shifts in the world economy, the costs of world war, and an international critique of 'colonialism' developed after 1945 and vociferously promoted in the United Nations in the context of the

[40] L. P. Curtis, Jnr., *Coercion and Conciliation in Ireland, 1880–1892: A Study in Conservative Unionism* (Princeton, 1963), pp. 408–10.

[41] Speech by Lord Cromer, 28 Oct. 1907, Cromer Papers, F[oreign] O[ffice] 833/25, p. 99; speech by Lord Curzon, 28 March 1892, *Parliamentary Debates*, III (Lords), cols. 65–67; S. Gopal, *British Policy in India, 1885–1905* (Cambridge, 1965), p. 297; see also R. L. Tignor, *Modernization and British Colonial Rule in Egypt, 1882–1914* (Princeton, 1966).

cold war. If there was any international competition it was, after 1959, a scramble to dismantle the Empire and not be left in the last ditch with Portugal. Meanwhile, both before and after 1914, what was striking about the British Empire was not its slow or continuous decline, but its continuing transformations and renewals. The challenges of the twentieth century, many of them skilfully identified by the Edwardians, were tackled resourcefully, and not always unsuccessfully.

Select Bibliography

D. George Boyce, ed., *The Crisis of British Power: The Imperial and Naval Papers of the Second Earl of Selborne, 1895–1910* (London, 1990).

John Eddy and Deryck Schreuder, eds., *The Rise of Colonial Nationalism: Australia, New Zealand, Canada, and South Africa First Assert Their Nationalities, 1880–1914* (Sydney, 1988).

Charles Sydney Goldman, ed., *The Empire and the Century: A Series of Essays on Imperial Problems and Possibilities by Various Writers* (London, 1905).

Ronald Hyam, *Elgin and Churchill at the Colonial Office, 1905–1908: The Watershed of the Empire-Commonwealth* (London, 1968).

A. F. Madden, 'Changing Attitudes and Widening Responsibilities, 1895–1914', in E. A. Benians and others, eds., *Cambridge History of the British Empire*, Vol. III, *The Empire-Commonwealth, 1870–1919* (Cambridge, 1959), chap. 10.

Ged Martin, 'The Idea of "Imperial Federation"', in Ronald Hyam and Ged Martin, *Reappraisals in British Imperial History* (London, 1975), chap. 6, pp. 121–38.

Bernard Porter, *Critics of Empire: British Radical Attitudes to Colonialism in Africa, 1895–1914* (London, 1968).

——'The Edwardians and Their Empire', in Donald Read, ed., *Edwardian England* (London, 1982).

G. R. Searle, *The Quest for National Efficiency: A Study of British Politics and Political Thought, 1895–1914* (London, 1971).

Nicholas Tarling, ed., *Cambridge History of Southeast Asia*, Vol. II, *Nineteenth and Twentieth Centuries* (Kuala Lumpur, 1992), chaps. by C. A. Trocki and R. E. Elson.

3

A Third British Empire? The Dominion Idea in Imperial Politics

JOHN DARWIN

In the twentieth century, as in the eighteenth, the cohesion of the British Imperial system in a highly unstable environment was the central problem of Imperial politics. Few world empires escape for very long the threat of dissolution from external attack or internal disruption. The longevity of British imperialism owed much to the forces of economic and cultural attraction which underpinned its political expansion as well as to the great demographic tide which had flowed out from the home islands after 1815. But it also depended upon holding an exceptionally delicate balance between the conflicting interests of what had become by 1914 a huge and extremely variegated Empire.

To survive at all as a political unit, the Imperial system had two fundamental requirements: an effective means of Imperial defence and the co-operation of political allies in all its assorted colonial and semi-colonial hinterlands. Without the loyalty or collaboration of settlers, sultans, sheikhs, chiefs, zamindars, nawabs, and 'creole' or 'Anglo-Oriental' élites in the Caribbean, West Africa, and South Asia, the Second British Empire would have suffered the same fate as the First. But collaboration abroad was only part of the Imperial problem: there also had to be collaboration at home. Imperially minded interests in Britain needed friends and allies in domestic politics prepared to meet the costs of Empire—especially its defence costs. Time and again, they also needed supporters who would accept the constitutional and ideological flexibility needed in the management of Imperial politics and for the containment of colonial nationalism. It was for this latter reason that the 'Dominion Idea' came to play such an important part in the construction of a Third British Empire in the twentieth century.

The fullest scholarly treatment of Britain's relations with the White Dominions between the wars is R. F. Holland, *Britain and the Commonwealth Alliance, 1918–1939* (Basingstoke, 1981). The indispensable account of inter-war Imperial politics is John A. Gallagher, *The Decline, Revival and Fall of the British Empire: The Ford Lectures and Other Essays*, ed. Anil Seal (Cambridge, 1982). Some of the ideas in this chap. can be found in an earlier form in John Darwin, 'Imperialism in Decline?' *Historical Journal*, XXIII, 3 (1980), pp. 657–79 and 'Durham in the East? India and the Idea of Responsible Government, 1858–1939', *Journal of Canadian Studies*, XXV, 1 (1990), pp. 144–61.

The mid-Victorians had solved the problem of Imperial cohesion by a bold series of pragmatic compromises. Discarding the fiction of cultural unity which had been the principle of adhesion in the First British Empire, they presided robustly over a tripartite world system. In the settlement colonies a wide local autonomy (reserving mainly defence, external relations, and constitutional change to the Imperial centre) had been conceded by the 1850s (somewhat later in South Africa). Here, strategic dependence, demographic links, cultural ties, and economic attraction coexisted amicably with strong provincial identities within the capacious framework of responsible government. In the dependent Empire and India, where economic and cultural attraction could not be relied upon, Imperial control deployed a variable mixture of coercion and collaboration. In India, British rule required a despotic edge to extract military resources and impose an open economy in the interests of Lancashire. But the Raj also became increasingly alert to the social fears of the rural élites upon whose co-operation it chiefly depended, and devised an elaborate system for consulting the mosaic of castes, communities, religions, and interests which made up its fragmented vision of Indian society. The third mode of British imperialism was 'informal empire', a vast residual category comprising spheres of interest and influence as diverse as Argentina, Egypt, and the Yangtze valley. Here, where annexation was impracticable or superfluous, commercial or strategic interests were sustained by private enterprise or an erratic combination of diplomacy and force. The supreme virtue of this eclectic approach was that it allowed the politicians at home to reconcile a voracious expansionism with fiscal parsimony and free-trade economics. Both were regarded as essential to the political and social stability of a rapidly industrializing economy under conditions of representative government.

The Second British Empire fashioned by the Victorians had been flexible enough to accommodate the great expansion of tropical Empire after 1870. But by the turn of the twentieth century its stability was under attack from many quarters. The profound sense of strategic insecurity which surfaced during the South African War implied that the sprawling decentralized Empire of the Victorians was a luxury that could no longer be afforded. Imperial defence demanded closer Imperial co-ordination to help defray its escalating costs. In the White Dominions, the conventional limits of responsible government, especially in external affairs, were challenged by colonial leaders whose sub-imperialist ambitions and racial fears demanded a larger voice in Imperial foreign policy. This new colonial assertiveness was complicated by two somewhat contradictory impulses: an awakening sense of British or perhaps 'Britannic' identity, the product of social change, ethnic anxiety, and the excitement of the Boer War; and the mobilization of French Canadians and Afrikaners against fears of political submergence or cultural absorption.[1] In India, the administrative despotism of the 'guardians' came under increasing attack from the Western-educated élite whose leaders denounced the 'Unbritishness of British rule' as well as from cultural nationalists whose objections to British rule were more fundamental. Their fusion in the struggle against the partition of Bengal helped propel the Edwardian Raj towards enlarging Indian political participation, while fiscal and administrative pressures encouraged it to toy with schemes for provincial devolution. The third source of Imperial discontent was to be found at home in the metropole. There the Victorian Imperial regime was denounced by a vociferous campaign calling for Tariff Reform and what Milner called the 'unity of the British race'—a reunion of the 'British nations' in a grand Imperial federation.

For all the Edwardians' constitutional experimentation in India and South Africa and the Imperial confabulations in 1907, 1909, and 1911, the essential character of the Victorian Imperial system survived almost unaltered until the First World War. There was no general redefinition of Dominion Status, no reconstruction in India, no abandonment of free trade, no Imperial federation. The Edwardian stalemate also precluded activating Irish Home Rule. The log-jam was broken only by the war, whose corrosive effects broke over the Second British Empire as much as they did over the *anciens régimes* of continental Europe. The result was not to shatter Imperial power as it was shattered in Russia, Austria-Hungary, Germany, and Turkey. But the dynamic phase of Imperial politics between 1917 and 1926 progressively demolished the Second British Empire and ushered in a new Imperial system. In that short period the constitutional status of the White Dominions was redefined; the political foundations of British India were transformed, projecting its eventual elevation to Dominion Status; the Union dissolved and an Irish Dominion set up; a new Middle East empire acquired; and crucial decisions taken on the political future of West, East, and Central Africa. Nor was the Imperial centre exempt from this new age of flux. After 1918 a mass electorate, unemployment, and financial stringency transformed the domestic political stage where Imperial interests had to be defended, and slowly cleared the way for the overthrow of free trade. By 1931, the year of the Import Duties Act, the Statute of Westminster, the Second Round Table Conference, and going off the gold standard, scarcely any important feature of the mid-Victorian Imperial regime remained.

In the twentieth century British world power came to depend more and more upon partnership with the White Dominions. By contrast with the nineteenth

[1] See Carl Berger, *The Sense of Power: Studies in the Ideas of Canadian Imperialism, 1867–1914* (Toronto, 1970); John Eddy and Deryck Schreuder, eds., *The Rise of Colonial Nationalism: Australia, New Zealand, Canada and South Africa First Assert Their Colonial Nationalities, 1880–1914* (Sydney, 1988).

century, when they were regarded in London as so many liabilities, in the era of the two world wars their economic resources, manpower reserves, and political fidelity turned them into vital Imperial assets. Not surprisingly, many of the most thoughtful British imperialists came to regard Anglo-Dominion relations as the key Imperial problem, and their continued adhesion to the principle of Imperial unity as worth almost any constitutional concession.

If British leaders had doubted the military value of Dominion assistance before 1914, by the middle of the war they had learnt their lesson. Collectively, the Dominions contributed armies as large as those of India, which had a population more than twenty times greater.[2] Canada alone was to send some 400,000 men to the Imperial war effort, sustaining casualties equal to those of the United States. Australian and New Zealand troops in the Middle East, South African in East Africa, as well as on the Western Front were an indispensable addition to British and Indian military power—regarded before 1914 as the Empire's defensive backbone on land. Australia, South Africa, and New Zealand also undertook regional military campaigns against German possessions in South-West Africa and the South Pacific. Because their foreign relations were an Imperial prerogative, the Dominions had found themselves at war with the Central Powers involuntarily. But the scale of their military contribution and its management were a different matter: inevitably they became the central issue of Dominion politics. In South Africa, Botha's invasion of South-West Africa was the pretext for a major Afrikaner revolt which threatened briefly to explode into civil war.[3] Even after its suppression, the sharp growth in nationalist (that is, anti-imperial) sentiment made overt subservience to Imperial direction politically undesirable. In Australia, which shared with New Zealand the travails of Gallipoli and whose economy was acutely dependent upon the economic and financial management of the war in London, W. M. Hughes, the Prime Minister, combined a passionate rhetoric of Britannic unity with the conviction that a fundamental Imperial reorganization was required.[4] In Canada, after the early phase of patriotic enthusiasm, commitment to the war increasingly demanded a sense of *national* involvement: it was no longer enough to be a loyal colonial auxiliary.[5] Each of the larger Dominions had its own urgent reasons for assuming a more visible part in the overall direction of the Imperial war effort.

Although both Robert Borden, Prime Minister of Canada 1911–20, and Hughes had been allowed to attend meetings of the British Cabinet in 1915 and 1916, it was

[2] See below, pp. 117–19.

[3] South African Government, U[nion] G[overnment] 46; 1916 *Report of the Inquiry into the Recent Rebellion in South Africa*, pp. 82–83.

[4] L. F. Fitzhardinge, *The Little Digger, 1914–1952* (Sydney, 1979), pp. 83–89.

[5] R. M. Bray, 'The English-Canadian Patriotic Response to the Great War', *Canadian Historical Review*, LXI, 2 (1980), pp. 97–122.

David Lloyd George's palace revolution in December 1916 which opened the way for a recognition of Dominion nationhood. Lloyd George's programme was the unlimited mobilization of British and Imperial resources to win the war. He, perhaps with an outsider's grasp of Dominion feeling, saw realistically that deeper Dominion sacrifices made the fuller political involvement of their leaders vital. Significantly, he recruited to his War Cabinet the Ishmaelite of Edwardian politics, Lord Milner, who stood for full economic organization at home and recognition of Dominion influence in a reconstructed Empire. When Dominion leaders were invited to London early in 1917, they seized the opportunity to assert a new theory of Dominionhood. Rejecting Milnerite ideas of Imperial federation, they called for 'full recognition of the Dominions as autonomous nations of an Imperial Commonwealth, and of India as an important portion of the same...', and demanded 'the right of the Dominions and India to an adequate voice in foreign policy...'. These claims were embodied in the celebrated Resolution IX of the Imperial War Conference, which looked forward to a full post-war overhaul of the Imperial constitution.[6]

The immediate preoccupation of Dominion Premiers in 1917 had been the enhancement of their own status as war leaders facing mounting social and ethnic stresses at home as the effects of the military struggle became more pronounced. It was natural that they should lay greatest emphasis upon sharing in the strategic and diplomatic direction of the war effort. At the Armistice, the Imperial War Conference which had sat again in 1918 transmuted itself into the British Empire Delegation at the peace conference. But with the signature of peace in June 1919, Dominion interest in the co-ordination of foreign policy waned rapidly. The project for a grand conference to redefine Imperial relations was abandoned. The fiasco of Churchill's call for Dominion military help during the Chanak crisis in September 1922 prompted the sharp assertion of a Dominion's claim to conduct its own foreign policy by the Canadian government of William Lyon Mackenzie King. Appeals for Dominion contributions to post-war Imperial defence fell on deaf ears. By 1923–24 it had been established that the Dominions were not bound by treaties signed only by the Imperial government; that they could sign treaties on their own behalf—as in the Canadian–American Halibut Treaty of 1923; and despatch diplomatic agents to foreign countries. Only Australia showed any enthusiasm for the better liaison between British and Dominion foreign policy provided for in 1923. In 1926 the lapidary phrases of the Balfour Report on Inter-Imperial Relations, written largely at South African and Irish behest, affirmed the

[6] Frederick Madden and John Darwin, eds., *Select Documents on the Constitutional History of the British Empire and Commonwealth*, Vol. VI, *The Dominions and India Since 1900* (Westport, Conn., 1993), p. 42.

equal constitutional status of the Dominions with the Mother Country, admitted their *right* to a full external personality, and by recognizing their association with the Empire as voluntary, implicitly conferred their right to secede. Between 1917 and 1926 the White Dominions had made, in constitutional theory, an exceptionally rapid progress from autonomy to equality.[7] In 1931 the Statute of Westminster set the seal on the new conception of Dominion nationhood by renouncing the Imperial Parliament's right to legislate for the Dominions unless at their explicit request. Dominion 'independence' seemed complete.

The real meaning of the celebrated formula of the Balfour Report—that the Dominions were 'autonomous communities within the British Empire, equal in status, and in no way subordinate one to another in any aspect of their domestic or external affairs'—was the imperative need of South African and Irish leaders, with the benign support of Mackenzie King, to widen consensus within their fragile polities. The supreme virtue of Dominion Status as it was defined between 1926 and 1931 lay for them in its plasticity. It enabled them to tread the finest of lines between public deference to Imperial unity—expressed primarily through allegiance to the common monarchy—and the rhetorical assertion of national independence. But in the other Dominions much of the wordplay which had preoccupied Hertzog of South Africa and O'Higgins, the Deputy Premier of the Irish Free State, in 1926 was of little relevance. Canadian fears of renewed Imperial centralism had been largely assuaged in 1923. In Australia, New Zealand, and Newfoundland there was less concern to fend off the Imperial embrace than to keep open the channels of influence to Imperial policy. Hence the Statute of Westminster was eagerly endorsed in Dublin and Pretoria, carefully emasculated in Canada, and comprehensively ignored in Australia and New Zealand.[8]

This was a curious anticlimax to twenty years of constitutional debate. But it would be wrong to see the constitutional compromise embodied in the Balfour Report and the Statute of Westminster as the result of London's resistance to a real Dominion breakaway. British reactions (outside the bureaucratic vested interests) were notably sympathetic to Dominion aspirations. Nor was this surprising. The most ardent protagonists of closer unity between Britain and the White Dominions who were to be found among former Milnerites and Tariff Reformers enthusiastically supported the Balfour formula and the recognition of Dominion nationhood. Adapting Milner's own arguments (Milner himself had died in 1925), they reasoned that the ultimate reunion of the 'British nations'—to which they still looked forward—could only take place once the Dominions were recognized

[7] The best recent treatment is Philip G. Wigley, *Canada and the Transition to Commonwealth: British Canadian Relations, 1917–1926* (Cambridge, 1977).

[8] At the express wish of Canadian leaders, Section 7 of the Statute reserved the power of constitutional amendment in Canada to the Westminster Parliament. This power was not 'patriated' until 1982.

(and regarded themselves) as British peoples on a par with those of the United Kingdom.[9] For this school, the adoption of Imperial Preference in 1932 was a key step towards British reunion. But whereas before 1914 the tariff component of Imperial unity had aroused violent opposition in Britain, by 1932 it was no longer at odds with the most powerful economic interests. Britain's commercial gains from the Ottawa system may have been less than was hoped, but Imperial Preference averted the risk that the Dominions would default on their sterling loans or embark on risky autarkic experiments that would damage British trade. Monetary co-operation under the aegis of the Bank of England was strengthened and British investment in South Africa, politically the least friendly of the overseas Dominions, grew rapidly with the second gold boom after 1933. At home, Imperial Preference offered a marriage of convenience to domestic economic interests whose real aim, as in agriculture, was protection against all foreign competition. Nor did the concession of full control over external relations seem likely to endanger Dominion co-operation when it really mattered. For all the anxious bureaucratic debate about diplomatic unity in the early 1920s, policy-makers displayed by the later 1930s an insouciant confidence that in a 'general war', all the Dominions would acknowledge that their own interests were as much at stake as Britain's.[10] Theoretical control over their foreign policies would not preclude, might even encourage, wholehearted acceptance that their Imperial obligations were the best guarantee of their safety. In this way, instead of being the 'monstrous empire' denounced by the French Canadian nationalist Henri Bourassa during the First World War, the British Imperial system would have become reassuring and indispensable.

Underlying these rationalistic calculations were assumptions whose influence on British attitudes is harder to weigh but wrong to discount. Indeed, it seems likely that they helped to promote the strongly positive view of the Dominion experiment across much of the political spectrum in the inter-war years. Fundamentally, these assumptions were cultural rather than political, economic, or strategic. The most articulate protagonists of the Dominion Idea in Britain insisted that the Empire offered a capacious mould into which the special identities of the Dominions could be poured. Like Britain, herself a four-nation state, they were synthetic nations united through common adherence to British ideals and institutions.[11] It was this institutional inheritance from Britain that formed the

[9] See the views set out in his book by the Rt. Hon. L. S. Amery, MP, *The Forward View* (London, 1935).

[10] For this view, Dominions Secretary to Foreign Secretary, 23 March 1938, D[ominions] O[ffice] 114/94.

[11] For the composite character of the United Kingdom, see R. Coupland, *The Empire in These Days: An Interpretation* (London, 1935) chap. 1; and of the White Dominions, Amery, *Forward View*, p. 164.

only foundation for nation-building in societies without a common indigenous culture. Provided that the tendency towards an introverted separatism could be held at bay, the 'compromising, conservative, adaptable English temper' would readily fuse with other traditions to form a composite 'Britannic' culture (the Imperial counterpart to the home-grown amalgam of 'Britishness') progressive, outward-looking, and internationally minded.[12] For as long as Britain remained a world power, exercised her economic functions as the world's banker, investor, supplier, and market-place, and sustained a vigorous Imperial culture, the Dominions' march towards modernity would draw them closer to Britain and strengthen their Britannic character.

Dominionhood was thus to be a distinctive blend of national status and Imperial identity. To its British apologists it seemed to offer the Dominions an influence and security as 'imperial nations' far above what small states could expect in a world of Great Powers.[13] But it would be wrong to see the new terms of the Dominion relationship as the magnanimous gesture of the weary titan. Nor is the settlement of 1926–31 to be regarded as a divorce *nisi* while the Dominions waited impatiently for 'complete independence'. The new Dominionhood was not the most that the Dominions could extract from the grudging Imperial centre: it was the most that the internal politics of the Dominions themselves would permit.

There were several reasons for this. All the Dominions were heavily dependent upon Britain as a market; even Canada exported as much to Britain in 1938 as to the United States. As other markets were closed against their commodities, this dependence seemed unlikely to lessen. All of them looked to Britain as a prime source of development capital: even in Canada, long exposed to American capital exports, British investment still amounted to two-thirds the American total in the 1930s and was especially prominent in the railway system.[14] The imperialism of free trade gave way after 1932 to a new mixed Imperial economy combining elements of multilateralism, monetary co-ordination, Imperial Preference, and domestic (British) protection. Imperial economic relations entered a phase of state planning and politicization, not of disengagement or alienation, which spawned a novel culture of lobbying and inter-governmental negotiation.[15] All

[12] Amery, *Forward View*, p. 169

[13] For Amery's use of this epithet, see *Parliamentary Debates* (Commons), Fifth Series, CCLIX, col. 1200 (20 Nov. 1931); Amery, *Forward View*, p. 187.

[14] For British and American investment in Canada, see M. C. Urquhart and K. A. H. Buckley, *Historical Statistics of Canada* (Cambridge, 1965), p. 168. See chap. by David MacKenzie.

[15] For Imperial economic relations in the 1930s, see Ian M. Drummond, *Imperial Economic Policy, 1917–1939: Studies in Expansion and Protection* (London, 1974); R. F. Holland, 'Imperial Collaboration and the Great Depression: Britain, Canada and the World Wheat Crisis, 1929–35', *Journal of Imperial and Commonwealth History* (hereafter *JICH*), XVI, 3 (1988), p. 87; K. Tsokhas, 'Protection, Imperial Preference and Australian Conservative Politics, 1923–39', *JICH*, XX, 1 (1992), pp. 65–87.

the Dominions recognized their strategic interdependence with Britain: felt most strongly in Australia and New Zealand; resented most in the Irish Free State; accepted in Canada as the corollary of a heavy transatlantic commerce. Amongst the overseas Dominions, Canada, Australia, and New Zealand also regarded continued British immigration as an indispensable factor in their economic growth and, in Australia and New Zealand, for their national survival. 'Men, money, and markets' in varying combinations still bound the Dominions to Britain almost as much, if not actually more, than before 1914.

But there were other circumstances which helped to enfold the Dominions in a form of 'imperial nationhood'. One of the most powerful was what contemporaries sometimes called 'British race sentiment'—a phenomenon usually passed over by historians in embarrassed silence. It was not to be confused with subservience to Downing Street, let alone blind attachment to the values of Cheltenham: the overseas British generally had little sympathy for what they regarded as an over-rigid class system at home. Its real character approximated to what might be called 'Britannic nationalism'. It rested upon an aggressive sense of cultural superiority as the representatives of a global civilization then at the height of its prestige. It was constantly reinforced not only by new recruits from Britain itself but by a vast British-centred system of global communications transmitting news, opinion, values, and ideas. It was sharpened by competition and insecurity: against French Canadians and foreign migrants in Canada; Afrikaners and Indians in South Africa; threatening unseen Asiatic hordes in Australia and New Zealand. Far from subsiding tamely into indifference after 1918, Britannic nationalism appeared to thoughtful observers a dangerous obstacle to political stability in Canada and South Africa. To the historian Arthur Lower, a clearer assertion of Canada's separateness from Britain was vital if the Dominion was to escape recurrent bouts of the violent communal feeling inspired by Britannic loyalism in 1917—a view which led him, despite an intense attachment to Canada's 'British' character, to favour neutrality in the event of another war.[16] For the great majority of the English in South Africa, remarked Patrick Duncan (once a member of Milner's 'Kindergarten', now Smuts's principal lieutenant), Commonwealth membership 'is reinforced by race sentiment and is the outward and visible sign of our portion in that British stock which has spread its influence over so large a part of the earth'.[17] During the First World War, it had been 'English' South Africans who had been most vigorous in resisting the 1914 rebellion, and it was widely thought that

[16] Carl Berger, *The Writing of Canadian History: Aspects of English-Canadian Historical Writing, 1900–1970* (Toronto, 1976), p. 134.

[17] Memorandum by Patrick Duncan, 12 Sept. 1932. Patrick Duncan Papers, A 12.1.4, Jagger Library, University of Cape Town. The Kindergarten had been the coterie of young Oxford graduates recruited by Milner as administrative assistants in South Africa at the time of the Boer War.

they would fight rather than permit secession from the Empire. The intense feeling aroused during the controversy over the design of a new union flag in the later 1920s, and encouraged in the English-speaking press, seemed to confirm this impression.[18]

In Australia and New Zealand, where the predominance of communities drawn from the British Isles was not in question, Britannic nationalism took a different form. Both Dominions rejected ratification of the Statute of Westminster, formally because they held it to be an unnecessarily legalistic complication in Imperial relations, in reality because leading politicians in both countries thought little would be gained and much lost from emphasizing their constitutional separateness from the Mother Country.[19] The 'Bulletin' outlook in Australia (the *Bulletin* was a strongly 'nationalist' periodical) had helped to create a robustly undeferential attitude to Britain. But between the wars two overlapping schools of thought held sway in Australia's external relations. One, of which William Morris Hughes was a fluent spokesman, combined a forceful regionalist viewpoint with an unflinchingly populist devotion to 'White Australia'. The logic of this position was an unequivocal identification of Australia as a 'British nation', fully entitled to call upon the other states of the Britannic world, especially Britain, to help defend the British place in the southern sun. This view coincided with that of seeing Australia as the trustee of the interests of the 'British race' in the South Pacific. The other school, much less populist in tone, nevertheless shared much the same assumptions. Its leading figures exerted a powerful influence on Australia's foreign policy in the 1920s and 1930s. J. G. Latham, Sir Henry Gullett, Richard Casey, and Robert Menzies formed part of what an American Consul-General once angrily described as the 'Victorian clique': a conservative élite closely allied to Melbourne's financial and mining interests, Anglophile in tastes and education, and strongly Anglocentric in their business interests.[20] None of this precluded the aggressive pursuit of Australian economic interests in intra-Imperial bargaining at which Gullett was very successful; nor did it prevent Menzies from wishing to ratify the Statute of Westminster on legal grounds.[21] In New Zealand a similar attitude towards Britain prevailed, less emphatic in tone and qualified by the strong public commitment of Labour politicians to the ideals of the League and collective security.

In all four overseas Dominions British race sentiment was a political factor no government could ignore, and exerted a powerful if unpredictable influence.

[18] See H. Saker, *The South African Flag Controversy, 1925–28* (Cape Town, 1980).

[19] For the confused Australian reaction to the Statute, see W. J. Hudson and M. P. Sharp, *Australian Independence* (Carlton, Victoria, 1988), pp. 116–24.

[20] Norman Harper, *A Great and Powerful Friend: A Study of Australian Relations Between 1900–1975* (St Lucia, 1987), p. 75. A. W. Martin, *Robert Menzies: A Life*, 1 vol. to date (Carlton, Victoria, 1993), I, pp. 54–56.

[21] Hudson and Sharp, *Australian Independence*, p. 124.

Dominion Status, however, had been redefined mainly to appease cultural nationalism in Ireland, South Africa, and (to a much lesser extent) Canada. In retrospect, it has been easy to assume that in this case, as in others, appeasement was a failure. In both Ireland and South Africa, the triumph of irreconcilable nationalist sentiment was consummated in 1948 when Eire left the Commonwealth and the National Party at last formed a majority government in Pretoria. Between the wars, however, cultural nationalism had looked much less likely to alter the political orientation of any of the Dominions to a marked extent.

In Canada, French Canadian nationalism had reached a crescendo of intensity in the conscription crisis of 1917. Thereafter, no party leader as dependent as Mackenzie King upon French Canadian votes dared court the accusation that he was the lackey of British Imperialism. But King, whose private view was that Canada could not remain neutral in a war involving Britain, showed that controversy over Canada's status could be put to sleep by refusing to make any advance commitment of Canadian loyalty.[22] Despite the best efforts of the Abbé Groulx and the *Action française*, separatism made minimal electoral headway in Quebec after 1918. When Liberal rule was eventually overthrown in the province after three decades of rewarding partnership with Anglo-Saxon big business, it was replaced by the ex-Conservative Maurice Duplessis and the Union Nationale.[23] Duplessis rejected separatism in favour of an unbending defence of provincial autonomy. Henri Bourassa, the tribune of French Canadian *survivance*, repudiated separatism as theologically heterodox. Even the separatist manifesto *Notre avenir politique* (1922) displayed astonishing vagueness about the area, institutions, and policies of the future Quebec state, and a notable reluctance to explain how the Confederation of 1867 was to be demolished. Groulx and his followers preferred instead to await its spontaneous dissolution: 'Nous ne voulons rien détruire', said the Abbé, with a priestly disregard for the old saying about eggs and omelettes.[24] In South Africa, which was a union, not a federation, and where the Afrikaners formed an electoral majority in the white 'political nation', cultural nationalism posed a greater threat to the Imperial link. But even here, despite linguistic self-assertion and the demand for public-sector employment for indigent Afrikaners, there was ample evidence by the 1930s that much Afrikaner opinion had been mollified by the trophies of internal and external equality that Hertzog had captured. In 1931–33 fear of economic catastrophe overcame nationalist demands for a gesture of financial independence and South Africa followed

[22] H. Blair Neatby, *The Politics of Chaos: Canada in the Thirties* (Toronto, 1972), p. 170.

[23] B. St Aubin, *Maurice Duplessis et son époque* (Montreal, 1979), pp. 131, 197.

[24] 'We wish to destroy nothing.' See Lionel Adolphe Groulx, *Mes mémoires*, 4 vols. (Montreal, 1971), II, p. 303; S. Trofimenkoff, *Action française: French-Canadian Nationalism in the Twenties* (Toronto, 1975), pp. 90–99.

Britain into devaluation. With the Fusion of 1933–34 and the creation of the United Party under the leadership of Hertzog and Smuts, the 'purified' nationalism of Malan retreated to the redoubts of Poor Whiteism in the Free State and on the Karoo plateau.[25]

Even in Ireland, where cultural nationalism was deep-rooted, pervasive, and prestigious, its impact on the Imperial connection was curiously ambivalent. This was despite the fact that the peculiarities of Ireland's Dominion Status made it an easy target for nationalist criticism. The Anglo-Irish Treaty of 1921 declared that the Irish Free State would enjoy the same constitutional status as Canada. But what Lloyd George could give, he could also take away. The Treaty endowed Anglo-Irish relations with a fixity quite different from the conventional basis of Dominion Status elsewhere. It enshrined the oath of allegiance to a monarchical constitution (the King was head of state); an undertaking to pay the annuities—the annual charge arising from the land-purchase schemes originally financed by the British government; and the provision of three naval stations from which the Royal Navy could guard the Western Approaches at Cobh, Berehaven, and Lough Swilly. More poignantly, the Treaty's acceptance in Southern Ireland entailed the disavowal of the republican constitution proclaimed by Sinn Fein in 1919 and, bitterest pill of all, the reality of partition. Bearing on their back so large an Imperial hump, it was little wonder that the Treatyites took cover behind an enthusiastic Gaelicization and pushed their constitutional status to the limits of sovereignty. Ireland's separate nationhood had been effectively asserted, insisted the Free State foreign minister in 1931, and a constitutional monarchy was tantamount to a republic.[26] The Treatyites were swept away in 1932 as much by economic disaster as by nationalism. But despite the sound and fury of Eamon de Valera's onslaught on the oath and the annuities, recent scholarship has tended to stress both the cautious pragmatism behind his attempt to reconstruct the Imperial connection and his anxiety to heal the old split with the Treatyites.[27] De Valera was determined to remove the remaining symbols of Irish inferiority; but he rejected secession—he would have to be thrown out, he told the Dominions Office in 1936—and his new constitution in 1937 carefully preserved, through the device of external association, an impenetrable ambiguity over whether Eire was really a republic.[28]

[25] N. M. Stultz, *Afrikaner Politics in South Africa, 1934–48* (Berkeley, 1974), p. 57.

[26] Madden and Darwin, eds., *Select Documents*, VI, p. 578.

[27] The key work is Deirdre McMahon, *Republicans and Imperialists: Anglo-Irish Relations in the 1930s* (New Haven, 1984). For Malcolm MacDonald's belief that de Valera would stop at 'external association', J. Bowman, *De Valera and the Ulster Question, 1917–73* (Oxford, 1982), pp. 144–45. See chap. by Deirdre McMahon, esp. pp. 151, 153–54.

[28] McMahon, *Republicans*, p. 181. De Valera had developed a kind of nationalism that was not anti-imperialist, Sardar Patel caustically remarked.

In Ireland, South Africa, and Quebec, it might be argued, cultural nationalism was most often expressed as 'therapeutic anglophobia', in Roy Foster's vivid phrase.[29] It demanded respect for national symbols but was only spasmodically harnessed to the daily round of institutional politics. It was one thing to dream of an Afrikaner or Gaelic republic, but quite another to devise a new political architecture to express its ideals, let alone the machinery required to create a new national society. It may not be too cynical to suspect that, for many 'purified' nationalists, republicanism or separatism were ideals to be viewed much as St Augustine regarded chastity 'make us a republic—but not yet!'—especially since they were likely to impose even greater material sacrifices. It was an added paradox of Imperial politics that, where the republican flame burned brightest, secession from the Empire was likely to extinguish all hope of unifying the 'national domain': the High Commission Territories in South Africa; Ulster in Ireland. If anything, the dilemma was more painful in Ireland, the paradox more cruel. For any move towards overt republicanism and a Gaelic Catholic identity in the South risked further alienating the Northern Protestants. But what if partition was overcome? Reunion could only strengthen the anti-republican sentiment already powerful in the South and herald a drift back towards the tepid Home Rule-ism rejected by Sinn Fein in 1919.[30]

Territorial incompleteness in South Africa and Ireland dramatized a condition common to all the Dominions in different ways. Their constitutional legitimacy depended upon acts of the Imperial Parliament which could not easily be repudiated: a consideration of particular force in the federal Dominions of Canada and Australia and even in South Africa, where Natal secessionism was a periodic difficulty. In all the Dominions, parliamentary government had become strongly indigenized, even amongst ardent cultural nationalists. 'I am a Liberal of the British School,' declared Henri Bourassa, 'I am a disciple of Burke, Fox, Bright [and] Gladstone.'[31] In South Africa, parliamentarism (to whose novelty among Afrikaners some observers had attributed the 1914 rebellion) comfortably survived the fascist challenge of the Ossewa Brandwag movement in the late 1930s and the war crisis of 1939–40. Here, as in Ireland, republicanism faced strong resistance by the 1930s from those who regarded it as a retrograde step towards violence, extremism, and the attack on property and capital. To complicate matters further, parliamentary government in the Dominions was cast in a monarchical form, and it could even be argued that in bicultural communities such as Canada or South Africa the lack of any consensus on the nature of the 'state' made the monarchy the only available

[29] R. F. Foster, *Paddy and Mr Punch: Connections in Irish and English History* (London, 1995), p. 272.

[30] The 1937 plebiscite approved the new constitution by 150,000 votes in a ballot of 1.2 million.

[31] C. Murrow, *Henri Bourassa and French-Canadian Nationalism* (Montreal, 1968), p. 33.

focus of national loyalty. Irish abolition of the 'internal' role of the monarchy in 1937 was not a route the other Dominions could easily follow: it reflected the unique freedom of Eire from the federal, communal, and sentimental inhibitions deeply felt elsewhere. Eire was the exception that proved the Dominion rule.

On the eve of the Second World War the five Dominions could not realistically be portrayed as 'nations-in-waiting', poised to follow, when opportunity allowed, the American path to autochthonous independence. In each case, some combination of strategic vulnerability, communal division, constitutional fragility, economic dependence, and political tradition closed off the American exit. In Canada, Australia, and New Zealand, majority opinion was too deeply attached to 'Britannic' institutions, especially the Imperial monarchy, to contemplate such a step. It was no less true that the alternative extreme of Imperial federation, still cherished by Round Tablers in smoke-filled common rooms, was politically inconceivable. Like 'responsible government', Dominionhood was unsystematic and 'conventional', fashioned as much by the local requirements of Dominion politicians as by policy-makers in London. But ultimately it depended, as will be seen, upon Britain's capacity to play the strenuous role the Third British Empire of the twentieth century required of its metropole, as well as upon the loyalty, acquiescence, or conservatism of Dominion leaders.

The Victorians had expected little from the white colonies towards the defence of their Empire, but much from India. Consequently they had seen no reason to harmonize the Imperial status of the two colonial types they had created and had many objections to uniformity. Before 1914 India's constitutional evolution towards self-government enjoyed by the White Dominions was explicitly ruled out. From different parts of the political spectrum, the radical Secretary of State for India, John Morley, and Curzon, a former Viceroy, sneered at schemes of Imperial reconstruction which involved the Dominions but left out the Empire's 'largest and most powerful unit'.[32] It was true that in India itself the most articulate political figures organized into the Indian National Congress had made self-government on the White Dominion model the goal of political ambition. It was also true that within the Government of India British officials were coming to recognize that fiscal pressures and the intolerable burden of administrative centralization had made provincial devolution inevitable.[33] Moreover, to the official mind it was easier to envisage greater Indian political participation in a decentralized Raj. But this was a far cry from Dominionhood, let alone federal

[32] Earl of Ronaldshay, *The Life of Lord Curzon*, 3 vols. (1929), III, p. 24.

[33] *Report of the Royal Commission on Decentralization*, paragraphs 46–47; Viceroy to Secretary of State for India, 25 Aug. 1911 (the 'Delhi Dispatch'), *P[arliamentary] P[apers]* (1908), XLIV (4360); C. P. Ilbert, *The Government of India*, 3rd edn. (Oxford, 1916), Appendix III.

Dominionhood on the Canadian or Australian model. Ironically, just as provincial decentralization was becoming the bureaucratic panacea, non-intervention was adopted as the motto for relations with the Indian states: their political and administrative assimilation to British India was firmly rejected.[34]

The real barrier to India's becoming a Dominion was the uniquely close military and commercial integration between Britain and India. Unlike any White Dominion, India met the costs of an Imperial garrison comprising one-third of the British army, as well as supporting a colonial army of its own available for Imperial service. It was also denied the tariff freedom successfully asserted in the white colonies. It was hard to imagine any freely elected Indian legislature in which these Imperial prerogatives—both of the utmost significance to Britain's management of the Imperial system—would not come under immediate attack.

But in India, as well as in the White Dominions, the First World War washed away the political landmarks of the Second British Empire. By 1916 fear of civil unrest in an India stripped of British troops, the stigma of military failure in the Middle East, and anxiety to win over 'moderate' nationalists who had united behind the Lucknow Pact (demanding progress towards colonial self-government) led the Viceroy to importune London for a declaration of constitutional intent.[35] As in the case of the White Dominions, the upheaval in British domestic politics which brought Lloyd George to power made the Imperial centre much more amenable to change. The effect was redoubled in India's case by the appointment of Edwin Montagu, an Asquithian renegade whom Lloyd George was eager to capture, to the India Office. Montagu exploited his 'doctor's mandate' to supercharge the devolution favoured by the Indian government in a dramatic way. His declaration in August 1917 promised India progress towards 'responsible government'—the phrase by which white colony self-government was denoted—and, by clear implication, eventual assimilation to the ill-defined stature of Dominionhood.[36] India was admitted to the Imperial Conference—hitherto the preserve of the White Dominions—represented in the British Empire Delegation at Paris, and most bizarrely of all, became a non-self-governing member of the League of Nations.

The Montagu–Chelmsford reforms enacted in 1919 thus constituted an immediate reconstruction of Indian politics, but also a revolution of Indian expectations.[37] Montagu's radicalism has sometimes been seen as the statesmanlike anticipation of the multi-racial Commonwealth which emerged in the 1950s. It

[34] Speech by Viceroy, 3 Nov. 1909, OIOC R/1/1/4033 British Library, London; S. R. Ashton, *British Policy and the Indian States, 1905–1939* (London, 1976).

[35] Chelmsford to Montagu, 3 Jan. 1917, OIOC, Chelmsford Collection, MSS, Eur. E 264/51.

[36] *Parliamentary Debates* (Commons), Third Series, Vol. XCV col. 2205 (1917).

[37] For reforms during the First World War, see chap. 18 by Judith M. Brown.

is likely, however, that he himself expected Indian advance to be gradual and uncomplicated by the intrusion of mass politics or an aggressive cultural nationalism. India was to get Dominionhood on the instalment plan: meanwhile dyarchy would carefully reserve financial policy and internal security in British hands, as well as maintaining London's control over India's contribution to Imperial defence.

Almost immediately, however, the reforms were overtaken by the vast non-cooperation campaign launched by Gandhi in 1920—precisely the kind of cultural nationalist movement which they had been expected to head off. Intriguingly, Gandhi, like Bourassa, Hertzog, and de Valera, combined an intense cultural Anglophobia with a curious ambivalence towards British institutions and values—a combination so baffling that one Viceroy was reduced to classifying him as a bolshevik.[38] But it was far from clear that the astonishing subcontinental coalition with which Gandhi proposed to reclaim India from Western civilization would be more than a temporary aberration in Congress politics. Many of the most prominent politicians in British India abandoned Gandhianism at the first opportunity after 1922 in favour of the old programme aimed at wresting from the British 'responsible government' at the Indian centre and eventual Dominion Status. For politicians such as Das, Motilal Nehru, Sastri, Sapru, and Banerjea (not to mention Mohamed Ali Jinnah), mobilizing the subalterns was a dangerous distraction from the pursuit of self-rule. There was little likelihood of India's trying to leave the Empire, claimed Nehru, 'if she is treated fairly and on an equal footing with the [other] Dominions'.[39] This constitutionalist programme, in which Dominion Status had emerged as the goal around which Indian opinion could unite, was reaffirmed at the All-Parties Conference held at Lucknow in 1928 to pre-empt the findings of the Statutory Commission sent to assess India's readiness for further political advance.[40] To shore up the credibility of the embattled Indian constitutionalists against the revival of Gandhian civil disobedience, the Viceroy, Lord Irwin, issued in October 1929 the celebrated declaration confirming Dominionhood as the intended outcome of India's constitutional progress.

But what would Dominionhood amount to, and when would the British deliver it? The concession of an enlarged constitutional status to the White Dominions after 1917 was uncontroversial in British politics because no British interests were

[38] The fullest statement of Gandhi's cultural nationalism can be found in his *Hind Swaraj* [1909] (Ahmedabad, 1938).

[39] M. Nehru to the Editor, *The Pioneer*, 2 May 1928. R. Kumar and H. D. Sharma, eds., *Selected Works of Motilal Nehru*, 6 vols. (New Delhi, 1992–95), V, p. 308.

[40] On Indian opinion see Motilal Nehru to Gandhi, 2 Oct. 1928, in Kumar and Sharma, eds., *Selected Works*, V, pp. 368–70.

affected and no cultural taboos broken. Indian Dominionhood was problematic on both counts. Any reduction in India's share of Imperial defence costs would load fresh burdens on the rebellious British taxpayer. Nor would it be easy to explain to British opinion why an unrepresentative 'microscopic minority' of agitators and 'wire-pullers' whose social oppressions British rule was meant to parry (the conventional picture disseminated by old India hands) should be promoted so quickly up the constitutional ladder to equality with kith and kin.[41]

These contradictions were reconciled by British leaders with a sang-froid which now seems almost breathtaking. They assumed that the Indian political élite they intended to empower would show great patience to win such a tempting constitutional prize. India, argued Sir Malcolm Hailey, then regarded as the greatest official expert on Indian politics, could be granted responsible government at the centre subject to a long list of reservations, including defence. Eventually, a 'convention of non-interference' would confer on India a real status equivalent to that of the White Dominions, but only after a long period, 'owing to her peculiar circumstances and in the absence of that identity of interest with Great Britain which made the evolution possible in the case of the Dominions'.[42] Sir John Simon, the Chairman of the Statutory Commission, to whom Hailey was writing, was bitterly critical of Irwin's promise of Dominion Status, but he too regarded the eventual attainment of Dominionhood as the right solution for India. But he insisted that there could be no prescribed time-scale. The first step was to establish full responsible government in the provinces to drive out Gandhianism and demagogy. Only when the provinces, which should receive the widest autonomy as soon as possible, came together voluntarily to create a new federation—as had happened in Canada and Australia—should British control of India gradually be relinquished.[43] These were the Simon Commission's findings: but Simon's scheme was rejected as impossibly Fabian. Instead, London proposed in 1931 to set up an All-India Federation as soon as the princely states could be persuaded to join, on the premise that a federation in which power was shared between the princes, Muslims, and the Congress would be a reliable guardian of Imperial interests. But in the final version of constitutional reform imposed on India, extensive 'safeguards' were prescribed limiting the control of any future federal assembly over defence, external affairs, currency, and minorities, and reserving wide powers for the Viceroy. Full responsible government, remarked the parliamentary Joint Select Committee which approved the reform scheme, would be achieved 'by insensible

[41] A classic in this genre is Al. Carthill (pseud.), *The Lost Dominion: The Story of England's Abdication in India* (New York, 1925).

[42] Hailey to Simon, 29 Oct. 1928, Bodleian Library, Oxford, MSS, Simon, 63.

[43] Simon to Coupland, 1 July 1930; Simon to E. T. Scott, 5 July 1930. MSS, Simon 65.

degrees'. That, said the Committee, 'was the way by which responsible government actually grew up in Canada'.[44] In the interval, it was assumed, Indian leaders would have learned to shoulder the obligations of Dominion Status and imbibed its special ethos.

'Responsible government with safeguards' was ridiculed by Conservative die-hards as a sham.[45] But the real question was whether the 1935 Act would create the political conditions in which India would move towards voluntary participation in a Britannic community of self-governing states. The verdict of historians has been scathing. Certainly, by 1939 there had been little progress towards persuading the princely states to join the federal scheme—the prerequisite for advance at the Indian centre. The attitude of the Congress leadership was volatile. Jawaharlal Nehru denounced federation as 'slavery', and rejected Dominion Status as signifying membership of 'a certain European dominating group exploiting numerous subject people . . . the very order and forces of reaction against which we struggle'.[46] But Nehru could not persuade the Congress high command to boycott the elections of 1937, nor reject the eight provincial ministries its electoral victory had yielded. Amongst the Gandhians there were those who saw merit in office-holding as well as in rallying the subalterns. Even Gandhi seemed non-committal about India's eventual status. 'I asked him,' recorded the Viceroy, Lord Linlithgow, in August 1937, 'did he in this rough modern world want to sail off from the British Commonwealth of Nations? He gave no direct answer to this, but from his silence and his general reaction, I gathered he was very conscious of the difficulty of the point from his aspect.' But Linlithgow also noted that Gandhi remained 'implacably hostile to British Rule in India'.[47]

The two-year experiment in constitutional politics between 1937 and 1939 was in fact a trial of strength prematurely terminated by the outbreak of war. The British had hoped that the new Congress ministries in the provinces would swiftly declare independence from the high command, forcing Gandhi, Sardar Patel, Prasad, Nehru, and Subhas Chandra Bose into acceptance of the federal scheme. But despite much evidence of internal strains, the high command's grip, stringently supervised by Patel and Prasad, held firm.[48] The steady accretion of Congress

[44] *Report of the Joint Select Committee on Indian Constitutional Reform*, p. 24. *PP* (1933–34), XI, House of Commons, 5, Part 1.

[45] *Morning Post*, 22, 23 June 1933; A. B. Keith to Lord Lloyd, 26 March 1934. Lloyd of Dolobran Papers, GLLD 17/18, Churchill College, Cambridge.

[46] Speech by J. Nehru, n.d. but March 1937, OIOC, Haig Collection MSS, Eur. F 115/14–15.

[47] Note by Viceroy, 4 Aug. 1937, OIOC, Haig Coll. MSS, Eur. F 115/13.

[48] R. Coupland, *The Indian Problem: Report on the Constitutional Problem in India* (New York, 1944), Part 2, pp. 98–100. The course of provincial politics can be followed in N. B. Khare, *My Political Memoirs* (Nagpur, 1959), pp. 11–18; M. Chalapathi Rau, *G. B. Pant* (New Delhi, 1981); V. Damodaran, *Broken Promises: Popular Protest, Indian Nationalism and the Congress Party in Bihar, 1935–46* (Delhi, 1992).

power at the grass roots seemed irreversible, so that step by step British leverage over Indian politics would be surrendered. By January 1939, with the princes, Congress, and Muslim opinion all opposed to federation, the prospects of India's attaining the form of Dominionhood envisaged earlier in the 1930s appeared remote.[49]

If British plans had gone awry, it also seemed unlikely that the Congress would be able to impose its own preference for unitary government and 'complete independence': indeed, within the Congress there was no agreed alternative to federation.[50] The key provinces of Bengal and Punjab were beyond its control. Despite the high command's success in keeping its grip on the provinces, a tribute to Gandhi's prestige, the longer provincial autonomy continued the greater the danger that Congress would become a loose alliance of provincial forces and the provincial ministries mere 'hand-maids of... vested interests'.[51] Gandhi himself denounced the corruption, indiscipline, and 'decay' of the Congress.[52] Above all, the growing signs of communal antagonism warned against any facile optimism that Congress could attain its objects by force of will alone. It was freely recognized that British power, still based on a loyal army, made open confrontation impracticable. 'I fear we are rapidly heading for what might be called civil war in the real sense of the word,' wrote Nehru gloomily on the eve of war. 'Our future conflicts are never going to be on the straight issue of Indian nationalism *versus* British imperialism...'[53] Time may have been running out for the British, but it was also running out for the Congress.

Hence, the most likely outcome in India seemed an attempt to reach a new accommodation between the Congress and the Raj, perhaps by shortening the timetable for self-government, modifying the federal scheme, and revising the terms of Britain's military corvée on India. By the late 1930s the old British project of fashioning an imperially minded élite which would dish the Gandhians and embrace the financial and military burdens of the Imperial connection no longer looked very plausible. Nevertheless, without a profound revolution in world politics, there was good reason to suppose that whatever regime eventually emerged from the stalemate of 1937–39 would find a continued association with Britain, more or less on the Dominion model, the only feasible basis for self-government in a divided subcontinent and in a colonial world. After 1937, however, every calculation was vitiated by fear of impending war:

[49] Secretary of State for India to Viceroy, 24 Jan. 1939. Marquess of Zetland, '*Essayez*' (London, 1956), p. 247.

[50] Damodaran, *Broken Promises*, p. 158.

[51] J. P. Narayan to J. Nehru, 23 Nov. 1938, J. Nehru, *A Bunch of Old Letters* (Bombay, 1958), p. 296.

[52] In *Harijan*, 28 Jan. 1939.

[53] J. Nehru to Sri Prakasa, 15 Aug. 1939, in S. Gopal, ed., *Selected Works of Jawaharlal Nehru*, First Series, 15 vols. (New Delhi, 1972–82), IX, pp. 599–600.

reducing the scope for concession and sharpening the mood of expectation and uncertainty. Then, in September 1939, the Third British Empire entered its Awful Revolution.[54]

The worst nightmare for loyal exponents of the Dominion Idea was British involvement in a war whose purpose was unintelligible to Dominion (or Indian) opinion. To South African, Irish, and Canadian leaders it was especially important to claim (as they could after 1926) that never again would they be committed to war solely at Downing Street's command. But how easy would it be in practice to remain neutral in a conflict in which Britain was a belligerent? Dominion self-interest and British 'race-sentiment' were likely to foreclose the option for the overseas Dominions, if not for Ireland. Smuts had recognized the dilemma in 1917 and proposed a solution. It was vital, he argued, that British foreign policy become 'far simpler. In other parts of the Empire we do not understand diplomatic finesse.'[55] Simplicity meant a willingness to subscribe to declared doctrines and principles, since Dominion politics were inimical to the secrecy and deviousness of the official mind. In substance this implied a 'blue water' or 'oceanic' foreign policy and no entanglements in Europe—least of all in eastern Europe. If London ignored this rule, Dominion leaders would be exposed to the local charge that consultation through the Imperial Conference—the central institution of the Dominion system—was a sham. The brutal choice between loyal subservience and secessionist neutrality would be thrust upon them.[56]

Little wonder, then, that in September 1939 when the Polish guarantee (issued without Dominion consultation) led Britain into war for the integrity of an east European state—or so it appeared—there were cries of anguish in Canada, where they were quickly extinguished by loyalism, and in South Africa, where they were not. 'In spite of a quarter century of proclamation and achievement of equality and independent status,' fumed Oscar Skelton, the most senior official in the Canadian External Affairs Department, 'we have thus far been relegated to the role of a Crown Colony.'[57] In South Africa, Patrick Duncan, now Governor-General, furiously contemplated the political damage that British entry into war would inflict locally. 'It is nothing but a tragedy,' he wrote on 1 September, 'that Britain with all her world wide interests should be committed to war over Danzig or even over Poland.' Three days later he recorded: 'All my evil forebodings about the

[54] Edward Gibbon's evocative term for the downfall of the Roman empire in the West.

[55] Speech, 15 May 1917. J. C. Smuts, *Plans For a Better World* (London, 1942), p. 42.

[56] See the fears expressed in Mackenzie King's diary in Oct. 1935. Neatby, *The Politics of Chaos*, p. 170.

[57] Memorandum, 25 Aug. 1939. J. Munro, ed., *Documents on Canadian External Relations*, 16 vols. to date (Ottawa, 1972), VI, pp. 1247–49.

Polish guarantee are being fulfilled. The Fusion Cabinet is broken.'[58] The sense of betrayal was palpable.

In South Africa the war crisis was resolved by the formation of a new government under J. C. Smuts, while Hertzog withdrew into opposition. Even so, the parliamentary majority for war was narrow. But it was in India that the war did most damage to the inchoate, experimental fabric of the Third British Empire. Without some constitutional concession, Congress leaders could hardly overlook the danger that remaining in office would implicate them in the travails of the war effort. In October 1939 the Congress provincial ministries resigned in unison. In the desperate crisis of British Imperial power between May 1940 and the end of 1942, no compromise could be found to enlist Congress co-operation in exchange for constitutional advance. After the violent fiasco of Gandhi's Quit India movement, swiftly suppressed by the British, the Congress organization was banned for the duration of the war. None of this prevented the British from using India's manpower and industrial resources for the Imperial war effort in the Middle East and South-East Asia. But the political price was disastrously high. The Congress boycott heightened British dependence on Muslim goodwill, enlarged Muslim political aspirations, and deepened the communal chasm. The socio-economic effects of the war stimulated populist and communalist movements and threatened social order. The strain of war mobilization and direct rule exhausted the British administrative machine. Above all, the abortive Cripps Mission of 1942 had promised swift progress to Indian independence at the end of the war, scrapping the timetable and safeguards of the 1935 Act. The outcome is a familiar story: within two years of their victory in the Pacific war, the British conceded independence by partition on terms which abandoned virtually all prospect of India's playing its old role in Imperial defence and the Imperial economy. Diplomatic and commercial links lingered on, but by the early 1950s Anglo-Indian disengagement was all but complete.[59]

The effects of the war on Britain's relations with the White Dominions were more ambiguous but in the end no less destructive of the Dominion Idea. Imperial military weakness grimly revealed in the disasters of 1940–42 signalled a strategic revolution which ultimate victory could not reverse. Four of the five Dominions framed their own response to the wartime strategic balance: Canada, Australia, and New Zealand established ties of strategic dependence with the United States; Eire remained neutral. Triumph in 1945 restored British prestige, and Britain remained the most powerful state after the superpowers until the later 1950s.

[58] Duncan to Lady Duncan, 1 Sept. 1939, 4 Sept. 1939, Patrick Duncan Papers E. 10.19.1; E.10.19.4.

[59] Michael Lipton and John Firn, *The Erosion of a Relationship: India and Britain Since 1960* (London, 1975).

But, as Attlee recognized, the old system of Imperial defence could not be revived in a nuclear age when Britain also faced a Russian threat in Europe.[60] And because the Empire-Commonwealth could no longer offer an independent strategic umbrella to its member states, it lost its claim to a monopoly of their external commitments—a basic presumption of pre-war British–Dominion relations.

A strategic revolution thus destroyed one indispensable precondition of the Dominion Idea; an economic revolution destroyed the second. The devastating effects of the war on British trade, investments, and physical assets triggered the end of her threefold attraction for the economies of the Dominions and India, now her creditors not debtors. By the 1950s it had become as important for them to diversify their economic relationships as their strategic ones, since Britain could no longer adequately fill her old role as market, investor, and supplier. To recover Britain's commercial pre-eminence, British governments groped painfully towards sterling convertibility, eventually achieved in 1958.[61] It was too late. The end of twenty years of monetary isolationism revealed an economy too weak to resume its former functions. Talk of post-war 'recovery' was replaced by a new vocabulary of structural crisis. In 1965 the Labour Government's National Plan brought overseas investment to a shuddering halt and marked the onset of sterling's collapse as a reserve currency. The imperialism of free trade had turned at last into the imperialism of free fall.

Long before the final erasure in the mid-1960s of British pretensions to world power through a system of satellite states, the Third British Empire had broken up, an event presaged by the lapse of the old term 'Dominion' after 1947. Behind the confusion and cynicism of British Imperial thinking in the inter-war years had lain a half-realized grand design to build a new world-system dependent upon Anglo-Dominion and Anglo-Indian co-operation. The vehicle for their collaboration, available in several different models, was to be restyled Dominionhood, a permanent reconciliation of national autonomy and Imperial identity.

At the heart of the Dominion Idea was the belief that in colonial societies without a common culture, adherence to British institutions and ideas was the only possible foundation for nation-building. To a remarkable extent that idea had become entrenched even in the apparently inhospitable settings of Afrikanerdom and Indian nationalism. The corollary to this formed the key assumption of the Third British Empire: that the emergent Dominion states would lack the need,

[60] Memorandum by Prime Minister, Cabinet Paper (45) 44, 1 Sept. 1945, CAB 129/1.

[61] See Catherine R. Schenk, *Britain and the Sterling Area: From Devaluation to Convertibility in the 1950s* (London, 1994).

motive, or capacity to re-create themselves as separate nationalities on the classic European model. Instead they would draw closer to the Mother Country as the 'Britishness' of their culture and institutions was reinforced by the modernization of their political and economic life. Modernity and Britishness would coincide. Britain's world power, her central place in the international economy, and the vigour of her Imperial culture would supply the context for this grand Imperial reunion, whose institutional underpinnings, apart from the Imperial Conference, were left studiously vague.

In retrospect we can see that the Dominion Idea rested upon a remarkable foundation of cultural self-confidence. Although it had been shaken by war and depression, in the inter-war years a shared belief among British communities around the world in the supreme attractiveness of their institutions, ethos, literary culture, and forms of civility remained extraordinarily pervasive. To a large extent, no doubt, this was a function of the wealth and prestige of the metropole, where the importance of sustaining an Imperial culture was not overlooked. In the depths of depression, funds were found to launch a new Empire Service of the British Broadcasting Corporation.[62] The value of new means of communication to promote Imperial solidarity was explicitly recognized.[63] In Canada, the Canadian Broadcasting Corporation was established on the British model of a state-supervised public service, while the main cinema chain and the principal academic publisher were both owned by United Kingdom interests.[64] As in the strategic and economic spheres, it was perhaps the weakness and impoverishment inflicted by the war that belittled the pretensions and eroded the credibility of British cultural pre-eminence.

Over much of the former Empire, even perhaps in India, the passing of the Dominion Idea in its wider ideological form left few traces. But in its heartlands, the legacy of its demise has been more painful. In the White Dominions the decline of Britannic nationalism left an ideological void not easily filled—with variable consequences for their political stability and national identity. The path from Dominionhood to nationhood has not proved easy or natural. Nor is it as clear as it once seemed that Britain has escaped unscathed from the loss of a wider Britannic identity, or that shrugging off the Imperial burden has had the liberating and energizing effects once confidently predicted. Only now are we beginning to

[62] Asa Briggs, *History of Broadcasting in the United Kingdom*, Vol. II, *The Golden Age of Wireless* (London, 1965), pp. 270–309.

[63] See J. Coatman, *Magna Britannia* (London, 1935), pp. 289 ff. After a varied career as an Indian policeman, government information officer in India and academic, Coatman became a senior BBC mandarin.

[64] Robert Bothwell, Ian M. Drummond, and John English, *Canada Since 1945: Power, Politics and Provincialism* (Toronto, 1981), pp. 110–11; 114–16.

gauge the impact of the end of Empire on Britain's cultural confidence, social ethos, and institutional stability. In the end decolonization has come home to roost.

Select Bibliography

CARL BRIDGE, *Holding India to the Empire* (New Delhi, 1986).

R. CRAIG BROWN, *Canada, 1896–1921: A Nation Transformed* (Toronto, 1974).

P. J. CAIN and A. G. HOPKINS, *British Imperialism: Crisis and Deconstruction, 1914–1990* (London, 1993).

IAN M. DRUMMOND, *Imperial Economic Policy, 1917–1939: Studies in Expansion and Protection* (London, 1974).

JOHN A. GALLAGHER, *The Decline, Revival and Fall of the British Empire: The Ford Lectures and Other Essays*, ed. Anil Seal (Cambridge, 1982).

W. K. HANCOCK, *Australia* (London, 1930).

—— *Survey of British Commonwealth Affairs*, Vol. I: *Problems of Nationality, 1918–1936* (London, 1937); Vol. II: *Problems of Economic Policy, 1918–1939*, Part 1 (London, 1940), Part 2 (London, 1942).

R. F. HOLLAND, *European Decolonization, 1918–1981: A Survey* (London, 1985).

W. J. HUDSON and M. P. SHARP, *Australian Independence* (Melbourne, 1988).

WM. ROGER LOUIS, *In the Name of God Go! Leo Amery and the British Empire in the Age of Churchill* (New York, 1992).

FREDERICK MADDEN and JOHN DARWIN, eds., *Select Documents on the Constitutional History of the British Empire and Commonwealth*, Vol. VI, *The Dominions and India Since 1900* (Westport, Conn., 1993).

DEIRDRE MCMAHON, *Republicans and Imperialists: Anglo-Irish Relations in the 1930s* (New Haven, 1984).

NICHOLAS MANSERGH, ed., *Documents and Speeches on British Commonwealth Affairs, 1931–1953*, 2 vols. (London, 1953).

H. BLAIR NEATBY, *William Lyon MacKenzie King*, Vol. III, *1932–39: The Prism of Unity* (Toronto, 1976).

KEITH SINCLAIR, *A History of New Zealand*, 4th edn. (Harmondsworth, 1988).

LEONARD THOMPSON, *The Unification of South Africa, 1902–1910* (Oxford, 1960).

A. P. THORNTON, *The Imperial Idea and its Enemies: A Study in British Power* (London, 1959).

B. R. TOMLINSON, *The Indian National Congress and the Raj, 1929–1942: The Penultimate Phase* (Cambridge, 1976).

K. C. WHEARE, *The Constitutional Structure of the Commonwealth* (Oxford, 1960).

PHILIP G. WIGLEY, *Canada and the Transition to Commonwealth: British–Canadian Relations, 1917–26* (Cambridge, 1977).

4

The Metropolitan Economics of Empire

D. K. FIELDHOUSE

From the beginnings of European overseas colonization two issues have dominated assessment of its consequences. What benefits, if any, did the metropolis gain from possession of an Empire? What were the consequences of Empire for the colonies? They can be considered together as two sides of the same coin. But in this book they are separated. This chapter concentrates on the British side of the equation because B. R. Tomlinson extends the discussion into the post-colonial era.

It must be said at the start that it is impossible to draw up a reliable calculus of the benefits and disadvantages of Empire to an imperial state such as Britain without setting up a counter-factual: how might the British economy have performed had Britain possessed no colonies? It would be possible to do this, but it is beyond the scope of this study. The questions to be considered here are concrete rather than hypothetical. First, what advantages did the British desire or expect to obtain from their Empire[1] at different times between 1900 and decolonization in the two decades after 1945? Secondly, what devices did they adopt to ensure such benefits? Finally, what were the measurable results—the effects on the British economy—of its Imperial role and the policies it adopted?

During the twentieth century the British had to make a choice between an open, multilateral economic system, based on free trade between all countries, and a more or less closed Imperial economy.

In outline Britain's choice varied according to circumstance, and British minds turned to Empire as an economic support only in times of crisis. Before 1914, and despite the arguments of 'fair traders' and Chamberlainite supporters of Imperial Preference, the dominant view remained that the Empire was a particularly valuable part of the international economy, but that no attempt must be made

[1] In this chapter 'Empire' will be used as shorthand for 'Empire-Commonwealth', the cumbersome term used to indicate the dualism of the dependent colonies and the largely autonomous 'Dominions' before decolonization in the 1950s and 1960s. 'Commonwealth' has been used instead of Imperial in the tables when the source used the term and in the text only when referring to a statistical table.

artificially to increase its value. The First World War weakened this consensus, largely because of the huge economic and military contribution the Empire made to the British war effort.[2] The crisis generated what Sir Keith Hancock later called 'a kind of witch-doctoring, or ju-ju economics',[3] which propagated the idea that the Empire could be the salvation of Britain through protectionism and exploitation of tropical territories. Such ideas quickly petered out after 1919, and it was not again until after 1929, in the crisis of the Depression, that the Empire was seriously treated as an essential prop to the British economy. Finally, the much greater crisis of the Second World War and its aftermath raised Imperial expectations to their highest level, and these were sustained and acted on for two decades. It was only in the later part of the 1950s that the more enlightened sections of public and political opinion began to lose faith in the Imperial economy.

There were three main methods by which a modern Imperial state such as Britain might attempt to obtain special economic benefit from possession of colonies: by regulating their trade; by manipulating their monetary systems; and by investing in them. These will be described below. But there were others which cannot be considered here, both for reasons of space and because they are largely difficult to quantify. Imperial shipping could be subsidized by awarding mail contracts and be helped by the system of conferences which controlled rates and allocated business between national lines. Imposition of the Imperial language greatly facilitated commercial links and transactions. The consumption patterns of British expatriates influenced local tastes towards products of the metropolis. Education also influenced local preferences. It was probable that colonial governments would buy British.

Tariff Preferences, Export Duties, Quotas, and Bulk Buying

The earliest and always the most significant way in which Britain and other imperial states attempted to obtain a special economic advantage from their colonies was by controlling their trade. This could be done in two ways. First, colonial exports might be channelled to imperial markets by regulation or by differential export duties. Secondly, colonial markets could be reserved, either by lower import duties on goods coming from the favoured imperial source or by some form of physical control, typically licensing or imposing a quota.

Discriminatory export duties as a controlling device had a short life: they were imposed before and after 1914 on exported Malayan and later Nigerian tin ore to

[2] See in particular Avner Offer, *The First World War: An Agrarian Interpretation* (Oxford, 1989).

[3] W. K. Hancock, *Survey of British Commonwealth Affairs*, Vol. II, *Problems of Economic Policy, 1918–1939* (London, 1942), part 1, p. 108.

ensure work for the Empire smelting firms, in which they were successful; and again between 1919 and 1922 on palm kernels exported to Germany, when they proved an economic disaster and had to be withdrawn. Apart from tin, no export duties were imposed after 1922 apart from those used by colonial governments for revenue purposes, which were non-discriminatory.

Of the devices to protect Imperial markets, differential import duties (Imperial Preference) came first and lasted longest.[4] Britain received some preferences in Dominion markets and one or two colonies from the late 1890s, all on their initiative, but did not reciprocate until 1919, when she remitted part of the existing revenue duties on a few 'luxury' goods when imported from the Empire. It was not until 1920 that the British took the first step to benefit from their own export trade. The Colonial Office then invited all colonies and Protectorates, which were not for some reason debarred from doing so, to establish preferential rates of tariff on goods from all Empire sources. Only five complied: the West Indies, Cyprus, Fiji, Mauritius, and Gibraltar.

From a British standpoint this was a limited response. There were two main reasons. First, most of the African colonies, Protectorates, or Mandates were prevented from giving preferences by various international treaties or agreements. Secondly, none of the other dependencies was willing to do so, mainly because they could see no countervailing benefits in the British market. Conservative proposals in 1923 to extend preferences to Empire imports proved electorally disastrous: it was not until 1932, and as a consequence of the international recession, coupled with the Hawley–Smoot tariff in the United States and heavy protectionism elsewhere, that the National government was in a position to adopt general protection and thereby offer Empire Preference. The Import Duties Act in 1932 imposed a general 10 per cent import duty, but it gave permanent exemption of the duty to the colonies and temporary and conditional exemption to the Dominions, including both agricultural and industrial products. The implied condition was that Britain would expect new or increased preferences in Dominion and colonial markets. The new preferential system was negotiated at the Ottawa Conference of 1932, though precisely what concessions Britain should demand remained vague. As Ian M. Drummond has commented: 'The [British] delegation sailed with full power to negotiate—and in full confusion about the terms it might or might not accept.'[5]

[4] This account of Imperial Preference is based mainly on the following: F. V. Meyer, *Britain's Colonies in World Trade* (London, 1948); Hancock, *Problems of Economic Policy*, part 1; D. J. Morgan, *The Official History of Colonial Development*, 5 vols., Vol. I. *The Origins of British Aid Policy, 1924–1945* (London, 1980); Ian M. Drummond, *British Economic Policy and the Empire, 1919–1939* (London, 1972), and *Imperial Economic Policy, 1917–1939: Studies in Expansion and Protection* (London, 1974); Michael Havinden and David Meredith, *Colonialism and Development: Britain and its Tropical Colonies, 1850–1960* (London, 1993).

[5] Drummond, *Imperial Economic Policy*, p. 217.

The outcome of this confused and generally ill-tempered conference was extremely complicated. To oversimplify, the results can be summarized under two heads: what the British conceded, and what they received.

There were six main British commitments, most to the Dominions rather than to the rest of the Empire: free entry to UK markets for most Empire imports for varying periods; increased margins over foreign competitors on dutiable goods; no reduction in the general 10 per cent *ad valorem* duty on specified lists of foreign goods; fixed quotas on imports of meat products; and a number of concessions on luxury imports. Finally, the Dominions were promised that virtually all British dependencies would give the Dominions whatever preferences they gave Britain.

It is more difficult to generalize about what Britain obtained in return, because separate deals were made with each Dominion. Britain had hoped for a general reduction of Dominion preferential rates: she obtained much less, for the most part promises to maintain or increase the margin between preferential and most-favoured nation (mfn) tariffs, plus the 'domestic competitors' principle which committed the Dominions to fix duties on British goods at levels calculated to offset lower British costs rather than provide protection against them. But the dependencies could be dictated to. All colonies not prevented by international agreements were obliged to pass local legislation to generalize any preferences they already gave throughout the Empire and to give Empire imports a preferential margin over foreign goods. In fact relatively few colonies were affected by this. In Africa, only Sierra Leone, the Gambia, British Somaliland, and part of Northern Rhodesia were affected. The West Indies, Fiji, and Mauritius already gave various preferences, and these were now generalized: the Pacific Islands had to introduce them. The greatest effect was on British Malaya, Ceylon, and India: all were now forced to provide preferences.

In return the dependencies were given preferences in the British and Dominion markets. But most gained little further. Under the 1932 Import Duties Act they already had exemption from protective as opposed to revenue-producing duties, an appreciable concession. By far the most important new concession was on colonial sugar, which was given two special rates of preference above the preferential rate, partly tied to a quota. These lasted with variations until 1951, when they were replaced by the Commonwealth Sugar Agreement.[6]

Ottawa proved to be the high-water mark of British Imperial protectionism by tariffs. The preferences and duties were subsequently modified considerably, notably by the Anglo-American Trade Agreement of 1938; but most lasted into

[6] For a detailed account, see Meyer, *Britain's Colonies in World Trade*, pp. 93–94; D. J. Morgan, *Official History*, Vol. III, *A Reassessment of British Aid Policy*, pp. 117–28.

the 1960s, gradually eroded by inflation of specific margins, renegotiation, and cancellation by newly independent states. By 1966 it was calculated that the total effect of preferences was merely to redistribute some £36.5m a year among those involved. But long before then tariffs had taken second place as a device for controlling Imperial trade to two other devices: quotas on imports to the colonies, after 1939 to the sterling area generally, and bulk purchase of colonial exports by Britain.

Quotas, which allocated fixed shares of imports from different sources, were initially a response to the fall in British exports to the colonies, particularly in textiles, and the parallel rise in Japanese imports after 1929. In 1934, when other measures had failed to check the rise of Japanese goods, Britain resorted to quotas, which (unlike preferences) were legally, if not morally, compatible with open-door international commitments once agreements with Japan and France had been abrogated. Generally quotas were based on average imports from foreign countries during the period 1927–31, no country being allocated less than 2.5 per cent of the total. Nowhere except in Lancashire were quotas welcomed. They were deeply resented in the colonies and by British trading firms.

These quotas lasted into the early years of the Second World War, after which they became irrelevant as supplies of essential textile imports became scarce. But in a different form they were widely used to ration purchases by sterling-area countries from dollar sources into the 1950s.

Bulk-buying by the British government implied contracts to purchase the whole of a given crop from any country at a fixed price. It had been used during the First World War, when Britain had bought total export crops from the Dominions, and ended soon afterwards. But in and after 1941 bulk purchase came into its own. It began with British agreement to buy the whole British West African cocoa crop in 1939,[7] and by early 1941 had extended to virtually every category of British food and raw-material imports. Prices were negotiated with the colonial, Dominion, or other friendly governments, though in dependent territories which had no bargaining power they were set well and increasingly below world prices. The profit was taken by the relevant British ministry or marketing board.

Bulk purchase continued after the war under conditions of world shortage and British balance-of-payments problems, partly because the terms of trade were favourable to Britain. Some products were returned to free market operations as the terms of trade reversed; but in 1951 the Ministry of Food still operated sixty-four bulk purchase agreements, of which forty-nine were with Empire countries. They were gradually run down during the 1950s.

[7] See D. K. Fieldhouse, 'War and the Origins of the Gold Coast Cocoa Marketing Board, 1939–40', in Michael Twaddle, ed., *Imperialism, the State and the Third World* (London, 1992).

Currency and the Sterling Area

There were three main ways by which Britain could and did benefit from controlling the currencies of its Empire. First, imposition of the Imperial currency, sterling, on the dependencies, or establishment of a fixed exchange rate between sterling and the currency of a dependency, greatly facilitated intra-Imperial commercial dealings. Secondly, in the special case of dependencies whose currencies were managed in London, the substantial assets (gold, gilt-edged securities) which they were forced to hold in London as backing for their currencies constituted a forced loan to Britain at low rates of interest. Finally, the fact of a widely used Imperial currency, most of whose reserves were held in London, provided an important support for sterling as an international currency. During and after the Second World War Britain was also able to hold the hard-currency earnings of the Empire in support of the pound and to ration use of Empire balances to match the needs of the Imperial economy. Conversely, countries holding sterling benefited from the relative stability of the pound from 1947 to 1967, despite devaluation by 44 per cent in 1949. The British developed all three strategies in that order.

The first step was to establish uniform or tied currencies. Before 1900 the pound sterling was already the currency of the future southern Dominions, which retained parity with the pound until after the British devaluation of 1931. Canada and Newfoundland, however, used dollars related to those of the United States.

The movement towards uniformity in other possessions began in the 1890s as a result of wide fluctuations in the silver–gold ratio and the acquisition of many colonies in Africa and the Pacific which did not possess currencies of a European type. These dependencies fell into three main groups: rupee colonies, silver dollar colonies, and dependencies without a comparable currency system.

The rupee countries—India, Ceylon, Aden, British Somaliland, Mauritius, the Seychelles, British East Africa, and after 1918, Tanganyika—used the Indian silver rupee, inherited from the Mughals. It was an autonomous currency managed by the Indian government. In the early 1890s fluctuations in the silver–gold ratio caused great inconvenience, particularly in transfers both ways. In 1893, therefore, the value of the rupee was de-linked from the price of silver, so that exchange stabilized at about 1 shilling 4 pence by the end of the decade. Although not formally pegged, the rupee was managed by means of a gold exchange standard at about this rate until the First World War. For similar reasons the (Malacca) Straits dollar was managed at about $1 = 2 shillings 4 pence. After 1914 depreciation of sterling and increases in the price of silver again caused problems for both currencies. Finally in 1926, after sterling had reverted to gold, it was decided to peg the rupee to the pound at the controversially high rate of 1 shilling 6 pence, where it remained until the end of the colonial period. The Straits dollar, used in Singapore, Malacca, Penang, and Malaya, was also pegged to sterling.

For dependencies, mostly in Africa, which did not possess conventional currencies, the parallel solution was what became known as the Colonial Sterling Exchange Standard (CSES). Starting with West Africa in 1912, Currency Boards were set up in London, with agents in the colonies, Protectorates, and Jordan and Palestine, which supplied colonies, through the banks, with their own silver or copper coins, in exchange for colonial exports. These were distinct from British coins but were fully convertible at face value and needed no currency reserve. Paper money was issued by banks, but was not legal tender. Through the Crown Agents, who managed business matters in Britain for most dependencies, comparable currency arrangements were made for a number of other colonies.

The system changed in 1920, when the colonies followed Britain into a largely fiduciary currency with token coins, which required backing. Thereafter colonial currencies had 100 per cent cover in London in the form of bullion, or in government securities on which they received interest. By 1946 currency funds held in Britain amounted to £242.5m.[8] This backing was a significant advantage for Britain since it was mainly held in government stock that provided low yields and thus constituted an enforced loan to the metropolis; but it eventually became a matter of controversy. Although the colonies benefited by having a fully convertible currency, immune to speculation, and did not have to undertake conventional currency management (for which they were ill-equipped), it was argued in the 1950s that these colonies should not be required to maintain 100 per cent cover, and that these funds represented real colonial assets which were urgently needed for development.

The most important British currency device was the sterling area, which has been defined as 'a group of countries which were heavily dependent on the British market . . . did most of their trade in sterling, fixed their own currencies in relation to the pound, and held some or all of their reserves in sterling'.[9] Deriving from widespread use, by both colonies and many foreign states, of the pound sterling as a medium of exchange and of London as a place of deposit, after devaluation of the pound in 1931 it became a device for maintaining Britain's primacy as an international currency market and attracting reserves to back sterling. During the 1930s the sterling area consisted of most of the British Empire (excluding Canada, British Honduras, and Newfoundland), and also a number of other countries which were heavily dependent on the British market, including Argentina,

[8] Morgan, *Official History*, Vol. II, *Developing British Colonial Resources, 1945–1951*, p. 53.

[9] P. J. Cain and A. G. Hopkins, *British Imperialism: Crisis and Deconstruction, 1914–1990* (London, 1993), p. 79.

Denmark, Egypt, Eire, Estonia, Finland, Iraq, Latvia, Lithuania, Norway, Portugal, Sweden, and Siam (Thailand).

Until 1939 the sterling area was an open system. Members could withdraw their holdings or convert them into other currencies at will at the current sterling exchange rate. From 1939 this loose area was converted into a tightly structured bloc. Shorn of some foreign members, it became a method by which Britain could control resources for the war effort and post-war reconstruction. All hard-currency earnings by members of the area were pooled in London in an equalization account from which the Bank of England issued funds on demonstration of need. Moreover, Britain was able to spend almost unlimited sums within the sterling area, mainly for war purposes, without exporting goods in compensation. Britain's total overseas deficit on current account during the war was some £10bn. About half of that was met by American Lend-Lease, part by sale of British assets overseas, and some £3.7bn by unrequited sterling credits. Of the sterling credits £2,348m came from the sterling area.[10] This created sterling balances far larger than those members with autonomous currencies had previously kept.

Such borrowing and disinvestment left Britain with huge post-war debts: in 1950 her net overseas assets were −£0.58bn, as compared with over £5bn in 1938. But holding the debts in this form had three main advantages. Most of them had been converted into British gilts, which offered a low rate of interest. Secondly, Britain was in a relatively strong position to decide the rate at which the debts were run down, though she had limited control over some member states, notably Argentina and Australia. Finally, Britain was able to impose trade discrimination by member states in favour of each other and against the dollar area. The premature convertibility of sterling in 1947, which virtually exhausted the 1945 United States loan, followed by the devaluation of the pound in 1949, demonstrated the importance of this factor. Meantime sterling continued to act as a major international currency, though it relied increasingly on voluntary new deposits in London, which in turn depended on attractive rates of interest with their potentially deflationary effects on the British domestic economy. Sterling became fully convertible in 1958, but in 1967 sterling area desposits in London were £2,982m, plus £2,167m held by non-sterling countries.[11] Devaluation of the pound in that year dealt a serious blow to sterling: a number of countries began to keep their overseas assets in other countries or forms. The sterling area was formally wound up in 1972.

[10] Bank of England *Statistical Abstract*, no. 1, 1970, pp. 125–43, quoted in J. D. B. Miller, *Survey of Commonwealth Affairs: Problems of Expansion and Attrition, 1953–1969* (London, 1974), p. 297.

[11] Ibid.

Capital Investment in the Empire

It is not immediately clear how possession of an overseas Empire might benefit a capital-exporting country such as Britain. Capital, unlike commodities or people, is normally extremely mobile: one does not need to own a place to invest in it or lend it money. Empire, therefore, was likely to have a marginal effect on overseas investments. In this account the main aim is to discover how specially important, if at all, the Empire was to British overseas investment in the twentieth century.[12]

In 1914 the nominal value of accumulated British called-up capital, home and overseas, amounted to some £5,783m. Of that total £1,828m (31.6 per cent) was in the UK, £2,467m (42.6 per cent) in foreign countries, and £1,148m (19.8 per cent) in the British Empire.[13] Of the 'Empire' total, the vast majority—£1,045m—had gone to the Dominions, whose fiscal and political autonomy enabled them to borrow and invest as they pleased. By contrast, India, a captive market, had borrowed only £286.5m and the whole of the rest of the Empire another £156.1m. Clearly, political subordination was not the main criterion for British lending.

That does not, however, imply that the Empire offered no special advantages to British investors. First, security in the Empire was much greater than in most other parts of the world. Rather more than half the Empire total consisted of borrowing by colonial governments, and these were virtually gilt-edged (government-guaranteed) stock under the Colonial Stocks Act, 1900.

Secondly, the development patterns of the pre-1914 Empire, particularly of the future Dominions, fitted conveniently with the needs of British investors. Thus, it has been argued that the surges in development spending, particularly on railways and other public utilities, and the expansion of agriculture between roughly 1870 and 1914, provided particularly good opportunities for British investors, possibly offsetting limited investment opportunities in Britain and thus the danger of 'oversaving'.[14]

There is less certainly about British overseas investments in the post-1919 period.[15] But on two matters there is no doubt. First, between the wars and later,

[12] There is a large critical literature on the size and distribution of British overseas investment before 1914. The following statistics are taken from Lance E. Davis and Robert A. Huttenback, with the assistance of Susan Gray Davis, *Mammon and the Pursuit of Empire: The Political Economy of British Imperialism, 1860–1912* (Cambridge, 1986). Where various estimates are given I have adopted the intermediate estimate.

[13] Davis and Huttenback, *Mammon and the Pursuit of Empire*, Table 2.1, pp. 40–41. There are discrepancies both in the totals and the percentage distribution, presumably representing 'unknown' distribution, as in Table 2.3, p. 46.

[14] Michael Edelstein, *Overseas Investment in the Age of High Imperialism: The United Kingdom, 1850–1914* (London, 1982). See particularly part 3.

[15] See B. R. Mitchell, *British Historical Statistics* (Cambridge, 1988), pp. 872–73; R. C. O. Matthews, C. H. Feinstein, and J. C. Odling-Smee, *British Economic Growth 1856–1973* (Oxford, 1982), Table 14.7;

new net overseas investment became much less important in proportion to the British gross domestic product (GDP). Between 1891 and 1913 this had averaged 5.0 per cent of GDP, rising to a unique 8 per cent from 1911 to 1913. Between 1921 and 1929 the figure had dropped to 2.2 per cent and it was -0.9 per cent from 1930 to 1938. Between 1952 and 1964 it was 0.6 per cent.[16]

Secondly, the distribution of new capital issues between the Empire and foreign countries changed significantly after 1920. In 1910–14 average new overseas capital issues were 39.1 per cent Empire and 60.9 per cent foreign. Between 1919 and 1923 the ratio was 66.4 to 33.6; in 1924–28, 58.8 to 41.2; in 1929–33, 69.6 to 30.4; and in 1934–38, 86.2 to 13.8.[17]

This constituted a sea-change in the pattern of British overseas investment. The reasons are both negative and positive. Negatively, New York could now offer generally lower interest rates to foreign governments with satisfactory credentials. The great age of railway building, the main object of British foreign investment before 1914, was now over. The British government, in support of sterling, imposed controls on lending to foreigners, partial during the 1920s, almost total after 1931 until late in the 1950s, and selective in the 1960s and 1970s.[18] Positively, during the 1930s the Empire was even more attractive to investors in government and municipal stock because of their greater security at a time when many foreign governments were defaulting on payments of interest or sinking funds liabilities. Not a single colonial or Dominion government did so. This shift from foreign to Imperial lending did not, however, affect private company issues as much as it did government issues: between 1918 and 1931 companies operating in the Empire raised only 52 per cent by value of new overseas company issues made in London, whereas 75 per cent of new government issues were made to colonial or Dominion governments.[19]

These figures suggest that the Empire became far more important for the British capital market between the wars, and became still more important after 1945.[20] Moreover, since some at least of these new issues within the Empire were linked to demand for the commodities that British industry, still highly geared to export

C. H. Feinstein, *National Income, Expenditure and Output of the United Kingdom, 1855–1970* (Cambridge, 1972), Table 16, p. 40; and John Michael Atkin, *British Overseas Investment, 1918–1931* (New York, 1977), Table 31, p. 231, for contrasting estimates of the balance of payments and net investment abroad during this period.

16 Matthews, Feinstein, and Odling-Smee, *British Economic Growth*, Table 14.7, p. 442.

17 Cain and Hopkins, *Crisis and Deconstruction*, Table 3.7, p. 45.

18 A. K. Cairncross, *Control of Long-Term International Capital Movements* (Washington, 1973), pp. 55–68.

19 Atkin, *British Overseas Investment*, p. 161.

20 Ibid., p. 164, provides a good assessment of the change.

production, could supply, it is at least possible that capital export within the Empire was beneficial to Britain's industrial economy.[21]

It is impossible confidently to generalize about the results for Britain of possessing an Empire, or of the various devices adopted to maximize benefits, over the whole period from 1900 to the 1960s. As Jacques Marseille has brilliantly demonstrated for France, the economic relevance of colonies to a metropolis changes constantly.[22] It is, therefore, proposed to use a matrix, in which time is balanced against function in each main period.

Before 1914

It has always been conventional to assume that a sheltered Imperial trading system would benefit the metropolis by maximizing exports and by providing ample and possibly cheaper imports. Moreover, trade might generate demand for development capital and provide invisible earnings from interest, dividends, shipping, and other commercial services. Did Empire provide these commercial advantages before 1914?

In 1913 37.2 per cent of total British exports were to the Empire and 24.9 per cent of British imports came from the Empire. British exports to the Empire were then worth £195.3m and imports from the Empire £191.4m. This rough balance on visibles contrasted with foreign trade, in which Britain then had an adverse visible balance of £247m.[23]

A more useful measure of Empire trade is provided by the proportion of particular goods Britain drew from or sent to the Empire. Table 4.1 lists the more important of both these.

These figures suggest some interesting conclusions. First, while the Empire provided half or more of a number of staple imports, it was a limited provider of others, including (Empire proportion in 1913) iron ore (18.4 per cent), copper (37.4 per cent), mineral oils (7.6 per cent), sugar (8.7 per cent), meat (24.7 per

[21] Atkin, *British Overseas Investment*, p. 248. P. Svedberg has argued in 'Colonization and Foreign Direct Investment Profitability', in John Black and John H. Dunning, eds., *International Capital Movements: Papers of the Fifth Annual Conference of the International Economics Study Group* (New York, 1982), that the British provided about 96% of direct investment made in the colonies before 1939, contrasted with only 44% in all Lesser Developed Countries (LDCs), attributing this to a variety of influences which deterred foreign investors in British possessions. Also that the British colonies provided a higher rate of return to all investors than other similar economies. After independence both advantages largely disappeared.

[22] *Empire colonial et capitalisme français: Histoire d'un divorce* (Paris, 1984); 'The Phases of French Colonial Imperialism. Towards a new Periodization', in A. N. Porter and R. F. Holland, eds., *Money, Finance and Empire, 1790–1960* (London, 1985).

[23] Taken from Werner Schlote, *British Overseas Trade from 1700 to the 1930s* (Oxford, 1952), appendix, Tables 21, 22.

TABLE 4.1. *The Empire share of major British imports and exports, 1913*

Imports to Britain	£m	%	Exports of British goods	£m	%
Total	769	100.0	Total	525	100.0
Empire	191	24.9	Empire	195	37.2
Foodstuffs			Textiles		
wheat		48.5	cotton goods		51.7
rice/ground rice		60.1	clothing (all)		68.6
tea		87.3	Other manufactures		
cocoa		50.9	hardware, cutlery		57.2
spices		72.2	copper and brass		64.8
cheese		81.7	locomotives		58.6
Raw Materials			railway carriages		58.4
tin (smelted)		94.8	motor vehicles		67.4
wool		80.2	electrical engineering		61.6
jute (raw)		99.4	paper, paper goods		62.0
oilseeds		53.3			
rubber (raw)		57.2			
cotton (raw)		3.0			
iron ore, etc.		8.4			

Source: Schlote, *British Overseas Trade*, app. Tables 21, 22.

cent), butter (19.0 per cent), leaf tobacco (0.9 per cent), and raw cotton (3.0 per cent). Clearly, the Empire could not make Britain independent of foreign supplies of vital imports. Moreover, only smelted tin provided Britain with any price advantage over foreign consumers due to the export duty.

The picture is different for British exports, for here the Empire provided markets for half or more of British exports of certain key manufactured products. The largest single export in 1913 was cotton piece goods, worth £97.7m, and more than half went to Empire markets: India was the largest single British customer, importing manufactured textiles of all kinds in 1913 worth £40.7m out of total textile exports of £186.4m, or 21.8 per cent. India was also an important market for machinery (£4.5m out of £33.6m), and locomotives and railway carriages (£2.2m out of £7.0m).[24] The only substantial British exports which did not go predominantly to Empire markets were coal and its by-products, woollens, cotton yarn, machinery, steamships, and pottery and porcelain.

It is, therefore, arguable that before the First World War, and without preferential duties, the Empire was well matched to the needs of the main British industries of the period. Except in Canada, there were few really competitive

[24] Ibid., appendix, Table 25.

Empire industries. In the special case of capital goods, it was axiomatic, though unpopular in India, that governments would order from Britain. Other factors tending to bias Empire imports towards Britain included the preference of British or British-owned trading firms, including Indian managing agencies; pegged currency rates; the convenience of language; and familiarity with British products, particularly important in the case of technical goods such as mill machinery.

An alternative, though imprecise, measure of the commercial value of Empire to Britain before 1914 is the extent to which British capital exports benefited British manufactured exports. The evidence is set out in Table 4.2.

The general conclusion suggested by these figures is that capital investment in the Empire before 1914 provided no great special benefits to British commerce. On the import side there was little correlation between proportions of British Imperial investment and imports. The Empire was more useful as a market, particularly for major products that were facing intense foreign competition, and here the investment–trade ratios were almost identical. But it is unlikely that large Imperial investment played a direct role in this, except in the special case of railways.

Between the Wars

The Empire played a greater role in Britain's trade after 1919. The Empire's share of British exports rose from an average of 35.0 per cent between 1909 and 1913 to 37.2 per cent in the later 1920s and to 41.3 per cent between 1934 and 1938. In the same

TABLE 4.2. *British investment and trade with the Empire in 1913*

	Capital exported c.1914[1]		Imports to UK in 1913[2]		Exports from UK in 1913[3]	
	£m	%	£m	%	£m	%
Total	3,956	100.0	768	100.0	525	100.0
Foreign	2,468	62.4	577	75.1	330	62.8
Empire	1,488	37.6	191	24.9	195	37.2
Dominions	1,045	26.4	103	13.2	92	17.5
India	286	7.2	49	6.3	70	13.4
Colonies	156	3.9	39	5.1	33	6.3

Sources: [1] Accumulated overseas capital stock, based on Davis and Huttenback, *Mammon and the Pursuit of Empire*, Table 2.1, pp. 40–1, intermediate estimate. There appears to be a typographical error in the total given for Empire investment: I have added the private and government figures to give a corrected total.

[2] Based on Schlote, app. Tables 21 and 24.

[3] Based on Schlote, app. Tables 22 and 25.

periods the Empire share of British imports increased from 26.9 per cent to 32.9 per cent and 41.2 per cent.[25] At first sight these seem evidence that Britain had been successful in creating an Imperial economy. Yet, as these figures and Tables 4.3 and 4.4 demonstrate, the benefit was limited.

First, the proportionate increase in Empire imports to Britain–about 14 per cent between 1914 and 1938—was far greater than the increase in British exports to the Empire, about 6 per cent. The increase in Empire imports was largely the result of the advantages given to the Dominions at the Ottawa Conference: their share of British imports increased from 14.3 per cent to 24.3 per cent in those years, though there were other beneficiaries, the most important being Empire sugar producers, whose share of the British market increased from 8.7 per cent to 64.2 per cent between 1913 and 1934. It is difficult to see any direct advantage to Britain in these changes, apart from a possible saving of foreign exchange. Indeed, their main effect was to raise prices to British consumers above what they might have been in a free market.

TABLE 4.3. *The Empire share of major British imports and exports, 1934*

Imports to Britain	£m	%	Exports from Britain	£m	%
Total	727	100.0	Total	378	100.0
Empire	257	35.3	Empire	166	44.0
Foodstuffs			Textiles		
wheat		63.3	cottons		53.2
tea		88.9	woollens		37.7
cocoa		90.7	art. silk		69.4
spices		77.6	Other Manufactures		
sugar, raw		64.2	iron products		55.3
meat, etc.		32.1	hardware, etc.		63.8
butter		53.5	copper/brass		68.2
cheese		88.9	machinery		51.2
Raw Materials			locomotives		65.3
copper, ore		80.0	carriages		68.3
copper, smelted		47.4	motor vehicles		71.7
tin, smelted		60.3	steamships		47.0
lead		89.4	electrical engineering		61.1
min. oils		5.9	rubber tyres		50.3
raw cotton		17.1	tobacco products		64.0
wool		83.4			
jute, raw		98.8			
oilseeds		60.5			
rubber, raw		79.7			

Sources: Imports, Schlote, *British Overseas Trade*, app. Table 21. Exports, ibid, app. Table 22.

[25] Cain and Hopkins, *Crisis and Deconstruction*, Table 3.3.

TABLE 4.4. *British overseas investment (1936) and trade with the Empire (1934)*

	Quoted overseas securities 1936		Imports to UK		Exports of UK	
	£m	%	£m	%	£m	%
Total	3,240	100.0	727	100.0	378	100.0
Foreign	1,259	38.9	470	64.6	212	56.1
Empire	1,981	61.1	257	35.3	166	43.9
Dominions	1,342	41.4	157	21.6	88	23.3
India[1]	438	13.5	42	5.7	37	9.8
Colonies[2]	201	6.2	58	7.9	41	10.8

Notes: [1] India and Ceylon for investment, India only for trade.
[2] Colonies include Ceylon for trade

Sources: 1. Investment: Thomas Balogh, *Studies in Financial Organization* (Cambridge, 1947), Table 48, p. 254. These are based on Sir R. Kindersley's estimates. They probably grossly understate the capital stock since they took account only of quoted securities, excluding unquoted securities, and other assets, notably those of private companies. Feinstein, *National Income, Expenditure and Output*, gives £5.1bn for total net overseas assets in 1938, but not their distribution. A. R. Conan, *Capital Imports into Sterling Countries* (London, 1960), p. 85, estimates total UK investment in the Empire in 1938 at £2175m.
2. Trade: Schlote, *British Overseas Trade*, app. Tables 21,22,23.

Secondly, therefore, any benefits Britain gained must have come in other ways: from sustaining the Empire market for British-manufactured exports, enabling the Empire to meet its debt obligations, and providing other invisible earnings, such as from shipping and insurance. The British export economy suffered badly in the 1930s: in 1934, while the value of imports had hardly changed since 1913, that of exports had declined by 28 per cent. Exports to the Empire had also droped absolutely, but there the decline was only 15 per cent. Overall in 1937 Britain had a favourable balance of trade in manufactures with the Empire of £156.2m, contrasted with a small adverse balance with all foreign countries of £1.9m.[26]

The Empire, therefore, buffered the British export economy. It is, however, arguable that the greatest benefit Britain received from the Empire in this period came from the relative security of capital investments, particularly debt servicing, rather than from trade. Table 4.4 shows how important the Empire, and particularly the Dominions, became after 1918. By 1936 the ratio of quoted British overseas securities relating to the Empire and foreign countries had been reversed since 1914: it was now 61.1 per cent to 38.9 per cent, due in part to the liquidation of most United States bonds during the First World War. Since Britain depended heavily on income from overseas investments, the constancy of colonial and Dominion debt servicing in the 1930s was important. Indeed, repayments on overseas loans

[26] Cain and Hopkins, *Crisis and Deconstruction*, Table 3.4.

were far greater than new overseas lending. Thus, by helping, through her trade policies, to keep the colonies and Dominions solvent during the recession, Britain received an indirect reward.

On the other hand, there is no evidence that investment in the Empire had any direct effect on British exports: as Table 4.4 shows, while in 1936 the Empire held over 61 per cent of quoted British overseas securities, in 1934 it took only about 44 per cent of British exports, substantially down from 1913. The Dominions held 41.4 per cent and India some 13.5 per cent of British investment but bought only 23.3 per cent and 9.8 per cent respectively of British exports. Only the rest of the British Empire had a higher percentage of British exports than its holding of British capital. The reason for this is that most of the new lending of the 1920s was to governments or public authorities: between 1918 and 1931 these took £591m out of an Empire total of £850m (69.5 per cent), as contrasted with a mere £36m (4.2 per cent) for railways and £258.7m (30.4 per cent) for other company issues.[27] Since this public borrowing was now seldom used for capital imports from Britain, it was unlikely to have any significant impact on British exports.

After the Second World War

The two decades after 1945 saw both the peak of the Imperial economy as it had been constructed after 1931 and also the start of its terminal decline. Tables 4.5 to 4.9 provide evidence on trade, the balance of payments, and the relative importance of capital investment in the Empire-sterling bloc.

These statistics raise two major questions. First, what advantages did Britain receive from its control over the Empire-sterling area? Secondly, what longer-term effects did this highly protective structure have on the British industrial economy?

On the first point, there can be no doubt that in the critical decade after 1945 the Empire was vital to Britain's short-term position. Table 4.5 shows that in 1948 the Empire provided 45 per cent and in 1954 48.3 per cent of British imports, paid for in sterling and so saving hard currency, and that in the same years it took 46.1 per cent and 48 per cent respectively of British exports. More importantly, Table 4.6 shows that throughout the post-war period the sterling area kept the British balance of payments more or less in balance. Significantly, the main surplus from the sterling area came from invisible earnings rather than from visibles, which were normally roughly balanced.

Paradoxically the Empire-sterling area's earlier importance is highlighted by considering why it became much less important by the early 1960s. Table 4.5 shows that by 1965 Western Europe had virtually caught up with the sterling area and had overtaken the Commonwealth as a source of imports and as a market for British

[27] Atkin, *British Overseas Investment*, Table 14.

TABLE 4.5 *British overseas trade, 1948–1965: sterling area and Commonwealth share of total UK exports and imports*

	1948		1954		1960		1965	
	£m	%	£m	%	£m	%	£m	%
A. Imports to the United Kingdom								
Total	2,077	100.0	3,379	100.0	4,655	100.0	5,763	100.0
Sterling area	755	36.4	1,501	44.4	1,582	34.0	1,812	31.4
Non-sterling	1,322	63.6	1,878	55.6	3,073	66.0	3,951	68.6
Dollar area	483	23.2	620	18.3	950	20.4	1,132	19.6
Western Europe	427	20.5	818	24.2	1,136	24.4	1,762	30.6
Rest of World	433	20.8	440	13.0	987	21.2	1,157	20.1
Commonwealth	933	44.9	1,634	48.3	1,510	32.4	1,720	29.8
Dominions	533	25.7	769	22.7	898	26.6	1,066	18.5
India/Pakistan	107	5.1	174	5.1	178	3.8	155	2.7
West Germany	30	1.4	78	2.3	183	3.9	265	4.6
B. Exports (includes re-exports) from the United Kingdom								
Total	1,639	100.0	2,775	100.0	3,789	100.0	4,897	100.0
Sterling area	794	48.4	1,347	48.5	1,465	38.5	1,676	34.3
Non-sterling	845	51.6	1,428	51.5	2,324	61.5	3,221	65.7
Dollar area	173	10.5	375	13.5	596	15.7	729	14.9
Western Europe	407	24.8	776	28.0	1,009	26.6	1,593	32.5
Rest of World	266	16.2	277	10.0	719	19.0	899	18.3
Commonwealth	757	46.1	1,333	48.0	1,353	35.7	1,365	27.9
Dominions	440	26.8	692	24.9	750	19.8	884	18.0
India/Pakistan	114	6.9	161	5.8	190	5.0	164	3.3
West Germany	25	1.5	71	2.5	163	4.3	255	5.2

Notes: 1. There are some inconsistencies in the data on which this Table is based. The regions changed slightly over this period: e.g. 'Western Europe' was listed as 'OEEC and dependencies' before 1960 and the sterling area lost Iraq in 1959. There are other changes in the figures for overlapping years in the Board of Trade figures. Moreover these figures sometimes differ from those given in other sources. The Table must therefore be taken as a broad indication of trends. 2. The 'Dominions' consist of Canada, Australia, South Africa, and New Zealand to correlate with those in previous Tables.

Sources: Board of Trade, *The Commonwealth and Sterling Area, 1951–1954* and *The Commonwealth and Sterling Area, 1965*. Individual countries are taken from *Annual Abstract of Statistics*, 1959 and 1967

exports. Meantime, between 1953 and 1961 Britain's share of manufactures imported by sterling countries declined from 61.4 per cent to 43.4 per cent.[28] Why did this significant decline take place? What light does it throw on the benefits resulting from previous British dominance of the Empire-sterling area markets?

[28] Much of the following two paragraphs derives from a paper published by the National Economic Development Council (actually written by M. FG. Scott), *Export Trends* (London, 1963).

TABLE 4.6. *United Kingdom balance-of-payments by region, 1946–1962* (£m—figures in brackets = deficit)

	Dollar area	Other western hemisphere	OEEC	Other non-sterling	Sterling area	Non-territorial	Total
A. Balance of current transactions, including defence aid (net), 1946–1955							
1946	(301)	(24)	80	(17)	(28)	(8)	(278)
1947	(510)	(65)	6	11	127	(12)	(443)
1948	(252)	(38)	88	(42)	254	(9)	1
1949	(296)	62	(16)	(8)	293	(4)	31
1950	(88)	26	115	(35)	287	(5)	300
1951	(436)	3	(197)	(101)	335	9	(403)
1952	(173)	93	(31)	1	363	(6)	247
1953	(4)	(24)	86	(13)	157	(14)	188
1954	(68)	8	38	(19)	278	(9)	228
1955	(205)	0	(51)	(42)	225	(6)	(79)

	Non-sterling				Sterling				
	Imports	Exports	Invisibles net	Total non-sterling balance	Imports	Exports	Invisibles net	Total sterling balance	Total balance-of-payments
B. The sterling area and the British balance of payments on current account, 1956–1962									
1956	2,092	1,949	79	(64)	1,370	1,458	213	301	237
1957	2,166	2,036	40	(90)	1,407	1,479	281	353	263
1958	2,113	1,973	7	(133)	1,247	1,434	288	475	342
1959	2,272	2,152	(39)	(159)	1,345	1,370	274	299	140
1960	2,705	2,274	(200)	(631)	1,401	1,454	306	359	(272)
1961	2,619	2,465	(165)	(319)	1,394	1,418	261	285	(34)
1962	2,654	2,631	(120)	(143)	1,405	1,360	262	217	74

Sources: A. *United Kingdom Balance of Payments 1946–1956*, Cmnd. 122 (London, 1957). B: For 1956 and 1957: *United Kingdom Balance of Payments 1956–1958*, Cmnd. 700 (London, 1959); for 1958–62: *United Kingdom Balance of Payments 1963* (London, 1963).

It is clear that the reduction in Britain's share of these markets was integral with Britain's decline in the world league of exporters of manufactures. The critical period appears to have been after 1953. In that year Britain's share of world exports of manufactures was 21 per cent (in 1938 it had been 22.1 per cent): in 1961 it was 15.7 per cent. By far the largest drop was in the sterling area: from 57.8 per cent to 43.2 per cent in these years. This was not due to any major change in Imperial Preferences, which still applied to some 49 per cent of British exports to the Empire in 1958, providing an average margin of perhaps 12 per cent, down only from about 14 per cent in 1948. It was only after 1958 that Australia and New Zealand made agreements freeing them from the 1932 arrangements.[29] By far the

[29] See Sir Donald MacDougall and R. Hutt, 'Imperial Preference: A Quantitive Analysis', *Economic Journal*, LXIV (1954) pp. 233–57.

TABLE 4.7 *The quality of British exports of UK-manufactured goods to sterling and non-sterling markets, excluding re-exports, 1951–1954 & 1960–1962, showing the share of different categories of British manufactured exports as a percentage of total exports of manufactures (col. 5) and of all goods (col. 7)*

	Chemicals %	Machinery and transport %	Textiles %	Other manufactures %	Total manufactures £ m	Manufactures as % of total exports 5/7%	Total exports[1] £m
A. 1951–1954							
Sterling Area							
1951	8.4	39.4	23.7	28.5	1,166	89.0	1,312
1952	8.5	43.6	16.9	31.0	1,099	86.5	1,271
1953	8.2	44.7	17.0	30.1	1,067	85.1	1,254
1954	9.1	45.1	16.3	29.5	1,136	85.4	1,339
Non-Sterling Area							
1951	9.1	41.8	19.0	30.2	1,028	81.0	1,269
1952	8.7	46.6	14.4	30.2	1,042	79.3	1,314
1953	8.6	45.1	14.1	32.2	1,032	77.7	1,328
1954	9.7	34.7	10.5	31.5	1,035	77.0	1,344

	Metals %	Engineering products %	Textiles (excluding clothing) %	Other manufactures %	Total manufactures £ m	Total manufactures as % of total exports to each area 5/7%	Total exports[1] £m
B. 1960–1962							
Sterling Area							
1960	14.4	51.3	9.8	24.5	1,258	88.0	1,429
1961	14.6	51.7	9.2	24.5	1,227	87.6	1,400
1962	13.3	53.0	8.8	25.0	1,176	87.6	1,342
Western Europe							
1960	17.3	50.3	8.1	24.3	807	78.3	1,030
1961	16.4	54.2	7.2	22.2	971	81.4	1,192
1962	16.5	54.3	7.0	22.2	1,089	80.1	1,360
North America							
1960	12.5	56.4	9.4	21.6	445	82.0	543
1961	10.9	55.0	9.2	24.6	402	79.6	505

Note: [1]Total exports, including food, beverages and tobacco; basic materials; and mineral fuels and lubricants.

Source: *Annual Abstract of Statistics (AAS)* 1955, 1963. The categories in 'Total exports' in A and B differ because the format of the *AAS* tables changed.

most likely cause was the rapid rundown of the whole apparatus of controls and quotas, including progressive liberation of sterling balances and the end of quotas on imports from non-sterling countries, which for the first time since 1939 enabled

TABLE 4.8. *Investments in, and trade with, the Commonwealth and world, 1956* (British-held securities at nominal balance sheet value; imports; and exports)

	Securities		Dividends and interest total yield		Imports		Exports	
	£m	%	£m	%	£m	%	£m	%
World								
Total	2,110	100.0	223.0	10.6	3,861	100.0	3,143	100.0
Government and Municipal loans	732	34.7	27.0	3.6	n/a	n/a	n/a	n/a
UK-registered companies	753	35.7	12.3	16.3	n/a	n/a	n/a	n/a
Overseas-registered companies	625	29.6	73.0	11.7	n/a	n/a	n/a	n/a
Foreign countries								
Total	614	29.1	50.0	8.1	2,143	55.5	1,711	51.4
USA	173	8.2	23.0	13.3	408	10.5	243	7.7
Argentina	34	1.6	7.0	2.0	92	2.4	18	0.6
Commonwealth								
Total	1,221	57.9	117.7	9.6	1,718	44.5	1,432	45.6
South Africa	156	7.4	19.5	12.5	91	2.3	154	4.9
CAF	130	6.2	17.7	13.6	108	2.8	58	1.8
India	65	3.1	10.8	16.6	141	3.6	168	5.3
Pakistan	11	0.5	2.6	23.6	23	0.6	34	1.1
Malaya	72	3.4	14.7	20.4	43	1.1	40	1.3
Australia	335	15.9	17.2	5.1	236	6.1	239	7.6
New Zealand	93	4.4	4.3	4.6	197	5.1	127	4.0
Canada	188	8.9	12.5	6.6	344	8.9	178	5.6
Other Commonwealth	171	8.1	18.4	10.6	535	13.8	434	13.8
Old Dominions	772	36.6	53.5	6.9	868	22.5	698	22.2
Unclassified by area								
Total	276	13.1	55.7	20.2	n/a	n/a	n/a	n/a

Notes: 1. The figures for overseas investment are for nominal capital values, not market values or the value of assets. They therefore do not show the full current value of British foreign investment.
2. Overseas currencies are converted into sterling at end-of-year exchange rates.

Sources: 1. For securities and interest and dividends, *Annual Abstract of Statistics*, 1958, Table 281. This is last time such data were printed in the *Abstract*. 2. Trade: *Annual Abstract of Statistics*, 1960, Tables 266, 267.

sterling countries to shop around for the best and cheapest goods in the world market. It was at this point that limitations of the British industrial economy had a major visible effect for the first time since 1932: lagging design and quality, slow delivery dates, lack of salesmanship, insufficient investment in research and development, and prices rising about 1 per cent faster that those of competitors. In

TABLE 4.9. *Net operating assets (NOA) and profitability (annual averages 1955–64) of British direct investment in fifteen countries and nine-year additions to net operating assets*

	Net operating assets (£m)	Pre-tax profitability (%)	UK stake (£m)	Post-tax profitability UK group (%)	1955–1964 addition to NOA (£m)
Germany	29.6	47.8	27.8	22.8	44.8
Malaysia	24.0	36.6	19.7	26.9	13.5
Italy	8.2	26.9	6.0	12.3	8.0
India	90.7	21.2	70.3	8.6	70.4
Ghana	22.1	20.0	21.3	10.6	(0.1)
Brazil	27.4	16.8	24.0	5.3	8.9
South Africa	97.2	14.3	96.7	10.5	34.9
Australia	199.3	14.3	154.5	7.9	170.6
USA	279.4	13.0	207.6	8.3	101.9
Jamaica	8.3	11.9	5.2	8.4	7.0
Canada	287.6	8.9	166.4	5.5	201.8
Nigeria	51.2	7.6	49.5	4.7	14.5
Argentina	14.5	7.5	13.7	1.6	14.3
France	23.3	7.4	14.5	1.9	16.6
Denmark	5.5	6.5	4.4	5.3	6.3
Total 15 countries	1,168.2	14.2	881.6	8.4	713.3
Rest of World	274.0	15.8	225.6	8.9	n/a
Total World	1,442.2	14.5	1,107.2	8.5	n/a

Notes: 1. 'Net operating assets' here means all the assets of a business, other than trade investment, less current liabilities other than to the British parent. 2. 'UK Stake' means the net operating assets of all overseas enterprises that were owned or substantially owned and controlled by a British registered company and represented the total net operating assets of these enterprises plus the value of trade investments, less minority interests in them and non-current liabilities.

Source: W. B. Reddaway, *Effects of U.K. Direct Investment Overseas: An Interim Report* (Cambridge, 1967), Tables 4.5 and 4.6.

short, once deprived of the protection provided by world shortages and economic regulation within the sterling area and Empire, the British industrial economy had to face up to its own competitive weakness.

This has two possible implications for assessment of the economic value of the Empire-sterling area to Britain. On the one hand, it is clear that for over two decades after 1932 these were the lifeline which kept the British export economy, and therefore the balance-of-payments and sterling, above water. This suggests that it was in these two and a half decades that Britain obtained the greatest benefit from its Empire. Yet, on the other hand, when the lifeline broke this dependence proved to have been only a short-term palliative. This raises two important questions. Did the existence of relatively soft sterling markets for British manufactures have a debilitating effect on British industry, enabling static firms and products to survive when they should have given place to more progressive enterprises and higher technology? And did the fact that the majority of new British overseas investment in this period was in the Empire (largely because investment in the sterling area was virtually free while that elsewhere faced obstacles), result in higher or lower returns than it might have done if invested elsewhere, and did it benefit British exports?

Table 4.7 attempts to throw light on the first question by analysing the 'quality' of British exports within and outside the sterling area in the early 1950s and early 1960s, taking 'quality' crudely to imply products which involved high rather than low technology, especially capital goods, and which pointed to future growth rather than earlier industrial development. At first sight the table suggests two significant conclusions. Manufactured exports constituted a higher proportion of total exports to the sterling area than to the rest of the world. Also, assuming 'machinery and transport' in the first period roughly equates with 'engineering goods' in the second, these provided an increasing proportion of manufactures exported to the sterling area: 39.4 per cent in 1951, rising to 45.1 per cent in 1954 and to 53 per cent in 1962. In both periods these proportions were similar to those for the non-sterling area. The same is true of other manufactures, which may indicate that British exports to the sterling area were not qualitatively inferior to those elsewhere. Conversely, there was a significant decline in the absolute and relative importance of textile exports, which may be taken as the main symbol of the traditional British export economy.

There is, however, an alternative interpretation of the trends. Even if these capital goods continued to provide more than half of total British manufactured exports to the sterling area, British exports had a declining share of every category to the non-OECD (Organization for Economic Cooperation and Development) sterling area between 1953 and 1961, and of all but two categories (drugs and power machinery) to the world as a whole. Moreover, apart from textiles and pottery, the largest proportionate drop in these years in exports to the sterling area was in electrical machinery, metalworking machinery, scientific instruments, rubber manufactures, and road motor-vehicles. These were precisely the goods in which an advanced industrial country would have expected to have remained in the forefront: yet, once the sterling area was free to buy where it pleased, most of its members chose not to buy British. This suggests that these two decades of feather-bedding had blunted the edge of British industry: that poor research and development were affecting design; that salesmanship and delivery periods were lax; and that rising wage costs in Britain (due more to slow increase in productivity rather than to rising wages) were making British goods less competitive on price.

Finally, what of the effects of investment in the Empire-sterling area? Tables 4.8 and 4.9 set out some of the available (and somewhat uncertain) data for the 1950s and early 1960s.[30]

First, after 1945 overseas capital was much less important for the British economy than it had been in any previous modern period. Thus net overses property income constituted 9.1 per cent of the British GNP in 1913, 5.9 per cent in 1929, 4.5 per cent in 1937, 3.6 per cent in 1950, but only 1.1 per cent in 1955 and 1960, rising to 1.5 per cent in both 1965 and 1970.[31] By another test, in 1913 net overseas assets represented 33.9 per cent of total UK reproducible assets at home and abroad. In 1937 this had dropped to 17.6 per cent. In 1955 it was 0.4 per cent and in 1964 1.8 per cent.[32] Between 1956 and 1971 the total net outflow of new long-term investment from Britain was only £636m.[33]

But if overseas investment and its proceeds were relatively less significant for the British economy after 1945, they were still important to the balance of payments. Here the Empire continued to play a major role. Table 4.8 shows that in 1956 about 58 per cent of total UK owned securities overseas was in Empire countries. This, however, did not continue after 1960. Between 1960 and 1971 total gross new investment in the overseas sterling area was £2,603m, compared with £3,005m in non-sterling countries.[34]

Profitability was another matter. Table 4.8 shows that in 1956 the average rate of return on securities in the Empire at 9.6 per cent was well above that on officially recorded foreign securities, though below the global figure, which includes a substantial balancing 'unclassified' element at 20.2 per cent. But in three of the British Dominions with the largest British investment the return on nominal values was comparatively low: 4.6 per cent in New Zealand, 5.1 per cent in

[30] There are major contrasts in three estimates of the net asset value of British direct overseas investment in the early and mid-1960s. *Board of Trade Journal* for 7 Aug. 1964, p. 293, gave a total book value of £3,117m, excluding oil and insurance, for 'the total net assets of overseas subsidiaries and branches attributable to parent companies' in 1962. Lynden Moore, *The Growth and Structure of International Trade since the Second World War* (Brighton, 1985), Table 10.4a, estimated a total, also excluding oil and banks, of £4.2bn for 1966 ($11.8bn). But W. B. Reddaway, *Effects of U.K. Direct Investment Overseas: An Interim Report* (Cambridge, 1967), Tables iv. 5 and v. 3, gave £1,442.2m as the total value of 'net operating assets' and £1,492.9m. for the book value (market value £2,025.6m) of British overseas direct investment, excluding oil and insurance, at the end of 1964. There must be a basic difference in how these figures were calculated. I have adopted Reddaway in the text mainly because his total for the book value of overseas direct investments at the end of 1955 (£791.1m) is close to the last British *Annual Abstract of Statistics* (London, 1958), estimate for 1956 of £756m for the nominal capital value (share and loan capital) of the overseas investments of all UK registered companies. In addition the *Abstract* gave £619m for the capital of British companies registered overseas at that date.

[31] Mitchell, *British Historical Statistics*, pp. 829–30.

[32] Matthews, Feinstein, and Odling-Smee, *British Economic Growth*, Table 5.3.

[33] Cairncross, *Control of Long-term International Capital Movements*, Table 4.1.

[34] Ibid.

Australia, and 6.6 per cent in Canada. This was because most of the British investment in these countries was still in Dominion government stock paying low interest, or in portfolio investments. By contrast, in countries such as India and Pakistan (which had written off their long-term public debt during the Second World War), South Africa, Malaya, and the Central African Federation, where the majority of the investment was direct, the yield was much higher.

This suggests that after 1945 one main benefit of Empire countries for Britain lay in the opportunities they presented for business investment within the sterling area, where restrictions on British investment were slight and investors did not have to pay a premium on foreign exchange. Neverthess, as can be seen from Table 4.9, the highest average pre-tax profits on operating assets for 1955–64 came from Germany, with Italy in third place, interleaved by Malaysia in second and India in fourth place. Moreover, in that decade the greatest proportionate increase in the net operating assets of British companies abroad came in two non-Empire countries—Germany with 302.1 per cent, and Denmark with 218.2 per cent. By the mid-1960s, and increasingly after the end of the sterling area in 1972, British direct investment was shifting from the Empire to Europe as the new focus of British economic activity.

Is it possible usefully to define what economic benefits Britain obtained from her overseas Empire during the first six decades of the twentieth century? Ignoring non-commercial aspects such as the cost of Imperial defence, which may well have outweighed economic benefits, particularly during and after the Second World War, the evidence suggests that the Empire always provided benefits for Britain, but that these were different in each of the three main periods after 1900 and had increasingly adverse long-term effects.

Before 1914 the Empire was not in any way essential to the British economy but provided some tangible benefits. It was relatively unimportant as a source of imports, but an important market for certain key British manufactures which faced increasing competition in foreign markets. Moreover, Britain's visible trade with the Empire was generally more or less in balance and favourable balances with India helped to balance Britain's international accounts. The Empire provided a particularly safe haven for investment and was able to take British funds at various times when other countries could not do so. The really critical fact is that whatever benefits the Empire then provided were largely unqualified. Despite limited preferences in some Dominion markets and the enforced open door in India and the colonies, Britain's economic role in the Empire was not artificial. It accurately reflected Britain's still dominant world-trading and investing position and probably had few adverse consequences for the domestic economy.

Between the wars the picture becomes more complicated. The Empire became even more proportionately important as a market for British exports, but this was increasingly artificial and ambiguous. Whereas before 1930 British imports from and exports (including re-exports) to the Empire roughly balanced, from 1931 to 1939 Britain had a consistent and sometimes large adverse balance on visibles with the Empire and the sterling area. This, in fact, was essential to enable overseas components of the Empire to meet their debt obligations and pay for other invisibles. But it meant that Britain had to accept a deficit on her visible trade with the Empire in order to ensure that she continued to profit from invisibles. She had also to continue to lend to them. It was a crude balancing act, probably beneficial to both Britain and her overseas partners in that time of crisis, potentially enervating to all parties in the long term.

Finally, during the period of prolonged war and post-war crisis between 1939 and the early 1950s, the Empire and sterling area were of greater short-term economic, as well as political, value to Britain than at any previous time. This was largely due to the devices adopted to protect Empire-sterling area markets, and for the time being it achieved its objectives. The sterling area, in particular, was critical for preserving London's place in the international monetary system, with its major contribution to invisible earnings. But by the later 1950s these benefits were waning as sterling markets became increasingly open to competitors and the British share of their imports declined.[35] By then the sterling area had passed its time of maximum utility as the world moved into its period of most rapid recorded growth. It was not surprising that by 1963 the British government had decided that it was time to abandon that ship and attempt to climb aboard another, though it was ten years before they were welcomed on board the European Community.

Overall, then, it would seem that the Empire made a significant, if ambiguous, contribution to the British economy in the twentieth century. Yet there remains a central question which this study has not attempted to answer. If Britain had not possessed an Empire or controlled the sterling area, what might have been the consequences for her own economy? Without sheltered markets might her industries have become more internationally competitive in the long run, though they would have suffered severely during the periods of recession? Without secure Imperial fields for investment might she have invested more in domestic growth? Without the need to bolster sterling by relatively high domestic interest rates, might the British industrial economy have been more innovative and competitive?

[35] Catherine R. Schenk, *Britain and the Sterling Area: From Devaluation to Convertibility in the 1950s* (London, 1994), chaps. 3 and 6, strongly challenges the traditional idea that feather-bedding by the sterling area and Commonwealth was in any way responsible for British industrial decline in this period.

In short, it remains quite unclear how Britain might have prospered without her Imperial crutches after 1914. The post-imperial recovery of Japan suggests one possibility, the record of other post-imperial states quite another.

Select Bibliography

JOHN MICHAEL ATKIN, *British Overseas Investment, 1918–1931* (New York, 1977).

P. J. CAIN and A. G. HOPKINS, *British Imperialism: Innovation and Expansion, 1688–1914* (London, 1993).

—— *British Imperialism: Crisis and Deconstruction, 1914–1990* (London, 1993).

A. K. CAIRNCROSS, *Control of Long-Term International Capital Movements* (Washington, 1973).

ARTHUR ROBERT CONAN, *Capital Imports into Sterling Countries* (London, 1960).

JOHN DARWIN, *Britain and Decolonisation: The Retreat from Empire in the Post-War World* (London, 1988).

LANCE E. DAVIS and ROBERT A. HUTTENBACK, with the assistance of SUSAN GRAY DAVIS, *Mammon and the Pursuit of Empire: The Political Economy of British Imperialism, 1860–1912* (Cambridge, 1986).

IAN M. DRUMMOND, *Imperial Economic Policy, 1917–1939: Studies in Expansion and Protection* (London, 1972).

MICHAEL EDELSTEIN, *Overseas Investment in the Age of High Imperialism: The United Kingdom, 1850–1914* (London, 1982).

W. K. HANCOCK, *Survey of British Commonwealth Affairs*, 2 vols. (London, 1937–42).

MICHAEL HAVINDEN and DAVID MEREDITH, *Colonialism and Development: Britain and its Tropical Colonies, 1850–1960* (London, 1993).

JACQUES MARSEILLE, *Empire colonial et capitalisme français: Histoire d'un divorce* (Paris, 1984).

R. C. O. MATTHEWS, C. H. FEINSTEIN, and J. C. ODLING-SMEE, *British Economic Growth, 1856–1973* (Oxford, 1972).

F. V. MEYER, *Britain's Colonies in World Trade* (London, 1948).

J. D. B. MILLER, *Survey of Commonwealth Affairs: Problems of Expansion and Attrition, 1953–1969* (London, 1974).

B. R. MITCHELL, *British Historical Statistics* (Cambridge, 1988).

D. J. MORGAN, *The Official History of Colonial Development*, 5 vols. (London, 1980).

TIM ROOTH, *British Protectionism and the International Economy: Overseas Commercial Policy in the 1930s* (Cambridge, 1993).

CATHERINE R. SCHENK, *Britain and the Sterling Area: From Devaluation to Convertibility in the 1950s* (London, 1994).

WERNER SCHLOTE, *British Overseas Trade from 1700 to the 1930s* (Oxford, 1952).

5

The British Empire and the Great War, 1914–1918

ROBERT HOLLAND

'The truth is,' Sir Henry Campbell-Bannerman wrote in 1903, 'that we cannot provide for a fighting empire, and nothing will give us the power. A peaceful empire of the old type we are quite fit for.'[1] This classic Liberal statement of Imperial belief touched on the dominant question embedded in British political culture at the outset of the twentieth century. During the Great War of 1914–18 that question was reopened and its implications pursued more rigorously than during the localized South African conflict, which had formed the basis of Campbell-Bannerman's judgement. Could the vast but disaggregated resources of the Empire be brought to bear on the single, compelling objective of victory? Or would the pressures lead to its constituent parts flying off at tangents from the main goal? This chapter will trace the impact of the wartime experience on the British Empire as a system of power, and suggest where between these two extremes the Imperial or colonial outcome of the war came to rest.

In 1904 War Office planners in London predicted that a conflict between Germany and Britain would be 'a struggle between an elephant and a whale in which each, although supreme in its own element, would find it difficult to bring its strength to bear on its antagonist'. Whether Britain could transform itself into a continental elephant, instead of being constrained into an Imperial and aquatic role, was also profoundly at issue between 1914 and 1918. Meanwhile, it was significant that the first British shots on land were fired by a small British West African Force on 12 August as it closed in on the German wireless station at Kamina in Togoland. The rash of six colonial campaigns in Togoland, Cameroon, East Africa, South-West Africa, New Guinea, and Samoa marking the early phases of war has been attributed to the need to disrupt Germany's far-flung cable communications on which the effectiveness of her commerce-destroyers depended. The ensuing destruction of the *Emden* (sunk by HMAS *Sydney*, which came directly under Admiralty control on the outbreak of war) in the Indian Ocean on 9 November 1914, of Admiral Graf von Spee's elusive squadron

[1] Quoted in A. J. Spender, *The Life of Sir Henry Campbell-Bannerman*, 2 vols. (London, 1923), II, p. 88.

in the Battle of the Falklands on 8 December 1914, and the *Königsberg* in the Rufiji River in East Africa on 11 July 1915, assured the maritime security of the British Empire. Practical necessity, however, was allied to a determination to gain colonial acquisitions while a war of uncertain duration afforded the opportunity. Whatever the motive, it was in keeping with traditional ways of British warfare that, even while the first divisions were struggling across the English Channel, forces on 'great and urgent imperial service' had already swung into flexible and highly dispersed action beyond Europe.

This colonial belligerency took place against the background of enthusiastic manifestations of Imperial solidarity. Such responses were most marked in those colonies of overseas settlement in which pan-British sentiments remained entrenched. The pledge of Andrew Fisher, leader of the Labor Party, that Australia would give 'our last man and our last shilling' to the common struggle, has been much quoted. Fisher was Scottish-born and susceptible to the sudden pull of Imperial patriotism. Yet similar refrains came from those of very different backgrounds. The leader of the Canadian Liberal party, and long-time hero of Quebec, Sir Wilfrid Laurier, asserted that, 'if in what has been done or in what remains to be done there may be anything which in our judgement should not be done or should be differently done, we raise no question, we take no exception, we offer no criticism, so long as there is danger at the front'. Such vibrations penetrated through many layers of Imperial society. In the Legislative Council in Delhi officials as well as unofficial members vied with one another in expressions of loyal enthusiasm and approved military aid which, C. E. Carrington remarks, the British government 'would not have dared to demand'.[2] The *Lagos Weekly Record* promised to abandon its plaintive tone towards Lord Lugard's autocratic administration in Nigeria. Only in 'Occupied' Egypt, where the Council of Ministers approved a *de facto* state of war on 5 August, was there a striking absence of protestations of loyalty, though the tranquillity of Cairo was taken in London to signify an easy compliance rather than the 'bitter if silent hatred' identified by some observers.[3]

Of course, what the populations in India or Egypt really made of these events is unknowable, just as the true feelings of British democracy cannot satisfactorily be defined. Conditions within the Empire were so varied that generalizations are always difficult; the pan-Britishness of the Dominions was replicated elsewhere only in cantonal miniatures. Yet certain shared pressures are discernible. Ernest Scott, the official civil historian of wartime Australia, pointed out that the unanimity with which Australian opinion greeted its engagement alongside the Mother

[2] C. E. Carrington, 'The Empire at War, 1914–18', in E. A. Benians and others, eds., *Cambridge History of the British Empire*, 9 vols. (Cambridge, 1929–59), III, p. 606.

[3] Lieut.-Col. P. G. Elgood, *Egypt and the Army* (Heliopolis, 1928), p. 1.

Country 'was a political fact of the utmost importance... In the circumstances which then prevailed... the slightest faltering would have been detected and denounced. No party could have survived in whose ranks a suspicion of weakening was apparent.'[4] Throughout the Empire, including Britain, there was undoubtedly in August 1914 an acute apprehension of being on trial. The instinctive reaction was not to put a foot wrong. This explains why Opposition leaders in the Dominions, and black journalists in Lagos, quickly made sound and unimpeachable utterances. That the outbreak of war fed a need to defend positions held within the complex hierarchies of the Empire was to underpin some of the contradictions that became evident once the costs of war also became apparent. At the start, however, it was not really so surprising that the Melbourne Celtic Club declared its support for the war; that the annual Indian National Congress in Madras during December 1914 was desultory and poorly attended; or that it was a descendant of the Prophet in Khartoum who helped to inaugurate *The Sudan Book of Loyalty*.

As an illuminating survey of the Empire's part in the Great War emphasizes, the despatch of Expeditionary Forces to Europe was 'the most obvious expression of the Empire's war effort'.[5] Yet the initial response of the authorities in London to such offers was often equivocal. The Army Council did not leap at the chance when the Australian government telegraphed on 3 August its preparedness to send and finance an expeditionary contingent, preferring instead to integrate Australian and New Zealand troops piecemeal into British formations. Charles Bean, Australia's official military historian, held that if the Army Council had prevailed 'there would have been no Anzac Corps'.[6] The only regular troops in the overseas Empire immediately available to the British Liberal government in August 1914 were those of the Indian Army. Even in this case, the Viceroy, Lord Hardinge, had to plead with the Home authorities to use them in Europe, since not to do so would be seen as a slight to Indian loyalty. This attitude is explained by the War Office's wariness of being embroiled in hasty improvisations, and its determination to maintain tight control of the military machinery. In Imperial terms, none the less, it also reflected a belief that it was the duty, and the *right*, of Britain to shoulder the main burden of the fighting, and for the rest of the Empire to accept a supplementary role. The war was eventually to modify this patrician logic. In the interval, it was telling that, when the First Canadian Division crossed to France at

[4] Ernest Scott, *Australia During the War* (Sydney, 1936), pp. 23–24.

[5] Gregory Martin, 'Financial and Manpower Aspects of the Dominions' and India's Contribution to Britain's War Effort, 1914–19', unpublished Ph.D. thesis, Cambridge, 1987, p. 6.

[6] C. E. W. Bean, *Official History of Australia in the War of 1914–18*, Vol. I, *The Story of Anzac from the Outbreak of War to the End of the First Phase of the Gallipoli Campaign, May 4 1915* (1921; Sydney, 1933), p. 32. 'Anzac' was the term coined in Egypt to connote the Australian and New Zealand Army Corps.

the beginning of March 1915, it was despatched alongside a motley group of Territorials and assigned a place on the left flank of the Allied line next to a detachment of French colonial troops from Algeria.

The allocation of parts within the traditional structure of the Empire was central to conceptions of the Imperial war effort (Table 5.1). Bean, for example, began his monumental account with the observation that Australia and her armed forces 'fitted into the larger role of the whole British people much as the part of Britain fitted into the great drama enacted by the "full cast" of the Allies'.[7] But this vision of the clockwork Empire at war obscures the anxiety on the part of Dominion and colonial cadres to resist any demotion within the system of power and protection to which they belonged. In Canada's case, which had so recently been rocked by a scare of 'annexation' to the United States, the sudden advent of war presented a challenge to preserve her status as the senior Dominion within the British Empire.

TABLE 5.1. Population at 1914, and military personnel overseas, and casualties, 1914–1918.

	Estimated population in 1914	Troops sent abroad	Killed, died, and missing
British Isles	46,000,000	5,000,000	705,000
Canada	8,000,000	458,000	57,000
Australia	5,000,000	332,000	59,000
New Zealand	1,100,000	112,000	17,000
South Africa (whites only)	1,400,000	136,000	7,000

Note: All statistical aggregates and breakdowns relating to British Empire forces between 1914 and 1918 are fraught with difficulties. For example, many overseas personnel served in British units; many Britons served with overseas units. The following gives only a rough guide to various war efforts in manpower. The Indian Army recruited 826,868 combatants and 445,592 non-combatants, including Imperial Service Units. India also sent 54 labour corps to France, and 19 labour corps and 12 porterage corps to Mesopotamia (*c*.100,000 in all). Indian Army casualties were officially estimated at 64,449 killed and 69,214 wounded. At the Armistice 943,344 Indian troops were serving in major theatres abroad distributed as follows: France (14.1%), East Africa (5.0%), Mesopotamia (62.4%), Egypt (12.3%), Salonica (1.0%), Aden and the Gulf (5.2%). The tabulation relates to the manpower of the British Isles and the four main Dominions.

The figure for South Africa includes 50,000 troops used in German South-West Africa. In addition, 44,000 black South Africans served in labour brigades in France (casualties were high, though no data is available). Newfoundland (technically a Dominion at this time) recruited 9,256, of whom 1,082 were killed (this does not allow for Newfoundlanders serving with the Canadian forces). An official estimate of the *Combatant Manpower of the Native Races of West Africa* (1923) stipulates the following territorial contributions (West Africa Frontier Force and Carrier Corps combined): Nigeria (43,043), Gold Coast (11,487), Sierra Leone (13,865), and Gambia (426). No aggregate figure for recruitment or mortality amongst colonial and Protectorate forces is available; on mortality, any statistic would anyway pale besides other war-related deaths in the general populations over the period.

[7] Ibid., p. xliv.

The Canadian Expeditionary Force was the first to be despatched in early October 1914. Whereas some other Imperial possessions had only their men to give, Canada was eager to demonstrate that she could do more: the government in Ottawa immediately provided Britain with a million bags of flour at a juncture when keeping supplies moving was as important to the Empire as anything happening in France. Before long, shells were to follow the flour; Canada was thereafter the only Dominion to make an *industrial* contribution to the war. One-third of the British army's munitions in France during 1917–18 were Canadian-made. Canada's drive to enhanced seniority after August 1914 suggested a link between status and contribution that operated throughout the Imperial system.

The relationship between status and war contribution was inevitably shaped by local context. South Africa offers a notable illustration. A society in which Britain had recently been at war with a large part of the European population could not be expected to relate to this new and grander conflict quite as did other Dominions. The rebellion by Afrikaner intransigents in October 1914—touched off by resentment at the commandeering of white troops to conquer German South-West Africa—swiftly made this clear. The Governor-General in Pretoria, Sydney Buxton, constantly reiterated afterwards that the British stake in the country depended on maintaining the Prime Minister, General Louis Botha, in power, and not pressing him into actions likely to jeopardize the Imperial connection. The British government broadly accepted this analysis. 'We may be thankful for what we are getting,' Buxton advised in January 1916. The Governor-General always carefully distanced himself from the raucous calls of British 'Loyalists' for a bigger and more controversial contribution to the war. This was not the only instance where extreme loyalism was an embarrassment to the British authorities. In short, between 1914 and 1918 Britain was above all concerned to preserve the gains she had made in South Africa in 1899–1902.

What Britain gained in South Africa was the conquest of German South-West Africa by Defence Force conscripts, and an Expeditionary Force diverted to East Africa at the end of 1915 to pursue a campaign that had languished after the British–Indian assault on the port of Tanga had gone disastrously wrong on 2–5 November 1914. Beyond this contribution, all South African military personnel abroad were volunteers, including the detachment which helped reduce the rebellious Senussi tribesmen in Tripolitania, and the single infantry brigade sent at the outset to France (the latter designated as Imperial troops and paid for by Britain). Only when the British government agreed to make up the difference between Union and British rates of pay was it possible, once the exhausted South Africans withdrew from East Africa in early 1917, to send a portion of the troops thus released to the Western Front. More than any other Dominion, South Africa's involvement in the war could be measured in cash. Yet the ambiguity of her position went deeper. Where other Dominions developed a rhetoric in which a distinctive nationality was 'blooded' by heroism at the Front—the Australians at Gallipoli (April–December 1915), the Canadians at Vimy Ridge (April 1917)—the exploits of the South African Brigade in the defence of Delville Wood (July 1916) went largely unheralded. As for the Union's black citizens, they were barred from military service, and only allowed to go to France in the South African Native Labour Contingent under strict conditions, including segregation in compounds. The 615 black South Africans who drowned when the troopship *Mendi* foundered off the Isle of Wight on 21 February 1917 received scant commemoration beyond their home towns until Queen Elizabeth II unveiled a memorial in Soweto seventy-eight years later. This was a token of how South African participation in the Empire crusade of 1914–18 was qualified, subdued, and sometimes covert.

General J. C. Smuts's elevation as a senior Imperial statesman was not thereby thwarted. He enjoyed an almost unique prestige within the British establishment. As Botha's position weakened (he was bitterly criticized at the October 1915 general election by Afrikaner Nationalists), and his health deteriorated, Britain's political investment shifted to Smuts. The latter's promotion to command the East African theatre in January 1916 was a stage in this process. Although he did not enjoy overwhelming success in his harrying of the German forces ably led by General Paul von Lettow-Vorbeck, at least he endured no significant defeat (see Map 5.1). The climax of Smuts's wartime career came when he was asked to stay on in London after the Imperial War Conference of 1917 to assume a number of high political assignments. In no other Dominion did the local war effort hinge so largely on one personality. Yet the war also led to divisions in white society. The 1915 election showed that half of all Afrikaners opposed the war. Afterwards, the option of Dominionhood propagated by Botha and Smuts was countered by an Afrikaner reaction, defined not least in linguistic and cultural terms, led by J. B. M. Hertzog. By 1917 Hertzogite Nationalism had adopted a secessionist and republican ideology opposed to the Imperial and Commonwealth connection. In South Africa the same principle was at work as elsewhere in the Empire: the more pressing the demands of an Imperial war became, the more tangled were the internal configurations.

It was a German interest to sustain operations outside Europe after August 1914 for the simple reason that naval control would allow the British to transfer soldiers to France while German defence forces were stranded. Anglo-French troops very quickly crushed German resistance in Togoland. Cameroon proved a tougher proposition. Although Duala and its wireless station was easily reduced after a naval attack on 27 September 1914, German forces put up a prolonged rearguard action before slipping over the frontier into Spanish Guinea on 15 February 1916.

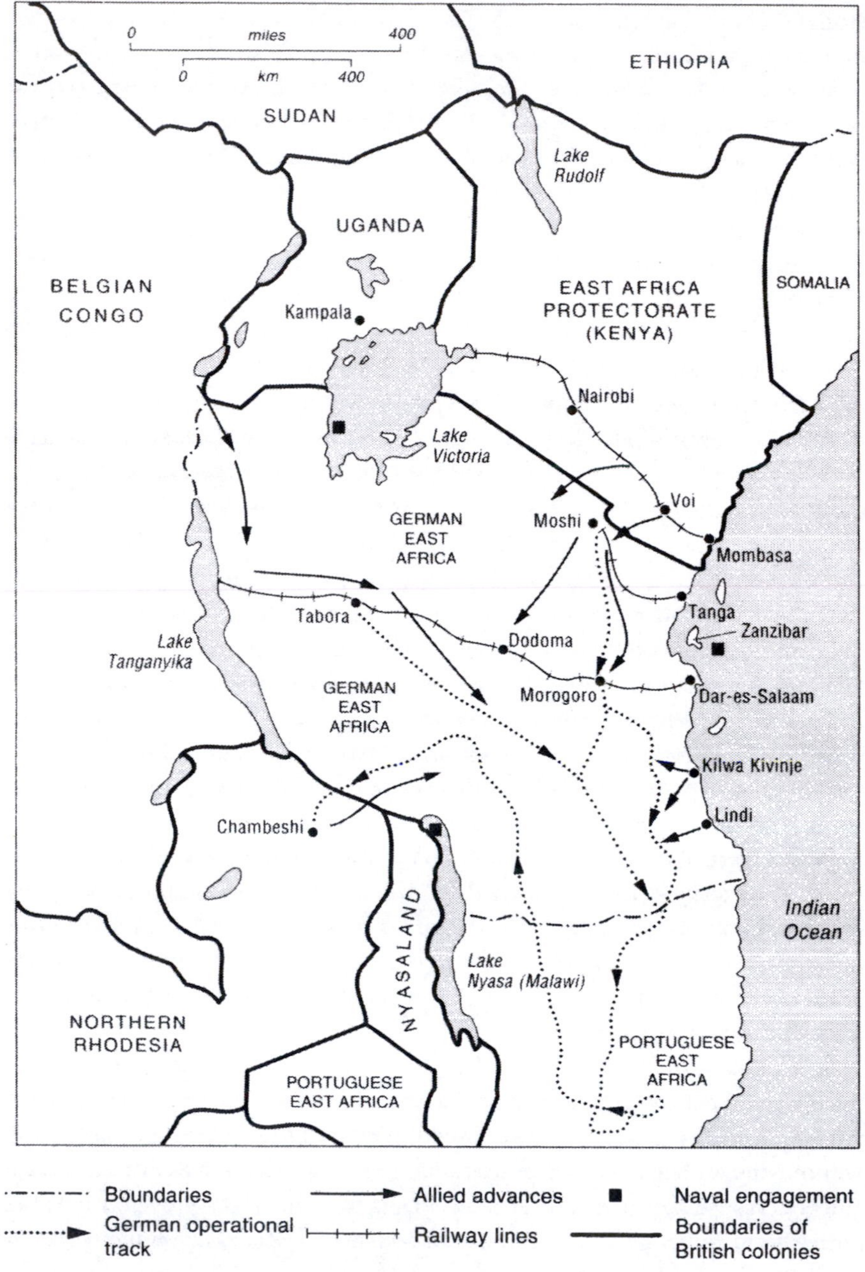

MAP 5.1 The First World War in East Africa

Even then the Germans blamed their disarray not on the local superiority of their European enemies but on 'native treachery and betrayal'—an early colonial version of the 'stab in the back'. Meanwhile, the British and French argued over the division of the West African spoils in a rekindling of the spirit of the Partition of the late nineteenth century. Outside Europe (as, doubtless, inside it) there was not one Great War, but many wars; and in Africa there was, in essence, a recommencement of nineteenth-century Scramble by other means (the pacification of Darfur in the Sudan in 1916 belatedly completed the reconquest of the Sudan). Galling though it was to some, the British Cabinet eventually decided to palm France off with the lion's share of the Cameroons in order to vitiate any claims she might have in East Africa as the greater Nile valley began to loom large in British strategy. By 1916 there was a swing to the East in Britain's African Empire.

Significantly, there were no large-scale revolts in British colonial Africa, though the Chilembwe Rising in Nyasaland was potent in its mixture of racial and millenarial emotions. In West Africa there were many localized disturbances, as in Nigerian Egbaland, often related to protests in neighbouring French colonies against mass conscription. Overall, however, the war was the occasion of such troubles, not their cause.[8] Black 'mahdism' never materialized, despite fears arising from hostilities with the Turkish caliphate, just as the jihad (holy war) never got under way in the Arab world. Some Nigerian opinion saw the war as a welcome opportunity to conquer the Cameroons—a testimony to the intractable parochialisms of empires at war. The sparsity of physical resistance to the war effort was not unique to Africa: in India and Egypt violent troubles did not explode until afterwards. This may be explained by the sheer momentum of the war machinery. The flexibility and logistical advantages enjoyed by the Imperial power are suggested by the episode in which the Indian Army's Fifth Light Infantry, having mutinied in Singapore and killed many of its British officers, was promptly despatched to West Africa as a policing unit. Yet the most profound currents set in motion after 1914 ultimately transcended such constraints. As Sir Harry Johnston, the veteran Victorian Proconsul, told the African Society presciently in March 1919, the war had marked the 'beginning of revolt against the white man's supremacy' in Africa.

Britain might not have succeeded in chasing General von Lettow-Vorbeck's makeshift but resilient force out of East Africa (it finally crossed the Rovuma into Portuguese territory at the end of November 1917) without the assistance of Indian Army cadres, just as later Britain could not have occupied so much of the Levant without Indian help. But between 1914 and 1918 the Indian jewel in the British Imperial crown lost some of its lustre. This was not a development that could have been anticipated in 1914. Then India had stood out as the only major military asset

[8] Akinjide Osuntokun, *Nigeria in the First World War* (London, 1979), pp. 132–33.

in the overseas Empire. It has been estimated that during autumn 1914 one-third of British forces in France were from India (either Indian Army troops or British army personnel drawn from Indian garrisons). An Indian Expeditionary Force entered Basra on 22 November 1915 and began to breath life into the dream of tacking the Gulf and its environs on to the Raj. In January 1916, while the newly arrived Australians began to train in and around Cairo, Indian soldiers manned the defences of the Canal and fought off the approach of the Turkish army. There followed, however, a string of setbacks; and in the Great War disappointments were often the cue for scapegoating. The botched landing at Tanga—in which, it was alleged, the Germans had sent their attackers into panic-stricken retreat by placing beehives in the banana plantations through which the latter advanced—led to such backbiting. 'I doubt if half the Indian Army are reliable under modern fire', the irascible Colone Richard Meinertzhagen noted in a diary awash with racist language.[9] Such griping came to be widespread in British military circles. Where Gallipoli ministered to the reputations of the Anzacs (Australian and New Zealand Army Corps), for the Indian troops involved it rubbed off less laudably. The Indian Army's performance on the Western Front was often considered wanting. This was brought to a climax by the jolts which followed the Indian Army's advance up the Euphrates after mid-November 1915, culminating in the humiliating surrender of General Townshend's British–Indian army at Kut in September 1916. The damning Report of the Commission of Enquiry into the Mesopotamian disaster (June 1917) led to the resignation of the Secretary of State for India, Austen Chamberlain. The Report's severest strictures were reserved for the Government of India and its military servants. As a later historian observed, 'The Indian Army had proved unable to administer what it was not designed to administer . . . a war overseas on a grand scale'.[10]

India during the Great War, indeed, functioned efficiently as the 'barrack in the Eastern seas' decreed by established Imperial doctrine. Her massive recruitment, straining under the philosophy of 'martial races', was reformed and reinvigorated after 1916. The true worth of the Indian Army to Britain lay in its reserve role that allowed other troops to be diverted to France from such theatres as East Africa, Egypt, and Palestine. In retrospect, Sir Charles Lucas reckoned that India's contribution stood comparison 'not only with what the Dominions accomplished in the way of improvising their contingents but with the Mother Country's effort in raising, training and equipping the "New Armies"'.[11] Yet this was to contradict the expectations that British strategists had of the greatest of dependencies. A certain

[9] Richard Meinertzhagen, *Army Diary* (London, 1960), p. 89.
[10] Carrington, 'The Empire at War, 1914–18', p. 610.
[11] Sir Charles Lucas, *The Empire at War*, 5 vols. (Oxford, 1926), V, p. 201.

rift emerged between London and Delhi, as it did between Delhi and Cairo, where a new nexus of British expansionists sought to challenge the Government of India's monopoly in Arabia and the Gulf. As the stakes of war had risen, Viceroy Hardinge and his colleagues concentrated on what mattered to them more than anything else—the security of the Raj and the 'placid, pathetic contentment' of its subjects. They believed that India already carried more than her fair share of the Empire's military burdens. Even before the war, India defended vast frontiers; by comparison, Dominion and colonial military expenditures were puny. If others started to catch up in this respect, it was because they had a long way to go. Nor did India only contribute her manpower. Pressed by the British Treasury, the Government of India risked the outrage of nationalists by donating a 'sweetener' of £100m ahead of the 1917 Imperial War Conference. None of this managed to satisfy the 'very exaggerated notions of what India can do', as Austen Chamberlain complained to Hardinge's successor, Lord Chelmsford. Arguably more might have been squeezed out of India had she *not* been a dependency, since fear of arousing unrest in an autocracy was as constraining as the opposite problem of eliciting co-operation from free citizens. However that may be, among the British and Indians embroiled in the governance of the Raj there emerged 'a resistance to accepting what were the inescapable demands of total war. By 1917 they had together arrived at this new phase of conflict.'[12]

At issue was the equation between war contribution and status within the Empire. Indeed, out of the fog of war there emerged a tacit principle: 'no contribution without representation.' Certainly from an early point, those concerned with Indian policy were conscious that the larger the contribution to the war, the more tangible had to be the rewards. This led to a curious phenomenon: the most conservative elements in Indian administration tended to be wary of bidding up India's role in Imperial belligerency while those *least* committed to the status quo supported a thoroughgoing exploitation of Indian manpower and resources. Where older hands hesitated, Edwin Montagu had an unconcealed distaste for the traditional Raj which led him, as Chamberlain's successor at the India Office, to expand the limits of war mobilization. The possible rewards for Indian co-operation were several. There was the prospect of improved job opportunities at senior levels in the civil service and the army (King's Commissions in the latter were theoretically opened up to Indians, although by November 1918 only a handful had been approved). India gained a place at the Imperial Conference in 1917, with two Indians in Delhi's delegation. There was the expansion of India's sway abroad, principally in Mesopotamia and East Africa (though the surrender of Indian troops at Kut prejudiced the first, while European settlers were

[12] Martin, 'Financial and Manpower Aspects', p. 57.

eventually to slam the door on the second). But in the end there was no substitute for the ultimate prize of political and constitutional advance to self-government—or at least some generous declaration of intent in this regard to rally moderate opinion. Once such a declaration was made, however, could the pace of advance be controlled? And would it not precipitate a flood-tide of aspirations going well beyond the Government of India's capacity to satisfy? These were the basic issues infusing British debates about wartime India. It was the belief, as Lloyd George put it, that India could and would do more for the war effort 'if her warm heart is touched', which lay behind the Montagu Declaration of 20 August 1917 establishing 'Responsible Government' as the Indian goal. But still more powerfully than in Africa, events after 1914 had effects that engulfed Imperial policy. Lord Curzon, a member of the War Cabinet from 1916, observed disapprovingly: 'In the course of the war forces have been let loose, ideas have found vent, aspirations have been formulated, which were either dormant before or which in a short space of time have reached an almost incredible development.'[13]

There was one way of countering this distintegration: repression. As the war went on, reform and repression became twin poles of British Indian policy. The Defence of India Act, 1915, was based on the essentially psychological principle that drastic legal powers reduced the number of troops required to guarantee internal security (though the Delhi authorities tried to hoard British troops, while sending Indian effectives abroad). It was a preoccupation with ensuring repressive powers after the war that lay behind the setting up of the Rowlatt Sedition Committee in 1918, with ill-fated consequences. Nor was India unique in exhibiting a link between the dynamics of war and the logic of coercion. In Egypt martial law, introduced in November 1914, was applied with increasing stringency, and in this case repression was not offset by the constitutional vistas spread before Indians. Once the pressures of war—with their tense equilibrium—lifted, the British were faced in both India and Egypt with widespread troubles that only a policy of 'paying out rope, and hitting the agitator hard' was able to contain.[14]

Nevertheless, up until 1916 the demands made by Britain on her Empire were limited. Prime Minister H. H. Asquith's proclivity for 'business as usual' at home found an Imperial expression. He had little inclination to involve the Dominions in British policy-making, and when Sir Robert Borden, the Canadian Prime Minister, complained about this treatment, he was deflected in a ham-fisted way. Excellent though the *idea* of giving the Dominions a voice in British counsels might be, Asquith told Borden, nobody had yet thought of a *way* to do so. Asquith held to the classic Liberal belief that the more artificially one tried to bring about

[13] Algernon Rumbold, *Watershed in India, 1914–22* (London, 1979), p. 91.

[14] Ibid., p. 48.

Imperial unity, the more certainly disunity would result. Once, however, Asquith's Coalition ministry had reluctantly moved towards compulsion in Britain with the Military Service Act in January 1916, new benchmarks were set for Empire contributions to the war effort. New Zealand was the first Dominion to adopt conscription in July 1916; a new national registration scheme was introduced in Canada (though conscription proper was not implemented until after the general election of December 1917); while on 28 October 1916 Australia held the first of two wartime referendums on compulsory military service overseas. The crucial watershed in the British conduct of the war came, both at home and in the Empire, with Asquith's replacement by Lloyd George in December 1916. Where Asquith clung to the residues of 'normalcy', Lloyd George savoured the emergency of war. It has been said that the new Prime Minister regarded the Dominions with 'a sympathetic eye';[15] it might also be described as the hard, covetous gaze of the recruiting-sergeant. The Empire, in short, was to underwrite the extended belligerency on which the Lloyd George coalition was based. For this reason, it was after December 1916 that Imperial War Conferences were convened, an Imperial War Cabinet set up, an Imperial Development Board established, and Imperial statesmen such as Curzon and Lord Milner brought back into government. Before December 1916 Britain was at war, assisted by her Empire; subsequently the Empire was at war, orchestrated by Britain much more as a *primus inter pares*.

It is tempting to see in this an imperialization of the British polity under the stress of war. Yet such an insight would be superficial. Curzon and Milner were promoted because of their reputation as organizers, not because of their Imperial beliefs as such. Lloyd George exploited them much more than they were able to use Lloyd George. This was emblematic of a more basic truth. The 'Welsh Wizard' did not seek to nurture the cause of Empire while pursuing all-out war; rather, he drained off whatever the Empire had to give for the purposes he had in hand—what a later generation would recognize as asset-stripping. Already by 1916 the fiscal effects of war were seen as auguring destruction for an English rural order based on country houses and great estates. In Britain's overseas realm, as at home, total conflict promised to buckle and break the existing equipoise. It was because many Tories suspected the true nature of Lloyd George's ideals that they felt deeply uneasy, even while rallying to his energetic leadership.

If the escalation of an Imperial war effort had ambiguous effects in Britain, so it did in the old Dominions. As usual, Canada rose pre-eminently to the challenge. Or rather, *English* Canada did, since from August 1914 the rhetoric of war was hitched to the Protestant, social-gospel, and materialist ideals of Anglophone society. Robert Borden's erratic, some said mad, Minister of Militia, Sam Hughes,

[15] Carrington, 'The Empire at War, 1914–18', p. 631.

was famously prejudiced against his French compatriots. French-Canadians were forbidden their own units, and a Methodist minister was appointed as Director of Recruiting in Montreal. 'This difficulty', two Canadian historians have written, regarding the low level of French-Canadian enlistment, 'merely revealed a problem rooted deep in the history of the [Canadian] militia.'[16] In fact, the overwhelmingly rural character of Quebec goes some way towards explaining the problem of recruiting in that province; while outside Quebec, once the great flood of British-born volunteers had subsided, the 'native' English-speaking stock of the Dominion also showed a relative disinclination to leave civilian pursuits. Nevertheless, over the course of the conflict, French-Canadians, who constituted around 35 per cent of the population, provided only 5 per cent of the Canadian Expeditionary Force personnel. Such data gave a field-day to Anglophone critics at a time when chauvinism proliferated.

This is not to say that French-Canada opposed participation in the war. Laurier's Imperial 'loyalty' has been noted. The Catholic hierarchy, with a tradition of cleaving to the British connection as a bulwark of its rights, supported the war; only one Francophone newspaper, *Le Devoir*, dissented. But gradually the extent of Canadian involvement tipped the balance of Quebec feeling. The erosion of French educational rights in Ontario, sectional currents amongst the lower clergy and professional classes, and the looming shadow of conscription all served to intensify this process. The confirmation of conscription in the general election of December 1917 that returned a Union government under Borden's leadership—an election that simultaneously set English and French against each other to a degree unknown since the Riel Rebellion of 1885—meant that the separatist Henri Bourrassa displaced Laurier as the acknowledged leader of Quebec. The election also set in train a sequence of events culminating in the anti-recruiting riots (including four fatalities) in Quebec City in March 1918. The ideas and rhetoric of a new Canadian autonomy, even nationhood, consecrated by the shedding of the Canadian Expeditionary Force's blood overseas, had led, perversely, to Canadians firing upon *Canadiens* at home. The war, then, divided and alienated, just as it united and recruited, within the British Empire. In Canada there arose 'a series of hard, competing regional, class, and ethnic interests. These had been present before the war, but in muted form. The war years, after the initial optimism about the country's unity of purpose had worn thin, exacerbated the old tension between French and English, between new and old Canada, between classes, and between city and country.'[17] This logic of escalating tensions was replicated elsewhere in the British Empire, just as it was in other belligerent empires between 1914 and 1918.

[16] R. C. Brown and Ramsay Cook, *Canada, 1896–1921: A Nation Transformed* (Toronto, 1974), p. 262.

[17] Ibid, p. 303.

Despite these internal fractures that were to shape Canadian politics for many years to come, the adoption of conscription confirmed the Imperial record of the Dominion and helped the Canadian Expeditionary Force to maintain its Divisions in France up to full strength for the rest of the war. In the case of Australia, there was a different twist. Despite the 8,141 Australian dead during the Gallipoli venture, there were occasional murmurings about the thoroughness of her commitment to the struggle. The Governor-General, Sir Ronald Munro-Ferguson, in contrast to the sympathetic role played by Buxton in South Africa, became increasingly acerbic in his reportage to Whitehall. At first this criticism focused on Australian state governments' persistence in making calls on the creaking London money market for non-military purposes. Nor was Munro-Ferguson appeased when it was pointed out that, under the Commonwealth constitution, the Federal authorities had no power to curb this. Trade matters also sometimes chafed Anglo-Australian relations. Although the depredations of German U-boats, and consequent shortage of tonnage, made it more sensible to rely on supply from Canada, the British government felt compelled to buy up Australian wheat and wool in order to stop the farmers going sour on the pro-war government of William M. ('Billy') Hughes. Many of these purchased supplies were left to rot by railway-sidings in Australia. War taxes began to affect sentiment, as they did in Britain. 'Things are not going too well in the Dominions,' Bonar Law, the Secretary of State for the Colonies, commented in December 1916, 'and there is especially an ugly spirit in Australia.' Whether Australians really *were* prepared to sacrifice their last man and last shilling to the Empire's cause was being tested.

It was men, not shillings, that was the true test of 'loyalty', and Bonar Law's comment came in the wake of the resounding 'No' given by the Australian electorate to the question on conscription put to it by the Hughes government in October 1916. Recruitment in Australia had tailed off from late 1915 onwards and was not helped by the long casualty lists of Gallipoli. As a result, the Australian Imperial Force (AIF) Divisions on the Western Front were gradually starved of drafts, and had, allegedly, to be 'nursed' by the High Command since they could not be kept permanently in the line. In fact the problem of recruiting had little to do with an 'ugly spirit'. It was simply that in Australia, as elsewhere and roughly at the same time, diminishing returns set in after the early flood of volunteers, composed of the ultra-patriotic, British-born, or unemployed, had exhausted itself. Nevertheless, the Australian failure of conscription (repeated on 20 December 1917, when the 'No' majority increased further) provided ammunition for those disposed to carp. Problems of finance and manpower apart, Australian troops got a reputation for rowdiness in Egypt that afterwards stuck. At the same time, Australia was the only Dominion that refused to allow its personnel to come under the British Army Act (and hence subject to court martials for desertion), which attracted some notice. Dissatisfaction naturally worked both ways. Prejudicial images of 'shirkers' in Britain—whether conscientious objectors, trade unionists, or Irish—translated themselves into sporadic Australian apprehensions that the Mother Country was failing her maternal responsibilities. Although Bean's official history later steered clear of expressing views about the quality of Britain's military leadership, his private diaries in France reveal that he fully shared the widespread Australian disillusionment on this matter. Prolonged war habitually corrodes allies, even Imperial allies, just as it intensifies the bitterness of enemies.

In voting down conscription twice, the Australian electorate certainly did not vote against the war as such. Between the two referendums, the Australian electorate gave a thumping victory to Hughes in a general election during which he campaigned unambiguously on a win-the-war ticket. 'Australians did not want to be forced to enlist,' the historian Carl Bridge has commented, 'but they did want to continue the war to the bloody end. Far from voting against the war, they voted to continue to wage it in their own democratic way.'[18] It is not even certain that Canada's war effort was more intensive than that of Australia. Although the former did eventually apply conscription after December 1917, it did so by granting so many exemptions—not least following the protests of many Western farmers, fearful about the loss of family labour—that the effect was all but cancelled out. Indeed, Australia's voluntary rate of enlistment in the population (7.5 per cent) was higher than Canada's conscripted rate (7.0 per cent).[19] Not only did the Australian Imperial Force give 'added value' in Imperial terms by service in a number of theatres (the Pacific, Gallipoli, Egypt, and Palestine as well as France), but on the Western Front it was a combatant force *par excellence*, with a 65 per cent likelihood of being killed, compared to 59 per cent for New Zealanders, 51 per cent for the British, and 49 per cent for the Canadians. As for finance and trade, Australia's debt structure—still, unlike Canada's, not fully recovered from the recession of the 1890s—was such that Britain simply had to go on extending loans and buying commodities if the country was not to grind to a halt. Even the British Treasury accepted that Australia, in the last analysis, 'must be financed'. Most profoundly of all, none of the Dominions, least of all Australia, could cease functioning as settler societies simply because they were at war, any more than Britain could cease to be an industrial state. In the end, there is little point in comparing the war efforts within the British Empire since the conditions of each component were so different. Nevertheless, the fact that contemporaries sometimes did so highlighted one of the dangers the war posed in Imperial relationships.

[18] Carl Bridge, 'The Reason Why: Australia and the Great War', *Quadrant* (April 1994), p. 12.
[19] Ibid.

The tyranny of distance inevitably lay behind these immanent differences. 'We arrived in the throes of a Provincial election,' a British official touring with the Dominions Royal Commission wrote from Prince Rupert in Canada in September 1916, 'to which, to all appearances, far more local interest attaches than to the most exciting incidents of the war.'[20] Distance, logically enough, played an even more formative role in shaping Australian responses. The Premier of New South Wales told the British Treasury that sheer physical separation meant that an equivalent measure of sacrifice could not be expected from the two countries. The effects of distance could be variously interpreted. Bean later argued that it provided the full measure of the 'idealism of their [Australasian] motives' in sending Expeditionary Forces to help the faraway Mother Country.[21] Even the physical separation of Britain from France involved differences of attitude. It was commonly said in 1916 that Londoners were going to the Essex seaside in greater droves than before August 1914. In the Great War there were many forms of escape. The very fact that the war was so largely concentrated near one part of the Empire came ultimately to exert a centrifugal strain.

The complicated currents operating within the wartime Empire were evident from the start, when the Dominions, even while being carried along on a tide of sublimated 'loyalty', invariably insisted on their Expeditionary Forces retaining separate identities at the Front (a separation which could have little meaning behind the Front, given the intermingling of logistical arrangements). General C. Bridges, Inspector-General of the Australian Military Forces in August 1914, insisted during his negotiations with the British Army Council that there be an 'Australian' Division, thereby becoming the real father of the Australian Imperial Force (killed at Gallipoli, Bridges was the only Australian serviceman whose body was taken home during the war). Not only did the authorities in Ottawa similarly insist that their Divisions (eventually numbering four in France, with a fifth remaining in England) constitute a Canadian Corps, but Sam Hughes as Minister of Militia rarely lost a chance to promote Canadians to staff posts in the Canadian Expeditionary Force. 'It is discreditable', Hughes laid down, 'to have British officers run the [Canadian] Army Corps and Divisional positions. It would be insulting to have them brought into the Brigades.'[22]

That the Dominions' political and military leaders had minimal say in operational matters—Hughes recalled that he was never consulted about any military decision in the first three years of war, while the consultative Committee of Imperial Defence was abolished when war broke out—made Dominion policy-

[20] Stephen Constantine, ed., *Dominions Diary: The Letters of E. J. Harding, 1913–16* (Halifax, 1992), p. 286.

[21] Bean, *The Story of Anzac*, p. xlvii.

[22] A. J. M. Hyatt, *General Sir Arthur Currie* (Toronto, 1987), p. 51.

makers all the more determined to protect the confined realm over which they presided. The resulting differentiation of 'British' identities took various forms, some more consequential than others. It had a physiognomic dimension. Numerous accounts stressed the tanned muscularity of members of the Australian Imperial Force once it arrived in Egypt, especially compared to the scrawny features of the Lancashire Fusiliers. There was also a sartorial factor: the stiff, round hat-brims and sharp smartness of the Canadians, the soft felt hats with a slight twist on the left of the more casual Australians, the short peaked hat and endless dull khaki of the British. Before long these differences extended to certain styles of belligerency and endurance. The British 'Tommy' was persistent, obedient, and with a dark, understated humour that went with his acceptance of being the first over the top. The Australians and Canadians might not be so easily led, or sacrificed, but they emerged as 'crack' troops, to be conserved for assaults against the vital points on the German line. Only the Canadians, it was said at the time, could have taken the village of Passchendaele after some of the hardest fighting on the Western Front. Certainly, Field Marshal Douglas Haig considered the Dominion formations to be his most prized asset, with perhaps the New Zealand Divisions the finest of all. Some pointed out that the effectiveness of the Australian and Canadian shock formations hinged on British forces taking the brunt of early attacks. These images and assessments were nevertheless fixed by 1917–18, and in great wars it is ultimately the images which endure.

There was no such thing as an Australian, a Canadian, or a New Zealand army on the Western Front. There were Expeditionary Forces, with a variable number of Divisions functioning as Corps within the British armies in France. The single South African Brigade, following heavy losses in March–April 1918, was merged into the 9th Scottish Division. Although these were not fully-fledged national formations, Dominion forces did come to possess a large degree of autonomous leadership. The Canadians went furthest in this regard, being the only Dominion to exercise organizational oversight through the appointment of a Cabinet Minister in London alongside a Canadian Military Mission. Up until June 1917 the Canadian Corps was commanded successively by two British Generals, Lieutenant-General Sir Richard Alderson and General Sir Julian Byng. Byng had consistently sought to 'nationalize' the Corps by promoting Canadian officers. He was himself promoted to succeed General (later Field Marshal and Viscount) Allenby at the head of the 3rd British Army, and the post of Corps Commander fell to a Canadian, Lieutenant-General Sir Arthur Currie. Currie had been a professional officer before the war and was conscious of the risks to efficiency from any crude policy of 'nationalization' through staff appointments, Corps organization, and tactical doctrine. He none the less accentuated a strong sense of Canadian autonomy, which was gravely threatened during the German offensive in March 1918. Situated almost exactly between the two main thrusts of Ludendorff's attack, Field Marshal Haig sought to siphon off Canadian units to plug gaps elsewhere. Currie opposed this strongly. 'From the very nature and constitution of the organization it is impossible for the same liaison to exist in a British Corps as exists in the Canadian Corps,' he protested. 'My staff and myself cannot do as well with a British Division in this battle as we can do with the Canadian Divisions, nor can any other Corps do as well with the Canadian Divisions as my own.'[23] Haig resented Currie's intractability, and, as Currie himself admitted, it was only his status as a Dominion Corps Commander that prevented his dismissal. His confession throws an interesting light on Dominion autonomy. In the event, the Canadian Expeditionary Force, like the Australian Imperial Force, retained its intregrity right through to the Armistice.

The Australian experience in this connection was more mixed. The five Australian Divisions in France were not grouped into a Corps until November 1917. The British Commander of the Australian Imperial Force, General Sir William Birdwood, 'did little to press the claims of Australians to positions on the staffs of British formations although he was quick to place British officers on Australian staffs'.[24] Although there was some justification for this at first, when there was a shortage of trained Australian officers, it obviously became less so as time went on. In May 1918, however, Birdwood replaced General Sir Hubert Gough at the head of the 5th British Army, to be succeeded by an Australian officer, General Sir John Monash. Australians simultaneously took over all the Divisional Commands. Not only did Monash emerge in the final months of the war as perhaps the finest commander on the Allied side—it was notable that before the war he had been a civilian. Only in Dominion ranks could there be found an exception to the rule, propagated by Lloyd George but violently repudiated by the British military establishment, that the cream of civilian talent and originality was not allowed to rise to the top in the British armies between 1914 and 1918. Imperial diversity was also reflected in those colonial units absorbed into British structures on the Western Front and elsewhere: the Newfoundland Regiment (its officers virtually wiped out on the Somme), the Rhodesian Regiment, the Gold Coast Regiment, with a distinguished record in East Africa, and the six battalions of the British West Indies Regiment, to name a few. Shades of an informal empire showed themselves in the services rendered in France by a South American volunteer force gathered together in King Edward's Horse.

If Dominion Expeditionary Forces evolved a certain resilient autonomy of their own, what of the higher management of the war? As one historian has noted, the

[23] Hyatt, *General Sir Arthur Currie*, p. 103.

[24] Jeffrey Grey, *A Military History of Australia* (Cambridge, 1990), p. 108.

outbreak of the war 'stimulated strongly regressive attitudes in the British Government'.[25] Although the latter was scrupulous after 3 August 1914, in framing British war legislation which did not infringe on Dominion competence, the fact of belligerency revealed the constitutional realities of the British Empire. When Borden visited London in the early summer of 1915, he complained that 'after six weeks he had uncovered no helpful information relevant to the war effort';[26] he was not much wiser after becoming the first Dominion Premier to be invited to attend a British Cabinet meeting on 14 July 1915. Deflecting such feelings, in Borden's words, of being 'toy automata' was one of Lloyd George's priorities after December 1916. Not only did Lloyd George call, as Asquith had avoided, an 'ordinary' Imperial War Conference (21 March–27 April), which passed a resolution looking forward to a clarification of the Dominions' constitutional status after the war; he arranged a series of special meetings of the War Cabinet to which Dominion Premiers were invited. Imperial Federationists greeted this as the beginning of a new Imperial executive. In fact, this body did not really formulate war policy and spent much of its time discussing post-war problems. Otherwise it was a glorified version of the 1911 Conference, with Lloyd George according the Dominion leaders a full briefing and some 'candid revelations'. The Dominions came to be associated with the higher command of the war, and helped to sustain its legitimacy, but at no point did they penetrate its innermost machinery. If they developed after August 1914 into 'junior but sovereign allies', that sovereignty remained significantly qualified by custom and the pace of events.

The war, therefore, did not spawn new Dominion nations in the way that simplified commentaries afterwards assumed. On the Western Front, the qualified autonomy of Dominion Expeditionary Forces was not allied to any larger political agenda of which Currie or Monash would have been conscious. When Charles Bean, at the end of his classic volume on the Anzacs at Gallipoli, posed the vital question as to what motive sustained the Australians and New Zealanders through the struggle, he dismissed such possibilities as love of a fight, hatred of the Turk, loyalty to Britain, or even pure patriotism 'as it would have been had they fought on Australian soil'.[27] Instead, Bean found the key in the Anzac sense of 'mateship', or the 'very mettle of the men themselves'. This rings true in its suggestion of how front-line experiences went deeper than the surface layers of regiment, nation, or Empire. For Dominion societies more generally, the effects of the war on self-images and perceptions were not clear-cut. 'The Great War brought Canadians to Europe, but left Europe remote to Canadians,' the Canadian historian James Eayrs

[25] Philip G. Wigley, *Canada and the Transition to Commonwealth: British–Canadian Relations, 1917–26* (Cambridge, 1977), p. 22.

[26] Ibid., p. 23.

[27] Bean, *The Story of Anzac*, p. 606.

has commented.[28] It did not create a Canadian, still less an Australian, identity that could yet be fully separated from the matrix of the British Empire. Perhaps the best, if necessarily ambiguous, conclusion has been that of W. K. Hancock, who began his survey of the inter-war Commonwealth by remarking on the 'heightened self-consciousness' with which the Dominions emerged from the experience of 1914–18.[29] Certainly, as the Paris Peace Conference soon illustrated, these burgeoning states were now well placed to have it both ways: to enjoy the benefits of Imperial partnership and yet increasingly to assert a measure of independence whenever it suited their interest. Perhaps this explains why the Dominion Status foreshadowed in 1917 was to prove a relatively comfortable constitutional halting-place until another great war was to upset the balance anew.

If new nations, however roughly and imperfectly, were being formed in settler Dominions, much older cultures were being brought within new and enlarged Imperial frontiers. The war brought to birth a fresh British Empire in the Middle East. This development was triggered by the war with Turkey, which began on 5 November 1914. Almost simultaneously the British government regularized her occupation in Egypt, not by annexation or by making Egypt self-governing, as it might have, but by declaring a Protectorate and thereby seizing the titular over-lordship from Turkey. This may have been the worst of all courses of action, since its very vagueness increased misunderstandings on all sides, but it allowed the British to tighten their effective control over the country. Thereafter, they stood on the defensive along the Suez Canal, fending off sporadic Turkish attacks, fomenting revolt in the Hejaz that finally broke out in June 1916, and above all, constructing a great new strategic base at Suez, 'unprecedented in the sheer magnitude of its logistics, involving water-supply, metalled roadways in the sand, floating bridges in the Canal itself, and entrenchment and wiring on an enormous scale... a bottomless sinkhole for imperial resources and manpower'. A Suez 'fixation' thus came into being that was vitally to affect Britain's Imperial consciousness in the years ahead.[30]

Like its Indian counterpart, the British civil and military establishment in Egypt was essentially static, though that did not prevent many military decorations, including the highest, the Victoria Cross, being won by members of the 'Egyptian' staff. Yet there gradually arose an expansionary impulse whose political exhilaration derived from an awareness of the easy prizes to be had if only the Turkish empire could be knocked over. The establishment of the Bunsen Committee in London during April 1915 began the process of reviewing Turkish spoils,

[28] James Eayrs, *In Defence of Canada: Appeasement and Rearmament* (Toronto, 1980), I, p. 3.

[29] W. K. Hancock, *Survey of Commonwealth Affairs*, Vol. I, *Problems of Nationality, 1918–36* (London, 1937), p. 1.

[30] Howard M. Sachar, *The Emergence of the Modern Middle East, 1914–18* (New York, 1969), pp. 43–44.

temporarily finding expression in the Sykes–Picot Agreement of early 1916, which hypothetically carved up the Levant on Anglo-French lines. The more dismal the stalemate in France, the more alluring this Eastern promise became, and as the Turkish presence wobbled in the face of a British-inspired Arab rebellion, the idea circulated that what might eventually be lost in Alsace, Poland, or Serbia could be recouped, to British benefit at least, in the Middle East.

In this area of policy, too, Lloyd George's elevation to Prime Minister was a crucial watershed. Having gained power on the basis of winning the war at all costs, he set out to re-configure the conflict in ways that were sustainable and capable of yielding to Britain the prizes that might make peace acceptable. Winston Churchill later summed up the dilemma as 'To attack the strong or to attack the weak,' and it was Lloyd George's attempt to switch the balance of British aggression from the Germans to the Turks that underlay his bitter rivalry ('Easterners' versus 'Westerners') with the Army High Command. In April 1917 the British Cabinet ordered an offensive into Palestine, and when this had a faltering start under General Sir Archibald Murray's leadership, the latter was replaced by General Allenby. Allenby was a cavalryman, an advocate of mobility frustrated by the fighting in France, and a volcanic personality. His instructions were to conquer Jerusalem by Christmas, and this he did when the Turks suddenly abandoned the Holy City on 9 December 1917. The Arab mayor found it difficult to find a taker for the keys, being refused by two abashed sergeants of the London Regiment before a Major-General accepted this illustrious gift on Allenby's behalf. As the Dome of the Rock came under the Union Jack, the bells of Westminster Abbey were rung out for the first time since the war began. This was, for Britain, the climax of the conflict in the Eastern world.

After the capture of Jerusalem, Lloyd George's Eastern vision was to ensure that Britain 'shall be there by right of conquest, and shall remain'. Allenby was ordered to advance on Amman and then Damascus. The pace of this offensive regardless of all difficulties (especially resented by the Australian mounted forces), the corpses of camels dead from exhaustion, the use of aerial bombing to smash the remnants of the Turkish presence (beginning a long history of British air-policing in the region), all testified to Allenby's, and Lloyd George's, impatience. Remaining in the Arab world, however, required pliable and, it was hoped, impressionable partners. It was in these final phases of the war that Lloyd George bought off the French with Lebanese and Syrian spheres of influence and a residual role as the protector of the Latin Churches, and at the same time aligned Britain with Zionism (encouraged by the Balfour Declaration on a Jewish 'Homeland' in Palestine issued on 2 November 1917) and with the Hashemite dynasty, the latter under the guidance of that quintessential British hero of the Great War, Lawrence of Arabia. Strikingly, no such British legend emerged from the Western Front. This new imperium with its experimental foundations was still being forged when Turkey suddenly sued for peace on 30 October 1918. In the words of C. E. Carrington, the supremacy of British armies throughout the world of Islam from 'Stamboul to Singapore . . . was perhaps the most astonishing consequence of the war'.[31] Certainly, it was the one that stored up most troubles and embarrassments for the future.

If in the disintegrating Ottoman world Lloyd George and Allenby had found the kind of war the British wanted to fight in the first place—one of movement, of triumphs, and of prestige—the parallel events in France were more sombre. Above all, the German offensive beginning on 21 March 1918, which aimed specifically at Haig's armies, came alarmingly close to sending the British formations into headlong retreat. It not only brought about a crisis in Allied relations, but also threatened a crisis in Imperial affairs. When the Imperial War Conference met in London in June 1918, it was 'charged with recriminations and serious Dominion misgivings'.[32] Borden warned that the Americans, whose troops were now pouring into France as an Associated, but not Allied, power, were 'in earnest and they and Canada will unite and win the war unless some of you mend your ways'.[33] It was in the wake of Germany's desperate attack that the heightened pressure of the recruiting machines from Montreal to Dublin disturbed, and sometimes upset, the delicate balances of internal Imperial politics. Lloyd George resorted to a personal appeal to India to become the 'bulwark of Asia'. At a special War Conference in Delhi in April 500,000 more recruits were promised. Ironically, India was emerging in the crisis of 1918 as what she had been in the crisis of 1914: the only preponderant military asset the British possessed outside the United Kingdom. Thoughts even began to turn to the exploitation of African military manpower on the French model. In the event, the German offensive petered out after mid-July; and in the rolling counter-offensive British Empire forces played a leading role. The Canadian Expeditionary Force, which suffered 42,000 casualties over the last four months of the conflict, was in the forefront at the Battle of Amiens, which began on 8 August and inaugurated the final trauma of Wilhelmine Germany. The British Empire had finally won through, though not with the triumphant éclat of 1763 or 1815. If the Armistice had not supervened so unexpectedly on 11 November 1918 and if the war had ground on into 1919–20, it seems highly probable that the mounting pressures would have enforced a radical change in many of its most important relationships (see Table 5.2).

Just as the Great War was for Britain too complex an experience in human terms ever to be satisfactorily reconstructed by historians, so its Imperial dimension

[31] Carrington, 'The Empire at War, 1914–18', p. 640.

[32] Wigley, *Canada and the Transition to Commonwealth*, p. 29.

[33] Ibid., p. 61.

TABLE 5.2. *Deployment of British and Imperial fighting formations on the various fronts at 1 November 1918*

	British		Dominion		Indian		
Fronts	Cavalry	Infantry	Cavalry	Infantry	Cavalry	Infantry	Total
France	3	51	—	10	—	—	64
Italy	—	3	—	—	—	—	3
Palestine	—	1	2	—	2	6	11
Salonika	—	4	—	—	—	—	4
Mesopotamia	—	1	—	—	1	4	6
India	—	3	—	—	—	3	6
East Africa	—	—	—	—	—	—	2*
UK	1	4	—	—	—	—	5
Total	4	67	2	10	3	13	101

* In East Africa the colonial troops, the King's African Rifles, numbering some 10,000, were active in 1918, see H. Moyse-Bartlett, *A Study of the History of East and Central Africa, 1890–1945* (Aldershot, 1956), p. 413.

cannot be reduced to a formula. It united and divided; it fuelled British solidarities, and defined emergent nationalities; it was driven by continental commitment, yet it reinforced a bias beyond Europe; it encouraged the liberality of reform, but accentuated the temptation of repression. Above all, it left individuals and societies in the 'British' world exhausted and introspective compared to the exuberant outbursts that had once characterized the Imperial generation of 1914. 'The war was one thing,' Milner remarked in the wake of the Armistice,'... a perfectly tremendous strain, but one was carried along by the bigness of the thing.... Now comes the inevitable slump.'[34] The Empire, like its citizens, consenting and otherwise, had also been carried along by the war's immense momentum. As 1919 dawned on an Empire once more at peace, it remained to be seen what forms the renewal of Rudyard Kipling's Imperial 'Recessional' would take.

[34] Quoted in Brian Gardner, *Allenby* (London, 1965), p. 252.

Select Bibliography

C. E. W. BEAN, *Official History of Australia in the War*, Vols. I–VI (Sydney, 1933).

JUDITH M. BROWN, 'War and the Colonial Relationship: Britain, India, and the War of 1914–18', in M. R. D. Foot, *War and Society* (London, 1973).

B. C. BUSCH, *Britain, India and the Arabs, 1914–21* (Los Angeles, 1971).

C. E. CARRINGTON, 'The Empire at War, 1914–18', in E. A. Benian and others, eds., *Cambridge History of the British Empire*, 9 vols. (Cambridge, 1919–59), II, pp. 605–44.

Lieut.-Col. P. G. ELGOOD, *Egypt and the Army* (Heliopolis, 1928).

JEFFREY GREY, *A Military History of Australia* (Cambridge, 1990), pp. 87–124.

N. G. GARSON, 'South Africa and World War One', *Journal of Imperial and Commonwealth History*, VIII, I (Oct. 1979), pp. 68–85.

GLENFORD D. HOWE, 'West Indies and World War One: A Social History of the British West Indies Regiment', unpublished Ph.D. thesis, London 1994.

A. J. M. HYATT, *General Sir Arthur Currie* (Toronto, 1987).

DAVID KILLINGRAY, 'The Idea of a British Imperial African Army', *Journal of African History*, XX (1979), pp. 421–36.

WM. ROGER LOUIS, *Great Britain and Germany's Lost Colonies, 1914–1919* (Oxford, 1967).

Sir CHARLES LUCAS, *The Empire at War*, Vols. I–V (London, 1926).

GREGORY MARTIN, 'Financial and Manpower Aspects of the Dominions' and India's Contribution to Britain's War Effort, 1914–19', unpublished Ph.D. thesis, Cambridge, 1987.

DESMOND MORTON, 'Junior but Sovereign Allies: The Transformation of the Canadian Expeditionary Force, 1914–18', *Journal of Imperial and Commonwealth History*, VIII, 1 (1979), pp. 56–67.

AKINJIDE OSUNTOKUN, *Nigeria in the First World War* (London, 1979).

Sir ALGERNON RUMBOLD, *Watershed in India, 1914–27* (London, 1979).

HOWARD M. SACHAR, *The Emergence of the Modern Middle East, 1914–18* (New York, 1969).

ERNEST SCOTT, *Australia During the War* (Sydney, 1936).

GEORGE SHEPPERSON and THOMAS PRICE, *Independent Africa: John Chilembwe and the Origins, Setting and Significance of the Nyasaland Native Rising of 1915* (Edinburgh, 1958).

PHILIP G. WIGLEY, *Canada and the Transition to Commonwealth: British–Canadian Relations, 1917–26* (Cambridge, 1977).

6

Ireland and the Empire-Commonwealth, 1900–1948

DEIRDRE MCMAHON

Nationalists of the generation born in the 1870s and 1880s played prominent parts in the Irish independence movement immediately before and after 1916. These new nationalists differed from their predecessors in their concern for Irish identity, a reaction to what they considered to be the insidious Anglicization of Ireland. For them the regeneration of the nation would be achieved by political, social, and economic self-reliance, wiping out the dispiriting memories of famine, emigration, and sterile political divisions. Their activity must be seen in the context of the nineteenth century.

In 1914 Ireland awaited its first measure of self-government since 1800. In the six decades since the Great Famine of the 1840s the country had undergone a social and economic revolution. The 1911 census figures, the last before independence, showed that the rate of population decline had dropped to its lowest level since 1851–1.54 per cent. Emigration had also halved since its peak in the 1880s. Nearly 50 per cent of the population was engaged in agriculture. The most industrialized part of the country was in north-east Ulster. Since 1881 a series of land purchase acts had revolutionized land tenure in Ireland, and by 1914 nearly two-thirds of tenant farmers had purchased their holdings. The losers in this revolution were the agricultural labourers whose numbers were a fifth of their 1.3 million in 1841. The decline in the rural population was reflected in the increasing urbanization of the population. In 1911 over one-third lived in towns and cities. Many lower-middle-class Catholics, urban and rural, benefited from the social and economic advances of the decades before 1914. The 1878 Intermediate Education Act and the 1908 Irish Universities Act had opened up secondary and third-level education for them, and they gradually achieved greater representation in the professions and the civil service.

The new, more self-assertive generation of nationalists was watched with some apprehension by the Roman Catholic Church. Nearly 75 per cent of the population was Catholic; the Church of Ireland (Anglican) accounted for 13 per cent, the Presbyterians for 10.5 per cent, and the Methodists for 1.42 per cent. The Protestant denominations were most strongly represented in the province of Ulster. The

Catholic Church in Ireland had the overwhelming loyalty of its flock, unlike some of its European counterparts, which faced strong anticlerical movements because of their support for unpopular regimes. In many ways it functioned as an alternative government in Ireland and had a huge political, social, cultural, and educational influence on the lives of its congregation. The Church supported the demand for Home Rule but opposed more revolutionary forms of nationalism, fearing not just the disorder and chaos of revolution but also the rise of the anticlericalism it had so successfully avoided. Church leaders had acute political antennae, and as the Irish political temperature rose in 1914 they adopted a watching and waiting game to see what would emerge from the new order.

The final contours of Home Rule were still unclear by the time it was finally enacted on 18 September 1914. Would it include all thirty-two counties or would it exclude the predominantly Protestant and unionist counties of north-east Ulster which were resolutely opposed to Home Rule? If there were to be exclusion, how many counties should be excluded, four, six, or nine? The attempts to resolve these questions had brought Ireland to the brink of civil war in 1914. Ulster unionists opposed Home Rule because they believed it would threaten their economic prosperity and ensure the dominance of the Roman Catholic Church. The unionists' political allies in Britain, the Conservative Party, saw Home Rule as a threat to the Empire and to British security. The Home Rule Bill was enacted but was suspended until the end of the European war, when the Ulster problem would be dealt with. On 20 September 1914 the leader of the Irish Parliamentary Party at Westminster, John Redmond, pledged Irish support for the war. Redmond's brother William, MP for East Clare, explaining why he joined up at the age of 53, wrote that 'Canada and Australia and New Zealand have been our loyal friends in our hour of strife. Their parliaments and their statesmen have ever pleaded our rights... Are we to leave these people who are our friends without our aid? If we did so, we should be justly disgraced.'[1] Redmond's invocation of the Dominions is revealing of the extent to which even nationalist Irish politicians at this time thought in Imperial terms. This perception of a Home Rule Ireland in a Dominion context was important both in the emergence of Irish autonomy and the constitutional development of the Commonwealth.

The passing of the Home Rule Act did little to quell political unrest in Ireland. Redmond's speech led to a split in the Volunteers, the paramilitary force founded by Eoin MacNeill in 1913 to reinforce the demand for Home Rule. A majority of the Volunteers, approximately 150,000, supported Redmond, with the remainder,

[1] Terence Denman, *A Lonely Grave: The Life and Death of William Redmond* (Dublin, 1995), p. 85.

approximately 7,500, siding with MacNeill who opposed Redmond's speech. The result was that MacNeill's Volunteers swung the balance in Ireland against Home Rule, as the MP Stephen Gwynn recognized: 'The pick of the young and keen who were with us [in favour of Home Rule] went off to the war; the young and keen who stayed kept up an organization with very different purposes.'[2]

There was also in Ireland an anti-war movement, which contributed to the development of nationalist sentiment. This movement was able to draw on its experience fifteen years before, during the South African (Boer) War, which was a seminal event for Irish nationalism. The Irish Transvaal Committee of 1899 had members who were still active in 1914, although some, William Redmond and Thomas Kettle, were now supporting the war; the others included W. B. Yeats, Arthur Griffith, and Maud Gonne. Three of the men executed after the 1916 rising, Thomas Clarke, James Connolly, and John MacBride, were all active in the pro-Boer movement, MacBride being one of the leaders of the Irish Brigade. The extent and effectiveness of the nationalist opposition to the Boer War disturbed the authorities at the time, causing fears of rebellion.[3]

Within his own party, Redmond found lukewarm attitudes to the war that broke out in 1914. Recruiting soon became a bone of contention. The War Office refused to arm and equip Redmond's Volunteers and delayed granting them the same status and privileges as the Ulster Volunteers, founded to resist Home Rule. Dismayed, Redmond warned the Prime Minister, H. H. Asquith, of the impression this would create in Ireland, but to no avail. Speaking in the House of Commons in October 1916, as the political ground was already shifting beneath him, Redmond complained bitterly that his efforts 'were thwarted, ignored, and snubbed'.[4]

Despite the problems, initial recruitment was creditable. Between 4 August 1914 and 30 April 1915, 42, 301 men volunteered in the twenty-six counties excluding the six predominantly unionist counties of Ulster. By February 1916, 95,000 had enlisted, including 25,000 from the Ulster Volunteer Force. Dublin was consistently better than Belfast for recruiting, probably because of higher unemployment. In this period recruitment was nearly as high in Ireland as in the rest of the United Kingdom, although there were marked regional differences and, as also happened in the United Kingdom, there was a sharp drop in enlistment after the first rush. Conscription was introduced in March 1916 but was not applied to Ireland, thus highlighting Irish reluctance. It is more useful to compare Ireland's recruiting record with the other Dominions. The comparison reveals that the

[2] Stephen Gwynn, *John Redmond's Last Years* (London, 1919), p. 166.

[3] Donal P. McCracken, *The Irish Pro-Boers, 1877–1902* (Johannesburg, 1989).

[4] John Redmond, 18 Oct. 1916, *Parliamentary Debates*, LXXXVI (Commons), col. 582.

percentages of the white male population which joined up in 1914–18 were 19 per cent for New Zealand, and 13 per cent each for Canada, Australia, and South Africa. For Ireland it was 6 per cent.[5]

The disillusionment with the war, which was reflected in the recruiting figures, had complex causes: they included not merely annoyance at the conduct of the recruiting campaign, but foreboding at the formation of the coalition in May 1915 which saw opponents of Home Rule in the British Cabinet. Following the losses incurred by the 10th (Irish) Division at Gallipoli there was a belief that Irish units were bearing the brunt of casualties (a complaint also heard during the Boer War). Falling Irish recruitment fuelled anti-Irish comments in the British press.

The 1916 rebellion was not the only Imperial disturbance during the war. There was also the Afrikaner rebellion in October 1914 and unrest in Nigeria, India, and Egypt. But the Irish uprising came at a critical point of the war and, because of the need to reassure American and Dominion opinion, the British government played down the true extent of rebellion. The treatment meted out to the rebels seemed all the more extreme. There were sixteen executions, which had a radicalizing effect, but the scale of the deportations and arrests, over 3,500, had an even greater impact. Hundreds were released within weeks, but the fact that the government had arrested so many people on insufficient evidence hardly inspired confidence. Bishop O'Dwyer of Limerick compared the fate of the rebels to that of the 'buccaneers' of the Jameson Raid. John Dillon, Redmond's deputy, drew another South African parallel: Botha's magnanimous treatment of the recent Afrikaner rebels.[6]

The ripple effects of the rebellion were soon felt among the Irish communities in the Empire. The Australian Irish Catholics had long been substantial contributors to the Irish Party which supported the Australian Commonwealth Act in the House of Commons. The Home Rule crisis made its presence felt in Australia, with large rival demonstrations in 1914 in Sydney and Melbourne. Home Rule was welcomed by the Australian Irish because it helped them to reconcile their various loyalties; they could be loyal to Australia, Ireland, and the Empire at the same time without too much conflict. The rising destroyed this fragile unity by posing loyalty to Ireland as antithetical to other loyalties. The initial reaction to the rising had been one of condemnation, especially from the Catholic bishops, but the executions changed this. Reservations about the rising remained, but there was disillusionment both with the Irish Party, which had clearly misled the Australian

[5] Keith Jeffery, 'The Irish Military Tradition and the British Empire', in Jeffery, ed., *'An Irish Empire'? Aspects of Ireland and the Empire* (Manchester, 1996), pp. 97–98.

[6] Charles Townshend, 'The Suppression of the Easter Rising', *Bullán*, I (1994), p. 28.

Irish about the real situation in Ireland, and with British rhetoric about fighting for small nations. The Irish were portrayed as disloyal and seditious. Anti-Irish feeling increased because of the prominent role the Irish played in the anti-conscription campaigns, notably Archbishop Mannix of Melbourne, who ignored Vatican instructions not to get involved.[7] The Australian Prime Minister, W. M. Hughes, blamed the Irish for the defeat of the first conscription referendum in October 1916 and urged David Lloyd George, the British Prime Minister, to seek a settlement, though without much success.[8] A second conscription referendum was defeated in December 1917.

The New Zealand Irish also faced allegations of treason and disloyalty. When conscription was introduced in May 1916, controversy arose over the conscription of Catholic clergy and seminarians. These events increased sectarian tensions, and in July 1917 the Protestant Political Association was founded with support from the Orange Order in New Zealand. The following month the editor of *The Green Ray*, which had close links with the New Zealand Labour Party, was imprisoned for sedition. The magazine was suppressed by the government the following year.[9]

The lowest point of Irish recruiting was reached in the six-month period February–August 1917. Conscription was announced in April 1918 but was never implemented, because of political unrest. Nevertheless recruiting improved, with a marked increase in the last three months of the war which was due to a special recruiting campaign and to domestic social and economic pressures. Still, there was distrust of Irish soldiers after 1916. Although there was little support for the rising among Irish soldiers, the executions caused concern. Catholic Irish soldiers, like their Dominion comrades, were generally regarded as shock troops with a reputation for indiscipline, but in the Irish case there were additional doubts about their loyalty stirred not only by the rising but by Roger Casement's attempt to raise an Irish Brigade from Irish prisoners-of-war in Germany. In March 1918 the casualties suffered by the 16th Division led to insinuations that the men had been weakened by political disaffection. In fact they were tired, under-trained, and holding poor positions.[10]

The Irish war memorial at Islandbridge lists 49,400 dead. Historians have written of the 'amnesia' in Ireland about the First World War, of which the memorial itself is a graphic example.[11] It was gradually moved away from the centre of Dublin to avoid the rowdy demonstrations which occurred for years on

[7] Patrick O'Farrell, *The Irish in Australia* (Kensington, NSW, 1987), pp. 252–73.

[8] Jeffery, 'Irish Military Tradition', p. 110.

[9] Richard P. Davis, *Irish Issues in New Zealand Politics, 1868–1922* (Dunedin, 1974), pp. 190–98.

[10] Terence Denman, *Ireland's Unknown Soldiers: The 16th (Irish) Division in the Great War* (Dublin, 1992), pp. 153–70.

[11] Keith Jeffery, 'Irish Culture and the Great War', *Bullán* I (1994), pp. 87–96.

Armistice Day. Official amnesia there certainly was, but at individual and family levels the picture was more complicated and many of those subsequently involved in the war of independence, and the civil war, had close connections with the Great War.

In December 1918 Sinn Fein won seventy-three seats in the general election, annihilating the Irish Party. In January 1919, in line with the party's policy of abstention from Westminster, those Sinn Fein TDs (MPs) who were not in jail or on the run gathered in Dublin to set up their own Assembly, Dáil Éireann, and to declare a republic. The unionist *Irish Times* described these proceedings as 'a solemn act of defiance of the British Empire by a body of young men who have not the slightest idea of that Empire's power and resources'. Other observers suspected that the new Sinn Fein and its leaders presented a far more sustained threat than any of their predecessors. The establishment of the Dáil and the Republic was followed by the setting up of Dáil departments with the avowed aim of supplanting the British administration in Ireland. The opening shots of a two-and-a-half-year guerrilla war were fired by the Irish Republican Army (IRA) on the very day the Dáil first met. With this attack, Sinn Fein threw down the gauntlet. The British authorities were hampered by their ignorance of the new party and its leaders. Eamon de Valera, President of Sinn Fein and of the new Republic, was to spend eighteen months in America in 1919–20 raising millions of dollars for the Republic and trying, unsuccessfully, to secure recognition from the American government. In his absence Arthur Griffith, founder of Sinn Fein in 1905, was Acting President, but effective power in both the administrative and military spheres rested with Michael Collins, Minister of Finance in the Dáil, and director of both intelligence and organization for the IRA.

In September 1919 both Sinn Fein and the Dáil were proscribed, but British policy remained in limbo. The result of the British Cabinet's deliberations in 1919–20 was the Government of Ireland Bill, which proposed two parliaments in Ireland, one for the twenty-six predominantly nationalist counties of the south and west, another for the six predominantly unionist counties of the north-east. The powers of the proposed parliaments were so circumscribed that Sinn Fein paid little attention as the bill trundled its way through Parliament, finally becoming law in December 1920. However, Ulster Unionists were more alert to its potential for effecting partition.

The British campaign in Ireland of 1919–21 suffered from constantly shifting policies and tactics. As happened later in India with the Congress Party, there was a reluctance to recognize the representative character of Sinn Fein. Political containment was the aim. There was a pervasive belief that the trouble was caused by a few malcontents and that once they were under control the cowed moderate majority would emerge—an enduring theme in later colonial emergencies.[12] For two and a half years the British Cabinet dithered, vacillating between heavy-handed repression and persisting with its Government of Ireland Bill. This confusion was repeated at Dublin Castle, which rapidly buckled under the onslaught of a determined guerrilla war.

Dublin Castle contrasted vividly with the quality of colonial administration elsewhere in the Empire. Its atmosphere was preserved in the memoirs of the last generation of administrators who presided over it. Maurice Headlam, appointed Treasury Remembrancer (representative) for Ireland in 1912, had failed the Indian Civil Service examinations and only accepted the post in Dublin because he could fish in his spare time. Headlam was convinced that Home Rule was a danger to the Empire, and decided to flout the civil service rules on taking part in politics since in his view in Ireland it was not politics but 'flagrant disloyalty to the Crown'.[13] One of his subordinates later wrote that Headlam's memoirs 'leave a bad taste in the mouth of any ex-British civil servant'.[14] The criticism implies that Headlam's interventionist attitude was perhaps more characteristic of the colonial service than the British civil service. Headlam's views were shared by other senior officials at the Castle, Sir Henry Robinson, President of the Local Government Board, and Sir John Taylor, Assistant Under-Secretary. They distrusted Catholics in the administration and did their best to isolate them. They grossly underestimated the strength of Sinn Fein and regarded the Government of Ireland Bill 'as a kind of side-show, an excrescence which need not be taken seriously, and which would shortly be ruthlessly removed by a Conservative knife'.[15]

In the spring of 1920 Sir Warren Fisher, Permanent Under-Secretary at the Treasury, was sent by Lloyd George to investigate the Castle administration. Fisher described it as 'almost woodenly stupid and devoid of imagination. It listens solely to the Ascendancy party and . . . never seemed to think of the utility of keeping in close touch with opinions of all kinds.'[16] Headlam and Taylor were sent back to England, Headlam ending up in the appropriate backwater of the National Debt Office, where he wrote embittered articles on Ireland for Lady Milner's *National Review*. The arrival of the new brooms of Sir John Anderson (whose Irish experience later stood him in good stead when he was Governor of Bengal in the

[12] For example, on Cyprus and Ireland see Harold Nicolson, *Diaries and Letters, 1945–62* (London, 1968), p. 303.

[13] Maurice Headlam, *Irish Reminiscences* (London, 1947), p. 196.

[14] G. C. Duggan, quoted in John McColgan, *British Policy and the Irish Administration, 1920–22* (London, 1983), p. 13. Duggan was later Comptroller and Auditor-General for Northern Ireland.

[15] 'Periscope' [G. C. Duggan], 'The Last Days of Dublin Castle', *Blackwoods' Magazine*, CCXII (Aug. 1922), p. 141.

[16] McColgan, *British Policy*, p. 8.

1930s) and Alfred Cope meant that a vastly more streamlined and efficient administration was handed over to the new Irish state in 1922.

The tardiness in appreciating the real strength of Sinn Fein was repeated with the IRA. Restoration of law and order was a mantra faithfully echoed by ministers in Parliament and the press, but what did this mean in the Irish context? In Ireland, and later in Palestine, Malaya, and Kenya, the attitude of the civilian population was crucial, but in Ireland attempts to win over the civilian population were effectively nullified by the hostility shown towards the Irish by the military establishment. These attitudes permeated down the ranks. Most soldiers avoided contact with the Irish people, regarding them all as 'Shinners' (Sinn Feiners). The IRA's targeting of the Royal Irish Constabulary (RIC) gradually dried up the amount of intelligence reaching the authorities. To ease the problem the Cabinet sanctioned the enlistment of ex-servicemen into an auxiliary division of the RIC. The Auxiliaries, as well as the famous all-purpose force known as the Black and Tans, were intended as a third force between the army and the police but were distrusted by both. The Inspector-General of the RIC predicted that the recruitment of non-Irish ex-servicemen with combat experience would not only be useless but dangerous in such a volatile atmosphere. So it proved. The Auxiliaries and the Black and Tans ended up as crude instruments of repression against the civilian population.[17]

The Foreign Secretary, Lord Curzon, proposed what he termed 'Indian' measures to the British Cabinet in May 1920 which would include fining towns and villages and blockading districts by British forces.[18] But in the aftermath of the Amritsar massacre in April 1919, India was hardly a suitable model. It revealed, as one historian has noted, the peculiarly ambiguous position of Ireland not only in 1919–21 but fifty years later when the Northern Ireland troubles erupted: 'Ireland still seems to be at once too metropolitan to permit the colonial-style departures from the "British way" which might allow some sort of forcible pacification, and too colonial to compel absolute adhesion to British standards.'[19] The Black and Tans and Auxiliaries became a model for third forces in other Imperial trouble-spots. Indeed, when they were disbanded they provided many of the recruits for the new Palestine Gendarmerie and for the Royal Air Force's armoured companies in Iraq. But they were also a symbol of the vacuum at the heart of Imperial defence policy after the war. That the Black and Tans could be transplanted to Palestine and Mesopotamia indicated that British policy-makers regarded them as an all-purpose tool to counter the different manifestations of violent nationalism.[20]

[17] Charles Townshend, *The British Campaign in Ireland, 1919–21* (Oxford, 1975), pp. 106–16.

[18] Keith Jeffery, *The British Army and the Crisis of Empire, 1918–22* (Manchester, 1984), p. 86.

[19] Charles Townshend, *Britain's Civil Wars: Counterinsurgency in the Twentieth Century* (London, 1986), p. 72.

[20] Jeffery, *British Army*, pp. 73–74.

'If we lose Ireland we have lost the Empire.'[21] This was the gloomy pronouncement of the Chief of the Imperial General Staff, Field-Marshal Sir Henry Wilson. So it seemed to British ministers as they wrestled with simultaneous unrest in Ireland, India, and Egypt. There was a clear interplay between each theatre as events moved to a climax in 1921–22. The Government of India Act was passed shortly before the Government of Ireland Bill was being drafted. The Amritsar massacre had strong Irish overtones. General Reginald Dyer of the Indian Army (who was responsible for the massacre) and Sir Michael O'Dwyer (the Governor of the Punjab, who approved Dyer's action) both had Irish connections. Dyer received staunch support from Sir Henry Wilson and also from Ulster Unionists in Parliament, notably Sir Edward Carson. After the Amritsar debate in July 1920, nearly all the anti-government votes were cast by coalition Unionists, with a preponderance of Ulster MPs.[22] The Secretary of State for India, Edwin Montagu, warned the Cabinet in October 1920 that the scale of the problems in Ireland would be dwarfed by the potential threat in India: 'a campaign comparable to the Sinn Féin campaign in Ireland would be almost impossible to deal with except by punishment and revenge, certainly not by prevention.'[23]

In Egypt the Lord Milner mission had important implications for Ireland. Milner had been a fierce opponent of Home Rule in 1913–14. Yet five years later, as Secretary of State for the Colonies, he concluded that concessions must be made to Egyptian nationalism. The memorandum of his talks with Saad Zaghlul, leader of the Wafd, the Nationalist Party in Egypt, in the summer of 1920 caused consternation among British ministers, especially Winston Churchill, Secretary for War, and Montagu. Churchill protested that giving Egypt sovereign status outside the Empire was a bad example to both India and Ireland: 'If we leave out the word "Egypt"... and substitute... "Ireland" it would with very small omissions make perfectly good sense, and would constitute a complete acceptance of Mr de Valera's demands.' Montagu was equally critical. 'The extremists of India are ignored and I understand that nobody disputed the wisdom of doing so. In Egypt the treaty is made with extremists. I... can find nothing which makes it possible to negotiate with Zaghlul which does not, at least, point the way to negotiation with De Valera or Gandhi.'[24]

Sinn Fein leaders were interested in events elsewhere in the Empire. In July 1919 Archbishop Cyrillus of the Cyprus Mission in London sent Michael Collins three

[21] Wilson to Arnold Robertson, 30 March 1921, in Keith Jeffery, ed., *The Military Correspondence of Field-Marshal Sir Henry Wilson, 1918–22* (London, 1985), p. 250.

[22] Derek Sayer, 'British Reaction to the Amritsar Massacre, 1919–20', *Past and Present*, CXXI (1991), pp. 130–64.

[23] Jeffery, *British Army*, p. 104.

[24] Ibid., pp. 115–16; John Darwin, *Britain, Egypt and the Middle East: Imperial Policy in the Aftermath of War, 1918–22* (London, 1981), pp. 110–11.

pamphlets about the situation on the island, which had been acquired by Britain in 1878 and annexed in 1914. The title of one of the pamphlets, *Cyprus Trusts in British Justice*, led Collins to reply caustically to the Archbishop: 'Your reliance on British justice and British fair play is entirely misplaced. Wherever in the world you should look for justice and fair play, that place is certainly not the centre of the British Empire.'[25] Arthur Griffith had long been interested in Indian nationalism, especially the Swadeshi movement, and corresponded with several Indian journals. In 1907 Jawaharlal Nehru, then a young student, visited Dublin and thought Sinn Fein 'a most interesting movement... Their policy is not to beg for favours but to wrest them. They do not want to fight England by arms but "to ignore her, boycott her and quietly assume the administration of Irish affairs"... Among people who ought to know, this movement is causing... consternation. They say that if its policy is adopted by the bulk of the country English rule will be a thing of the past.'[26]

South Africa aroused most interest among Sinn Fein leaders. Memories of the Boer War were vivid even among those who had only been children at the time. Collins had enormous admiration for the Boer guerrilla leader Christian de Wet, with whom he briefly corresponded before de Wet's death in 1922. 'Your great fight', Collins wrote to him, 'was the earliest inspiration of the men who have been fighting here for the past two years... They were all on your side.'[27] Arthur Griffith had spent several years in South Africa just before the Boer War and keenly admired the Boer leaders, especially Paul Kruger. When Griffith founded Sinn Fein in 1905 he had set out his theory of an Anglo-Irish dual monarchy based on the Austro-Hungarian model. Like John Redmond, Griffith wanted Ireland to be recognized as a co-equal Mother Country of the Empire; but there was considerable general ambivalence in the post-1916 period when Sinn Fein embraced a wide political spectrum, from radical republicans to moderate nationalists. For republicans, the Republic established in January 1919 was now a fact. Its departments and courts were functioning, to a greater or lesser extent, in most of the country. As the war intensified, the question of the relationship with the Empire was put in abeyance.

The conflicting ideas in the evolution of an Irish settlement were symbolized by two remarkable men, Erskine Childers and Lionel Curtis, who had known each other since their schooldays at Haileybury and whose paths had crossed and criss-crossed since then. Childers was Anglo-Irish and his support for Home Rule,

[25] Michael Collins to Archbishop Cyrillus, 28 July 1919, DE2/510, National Archives Ireland, Dublin.

[26] Jawaharlal Nehru to Motilal Nehru, 7 Nov. 1907, quoted in S. Gopal, ed., *Selected Works of Jawaharlal Nehru*, First Series, 15 vols. (New Delhi, 1972–82), I, pp. 37–38.

[27] Collins to de Wet, 21 Sept. 1921, Piaras Béaslaí Papers, National Library of Ireland.

Sinn Fein, and later the republican side in the Irish civil war, was not unique to his class. He had been preceded on that path by his cousin and close friend Robert Barton, who had resigned his army commission after the 1916 rising. The Boer War was a defining experience for Childers. He strongly disapproved of the policies pursued in South Africa by Sir Alfred Milner, who had drawn into his circle friends and contemporaries of Childers, among them Basil Williams, who later wrote the life of Cecil Rhodes, and Lionel Curtis. Childers converted to Home Rule in 1908 and became its most able intellectual protagonist. In *The Framework of Home Rule* (1911) he put the case for a moderate Home Rule Bill and discussed colonial parallels in Canada, Australia, and South Africa, parallels about which Childers was later distinctly dubious.

The Round Table, founded in 1910 by Lionel Curtis and Philip Kerr, was to have a close involvement in Irish affairs over the following decade and more. Three of its most prominent members, Curtis, Kerr, and Edward Grigg, were Secretaries to the British delegation during the 1921 Anglo-Irish Treaty negotiations; a fourth, Richard Feetham, chaired the ill-fated boundary commission in 1924–25. Not for nothing was Curtis nicknamed 'the Prophet'. His biographer refers to his faith in the 'Hegelian destiny of the English-speaking peoples to elevate the world and lead it to Utopia'.[28] Where did Ireland fit into this lofty scheme? Childers believed that beneath the high-flown rhetoric there lurked old-style imperialism cloaking itself in new forms.

Curtis's involvement with Irish affairs transformed his views on the Commonwealth but did not noticeably deepen his understanding of the nature of Irish nationalism. He frequently expressed his exasperation with the Irish preference for American models.[29] Curtis believed that once the case for separation was argued on its merits, 'it will fail in the minds of all reasonable men through its manifest impossibility and its own inherent weakness'.[30] Curtis was making some characteristically sweeping assumptions, but in envisaging a solution in which Ireland would become a self-governing unit within a federated Empire, he was considerably in advance of British policy.

Dominion Home Rule emerged tentatively as a solution. But what did it mean? The very term was contradictory and implied a confusing hybrid of Home Rule and Dominion status. Conservative leaders such as Walter Long and Andrew Bonar Law were emphatic that it could never be conceded to Ireland. This remained the position until July 1921. Until then British policy was firmly rooted in the Government of Ireland Act. The Rubicon was reached in May–June 1921,

[28] Deborah Lavin, *From Empire to International Commonwealth: A Biography of Lionel Curtis* (Oxford, 1995), p. 330.

[29] Lionel Curtis, *The Commonwealth of Nations* (London, 1917), p. 496.

[30] 'Ireland and the Empire', *Round Table*, XXIV (Sept. 1916), p. 649.

when the elections for the Southern Ireland Parliament, set up under the Government of Ireland Act, returned 124 Sinn Fein members. Opinion in the British Cabinet was gradually shifting towards a truce, but Lloyd George believed that a truce would only lead to negotiations which in turn would lead to a Dominion settlement. But the commander in Ireland, General Sir Nevil Macready, warned ministers that the choice was now 'all out' or 'get out'. On 2 June 1921 the Cabinet decided to introduce full-scale martial law on 14 July.[31]

On 22 June 1921 George V opened the new Northern Ireland Parliament in Belfast with a plea for reconciliation which finally spurred British ministers to seek a truce with Sinn Fein. The moving spirit behind the King's speech was the South African Prime Minister, J. C. Smuts, who was in London for the Imperial Conference. Smuts wanted the speech to go further and promise Dominion Status, but this was firmly rejected by Lloyd George. On 25 June, however, de Valera was invited to London for negotiations and a truce was finally agreed on 11 July.

The Imperial Conference opened two days before the King's speech in Belfast. Dominion leaders were anxious to see an end to the war because of the unwelcome tensions it had caused in their countries, particularly Australia. Irish independence would never have achieved the importance it did in Australia without Archbishop Mannix. Most of his fellow bishops and clergy would have preferred to ignore it, but after Sinn Fein's victory in 1918 this was impossible. The Irish Race Convention held in Melbourne in November 1919 was attended by almost the entire Australian hierarchy. It was chaired by T. J. Ryan, ex-Premier of Queensland and leader of the federal Labor Party. The following year, at a meeting of the Victoria Irish–Ireland League, Hugh Mahon, Labor MP for Kalgoorlie, attacked 'this bloody and accursed despotism' and was expelled from the House of Representatives.[32]

In New Zealand the Irish question also caused unrest. Efforts to secure a resolution on Irish self-determination from the House of Representatives failed, in contrast to the other Dominion legislatures. The William Massey government banned Sinn Fein, but branches of the Irish Self-Determination League set up in Australia were also quickly established in New Zealand. Substantial sums were raised: £6,000 by December 1920, of which £2,000 came from Wellington. In 1921 a further £2,000 was contributed for relief in the Belfast riots. As in Australia, most of the Catholic bishops were reluctant to get involved, rightly fearing a rise in the sectarian temperature, but with an overwhelmingly Irish flock, they had little choice. In 1920 the Marriage Amendment Act was passed which legislated against

[31] Thomas Jones, *A Whitehall Diary*, Vol. III, *Ireland, 1918–25*, ed. Keith Middlemas (Oxford, 1971), pp. 63–74; Sir Nevil Macready, *Annals of an Active Life*, 2 vols. (London, 1924), II, p. 565.

[32] O'Farrell, *Irish in Australia*, pp. 278–88.

the Catholic Church's *Ne temere* decree on mixed marriages. In 1922 Bishop James Liston of Auckland was prosecuted for sedition after he attacked British policies in Ireland, but the prosecution was quashed by the Supreme Court which ruled that it did not amount to sedition in New Zealand.[33]

In view of these events, it was not surprising that Dominion leaders wanted to see an end to the Anglo-Irish war and made their views known to the British government. But did they regard Ireland as a Dominion? Smuts's plans for enhancing Dominion autonomy and co-operation foundered on the reluctance of Britain and the other Dominions, particularly Australia, to define Dominion Status. It was remarkable that although Dominion Status was offered to the Irish on 20 July, while the Imperial Conference was still sitting, none of the Dominion leaders apart from Smuts was formally consulted about the offer. After sitting for seven weeks the Conference decided that it would not after all define the mysteries of Dominion Status, preferring plasticity to precision.[34] This missed opportunity had serious consequences for the Irish negotiations that started two months later. It also made Smuts's attempts to persuade the Irish of the benefits of Dominion Status appear unconvincing. Nobody was less convinced than Erskine Childers.

Childers later stated that he had 'passed through the Dominion phase years before, discarded it and sworn allegiance to the established republic'.[35] He had a distinguished record in the First World War, but in 1919 the pace of events in Ireland drew him increasingly to Sinn Fein. His cousin, Robert Barton, was elected a Sinn Fein TD in 1918 and became a member of the first Dáil Cabinet. In the summer of 1919 Michael Collins and Arthur Griffith asked Childers to go to Paris to help present Ireland's case at the Peace Conference. He was deeply disillusioned by the proceedings there. While in Paris he met Philip Kerr and Lionel Curtis, who were with the British delegation. Curtis, he noted, was more reactionary than Kerr and 'seemed impervious to the idea that it [Ireland's Case] is other than an intellectual exercise for constitutional experts, like South Africa and India (in both of which he has taken a large part), and [is] obsessed by the partition idea and of aiming at a solution through UK devolution. I have rarely seen the English—hypocrisy is quite the wrong word—impenetrable egotism in such an insolent, anti-Irish form . . .'[36]

[33] Davis, *Irish Issues in New Zealand*, pp. 201–05. In 1968 Archbishop Liston, as he then was, was awarded the CMG.

[34] David Harkness, 'Britain and the Independence of the Dominions: The 1921 Crossroads', T. W. Moody, ed., *Nationality and the Pursuit of National Independence: Historical Studies*, XI (Belfast, 1978), pp. 141–59.

[35] F. M. A. Hawkings, 'Defence and the Role of Erskine Childers in the Treaty Negotiations of 1921', *Irish Historical Studies*, XXII (1980–81), p. 252.

[36] Erskine Childers to Mary Alden Childers, 17 Sept. 1919, MS 7852–5, Childers Papers, Trinity College, Dublin.

After de Valera's return from America in December 1920, Childers's influence gradually moved beyond propaganda work when de Valera came to rely on his advice and experience. As is clear from Childers's papers, he played a significant role in the evolution of external association, a concept de Valera had begun to explore in America. De Valera and Childers both believed that for reasons of geography and self-interest Britain would never treat Ireland on the same basis as the overseas Dominions. Sovereignty and secession were not bargaining counters but fundamental rights. This point was underlined when Smuts visited Dublin in early July 1921 to persuade de Valera to accept Dominion Status, urging de Valera not to press for a republic. When de Valera replied that the choice was for the Irish people, Smuts countered: 'the British people will never give you this choice. You are next door to them.'[37]

Childers accompanied de Valera to London for the first meeting with Lloyd George on 14 July 1921. Their meetings were inconclusive, but six days later Lloyd George made the first offer: Dominion Status involving membership and allegiance to the Crown but with six provisos, four of which related to defence and the other two to protective tariffs and a share of the public debt. The settlement would be embodied in a treaty which would also fully recognize the existing powers and privileges of the Northern Ireland Parliament. These terms disappointed even Smuts, who nevertheless told de Valera not to be too gloomy and to take what was offered. In his reply on 10 August de Valera asserted Ireland's inalienable right to realize her own destiny. Dominion Status for Ireland was illusory: 'Our geographical position is made the basis of denials and restrictions unheard of in the case of the Dominions.' As for partition: 'We cannot admit the right of the British Government to mutilate our country.' On the other hand, de Valera expressed his willingness to enter into a treaty of free association with the British Commonwealth.[38]

In these first two exchanges the essentials were set out. In the ensuing correspondence neither side would budge, for both men knew what was at stake. When stalemate was reached at the end of September after a protracted correspondence, Lloyd George issued a fresh invitation to negotiations without preconditions to ascertain 'how the association of Ireland with the community of nations known as the British Empire may best be reconciled with Irish national aspirations'.[39]

The negotiations which led to the signing of the Anglo-Irish Treaty have been described in the diaries and memoirs of the period and in Lord Longford's classic

[37] Jones, *Whitehall Diary*, p. 83.

[38] Dáil Éireann, *Official Correspondence Relating to the Peace Negotiations June–September 1921* (Dublin, 1921), pp. 6–11.

[39] Dáil, *Official Correspondence*, pp. 23–24, 29 Sept. 1921.

study, *Peace by Ordeal* (1935). The Irish delegates included Griffith, Collins, and Robert Barton. Childers was the Secretary. The principal British delegates were Lloyd George, Austen Chamberlain, Winston Churchill, and Lord Birkenhead. The roster of Secretaries included Philip Kerr, Edward Grigg, and Thómas Jones, who was Lloyd George's right-hand man throughout the negotiations. Lionel Curtis had just been elected to a fellowship at All Souls College, Oxford, when he was summoned by Lloyd George to become the constitutional adviser to the British delegation.

Childers, who had briefed himself thoroughly in recent writing about the Commonwealth, had a good idea what to expect from Curtis. The irony of Curtis and Childers being seated on opposite sides of the negotiating table was not lost on contemporaries. In a letter to Grigg, F. S. Oliver, the *éminence grise* of federalism, expressed the hope that 'the collision of the prophet and the ghazi . . . will, I trust, finally disrupt the proceedings . . . The selection is a shot of grim humour that does Providence infinite credit.'[40]

Allegiance to the Crown, membership of the Empire-Commonwealth, and defence guarantees were the core of the British demands. Lloyd George suggested that Curtis and Childers draft a statement on Dominion Status, a suggestion which proved impossible. Both men wrote separate memoranda, though Childers did not submit his to the British delegation. Curtis's document was a sweeping *tour d'horizon*, Dominion by Dominion. Status was fundamental, Curtis wrote: 'If I am asked then, to say what the status of a Dominion is so far as matters domestic to itself are concerned, I am forced to answer that it is exactly the same as the status of the United Kingdom.' Why, it might be asked, did he have to be forced to answer? 'The position', Curtis continued, 'can only be described as it is today without attempting to conjecture what it may become.'[41] Curtis clearly thought that such conjecture was undesirable, but since Dominion Status was the British desideratum, the failure to define what it meant and what it would mean was evasive. After all, the Irish had not asked for Dominion Status. For all Curtis's embroidery, there was a hollowness which critics like Childers discerned. Childers emphasized that Ireland could not rely on an unwritten British constitution, the interpretation of which would always rest with British jurists.

If Dominion Status was never exactly defined, then this was also true of the alternative presented by the Irish delegates—external association. It was not until 24 October, nearly two weeks after the start of the negotiations, that the first concrete formulation of external association was given to the British delegates. Ireland would adhere for certain purposes to the Commonwealth, these purposes

[40] Lavin, *Curtis*, p. 187.

[41] Memorandum on Dominion Status, 17 Oct. 1921, DE2/304: 1, National Archives Ireland, Dublin.

being defined as peace and war, defence, and political treaties. The King would be recognized as the head of the association.

After weeks of tense negotiations the Anglo-Irish Treaty was signed on 6 December 1921. It established the Irish Free State as a self-governing Dominion within the British Commonwealth. The first four articles defined the relationship with Britain and the Commonwealth. The Free State would have the same constitutional status as Canada; the Crown would be represented by a Governor-General; members of the Free State Parliament were to take an oath of allegiance. Articles 6 and 7 concerned coastal defence and the permanent facilities required by the British government. Partition was not broached, but Article 12 provided for the setting up of a boundary commission. The administrative arrangements included the establishment of a provisional government pending the drafting of a new constitution.

During the bitter debates on the Treaty which took place in December and January, de Valera tried to reconcile the differences between the Treaty and the proposals for external association in what became known as Document No. 2 (Document No. 1 was the Treaty). Although many of the provisions were identical, the differences were fundamental. There was no oath and no Governor-General; defence facilities similar to those of the Treaty were conceded, but only for a period of five years. There were also differences on Northern Ireland. Document No. 2 was withdrawn before it could be considered by the Dáil, but its significance for the future history of the Commonwealth was to be as momentous as that of the Treaty itself.

The terms of the Treaty in the British view were such an advance that the closeness of the Dáil vote, 64 for to 57 against, was an unwelcome surprise for British ministers. For the Treaty's Irish opponents the terms were bad enough, but even more humiliating were the circumstances under which it had been signed. On 5 December, as the fate of the negotiations hung in the balance, Lloyd George had threatened the wavering Irish delegates with immediate war if they did not sign. The threat was not a rhetorical flourish as it has sometimes been interpreted. In 1928 Curtis was clearly aware of the sensitivity of the issue when he reproached Churchill for revealing the ultimatum in his memoirs.[42] For opponents of the Treaty the fact that the delegates signed under duress made the document morally worthless, a view from which de Valera never wavered.

In January the Provisional Government was established, with Michael Collins as chairman. Drafting of the constitution also commenced. The Treaty was passed by both Houses of the British Parliament in March 1922. Lionel Curtis played a vital

[42] Correspondence between Curtis and Churchill, Dec. 1928, MSS Curtis 90, Bodleian Library, Oxford.

role in the implementation of the Treaty. He joined the Irish branch of the Colonial Office. He vigilantly guarded against possible amendments to the Treaty. To this end he ensured that the draft constitution was vetted by the British government before finally being ratified by the British Parliament, a move Collins strongly resisted. The Irish, Curtis observed, were still regrettably influenced by American ideas, especially the theory that the people were the source of authority.[43]

Curtis distrusted Collins but never appreciated the pressures the Irish leader faced as civil war loomed in Ireland. Eventually Collins bowed to British pressure on the draft constitution, which in its final form contained a clause that any provision or amendment of the constitution in conflict with the Treaty would be void. The pro-Treaty party was successful in the elections of June 1922. Two weeks later Collins finally moved against splinter IRA units occupying the lawcourts in Dublin, thus precipitating the civil war. Curtis and British ministers were nevertheless privately relieved when Collins was killed in August 1922. Curtis later described Collins patronizingly as the 'corner-boy in excelsis'.[44] Collins's successor, W. T. Cosgrave, was regarded as more reliable and Curtis had a warm regard for him. From his position in the Colonial Office, Curtis frustrated diehard attempts to wreck the Treaty after Lloyd George left office in October 1922. Curtis was instrumental in seeing that the boundary commission was set up and in the appointment of the commission chairman, his old friend Judge Richard Feetham from South Africa. The collapse of the commission was a disappointing epitaph for Curtis's involvement in Irish affairs. He returned to All Souls and a prolific writing career. When de Valera later began his assault on the Treaty in 1932, Curtis declared sternly that he must be resisted. In 1937 he published the second volume of his *Civitas Dei*, chapter 63 of which was 'The Irish Free State 1905–26'. He drew a veil over Irish affairs after 1926; it was the end of Irish history as far as Curtis was concerned. British ministers could not afford the luxury of such oblivion. For them 1937 was the year of de Valera's new constitution, which finally obliterated the edifice so carefully constructed by Curtis in 1922.

The signing of the Anglo-Irish Treaty had profound repercussions in the wider Imperial sphere. To the relief of the other Dominions, Irish agitation subsided and following the civil war there was a positive revulsion against violence in the Irish diaspora. But in Egypt and India the Irish Treaty had unforeseen consequences. In the autumn of 1921 British ministers faced negotiations not only with the Irish but with the Egyptians led by the Prime Minister Adli Pasha Yaghan. In both sets of negotiations the problem was similar: how far could nationalist demands be met?

[43] Lavin, *Curtis*, pp. 194–203. On the drafting of the 1922 Constitution see files P4/299–311, 838–50, 1249–52, Hugh Kennedy Papers, University College Dublin Archives Department.

[44] Lavin, *Curtis*, p. 203.

Ministers were aware that hostile elements in the British Conservative Party were monitoring both sets of negotiations in case unacceptable concessions were made. H. A. L. Fisher, the historian and a member of the Cabinet's Egyptian committee, compared Adli with Redmond and Zaghlul with Collins, and feared that Ireland was preventing Lloyd George from making concessions on Egypt.[45] Zaghlul was deported to the Seychelles in December 1921 but, like de Valera, who was on the run and in jail during 1922–24, his disappearance from the scene was temporary.

The Irish negotiations also caused ripples in Indian affairs. As disorder escalated in the wake of the non-cooperation movement, British ministers pressed the Government of India to arrest Gandhi. Many Conservative MPs were emphatic that the surrender to Sinn Fein must not be repeated with Gandhi and the Congress Party, particularly since it was increasingly obvious by early 1922 that the Irish Treaty, which had caused such dissension in the Conservative Party, far from bringing peace, seemed to be hastening civil war. The Government of India was reluctant to arrest Gandhi, fearing major disturbances, but to Conservative backbenchers this was all too reminiscent of the dithering with Sinn Fein. Gandhi was arrested on 9 March.[46]

There were other lessons learned from the Irish settlement. Ulster became a beacon for many white settlers as the pace of colonial independence quickened. In Kenya the vigilance committees organized to resist equal voting rights for Indians were modelled on the Ulster Volunteer Force. Ulster links with Rhodesia were particularly strong. The parallels with Ulster became uncomfortably close in the 1960s. White Rhodesians, like Ulster Unionists, drew a clear distinction between the Crown and the British government. When the Unilateral Declaration of Independence (UDI) was declared in 1965 there were uneasy references to the Curragh incident in 1914. Speculation arose whether British officers would be willing to crush UDI. In the early 1960s Sir Edgar Whitehead, Prime Minister of Southern Rhodesia, advocated his country's incorporation into the United Kingdom on the same terms as that of Northern Ireland, with Rhodesia retaining a government in Salisbury but with representation at Westminster. This would have made black Rhodesians, like Northern Ireland Catholics, a permanent minority in the United Kingdom. For some Tory MPs, Rhodesia was Ulster writ large. The historical parallels were reinforced when Bonar Law's son, Lord Coleraine, in the House of Lords, gave his support to Ian Smith. The British Prime Minister, Harold Wilson, later commented on the comparison between Rhodesia and Northern Ireland.[47]

45 Darwin, *Britain, Egypt and the Middle East*, pp. 40–42.

46 Sir Algernon Rumbold, *Watershed in India, 1914–22* (London, 1979), pp. 273, 281–88.

47 Donal Lowry, 'Ulster Resistance and Loyalist Rebellion in the Empire', in Keith Jeffery, ed., *'An Irish Empire?': Aspects of Ireland and the British Empire* (Manchester, 1996), pp. 191–215.

Irish statesmen made a creative contribution to Dominion Status at the Imperial Conferences of the 1920s.[48] The report of the 1926 Imperial Conference stated, in what became known as the Balfour Report, that the Dominions were 'autonomous communities... equal in status, in no way subordinate one to another in any aspect of their domestic or external affairs, though united by a common allegiance to the Crown, and freely associated as members of the British Commonwealth of Nations'. It was the long-awaited definition of Dominion Status, but in Ireland the reaction outside government circles was one of indifference. Dominion Status never aroused popular interest in Ireland; it came too late, it was imposed, and it was accompanied by partition and civil war. The achievements of the Irish government in the 1920s seemed to count for little when in November 1931 Churchill (by now a Conservative) and other diehard MPs tried to exclude the Free State from the jurisdiction of the Statute of Westminster, which freed Dominion Parliaments from the last legislative shackles of Westminster. They were unsuccessful, and the Free State became the first Dominion to adopt the Statute.

Three months later in February 1932 de Valera came to power, and within days introduced a bill to abolish the oath of allegiance and the clause in the 1922 constitution which stipulated that any provision of the constitution in conflict with the Treaty was void. He also disputed several substantial payments to Britain. When retaliatory tariffs were imposed, the dispute escalated into a six-year 'economic war', a misnomer, since political, constitutional, and defence questions were soon entangled. The British government mobilized Dominion opinion against de Valera, but this only antagonized and set him against the Commonwealth at the very moment he took office. In any event, the Canadian and South African responses were disappointing to the British government, so much so that the Dominions were not consulted on Ireland again for five years.[49] Once de Valera started to dismantle the Treaty, the cracks papered over in 1922 began to appear. To the indignation of British ministers who negotiated with him, he resurrected the alternative scheme for free association with Britain known as Document No. 2 as a basis for a new Anglo-Irish settlement. It was widely believed in British government circles in 1932 that de Valera would not last six months, but when he won an overall majority in a subsequent election in January 1933, the Treaty as the basis for Anglo-Irish relations was doomed.

[48] The Irish contribution to the Commonwealth in the 1920s has been discussed by D. W. Harkness, *The Restless Dominion* (London, 1969). There is a contrasting view in Ged Martin, 'The Irish Free State and the Evolution of the Commonwealth 1921–49', in Ronald Hyam and Ged Martin, eds., *Reappraisals in British Imperial History* (London, 1975), pp. 201–23.

[49] Memoranda and Correspondence Relating to the Dominions, March–April 1932, CAB[inet] 27/525, ISC (32) 3, 6, 10.

Officials at the Dominions Office showed a willingness to recognize that the Treaty was dead, but with initiative at ministerial level moribund, there was little they could do. De Valera decided to move ahead unilaterally with his new constitution, an outline of which he sent to the Dominions Secretary, Malcolm MacDonald, in June 1936. The Cabinet's Irish Situation Committee had lengthy discussions about Dominion Status.[50] De Valera had told MacDonald that the Crown would be eliminated from the Free State's internal affairs but that in matters of common concern the Free State would co-operate fully. For years, he told MacDonald, the British government had insisted on outdated forms. He thought his proposals were consistent with staying in the Commonwealth, but if the British thought otherwise they 'would have to throw them out'.[51] This was the dilemma facing the British government in 1936–37. De Valera's rejection of allegiance put him outside the Commonwealth, but as one minister (Walter Elliot) observed to the Irish Situation Committee, since the Free State was willing to recognize the King as the head of the association it was something more than a foreign country. Document No. 2 adequately covered the King's position, and in Elliot's opinion 'it was a mistake to treat that document as serving no useful purpose'.[52]

The issue of allegiance remained fundamental. In December 1936, during the Abdication crisis, de Valera passed the External Relations Act, which recognized the King for certain limited purposes in external affairs. It was much more negative and restricted in scope than Document No. 2 and it did not conform to the definitions of Dominion Status so laboriously worked out by the Irish Situation Committee. The Dominions were consulted about the External Relations Act and the new constitution. All favoured acceptance. Hertzog, for example, declared that if the Free State decided to become a republic, it could remain in the Commonwealth as long as the King remained the symbol of co-operation.[53]

De Valera's constitution was passed by referendum in July 1937 and became law at the end of the year. Four months later, the six-year dispute ended when de Valera and the British government concluded a new Anglo-Irish agreement. The economic dispute was settled and the ports that had been retained under the 1921 Treaty were returned unconditionally, thus facilitating Irish neutrality a year later. To de Valera's great regret, there was no progress on partition.

The fate of Dominion Status as applied to Ireland had many lessons for British statesmen and officials, particularly its suitability for countries which were not 'natural'

[50] Meetings of the Irish Situation Committee, June–July 1936, CAB 27/524.

[51] Memorandum by Malcolm MacDonald, July 1936, CAB 27/527, ISC (32)108.

[52] Meeting of the Irish Situation Committee, 22 July 1936, CAB 27/524.

[53] Dominion telegrams, 15, 27 Feb., 1 March 1937, CAB 24/268, C. P. 91(37); note of meeting with Dominion Prime Ministers, 14 June 1937, D[ominions] O[ffice] 35/891, XI, 82.

Dominions. In 1929, eight years after Ireland, Dominion Status became the declared goal of British policy in India but the lessons so painfully learned from Ireland were only partially absorbed, in part because Irish and Indian affairs were dealt with by separate departments. The Dominions Office and the India Office were 'divided geographically only by the width of a Whitehall quadrangle . . . [with] surprisingly little contact and a marked difference of outlook'.[54] The shadow of Ireland nevertheless hung heavily over the debate on India in the 1930s, and the Secretary of State for India, Lord Zetland, attended the meetings of the Irish Situation Committee in the summer of 1936 when Dominion Status was being discussed.

The volumes of *The Transfer of Power* in India are dotted with references to Ireland. Leopold Amery, the Secretary of State for India, acknowledged in 1942 that an imposed constitution was unworkable and saw ominous parallels between Nehru and de Valera, though he conceded that de Valera 'evidently has some executive ability'.[55] In February 1945 Amery submitted a memorandum to the Cabinet's India Committee which contained an appendix entitled 'The Problem of an Anglo-Indian Treaty', written by an unidentified adviser. It examined the precedents for a treaty and in effect contributed the most comprehensive post-mortem on the Irish Treaty undertaken by the British government. In retrospect some of the clauses of the Irish Treaty were seriously flawed. The Irish experience showed that enshrining allegiance in a set form was dangerous. The financial disputes with de Valera made it advisable to discharge all financial liabilities by the time a treaty came into force. On defence, although the return of the Treaty ports in 1938 was opposed by Churchill, the report concluded that 'possibly a "not unfriendly" Eire added to the power of the Navy, and the existence of "Northern Ireland" . . . helped to deter Hitler from a descent on that country'. The protection of minorities in the Irish Treaty could be useful for India; Article 16 on religious discrimination 'appears to have been, on the whole, respected in both areas, perhaps because reprisals are easy', a conclusion open to contention in both parts of Ireland. On the question of a repugnancy clause [which stipulated that any provision of the Irish constitution in conflict with the Treaty was invalid], the memorandum noted that the objection in the Irish case was founded on the theory that Ireland had always been a sovereign state. 'It is to be hoped that such a theory will not be so passionately held in regard to India, and in this view it seems proper that the doctrine of repugnancy should be in some form or other recognized and maintained for whatever period the Treaty or Treaties remain valid.' The memorandum ascribed the frustrated expectations of the Irish Treaty to:

[54] Nicholas Mansergh, *Survey of British Commonwealth Affairs: Problems of External Policy, 1931–39* (London, 1952), p. 271, n. 1.

[55] Press conference, 7 April 1942, in Nicholas Mansergh and others, eds., *The Transfer of Power*, 12 vols. (London, 1970–83), I, p. 677; Amery to Linlithgow, 24 July 1942, *Transfer of Power*, II, p. 455.

the survival and ultimate predominance of a party unwilling to forget the past or abandon the political theory that the State of Eire rests, not on agreement between two political entities previously in union, but on the natural right of a nation to self-determination... Although it is to be hoped that the settlement between Great Britain and India will not be preceded by a 'Black and Tan' campaign or followed by a Civil War, it is impossible to rule out the likelihood of a body of opinion in India intensely critical of the terms of a Treaty confirming the settlement.[56]

The consequences of partition were not mentioned in this historic comment. Smuts was alive to the danger and had warned Churchill in March 1942 that if 'Irish tactics' of partition were followed then India might decline a free constitution and with much public sympathy.[57] In Ireland and India power was transferred in a political triangle consisting of a nationalist majority at its base, with a recalcitrant minority and the departing Imperial power on each side. In Ireland it was divide and depart; the British settled with the minority before they settled with the nationalist majority. In India there was the same triangle (though complicated by the existence of another substantial minority, the Sikhs), but partition and withdrawal were simultaneous. In Ireland partition was seen by both the British government and the new Free State as a temporary measure, but as it became more deep-rooted the resentment it engendered was a source of instability for every Irish government after independence. It left them open to republican charges that they had sold out on Ulster. In India the legacy was even more unstable. Two wars with Pakistan in 1965 and 1971, were followed by Pakistan itself splitting up. There was also the long-running dispute over Kashmir.

In India the partition of 1947 was the price of independence and there were few illusions that it was temporary. But that did nothing to lessen the resentment that British policies had encouraged Muslim and Unionist resistance to the new states. In both countries boundary commissions determined disputed frontiers. In India this led to bloodshed and huge movements of population; in Ireland the border was unchanged, preserving in stone the political, religious, social, and economic tensions of an ill-thought-out partition. Unlike the Muslims, most Ulster Unionists did not think of themselves as a separate nation, but in both cases their leaders, Sir Edward Carson and Muhammed Ali Jinnah, became prisoners of policies initially adopted as tactical devices.[58]

In the autumn of 1946 the question of India's future relations with the Commonwealth became urgent. As the India Office pondered what course to

[56] Memorandum by Amery, appendix, 1 Feb. 1945, *Transfer of Power*, V, pp. 503–16.

[57] Smuts to Churchill, 5 March 1942, *Transfer of Power*, I, p. 327.

[58] T. G. Fraser, *Partition in Ireland, India and Palestine* (London, 1984); Nicholas Mansergh, *The Prelude to Partition: Concepts and Aims in Ireland and India* (Cambridge, 1978).

recommend to the government, Ireland was a painful precedent. The India Office asked other government departments whether it was in the interests of the Commonwealth that India should remain within it. The question had been debated exactly ten years before with de Valera's new constitution. The obvious answer was 'yes', but there was a danger that India might become 'a larger and noisier Southern Ireland' and be more of an embarrassment than an asset. The alternative would be a new variant of Dominion Status which could accommodate a republican India, but allegiance to the Crown was still vital. The consensus was that there was no need to tolerate the same unsatisfactory relationship with India; the Irish precedent should be avoided at all costs. But it could not be.[59]

The India Independence Act created two independent Dominions which, unlike the Free State in 1922, were given the choice of remaining in the Commonwealth. This was not finally decided until April 1949, but the intervening twenty months witnessed two events of ironic symmetry: republican India's accession to the Commonwealth and republican Ireland's secession.

In February 1948 de Valera was defeated by a coalition led by John A. Costello of Fine Gael, who had frequently expressed his dislike of the ambiguity of the External Relations Act. The Minister of External Affairs, Sean MacBride, was the leader of one of the other coalition parties, the republican Clann na Poblachta founded in 1946. MacBride was the son of John MacBride, one of the leaders of the Irish Brigade in the Boer War who had been executed in 1916, and of Maud Gonne MacBride, who had also been a leading pro-Boer.

Rumours of the repeal of the External Relations Act surfaced in the months after the new government took office. The course of events is still controversial, but the evidence suggests that, although it had been discussed by the Irish Cabinet, nothing had been decided by the time Costello visited Canada in September 1948. On 7 September, to the astonishment of his Canadian hosts, Costello announced not only the repeal of the External Relations Act but that Ireland would also be leaving the Commonwealth. The suddenness of the announcement provoked an enduring controversy. Costello maintained that it was a decision agreed by the Cabinet. If so, it reflected even more unfavourably on his government, since the Irish archives reveal that there was little preparation for a major step which was bound to have serious consequences on citizenship and trade. Since secession from the Crown did not necessarily mean leaving the Commonwealth, particularly now that the Indian position was under discussion, Costello had certainly burned his boats. De Valera, who had recently visited Nehru in New Delhi, was much more aware of the Indian dimension.

[59] R. J. Moore, *Escape from Empire: The Attlee Government and the Indian Problem* (Oxford, 1983), pp. 227–31.

Prime Minister Clement Attlee and his ministers were in a dilemma. They were annoyed by the cavalier manner of Costello's announcement, but as in 1937 the Dominions would have to be consulted about the Irish action. Attlee hoped that they would dissuade the Irish from repeal, and in October 1948, taking advantage of the Commonwealth Conference in London, a meeting was held in Chequers with British, Irish, and Dominion representatives. The Dominions were those which had large Irish populations—Canada, Australia, and New Zealand; there were no representatives from South Africa or from the new Asian Dominions. It was Attlee's intention to stress the serious consequences of repeal, especially for citizenship and trade. He and the other British representatives evidently assumed that the other Dominions would fall into line, but they soon realized their mistake. The Canadian Prime Minister, W. L. Mackenzie King, hoped that the Irish could be brought into effective, if not formal, membership of the Commonwealth. The New Zealand Prime Minister, Peter Fraser, revealed unsuspected links with Ireland when, at the beginning of the Chequers meeting, he asked after MacBride's mother whom he remembered from anti-war meetings during the Boer War.[60] The Australian representative at the meeting, the deputy Prime Minister Dr Herbert Evatt, had, like Mackenzie King, already urged Attlee to explore newer forms or symbols, even if they were unorthodox.[61]

The Dominion representatives all took the view that, as it was desirable to maintain Irish links with the United Kingdom and the Commonwealth, Ireland should not be treated as a foreign country. Following another meeting in November 1948, Costello was able to announce to the Dáil when introducing the Republic of Ireland Bill that reciprocal arrangements would come into force with Britain and the Commonwealth for citizenship and trade purposes.[62] Under the 1948 British Nationality Act, Irish citizens were not treated as aliens and retained full residence and voting rights.

That the Irish government emerged so unscathed was due entirely to the good offices of the other Dominions. But there was a sting in the tail. At midnight on 17–18 April 1949 Ireland left the Commonwealth and became the Republic of Ireland. Five days later at the Commonwealth Conference in London, the Indian government affirmed its desire to continue full membership in the Commonwealth and to accept the King as 'a symbol of the free association of its independent member nations'. Ten days later, on 3 May, the British government published its Ireland Bill,

[60] *Irish Times*, 1–2 Jan. 1979. Fraser asked after the family of another executed 1916 leader, James Connolly, whom he had also known. Attlee was disconcerted by these revelations.

[61] John O'Brien, 'Australia and the Repeal of the External Relations Act', Colm Kiernan, ed., *Australia and Ireland, 1788–1988*, (Dublin, 1986), pp. 252–66; F. J. McEvoy, 'Canada, Ireland, and the Commonwealth: The Declaration of the Irish Republic, 1948–49', *Irish Historical Studies*, XXIV (1985), pp. 506–27.

[62] John A. Costello, 24 Nov. 1948, *Dáil Éireann Parliamentary Debates*, CXIII, cols. 380–83.

the legislative response to the Irish departure from the Commonwealth. The special citizenship and trade arrangements were confirmed, but there was also a clause which declared that 'in no event will Northern Ireland or any part thereof cease to be . . . part of the United Kingdom without the consent of the Parliament of Northern Ireland'. In effect this clause transferred the veto on Irish unity from Westminster to Belfast. The Republic had come—but at a price.

Select Bibliography

PAUL CANNING, *British Policy Towards Ireland, 1921–41* (Oxford, 1985).

RICHARD P. DAVIS, *Irish Issues in New Zealand Politics, 1868–1922* (Dunedin, 1974).

W. K. HANCOCK, *Survey of British Commonwealth Affairs: Problems of Nationality, 1918–36* (Oxford, 1937).

D. W. HARKNESS, *The Restless Dominion: The Irish Free State and the British Commonwealth of Nations, 1921–31* (London, 1969).

KEITH JEFFERY, *The British Army and the Crisis of Empire, 1918–22* (Manchester, 1984).

—— ed., *'An Irish Empire?': Aspects of Ireland and the Empire* (Manchester, 1996).

JOHN KENDLE, *Ireland and the Federal Solution: The Debate over the United Kingdom Constitution, 1870–1921* (Kingston, Ontario, 1989).

Lord LONGFORD (FRANK PAKENHAM), *Peace by Ordeal* [1935], 5th edn. (London, 1992).

DEBORAH LAVIN, *From Empire to International Commonwealth: A Biography of Lionel Curtis* (Oxford, 1995).

DONAL MCCRACKEN, *Southern African–Irish Studies*, 2 vols. (Durban, 1991–92).

DEIRDRE MCMAHON, *Republicans and Imperialists: Anglo-Irish Relations in the 1930s* (New Haven, 1984).

NICHOLAS MANSERGH, *Survey of British Commonwealth Affairs: Problems of External Policy, 1931–39* (Oxford, 1952).

—— *The Commonwealth Experience*, 2nd edn. (London, 1982).

—— *The Unresolved Question: The Anglo-Irish Settlement and its Undoing, 1912–72* (London, 1991).

ROBERT O'DRISCOLL and LORNA REYNOLDS, eds., *The Untold Story: The Irish in Canada*, 2 vols. (Toronto, 1988).

PATRICK O'FARRELL, *The Irish in Australia* (Kensington, NSW, 1987).

CHARLES TOWNSHEND, *Britain's Civil Wars: Counterinsurgency in the Twentieth Century* (London, 1986).

7
Migrants and Settlers

STEPHEN CONSTANTINE

The size of the Empire and the volume and variety of its people much impressed the British at the beginning of the twentieth century. Recent expansion had sent the cartographers back to their maps to colour in yet more of the earth's surface in shades of pink. Typical of the popular product was *The Royal Primrose Atlas*, published by the soap manufacturer John Knight Ltd. in 1913, which placed between the advertisements for soap not only maps but statistical data. Highlighted was the population of Britain and the Empire, totalling, it claimed, 396 million and thereby outnumbering the assets of Germany and its colonies (71 million), the United States (84 million), France and the French Empire (93 million), Imperial Russia (130 million), and even China (358 million).

Moreover, the integration of, eventually, about one-quarter of the world's land surface into what purported to be a single polity seemed to British observers to open up dizzying possibilities of enhanced global mobility for the ethnically diverse peoples of the Empire. The British Nationality and Status of Aliens Act in 1914 clarified the definition of British citizens to include 'any person born within His Majesty's dominions and allegiances', and by implication confirmed their right of entry into Britain. There also seemed a prospect of free movement into and between other Imperial territories. Certainly there was much evidence of past mobility, through temporary migration or permanent settlement. Early in the new century it was collected statistically into a *Census of the British Empire*, whose tables recorded the dispersal of people from the British Isles to the colonies of white settlement and elsewhere; the diaspora, especially of Indians, black Africans, and Pacific Islanders, to Imperial territories outside their homelands; and some influx of the colonial-born into Britain.[1]

It was easy too for the British at the opening of the century to fit these movements into a metropolitan-centred economic concept of Empire. The historic role of Britain had evidently been to despatch supplies of labour and skills as well as

[1] *P[arliamentary] P[apers]* (1905), CII, Cd. 2660, pp. xxix–xlix; Colin Newbury, 'The March of Everyman: Mobility and the Imperial Census of 1901', *Journal of Imperial and Commonwealth History*, XII (1984), pp. 80–101.

capital from the Imperial core to the colonial periphery. Emigrants to the white settler societies had increased the output and export of their principal products by farming, forestry, or mining. In India and the Colonial Empire, permanent and transient immigrants from Britain formed a managerial élite as planters, mine-owners, and traders, assisted by the official administrative class. Moreover, the functions of expatriates had often included the moving of indigenous workers long distances into British-managed plantations and mines. Obligations and sometimes opportunities created by Imperial intrusions had also resulted in independent migrations across colonial borders of, for example, African and Indian labourers and traders. In sum, adjustments in the distribution of local labour seemed to have perfected the primary-producing status of the overseas Empire and its integration with a Britain increasingly committed instead to industry, finance, and commerce.

Of course, such an assessment caricatures the economic complexity of the Empire by 1900 and ignores the reliance of some Empire producers and consumers on world and not just Imperial markets, the quasi-autonomy of some regions, and the drift of labour (including immigrants) in the white settler societies towards services and manufacturing and into urban settings. Nevertheless, at a high level of generalization and from the British perspective, the demographic and economic interpretation embedded in John Knight's *Atlas* of 1913 did not mislead. The consequence for consumers in Britain of the shifts of entrepreneurs, administrators, and workers out to and around the Empire was tea from Ceylon, cocoa from the Gold Coast, sugar from Mauritius, bananas from Jamaica, sago from Malaya, wheat from Canada, and New Zealand lamb for dinner. Industry absorbed palm-oil from Nigeria, wool from Australia, cotton from the Sudan, and metal ores from Northern Rhodesia. The gold of South Africa sustained the flows of Imperial and international commerce and enriched the City.

The essentials of this system, and the role of migration and settlement in its sustenance, continued deep into the twentieth century. The maintenance, even intensification, of Imperial connections is suggested by the continuing flows of emigration from Britain. The available statistics are unfortunately flawed. The most consistent set records the movement of British nationals (including other Empire subjects) between United Kingdom ports and extra-European territories (that is, outside the continent and also the Mediterranean and Black Sea) from 1876 to 1962. But these are figures of all ships' passengers and therefore include not just migrants but increasing numbers of temporary departures, including tourists. Moreover, the totals exclude, later, the growing volume of air passengers. Only during 1912 were attempts begun to distinguish separately the number of migrants, defined as those intending to take up residence for at least one year. Difficulties remained, including the inability to register those who subsequently changed their intentions and the failure still to record those travelling by air. Table 7.1 summarizes the figures from 1876 to 1912 using the passenger totals. Table 7.2 completes the sequence to 1963 but using the migration figures.

Table 7.1 shows that from 1900 the average annual flow of outward passengers (including migrants) was rising. Outward emigrants, numbered in Table 7.2, were naturally fewer, but 389,394 in 1913 alone, the first full year of recording, is

TABLE 7.1. *Passengers of British nationality from UK to extra-European destinations, 1876–1912*

Years	Outward		Net Movement	
	Total	Average	Total	Average
1876–79	481,840	120,460	−253, 666	−63, 417
1880–84	1,312,207	262,441	−992, 622	−198, 524
1885–89	1,255,754	251,151	−807, 590	−161, 518
1890–94	1,011,509	202,302	−480, 794	−96, 159
1895–99	780,572	156,114	−282, 697	−56, 539
1900–04	1,077,587	215,517	−518, 641	−103, 728
1905–09	1,534,854	306,971	−799, 977	−159, 928
1910–12	1,320,041	440,014	−764, 003	−254, 668

Source: N. H. Carrier and J. R. Jeffery, *External Migration: A Study of the Available Statistics, 1815–1950* (London, 1953), pp. 90–91.

TABLE 7.2. *Emigrants of British nationality from UK to extra-European destinations, 1913–1963*

Years	Outward		Net Movement	
	Total	Average	Total	Average
1913–14	604,287	302,144	−414, 116	−207, 058
1915–19	297,397	59,479	−33, 029	−6, 606
1920–24	1,070,333	214,067	−723, 167	−144, 633
1925–29	741,220	148,244	−462, 785	−92, 557
1930–34	208,942	41,788	113,405	22,681
1935–38	125,525	31,381	51,200	12,800
1946–49	590,022	147,506	−349, 579	−87, 395
1950–54	726,800	145,360	−372, 200	−74, 440
1955–59	600,500	120,100	−279, 500	−55, 900
1960–63	378,100	94,525	−99, 100	−24, 775

Source: G. F. Plant, *Oversea Settlement* (London, 1951), pp. 174–75; B. R. Mitchell, *International Historical Statistics, Europe, 1780–1988* (London, 1992), p. 135. Figures exclude departures from Irish Free State ports after 1923.

remarkably high. Emigration after the First World War fell below this peak, but in taking a longer perspective it is important to compare like with like. Assuming that the proportion of emigrants among passengers was the same before 1913 as after, we can estimate the total number of emigrants for the decade 1900–09 as 1,670,198; and that figure is exceeded by the 1920–29 total of 1,811,553. Although emigration declined in the late 1920s and especially in the 1930s, there was another surge in the late 1940s and 1950s. The inclusion of air passengers would boost these later totals. True, net movements of migrants were generally lower after the First World War than before, but with the distinctive exception of the 1930s, they remained strongly outwards and once more became substantial after the Second World War.

Like earlier emigrants, those leaving after 1900 were largely aged under 30 (over 70 per cent before the First World War). An increasing proportion of the adult emigrants was female, though there were year by year variations and differences according to national origin within the United Kingdom. Except in the 1930s, a growing number were children. There were also some significant shifts in the occupations of those economically active. As Table 7.3 indicates, the proportions

TABLE 7.3. *Occupational distribution of UK adult emigrants, 1912–1949* (%)

	England and Wales					Scotland				
	1912–13	1921–24	1925–30	1931–37	1949	1912–13	1921–24	1925–30	1931–37	1949
Males										
Commerce, Finance, Professions, etc.	20.8	25.1	29.5	55.4	37.5	21.1	14.8	19.1	41.3	25.9
Mining, Quarrying		6.1	8.2	3.0	1.6		8.8	11.9	3.2	2.8
Metal and Engineering		14.5	13.4	17.4	13.7		27.0	17.2	24.4	15.3
Building		2.5	2.2	1.6	5.5		3.5	2.7	2.2	7.3
Others		13.0	10.4	7.4	20.4		16.2	14.6	12.1	24.6
Total Skilled Trades	36.1	36.1	34.2	29.3	41.2	47.6	55.6	46.4	41.9	49.9
Transport and Communications		4.8	4.4	3.7	5.4		4.5	4.9	3.3	7.0
Agriculture	20.9	21.9	23.6	10.2	8.8	19.0	16.1	18.6	11.6	9.0
Labourers (other than agriculture and transport)	22.2	12.1	8.2	1.3	7.1	12.3	9.1	11.1	1.9	8.2
Females										
Commerce, Finance, Professions, etc.	11.6	33.6	37.3	68.4	74.2	9.4	29.5	29.1	57.5	70.0
Clothing Trades	13.4	7.4	5.6	3.3	7.2	19.1	8.9	6.9	4.8	7.9
Domestic, Hotel etc., Service	75.1	59.0	57.1	28.3	18.7	71.5	61.7	64.0	37.7	22.1

Source: N. H. Carrier and J. R. Jeffery, *External Migration: A Study of the Available Statistics, 1815–1950* (London, 1953), pp. 124–25.

of male emigrants who were labourers or in agriculture and of females who were domestic servants or in the clothing trades had fallen by mid-century, while the shares of skilled tradesmen (after a setback in the 1930s) and more especially of white-collar workers and professionals, both male and female, had generally risen.

Even more remarkable was the shift in destinations. In the 1880s and 1890s about two-thirds of passengers from Britain had departed for the United States, but as Table 7.4 shows, the foreign share of departing passengers and then of emigrants fell markedly in the new century. This redirection was not solely due, as is sometimes claimed, to the operation of national immigration quotas by the United States government from 1921 to 1965, since except in the mid-1920s the number of British immigrants fell far below their allowance. More positive reasons must be found for the substantial rise in the proportions choosing Empire destinations, a lift from barely one-third in the later nineteenth century to around four-fifths. From 1946 to 1963, over 82 per cent of emigrants leaving by sea went to Empire-Commonwealth countries.[2]

Overwhelmingly, emigrants from Britain were heading for the existing white settler societies. It was especially the attraction of Canada which boosted the share of the Empire before the First World War and which sustained the high emigration rate until the 1930s. However, Australia and to a lesser extent New Zealand also increased their appeal just before 1914 and maintained it thereafter. The totals for South Africa were comparatively small before 1914 and only modest in the 1920s, though numbers held up much better than elsewhere in the 1930s and reached unusual heights in 1947–48. Between 1948 and 1957 emigrants from Britain to

TABLE 7.4. *Extra-European destinations of British nationals: passengers, 1900–1912, emigrants, 1913–1949*

	All Empire		British North America		Australasia		Rest of Empire		Foreign	
1900–04	465,924	(43.2%)	189,826	(17.6%)	70,902	(6.6%)	205,196	(19.0%)	611,663	(56.8%)
1905–09	831,293	(54.2%)	515,720	(33.6%)	130,426	(8.5%)	185,147	(12.1%)	703,561	(45.8%)
1910–12	896,260	(67.9%)	527,997	(40.0%)	223,271	(16.9%)	144,992	(11.0%)	423,781	(32.1%)
1913–14	423,802	(70.1%)	269,424	(44.6%)	111,332	(18.4%)	43,046	(7.1%)	180,485	(29.9%)
1915–19	202,888	(68.2%)	113,620	(38.2%)	39,391	(13.2%)	49,877	(16.8%)	94,509	(31.8%)
1920–24	743,060	(69.4%)	383,868	(35.9%)	233,468	(21.8%)	125,724	(11.7%)	327,273	(30.6%)
1925–29	576,146	(77.7%)	261,477	(35.3%)	213,412	(28.8%)	101,257	(13.7%)	165,074	(22.3%)
1930–34	151,367	(72.4%)	46,208	(22.1%)	36,568	(17.5%)	68,591	(32.8%)	57,575	(27.6%)
1935–38	103,860	(82.7%)	10,673	(8.5%)	25,550	(20.3%)	67,622	(53.9%)	21,665	(17.3%)
1946–49	466,362	(79.0%)	130,534	(22.1%)	137,642	(23.3%)	198,186	(33.6%)	123,660	21.0%)

Source: G. F. Plant, *Oversea Settlement* (London, 1951), pp. 175–80.

[2] W. D. Borrie, *The Growth and Control of World Population* (London, 1970), p. 100; see also B. R. Mitchell, *British Historical Statistics* (Cambridge, 1988), p. 84, for figures from 1964 to 1980.

Canada totalled 431,993, to Australia 413,836, to New Zealand 108,612, and to South Africa 71,551.[3]

The 'Rest of Empire' totals in Table 7.4 include widely scattered groups who settled or took up temporary residence in the dependent Empire. For example, the census in 1931 counted 6,533 people of British origin in British West Africa, nearly two-thirds in Nigeria. There were 8,507 British-born nationals in Kenya in 1931, 4,225 in Northern Rhodesia, 2,552 in Tanganyika, 1,167 in Uganda, and 1,138 in Nyasaland, plus fifty-six sweating it out in Somaliland: a total in East Africa of 17,615. Kenya's European and Eurasian population had been a mere 596 in 1902. Southern Rhodesia received increased cohorts of immigrants direct from Britain (and others indirectly from elsewhere in southern Africa) after the First World War, 2,181 in 1920 alone, and more arrived after the Second World War. British India continued to attract British personnel, though in diminishing numbers: the Indian census of 1921 recorded 116,000 born in the British Isles. Others pitched up in South-East Asia, the Pacific Islands, and the West Indies.[4]

Personal testimony, largely derived from inquiries after 1945, naturally confirms that emigrants expected their moves to be economically and socially beneficial to themselves and their families. In a sample survey of emigrants to Australia in 1959, 74 per cent of the married men and 63 per cent of married women said their first reason for emigrating was in the expectation of better opportunities for themselves or their children.[5] Moreover, Gallup polls in this period revealed where people expected advantages to lie: on seventeen occasions between 1948 and 1975 usually 30–40 per cent of respondents expressed a wish to settle in another country, and the preference for the Commonwealth was always overwhelming.[6]

While individual decisions to emigrate often seem specific and personal, overcrowded labour markets in Britain prompted a response. Certainly, downturns in the trade cycle affected labour's prospects, with, for example, high levels of unemployment peaking in 1908, 1921, and 1931. Demobilization and adjustments to a peacetime economy in 1918–19 and 1945–46 also caused moments of difficulty, and there was renewed anxiety from the late 1960s. However, volumes of emigration from Britain do not correlate easily with cyclical shifts in the domestic demand for labour. Most obviously, emigration fell markedly in 1931 even though unemployment rose sharply. Moreover, rates of emigration revived after 1945 and remained high through the 1950s and 1960s even in a period of generally full

[3] R. T. Appleyard, *British Emigration to Australia* (London, 1964), p. 23.

[4] R. R. Kuczynski, *Demographic Survey of the British Colonial Empire*, 3 vols. (London, 1948–53); Imre Ferenczi, ed., *International Migrations*, Vol. I, *Statistics* (New York, 1929).

[5] Appleyard, *British Emigration to Australia*, p. 165.

[6] George H. Gallup, *The Gallup International Public Opinion Polls: Great Britain, 1937–1975*, 2 vols. (New York, 1976).

employment: in these decades rising expectations leading to frustrated ambitions in a society still markedly resistant to upward social mobility may account for the sense of overcrowding in the labour market.

In addition to cyclical movements in the national economy, there were, however, structural shifts which troubled particular occupations. They were due, in general, to increases in the international supply of competitive products, changes in consumer taste, and the spread of labour-saving means of production. Structural stresses at the beginning of the century were still affecting, for example, the demand for rural labour and the profitability of farming, and a proportion of agricultural workers and some landowners were inclined to quit. The latter were also affected after the First World War by a further downturn in agricultural prices and higher levels of taxation. This century has also seen the marked scaling down in the size of the staple Victorian industries of coal, cotton, iron and steel, and shipbuilding, notoriously between the wars. Even in the buoyant 1950s and 1960s reductions in textiles, heavy engineering enterprises, and the railway network obliged those made redundant to change jobs—or move. It has also been argued that the expansion of education from the late nineteenth century was increasing the potential recruits for white-collar clerical work and for the professions more rapidly than even those fast-expanding occupations could absorb.[7]

It did not, of course, follow that all those whose present livelihood or future expectations were threatened would respond by emigrating, but particular regions where stresses were most keenly felt seem to have suffered most losses. Scotland and Ireland lost a higher proportion of their population than did England. For example, between 1921 and 1931 net migration out of England averaged just 5 per 10,000 of the population, but from Scotland as many as 80 and from Northern Ireland 82. Indeed, Scotland and Ireland (north and south) experienced an absolute fall in their populations between 1921 and 1931. But much of this exodus was internal migration to the faster-growing English parts of the British economy in the Midlands and the south-east. It was, therefore, similar to shifts from northern England and from South Wales, which also experienced the loss of some of their young workforce. Only a proportion of these dislocated workers from the outer regions of Britain took the still bolder step of migrating overseas, either directly or at one (or more) remove as step migrants who first migrated within Britain before finally moving overseas. Nevertheless, the immigration records and census reports of Empire-Commonwealth countries do record disproportionate rates arriving from some regions of Britain. For example, by 1931 the number of those born in England and Wales and living in Canada had risen to

[7] Frank Musgrove, *The Migratory Elite* (London, 1963).

746,000, but those from far less-populated Scotland to 280,000 and the Irish-born to 108,000.[8]

Occupational and social opportunities in the Empire were, however, also needed to tug migrants overseas. The Empire territories which drew in personnel from Britain obviously differed widely, but in terms of labour markets they conformed broadly to two types. On the one hand, in India and the Colonial Empire after 1900 a dual labour market operated by which the manual workers needed by the economy were not imported from Britain (some skilled trades excepted) but were largely recruited from within the indigenous population or were obtained cheaply from non-European external sources. Recruits from Britain were therefore mainly confined to superior administrative, professional, and managerial posts, and tended to be of good educational background and high social status. Analysis of the recorded careers of graduates from Oxford men's colleges may show a decline between 1874–1914 and 1918–38 in the percentage from Balliol who went to work in the Empire (all parts), from 27 per cent to 18 per cent, but the percentages from Keble remained a steady 20, and from St John's there was only a mild reduction from 17 per cent to 15 per cent. India at the beginning of the century was still attracting the largest share of such young men, although constitutional change and Indianization within the Indian Civil Service reduced the volume long before 1947. As compensation, the first half of the twentieth century saw a marked though irregular growth in recruiting to the Colonial Service, providing opportunities in administration and eventually in educational, scientific, and technical services. Recruits totalled 4,616 in the period 1919–30, a mere 1,887 during the rest of the depressed 1930s, but a further 7,735 from 1940 to 1950.[9]

In addition, the private sector in India and the Colonial Empire provided other career openings for a similar élite. Overseas branches of British banks, shipping lines, and other businesses certainly recruited some local staff, but senior personnel especially were predominantly British expatriates.[10] Similarly, the exploitation of Northern Rhodesia's mineral resources drew in skilled manual workers from Britain, but especially professional mining engineers and managers. The European population was a mere 4,182 in 1924 before the copper deposits were located, but had risen to 13,846 by 1931, of whom 4,219 had been born in the British Isles (and most of the rest in South Africa).[11] Similarly, the new settler communities being

[8] N. H. Carrier and J. R. Jeffery, *External Migration: A Study of the Available Statistics, 1815–1950* (London, 1953), pp. 14–15.

[9] Richard Symonds, *Oxford and Empire: The Last Lost Cause* (London, 1986), pp. 184–202, 306–08; Sir Ralph Furse, *Aucuparius: Recollections of a Recruiting Officer* (London, 1962), Appendix 1.

[10] See, for example, D. K. Fieldhouse, *Unilever Overseas: The Anatomy of a Multinational, 1895–1965* (London, 1978), esp. pp. 191–97, 331–32, 367–68.

[11] Kuczynski, *Demographic Survey*, II, pp. 417–19, 475.

formed in Kenya and Southern Rhodesia especially after the First World War were largely drawn from Britain's cohorts of distressed landowners, former military officers, ex-public schoolboys, hard-pressed middle-class professionals, and twigs from the branches of the aristocracy.[12] Nor should we overlook the development by missionary societies of medical and educational services in India and the dependent Empire. They often provided exceptional careers for well-educated (and often single) middle-class women, whose chances in Britain remained severely constrained during at least the first half of this century. For them, the Empire provided remarkable opportunities to exercise authority.[13]

The Dominions constituted the second kind of labour market. With the very considerable exception of the Union of South Africa, whose labour market shared characteristics with colonial Africa, they were unable to tap an adequate indigenous labour force and were either dependent on the natural increase of existing settler stock or on the immigration of 'new chums'. In practice, the expansion and the diversification of settler economies in the twentieth century tended to require immigrants in both larger numbers and of a greater occupational variety. Such supplies were introduced in waves, which largely reflected fluctuations in the prices of the Dominions' principal exports on the international market. Overseas earnings affected profits, capital investments (whether raised locally or borrowed from abroad), wages, and thus labour demand. Early in the century, for example, large volumes of British capital attracted to Canada by the opening of the prairies generated a demand for immigrants from Britain. Likewise, in the 1920s sales of Australian wheat and wool and New Zealand pastoral products prompted efforts to raise capital, extend the area of cultivated land, and encourage immigration. South African immigration was affected by volumes of world trade which determined the price of gold and hence investment levels and labour demands, with better results in the 1920s and 1950s than in the 1930s.[14] But these cyclical variations—and others caused by the interruption of two world wars—better explain the fluctuations in the volume of emigration from Britain than the initial redirection and the widening occupational range of the migrants.

Longer-term structural shifts were also at work. The Dominions from the early twentieth century were developing into multi-sectored economies. Diversification broadened labour needs and increased the appeal of these societies to immigrants

[12] David Cannadine, *The Decline and Fall of the British Aristocracy* (New Haven, 1990), pp. 438–43; C. J. Duder, 'Men of the Officer Class: The Participants in the 1919 Soldier Settlement Scheme in Kenya', *African Affairs*, LXLII (1993), pp. 69–87.

[13] Symonds, *Oxford and Empire*, pp. 203–312; Musgrove, *Migratory Elite*, pp. 31–43; Pat Barr, *The Dust in the Balance: British Women in India, 1905–1945* (London, 1989). See below, pp. 395–96.

[14] See also the graph plotting the inverse relationship between unemployment rates in Canada and immigration 1951–78, in Huw R. Jones, *A Population Geography* (London, 1981), p. 263.

drawn from an urbanized society such as Britain's and practised in a wide range of trades and professions. Primary production in the Dominions was itself generating demand for other skilled workers in trade and transport, in financial services, and in industrial processing. Moreover, populations were concentrating in large cities such as Toronto, Melbourne, and Johannesburg, and this relocation attracted migrants with experience as skilled manual workers, clerical staff, technicians, and professionals into the construction industries, public utilities, and such services as education and health. Many of those Oxford graduates, for example, and others from medical schools in England and Scotland were finding attractive openings overseas in schools, new universities, and hospitals.

There is also no doubt that United Kingdom citizens were highly privileged as Empire migrants, especially when seeking entry to the white settler societies. It is true that these nations early adopted controls over immigration as one feature of their nation-building, but until quite recently their grounds for excluding immigrants from the British Isles were principally to bar the sick and political dissidents as well as those likely to become a public charge. Otherwise, British immigrants enjoyed a remarkable freedom of entry.

Even more indicative of the assumed harmony of interest between British emigration and Dominions immigration were efforts to promote and sustain that intimacy by intervention in the migrant labour market in order to divert flows, increase volumes, and recruit preferred personnel. The principal operators before the First World War, continuing their past activities, were the Dominions governments. In 1904, for example, New Zealand's Agent-General launched another recruiting campaign in Britain, using press and pamphlet advertising and offering cheap passages for those selected. Agents working for the Canadian government and for the Australian states were similarly active, and part of Sir Alfred Milner's reconstruction programme when High Commissioner in South Africa after the Boer War was to promote the increased immigration of British stock.[15]

The Imperial government's contribution before 1914 was largely limited to the Emigrants' Information Office (set up in 1886), which confined itself to advising and even warning prospective emigrants. The only official financial support for emigration was via the modest operations of the Poor Law, which from 1900 to 1913 assisted the emigration of just 9,472 people, of the Reformatory and Industrial

[15] J. S. McBean, 'Immigration into New Zealand, 1900 to 1915', unpublished MA thesis, Wellington, 1946; Donald F. Harris, 'The Work of Canadian Emigration Agents in Shropshire, 1896–1914', Dacsub Papers, University of Birmingham, 1991; Geoffrey Sherington, *Australia's Immigrants*, 2nd edn. (Sydney, 1990), p. 96; M. Streak, *Lord Milner's Immigration Policy for the Transvaal, 1897–1905* (Johannesburg, 1970).

Schools Act of 1891 and the Children's Act of 1908, which helped 3,097 cases abroad between 1900 and 1914, and of the Unemployed Workmen's Act of 1905, which had disposed of 27,465 by 1914. These efforts were overshadowed by British-based charities, such as the East End Emigration Fund and the Salvation Army, which raised considerable amounts of money to despatch their 'clients', in some cases after modest training, to new lives in new homes in the overseas Empire. Philanthropists and imperialist bodies such as the Royal Colonial Institute had tried since the 1880s to persuade the Imperial government to co-operate, preferably financially, with their efforts and with those of the Dominions, but even a highly publicized conference in 1910 failed to convince.[16]

Furher lobbying by the Royal Colonial Institute, pressure from Milner and Amery at the Colonial Office, and especially the Cabinet's concerns about post-war demobilization led to the establishment of the Oversea Settlement Committee in 1919 and the offer of free passages to Empire destinations for British ex-service personnel and their families. Altogether, between 1919 and 1924 this scheme assisted the departure of 86,027 people at a cost of £2,418,263. Australia accepted 37,576 immigrants, Canada 26,905, New Zealand 13,349, South Africa and Rhodesia 6,064, and 2,133 went to other Empire destinations, especially Kenya.[17]

This gesture formed the precedent for the rather more formidable commitment, accepted in principle by the Imperial Conference in 1921, which achieved legislative shape in the Empire Settlement Act of 1922. The Imperial government agreed to spend up to £3 million a year for fifteen years to help emigrants with the costs of passages and settlement, on the basis of sharing expenses with the governments of the Dominions (and of Southern Rhodesia) and with approved charities. Results fell far below intentions, but between 1922 and 1936 British expenditure amounting to £6,099,046 assisted the emigration of 405,230 people, or 36 per cent of the total volume of Empire migrants in those years, of whom 186,524 went to Canada, 172,735 to Australia, 44,745 to New Zealand, and just 1,226 to South Africa and Southern Rhodesia. Roughly one-third were males aged 12 or over, one-third females 12 or over, and one-third children under 12, suggesting that assistance and selection had effected a more even balance than among emigrants in general.[18]

[16] Keith Williams, '"A Way Out of Our Troubles": The Politics of Empire Settlement, 1900–1922', in Stephen Constantine, ed., *Emigrants and Empire: British Settlement in the Dominions between the Wars* (Manchester, 1990).

[17] Kent Fedorowich, *Unfit for Heroes: Reconstruction and Soldier Settlement in the Empire Between the Wars* (Manchester, 1995).

[18] Sidney Wertimer, 'Migration from Britain to the Dominions in the Inter-War Years', unpublished Ph.D. thesis, London, 1952; Plant, *Oversea Settlement*; Michael Roe, *Australia, Britain and Migration, 1915–1940* (Cambridge, 1995); Constantine, ed., *Emigrants and Empire*.

These efforts to assist Empire migration assumed that a natural harmony existed or could be engineered between the respective migration needs of Britain and of the overseas Empire.[19] One argument was demographic, that Britain was overcrowded, with population densities far higher than those of the underpopulated Dominions. Statistics were much employed, one writer in 1922 calculating, for example, that there were 650 people per square mile in England but in New Zealand 11.7, in Canada 2.5, and in Australia and South Africa a mere 1.8 (conceding that the Dominions figures counted 'white people' only).[20] The perceived consequences in Britain were recurrent high levels of unemployment, casual work, depressed wages, slum housing, degradation, and immorality. Such concerns prompted the efforts of charities. Cabinet ministers also accepted the thesis in 1919, when demobilization left people out of work, and in late 1920, when cyclical depression had driven up the numbers claiming (expensive) unemployment benefits. Meantime, underpopulation in the Dominions constrained their further economic development, limited their domestic markets, kept wages artificially high, left taxpayers with immoderate per capita burdens trying to support large national overseas debts, denied economies of scale in running public services, and even, some claimed, stunted the cultural development of under-endowed communities.

Another demographic argument was derived, rather shakily, from the perceived 'excess' of women in Britain and the greater proportion of men to women in the Dominions. The Dominions Royal Commission calculated that in 1911 in England and Wales there were 'at least 346,000 women of ages suitable for migration with no statistical prospect of marriage'.[21] A transfer would enable such women to fulfil their biological destinies and boost rates of natural increase in the overseas Empire. After the Boer War, special efforts had been made to encourage the migration of women to South Africa, partly to meet a demand for their labour but also in a vain effort to secure the political future for British interests by promoting marriage and outbreeding the Boers. The other Dominions also set out to entice single women with much-reduced or free passages and offers of employment, largely as domestic servants. The Imperial government endorsed the strategy, and from 1919 funded the Society for the Oversea Settlement of British Women largely to organize their selection and safe despatch.[22]

Philanthropists and governments also assumed that migrants from industrial Britain could and should be resettled in the rural Empire. Their labour would

[19] Stephen Constantine, 'Emigration and Social Reform, 1880–1950', in Colin G. Pooley and Ian D. Whyte, eds., *Migrants, Emigrants and Immigrants: A Social History of Migration* (London, 1991).

[20] J. Saxon Mills, 'Unemployment and the Empire', *Contemporary Review*, (March 1922), p. 317.

[21] *Final Report*, *PP* (1917–18), X, Cmd. 8462, p. 96.

[22] Una Monk, *New Horizons: A Hundred Years of Women's Migration* (London, 1963); Janice Gothard, '"The Healthy, Wholesome British Domestic Girl": Single Female Migration and the Empire Settlement

boost primary production, but they would also flourish morally and recover physically once transferred away from urban environments thought to be exceptionally debilitating of mind and body. One practical consequence was expected to be the increase and maturing in the healthier environment of the Empire of that racial stock upon which the Imperial government needed to draw for military purposes. Thus economic, ideological, and military arguments lurked behind the decision-making which saw the British government agree to fund, under the Empire Settlement Act, expensive land-settlement schemes in Western Australia, Victoria, New South Wales, New Brunswick, and elsewhere. Moreover, the same mixed rationale explains the efforts to pluck young children (and not only orphans) out of British slums before they were too badly damaged and to resettle them for regeneration in the Dominions. Canada took most (not least because their labour was cheap and appropriate for farm work) until 1925, after when only those aged over 14 were accepted. But others continued to be sent to Southern Rhodesia, New Zealand, and especially to Australia, where the last cohort, from Dr Barnardo's Homes, arrived by air in 1967.[23]

Disappointment with the land-settlement schemes was followed in the 1930s by more realistic assessments of the environmental capacity of the Dominions to absorb large numbers of immigrants and by growing doubts about the demographic capacity of Britain to supply emigrants. Many observers were persuaded that the era of mass migration was over. But the Empire Settlement Act was renewed in 1937, 1952, and 1957, and as the Commonwealth Settlement Act in 1962 and 1967, to expire finally only in 1972. Admittedly, the financial contributions of Britain's government were reduced until they became merely notional, but the governments of Australia, New Zealand, and Canada (though after 1948 not South Africa) preserved, after the Second World War, the privileged status of British immigrants. Security concerns, prompted by the recent war against Japan, added an extra incentive to 'populate or perish', and preferably from British stock. Assisted-passage schemes were revived by Australia and New Zealand in 1947 and by Canada in 1951. Vigorous advertising ensured that emigration to the Empire-Commonwealth remained a perceived option for unsettled members of Britain's labour force.[24]

Act, 1922–1930', in Constantine, ed., *Emigrants and Empire*; Brian L. Blakeley, 'The Society for the Oversea Settlement of British Women and the Problems of Empire Settlement, 1917–1936', *Albion*, XX (1988), pp. 421–44; Jean Jacques Van Helten and Keith Williams, 'The Crying Need of South Africa: The Emigration of Single British Women to the Transvaal, 1901–10', *Journal of Southern African Studies*, X (1983), pp. 17–38.

[23] Gillian Wagner, *Children of the Empire* (London, 1982); Joy Parr, *Labouring Children: British Immigrant Apprentices to Canada, 1869–1924* (London, 1980).

[24] Reg Appleyard, *The Ten Pound Immigrants* (London, 1988); Stephen Constantine, 'Immigration, Population and New Zealand's Destiny', *British Review of New Zealand Studies*, III (1990), pp. 16–26; Anthony H. Richmond, *Post-War Immigrants in Canada* (Toronto, 1967).

Privileged status was also enjoyed by migrants moving between the Dominions during the first half of the century, strengthening the perception of Empire as a zone of free labour mobility. Transfers across the Tasman Sea between Australia and New Zealand remained particularly strong, reflecting largely the oscillating opportunities perceived in the two Dominions as their programmes of land settlement, mining development, manufacturing, and urban expansion unfolded. By 1936 there were 42,000 Australians in New Zealand (and 6,000 in South Africa, 3,000 in Canada, and 1,000 in Southern Rhodesia and East Africa). In 1951 there were 35,000 Australians in New Zealand and 45,000 New Zealanders in Australia. Modest numbers of the Dominions-born also made careers for themselves in India and the Colonial Empire. In addition there were British-born emigrants to one Empire destination who subsequently moved to another.[25]

While there was transverse movement around the Empire's periphery, there was also migration, temporary and permanent, from the white settler societies at the periphery to the Imperial core. The census of 1931, for example, counted 92,745 people born in the four Dominions and resident in England and Wales. Such immigrants included the highly talented: the cultural hegemony of Imperial Britain was exemplified by the centripetal forces that drew them in. Until late in the twentieth century Britain remained the principal place for many born overseas to complete their academic and professional training. Between 1903 and 1953 over 2,500 Rhodes Scholars (including many Americans and some Germans) passed through Oxford. Others in substantial numbers attended other British universities and especially medical colleges. Some of the British-trained colonial-born were recycled within the Empire and, for example, entered the Colonial Service. Others remained in Britain as the most prestigious venue in which to exercise their talents. They included, from Australia, the classicist Gilbert Murray, the pathologist Howard Florey, the brain surgeon Hugh Cairns, the political scientist Kenneth Wheare, and (for a period) the historian Keith Hancock. The physicist Ernest Rutherford left New Zealand and went to Cambridge in 1895, moved to McGill in 1898, then to Manchester in 1907, and back to Cambridge in 1919. By 1953, twenty-three Rhodes scholars (including nine Australians) had became Fellows of Oxford Colleges.[26]

These Dominions-born immigrants are included in the total volumes of arrivals from the Empire listed in Table 7.5. The figures confirm the fluency of movement to and from the Empire-Commonwealth and further imply its unity. These totals also include large numbers of British-born migrants returning home. Settlers who

[25] T. E. Smith, *Commonwealth Migration* (London, 1981), pp. 20–21; A. H. McClintock, ed., *An Encyclopaedia of New Zealand*, 3 vols. (Wellington, 1966), II, pp. 137–38.

[26] Symonds, *Oxford and Empire*, p. 166.

TABLE 7.5. *Arrivals of British nationals from extra-European destinations: passengers, 1900–1912, emigrants, 1913–1949*

Years	All Empire		British North America		Australasia		Rest of Empire		Foreign	
1900–04	226,980	(40.6%)	63,022	(11.3%)	44,774	(8.0%)	119,184	(21.3%)	331,966	(59.4%)
1905–09	377,309	(51.3%)	150,596	(20.5%)	53,734	(7.3%)	172,979	(23.5%)	357,568	(48.7%)
1910–12	307,012	(55.2%)	143,990	(25.9%)	45,051	(8.1%)	117,971	(21.2%)	249,026	(44.8%)
1913–14	136,022	(71.5%)	59,972	(31.5%)	31,192	(16.4%)	44,858	(23.5%)	54,149	(28.5%)
1915–19	193,406	(73.2%)	100,994	(38.2%)	28,637	(10.8%)	63,775	(24.1%)	70,962	(26.8%)
1920–24	257,905	(74.3%)	89,839	(25.9%)	57,588	(16.6%)	110,478	(31.8%)	89,261	(25.7%)
1925–29	213,721	(76.8%)	65,088	(23.4%)	53,541	(19.2%)	95,092	(34.2%)	64,714	(23.2%)
1930–34	242,380	(75.2%)	83,370	(25.9%)	58,825	(18.3%)	100,185	(31.1%)	79,967	(24.8%)
1935–38	139,874	(79.1%)	36,130	(20.4%)	26,968	(15.3%)	76,766	(43.4%)	36,851	(20.9%)
1946–49	207,403	(86.3%)	31,326	(13.0%)	29,138	(12.1%)	146,939	(61.1%)	33,040	(13.7%)

Source: G. F. Plant, *Oversea Settlement* (London, 1951), pp. 175–80. Figures exclude arrivals at Irish Free State ports after 1923.

could not settle, the disillusioned, and the defeated must be counted among them. Numbers rose during the 1930s when economic conditions in the overseas Empire were worse than in Britain. In that decade the Canadian government deported immigrants who fell upon public relief.[27] Others, in all periods, returned not because they were economically defeated but because they, or their families, could not adjust socially to cultures which may have been British-derivatives but which were also distinctive.[28]

It would, however, be wrong to assume that those who returned were simply those who had failed to make good as Empire settlers. Returned migrants included those for whom emigration from Britain had only ever been intended as a stage in their life-cycles. This was most obvious among those in the services or in official administrative posts whose career trajectories took them overseas either for fixed periods or for lifetime careers, but whose expectations always were to return to and certainly to retire in Britain. Similarly, many in business and the professions might expect a temporary posting to work in an overseas branch or to fulfil an overseas contract in the Empire. The noticeably higher average age of immigrants compared with emigrants in the first half of the century also suggests that some of those who emigrated to the Dominions, and who settled, worked, and raised families, nevertheless returned 'home' to Britain in their twilight years. Some young adults, usually single, took advantage of assisted-passage schemes like the

[27] Henry F. Drystek, '"The Simplest and Cheapest Mode of Dealing with Them": Deportation from Canada before World War II', *Histoire Sociale—Social History*, XV (1982), pp. 407–41.

[28] For oral testimony see Betka Zamoyska, *The Ten Pound Fare: Experiences of British People Who Emigrated to Australia in the 1950s* (London, 1988) and Barry Broadfoot, *The Immigrant Years: From Europe to Canada, 1945–67* (Vancouver, 1986).

£10 fare to Australia in the 1950s to get abroad and see the world (or at least Australia) for a couple of years, before returning to Britain to settle down. Such temporary migrants may not have been popular with immigration authorities, but their progress to and from the Dominions strengthens the notion that the Empire was an integrated zone of easy labour mobility.[29]

There is also evidence that opportunities for labour (and for entrepreneurs) continued after 1900 to carry indigenous subjects of the overseas Empire across borders into other Imperial territories. Much of this migration formed the other half of a dual labour market invariably segregated by race: it needs to be set alongside the simultaneous recruiting, already discussed, of an administrative, professional, and managerial élite mainly from Britain.

For example, systems of indentured labour persisted into the early twentieth century.[30] The purpose was to provide white colonial entrepreneurs with the labour not locally accessible which was deemed essential for commercial viablity using labour-intensive methods of primary production. The system of recruiting young male Pacific islanders for work in the Queensland sugar plantations, which began in 1863, may have been prohibited by Australian legislation in 1901, but the last contracts only expired in 1906. By then a recorded 62,542 workers had been employed. Undoubtedly, these were 'free' workers exploiting an economic opportunity, but equally their recruitment was a consequence of obligations imposed upon them in their home islands by an alien cash economy, and by the diminution of other economic openings often as a result of Imperial impact.[31]

The Empire's ethnic geography was permanently affected by the larger movements out of India. A regulated system for recruiting indentured Indian labourers to work under white supervision on sugar, coffee, tea, cotton, and rubber plantations in the West Indies, British Guiana, Mauritius, Fiji, Malaya, and Natal had been developed since the 1830s. Less formally, many others migrated to Ceylon and Burma. Indentured labourers also worked in the coal mines and as domestic servants in Natal, and more were brought into East Africa from 1896 (mainly from the Punjab) to construct and maintain the Uganda Railway (in aggregate nearly 40,000 by 1922). They were attracted by the wages offered, but also

[29] Carrier and Jeffery, *External Migration*, esp. pp. 48–49, 54; Richmond, *Post-War Immigrants in Canada*, pp. 229–52; R. T. Appleyard, 'The Return Movement of United Kingdom Migrants from Australia', *Population Studies*, XV (1962), pp. 214–25, and 'Determinants of Return Migration—A Socio-Economic Study of United Kingdom Migrants Who Returned from Australia', *Economic Record*, XXXVIII (1962), pp. 352–68.

[30] David Northrup, *Indentured Labor in the Age of Imperialism, 1834–1922* (Cambridge, 1995).

[31] Adrian Graves, 'The Nature and Origins of Pacific Islands Labour Migration to Queensland, 1863–1906', in Shula Marks and Peter Richardson, eds., *International Labour Migration: Historical Perspectives* (London, 1984); O. W. Parnaby, *Britain and the Labor Trade in the Southwest Pacific* (Durham, NC, 1964).

prompted by increased taxation in India, by diminishing opportunities for agricultural and craft employment at home, and by population pressure. Objections, especially from Indians, to the circumstances of recruitment and to working conditions obliged the British Government of India to regulate, and eventually in 1917, to prohibit further indentured labour by Indians overseas and to exercise thereafter a closer supervision over other emigrant workers. Migrants were mainly single men, and most (at least of those who survived often arduous working and living conditions) were repatriated on completion of contracts.

However, others stayed, and contracted labour also came to include women and family groups, so that large Indian populations accumulated overseas. Other Indian workers and entrepreneurs also moved independently into some of these transplanted communities. For example, for a period Indian craftsmen and small businessmen could follow freely their compatriots into Natal. By 1912 there were about 120,000 Indians in Natal. Others crossed the Indian Ocean to seize the entrepreneurial opportunities presented by the opening under British colonial control of East African markets among both black Africans and white settlers. As a result, by 1931 there were 39,644 Indians in Kenya, of whom 25,590 had been born in India; plus 23,422 in Tanganyika, including 13,742 Indian-born; and 13,026 in Uganda, of whom 9,161 were immigrants from India. From 1909 until 1938 Malaya even provided free passages to attract workers to the rubber plantations, 729,261 between 1920 and 1939. By 1917 there were also 358,000 Indian immigrants in Ceylon, and large numbers continued to arrive. Indian migration to Burma similarly continued, though mainly as seasonal harvest workers. Among so many Indian emigrants there were entrepreneurial success stories, such as Deroda Shamji Haji in East Africa.[32] Some professional men, not least the lawyer M. K. Gandhi in Natal, also made their mark. But Indian immigrants mainly became established in subordinate capacities as traders, clerical workers, and artisans in an Imperial economy managed by Europeans.[33]

Africans too were prompted or provoked to migrate by the Imperial presence. Modern communications (by rail, road, and eventually by air) spread knowledge of opportunities and facilitated movement, but as elsewhere, localized population growth, land confiscations, and increased colonial taxation also drove many workers into the cash economy and into long-distance migration. Some West Africans, it is true, were alert without coercion to the chances created by trade with

[32] See also the case of Visram below, p. 534.

[33] Hugh Tinker, *A New System of Slavery: The Export of Indian Labour Overseas, 1830–1920* (London, 1974); Colin Clarke, Ceri Peach, and Steven Vertover, eds., *South Asians Overseas: Migration and Ethnicity* (Cambridge, 1990); Robert G. Gregory, *India and East Africa* (Oxford, 1971); B. C. Roberts, *Labour in the Tropical Territories of the Commonwealth* (London, 1964), pp. 354–55; Kuczynski, *Demographic Survey*, II, pp. 162, 261, 356.

the Europeans. One response in the Gold Coast was migration, land settlement, and the development of cocoa as an export crop. Others sought out employment in the gold-mines of the Gold Coast and the tin-fields of Nigeria, on public works, and later in West Africa's expanding towns.[34] Africans from Nyasaland and elsewhere similarly migrated to the labour opportunities offered by the development of copper mining in Northern Rhodesia especially in the 1920s. By 1931, still more, totalling 49,487 men from Nyasaland and 35,542 from Northern Rhodesia, were working in Southern Rhodesia, especially for white-run farms and mining companies.[35]

The largest and most persistent movement of migrant workers, however, was drawn into the Union of South Africa to work especially in the gold-mines of the Rand, where the dual labour market system was most starkly established. The status distinguishing white from black labour forces was set out formally by the Mines and Works Act of 1911 and confirmed in its later derivatives. In so far as South Africa's premier industry was simultaneously tapping into British labour supplies, it was attracting skilled employees, for example mining engineers, managers, and the professionally qualified. But to maintain their profits the companies also had to bring in the supplies of cheap, black, unskilled labour which they were unable to obtain sufficiently from within the Union (in spite of local legislative and fiscal pressures). The Chamber of Mines set up the Witwatersrand Native Labour Association in 1900 to bring in workers largely from Nyasaland, Northern Rhodesia, Tanganyika, and Mozambique, though horrendous death rates among workers from tropical territories caused a suspension of recruiting north of a latitude of 22° S. from 1913 to 1933. The Native Recruiting Corporation, created in 1912, tapped supplies in the High Commission Territories. Of the total of 305,000 black employees of the Chamber of Mines in 1946, 16.6 per cent came from the High Commission Territories and 10.6 per cent from the north (17.9 per cent by 1956). The short-term contracts available to black employees in the gold-mines offered some rewards, financially and socially, but since real earnings for black workers in 1969 were no higher and possibly lower than in 1911, these were in material terms marginal and always incidental.[36]

Further possibilities of labour mobility within the twentieth-century Empire were apparently revealed by the immigration into Britain of workers of non-

[34] A. G. Hopkins, *An Economic History of West Africa* (London, 1973), pp. 217–18, 222–25, 241–42; Michael Crowder, *West Africa Under Colonial Rule* (London, 1968), pp. 336–42.

[35] Kuczynski, *Demographic Survey*, II, pp. 447, 557; J. M. MacKenzie, 'Colonial Labour Policy in Rhodesia', *Rhodesia Journal of Economics*, VIII (1974), pp. 1–15.

[36] Francis Wilson, *Labour in the South African Gold Mines, 1911–1969* (Cambridge, 1972); Martin Legassick and Francine de Clercq, 'Capitalism and Migrant Labour in Southern Africa', in Marks and Richardson, eds., *International Labour Migration.*

European ethnic origin from, especially, the West Indies and the Indian subcontinent.[37] Black people and even black communities had long been a feature of British society, especially in seaports such as Liverpool.[38] But volumes increased rapidly after 1945 when the British deceleration of growth in population and therefore in the labour supply was coupled with an unusually high demand for labour, especially in housing construction, in transport, and in other public services. Especially by the 1950s, the core economy was being served by labour drawn from the New Commonwealth periphery. The census of 1961 estimated the 'coloured' population of Great Britain to have risen in a decade from 74,500 to 336,000, to include 171,800 West Indians, 81,400 Indians, 24,900 Pakistanis, and 19,800 from West Africa. Most of these were classified as unskilled or semi-skilled workers, but some from the start and others in due course demonstrated entrepreneurial skills, and a minority held academic and professional qualifications. The last especially resembled those Old Commonwealth immigrants, coming to Britain to exercise their talents in what they hoped would be a more rewarding environment. Also like other migrant streams, New Commonwealth immigrants were at first disproportionately young males, but the balance of gender became more equal, divided families were reunited, and new family groups were formed. Migrants became settlers. Their presence may seem final evidence that in the twentieth century the British Empire-Commonwealth operated as an integrated labour market, which shifted around the labour and skills required to service especially the producing and consuming needs of the Imperial metropolis.

It is important, however, not to exaggerate the coherence of the Empire at any period as a region of labour mobility. In the first place, it was never, of course, a self-contained and closed community. Rather, workers and employers in Britain specifically and in the Empire in general operated within a wider global labour market from which they could not be, nor would wish to be, entirely sealed off. For example, while it is true that the percentage of British emigrants who were retained within the formal boundaries of the Empire-Commonwealth grew, many continued to shift outside in pursuit of economic, social, or personal goals. Until very recently only modest numbers of permanent emigrants moved across the yawning chasm of the narrow English Channel to continental Europe, but large numbers moved easily across the wider Atlantic to the United States. Many Empire emigrants joined them, especially from Canada. Similarly, Indian labourers opted in large numbers for work outside the formal British Empire, including 100,000 in

[37] Colin Holmes, *John Bull's Island: Immigration and British Society, 1871–1971* (London, 1988); Ceri Peach and others, 'Immigration and Ethnicity', in A. H. Halsey, ed., *British Social Trends since 1900* (London, 1988), pp. 561–615.

[38] On blacks in Britain see Vol. II, pp. 468, 471, 474.

Thailand by 1934. Since 1967 many more from the British West Indies have gained entry to the United States.[39] Regional economic pulls frequently tugged more strongly than Imperial ties and certainly than Imperial sentiment.

At the same time, the Empire's boundaries were also penetrated by migrants from outside. Britain itself may have tightened its controls over 'alien' immigrants from 1905, initially to restrict the influx of impoverished East European Jews, but substantial European immigrant communities (Germans, Italians) were a feature of British society, and they were increased between 1946 and 1951 by refugees from war-torn Europe, ex-prisoners of war, and recruited labourers, totalling 350,000. Even after Eire left the Commonwealth in 1948, the Irish retained privileged entry into Britain, and indeed they were outstandingly the largest cohort of immigrants between 1945 and 1960 and brought the total number of Irish-born in England and Wales to almost 1 million.[40] Similarly, Lebanese from the Eastern Mediterranean became a significant presence in British West African colonies after 1900, established initially as petty traders but advancing often to form a substantial commercial middle class.[41] Few of the 407,984 Jewish immigrants into British-controlled Palestine between 1923 and 1947 arrived from British Empire sources.[42] Such was the volume of Chinese migration into British Malaya, alongside the Indians, that by 1945 Malays found themselves a minority. By 1961 half the population of Hong Kong had been born in mainland China.[43] Earlier in the century, the labour needs of the Rand had persuaded Milner to introduce Chinese workers as indentured labourers: 64,000 were brought in from 1904 to 1907. But by far the largest external reserve army of labour for South Africa was located in Portuguese Mozambique.[44]

Still more detrimental to Empire self-sufficiency were the active efforts made by Dominions governments to attract white settlers from outside Britain. Canadian authorities, despairing of obtaining adequate numbers from farming backgrounds from Britain to open up the prairies, set out from 1896 to supplement supplies from the United States and more innovatively from Eastern Europe: parts of the West became characteristically multicultural.[45] The precedent was followed by

[39] Smith, *Commonwealth Migration*, pp. 21, 165; Franklin D. Scott, ed., *World Migration in Modern Times* (Englewood Cliffs, NJ, 1968), pp. 121–22.

[40] Holmes, *John Bull's Island*; Peach and others, 'Immigration and Ethnicity'.

[41] R. Bayly Winder, 'The Lebanese in West Africa', *Comparative Studies in Society and History*, IV (1961–62), pp. 296–333; Crowder, *West Africa*, pp. 293–98.

[42] W. S. and E. S. Woytinsky, *World Population and Production: Trends and Outlook* (New York, 1953), pp. 104–05.

[43] Ibid., pp. 69–70; Borrie, *World Population*, pp. 118, 121.

[44] T. R. H. Davenport, *South Africa: A Modern History*, 3rd edn. (London, 1987), pp. 521–22; Wilson, *South African Gold Mines*, p. 70.

[45] Gerald Friesen, *The Canadian Prairies: A History* (Toronto, 1984), pp. 242–73.

Australia from 1947 and more modestly by New Zealand from 1950, when assisted passages were offered to migrants from Northern Europe (especially the Netherlands) and later from Southern Europe (Italy, Greece).[46] South Africa, especially under Nationalist governments from 1948, had no qualms about welcoming qualified immigrants from continental Europe.[47] The Dominions also responded to national labour needs as well as humanitarian appeals by accepting from continental Europe after the war large numbers of 'displaced persons', of whom 182,200 went to Australia and 123,500 to Canada. Such immigration flows made a marked impression on the complexion of these erstwhile British components of the Empire-Commonwealth. Until 1891, only one in ten of immigrants to Australia from Europe did not come from Britain, and until 1940 only one in five, but from 1947 the proportion rose to two out of every three.[48]

Yet more radical was the belated willingness of the 'white' Commonwealth to accept settlers from outside Europe. Although, as suggested, the Empire might be presented as a zone inviting free labour mobility, this ideal had never in practice been fully realized. Migrants of British stock had been privileged, but non-European peoples had traditionally experienced severe constraints on their freedom of entry.[49] For most of this century, discrimination by the white settler societies against all 'Asiatics' was not even relaxed for those of Empire origin. Objections to their admission were vigorously expressed, for example, by trade unions and organizations of ex-servicemen, and endorsed by aspirant politicians. Some employers short of labour favoured allowing in cheap supplies from Asia, but most shared prevailing racist assumptions and adapted their business to cope. Although the roots of prejudice lay deep in the nineteenth century, legislative controls became tighter later. Natal in 1897 was the first colony to adopt language tests (in any European language of the immigration authorities' choice) in order to bar entry on supposedly non-racial grounds to non-Europeans, and this technique was then generalized throughout South Africa and endorsed by the Union in 1913. It was employed by New Zealand from 1899, by several Australian colonies from 1898, and by the new Commonwealth of Australia from 1901, while Canada tightened its own deterrent legislation especially in 1910. Proclamations of

[46] Smith, *Commonwealth Migration*, esp. pp. 16–17 and 40; Brian Murphy, *The Other Australia* (Cambridge, 1993); Ruth Farmer, 'International Migration', in R. J. Warwick Neville and C. James O'Neill, eds., *The Population of New Zealand* (Auckland, 1979).

[47] L. Katzen, 'South African Immigration and Emigration in the Post-War Period', *International Migration*, I (1963), pp. 202–10.

[48] Borrie, *World Population*, pp. 96, 103–12; J. A. Jackson, *Migration* (London, 1986), p. 26.

[49] Robert A. Huttenback, *Racism and Empire: White Settlers and Colored Immigrants in the British Self-Governing Colonies, 1830–1910* (Ithaca, NY, 1976); Hugh Tinker, *Separate and Unequal: India and the Indians in the British Commonwealth, 1920–1950* (London, 1976); P. S. O'Connor, 'Keeping New Zealand White, 1908–1920', *New Zealand Journal of History*, II (1968), pp. 41–65.

Imperial unity during the First World War were mocked by the Imperial Conference's approval in 1918 (reaffirmed in 1921 and 1923) of the right of the self-governing Dominions to determine through immigration controls which ethnic groups were acceptable as settlers. While methods to deter and exclude prospective non-European immigrants were subsequently modified, opportunities for entry remained limited, and popular prejudice was slow to diminish. Indeed, the commitment to 'White' Australia, New Zealand, and Canada, and to 'white' supremacy in South Africa, was increased by anxieties about Japanese imperialism and the experience of the Second World War. Although certain categories of non-Europeans were subsequently allowed in, such as modest numbers of refugees, ethnic discrimination was only formally abolished by Canada in 1962, by Australia in 1973, by New Zealand in 1987, and by South Africa not at all before the fall of apartheid. Recent inflows of migrants to the former white Dominions from Asia and to a lesser extent from Africa and the West Indies came too late to refurbish the image of the Empire-Commonwealth as a zone of perfect labour mobility.

The Imperial government had ostensibly adhered to a concept of racial equality throughout the Empire, although it had been a colluding observer of the measures taken by the self-governing Dominions, and sometimes a more active adviser. But the Imperial government could afford to register discomfort with Dominions regulations because initially only the white settler societies overseas and not Britain were likely to attract mass migration from Asia. As noted earlier, the right of free entry of all Empire subjects into Britain was a founding Imperial principle, endorsed again as recently as 1948 in the British Nationality Act. But this liberality lasted only until large numbers began to avail themselves of that right. When immigration from the New Commonwealth increased rapidly from the late 1940s, the Imperial government's open door policy began to swing shut. New Commonwealth immigrants even by the mid-1970s still constituted only 3.3 per cent of the total population, but their clustering in particular districts of industrial cities and often in particular trades made them more conspicuous. Certainly the volume of immigration by young adults increased locally the demands on housing and social services, but public and political attention was focused on minority ethnic groups largely when they were perceived by the British-born as competitors in the labour market, and when political capital was made out of racial conflicts. The Commonwealth Immigrants Act of 1962 was introduced to reduce the inflow of those without British passports. But the Act of 1968 even restricted the rights of those (especially from East Africa) who were holders of British passports but who were not born in Britain or whose parents or grandparents were not born there. Discriminatory restrictions on the free flow of Commonwealth citizens into the former Imperial motherland marked a signal step away from Imperial integrity. It is a measure of the end of Empire that the Immigration Act of 1971 virtually removed the distinction between Commonwealth and foreign immigrants. Entry to Britain has since been eased only for members of the European Community.[50]

A further mark of the end of Empire was exemplified by the changed relationship between Britain and the white Commonwealth in the allocation of labour between them. The model of free labour mobility at the beginning of the century, upon which much Imperial thinking was initially based, assumed a complementarity between the economic interests of the core and of the periphery. As mentioned earlier in this chapter, even in 1900 this was a summation of Imperial economic relations which strained to incorporate all their complexity. Moreover, as the century developed critical observers began to query the supposed harmony of interests in the flows of migration from Britain to the Dominions.

For one thing, demographic competition replaced complementarity. As the rate of natural increase declined in Britain, commentators by the 1930s and 1940s began to predict an absolute fall in population size. Certainly the population was ageing: the number of young people aged 0–19 in England and Wales fell from 13,792,000, or 42.4 per cent of the total, in 1901 to 12,396,000, a mere 28.9 per cent, by 1951. The comparable percentages for Scotland were 43.6 per cent and 31.7 per cent.[51] The white settler societies might in general be anxious to recruit immigrants from Britain, but it was less apparent that Britain could afford to let them go. Those most susceptible to the pull of migration were young adults in whom Britain had invested national resources in their upbringing, welfare, and especially education—yet their active working careers might be spent abroad.

In addition, Commonwealth countries may have continued for a while to favour immigrants from the British Isles (including Eire), but it was immigrants with skills or capital whom they were increasingly anxious to recruit. Moreover, although their national economies and especially their exports still relied heavily upon primary production, agricultural activities were less and less labour-intensive: the tractor, the aerial crop dresser, mechanical shearing, and other techniques had reduced the labour needs of agri-businesses. Rather, it was migrants whose qualities were best fitted to modern manufacturing and service industries who were most in demand. These shifting requirements determined who would be offered assisted passages and who among the unassisted would be admitted on occupational grounds. As a result, in comparison with the occupational structures of the country from which they came and of those to which they were going, post-war migrants were disproportionately proprietors, white-collar workers (professionals, managers, and clerical staff) and skilled manual workers (engineers, electricians, and building craftsmen). Table 7.6 provides a representative comparison.

[50] Kathleen Paul, 'The Politics of Citizenship in Post-War Britain', *Contemporary Record*, VI (1992), pp. 452–73; Smith, *Commonwealth Migration*, pp. 96–120.

[51] A. H. Halsey, ed., *Trends in British Society since 1900* (London, 1972), p. 33.

TABLE 7.6. *Occupational groups, male and female*

British Emigrants, 1946–1949 (%)			*Census of Great Britain, 1951* (%)		
Proprietors, etc.		16.2	Employers and Proprietors		5.0
White-Collar Workers		44.1	White-Collar Workers		30.9
Professions	17.2		Higher Professions	1.9	
Semi-Professions	10.4		Lower Professions	4.7	
			Managers and Administration	5.5	
			Foremen and Inspectors	2.6	
			Salesmen and Shop Assistants	5.7	
Clerical Workers		16.5	Clerical Workers	10.4	
Manual Workers		39.8	Manual Workers		64.2
Skilled	26.5		Skilled	24.9	
Semi-Skilled	7.5		Semi-Skilled	27.2	
Unskilled	5.8		Unskilled	12.0	

Sources: Julius Isaac, *British Post-War Migration* (Cambridge, 1954), p. 53; A. H. Halsey, ed., *Trends in British Society Since 1900* (London, 1972), p. 113.

Especially since the Second World War, therefore, the modern economies within the Commonwealth have been competing on increasingly equal terms with Britain—and indeed with the United States—for that most valued commodity, skilled labour. Instead of an Imperial periphery centred around a British core, there had evolved a single international economy. And the key players, the British among many, sought out, selectively, the migrants they needed. Valued though Britain remained as a supplier to the rest of the Commonwealth, it was no longer a sufficient source, as the recruiting of talent from elsewhere in Europe and then from the rest of the world revealed. Those wanted were not masses to fill empty spaces and man labour-intensive businesses, but skilled employees, trained professionals, and those rich in capital.

Select Bibliography

R. T. APPLEYARD, *British Emigration to Australia* (London, 1964).

PAT BARR, *The Dust in the Balance: British Women in India, 1905–1945* (London, 1989).

BRIAN L. BLAKELEY, 'The Society for the Oversea Settlement of British Women and the Problems of Empire Settlement, 1917–1936', *Albion*, XX (1988), pp. 421–44.

N. H. CARRIER and J. R. JEFFERY, *External Migration: A Study of the Available Statistics, 1815–1950* (London, 1953).

STEPHEN CONSTANTINE, ed., *Emigrants and Empire: British Settlement in the Dominions Between the Wars* (Manchester, 1990).

KENT FEDOROWICH, *Unfit for Heroes: Reconstruction and Soldier Settlement in the Empire Between the Wars* (Manchester, 1995).

COLIN HOLMES, *John Bull's Island: Immigration and British Society, 1871–1971* (London, 1988).

JULIUS ISAAC, *British Post-War Migration* (Cambridge, 1954).

SHULA MARKS and PETER RICHARDSON, eds., *International Labour Migration: Historical Perspectives* (London, 1984).

UNA MONK, *New Horizons: A Hundred Years of Women's Migration* (London, 1963).

G. F. PLANT, *Oversea Settlement* (London, 1951).

COLIN G. POOLEY and IAN D. WHYTE, eds., *Migrants, Emigrants and Immigrants: A Social History of Migration* (London, 1991).

ANTHONY H. RICHMOND, *Post-War Immigrants in Canada* (Toronto, 1967).

MICHAEL ROE, *Australia, Britain and Migration, 1915–1940* (Cambridge, 1995).

GEOFFREY SHERINGTON, *Australia's Immigrants*, 2nd edn. (Sydney, 1990).

T. E. SMITH, *Commonwealth Migration* (London, 1981).

HUGH TINKER, *A New System of Slavery: The Export of Indian Labour Overseas, 1830–1920* (London, 1974).

GILLIAN WAGNER, *Children of the Empire* (London, 1982).

FRANCIS WILSON, *Labour in the South African Gold Mines, 1911–1969* (Cambridge, 1972).

BETKA ZAMOYSKA, *The Ten Pound Fare: Experiences of British People Who Emigrated to Australia in the 1950s* (London, 1988).

8

Critics of Empire in Britain

NICHOLAS OWEN

'Few, if any, pronounced anti-imperialists exist,' wrote the British Proconsul Lord Cromer in 1913, 'but a wide divergence of opinion prevails as to the method of giving effect to an imperial policy.'[1] Such a comment might easily be dismissed as proconsular short-sightedness. It reveals, however, a problem familiar to all historians of the British Empire: the ambiguity of the terms 'imperialist' and 'anti-imperialist'. Both are porous terms: disputed territory on which both combatants and conflict may vary with circumstances of geography and history. Did anti-imperialism merely mean resistance to the annexation and direct rule of colonies in the non-European world, or did it also entail opposition to the strengthening of links with the semi-autonomous White Dominions or to the 'informal empire' of commerce and trading privileges enjoyed by the British in Argentina, China, and elsewhere? Which manifestations of British power and influence were unacceptable? The coercive policing? The 'advice' offered by British representatives to indigenous rulers? The proselytizing of missionaries and teachers? The operations of traders and the investments of venture capitalists? The 'protection' afforded by the Royal Navy? Even during the period 1900–64, the constituent elements of 'imperialism' altered greatly, forcing compensating shifts in what composed 'anti-imperialism'. Like all movements of protest, 'anti-imperialism' was forced to be as multifaceted and mutable as its opponent.

1900–1918

The critique of Empire fashioned at the turn of the century in response to the South African (Boer) War and the programme of 'constructive imperialism' championed by Joseph Chamberlain owed much to its nineteenth-century inheritance. The war reinforced the beliefs of critics that the old imperialism of emigration and free trade was giving way to a more aggressive alternative. Radicals had long regarded the chartered company as inefficient and irresponsible, motivated

[1] Quoted in Bernard Porter, *The Lion's Share: A Short History of British Imperialism, 1850–1900* (London, 1975), p. 194.

less by the desire to expand free trade, still less by concern for the welfare of colonial inhabitants, than by the search for profit. But the war demonstrated that imperialists had acquired a new ability to stir up an emotional jingoism in the popular press and even to manipulate foreign policy in their own private interests. Overseas, the new imperialism might antagonize foreign rivals prepared to exploit the defensive problems of an over-extended Empire. Worse still, authoritarian viruses contracted in the Empire might infect politics at home. An expanded Imperial army, perhaps even conscription, would not merely be financially imprudent. It would encourage a lack of respect for hard-won political liberties, especially if, as Alfred Milner and George Curzon desired, it were to be accompanied by modifications of the parliamentary system designed to prevent internal divisions from hampering the single-minded pursuit of national advantage.

Such condemnations, however, were no substitute for a positive response to the prospect of isolation in an unfriendly and predatory world that so tortured Edwardian élites. The dated Cobdenite formula of *laissez-faire* and non-intervention were plainly inadequate solutions in a world, in Lord Rosebery's phrase, that had been 'marching and revolving'.[2] In response, the political economist and writer J. A. Hobson combined the old Radical critique of Empire with an analysis of the contemporary twist it had taken. Hobson argued that maldistribution of wealth at home meant that domestic markets were characterized by under-consumption. Since excess savings could not be profitably invested in these artificially saturated markets at home, they were forced to seek less dependable outlets overseas. This new imperialism was manipulated by parasitic interests: arms manufacturers and shippers, aristocrats anxious to find jobs for less talented sons in military or colonial civil services or as planters, ranchers, or missionaries. Co-ordinating their activities were international financiers whose interests were only indirectly responsive to British interests. But while only a narrow coterie benefited from Empire, its costs were borne by the nation as a whole. Empire, for Hobson, was not good political economy. Indirect methods of control were always liable to collapse into formal rule under the weight of crises, which Britain's enemies would be sure to provoke. Indeed, even had other countries acquired the burden of developing the colonies, Britain, as a free trading nation, would still have benefited indirectly from the opening up of new markets and might thereby have as great a colonial trade as it did at lower cost.

The new imperialism fared still worse when tested against Hobson's ethical principles. At home, it fostered the survival of unaccountable and illiberal forces: the feudal anachronism of unearned wealth, the irrational snobberies of London and the stockbroker belt, and the indoctrination of British public schoolboys with

[2] Quoted in Martin Pugh, *The Making of Modern British Politics, 1967–1939* (Oxford, 1982), p. 93.

military values and 'primitive lusts of struggle, domination and acquisitiveness'.[3] It hampered the advance of progress and democratic reform, as imperialists bought influence in Westminster and Fleet Street, tugged the strings of secret diplomacy, and wrapped their private interests in the flag of patriotic defence. However, despite his distrust of the 'civilizing mission', Hobson held that the solution to the colonial problem did not lie simply in the abandonment of Empire and a reversion to 'Little Englandism'. Applying his cherished criteria of rationality, efficiency, and the common good to colonial management, he concluded that capitalist development of colonial territories was permissible on the grounds that resources did not belong to the colonized any more than they did to the colonizer, but to those who could make best use of them. Since such 'sane and legitimate imperialism' could not be left to the unaccountable and selfish play of private interests, it must be controlled by the state and supervised by international organizations.

Hobson's theory of Empire was general in its application and concerned largely with the implications of the new imperialism for domestic political economy. The critique offered by E. D. Morel and the Congo Reform Association, by contrast, was concerned with the manifestation of imperialism in a specific arena: that of western and central Africa, and focused less on the metropole than on the results of Empire for colonial societies. Morel held that concessions or monopolies undermined indigenous traditions and cultures, and prevailed, especially in the Congo of King Leopold, only by savage repression. At first Morel placed his faith in free-traders, especially the Liverpool companies, to regulate the internal politics of Africa, on the grounds that they alone possessed the necessary local experience and willingness to restore the free-trading and property rights of the native population. Later, worried that the traders were more interested in breaking the hold of colonial monopoly than in nuturing native self-development, Morel accepted the necessity for the state to play a larger role in licensing companies and making certain that they respected peasant proprietorship.

The criticisms offered by Hobson and Morel thus fell short of an outright condemnation of imperialism. Rather, they censured the unprincipled turn that the Empire had taken. It should resist further acquisitions, but it was not obliged to give up those areas already annexed. Efficiency demanded that colonial estates be developed by Europeans. The task, however, should not be left to private companies and fortune-hunters but to an enlightened and disinterested authority emanating from the 'higher races', which would act in the interests both of the native population and of the wider world community. In this sense Hobson and Morel prepared the ground for theories of Imperial trusteeship.

[3] J. A. Hobson, *Imperialism: A Study* (1902; London, 1948), pp. 233–34.

For the critics of Empire to be politically effective, they had not merely to develop an ideological critique of imperialism, but also to harness their cause to the party system. This could only be done at the cost of bending and reshaping anti-imperialism in the interests of party unity and electoral appeal. Party reactions to the South African War demonstrated that anti-imperialism might only be hitched to the Liberal waggon provided it did not interfere with the transport of more important cargo. The 'Mafficking' crowds of May 1900, the attacks on 'pro-Boer' homes or political meetings, and the election result that followed made clear the danger that a politically unsophisticated electorate might easily be swayed by crude popular imperialism. To oppose the war outright was to court the charges of being unpatriotic and of having encouraged enemies overseas, and of having betrayed the British settlers in the Transvaal gold-fields. Official Liberal opposition thus confined itself to attacks on Kitchener's 'methods of barbarism' and charges of hypocrisy, military incompetence, and waste. These charges were directed mainly at speculators and financiers on the Rand rather than the government or the British settlers. Though such a campaign found no shortage of targets, it was hard to maintain against those who pointed out that its logical conclusion was not anti-imperialism, but the redoubling of efforts through army reorganization and the breeding of a healthier stock of recruits to the Imperial cause.

Through the influence of the Fabian Society, these tensions found their way into the nascent Labour Party. Some Fabians saw imperialism as a necessity in an era of fiercely competing nation-states, to be pursued in the name of 'national efficiency' and turned, where possible, into progressive channels. For others, attachment to the Imperial cause was purely opportunistic: the product of the Fabian technique of permeating official opinion by tactical persuasion rather than frontal attack. The rising imperialist tide could not be turned back, and by lashing their domestic reforms to the raft of Liberal Imperialism, it was hoped, they too might be carried along with it. To others still, Empire was attractive because it offered a testing-ground in which Fabian ideas of scientific planning might be tried out. However, other Fabians found this medicine too strong, and favoured recasting the old Gladstonian demands for liberal values to inform Britain's international activities. The South African War drove this Imperial wedge firmly into the Society, splitting those who saw it as regrettable but unavoidable from the minority who saw it as morally unacceptable.

This minority position was also adopted by many of those associated with the Independent Labour Party (ILP). Drawing on a variety of influences, which extended from Marxism to Methodism, ILP thought on Imperial questions was eclectic, but perhaps best distinguished as internationalist and pacifist, or at least anti-militarist, in its leanings. Its Marxist heritage offered only a partial and cramped account of imperialism. In part this was because neither Marx nor Engels had placed much faith in the contribution that the colonized might make to the socialist revolution. Indeed, Marx himself had famously expressed the belief that whatever England's crimes in India, the destruction of its 'oriental despotism' had made it 'the unconscious tool of history'.[4] The party voiced many of the concerns developed by Hobson and Morel, especially with regard to economic exploitation. Its influence before 1918, however, was limited by the exclusion of Labour from political power at Westminster and by the diversion of its leaders' energies into domestic and European affairs. Its humanitarian leanings led it, as they did Morel, to favour not the abolition of the colonial system, but the extension of native rights. This ambivalent ideological inheritance is perhaps the most important reason why the early Labour Party exhibited an equivocal stance on questions of Empire.

Distaste for certain features of the Edwardian Empire should not, therefore, be equated with anti-imperialism. Unease over the handling of the South African War merely indicated that where disproportionate military demands from one part of the Imperial system forced the abandonment of orthodox finance, and where such costs were incurred unnecessarily as the result of senseless errors and humiliating defeats, imperialists would expose a limited front to attacks from their critics. Nor can the failure of the 'constructive imperialism' proposed by Joseph Chamberlain in 1903 be taken to indicate the unpopularity of imperialism. Rather, it illustrated the lack of widespread support for a particular, insular, and exclusive conception of Empire.[5] Provided imperialism could recast itself in a form which avoided these unpopular implications, there seemed little reason why it should not brush off the attacks of its critics.

1918–1940

The strains of debt imposed by the First World War on Britain's national economy and the post-war intensification of nationalist unrest in the Empire prompted a far-reaching reappraisal of British commitments after 1918. It led to the scaling down of Imperial ambitions in the Middle East, political concessions in India and Ireland, and the stern pruning of defence spending. Central to the new strategy was the premise that Imperial expenditure must not be permitted to rise high enough to frustrate the expectations of social reform created by an enlarged electorate and a more powerful labour movement. Whitehall policy-makers were determined to avoid prolonged military actions and to place greater emphasis on the notion of Imperial trusteeship. Old Milnerite imperialist justifications

[4] Karl Marx and Friedrich Engels, *On Colonialism* (Moscow, 1959 edn.), p. 41.

[5] See Vol. III, chap. by E. H. H. Green.

for Empire phrased in terms of racial patriotism increasingly gave way to more subtle and persuasive claims. Fresh justification for colonial administration was provided by the theory of the Dual Mandate, which claimed that British trading interests and the moral and material progress of West African peoples were not conflicting but mutually supporting, and therefore for the good of the civilized world. Its champion, Frederick Lugard, also insisted that these interests could be safely managed for the benefit of all within a framework of Indirect Rule which, beneath an overarching structure of orderly administration, left existing native authorities subordinate but largely intact. Lionel Curtis and others associated with the Round Table movement argued that Britain had a duty to share the fruits of its successful constitutional evolution (in particular, the rule of law and free political institutions) across the Empire, thereby transforming it by gradual stages into a multiracial Commonwealth.

As an exercise in retrenchment and redeployment rather than the prelude to Imperial retreat, the reinvention of imperialism as trusteeship had more to do with financial stringency at home and crises of authority on the periphery than to any sudden triumph of liberal opinion. Indeed, it now became harder for the anti-imperialist case to gain acceptance. As military cuts ruled out further annexations, imperialists could no longer be pilloried as reckless expansionists. In establishing liberal goals for the Commonwealth, imperialists lessened their dependence upon dubious claims of racial superiority and forced their critics into the uncomfortable position of arguing that Britain lacked the capacity to promote good government. In placing the principles of racial equality, native paramountcy, and economic and social development before the eventual granting of self-government firmly in the trust of the Imperial power, pro-Empire advocates strengthened their defences against the charge that Empire meant only exploitation of colonial labour for the enrichment of its white races. Lugardian Indirect Rule promised to protect the customary rights of native producers against the intrusion of the planter economy almost exactly as Morel had demanded. Hobson's charges, too, were blunted. Since the methods of imperialism under the guise of trusteeship were designed to be unprovocative, Empire would require few resources from British taxpayers, and fewer still as the trust was discharged. Trusteeship imperialism, far from corrupting the political freedoms of the metropole as radicals had feared, offered an attractive vision of Empire as a kind of training academy in liberal democracy and of the spread of little Westminsters across the globe. The gap between 'imperium' and 'libertas' that had provided the point of leverage for pre-war anti-imperialists was now welded tightly shut.

What could critics do but welcome these developments? The ideal of trusteeship 'served to convert the anti-imperialists of one generation into the imperialists of the next'.[6] But trusteeship imperialism *could* be attacked by pointing out how far practice fell short of principle. This was the burden of a disparate group of disaffected officials, many of whom had left colonial service frustrated with the limitations on their work and prepared to break the unwritten rule of public silence. The most prominent were Norman Leys, William McGregor Ross, F. H. Melland, Sir John Maynard, and Sydney Olivier. With activists and publicists, such as C. R. Buxton, whose unhappiness with the unprincipled path followed by the Liberal Party on the outbreak of war had driven them leftwards, and a sprinkling of progressive academics such as W. M. Macmillan, they congregated in the Labour Party's Advisory Committee on Imperial Questions. This body had been established by Sidney Webb, himself an ex-servant of the Colonial Office, to provide trade-union MPs with briefings. Its Secretary was the former colonial civil servant Leonard Woolf, whose Bloomsbury publishing firm disseminated many of the writings of the group.

These critics offered two main arguments against trusteeship imperialism. The first was that in east, central, and southern Africa, the regions in which many of them had worked, the principle of trusteeship had been traded away in a corrupt alliance between conservative politicians at home anxious for Empire on the cheap and local settlers and capitalists keen to establish white dominion. Leys denied that the interests of Africans and settlers in Kenya meshed easily, as the Dual Mandate suggested. Africans had been deprived of their lands and reduced to the status of right-less tenants and migrant labourers. Leys demanded that the Colonial Office insist on the paramountcy of native welfare. These criticisms achieved some degree of success in foiling plans for a closer union under white supremacy in East Africa, although the need to appease the India Office, and Indian nationalists, for the refusal of their demands for a common electoral roll and the opening of the white highlands to Indian colonists seems to have carried as much weight as the arguments of liberal critics.

Secondly, critics argued that Indirect Rule had served to retard economic and social development of the colonies. The principles of 'protecting' and 'preserving' native custom had been upheld by Governors, but little had been done about poverty, ignorance, and disease. Indirect Rule had proved incapable of adapting to new tasks, and it clearly failed to promote the diversification of colonial economies needed to cope with the collapse of world commodity prices. The solution to these problems, it was argued, was economic self-development. Woolf suggested that the colonial administrations should not promote metropolitan economic interests but become development trustees for the native population. The profits of state-

[6] R. E. Robinson, 'The Moral Disarmament of African Empire, 1919–1947', *Journal of Imperial and Commonwealth History* (hereafter *JICH*) VII (1979), p. 88.

led development might be ploughed back into education and training. By the mid-1930s, armed with new economic theories, critics argued for even more energetic development. In *Warning From the West Indies* in 1936, Macmillan argued powerfully that negative trusteeship had failed in the Caribbean. It had provided legal freedoms and rights but no economic infrastructure or welfare services. The results were low wages and labour unrest, which could only spill over into political dissent since the colonial regime lacked a popular base.[7] Land should be allocated fairly, but for reasons of efficiency should be farmed by state-sponsored collectives growing crops for subsistence as much as for export. There should be investment in industrial development and public works to reduce unemployment. Education should be improved, and agricultural research carried out to raise farm productivity. Health and social services should be provided to improve the condition of the workforce.

On two further questions, the critics were more divided. The first was that of political development. It was generally held that colonial civil services should be opened up to indigenous candidates, who, once trained in the skills of development, would take their place in colonial administration. But the question of how, in the absence of democracy, such administrators should be made accountable was more difficult. The critics were as one in condemning those colonial Governors who regarded the growth of political consciousness as seditious. Leys and Macmillan argued that political participation must be widened to encompass not merely feudal chiefs, but also rising educated classes. Where Morel and Lugard had only wanted technical training for Africans to enable them to be better peasant producers, Woolf and Buxton argued for the expansion of higher education. Nevertheless, healthy political development required a period of apprenticeship, during which constitutional advances could not simply be exported ready-packed to the colonies according to a pre-planned time-scale. They must grow naturally out of economic and social advances and the evolution of classes, interests, and parties that would follow. To transfer power prematurely would be to leave the colonized at the mercy of indigenous élites and foreign exploiters.

There were also divisions over the question of whether the colonial trust should be internationalized. One of the significant contributions to the Labour Party Advisory Committee on Imperial Questions imported by Liberal refugees such as H. N. Brailsford and Woolf was a commitment to ideas of international organization. Brailsford and Hobson had favoured the placing of colonies under international supervision, an ambition which was partly realized in the establishment of the Permanent Mandates Commission of the League of Nations. To Hobson, internationalization would establish a wider and more responsive trusteeship,

[7] W. M. Macmillan, *Warning From the West Indies: A Tract for Africa and the Empire* (London, 1936).

insulated from the selfish claims of national advantage. But to others, such as Macmillan and Olivier, it placed too much faith in the benevolence of other nations and the power of international organizations. These reservations gained force through the 1920s, when the League failed to fulfil the internationalists' expectations and European colonial systems proved resilient to internal and external criticism. Woolf feared that internationalization of the trust would simply collapse into a form of collective colonialism, replacing national empires with an internationalized one.[8] For those critics anxious to see colonial governments introduce plans for state-led development, it was hard to accept the principles of the 'open door' and minimal interference under which League Mandates operated.

Overlapping with the experts of the Labour Party Advisory Committee, but distinctive in approach, were missionary and church groups. For many, though not all, missionaries the egalitarian basis of the faith had always been in conflict with the assertions of white supremacy at the heart of imperialism. In multiracial societies missions had long favoured native welfare more than European commercial interests. Through John Harris, from 1909 the Parliamentary Secretary to the Anti-Slavery and Aborigines Protection Society, MPs had been presented with petitions against forced labour and colonial atrocities. But since missionaries had to operate primarily under colonial rule, their criticism was often heavily qualified. The scope of missionary opportunity and the possibility of rectifying abuses was defined by the extent of British influence. Mission privileges and operational effectiveness depended upon the infrastructure and tolerance offered by local administrators. While this did not deter quiet lobbying, it was often a sufficient check to public radicalism and had in the past fractured the unity of humanitarian lobbies.

The effectiveness of British missions also depended on coming to terms with the emergence of nationalist politics, without which church schools would be boycotted and ground lost to numerically and financially stronger American rivals. With the deterioration of race relations in settler-dominated parts of Africa after 1920, several missionaries and also J. H. Oldham, Secretary of the International Missionary Council, held that the stability of multiracial societies, and hence their openness to evangelism, depended on ending economic exploitation and racial discrimination. Without reform, Christianity would simply be rejected as a white man's religion. Church leaders in Kenya, with Oldham at their head, lobbied Parliament against forced labour, much as Christian humanitarians had a century earlier against slavery, and helped to slow the drift of power to white settlers.

Of course, this did not make such missionaries opponents of white settlement or of Imperial government. Indirect Rule fitted well with scepticism about the

[8] Leonard Woolf, *Imperialism and Civilization* (London, 1928).

pliancy of colonial societies and the guilt many felt about the intolerant proselytizing of their predecessors. Missionaries hoped to graft Christian ideals on to what they felt they had identified as the positive features of African tribal life: the sense of mutual dependence and what they believed to be a childlike spirituality. Mission groups were keen to see greater educational and spiritual content infused into the trust, in the hope of building self-governing churches. But they were more conservatively minded about the statist plans of developers such as Macmillan and Woolf. State administrators, in the missionary view, should serve primarily to shield the colonized against the exploitation of outsiders, to alleviate grievances, and to provide a structure of law and order in which the work of mission schools and hospitals could be carried out. They should not undertake active development work themselves. Education should not aim to create westernized élites, for in dragging the colonized out of their traditional social milieu, it might breed discontented 'agitators'. Whether the unexpectedly vehement voice of nationalist protest that emerged from many of the mission-educated was an indication of success or failure was a question that deeply divided missionaries. In Kenya, some were prepared to sponsor constitutional nationalists, provided their actions were compatible with Christian ethics, while others, deploring the politicization of the African church, sided with Imperial authority in crushing the more radical Kikuyu activists. In India, Christian theologians were no less divided over whether Gandhi and Congress constituted a threat to the fulfilment of the Christian purposes they saw entrusted to the British Raj or, as the missionary C. F. Andrews believed, a means of arresting the moral atrophy of Empire.

The most extreme challenge to the ideals of trusteeship came at the end of the 1930s from another group. Where liberals had argued that the trust was being realized in the wrong way, radical critics dismissed the whole notion of trusteeship. Imperial and native interests were inherently and incorrigibly in conflict. The consensus sought by advocates of the Dual Mandate or paternalist development was therefore unattainable without surrender of the trust and the transfer of power from British hands on the basis of self-determination. Radical critics were therefore uninterested in the idea of colonial reform, an orientation which set them firmly apart from other critics. For Leonard Barnes, a former Colonial Office civil servant and journalist, the problems of the dependent territories could not be solved by outsiders. There might still be a role for the British after independence, but only as 'simple educationalist, co-operator and missionary in the widest sense'.[9] Barnes favoured a transitional stage of rapid socialist modernization in Africa, with capital provided either by a board responsible to the British Parliament, or by an international body supervising its investments in the interests of

[9] Leonard Barnes, *The Duty of Empire* (London, 1935), p. 288.

the colony rather than those of its creditors. All land should be nationalized and redistributed, with cheap loans provided for African farmers, and the government in control of Western mineral interests. But in a claim which distanced him from the advocates of development in the Labour Party, Barnes also insisted on the granting of political rights. The franchise should be extended to all literates, and laws that prevented political activity lifted, with the intention of transferring power to African hands as soon as possible.

Other radical critics, especially those convinced by Lenin's claim that imperialism, far from being an unfortunate quirk of capitalism, was an inevitable feature of it, believed that Imperial rule could not be turned in progressive directions, even as Barnes suggested, because it was inherently exploitative. For Rajani Palme Dutt, the British Empire was no more than 'conquered territory added to the estates of the British bourgeoisie for the purpose of large-scale exploitation'.[10] Colonial development was dictated by the demands of British capital and could not flourish short of the achievement of independence. The colonized would therefore have to effect their own liberation. This required reconsideration of the tactics of metropolitan sympathizers and the assumption, long held even on the left, that only political change at the metropole could win the battle against Empire.

As before the war, campaigners found that, once translated into terms that parties of the left could accept, something of anti-imperialism was lost. In the first place, it was likely to conflict with more pressing economic interests. There was trade union support for regulation of colonial labour, rooted in fear of competition from unorganized workers. The Dominions offered possibilities for emigration and employment to recession-hit industrial workforces. Among workers in those industries which were primarily export-oriented and therefore drew sustenance from the free-trade Empire, a category which included iron and steel, shipbuilding, cotton, coal, and defence supplies, there was limited support for tariffs to protect home industries in the transition to socialism. But few trade unionists were converted to the cause of 'Empire Free Trade', partly because of its potential effect on prices and partly because it was so clearly a poor substitute for much-needed reforms in the domestic economy. Although in 1932 the Trades Union Congress formally supported 'Empire Free Trade', it abandoned it swiftly once it became obvious that, hedged about by the divergent needs and economic nationalisms of the Dominions, it did not offer any real escape from the industrial slumps and job losses.

Despite the efforts of 'Empire Socialists', most workers were indifferent or apathetic to questions of Empire, which seemed to have little bearing on questions

[10] John Callaghan, 'The Heart of Darkness: Rajani Palme Dutt and the British Empire—A Profile', *Contemporary Record*, V (1991), pp. 257–75.

of domestic reform. Any Indian policy could be defended to a working-class audience, the Labour Secretary of State for India, William Wedgewood Benn (later Lord Stansgate), cheerfully admitted in 1930. They were 'a mixture of ignorance... and idealism, always with racial prejudice ready to be excited, so that the ground is indeed clear for any argument'.[11] Many Labour MPs regarded the Empire either as insignificant to Labour's domestic programme or little more than a corrupt conspiracy to extract wealth from the colonies to prop up the capitalist system at home and blur the otherwise clear lines of class struggle. To the annoyance of those who wished to alleviate the slums of Empire, MPs were reluctant, especially during periods of high unemployment, to see money spent overseas which could be better spent, for example, in the East End.

Even in power, Labour's performance was disappointing. The restraints of minority government and its leaders' desire to be seen as 'responsible' dragged it into support for bipartisan policies. At the head of an inexperienced government, but one with a social programme to implement, Ramsay MacDonald had no intention of jeopardizing Labour's chances of securing a majority at the next election by risky policies in the Empire. Thus the hopes of liberal critics that Labour would grant equal rights and political opportunities in East Africa and the Rhodesias were thwarted by the fear of losing the loyalties of white colonists throughout Africa and of alienating party groupings at Westminster with which Labour felt obliged to co-operate.

Labour's traditions of parliamentarism and gradualism affected not merely the party's unwillingness to strike out on Imperial issues independently from the Liberals at Westminster. They also coloured perceptions of colonial nationalism. From 1909 to 1920 a succession of Labour visitors to India had set down their thoughts on the nature of healthy political development. For Keir Hardie, the devolution of political power to village councils would ensure that the urban lawyers and doctors who made up the Congress movement were brought face-to-face with the problems of the rural poor. Sidney and Beatrice Webb hoped to see co-operation between the Congress and sympathetic British officials in local schemes of social improvement, through which Indians might acquire the skills to run a modern, interventionist state. For his part, Ramsay MacDonald regarded Congress as only at the first stage of its development, comparing its proposals to the narrow, class-bound demands of the mid-Victorian Liberal Party. Indian nationalism should follow the same lines of political evolution as the movement for labour representation had at home. Congress should carve out a broader-based political support among Indian workers and peasants, reduce its dependence on

[11] Benn to Irwin, 20 June 1930, Irwin Papers, OIOC, British Library, MSS Eur C. 152/6.

middle-class activists, and campaign not merely for political independence but for social reform to raise the condition of India's underprivileged.

The failure of the Gandhian Congress to evolve along such lines distressed many senior Labour figures. Many, especially in the trade unions, doubted whether Congress was truly interested in socialism. Its demands for independence seemed too closely entwined with the vested interests of the Indian middle classes and too bound up with impractical Gandhian ideas to act as an instrument for genuine industrial and economic change. Congress chose to adopt strategies of non-cooperation and civil disobedience which were strongly at odds with Labour's own ideas of responsible political action. To those, such as Harold Laski, who regarded the Labour Party primarily as a moral crusade of protest and dissent, such tactics were legitimate, even inevitable. But to those for whom the Labour Party existed primarily to achieve practical reforms, it was vital that Congress adopt similarly responsible methods. It should work through Parliament rather than through direct action, and through constructive action by local councils and trade unions rather than agitation. The Congress high command seemed to Labour leaders in Britain to demonstrate all the worst faults of the irresponsible politician: unwilling to give ground in negotiations, but unreliable once settlements had been reached; reluctant to shoulder the burden of administration, but happy to wield unaccountable power from the sidelines; prepared to raise popular emotions through demagoguery and agitation, but capable only of floundering blindly in the wake of those they had inspired when public order collapsed as a result. It was all quite alien to the rigid party discipline and solidarity the British labour movement expected of itself. In government, Labour ministers were ready to deal firmly with civil disobedience and, as late as 1943, worked on plans to undermine the Congress leadership and remould Indian nationalism into a more acceptable form. Despite Congress having been founded some fifteen years before their own party, Labour leaders saw it as a junior partner in need of education in the art of good government. They seldom questioned whether tactics designed to advance the interests of uniquely class-conscious workers in an industrial society, whose ruling classes generally eschewed repression, were appropriate for the divided mix of classes and interests over which Congress presided.

British trade-union leaders offered a similarly paternalistic education to their colonial counterparts. Unions in the colonies seemed too prone to spontaneous and undisciplined outbreaks of labour unrest, their leadership dominated by lawyers or even employers rather than workers, and their work characterized by political objectives that ranged too far beyond wage-bargaining. British labour leaders, therefore, acted to sponsor less militantly nationalistic alternatives, such as the All-India Trade Union Congress. In the late 1940s they assisted the

Colonial Office to ensure that British models of union organization were employed in the regulation of colonial industrial relations.

Given its commitment to international struggle, the Communist Party of Great Britain proved less vulnerable than Labour to the appeal of a specifically British mission in the colonial world. Its primary aims included the propagation of Lenin's notion of imperialism as characteristic of monopoly capitalism, and the establishment of a network of political organization in the colonies. Yet it proved hard for many to comprehend the numerous ambiguities of Lenin's theory, let alone its applicability to British situations. Leninist interpretations only gained credibility when they could be reconciled with earlier liberal and humanitarian traditions of resistance to imperialism. Since so little of the colonized world was industrialized and so much had yet to produce the class conditions ripe for effective party work, the Communists concentrated their extra-metropolitan efforts on India, where Philip Spratt, Ben Bradley, and Lester Hutchinson built up Communist support in the unions of Bombay and Madras. Their imprisonment on conspiracy charges in 1933 made clear how little tolerance the Raj was prepared to offer Communist anti-imperialism. It also provided the party in Britain with the opportunity to embarrass the Labour leaders, who had proved unwilling to interfere with the trial when in office. Indeed, in Britain the Communist Party could boast an impressive range of expertise on colonial questions, and it was dedicated to a greater degree than other labour organizations to publicizing among students and workers its view of colonial conditions. But its anti-imperialism was handicapped by the shifting priorities of the Comintern, which increasingly sublimated the fight for social revolution in the colonies to the overriding needs of Stalinist foreign policy.

Frustrated by the dilution of their ideas by metropolitan political parties, anti-imperialist groups often preferred to keep their distance. The success of Morel's Congo Reform Association had earlier illustrated the possibility that single-issue campaigns, with effective and industrious leadership, could influence metropolitan opinion while remaining independent of party ties. After 1918, the bulk of anti-colonial activity was carried out by many such groups, mainly London-based, which often focused on the problems and interests of single territories, their influence rising and falling with the salience of issues and crises. But campaigning outside the party system presented its own difficulties. Anti-colonial campaigns depended for prominence on a narrow stratum of public figures who, however sincere, were frequently over-committed or uninfluential. Often racked by chronic financial crises, they relied, in large part, on a floating body of industrious but volatile students and political activists. They were also regularly harassed by the police when, and sometimes even before, their activities spread outside the metropole. Even the task of assembling accurate information was a perpetual struggle to disentangle contradictory reports, which often emerged twisted and partisan from the colonies, whether this was the work of nationalists anxious to exaggerate the scale of brutalities and of their political support, or of unsympathetic colonial officials ready to censor messages and ban fact-finding tours on the grounds that they might excite dissent. There were frequently divisions within the organization over questions of whether to adopt the tactics of quiet lobbying in Whitehall or to sacrifice private influence for the gains of public protest. There was also the question of how to establish links with anti-colonial nationalist movements. In the absence of nationalist agitation, was it the role of metropolitan anti-colonial campaigners to sponsor its emergence? Where nationalist movements existed, should London-based sympathizers direct the independence struggle, assist as partners, or merely act as their metropolitan arm? In plural societies, how should sympathizers choose between rival nationalist groups? Too close an identification with the opponents of British rule overseas, as 'pro-Boers' had found, risked accusations that anti-imperialists stirred up nationalist agitation rather than responding constructively to it. While such problems made all the more remarkable the degree of commitment such groups showed to their respective causes, it was not surprising that many came to consist of little more than one man and his duplicator.

Building organizations dedicated to a broad range of colonial issues was also problematic because 'imperialism' was simply too distant and perhaps too abstract a phenomenon to campaign against. One exception was the International African Service Bureau, which emerged from the diagnosis by C. L. R. James, George Padmore, and others that colonial liberation was the key to world revolution, but that this could not be achieved through a Communist Party dominated by Soviet concerns or by the paternalist Labour Party. Asserting the unity of the African diaspora, the Bureau succeeded in bringing together a wide range of groups under the banner of Pan-Africanism. Smaller London-based groups, such as the West African Students' Union, offered a meeting-place where anti-colonial nationalists could lobby British activists. In this way, the metropole served as a 'junction-box' in which visiting nationalists could share ideas with each other and with British radicals. The culmination of this activity, the 5th Pan-African Congress at Manchester in October 1945, was distinctive in the number, range, and eminence of its delegates, as well as in the radicalism and confidence of its demands. Yet the Congress marked an end rather than a beginning: as Pan-Africanism reverted from the diaspora to the continent itself, divergences of outlook and strategy were plainer to see, and its significance lay less in its effect on metropolitan radicals than on the numerous delegates who went on to be significant figures in independence movements.

Attempts to build an international front against colonialism were repeatedly unsuccessful. For many British anti-colonialists, from the Fabian Arthur Creech Jones to the Marxist John Strachey, there was a powerful national responsibility to resolve colonial problems, which could not be left to critics of other nations, no matter how well-intentioned. It was this belief, combined with distrust on the left for the intentions of American capital, that accounts in large part for the almost total absence of transatlantic co-operation. Other experiments were defeated by factionalism on the left. Despite some popular campaigning against the trials of the Indian Meerut trade unionists and some fruitful attempts to bring colonial émigrés into contact with the British left, the League Against Imperialism founded in 1927 was dogged from the start by sectarian squabbles between its Comintern sponsors and Labour and ILP delegates. Effectively reduced after 1932 to its British section and the individual efforts of its Secretary, Reginald Bridgeman, the League never proved able to concert a united front against imperialism. Later attempts to breathe life into international organization got little further. The Congress of Peoples Against Imperialism aimed to link up western European advocates of a 'third force' with anti-colonial nationalist movements from Asia and Africa, but it was stultified at its headquarters by shortage of funds, political restrictions on its activities in the colonies, disunity in the French left, Trotskyite infiltration in its London branch, and disagreements over Soviet imperialism and the legitimacy of armed struggle.

1940–1964

During the Second World War, far-reaching adjustments in colonial policy gave effect to many of the proposals by Woolf and Macmillan, especially on questions of development and welfare. The recruitment of experts to assist the Colonial Office in its plans and the entry of the Labour Party into the Coalition government in May 1940 gave the critics grouped around the Party Advisory Committee and the newly established Fabian Colonial Bureau under Creech Jones and Rita Hinden an unprecedented opportunity to influence policy. With Labour's election victory in 1945 and the appointment of Creech Jones as Colonial Secretary the following year, still closer co-operation between critics and officialdom was achieved. As critics had urged, the British state took control of colonial development and attempted to force a programme of rapid modernization on the economies of the dependent Empire, in part through investment in agricultural production.

Yet the price of influence was compromise. During the war, the Colonial Office was moved less by the critics' convictions than by the need to mobilize colonial resources, to check the consequent unrest, and to refine Britain's liberal intentions sufficiently to deter her American allies from imposing their proposals for international trusteeship. Singularly little success was achieved in alerting officials to the narrowness and inadequacy of the representative foundations on which schemes of development and welfare were to be built, and the consequent need to promote socio-economic advance and political progress in tandem rather than sequentially. When Labour took office, colonial reform was cut and shaped to fit new economic and strategic priorities. To patch its war-damaged economy sufficiently to sustain promised welfare improvements at home, Labour needed to reclaim and develop its old markets and suppliers without incurring costly overseas expenditure and thereby increasing its dependence upon dollars. Ministers thus felt obliged to gear development policy to metropolitan needs. The demands of the cold war also ended Attlee's attempt to overhaul Britain's Imperial commitments in the Middle East with a view to swift economies. Although India, Pakistan, Burma, and Ceylon achieved independence, it was clear that this was not intended as a prelude to general decolonization. In Africa, in line with their earlier feelings about Indian nationalism, Labour ministers hoped to use local government as a means of diverting nationalists from agitation towards constructive 'nation-building' tasks, with political independence a distant prospect.

For the Fabian Colonial Bureau, such delays were unavoidable if power were to be transferred in such a way as to promote healthy progress after independence. Radical critics, however, dismissed the idea that colonies must 'mature' under British guidance before they were fitted for self-government. Among the most prominent critics was the ex-ILP General Secretary Fenner Brockway. For Brockway, the colonial question could be reduced to a single principle: the right of colonized nations to self-determination. He believed that the world was witnessing a colonial revolution, as nationalists in practically all European colonies united behind this great simplifying demand. Unless it were met, even the extended forms of trusteeship favoured by the Fabians would prove incapable of promoting real development. Firm dates should, therefore, be set for transfers of power in Asia and Africa. Should Britain and its colonies seize this opportunity swiftly, they might become a 'Third Force' in world affairs, with greater moral authority than either American capitalism or Soviet communism. Brockway found allies both among the Labour left and among the increasing number of academics, activists, and journalists working on African politics and history. Basil Davidson argued that development could not be imposed by British officials, however well-intentioned, but only by fostering an 'African socialism'. Particularly troubled by the political ambitions of white settlers in Africa, such critics made resistance to the creation of the Central African Federation and support for the exiled Bechuanaland chief Seretse Khama the focus of their demands for racial equality.

At first, the activities of these individuals were channelled through a number of liberal groups, including Michael Scott's Africa Bureau, the National Peace Council, the Union of Democratic Control, and a succession of protest groups dedicated to single issues. But the advantages of consolidation soon became clear. While anti-colonial energies were dispersed among rival groups, too much work was duplicated and the focus of the anti-colonial message was lost in obscure discussions of specific cases and situations. Some of these deficiencies were rectified in 1954 when the activities of smaller groups were merged with the remnants of the London Branch of the Congress of Peoples Against Imperialism in the Movement for Colonial Freedom (MCF). The movement differed from the Fabian Colonial Bureau both in its guiding principles and its methods. The main difference was simply one of pace. The Movement held that Fabian 'nation-building' could only begin once the colonial relationship itself had been broken through the grant of full and equal political rights. Thus, it worked less on solving the particular socio-economic problems of individual colonies than on putting forward a wide-ranging critique of colonialism, in the belief that anti-colonial struggles were both interdependent and irreducibly political. There was even a Hobsonian echo in the claim of its Treasurer, Anthony Wedgwood Benn, that ending imperialism was a prerequisite to extending democracy at home. These intentions led to new methods and organization. At home, the MCF aimed to challenge ministers rather than lobby them privately, and to extend its influence beyond the small, well-informed metropolitan audience reached by the Fabians. Questions in the Commons were used as a starting-point for wider public campaigns. The Movement also made contacts more with the nationalists themselves than, as had the Fabians, with their Liberal sponsors among colonial administrators. The purpose of such links was less to educate nationalists than to provide a platform and audience for listening to what they wished to say. The possibility that this would, as the Fabians feared, lead to accusations of publicizing extremism was welcomed as a means of exposing official intolerance.

In the Attlee era, relations between the critics and the Labour Party leadership were sometimes frosty. This was partly due to cold war considerations. In Malaya, Labour's official spokesmen confined themselves to vigorous protests over police brutality rather than support for the Communist-dominated nationalist movement. This suspension of the constitution of British Guiana in 1953 split the Party, largely on the issue of whether to support the popularly elected but anti-democratic Peoples Progressive Party government. Nationalists who employed direct action were also given short shrift. Supporting them attracted accusations that Labour pandered to the intransigent, just as echoing the censure emanating from the United Nations or Moscow ran the risk of seeming to run the country down in public. It was for these reasons, among others, that before the invasion of

Suez in November 1956 Hugh Gaitskell was cautious about condemning Anthony Eden's Egyptian policies, and in 1958 refused to be drawn into supporting the Greek Cypriots' demand for *enosis* (union with Greece). In Central Africa, the Labour Party leaders, while insistent that the white settlers should sweeten the medicine of federation, still believed it good for dissenting Africans to swallow. In 1956 Labour remained committed to equality between races in plural societies rather than majoritarian democracy, a stance which was bound to favour white minorities.

By the late 1950s, however, the Movement for Colonial Freedom had come to dominate Labour's anti-colonial activity. This was partly a result of effective organization. Although the MCF was never a mass movement (most of its 3 million members were simply affiliated through unions or local parties), it proved successful in supplanting the Fabian Colonial Bureau as the main forum of colonial policy-making within the party apparatus and Parliament. These victories owed much to the fact that those who sought to control the rate of political change were now thoroughly on the defensive. The challenge of nationalism had grown much more rapidly than expected. The use of emergency powers in response to crises gave fresh credibility to the critics' claims that colonialism depended on repression. The advance of anti-imperialism in British politics had long depended on the intermittent jolts provided by crises and scandals. Sudden and shaming incidents were much better than abstract arguments at alerting British voters to the harsh face of colonialism. As a display of obsolete and ineffective imperialism, the Suez crisis could hardly be bettered. In the past the impact of lesser crises had usually been short-lived and easily deflected by promises of reform. Further crises in rapid succession, such as the Nyasaland Emergency of March 1959, the Hola Camp atrocities in July 1959, and the Sharpeville massacre of March 1960, all combined with persistent repression in Cyprus to turn a sequence of irregular shocks into unremitting pressure. This was of crucial importance in enabling anti-colonialists to sustain the momentum of their campaign. It gave them an opportunity to tap the sympathies of hitherto undecided audiences such as church groups and university students. It enabled them to turn the tables on those opponents who had argued that the colonial framework was a guarantee of public order. They could also point to a widening international consensus that the repression of colonial dissent had become illegitimate and as such damaging to Britain's reputation at the United Nations and elsewhere. The same thinking also persuaded a large cohort of Labour MPs that only independence at an early date would avert a series of futile colonial wars. Now even those traditionally cautious about the unpopularity of attacking the Empire and those bored by colonial affairs saw in anti-colonialism a political weapon to divide the Conservatives, win the moral high ground, and rally the otherwise divided Labour Party.

For practically the first time, therefore, anti-colonialists found renewed moral strength, effective political organization, and a reliable party to support their attack. Yet even as they held the 'moving target of Empire' in their sights, it had begun to slow down and crumble before their eyes. The 'moral disarmament' of Empire interlocked powerfully with a new sense of its economic and strategic redundancy. Britain's changing diplomatic needs dictated greater reliance upon American support and the preservation of Commonwealth unity. Her economic weakness demanded investment and modernization at home, shifting the balance of exports away from colonial economies with painfully slow growth rates towards the advanced economies of western Europe, and a reduction in the burden of overseas expenditure, especially on defence. Taken together, these made a good general case for replacing an Empire based on conventional colonial rule with a system of informal influence.[12] Its metropolitan dimension lay in the fears of policy-makers that, as nationalists drove up the cost of colonial policing, repression threatened to become costly for taxpayers and consumers at home. Unconsulted and unaware that their preferences entailed Imperial contraction, these were the critics of Empire who ultimately mattered most. At the moment of their greatest triumph, therefore, the critics of Empire were aware that they were riding a wave that their actions had not created.

Metropolitan Anti-Imperialism in Retrospect

Despite the efforts of some of its supporters to build an international anti-colonial front in the belief that national struggles against imperialism were interdependent, the character of British anti-imperialism was profoundly shaped by metropolitan political institutions and a traditional and insular political culture. Many of its supporters and most of its activists were members of an élite: middle-class intellectuals, journalists, party workers, academics, and retired officials, all of whom in a sense were the residue of the pre-1914 war Liberal punditry. They had inherited many of the tenets of Radical thought on Empire from their nineteenth-century forebears, and even as late as the 1950s, leading critics such as Wedgwood Benn (later Tony Benn) talked proudly of their legacy from Cobden and Bright. If 'nation' and 'Empire' were to be prised apart, anti-imperialists found, like the anti-slavery campaigners before them, that it was politic to appeal to feelings that the excesses of imperialism were un-British. Even in their anti-imperialism, the British might set an example to the rest for the world.

[12] For these themes, see esp. Wm. Roger Louis and Ronald Robinson, 'The Imperialism of Decolonization', *JICH*, XXII, 3 (Sept. 1994), pp. 462–511.

Anti-imperialists also dwelt more on Britain's moral responsibility for the welfare of the colonized than on the economic redundancy of Empire for the metropole. The motive force of British anti-imperialism was emotional commitment rather than ideology, and its unity was based on ethical ideals rather than shared economic interests. There were a number of reasons for this. The dominant theories of economic imperialism were Marxist in origin and, as such, suffered in Britain from the absence of a mass Marxist party to spread them widely. Moral arguments, by contrast, had strong roots in the religious and humanitarian traditions of the British labour movement. Economic appeals also threatened, as moral exhortation did not, to fragment support on the left. Those who wished to argue that the working class did not benefit from the Empire were countered by those, such as George Orwell, who believed that without it Britain would be reduced to 'a cold and unimportant little island where we should all have to work very hard and live mainly on herrings and potatoes'.[13] More practically, economic exploitation was also generally less visible than the atrocities upon which the moral critique rested and, as such, formed a weaker basis for public campaigns.

The campaigning of anti-imperialists was uphill work: it was hard to fill meeting halls except when severe colonial crises broke through the crust of public indifference; it was hard to get reliable information from public officials; it was hard to raise funds. Their political significance thus depended largely on their ability to capture support within parties. But this inevitably entailed compromise with other conflicting priorities, in particular domestically oriented ideologies, electoral imperatives, and economic interests. Compared to their French counterparts, which often found it easier to penetrate metropolitan party politics because of the direct representation of colonies in the Parisian National Assembly and the existence of a weak multi-party system, British pressure groups lobbied a legislature well insulated against disturbance by colonial issues and dominated by a smaller number of strong, disciplined parties. This stifled anti-imperialist debate by making the force of its campaigns dependent upon their implications for domestic calculations and hard to broaden into a wide-ranging critique of Empire.

In particular, the character of the British labour movement was influential. Though naturally sympathetic to the victims of Imperial power, it tended none the less to view anti-colonial nationalism through the prism of its own experiences. To those who had won acceptance for the Labour Party through coming to terms with capitalism in Parliament and demonstrating their fitness to govern to local electorates, there could be no short cuts to political maturity. This more frequently

[13] Quoted in Paul M. Kennedy, *Strategy and Diplomacy, 1870–1945: Eight Studies* (London, 1983), pp. 139–40.

meant a preference for movements which had proved their representativeness and progressive intentions, and shown themselves prepared to negotiate with the British in the interest of gradual reform, than for those impatient for power, defiant of foreign rule, and prepared to resort to civil disobedience. The inner workings of the 'dominant parties' that often led anti-imperialist struggles were more complex than this typology allowed, and could only be poorly understood by those anxious to squash them into the moulds of Western, and usually British, experience. Effective links with colonial nationalist groups were often retarded by the desire of nationalists for independence of action and metropolitan anti-colonialists for respectable clients.

Whatever the tactical sense of these strategies, they were ultimately restrictive. The insularity of metropolitan anti-imperialism meant that its attacks ran parallel, unsynchronized and unintegrated with those of the international critics of colonialism at the United Nations and elsewhere. Since anti-imperialism depended upon the ability of critics to demonstrate that Empire threatened interests at home, it was hard to rouse enthusiasm except at times when Imperial crises interlocked with domestic ones. Success also seemed to require finding a way to attack the Empire obliquely, for neither the interests of British settlers nor the integrity of British administrators could be attacked directly. Most of Morel's achievements, after all, had been due to confining his criticisms to the redress of abuses which were primarily those not of Britain but of King Leopold's Congo. Concentration on the moral case meant that anti-imperialism could be turned more readily into the channels of Imperial reform than into those of decolonization. If the trust was being betrayed, it scarcely made sense to throw it aside for less worthy rivals.

The task was made harder still by the ability of imperialism to renew itself in fresh guises. The rapidity of these shifts often left anti-imperialists employing categories that were outdated. It was also one reason why the ability of critics to gain advantage in public debate was so much stronger when imperialists forgot themselves and reverted to their old, bad ways, as at Amritsar, Suez, or Hola. It was only when imperialism ceased to be able to reinvent itself—or perhaps, as some critics bitterly observed, could only reinvent itself at the cost of transferring power—that it presented a target that anti-imperialists could seriously damage.

Not even the most radical critics foresaw the suddenness and completeness with which British influence in its former colonies collapsed in the wake of the transfers of power. Indeed, most thought that the relationship would be revitalized once it was purged of colonialism. This alone should make us wary of attributing decolonization to metropolitan anti-imperialism. By publicizing colonial excesses, the critics had successfully pointed out the discrepancies between the public face of British colonialism and the seamy and brutal side of its methods of rule. In this way, they had promoted a kind of 'accountability by proxy',[14] forcing, as far as constitutional conventions permitted, those whose actions were only indirectly answerable, if at all, to those they governed, to defend themselves in public. These were tactics which were much more effective at handling individual abuses, such as infringements of civil liberties, than they were at undermining the Imperial system.

For their Conservative advocates, transfers of power were a means of propping up British influence in the world, a recognition, not of the wrongness of colonial rule, as critics of the left had argued, but merely of its futility. Decolonization, when it came, and inasmuch as it was a product of metropolitan recalculations, owed more to the unwillingness of politicians to devote the resources necessary to repress or reward the colonized in the interests of prolonging direct rule than to the claims of its ethical unacceptability on which the critics of Empire had largely based their case. Their engagement with imperialism at the metropole, like its counterpart at the colonial periphery, had thus scarcely ever resembled a pitched battle. It was rather a series of limited skirmishes in which critics of Empire, frequently under-equipped and internally divided about their purpose, harried an enemy of bewildering mutability and resourcefulness, and capable of ceding ground unexpectedly and regrouping elsewhere.

[14] Stephen Howe, *Anticolonialism in British Politics: The Left and the End of Empire, 1918–1964* (Oxford, 1993), p. 327.

Select Bibliography

John Callaghan, 'The Communists and the Colonies: Anti-imperialism Between the Wars', in Nina Fishman and others, eds., *Opening the Books: Essays on the Social and Cultural History of British Communism* (London, 1995).

John Darwin, *The End of the British Empire: The Historical Debate* (Oxford, 1991).

D. K. Fieldhouse, 'The Labour Governments and the Empire-Commonwealth', in Ritchie Ovendale, ed., *The Foreign Policy of the British Labour Governments, 1945–1951* (Leicester, 1984), pp. 83–120.

John E. Flint, 'Macmillan as a Critic of Empire: The Impact of an Historian on Colonial Policy', in Hugh Macmillan and Shula Marks, eds., *Africa and Empire: W. M. Macmillan, Historian and Social Critic* (London, 1989), pp. 212–31.

David Goldsworthy, *Colonial Issues in British Politics, 1945–1961* (Oxford, 1971).

—— 'Britain and the International Critics of British Colonialism, 1951–56', *Journal of Commonwealth and Comparative Politics*, XXIX (1991), pp. 1–24.

Partha S. Gupta, *Imperialism and the British Labour Movement* (London, 1975).

Penelope Hetherington, *British Paternalism and Africa, 1920–1940* (London, 1978).

J. A. Hobson, *Imperialism: A Study* (1902; London, 1948).

STEPHEN HOWE, *Anticolonialism in British Politics: The Left and the End of Empire, 1918–1964* (Oxford, 1993).

MILES KAHLER, *Decolonization in Britain and France: The Domestic Consequences of International Relations* (Princeton, 1984).

WM. ROGER LOUIS, *Imperialism at Bay, 1941–1945: The United States and the Decolonization of the British Empire* (Oxford, 1977).

—— and JEAN STENGERS, eds., *E. D. Morel's History of the Congo Reform Movement* (Oxford, 1968).

BERNARD PORTER, *Critics of Empire: British Racial Attitudes to Colonialism in Africa, 1895–1914* (London, 1968).

—— 'Fabians, Imperialists and the International Order', in Ben Pimlott, ed., *Fabian Essays in Socialist Thought* (London, 1984).

RICHARD PRICE, *An Imperial War and the British Working Class* (London, 1972).

PAUL B. RICH, *Race and Empire in British Politics* (Cambridge, 1986).

BRIAN STANLEY, *The Bible and the Flag: Protestant Missions and Imperialism in the Nineteenth and Twentieth Centuries* (Leicester, 1990).

A. P. THORNTON, *The Imperial Idea and Its Enemies: A Study in British Power* (London, 1959).

9

The Popular Culture of Empire in Britain

JOHN M. MACKENZIE

From the perspective of the late twentieth century, it is hard to recognize the pervasiveness and power of the British Empire in the thought and imagination of many sections of the British public. Yet there have been echoes in the Falklands War in 1982; there has been the continuing fascination of the entertainment media with many aspects of the Imperial experience; and most recently there has been the prominence given to the handover of Hong Kong to China in 1997. Serious and scholarly interest in Imperial matters has also led to the development of programmes to collect oral, visual, and written material about colonial experiences while a Museum of the British Empire and Commonwealth has been established in Bristol. In still wider perspective, British officials such as those at the Colonial or India Offices were not the only people to be connected to the enterprise of Empire. Many more British people had a knowledge of the Empire because of personal, professional, religious, and cultural experiences.

Thousands of British families had friends or relatives who had emigrated to the Dominions, or who had served or were serving in other parts of the dependent Empire as civil servants, teachers, missionaries, engineers, or in such technical trades as driving locomotives, and of course as soldiers in the British army. Imperial perceptions were not confined to Cheltenham and other genteel places where retired Imperial servants congregated. All social classes were influenced in different ways. The churches of the country and their Sunday schools were a constant source of information about Empire, as missionaries 'on furlough' preached about their work, showed magic-lantern slides, and urged their hearers to contribute generously to medical, educational, and evangelical work throughout the Empire. The missionary commitment to medicine as well as educational work helped to popularize the notion that Western medicine and Western-trained doctors were heroically tackling the most feared tropical diseases and the scourge of maternal and infant mortality. Medicine was thus seen to parallel the perceived moral and spiritual force of the work of Christian missions.

In the various institutions of higher education, Empire was also a pervasive theme—through the teaching of specifically Imperial history, through the university-based training of new cohorts of civil servants in such disciplines as law and languages, and through the teaching of technical skills intimately linked to the Imperial experience. As well as medicine and hygiene, these included forestry, agriculture, surveying, engineering, and anthropology.

The Empire increasingly came to the British public in new and often dramatic ways: through the cinema newsreel and through the press, with its coverage of colonial crises and constitutional developments. British people were, for example, well aware of the 1919 Amritsar shooting in northern India, which generated heated domestic debate. As constitutional reform and eventually decolonization became imminent, the British people were aware of Asian and African politicians visiting London for Round Table Conferences. Among the earliest of such visitors was Mahatma Gandhi, who in 1931 took care to stay in London's East End and to visit the cotton mills as well as to talk in universities and schools. By so many and varied means did the Empire become an integral aspect of British culture and imagination.

There were also specific ways in which groups and individuals sought to popularize Empire more consciously. These included great public exhibitions, consumer propaganda, popular literature, particularly adventure stories written for boys and girls, and 'imperial cinema', both in the shape of newsreels and educational productions, and through romantic and adventure stories. These expressions of popular culture and experience form the main theme of this chapter.

The idea for the Wembley Exhibition is the first important manifestation. It had been mooted by the British Empire League as early as 1902. In 1913 it was the former Canadian High Commissioner in London, Donald Smith, Lord Strathcona, the celebrated veteran of the Hudson's Bay Company and the Canadian Pacific Railway, who now revived the notion of an officially sanctioned exhibition of Empire. The scheme was delayed by the First World War, but in 1919 it was resurrected. The Prince of Wales, the future Edward VIII, became president of the general committee appointed to plan the exhibition, and the government of David Lloyd George gave the project official recognition. It gradually developed a new significance: to restore national and Imperial confidence after the war and to proclaim the economic importance of Empire to the British. This was emphasized by inviting only territories of the British Empire to participate.[1]

By 1921 financial guarantees totalling £2.2 million, roughly half from the British government, were promised. A 216-acre site was purchased at Wembley in North London, and the Prince of Wales, in a speech to the Imperial Conference of

[1] Many themes discussed in this chapter are explored in greater depth in John M. MacKenzie, *Propaganda and Empire: The Manipulation of British Public Opinion, 1880–1960* (Manchester, 1984). John E. Findling and Kimberley D. Pelle, eds., *Historical Dictionary of World's Fairs and Expositions, 1851–1988* (Westport, Conn., 1990), pp. 235–38.

Dominions Prime Ministers, announced that a 'great national sports ground' would be constructed on the exhibition site and opened with the Football Association Cup Final in 1923. Thus, Britain's national sport with the widest working-class following would draw the public's attention to Wembley and its exhibition. Eventually inaugurated on 23 April 1924 (St George's Day) by King George V the exhibition attracted 17,403,267 visitors in 1924 and 9,699,231 visitors during its second and final year, 1925.

The official guide described Wembley's primary purpose as:

> To find, in the development and utilization of the raw materials of the Empire, new sources of Imperial wealth. To foster inter-Imperial trade and open fresh world markets for Dominion and home products. To make the different races of the British Empire better known to each other, and to demonstrate to the people of Britain the almost illimitable possibilities of the Dominions, Colonies, and Dependencies overseas.[2]

The guide emphasized that the entire Empire would be accessible in miniature on a single site. The buildings of the exhibition, constructed largely in the new technique of ferro-concrete on a framework of steel, included Palaces of Engineering, Industries, and Arts, a mock-up of a coal-mine, and pavilions for almost every territory of the Empire, some of them (such as those for India, Ceylon, Burma, the West African colonies, and South Africa) designed to represent examples of local architecture. In addition, there was a forty-acre amusement park. As in its nineteenth-century predecessors, there were also on view indigenous peoples, or 'races in residence' as they were described, most of them demonstrating local crafts and manufacturing techniques. These included 175 Chinese active in the Hong Kong exhibit, as well as seventy representatives of the Yoruba, Fante, Hausa, and Mende peoples in the West African pavilions.

The exhibition also included environmental, technical, and medical displays, in which Imperial rule could be portrayed as having made significant advances.[3] The inter-war years were to be a period when experts were employed throughout the Empire in such fields as agriculture, forestry, entomology, and zoology, as well as the human sciences of anthropology, dietetics, and health. Such expertise was to have a considerable impact upon Britain. The successes of tropical medicine, symbolized by Ronald Ross's discovery of the role of mosquitoes in the transmission of malaria and the founding of schools of tropical medicine in London and Liverpool at the end of the nineteenth century, helped to enhance the confidence

[2] Publicity leaflet, British Empire Exhibition (Wembley, 1924); *British Empire Exhibition, 1924, Official Guide* (London, 1924).

[3] For alternative views, see David Arnold, ed., *Imperial Medicine and Indigenous Societies* (Manchester, 1988); Andrew Cunningham and Bridie Andrew, eds., *Western Medicine as Contested Knowledge* (Manchester, 1997).

and dominant practices of Western medicine. The Indian forestry service influenced the founding of the first university forestry departments in Britain.

Few members of the general public and even of the élite would have been aware of the manner in which the Empire was influencing the Mother Country. Indeed, in general terms it is difficult to judge the extent of the public impact of Wembley. It was heavily satirized in its own day, by Noel Coward among others, and many implied that for the most it was no more than a vast entertainment. Yet it featured prominently in popular songs of the period. Large quantities of ephemera and of souvenirs were produced and sold.[4] Newspapers produced special issues, and children's annuals and comics, including Frank Richards's celebrated 'Billy Bunter' stories in the *Magnet*, portrayed it as one of the wonders of the age.[5] Radio made much of the exhibition and considerable film footage was produced for the newsreels. The fact that West African students complained about the portrayal of the alleged racial characteristics of Africans indicates that they certainly thought that it had some effect on public opinion.[6] The sheer scale of its exhibits may well have blunted its impact for individual visitors, but few can have left it without some sense of the continuing power and significance of the British Empire, of its economic advantages, and of the opportunities for emigration.

Throughout the inter-war years, the authorities in Britain and elsewhere continued to be convinced of the value of Imperial exhibitions as a source of propaganda. The French exhibited their empire in Paris in 1925 and 1931 while in the British Empire there were major exhibitions in Dunedin, New Zealand, in 1925–26, and Johannesburg in 1936–37. In Britain, the last in the long series of Empire exhibitions took place in Glasgow in 1938.

Just as Wembley serves as the first example of putting the Empire on display during the inter-war years, the Glasgow Exhibition represents the problems of promoting the Empire at the end of this period. The idea for a Glasgow Exhibition was conceived in 1931 at the height of the depression in a conscious effort to promote employment and advertise the industries of Scotland. In some ways it acted as the climax of many years of intensive propaganda from the Imperial Economic Committee, the Empire Marketing Board, and the Imperial Preference movement.

The organizers of the exhibition had five main objectives: to illustrate the progress of the British Empire; to reveal its resources and potentialities; to stimulate Scottish trade and industry and direct attention to Scotland's historical and scenic attractions; to foster Empire trade and closer friendship among the

[4] Many of these can be seen in the collections of the Grange Museum of Local History, London.

[5] John M. MacKenzie, ed., *Imperialism and Popular Culture* (Manchester, 1986), p. 8; the *Magnet*, 11 Oct. 1924.

[6] For the correspondence on West African complaints see C[olonial] O[ffice] 555/7, 1924.

peoples of the Commonwealth of Nations; and to emphasize the peaceful aspirations of the peoples of the British Empire.[7] The Scottish dimension was emphasized through major exhibits on heavy engineering, transport, and other staple industries of Scotland as well as upon Scottish 'heritage' and its potential for tourism. Many of the features of Wembley were reproduced, although by the 1930s the architectural style was now a modern Art Deco. The exhibition demonstrated how the Scots had developed their own special relationship with Empire. Such ideas were embraced by Scottish political opinion ranging from Unionism to Scottish Nationalism.[8] The Glasgow Exhibition attracted 12,593,232 visitors, as well as 600,000 to events at the nearby Ibrox Stadium. By 1938 propaganda techniques, publications, and the media had become a great deal more sophisticated than in 1924–25. Newsreels featured the opening of the exhibition by King George VI and Queen Elizabeth. The British Broadcasting Corporation (BBC) carried radio features on the exhibition to a large proportion of British homes.

Although the British Empire exhibitions at Wembley and Glasgow were spectacular and costly events, information about colonial products and trading relationships was conveyed through many other displays. This was an important period in the development of propagandist organizations, culminating in the founding of the British Council in 1934.[9] During and after the First World War a whole series of bodies was established to develop the Imperial economic relationship, including the British Empire Producers Organisation (1916), the Empire Resources Development Committee (also 1916), the Empire Development Parliamentary Committee (1920), the Empire Development Union (1922), the Empire Industries Association (1924), and the Empire Economic Union (1929).

Much of this work achieved its most notable public prominence through the creation of the Empire Marketing Board in 1926, the brainchild of the Colonial and Dominions Secretary, Leopold Amery. This Board was partly designed to counter the continuing failure of Tariff Reform and Imperial Preference in the elections of the early 1920s as well as the influence of Winston Churchill, then as always a free trader, at the Treasury after 1924. It secured a considerable degree of cross-party support until its demise in 1933, when the Ottawa Agreements were judged to have

[7] Perilla Kinchin and Juliet Kinchin, *Glasgow's Great Exhibitions, 1888, 1901, 1911, 1938, 1988* (Wendlebury, 1988), pp. 127–67; Findling and Pelle, eds., *Historical Dictionary*, pp. 291–92; *Empire Exhibition, Scotland, 1938, Official Guide* (Glasgow, 1938).

[8] John M. MacKenzie, 'On Scotland and the Empire', *International History Review*, XV, 4 (1993), pp. 714–39. Among contemporary works, Andrew Dewar Gibb, *Scottish Empire* (London, 1937). See also R. Coupland, *Welsh and Scottish Nationalism* (London, 1954), in which Coupland argued that Irish independence need not lead to the break-up of the United Kingdom. For Ireland, see Keith Jeffery, ed., '*An Irish Empire*'? *Aspects of Ireland and the British Empire* (Manchester, 1996).

[9] Philip M. Taylor, *The Projection of Britain: British Overseas Publicity and Propaganda, 1919–39* (Cambridge, 1981).

made its continuing existence unnecessary. It spent almost £2 million on research and marketing services connected with Imperial products and over £1 million on publicity. Few people were untouched by its activities in some shape or form. Its exceptionally talented staff employed every propaganda technique of the time, and much of the press willingly participated in its advertising campaigns. The BBC also broadcast a large number of talks on Empire Marketing Board themes. Booklets, pamphlets, and postcards were published. Documentary films were produced, and the most notable poster artists of the time were commissioned to design advertising posters for the London Underground. Throughout the country contacts were made with literary societies, the Young Men's Christian Association, Women's Institutes, schools, colleges, Rotary Clubs, and Grocers' Associations, and lectures were given in public libraries.[10]

Special displays were mounted at over seventy exhibitions in the period, including Industries' fairs, Ideal Home exhibitions, Bakers', Confectioners' and Grocers' exhibits as well as exhibitions with Empire themes in Belfast, Edinburgh, Liverpool, Birmingham, and Cardiff. In 1930 alone, 200 British Empire shopping weeks were organized in sixty-five towns. The tradition of smaller-scale Imperial exhibitions included 'Peeps at the Colonial Empire', which was held in Charing Cross underground station in London in 1936, and the 1944 touring Colonies Exhibition, sponsored by the Colonial Office and the Ministry of Information. In all of this the government sought to convey the message that the British Empire constituted a single family of diverse yet united peoples. Although the public impact is difficult to gauge, it certainly contributed to a national and cross-party sense that the British Empire retained its influence and significance in the world and that it constituted an economic and political complex which the British themselves would ignore only at their peril.

The direct appeal of Empire to women was probably greater in this period than in any other. Through government propaganda women were encouraged to buy Empire products, though in practice their purchasing behaviour was no doubt governed more by price than Imperial sentiment. The Wembley Exhibition had a Women's Section and a Women's Week. The Glasgow Exhibition had a separate Women's Pavilion illustrating the work, products, and crafts of women throughout the Empire.[11] Women were increasingly active in the various colonial societies, such as the Victoria League founded by women during the Boer War, the Royal Empire Society (formerly the Royal Colonial Institute), the Overseas League, the Royal Geographical Society, the British Empire League, and in missionary,

[10] Stephen Constantine, '"Bringing the Empire Alive": The Empire Marketing Board and Imperial Propaganda, 1926–33', in MacKenzie, ed., *Imperialism and Popular Culture*, pp. 192–231; and *Buy and Build: The Advertising Posters of the Empire Marketing Board* (London, 1986).

[11] *Empire Exhibition, Scotland 1938*, pp. 161–63.

humanitarian, and educational circles which sent increasing numbers of women overseas to work in the Empire. A female intellectual and political élite had also become extremely active in Imperial causes.[12]

There is a paradox about these activities during these years. On the one hand, the growth in numbers and range of activities of the wide variety of Imperial societies represented a great deal of energy. One Dominions Secretary, J. H. Thomas, pointed out in 1932 that there were thirty-three Imperial and patriotic societies.[13] Many attempts at amalgamation failed, and such diversity would ultimately prove a great weakness. On the other hand, anti-Imperial sentiment was equally fragmented, and radical groups supporting anti-colonial policies tended to be small and often 'marginal to the political process'.[14] Nevertheless, intellectuals and nationalists from the Indian and dependent Empire were able to make contact with sympathetic individuals and factions as well as with each other, and the interaction had considerable significance for future decolonization.[15]

That the cultural, political, and economic relations of the Empire were somehow regarded as above controversy and party politics is well illustrated by the attitude of the BBC. The Corporation, founded in 1923 and dominated until 1938 by its first Director-General, John Reith, viewed the Empire as a significant source of broadcasting material and a topic of central concern to national life, one which could be turned to nationalist, moral, and quasi-religious ends. Reith had an almost mystical approach to the Empire, which he regarded as the most successful example of internationalism and peaceful coexistence in modern times. In this his thinking was close to that of such diverse figures as J. C. Smuts, Robert Baden-Powell, and George Bernard Shaw. It followed that the medium of radio could contribute to the cohesion of British subjects and of the worldwide family of English-speaking peoples. One of the first successful outside broadcasts was that of the opening speech of George V at the Wembley Exhibition in 1924. Thereafter the BBC was involved in every national event and in the many pageants and exhibitions which contributed to the Imperial ethos. It carried special Empire Day programmes, and frequently broadcast talks, features, and poetry relating to the Empire. In 1932 it began a tradition of Christmas broadcasts associated with the

[12] Barbara Bush, '"Britain's Conscience in Africa": White Women, Race and Imperial Politics in Inter-War Britain', in Clare Midgley, ed., *Gender and Imperialism* (Manchester, 1997).

[13] Trevor R. Reese, *The History of the Royal Commonwealth Society, 1868–1968* (London, 1968), pp. 158–59.

[14] Stephen Howe, *Anticolonialism in British Politics: The Left and the End of Empire, 1918–1964* (Oxford, 1993), p. 309. See also Partha Sarathi Gupta, *Imperialism and the British Labour Movement, 1914–1964* (London, 1975) and David Goldsworthy, *Colonial Issues in British Politics, 1945–61* (Oxford, 1971). See chap. by Nicholas Owen, esp. pp. 207–10.

[15] C. L. R. James, *Beyond a Boundary* (London, 1963) offers some of the flavour of this period.

King's Christmas messages, which included contributions from colonial territories around the world.[16]

This tradition was sufficiently well-entrenched to survive Reith's departure from broadcasting. In the final years of the Second World War annual Festivals of Empire were broadcast from the Royal Albert Hall. The Christmas Empire programmes continued into the 1950s, narrated by distinguished actors such as Laurence Olivier, Robert Donat, and John Gielgud, with specially commissioned music by leading composers of the day, such as William Alwyn, Benjamin Britten, and Walter Goehr. These programmes projected a confident, mutually beneficial, economic imperialism. In 1947, for example, the groundnuts scheme in Tanganyika was described as offering 'solid ground for hope, hundreds of miles of jungle cleared by science and the bulldozer with a real promise of a better life for African and European'.[17] In broadcast programmes and in the *Radio Times*, one of the conspicuous publications of the period, the image conveyed of Empire was one of peace and economic regeneration contrasted with the old Empire of conquest and settlement.

By 1939 there were 9 million wireless licences in Britain, probably providing access to radio to almost everyone in the country.[18] The *Radio Times* sold nearly 3 million copies per week, and both the magazine and the medium it represented were particularly influential at such moments as the death and funeral of George V and the coronations of George VI in 1937 and of Elizabeth II in 1953, all of which were strikingly Imperial occasions. From the time of the first audience research in the second half of the 1930s, it is apparent that the national flagship programmes, particularly the Christmas Day broadcasts, which always contained material from the Empire, had an exceptionally wide following. They also secured large listener figures throughout the Empire and were heard and appreciated in the United States.[19]

A number of institutions and organizations founded in the Victorian period of Empire achieved their greatest success during this period. Such a body was the Imperial Institute in South Kensington. Founded after the Colonial and Indian Exhibition of 1886 and the Jubilee of 1887, funded by public subscriptions from throughout the Empire, and opened in a grand Imperial ceremony in 1893, the Institute had nevertheless not achieved high public recognition before 1914. Its

[16] John M. MacKenzie, '"In Touch with the Infinite": The BBC and the Empire', in MacKenzie, ed., *Imperialism and Popular Culture*, and 'Propaganda and the BBC Empire Service', in Jeremy Hawthorn, ed., *Propaganda, Persuasion and Polemic* (London, 1987).

[17] *Radio Times*, 19 Dec. 1947, p. 21.

[18] For statistics of licences and sales of the *Radio Times*, see Asa Briggs, *The History of Broadcasting in the United Kingdom*, 2 vols. (Oxford, 1965), II, pp. 253 and 281; also Mark Pegg, *Broadcasting and Society* (London, 1983), pp. 7 and 106.

[19] Information on American reactions to these broadcasts can be found in the BBC Written Archives, Caversham, R34/213/1 and R19/166.

elaborate and costly building, erected where Imperial College of the University of London now stands, created financial problems from which the Institute never wholly escaped. After 1923 it was saved by large donations from a number of industrialists, such as the metallurgist and steel-maker Sir Robert Hadfield and the oil millionaires, Viscounts Cowdray and Wakefield. After 1924 it was described as taking on the role of a permanent 'Wembley', and it became closely associated with the work of the Empire Marketing Board, which raised the money for a cinema in the Institute. Using more modern exhibition and propaganda techniques, the Institute attracted a steadily rising attendance, and achieved figures in excess of 1 million visitors a year in the early 1930s. It also established close connections with other Imperial societies, schools, youth organizations, the General Post Office, the Central Film Library, and various propagandist bodies. It published leaflets, pamphlets, and postcards relating to the Empire and its products.[20] Many of its visitors, including schoolchildren and servicemen during the war, were involuntary ones. However, the Imperial Institute was unquestionably more successful in the inter-war years than at any other time. After the Second World War the government announced its closure in 1955, but it was later resurrected as the Commonwealth Institute in Kensington High Street.

Compared with the BBC, the exhibitions, and the Marketing Board, the Imperial Institute had a relatively restricted influence on popular opinion. Although it did establish travelling exhibits and local agencies, it reached relatively few people outside London and had to compete with many more-popular attractions in the capital. Even within the South Kensington museum district it was overshadowed by the popular Natural History Museum or the Victoria and Albert, itself closely associated with India. Other media, including school textbooks, juvenile journals and literature, youth organizations and their publications, and above all the cinema, had a much more widespread effect. The rest of this chapter will be devoted to these educational and cultural expressions of Empire.

The teaching of Imperial ideas in schools did not arise immediately from the 'New Imperialism' of the 1870s and 1880s. Although there were texts in the nineteenth century for teachers and pupils on the development of the British Empire, it was not until the 1890s that education codes and teacher manuals began to stress the importance of the Empire and its associated adventure tradition in conveying concepts of national identity and pride to schoolchildren. From that period, the Empire became a focus for teaching in geography, history, aspects of English

[20] John M. MacKenzie, 'The Imperial Institute', *The Round Table*, CCCII (1987), pp. 246–53; for some of the Institute's technical work, see Michael Worboys, 'The Imperial Institute: The State and the Development of the Natural Resources of the Colonial Empire, 1887–1923', in MacKenzie, *Imperialism and the Natural World* (Manchester, 1990) pp. 164–86.

(readers often included Imperial poetry and prose), and religious studies. Geography had a notable immediacy because of exploration and the consequent discussion of natural resources, the character of indigenous peoples, and the capacity of technology to exploit global riches.[21]

It was this sense of a historic geographical mission, sometimes traced to medieval times, sometimes to the heroic era of the Tudors and Stuarts, which was conveyed in so much Imperial poetry, including that of Tennyson, Kipling, Newbolt, Austin, Noyes, and Masefield. Similarly, the fiction of Empire, particularly that of Captain Marryat, W. H. G. Kingston, R. M. Ballantyne, Henry Rider Haggard, G. A. Henty, and R. L. Stevenson was regarded as suitable reading material for the young by day schools, Sunday schools, and youth organizations. The history and the contemporary life and work of the Christian missions could also be linked to the same national enterprise: the lives of Christian heroes, such as David Livingstone, General Charles Gordon, Mary Slessor, and many others continued to be related to the adventure tradition in pursuit of the moral examples and self-sacrifice associated with the Empire.

Although a generation of scholars was beginning to react against it, Sir John Seeley's *The Expansion of England* of 1883 remained in print. His vision of Empire as the logical and inseparable outcome of English dominance within Britain had a considerable influence on teachers and school textbooks.[22] Although many school texts reflected changing conditions in emphasizing the internationalist and trusteeship aspects of the Imperial mission, others upheld the view that the Tudor period marked the origins of the British Empire, or insisted that the eighteenth century should be studied essentially as an era of colonial wars.[23] The vast majority of publishers continued to take a pride in Empire for many decades thereafter. There are few, if any, dissident voices within school geography and history texts, for to take a contrary line would inevitably have been seen as unpatriotic. No school or local authority could take such a risk.[24] The satirical work, *1066 and All*

[21] Valerie E. Chancellor, *History for their Masters* (London, 1970) and Kathryn Castle, *Britannia's Children: Reading Colonialism Through Children's Books and Magazines* (Manchester, 1996).

[22] J. R. Seeley, *The Expansion of England* (London, 1883). Interestingly, Seeley was also influential in Germany, where his selection of historical writings to illustrate the emergence of the British as an Imperial power was seen as a valuable example of the uses of history for the service of the modern state: G. A. Rein, *Sir John Robert Seeley: A Study of the Historian*, ed. and trans. by John L. Herkless (1912; Dover, NH, 1983). See also Peter Burroughs, 'John Robert Seeley and British Imperial History', *Journal of Imperial and Commonwealth History* (hereafter *JICH*), I (1972–73) pp. 191–211; and H. John Field, *Toward a Programme of Imperial Life* (Oxford, 1982).

[23] Catherine B. Firth, *The Learning of History in Elementary Schools* (London, 1932), p. 208; C. F. Strong, *Today Through Yesterday*, 3 vols. (London, 1935) among many other textbooks pursuing an Imperial approach to British history in the period.

[24] In 1934, however, the education committee of the Labour-controlled London County Council instructed its schools that Empire Day should henceforth be known as Commonwealth Day. The

That, first published in 1930, was reacting against a tradition of history teaching in the period.[25]

Imperial studies had also become more common in universities. The Rhodes and Beit Trustees had been active in funding chairs and lectureships in London and Oxford. The Colonial Service increasingly sent recruits for language, anthropological, and other training to these institutions of higher education, as well as to the recently founded School of Oriental and African Studies. As in technical and medical services, the old traditions of amateurism were being replaced by attempts to develop professionalism in the colonial world, though most historians of Empire, such as A. P. Newton, Basil Williams, and Sir Reginald Coupland, continued to write within an Imperial moralistic tradition.

If school texts and most university studies reveal little hint of anti-Imperial sentiment or the rise of colonial nationalism until well after the Second World War, juvenile literature continued to exploit many of the themes which had made it such a successful area of publishing in the late nineteenth century. Celebrated journals and comics, such as the *Boy's Own Paper, Gem, Magnet*, and *Union Jack*, continued publication throughout this period and carried many of the same sort of adventure stories set within the colonial context as they had done in the last decades of the nineteenth century. While many more boys from the Dominions, and also India, began to appear at Frank Richards's Greyfriars School, they still embarked on colonial adventures in Africa, Canada, and elsewhere during the holidays.

These nineteenth-century favourites were joined by a new breed of comics, published by D. C. Thomson of Dundee (with five new titles in the 1920s and 1930s) and a rival, the Amalgamated Press. It has been estimated that each of these papers sold some 600,000 copies to 1.5 million readers among boys and girls during these years.[26] While such genres as science fiction became more popular, colonial wars continued to be fought out in their pages until the 1950s. At the same time, the popularity of G. A. Henty and rivals such as Gordon Stables and F. S. Brereton remained strikingly high.[27]

Henty was something of a publishing phenomenon. In the 1950s Agnes Blackie estimated that her family's publishing house had sold up to 25 million copies of his

Empire Day Movement raised the matter in the Commons, arguing that 'Commonwealth' referred to only one part of the Empire, the Dominions. Reese, *Royal Commonwealth Society*, p. 157.

[25] W. C. Sellar and R. J. Yeatman, *1066 and All That* (London, 1930).

[26] Joseph McAleer, *Popular Reading and Publishing in Britain, 1914–1950* (Oxford, 1992).

[27] Guy Arnold, *Held Fast for England: G. A. Henty, Imperialist Boys' Writers* (London, 1980); Patrick A. Dunae, 'Boys' Literature and the Idea of Empire, 1870–1914', *Victorian Studies*, XXIV (1980), pp. 105–21; Jeffrey Richards, ed., *Imperialism and Juvenile Literature* (Manchester, 1989); Joseph Bristow, *Empire Boys: Adventures in a Man's World* (London, 1991).

titles, all of which remained in print until comparatively recent times.[28] A large proportion of Henty's full-length stories for children took events from the history of the Empire for their text. Henty's standard technique was to inject youthful fictional characters into historic events, thus providing his readers with the feel for great moments of Imperial history, and offering opportunity for moral uplift through contact with exemplary figures from the past. Geographical remoteness often substituted for chronological distance. Henty's procedures were imitated by many other writers, and the form of his titles, such as *With Clive in India*, *With Kitchener in the Soudan*, and *With Roberts to Pretoria* was adopted by journalists, missionary writers, and film-makers for descriptions of campaigns, memoirs, and travelogues.

Henty received the approval of missionary societies, school headmasters, and newspaper editors. Celebrated figures testified to his power in framing their world view. These included Field Marshal Montgomery, Harold Macmillan, Lord Home, J. Paul Getty, the historian A. J. P. Taylor, trade-union leader Tom Jackson, and the industrialist Sir John Harvey-Jones. In 1963 the Bishop of London said in a speech to the House of Lords that he still had Henty in his system.[29] A. J. P. Taylor attempted to separate Henty's historical account from his imperialism, but in truth the two were inseparably intertwined. Colonial campaigns represented the conflict of good and evil, the moral force of superior character. Violence became necessary as a means to progressive ends, and overcoming those who were racially disadvantaged. The reconciling of character and violence was closely bound up with Social Darwinian notions of racial inferiority.[30] These concepts were reflected in a new genre of Imperial flying stories by W. E. Johns, Percy F. Westerman, and George E. Rochester that featured patriotism, xenophobia, and global conspiracies.[31] Similar stories for girls linked opportunities for the independent action of females to continuing subordination to male power and the maintenance of the domestic virtues.[32]

Henty's racial message, formed in the atmosphere of 'scientific' racial beliefs of the late nineteenth-century, was carried forward well into the twentieth. Such

[28] Agnes C. Blackie, *Blackie and Son: A Short History of the Firm, 1809–1959* (London, 1959). If this estimate seems rather high, a 1952 figure of 3,514,000 copies seems rather low: Robert L. Dartt, *G. A. Henty: A Bibliography* (Altrincham, 1971), p. v.

[29] Jeffrey Richards, 'With Henty to Africa', in Richards, *Imperialism and Juvenile Literature*, p. 73; 'The World of Henty', BBC Radio 4, 23 Dec. 1982; see also J. S. Bratton, *The Impact of Victorian Children's Fiction* (London, 1981), p. 200.

[30] See Kathryn Tidrick, *Empire and the English Character* (London, 1990).

[31] Dennis Butts, 'Imperialists of the Air-Flying Stories, 1900–50', in Richards, *Imperialism and Juvenile Literature*, pp. 126–43.

[32] J. S. Bratton, 'British Imperialism and the Reproduction of Femininity in Girls' Fiction, 1900–1930', in Richards, *Imperialism and Juvenile Literature*, pp. 195–295.

racial views were somewhat more muted in school textbooks, and in the Empire 'annuals' which became a feature of publishing in the inter-war period. These annuals first appeared at the end of the nineteenth century; indeed, Henty founded two of them. The publisher Ward Lock issued the *Wonder Book of the Empire* before the First World War and it reached its fifth edition just after it. By the 1930s it had been joined by the *New Empire Annual* and *The Empire Annual for Girls*. These were designed for the extensive prize and present market. They contained stories of Imperial adventure, descriptions of campaigns, geographical material, factual accounts of settler life, and portrayals of 'picturesque and primitive native life'. They continued to be published well into the 1950s.

The audience for such materials could be found among the youth organizations which had mushroomed before 1914. After the war, the Boy Scouts, the Girl Guides, and the Boys' Brigade grew in popularity and developed an international profile. It has been argued that the Scouts and Guides became less imperial and militaristic, more concerned with internationalism and the maintenance of peace after the First World War.[33] Although this may be true, it is also clear that the ideals of Empire remained the model and were regarded as in no way incompatible with international idealism. The founder of the Scouts, Baden-Powell, viewed the Empire as a model for world integration and peace. Attempts in the 1920s to found alternative youth groups, such as the Kibbo Kift and the Woodland Folk, designed to be environmental, rural, non-military, co-educational, mystical, and in some respects quasi-socialist bodies, were largely unsuccessful.

In these years the Empire essay competitions of the Royal Colonial Institute (from 1928 the Royal Empire Society and later the Royal Commonwealth Society), which had been notably unsuccessful before the First World War, attracted large numbers of entries. Membership of the Royal Colonial Institute reached record peaks in 1930 and 1939 when the Society took on prime responsibility for Imperial studies.[34] Under the aegis of the Empire Day Movement, Empire Day on 24 May was more consistently observed by larger numbers of schools and organizations than it had been previously. It received a considerable impetus from rallies at the Wembley Exhibition and the interest of the BBC and the Empire Marketing Board. It was stimulated further after the outbreak of the Second World War.[35] The rival

[33] Allen Warren, 'Citizens of the Empire: Baden-Powell, Scouts and Guides, and an Imperial Ideal', in MacKenzie, ed., *Imperialism and Popular Culture*. See also Tim Jeal, *The Boy-Man: The Life of Lord Baden-Powell* (New York, 1990), and contrast with J. O. Springhall, 'The Boy Scouts, Class and Militarism in Relation to British Youth Movements, 1908–1930', *International Review of Social History*, XVI (1971), pp. 125–58.

[34] Reese, *Royal Commonwealth Society*, pp. 134, 138–39, 144, and *passim*.

[35] John Springhall, 'Lord Meath, Youth and Empire', *Journal of Contemporary History*, V, 4 (1970), pp. 97–111. For the Empire Day Movement in Ireland and its connections with Ulster loyalism, see David H. Hume, 'Empire Day in Ireland, 1896–1962', in Jeffery, *'An Irish Empire?'*, pp. 149–68.

Empire Youth Movement was founded as late as 1937 by a Canadian, Major Ney, who had been inspired by a large rally of Imperial youth at the Royal Albert Hall in association with the Coronation. The movement had wildly extravagant and unrealizable ambitions, but for a time it was remarkably successful. Helped by the outbreak of a new world war and by a fresh upsurge of Imperial and patriotic fervour, it collected extensive funds from companies and other sources, held annual rallies in Britain and the Dominions, won over the BBC and the older youth organizations, and was patronized by members of the royal family. It produced a publication entitled *The Great Crusade of Youth*, and continued to be active until the 1950s.

The celebration of Empire Day became an annual event in the majority of schools, and was fostered by features on the BBC and in the *Radio Times*. It was enhanced by marches and band performances in most towns. Perhaps its main impact was in offering a half-day holiday from school. The Empire Youth Movement and its observances never had the same impact and was restricted to a privileged few in the cities and towns in Britain and the Dominions. Yet these movements grew during this period, and secured more extensive funding and support. Their lavish annual reports and other publications indicate that the ideology of Empire was not experiencing a sudden and dramatic death. On the contrary, the international economic crisis and the continuing desire for security at home and Empire abroad seem to have created an Indian summer in the dissemination of Imperial ideas. There was a continuing disposition to turn national and royal events into great Imperial extravaganzas.

The most powerful influence on the public's views on the Empire was that of the cinema. Although moving film had its origins in the 1890s, it was in the inter-war years that the technology of film-making and cinema buildings came of age. In 1926 there were 3,000 cinemas in Britain; by 1938 there were nearly 5,000. By 1940 ticket sales had passed the 1,000 million mark.[36] The revolutions of sound, and by the end of the 1930s colour, larger screen sizes, as well as the provision of longer reels and multiple projectors helped to develop this popularity. Technically sophisticated cinemas ensured that continuous, lengthy, and dramatic presentations were possible. Yet, despite its new technology, film was a remarkably conservative medium. The standard entertainment forms of the nineteenth century, including the military spectacles performed in some theatres and circus rings, the tradition of spectacular theatre, elements from the music hall, panoramas, and above all melodrama, now became the subject of the very films which had supplanted them.[37] Moreover, the cinema in Britain was as tightly controlled as

[36] Jeffrey Richards, *The Age of the Dream Palace: Cinema and Society in Britain, 1930–39* (London, 1984), pp. 11–12.

[37] Jeffrey Richards, *Visions of Yesterday* (London, 1973), Part 1, 'The Cinema of Empire'.

the nineteenth-century theatre had been, perhaps more so. From 1912 the British Board of Film Censors maintained a tight grip on what could and could not be shown in cinemas in Britain, thus ensuring ideological safety and the avoidance of controversial topics, just as in the case of the theatrical licensing system of the Lord Chamberlain.[38]

The propaganda value of film became obvious at an early stage. The Boer (South African) War was featured prominently in early newsreels and documentaries, and film was extensively used for propaganda purposes during the First World War. By the inter-war years politicians and others assessed the potential of film in pursuing the Imperial cause. In 1926 several Dominion Premiers agreed that 'wholesome imperial sentiments' could be disseminated through film. A subcommittee report proposed that cinema was 'not merely a form of entertainment' but also a 'powerful instrument of education', which 'even when . . . not used avowedly for purposes of instruction, advertisement or propaganda . . . exercises a great influence in shaping the ideas of the very large numbers to whom it appeals'.[39] Throughout the 1930s government departments continued to be interested in the propaganda potential of films. In 1938 a committee under the chairmanship of Sir Robert Vansittart, the Permanent Under-Secretary at the Foreign Office, suggested that feature films were more effective in influencing audiences than documentaries, since 'they strike subconscious chords and reinforce or modify prejudices or opinions already held, and thus in the long run make a more lasting impression'. After leaving the Foreign Office and becoming involved in commercial film-making, Vansittart wrote the script for the film *Sixty Glorious Years* (1938), which celebrated the reign of Queen Victoria.[40]

The relative influence and ideological substance of both documentaries and feature films in the period have been much debated. Films of 'actuality' had been made early on. The subjects of nineteenth-century panoramas, magic-lantern shows, and illustrated journals such as *The Illustrated London News* and the *Graphic* were now presented on celluloid: journeys in exotic parts of the globe, anthropological accounts of other peoples, colonial products and their relation to the home economy, big-game hunting, and company advertising. Before the First World War the British North Borneo Company paid for films to illustrate its work in the East. 'Travel industrials' were made featuring, for example, seal-hunting off

[38] Jeffrey Richards, 'The British Board of Film Censors and Content Control in the 1930s: Images of Britain', *Historical Journal of Film, Radio and Television* (hereafter *HJFRT*), I (1981), pp. 95–116; Richards, *Age of the Dream Palace*, pp. 134–52.

[39] Constantine, 'Bringing the Empire Alive', p. 208.

[40] Jeffrey Richards, '"Boy's Own Empire": Feature Films and Imperialism in the 1930s', in MacKenzie, *Imperialism and Popular Culture*, pp. 152–53.

Newfoundland, whaling off Natal, and date-growing in Egypt. Cadbury's made a film on the Gold Coast cocoa bean and its manufacture into chocolate in their model factory and village at Bourneville.[41]

The documentary came into its own in the inter-war years. Numerous documentary accounts, many with colonial settings, were made in the 1920s. In that decade the British documentary film movement began to emerge as a significant source of innovative film materials. Sir Stephen Tallents, Secretary of the Empire Marketing Board, and later head of public relations at the Post Office and the BBC, was aware of the power of film and made sure that the Marketing Board made some use of its potential.[42] Documentary techniques were developed and promoted by such producers as John Grierson, Paul Rotha, and Basil Wright. These producers have been portrayed as radical figures, and it is true that some of them had moderate left-wing sympathies, but the films they made showed little disposition to undermine either the British establishment view or the colonial relationship. They tended to attack feature films, particularly those that came from Hollywood, but many of their own documentaries were commissioned by the Empire Marketing Board, the General Post Office, colonial governments, or international companies such as Shell, Anglo-Iranian, Imperial Airways, and Imperial Chemical Industries. Films such as *Gold Coast Cocoa* (1930), *Lumber* (1931), *Cargo from Jamaica* and *Song of Ceylon* (both 1933), and *Windmill in Barbados* (1934) were designed to illustrate the economic interdependence of Britain and the Empire. *Air Post* (1934) and *African Skyways* (1939) were among several films made for Imperial Airways. *Five Faces* (1938) was made for the Malayan colonial authorities, *Men of Africa* (1939), one of the most overtly propagandist of all these films, was made for the Colonial Office to celebrate the work of colonial officials.[43] A film was also made of the remarkable Hendon Air Pageants which took place between 1920 and 1937. A prime attraction at one of these was the mock bombing of 'native' villages to illustrate the use of air power in colonial policing.[44]

41 For accounts and listings of these early Imperial films, see Rachael Low and Roger Manvell, *The History of the British Film, 1896–1906* (London, 1948), and Rachael Low, *The History of the British Film, 1914–18* (London, 1950) and *The History of the British Film, 1918–1929* (London, 1971). See also A. D. Roberts, 'Africa on Film to 1940', *History in Africa*, XIV (1987), pp. 189–227 and 'Non-Fiction Film of Africa before 1940', *HJFRT*, VIII, 2 (1988), pp. 203–06.

42 Constantine, 'Bringing the Empire Alive', pp. 208–10; S. G. Tallents, *The Projection of England* (London, 1932).

43 Rachael Low, *Documentary and Educational Films of the 1930s* (London, 1979).

44 For the Hendon Pageants and films associated with them, see David Enrico Omissi, 'The Hendon Air Pageant, 1920–37', in John M. MacKenzie, ed., *Popular Imperialism and the Military* (Manchester, 1992), pp. 198–220; and Michael Paris, *From the Wright Brothers to Top Gun: Aviation, Nationalism and Popular Cinema* (Manchester, 1995), p. 105.

Such films, among many others, were shown in schools, to youth organizations, at the Imperial Institute cinema, and countless other informal locations. But there is little doubt that, important as the documentary film movement was in artistic and cultural terms, its products had only a slight public impact as compared with the immensely popular feature films of the period. Here too it is striking that the British Empire offered a key subject for cinematic treatment. These films were heavily dependent on the work of popular writers. Thus, the fiction of A. E. W. Mason and Edgar Wallace featured prominently, as did material derived from Francis Yeats-Brown and Rudyard Kipling. The Empire offered a seemingly consensual and uncontroversial source of subjects, likely to secure the approval of the film censors. On the other hand, anything tending to denigrate white officials, degrade white women in the tropics, or emphasize conflict and resistance in the Empire was likely to be banned. Attempts to make films about the Indian Mutiny, for example, were thwarted because of the effect they might have on contemporary Indian audiences.[45] The censors were well aware that the cinema effectively made all the world a screen.[46] The Empire could be depicted as a source of adventure and romance, a location for moral redemption, heroic action, and military success. There were obvious parallels between the highly popular 'Western' tradition in the cinematic celebration of American history and the Imperial adventures of the British. Not least, there were virtually no pressure groups prepared to complain about the stereotypical and unflattering depiction of indigenous peoples on the screen.

Films with an 'Imperial' content attracted an immense public. The tradition of using the works of popular writers or of celebrating heroic patriotic action overseas began early and continued in the inter-war period (for example, A. E. W. Mason's *The Four Feathers* was first made during the First World War, Rider Haggard's *She* was filmed in 1925, and a film about Livingstone was produced in the same year). The 1930s became the classic decade of Imperial spectaculars. Hollywood companies were as active as British film-makers in celebrating the Empire. Paramount's *The Lives of a Bengal Lancer* (1935, only loosely based on Francis Yeats-Brown's book, *Bengal Lancer*, published in 1930) was a blockbusting success on both sides of the Atlantic and stimulated many imitations. Cinemagoers seemed to be enthralled by melodramatic actors clothed in colourful, and often inauthentic, uniforms in exotic settings. Other Imperial epics flowed,

[45] Richards, 'Boy's Own Empire', p. 153.

[46] Tallents argued for the need to 'throw a fitting presentation of England upon the world's screen': *Projection of England*, p. 39. Recent work suggests that there was a continuing realization of the need to manipulate the media, including newsreels, during the counter-insurgency campaigns of the 1940s and 1950s: Susan L. Carruthers, *Winning Hearts and Minds: British Governments, the Media and Colonial Counter-Insurgency, 1944–1960* (London, 1995).

slightly incongruously, out of Hollywood, such as *Clive of India* (1935), *Wee Willie Winkie* (1937), *Storm over Bengal* (1938), *The Sun Never Sets*, *Gunga Din*, and *Stanley and Livingstone* (the last three all 1939).

In Britain, Alexander and Zoltan Korda made *Sanders of the River* (after a novel by Edgar Wallace, 1935), *The Drum* (1938), and *The Four Feathers* (1939, both after A. E. W. Mason), while Michael Balcon at Gaumont British produced *Rhodes of Africa* and *The Great Barrier* (both 1936), as well as *King Solomon's Mines* (after Rider Haggard, 1937). Noted stars acted in Imperial extravaganzas: on the British side Gracie Fields appeared in a musical, *We're Going to Be Rich* (1937), set in the South African gold-fields, and on the American the child star Shirley Temple appeared in *Wee Willie Winkie*, *Susannah of the Mounties*, and *The Little Princess* (all 1939). The tradition was maintained by *The Four Just Men* (1939), based on an Edgar Wallace thriller about a plot to seize the Suez Canal, and such Kipling material as *Elephant Boy*, the *Jungle Book* (1942), and *Soldiers Three* and *Kim* (1951). So successful was the 1930s' formula that it continued through the 1950s and 1960s, with such successes as *Storm over Africa* and *Storm over the Nile* (1953 and 1955), *Khyber Patrol*, *King of the Khyber Rifles*, and *West of Zanzibar* (all 1954), *North-West Frontier* (1959), *Zulu* (1963), and *Khartoum* (1966), to mention only a few.

Such films represented an extraordinary Indian summer in the popular culture of Empire. They all projected myth rather than reality, an adventure tradition suffused with an ideology dating from the 1890s: with a sense of mission, and of economic opportunity, of the superiority of Western science, technology, administrative, and military capacity with all its attendant racial prejudice. Films in the context of Empire offered their vast audiences not only escapist entertainment but also a sense of security, as well as feelings of pride and achievement. They reflected assumptions of racial and cultural superiority. They constituted the most significant evidence for the argument that the public was little infected with anti-Imperial sentiment. The emotional power of these films was great. Even Bertolt Brecht found himself being seduced by *Gunga Din*, and a critic in the *New York Times* described *The Four Feathers* as 'an imperialist symphony'.[47] George Orwell regarded the movies and the radio as two of the prime reasons for the absence of true working-class dissent within Britain.[48]

In his analyses of British society in this period, Orwell noted that a chasm had opened up between the ideas of the intelligentsia and the cultural interests of the masses. Among the latter, he singled out patriotism, the Empire, breeding, honour, and discipline, all suffused with reverence for the monarchy.[49] Thus, it

[47] Richards, 'Boy's Own Empire', pp. 144–45.

[48] George Orwell, *The Road to Wigan Pier* (London, 1937), chap. 5, p. 80.

[49] George Orwell, *Collected Essays, Journalism and Letters*, eds. Sonia Orwell and Ian Angus, 4 vols. (Harmondsworth, 1970), I, p. 564.

seems to be one of the apparent curiosities of British Imperial history that, when the Empire encountered the economic, political, and constitutional crises that would ultimately bring it down, British domestic culture came to emphasize colonial relationships as never before. There were several reasons. There is often a time-lapse in ideas filtering into popular culture. New entertainment technologies, such as cinema and radio, cling to tested ways to ensure their success. The practitioners of the techniques of propaganda, advertising, and public relations stuck to eternal verities around which a national consensus had formed. It was, after all, an ethos which could be portrayed as combining both a national and an individual ethic. The loss of this moral force may well have been a vital contributor to the acceptance of decolonization.[50]

All this is not to suggest that a gullible public was duped. No one forced people to visit exhibitions, purchase comics, journals, and books, participate in pageants, national ceremonies, or Empire Day Movement activities, switch on their radios, or flock to the cinema. People were partly conditioned by a rise in living standards. The public sought consolation in what often felt like threatening times, and had the sense of participating in a worldwide enterprise which seemed, despite the intellectual jeremiads of the day, to represent success. The realm of politics and ideology were inseparably linked to the Empire.

One acute social observer, looking back from the vantage-point of the 1980s, remembered that his village classroom as a boy in the 1920s 'was steeped in officially sanctioned nationalism. The world map was red for the Empire and dull brown for the rest, with Australia and Canada vastly exaggerated in size by Mercator's projection. The Greenwich meridian placed London at the centre of the world. Empire Day and 11 November [Armistice Day marking the Allied victory at the end of the First World War] ritualized an established national supremacy.'[51] At the time when this memory was recorded the processes of decolonization had already eroded most of the specifically Imperial aspects of popular British culture. The longer-term legacies of colonial connections, however, were significantly changing the face of British society. After the Second World War waves of immigrants from the West Indies, and then from India, Pakistan, and eventually Bangladesh (formerly East Pakistan), settled in Britain, clustering in its big urban areas. As a result, despite tightening controls on new immigration, Britain became increasingly a multi-ethnic society. This ethnic diversity became even more manifest with the birth of second and third generations of once-immigrant families. The cultural repercussions of migration were soon clearly visible—in

[50] R. E. Robinson, 'The Moral Disarmament of African Empire, 1919–47', *JICH*, VIII, 1 (1979), pp. 86–104.

[51] The sociologist A. H. Halsey in a radio talk, later published in the *Listener*, 6 Jan. 1983, p. 10.

the building of Hindu temples and of mosques, in the change in school curricula to acknowledge the multiracial and multi-religious origins of pupils, in the burgeoning of Indian and Pakistani corner shops and restaurants, and, more darkly, in the growth of racial tensions. Ironically, a post-colonial metropolitan society and culture now found itself more deeply marked by the long-term effects of Imperial connections than in earlier generations when Empire seemed real but remote.

Select Bibliography

SUSAN L. CARRUTHERS, *Winning Hearts and Minds: British Governments, the Media and Colonial Counter-Insurgency, 1944–1960* (London, 1995).

KATHRYN CASTLE, *Britannia's Children: Reading Colonialism through Children's Books and Magazines* (Manchester, 1996).

STEPHEN CONSTANTINE, *Buy and Build: The Advertising Posters of the Empire Marketing Board* (London, 1986).

R. COUPLAND, *Welsh and Scottish Nationalism* (London, 1954).

ANDREW DEWAR GIBB, *Scottish Empire* (London, 1937).

PAUL GREENHALGH, *Ephemeral Vistas: The Expositions Universelles, Great Exhibitions and World's Fairs, 1851–1939* (Manchester, 1988).

STEPHEN HOWE, *Anticolonialism in British Politics: The Left and the End of Empire, 1918–1964* (Oxford, 1993).

C. L. R. JAMES, *Beyond a Boundary* (London, 1963).

KEITH JEFFREY, ed., *An Irish Empire? Aspects of Ireland and the British Empire* (Manchester, 1996).

JOHN M. MACKENZIE, *Propaganda and Empire: The Manipulation of British Public Opinion, 1880–1960* (Manchester, 1984).

—— ed., *Imperialism and Popular Culture* (Manchester, 1986).

—— ed., *Imperialism and the Natural World* (Manchester, 1990).

—— ed., *Popular Imperialism and the Military, 1850–1950* (Manchester, 1992).

TOM NAIRN, *The Break-Up of Britain: Crisis and Neo-Nationalism* (London, 1981).

TREVOR R. REESE, *The History of the Royal Commonwealth Society in Britain, 1868–1968* (London, 1968).

JEFFREY RICHARDS, *Visions of Yesterday* (London, 1973).

—— *The Age of the Dream Palace: Cinema and Society in Britain, 1930–1939* (London, 1984).

—— ed., *Imperialism and Juvenile Literature* (Manchester, 1989).

PHILIP M. TAYLOR, *The Projection of Britain: British Overseas Publicity and Propaganda, 1919–39* (Cambridge, 1981).

KATHRYN TIDRICK, *Empire and the English Character* (London, 1990).

10

Colonial Rule

JOHN W. CELL

The outstanding feature of British colonial governance was its remarkably small component of civil servants from the metropole. On the eve of the Second World War the élite administrative division of the colonial service in Africa, including District Officers and central secretariats but not railway, agriculture, or other specialist departments, numbered slightly more than 1,200 men. These were spread over more than a dozen colonies covering nearly 2 million square miles, with an estimated population of 43 million.[1] Kenya averaged 19,000 people per administrator, Nigeria 54,000. The Sudan Political Service, which reported to the Foreign Office, had some 125 senior officials for a territory twice the size of the American state of Texas.[2] For a population of 353 million, the Indian Civil Service (ICS) had a maximum strength of 1,250 covenanted members,[3] whereas the relatively well-manned Malayan Civil Service possessed some 220 élite administrators for a mere 3.2 million people.[4]

The several Imperial services had different modes of selection. Ever since the British governmental reforms of the 1850s the Indian Civil Service had required a competitive examination, as did Hong Kong's and Ceylon's, while the Malayan, Sudan, and other colonial services in Africa were all chosen without one. The 'competition wallahs' in the ICS were somewhat stronger academically, came from a slightly wider range of public schools and universities, and had fewer athletes,

[1] These included Nigeria, the Cameroons, Gold Coast, Sierra Leone, the Gambia, Kenya, Uganda, Somaliland, Tanganyika, Zanzibar, Northern Rhodesia, Nyasaland, and the three High Commission Territories of Basutoland, Swaziland, and Bechuanaland in South Africa. The internally self-governing colony of Southern Rhodesia, controlled by its local white population, had its own Department of Native Affairs.

[2] Anthony H. M. Kirk-Greene, 'The Thin White Line', *African Affairs* (hereafter *AA*), LXXIX (1980), pp. 25–44, and 'The Sudan Political Service: A Profile in the Sociology of Imperialism', *International Journal of African Historical Studies*, XV (1982), pp. 21–48.

[3] David C. Potter, *India's Political Administrators, 1919–1983* (Oxford, 1986), chap. 1. Covenanted members had sworn to accept the pension of the East India Company (and after 1858, when the Company was abolished, of the Crown) rather than accept fees of office.

[4] J. de Vere Allen, 'Malayan Civil Service, 1874–1941: Colonial Bureaucracy-Malayan Elite', *Comparative Studies in Society and History*, XII (1970), pp. 149–78.

but more Irish and Scots. If the non-examination services were more homogeneous, however, with a stronger concentration from the south of England, they were also more flexible. Neither Sir Donald Cameron nor Sir Alan Burns, for instance, two of the most capable African Governors of the inter-war period, had been to an élite school or to university, having worked their way up from junior appointments in the West Indies.[5]

The examination variable notwithstanding, the British members of the Imperial services were much alike, overwhelmingly from the upper-middle and professional classes. Their schools were aptly called factories for gentlemen: curricula dominated by classics and mathematics, games, teamwork, exaggerated masculinity, cold showers, and stiff upper lips. The fagging system was supposed to teach boys to obey, punish, encourage, and rule.[6] The British élite educational system was shaped to produce generalists rather than technical specialists: men equipped to become Imperial mandarins or military officers.

Studies in the sociology of imperialism have stressed the authoritarian, hypermasculine, militaristic backgrounds of overseas officials. Yet the same class structure and educational system produced not only the Imperial governing élite but bankers, church officials, government ministers, and civil servants in British domestic society. Young men attracted to careers overseas may have been a little more inclined towards autocratic ways than those who stayed home. What mattered more, however, was what happened to them when they got there.

The most important fact was lonely responsibility. 'I've been four months alone now,' the future novelist Joyce Cary wrote to his wife from Northern Nigeria in 1917, 'but I haven't been unhappy.' He had found out a lot about himself: 'One does in solitude. I often wondered how I should stand being alone.' His rudimentary knowledge of local languages and his detached position had kept him from exchanging 'a word of rational conversation since May, and this is getting on to the end of September'.[7] Leonard Woolf, who later wrote books denouncing economic imperialism, made no apologies for his youthful stint in Ceylon, not that he had done anything to regret. He recalled having been assigned to a religious festival that drew pilgrims from all over South India, the assumption being that

[5] Robert Heussler, *Yesterday's Rulers: The Making of the British Colonial Service* (Syracuse, NY, 1963); Ralph Furse, *Aucuparius: Recollections of a Recruiting Officer* (London, 1962); Potter, *India's Political Administrators.*

[6] Philip Mason, *The English Gentleman: The Rise and Fall of an Ideal* (London, 1982), p. 170; Rupert Wilkinson, *Gentlemanly Power: British Leadership and the Public School Tradition* (London, 1964); Simon Raven, *The Decline of the Gentleman* (New York, 1962); James A. Mangan, ed., *Benefits Bestowed: Education and British Imperialism* (London, 1988). On universities, see Sheldon Rothblatt, *The Revolution of the Dons: Cambridge and Society in Victorian England* (London, 1968); Richard Symonds, *Oxford and Empire: The Last Lost Cause* (London, 1986).

[7] Molly Mahood, *Joyce Cary's Africa* (Boston, 1965), pp. 39–40.

because a single white man was on hand, somehow order would prevail—and somehow it did.[8] Sir Frank Swettenham said much the same about the Residency System in Malaya: a British officer would 'be sent into a country where white men were unknown; where everything that could be wrong was wrong'—lawless, undeveloped, unpoliced, anarchic, tyrannical. 'It was apparently conceived that . . . the single white man would reduce everything to order by the exercise of tactful advice.'[9]

Even if a man had been so inclined, what has been called the dominance–dependency complex would have been hard to avoid. In India, where caste and client networks had existed for centuries, henchmen would mysteriously attach themselves, ready to do whatever might be wanted.[10] In Africa the racial hierarchy had much the same effect. In combination with lonely responsibility, the habit of command helped mould an authoritarian personality, accustomed to giving orders and having them obeyed.

At 29, for example, Malcolm Hailey (who was to become both an Indian Governor and editor of *An African Survey*) was sent to develop a new canal colony on the Jhelum River in what is now Pakistan. He was in charge of everything: surveying, selecting colonists from other regions in the Punjab, choosing town sites, collecting taxes, developing a seed farm, overseeing anti-plague measures, warning against possible unrest. Virtually autonomous, speaking English only with his wife, this was Hailey's formative experience. It made him an Imperialist.[11]

Underpinning, but also somewhat counteracting, the authoritarian motif was the need to work with local authorities. The concentrated, overpowering force that reinforced colonial rule was usually remote. If officials called upon it frequently, there would be questions. They therefore had to learn to make concessions, not to give orders unless reasonably confident they would be obeyed. With so few administrators and so much ground to cover, even inexperienced officers received wide latitude, and ordinarily their superiors were supposed to back them up. Although continuity was the ideal, in practice illnesses, leaves, or promotions caused such rapid turnover that officers rarely stayed in the same district more than a year or two.

Although their backgrounds and job experiences were much alike, in two ways the various Imperial services did differ markedly. The first was the number of indigenous members. Although admission into the Indian Civil Service had been

[8] Leonard Woolf, *Growing: An Autobiography of the Years 1904–1911* (New York, 1962).

[9] Frank Swettenham, *British Malaya: An Account of the Origin and Progress of British Influence*, revised edn. (London, 1948), pp. 213–14.

[10] Philip Mason, *A Shaft of Sunlight: Memoirs of a Varied Life* (London, 1978), p. 97.

[11] John W. Cell, *Hailey: A Study in British Imperialism, 1872–1969* (Cambridge, 1992), chap. 2.

formally race-blind ever since Queen Victoria's Proclamation of 1858, such devices as holding examinations in England and lowering the age limits had kept non-British entrants to a trickle. In partial fulfilment of the wartime pledge that the country would evolve toward Dominion Status, however, the Government of India in 1919 committed itself to gradual Indianization of both the ICS and the officer corps of the Indian Army. Although to nationalist ears the pace sounded ludicrously slow—the target being somewhere in the mid-1980s—by 1939 about one-quarter of the ICS was Indian and by 1947 over half. In Ceylon (now Sri Lanka), placed under the Colonial Office in 1808, the pattern was similar: token local appointments until after the First World War, then an indigenization programme resulting in a Ceylonese majority by 1940.[12] In Malaya, another Colonial Office responsibility with Indian origins, the indigenization of the élite Malayan Civil Service had gone slowly before the Japanese conquest in 1942. There was, however, a separate Malayan Administrative Service, begun in 1910, restricted to Malays despite the large Chinese population.[13]

The African case was entirely different. Until after the Second World War British colonies in East and Central Africa had no Africans above the level of minor clerk. Although education and other specialist departments in West Africa and the Sudan did contain a few, their presence in important posts had actually declined since the 1890s. Despite the recommendations of the Hailey Report of 1941, which urged the appointment of Africans to all layers and sectors of the administration, little happened until the 1950s.[14]

The second crucial variable was the size of the supporting bureaucracies. If to the 1,200 élite administrators in Britain's African colonies (excluding Sudan and Southern Rhodesia) were added police and specialist departments, the number of European employees by the late 1930s still came to slightly below 8,000. No count was ever made of the total number of Africans in government service (clerks, messengers, and so on): say 30,000–40,000? According to the 1931 census India had as many as a million government workers, making the covenanted ICS a minuscule .001 per cent of the total, more like a spider's web than Lloyd George's metaphor of a steel frame. That huge discrepancy between India and Africa was the difference between direct and Indirect Rule.

[12] Charles Collins, 'Ceylon: The Imperial Heritage', in Ralph Braibanti, ed., *Asian Bureaucratic Systems Emergent from the British Imperial Tradition* (Durham, NC, 1966), pp. 444–84.

[13] Robert O. Tilman, 'Bureaucratic Development in Malaya'; Braibanti, *Asian Bureaucratic Systems*, pp. 550–604; Allen, 'Malayan Civil Service'. See the classic comparative works by Rupert Emerson, *Malaysia: A Study in Direct and Indirect Rule* (New York, 1937), and J. S. Furnivall, *Colonial Policy and Practice: A Comparative Study of Burma and Netherlands India* (Cambridge, 1948).

[14] W. Malcolm Hailey, *Native Administration and Political Development in British Tropical Africa*, ed. A. H. M. Kirk-Greene (Nendeen, 1979). Two Africans did become District Officers in the Gold Coast during the Second World War.

Direct rule was the system in two-thirds of the Indian continent (or 'British India'). Its huge, multi-layered bureaucracy, comparable in size to those of the Tsarist Russian or Chinese empires, incorporated a vast array of village headmen, record-keepers, and other Indian officials, with central, provincial, district, and local services linked together in an unbroken hierarchy. Authoritarian in origin, in the late-nineteenth century the structure gradually began to incorporate quasi-representative reforms. In the 1870s came municipal and district boards, at first nominated but increasingly elective, and with expanding patronage. There were also central and provincial Legislative Councils. These too began with government officials in the majority, gradually adding appointed and then elected non-official members.

Under the Government of India Act of 1919 the provinces moved part-way towards autonomy in a system known as Dyarchy, which made ministers in provincial government responsible to the legislature for education, public works, and other such departments, with officials remaining in charge of crucial ones such as Finance and Home (including police). In the central Government of India the Viceroy's Council (analogous to the British Cabinet) remained an appointed body, but faced an elected majority in the Indian Legislative Assembly. (After 1922 the Law Member was an Indian.) Under the constitution of 1935 the provinces obtained full responsible government, with Governors taking the advice of ministers able to command the confidence of the legislature. The central government remained unchanged.

Ceylon had comparable features—a hierarchical structure linking centre to province to district, incorporating Ceylonese headmen and other local officials; municipal and district boards; an increasingly elective Legislative Council—but without the huge bureaucracy of India.[15] Although Ceylon's constitutional history was also comparable to India's, much of it was actually *anti*-Indian. The Donoughmore constitution of 1929, modelled on the London County Council system of English local government, attempted to prevent the colony's communal problem from exploding and to avoid what seemed to be the unsuitability for Asia of the Westminster model of party government. Like the Government of India Act of 1935, that constitution was a detour. During the war Ceylon resumed its comparatively unruffled march toward responsible government; in 1948 it became independent within the Commonwealth—all largely because it was next to India.

Apart from small but densely populated commercial enclaves (Hong Kong or Singapore) or strategic outposts (Gibraltar or Cyprus), everywhere else in the dependent Empire had some kind of indirect rule. Although the basic definition of

[15] See K. M. de Silva, *A History of Sri Lanka* (Berkeley, 1981), and Sir Charles Jeffries, *Ceylon: The Path to Independence* (New York, 1963).

the indirect method seems simple enough—'systematic use of the customary institutions of the people as agencies of local rule'—the variations were considerable.[16]

Variations of Indirect Rule

The Indian princely states covered a third of the Indian Empire, ranging from large, important entities such as Kashmir or Hyderabad to tiny principalities with populations under 100,000. Before the Mutiny of 1857–58 the East India Company, thirsty for additional sources of revenue, had absorbed Indian polities at a rapid pace. Afterwards, most of the princes having refused to join the insurrection, annexations ceased abruptly.[17] As nominally autonomous 'native states' they administered themselves under British paramountcy, Residents (members of the Indian Political Service reporting to the Government of India's Political Department) being assigned to them as advisers. The states were outside the Government of India's tax base; their autocratic character insulated most of them from nationalist agitation; and they contributed substantially to the Indian Army. Ordinarily Residents were told to interfere cautiously and sparingly, and above all not to cause the prince to lose face with his subjects. Depending on personalities, circumstances, and government policy, relationships between Residents and princes varied enormously.[18]

Despite the assurance that Britain would not ordinarily annex states, there were limits to non-intervention. The best-known test case involved the Nizam of Hyderabad. During the First World War, when Indian troops (including a substantial number of Muslims) fought mainly in the Middle East against the predominantly Muslim forces of the Ottoman empire, the British obtained from the Nizam a declaration that, although the Sultan of Turkey was the head of World Islam, the conflict was a political one, lacking the religious sanction of a holy war (jihad). After the war the Nizam tried to claim special status as an ally, meaning that on internal matters he could parley with the Viceroy on equal terms, disagreements being submitted to an independent tribunal. Lord Reading, the Viceroy, called his bluff. Although the British might be reluctant to intervene, he

[16] W. Malcolm Hailey, *The Future of Colonial Peoples* (London, 1944), pp. 45–46.

[17] Thomas R. Metcalf, *The Aftermath of Revolt: India, 1857–1870* (Princeton, 1964).

[18] Robin Jeffrey, ed., *People, Princes and Paramount Power: Society and Politics in the Indian Princely States* (Delhi, 1978); Ian Copland, *The British Raj and the Indian Princes: Paramountcy in Western India, 1857–1930* (Bombay, 1982); Barbara N. Ramusack, *The Princes of India in the Twilight of Empire: Dissolution of a Patron–Client System, 1914–1939* (Columbus, Oh., 1978); Terence Creagh Coen, *The Indian Political Service: A Study in Indirect Rule* (London, 1971); Michael Fisher, *Indirect Rule in India: Residents and the Residency System, 1764–1858* (Delhi, 1991).

declared, their paramountcy was supreme, indivisible, and not based on specific treaties.[19]

Although in the long run they failed to exploit the long struggle between the government and the Indian National Congress, the princes gained considerable room to manœuvre. A Chamber of Princes, created in 1921, met irregularly, was weakened by personal jealousies, had no legislative power, refused to have its proceedings published, and ultimately came to little. At the Round Table Conference of 1930 the princes seized the initiative by proposing an All-India Federation. According to the subsequent Government of India Act of 1935, which left them free to enter or remain outside the eventual Dominion, their representation would have been weighted so heavily that (unless the constitution were amended, a process requiring a huge majority) Congress would have been prevented from *ever* obtaining a majority in the central legislature. Nevertheless, despite the strong manpower and financial contribution of their states during the Second World War, the princes entered the partition era without their future guaranteed. In the end, in a masterpiece of obfuscation at a press conference in June 1947, Lord Mountbatten (who had been at school with several of them) gave the princes short shrift. 'I am not trying to be funny,' he explained disarmingly. 'If there is one India then we can transfer power to one India. If there are two parts, then we must transfer power to two parts. What else can we do?'[20]

Malaya also had a Residency System, modelled after the Indian princely states, with British officers serving as advisers to the sultans' courts. As in the Indian states the relationship between sultans and Residents varied widely. Residents having 'been placed in the Native States as advisers, not as rulers', the Colonial Office warned in the 1870s, 'if they take upon themselves to disregard this principle they will assuredly be held responsible if trouble springs out of their neglect of it'. That was all very well, an early Resident reflected, except that 'we must first create the government to be advised'. In practice, another explained, 'instead of the Sultan carrying on the administration with the advice of the Resident', apart from matters affecting Islamic religion and custom, the Resident actually conducted the government, referring to the sultan only occasionally.[21]

The closest African approximation to the Malayan system was in the kingdoms of Buganda and Bunyoro, both in the East African Protectorate of Uganda, where native authorities were not incorporated into the British governing structure. It

[19] C. H. Philips, *The Evolution of India and Pakistan, 1858–1947: Select Documents* (London, 1962), pp. 429–31.

[20] 19 June 1947, Nicholas Mansergh and others, eds., *The Transfer of Power*, 12 vols. (London, 1970–83), XI, pp. 114–22. See also Ian Copland, *The Princes of India in the Endgame of Empire, 1917–1947* (Cambridge, 1997).

[21] Simon Smith, *British Relations with the Malay Rulers from Decentralization to Malayan Independence, 1930–1957* (Kuala Lumpur, 1995), p. 4.

was direct rule by the chiefs (such as the Kabaka of Buganda), subject to British overrule (including removal).[22]

Another type of indirect governance was found in early toeholds in West Africa, notably Cape Coast Colony in the Gold Coast (now Ghana) and the island of Lagos off the Niger coast. These colonies had Legislative Councils with nominated, non-official members who regarded themselves as a loyal opposition, as well as newspapers critical of government. A few Africans held important administrative positions.[23]

Yet another version of Indirect Rule developed with respect to the loosely organized, so-called stateless peoples of Southern Nigeria, Kenya, or Tanganyika, whose political institutions had either remained rudimentary or been destroyed by European military action. Here 'foreigners' (such as the Akidas, or military functionaries, under German rule in East Africa) or relatively unimportant individuals (such as the warrant chiefs in Southern Nigeria) were imported or raised above their former stations. Again, purists would have resisted including such examples under Indirect Rule—but neither were they direct.

Provided a loose model is adopted, provided the emphasis is placed on 'indirect' rather than on 'administration', then of course the British practised it very widely indeed throughout the Middle East and elsewhere, especially in the Muslim World.[24] Except in Palestine, where the territory was so sharply contested between Arabs and Jews, it would have been hard to find much that resembled what Lugard or the mid-Victorian Governor Sir George Grey would have called 'native administration'. But that was also true of Malaya and the Indian princely states.

By far the best-known form of Indirect Rule was found in Northern Nigeria, comparable versions being found in the Northern Territory of the Gold Coast, the Mandate of Tanganyika, the southern Sudan, Barotseland in Northern Rhodesia, Matabeleland in Southern Rhodesia, the three British High Commission Territories (Basutoland, Bechuanaland, Swaziland), as well as Zululand and Transkei in South Africa proper. In this category strong Native Authorities were incorporated into the British (or South African) governing structures, running along what were said to be authentic African lines. These authorities ordinarily possessed native treasuries, with chiefs exercising varying degrees of financial autonomy; advisory councils composed of sub-chiefs or leading elders; and courts, where certain classes of cases were tried according to traditional law and custom and (much to the displeasure of British-trained African lawyers) without recourse to legal forms

[22] D. Anthony Low and R. Cranford Pratt, *Buganda and British Overrule, 1900–1955* (London, 1960); D. A. Low, *Buganda in Modern History* (Berkeley, 1971); Michael Twaddle, *Kakunzulu and the Creation of Uganda, 1868–1928* (London, 1993).

[23] Martin Wight, *British Colonial Constitutions* (Oxford, 1947).

[24] See chap. by Francis Robinson, esp. pp. 407–411.

or counsel. During its heyday the structures and processes of Indirect Rule were the subject of painstaking scrutiny and comparison. After the Second World War, as the author of the last comprehensive survey put it, the precise details were already of little more than antiquarian interest.[25]

Traditionally the credit for developing Indirect Rule has gone to Frederick (later Baron) Lugard, who served as High Commissioner of the Northern Nigerian Protectorate (1900–06) and, after an interval in Hong Kong, as Governor-General of Nigeria (1912–18). By the end of his first appointment in 1906, according to his biographer, Margery Perham, he had created 'the most comprehensive, coherent, and renowned system of administration' in British Imperial history.[26] In his second posting, charged with amalgamating the whole of Nigeria, he was admittedly less successful, hampered by his impatience and lack of understanding of the southern and western regions. Even so, Perham insisted, his great contribution could not be denied.

Not the least of Lugard's achievements, Perham argued, was in being so widely imitated. In Tanganyika his former lieutenant, Sir Donald Cameron, developed Indirect Rule primarily as a counter-force to the white settlers of Kenya. In the late 1920s Sir John Maffey, who had previously served with the Government of India's Political Department, instituted the system in the Sudan. Meanwhile Lugard's classic book, *The Dual Mandate* (1922), which held that 'civilized' peoples had the obligation both to develop the resources of backward areas and to protect their indigenous inhabitants, had consolidated his reputation. For nearly two decades, until he was replaced by Lord Hailey in the late 1930s, he was the leading standard-bearer of Britain's Africanist establishment. Indirect Rule became *the* hallmark of British tropical Africa, hailed as a humane and far-sighted alternative to either the policy of assimilation of the French and Portuguese or the doctrine of segregation in southern Africa.

After a quarter-century of revision not much of the Lugard myth is left.[27] By no means a great or even a competent administrator, his detractors contend, he was

[25] W. Malcolm Hailey, *Native Administration in the British African Territories*, 5 vols. (London, 1953–55). See also the first edition of Lord Hailey's *An African Survey: A Study of Problems Arising in Africa South of the Sahara* (Oxford, 1938); Frederick D. Lugard, *Political Memoranda: Revision of Instructions to Political Officers on Subjects Chiefly Political and Administrative*, 3rd edn. (London, 1970); Sir F. D. Lugard, *The Dual Mandate in British Tropical Africa* (London, 1922); Lucy P. Mair, *Native Policies in Africa* (London, 1936); and Margery Perham, *Native Administration in Nigeria* (London, 1962). There are useful documents in S. R. Ashton and S. E. Stockwell, eds., *Imperial Policy and Colonial Practice, 1925–1945*, British Documents on the End of Empire Project (BDEEP) Series A, (London, 1996), Part 1, chap. 3. For a revealing fictitious account of the operation of a Nigerian Native Authority, see Joyce Cary's novel, *Mister Johnson* (New York, 1951).

[26] Margery Perham, *Lugard*, 2 vols. (London, 1956–60), II, p. 138.

[27] I. F. Nicolson, *The Administration of Nigeria: Men, Methods and Myths* (Oxford, 1969); John E. Flint, 'Nigeria, The Colonial Experience from 1880 to 1914', in L. H. Gann and Peter Duignan, eds.,

actually a skilful propagandist. To that end he was fortunate to have a well-connected journalist, Flora Shaw, as wife, and the foremost Africanist of her generation, Margery Perham, as protégé and biographer. Above all, Lugard was an autocrat, obsessed with removing any and all obstacles to his authority. He found the Muslim emirs of the North attractive because they too were autocratic and because, as conquering aliens from the Sudan, they depended on the British to maintain them. By every normal test of colonial government, the revisionists contend—finance, trade, industry, education, public health—Northern Nigeria was a failure, especially compared to the more prosperous, less militarist administrations in the west and south. In those areas indirect rule meant not incorporating a ruling class into an authoritarian chain of command but the humbler, if more exacting, task of getting along with Africans in power. Although the fact was disguised by the selection of Lugard to direct the operation, the imperative reason for amalgamation was to enable the despised but financially solvent South to subsidize the venerated but bankrupt North. Lugard's *Dual Mandate* has also been demolished, found to be full of petty, long-standing feuds with the Colonial Office and colleagues, strong prejudice against educated Africans, and racialist views that read strangely even for the 1920s.

The earlier version of the spread of Indirect Rule has also been revised. In Northern Nigeria, at least, Lugard had no alternative. That was not the case in the Sudan, where native authorities had been employed ever since the beginning of the Anglo-Egyptian Condominium in the 1890s. When Sir John Maffey instituted the system formally in the 1920s, his motive was to seal off the backward South from the advanced North, and the whole territory from the still more rebellious Egyptians. Indirect Rule would buy time, Maffey explained, splitting the South into 'nicely balanced compartments, protective glands against the septic germs' that would 'inevitably be passed on from the Khartoum of the future'.[28] The point being to exclude Northerners, who could have been hired for less, the number of *British* officials actually increased. In the Sudan Indirect Rule, therefore, turned out to be more expensive.

Contemporaries would have broken this broad grouping into at least two subcategories: one for West Africa, the other for South and East. Indeed, the

Colonialism in Africa, 1870–1960, 5 vols. (Cambridge, 1969–75), I, pp. 220–60; Flint, 'Frederick Lugard: The Making of an Autocrat, 1858–1943', in Gann and Duignan, eds., *African Proconsuls: European Governors in Africa* (New York, 1978), pp. 290–312; Adiele Afigbo, *The Warrant Chiefs: Indirect Rule in Southeastern Nigeria, 1891–1929* (New York, 1972); Joseph Atanda, *The New Oyo Empire: Indirect Rule and Change in Western Nigeria, 1894–1934* (New York, 1973); Mary Bull, 'Indirect Rule in Northern Nigeria, 1906–1911', in Kenneth Robinson and Frederick Madden, eds., *Essays in Imperial Government Presented to Margery Perham* (London, 1963), pp. 47–87.

[28] Martin Daly, *Empire on the Nile: The Anglo-Egyptian Sudan, 1898–1934* (Cambridge, 1986), p. 366.

comparison between Northern Nigeria (where Muslim emirs, often in walled cities, ruling over a conquered population, applying direct taxation and Islamic law) and the Transkei (lying between two large zones of white settlement, functioning as an impoverished labour reserve, with no hope of autonomy) does seem somewhat strained. Yet the High Commission Territories, Tanganyika, and Matabeleland all differed from both the Nigerian and Transkeian models—as well as from each other.

On balance, Indirect Rule was inefficient and unprogressive, but (the example of Sudan notwithstanding) relatively inexpensive. It had no role for educated Africans. Moreover, confined as it was to local authorities possessing little or no connection to the central administration, it had no relevance to the political future of independent African states—a point Africans understood clearly. The fact that it became known as the arch-antithesis of segregation was more the achievement of Margery Perham herself than of the Governors about whom she wrote. Finally, as some observers noted at the time, the primary importance of Indirect Rule was not as a system but a philosophy, a justification for the British colonial order in tropical Africa.[29]

It is easy to take the categorization of 'native administration' much too seriously. The main point is not the precise gradations of indirect governance, or even whether control was direct or indirect. It was the adoption across virtually the entire dependent Empire of one or another version of the basic hierarchical structure that has been common to all empires: Mughal, Ottoman, Chinese, or Russian land agglomerations, as well as the French, Dutch, or Spanish seaborne varieties. 'It was a prefectural administration,' one historian has written, 'staffed by an élite cadre of political officers acting as direct agents of the central government and exercising diffuse and wide-ranging powers within the territorial subdivisions.'[30]

The prefectural system works like a military chain of command. Although British colonial officials were ultimately subject to ministers responsible to a democratically elected Parliament, perhaps their temperaments but more probably their early job experiences bent them in an authoritarian direction. Nor did they necessarily represent social forces or classes dominant at home. Although some of them did fit the model of an atavistic warrior class, they were more likely to be aspiring gentry.[31] Their primary loyalty was to the largely self-defined missions of their services, in communities they helped to imagine called 'India',

[29] W. Malcolm Hailey, 'Some Problems Dealt with in the "African Survey"', *International Affairs*, XVIII (1939), pp. 194–210.

[30] Bruce Berman, *Control and Crisis in Colonial Kenya* (London, 1990).

[31] Joseph Schumpeter, *Imperialism and Social Classes* (New York, 1951).

'Nigeria', or 'Palestine'. They were élite administrators: gentlemen first, capitalists (if at all) a distant second.

Like feudalism, prefectural systems contain persistent structural tension between centre and periphery. (Indeed, the break-out by the Nawab of Bengal from the Mughal Emperor in Delhi in the mid-eighteenth century had given the East India Company its chance in the subcontinent in the first place.)[32] Empires have tried to solve the problem in various ways: choosing bureaucrats from alien ethnic or religious groups, circulating them frequently, even requiring them to be slaves or eunuchs. The Chinese and Mughals, as well as the Indian Civil Service, had candidates spend years preparing for competitive examinations, the purpose being not only to select the most able young men but to ensure their indoctrination. Although the headstrong 'man-on-the-spot' is a mainstay of British Imperial history, in the twentieth century improving communications ordinarily kept insubordination in check.

In India the decision to retain princely states was a political choice. In Africa, except for Egypt and the northern Sudan which (like India) possessed large educated classes, or South Africa and Southern Rhodesia with their substantial white minorities, the option of using local people to operate a large, direct, centralized administration did not exist. Some sort of indirect approach was ubiquitous, not only for the British, who made a virtue of it, but for the French or Portuguese, who did not. If colonial officials thought traditional structures too weak (or too dangerous), they might promote local men from obscurity or bring in outsiders. But that was comparatively rare.

Service Ideologies

Like other colonial rulers, the British developed stereotypes of indigenous peoples, which they used to maintain alliances with some groups and deny the legitimacy of others. Well-known favourable examples included the so-called martial races (Punjabis in India, Masai in Kenya, or Muslim Northerners in Nigeria), as opposed to educated lawyers or journalists (the Indian 'babu', the African 'mission boy'), who were portrayed as effeminate, speaking exaggeratedly correct English, and thinking themselves above manual work (as, of course, did the white man in the tropics). Over time these stereotypes took on lives of their own, becoming formidable mechanisms of manipulation.[33]

[32] C. A. Bayly, *Imperial Meridian: The British Empire and the World, 1780–1830* (London, 1989).

[33] The classic work is Edward M. Said, *Orientalism* (New York, 1978). On gender: Anne McClintock, *Imperial Leather: Race, Gender, and Sexuality in the Colonial Conquest* (London, 1995). On India: Ronald Inden, *Imagining India* (Oxford, 1990); Bernard S. Cohn, *An Anthropologist among the Historians and Other Essays* (Delhi, 1987) and *Colonialism and its Forms of Knowledge: The British in India*

More broadly, Britain's Imperial services needed rationales to reinforce morale and justify to outsiders what it meant to be 'something in India' or Africa. Such doctrines needed to be not only morally defensible but intellectually respectable, compatible with prevailing scientific and especially anthropological ideas. During the century before the Second World War, at which time the explosion of colonial nationalism threw imperialism in all its guises on the defensive, two doctrines were outstanding. The first, which had its heyday in nineteenth-century India, was the social-evolutionary theory centring on the village community. The second, which in some ways was a direct descendant, prevailed in British West Africa and other colonies where white settlers did not gain substantial power. It was Indirect Rule, supported by the functional school of anthropology. Into these ideologies Imperial civil servants were inducted in various ways: in examinations, in probationary years at university, or in Margery Perham's Oxford summer school sessions for officials on leave from Africa.

In the evolution of British efforts to understand, stereotype, and therefore manipulate 'India', the concept of an ancient and ideal village-community (*panch*) had a long run. Once upon a time, it was said, in the distant Aryan past, small and isolated agrarian communities had governed, taxed, defended, and adjudicated themselves. Moreover, in some places, where conquerors had not taken over, imposing both authoritarian rule and alien concepts of governance, those communities still functioned. Theirs was the authentic Indian way. During the late eighteenth and early nineteenth centuries such 'Orientalists' as Sir Thomas Munro and Sir Charles Metcalfe pressed the doctrine into service on behalf of the *ryotwari* system of land tenure against its primary competitor, the *zamindari* system associated with the so-called Permanent Settlement of Lord Cornwallis during the 1790s in Bengal. Later they employed it in resisting the Utilitarian campaign in favour of westernization, which was highlighted by Sir Thomas Babington (later Lord) Macaulay's famous education Minute of the early 1830s.[34]

The village community doctrine gained new strength as part of the general recoil against cultural intervention that set in after the great Indian Mutiny of 1857–58. Although many writers were cited, including the American anthropologist Lewis Morgan, the primary exponent was Sir Henry Maine, author of the

(Princeton, 1996); and Thomas R. Metcalf, *Ideologies of the Raj* (Cambridge, 1994). On Africa: V. Y. Mudimbe, *The Invention of Africa* (Bloomington, Ind., 1988). The list could be extended considerably.

[34] The classic work is Eric Stokes, *The English Utilitarians and India* (Oxford, 1959). Very briefly (and somewhat oversimplified), under the *ryotwari* system cultivators were treated as tenants of the state, paying taxes directly to the government, who revised assessments more or less annually according to crop yields. Under the *zamindari* system big landlords (called *zamindars* or, in Oudh, *talukdars*) collected rent from their tenants, paying a fixed proportion to the state in the form of revenue, making them tax-farmers. *Zamindari* was located in the North-East (Bengal, Bihar, Uttar Pradesh); *ryotwari* in the South, the West (Bombay) and the Punjab.

influential *Ancient Law*. During the 1850s, sandwiched between appointments at Oxford and Cambridge, where many Indian Civil Service probationers attended his courses, Maine was Law Member of the Viceroy's Council. His central idea was that the village community was the primordial unit not merely for India but throughout Indo-European societies—or Aryan, as they were usually called. In Europe the ancient prototype had long been superseded. In India it could still be observed, still in good working order. In their ideal form such communities were miniature republics: self-contained, self-sufficient, self-regulating. Other villages had evolved into little kingdoms, having been taken over by outsiders who owned the means of production and governed despotically. The Indian village, Maine insisted, was much like the German or Scandinavian *mark*, the venerable forest settlement where the seeds of Western democracy had originally been sown.[35]

Like Marx's scheme of successive historical epochs based on dominant modes of production, Maine's village community was a simple comparative formula with considerable explanatory power. Since societies in different parts of the world were supposed to have gone through the same broad evolutionary stages, contemporary India held the keys to the past of Europe itself. In India the forces could be observed at first-hand that had shaped the great historical transitions: from *mark* to manor, from lordship to kingship, from communal to private property, from custom to law, or, in Maine's famous phrase, from status to contract. Like the tribal stereotype later on in Africa, the village community model enabled District Officers to work confidently at a local level—given the realities of communications, the only level practical—with tangible, manageable units that could be seen, surveyed, counted, and smelled, all within the relatively confined boundaries of their own jurisdictions. With its aid they could find the pulse of India. And what could be felt could be controlled. Breaking a civilization down into component parts made it easier to reify or construct other units, such as caste, ethnic, or religious communities, which could be played off against one another in the common Imperial tactic of divide and rule.[36]

For Indian civil servants of the late nineteenth century Maine's village community concept was intellectually attractive. It transformed what would otherwise have been the humdrum busy work of surveying and counting into

[35] Henry Maine, *Ancient Law: Its Connection with the Early History of Society and its Relation to Modern Ideas* (1861; Boston, 1963), and *Village-Communities in the East and West*, 7th edn. (London, 1895); Lewis Morgan, *Ancient Society* (1878; Cambridge, Mass., 1964). Clive Dewey, 'The Influence of Sir Henry Maine on Agrarian Society in India', in Alan Diamond, ed., *The Victorian Achievement of Sir Henry Maine* (Cambridge, 1991), pp. 353–75, and *The Settlement Literature of the Greater Punjab: A Handbook* (New Delhi, 1991); J. W. Burrow, *Evolution and Society: A Study in Victorian Social Theory* (Cambridge, 1966).

[36] This is the point of departure of the prolific and important Subaltern School. See the series of *Subaltern Studies* (1982–), ed. Ranajit Guha, and others, and particularly Gyanendra Pandey, *The Construction of Communalism in Colonial North India* (Delhi, 1990).

exciting pioneering research. For each village officers mapped out detailed records of rights: ownership, landlordship, tenancy, and land left in common. Their Settlement Reports (or tax assessments), some of which rank as anthropological classics, were supposed to make it possible to reconstruct and reconnect long-separated segments of the Indo-European past. The village community doctrine was also central to the long, intense debate over what tended to be transfers of land from long-standing agricultural to moneylending classes, British law having unfortunately upset the balance in favour of the latter. The result was a series of agrarian laws designed to protect 'agriculturalists', often patterned on those in Ireland, notably the Deccan Agriculturists' Relief Act (1879), the Bengal Tenancy Act (1885), and the Punjab Alienation Act (1900).[37] Some measures tried to prevent tenant revolts by regulating rent increases; others prohibited landowners whose caste names appeared on lists of hereditary agricultural 'tribes' from contracting mortgages that might result in foreclosure; still others authorized courts to administer debt-ridden estates. This legislation, which would echo loudly in Egypt, Palestine, and tropical Africa, revealed the paternal, pro-agrarian, even anti-capitalist face of British colonialism.[38]

The African counterpart of Maine's village community concept was the doctrine of Indirect Rule, supported intellectually by the functional school of anthropology most closely associated with Bronislaw Malinowski of the London School of Economics. The organizational base was the Institute of African Languages and Cultures, founded in the 1920s by the missionary leader Joseph Oldham, in partnership with the ubiquitous Lugard. Malinowski gave the enterprise academic connections and prestige. African societies could accept some changes, he argued, provided they were not incompatible with the still-functioning but fragile whole of primitive society, and provided they were implemented slowly. If anthropologists were given employment, he promised, or at the least research grants, they could provide colonial governments with valuable practical advice. In 1927, skimming through Lugard's *Dual Mandate* before talking with the author, Malinowski noted tersely that if the Proconsul 'had wanted to control Scientific Anthrop[ology] so as to fit into his Imp[erial] idea ... he couldn't have done anything but to create [the] Functional School'. Indirect Rule was a 'Complete Surrender to the Functional Point of View'. Or was it the other way around?[39]

[37] Dewey, *Settlement Literature*; Thomas R. Metcalf, *Land, Landlords and the British Raj* (Berkeley, 1979); Septimus Thorburn, *Musulmans and Money-Lenders in the Punjab* (1886; Delhi, 1983).

[38] Cell, *Hailey*, pp. 276–78.

[39] Bronislaw Malinowski, 'Practical Anthropology', *Africa*, II (1929), pp. 22–38; George Stocking, Jr., ed., *Functionalism Historicized: Essays on British Social Anthropology* (Madison, 1984); Stocking, ed., *Colonial Situations: Essays on the Contextualization of Ethnographic Knowledge* (Madison, 1991); Henrika Kuklick, *The Savage Within: The Social History of British Anthropology, 1885–1945* (Cambridge, 1991);

Malinowski's special pleading notwithstanding, the practical effect of anthropologists was mixed. Some practitioners, notably Godfrey Wilson of the Rhodes–Livingstone Institute in Northern Rhodesia (Zambia), carried out important research on such problems as conditions in copper-mines or the impact of migrant labour on the African family, and reached conclusions that were highly unpopular with powerful white interests. Other anthropologists coerced reluctant informants or provided their government employers with valuable military intelligence. Overall, the practical impact was limited. Colonial officials tended to distrust academics, who in the official view were always criticizing, preferred small, apparently insignificant subjects, and took an unconscionably long time to obtain results.

As Lugard's largely sympathetic biographer, as well as author of a large number of important studies of contemporary 'native administrations', Margery Perham tied herself closely and enthusiastically to the doctrine of Indirect Rule. Having attended Malinowski's seminars, she popularized his 'functional ideas'. Whereas anthropologists for the most part maintained an arms-length relationship with colonial officers, hers could hardly have been closer: teaching them in probationary courses and summer schools at Oxford, touring with them, working on confidential files in their offices, and carrying on extensive professional correspondence. She taught numerous Africans, including Kofi Busia and Tom Mboya, and corresponded with them as well. She served on numerous Colonial Office committees, especially on education. Whereas Malinowski's influence was entrepreneurial and somewhat fleeting, hers was solid and enduring. Through her books, radio broadcasts, and especially her frequent letters to *The Times*, she was a fervent colonial reformer. Sometimes she criticized, but not much. More than any other person, she raised her country's consciousness of Africa.[40]

The philosophy of Indirect Rule thrived in the tropical dependencies of West Africa, places with climates unattractive to Europeans, with cash-crop

Adam Kuper, *Anthropologists and Anthropology: The British School, 1922–1972* (New York, 1975); Talal Asad, ed., *Anthropology and the Colonial Encounter* (Atlantic Highlands, NJ, 1973); A. D. Roberts, 'The Imperial Mind', in Roberts, ed., *The Colonial Moment in Africa* (Cambridge, 1990), VII, pp. 24–76; Martin Chanock, *Law, Custom and Social Order: The Colonial Experience in Malawi and Zambia* (Cambridge, 1985), chap. 2; John W. Cell, 'Lord Hailey and the Making of the African Survey', *AA*, LXXXVIII (1989), pp. 481–505. For a sharp rebuttal of Malinoski's views by an anthropologist, which focuses on the personalities and motives of the anthropologists themselves, see Jack Goody, *The Expansive Moment: The Rise of Social Anthropology in Britain and Africa, 1918–1970* (Cambridge, 1995).

[40] In addition to her two-volumed biography of Lugard, see particularly *Native Administrations in Nigeria* (London, 1937); the collection of articles and letters to newspapers in *The Colonial Reckoning: The End of Imperial Rule in Africa in the Light of British Experience*, 2 vols. (London, 1962); and the post-mortem symposium volume edited by Alison Smith and Mary Bull, *Margery Perham and British Rule in Africa* (London, 1991).

economies centred on peasant production. From there it spread to the Sudan and the East African colonies of Uganda and Tanganyika. The doctrine (as opposed to the practice) did not take root in colonies of settlement: South Africa, Southern Rhodesia (Zimbabwe), or Kenya. In this second, distinctly different part of Africa, where expansionists such as Cecil Rhodes, Leopold Amery, and Jan Smuts envisioned new white Dominions, the prevailing theme was segregation.

During the 1930s, and especially after the Second World War, when the colonial reform movement in Britain confronted an insurgent Afrikaner National Party intent on taking segregation—apartheid—to its logical conclusion, the two traditions came to represent increasingly hostile camps. Earlier in the century the relationship had been more complementary than antagonistic. The two schools employed a common vocabulary, shared assumptions about race and culture, and drew on the same bank of anthropological theory. In its early stages, indeed, the doctrine of segregation was quite as much British as Afrikaner.[41] Typically, Afrikaners had practised slavery and other direct, vertical forms of dominance (*baaskap*) rather than the indirect, horizontal varieties that, at least in theory, were characteristic of segregation. Afrikaners had also been less fussy about disguising their intentions.

Until well into the twentieth century the South and West African schools of African administration remained closely intertwined. Lugard recommended racial segregation throughout the tropics, for example, and though he did so on grounds of health, especially as a means of combating malaria, White Man's Countries used that pretext too.[42] Nor were well-intentioned people restricted to West Africa. In South Africa the predominantly English-speaking members of the Native Affairs Department carried on the relatively liberal Cape tradition, striving to maintain at least a modicum of interracial balance.[43] If assumptions about the future of Africans were set aside, and before the Second World War those were not all that different either, Bantustans and indirectly ruled tropical colonies had a great deal in common.[44] All of them claimed to be helping Africans develop on 'their own

[41] David Welsh, *The Roots of Segregation: Native Policy in Natal, 1845–1910* (Cape Town, 1971); Martin Legassick, 'The Making of South African "Native Policy"', and 'The Rise of Modern South African Liberalism', Institute of Commonwealth Studies, University of London, 1972–73; John W. Cell, *The Highest Stage of White Supremacy: The Origins of Segregation in South Africa and the American South* (Cambridge, 1982).

[42] Maynard Swanson, 'The Sanitation Syndrome: Bubonic Plague and Urban Native Policy in the Cape Colony, 1900–1909', *Journal of African History*, XVIII (1977), pp. 387–410.

[43] Saul Dubow, *Racial Segregation and the Origins of Apartheid in South Africa, 1919–36* (London, 1989).

[44] John E. Flint, 'Planned Decolonization and Its Failure in British Africa', *AA*, LXXXII (1983), pp. 389–412.

lines'. All of them were small-scale and static. All of them assumed a lengthy period of dependency. None of them had a place for educated Africans.

In 1940 the Secretary of State for the Colonies, Malcolm MacDonald, asked Lord Hailey to make a tour of Britain's colonies. The secret part of the assignment (which was not covered in the published version of his report that was distributed confidentially to colonial officials), was to assess the advisability of the proposed amalgamation of Southern and Northern Rhodesia, the former an internally self-governing colony dominated by settlers, the latter a British Protectorate (with a significant white population), which was supposedly dedicated to the principles of trusteeship. In fact, Hailey discovered, the White Man's Country was spending a good deal more on education, health, and other development programmes. Only if assumptions about the future of the country remaining under white control were taken into account could Southern Rhodesia's policies be faulted.[45]

Where, MacDonald asked Hailey to determine, was Indirect Rule going?[46] Hailey's simple answer was 'nowhere'—and historians have largely confirmed his verdict. Why, then, did a generation of colonial officials, as well as thoughtful, liberal-minded people such as Margery Perham, paint such an optimistic picture? One reason is the widespread disillusion of inter-war Europeans with Western civilization. Better to retain African customs and institutions, they often concluded, modifying slowly and cautiously. Indirect Rule was like scaffolding around a building, Perham put it, the impermanent external planks European, the permanent structure African. One day, the core having proved capable of standing on its own, the scaffolding would be removed. Africans should not be allowed to become pseudo-Europeans, both Lugard and General Smuts insisted; instead, they should 'evolve on their own lines'.[47] Having been a critic of Indirect Rule in the 1930s and early war years, Hailey became a defender, his reason being strong and (it turned out) well-founded doubts about the suitability of the Westminster model for Africa, especially the concept of a loyal opposition.

A second reason for the longevity of Indirect Rule was that, like the earlier village community doctrine in India, it bolstered the morale of the colonial service. Lugardism gave local officials 'a fascinating job to do', Frederick Pedler of the Colonial Office observed, a sense of mission, a belief that they were doing something important, instead of simply holding power until Africans became sufficiently advanced in the techniques of political agitation to make it clear that the time had come to leave. Like the village community formula, the model of the 'tribe' reduced the huge, complex, baffling continent of Africa to a small scale, one

[45] Hailey, *Native Administration and Political Development.*

[46] Ashton and Stockwell, eds., *Imperial Policy*, I, Docs. 55 and 56.

[47] J. C. Smuts, *Africa and Some World Problems* (Oxford, 1930).

well within the compass of ordinary District Officers, enabling them to 'see results inside the sphere of [their] own activity'.[48] As Hailey's wartime report warned, however, nationalism was rooted in the soil of all colonial societies, Asian or African alike. Any form of governance that contained no place for educated Africans would become obsolete very soon. Indeed, once the British began to think at all seriously about the possibility of African self-government, Indirect Rule was discarded.[49]

By the 1890s investigators in India had uncovered such a wide assortment of types of villages as to raise doubts about whether any such thing as a model village community had ever existed at all. Maine's doctrine, therefore, began to lose much of its intellectual attraction for British officials. Ironically, Gandhi gave the idea a new lease of life. Much the same thing happened to anthropological theory in Africa. With its emphasis on little democracies, largely self-sufficient and self-contained, land and other means of subsistence being held in common, the language of Indirect Rule bore a striking resemblance to that of African socialism. It was both fascinating and troubling to see the scepticism of a Lugard or a Hailey about whether Africans could manage a Western-style political system being repeated in almost identical terms by politicians justifying *de jure* one-party rule as the 'traditional', authentic African way.

Although the importance of Indirect Rule as a working administrative system was limited, in other ways its impact was considerable. It severely curbed the political experience of future African or Asian leaders. When members of the educated, westernized élite took control, as they did nearly everywhere, they were experts on how to organize political parties or lead military manœuvres, but not on how to govern and certainly not on how to tolerate a loyal opposition. Indirect Rule also built up some groups at the expense of others. The Residency system in Malaya, for example, enhanced the power of the sultans against chiefs in the second tier.[50] Except for their alliance with the British, the Muslim emirs of Northern Nigeria might well have been forced to retreat.

Moreover, the practitioners of Indirect Rule oversimplified and stereotyped groups and institutions. African historians agree that traditional identities and allegiances were much less fixed and permanent than was formerly supposed. Colonialism in general, and Indirect Rule in particular, lumped all Africans into

[48] Pedler note, 11 March 1946, C[olonial] O[ffice] 847/25/7.

[49] Circular No. 41, 25 Feb. 1947. This and other documents are printed in Ronald Hyam, ed., *The Labour Government and the End of Empire, 1945–1951*, BDEEP, 4 vols. (London, 1992), I, 112–57. See also Ronald Robinson, 'Why "Indirect Rule" has been Replaced by "Local Government" in the Nomenclature of British Native Administration', *Journal of African Administration*, II, 3 (1950), pp. 12–15.

[50] J. M. Gullick, *Rulers and Residents: Influence and Power in the Malay States, 1870–1920* (Singapore, 1992).

artificially constructed units called 'tribes', a word implying something too large and formal for some African political systems, too small and informal for others.[51]

Except in the purest type of settlement colonies, such as Australia or the United States, where indigenous peoples were decimated to a degree approaching political and demographic extinction, colonial domination required collaboration, which in turn shaped the character and operation of the regime.[52] Although the existence of collaborators might be inevitable, their identity was often a matter of choice. Sometimes they were the new comprador class, a modernizing élite, Western-educated, in many ways like the Europeans themselves, such as the so-called *bhadralok* in early-nineteenth-century Bengal or the educated, often Christian Africans of late-nineteenth-century Lagos.

At least until experience taught them otherwise, such people were likely to favour British expansion. Hoping the colonial state would attack reactionary leaders, customs, and institutions, thereby providing a short cut toward their goal of a modern, progressive nation, they saw themselves as the natural allies of the colonizers as well as their successors.[53] Many from this class, such as the ubiquitous Igbo clerks in Northern Nigeria and the still more numerous native officials in India, did indeed work for the British. Moreover, in the long run it was Western-educated leaders who proved most adept at organizing political parties, promoting agitation, and taking control of state structures after the Europeans had departed.

During the colonial era itself, however, Western-educated élites were usually bitterly disappointed. Instead of removing reactionaries from positions of authority, the British tended to uphold them. How ironic, observed Jawaharlal Nehru, the product of Harrow and Cambridge, to see representatives of the dynamic, progressive West allying themselves with the princely and landlord classes, the most conservative components of the static, backward East.[54] However it might be disguised with anthropological jargon, indirect rule in all its forms—Indian princely states, Malayan sultanates, Nigerian emirates, African kingdoms in Uganda—sought to freeze colonial societies, to slow and control the pace of change. Its long-term positive influence was limited.

The last of the Imperial service ideologies was that of the Commonwealth itself. This was a vision of emerging nationhood for which the models were the white

[51] Elizabeth Colson, 'African Society at the Time of the Scramble', in Gann and Duignan, eds., *Colonialism in Africa*, I, pp. 27–65.

[52] Ronald Robinson, 'Non-European Foundations of European Imperialism: Sketch for a Theory of Collaboration', in Roger Owen and Bob Sutcliffe, eds., *Studies in the Theory of Imperialism* (London, 1972).

[53] Flint, 'Nigeria: The Colonial Experience'.

[54] Jawaharlal Nehru, *The Discovery of India* (London, 1936).

Dominions of the nineteenth and early twentieth centuries. Having been formalized only after the First World War in the Balfour definition of 1926 and the Statute of Westminster of 1931, Dominion Status had been promised to India in 1929 and then confirmed in 1942. By then the language of the Commonwealth was already beginning to be applied to Africa–but tentatively, in relation to a still-distant future.

The idea of the Commonwealth was closely linked to a still more venerable doctrine, that of trusteeship, the origins of which can be found in Edmund Burke's impeachment campaign against Warren Hastings of the East India Company in the late eighteenth century and the anti-slavery crusade of the early nineteenth.[55] After the First World War the concept had resurfaced in the League of Nations Mandates system, which attempted to disguise what was actually a reasonably straightforward transfer of colonies from losers to winners. Still later the word 'partner' was substituted for 'trustee', the latter having been discovered to have disconcertingly paternalist implications. Like other ideologies, that of the Commonwealth was partly myth—but since normal, ordinarily well-meaning individuals believed in it, it did shape behaviour.

In 1953 Lord Hailey was asked to state, in a five-minute radio broadcast, 'What I Believe'. Although he had once been religious in the usual sense, he said, his long Asian experience had given his beliefs a secular, even sociological basis—for he had known many moral individuals, from many faiths, so that morality did not seem to be grounded in any particular religion. 'I believe', he said, that 'we must look to the moral or social code which has been developed by human society as one of the instruments of its own improvement.' He had been struck by how 'a code of behaviour starting in a family group will in time be adopted as the code of a tribe or of a larger unit of society'. He had 'seen groups of different origin united for the first time in a nation', held together by such a social code. He left unspoken his own role: holding the ring while new societies, or old ones that had disintegrated, prepared to stand by themselves as modern nations.

'Let me join with the Psalmist', concluded the last of the great British Imperial Proconsuls, 'in thanking Providence for the diversity of its creatures.'[56] A listener familiar with Lord Hailey's career might have recognized the Commonwealth. It was an idea in which, by the 1950s, many of the British people and their governing class no longer believed. The speaker's generation had devoted their lives to it.

The Commonwealth vision came closest to realization at a time when the British Empire itself was nearing its end in the 1950s. Once again, ideology served

[55] In Vol. III, see chap. 10 by Andrew Porter, esp. pp. 198–203, 220.

[56] 29 June 1953. Transcript in Hailey Papers, Rhodes House, Oxford, MSS Brit. Emp. s 339. The broadcast was in a series introduced by the American correspondent Edward R. Murrow.

to mystify reality. Many British officials were uncomfortable serving under African ministers; there were fears of an exodus so severe that it might cause administrative collapse; sobering reports described the lack of competence and integrity of African politicians and administrators, notably in the police and the military; fairly precipitous haste was being dressed up to look like measured, stately transition.[57] Although the British withdrawal from the east and central African colonies came only a few years later than in the West, there the decision to leave was a snap one, prompted in part by the long and never quite completed suppression of the Mau Mau insurrection in Kenya. Given a little more than a decade in West Africa, compared with only two or three years in the East, British officials had no choice but to train their successors to sail without them into uncharted, turbulent waters. They have often been accused of setting the compass in a neo-colonialist direction. In fact, the colonial administrators themselves were largely unconcerned with economic matters outside their own districts. They were often passionately committed to the success of the independent countries they left behind.[58]

[57] See the report by F. E. Cumming-Bruce on the future of the Gold Coast, 19 Aug. 1955, in Richard Rathbone, ed., *Ghana*, BDEEP, 2 vols. (London, 1992), II, pp. 157–63.

[58] See John Smith, *Colonial Cadet in Nigeria* (Durham, NC, 1968); A. H. M. Kirk-Greene, ed., *Crisis and Conflict in Nigeria* (Oxford, 1971).

Select Bibliography

ADIELE E. AFIGBO, *The Warrant Chiefs: Indirect Rule in Southeastern Nigeria, 1891–1929* (New York, 1972).

JOHN W. CELL, *Hailey: A Study in British Imperialism, 1872–1969* (Cambridge, 1992).

TERENCE CREAGH COEN, *The Indian Political Service: A Study in Indirect Rule* (London, 1971).

MICHAEL CROWDER, *West Africa Under Colonial Rule* (London, 1968).

M. W. DALY, *Empire on the Nile: The Anglo-Egyptian Sudan, 1898–1934* (Cambridge, 1986).

RUPERT EMERSON, *Malaysia: A Study in Direct and Indirect Rule* (New York, 1937).

JOHN E. FLINT, 'Nigeria: The Colonial Experience from 1880 to 1914', in L. H. Gann and Peter Duignan, eds., *Colonialism in Africa, 1870–1960*, 5 vols. (Cambridge, 1969– 1975), I, pp. 220–60.

J. S. FURNIVALL, *Colonial Policy and Practice: A Comparative Study of Burma and Netherlands India* (Cambridge, 1948).

J. M. GULLICK, *Rulers and Residents: Influence and Power in the Malay States, 1870–1920* (Singapore, 1992).

W. MALCOLM HAILEY, *Native Administration and Political Development in British Tropical Africa: Report 1940–1963*, ed. A. H. M. Kirk-Greene (Nendeen, 1979).

ROBERT HEUSSLER, *Yesterday's Rulers: The Making of the British Colonial Service* (Syracuse, NY, 1963).

JOHN ILIFFE, *A Modern History of Tanganyika* (Cambridge, 1979).

ROBIN JEFFREY, ed., *People, Princes and Paramount Power: Society and Politics in the Indian Princely States* (Delhi, 1978).

A. H. M. KIRK-GREENE, ed., *The Principles of Native Administration in Nigeria: Selected Documents, 1900–1947* (London, 1965).

Sir F. D. LUGARD, *The Dual Mandate in British Tropical Africa* (London, 1922).

I. F. NICOLSON, *The Administration of Nigeria, 1900–1960: Men, Methods, and Myths* (Oxford, 1969).

MARGERY PERHAM, *Lugard*, 2 vols. (London, 1956–60).

—— *Native Administration in Nigeria* (1937; London, 1962).

DAVID C. POTTER, *India's Political Administrators, 1919–1983* (Oxford, 1986).

BARBARA N. RAMUSACK, *The Princes of India in the Twilight of Empire: Dissolution of a Patron–Client System, 1914–1939* (Columbus, Ohio, 1978).

11

Bureaucracy and 'Trusteeship' in the Colonial Empire

RONALD HYAM

How was the central bureaucracy of the Empire organized, and what was its role?[1] Colonial affairs had been dealt with in Whitehall by a Secretary of State since 1768, though sometimes in combination with other ministerial portfolios. Towards the end of the eighteenth century the Secretaryships of War and Colonies were combined and not finally separated until 1854. At this time the Colonial Office operated out of 12 Downing Street, a seriously dilapidated building, later pulled down and replaced by the Whips' Office. In 1875 the Office was moved to the north-east corner of the prestigious block containing the Home, Foreign, and India Offices. There was a further move to Great Smith Street in 1945. Plans for a grand new Colonial Office building in Parliament Square were abandoned in 1954 because of Winston Churchill's objection—not on the grounds that the Empire was contracting, but that it would ruin his own grandiose scheme for an enlarged Parliament Square, 'to be laid out as a truly noble setting for the heart of the British Empire'.[2] Before the routine use of the typewriter and telegraph from the 1890s, the Colonial Office was a sleepy, humdrum place. It was also, before the arrival of Joseph Chamberlain (Secretary of State, 1895–1903), a political backwater. In 1870 incoming communications totalled a mere 13,500 items. By 1900 this had risen to 42,000 and by 1905 to 50,000 a year. It was one of the smallest departments in Whitehall, with a staff of 113 by 1903. Numbers were to increase, although the Office remained comparatively small:

1935	1939	1943	1947	1954	1964
372	450	817	1139	1661	530

[1] Sir Charles Joseph Jeffries, *Whitehall and the Colonial Service: An Administrative Memoir, 1939–56*, Institute of Commonwealth Studies Paper, no. 15 (London, 1972); Joe Garner, *The Commonwealth Office, 1925–68* (London, 1978); R. B. Pugh, 'The Colonial Office, 1801–1925', in E. A. Benians and others, eds., *Cambridge History of the British Empire*, Vol. III, *1870–1919* (Cambridge, 1959), pp. 711–68; Ronald Hyam, 'The Colonial Office Mind, 1900–14', *Journal of Imperial and Commonwealth History*, VIII (1979), pp. 30–55, reprinted in Norman Hillmer and Philip G. Wigley, eds., *The First British Commonwealth: Essays in Honour of Nicholas Mansergh* (London, 1980); *The Colonial Office List* (London, annually), *passim*.

[2] David Goldsworthy, ed., *The Conservative Government and the End of Empire, 1951–1957*, British Documents on the End of Empire Project (BDEEP) (London, 1994), II, pp. 87–89.

Of these only about 70 were administrative grade secretaries (1930s).

In response to criticism that the Colonial Office was insensitive to the emerging and developing self-governing communities (Canada, Australia, New Zealand, and South Africa), a separate Dominions Department was established within the Office in 1907. This led eventually to the creation of a separate Secretaryship of State for Dominion Affairs in 1925, but until 1930 the post was held by the Secretary of State for the Colonies, L. S. Amery. The two posts remained distinct after 1931 until they were recombined in 1962 in the person of Duncan Sandys. Meanwhile the Dominions Office was renamed the Commonwealth Relations Office in 1947, when it took over residual India Office work after independence. Probably only at this point did the 'Dominions Office' (DO) acquire any real sense of purpose, even though Kashmir was to provide plenty of headaches in Commonwealth relations. A merger took place between the Colonial Office (CO) and the Commonwealth Relations Office (CRO) in 1966. Two years later a final merger with the Foreign Office (FO) established the Foreign and Commonwealth Office (1968). These changes were not uncontested. Cabinet Secretary Norman Brook, as early as 1956, was in favour of a united 'Department of Commonwealth Affairs', which would get rid of the word 'Colonial', fast becoming a term of abuse. He thought Australia and New Zealand were now mature enough not to feel threatened by this change, and all ought to appreciate the need to dispel criticism of colonial policy. Neither Office was enthusiastic, but it was increasingly recognized that there were problems in maintaining the post-1925 structure. By 1958 Alan Lennox-Boyd (Secretary of State, 1954–59) believed 'we should be thinking in terms of an ultimate merger' of colonial and Commonwealth affairs. In 1959 High Commissioners were asked for their views about the suggested amalgamation. All believed Commonwealth governments would regard being linked with colonial territories unfavourably: it would be a retrograde act which might increase the taint of 'colonialism'. (Only the government of the Central African Federation welcomed it, as leading to the disappearance of its bogey, the Colonial Office.) The High Commissioners warned that the result would probably be that the Commonwealth governments would bypass the new office and deal directly with the Foreign Office. The existence of a separate office, they argued, was living proof of the importance attached to the Commonwealth connection, and Commonwealth relations were, after all, supposed to be 'different in kind' from foreign relations.[3] However, by the end of 1962 the winding up of the Colonial Empire had proceeded to such an extent that the Prime Minister, Harold Macmillan, was in favour of amalgamating the two. Meanwhile, the Plowden Committee had tentatively

[3] Goldsworthy, *Conservative Government*, II, pp. 89–92; D[ominions] O[ffice] 35/7999, no. 18, and C[olonial] O[ffice] 1032/147, no. 161.

recommended amalgamation of the Commonwealth Relations Office and Foreign Office as the two 'diplomatic' departments, engaged on different work from the Colonial Office's 'administration' of dependencies. But Macmillan was vehemently opposed to this further merger: 'No. I think the Plowden Ctee. are on the wrong track *altogether*: I should *oppose* strongly merg[ing] Commonwealth with FO. *Politically*, it would be worse for us than the Common Market.'[4] An incoming Labour government after 1964 thought differently. The establishment of the Commonwealth Secretariat in 1965 (on Afro-Asian initiative) also fundamentally changed the situation.

Until 1925, when the separate Dominions Office was created, the work of the Colonial Office was subdivided essentially along geographical or regional lines, and these country departments were relatively self-contained. The role of the Office was supervisory. Colonies were not *administered* from London, 'the one rank heresy which we all shudder at', but by their Governors on the spot. Governors, however, acted under a general metropolitan supervision. The feasibility of a Governor's proposals would be assessed by the Colonial Office, whose officials saw their task as being 'an essential function of cautious criticism'. They were unperturbed by the argument that they lacked practical experience and firsthand knowledge of particular colonies: 'one can criticize a pudding without being a cook' (Charles Strachey). From the 1930s the Colonial Empire gradually began to be seen more as a whole, and as a stage upon which more interventionist and generally applicable policies might be evolved, beginning with Colonial Development and Welfare. Attempts at regional co-ordination increased. Administration became more and more complex and technical. Accordingly, the subject departments became more important. There had long been a General Department, dealing with promotions and transfers in the Colonial Service, postal communications and copyright inventions, uniforms and flags; only to a limited extent was it genuinely concerned with general policy. The Personnel Division was created in 1930, and the General Department developed its subject functions which then again subdivided, starting with the Economic Department (trade, colonial products) in 1934, followed by International Relations (dealing with the League of Nations Mandates), Defence, Social Service (labour, education, and health), and Development. By 1950 there were twenty-one subject departments as against eight geographical departments. A parallel development was the increase in specialist advisers. There had been a legal adviser since 1867. The Secretary of the Advisory Committee on Native Education in Tropical Africa became in 1934, in effect, the Educational Adviser. A Chief Medical Adviser was appointed in 1926, an Economic and Financial Adviser in 1928, a Fisheries Adviser in 1928, an Agricultural

[4] Minute by Macmillan, Dec. 1962, PREM[ier] 11/3816.

Adviser in 1929, an Animal Health Adviser in 1930, and a Labour Adviser in 1938. By 1960 there were thirty scientific and technical advisers, and twenty-three advisory committees. All these changes were reflected from the late 1930s in subject files becoming increasingly the focus of business, until by 1950 there were about three times as many subject files as country files. The country or geographical classes of records between 1925 and 1954 are now represented in the Public Record Office by about 55,000 surviving files for thirty years, while the subject classes for the period 1939 to 1954 alone are represented by 31,000 files for fifteen years. Co-operation between geographical and subject departments remained close. Ministers, when they took decisions, were usually advised not simply by one of the geographical departments or one of the subject departments but by both working together. And the country departments remained more important politically than the mere statistics suggest.[5]

Was there in the Colonial Office an 'official mind' on Empire problems? Although technically only the instrument of the Secretary of State, 'as a continuous institution it had in fact a corporate "mind" of its own, built up on its long tradition, the experience and personal characteristics of its staff, and the effectual influence of its constant and intimate contact with the Colonial Service'.[6] By contrast, it would have to be a powerful Secretary of State who could impose his own policy on all but a highly selected number of individual issues. The vast majority of files only went to the Secretary of State at the discretion of officials. Changes of government were seldom a problem. Political bipartisanship generally prevailed, although apparently fractured from 1964. Before then little adjustment to new parties in power was required. Temperamental differences between ministers of whatever political colour were more important, as garrulous character succeeded taciturn, slave-driver replaced indulgent, intellectual followed near-illiterate, or lazy amateur succeeded dedicated professional. Like all civil servants, Colonial Office officials were expected to be unbiased politically. However, in the broadest terms, the 'mind' of the Colonial Office was humane and progressive, unable to identify with extreme right-wing attitudes to Empire. They were proud of the Empire, but also sceptical about it. They were happiest and worked most effectively under radical administrations, such as that of the Liberal government of 1905 to 1915 and the Labour government of 1945 to 1951.

It is manifestly the case, however, that there was never a time in the twentieth century when the Colonial Office staff was of a single mind. As in all small

[5] Anne Thurston, ed., *Records of the Colonial Office, Dominions Office, Commonwealth Relations Office and Commonwealth Office*, BDEEP (London, 1995), pp. 1–29; see also a major memorandum by C. J. Jeffries, Nov. 1942, 'A Plan for the Colonial Office', in S. R. Ashton and S. E. Stockwell, eds., *Imperial Policy and Colonial Practice, 1925–1945*, BDEEP (London, 1996), I, Doc. 4.

[6] Jeffries, *Whitehall and the Colonial Service*, p. 72.

communities of intelligent people, there were tensions and strongly argued disagreements which could quickly acquire a personal dimension. The argumentativeness of its officials was remarked on ruefully by a new Permanent Under-Secretary, Sir Francis Hopwood, coming in from the outside in 1907, who found he suffered a lot and wasted too much time every day 'endeavouring to convince or coerce' the remarkable 'self-confidence in opinion' of those below him. Chamberlain, he believed, had to a certain extent 'fomented contentiousness'. In a later generation there were marked differences of approach between traditional conservatives such as Sir Hilton Poynton and Sir John Martin, and radical Young Turks such as J. S. Bennett. Nevertheless, the atmosphere was clubbish and donnish. It was also rather patronizing towards public opinion and pressure groups. Officials were generally impatient of humanitarian and missionary pressure. This was not because they did not care about human rights; on the contrary, they regarded themselves as the true and efficient guardians of 'the moral tradition', to which outside bodies, with imperfect access to full information, could add little. Too often the representations of the latter seemed inaccurate, exaggerated, sentimental, and unrealistic. And where matters of high policy, like strategic considerations or delicate diplomatic relations, were concerned, it was not possible to provide proper and convincing explanations.

These officials were a true élite of scholar-official mandarins. They were clever men, richly furnished with ability. Many of them passed high in the open competition for the Home Civil Service, some of them head of their year, among them C. P. Lucas, S. Olivier, W. A. Robinson, and A. B. Keith, the last-named passing in 1901 with more than a thousand marks more than any previous candidate. Keith had an Oxford triple first on top of his previous first-class degree from Edinburgh; he took a law doctorate by thesis in 1907, and became a Professor of Sanskrit and Comparative Philology, as well as an acknowledged authority on the constitutional history of the Empire. First-class degrees were common (unlike the Colonial Service, dominated by the 'Blues and 2.2s'). Of the later generation, J. S. Bennett had a double-starred first in History from Cambridge, the kind of result which ranks him with such professorial luminaries as Eric Hobsbawm, Sir John Elliott, or Quentin Skinner. Andrew Cohen was within six marks of first place in the 1932 entry, but had sixty marks deducted for 'bad handwriting' (he practised a large, vague script which looked like gothicized Hebrew with all the diacriticals omitted), a penalization which demoted him to fourth place. Kenneth Robinson left for an academic career which embraced the Directorship of the Institute of Commonwealth Studies in London and Vice-Chancellorship of the University of Hong Kong.

Almost the entire routine of the Colonial Office consisted in the circulation of paper among its officers in strict hierarchical sequence, each person recording his—it was usually his—opinion in minutes. Minuting tended to be more extensive and meticulous than it was in the sparser, less reflective Foreign Office tradition. Minuting is a more time-consuming process than might be thought, as it required good composition combined with mastery of a lot of documentation. But in this painstaking way the Colonial Office was able to function efficiently as a memory-system of data storage and retrieval, as hard-working officials recorded the reasoning behind decisions and made themselves able to give an expert opinion or draft appropriately worded despatches reasonably quickly, make precedents available, and warn politicians of actions already proved futile.

One aspect of bureaucracy which became increasingly central as the twentieth century progressed was interdepartmental relations. In the early days it had not much troubled the Colonial Office what other government departments thought about the Empire. The relationships which came to matter were principally those with the Foreign Office, Commonwealth Relations Office, and Treasury. The approach of the Foreign Office was radically different, its main interest being in diplomatic accommodations without the responsibility of actually running any territories. All too often it seemed to think the Colonial Office could well afford to make gestures within the Colonial Empire in order to make its own general task in the international arena simpler. The Colonial Office often felt it got no help from the Foreign Office permanent officials, and frequently a good deal of hindrance, since they seemed to regard colonial matters as rather a nuisance, especially as they appeared not to be much concerned to stand up for British rights, let alone those of the inhabitants of colonial territories. The Foreign Office thought the Colonial Office too legalistic, and rather resented the fact that British Honduras bedevilled 'normal' relations with Guatemala, or the Falkland Islands with Argentina. Above all, they were annoyed that Cyprus upset relations with Greece. The Foreign Office view tended to be that British policy itself caused discontent in Cyprus because of an unduly high-and-mighty attitude emanating from Government House, Nicosia (but then, the Colonial Office would have agreed with that). They also thought the Colonial Office attitude too ambivalent: was *enosis* (union with Greece) a serious problem or not? ('The Colonial Office are supreme wishful thinkers.') There was a major disagreement between the Foreign Office and Colonial Office about the recognition of the Yemen Republic in 1963, with the Foreign Office much more disposed to be nice to the 'Nasserite' Yemenis, and the Colonial Office evaluating the question from the narrow standpoint of the Aden base. The Foreign Office was contemptuous of the Colonial Office's reluctance to see it move into a more significant role in African policy. They thought the Colonial Office 'Bourbon-minded' in resisting a more planned and interdepartmental approach. In 1949 the Foreign Office suggested there should be a Nile Valley Board (made up of Egypt, Sudan, Ethiopia, Uganda, and the Belgian Congo) to sort out the problems of the Nile waters, foster good relations with Egypt, and generally improve the British reputation at the United Nations. But to Cohen and the Colonial Office this was wholly disadvantageous to East Africa: 'we cannot sacrifice the interests of colonial territories for these purposes.' It was not in Uganda's interest to risk Egyptian and Ethiopian interference. Hilton Poynton agreed: 'This is a characteristic piece of Foreign Office nonsense. I agree that it should be vigorously opposed.'[7]

Differences of approach with the Commonwealth Relations Office are best illustrated with reference to two major surveys conducted at the request of the Prime Minister in 1957 and 1959, entitled respectively 'Future Constitutional Relations with Colonies' and 'Future Policy Study, 1960–1970'. In response to the former (vulgarly known as Macmillan's 'profit and loss account'),[8] the Commonwealth Relations Office indicated that it would like Britain to divest herself of responsibility for the Solomon Islands and the New Hebrides (a Condominium with France), which could be more sensibly administered by Australia and New Zealand. The Colonial Office could not see this working and doubted whether it would be in accordance with 'the wishes of the natives'. Two years later Macmillan himself raised the matter again, after 'some interesting' representations from the Duke of Edinburgh who had just visited the Pacific. Macmillan agreed there was 'much to be said for a rationalization of colonial responsibilities' in the South-West Pacific. Australia spent more on her dependent territories than Britain did per head, and if she were interested in taking over, this could be of advantage to the peoples involved. A transfer 'within the Commonwealth' would involve no loss of prestige. The New Hebrides were of no importance to Britain. If the British held on they would have to spend more on them: 'otherwise the disparity between our standards and those of the Australians and the French will become so marked that the inhabitants may become disaffected'. If the Gilbert and Ellice Islands could be rejoined to Fiji, a 'general co-ordination' of dependencies in the region might be secured.

Such arguments were familiar to the Commonwealth Relations Office, and had been mooted by them before, but for the most part, and certainly since 1952, Australia had seemed reluctant to take on new responsibilities. Macmillan's interest polarized departmental attitudes sharply. The Colonial Office took its stand on 'trusteeship': the people themselves must choose for themselves when they had

[7] Ronald Hyam, ed., *The Labour Government and the End of Empire, 1945–1951*, BDEEP (London, 1992), II, pp. 278–82, 459–65, and III, p. 83 (for Foreign Office attitudes); for the Yemen, see CAB[inet] [Office] 134/2371, OP(63)2 and 4 (Feb. 1963).

[8] A. G. Hopkins, 'Macmillan's Audit of Empire, 1957', in Peter Clarke and Clive Trebilcock, eds., *Understanding Decline: Perceptions and Realities of British Economic Performance: Essays in Honour of Barry Supple* (Cambridge, 1997), chap. 11, pp. 234–60.

been brought to a sufficient stage of political and economic advancement. The Commonwealth Relations Office focused on the admitted poor reputation of European rule in these territories: the 'Pandemonium' of the New Hebrides, and the 'discreditable backwater' of the Solomons; and argued that it was a nonsense for six Western powers to be exercising jurisdiction in the South Pacific. John Chadwick of the Commonwealth Relations Office minuted:

> This has now become an open battle between the Colonial Office paternalists who wish to retain control until they have led their South Seas protégés into the best of all possible worlds, and CRO devolutionists, who believe in the lessons of geo-history and see some chance of lessening the white man's burden... It is clear that we and the CO are poles apart.

A special committee of ministers discussed the issue in July 1959. The principal points made were that Britain could not indefinitely undertake the financial commitment of administering territories of no particular strategic significance, especially where they could be more appropriately administered by other Commonwealth countries; but the peoples might not welcome transfer and the French might not agree. The Prime Minister then directed the matter to be remitted to the 'Future Policy Study' group of officials—which in the event could make no clear recommendation because of the continuing irreconcilability of views between the Colonial Office and Commonwealth Relations Office, but they did incline to the Colonial Office basic arguments of 'moral responsibility' and allowing the wishes of the inhabitants to prevail.[9]

The production of this 'Future Policy Study' paper provided a major occasion for interdepartmental co-ordination, particularly over perceptions of the future of the Commonwealth, the most contentious section as originally drafted by the Commonwealth Relations Office. Both the Colonial Office and the Foreign Office felt the Commonwealth Relations Office exaggerated the importance of the Commonwealth as a factor in British relations with the United States when they argued that Americans listened to the British *because* of the Commonwealth. The Commonwealth Relations Office draft also seemed to contain too much special pleading and too much optimism about the value of economic ties to the United Kingdom for future African states. But a lot of the imprecision of the Commonwealth Relations Office paper arose from internal disagreements within that office. The Foreign Office view was that the Commonwealth was not a possible source of power (as the United States was and Europe might be) for Britain, but was nevertheless important as an instrument of such limited power as Britain still had. The Colonial Office valued the Commonwealth highly, but to some extent simply because it was a non-American grouping in international affairs. However,

[9] Minutes by Macmillan, M.213/59, 16 June 1959, and J. Chadwick, 8 Oct. 1959, DO 35/8095; see also CAB 134/1551, CPC(57)27 and CO 1036/781, no. 1.

these differences of official perception were ironed out, and the final version of the paper on the future of the Commonwealth was accepted by the Colonial Office officials as 'very satisfactory'. They too believed that the Commonwealth was of great significance in the crucial matter of relations between advanced and under-developed nations: that it was the only alternative to the growing political and economic deterioration of Britain, as well as a useful instrument of Western influence in the global struggle against Communism. Moreover, its very existence provided a good answer to the charge of 'colonialism', and it enabled emerging nations to begin to learn about international relations within 'a sort of family circle'. By 1962, when the Commonwealth had changed from a cohesive and small group of relatively large countries into a large association of mainly small states, the value of the Commonwealth—according to Norman Brook—was that it was a means of attracting Western as opposed to Communist allegiance, and might make a valuable contribution to world peace if Britain could reduce racial tension in the world by co-operation within this multiracial organization. 'Two-tier' concepts of the Commonwealth, with different levels of participation for the old 'white' members and the new Afro-Asian ones, were firmly rejected by the officials.[10]

There were departmental differences, too, about how to treat the United Nations. The Foreign Office and Commonwealth Relations Office felt that the collapse of the United Nations would be disastrous, and Britain must not let her discontent with it lead to policies which might damage it. They wanted a more robust attitude to colonial problems when these were debated at the United Nations: the British delegation should be more active and publicize the British case more effectively, instead of thinking more in Colonial Office terms of disdainful silence or walkouts. They thought the Colonial Office attitude—at least as exemplified by Hilton Poynton, obsessed with resisting the United Nations and seeing no real need to work either with it, the United States, or even the Commonwealth—profoundly unsatisfactory and legalistic. Some years of interdepartmental debate (defy or co-operate?) reached a climax in 1962.[11]

After the Foreign Office and Commonwealth Relations Office, the other main department the Colonial Office dealt with was the Treasury—a relationship in which the Colonial Office is commonly supposed to have been at a disadvantage. Things were not quite as difficult as might be thought. The Treasury had no

[10] CAB 129/100, C(60)35; minutes by I. Watt, 11 Feb. and 11 June 1958, CO 1032/167; CO 1032/174; officials' report on 'The Evolution of the Commonwealth', April 1962, CO 1032/226; F[oreign] O[ffice]371/135623, no. 1; FO 371/135624, no. 9; FO 371/143705, no. 51; minute by P. E. Ramsbotham, 22 Sept. 1959, FO 371/143707, no. 72.

[11] Sir Hugh Foot to Sir Patrick Dean, 16 March 1962, FO 371/166820, no. 70; see also FO 371/166819, FO 371/166824, and FO 371/172591, nos. 16, 17 and 19 (1963).

positive input into colonial policy. It simply reacted to proposals. In the vast majority of cases all it had to do was declare 'no Treasury interest'. What it did do was to provide funding for colonial projects, and its scrutiny then was, quite properly, rigorous. But it certainly was not the case that the Colonial Office pressed for the expenditure of limitless sums of money. Before 1940 its own fundamental principle was that the 'colonies should pay for themselves', usually by taxation. When the Colonial Office got into a serious argument with the Treasury it was because it felt compelled to do so, and on the whole the Treasury respected this and its response was not necessarily unsympathetic. The testimony of a notable Deputy Under-Secretary, Sir Charles Jeffries, throws useful light on this. He described Treasury officials as always courteous and helpful, but naturally 'some were more inclined than others to take a real interest in colonial affairs', which often raised questions 'for which normal "Treasury practice" did not provide clear answers'. Even in the titanic debate over the funding of pensions for the new Overseas Civil Service (HMOCS) between 1955 and 1961, the Treasury officials were, Jeffries found, 'anxious to be as helpful as possible within the limits of what they regarded as the correct approach'. And in the end, 'the Colonial Office substantially achieved all that it had fought for over the years' in the scheme established under the Overseas Service Aid Act (1961).[12]

It has often been argued that the Colonial Office lacked respect in Whitehall, that it suffered from 'political weakness'. Such an interpretation would seem hard to sustain in the light of detailed examination of the evidence. How did this evaluation come about? In part because influential Prime Ministers, such as Attlee or Macmillan, are supposed to have had a low opinion of the Colonial Office. We must be careful not to rip out of context their occasional acid comments on particular personalities or issues. Attlee did not get on at all well with Arthur Creech Jones (Secretary of State, 1946–50), essentially because he could not stand his talkativeness. Macmillan as Foreign Secretary despaired of the 'Byzantine ways' of the Colonial Office department which handled Cyprus; but his very choice of adjective shows that it was not meant to be a *general* comment on the Colonial Office. Indeed his assessment of it, based on his experience as Parliamentary Under-Secretary in 1942, praised it as a small, tightly knit department, with intelligent, devoted, conscientious officers.[13] No convincing generalization that the Colonial Office was not highly regarded by ministers can be constructed: rather the reverse, since the ministers usually expressed themselves well satisfied with the service they received. From the perspective of officials themselves,

[12] Jeffries, *Whitehall and the Colonial Service*, pp. 27–28; Goldsworthy, *Conservative Government*, II, pp. 111–38.

[13] Harold Macmillan, *The Blast of War, 1939–1945* (London, 1967), p. 163; Alistair Horne, *Macmillan, 1894–1956: Volume I of the Official Biography*, (London, 1988), I, p. 365 [2nd Vol: *1957–1986*, 1989].

obviously they preferred a boss who effectively fought the Colonial Office corner at the Cabinet. If Creech Jones could not always do so against Foreign Secretary Ernest Bevin, that was not an unusual situation, for not even Attlee himself could automatically prevail against such a heavyweight opponent. The Colonial Office was certainly powerful enough to impose its views and even take advantage of the change of government in 1951 from Labour to Conservative. A declaration of continuity of policy initiated by Andrew Cohen went ahead despite the disinclination of Churchill to endorse it. The civil servants' project (also masterminded by Cohen) for a Central African Federation was pushed forward relentlessly, and their notions of how best to treat Seretse Khama (heir to the Bangwato chieftainship in Bechuanaland) were imposed on new ministers with vigorous determination.[14]

It will now be appropriate to examine the doctrines of the Colonial Office, and its principal contributions to policy-making. Its doctrines were famously embodied in the term 'trusteeship', which in the post-war era was elided into 'partnership', 'multiracialism', and finally 'non-racialism'.[15]

Edmund Burke declared in 1783 with respect to India:

> all political power which is set over men, being wholly artificial, and for so much a derogation from the natural equality of mankind at large, ought to be some way or other exercised ultimately for their benefit ... such rights ... are all in the strictest sense a *trust*; and it is in the very essence of every trust to be rendered accountable.

This was the first occasion upon which governmental 'trust' doctrines were applied to dependencies. The idea was refined by Lord Macaulay and J. S. Mill in ways which envisaged self-government as the desirable long-term outcome of the 'trust'. In the government of dependencies, said Mill, unless there was some approach to facilitating a transition to a higher stage of improvement, 'the rulers are guilty of a dereliction of the highest moral trust which can devolve upon a nation'. Macaulay looked forward to the day when India should be independent. These doctrines, especially as reinforced by anti-slavery ideologies and evangelical missionary religion, had some real and positive influence on the conduct of

[14] Goldsworthy, *Conservative Government*, II, pp. 1–2; R. Hyam, 'The Political Consequences of Seretse Khama: Britain, the Bangwato and South Africa, 1948–52', *Historical Journal*, XIX (1986), pp. 921–47, and 'The Geopolitical Origins of the Central African Federation: Britain, Rhodesia and South Africa, 1948–53', ibid., XXX (1987), pp. 145–72.

[15] Ronald Robinson, 'The Moral Disarmament of African Empire', *Journal of Imperial and Commonwealth History*, VIII (1979), pp. 86–104, reprinted in Hillmer and Wigley, eds., *The First British Commonwealth*; Kenneth Robinson, *The Dilemmas of Trusteeship: Aspects of British Colonial Policy Between the Wars* (Oxford, 1965). For nineteenth-century trusteeship see Vol. III, chap. 10 by Andrew Porter.

government policy of the Empire in the 1830s—the climax of a genuine period of humanitarian doctrines, when a concern for 'aboriginal rights' was manifestly prominent. Such rights were rather more equivocally set forth in the Treaty of Waitangi (1840) with the Maoris of New Zealand, and thereafter were harder to assert in the face of proliferating disillusionment in non-European capacities and amenability—a disillusionment which reached its climacteric as a result of the Indian Mutiny-Rebellion of 1857. Later-Victorians might still recognize their 'trust' in a paternalistic and protective way, but its positive and progressive elements (as added by Macaulay and Mill) were at a discount. They began to revive only after 1905, but if there were then some 'gains' towards a less negative trusteeship, there were also some notable 'losses' in terms of promoting self-government in white minority hands in South Africa in 1909–10. Only from 1923, after similar gains for white settlers in Southern Rhodesia, were the more positive aspects of the 'trust' gradually consolidated.

Trusteeship in the early years of the century was in constant counterpoint with the parallel policies of increasing deference to the principles of white self-government. This was especially the case with the terms of the South African transfer of power, but also there was a soft-pedalling of Imperial protest at the immigration-restriction policies of the Dominions. The desire of Indians to emigrate freely within the Empire posed a difficult issue, as white regimes everywhere wished to exclude them. Whose loyalty was government to forfeit: Indian or European? There was a genuine fear in Whitehall that an attempt to stop restriction of immigration would set up a movement of secession from the Empire; some Australians, indeed, had already muttered threats about breaking with the Empire if thwarted. When the Colonial Office in 1905 (under Alfred Lyttelton) had tried to get self-governing colonies to reserve for Imperial consideration all bills containing provisions based on race and colour distinctions, there was uproar. Thereafter an uneasy compromise was worked out. The Dominions found means of discrimination based on vague grounds of 'unsuitability' rather than express prohibition of racial categories. The Imperial government was obliged to admit the right of self-governing colonies to exclude those it did not wish to receive, but tried to see that the way they did it did not cause needless offence or hardship, or involve Britain in 'diplomatic' difficulties with India or Japan; they would continue to make selective representations against racial discrimination even if they could not veto offensive legislation; but they knew they must not preach, as that would cause friction and so be counter-productive.

Some definite victories for trusteeship were achieved outside the strictly colonial field. It was agreed to stop selling opium to China from 1907. In 1917 Indian indentured labour—which had been such a central feature of the Imperial enterprise since the 1830s—was terminated. But this chapter is concerned with colonial policy and the revival of trusteeship from 1905.[16] Under the Liberal government, bureaucratic heavy-handedness came under attack everywhere, from Curzon's India to Milner's Transvaal. Stern rebukes were issued to Captain Ewart Grogan (President of the Colonists' Association of Kenya), who flogged some Kikuyu men outside the Nairobi courthouse in 1907 for having jolted a rickshaw carrying white women. Colonel Montgomery (Conservator of Kenya forests) was also taken severely to task for saying 'natives did irretrievable damage to forests, and whilst the natives themselves could always be replaced, with trees it was different, for it cost much money to plant a forest'. A closer watch was kept on forced labour and flogging, although the former was not effectively brought under control until 1921. The Colonial Office would not accept a political argument for pulling administration out of any part of the newly acquired territories in Africa, not even the unproductive hinterland of Somaliland: 'we have undertaken the responsibility before the world of gradually introducing order and settled government . . . and to withdraw our civilizing agents . . . is a renunciation of our mission which is not admissible' (W. D. Ellis). Nor would they co-operate with the Foreign Office in a diplomatic deal with France involving the handing over of the Gambia, asserting the need to have the consent of the inhabitants. In Nigeria they put (Lord) Lugard on a much tighter rein. In Southern Rhodesia they vetoed restrictions on Asian immigration. They refused permission for large-scale European plantations even to respected firms such as W. H. Lever, the soap manufacturer, in West Africa. This foreshadowed the rebuff to Bovril, denied ranching access to Bechuanaland in 1919. African colonies, officials believed, were administered 'first of all and chiefly in the interests of the inhabitants of the Territories; and secondly in accordance with the views of people in this country (and not a small and interested section of them [the merchants] represented in Parliament)' (R. L. Antrobus, Assistant Under-Secretary). The first consideration was 'to do what was best for Africa', and trusteeship came before development. Not that development was entirely neglected. In July 1906 a circular despatch was issued to promote the work of development through the revamped Scientific and Technical Department of the Imperial Institute. At this date, however, development meant measures to combat disease and improve transport rather than a comprehensive infrastructural programme.

Interlocking with trusteeship were policies of Indirect Rule and promoting peasant cultivation. Central to all of this was the report of the Northern Nigeria Lands Committee (1908) and the resulting Land and Native Rights Proclamation of 1910, an important measure which secured non-alienation of African land,

[16] Ronald Hyam, *Elgin and Churchill at the Colonial Office, 1905–08: The Watershed of Empire-Commonwealth* (London, 1968), esp. pp. 468–74.

leasehold in preference to freehold, and African priority in undisturbed use. Africans were encouraged to initiate commercial development wherever there were no settlers, especially in cotton growing in Southern Nigeria, Uganda, and in the Sudan, where there was a massive scheme at Gezira. Cocoa was also successfully developed by peasant production in the Gold Coast (Ghana). Broadly speaking, the African policy of the Colonial Office before the First World War was anti-settler and pro-African, in favour of 'rule through chiefs' and the development of traditional organization, was wary of chartered companies, excessive expenditure, and indentured labour, and was opposed to 'punitive expeditions', monopolies, and concession-hunting. As a former Governor, Lord Lugard famously summed up this version of trusteeship as a 'Dual Mandate', with Britain as trustee to civilization for the development of resources, and to the natives for their welfare.[17]

The story of trusteeship between the wars was essentially played out through eight separate pronouncements about the future of East and Central Africa, especially Kenya and the Rhodesias (Zambia and Zimbabwe), which had the most vociferous settler communities. Analysis of these documents cannot be avoided. As Lord Vansittart of the Foreign Office has written, this was a generation which 'paddled in a purée of words and hoped to catch a formula'. These pronouncements reflected the tussle for control between conflicting interests: officials as trustees, Parliament as watchdog, the settlers, and the Government of India.[18]

Churchill's statement, 1922: Churchill was Secretary of State, 1921–22. He declared: 'We do not contemplate any settlement or system which will prevent . . . Kenya . . . from becoming a characteristically and distinctively British Colony, looking forward in the full fruition of time to responsible self-government.' This was not actually quite so much of a charter for settler self-government as it appeared, and it was balanced by a call for a common electoral roll to be established. The Indian community would be the principal beneficiary, and the settlers were furious.

[17] F. D. Lugard, *The Dual Mandate in British Tropical Africa* (London, 1922), pp. 282–94, 391.

[18] R. Vansittart, *The Mist Procession: The Autobiography of Lord Vansittart* (London, 1958), p. 484; Robert G. Gregory, *India and East Africa: A History of Race Relations Within the British Empire, 1890–1939* (Oxford, 1971); Edna Bradlow, 'The Evolution of "Trusteeship" in Kenya', *South African Historical Journal*, IV (1972), pp. 64–80; J. G. Kamoche, *Imperial Trusteeship and Political Evolution in Kenya, 1923–63: A Study in the Official Views* (Washington, 1981); R. I. Rotberg, 'The Federal Movement in East and Central Africa, 1889–1953', *Journal of Commonwealth Political Studies*, II (1964), pp. 141–60; Robert M. Maxon, *Struggle for Kenya: The Loss and Reassertion of Imperial Initiative, 1912–1923* (London, 1993). For Amery and Kenya, see Wm. Roger Louis, *In the Name of God, Go! Leo Amery and the British Empire in the Age of Churchill* (New York, 1992), pp. 94–99; for Churchill and Kenya, see Ronald Hyam, 'Churchill and the Empire', in Wm. Roger Louis and Robert Blake, eds., *Churchill* (Oxford, 1993), esp. pp. 175–79.

The Devonshire Declaration, 1923: the Duke of Devonshire was Secretary of State, 1922–24. This declaration reversed Churchill's approach by giving less to Indians and more to Africans: 'His Majesty's Government regard themselves as exercising a trust on behalf of the African population, and they are unable to delegate or share this trust, the object of which may be defined as the protection and advancement of the native races.' There followed words about 'the mission of Great Britain' to work continuously for 'the training and education of the Africans towards a higher intellectual, moral and economic level' than that which they had reached. And finally there was one of the most famous and powerfully worded declarations of Imperial policy ever made:

> Primarily Kenya is an African territory, and His Majesty's Government think it necessary definitely to record their considered opinion that the interests of the African natives must be paramount, and that if, and when, those interests and the interests of the immigrant races should conflict, the former should prevail.

Amery's White Paper, 1927: L. S. Amery was Secretary of State, 1924–29. Amery had a more political programme than was common among Colonial Secretaries. He proposed to do what the Devonshire Declaration had expressly forbidden: to share the trust with the settlers. This was known as the 'dual policy', and it seemed to give as much weight to European settler interests as to trusteeship for Africans. He was also keen to promote closer association between the East African dependencies and also the Central African territories.

The Hilton Young Report, 1929: Sir Edward Hilton Young was a former Liberal junior minister and Chief Whip, now moving to the Conservative side. His committee was hijacked by Sir George Schuster (Colonial Office Financial Adviser) and J. H. Oldham (Secretary to the International Missionary Council), and the majority report (which Hilton Young himself did not sign) rejected the idea of self-government for Kenya on the Southern Rhodesia model. It rejected also a closer union under white domination for the territories both of East and Central Africa, and instead looked to an imperially directed co-ordination of trusteeship policy. This meant: 'the creation ... of a field for the full development of native life as a first charge on any territory; the government ... has the duty to devote all available resources to assisting the natives to develop it.' The report was also significant for introducing a new concept, of which much was to be heard in future: 'what the immigrant communities may justly claim is partnership, not control.'

The Passfield 'Memorandum on Native Policy in East Africa', 1930: Lord Passfield, formerly Sidney Webb, was Labour's Secretary of State, 1929–31. His paper tried to reconcile previous statements by promoting the fiction that the 'dual policy' of looking to settler interests was 'in no way inconsistent with trusteeship', but the emphasis was primarily on the paramountcy of African interests.

The Passfield Statement on Closer Union, 1930: to the disgust of the Kenya settlers, this revived the Churchillian proposal of a common roll franchise for all races, based on educational attainments. The two Passfield White Papers together were denounced by the settlers as 'black papers'.

The Parliamentary Joint Select Committee Report, 1931: this asserted that the East-Central African question had become 'a test case of imperial statesmanship in harmonizing the separate interests . . . of different races'. It glossed 'paramountcy' as meaning that African majority interests 'should not be subordinated to those of a minority belonging to another race, however important in itself'. The Report was not in favour of East African Closer Union, and it affirmed a continuation of the 'dual policy', 'the complementary development of the native and non-native communities'. This was how the Kenya issue was more or less left for the 1930s.

The Bledisloe Commission Report, 1939: Viscount Bledisloe was formerly Parliamentary Secretary to the Ministry of Agriculture, and Governor-General of New Zealand, 1930–35. He was asked in 1935 to investigate whether some form of closer association or co-operation between Northern and Southern Rhodesia was desirable or feasible, 'having due regard to the interests of the inhabitants irrespective of race, and the special responsibilities of the government for African interests'. He took such a long time to report that he acquired the nickname 'Bloody-slow'. The eventual conclusion was that the only argument against amalgamation was the difference in native policies of the two Rhodesias, with Northern Rhodesia following Colonial Office doctrine: 'It is the fear that the balance is not fairly held between the two races in Southern Rhodesia that alone prevents a recommendation being made for immediate amalgamation.' That single obstacle was of course received as decisive in Whitehall. Bledisloe recommended economic co-operation and a political standstill.

The upshot of the battle of words was clearly resolved in favour of trusteeship and against the settler aspirations in Kenya. It was, however, a hollow victory, because it proved impossible to get the resolutions implemented. With the exception of the statements of Amery, and of Churchill to a lesser extent, these pronouncements represent a consistent Colonial Office view. The Devonshire Declaration of 1923 clearly stands out as historically central and significant, however difficult to turn into effective practical results in the short term. It was a courageous statement which, whatever the equivocations, represented the moment from which Kenya would develop into a black state. The retreat from a settler state, however discontinuous, had publicly begun. It was not an entirely new departure, but picked up a thread inherent in British policy for Kenya since the Foreign Office in 1904 had instructed its officers: 'the primary duty of Great Britain in East Africa is the welfare of the native races.'

Why, then, was it so hard to make trusteeship stick in Kenya? The settlers were strong-willed and often intimidating, and they successfully 'captured' Governors selected to control them. Governors with impeccable records in defending native rights elsewhere (Girouard in Nigeria, Mitchell in Fiji) soon succumbed to this bluff and intimidation. Only Sir Joseph Byrne (1931–37) is generally reckoned to have achieved anything like resistance to their seductive pressure. Under provocation, intimidation could mean actual threats of rebellion, as in 1922–23 against putting Indians on a common roll franchise. The Devonshire Memorandum itself held that it was out of the question to use force against the settlers, many of whom were ex-soldiers: it would be costly and unedifying; anything like a blockade to cut trade facilities would be damaging to the entire Indian community, and to Uganda; blacks could not be used to suppress whites. These considerations made Passfield's papers more equivocal than they would otherwise have been. In 1942 Sir Arthur Dawe of the Colonial Office wrote: 'The lesson of 1923 is always there . . . it seems unthinkable that any British government would bring military force to bear upon a community of our own blood who have supported the British cause splendidly in this and the last war.' Compromises *tended* to favour the settler interest, and all the while there was a fear of driving them into the arms of South Africa.[19]

Yet in a fundamental sense Whitehall was never wholeheartedly behind the Kenya settlement, even if it acknowledged some obligations. As early as 1908 a junior Colonial Office official had adumbrated a scheme of wholesale repatriation: 'It would probably pay the British taxpayer to repatriate all the whites and forbid their entry except on payment of a heavy poll-tax' (W. D. Ellis).[20] In 1923 Viscount Peel told a settler delegation directly, 'I think the best solution of this trouble is to buy you all out'. In 1928 he said privately that he had never negotiated 'with a more stiff-necked or unreasonable set of people'. Harold Macmillan, as Parliamentary Under-Secretary of State in 1942, concluded that Kenya was 'not a white man's country' and there would be a clash in which the government would be torn between the rights of the settlers and their obligations to the natives. The solution, he believed, was to buy out the whites and give land back to the Africans; there might be land nationalization into state and collective farms run by such farmer-settlers who were serious and efficient. This would be expensive, 'but it will be less

[19] E. A. Brett, *Colonialism and Underdevelopment in East Africa: The Politics of Economic Change, 1919–39* (London, 1973), pp. 171–212; C. P. Youé, 'The Threat of Settler Rebellion and the Imperial Predicament: The Denial of Indian Rights in Kenya, 1923', *Canadian Journal of History*, XII (1978), pp. 347–60; D. Wylie, 'Confrontation Over Kenya: Colonial Office and its Critics, 1918–40', *Journal of African History*, XVIII (1970), pp. 427–47.

[20] Hyam, *Elgin and Churchill at the Colonial Office*, p. 413.

expensive than a civil war'.[21] After 1945, however, when the Labour Party suggested something similar, Cohen was adamant that it was now too late for such drastic measures, and persuaded Creech Jones that the Kenya problem could not be solved by dramatic gestures of this kind. Instead, an appeal was made to the settlers to see the wisdom and decency of a policy of multiracialism. In the wake of Mau Mau, this bore fruit in the shape of Michael Blundell and his New Kenya Party. The Lyttelton Constitution of 1954 finally ruled out for all time the prospect of self-government for the Kenya Europeans alone. The officials' report, 'Future Constitutional Development of the Colonies' (1957), described Kenya as an 'unstable multi-racial society... the task of statesmanship in the next decade is to manipulate European fears, Asian timidity and African impatience to a delicate but changing balance which allows no member of the team to run off the field'. The whole of East Africa was seen in the Colonial Office at this date as 'the testing ground for the possibility of multi-racial or non-racial development'.[22]

The success of the Colonial Office in blocking the amalgamation of the Rhodesias meant that after the war the settlers switched their objective to a federation of the Rhodesias and Nyasaland. This was, perhaps, only a partial victory for trusteeship in Central Africa. Whatever their reservations, officials in the Colonial Office and Commonwealth Relations Office thought there were good arguments for a link-up which would act as a counterpoise to South African expansion and retain some formal elements of Imperial control over African affairs.[23]

Although the issues of trusteeship for East and Central Africa between the wars were fought out in the public arena, there was another equally important battle raging mainly behind the scenes. This concerned the High Commission Territories of Basutoland, Bechuanaland, and Swaziland. From 1925 these became the responsibility of the Dominions Office, and second only to Ireland as its principal problem. The continual frustration by the Colonial Office and the Dominions Office of aspirations passionately espoused by all South African governments for fifty years was a notable tribute to Imperial trusteeship. In the early years at least it was trusteeship maintained in default of any public knowledge of, or interest in, the question, which only emerged after 1933.[24]

[21] Macmillan to G. Gater, 15 Aug. 1942, commenting on A. J. Dawe, 'A Federal Solution for East Africa' (July 1942), CO 967/57, printed in Ashton and Stockwell, *Imperial Policy*, I, Docs 65 and 66; Macmillan, *Memoirs*, Vol. VI, *1961–63* (London, 1973), p. 289.

[22] Hyam, *Labour Government*, III, pp. 14–15; CAB 134/1551, CPC(57)27.

[23] Martin Chanock, *Unconsummated Union: Britain, Rhodesia and South Africa, 1900–45* (Manchester, 1977); H. I. Wetherell, 'Britain and Rhodesian Expansionism: Imperial Collusion or Empirical Carelessness?', *Rhodesian History*, VIII (1977), pp. 115–28; R. E. Robinson, 'The "Trust" in British Central African Policy, 1889–1939', unpublished Ph.D. thesis, Cambridge, 1950.

[24] Garner, *Commonwealth Office*, pp. 134–36; Ronald Hyam, *The Failure of South African Expansion, 1908–48* (London, 1972), and 'The Politics of Partition in Southern Africa, 1908–61', in Ronald Hyam

The problem was as follows. The schedule to the South Africa Act (1909) provided for a possible transfer of the administration of the three Territories to the Union. Section 151 was purely permissive; transfer was essentially conditional, and no date was specified. Moreover, important pledges were given during the passage of the Act through the British Parliament that Africans would be consulted and their opinion 'most carefully considered'. It was never clearly explained what this meant: 'consultation means consultation.' Equivocation was part of the tactics; another was playing for time. Since South African native policies got progressively tougher, beginning with the Land Act of 1913, there was never any serious hope that the Colonial Office or Dominions Office would be willing to hand over its trusteeship to South Africa. Accordingly, the Colonial Office took issue with Viscount Gladstone, the first Governor-General, over his apparent unawareness that 'it is the natives who really count'. Gladstone seemed to contemplate transfer as something to be prepared for rather than staved off. Overtures were received from the South African government, broadly divided into five main sets: 1911–13 (Botha), 1919–23 (Smuts), 1924–27 (Hertzog), 1932–39 (Hertzog again), and 1939 (Smuts). But even after 1948, all Prime Ministers (Malan, Strijdom, Verwoerd) until 1961 (when South Africa left the Commonwealth) still hoped to secure substantive negotiations. Despite some differences between British politicians, officials to a man consistently opposed any change in the status quo. The most anyone was ever prepared to contemplate was an experimental transfer of Swaziland before 1925. What they achieved was a containment of South Africa within its boundaries of 1909. Whether this could be made permanent was in doubt as late as the mid-1970s. In dealing with the evil of apartheid, containment of its boundaries was the most effective contribution Britain could have made, and by the end of the 1960s British policy had allowed the emergence of three successful independent states (Lesotho, Botswana, and Swaziland). This was trusteeship exercised at the expense of Imperial political advantage. Britain risked the hostility of white South Africans whose loyalty hung in the balance. No comparable advantage could be expected from the goodwill of small African communities enmeshed in the southern African geopolitical structure. Britain's resistance to Union demands was played from a position of steadily decreasing strength. Britain could so easily have bought the favour and co-operation of the South African government, which economic and strategic interests required, by relinquishing the High Commission Territories, since these were a drain rather than an asset, in no sense valuable as showpieces of Empire—it was feared any

and Ged Martin, *Reappraisals in British Imperial History* (London, 1975), pp. 187–200; J. E. Spence, 'British Policy Towards the High Commission Territories', *Journal of Modern African Studies*, II (1964), pp. 221–46.

development of their resources would only make them more attractive to the Union. They were, therefore, largely left alone as backwaters.

It was precisely in this contradiction—that development seemed incompatible with active trusteeship—that the weakness of the doctrine was revealed, and it is this which explains its transmutation into multiracial 'partnership'. Protection from exploitation was no longer enough. As Secretary of State Oliver Stanley declared in 1943: 'Some of us feel now that the word "trustee" is rather too static in its connotation, and that we should prefer to combine with the status of trustee the position also of partner.' A little earlier, the Under-Secretary, Macmillan, had declared that the 'governing principle of the Colonial Empire' should be 'the principle of partnership between the various elements composing it'. This exceedingly general proposition soon became refined in East and Central Africa in an idiomatic sense, where it meant partnership between the different sections of the community. Great faith was pinned upon 'a genuine partnership between Europeans and Africans' in producing prosperity and concord. The planners here did not favour in East Africa either an African or a European nationalism as the basis for the future, believing that one group or the other would always feel threatened by it. Partnership was thus a device to promote stability. There was a definite fear that the progressive withdrawal of European influence might cause the whole central area of the continent to fall into great disorder, which would not be in anybody's interest. It was in regard to the Central African Federation established in 1953 that 'partnership' was most ardently invoked: but the invocation was one more likely to be made by politicians than officials. The civil servants had propounded the theory that the expansionist pressure of a militant National Party in South Africa and its apartheid doctrines had to be counterbalanced by keeping an active loyal 'British' state on its border, in which the relationship between Europeans and Africans would be progressively improved, and the 'share of the Africans in the political and economic life of the territories . . . progressively increased under the policy of partnership'. It was not to be, and the special association of 'partnership' with the Federation discredited it.[25]

Meanwhile, outside the East-Central African area, trusteeship still held sway. It was particularly in evidence in the arguments advanced by the civil servants in 1957 to discourage Macmillan from offloading colonial responsibilities. Often enough in 1957 they relied on arguments about the need to maintain 'global prestige', but where these manifestly could not apply they fell back on the 'abdication of moral responsibility'. It would be deplorable, discreditable, and dangerous, they said, to allow colonies to degenerate into chaos, as would happen in the Seychelles, the Solomons, and the Gilbert and Ellice Islands. In other cases, such as Mauritius

[25] Lord Hailey, *An African Survey Revised, 1956* (Oxford, 1957), pp. 185–87.

and Fiji, there were delicate racial problems which Britain must accept the responsibility of having created in the first place by the introduction of Indian labourers.[26]

By the end of 1959 the doctrinal emphasis had shifted again to 'non-racialism'. In the officials' paper 'Africa in the Next Ten Years', it was asserted: 'East Africa must be non-racial, where minorities can contribute.'[27] The future of the High Commission Territories was also from about this date considered to be 'non-racial'. When the 'Future Policy Study' paper was being prepared, C. Y. Carstairs of the Colonial Office thought it was a good opportunity to reaffirm trusteeship doctrines. Something needed to be included in any statement of the aims of government policy which recognized that: 'In terms of practical politics a large section of opinion in this country will never be easy if it feels that our liberty or property depend directly or indirectly on the servitude or property of others; and a policy which gives rise to such feelings will for that reason not in the long run be capable of steady and effective pursuit.' This was not, Carstairs argued, mere sentimentality, and to ignore it was 'inverted sentimentality': public opinion had a right to feel government was doing what it reasonably could to put an end to possible abuses.[28]

From the 1950s the context within which trusteeship could still be invoked was entirely different, and the emphasis was much more on its positive aspects. A new and forward policy emerged from about 1940. Lord Hailey urged the application to the Empire of the expanded role of the state which had developed in Britain herself during the 1930s Depression. With the full backing of the Colonial Office, Secretary of State Malcolm MacDonald was determined to align trusteeship to a more active development policy in a new Colonial Development and Welfare Act. Gerard Clauson of the Colonial Office described the two motives behind this as 'to avert possible trouble in certain colonies where disturbances are feared if something is not done to improve the lot of the people', and 'to impress the world with our consciousness of our duties as a great Colonial Power'. MacDonald was anxious to make the colonial position in wartime unassailable. It was 'essential to get away from the old principle that Colonies can only have what they themselves can afford to pay for'. Without such action 'we shall deserve to lose the Colonies and it will be only a matter of time before we get what we deserve'. The introduction of 'welfare' as well as 'development' would provide the genuineness of more altruistic purpose. It was not easy to persuade the Treasury about this new dimension. The Colonial Office had to fight to keep the word 'welfare' in the title of the Act. But by 1944 even Treasury officials were persuaded that 'as regards

[26] CAB 134/1551, CPC(57)27. [27] May 1959, FO 371/137972, no. 27, AF(59)28.
[28] CAB 129/100, C(60)35; CO 1032/172, no. 102.

the money we are conscious that we must justify ourselves before the world as a great Colonial power'.[29]

There is no doubt that, as Wm. Roger Louis writes: 'The Second World War witnessed a moral regeneration of British purpose in the colonial world.' With the impetus of MacDonald's achievement behind them, together with better information in the shape of Lord Hailey's *An African Survey* (1938) and the stimulus of Lord Moyne's damning report on the West Indies (1939), the Colonial Office officials entered enthusiastically into the task of redefining colonial policy.[30] This in itself marked a dramatic shift. Formerly the initiative was allowed to rest with innovative Governors such as Lugard of Nigeria and Cameron of Tanganyika. Now, as Cohen put it, 'we cannot afford to leave this vital matter to the chance of new Lugards and Camerons coming forward in the future'. The Colonial Office must itself define a centrally determined and generally applicable clear policy. This became 'political advancement', the key to which was to look upon African administrations as local authorities, 'in broadly the same relationship to central government as local authorities in this country'; to provide 'a balanced system of political representation for the traditional and non-traditional elements of African opinion', a pyramidal chain of representation leading up to the Legislative Councils and national self-government. The Colonial Office recognized that more social services and educational facilities would have to be provided. They acknowledged they had to respond to 'a rapidly increasing political consciousness among Africans' (Cohen), as well as international opinion reinforcing 'pressures towards the immediate implementation of trusteeship obligations' (R. E. Robinson).[31] Officials after 1945 saw themselves as engaged not only on what they called 'a new policy for Africa', but also 'a gigantic experiment', 'a worldwide experiment in nation building' (H. T. Bourdillon). The central aim of policy as they redefined it was to lead all but the smaller isolated colonies into self-government as soon as possible (though that was not expected to be soon), and to consolidate links with Britain on a permanent basis, so that ex-colonies would remain in the Commonwealth. 'In this conception of the evolving Commonwealth,' wrote Bourdillon,

[29] Stephen Constantine, *The Making of British Colonial Development Policy, 1919–40* (London, 1984); John W. Cell, *Hailey: A Study in British Imperialism, 1872–1969* (Cambridge, 1992), pp. 136–37; Joanna Lewis, 'The Colonial Politics of African Welfare, 1939–52: A Crisis of Paternalism', unpublished Ph.D. thesis, Cambridge, 1993, pp. 35–37.

[30] Wm. Roger Louis, *Imperialism at Bay, 1941–45: The United States and the Decolonization of the British Empire* (Oxford, 1977), pp. 101–03; J. M. Lee and Martin Petter, *The Colonial Office, War, and Development Policy: Organisation and Planning of a Metropolitan Initiative, 1939–45*, Institute of Commonwealth Studies Paper) no. 22 (London, 1982); Nicholas J. Westcott, 'Impact of the Second World War on Tanganyika, 1939–49', unpublished Ph.D. thesis, Cambridge, 1982, pp. 230–76; Ashton and Stockwell, *Imperial Policy*, II, docs. 100 and 101.

[31] Hyam, *Labour Government and the End of Empire*, I, pp. 103–09 (memorandum by A. B. Cohen, 3 April 1946), pp. 153–59 (memorandum by R. E. Robinson, n.d., 1947).

'I see the boldest stroke of political idealism which the world has yet witnessed, and on by far the grandest scale'; this great experiment was something 'surpassing in importance any of the much publicized political experiments indulged in by the Soviet Union or anybody else'.[32] Poynton declared at the United Nations: 'the present time is one of unprecedented vigour and imagination' in British colonial policy, 'one cheerful thing in a depressing world'. A carefully considered formulation of policy by the Colonial Office (probably drafted by Cohen) in 1948 was certainly high-minded:[33] 'The fundamental objectives in Africa are to foster the emergence of large-scale societies, integrated for self-government by effective and democratic political and economic institutions both national and local, inspired by a common faith in progress and Western values and equipped with efficient techniques of production and betterment.'

From 1945 onwards the Colonial Office was fully aware that a major task would be to come to terms with African nationalism. They had not previously thought much about this problem, as British attitudes to colonial nationalism had originally been responses to it in Ireland, India, and Egypt. Lessons of Asian and Arab nationalism had been learned fast after 1945, and by the 1950s there was a considerable body of accumulated experience to draw upon. It was clear that Britain's limited economic resources made it impossible to resist nationalists everywhere; that strategic bases could not effectively be held without local goodwill, and that it was difficult to withhold equal concessions from similar states (especially if neighbours). Experience also suggested the importance of recognizing not only what was feasible, but of keeping the initiative. One had to keep one jump ahead of nationalists, make timely and graceful concessions from a position of control, show willingness to modify ideal timetables in response to circumstances, be prepared to go faster rather than slower, avoid giving too little and too late; and recognize the fundamental need to decide who the 'moderates' were, then back them and outmanœuvre the 'extremists'; and generally find ways of turning nationalism to constructive account. In response to what the Colonial Office thought an unimpressive Foreign Office paper on 'The Problem of Nationalism' (1952), Trafford Smith summed up their view: 'the important ways in which we should deal with nationalism, both inside and outside the Colonial sphere, are those which depend on publicity and propaganda, especially in the United States and the United Nations, and not by thinking in Edwardian terms of the use of military and economic power which we no longer possess.'[34]

[32] Hyam, *Labour Government*, pp. 320–26 (memorandum by H. T. Bourdillon, 10 May 1948), and Intro., pp. xxix–xxxiv.

[33] Speech by A. H. Poynton at United Nations, 3 Oct. 1947, CO 847/36/4, no. 27; paper to Cambridge Summer School, CO 852/1053/1, CSC(48)4.

[34] Minute by Trafford Smith, 22 July 1952, CO 936/217.

As the end of Empire approached, Sir Charles Jeffries described the 'Colonial Office mind' as united on the proposition that: 'the colonial episode would only have made sense if it resulted in the new countries and the old country continuing as friends and partners when the ruler–subject relationship should come to an end. They should at least be started off with a democratic system, an efficient judiciary and civil service and impartial police.'[35] The Colonial Office was anxious not to be rushed. A 1959 statement prepared for the Secretary of State contained the following assertion on East and Central Africa: 'We are not prepared to betray our trust by leaving off our work before it is properly finished.'[36] This involved trying to ensure there were in place a good honest political system, rights for all, reasonable standards of living, and trained civil servants. William Gorell Barnes defined the task in East Africa at the end of 1960: 'to regulate the pace of political development so that it was fast enough to satisfy the African desire for self-government but not so fast as to jeopardize economic progress or the security situation.'[37] As late as 1960 in West Africa residual trusteeship notions made Colonial Office officials reluctant to contemplate the independence of a tiny state like the Gambia, even in some form of association with another country, Senegal being the most likely candidate (an association which would take it out of the Commonwealth). The Gambia was costing Britain too much in grants-in-aid, Christopher Eastwood wrote:

> But of course mercenary considerations are by no means all. It would be no light matter for the UK to divest itself of a country which had been associated with it for very many years, and like marriage it is not an enterprise to be lightly or inadvisedly embarked on.[38]

Gambia achieved independence on its own in 1964.

In the end, of course, the imperatives of decolonization, the growing force of the 'wind of change', simply overwhelmed the maintenance of trusteeship. The Colonial Office would have preferred a little more time to prepare states for independence, but it did not think that the process up to 1964 had been disastrously rushed.

[35] Jeffries, *Whitehall*, p. 73. [36] CO 1027/177, no. 11. [37] FO 371/146504, no. 30.
[38] C. G. Eastwood to E. B. Boothby (FO), 2 Dec. 1960, FO 371/146485, no. 20.

Select Bibliography

S. R. Ashton and S. E. Stockwell, eds., *Imperial Policy and Colonial Practice, 1925–1945*, British Documents on the End of Empire Project (BDEEP) (London, 1996).

Martin Chanock, *Unconsummated Union: Britain, Rhodesia and South Africa, 1900–45* (Manchester, 1977).

JOE GARNER, *The Commonwealth Office, 1925–68* (London, 1978).

DAVID GOLDSWORTHY, ed., *The Conservative Government and the End of Empire, 1951–1957*, British Documents on the End of Empire Project (BDEEP) (London, 1994).

ROBERT G. GREGORY, *India and East Africa: A History of Race Relations within the British Empire, 1890–1939* (Oxford, 1971).

RONALD HYAM, *The Failure of South African Expansion, 1908–48* (London, 1972).

—— 'The Colonial Office Mind, 1900–14', in Norman Hillmer and Philip G. Wigley, eds., *The First British Commonwealth: Essays in Honour of Nicholas Mansergh* (London, 1980), pp. 30–55.

Sir CHARLES JEFFRIES, *Whitehall and the Colonial Service: An Administrative Memoir, 1939–56*, Institute of Commonwealth Studies Paper, no. 15 (London, 1972).

J. M. LEE and MARTIN PETTER, *The Colonial Office, War, and Development Policy: Organisation and Planning of a Metropolitan Initiative, 1939–45*, Institute of Commonwealth Studies Paper, no. 22 (London, 1982).

WM. ROGER LOUIS, *Imperialism at Bay, 1941–1945: The United States and the Decolonization of the British Empire* (Oxford, 1977).

ANDREW ROBERTS, 'The Imperial Mind', chap. 1 of A. D. Roberts, ed., *The Cambridge History of Africa*, Vol. VII, *From 1905 to 1940* (Cambridge, 1986), pp. 24–76.

KENNETH ROBINSON, *The Dilemmas of Trusteeship: Aspects of British Colonial Policy Between the Wars* (Oxford, 1965).

RONALD ROBINSON, 'The Moral Disarmament of African Empire', in Norman Hillmer and Philip G. Wigley, eds., *The First British Commonwealth: Essays in Honour of Nicholas Mansergh* (London, 1980), pp. 86–104.

12

'Deceptive Might': Imperial Defence and Security, 1900–1968

ANTHONY CLAYTON

> ... the deceptive might of an Empire which continued to expand until 1919 but which cost more to defend than it contributed to national wealth.
>
> (Margaret Thatcher)[1]

> It is possible to have separate fleets in a United Empire but it is not possible to have separate fleets in a United Empire without having a common foreign policy—the creation of separate fleets has made it essential that the foreign policy of the Empire should be a common policy.
>
> (Sir Edward Grey, Foreign Secretary, 1911)[2]

Grey's observation, made to a meeting of the Committee of Imperial Defence at which Dominion delegates to the 1911 Imperial Conference were present, encapsulates the major conflicting themes of Imperial foreign and defence policies up to the end of the Second World War. The conference agreed to give priority to maritime strategy. Even in the early years of the twentieth century, however, tensions were already emerging between Dominion and British policies as well as within the defence establishment itself. Yet in the years prior to 1914, the mismatch between strategy and actual power did not seem to be of fundamental significance. After the First World War the tension became increasingly acute, in part because of shifting Dominion aims.

The menace of Wilhelmine Germany with her High Seas Fleet could clearly be seen as the main danger to the whole Empire. The alliance with Japan in 1902 and the agreements with France in 1904 and Russia in 1907 permitted naval concentration in home waters. The extension of Britain's administration of Egypt into Sinai shielded the Suez Canal. The Agadir crisis of 1911 led to an acceptance of a European continental commitment for the British army. Canada had sounded

[1] Margaret Thatcher, *The Downing Street Years* (London, 1995), p. 5.

[2] G. P. Gooch and Harold Temperley, eds., *British Documents on the Origins of the War, 1898–1914* (London, 1927–). For a more general examination see D. C. Watt, 'Imperial Defence Policy and Imperial Foreign Policy, 1911–1949: A Neglected Paradox?', *Journal of Commonwealth Political Studies*, I (1963), p. 266.

warnings, later modified, that she might not feel herself bound automatically to enter a British war. Australia, concerned with the rising naval power of Japan, had decided to build up a small Australian navy rather than contribute ships for absorption by the Royal Navy. Overall, however, Grey by 1914 could count on general Dominion support for foreign policy. The Committee for Imperial Defence, if not able to create an Imperial general staff, was able to co-ordinate preparatory work and ensure standardization of equipment and training. All the Dominions agreed that the defence of the metropole was paramount. If the metropole fell, the Dominions could not long survive. The defence of both metropole and Empire depended upon sea power.

Foreign and Defence Policies to 1939

The major Imperial consequences of the First World War have been summarized in chapter 5. Some were paradoxical. The Dominions had assumed a measure of joint responsibility with Britain for strategy and policy. This had enhanced Imperial sentiment and recognition of what a united Empire could achieve. At the same time, however, shared responsibility had fundamentally altered the relationship between Britain and the Dominions. The shift was augmented by the victorious emergence of the Irish Free State in 1921.

The new pattern was evident in 1919 at the Paris Peace Conference, where the Dominions and India were all represented in the British Empire delegation. Britain would have to continue to heed Dominion opinion and advice if she were to claim to speak for the Empire as a whole. Dominion opinion and advice, however, was in large part the product of each Dominion's fluctuating domestic policy and regional concerns. Although Dominion opinion necessarily reflected such diverse views as those of Afrikaners and French Canadians, it still contained a large measure of Imperial kith and kin sentiment. The shared suffering of 1914–18, and the hard fact that the destruction of Britain's still formidable naval and military power would leave the Dominions dangerously isolated, ensured a continuing, if ill-defined, Imperial dimension in foreign and defence policy. There followed a loose agreement on the major threats. The Dominions still looked to London for leadership. But the Dominions' new regional anxieties and interests before long led to divergence from Britain in foreign and defence perceptions, and thus the mismatch in foreign policy between Britain and the Dominions. Although there was general agreement on threats and an overarching defence framework, there was a disparity in foreign and defence priorities and needs, and in allocation of resources. Britain's global presence, indicated by the vast areas of the earth's surface coloured red on the map, created an illusion of global strength which in practice served to obscure realities.

Early indications of the consequences of these growing divergences were visible in disagreements over specific actions to be taken in the years from 1920 to 1922. The post-war hopes for a British-led Imperial foreign and defence policy first ran into difficulties when Canadian units withdrew from the Allied forces which had intervened against the Bolsheviks in Russia. There followed the more serious issue in 1921 of the ending of the Anglo-Japanese Alliance. Australia and New Zealand argued in vain for renewal; Canada was opposed.[3] The 1922 Chanak crisis, in which Canada and South Africa refused to promise any military support, could not be dismissed, as many in Britain hoped, as an aberration. For the remainder of the decade no major issues arose since there was no perceived opponent. In its strength the Empire could enjoy the luxury of being the world's only superpower, other contenders being preoccupied with internal affairs. The challenge of the aggressor nations in the early and mid-1930s, however, highlighted the mismatches in aims between the metropole and the Dominions, with the pressures of the Depression and rising costs of rearmament adding to the difficulties. In the critical pre-1939 years Britain was herself divided over how to frame Imperial foreign policies to meet aggressors; inevitably, military responses were limited.

Despite the absence of an agreed foreign policy, British defence policy reflected a much stronger measure of agreement. Although hopes for an 'Imperial Fleet' were dashed and tensions over priorities caused controversy, there did exist an over-arching solidarity between Britain and the Dominions. This was well summarized by Canada's W. L. Mackenzie King, the most independent-minded Dominion Prime Minister in matters of defence, who stated at the 1937 Imperial Conference that if Germany should ever attack Britain all the Dominions would come to her aid.[4] Much of this harmony in defence affairs was the outcome of the work of the Committee of Imperial Defence, in particular of the contacts, negotiating skills, and visits of its tireless Secretary until 1938, Sir Maurice Hankey.

After 1918 the dimensions of British naval strategy were altered by changing technology and economic needs. Middle East oil was important generally for internal combustion engines, for shipping, and specifically for the Royal Navy. Malaya was important for rubber. The Suez Canal and Singapore assumed a new significance at a time when Japan's ambitions posed a totally new Far Eastern threat to the Empire, creating later the insoluble major mismatch between needs and resources. The key force, despite obsolescence and reductions, remained the Royal Navy. After the abrogation of the Anglo-Japanese Alliance in 1921, almost one-half of the Royal Navy was stationed in the Mediterranean. Australia was

[3] Stephen Roskill, *Naval Policy Between the Wars*, 2 vols. (London, 1968), I, pp. 72, 292–93, 296–97, 300, and 315–17.

[4] Stephen Roskill, *Hankey, Man of Secrets*, 3 vols. (London, 1970–74), III, p. 281.

assured that the main fleet would arrive at Singapore within seventy days of a Japanese attack. All ships were given roles for such a contingency and refuelling facilities were prepared. The squadron stationed at Hong Kong, designed primarily to watch China and to serve as a tripwire against Japan, remained relatively small so that it would not be viewed by Japan as a provocation. The decision to build a naval base at Singapore was taken in 1921, but work was slow and interrupted. It was paid for in large part by contributions from the Straits Settlements and New Zealand. It quickly became another case of clash between Imperial defence needs and political quests for cuts in British foreign policy and defence costs. Work on the base was reduced in 1924–26 and only properly began in 1928. Despite further contributions from Hong Kong and the Federated Malay States, it slowed again in 1929.[5] The arguments ranged over cost, land and air vulnerability, and a proposed cheaper option of a large Royal Air Force (RAF) base. Australia and India both refused contributions. The leased naval facility at Wei-hai-wei was terminated and returned to China in 1930.

The British army reverted to its late-nineteenth-century role of a professional field army for Asia but not Europe. It was structured to meet what was considered the most likely military danger, a Soviet threat to India. In addition to its strategic role, the army could reinforce colonial authorities at times of unrest.[6] The British army in the inter-war years had a strength of about 180,000. Approximately one-third of the army, no less than forty-five battalions and six cavalry regiments, was stationed in India. Smaller garrisons served in Egypt, Sudan, Palestine, Singapore, Hong Kong, Shanghai, Jamaica, Malta, Gibraltar, and later Cyprus. The four, later five, divisions remaining in Britain were all under strength.

The recently formed Royal Air Force faced a battle to survive.[7] A high policy debate raged over the capacity of strategic bombing to win wars and in particular to destroy navies. In this controversy the RAF was held in check by the navy's champion, Admiral Earl Beatty, who argued successfully for a strong cruiser fleet to protect seaborne trade. The RAF's aggressive chief, Sir Hugh Trenchard, then championed the cause of air power in Imperial policing, based primarily on success in Iraq.[8] By the end of the 1930s RAF squadrons were serving in India, Iraq, Palestine, Malta, Aden, and Singapore.

[5] W. David McIntyre, *The Rise and Fall of the Singapore Naval Base, 1919–42* (London, 1979), chaps. 2–5.

[6] Field Marshal Lord Carver, *The Seven Ages of the British Army* (London, 1986), p. 223. Especially for the Soviet threat to India, see Brian Bond, *British Military Policy Between the Two World Wars* (Oxford, 1980), and Keith Jeffery, *The British Army and the Crisis of Empire, 1918–1922* (Manchester, 1984).

[7] Malcolm Smith, *British Air Strategy Between the Wars* (Oxford, 1984).

[8] For a more detailed look see David E. Omissi, *Air Power and Colonial Control: The Royal Air Force, 1919–1939* (Manchester, 1990).

The peacetime land and air forces of the Dominions remained small. The only significant contribution to Imperial security was that of Australia's cruiser squadron.[9] This squadron remained under tight local control, in contrast to New Zealand's more flexible approach with its much smaller naval force. British forces in Africa were also minor. No British units served in sub-Saharan Africa. The few small units of African troops remained under strength until the late 1930s.

After the First World War the Indian Army was reorganized for deployment on the frontiers (and to enter Afghanistan if necessary) and to provide internal security brigades. Its strength was slightly reduced from pre-1914 totals to 107 infantry battalions and twenty-one cavalry regiments.[10] This strength, still very large, was part of the Imperial military and strategic design, and was visible evidence of the strength and solidity of British rule. The regiments were recruited principally from the northern Indian peoples, perceived as the 'martial races'; the ten Gurkha regiments were recruited in Nepal. Almost all the Indian regiments were structured into different ethnic sub-units. Competition among the sub-units greatly increased their efficiency. The decade also saw the beginning of systematized training of Indian officers for the army. In addition to the formal Indian Army there were reserves, frontier levies, and barrack police totalling approximately 100,000 men. There were also the small forces of the Indian princely states, which varied greatly in size and quality.

In the deteriorating international situation of the 1930s the Dominions shared British reluctance to face up to the emerging triple threat from Japan, Italy, and Germany.[11] There were differences of opinion on the most immediate of the threats. These differences were compounded by doubts about the probability of all three aggressors acting together simultaneously and by different assessments in each Dominion. None approved any project for a British European military commitment.

As late as 1937 Canada, though willing to support Britain, was unwilling to promise an automatic response to a European war, and her rearmament was belated. Increasing nationalist sentiment in South Africa produced some sympathy for Germany and little for British Imperial ideals. South Africans were, however, concerned over Italy's attack on Ethiopia and over problems created by the more extreme Nazi sympathizers at home and in South-West Africa. Austra-

[9] A complete survey of all the forces of the Empire and commitments undertaken in the 1919–39 era is set out in Anthony Clayton, *The British Empire as a Superpower, 1919–39* (London, 1986).

[10] T. A. Heathcote, *The Military in British India* (Manchester, 1995), pp. 241–42. The combined total of 'The Army in India', the British General Staff term, was approximately 210,000 soldiers, 60,000 British, 150,000 Indian.

[11] Lawrence R. Pratt, *East of Malta, West of Suez: Britain's Mediterranean Crisis, 1936–1939* (Cambridge, 1975).

lia's fears centred on Japan.[12] There was growing scepticism about British ability to deploy a powerful enough navy in time, or even at all, to defeat Japan.[13] By 1939 Australian anxieties had greatly increased. The British undertaking to provide a fleet within seventy days from the start of any hostilities had extended to ninety. Australia's response was to strengthen her cruiser squadron rather than to help meet the costs of the Singapore base. New Zealand was generally less overtly critical of apparent British weaknesses, at least in part to assert her separate identity from Australia. New Zealand had, however, lodged objections to the 1931 British Labour government's decision to halt construction work at Singapore. Practical co-ordination among the Dominions was pushed in projects such as the Empire Air Training Scheme developed with Canada, in port modernization in South Africa, and in the unobtrusive development of shadow industries that could be converted in wartime to military use.

For India and the colonies, steps were taken in response to emerging threats from Italy, Japan, and ultimately from Germany. In the 1930s the Indian Army began a process of modernization. India was now allowed its own artillery and air force. If India's role in the First World War had been largely that of an Imperial reserve, this was not to be so again. By August 1939 combat-ready Indian Army brigades, in response to threats from Japan and Italy, were already on their way to Malaya and East Africa. In the colonies, African battalions were converted to field units while Italian subversive activity in Malta and Aden was kept under careful surveillance. In Egypt, British forces were moved to the Libyan border and plans were prepared for operations against the Italian navy. These included an aircraft-carrier strike on Taranto, a port and naval base in southern Italy. The plan was put to use in 1940.

In Britain herself, anti-militarism and appeasement slowed the pace of re-armament until 1936. It would seem that until 1937–38 the views of Prime Minister Neville Chamberlain prevailed: if attempts to placate Germany and Italy failed, Germany would be kept at a distance by France; the Japanese could never be stopped in China and probably not in Malaya, but any Japanese threat to Australia might draw America into war; India could protect herself; and British home and maritime defence could be secured by ships and relatively inexpensive fighter and coastal reconnaissance aircraft. The consequences of a collapse of France were never contemplated. But the events of 1938 and early 1939 shattered this insular approach. Preparations for war in Europe, including development of a field army, were reluctantly begun—sometimes at the expense of Imperial defence. France

[12] Henry P. Frie, *Japan's Southward Advance and Australia* (Honolulu, 1991).

[13] See Ian Hamill, *The Strategic Illusion: The Singapore Strategy and the Defence of Australia and New Zealand* (Singapore, 1981).

faced a naval threat from both Germany and Italy, and the British government consequently came under great pressure not to weaken its fleets in European waters. As a result, the Far East naval squadrons were not strengthened. Work resumed on the Singapore naval base in response to the Japanese threat, but did so on a reduced scale. The great dry dock was completed in 1938, but the landward defence for the base remained neglected.

Military reaction to the aggressors accordingly reflected the weakness of the Empire in face of the triple threat and the divergences between the priorities of the different parties. Japanese aggression was still met only by the defence of British interests in China.[14] In the Ethiopian crisis, although Australia and New Zealand contributed ships to the massive naval concentration, no action followed.[15] The navy feared that ships damaged in a conflict with Italy would not be available for use against Japan. To complicate matters further, France was opposed to war. Britain's decision not to act against German re-entry into the Rhineland was in part influenced by Dominion opposition to intervention. The Sudeten crisis of 1938 revealed disunity. South Africa and Canada both made it clear that they would not go to war. Their attitudes thereby reinforced domestic British preference for appeasement. Only the events of 1939 were sufficiently grave to draw strings of Imperial sentiment together and to enable an Empire united to go to war.

All three British services in the 1930s were the victims not only of financial stringency but also of their own circumstances. The navy remained haunted by the inhibiting memories of exploding capital ships at Jutland. The RAF and the army were constrained by the priorities given to light bombers and light tanks suitable only for Imperial security.[16]

In August 1939 the army possessed only sixty available infantry battle tanks. Consequently, the British Expeditionary Force sent to France in the following month comprised four infantry divisions, inadequately equipped, with no armoured formation.[17] An offsetting bonus, however, was the high standard of individual training and shooting within the army, a consequence of service on the North-West Frontier of India. It can perhaps also be claimed that Imperial experience gave senior British officers a wide vision and a political awareness, both of which proved invaluable in the Second World War. On the other hand, the techniques of lower-level purely military intelligence suffered, since in colonial

[14] Martin Brice, *The Royal Navy and the Sino-Japanese Incident, 1937–41* (London, 1973), details British reactions.

[15] See esp. Arthur J. Marder, *From the Dardanelles to Oran: Studies of the Royal Navy in War and Peace, 1915–1940* (London, 1974).

[16] Harold R. Winton, *To Change an Army: General Sir John Burnett-Stuart and British Armoured Doctrine, 1927–1938* (Lawrence, Kan., 1988); Uri Bialer, *The Shadow of the Bomber* (London, 1976).

[17] Bond, *British Military Policy*, p. 328.

situations intelligence work had fallen to the police. In Britain, manpower was available in almost the required totals. The unemployed joined the forces in large numbers for a square meal: many were undernourished and required special feeding and training. For the ambitious middle classes, Empire offered adventure and upward social mobility.

Internal Security, 1918–1939

The years prior to 1914 had seen no nationalist unrest of any security significance in India or the Colonial Empire. After the end of the First World War, however, nationalist challenges increasingly threatened not only local but wider Imperial security, as unrest often erupted in territories of especial economic or strategic significance. In the inter-war years British response to unrest or rebellion was a resolute defence of Imperial rule in the territory concerned.

In the 1919–39 era the main areas of unrest were in the Middle East and India (see Map 12.1). In the Middle East the causes included resentment that independence had not been granted in the post-war peacemaking. Other causes were exploitation during the war, British support for the landed classes, and Jewish immigration in Palestine. Revolt began in Egypt in 1919 with a small uprising put down with relative ease. In 1921 the nationalist leader Saad Zaghlul was arrested, but for the rest of the decade calm was secured by the granting of 'flag independence' in 1922, together with the display of power by warships and troops on further occasions of rioting. In 1920 there was a more serious, large-scale, 130,000-strong Arab uprising in Iraq, at the time a British mandated territory, which required fifty-one battalions to contain it.[18] The power of the insurgents and, later in the decade, that of both Turkish irredentists and local secessionists in the oil-producing Mosul and the Kurd areas, were all broken primarily by RAF bombing and machine-gunning.[19] The combination of aircraft, armoured cars, and locally recruited units or levies also secured British dominance when challenged by incursions into Palestine, Transjordan, or Iraq by armed raiders from Arabia. This mix of armed forces also secured the autonomy of Kuwait in 1927–29, and was applied with equal success against rebels in the Aden hinterland. Only two uprisings in the Middle East required a heavier deployment of force, the Sudan military mutiny of 1924 and the 1929 Arab uprising in Palestine.[20] The former was

[18] General Sir Aylmer Haldane, *The Insurrection in Mesopotamia, 1920* (London, 1923), outlines the operations.

[19] Air Marshal Sir John Salmond, 'The Air Force in Iraq', *Journal of the Royal United Services Institution*, LXX (1925), pp. 483–98.

[20] Accounts of these appear in Major-General Sir Charles W. Gwynn, *Imperial Policing* (London, 1934), chaps. 7 and 9.

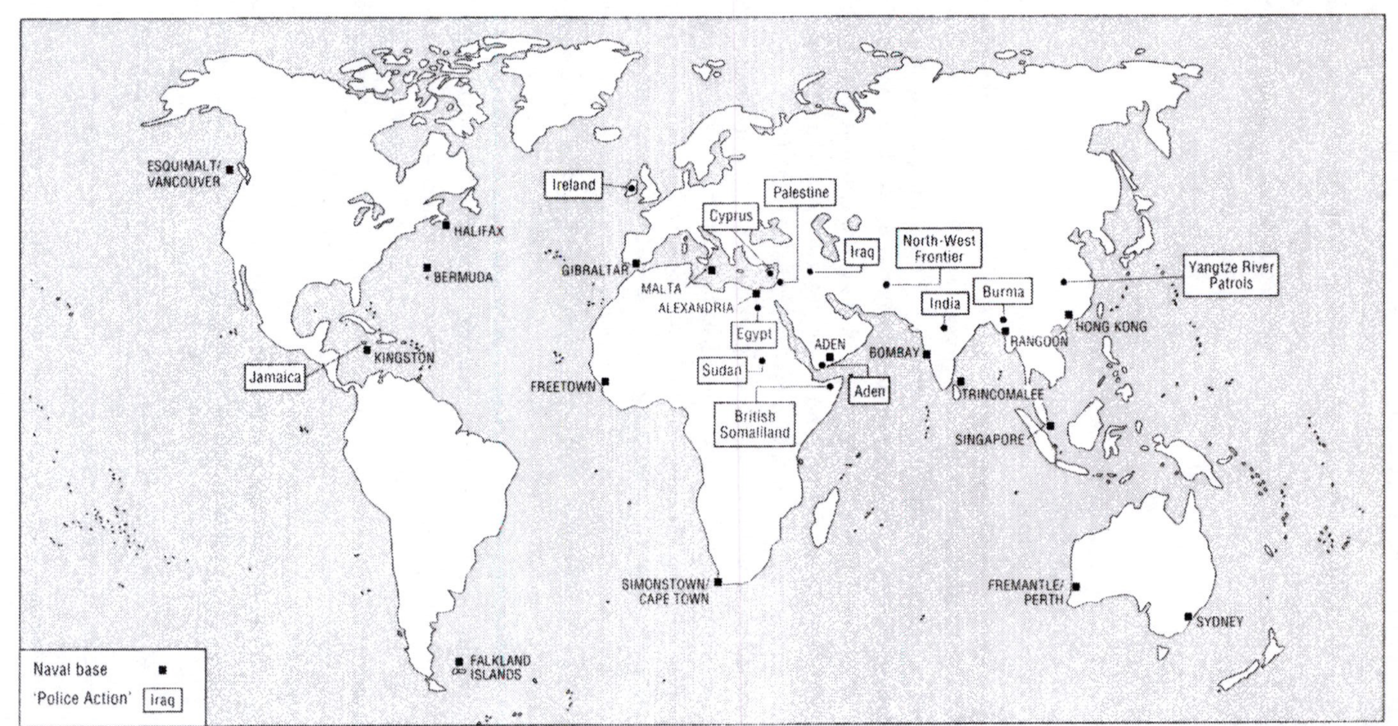

MAP 12.1. Police Action involving Military or Naval Deployment between the Wars, 1919–1939

followed by prolonged small-scale operations in the Upper Nile. The Palestine uprising required troop reinforcements transported in warships from Egypt. Notably effective also were the partly European Palestine Police and the Arab Legion, the latter based in the British client state of Transjordan. By the end of the decade British hegemony appeared solidly established, and the rival Hashemite and Saudi dynasties seemed reconciled, at least temporarily, at a meeting aboard a British sloop.

Almost immediately after the Armistice of 1918 India faced the double challenge of nationalist protest and Afghan invasion. The nationalist movement in India was fuelled by wartime hardship and resentment against repressive anti-sedition legislation. Mahatma Gandhi's response was *satyagraha*, the non-cooperation movement, largely Hindu but also Muslim-supported. Intended to be non-violent, the movement nevertheless led to disturbances in the Punjab and elsewhere. Rioting and disorders were followed by firm repression. In the mistaken belief that all Muslims would rise in support, the Emir of Afghanistan launched a powerful military invasion into the North-West Frontier Province and Baluchistan in 1919. After some heavy fighting the Afghans were defeated and India's frontiers were restored. The war, however, ended any hope of Afghanistan becoming a client state. For the remainder of the decade the Frontier Province and Baluchistan were the scene of ongoing, limited-scale operations against skilful Pathan guerrillas. British, Indian, and Gurkha battalions, Scout gendarmerie units, and irregular levies as well as those supported by the RAF all operated in harsh mountainous areas described, accurately, as 'non-administered'. Defence was based on massive forts, the largest of which, Razmak, could accommodate two brigades, though its normal garrison was three battalions.[21]

In the subcontinent itself the non-cooperation movement became entangled with other violent protests: the 1919–21 Muslim Khalifat movement, the 1921 Moplah peasant uprising in south-west India, the 1922 Akali Sikh movement. There were attacks on police and government stations in Madras in 1922–23 and Bengal from 1924.[22] As the decade progressed rioting and killings became increasingly 'communal', arising from the tensions of poverty as well as nationalism, but requiring considerable police and military effort to contain. India's north-east frontier and Burma were also the scenes of local violence. The years 1928–29 saw a return to sporadic but widespread violence, which the British promise of 1929 for a grant of Dominion Status and a constitutional conference failed to satisfy.

Elsewhere in the Empire the final suppression in 1919 of the revolt in British Somaliland was only achieved after a sharp campaign in which RAF aircraft

[21] Major General J. G. Elliott, *The Frontier, 1839–1947* (London, 1968), pp. 49–51.

[22] See Gwynn, *Imperial Policing*, chap. V.

demonstrated considerable skill. The Colonial Office saw the campaign as a model. At £70,000 it was the least-expensive Imperial campaign on record. In the East and West African territories small-scale resistance or unrest was usually caused by labour protest, opposition to taxation or chieftaincy appointments, local ethnic clashes, or prevention of cross-frontier raiding. These disturbances were generally controlled by small police forces, but sometimes required the support of local African battalions. Unrest in Trinidad and British Honduras in 1919 and in Singapore in 1927 was checked by the police, but control over disturbances in Sarawak in 1923 and in Hong Kong in 1925 necessitated military support, and in Malta in 1919, support from warship crews. New Zealand naval personnel suppressed Mau insurgency in Samoa, though it was to surface again in the 1930s. Australian sailors were used to reassert British Imperial authority in the New Hebrides in 1920 and the Solomons in 1927, and Australian authority in Papua and New Britain in 1926–29. In 1926–27 a large British force, including Indian troops, was despatched to join a multinational force in Shanghai, where warlord fighting threatened the International Settlement.[23] By the end of the decade, however, Indian troops were stationed outside the subcontinent only in Aden and Hong Kong.

The control of the Empire and repression of insurrection was secured by new technology without which the British might have been forced to abandon several areas, including part of the Middle East. Foremost was the use of air power for reconnaissance, supply, and attack. The bombing of dissidents, at times ruthless, ensured British authority at immense savings of manpower.[24] The garrison of Iraq, supported by twenty-three British and Indian battalions in May 1921, was reduced to two battalions by 1928. This was particularly fortunate for the British because the use of Indian Army battalions outside India now aroused political protests in India. Air bombing was remote, and its effects could often be concealed from critics, both metropolitan and local. On occasion the effect was enhanced by the use of delayed-action bombs, but the use of poison gas was never sanctioned. Other developments included the much swifter local movement of troops to the scene of conflict by motor lorry, first demonstrated in repelling the Afghan invasion of 1919, the air movement of troops, used increasingly in Iraq, and the transport of troops by sea aboard the faster warships of the period. Developments in wireless technology and aircraft signals facilitated command and control.

At the same time democratic accountability in Britain, real if incomplete, soon imposed restraints, usually in the form of Parliamentary Questions or debates on the uses of force. The massacre at Amritsar in 1919, when British troops fired on an angry but unarmed crowd, occasioned political repercussions both in India and Britain. Military tactics and training evolved on principles of displays of power by

[23] See Gwynn, *Imperial Policing*, chap. 8.

[24] See Omissi, *Air Power* chaps. 1–3.

ships, aircraft, and 'flag marches' by troops in the hope that conversion of power into force would not be necessary. When force was used in the 1920s, it involved minimum numbers and where possible locally recruited units. Such use was only in accord with the wishes of the local administration and with strict rules governing crowd-control and clear warning before firing commenced. The severity of aircraft bombing was scaled down to intimidating 'air control' flights. Those targeted in any case developed their own early warnings as well as evacuation and decoy counter-measures.

The 1930s were very different. Imperial hegemony was now seriously challenged by the dictator nations. At the same time the Empire also faced, in several territories, more sophisticated insurgency fuelled in part by the hardship of the Depression years. Britain's ability to control events was undermined by her own economic problems, the costs of rearmament, anti-militarism, and increasing self-doubt over the propriety of defending or even retaining the Empire. Nevertheless, the more numerous and threatening security problems of the decade saw the development of counter-insurgency operational techniques based on experience. Stress was laid on intelligence, collective communal punishment, cordon and search tactics, and the strict control over orders to shoot.[25]

In the case of the Indian Empire the challenges on the North-West Frontier, 'The Grim' to generations of British soldiers, escalated into limited conventional war. Ever-larger forces were required in operations against the Red Shirt followers of the Haji of Turungzai and the Fakir of Alinghar and, from 1936, the Fakir of Ipi. By 1937 50,000 soldiers, artillery, light tanks, and aircraft were committed.[26] The Haji's raids of 1930 were timed to coincide with the nationalist civil disobedience campaign, and resulted in mass arrests throughout India. Gandhi's release from prison in January 1931 secured a brief cessation of unrest, but civil disobedience was renewed in 1932–33. The disturbances in the last pre-war years increasingly reflected communal tensions and competition for local power, and, in Bengal, the calculated use of terror. In Burma too, British rule was challenged by frequent nationalist rioting, by a jungle guerrilla rebellion from 1930 to 1932, and in the last years of the decade by student revolts and the wider-based *Thakin* movement.[27]

The Great Depression exacerbated security problems in many colonies or created new ones. Local unrest in the West Indies and in British Honduras from 1930 to 1934 was followed by protest in the Leeward Islands, in Trinidad, and in St Lucia in 1935. All these events culminated in mass demonstrations in Trinidad and Barbados in 1937, in British Guiana in 1938, and finally with riots in Jamaica in 1938.

[25] Two War Office publications, *Notes on Imperial Policing* (1934) and *Duties in Aid of the Civil Power* (1937), were the official manuals; Gwynn, *Imperial Policing*, chaps. 1, 2, is also useful.

[26] Gwynn, *Imperial Policing*, chap. 10; Elliott, *The Frontier*, pp. 181–88, 270–81.

[27] John F. Cady, *A History of Modern Burma* (Ithaca, NY, 1958), pp. 309–17, 375–83.

These were all contained by police, local militia, troops, and warship crews. In Africa military units were used to depose a regent (Tshekedi Khama) in Bechuanaland. Other African colonies also experienced forewarnings of difficulties to come. To the ongoing unrest caused by local issues, ethnic and industrial, were now added events such as the 1935 strikes by African mine-workers in Northern Rhodesia, the 1939 Mombasa strike, and the tensions created by the Gold Coast cocoa growers' boycott. The Italian attack on Ethiopia in 1935–36 created refugee problems in northern Kenya. Small-scale security operations continued in several remote areas of the Sudan, military support for the police was necessary in Ceylon and Mauritius, while subversive movements appeared in Singapore, Fiji, and Sarawak. Even more serious trouble had erupted in 1931 in Cyprus where a movement seeking *enosis* or union with Greece was suppressed by troops and warship crews.[28]

In the Middle East British hegemony proved increasingly difficult to maintain, and the means employed more questionable. In Egypt, after an outbreak of nationalist rioting in 1930 was contained by troops and warships, British political manipulation secured a docile client government until further disorders in 1935. A new and, at the time, well-received Anglo-Egyptian Treaty of 1936 actually perpetuated Egypt's client status. The continuing British military presence was compensated for by League of Nations membership. Iraq, another British client, experienced violence after independence in 1932. The Sunni Baghdad governments, first civil then military, remained dependent on the RAF against Kurdish insurrection, but they soon turned to oppression of Kurds, Assyrian Christians, and Shia Muslims. Britain's need for oil forced her to tolerate these Iraqi actions. After several internal coups, some form of order was temporarily restored from 1938 by the pro-British Nuri es-Said. The combination of air control and local regiments or levies continued to protect Transjordan against destabilizing raids. (Sir) John Glubb, the British commander of the 'Desert Patrol' and later of the Arab Legion, saw his role as psychological as much as military. He aimed to convert the desert Arabs, by their own choice, from a life of violence.[29] In this he was successful, gaining the confidence of the Emir of Transjordan, Abdullah, who was later to prove of great importance. In 1934 a treaty with Yemen ended the external threat to the Aden hinterland. The 'air blockade' tactic for controlling movement to and from particular areas, however, remained necessary within the Protectorate.

It was the uprising in Palestine in 1936–39 that most seriously jeopardized the British structure of control in the Middle East.[30] Palestine was second only to

[28] Gwynn, *Imperial Policing*, chap. 12.

[29] James Lunt, *Glubb Pasha: A Biography. Lieutenant-General Sir John Bagot Glubb, Commander of the Arab Legion, 1939–1956* (London, 1984), chaps. 5–6.

[30] Michael J. Cohen, *Palestine: Retreat from the Mandate* (London, 1978), chaps. 1–5, provides a valuable account of the events.

Egypt in importance both as a base for arriving Indian troops, if Italy threatened control of the Eastern Mediterranean and the Red Sea, and as the terminal for the Haifa oil pipeline. Accelerating rates of Jewish immigration, followed by Jewish acquisition of property and land, created Arab resentment. The resulting riots and killings of the early 1930s turned to full rebellion guided by the Mufti of Jerusalem in April 1936. Initial violence was reduced by the October 1936 promise of a Royal Commission. During this lull, lasting to the summer of 1937, violence remained sporadic as mutual suspicions worsened, but Britain, freed from the Ethiopian crisis, was able to deploy sufficient troops. Drawn from among these were the Special Night Squads. The British army's first special forces, they represented the forerunners of the later Special Air Service Regiments. The Special Night Squads were the brainchild of Orde Wingate, who later achieved fame in Burma during the Second World War as leader of the 'Chindit' long-range penetration groups.[31] Their role was pursuit, patrolling, ambush, and intelligence-gathering.

The report of the Royal Commission (Peel Commission) approved by the Colonial Office but opposed by the Foreign Office, envisaged partition, thus arousing renewed Arab anger. The British had to face a violent campaign of killings, burnings, ambushes, and rail and pipeline sabotage at a time when troops had to be withdrawn because of the Sudeten crisis in 1938. Control of the rural areas was lost, or passed into the hands of Jewish irregulars. Arab propaganda and the charisma of one insurgent leader, Fawzi Kauwakji, attracted recruits from the entire Arab world. The Munich Agreement of September 1938 released more troops, and the garrison, now some twenty regiments, was able to contain the Arab uprising. To retain the increasingly reluctant support of Iraq and Saudi Arabia, a new policy statement was prepared and issued in May 1939 that curtailed Jewish immigration into Palestine. This in turn intensified a Jewish terrorist campaign that had begun earlier. Only the outbreak of the Second World War brought about a truce. Overall Britain was fortunate that, despite the tensions caused by the Jewish freedom fighters, her clients and allies in the Middle East remained supportive. The visible strength of the Royal Navy in the Mediterranean was an important element in securing this support.

Defence and Security after 1945

The post-war foreign and defence policies of Britain extended further the dilemma of mismatch between needs and resources for another twenty-five years. Britain herself was financially exhausted. Her people had voted for the promised welfare state and a Labour government. At the same time a massive Soviet continental threat, directly affecting Britain herself, was emerging against which costly nuclear

[31] Trevor Royle, *Orde Wingate: Irregular Soldier* (London, 1995).

weaponry was seen as an essential counter. But Britain's worldwide commitments in 1945 were supported by over 2 million men under arms. Labour politicians, notably the Foreign Secretary, Ernest Bevin, and military commanders (once again mindful of Dominion manpower) argued for a revived Imperial defence policy as essential for continuing Great Power status.[32] This was to be based on 'world zones', including one in East Asia and one in the Middle East. Strengthening the latter to secure oil routes was of particular importance. Both zones were to be supported by Australia, New Zealand, and South Africa.[33] The Chiefs of Staff initially rejected any permanent European continental commitment.

The Prime Minister, Clement Attlee, was at first sceptical. He correctly foresaw Indian independence and the consequent loss of Indian military manpower. In March 1946 he wrote perceptively that '... we shall have to consider the British Isles as an easterly extension of a strategic arc the centre of which is the American continent more than as a power looking Eastwards through the Mediterranean and the East'.[34] Though he later modified these views, he opposed costly strategies. He was supported by the Treasury ministers, who pointed out the huge discrepancy between Britain's military commitments and her financial resources; by other ministers who appreciated that colonial empires were becoming anachronistic, and by those within the military, led by Field Marshal Viscount Montgomery, who argued that priority must be given to a continental commitment with an army- and not a navy-based strategy.[35] Significantly, the Committee of Imperial Defence was not reformed, though consultation continued.

As the cold war intensified, it strengthened the hands of Bevin and the Chiefs of Staff both in overall strategy debate and in claiming a need to retain strategically important British possessions such as Malaya in the face of insurgency. A parallel belief that Britain's economic decline was temporary led to a succession of compromises that resulted in periodic and precipitate changes in defence and colonial policies. The continuing economic weakness, too, necessitated a greater reliance on the United States for financial support. Initially this 'Special Relationship' was seen in Britain as a partnership between equals. Responsive to domestic attitudes, the Dominion governments were increasingly uninterested in general defence policy outside their own geographic regions as contrasted with the

[32] Correlli Barnett, 'The British Illusion of World Power, 1945–50', *Royal United Services Institute Journal* (Oct. 1995), pp. 57–64, and the introduction and documents in Ritchie Ovendale, *British Defence Policy since 1945* (Manchester, 1994), set out the issues.

[33] Ritchie Ovendale, *The English-Speaking Alliance* (London, 1985), p. 275 notes the South African Premier Malan's respect for Bevin.

[34] Ronald Hyam, ed., *The Labour Government and the End of Empire, 1945–1951*, British Documents on the End of Empire Project (BDEEP), Series A, 4 vols. (London, 1992), III, p. 213.

[35] See Michael Howard, *The Continental Commitment: The Dilemma of British Defence Policy in the Era of the Two World Wars* (London, 1972).

American concern over European and even global security. Only the Korean War, when Commonwealth forces assembled from every self-governing territory except Pakistan and Ceylon, recaptured the pre-1945 years of Imperial unity.

The new relationship with the United States also reflected the importance that the Americans attached to a politically strong Britain as a partner in the cold war. It amounted to a grand strategy, never formally set out but tacitly agreed upon, that the United States would not complicate British colonial policies provided these were liberal. Policies would be followed that aimed at independence, which would come sooner for client states and later for colonies. All would be linked, if possible, in American, British, and Dominion security treaty systems. Of these systems, the 1949 North Atlantic Treaty Organization (NATO) was in time to become pre-eminent. The new emphasis was first displayed in the 1950 Defence White Paper, followed later in the same year by a specific acceptance of a land-force commitment in Europe. At the same time the United States Navy supplanted the Royal Navy as the major force in both the Mediterranean and the Atlantic. While the US Navy defended the British Isles as part of its role in NATO, it was not committed to the defence of other British territories. The Labour government had to draw on Conservative parliamentary support to extend wartime conscription, which was necessary for the army to meet the combination of colonial and continental commitments.

In 1950 a British 'Global Strategy' paper was conceived in terms of a deterrent phase in the cold war secured by an American nuclear umbrella in the form of American bomber squadrons based in Britain. These aircraft in fact arrived during the tension over the Berlin airlift in 1948–49. Under the Conservative government of 1951–55 there followed a succession of Defence Reviews, each attempting to balance inter-service arguments while edging away from any colonial dimension in policy. Weight was necessarily laid upon the available resources, which were constrained by the spiralling costs imposed by advances in technology. Increasing attention was paid to NATO and to nuclear and ballistic missile capabilities. These policy shifts emphasized that defence was centred on the metropole and that the Dominions would be left to negotiate and secure their own regional arrangements. Notable among the reviews were the 1952 Defence White Paper that marked the end of ambitious Royal Navy construction projects, the transfer of the Simonstown naval base to South Africa in 1955, and Duncan Sandys's 1957 White Paper that strongly emphasized nuclear deterrence, announced the end of conscription, and foresaw further moves away from a maritime strategy and from any assertion of a primary importance for the Middle East.[36] These developments all arose from

[36] On Simonstown, see Peter James Henshaw, 'The Transfer of Simonstown: Afrikaner Nationalism, South African Strategic Dependence, and British Global Power', *Journal of Imperial and Commonwealth*

the mismatch between resources and commitments that was not to be resolved until the next decade.

The internal security challenges within colonial territories must, therefore, be seen within the context of fears that the colonies would become ideological battlefields in the cold war.[37] Before 1939 the aim of robust 'imperial policing' had been the maintenance of political control, or in the Middle East of hegemony, but by the early 1950s such aims were outdated. In areas of disturbance or open rebellion, now described in low-key terms as 'emergencies', security operations were designed to gain time and, with regained initiative, to find new 'moderate' allies and marginalize 'extremists', if necessary by force. Marginalization was also useful for political presentation, as it appeared to justify military action.[38] Time gained could also be used for political, economic, and social restructuring aimed at creating the new moderate interlocutors who would co-operate in the preservation of Britain's long-term economic and strategic interests after independence. Accordingly, during the years of decolonization British governments, whether Labour or Conservative, made it clear that while they were not prepared to be summarily ejected from any colony, they would use their still-considerable powers to influence the nature of change, if not the ultimate goal, for metropolitan or for local reasons. The events were in consequence a disjointed sequence of pragmatic local responses to challenges. They are best described by region rather than in chronological order (see Map 12.2).[39]

Perhaps no available military force could have prevented the ethnic violence in the Punjab and Bengal that accompanied the independence and partition of India and Pakistan. British personnel were forbidden to assist either side in the Kashmir crisis or in later India–Pakistan conflicts, though the British tilted towards Pakistan. By March 1948 all British troops had left both the subcontinent and Burma. The Malayan insurgency, with its threat to rubber supply and dollar earnings, however, retained in South-East Asia powerful British forces committed to military operations against insurgents, who were described somewhat loosely as 'C.T.s', Communist terrorists. These operations lasted twelve years and at their peak involved 35,000 troops and 73,000 police. An exceptionally able military High Commissioner from 1952 to 1954, General Sir Gerald Templer, was the principal

History, XX, 3, pp. 419–44. On the navy generally, Eric Grove, *From Vanguard to Trident: British Naval Policy Since World War Two* (Annapolis, 1987).

[37] See John Kent, *British Imperial Strategy and Origins of the Cold War, 1944–1949* (London, 1993).

[38] Frank Furedi, 'Creating a Breathing Space: The Political Management of Colonial Emergencies', in Robert Holland, ed., *Emergencies and Disorder in the European Empires After 1945* (London, 1994), pp. 89–106.

[39] General Sir William Jackson, *Withdrawal from Empire* (London, 1990) provides a comprehensive military account.

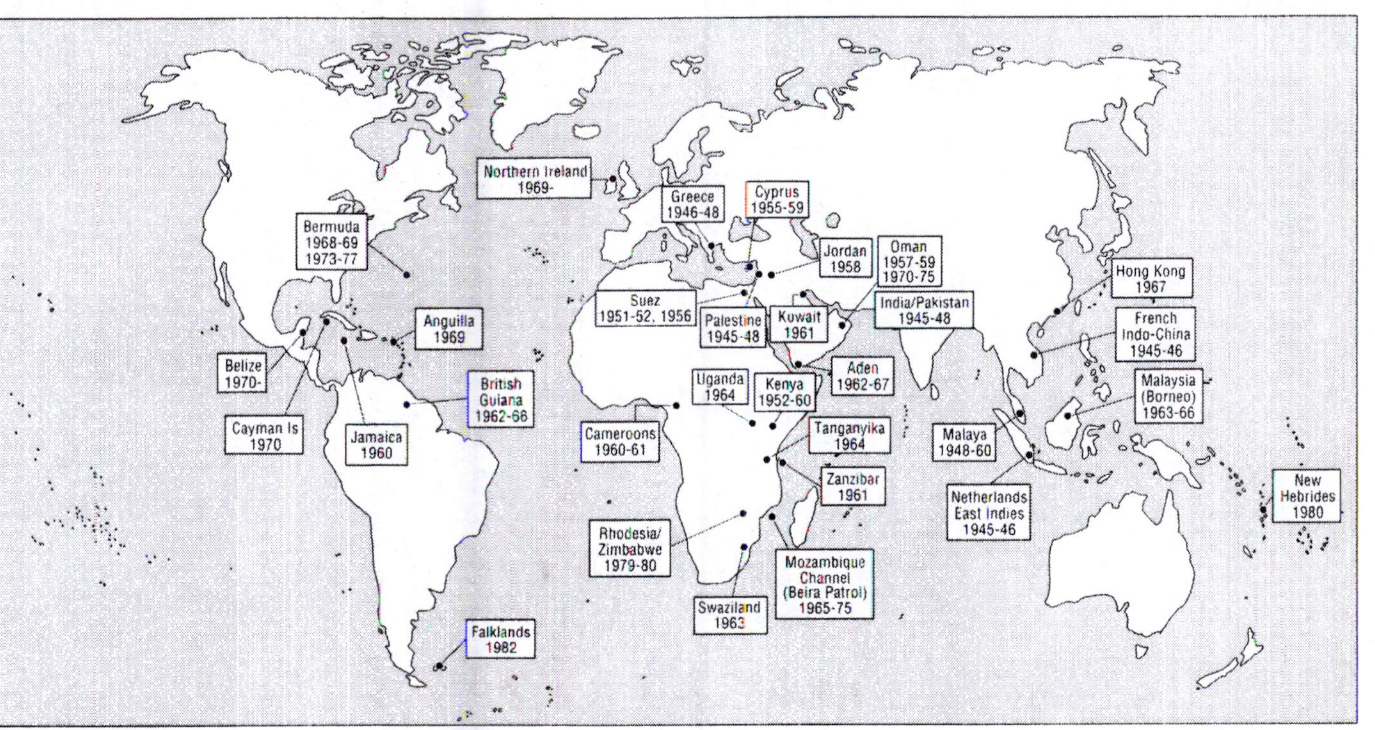

Map 12.2. British Emergencies and Operations since 1945

architect both of the military victory and of the effective mobilization of local political and popular support.[40] A vital ingredient of this success was the policy of 'villageization', the large-scale movement of plantation labour from scattered jungle-fringe settlements into well-policed and administered villages from which the insurgents could no longer draw support.

In the Middle East in 1945 Palestine and Egypt were seen as the foundations on which British power would rest.[41] Palestine was to be a bomber base in case of war with the Soviet Union and a station for a cold war strategic reserve. Egypt and the Suez Canal were seen as indispensable for the transport of oil supplies from the Persian Gulf and specifically for control of the Abadan oil refinery in Iran. Middle Eastern oil was essential to maintain the viability of sterling. Middle Eastern countries, however, were quick to notice that the Royal Navy no longer dominated the Eastern Mediterranean.

The first major challenge was the Jewish rebellion in Palestine that erupted on 31 October 1945.[42] Violence worsened with a sophisticated campaign of urban bombings, sabotage, and assassinations by the 45,000 strong Jewish people's defence force, the Haganah, and two aggressive commando groups, Irgun Zvai Leumi, 2,500 strong, and Lachmi Heruth Israel (Stern Gang) of some 600. Their common ambition, an Israeli state, was contrary to the British policy in 1945–46 of a binational state. The campaign for a Jewish state was supported by massive propaganda, particularly in the United States, whose pressures on the British government to permit mass Jewish immigration into Palestine greatly added to Britain's difficulties. The British garrison, although 100,000 strong, was war-weary and often ineffective in security operations. The navy, however, functioned efficiently in intercepting numerous illegal immigrant ships that attempted, often with French, Italian, or American help, to land large numbers of Jews in excess of the permitted quotas. The British naval policy in particular attracted wide criticism. The British government tried in vain to secure agreement between Jews and Arabs for the binational state. In February 1947, in mounting despair, and appalled by the cost of the campaign, London announced that it was passing the problem to the United Nations for solution. Under pressure from both the United States and the Soviet Union, and to the chagrin of Britain, the United Nations recommended partition. This proposal, announced in November, was the signal for both Jews and Arabs to turn to arms. In disgust Britain announced that she

[40] Lawrence James, *Imperial Rearguard: Wars of Empire, 1918–95* (London, 1988), pp. 136–57; John Clarke, *Templer: Tiger of Malaya* (London, 1985), chaps. 9–12.

[41] See Michael Cohen, *Fighting World War Three from the Middle East: Allied Contingency Plans, 1945–1954* (London, 1997).

[42] David A. Charters, *The British Army and Jewish Insurgency in Palestine, 1945–47* (Basingstoke, 1989), provides the best account of this campaign.

would end the mandate in May 1948. This was followed by localized but bloody civil war between Jews and Arabs. Residual British security collapsed as troops moved out, area by area. Britain's hopes that the Arabs would secure possession of sufficient land, and so retain goodwill towards Britain, were dashed by the incompetence of the Arab armies in the post-independence conflict, in spite of some covert British aid.

Withdrawal from Palestine sharpened debate over the British military presence in Egypt.[43] Some Labour ministers, including at first Attlee, were in favour of conceding Egypt's request of 1946 for a withdrawal of troops and of concentrating on a new defence line from East Africa to the Gulf. The military, however, argued that a strong presence in the Canal Zone remained essential to contain Soviet designs. These views were supported by more traditional and Conservative political leaders, for whom control of the Suez Canal had become a symbol of British virility. A loosening of control would be seen as evidence of decline, with ripple effects elsewhere. Such attitudes towards Suez were to develop into the self-deluding view that any Egyptian leader who challenged them would present a mortal danger to Britain and have to be neutralized. Attlee recognized these pressures, but negotiations with the Egyptian government on conditions for troops remaining anywhere in the country made no real progress. A shooting and sabotage campaign against British forces in the Canal Zone opened with covert Egyptian government support. The fighting intensified in 1951 and by early 1952 required 80,000 troops to garrison the Zone.

The Churchill government that came to power in 1951 was divided. The Foreign Secretary, Anthony Eden, argued for a negotiated withdrawal with the right to return in the event of war, while the Treasury pressed for large cuts in military expenditure. New negotiations with Egypt resulted in an agreement in 1954 that British troops would be withdrawn with a right to return, and that the base installations would be maintained by British civilians. Churchill's initial objections were assuaged by his vision of a more favourable overall international situation that followed the American explosion of the hydrogen bomb, American aid to Iraq, and Yugoslavia's quarrel with Stalin.

American diplomacy had facilitated the Egyptian agreement, as it had in the crisis following the Iranian government's nationalization in 1951 of the British-owned Abadan oil installations. The nationalization had led to vain military threats from Britain. The United States counselled caution and eventually masterminded the political and commercial solution of the 1954 Consortium Agreement,

[43] A valuable summary of the debate appears in John Kent, 'The Egyptian Base and the Defence of the Middle East, 1945–54', in Holland, ed., *Emergencies and Disorder*, pp. 45–65. The main documents arising from the debate are reproduced in Ronald Hyam, ed., *The Labour Government*, III, pp. 273–82.

which broke the British oil monopoly and allowed American participation. This solution was, however, seen by many, especially within the British military, as one more step towards the replacement of British by American hegemony.

The Suez crisis of 1956, following Egyptian military contacts with the Soviet Union and President Nasser's defiant nationalization of the Suez Canal Company, opened a more obvious Anglo-American rift. Gamal Abdel Nasser's action reawakened Conservative suspicions and reservations over withdrawal from Egypt. Eden, now Prime Minister, believed that he had been betrayed, and he saw in Nasser a Soviet-backed 1930s-style dictator posing a mortal threat. In this view Eden was encouraged, for their own reasons, by both France and Israel, and by considerable public sentiment that resented British decline and hoped for some reassertion of British power. A massive Anglo-French armada seized Port Said in November 1956. The hope was that Nasser would then fall. United Nations criticism contributed to the decision by Britain and France to halt and later to evacuate their forces. The United States had applied heavy economic pressure while Canada had proposed an international force. Within the Commonwealth the expedition was supported fully only by Australia and tepidly by New Zealand. It was strongly opposed by India and within Britain herself by the Labour Opposition. Despite the rift, the Anglo-American partnership was quickly restored, although after Suez the United States watched British policies more critically. The need for the British and Americans to close ranks was emphasized by threats from Moscow during the crisis and by the brutality of the Soviet repression of the Hungarian uprising.

Britain's involvement in the Suez attack first led to her withdrawal from Jordan in 1956–57 and then sealed the fate of the pro-British government of Nuri es-Said in Iraq, which was overthrown in 1958. The intervention by British troops in 1958 in Jordan and Oman represented an attempt to restore respect for Britain at a time when American troops were committed in Lebanon. Overall, however, the Suez crisis represented the effective end of the British era in the Middle East and brought home to the British government the reduction of British power and influence.[44]

Britain had simultaneously to cope with a major insurrection in another strategically sensitive area, Cyprus. In 1955 the Ethniki Orhanosis Kyrion Agoniston (EOKA) movement in Cyprus, led by an able former Greek army officer General Georgios Grivas, opened an urban and mountain terror campaign aimed at union with Greece. EOKA was violently opposed by the Turkish minority. The campaign was marked by EOKA's intimidation and infiltration of the largely Greek Cyprus police force and violence on both sides, which took the form of

[44] Selwyn Lloyd, *Suez 1956* (London, 1978), pp. 251–52.

bombings by EOKA and severe interrogations by the security forces. The effort against EOKA involved a 30,000 strong British garrison and an imported force of British police.[45] Finally, in 1959, an international conference in Zurich, the result of American diplomacy through NATO, prepared a constitution providing for independence, but not union with Greece, and the retention by Britain of small base enclaves. The solution satisfied the reduced needs of the British. The Greeks accepted it reluctantly as a lesser evil than partition.

Britain's last colonial campaign in the Middle East was in Aden, also still perceived as strategically important.[46] The territory had seen small-scale violence in 1947 and rather larger-scale insurrection, requiring British troops, in 1955. British policy from 1959 was to create an economically and politically viable Federation of Southern Arabia in which the more moderate chieftains of the barren hinterland would check the radical nationalism of the prosperous Aden port area. Aden had reluctantly agreed to join the Federation in 1963, but in that year there erupted near the Yemen border a two-year long guerrilla campaign supported by Egypt. This campaign was contained by British and Federation troops. Britain later promised the Federation independence with a continued British military presence. In 1964, however, the insurgency movement, notably the National Liberation Front, launched violent attacks in Aden itself. In 1966 the re-elected British Labour government cancelled the proposed British military support. At the same time a rival, Egyptian-backed, insurgency movement, the Freedom and Liberation of Occupied South Yemen (FLOSY) also appeared. The hinterland chieftains changed alliances or were killed, and some, but not all, of the Federation forces defected. Britain was forced into a military withdrawal in November 1967. After Suez, British policy in the Middle East had little hope of long-term success and the policy-changes merely ensured total failure.

In most of the remaining Colonial Empire political emergencies were small-scale, but a major exception was in Kenya, where the Mau Mau uprising opened in 1952 and lasted effectively for four years. Mau Mau drew its members from the landless, the exploited urban workers, and evicted 'surplus' labour from settler farms, almost all Kikuyu or Kikuyu-related peoples. The Mau Mau movement was greatly strengthened by the arrest of Jomo Kenyatta, the foremost nationalist leader. Some 12,000 British and African troops, a greatly expanded police force, and local Kikuyu irregulars were required to suppress the rebellion. The RAF attempted to reassert its pre-war policing role, but its bombing campaign achieved little. The fighting was marked by violence on both sides. Much of Mau Mau

[45] David M. Anderson, 'Policing and Communal Conflict: The Cyprus Emergency, 1954–60', in Holland, ed., *Emergencies and Disorder*, pp. 177–207.

[46] Julian Paget, *Last Post: Aden, 1964–67* (London, 1969).

strategy was based on terror. On the government's side excesses were committed almost entirely by the irregulars or local whites, in disregard of the strict orders by the Army Commander, General Sir George Erskine.[47] Heavy political criticism, in particular over the deaths of prisoners at Hola Camp, contributed to changes in Conservative colonial policies at the end of the 1950s. The campaign's end, and lack of support from other Kenyan ethnic groups, was the result of political, economic, and social reforms which reflected British acceptance that future British interests lay in an African rather than a white settler economy. Providing a stabilizing presence in a time of rapid change, British troops remained in Kenya until 1964.

The events of another episode developed into a far wider significance with the Unilateral Declaration of Independence by Rhodesia in 1965. Unrest in the Federation of Rhodesia and Nyasaland had begun with the 1959 disturbances and emergencies in Nyasaland. The ending of British conscription and the example of the French experience in Algeria discouraged the Macmillan government from any thought of preserving the Federation by force. London threatened air attacks to pressure the white settlers and their political leadership to accept constitutional change. The threat of air attacks signalled London's acceptance of dissolution. The changes desired by Britain would lead to political control by the African majority and ultimately to the breakup of the Federation in 1963. A major difficulty for London was that the Federal Army was effectively under local white control, as was Southern Rhodesia's army at the time of the territory's subsequent declaration of independence. The British government appreciated that, even if troops could be made available, military action against Southern Rhodesia would be unacceptable in Britain. Action was limited to the largely futile despatch of aircraft to protect Zambia and of frigates to blockade Mozambique ports. Rhodesia's illegal independence was finally brought to an end in 1980 as a consequence of increased insurgent strength following the Portuguese revolution in the mid-1970s and the withdrawal of South African support, as well as international, political, and economic pressure.

Small contingents of British troops were used to preserve security in British Honduras (from 1948), Grenada and Antigua (1952), British Guiana (1953, 1962–66), the Bahamas (1958), Jamaica (1960), Nigeria for the Southern Cameroons plebiscite (1960–61), Zanzibar (1961), Swaziland (1963), Mauritius (1965, 1968), Hong Kong (1967), Bermuda (1968, 1969, 1973, 1977), Anguilla (1969), and Cayman (1970).[48] Generally, however, emergencies created by nationalist challenge or intercommunal tensions were contained by local police forces, supported when necessary by local colonial military units.

[47] Anthony Clayton, *Counter-Insurgency in Kenya, 1952–56* (Manhattan, Kan., 1984), pp. 38–39; Michael Dockrill, *British Defence Policy Since 1945* (Oxford, 1988), pp. 78, 89.

[48] John Pimlott, *British Military Operations, 1945–1984* (London, 1984), pp. 6–7.

Some military commitments remained. In 1961 British troops were sent to Kuwait to forestall an Iraqi attack. More important was the 1963–66 campaign to secure the Borneo regions of Malaysia against Indonesian infiltration and, on occasion, against attacks by Indonesian regular forces on the Malay Peninsula itself.[49] The campaign was conducted with notable professionalism and involved some 27,000 British servicemen together with Malaysian and New Zealand units. A final, again well-executed campaign to secure a former dependency and now an ally was that waged by British forces in 1970–75 in Oman, where the Sultan's authority was challenged by rebels in the Dhofar Province.[50] British troops also secured the newly independent governments of Tanganyika (Tanzania), Uganda, and Kenya against army mutinies in January 1964 as well as the integrity of British Honduras (Belize) against recurrent Guatemalan designs.

The conduct of counter-insurgency operations evolved from the operational art of the 1920s and 1930s to a full military doctrine by the late 1950s and 1960s. The chief theoretician was Sir Robert Thompson, who set out basic principles: clear political aims of establishing and maintaining a free, independent, and united country, with political and economic viability; respect for the rule of law and prevention of excesses by either side; an integrated civil, military, intelligence, and police strategy aimed primarily at defeating political subversion as the cause of insurgency rather than the insurgents themselves; and finally, the security of bases essential for any long-drawn-out campaign.[51]

In colonial campaigns, four advances in technology assisted security forces: troop-carrying aircraft which could transport units in a matter of hours; the helicopter, with its ability to fly in troops as rapid reaction to an insurgent attack or to prepare an ambush, and also to provide logistical support; advances in electronic warfare technology, in particular radar surveillance of movements and signals interception; and the navy's riposte to the RAF, commando aircraft-carriers, from which Marines could be lifted by helicopter. In the British army the Special Air Service regiment and the Intelligence Corps were developed to play increasingly significant roles. In most colonies, also, police Special Branches (political surveillance) were developed, in some of which a British Security Service official was stationed. Police forces had to be expanded to provide for mobile force units for rapid deployment in areas of unrest. Notably effective in Kenya and Cyprus also were 'counter-gangs' whose members were drawn from loyalists or 'turned' insurgents.

[49] Gregory Blaxland, *The Regiments Depart* (London, 1971), chap. 14.

[50] John Akehurst, *We Won a War: The Campaign in Oman, 1965–75* (Salisbury, 1982).

[51] Sir Robert Thompson, *Defeating Communist Insurgency: Experiences from Malaya and Vietnam* (London, 1966), pp. 50–58.

The cost of this air and naval equipment, of the Aden campaign, of the garrisons in South-East Asia and of the Rhine army, and of a second generation of nuclear-deterrent weapons became intolerable by the early 1960s. Left-wing figures in the Labour Party, some of Cabinet rank, pressed for drastic reductions. Although as late as 1966 Labour's Prime Minister, Harold Wilson, was still asserting that Britain's frontier was on the Himalayas, the reality, that Britain's economic decline was structural and not simply the consequences of the costly world war and subsequent misfortunes, was now inescapably clear and was to be highlighted by the sterling crisis in the autumn of 1964. The Labour government, re-elected in late 1966, faced additional problems following the 1967 closure of the Suez Canal necessitating oil purchases in dollars, and also industrial disputes. Devaluation of the pound became necessary. In these circumstances Britain was forced to undertake a further series of Defence Reviews, more fundamental than any of their predecessors, culminating in the 1968 decision to withdraw all British forces east of Suez by the end of 1971, so fulfilling Attlee's 1946 prophecy.[52]

The 1968 decisions constituted the end of strategies of Imperial defence and security, but there was to be an epilogue. In 1982 the Argentine dictator Galtieri occupied the Falkland–Malvinas Islands. The Royal Navy, facing a further defence review that strengthened the army at its expense, and recognizing the political vulnerability of the Prime Minister, Margaret Thatcher, seized the opportunity to reassert traditional maritime power.[53] The United States remained overtly, and more importantly covertly, supportive. Despite the distance and logistical difficulties, the Falklands were quickly recaptured by a task-force of British warships and troops. In support, New Zealand volunteered a frigate to release a British vessel for the South Atlantic. The naval strategy, the British refusal to be forcibly ejected from a colony, and New Zealand's gesture briefly echoed Sir Edward Grey's remarks on Imperial fleets and a common policy.

[52] On the withdrawal East of Suez, see esp. Philip Darby, *British Defence Policy East of Suez, 1947–1960* (London, 1973); on the Gulf region, J. B. Kelly, *Arabia, the Gulf, and the West* (London, 1980).

[53] Admiral Sir Henry Leach, *Endure No Makeshifts* (London, 1993), pp. 197–230.

Select Bibliography

BRIAN BOND, *British Military Policy Between the Two World Wars* (Oxford, 1980).

MICHAEL (Field Marshal Lord) CARVER, *Tightrope Walking: British Defence Policy Since 1945* (London, 1992).

Admiral of the Fleet Lord CHATFIELD, *It Might Happen Again* (London, 1947).

ANTHONY CLAYTON, *The British Empire as a Superpower, 1919–39* (London, 1986).

JOHN GOOCH, *The Plans of War: The General Staff and British Military Strategy, c.1900–1916* (London, 1974).

ANANDEWARAP GUPTA, *The Police in British India, 1861–1947* (New Delhi, 1979).

Sir CHARLES GWYNN, *Imperial Policing* (London, 1934).

T. A. HEATHCOTE, *The Military in British India* (Manchester, 1995).

ROBERT HOLLAND, ed., *Emergencies and Disorders in the European Empires After 1945* (London, 1994).

General Sir WILLIAM JACKSON, *Withdrawal from Empire* (London, 1990).

—— and Field Marshal Lord BRAMALL, *The Chiefs: The Story of the United Kingdom Chiefs of Staff* (London, 1992).

KEITH JEFFERY, *The British Army and the Crisis of Empire, 1918–22* (Manchester, 1984).

Sir CHARLES JEFFRIES, *The Colonial Police* (London, 1952).

WM. ROGER LOUIS and ROGER OWEN, eds., *Suez 1956: The Crisis and Its Consequences* (Oxford, 1989).

Major-General JAMES LUNT, *Imperial Sunset: Frontier Soldiering in the 20th Century* (London, 1981).

THOMAS R. MOCKAITIS, *British Counter-Insurgency, 1919–60* (London, 1990).

W. DAVID MCINTYRE, *The Rise and Fall of the Singapore Naval Base, 1919–1942* (London, 1979).

RITCHIE OVENDALE, *British Defence Policy since 1945* (Manchester, 1994).

JOHN PIMLOTT, ed., *British Military Operations, 1945–1984* (London, 1984).

STEPHEN ROSKILL, *Hankey, Man of Secrets*, 3 vols. (London, 1970–74).

13

The Second World War

KEITH JEFFERY

In September 1939 the New Zealand light cruiser HMS *Leander* called at Fiji to deposit two 4.7-inch guns. In great secrecy they were lifted off the ship and mounted at Suva Battery for the defence of the harbour. The clandestine nature of the operation was understandable for reasons of wartime security, but more importantly, it was essential because the guns themselves were dummies. Not until the end of year were they replaced by genuine ones.[1] Thus did one corner of the British Empire prepare for battle in 1939. Thus perhaps too did the Empire as a whole engage in the war, beginning with a demonstration of unity and strength, but unsupported by actual power until later in the conflict. The British Empire was sustained in large measure by the convenient belief held by non-British people that armed forces could be summoned up at will for immediate deployment in any part of the world.[2] For most of the Empire's history this was indeed a fantasy. It was certainly so in times of peace. Only in war, most clearly during the Second World War, did the Empire approach the otherwise mythical status of a formidable, efficient, and effective power system, prepared to exploit its apparently limitless resources, and actually able to deploy forces throughout the world.

The Second World War marked the greatest and the ultimate 'revival' of the British Empire.[3] In the short term, at least, the impact of war did much to strengthen the Imperial system. The accession of that ardent imperialist, Winston Churchill, to the British premiership in May 1940 meant that the war effort was

[1] R. A. Howlett, *The History of the Fiji Military Forces, 1939–1945* (London, 1948), pp. 14–15.

[2] Ged Martin, 'Was there a British Empire?', *Historical Journal*, XV (1972), pp. 562–69.

[3] See John Gallagher, *The Decline, Revival and Fall of the British Empire: The Ford Lectures and Other Essays*, ed. Anil Seal (Cambridge, 1982), pp. 139–41. Other accounts of the Empire in the Second World War on which I have drawn are: Nicholas Mansergh, *Survey of British Commonwealth Affairs: Problems of Wartime Co-operation and Post-War Change, 1939–1952* (London, 1958) and Glen St. J. Barclay, *The Empire is Marching: A Study of the Military Effort of the British Empire, 1800–1945* (London, 1976), pp. 142–219. The best general sources for the war are: Peter Calvocoressi, Guy Wint, and John Pritchard, *Total War: The Causes and Courses of the Second World War*, 2nd edn., 2 vols. (Harmondsworth, 1989); Gerhard L. Weinberg, *A World at Arms: A Global History of World War II* (Cambridge, 1994); and I. C. B. Dear, ed., *The Oxford Companion to the Second World War* (Oxford, 1995).

emphatically defined in Imperial terms. In his first speech as Prime Minister, Churchill bluntly told the House of Commons that the aim of his government was simply 'victory'. Otherwise there would be 'no survival for the British Empire, no survival for all that the British Empire has stood for'. In August the same year, he reported that 'the British nation and the British Empire, finding themselves alone, stood undismayed against disaster'. More bullishly, in December 1941, he told the United States Congress 'that the British Empire, which many thought eighteen months ago was broken and ruined, is now incomparably stronger, and is growing stronger with every month'.[4]

This resurgence of Imperial rhetoric was partly wartime bombast. Imperial propaganda, too, was required to help keep parts of the Empire sweet. In 1943 George Orwell, in a broadcast to America, said that it was 'politically necessary to flatter the Dominions, which involves playing down the British'. As a result, he continued, 'the Germans are able to say plausibly that Britain's fighting is done for her by colonial troops, but this is held to be a lesser evil than offending the Australians, who are only very loosely attached to the Empire and culturally hostile to Britain'.[5] Yet the rhetoric also placed the Empire unequivocally behind the cause of democracy and freedom, and, broadly speaking, there was an extraordinary acceptance and even enthusiasm for the war effort across the Empire. The general nature of British imperialism, with its peacetime free press, civil rights, habeas corpus, cultivation of élites, and promises, however vague, of ultimate self-government, paid enormous dividends during the war.

The way the constituent parts of the Empire went to war in 1939 is quite revealing about the relationships that existed between the 'Mother Country' and its Imperial possessions. As in 1914 the 'old' Dominions rallied round, though not quite so unquestioningly as before (Map 13.1). The technicalities of declaring war, moreover, demonstrated the vagueness of the legal relationship between the Dominions and Britain, despite the fact that the Statute of Westminster in 1931 had provided for full autonomy. Australia was the first to join Britain at war. The Prime Minister in Canberra, Robert Menzies, a lawyer, took the view that King George VI's declaration of war involved all his subjects throughout the Empire. Thus, once Britain was at war, so was Australia. New Zealand took a few hours longer, during which time the Prime Minister, M. J. Savage, consulted his Cabinet colleagues and secured a proclamation from the Governor-General formally declaring a state of war. In South Africa the anti-British Prime Minister, General J. B. M. Hertzog, proposed

[4] 13 May, 20 Aug. 1940, and 26 Dec. 1941: Robert Rhodes James, ed., *Winston S. Churchill: His Complete Speeches, 1897–1963*, 8 vols. (London, 1974), VI, pp. 6220, 6263–64, 6539.

[5] 'Letter from England' to *Partisan Review*, 3 Jan. 1943, in Sonia Orwell and Ian Angus, eds., *The Collected Essays, Journalism and Letters of George Orwell*, 4 vols. (Harmondsworth, 1970), II, pp. 321–22.

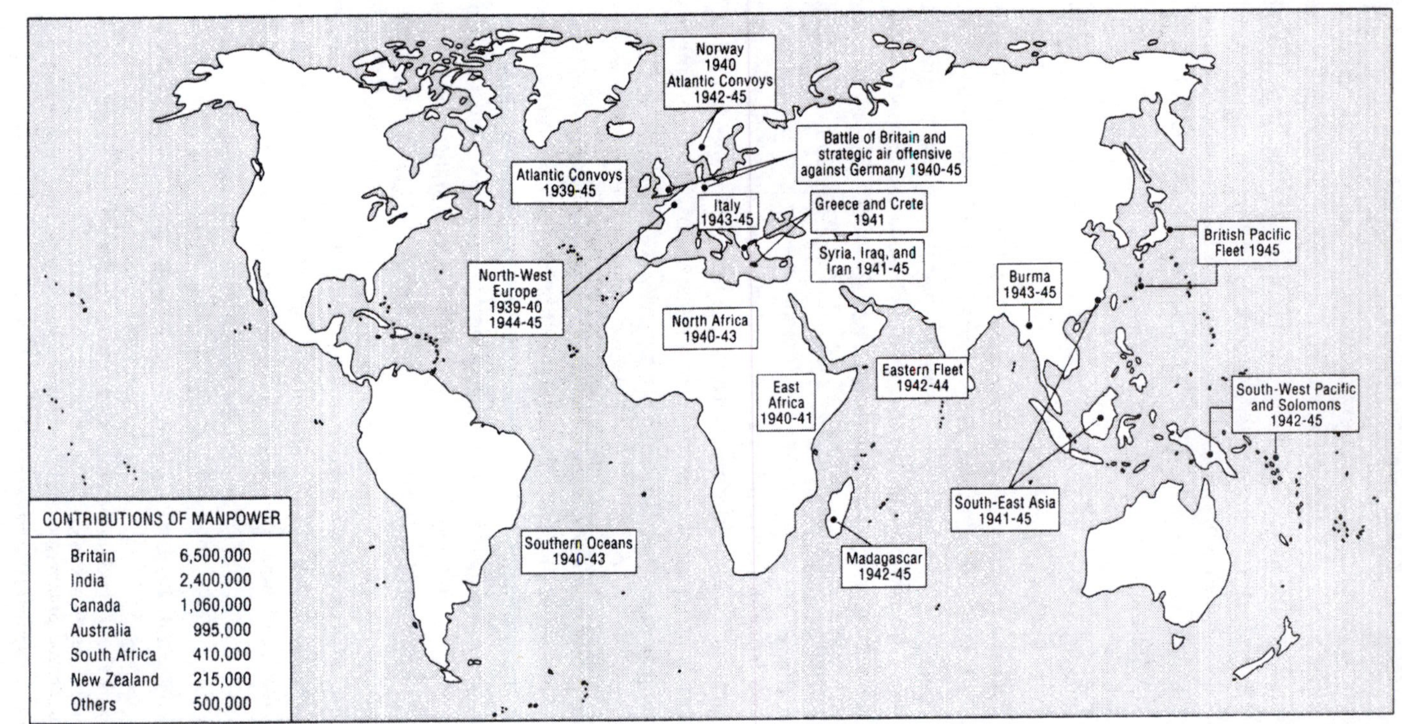

Map 13.1 Main Theatres of British, Commonwealth, and Colonial Operations, 1939–1945

remaining neutral, while his deputy, General J. C. Smuts, opted for war. The matter went before the Union Parliament, which divided eighty votes to sixty-five in favour of Smuts. South African neutrality would have had a calamitous strategic effect on the war effort. In the last real exercise of British imperialism in South Africa, the Governor-General used the royal prerogative to refuse Hertzog's request for a general election. Smuts subsequently formed an administration and remained in office throughout the war.

Canada technically remained neutral for a week after Britain had gone to war. As one historian has observed, 'domestic politics demanded that at least the appearance of free choice be preserved'. Mackenzie King, the Canadian Prime Minister, broadcast on 3 September 1939, saying that 'Canada would go to war, but it would be up to Parliament to decide the form and scope of Canadian participation', and the formal agreement to declare war was not completed until 10 September.[6] Significantly, when the Italians declared war on Britain and France the following June, the Dominions responded without any hesitation. Within a day, almost all of them were at war with Italy, which posed a clear threat to British interests in the Mediterranean.

One newer Dominion, Ireland, remained neutral, and thus demonstrated the full implication of the Statute of Westminster, which had effectively established the right of secession from the Empire. This was recognized by the German Minister in Dublin, Eduard Hempel, the only German diplomat to be accredited to a Commonwealth country during the war. Hempel recommended to Berlin on 8 October 1939 that Germany continue 'to support consolidation of Irish neutrality and independence on a broad national basis, which is also important in its effect on the Dominions, India, and America as a symptom of the loosening ties of Empire'.[7]

Hempel's identification of 'loosening ties of Empire' was wholly fanciful, in the short term at least. On the contrary, in 1939 the tide flowed strongly in the other direction. As Elizabeth Monroe remarked, Hitler's war was a 'tonic' to Imperial fervour, 'not merely in terms of mutual defence, but of exhilaration'.[8] On 3 September Robert Menzies assured his fellow-Australians that there was 'unity in the Empire ranks—one King, one flag, one cause'. The Labor Opposition promised to 'do all that is possible to safeguard Australia and at the same time... do its utmost to maintain the integrity of the British Commonwealth'.[9]

[6] J. L. Granatstein, *Canada's War: The Politics of the Mackenzie King Government, 1939–1945* (Toronto, 1990 edn.), pp. 5–18.

[7] Mansergh, *Survey, 1939–1952*, p. 60; Robert Fisk, *In Time of War: Ireland, Ulster and the Price of Neutrality, 1939–45* (London, 1983), p. 135.

[8] Elizabeth Monroe, *Britain's Moment in the Middle East, 1914–71*, 2nd edn. (London, 1981), p. 148.

[9] Barclay, *The Empire is Marching*, pp. 142–43.

Prime Minister Savage similarly expressed solidarity of New Zealanders with the Mother Country: 'We range ourselves without fear beside Britain. Where she goes, we go, where she stands, we stand.'[10]

The test of these uplifting sentiments lay in the practical assistance that the Empire was prepared to contribute to the war effort in manpower, money, and material. In fact, the Dominions' contribution, even that of the 43,000 Eire citizens who joined the British forces, was very considerable. The first Canadian service personnel, of whom there were eventually nearly half a million, reached Britain in December 1939. In January 1940 Australia and New Zealand each agreed to send a division to the Middle East. The Australian army contribution, in what was significantly called as in the First World War the 'Australian Imperial Force', eventually reached seven divisions. A total of some 558,000 Australians served in all branches of the forces overseas, of whom 27,000 did not return.[11] The New Zealanders and the South Africans sent two divisions each, the former to fight in North Africa, Italy, and the Pacific, the latter initially to fight only in the African continent, but eventually in Italy as well. Happily for the British Treasury, it was established at the start that the Dominions themselves would take complete financial responsibility for their contingents in the field.

The Dominions also raised substantial numbers of air force personnel, many of whom served in the Royal Air Force and who were among the first Imperial servicemen actually to fight in the war. An important Dominion contribution was made in the 'British Empire Air Training Scheme', called the British *Commonwealth* Air Training Plan from June 1942, which trained 169,000 personnel, of whom 75,000 were pilots. Although flying-schools were set up in Australia, New Zealand, South Africa, and Southern Rhodesia, the largest share was taken by the Canadians, for whom the enterprise constituted a major contribution to the Allied war effort. Over 116,000 people passed through Canadian hands, and Ottawa shouldered $1.6 billion of the total $2.2 billion cost of the scheme.

Maritime contributions were also made by the Dominions, whose naval forces, at least in the early stages of the war, tended to be more fully integrated into the Royal Navy than were air or army units into their British equivalents. The New Zealand Naval Forces were not styled Royal New Zealand Navy until September 1941. As was the case with the other arms, from time to time the British High Command found that Dominion units were less amenable to direction than their own. On 3 September 1939 in Portsmouth Harbour, England, some members of a scratch crew of South Africans on the monitor HMS *Erebus*, refused duty on the

[10] F. L. W. Wood, *The New Zealand People at War: Political and External Affairs* (Wellington, 1958), p. 11.

[11] Gavin Long, *The Final Campaigns* (Canberra, 1963), pp. 633–64.

grounds that South Africa was not yet at war.[12] The most important Dominion naval commitment was that of the Royal Canadian Navy in the North Atlantic where by the end of the war the Canadians, with the third largest Allied navy, were primarily responsible for convoy protection duties against German U-boats.

The Colonial Empire assumed belligerent status along with Britain, a process that was accompanied by protestations of support for the Imperial war effort from both British administrators and some local leaders. On 27 September 1939 the Honourable Adeyemo Alakija moved a motion in the Nigerian Legislative Council pledging the colony's support for the British government in the war, 'a war', he said, 'which this time is not going to be a war to end all wars, but a war which will ensure to the human race perpetual peace and freedom'. 'Carry on Britain!' went a telegram the following summer, 'Barbados is behind you!'[13] Some colonial groups went on to make apparently spontaneous contributions to the war effort. In Northern Nigeria the Provincial Committee of the city of Kano raised £10,290 for the purchase of a Spitfire fighter and another gift was received from Sierra Leone 'in grateful recognition of the great benefits which Sierra Leone has received during the last 135 years under the British flag'.[14]

In the case of India the Viceroy, Lord Linlithgow, closely followed the 1914 precedent and declared war without consulting any Indian political representatives. As Nicholas Mansergh observed, the way India went to war underlined 'not so much the measure of autonomy India had so far acquired as the extent of her dependence'.[15] How India as a state, though not as a nation, was committed to the war greatly offended Indian nationalists. 'It hurt,' said Jawaharlal Nehru.[16] Yet many, including Nehru, sympathized with the broad war aim of defeating fascism. Two days after the declaration of war, Mahatma Gandhi told the Viceroy that he viewed the war 'with an English heart' and would personally favour unconditional support for the Allies.[17] Nevertheless, the main vehicle for Indian nationalist opinion, the Congress Party, followed the harder, Nehru line and, pending a clear British commitment to Indian independence, withdrew from any active participation in the Government of India, and became progressively more intransigent on the national issue as the war continued.

[12] H. J. Martin and Neil D. Orpen, *South Africa at War: Military and Industrial Organisation and Operations in Connection with the Conduct of the War, 1939–1945* (Cape Town, 1979), pp. 22–23.

[13] G. O. Olusanya, *The Second World War and Politics in Nigeria, 1939–53* (Lagos, 1973), pp. 43–44; James Morris, *Farewell the Trumpets: An Imperial Retreat* (Harmondsworth, 1979), p. 432.

[14] Peter B. Clarke, *West Africans at War, 1914–18, 1939–45* (London, 1986), p. 22; Ernest Barker, *The Ideas and Ideals of the British Empire* (Cambridge, 1942), pp. 163–64.

[15] Nicholas Mansergh, *The Commonwealth Experience* (New York, 1969), p. 295.

[16] Mansergh, *Survey, 1939–1952*, p. 4.

[17] Manzoor Ahmad, *Indian Response to the Second World War: A Political Study* (New Delhi, 1987), p. 6.

But these political differences did not prevent a huge mobilization of Indian manpower and resources. By 1945 about 2.25 million Indians were serving in the armed forces, and the whole country had become a vast supply base for Allied operations both for the Middle East and Asia. In one significant respect, the Indian provision of troops for the Imperial war effort differed from that of the Dominions. Under an agreement concluded in November 1939, the British government promised to pay for all defence expenditure that was not purely Indian. In practice this meant that London would meet the additional costs incurred in India for the expansion of Indian armed forces during the war as well as the expenses of Indian forces and military equipment used beyond the frontiers of India. Thus, for example, Indian troops in North Africa and Burma were paid for by the British Exchequer.

Although the high level of mobilization in India was not wholly matched in the Colonial Empire, after the end of the war the Colonial Office calculated that some 374,000 Africans had been recruited into the armed forces,[18] of whom nearly 7,000 died. An estimated 15,000 colonial seamen served in the merchant navy, and of 30,000 British merchant seamen who perished in the war an astonishing 5,000 were believed to have been of colonial origin. In explanation for such a high casualty rate, it was offered that colonial personnel were largely employed in the engine rooms of the old coal-burning ships.[19] It is an apt allegory of the role of 'colonials' in the Second World War, and perhaps the Empire in general: in the engine room, doing dirty, manual work, stoking the fires; and when a crisis comes, trapped and suffering disproportionate casualties.

On the domestic fronts, there was a widespread recruitment of labour into agriculture, industry, and services supplying the war effort. Forced labour was imposed in a number of African colonies. In Tanganyika, for example, 84,500 people were conscripted to work on farms and estates, producing sisal, rubber, pyrethrum, and other agricultural products. Between April 1942 and April 1944 100,000 peasants in Northern Nigeria were conscripted to work in the open-cast mines of the Jos Plateau, to produce urgently needed tin after the loss of Malayan supplies following the Japanese invasion in December 1941.[20] Substantial move-

[18] Taking into account the great number of non-combatants, David Killingray has suggested that 'well over half a million soldiers' were recruited by the British. See David Killingray, 'Labour Mobilisation in British Colonial Africa for the War Effort, 1939–46', in David Killingray and Richard Rathbone, eds., *Africa and the Second World War* (London, 1986), p. 71.

[19] *The Colonial Empire (1939–1947)*, pp. 9–10, [Cmd. 7167], *Parliamentary Papers* (Commons), 1946–47, x, 415–16. This paper contains a useful, wide-ranging survey of the Colonial Empire's war effort, upon which I have drawn in this chapter.

[20] Nicholas Westcott, 'The Impact of the Second World War on Tanganyika, 1939–49', in Killingray and Rathbone, *Africa and the Second World War*, pp. 143–59; Killingray, 'Labour Mobilisation', p. 89.

ments of labour also occurred: over 50,000 West Indians went to the United States to work in agriculture and war industries, and rather smaller numbers came to Britain. The recruitment of personnel, both civil and military, in the West Indies illustrates some of the tensions that emerged when institutional, and, no doubt, personal, prejudices came up against the pressing need to exploit the Empire's resources to the utmost. Although in October 1939 the armed services formally abandoned the existing colour bar against non-white officers, in January 1940 the Colonial Office stated that colonial governments had 'been informed that it is not desired that non-European British Subjects should come here for enlistment'. Ironically, a substantial number of West Indians enlisted freely in the Canadian forces and ended up serving in Britain. The growing demands of war brought some modification of the position. From 1943 the Royal Air Force recruited some 6,400 West Indians, of whom over 800 served as aircrew, but the British military authorities in both India and Italy refused to accept a West Indian infantry regiment raised in 1944. Only after the Colonial Office had insisted that the unit be employed in an operational theatre was it sent to Europe, too late to fight. Civilian deployment was less problematical. Several hundred Caribbean workers went to munitions factories in England, and 900 or so foresters from British Honduras worked in Scotland in 1941–43.[21]

There was also an ideological mobilization that reflected the fact that the Second World War was seen as a crusade on behalf of freedom and democracy against the uniquely evil forces of fascism. In the autumn of 1939 the Colonial Office set up a public relations department that worked, not always amicably, with the Ministry of Information on Imperial propaganda. An Empire publicity campaign in 1940 sought to sell the message that Britain's colonies were 'loyal and happy under our rule and helping us to the limit of their resources'. The fall of Singapore in February 1942, which was partly blamed on a failure of the Malays to fight with the British, prompted a review of propaganda that led to the idea of 'partnership' with colonial peoples becoming the new 'credo of empire'. Full use was made of the technological means of transmitting ideological propaganda and information. In 1942 the British Broadcasting Corporation established a regular 'West Indies Radio Newsletter', broadcast from the United States. The same year the 'Mobile Propaganda Unit' of the East African Command was set up in Nairobi. It toured the region 'with a kind of military circus, an Africanized version of the Edinburgh tattoo'.[22] The printed word was also used. In Tanganyika 15,000 copies of a weekly news-sheet, *Habari za Vita* (News of the War) were distributed. The

[21] Marika Sherwood, *Many Struggles: West Indian Workers and Service Personnel in Britain (1939–45)* (London, 1985), pp. 3–5, 38–45, 50, 84, 93–124.

[22] Rosaleen Smyth, 'Britain's African Colonies and British Propaganda during the Second World War', *Journal of Imperial and Commonwealth History*, XIV (1985), pp. 65–82.

Axis Powers used these techniques as well. In mid-1942 at the time of the fall of Tobruk, German and Italian radio propaganda was specifically aimed at Indian troops in North Africa, though not to any great effect.[23] With equipment supplied by the Japanese, Subhas Chandra Bose's Indian National Army also set up broadcasting stations in Singapore and Rangoon.

Ideology was a double-edged weapon. At the outbreak of the war the Ministry of Information in London considered that the dissemination of war propaganda might be restricted in some colonies. For 'particularly backward communities living in virtual isolation', the Ministry argued that 'it would be wiser to leave them alone and not to risk distorting their minds'.[24] The contrast between the ostentatious adoption of freedom and democracy as British and Allied war aims and the actual maintenance of Imperial rule was not lost on nationalists, or any politically aware person, in the Empire. In March 1940 at the Congress meeting at Ramgarh, Bihar, the President of the party, Maulana Abdul Kalam Azad, declared: 'India cannot endure the prospect of Nazism and Fascism, but she is even more tired of British imperialism.'[25] In August 1941 the *Nigerian Eastern Mail* asked: 'What purpose does it serve to remind us that Hitler regards us as semi-apes if the Empire for which we are ready to suffer and die, for whom we poured our blood and drained our pockets in 1914 and for which we are draining the same today, can tolerate racial discrimination against us?'[26] The much-publicized Atlantic Charter of August 1941, in which Article 3 affirmed the 'rights of all peoples to choose the form of government under which they will live', posed a particular problem for the British Empire. Churchill, however, saw no conflict and somewhat complacently told the House of Commons, 'British policy towards the colonies was covered by declarations in harmony with the Atlantic Charter.'[27] By explicitly associating Britain and the United States together, the Charter also enhanced the tendency of Americans to press for reforms within the Empire. As *Life* magazine put it in October 1942: 'One thing we are sure we are *not* fighting for is to hold the British Empire together.'[28]

On an organizational level, various attempts were made to provide for the effective co-ordination of the Imperial war effort. The idea of an 'Imperial War

[23] Axis attempts to enlist Indian allies are fully covered in Milan Hauner, *India in Axis Strategy: Germany, Japan and Indian Nationalists in the Second World War* (Stuttgart, 1981).

[24] Quoted in Clare Thomas, 'Colonial Government, Propaganda and Public Relations and the Administration in Nigeria, 1939–51', unpublished Ph.D. thesis, Cambridge, 1986, p. 29.

[25] Ahmad, *Indian Response*, p. 17.

[26] Olusanya, *The Second World War and Politics in Nigeria*, p. 60.

[27] For the impact of the Atlantic Charter, see Wm. Roger Louis, *Imperialism at Bay, 1941–45: The United States and the Decolonization of the British Empire* (Oxford, 1977), chap. 6, and David Reynolds, *The Creation of the Anglo-American Alliance, 1937–41: A Study in Competitive Co-operation* (Chapel Hill, NC, 1981), pp. 259–61.

[28] Quoted in Louis, *Imperialism at Bay*, p. 198.

Cabinet', as in the First World War, was emphatically rejected by W. L. Mackenzie King of Canada, partly because improvement in communications, most notably the telephone, facilitated intra-Commonwealth consultation and partly because he, and Smuts, felt that the decentralized nature of the 'Commonwealth system' was better suited to waging a worldwide war and maintaining autonomy. Most importantly, he believed that any Imperial executive would diminish Canada's sovereign power. A high level of consultation, however, was maintained through ministerial conferences (including a Prime Ministers' Meeting in 1944 and ministerial meetings before the 1945 San Francisco United Nations Conference), daily cables of information from London to the Dominion capitals, and regular briefings from the Dominions Secretary and others to the Dominion High Commissioners. From time to time, moreover, Dominion representatives and visiting ministers were invited to sit in on the British War Cabinet. Even so, these arrangements did not always run smoothly. Australia and New Zealand complained about the despatch of their forces to Greece in the spring of 1941 without proper consultation. Injury was added to insult when the Greek campaign ended badly.

Regional functional networks were also set up, including the 'Eastern Group Supply Council' that the Viceroy of India, Lord Linlithgow, proposed in June 1940 should co-ordinate 'the armament industries of Australia, New Zealand, South Africa and India'. Linlithgow's idea was that India, by virtue of its geographical position and economic resources, should be the centre of this organization. Although the Australians were reluctant to subordinate themselves to Indian direction, for a year or two the Council worked well in rationalizing the purchase and supply of various strategic commodities. While it operated, the main beneficiaries were India and South Africa. After the outbreak of the Pacific War, Australia, the United States, and other allies formed a new Supply Council for the Pacific Area.[29] Other regional groupings such as the East African Governors' Conference, the West African Produce Control Board, and the Middle East Supply Centre sought to oil the wheels of British co-ordination.[30] As with the Pacific supply arrangements, however, the exclusively British nature of these organizations was diluted by the participation of the United States, which increasingly reflected the latter's status as senior partner in the anti-Axis alliance. In some cases, the Americans had to be included from the beginning, as with the Anglo-American Caribbean Commission established in 1942 which 'served mainly as a

[29] Johannes H. Voigt, *India in the Second World War* (New Delhi, 1987), pp. 79–81; 'The South African Economy during the Second World War' [by H. M. Robertson and others], Union of South Africa, *Official Year Book of the Union*, no. 29, 1956–57, p. 819.

[30] West Africa also provided staging posts for men and materials on the way to North Africa and India; see below, p. 522.

co-ordinating supply agency for British and American Caribbean territories'.[31] Such organizations as these demonstrated the extent to which, under the immense challenges of 'total war', the British Empire could no longer operate on a unilateral basis.

While John Gallagher has suggested that 'the period of European civil war to 1941' was less important for the British Empire than 'the spread of fighting later to a world-wide scale',[32] it can be argued that the most vital theatre of operations was always in Western Europe. For the British government the first priority, above all other Imperial interests, was always the protection of the United Kingdom itself. As Churchill unequivocally put it in January 1941, 'the task of preventing invasion, of feeding the Island, and of speeding our armament production must in no way be compromised for the sake of any other objective whatsoever'.[33] It might, moreover, be hazarded that the defence of Britain was essential to the survival of the British *Empire*, but not that of the British *Commonwealth*, bearing in mind, among other things, the plan to evacuate the royal family to Canada should Britain fall. It could also be said that the fall of France in 1940 had an absolutely crucial effect on the Empire's war. Nicholas Mansergh, in typically elegant prose, noted that the Germans' 'triumphant sweep across northern France in those lovely summer days of 1940 destroyed many things which even victory could never restore'.[34] There was a psychological cost, to be sure, but also, as Smuts argued in October 1942, there was the fact 'that the almost total loss of the entire Allied possessions in the Far East and in South-East Asia was due to the fall of France'. The subsequent Vichy government in French Indo-China 'opened the door' for the Japanese to Singapore, Siam, Malaya, and Burma.[35] By this analysis Hong Kong would have fallen to the Japanese anyway, but if France had not surrendered, perhaps not Singapore.

Two positions were seen as of surpassing significance for the survival of the Empire: Suez and Singapore. Just four days after the outbreak of war, the Chief of the Imperial General Staff (CIGS), Sir Edmund Ironside, reflected that Britain's strategy in the Middle East had to be 'Imperial strategy'. 'The Suez Canal', he stated, 'is the centre of the British Empire.' He wanted to concentrate in Egypt, Palestine, and Iraq such forces as could be spared from India, together with any

[31] Elizabeth Wallace, *The British Caribbean: From the Decline of Colonialism to the End of Federation* (Toronto, 1977), pp. 52–53.

[32] Gallagher, *Decline, Revival and Fall*, p. 139.

[33] Prime Minister to Chiefs of Staff, 6 Jan. 1941, in Winston S. Churchill, *The Second World War*, 6 vols. (London, 1948–54), III, *The Grand Alliance*, p. 10.

[34] Mansergh, *Survey, 1939–1952*, p. 190.

[35] Ibid., p. 191.

Australian, New Zealand, or South African units that might be made available.[36] Singapore had its claims too, but the assurances London had given to Australia and New Zealand in the 1930s, that in the event of Japanese aggression substantial naval reinforcements would be sent to the Far East, evaporated with the fall of France. In mid-June 1940 the British guarantees were abandoned and replaced by a Micawber-like faith that the Americans might bail out the Empire. 'Without the assistance of France,' London told Canberra and Wellington, 'we should not have sufficient forces to meet the combined German and Italian navies in European waters and the Japanese fleet in the Far East. In the circumstances envisaged, it is most improbable that we could send adequate reinforcements to the Far East. We should therefore have to rely on the United States of America to safeguard our interests there.'[37] This realistic appreciation of the situation rattled the Australians, and they had to be mollified by a promise from Churchill that in the event of an actual Japanese invasion of either antipodean Dominion, 'we should then cut our losses in the Mediterranean and proceed to your aid, sacrificing every interest except only the defence and feeding of this Island on which all depends'.[38] In the meantime, the Australians were asked to provide reinforcements of their own for Singapore.

During 1941 the continuing importance of Singapore was stressed. In May, discussing 'the relation of the Middle East to the security of the United Kingdom', Ironside's successor as CIGS, Sir John Dill, re-emphasized that it was Britain 'and not Egypt that [was] vital, and the defence of the United Kingdom must take first place. Egypt was not even second in order of priority, for it has been an accepted principle in our strategy that in the last resort the security of Singapore comes before that of Egypt.'[39]

In the absence of any direct Japanese aggression, however, British and Imperial resources were concentrated first for the defence of Britain against invasion and then in the Mediterranean theatre. Following the Dunkirk evacuation in June 1940, units from the 1st Canadian Division were sent to France to bolster continuing resistance to the German advance, but these troops were rapidly withdrawn again when France collapsed completely. Joined by a second division during the summer of 1940, the Canadian army formed an important part of the British home defence forces. In the meantime parts of the Australian and New Zealand divisions, which had been despatched early in 1940, were diverted to Britain. The bulk

[36] *The Ironside Diaries, 1937–40*, eds. Roderick Macleod and Denis Kelly (London, 1962), p. 105.

[37] 14 June 1940, quoted in W. David McIntyre, *The Rise and Fall of the Singapore Naval Base, 1919–1942* (London, 1979), p. 164.

[38] 11 Aug. 1940, ibid., p. 171.

[39] Churchill, *Second World War*, III, *The Grand Alliance*, p. 375.

of the forces, however, was concentrated in North Africa and the Middle East where they were to play a major part in the campaigns of 1940–43.

The East African campaign of 1940–41, which followed Italy's declaration of war in June 1940, had a strikingly Imperial aspect, involving troops from Britain, India, Africa, and even two detachments of Cypriot personnel. After the Italians had captured British Somaliland, a predominantly Indian Army force, which included some Sudanese units, attacked the Italian positions in Ethiopia from the Sudan while a force, comprising troops from the King's African Rifles (raised in East Africa) and the Royal West African Frontier Force, as well as South African and Southern Rhodesian soldiers, invaded from Kenya. In four months the Italians were soundly defeated. Other welcome victories were won against the Italians in the Western Desert. After the German Afrika Corps arrived at the beginning of 1941, however, the pendulum swung so far against the British that even Egypt came under threat. In June 1942, as British forces were withdrawing to El Alamein, Dan Pienaar, commanding the 1st South African Division, said: 'If Alamein goes, Egypt goes. If Egypt goes, the Middle East goes and what about the British Empire?'[40]

But the Middle East did not fall. For two years from the summer of 1940 the vital 'fortress colony' of Malta held out against persistent Axis attacks and thus helped to secure Britain's position in the Mediterranean. From the autumn of 1942 the British Eighth Army, which included a division each from Australia, India, New Zealand, and South Africa, gradually drove the enemy back until, with the help of Anglo-American forces advancing from Morocco and Algeria, the Axis powers were expelled from North Africa in May 1943. The Second World War saw a marked revival of the British Empire in the Middle East. Not only was the Suez Canal confirmed as vital for the Imperial line of communications; Middle Eastern oil was also of immense strategic importance. During 1941 Iraq, Syria, and Iran were all invaded and occupied by British troops, who were joined in Syria by Free French and in Iran by Soviet forces. Egypt, while nominally independent, was dominated by the British, who forced the King to dismiss a pro-Axis Prime Minister in 1942. For a few years, indeed, Cairo was the military capital of the British Empire.[41]

The worst British defeats of the war occurred in the East following the Japanese attack on Pearl Harbor on 7 December 1941, which brought the United States into the war. Within six hours of the first Japanese bomb falling on Hawaii, Hong Kong was under siege, and within another twenty-four hours Canadian soldiers, who had been in the colony scarcely three weeks, and who were the first Canadian troops to see action in the war, were retreating from their initial line of defence

[40] Lavinia Greacen, *Chink: A Biography* (London, paperback edn., 1991), p. 212.

[41] Morris, *Farewell the Trumpets*, p. 438.

above Gin Drinkers Bay in the New Territories. Nearly a fortnight's stiff resistance by the heavily outnumbered British, Indian, Canadian, and locally raised forces ultimately proved futile and the colony surrendered on Christmas Day.

To the south-west, Japanese landings in Malaya actually started just before the Pearl Harbor attack.[42] The defence of Malaya and Singapore was entrusted to a characteristically motley collection of Commonwealth forces. On land there were British and Indian Army formations, two Australian brigades, 17,000 Malaysian volunteers, and five units from the Indian princely states. At sea British vessels, including the capital ships *Prince of Wales* and *Repulse*, were joined by an Australian destroyer. The territory's air defence was shared mainly by British and Australian formations, along with two New Zealand units. Although in its extent and variety the force defending Malaya seemed abundantly to represent the deep reserves of strength the Empire could call upon, ironically one of its many weaknesses lay in the very disparity and incoherence of the force. Despite some stout resistance, the British were driven out of Malaya by the end of January 1942 and Singapore surrendered on 15 February. One hundred and thirty thousand British subjects were captured by the Japanese, including 14,000 Australian, 16,000 British, and 32,000 Indian troops.

The fall of Singapore—the 'Yorktown of the British empire in Asia'[43]—was described by Churchill with typical certainty as 'the worst disaster and largest capitulation in British history'.[44] But it was not so much Britain as the British Empire, with all that that term connoted, that failed in 1941–42. 'The fall of Singapore', declared Subhas Chandra Bose in a broadcast from Germany, 'means the collapse of the British Empire, the end of the iniquitous regime which it has symbolised and the dawn of a new era in Indian history.'[45] This prediction, although premature, was not wholly wrong. The cataclysmic blows struck by the triumphant Japanese in Hong Kong, Malaya, Singapore, and Burma grievously undermined the myth of European invincibility. In the Far East the British Empire 'depended on prestige', wrote Sir Frederic Eggleston, the Australian Minister in Chunking at May 1942. 'This prestige has been completely shattered.'[46]

Yet the Empire itself survived. Although the Japanese reached the gates of India, they were decisively defeated in the Battle of Imphal (March–June 1944). The Burma campaign was a triumph for British Imperial forces, most notably the

[42] Because the International Date Line runs between Hawaii and Malaya, the former was bombed on 7 December while the latter, an hour or so earlier, was attacked on 8 December. See the timetable in McIntyre, *Rise and Fall*, pp. 192–93.

[43] Nicholas Tarling, *The Fall of Imperial Britain in South-East Asia* (Singapore, 1993), p. 140.

[44] Churchill, *Second World War*, IV, *The Hinge of Fate*, p. 81.

[45] Hauner, *India in Axis Strategy*, p. 427.

[46] Quoted in Christopher Thorne, *Allies of a Kind: The United States, Britain, and the War against Japan, 1941–1945* (London, 1978), p. 206.

Indian Army. But troops from other parts of the Empire brought their own particular qualities to the battlefield. In January 1944 men of the Royal West African Frontier Force secured the surrender of some Japanese soldiers—at that time an almost unprecedented occurrence. The reason given was that the Japanese 'believed African troops ate the killed in battle, but not prisoners. They feared that, if eaten by Africans, they would not be acceptable to their ancestors in the hereafter.'[47]

In the west, the tide turned in North Africa at the second Battle of El Alamein in late 1942. In the summer of 1943 the Eighth Army, now joined by a Canadian division, began to fight in Italy. The Canadians had been among the first Commonwealth contingents to arrive in Britain but had been left in frustrating inactivity. Pressure from Ottawa for their troops to see action, however, led to men of the 2nd Canadian Division being used in the disastrous raid on Dieppe in August 1942. The Canadians played a major part in Operation Overlord—the invasion of Europe—launched on 6 June 1944. Above all, however, the Canadians' chief contribution to the war effort was their part in securing the most important strategic link of all: the Atlantic supply route between North America and Europe. From the beginning of 1942 the Royal Canadian Navy took increasing responsibility for 'mid-ocean escorts' of North Atlantic convoys, becoming solely responsible in the summer of 1944.[48] In both world wars the maintenance of this route ensured that the British Empire ended up on the winning side.

What impact did the Second World War have on the Empire? It is possible to argue that the war caused no substantive change; it merely accelerated and accentuated existing trends. In terms of constitutional development, so this argument goes, self-government and independence would have happened anyway. The war, if it had any real impact at all, simply affected the timing of these reforms. In contrast to this approach, it may be that the war produced objective changes that would not otherwise have happened; that the war made things significantly different. Certainly, at the time many observers felt that the sheer scale of the conflict was irrevocably changing the Empire. In 1942 the Governor of Uganda, Sir Charles Dundas, comparing the war to that of 1914–18, asserted that it would have 'an even more rousing influence, chiefly political and social, and it will be sheer blindness not to foresee the logical consequences'.[49]

[47] A. Haywood and F. A. S. Clarke, *The History of the Royal West African Frontier Force* (Aldershot, 1964), pp. 385–86.

[48] See Marc Milner, *North Atlantic Run: The Royal Canadian Navy and the Battle for the Convoys* (Toronto, 1985).

[49] Dundas to Colonial Secretary, 1 June 1942, quoted in Pearce, *The Turning Point*, p. 42.

Constitutional change is easy to map, since it played a relatively small part in Imperial wartime policy-making. In the dependent Empire, domestic politics, with a few significant exceptions, were generally kept in a kind of suspended animation. Pending the end of the war, governments throughout the Empire went to sometimes extravagant lengths to suppress domestic criticism. In Canada and Australia the (pacifist) Jehovah's Witnesses were proscribed. Much more seriously, the 'Quit India' movement in 1942, which produced the gravest challenge to British rule since 1857, was swiftly and unambiguously crushed by the authorities in New Delhi.

The only major constitutional alteration during the war occurred in Jamaica, which was granted full internal self-government in 1944 with a House of Representatives elected by universal adult suffrage. New constitutions in British Guiana, the Gold Coast, and Nigeria established Legislative Councils with, for the first time, unofficial majorities. In 1940 and 1942 constitutional schemes offering 'Dominion Status' to India were put forward, reflecting both the extent of internal political challenge to the Raj and the vital military and strategic importance of the subcontinent. In July 1943 the Secretary of State for the Colonies, Oliver Stanley, told Parliament that the British government was 'pledged to guide Colonial people along the road to self-government within the framework of the British Empire'.[50] Stanley disingenuously claimed that this had always been British policy, but it had never hitherto been stated in such unequivocal terms.

It may be, however, that the precise *nature* of proposed constitutional and political change was affected by the war and wartime conditions. It has been argued, for example, that the *war* made partition inevitable in India and that British techniques of divide and rule that were applied to sustain the war effort favoured the Muslim League at the expense of Congress. Writing in the winter of 1944–45, one observer asserted that the expanding Muslim bourgeoisie, itself underpinned by the flourishing wartime economy, was sharpening Muslim separatism.[51] The general impact of the conflict and the demands imposed by the Government of India in the interests of the war were clearly destabilizing. 'The convulsions and constraints of the war', wrote Manzoor Ahmad, 'produced fragmentation in the Indian political set-up and brought to the surface disruptive and disintegrating forces undermining national unity.'[52] In the view of another historian, the war 'finally broke the hold of the leaders of Congress and the Muslim

[50] 13 July 1943, *Parliamentary Debates*, CCCXCI (Commons), col. 48; see Louis, *Imperialism at Bay*, chap. 15.

[51] Wilfred Cantwell Smith, *Modern Islam in India*, 2nd edn. (London, 1946), pp. 189–93, 272–76.

[52] Ahmad, *Indian Response to the Second World War*, p. 256.

League over their respective followings', and also deprived the British of that 'initiative and ability to control events which was the vital underpinning of their plans to advance India to the status of a Dominion'.[53]

For the 'old' Dominions, the war, as the First World War had done, did much to enhance their autonomy. The war enabled Canada to carve out 'a new stature as a middle power'. In 1939, argues John Granatstein, Canada was 'a colony in everything but name'. Six years later 'the nation, for a brief period, was as independent and powerful as it would ever be'.[54] The way in which the war was fought, particularly after the United States entered the conflict, widened the Dominions' diplomatic horizons and forged new alliances, sometimes in conjunction with Britain, but in some cases involving the Dominions alone. The intra-Imperial links and the exclusive, bilateral relationships that individual Dominions had with London, and that collectively constituted the 'Empire' before 1939, were supplemented, perhaps even superseded, by new linkages with Washington, even before the United States became a belligerent. The Canadian–United States agreement made at Ogdensburg, New York, in August 1940 established a 'Permanent Joint Board on Defence'. This agreement, together with an economic arrangement concluded a year later at F. D. Roosevelt's residence at Hyde Park, inextricably linked the defences and economies of the two nations. Australia travelled a similar route. After the fall of Singapore, Australia itself feared invasion and gravitated closer than before towards the United States. From April 1942 the American General Douglas MacArthur took command of all Allied forces in the South-West Pacific area, and became the Australian government's chief military adviser. In effect, the Australian war effort was 'subsumed in the enormous US military machine'.[55]

The effect of the war as a catalyst for change can be observed in its social impact throughout the Empire. The expansion of economic activity, some measure of prosperity, and the presence of sometimes large numbers of service personnel in training camps and in transit certainly had an unsettling effect in many colonies. The strains of war contributed to a situation in the Bahamas that erupted into rioting during which three people died in Nassau in June 1942. The war had destroyed the tourist industry and thrown many Bahamians out of work. Although the construction of an Anglo-American military base offered the possibilities of employment, the contractors had determined only to offer low wages to local workers, who responded with protest. One skilled worker, urged with

[53] Nicholas Owen, 'War and Britain's Political Crisis in India', in Brian Brivati and Harriet Jones, eds., *What Difference did the War Make?* (Leicester, 1993), p. 108.

[54] Granatstein, *Canada's War*, p. x.

[55] Jeffrey Grey, *A Military History of Australia* (Cambridge, 1990), p. 177.

destroying a Union Jack, explained, 'I willing to fight under the flag, but I ain't gwine starve under the flag'.[56] In Kenya white settlers moaned about increasing African insolence. 'The chief cause of it', wrote one to the *Mombasa Times* in September 1942, 'is the misguided, over-zealous friendliness and undignified attitude of the Forces.'[57]

It has been argued that the experience of enlistment and military service, frequently overseas, had a 'modernizing' and radicalizing impact on those involved. Returning soldiers, for example, were often in the vanguard of demands for political change in the Colonial Empire. F. M. Bourret has stressed the 'psychological effect which wider contacts with world affairs' had upon West Africans. 'Though the number of Gold Coast servicemen was small in relation to the population,' she continues, 'their influence after demobilization was all out of proportion to their numbers.'[58] The pace of political reform in the colony was sharply accelerated following a wave of disturbances precipitated by a rally of ex-soldiers in Accra in February 1948. A government inquiry into the disturbances concluded that 'the large number of African soldiers returning from service with the Forces, where they had lived under different and better conditions, made for a general communicable state of unrest'. 'Such Africans,' continued the report, 'by reason of their contacts with other peoples including Europeans had developed a political and national consciousness.'[59]

Increased employment—there was a growing urban wage-earning class—and the acquisition of new skills in both civilian and military sectors were important in promoting African political consciousness. For Kenyan soldiers this development has been ascribed in part to military service: 'the acquisition of good health and simple technical skills from the army played a far larger part in the political awakening of the African masses than the occasional sight of militant nationalism in the Middle or Far East.'[60] In Tanganyika there was some agitation by demobilized soldiers. A group of ten ex-servicemen petitioned the colonial administration in July 1946, concerned that 'the freedom we have fought for is not going to be given to us ... The Tanganyika Government should realize that we have been fighting for our own freedom and not for imperial purposes.' Nevertheless, it appears that most of the returning African soldiers simply 'faded rapidly back to

[56] D. Gail Saunders, 'The 1942 Riot in Nassau: A Demand for Change?', *Journal of Caribbean History*, XX (1985–86), pp. 117–46.

[57] Anthony Clayton and Donald C. Savage, *Government and Labour in Kenya, 1895–1963* (London, 1974), p. 237.

[58] F. M. Bourret, *Ghana: The Road to Independence, 1919–1957* (Oxford, 1960), pp. 155, 165.

[59] *Report of the Commission of Enquiry into Disturbances in the Gold Coast, 1948, Parliamentary Papers*, Colonial 231 (London, 1948), p. 2.

[60] Clayton and Savage, *Government and Labour in Kenya*, pp. 233–34.

the land'. On balance, those who had stayed at home were more active in post-war politics than those who had served in the army during the war.[61]

The Japanese victories following Pearl Harbor provided new opportunities for armed opponents to British rule. The most outstanding example of this was the Indian National Army (INA) first commanded by Mohan Singh and later led by Subhas Chandra Bose. Canvassing for recruits among demoralized Indian prisoners-of-war captured in Malaya and Singapore, the nationalists secured quite a good response. Many men felt, in the words of one later INA brigade commander, that they had been 'handed over like cattle by the British to the Japs'.[62] By the summer of 1943 Bose had an army of 11,000, with a further 20,000 in training. But the INA did not achieve any great military success; its chief significance was to demonstrate quite explicitly to the British that Indian loyalty to the British Empire—even among soldiers—could not necessarily be relied upon in all circumstances. In occupied Burma, which was granted a measure of independence by the Japanese in 1943, the Burma National Army under its leader Aung San at first took the Japanese side but later defected to the Allies.[63] During the war the British themselves actually provided military training for some anti-imperialists. The Malay Chinese, Chin Peng, for example, among other Communists, was trained in subversion and sabotage techniques by the covert action specialists of Special Operations Executive for operations against the Japanese. As leader of the 'insurrection' in Malaya that commenced in 1948, Chin Peng used these very skills against the British, initially with some success.[64]

There were economic changes too. Industrial development and the exploitation of resources left many parts of the Empire more economically self-sufficient than before. The demands of the war stimulated Indian industrialization and prompted concern about the long-term damage this might do to British interests. In 1941 the leading industrialist, Lord Rootes, warned of 'the detrimental effects' of possible Indian automobile manufacturing on the British car industry 'in the period after the war'.[65] There was a massive expansion in the exploitation of tropical resources, especially after the fall of Malaya. Bulk-purchasing schemes were set up for almost all major exports, such as Northern Rhodesian copper, West Indian bananas, Palestine citrus, Ceylonese tea, and East African cotton and sisal. Although the increased demand for these commodities might bring local prosperity, some—for

[61] N. J. Westcott, 'The Impact of the Second World War on Tanganyika, 1939–49', unpublished Ph.D. thesis, Cambridge, 1982, pp. 294–98.

[62] Peter Ward Fay, *The Forgotten Army: India's Armed Struggle for Independence, 1942–1945* (Ann Arbor, 1993), p. 83.

[63] See below, pp. 479, 482.

[64] Brian Lapping, *End of Empire* (London, 1985), pp. 159–61.

[65] Voigt, *India in the Second World War*, p. 74.

example, much of the West African cocoa crop—were never exported at all. The purchases were simply made as an indirect subsidy to the growers in order to prevent social or economic hardship.[66]

Governments throughout the Empire became more interventionist in support of the war effort. Both the 'colonial state' and individual colonial administrations became more 'managerial'. The Tanganyikan government, for example, was under pressure from above—London urging it to deliver—and from below, as it became more indispensable to the running of the colonial economy and to the satisfying of internal economic and political demands.[67] The same processes are identifiable in India, where the recruitment and provisioning of armed forces, economic mobilization, rationing, and widespread requisitioning caused the state to penetrate more deeply than ever before into Indian society.[68] This growth of the state might not have happened without the pressures of war, which dramatically converted colonial governments into more-or-less enthusiastic Keynesians. The enhanced role of the state was certainly a continuing legacy of the war.

This was matched by the Colonial Office's growing conviction of the merits of government-sponsored 'development' and welfare schemes, which were intended to enhance economic efficiency and productivity, improve living standards, and, it was hoped, reduce social, and perhaps political, unrest in the colonies, while demonstrating to the world (especially the United States) Britain's commitment to what might be called 'constructive imperialism'. The 1940 Colonial Development and Welfare Act was a much-vaunted, though practically not very effective, demonstration of this new commitment. As the tide of war turned in the Allies' favour, these developments were intensified by a new 'colonial mission', articulated by Oliver Stanley into a bipartisan policy which sought to reshape the Imperial system on the basis of equal relationships and common economic and social benefits.

Sterling balances, and the sterling area, represented another legacy of the war, which in the case of India unambiguously demonstrated power shifts within the Empire.[69] The pressures of the conflict welded the rather loose pre-war sterling bloc into a closely integrated monetary association that survived for twenty years after the war. It also helped secure Britain's economic position in the world. But the sterling balances which Dominions and colonies alike built up in London reflected more clearly than anything else the cost of the war to Britain. As Lord

[66] J. M. Lee and Martin Petter, *The Colonial Office, War and Development Policy: Organization and Planning of a Metropolitan Initiative, 1939–45* (London, 1982), p. 74.

[67] See Westcott, 'The Impact of the Second World War on Tanganyika, 1939–49'.

[68] This is one of the main themes of Indivar Kamtekar, 'The End of the Colonial State in India, 1942–47', unpublished Ph.D. thesis, Cambridge, 1989.

[69] See chap. by D. K. Fieldhouse, esp. pp. 93–94, 95, 112.

Keynes put it, the 'principles of good housekeeping' had, for good reasons, been thrown 'to the winds' during the war, when British expenditure on defence and war supplies was almost entirely based on credit.[70] This resulted in territories which had owed Britain money before the war emerging as creditors in 1945. Arising from the 1939 Defence Expenditure Agreement, over £1,300 million of India's enormous contribution to the Imperial war effort was charged up to Britain.

The Second World War saw the apotheosis of the British Empire, yet it contained elements of both the best and the worst in the Imperial relationship. During the war it was clearly demonstrated that colonial control depended ultimately on force, albeit applied by Britain in pursuit of national survival. On one level, a seamless robe of force and coercion linked the British response to external and internal challenges. D-Day, El Alamein, and Imphal thus share an Imperial relationship with the suppression of the 1942 Indian uprising, the British occupation of Iraq, Syria, and Iran, and the shooting by police and military of strikers in the Northern Rhodesian Copper Belt in March 1940 or in the Bahamas in June 1942. The increased authoritarianism of wartime Imperial control was but one manifestation of 'rule by the sword'.

The corollary to this was that, where force failed—as in Asia—the Empire was gravely, if not fatally, injured. The failure by Britain to protect Imperial subjects had a long-term effect. In Sarawak, for instance, although a battalion of British-officered Punjabis held out after the Japanese landings from 19 December 1941 until 3 April 1942, the local people were consigned to almost four years of enemy occupation. 'For liberation from the "evil oppression" of the Japanese,' writes one historian, 'the people of Sarawak turned, not to the British, who had let them down, but to their own efforts as guerrillas . . . and to soldiers of the 9th Australian Division.'[71] But for some the shared experience of war appeared to have consolidated the Empire. In November 1946 Lord Alanbrooke, the wartime Chief of the Imperial General Staff, told the Royal Empire Society that the war had strengthened the 'family' bonds of the Commonwealth, and he expressed the hope that 'those bonds which have held this British family together will continue to grow in strength'.[72]

On the more positive side there was some constitutional advance. Self-government, the precise meaning of which remained unclear, was promised, most

[70] D. E. Moggridge, 'From War to Peace—The Sterling Balances', *The Banker*, CXXII, 558 (Aug. 1972), pp. 1032–35.

[71] A. V. M. Horton, 'A Note on the British Retreat from Kuching, 1941–1942', *Sarawak Museum Journal*, XXXVI, 57, New Series (Dec. 1986), pp. 241–49.

[72] Lord Alanbrooke, 'Empire Defence', *United Empire*, XXXVIII, 1 (Jan.–Feb. 1947), p. 4.

immediately to India, but the principle, though not the timing, was conceded for the Colonial Empire. 'Partnership' and 'colonial development' became maxims for the future. In part, these promises were prompted by the need to secure internal support for the war effort throughout the Empire and to reassure the Americans that the British Empire was not actually very imperial at all. There were those, however, who conceived a higher purpose for colonial development and self-government. The old Colonial Office hand, Sir John Shuckburgh, identified a 'new angle of vision' towards colonial problems, 'which, if it did not originate with the War, was greatly accentuated by wartime conditions and reactions'. He argued that European colonial administrators had now to 'collaborate with Colonial peoples, not, as in the past, merely to direct them . . . Inter-racial co-operation must be the keynote of Colonial policy.' 'We are', he concluded in his unpublished 'Colonial Civil History of the War', 'in fact engaged in a race against time; and the prize of victory will not be the perpetuation, but the honourable interment of the old system.'[73] Yet, honourable or not, the 'interment' of the British Imperial system was an inevitable consequence of the 1939–45 conflict. The means by which the immense resources of the Empire were channelled into an extraordinary collective war effort unleashed social and political expectations that in the end could not be accommodated, even within a reformed colonial system such as that envisaged by Oliver Stanley and his successors in the Labour government. Paradoxically, the ultimate cost of defending the British Empire during the Second World War was the Empire itself.

[73] John Shuckburgh, 'Colonial Civil History of the War', 4 vols. (Colonial Office, n.d.), IV, pp. 113, 118, 120. There are copies of this history in the Royal Commonwealth Society Library (now at Cambridge University Library), and the Institute of Commonwealth Studies, London.

Select Bibliography

GLEN ST J. BARCLAY, *The Empire is Marching: A Study of the Military Effort of the British Empire, 1800–1945* (London, 1976).

I. C. B. DEAR, ed., *The Oxford Companion to the Second World War* (Oxford, 1995).

JOHN GALLAGHER, *The Decline, Revival and Fall of the British Empire: The Ford Lectures and Other Essays*, ed. Anil Seal (Cambridge, 1982).

J. L. GRANATSTEIN, *Canada's War: The Politics of the Mackenzie King Government, 1939–1945* (Toronto, 1990).

JEFFREY GREY, *A Military History of Australia* (Cambridge, 1990).

DAVID KILLINGRAY and RICHARD RATHBONE, eds., *Africa and the Second World War* (London, 1986).

J. M. LEE and MARTIN PETTER, *The Colonial Office: War and Development Policy: Organization and Planning of a Metropolitan Initiative, 1934–45* (London, 1982).

WM. ROGER LOUIS, *Imperialism at Bay, 1941–45: The United States and the Decolonization of the British Empire* (Oxford, 1977).

NICHOLAS MANSERGH, *Survey of British Commonwealth Affairs: Problems of Wartime Co-operation and Post-War Change, 1939–1952* (London, 1958).

H. J. MARTIN and NEIL D. ORPEN, *South Africa at War: Military and Industrial Organisation and Operations in Connection with the Conduct of the War, 1939–1945* (Cape Town, 1979).

G. O. OLUSANYA, *The Second World War and Politics in Nigeria, 1939–53* (Lagos, 1973).

R. D. PEARCE, *The Turning Point: British Colonial Policy, 1938–48* (London, 1982).

CHRISTOPHER THORNE, *Allies of a Kind: The United States, Britain, and the War Against Japan, 1941–1945* (London, 1978).

JOHANNES H. VOIGT, *India in the Second World War* (New Delhi, 1987).

F. L. W. WOOD, *The New Zealand People at War: Political and External Affairs* (Wellington, 1958).

14

The Dissolution of the British Empire

WM. ROGER LOUIS

When the Cabinet in the aftermath of the Second World War came to grips with the problem of liquidating the British Raj in India, a consensus eventually emerged that is basic in understanding British motives and aims during the subsequent two decades of decolonization: 'withdrawal from India need not appear to be forced upon us by our weakness nor to be the first step in the dissolution of the Empire.'[1] There was a corollary: whatever the outcome, it would be presented to the public as the result of British policy. To the world at large, the British would be seen as remaining in control of events. History would record a commitment to self-government that had been planned and fulfilled. The British aimed to control their own destiny, presiding if possible over the rebirth of the Imperial system rather than its dissolution. As events transpired in the late 1940s and 1950s, they found that they had to reshape the old Imperial structure into a new framework of more or less equal partners. The British would secure the collaboration of moderate nationalists by yielding control before the initiative passed to irreconcilables. Influence would thus be retained by transferring power. Nationalism would be channelled into constructing nations in harmony with British interests. British imperialism would be sustained by means other than domination.

The actuality did not conform to the hope. The British lurched from one crisis to the next, sometimes turning adversity to advantage. The idea of ostensible equal partnership never quite overcame Asian and African scepticism. What emerged was mutual accommodation based on self-interest. With the general public, and later with some historians, the Whiggish idea of progress towards a goal met with some success. The archives now reveal an infinitely more complicated story,

A version of this chapter was delivered as the Cust Foundation Lecture at Nottingham University in April 1995.

[1] Cabinet Minutes (46) 108 Confidential Annex, 31 Dec. 1946, CAB 128/8. For critical discussion of the topics pursued in this chapter, see John Darwin, *Britain and Decolonisation: The Retreat from Empire in the Post-War World* (London, 1988); R. F. Holland, *European Decolonization, 1918–1981* (London, 1985); and the introductory chapter in Ronald Hyam, ed., *The Labour Government and the End of Empire, 1945–1951*, British Documents on the End of Empire Project (BDEEP), 4 vols. (London, 1992), I, pp. xxiii–lxxviii.

though with a consistent thread. Ultimately the aim of the post-war practitioners of British imperialism remained the same as that of their Victorian predecessors. The goal was not that Britain should sustain the Empire but that the Empire, in a new form, should continue to sustain Britain.

This chapter addresses itself to the critical cases of India, Palestine, Burma, Ceylon, Egypt, the Sudan, Malaya, the West Indies, and tropical Africa. Above all, it explains how the initial phase of disengagement, presided over by Clement Attlee, eventually found its culmination in the era of liquidation dominated by Harold Macmillan. There were three main periods. The first was that of the Labour government, 1945–51; the second that of the Tory governments of Sir Winston Churchill and Sir Anthony Eden, 1951–57; and the third that of Macmillan from 1957. With the exception of the Suez crisis of 1956, the hand was played with skill and determination, especially by two grand practitioners of decolonization, Lord Mountbatten, the last Viceroy in India, and Iain Macleod, the Secretary of State for the Colonies during the critical phase in Africa, 1959–61. Mountbatten's achievement was to disengage from India in a spirit of goodwill, with the two successor states of India and Pakistan remaining in the Commonwealth. In the intervening years between Mountbatten and Macleod, the Gold Coast, Malaya, and the Sudan became independent and the goal was set for Nigerian independence in 1960. Largely as a result of Macleod's momentum, all of Britain's remaining twelve African dependencies except Southern Rhodesia were independent by 1968. The number of people under British rule in the two decades after 1945 was reduced from 700 million people to 5 million, of which 3 million were concentrated in Hong Kong.

In the background lay the Anglo-American coalition, not merely during the Second World War but throughout the era of the cold war. American assistance allowed the British Empire to revive before it collapsed. The American support of the British Empire was an arrangement that neither side cared to publicize, the British because it was humiliating to be so dependent on the United States, the Americans because the support of empire seemed at variance with historic principles.[2]

There are two further essential points of background, but they are intangibles. The period after the Second World War was at once profoundly anti-imperial and, in the West, anti-Communist. The attitude of the American government revealed both strains of thought, which were not always complementary. In the American mind anti-Communism always prevailed over anti-imperialism and thus gave the British Empire, at least, an extended lease on life. Generally, it was an age in which

[2] For these themes see Wm. Roger Louis and Ronald Robinson, 'The Imperialism of Decolonization', *Journal of Imperial and Commonwealth History*, XXII; 3 (Sept. 1994), pp. 462–511.

the critics of British imperialism as well as the permanent officials of the Colonial Office hoped for gradual change, not a landslide into independence. In 1945 the independence of India could be seen on the horizon, but no one would have guessed that within the next two decades the British Empire would be in a state of dissolution. If anti-imperialism at first was merely an attitude held by certain enemies of the British Empire in America and in Asia and Africa, it became no less than a worldwide movement. Sir Robert Scott, an old China hand and Commissioner-General in South-East Asia in 1959, described the idea of 'anti-colonialism':

> It is a frame of mind, resentment at patronage, resentment at fancied Western assumptions of superiority whether in social status or culture, reaction to the Western impact on Asia in the past centuries. This frame of mind, expressed in terms of opposition to Western control or interference, explains the paradox of 'anti-colonialism' in countries that have never been colonies, directed against countries that have never had them.
>
> Americans are sometimes baffled to find that Asian sentiment towards Britain, the greatest colonial power of all, is apt to be more cordial than towards the United States despite their remarkable record of generosity and altruism in dealings with Asia.[3]

Though the British might take some comfort in sharing the brunt of anti-colonialism with the United States as well as with the European colonial powers, there could be no doubt that they felt increasingly embattled. Sir Hilton Poynton of the Colonial Office in 1960 reflected on 'South African riots . . . Congo . . . [the] future of Algeria. . . . [W]e have entered a period in which the international climate . . . has changed and has become a more decisive factor in those problems.'[4] With such troubles, it is not difficult to understand why some wondered whether the game was worth the candle. Yet the alternative was equally unbearable. The other intangible was the idea of Britain without an Empire, a Britain that might become, in the words of Sir Charles Johnston, the Governor of Aden, 'a sort of poor man's Sweden'.[5]

Throughout the era, the economics, the politics, and the military aspects of the Imperial crisis were all inseparable, but at the end of the war the overall crisis was first and foremost economic. John Maynard Keynes at the Treasury had already warned of a 'financial Dunkirk', and wrote that 'We cannot police half the world at our own expense when we have already gone into pawn to the other half.'[6] The British averted bankruptcy in 1946 only by the American loan of $3.5 billion, an amount at the time so large that it seemed to critics to imply dependence on the United States to the extent of reducing the British Isles to the status of an economic

[3] Scott to Macmillan, Secret, 13 Nov. 1959, F[oreign] O[ffice] 371/143732.

[4] Poynton circular, Secret and Personal, 29 Sept. 1960, C[olonial] O[ffice] 1015/2515.

[5] Johnston to Colonial Office, Secret, 16 July 1963, FO 371/168630.

[6] Memorandum by Keynes, Top Secret, 28 Sept. 1944, T[reasury] 160/1375/F17942/010/5.

satellite. American economic assistance enabled the British to maintain a troop level at 1.4 million men, but from the Mediterranean to South-East Asia the British were militarily overextended. British and Indian troops re-established colonial control over Malaya, which was vital to the British economic system because of dollar-earning tin and rubber. In South-East Asia generally, there were significant degrees of intervention. The British assisted the French in attempting to reassert control over Indo-China but after the initial reoccupation of the East Indies decided in principle against helping the Dutch oppose Indonesian nationalism. The Americans later vetoed the Dutch effort to reimpose colonial rule by threatening to cancel Marshall Aid, thus demonstrating the effectiveness and brutality, as the Dutch saw it, of superpower intervention in colonial affairs. The Labour government in the early post-war period felt compelled to take into account Indian as well as American sentiment. By 1946 the Indian Army could no longer be relied on. '[T]he Indian Army', according to the minutes of the Cabinet, '... could not fairly be expected to prove a reliable instrument for maintaining public order in conditions tantamount to civil war.'[7] India was becoming ungovernable, thus creating a political as well as a military problem of the first magnitude.

'[T]he really fatal thing for us', Lord Wavell wrote in early 1947, 'would be to hang on to responsibility [in India] when we had lost the power to exercise it, and possibly to involve ourselves in a large-scale Palestine.'[8] Wavell was Mountbatten's predecessor, who had been Viceroy since 1943. His political masters, particularly Attlee, did not believe that he had either the political skill or the imagination to rise to the occasion of extricating Britain from India, or that he could remain on good terms with the leaders of the Indian National Congress. Wavell had served previously as Commander-in-Chief in India, but had also spent a substantial part of his military career in the Middle East. He did not minimize the importance of keeping on good terms with the Congress, but he attached just as much significance to maintaining good relations with the 90 million Muslim minority in India, which was more than the combined population of the Arab states of the Middle East. He viewed Jawaharlal Nehru and Vallabhbhai Patel, and above all Gandhi, with distrust, which was one among several reasons why he came into conflict with Attlee. Another reason was Wavell's contingency planning, called the 'Breakdown Plan', for withdrawal in stages, if necessary, from hostile territory. The Prime Minister and others regarded the plan as defeatist, in part because of the assumption of antagonism. Wavell had taken steps of basic military precaution, but Attlee and his colleagues believed that he would drift into the very 'large-scale Palestine' that the British wanted to avoid at any cost.

[7] Cabinet Minutes (46) 104, Minute 3, Confidential Annex, 10 Dec. 1946, CAB 128/8.

[8] Wavell to H. M. King George VI, 24 Feb. 1947, in Nicholas Mansergh and others, eds., *The Transfer of Power, 1942–1947*, 12 vols. (London, 1970–83), IX, p. 807.

During the two simultaneous crises in India and the eastern Mediterranean, the members of the Labour government held certain assumptions so basic that they often remained unstated.[9] One axiom was the principle of refusal to be drawn into civil war, whether in India, Palestine, or Greece, and of refusing to impose settlements that would require British bayonets (and that would coincidentally increase the appalling balance-of-payments deficit). Another tenet was the supposition that tenacious reasoning could persuade nationalists to see that it would be in their own self-interest to retain the British connection. The leaders of the Labour government, again like their Victorian predecessors, believed in a harmony of interests. There were strong differences in judgement, however, among the three men who in different ways were crucial in making the ultimate decisions. These were Attlee, Ernest Bevin (the Foreign Secretary), and Sir Stafford Cripps (President of the Board of Trade from August 1945 and then Chancellor of the Exchequer from November 1947). Bevin was the strongest figure in the Cabinet. His influence prevailed in the Middle East and generally in foreign and colonial affairs, but it counted for little in India. Cripps had a long-standing interest in India since the 1930s and particularly since 1942, when Churchill sent him on an abortive mission to offer Indian independence after the war in return for wartime co-operation. Cripps was an austere man of towering intellect, and by reputation had the keenest legal mind in England. Apart from the economics of the sterling area, however, his concern with the Imperial system focused on India. Attlee was the only key figure whose grip extended to the Empire as a whole. Even so, he was not much interested in Africa. He was a man of quiet authority, competence, and decisiveness. He was prepared to retrench where necessary and determined to uphold Labour's pledges gradually to transform the Empire into a Commonwealth. But Attlee, and those in the Labour government generally, believed in reform and gradual progress, not liquidation. Most of them were as determined as their Tory counterparts to uphold the Empire's prestige.

Bevin opposed the plans for what he judged to be scuttle in India. He regarded Cripps as too pro-Congress, too committed to a policy of appeasement, and not sufficiently pro-Empire. In lines that provide an oblique comment on the state of British morale in 1946–47, the Foreign Secretary wrote to the Prime Minister about India and the Middle East:

I must express my strong views with regard to India . . . I have examined this problem in relation to Egypt, Palestine, the Middle East, and all the Arab States and Persia, and I cannot

[9] For India, see esp. R. J. Moore, *Escape from Empire: The Attlee Government and the Indian Problem* (Oxford, 1983); for the Middle East, Wm. Roger Louis, *The British Empire in the Middle East, 1945–1951: Arab Nationalism, the United States, and Postwar Imperialism* (Oxford, 1984).

help feeling that the defeatist attitude adopted both by the Cabinet and by Field-Marshal Wavell is just completely letting us down . . .

I can quite understand that with a mind like Wavell's the demoralisation of the whole of the Army and the Police must be inevitable and I would strongly recommend that he be recalled and that you find somebody with courage who, even if he were the last man left there, would come out with dignity and uphold the British Empire and Commonwealth.

Bevin in his frustration expressed fundamental perplexities. Linking the issue of the Empire's possible collapse with the problem of economic weakness, he commented on the consequences of Indian independence throughout the British Imperial system:

You cannot read the telegrams from Egypt and the Middle East nowadays without realising that not only is India going, but Malay[a], Ceylon and the Middle East is going with it, with a tremendous repercussion on the African territories. . . . As Foreign Secretary, I can offer nothing to any foreign country, neither credit, nor coal, nor goods . . . And on top of that, within the British Empire, we knuckle under at the first blow and yet we are expected to preserve the position.[10]

Attlee rejected this line of thinking out of hand. 'I must ask you if you are prepared to take the strong hand in India, to announce that we intend to stay there and to put in enough troops to enforce our rule? This is to go back on the pledges that have been given by Governments of every political colour.' On the other hand, Attlee agreed with Bevin about the Viceroy: 'Wavell has a defeatist mind and I am contemplating replacing him.'[11]

The critical period was December 1946–February 1947, when decisions were made during a savage winter of coal shortages, cuts in fuel and electricity, and limited supplies of food and milk. Two days after Christmas Attlee and Bevin not only agreed on the question of withdrawal from Greece but also on the issue of submitting the Palestine question to the United Nations. There was also significant consensus on Libya: 'The Prime Minister agreed [with Bevin] that if we had Cyrenaica, there would be no need to stay in either Egypt or Palestine.'[12] On 1 January Attlee and Cripps met with Mountbatten and discussed the termination of the British Raj. 'They offered me "carte blanche",' Mountbatten wrote to the King.[13] On 13 February the Cabinet decided to transfer power in India by June 1948.

Mountbatten exaggerated, as he did characteristically, about the 'carte blanche' accorded to him, but it is true that he had more latitude than Wavell. Attlee and Cripps continued to drive the discussions in the Cabinet's India and Burma

[10] Bevin to Attlee, Private and Confidential, 1 Jan. 1947, PREM[ier] 8/564.

[11] Attlee to Bevin, Private and Confidential, 2 Jan. 1947, *Transfer of Power*, IX, pp. 445–46.

[12] Note by J. N. Henderson, 28 Dec. 1946, FO 800/475.

[13] Mountbatten to H. M. King George VI, 4 Jan. 1947, *Transfer of Power*, IX, p. 453.

Committee that determined policy. The complaint against Wavell had been that he seemed to be moving towards withdrawal without first exhausting the possibilities of a political settlement, which Attlee and Cripps now systematically pursued with the leaders of the Congress and the Muslim League, even if it might lead in the end to the upheaval of partition. At this stage Mountbatten had virtually no influence on the shaping of British policy other than to insist on a hard-and-fast declaration of British intent to leave by a fixed date. He arrived in India on 27 March 1947. His megalomania, his self-serving accounts, and his doctoring of historical records must not be allowed to obscure his achievement. Some historians have judged him merely to have pursued the appeasement of Nehru and Patel, but this is to trivialize the complex set of issues. The key to the general problem was the nature of the central government. Jinnah might have settled for something less than a separate state provided he had parity at the centre, which the Congress would never have accepted.[14] Though Mountbatten initially shifted impetuously from one solution to the next with no motive other than expediency and the urge to further his own reputation, he came down decisively in favour of a strong centre and of shucking off the provinces that would form the state of Pakistan. His views coincided with those of Nehru and Patel, who now favoured partition as a means to secure a strong central government and to prevent the collapse of authority after the departure of the British.

Playing on Jinnah's anxieties that Pakistan might be left adrift beyond the Commonwealth, Mountbatten also manipulated the suspicions of the Congress leaders that the Americans 'wished to capture all the markets, to step in and take the place of the British'.[15] He was adroit in bringing home to the Indian leaders the perils of isolation as well as the dangers of Balkanization. He later used similar tactics with the princes, almost all of whom were bullied into accepting a lapse of sovereignty and into acceding to one of the two successor states. Within two weeks after his arrival, Mountbatten became convinced that the unity of India could not be held, and that the British would have to quit much sooner than June 1948. His acceleration of the date to 15 August 1947 was one way of winning the co-operation of the Congress, but the essence of his triumph was the acceptance by the leaders of both political parties in Britain, by Churchill and Eden as well as by Attlee and Cripps, and by the leaders of the Congress and the Muslim League, that India and Pakistan would remain in the British orbit on the basis of Dominion Status. Mountbatten clearly regarded the Commonwealth as the continuation of British imperialism by other means. When he learned that Nehru and Patel would be

[14] See Ayesha Jalal, *The Sole Spokesman: Jinnah, the Muslim League and the Demand for Pakistan* (Cambridge, 1985).

[15] Mountbatten paraphrasing Krishna Menon, 22 April 1947, *Transfer of Power*, X, p. 372.

prepared, in return for an early transfer of power, to muffle the Congress battle-cry of an 'independent sovereign Republic' and to embrace Dominion Status, as an interim measure at least, he described the prospect in ringing words as 'the greatest opportunity ever offered to the Empire'.[16]

In Palestine as well as in India the goal initially was to avoid partition. All efforts would be directed towards reconciliation. If the goal proved to be illusive, then the aim would be to cut losses strictly in terms of British self-interest. The quest for reconciliation can be seen in the work of the Anglo-American Committee of Inquiry in Palestine, 1945–46, and in the proceedings of the Cabinet Mission to India in 1946. When the British evacuated Palestine in the spring of 1948, the withdrawal was remarkably similar to the 'Breakdown Plan' drawn up by Wavell two years earlier in India. If there was one point more than any other that the Labour government consistently upheld, it was not to engage military units. Humanitarian considerations in India paled before that basic preoccupation, as they did in Palestine. The remarkable feature of these massive disengagements from India and Palestine, and, it should be added, Greece, is that British forces emerged virtually unscathed.

The British decided to withdraw from Palestine on 30 September 1947 in the wake of the sterling convertibility crisis and, more directly, the majority report of the United Nations Special Committee on Palestine recommending partition. According to the minutes of the Cabinet, Attlee stated that there was 'a close parallel' between the situation in Palestine and India. 'He did not think it reasonable to ask the British administration to continue in present conditions, and he hoped that salutary results would be produced by a clear announcement that His Majesty's Government intended to relinquish the Mandate and, failing a peaceful settlement, to withdraw the British administration and British forces.'[17] As in India, the pace quickened. The final date for termination of the Mandate was set for 15 May 1948, which became accelerated to the 14th. In contrast to the partition of India, there was no division of assets, no question of splitting an army, and no continuity of the civil service. Israel emerged on the field of battle as the successor state. From the British vantage-point nothing was left but 'the dismal wreck of Arab Palestine'.[18]

After Indian independence, the centre of gravity of the British Empire shifted to the Middle East and Africa, but, in John Gallagher's phrase, the sun never set on troubles throughout the world. Malaya remained the bastion of British economic power in South-East Asia. The aim, or the hope, according to Bevin and other optimists, was to create in Singapore the driving force in a new and vast market in

[16] Mountbatten to Ismay, Secret, 8 May 1947, *Transfer of Power*, X, p. 699.

[17] Cabinet Minutes (47) 76, 20 Sept. 1947, CAB 128/10. See below, pp. 504, 507.

[18] The phrase of Sir Michael Wright, 30 March 1949, FO 371/75064.

the Far East that would link Britain, Australia, New Zealand, Hong Kong, and India. With the beginning of the Communist insurgency in 1948, however, the British faced the danger of Malaya becoming 'a second Palestine'.[19] In the same year Burma achieved independence and left the Commonwealth, while Ceylon also achieved independence and became a Dominion. The watchword became 'more Ceylons and fewer Burmas'.[20]

The loss of Burma represented a severe economic setback because of its rice, oil, timber, and tin. The secession also constituted a symbolic loss keenly felt by the Labour government. Attlee again was directly involved from March 1946. One remarkable feature of his decisions is the extent to which he acted on the advice of Mountbatten, who until 1946 was Supreme Allied Commander South-East Asia. In attempting to salvage the situation that had gone from crisis to crisis since the end of the war, Attlee relieved the Governor, Sir Reginald Dorman-Smith, and, at Mountbatten's suggestion, appointed Major-General Sir Hubert Rance, who was much more sympathetic to Burmese national aspirations. From Rance's reports, Attlee knew of increasing Burmese disaffection, which had crystallized during the 1930s when peasant farmers protested against British commercial exploitation and more specifically against Indian moneylenders who had dispossessed them. The collapse in 1942, after the fall of Singapore and the Japanese invasion, destroyed an economic as well as a political system. Attlee calculated that the Burmese leader Aung Sang was a patriotic nationalist and not necessarily anti-British. He was the only person who might hold the country together and, in return for independence, perhaps keep Burma in the Commonwealth. Burma could not be held by force. According to Field Marshal Montgomery, if Burma were to rebel the British military would approach 'the position when we would no longer be able to meet our commitments'.[21] In a critical decision taken in December 1946, the Cabinet offered the Burmese the choice of whether or not to stay within the British system.[22] The offer of independence drew Churchill's wrath in the House of Commons in a famous rebuke to the Labour government:

> The British Empire seems to be running off almost as fast as the American Loan. The steady and remorseless process of divesting ourselves of what has been gained by so many generations of toil, administration and sacrifice continues. In the case of Burma... this haste is appalling. 'Scuttle' is the only word that can be applied.[23]

[19] Hyam, *The Labour Government*, I, p. xxvii.

[20] Memorandum for African Governors' Conference dated Nov. 1947, ibid., I, p. 288. See below, pp. 460–63, 477, 482–84.

[21] Hugh Tinker, ed., *Burma: The Struggle for Independence, 1944–1948*, 2 vols. (London, 1983 and 1984), II, p. 57.

[22] Cabinet Minutes (46) 107, 19 Dec. 1946, CAB 128/6.

[23] *Parliamentary Debates* (Commons), Fifth Series, CDXXXI, 20 Dec. 1946, cols. 2343 and 2350.

By early 1947 it was clear that Burma would break the tie with Britain. In July of the same year Aung Sang and most of the members of the Burmese Cabinet were assassinated. On 4 January 1948 Burma became a sovereign and independent republic. Attlee reflected that if the British had worked with Aung Sang from the start, 'I think Burma would have stayed in the Commonwealth'.[24] Attlee's experience with the problem of Burma cast a long shadow on all subsequent major decisions.

In the case of Ceylon, Attlee interfered less, partly because he judged that the nationalist leader D. S. Senanayake aimed at constitutional evolution as in the White Dominions, and believed in working with the British rather than against them. The Prime Minister kept a sharp eye on developments but left the Secretary of State for the Colonies, Arthur Creech Jones, to handle the negotiations in concert with the Commonwealth Relations Office. Creech Jones was a key figure in the shaping of Labour's conciliatory policy towards colonial nationalism. In his judgement, and generally that of the Colonial Office, the Ceylonese leaders feared domination by India, which worked to British advantage. Creech Jones further pondered the composition of the Ceylonese population. Among the predominant Sinhalese, there were large minorities of Tamils and Indian immigrants totalling some 30 per cent of the population. The Colonial Office accepted Senanayake's assurances of the viability of the plural society, which at the time seemed to be a reasonable assumption. The key to the general British assessment, however, was the economic appraisal. By contrast with the adverse economic circumstances in Burma, those in Ceylon were favourable. Patrick Gordon Walker at the Commonwealth Relations Office described Senanayake and his fellow conservative nationalists as 'extremely rich landowners with local power and influence comparable to a Whig landlord's in George III's time'.[25] The British thus had, in Ronald Robinson's phrase, a set of prefabricated collaborators, provided that power could be transferred sooner rather than later. Lord Soulbury, the chairman of a wartime commission on Ceylon, had written in 1945 about the historical lessons:

> Certain parallels can be drawn between Ceylon and Ireland. Many of the Ceylonese resemble the Irish in temperament and intelligence and like the Irish they have long memories. It would be a tragedy to repeat in Ceylon any of the colossal mistakes we have made in Ireland.
>
> The treatment of South Africa by the Liberal Government of 1906 is a much happier example. To hit the golden mean between caution and magnanimity is perhaps impossible but I believe that in the long run giving too much and too soon will prove to be wiser than giving too little and too late.[26]

[24] Kenneth Harris, *Attlee* (London, 1982), p. 361.

[25] Quoted in Darwin, *Britain and Decolonisation*, p. 105.

[26] Soulbury to Hall, 5 Oct. 1945, Hyam, *Labour Government*, I, p. 5.

When Ceylon became a Dominion in February 1948, a set of agreements established bedrock precedent for the Colonial Office. The same set of principles appeared in subsequent transfers of power. Britain preserved close links in foreign affairs and defence arrangements. The Royal Navy retained access to the magnificent naval base at Trincomalee.

In mainstream colonial affairs, Attlee's influence predominated in the Labour government and left a lasting mark. In the Middle East, however, he delegated authority to Ernest Bevin, who attempted with mixed success to create an extended system of client states on an Iraq–Jordan axis. One success was the creation of a veiled British protectorate in Libya in concert with the United Nations and with US economic and diplomatic assistance. In Egypt, Bevin failed to reach agreement on the evacuation of British troops from the Canal Zone or on the issue of the Sudan. His tenure as Foreign Secretary ended shortly before the nationalization of the Anglo-Iranian Oil Company on 2 May 1951 by the Prime Minister Mohammed Musaddiq. The loss of the refinery at Abadan represented an economic catastrophe valued at £120m, or the equivalent cost 'of retooling and modernising the coal industry' in Britain.[27] It was a further blow to the prestige of the Labour government, not least because of the precedent. If Musaddiq were able evict the British, what might be the repercussions at Suez? Attlee held the Cabinet steady, refusing to resort to force, though he was influenced by the American calculation that a British reoccupation of Abadan might provoke the Russians to occupy northern Iran. The Labour government acted consistently but acquired a further reputation of 'scuttle', the word again used by Churchill. 'How different would the position have been', he wrote, 'if the late [Labour] Government had not flinched . . . at Abadan.'[28]

Churchill believed that the base at Suez would continue to provide Britain with a commanding bastion in the Middle East regardless of the loss of India. As Prime Minister, 1951–55, he had a style that was at once determined, obstructive, and retrograde. He had no positive vision of the Colonial Empire other than as an adornment of British glory. He acquiesced in the face of persistent argument, however, and pragmatism flavoured his judgement. On large issues Churchill's decisions often proved to be sound. The other leading figures in Imperial affairs were Eden (Foreign Secretary), Lord Salisbury (Commonwealth Relations Secretary in 1952), Alan Lennox-Boyd (Secretary of State for the Colonies from 1954), and Harold Macmillan (Minister of Defence from 1954). Macmillan's ideas were representative. In 1951 he had warned during the Persian oil crisis that British withdrawal from Abadan would signify 'the collapse of British power and prestige

[27] Ministry of Fuel and Power, quoted in Louis, *British Empire in the Middle East*, p. 55.

[28] Minute by Churchill, 17 Aug. 1952, PREM 11/392.

in the East'.[29] In 1952 he described the choice confronting the British nation as one between 'the slide into a shoddy and slushy Socialism, or the march to the third British Empire'.[30] The Churchill government faced the legacy of the sterling crises of 1947, 1949, and 1951 as well as the consequences of rearmament during the Korean War and the cost of nuclear weapons. Despite economic weakness, Britain ostensibly remained a great world power as well as a great colonial power. Churchill and his colleagues aimed to regenerate Britain's power, to remain on good terms with the United States, to defend the Empire against Labour criticism, to prevail over Communist insurgents in Malaya, EOKA in Cyprus, Mau Mau in Kenya, and not least, to come to terms with the revolutionary government in Egypt.

The Egyptian revolution of 1952 fundamentally altered Britain's relationship, not merely with Egypt but also with the Sudan. King Farouk had regarded himself as King of the Sudan as well as King of Egypt. The military officers of the revolution broke the symbolic unity. General Mohammed Neguib, who was half-Sudanese, declared that one of the revolutionary goals was to guarantee Sudanese self-determination. At one stroke he transformed the situation. The British position in the Sudan had been secure as long as the Sudanese feared Egyptian domination. The Sudanese and the Egyptians now became comrades-in-arms against the British, thus destroying the collaborative basis of British rule. The Anglo-Egyptian agreement of February 1953 on self-determination in the Sudan prepared the way for the evacuation of British troops in Egypt. The Foreign Office made concessions in the Sudan that included a speeding up of the Sudanization of the administration, an international commission to supervise the process of self-determination by no later than the end of 1955, and a target date set for independence shortly thereafter. 'I think this price is worth paying,' wrote the Permanent Under-Secretary at the Foreign Office, Sir William Strang, about yielding to the Egyptian demands in the Sudan in order to resolve the problem of the Canal Zone.[31] The officers of the Sudan Political Service felt betrayed. The case of the Sudan reinforced the pattern of British decolonization. Calculations of strategic and economic self-interest would prevail over concern for the welfare of the inhabitants as viewed by those in the colonial administration. The Foreign Office dealt with the Sudan as 'the pawn in our Egyptian policy', the phrase of Margery Perham, the foremost academic authority on Africa, who hoped that Arthur Creech Jones, the former Colonial Secretary, would be sent to the Sudan to

[29] *Parliamentary Debates* (Commons), Fifth Series, CDXCI, 30 July 1951, col. 1059.

[30] Memorandum by Macmillan, 17 June 1952, in David Goldsworthy, ed., *The Conservative Government and the End of Empire, 1951–1957*, British Documents on the End of Empire Project (BDEEP), 3 vols. (London, 1994), III, p. 50.

[31] Minute by Strang, 4 Dec. 1952, FO 371/96915.

'do a Mountbatten' and persuade the Sudanese to remain in the Commonwealth.[32] The Foreign Office did not favour that or similar proposals, and the Sudanese themselves believed that the phrase 'Dominion Status' implied further British domination. So also did the Egyptians. The Sudan did not join the Commonwealth. From 1954 the Sudanese nationalists installed by the British gradually but effectively took control of the administration and remained favorably disposed. The transfer of power on 1 January 1956 was merely symbolic. The British left the Sudan as they had arrived in the late nineteenth century, for reasons that transcended the country itself, including Anglo-American motives of regional security and higher strategic aims in Egypt and the eastern Mediterranean.

In 1954 Churchill decided to evacuate troops from the Canal Zone and to redeploy forces elsewhere in the Middle East. 'He hates the policy of "scuttle" which the Foreign Office and Anthony [Eden] have persuaded him to accept about the Suez Canal,' his doctor, Lord Moran, recorded, 'but tries to console himself with the fact that the eighty thousand troops can be used elsewhere, and that it will mean a substantial economy.'[33] Nuclear weapons and other developments in military technology had rendered the base obsolete. The ominous significance of the hydrogen bomb weighed heavily in Churchill's decision, but so also did his instinct to hold on to the base at any cost. Eden and others, notably Lord Salisbury and General Sir Brian Robertson, had worked hard to woo him away from a diehard attitude against the Egyptians. They believed that Egypt could be reconciled. Eden put his own reputation at risk. Once regarded as the champion of anti-appeasement of Hitler, he now appeared to the hard right of the Tory party as the arch-appeaser of Gamal Abdel Nasser. By evacuating troops from the Canal Zone, Eden seemed to be sounding an Imperial retreat. He himself believed such criticism to be a caricature of his position, but in comparison with Churchill he did have progressive views. During the Suez crisis Eden responded with anger to the American accusation that old-fashioned colonialism motivated him. 'It was I who ended the "so-called colonialism" in Egypt,' he exclaimed![34]

Eden seldom articulated his ideas about the British Empire, but he believed in colonial evolution in the same way as did Alan Lennox-Boyd, though the latter devoted serious attention to the matter. Over decades or perhaps centuries, in Eden's view, colonial subjects would become able to manage their own affairs. He was the last Prime Minister to hold such a leisurely view. He approved the plans of the Colonial Office for federal systems in South-East Asia, the Aden Colony and

[32] Perham to R. C. Mayall, 23 June 1953; and to James Robertson, 27 Nov. 1952, Margery Perham Papers 536/5–7, Rhodes House, Oxford.

[33] Lord Moran, *Churchill: Taken from the Diaries of Lord Moran* (Boston, 1966), p. 513.

[34] Iverach McDonald and others, *The History of 'The Times'*, 6 vols. (London, 1935–94), V, p. 268.

Protectorates, East Africa, Central Africa, and the West Indies. The essential concept was that of shared wealth that would allow overall development. Eden thus held fairly enlightened views by the standards of his time. In 1956 he presided over a far-reaching reassessment of general policy that anticipated many of the economic and military measures of retrenchment pursued later by Macmillan. Eden's plans were stillborn because of the Suez crisis, which had its immediate origins in late 1955 in Nasser's acceptance of military assistance from the Soviet Union via Czechoslovakia. This was of revolutionary significance. It altered the existing balance of power in the Middle East and introduced the Soviet Union as a major contender for regional hegemony. The Czech arms deal liberated Nasser from the Anglo-American embrace. The stakes were high. This was one reason why Eden decided immediately to move against Nasser after the nationalization of the Suez Canal Company on 26 July 1956. He now attempted to prove that he could rise to the occasion in the tradition of Churchill, but he had a higher aim as well: Britain would demonstrate that she remained the pre-eminent regional power in the Middle East and, moreover, a great world power that could act, if necessary, independently from the United States.

The British prepared for the invasion of Egypt as if they were engaging German Panzer units during the Second World War. With more effective and more daring planning, and without the fatal misjudgement about the United States, the military operations in November 1956 might have been a success. Nasser might have been toppled, a more friendly regime in Cairo might have been installed, and the life of the British Empire might have been extended. But it is just as possible that the British might have turned the clock back to 1882 and might have poisoned sentiment throughout the colonial world, not merely against Britain and France but against the United States. In any event, Eden and Macmillan, now Chancellor of the Exchequer, did indeed make a monumental miscalculation, because President Dwight D. Eisenhower and Secretary of State John Foster Dulles believed that there would be a far-reaching anti-Western reaction. But what really irritated the Americans was the lack of consultation. Eden and Macmillan, as well as other members of the Cabinet, generally thought that the Americans did not want to know about the plans and would acquiesce in a successful operation. There is some evidence that this was actually true for Dulles but certainly not for Eisenhower, who was outraged. The Eisenhower administration waged virtual economic warfare against the British, forcing them and also the French and Israelis to withdraw. It was Eden, not Nasser, who was toppled. The significance is that the Suez venture demonstrated the dependence of Britain on the United States. Suez made plain for all to see that Britain was doomed both as a colonial power and as a world power unless she acted in concert with the United States. As Eden himself put it: 'we must review our world position and our domestic capacity more searchingly in the light of the Suez experience, which has not so much changed our fortunes as revealed realities.'[35]

There was a psychological dimension to the trauma of Suez that has a bearing on subsequent decolonization. Sir Charles Johnston, the Governor of Aden, expressed it in regard to the Middle East:

> [O]ne of the worst things that has happened to us . . . particularly since Suez, is that in the Middle East we have lost confidence in our ability to deal with situations. The loss of confidence is a very odd thing—it is something which has happened inside ourselves, and bears no particular relation to the facts as observed in the field. Our Suez fiasco seems, in effect, to have left a far deeper mark on ourselves than on the Arabs.[36]

Julian Amery, one of Eden's fiercest critics, then and forever after referred to Suez as a fatal turning-point in the history of the British Empire and as 'Britain's Waterloo'. Yet as he himself proved when he became Under-Secretary of State for the Colonies in the Macmillan government, Britain had not lost the will or the capacity to deal with colonial insurgency. What she had lost was the pretence of being a superpower.

In February 1957, in the wake of Suez, Harold Macmillan became Prime Minister. He was not committed to the Empire in the way that Churchill or even Eden had been. He was a political adventurer, able to change course 180 degrees if it served his purpose, as indeed he did during the Suez crisis, when he had been the most aggressive of all ministers at the beginning but then at the height of the emergency had urged an abrupt withdrawal. He aimed above all to recapture the benevolence of the United States and, equally, to avert a collision with African nationalism. Towards the beginning of his tenure he requested a balance sheet that would indicate whether specific colonies were a liability or an asset.[37] The result was indeterminate. There were too many intangibles and the military and strategic elements were intertwined with the economic. Macmillan, however, made up his own mind without the help of charts, graphs, and economic assessments. He eventually persuaded himself that the Colonial Empire was an albatross. He knew first and foremost that he could not get back on good terms with the Americans unless he demonstrated that the British were contrite and no longer possessed a Suez mentality. He recognized too that international sentiment against the colonial powers would continue to mount at a time when the British could least afford a prolonged military conflict. The British could still cope with limited colonial

[35] Eden, 'Thoughts', Secret and Personal, n.d. but Dec. 1956, PREM 11/1138.

[36] Johnston to Sir Roger Stevens, Personal and Confidential, 16 March 1961, CO 1015/2185.

[37] See Tony Hopkins, 'Macmillan's Audit of Empire, 1957', in Peter Clarke and Clive Trebilcock, eds., *Understanding Decline: Perceptions and Realities of British Economic Performance* (Cambridge, 1997).

insurgency, but they could not deal with major colonial warfare. The British Parliament and public would not tolerate it, nor could the economy sustain it.

Macmillan's conversion to liquidation came only gradually. In the two years from 1957 he responded sympathetically, if ambiguously, to the logic of the Chiefs of Staff and to certain officials in the Colonial Office and Foreign Office, that the British Empire might contract yet prove to be a durable force in the shape of a hard core of strategic bases through the Mediterranean to Aden, and through Africa from Freetown (Sierra Leone), Kano (Nigeria), and Mombasa (Kenya) to Aden and on to Singapore. The essential elements of the old Empire would be retained, not abandoned. Macmillan himself noted, 'we only need our "Gibraltars"'.[38] When Malta became independent in 1964, the Grand Harbour remained linked with Britain through a defence agreement. In the eastern Mediterranean, Cyprus remained indispensable. Julian Amery, who negotiated Cypriot independence in 1960, secured two sovereign enclaves and simultaneously worked to acquire a sovereign base in Aden, the point of connection between the Mediterranean, African, and Asian bases. Aden would be the keystone in the new Imperial system, the fortress protecting Britain's position in the Gulf regardless of Adeni or Arab nationalism. 'One of the greater heresies of contemporary thought is that a base is useless if situated amidst a hostile population,' Amery wrote.[39] He believed that Aden could be easily defended and devil take the hindmost. In the extensive controversy within official circles about the future of Aden, Amery found himself on the losing side. The British eventually pinned their hopes on Aden not as a sovereign base but, in the words of the Governor, as 'an independent and prosperous Arab State on terms of friendly partnership and association with us'.[40] The essential point of a harder, tougher Empire unified by strategic bases stretching from the Atlantic to the Pacific had an appeal to Macmillan as well as the permanent officials as they constructed the South Arabian Federation that allowed the British continued use of the Aden base after independence. But in 1967, in the wake of a severe sterling crisis and in the midst of revolution in the Aden peninsula, the British abandoned the base.

In South-East Asia as well as in Aden there emerged, in the phrase of Lord Selkirk, the Commissioner-General, the 'Grand Design' of federation.[41] A Scot and an intimate of Macmillan, Selkirk had served as First Lord of the Admiralty. He

[38] Harold Macmillan, *Riding the Storm, 1956–1959* (London, 1971), p. 692; Macmillan Diary, 10 Feb. 1959. (References to the Macmillan Diaries are to those in possession of Alistair Horne. I am indebted to Mr Horne for allowing me to read them. The Macmillan Papers are now in the Bodleian Library in Oxford.)

[39] Minute by Amery, 10 March 1959, CO 1015/1910.

[40] Johnston to C.O., Secret, 16 July 1963, FO 371/168630.

[41] Selkirk in a meeting with Lord Lansdowne and others, 4 July 1961, FO 371/159701.

saw the regional as well as the internal problems of Malaya and Singapore in clear perspective. After the collapse of the Dutch and French colonial empires, the British had survived as the paramount European power in South-East Asia. According to this interpretation, on the horizon stood the traditional Western foe with a new complexion—China as the 'Yellow Peril flecked with Red'. Under General Sir Gerald Templer the British had waged a successful campaign against Communist insurgents. The socially conservative rulers of Malaya were dependent on the British to end the emergency, but both nationalist parties, which united in an alliance, were anti-colonial as well as anti-Communist. When the Alliance Party led by Tunku Abdul Rahman captured fifty-one of fifty-two seats in the national election of 1955, the British reacted in the familiar paradigm of freedom sooner rather than later by granting Malayan independence in August 1957. They responded also to the leader in Singapore, Lee Kuan Yew, who according to Selkirk thought that the only way to secure the island's safety would be to construct a Malaysian federation. To balance the 1 million Chinese of Singapore, the British included Sarawak and Sabah in North Borneo. The Federation of Malaysia was born in September 1963. It had military as well as economic significance for the phoenix of British imperialism attempting to rise in Asia. The great military and naval base at Singapore would continue to command the gateway to the Pacific. British military and naval officers, who lamented the loss of Suez and even India, took a resolute stand. 'No further scuttle' became the watchword of the diehard military officers described by their critics as possessing 'the Singapore mentality'.[42] The creation of Malaysia, however, gave rise to protests from the Philippines and above all from Indonesia. During the era of confrontation with Indonesia, Macmillan believed that the Colonial Office and the Chiefs of Staff had overestimated British capacity to defend this last Imperial edifice. '[O]ur weakness in Singapore', he wrote in 1962, had not been accurately measured: 'The whole mood [of the Colonial Office] is based on a false assumption of our power.'[43]

According to Lord Selkirk, who placed Malaysian perplexities in grand historical perspective:

> From Trafalgar to the Entente Cordiale we were able to maintain peace in almost all parts of the world. Since then we have continued this policy, though with much less success, first in co-operation with the French and more recently in co-operation with the U.S.A. We have done this partly from a sense of duty and partly because of the inherent dependence of our economic position on world trade. But the means at our disposal have become less and less adequate to meet the commitments which we still retain.

[42] Sir Geofroy Tory (Kuala Lumpur) to Sir Henry Lintott, Secret and Personal, 3 April 1958, DO 35/10535.

[43] Minute by Macmillan, 21 June 1962, PREM 11/3867. 'I foresee a situation like that in Central Africa', Macmillan noted in his diary (24 March 1962).

> The result of this is that we are stretched to a point where our strength might snap under the strain, and indeed our present position would be highly perilous were it not for our basic dependence on the U.S.A.[44]

In South-East Asia and in the West Indies the British had to tolerate the twists and turns of American policy and what they believed to be its manifest hypocrisy. The Americans, Macmillan noted in his diary, 'are the first to squeal when: "decolonization" takes place uncomfortably near to them'.[45]

Macmillan wrote in 1962, when British Guiana threatened to become 'another Congo', and after the Federation of the West Indies had already collapsed. The two mainland colonies of Guiana and Honduras had rejected from the outset, in the words of a minister in the Colonial Office, 'the grand concept of Federation', but from 1958 to 1962 a precarious federal framework held together Jamaica, Trinidad, and Barbados as well as the smaller islands of the Leewards (Antigua, Monserrat, St Kitts) and the Windwards (Dominica, Grenada, St Lucia, St Vincent). Jamaica and Trinidad contributed 85 per cent of the federal budget in about equal measure. In an assessment that identified one of the underlying problems, Lennox-Boyd in 1959 pointed out that Jamaica would resist high taxation by the federal government while Trinidad would work towards increased federal powers. He commented too on another basic tension: 'the intense wish of the small islands to be placed on a footing within the Federation comparable with that of Jamaica, Trinidad and Barbados.'[46] Nevertheless, the Colonial Office believed that these problems and a multitude of others could be resolved. The aim, in the phrase of one official, was 'efficiency and economy'.[47] In this rational and laudable federal design, which reflected forty years of West Indian popular sentiment and a dozen years of careful planning, the wealth of Jamaica and Trinidad would help the smaller islands to move forward from economic and political stagnation and to launch a concerted attack against agricultural deterioration, illiteracy, malnutrition, and poverty. According to the Colonial Office vision, the Federation would promote a viable regional economy that would avert the danger of the islands becoming perpetual wards—loyal to Britain but a drain on the British economy.

[44] Selkirk to Macmillan, Secret, 14 Aug. 1961, PREM 11/3737.

[45] Macmillan Diary, 27 Sept. 1962. Dean Rusk, the US Secretary of State, had written earlier in the year that it would be impossible for the United States 'to put up with' an independent Guiana and that the Prime Minister, Cheddi Jagan, 'should not accede to power again' because of the danger of a regime sympathetic to both Cuba and the Soviet Union. Macmillan noted in anger: 'How can the Americans continue to attack us in the United Nations on colonialism and then use expressions like these which are not colonialism but pure Machiavellianism . . . it does show a degree of cynicism which I would have thought Dean Rusk could hardly put his pen to. He, after all, is not an Irishman, not a politician, nor a millionaire; he has the reputation of being an honourable and somewhat academic figure.' Minute by Macmillan, 21 Feb. 1962, PREM 11/3666.

[46] Minute by Lennox-Boyd, 23 June 1959, PREM 11/4598. See below, pp. 618–19; 620.

[47] Minute by Philip Rogers, 13 Nov. 1959, CO 1031/2574.

The Colonial Office recognized that local politicians would be reluctant to relinquish power to a federal government but would nevertheless hope to benefit from Commonwealth status. Julian Amery, who played a prominent part in West Indian affairs, believed that it would be 'absurd' to grant independence to the Federation without adequate financing for the central government. He wrote in 1959 that the year 1963 might be the earliest that independence would not be 'purely fictitious'.[48] Plans for an independent Federation, however, ended abruptly when in September 1961 the Jamaican referendum decided the issue. Jamaica would secede.[49] Macleod wrote to Macmillan: 'This is a most grievous blow to the Federal ideal for which we and enlightened West Indian opinion have striven for so many years'.[50] Lord Perth, Macleod's right-hand man at the Colonial Office, commented that 'the grand concept of Federation . . . is in ruins'.[51] 'This is all very sad,' reflected one of Macmillan's advisers. 'But once the Jamaica Referendum had gone against Federation it became almost inevitable that Trinidad would follow suit . . . [I]t is, alas, impossible to order people to behave sensibly.'[52]

In Africa too, federation emerged as a central theme in the era of dissolution, but the dilemmas of bringing an end to the Empire in tropical Africa must be seen in relation to pan-Africanism, which aspired to a federation of African states, and in relation to South Africa, increasingly isolated but defiant (see Map 14.1). When Macmillan embarked on his fateful tour of Africa in 1960, he first used the phrase 'wind of change' in Ghana in a speech that had been prepared before he left England.[53] The purpose was to align Britain with mainstream black African nationalism. When he used the phrase again in South Africa it left no doubt about British intent, but Macmillan himself still hoped to reconcile South Africa, not drive her out of the Commonwealth. When she departed in 1961, it was a melancholy day.[54] Nor could he take any pleasure in Ghana's ascendancy in the pan-African movement. Ghana had become independent in 1957, in the phrase of a Colonial Office official, 'with less bitterness' than virtually any other colony.[55] It seemed to vindicate the liberal policies initiated a decade earlier by Arthur Creech Jones and especially by his principal adviser on Africa, Andrew Cohen, as well as by

[48] Minute by Amery, 6 Aug. 1959, CO 1031/2311.

[49] For the collapse of the Federation see John Mordecai, *The West Indies: The Federal Negotiations* (London 1968), esp. the epilogue by W. Arthur Lewis; and Elisabeth Wallace, *The British Caribbean: From the Decline of Colonialism to the End of Federation* (Toronto, 1977).

[50] Minute by Macleod to Macmillan, 22 Sept. 1961, PREM 11/4074.

[51] Minute by Perth, 22 Nov. 1961, CO 1031/3278.

[52] Minute by T. J. Bligh, 31 Jan. 1962, PREM 11/4074.

[53] Richard Lamb, *The Macmillan Years, 1957–1963: The Emerging Truth* (London, 1995), has useful chaps. on Macmillan and Africa.

[54] 'A very sad day,' Lord Home wrote to Macmillan, '. . . with emotion overcoming reason.' 15 March 1961, PREM 11/3535.

[55] Minute by J. S. Bennett, 26 March 1957, CO 936/576.

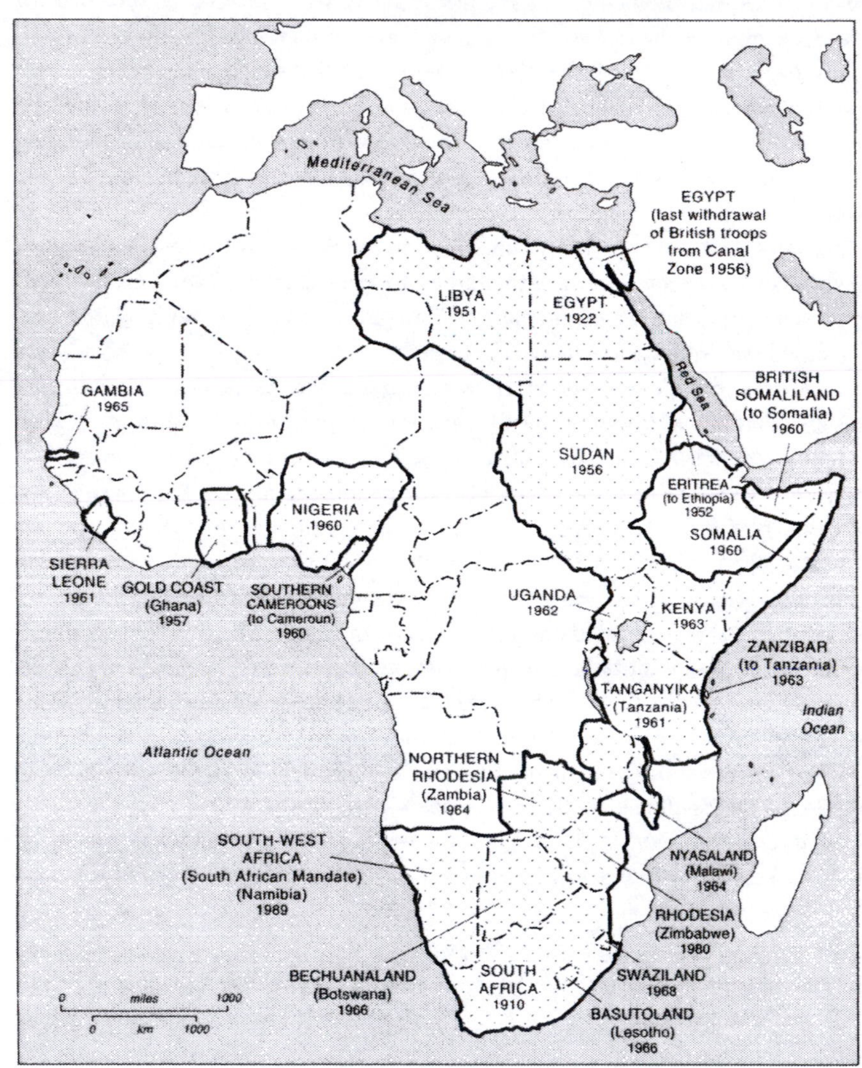

MAP 14.1. British Decolonization in Africa

the Governor of the Gold Coast (as Ghana then was), Charles Arden-Clarke, and by one of the principal British officials, Reginald Saloway, who had served in India and who drew parallels with the Indian freedom movement. Before Arden-Clarke arrived in the Gold Coast in the aftermath of the 1948 riots, Creech Jones told him that the colony stood on the edge of revolution. The Governor gave decisive support to the charismatic and erratic Kwame Nkrumah, the two of them guiding the colony to independence. At first the gamble seemed to pay off, but in the exuberant years of post-independence Ghana became the home of pan-Africanism and Nkrumah the spokesman for anti-colonialism and African unity. Ghana itself became an authoritarian state, described by some as 'totalitarian'. Lord Home, then Commonwealth Secretary, wrote that Nkrumah regarded himself 'as a Messiah sent to deliver Africa from bondage' and threatened to become the Nasser of black Africa.[56] According to John Russell, British Ambassador in Addis Ababa, another centre of the pan-African movement, the comparison with Nasser did not do Nkrumah justice:

> In comparison with Nkrumah, Nasser is a pale amateur in the export of African subversion. Nkrumah is the boy for us to watch...
>
> Nkrumah is our enemy, he is determined to complete our expulsion from an Africa which he aspires to dominate absolutely... We, being white, cannot hope to fight him openly in Africa. Ergo: we must find blacks who can; and although it would be counter-productive to damn them with our old colonial kiss, yet surely it is not beyond our ingenuity to find effective ways of affording them discreet and legitimate support?[57]

The answer in part seemed to lie in the neighbouring West African states—'Almost every other West African ruler is suspicious of Nkrumah's motives,' the High Commissioner in Ghana, (Sir) Arthur Snelling, wrote in 1961, 'and suspects that his advocacy of African unity springs mainly from a desire to be boss of something bigger than Ghana.'[58] The British saw the massive presence of an independent Nigeria as a bulwark against Nkrumah's expansionist aims.

In Nigeria, as in other parts of the continent, the British created a federation with the aim of establishing a viable sovereign state from which they could withdraw with dignity and retain economic and defence connections. At the time of independence in 1960, the Chiefs of Staff acquiesced in far less explicit guarantees than they had originally wanted. Even minimal base rights at Kano proved to be short-lived. Nigeria at least had existed as an amalgamated colony since 1914, and the Colonial Office thus found it easier there than elsewhere to implement the political formula of federation. After a review of the 1954 constitution, the key legislation defining the component powers of the Muslim north, the Yoruba west,

[56] Memorandum by Home, 1 June 1959, PREM 11/2588.

[57] Russell to R. A. Butler, Confidential, 31 Dec. 1963, FO 371/176507.

[58] Snelling to CRO, Secret, 5 Dec. 1961, CO 936/714.

and the Igbo east, the Nigerians in 1957 were promised independence in three years if they could work in harness within a federal system. The time seemed too compressed to allow much optimism. Why did the British accelerate the timetable so rapidly? Sir James Robertson, the Governor-General, in 1959 tended to believe that the explanation lay in the international climate of anti-colonialism rather than in the development of cohesive Nigerian nationalism:

The trouble is that we have not been allowed enough time: partly this is because we are not strong enough now as a result of two world wars to insist on having longer to build up democratic forms of government, partly because of American opposition to our idea of colonialism by the gradual training of people in the course of generations to run their own show: partly because of dangers from our enemies, the Communists, we have had to move faster than we should have wished.[59]

After independence, Nigerian federation remained a delicate plant, endangered by domestic violence in the Yoruba west and by regional tension. John Chadwick of the Commonwealth Relations Office wrote in 1964:

[T]huggery and even murder... [are] daily occurrences in the West, [and] it is difficult to believe that Nigeria is not about to embark on a period of intense internal strain.... Maybe corruption will eventually price itself out of the market. But its present alarming scale, coupled with such factors as unemployed graduates and school leavers in increasing numbers, oil revenues, tribalism, trade unionism flexing its untrained muscles—add up to major symptoms of internal strain.[60]

Nevertheless, Nigeria in the post-independence era seemed to be the most successful of the federal experiments. According to the Foreign Office balance sheet:

The West Indian Federation	a failure
Central Africa	a failure
Southern Arabia	future uncertain
Malaysia	future uncertain
Nigeria	perhaps the best hope of the lot, largely because Federation was a genuinely indigenous product. But still decidedly shaky.[61]

[59] Robertson to Christopher Eastwood, Secret and Personal, 26 June 1959, CO 936/572. Eastwood, an official of long experience, was not unduly concerned about democracy in the new states: 'The problem of finding an alternative Government to which the metropolitan ruler could transfer power, though it had proved acute in Ireland and India, was not arising to the same extent in African territories. There was a tendency towards authoritarianism in newly independent territories, but this was not necessarily a bad thing, since in the early days at least of independence, strong Government was vital.' CRO record of conversation, Confidential, 26 Nov. 1959, DO 35/10687.

[60] Memorandum by Chadwick, Confidential, 18 Sept. 1964, FO 371/176588.

[61] A. M. Palliser, 'Policy towards East Africa', Top Secret, 4 Feb. 1964, FO 371/176524.

The assessment might have included the earlier disappointments of federal solutions for India and Palestine before partition. It probably erred on the extent to which the Nigerian federation was an 'indigenous product' rather than one imposed by the British. In any event, the negative record did not inspire optimism about an East African federation.

After Iain Macleod became Secretary of State for the Colonies in October 1959, and even a year later, he regarded 'federation for East Africa... [as] a wonderful prize'.[62] His sense of realism prevailed. He saw that the Colonial Office could not impose federation. Its lure did not deflect him from bringing the East African territories to independence at a radically quick pace. His approach reflected his political philosophy, and his general outlook rekindled the idealism of the British Empire, especially among those of a younger generation or, as Macmillan put it, 'the younger men in the Party'.[63] A romantic Scot and an inspiring orator, Macleod possessed an acute intelligence and political agility that his critics denounced as deviousness. In speed and decisiveness, he was to Africa what Mountbatten had been to India. Just as Attlee and Cripps had allowed Mountbatten latitude, so Macmillan and R. A. Butler (then Home Secretary) sympathized with Macleod's aims and gave him room for manœuvre. The former Colonial Secretary, Lennox-Boyd, in 1959 had set dates for Tanganyika to achieve independence in 1970, Uganda in 1971, and Kenya in 1975. Macleod, though he was Colonial Secretary for only two years (October 1959–October 1961), set in motion Tanganyika's independence in 1961, Uganda's in 1962, and Kenya's in 1963. This was no less than a revolution in colonial affairs.[64] It astonished and dismayed many of his Conservative colleagues and caused Macmillan himself to believe that the Colonial Secretary had tilted too far in favour of African nationalism.

Macleod's achievement must be seen in the context of African nationalism in the early 1960s and against the background of Algeria, the Congo, and—the immediate link with East African independence—the rising expectations brought about by the reaffirmation of the United Nations in 1955 to grant independence to the trust territory of Somalia in 1960. 'Does the appeasement of Somalia', asked the Governor of Uganda, Sir Frederick Crawford, in 1958, 'outweigh the advantages of keeping East Africa British and giving it time to prepare properly for its future?'[65] How did officials in the Colonial Office answer that question? The answer is fundamental, because Macleod could not have brought about so dramatic a

[62] Macleod minute to Macmillan, 22 Nov. 1960, CO 1015/2340.

[63] Macmillan Diary, 22 Feb. 1961.

[64] Macleod later reflected in 1967: 'The change of policy that I introduced in October 1959 was, on the surface, mainly a change of timing. In reality, of course, it was a true change of policy...' Quoted in the excellent biography by Robert Shepherd, *Macleod: A Biography* (London, 1994), p. 164.

[65] Memorandum by Crawford, 26 Oct. 1958, CO 1015/1918.

shift without the support of his staff. In general the key officials agreed on the necessity to accelerate the pace. Sir John Martin, one of Macleod's most balanced advisers, perhaps the wisest, wrote that the Colonial Office had believed that 'the Mau Mau were "sub-human"' but later that the Colonial Secretary should press for 'the release of the man [Jomo Kenyatta] who, although not equally acceptable to all sections of the population, is unquestionably the national leader'.[66] Such views represented a revolution in Colonial Office thought running parallel with Macleod's ideas.[67] Though the Governor of Kenya, Sir Patrick Renison, continued to regard Kenyatta as 'darkness and death', even Renison eventually came round to the Colonial Office view and Kenyatta was released in August 1961. In Tanganyika, the Governor, Sir Richard Turnbull, warned that an improbable mixture of 'Mau Mau and Maji-Maji' would undermine British rule unless there were a rapid transfer of power. All political forces in the territory had united against the administration at the same time that the British felt increased pressure from the Trusteeship Council in the United Nations. At a high level of generalization, C. Y. Carstairs, an official with a philosophical turn of mind who often clarified unspoken assumptions, explained the underlying purpose not only in Tanganyika but in all remaining British dependencies: to discourage Tanganyika from travelling 'down the Ghana totalitarian road' and to encourage Julius Nyerere and other nationalists to take the path of 'collaboration with the U.K.'—'which is what we are seeking to substitute for control'.[68] Launching Tanganyika on a course of independence proved to be fairly easy for Macleod, in part because of the relatively small numbers of Europeans in the territory, only 22,330 versus the 68,000 settlers in Kenya. Macmillan wrote in his diary that Kenya 'is more difficult *at home* even than Central Africa', because the settlers were 'aristocratic and upper middle class' and had 'strong links with the City and the Clubs'.[69] By early 1961 the Prime Minister had begun to distance himself from the Colonial Secretary. 'Iain Macleod... undoubtedly has leaned over too far towards the African view.'[70] Macmillan wrote later in the year: 'If we have to give independence to Kenya, it may well prove another Congo. If we hold on, it will mean a long and cruel campaign—Mau Mau and all that.'[71] But by late 1961 the course set by Macleod was irreversible.

The finale came in central Africa with the collapse of the Central African Federation in December 1963, but the issues of eastern and central Africa were

[66] Minutes by Martin, 22 Dec. 1959, CO 1015/1518; and 29 Dec. 1960, CO 822/1910.
[67] e.g. Shepherd, *Macleod*, p. 168.
[68] Minute by Carstairs, 13 March 1961, CO 822/2063.
[69] Macmillan Diary, 20 Jan. 1961.
[70] Ibid., 22 Feb. 1961.
[71] Ibid., 19 Dec. 1961.

closely linked. In the summer before Macleod had become Colonial Secretary there had been two major crises arising from the death of eleven Mau Mau prisoners in the Hola Detention Camp in Kenya, and from the report by Justice (Sir Patrick) Devlin, who had described Nyasaland as a 'police state'. Both events caused controversy in Parliament. Macleod had to deal with the aftermath of the two crises simultaneously, attempting to reconcile white and African communities, but leaving no doubt that he would champion the principle of African majorities, or at least parity. Otherwise he would resign. He came into head-on collision with Lord Home (the Commonwealth Secretary), and later with Duncan Sandys (Home's successor in July 1960). In part the confrontation was institutional. The Federation had been formed in 1953 by amalgamating the territories of Southern Rhodesia (Zimbabwe), Northern Rhodesia (Zambia), and Nyasaland (Malawi). The aim was to create a multiracial society (in contrast with the apartheid of South Africa) and to establish an economically viable unit that would benefit both Europeans and Africans, but the latter viewed it as an attempt to reinforce white domination. The Colonial Office held responsibility for Northern Rhodesia and Nyasaland; the Commonwealth Relations Office had corresponding and overlapping responsibilities for the Federation and the self-governing colony of Southern Rhodesia. The two offices of state opposed each other with daggers drawn. Macleod collided also with Sir Roy Welensky, the Prime Minister of the Federation, whom Lord Salisbury and others to the right of the Conservative Party regarded as an honourable man betrayed by the Colonial Office and specifically by Macleod. Macmillan wrote in his diary in February 1961: 'We may have a Boston Tea Party (Welensky declaring the Federation independent and seizing the colony of Northern Rhodesia), or an African Blood-Bath (riots all over British Africa), accentuated if Colonial Secretary were to resign.'[72] What Macmillan feared most was an 'Algeria' in central Africa. He could not curb Macleod without risking an explosion in Africa as well as in Britain, in the House of Commons as well as in the Conservative Party. 'If Colonial Secretary had resigned,' Macmillan wrote of the crisis over parity in Northern Rhodesia in February 1961, 'I think Government would have fallen. All the younger men in the Party would have gone against us.'[73]

Macleod played a daring and ruthless hand. Three times he threatened to resign, pressing his luck against great odds and winning each time: in February 1960, to secure the release of Hastings Banda in Nyasaland in time to give evidence as a free man to the Monckton Commission inquiring into the future of the Federation; in February 1961, over the issue of equal power-sharing between blacks and whites in Northern Rhodesia; and in July 1961, to gain Kenyatta's freedom. In March 1961 Lord Salisbury had denounced Macleod for transforming the 'complete loyalty' of

[72] Macmillan Diary, 22 Feb. 1961. [73] Ibid.

the white Rhodesians into feelings 'of suspicion, of contempt, almost of hatred of the home Government'.[74] By July of the same year Macmillan could take no more. He appointed Macleod as Leader of the House of Commons and Chairman of the Conservative Party, replacing him as Colonial Secretary with Reginald Maudling, who sustained, however, the Macleod juggernaut. Nyasaland and Northern Rhodesia in effect seceded from the white-dominated Federation and became independent respectively as Malawi and Zambia in 1964. The Rhodesian issue took another sixteen years to resolve before Zimbabwe emerged as a sovereign state in 1980, but almost all other major British colonial dependencies achieved independence in the wake of the extraordinary speed with which Iain Macleod, with Macmillan's wavering support, hastened the end of a long and inevitable process.

The immediate causes of the end of the British Empire are to be found not only in the nationalist movements in Empire itself but also in the lessons learned from the Algerian revolution and in the danger of Soviet intervention in the Congo. It seemed altogether more prudent to settle with African liberation movements in eastern and central Africa before war broke out between blacks and whites or before the Africans turned to the Russians for sponsorship.

The longer causes can be located in the shift in the balance of power during and after the Second World War. At the international level the survival of the Empire had depended on the Anglo-American coalition. American aid indirectly supported the British colonial system in an age of superpowers. From 1947 to 1952 the post-war Empire regenerated on American wealth and power. Despite the tradition of anti-colonialism, the United States buoyed up the system for cold war purposes until the mid-1960s. Throughout recurrent and severe sterling crises, American dollars helped to sustain British power overseas by underwriting the balance-of-payments costs of British forces in NATO and thus, indirectly, the costs of overseas garrisons. Though the Americans protested against the discriminatory sterling area, they refrained from retaliating. In the last resort, the defence of the Empire against Soviet pressure depended on American strategic protection. There was an implicit theme in the Anglo-American colonial relationship. The British were expected to keep troops on the Rhine. The Empire and Commonwealth, backed by the American nuclear deterrent, would secure large regions in the Middle East, South-East Asia, and Africa. If the Americans looked forward to transforming the Empire in the long run into independent states within the Western alliance, in the short run they propped it up against the challenge posed

[74] *Parliamentary Debates* (Lords), Fifth Series, CCXXIX, 7 March 1961, col. 306. This is the famous speech in which Salisbury describes Macleod as a man 'of most unusual intellectual brilliance . . . [but] too clever by half'.

by the Soviet Union and Communist China. Paradoxically, one consequence was that the cold war sometimes presented nationalists with the opportunity of playing the superpowers against each other or against the British. Actual or prospective superpower intervention could increase nationalist prospects. As this chapter has demonstrated, the international climate thus expedited the advance to independence, but the circumstances varied from region to region, from colony to colony. With the United States and the Soviet Union competing against each other in the colonial world, the local strength of nationalism or insurgency often determined the actual timing of decolonization.

Select Bibliography

COLIN BAKER, *Retreat from Empire: Sir Robert Armitage in Africa and Cyprus* (London, 1998).

GLEN BALFOUR-PAUL, *The End of Empire in the Middle East: Britain's Relinquishment of Power in Her Last Three Arab Dependencies* (Cambridge, 1991).

JOHN DARWIN, *Britain and Decolonisation: The Retreat from Empire in the Post-War World* (London, 1988).

DAVID GOLDSWORTHY, ed., *The Conservative Government and the End of Empire, 1951–1957*, British Documents on the End of Empire Project (BDEEP), 3 vols. (London, 1994).

JOHN D. HARGREAVES, *Decolonization in Africa* (London, 1988).

R. F. HOLLAND, *European Decolonisation, 1918–1981* (London, 1985).

TONY HOPKINS, 'Macmillan's Audit of Empire, 1957', in Peter Clarke and Clive Trebilcock, eds., *Understanding Decline: Perceptions and Realities of British Economic Performance* (Cambridge, 1997).

STEPHEN HOWE, *Anticolonialism in British Politics: The Left and the End of Empire, 1918–1964* (Oxford, 1994).

RONALD HYAM, ed., *The Labour Government and the End of Empire, 1945–1951*, British Documents on the End of Empire Project (BDEEP), 4 vols. (London, 1992).

—— and WM. ROGER LOUIS, eds., *The Conservative Governments and the End of Empire, 1957–1963*, British Documents on the End of Empire Project (BDEEP), 4 vols. (forthcoming).

JOHN KENT, *The Internationalization of Colonialism: Britain, France, and Black Africa, 1939–1956* (Oxford, 1992).

WM. ROGER LOUIS, *The British Empire in the Middle East, 1945–1951: Arab Nationalism, the United States, and Postwar Imperialism* (Oxford, 1984).

—— and RONALD ROBINSON, 'The Imperialism of Decolonization', *Journal of Imperial and Commonwealth History*, XXII, 3 (Sept. 1994), pp. 462–511.

W. DAVID MCINTYRE, *Background to the Anzus Pact: Policy-Making, Strategy and Diplomacy, 1945–55* (London, 1995).

NICHOLAS MANSERGH and others, eds., *The Transfer of Power, 1942–1947*, 12 vols. (London, 1970–83).

R. J. Moore, *Escape from Empire: The Attlee Government and the Indian Problem* (Oxford, 1983).

Philip Murphy, *Party Politics and Decolonization: The Conservative Party and British Colonial Policy in Tropical Africa, 1951–1964* (Oxford, 1995).

Hugh Tinker, ed., *Burma: The Struggle for Independence, 1944–1948*, 2 vols. (London, 1983 and 1984).

Robert Shepherd, *Macleod: A Biography* (London, 1994).

B. R. Tomlinson, *The Political Economy of the Raj, 1914–1947: The Economics of Decolonization in India* (London, 1979).

15

Imperialism and After: The Economy of the Empire on the Periphery

B. R. TOMLINSON

This chapter deals with the economic history of the Imperial periphery—the overseas territories that were part of the British Empire in 1914—from the turn of the century to the present day. It examines the patterns and structures of economic activity within the Imperial economic system, both before and after the British crises of the 1930s and 1940s; in addition, it considers the problems faced by Commonwealth countries in securing growth and development in the much more complex circumstances of the post-Imperial global economy of the last three decades. Looking back on the economy of the Empire from a vantage-point at the end of the twentieth century, it is now clear that it was able to operate so successfully only because of a particular set of global and local circumstances. These circumstances were linked closely to the demands and levels of technological advance that emerged in Western Europe, especially in Britain, during the second half of the nineteenth century.

In 1900 much of the world's economic activity was closely linked to the needs and capacities of the industrial centres of Western Europe, which was structured through the liberal international economic system of low transport costs, a stable international currency regime based on the gold standard, free trade, free migration, and large flows of international investment that had developed during the latter half of the nineteenth century. This international system connected industrial producers and consumers in the core (Western Europe and, increasingly, the United States) with primary product suppliers in the periphery (the less developed world) through a network of infrastructure, transport systems, and technology provided largely by exports of British capital. In a sense, all of the world outside Europe had formed a periphery for the British economy for much of the nineteenth century, since Britain dominated so much of the international networks of trade and finance, drawing in imports of food and raw materials and pumping out industrial goods, capital, and colonists that gave shape to many parts of the world. By 1914 the development of other industrial economies in Europe and the United States meant that the British economy was only one among equals, but one that retained extensive links with the non-European world, and that still provided the strongest focal point for international economic interaction.

At the beginning of the twentieth century the British Imperial economy operated within the established liberal international system, and was heavily dependent on the institutions and economic vitality of the larger whole. In aggregate, the Empire was not of overwhelming importance to the British domestic economy during the course of the nineteenth or early twentieth centuries; for peripheral economies, too, Britain alone never provided an adequate focus for the external economic activity of her major colonies and dependencies. However, economic imperialism—the exercise of power in economic relations—did play some part in constructing and sustaining the international system at all times. Even the liberal international economy of the second half of the nineteenth century was underpinned, especially in Asia, Africa, the Caribbean, and Latin America, by a judicious use of formal and informal techniques of imperialism to provide appropriate public institutions and structures of sociopolitical and economic power within which such economic activity could flourish. After 1914 the importance of a self-conscious, discriminatory Imperial system increased as the strains imposed by the material and human costs of the First World War weakened the foundations of the established international system and the institutional networks that were integrated into it. In the 1920s, 1930s, and 1940s the world economy collapsed into regionalism, economic nationalism, autarky, and the desperate accumulation of resources for war and reconstruction. In the short term these events strengthened the Imperial economy as a viable basis for interregional integration, but as a new system of multilateral economic activity developed in the 1950s, Britain and her major colonies and ex-colonies began to disengage from each other in trade and investment once more, and British institutional structures lost their newfound rationale in the periphery as well as at the core.

The history of the British Empire as an economic phenomenon came to an end some time between 1967, when the detrimental effects of sterling's devaluation ended the currency's role as a reserve asset, and 1973, when Britain finally joined the European Economic Community and signalled clearly to her partners in the Commonwealth that her future role lay in Europe rather than as a global power. Over the last thirty years new patterns of trade and investment, driven by new types of technology and innovation, have fundamentally altered the shape and balance of international economic interaction once more. The pattern of international migration, trade, and investment that characterized the second half of the nineteenth and the first half of the twentieth centuries has been swept away by a greater variation and wider diffusion of economic activity throughout a globalized system of production and exchange. These latest developments have little or nothing to do with the conventional themes of Imperial economic history, but they explain why the Imperial economy, which seemed so strong in the middle decades of the twentieth century, was quickly abandoned thereafter by even its most enthusiastic supporters, and lost its function in an international system with very different dynamics of economic growth and opportunities for development.

The long trade boom in the second half of the nineteenth century offered considerable possibilities for growth in developing countries, since many areas contained large quantities of apparently underutilized land and labour with the potential to produce exports for the world market. But growth through such trade also had negative consequences. Extensive commercial networks already existed in many areas of Asia, Africa, and Latin America before the industrialization of Europe, which dealt mainly in relatively high-value manufactured or semi-manufactured goods. The expansion of international demand for primary produce over the course of the nineteenth century damaged existing patterns of production and exchange, and caused extensive structural changes in many localities and regions. In severe cases—such as on the plains of North America—the colonization of apparently unused resources of land for commercial farming destroyed entire cultures on which viable pre-existing socio-economic systems were based. Elsewhere, however, the increase in production and utilization of resources for export were maintained at less human cost. A much-cited case of such growth was that observed in South-East Asia in the quarter-century before 1914, where peasant export production of traditional crops expanded by using new land and underemployed labour, while mines and plantations used the same resources with the addition of imported capital.

The relationship between increased output of primary produce and the satisfactory development of peripheral economies was heavily influenced by the way in which individual territories were opened up to trade, and by the nature of the local response in terms of productivity, skills, and savings. The ecological, social, and political distinctions between the 'neo-European periphery' and the 'tropical periphery' in the nineteenth century can be seen as one crucial variable.[1] In the 'neo-Europes'—those parts of the world where it was relatively easy to adapt European techniques of industrial and agricultural production, and to utilize advances in labour and capital productivity developed in Europe—trade quickly expanded the market, inducing innovations, increasing productivity, augmenting savings and capital accumulation, and helping the transfer of technology, skills, and entrepreneurship, once the native peoples had been eliminated as obstacles to growth.[2] The production of export staples such as wheat, timber, wool, and meat

[1] On the use of these terms, see Vol. III, chap. by B. R. Tomlinson pp. 53, 55.

[2] In the United States, the largest of these neo-European countries, the rapid expansion of the domestic industrial economy determined the rate of economic transformation after 1860, ensuring that

for the international market played a significant role in stimulating local employment and investment, and augmenting the supply of capital and technology, especially in Canada, Australia, South Africa, and the River Plate countries of Latin America—all of which had close formal or informal political links with Britain.[3]

By contrast, export expansion was less dynamic and had fewer beneficial effects in the 'tropical periphery' of Asia, Africa, and most of Latin America, where European capital, technologies, colonists, and market structures could not be transplanted so easily. International demand for tropical foodstuffs and industrial raw materials certainly stimulated growth of some tropical economies, but this did not necessarily provide the best basis for their development over the long term. Apparent increases in output often occurred because the international market provided a 'vent for surplus'—employing previously underutilized land and labour with low productivity using static technology—rather than stimulating productivity increases brought about by continuous improvements in skills and technological advance. Land was cleared for peasant colonization or for plantations using cheap local labour and capital, while output growth for export and domestic consumption in the commercialized sectors of tropical economies depended on drawing in supplies of labour from the subsistence economy. The presence of cheap labour, and the absence of productivity increases in agriculture, resulted in a 'dualistic' form of development—one that rewarded domestic and foreign capital while ensuring that the income of many rural workers lagged behind the rate of profit. The result was worsening income distribution and increasing poverty in the countryside.[4]

The dynamic relationship between trade in primary produce and sustained economic growth in the periphery faltered significantly after 1914. The events of

trade was a contributory factor to economic growth, rather than its prime cause. See Irvin B. Kravis, 'Trade as a Handmaiden of Growth: Similarities between the Nineteenth and Twentieth Centuries', *Economic Journal* (hereafter *EJ*), LXXX (1970), pp. 850–72.

[3] Important theoretical insights into this process came with the development of 'staple theory' by economists in Canada, which suggested that successful producing and trading regions in the periphery were linked to the production of export staples for the international market. While 'staple theory' cannot explain all cases of development through trade, especially in export economies with a relatively large subsistence agriculture or with significant urbanization, it is still of some relevance when applied to the sparsely populated regions of North and South America and Oceania in the nineteenth century. See Melville H. Watkins, 'A Staple Theory of Economic Growth', *Canadian Journal of Economics and Political Science*, XXIX, 2 (1963), pp. 141–58, and Richard E. Caves, '"Vent for Surplus" Models of Trade and Growth', in Robert Baldwin and others, eds., *Trade, Growth and the Balance of Payments* (Amsterdam, 1971), pp. 403–42.

[4] There is a classic critique of the 'vent for surplus' model of growth through international trade in Hla Myint, 'The "Classical Theory" of International Trade and the Underdeveloped Countries', *EJ*, LXVIII (1958), pp. 317–37, and of dualistic development in W. Arthur Lewis, 'Economic Development with Unlimited Supplies of Labour', *Manchester School*, XXI (1954), pp. 131–91.

the First World War and its aftermath initially seemed to strengthen the link between export growth and increased output of primary produce. In the immediate aftermath of the war, many economies in the periphery were able to take advantage of rising demand in Europe, as the belligerents rebuilt their stocks of foodstuffs and raw materials. But the sharp depression of 1920–21 signalled problems of overproduction, and the gradual faltering of economic growth over the course of the 1920s, especially in Britain and Germany, the two largest importers of primary produce, underlined the dangers of excess supply. There was no major crisis for producers until the end of the decade, except for wheat-growers, but high levels of stockholding and heavy short-term borrowing were necessary to sustain prices in commodities such as wheat, coffee, tin, and rubber.[5] When international liquidity became constricted as a result of the short-term capital flows caused by the boom and bust on Wall Street in 1927–29, primary produce prices could no longer be sustained. The result was a cycle of balance-of-payments crises, currency devaluation, and market failures, exacerbated by declining terms of trade for the commodity producers, that culminated in the Great Depression of 1929–33.

The disruptions to peripheral economies caused by these events can be seen clearly in Figures 15.1 and 15.2, which provide a simplified but bold picture of the pattern of multilateral trade flows in the 1920s and 1930s. As before 1914, peripheral economies outside Europe were important to multilateral trade and payments in two main ways.[6] The regions of recent settlement such as Canada, Argentina, and Australasia (roughly equivalent to the neo-Europes defined above) supplied primary produce to Europe and imported significant amounts of industrial goods in return. They also relied on imports of long- and short-term capital from Britain and the United States to develop their resources and sustain the infrastructure of production and trade. The tropics of Asia, Africa, and most of Latin America supplied significant amounts of primary produce to all the industrial regions of the world, and represented the only area of the world with which Britain could earn a trade surplus, although this surplus was no longer as large in relation to Britain's deficits elsewhere in the world as it had been in the nineteenth century.

[5] For a convenient introduction to the literature on the origins of the Great Depression, see Peter Fearon, *The Origins and Nature of the Great Slump, 1929–1932, Economic History Society, Studies in Economic History and Social History* (London, 1979).

[6] By the 1920s the United States could no longer be classed as an economy of the periphery, and was well on the way to becoming the single most important influence on world stability, growth, and development. The United States was now a net exporter of capital, and had a significant balance-of-payments surplus sustained by exports of both primary produce and manufactured goods. Her economic growth and fluctuations had always depended significantly on internal forces, and these became important determinants of the cyclical behaviour of the international economy as a whole.

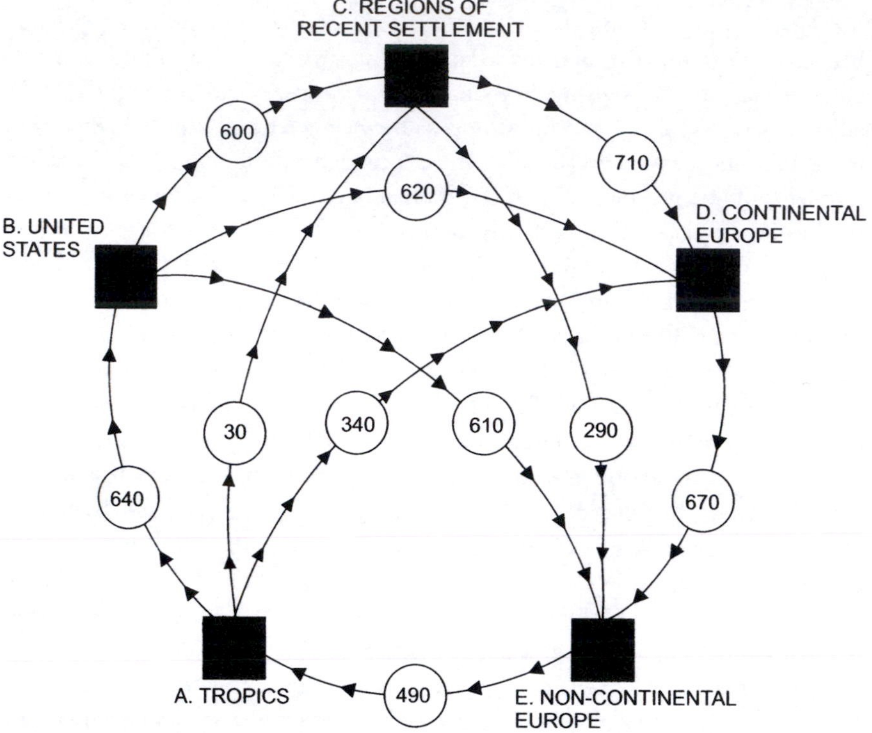

FIGURE 15.1. The system of multilateral trade, 1928

Note: The figures in circles represent the net export surpluses in $ million at 1928 rates of exchange, net of transport, and insurance costs.

Source: League of Nations, *The Network of World Trade* (Geneva, 1942), Diagram 9

The disturbed economic conditions of the early 1930s had important consequences for the pattern of international trade and payments that had been re-established in the 1920s. The imposition of tariffs in the United States in 1930 (the Hawley–Smoot tariffs) cut the links between the tropical economies and their most important single market, and also priced American farm produce out of European markets. One effect of this was to exacerbate the income and balance-of-payments difficulties already being suffered by peripheral economies, which led to a fall in demand for industrial products, especially from Britain, and to widespread fears of currency devaluation and default on their external debt which, in the case of the Empire, was mostly held in Britain. These problems contributed to the pressures that forced sterling off the gold standard in 1931.

The Great Depression of 1929–33 encouraged economic nationalists throughout the world in the belief that the benefits brought by an open economy, fixed exchange rates and a strategy of export-oriented growth through trade in primary

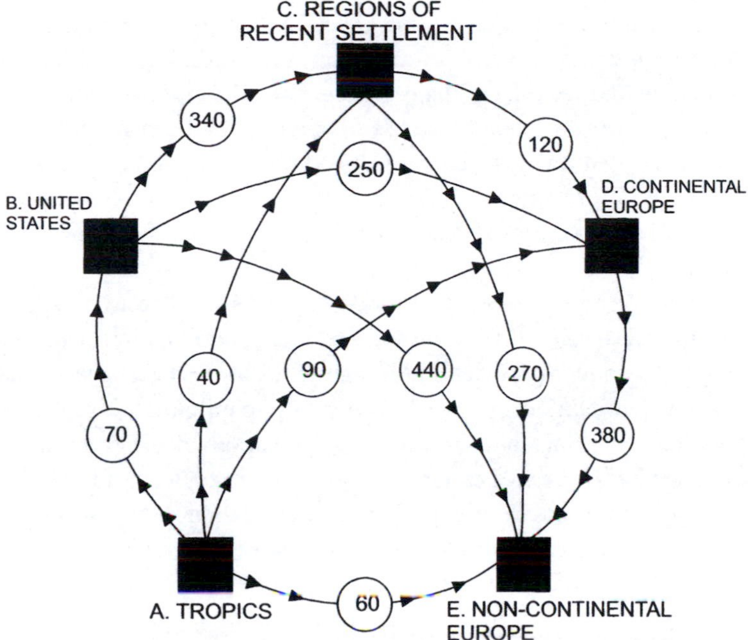

FIGURE 15.2. The system of multilateral trade, 1938

Note: The figures in circles represent the net export surpluses in $ million at official rates of exchange, net of transport, and insurance costs.

Source: League of Nations, *The Network of World Trade* (Geneva, 1942), Diagram 10

produce were ephemeral, and that economic recovery could best be achieved by partial withdrawal from the international system. Even in Britain, for so long the citadel of *laissez-faire* economic policies, the economic revolution of the 1930s led to import restrictions and tariffs, a managed exchange rate for sterling, and a search for preferential treatment in colonial economies. The imposition of tariffs under the Import Duties Act of 1932 made the levying of preferences possible, and Imperial Preference had been one of the great rallying-cries of the debate about Imperial economics since the 1890s. By the time of the Imperial Economic Conference held at Ottawa in the summer of 1932, the National Government in London had hammered out a new external economic policy in which the countries of the periphery were assigned an important and distinctive role. At Ottawa the Dominions and India were expected to open their markets to British industrial goods, by giving preferences to British exports over those from other industrial countries in return for free access to the British market for food and raw materials. Arrangements between Britain and her major Imperial trading partners were controlled along these lines, which were meant to set Britain's relations with the Dominions on a new basis. But, as subsequent events clearly proved, the British Empire was no longer a self-contained economic unit. Britain, the Dominions, and India all had diverse trading and manufacturing economies with complex requirements that could not be satisfied by simple models of Imperial preference. The attempt to create a semi-closed Imperial economy at Ottawa was doubly ironic, since perceptive observers at the time could see that the experience of international trade and finance in the 1930s proved conclusively that this sort of economic system was not viable.[7]

The Imperial economic ties of trade and finance that had been strengthened by the institutional changes of the 1930s were further intensified by the problems of financing the Second World War and post-war reconstruction between 1945 and the early 1950s. Britain's urgent need for men and equipment from the colonies and Dominions during the war led to the creation of a system of sterling balances—credits set up in London to pay overseas territories for the Imperial defence expenditure and the supply of strategic goods. Once the war was over, the legacy of these arrangements made it necessary for Britain to retain close contacts with her creditors, and to negotiate ways of conserving and controlling their sterling expenditure. Even more pressing was the problem of the dollar 'gap'. Britain was now desperate for food and capital equipment from the western hemisphere—primarily from the United States itself—which had to be bought in dollars. With her own dollar reserves and dollar investments already spent, and with the Anglo-American loan of 1946 proving to be largely inadequate, Britain's recovery depended in large part on the dollar-earning capacity of her colonial territories. As Table 15.1 shows, certain parts of the Empire ran significant balance-of-trade surpluses with the United States, and the dollars earned by these territories were put into an Empire dollar pool, administered in London, from which Britain drew freely to meet her own dollar deficit until the 1950s.[8]

The problems of economic co-operation within the Empire during the 1930s and 1940s had important implications for the process of political change that led to decolonization. The crisis of 1929–31 had brought a strong sense of Imperial economic solidarity, but the Ottawa Conference of 1932 had demonstrated to

[7] The classic work here is W. K. Hancock, *Survey of British Commonwealth Affairs*, Vol. II, *Problems of Economic Policy, 1918–1939*, Part 1 (London, 1942). For recent work that broadens and deepens the analysis, see Ian M. Drummond, *Imperial Economic Policy, 1917–1939: Studies in Expansion and Protection* (London, 1974); Tim Rooth, *British Protectionism and the International Economy* (Cambridge, 1992); and Catherine R. Schenk, *Britain and the Sterling Area: From Devaluation to Convertibility in the 1950s* (London, 1994).

[8] An excellent summary of the economic institutions of the British Commonwealth in the 1950s and 1960s, especially those of the sterling area, will be found in J. D. B. Miller, *Survey of Commonwealth Affairs: Problems of Expansion and Attrition, 1953–1969* (Oxford, 1974).

TABLE 15.1 *United States trade with sterling area countries, 1950* ($m)

	Exports	Imports
United Kingdom	511.3	334.8
Ceylon	6.3	65.9
India	212.4	259.4
Malaya and Singapore	19.7	308.6
Australia	100.4	141.0
New Zealand	26.6	64.3
South Africa	119.8	140.3
Gold Coast	5.6	61.1
Nigeria	5.7	34.8
Northern Rhodesia	2.1	29.6
Total £ Area	1,270.3	1,601.3

Note: Both exports and imports are listed (free on board).

Source: United Nations Statistical Office, *Direction of International Trade: Supplement, May 1952* (New York, 1952).

British policy-makers how difficult it was to win the wholehearted co-operation of Dominion politicians. Even India, the only participant at Ottawa that was still ruled directly by Britain, was able to take a semi-autonomous line in trade matters during the 1930s, especially over Imperial Preference in tariffs on steel and cotton goods. In monetary matters the British retained a greater capacity for command, and the Treasury and the Bank of England worked hard to set up reserve banks in the Dominions and India as a way of asserting informal control in defence of sterling. However, except in India (where the Reserve Bank's statutory commitment to a fixed sterling exchange rate of Rs.13.3 = £1 added fuel to a long-running dispute over exchange-rate policy), there was little opportunity in practice for banking imperialism to secure British interests in the Dominions during the 1930s.[9]

Within important territories in South Asia, South-East Asia, and West Africa, the economic dislocations caused by the Depression strengthened political nationalism by weakening the vertical linkages between landlord and tenant, creditor and debtor, farmer and agricultural labourer.[10] The crucial importance of certain

[9] For a case study of the informal imperialism of central banking, see P. J. Cain, 'Gentlemanly Imperialism at Work: The Bank of England, Canada and the Sterling Area, 1932–1936', *Economic History Review*, XLIX, 2 (1996), pp. 336–57. The classic contemporary account is A. W. F. Plumptre, *Central Banking in the British Dominions* (Toronto, 1940). On India, see G. Balachandran, 'Gold and Empire: Britain and India in the Great Depression', *Journal of European Economic History*, XX, 2 (1991), pp. 239–70, and S. L. M. Simha, *History of the Reserve Bank of India, 1935–1951* (Bombay, 1970).

[10] See the case studies in Ian Brown, ed., *The Economies of Africa and Asia in the Inter-War Depression*, (London, 1989) and Gareth Austin and Kaoru Sugihara, eds., *Local Suppliers of Credit in the Third World, 1750–1960* (Basingstoke, 1993).

colonies to the British balance of payments after 1945 raised the stakes over constitutional reform in West Africa and South-East Asia, and complicated Britain's relations with heavy dollar earners such as Kuwait. During the Second World War British colonial administrations in Africa and South-East Asia had regulated export prices and domestic money supply through a network of colonial Currency Boards and commodity control schemes. These remained in place during the 1940s and early 1950s, maintaining close institutional links between colonial export crops and currency arrangements and British firms and monetary institutions. Retaining such territories in the sterling area allowed London to keep control over their dollar earnings, and their internal monetary policies and export prices. However, the balance of any advantage to be gained from closer economic ties had to be weighed against the impossibility of restraining mass nationalism in the Gold Coast, and the need to retain the support of the Malay population against a Communist insurrection during the Emergency. Elsewhere in Africa, and in the Caribbean, where colonial development policies were belatedly brought into effect to boost the export potential of tropical economies to meet British needs for foodstuffs and raw materials, even mild intervention in economic affairs often had disruptive political consequences, and tended to undermine the paternalistic structures on which British authority had rested hitherto.[11] The coming of independence, in its turn, saw the partition of old colonies into new states, and encouraged closely linked groups of colonial territories to follow separatist policies of national economic development, which seriously disrupted regional economic integration in South Asia, the Caribbean, and East Africa. Political disturbances at independence, and even conflict or civil war within or between successor states, further weakened many of the internal and external connections that had been built up under colonial rule, notably in Nigeria.

The self-conscious 'Imperial' economy of the 1930s and 1940s was created by market failure and political desperation rather than consistent policy or self-sustaining developments in the economies of Britain and her dependencies. With the ending of the dollar problem, the revival of world trade, and the re-emergence of a multilateral payments system during the 1950s, the institutional structures of British and colonial overseas trade and finance were gradually liberalized. However, British colonial development policies in Africa and the Caribbean remained somewhat Empire-centric, and one effect of this was to sustain the pattern of economic activity that had been established in an Imperial

[11] On the interaction of political, economic, and social change in the major colonial regions during this period, see Ronald Hyam, ed., *The Labour Government and the End of Empire, 1945–1951*, British Documents on the End of Empire Project (BDEEP), Series A, 4 Parts (London, 1992).

context during the late nineteenth and early twentieth centuries well into the post-war era.[12] As a result, many Commonwealth countries still relied on a narrow range of primary produce for two-thirds to three-quarters of their commodity exports in the mid-1960s, as the trade data for the major exporting countries of the British Empire-Commonwealth summarized in Table 15.2 demonstrates. Furthermore, a relatively small number of Commonwealth producers remained major world suppliers of particular raw materials and foodstuffs, with Britain an important market, especially for temperate foodstuffs. The most intense Imperial trade relationships were in meat and dairy produce, especially between New Zealand and Britain. The dominance of the export sector in primary produce in the economies of Britain's colonies and ex-colonies in West Africa, South Asia, and South-East Asia was also the result of the colonial development schemes of the post-war years. However, political independence in these regions led inexorably to policies that discriminated against agricultural exports in favour of industry. In some places—Ghana, for example—this seriously damaged the rural economy without any effective compensation in other sectors; elsewhere, as in Malaysia, an effective industrial sector was created by a mixture of state-sponsored enterprise and foreign capital.

The economic history of Britain's ex-colonies changed in fundamental ways as the ties of Empire began to slacken and dissolve in the 1970s. Indeed, the modern economic history of Africa, South-East and South Asia, and the Caribbean can be said to have begun as their links to the British Empire came to an end. The break-up of the Imperial enclave within the international economy, as former colonies have disengaged their economic institutions from the failing British centre, opened up new opportunities for Commonwealth countries in trade, industrialization, and technical progress. Equally significant is that, for the first time since the end of the eighteenth century, the centre of gravity of the global economy has shifted decisively away from the Atlantic towards the Pacific Rim, and from Western Europe to the countries of East, South-East, and South Asia. In a very real sense, the whole global system based on a 'core' of industrial economies in Europe and North America and a 'periphery' of raw-material and primary producing economies in the rest of the world—within which the economy of the British

[12] As W. Arthur Lewis had pointed out in his 1950 report on *The Industrialization of the British West Indies*, Colonial Office officials held to 'the mystical view that the Almighty meant some countries to specialize in manufactures and others on agriculture'. Colonial territories were placed firmly in the latter category. Quoted in Barbara Ingham, 'The Manchester Year, 1947–58: A Tribute to The Work of Arthur Lewis', *Journal of International Development*, III, 5 (1991), p. 534. For a stimulating recent critique of orthodox economic analyses of the links between trade, liberalization, and development, see Erik S. Reinert, 'The Role of Technology in the Creation of Rich and Poor Nations: Underdevelopment in a Schumpeterian World', in Derek H. Aldcroft and Ross E. Catterall, eds., *Rich Nations—Poor Nations: The Long-Run Perspective* (Cheltenham, 1996), pp. 161–80.

TABLE 15.2 *Commodity composition of exports of selected sterling area countries, 1964* (%)

	Tropical beverages	Sugar	Meat	Dairy	Fruit	Cotton and wool	Jute	Rubber	Vegetable oil and oilseeds	Hides and Skins	Non-Ferrous metals	Manufactures	% of total exports
India	17					2	23		2	4		20	68
Pakistan						17	48			2		18	85
Ceylon	62							16	11				89
Malaysia					1			61	4		22	3	91
Hong Kong												91	91
Mauritius		94											94
Ghana	66												66
Nigeria	19					3		6	36	2	6		72
Uganda	58					24							82
Kenya	49												49
Zambia											92		92
Tanzania	18					13							31
South Africa		4			10	12				3	5	15	50
Australia		6	9	3	4	34				3	5	10	74
New Zealand			25	22	35					4		4	90
Fiji		82											82
Barbados		74											74
Guyana		34									12		46
Jamaica		26			11						43	8	88

Source: Alfred Maizels, *Exports And Economic Growth Of Developing Countries* (Cambridge, 1968), Appendices A–C.

Empire fitted so snugly from the late eighteenth century to the mid-twentieth century—has recently come to an end.[13]

The new opportunities provided by the global system for economic growth and development in the periphery during the last third of the twentieth century can be seen most clearly in trade and industrialization. Specific statistical estimates of the economic development of Commonwealth countries in the aggregate are not available for the period after decolonization. Instead, the argument must be based on the aggregate data that exist for the contemporary Third World as a whole, and by regions, on the assumption that the economic history of individual Commonwealth countries since 1960 has not been significantly different from others in their region. Using such data, it is possible to see that the pattern of economic activity across the world has changed fundamentally from that established by the international and Imperial economic system of the previous hundred years.[14] Global networks of trade, in particular, have evolved considerably. Since 1970 the growing sectors of world trade have been those concerned with exchanging manufactures for manufactures, rather than for primary produce: as Figure 15.3 shows, the major industrial economies of Western Europe and North America now trade between themselves in similar products, rather than trading substantially with other regions in complementary commodities. These changes have rewarded national economies in the periphery that can raise productivity by investment in technology and human capital. In successful developing countries over the last thirty years growth in output and in exports has been based on production of manufactured goods (resulting from investment in machinery and in the skills of the workforce), or on new sources of agricultural productivity (the result of 'Green Revolution' techniques and increased investment in agricultural capital goods). Such countries, mainly in East and South-East Asia, have been able to trade successfully with Europe and North America in manufactured goods, and have proved themselves competitive in global terms. One consequence is that Asia has now re-emerged as a region of renewed economic importance; whereas the region's share of world trade fell consistently from the early eighteenth century

[13] The economic history of trade and development outside Europe over the last two centuries is summarized in Patrick Karl O'Brien, 'Intercontinental Trade and the Development of the Third World Since the Industrial Revolution', *Journal of World History*, VIII, 1 (1997), pp. 75–133. On the most recent trends in international economic history, see Daniele Archibugi and Jonathan Michie, *Technology, Globalisation and Economic Performance* (Cambridge, 1997).

[14] A convenient summary of the very imperfect historical data that exist for individual Third World countries and regions for the twentieth century may be found in Paul Bairoch, *The Economic Development of the Third World Since 1900* (London, 1975). On the nineteenth century, see J. R. Hanson, *Trade in Transition: Exports from the Third World, 1840–1900* (New York, 1980); for a useful statistical digest of the Imperial economy, analysed in conventional terms, see Michael Havinden and David Meredith, *Colonialism and Development: Britain and its Tropical Colonies, 1850–1960* (London, 1993).

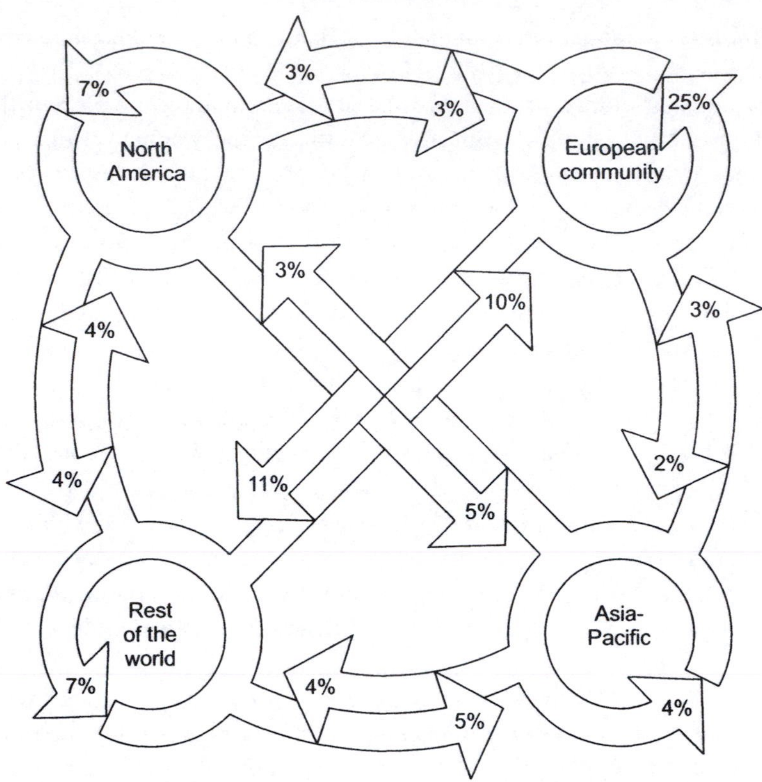

FIGURE 15.3. World exports within and between trading areas, 1990 (percentage share)

Note: North America 'bloc' is defined as Canada, Mexico, and the United States. European Community is EC-12. Asia-Pacific 'bloc' is Hong Kong, Japan, Malaysia, Republic of Korea, Singapore, and Thailand.

Source: United Nations, Department of International Economic and Social Affairs of the United Nations Secretariat, *World Economic Survey, 1991/92: A Reader* (New York, 1991)

until the early twentieth century, in the 1970s and 1980s it exceeded the level of the 1720s for the first time.[15] In the late 1990s current trade and payments crisis in the region has suggested that some of the policies on which this growth was built are not sustainable, but it has also underlined emphatically the importance of the region to the post-colonial global economy of the late twentieth century and beyond.

Another significant contrast between the underpinning structures of economic growth in the Imperial and post-Imperial decades of the twentieth century is shown by the pattern of agricultural expansion. Before 1914 the most rapidly

[15] See Carl-Ludwig Holtfrerich, 'Introduction: The Evolution of World Trade, 1720 to the Present', in Carl-Ludwig Holtfrerich, ed., *Interactions in the World Economy: Perspectives from International Economic History* (London, 1989), pp. 1–23.

expanding economies on the periphery were those—like the United States—that opened up new croplands using imported capital and labour. However, the link between an expanding agricultural frontier and economic growth has been broken decisively in the twentieth century. As Tables 15.3 and 15.4 make clear, the world's croplands increased three times in area between 1850 and 1980, but the percentage farmed by Europeans (in Europe, North America, Russia/Soviet Union, Australia, and New Zealand) declined from 57 per cent in 1920 to 43 per cent in 1980. Since 1950 the heavily populated countries of Africa, South Asia, and China have

TABLE 15.3. *Expansion of land use, 1850–1980* (percentage increase or decrease in cropland area, by region)

	1850–1920	1920–50	1950–80
Tropical Africa	54.4	54.5	63.2
North Africa/Middle East	59.3	53.5	62.1
North America	258.0	15.1	−1.5
Latin America	150.0	93.3	63.2
China	26.7	13.7	24.1
South Asia	38.0	38.8	54.4
South-East Asia	200.0	66.7	57.1
Europe	11.4	3.4	−9.9
USSR	89.4	21.3	7.9
Pacific developed countries	216.7	47.4	107.1
TOTAL	70.0	28.1	28.3

TABLE 15.4. *Distribution of world croplands, 1850–1980* (%age by region)

	1850	1920	1950	1980
Tropical Africa	11	10	12	15
North Africa/Middle East	5	5	6	7
North America	9	20	18	14
Latin America	3	5	7	9
China	14	10	9	9
South Asia	13	11	12	14
South-East Asia	1	2	3	4
Europe	25	16	13	9
USSR	18	19	18	16
Pacific developed countries	1	2	2	4
TOTAL (million ha.)	537	913	1,170	1,501

Source: Calculated from B. L. Turner and others, *The Earth as Transformed by Human Action: Global and Regional Changes in the Biosphere over the Past 300 Years* (Cambridge, 1990), Tables 10.1 and 10.2.

maintained their agricultural expansion, while North America and Russia/ Soviet Union have finished the process of land colonization that accompanied their economic growth in the nineteenth century. The highest yields in contemporary farming come from the most intensive agriculture. The Western European model of capital-intensive and land-intensive food-grain production based on industrially derived inputs such as fertilizers, tractors, and pesticides is mirrored in Japan and other parts of East Asia. By contrast, the majority of peasant-based agricultural systems in mainland Asia and Africa have relatively little land per head, a relatively large proportion of the labour force dependent on rural employment, and relatively low levels of investment and productivity.[16]

Perhaps the best indicator of the pace of economic change in major regions of the periphery, and of the possibilities for economic development opened up in the post-Imperial world economy of the last thirty years, is provided by estimates of energy use. The process of technological development since the industrial revolution has been largely based on the intensive use of the earth's accumulated stocks of solar energy, stored in the form of fossil fuels: thus, energy consumption provides the best measurement of technological change (and hence, investment and productivity), as well as of levels of industrialization and the internal mobility of goods and people, in modern industrial and post-industrial economies.[17] Estimates of national energy consumption are based on measurements of total domestic energy supply, summarized in Table 15.5. These show that in the early 1970s, at the close of the British Imperial age in international economic history, the developed, industrialized, market-based economies of the twenty-three member-countries of the Organization for Economic Co-operation and Development (OECD) consumed two-thirds of world energy production, demonstrating their dominance of the world's industrial and transportation systems in the first six decades of the century.[18] By contrast, the developing countries of the non-European periphery in Africa, Latin America, Asia, and the Middle East consumed about one-sixth of the total. During the 1970s and 1980s, however, this established

[16] For a summary of indicators of agricultural structure and performance, see World Resources Institute, *World Resources, 1990–91* (Oxford, 1990), Tables 17.1, 17.2, 18.1, and 18.2.

[17] For a provocative introduction to these issues, see E. A. Wrigley, 'Reflections on the History of Energy Supply, Living Standards and Economic Growth', *Australian Economic History Review*, XXXIII, 1 (1993), pp. 3–21. A useful introduction to the use of energy-mapping in environmental history will be found in I. G. Simmons, *Changing the Face of the Earth: Culture, Environment, History* (Oxford, 1989).

[18] The Organization for Economic Co-operation and Development (OECD) consists of the major European economies—Austria, Belgium, Denmark, Finland, Germany, Greece, Iceland, Ireland, Italy, Luxembourg, the Netherlands, Norway, Portugal, Spain, Sweden, Switzerland, and the United Kingdom—plus the largest of those in the 'neo-European' periphery, Australia, Canada, New Zealand, and the United States, and two in Asia—Japan and Turkey.

TABLE 15.5. *Total primary energy consumption* (million tons of energy (t.o.e.) and % of world consumption).

	1971		1981		1991	
	million t.o.e	%	million t.o.e.	%	million t.o.e.	%
Africa	81.59	1.7	150.38	2.3	214.70	2.7
South Africa	45.98		68.93		95.29	
Latin America	175.35	3.6	308.40	4.8	399.69	5.0
Brazil	35.40		68.53		100.86	
Mexico	33.97		92.84		125.51	
Asia	408.62	8.4	715.73	11.2	1269.57	16.0
China	235.98		407.17		680.88	
India	63.61		104.16		192.88	
South Korea	16.53		43.09		101.68	
Middle East	53.54	1.1	143.22	2.2	237.57	3.0
Non-OECD Europe	240.77	5.0	342.38	5.3	299.74	3.8
(Former) USSR	770.16	15.8	1,131.04	17.7	1,336.57	16.9
Total non-OECD	1,730.06	35.6	2,791.22	43.6	3,757.77	47.4
Total OECD	3,135.45	64.4	3,612.05	56.4	4,164.75	52.6
WORLD TOTAL	4,865.51	100.0	6,403.27	100.0	7,922.52	100.0

Source: Calculated from International Energy Agency, *Energy Statistics and Balances of Non-OECD Countries, 1991–1992*, OECD (Paris, 1994), pp. 20–23.

pattern of economic activity changed fundamentally, and by 1991 non-OECD countries consumed almost half of the world's energy supplies, more than twice as much as they had twenty years before. In this period the share of the developing countries of the non-European periphery almost doubled, to a total of 27 per cent, with the largest new consumers in the Middle East and Asia.[19] Industrializing countries in Asia, notably South Korea, China, and to a lesser extent India, were the fastest-growing users of energy, and used this to expand their industrial and transportation sectors.[20]

Economic growth and economic expansion are slippery concepts, and it is dangerous to assume that an increase in either the extent or intensity of the production and exchange of material goods in a society necessarily reflects an improvement in the overall welfare of its members. Evaluating such issues means assessing the extent of economic 'development', a concept that incorporates qualitative change in economic performance representing, in turn, long-term improvements in productivity, income, and equity of distribution. It requires an element of qualitative, or even moral, judgement.[21] Conventional indicators of growth rely on measurements of Gross National Product (GNP) and GNP per head, but these beg many questions about the measurement of informal and non-monetized sectors of the economy, and about issues of distribution and welfare. To overcome this, other indicators have been devised—notably the Physical Quality of Life Index (PQLI) and the Human Development Index (HDI)—which seek to assess levels of socio-economic freedom and welfare by indicators based on national income, life-expectancy at birth, child survival rates, and educational attainment in literacy.[22] Such measurements are themselves the subject of considerable debate, but a complete account of the economic history of the British

[19] The significance of these figures is modified somewhat by evidence of increased efficiency in energy use in developed countries during the 1970s. Calculations of energy intensity in major economies (megajoules consumed per unit of GNP) suggest that Japan reduced its energy intensity by 30% between 1973 and 1985, while the United States, the United Kingdom, Italy, the Netherlands, and West Germany all reduced energy intensity by about 20%. See data from International Energy Agency, *Energy Conservation in IEA Countries*, OECD (Paris, 1987), reproduced in Nathan Rosenberg, *Exploring the Black Box: Technology, Economics and History* (Cambridge, 1994), Table 9.4.

[20] Taiwan does not appear in these statistics. In OECD economies secondary and tertiary sectors are by far the most intensive in their energy use. In 1991 the sectoral use of energy (as a percentage of total final consumption) was 33% for industry, 31% for transport, and 32% for other users, with agriculture consuming less than 2% of the total. See International Energy Agency, *Energy Statistics and Balances of OECD Countries, 1991–1992*, OECD (Paris, 1994) p. 20.

[21] See Gerald M. Meier, *Leading Issues in Economic Development*, 4th edn. (Oxford, 1984), pp. 5–9. The United Nations Development Programme's first *Human Development Report* in 1990 defined human development as the process of enabling people to have wider choices.

[22] The strengths and weaknesses of such measurements are summarized in Barbara Ingham, *Economics and Development* (London, 1995), chap. 1.

Empire in the twentieth century must try to take such concepts into account. For many observers today, both in the peripheral countries themselves and in the developed world, the central economic issue in the Third World is that of maximizing the life-chances of its millions of inhabitants. This, in turn, depends on the supply of basic needs and opportunities for personal fulfilment that come from the resources generated by economic activity inside and outside the world's developing countries.

There are no reliable estimates of levels of economic development or welfare over the long term for any of Britain's colonies in Asia, Africa or the Caribbean, or any aggregate data that can provide useful comparisons between regions or territories during the Imperial age. Contemporary development indicators for large and medium-sized Commonwealth countries in the 1980s and early 1990s are summarized in Table 15.6. These figures show that by far the highest levels of income, welfare, and intensity of economic activity are found in those territories that had been intensively settled by Europeans after 1800, and which had few pre-colonial inhabitants left alive by 1914. Countries such as Canada, Australia, and New Zealand, which had among the highest per capita incomes in the world at the end of the nineteenth century, have remained richly endowed throughout the twentieth century.[23] By contrast, Britain's ex-colonial territories in Africa and South Asia have experienced relatively high levels of poverty, and low levels of international trade and expenditure on welfare, with the Caribbean and South-East Asian Commonwealth countries, broadly speaking, somewhere in the middle. While it is dangerous to extrapolate such data backwards, it is very probable that the levels of magnitude that they suggest would hold true for the twentieth century as a whole, and probably for the nineteenth century as well.[24] This situation was not simply the result of the colonial system, but the suggestion remains that British rule did not leave a substantial legacy of wealth, health, or happiness to the majority of the subjects of the Commonwealth.

[23] The success of the ex-colonies of settlement in international trade and the export-led growth of the major economies of South-East Asia since 1960 suggest that there may be a positive correlation between high levels of GNP, large-scale participation in international trade, and high per capita expenditure on education, although no simple causal linkages in this relationship should be inferred from the data presented in Table 15.6.

[24] More impressionistic evidence for individual colonies confirms this—in colonial South Asia, for example, the increase in population after 1921 was not linked to any increase in the standard of living, while food-grain availability per head fell significantly between 1900 and 1947. See B. R. Tomlinson, *The Economy of Modern India, 1860–1970* (Cambridge, 1993), pp. 6–7, 30–32. One great advantage that the neo-European periphery of the nineteenth century held over today's Third World is that European settlers and European agricultural techniques could be used profitably there.

TABLE 15.6. *Economic and social indicators of development, 1985–1987*

	Population mid-1987 (ml.)	Per capita GNP 1985 ($)	Average annual growth rate of real GNP per capita 1965–85 (%)	Per capita public education spending 1983 ($)	Annual growth rate of population (%)	Value of exports per capita 1986 ($)	Value of imports per capita 1986 ($)	Physical Quality of Life Index (1985)	Human Development Index (1992)
Africa									
Gambia	0.8	230	1.1	14	2.1	86	210	28	0.083
Ghana (Gold Coast)	13.9	380	−2.2	5	2.8	63	63	55	0.310
Kenya	22.4	290	1.9	17	3.9	60	82	58	0.366
Malawi (Nyasaland)	7.4	170	1.5	5	3.2	38	39	37	0.166
Nigeria	108.6	800	2.2	16	2.8	81	52	47	0.241
Sierra Leone	3.9	350	1.1	10	1.8	45	46	26	0.062
South Africa	34.3	2,010	1.1	97	2.3	575	373	66	0.674
Tanzania (Tanganikya)	23.5	290	0.0	14	3.5	16	43	63	0.268
Uganda	15.9	220	−2.6	4	3.4	28	21	51	0.192
Zambia (N Rhodesia)	7.1	390	−1.6	32	3.5	97	83	62	0.315
Zimbabwe (S Rhodesia)	9.4	680	1.6	64	3.5	106	123	67	0.397
Asia									
Bangladesh (East Pakistan)	107.1	150	0.4	2	2.7	8	23	43	0.185
Burma (Myanmar)	38.8	190	2.4	4	2.1	13	17	71	0.385
Hong Kong	5.6	6,230	6.1	n/a	0.9	6,325	6,314	95	0.913

TABLE 15.6. *Continued*

India	800.3	270	1.7	8	2.1	13	24	55	0.297
Malaysia	16.1	2,000	4.4	141	2.4	859	672	81	0.789
Pakistan	104.6	380	2.6	8	2.9	32	51	43	0.305
Sri Lanka (Ceylon)	16.3	380	2.9	10	1.8	71	112	87	0.651
Singapore	2.6	7,420	7.6	339	1.1	8,560	9,810	91	0.848
Caribbean									
Bahamas	0.2	7,070	−0.5	n/a	1.8	3,245	11,110	89	n/a
Barbados	0.3	4,360	2.3	228	0.9	933	1,907	95	0.927
Belize (British Honduras)	0.2	1,190	2.7	n/a	2.7	420	675	86	0.665
Guyana (British Guiana)	0.8	500	−0.2	52	2.0	303	289	86	0.539
Jamaica	2.5	940	−0.7	102	2.0	233	388	92	0.722
Trinidad and Tobago	1.3	6,020	2.3	367	2.0	1,055	1,025	90	0.876
Oceania									
Australia	16.2	10,830	2.0	741	0.8	1,391	1,618	100	0.971
Fiji	0.7	1,710	2.9	115	2.3	353	541	83	0.713
New Zealand	3.3	7,010	1.4	391	0.8	1,797	1,817	96	0.947
Papua New Guinea	3.6	680	0.4	58	2.4	286	274	54	0.321
North America									
Canada	25.9	13,680	2.4	951	0.8	3,464	3,308	98	0.982
United Kingdom	56.8	8,460	1.6	482	0.2	1,885	2,224	97	0.962

Source: Cols. 1–8: calculated from Michael P. Todaro, *Economic Development in the Third World*, 4th edn. (London, 1989), Table A2.2. Col. 9: UNDP, *Human Development Report, 1992*, reproduced in Barabara Ingham, *Economics and Development* (London, 1995), Tables 1.7 and 1.8.

Select Bibliography

B. W. E. Alford, *Britain in the World Economy Since 1880* (London, 1996).

Paul Bairoch, *The Economic Development of the Third World Since 1900* (London, 1975).

Ian Brown, *Economic Change in South-East Asia, c.1830–1980* (Kuala Lumpur, 1997).

P. J. Cain and A. G. Hopkins, *British Imperialism: Crisis and Deconstruction, 1914–1990* (London, 1993).

Ian M. Drummond, *Imperial Economic Policy, 1917–1939* (London, 1974).

Economist Intelligence Unit, *The Commonwealth and Europe* (London, 1960).

W. K. Hancock, *Survey of British Commonwealth Affairs*, Vol. II, *Problems of Economic Policy, 1918–1939*, Part 1 (London, 1942).

Ronald Hyam, ed., *The Labour Government and the End of Empire, 1945–1951* British Documents on the End of Empire Project (BDEEP), Series A, 4 Parts (London, 1992).

Michael Havinden and David Meredith, *Colonialism and Development: Britain and its Tropical Colonies, 1850–1960* (London, 1993).

Calvin B. Hoover, ed., *Economic Systems of the Commonwealth* (Cambridge, 1962).

A. G. Kenwood and A. L. Lougheed, *The Growth of the International Economy, 1820–1990*, 3rd edn. (London, 1992).

Irving B. Kravis, Alan Heston, Robert Summers, and others, *World Product and Income: International Comparisons of Real Gross Product*, United Nations/World Bank (London, 1982).

W. Arthur Lewis, *Economic Survey, 1919–1939* (London, 1949).

Angus Maddison, *Monitoring the World Economy, 1820–1992*, OECD (Paris, 1995).

Alfred Maizels, *Industrial Growth and World Trade: An Empirical Study of Trends in Production, Consumption and Trade in Manufactures from 1899–1959* (Cambridge, 1963).

Lloyd G. Reynolds, *Economic Growth in the Third World, 1850–1980: An Introduction* (New Haven, 1985).

Peter N. Stearns, *The Industrial Revolution in World History* (Boulder, Colo., 1993).

Michael P. Todaro, *Economic Development*, 5th edn. (London, 1994).

Philip West and Frans A. M. Alting von Geusau, eds., *The Pacific Rim and the Western World: Strategic, Economic and Cultural Perspectives* (Boulder, Colo., 1987).

P. L. Yates, *Forty Years of Foreign Trade* (London, 1959).

16

Gender in the British Empire

ROSALIND O'HANLON

Once the intellectual high ground of an older political and military history, the British Empire has recently become remarkably hospitable terrain for the study of women and gender. As women have been restored to historical visibility across the field of British Imperial history, so the importance of gender as a wider social relation conditioning the lives of men as well as women has emerged ever more clearly. These perspectives have brought us new insights alike into imperial systems of extraction and their transformative effects on local social relations, into ideologies of empire in metropolitan as well as local contexts, and into structures of nationalist politics and anti-colonial struggle. For British Imperial governments, colonial states, and their local opponents alike, women's productive and symbolic potential were prizes to be fought over, and gender itself a powerful lever for the reordering of society.

This is a large and diverse field of historical experience, and part of the purpose of this chapter is to provide an overview of key parts of the field for historians accustomed to thinking that questions about women or gender are not pertinent to what they do, or of the view that such studies are still 'stuck in a specialized sub-branch of historical explanation'.[1] A comparative framework drawing together the varieties of metropolitan and colonial experience from the late nineteenth century also suggests new insights. This means a search not only for the undoubted diversities of Imperial strategy and colonial context, but also for the unities of ideology and practice which characterized British Imperial approaches to women and gender, unities which had consequences for the experience of men and women in colonial societies themselves.

[1] Ronald Hyam, *Empire and Sexuality: The British Experience* (Manchester, 1990), p. 16. A number of historians have taken issue with Hyam's refusal to place his study of sexual behaviour in the British Empire within the wider context of gender seen as a relation of power: see Margaret Strobel, 'Sex and Work in the British Empire', *Radical History Review*, LIV (1992), pp. 177–86, and Richard A. Voeltz, 'The British Empire, Sexuality, Feminism and Ronald Hyam', *European Review of History*, III, 1 (1996), pp. 41–44. Hyam's study was nevertheless a pioneering one in taking the connections between sexuality and Empire seriously.

Perhaps nowhere has the restoration of women to historical visibility within the British Empire been clearer than in the field of labour. A central preoccupation of British Imperial policy-makers and colonial governments alike lay in the effort to mobilize and discipline labour, as colonial economies were drawn into more global and capitalist systems of production and exchange. Of course, the timing of economic penetration varied substantially: many areas of British India, for example, were drawn into the international economy in the later nineteenth century, while, some of those of sub-Saharan Africa and South-East Asia were integrated only haltingly as late as the 1930s. Dramatic differences distinguished these economic relationships too, as elements of ecology and natural resources, population, transport, and political control combined to shape colonial economies and labour needs along different lines: from the techniques of forced cultivation and labour employed by the early African chartered companies, to the large-scale migration of young men called into being by the development of mining and plantation economies, and of a significant urban manufacturing sector in many parts of the Empire, and the promotion of cash-crop agriculture among peasant communities.

Despite this diversity, the problem for colonial states was in many cases the same: how to draw labour away from producing for family consumption into colonial infrastructural projects or production of commodities for the market. Most colonial states used taxation as an instrument in this process: by imposing a cash tax on their subjects, in the form of hut or head taxes, or taxes on essential commodities like salt, colonial states made it increasingly difficult for any of their subjects to subsist without access to cash, thus increasing the pressure on rural households to divert labour to cash crops, or to send some of their men to work in mines, plantations, European-owned farms, or urban industry to work for a money wage. Good prices for cash crops, together with the increasing availability of a range of petty European consumer goods, helped achieve the same result voluntarily, inducing many households in the 1920s before the Depression, and again from the 1940s, to divert increasing amounts of family labour away from subsistence production.[2] Changes in women's productive and reproductive labour lay at the heart of these processes of economic 'development'. From the southern states of Africa to the Indian Punjab, colonial pressures to draw labour out of the subsistence economy into production for the market helped to create a 'feminization of subsistence agriculture'. The migration of male labour to mines, plantations, and factories, together with the local expansion of cash crops threw much

[2] For good introductions to the vast regional literatures on these processes, see John Iliffe, *Africans: The History of a Continent* (Cambridge, 1995), chaps. 9–10; Nicholas Tarling, ed., *The Cambridge History of Southeast Asia*, Vol. II (Cambridge, 1992), chaps. 1–3; and B. R. Tomlinson, *The Economy of Modern India, 1860–1970* (Cambridge, 1993).

more of the burden of providing for family subsistence on to women. However, patterns of causality here were always complex and variable. The increasing sexual specialization of rural labour often reinforced pre-existing divisions, but along lines that were shaped by the particular fit between new cropping patterns and older rhythms of work.[3]

To these roles for women as labourers in the colonial economy were added many others. Women were not invariably identified with subsistence agriculture, nor were migrants always young males. Indian women as well as men migrated in search of work. They migrated within India, to the jute mills of Calcutta, to coal-mines in Bihar, tea gardens in Assam, and textile mills in Bombay. Following a Government of India ruling in the 1870s intended to promote the 'stabilizing' influences of family life, women also joined the stream of male indentured labour abroad.[4] Women's migration had its own distinctive patterns and imperatives. For single men, migration to the jute mills of Calcutta represented a strategy for family survival within a continuing network of kinship ties. For single women, migration was often a final response to familial rejection, and it marked the termination of those ties.[5]

Nor were the new urban economies of the twentieth-century Empire the exclusive preserve of men. The processes whereby men became wage labourers also drew women into urban economies and production for the market in quite particular ways: in the interstices of colonial economies, in the 'informal economy' of petty commerce, craft activity, and the provision of domestic and sexual services. Until quite recently many of these remained invisible to historians and policy-makers alike because of their informal and small-scale character. Thus, different forms of prostitution in the Kenyan capital of Nairobi allowed successful

[3] Esther Boserup, *Women's Role in Economic Development* (London, 1989), chap. 4. More recent studies of women's subsistence work are in Henrietta Moore, *Feminism and Anthropology* (Oxford, 1988), chap. 4; Sharon B. Stichter and Jane L. Parpart, *Patriarchy and Class: African Women in the Home and the Workforce* (Boulder, Colo., 1988); Claire Robertson and Iris Berger, eds., *Women and Class in Africa* (New York, 1986); and Elizabeth Schmidt, *Peasants, Traders and Wives: Shona Women in the History of Zimbabwe, 1870–1939* (London 1992). Excellent conceptual discussion of female farming in Africa is in Jane I. Guyer, 'Food, Cocoa and the Division of Labour by Sex in Two West African Societies', *Comparative Studies in Society and History*, XXII, 3 (1980), pp. 355–73, and by the same author, 'Female Farming in Anthropology and African History', in Micaela di Leonardo, ed., *Gender at the Crossroads of Knowledge: Feminist Anthropology in the Postmodern Era* (Berkeley, 1991), pp. 257–77. See also Olukemi Idowu and Jane Guyer, *Commercialisation and the Harvest Work of Women: Ibarapa, Oyo State, Nigeria* (Ibadan, 1991).

[4] Brij V. Lal, 'Kunti's Cry: Indentured Women on Fiji Plantations,' in J. Krishnamurti, ed., *Women in Colonial India: Essays on Survival, Work and the State* (Oxford, 1989), pp. 163–79; Hugh Tinker, *A New System of Slavery: The Export of Indian Labour Overseas, 1830–1920* (London, 1993).

[5] Samita Sen, 'Women in the Bengal Jute Industry, 1890–1930: Migration, Motherhood and Militancy', unpublished Ph.D. thesis, Cambridge, 1992. See also Dagmar Engels, *Beyond Purdah? Women in Bengal, 1890–1939* (Delhi, 1996), chap. 6.

women to accumulate sufficient capital to become house-owners in the city or, in the case of migrant women, to remit substantial savings to the family farm.[6] For women on the Zambian Copper Belt, the decision of some Northern Rhodesian mining companies from the late 1920s to encourage the presence of women and families in the mining compounds opened a wide range of economic opportunities for them, from sexual services to beer brewing, and selling vegetables, fish, and cooked food. Some were so successful that they were able to hire migrant men turned down by the mines for employment to work in helping them to grow produce in their own gardens.[7] Striking areas of success for women in commerce have also emerged in parts of western Africa, where they came to dominate many local markets in coastal Nigeria and Ghana, selling cooked foods, textiles, and craft products.[8]

It is clear, then, that women were not just the passive objects of colonial economic change, but responded ingeniously and often rather successfully to its challenges. However, a further and perhaps more fundamental insight emerges from this work. Historians have long been aware that capitalism could not simply remake indigenous social formations in line with its own needs; rather, these had a determining effect on the way that forces of capitalism were able to draw on, mould, and shape colonial economies. At many levels, women's productive and reproductive labour fed into these processes. This was particularly the case when colonial states began to try to manipulate women's labour, for this usually meant interfering in the internal relations of the household, and was thus likely to set off a wide range of unanticipated changes and resistances. The increased mobility of rural women and the more fluid urban societies that emerged on the Zambian Copper Belt brought a number of unanticipated problems to the mining companies and colonial government alike. To the chagrin of management, African women enthusiastically supported the major strikes of 1935 and 1940, as well as the activities of the African Mineworkers' Union established in 1949. The increased mobility of rural women in turn posed great problems for Northern Rhodesian government officials, more generally opposed to the establishment of a permanent

[6] Luise White, *The Comforts of Home: Prostitution in Colonial Nairobi* (Chicago, 1990).

[7] Geoffrey Chauncey, 'The Locus of Reproduction: Women's Labour in the Zambian Copperbelt, 1927–1953', *Journal of Southern African Studies*, VII, 2 (1981), pp. 135–64; Jane Parpart, 'Class and Gender on the Copperbelt: Women in Northern Rhodesian Copper Mining Communities, 1926–1964', in Robertson and Berger, *Women and Class in Africa*, pp. 141–60.

[8] Margaret Hay, 'Luo Women and Economic Change During the Colonial Period', and Claire Robertson, 'Ga Women and Socio-Economic Change in Accra, Ghana', both in Nancy J. Hafkin and Edna Bay, eds., *Women in Africa: Studies in Social and Economic Change* (Stanford, Calif., 1976); Janet MacGaffey, 'Women and Class Formation in a Dependent Economy: Kisangani Entrepreneurs', in Robertson and Berger, *Women and Class in Africa*, pp. 161–77. For southern Africa, see Tshidiso Maloka, 'Khomo Lia Oela: Canteens, Brothels and Labour Migrancy in Colonial Lesotho, 1900–1940', *Journal of African History* (hereafter *JAH*), XXXVIII (1997), pp. 101–22.

urban African population, and with their own set notions of the proper sphere and duties of women. Africans tied to the rural economy accepted Indirect Rule, while women in rural society could properly help in the costs of labour reproduction by providing low-cost support for youth and elders. Women's mobility also posed great problems for the colonial government's rural political allies amongst African elders and chiefs, who complained bitterly about their women running away to the Copper Belt. There ensued a lengthy and largely unsuccessful campaign to control the movement of African women into urban areas, by making marriage certificates issued by Native Authorities a requisite for being in urban areas, by limiting female income earning, and by passing more stringent laws against divorce and adultery.[9]

These themes emerge again and again in African colonial history from the late nineteenth century: the social strains placed on African households and marriage systems by labour migration, of enhanced female mobility as African women sought escape from heavier work burdens in mining compounds, towns, and mission stations, and an inter-war conservative backlash from local elders and colonial officials, alike concerned to preserve the control of rural patriarchs over women's labour and able to use the legal apparatus of the colonial state to do so. In these ways, women's labour was essential to colonial states' own designs for profit, but was so bound up with other aspects of social organization that attempts to draw on it set off much broader and less manageable social changes with important political implications. Gender could not be remade without unravelling much wider aspects of social organization.

As a key instrument in these diverse struggles, colonial law too appears more and more as a field where gender questions were important. For all of its localized variety, the history of British colonial lawmaking demonstrates a number of consistent themes, many of them inherited from the Indian Imperial experience. Most importantly, it became a commonplace amongst British colonial officials from the late eighteenth century that their task was not, in the main, to invent or import new laws for those they governed. Their duty was, rather, to discover the definitive version of indigenous law belonging to each community or people amongst the ruled, helped if necessary by local experts, and then to administer this law in a just and impartial manner. These Imperial fictions fitted in with that wider and familiar conception of Empire as Pax Britannica, and of colonial states not as innovators, but as the benevolent guardians of local systems of law and justice and neutral arbiters between their diverse and often fractious subjects. Change and progress in this picture were to come about less through the deliberate

[9] Parpart, 'Class and Gender on the Copperbelt'. For West African parallels, see Jean Allman, 'Rounding Up Spinsters: Gender Chaos and Unmarried Women in Colonial Asante', *JAH*, XXXVII (1996), pp. 195–214.

interference of the state, and more through the 'natural' forces of education, commerce, and contact with more advanced societies. Sometimes, of course, colonial states had deliberately to intervene, where local practices seemed particularly barbarous or offensive to natural justice, as in the Indian Age of Consent Act of 1891, or the early-twentieth-century colonial campaigns against the 'forced' marriage of African women.[10] In general, however, the presumption was that European legal norms should not be used routinely to regulate 'traditional' domestic and social institutions; the point, rather, was to uncover indigenous law and to administer it.

There were variations on these themes within the Empire and over time. In particular, the Government of India grew more hesitant in its legislative interventions after 1857, and more wedded to the belief that its task was to administer law to an essentially unchanging Indian society. Newer colonial states in early-twentieth-century Africa were rather more willing to use the law to affect social change, often in the belief that local African societies had not the weight of tradition to be disturbed and certainly in the knowledge that they would not face the kind of experienced and concerted conservative resistance encountered in India. But there were also common themes. The task itself of 'discovering' law always meant in practice quite profound innovation. This was partly, of course, because few of the 'societies' which came under British rule possessed abstract or generally accepted bodies of law that could simply be 'discovered' in this way, while many did not even recognize a discrete realm of 'law,' separate from custom and obligation and enforcible by the state. Thus, in seeking help from those whom they favoured as experts or specialists, colonial officials not only helped manufacture quite novel interpretations of law and its relation to wider social institutions and individuals, but sometimes unwittingly aligned themselves with one side or another in what were often pre-existing contests for legitimacy and power.

These processes of 'discovery' and codification took place from the 1890s in most parts of British Africa. Here too colonial officials set themselves to elicit the definitive 'customary' law applicable to each community under their jurisdiction, and here too 'tradition' was invented. Indeed, gender issues were often at the heart of colonial lawmaking, precisely because the consequences of colonial social change were often most profoundly felt within the household. These processes emerge clearly in the formation of customary law in colonial Malawi and Zambia. Colonial officials early congratulated themselves on establishing the free status of

[10] Mrinalini Sinha, *Colonial Masculinity: The 'Manly Englishman' and the 'Effeminate Bengali' in the Late Nineteenth Century* (Manchester, 1995), pp. 138–80; Martin Chanock, *Law, Custom and Social Order: The Colonial Experience in Malawi and Zambia* (Cambridge, 1995), p. 186, and Schmidt, *Peasants, Traders and Wives*, pp. 110–13.

women through enactments in 1902 and 1905 which made women's consent necessary for a legally recognizable marriage. But the same officials came increasingly to dislike the uses to which African women put their new independence. As rural wives of migrant men in particular found their work burdens growing, and themselves left unsupported with their husband's families for several months of the year, many took their complaints to the courts and to District Commissioners, or worse still tried to escape lineage authority altogether by taking the train or motor-bus to towns or mining compounds.[11] Lineage elders and migrant men themselves were also worried by their apparent loss of control over the women in whom their bridewealth had been invested. Migrant men's access to land also depended on women continuing to tend land in their absence.[12] It was out of these pressures, then, that 'customary law' emerged. The 1930s saw a series of measures designed to restrict women's mobility and marriage choices, and punish the men who violated others' rights in them.[13]

Studied from the perspective of gender, formal nationalist movements in the Empire have also begun to look different. It has become clear what a large and sometimes leading part women took in anti-colonial agitations of many different kinds. Women had their own political organizations within many formal nationalist movements, such as the All-India Women's Conference in India or the Kaum Ibu UNMO, the women's branch of the United Malays National Organisation.[14] Less formal roles could be just as effective, such as the women's dance groups that played a vital part in the early mobilizing of the Tanganyika African National Union, or the networks of rural women who sustained the struggle for independence in Zimbabwe through their work as smugglers and spies.[15]

Yet gender as a lever for social change could be unpredictable in its results for the critics of colonialism too. Institutional relationships were always a source of

[11] Chanock, *Law, Custom and Social Order*, pp. 146–59. For other examples of colonial 'customary law', see Sally Falk Moore, *Social Facts and Fabrications: 'Customary' Law on Kilimanjaro, 1880–1890* (Cambridge, 1986).

[12] Moore, *Social Facts*, pp. 172–91.

[13] Ibid., pp. 192–216. See also Marjorie Mbilinyi, 'Runaway Wives in Colonial Tanganyika: Forced Labour and Forced Marriages in Rungwe District, 1919–1961', *International Journal of the Sociology of Law*, XVI, 1 (1988) pp. 1–29.

[14] Aparna Basu and Bharati Ray, *Women's Struggle: A History of the All India Women's Conference, 1927–1990* (Delhi, 1990); L. Manderson, *Women, Politics and Change: The Kaum Ibu UNMO in Malaysia, 1945–1972* (Kuala Lumpur, 1980).

[15] Susan Geiger, 'Women in Nationalist Struggle: Tanu Activists in Dar es Salaam', *International Journal of African Historical Studies*, XX, 1 (1987), pp. 1–26 and 'Tanganyikan Nationalism as "Women's Work": Life Histories, Collective Biography and Changing Historiography', *JAH*, XXXVII (1996), pp. 465–78; Irene Staunton, *The War Experiences of Thirty Zimbabwean Women* (London, 1990); Leela Kasturi and Vina Mazumdar, eds., *Women and Indian Nationalism* (Delhi, 1994); Radha Kumar, *The History of Doing: An Illustrated Account of Movements for Women's Rights and Feminism in India, 1800–1990* (London, 1993).

tension, particularly when women's organizations clashed with conservative elements within the nationalist leadership. The Kaum Ibu UNMO in Malaya always sought to maintain its own independent agenda, focusing on women's education and the protection of women within marriage. Sometimes UNMO leaders supported their initiatives, as when Islamic religious teachers sought a ban on women's participation in public life. Yet there were clear limits to the independence of the women's organization. In 1956 the UNMO leadership acted decisively to expel one of its most assertive leaders, Khadijah Sidek, following her outspoken campaign to get UNMO to select more women as candidates in the elections of the previous year.[16] Differences of class and culture often compounded those of gender. In the pre-independence elections held in Lesotho in 1965, it was Basotho women's votes which brought the apparently conservative and Catholic-dominated Basutoland National Party to power, rather than the radical nationalist Basutoland Congress Party. Paradoxically, the Catholic Church and local institutions of hereditary chieftaincy offered women forms of empowerment and local protection not afforded by male political radicals, for whom authority in a 'modern' state belonged properly to Western-educated men, and who evinced ignorance and contempt for women's local needs.[17]

There were profound asymmetries too at the level of ideology. Reified images of women, particularly of women as mothers, were often central to the ways in which national or 'community' identities themselves were defined. In India, as elsewhere in the British Empire, colonial governments, missionaries, and paternalist reformers had long cited the 'debased' status of women as evidence of moral backwardness. Conversely, for many urban middle-class men, buffeted by forces of economic change and torn between conflicting cultural norms, 'woman' and 'home' came to stand as a tranquil refuge of unchanging 'tradition'. This created an intense focus on women and the home as realms of freedom and cultural integrity, beyond the reach of the colonial state. In India, Mahatma Gandhi identified what he saw as Indian women's particular capacity for suffering and self-sacrifice with the spirit of the Indian nation itself. Thus, India's 'weakness' was not passivity or 'effeminacy'. It was rather a distinctive form of spiritual vitality, a strength expressed not through brute aggression but through virtues of selflessness, loyalty, and compassion: virtues most naturally found in India's women. Women's practical roles as wives and mothers also meant that the evils of colonial rule hit them hardest: in the collapse of Indian handicrafts, in colonial taxes on

[16] Virginia H. Dancz, *Women and Party Politics in Peninsular Malaysia* (Singapore, 1987), pp. 87–96. For Khadijah Sidek's compelling memoirs, which she published under the name 'Ardjasni', see *Eastern Horizon*, I and II (1963–64).

[17] Marc Eprecht, 'Women's "conservatism" and the Politics of Gender in Late Colonial Lesotho', *JAH*, XXXVI (1995), pp. 29–56.

essential domestic items, in state profiteering from alcohol sales. Naturally, this elevation of 'feminine' virtues implied clear boundaries too. It meant that the conduct of Congress women activists themselves would be subject to particular scrutiny and regulation, as when Gandhi denounced a group of prostitutes who had organized themselves for local social work under Congress auspices.[18] These appeals, carefully constructed to maximize women's participation without threatening their primary identification with motherhood and family, brought women into Gandhian *satyagrahas* in great numbers. For all their implicit conservatism, they marked a presence and legitimacy in Indian public life that was quite new.

Such constructs were inevitably contested. Hindu revivalism similarly projected powerful images of woman as mother, protector of the home and sacred embodiment of national virtue, her body a pure space which had escaped the transformative effects of colonialism. But to this in the 1920s was often added a sharp communal twist. The ideology of many communalist organizations depicted Muslim men, as much as imported cultural norms, as the real danger to the Hindu woman's motherly virtue, their 'fertility' threatening to overwhelm her with numbers and their 'aggression' laying siege to her bodily purity.[19] For Muslims, the special status of women under Muslim personal law seemed to crystallize and guarantee the core values of Indian Muslim identity. This separate legal status formed the subject of bitter conflict from the mid-1930s, when Congress workers put forward plans for a uniform civil code.[20] It also proved one of the final blows to the cross-communal campaigning platform that the All-India Women's Conference had sought to establish since its foundation in 1926.

In these inter-war contexts, efforts to make women and the home into particular kinds of national icon were no longer primarily tactics against the colonial state. They represented rather the efforts of competing segments of the urban middle class to define 'the nation' in their own image, and to appoint themselves guardians of its political project. The demise of the formal colonial system, therefore, hardly dented these constructions of women as icons of nation and community. Indeed, the meanings of womanhood in India continue to be infused

[18] Madhu Kishwar, 'Gandhi on Women', *Economic and Political Weekly*, V (Oct. 1985), p. 1693.

[19] Urvashi Bhutalia, 'Communal Stereotypes and the Partition of India', in Urvashi Bhutalia and Tanika Sarkar, eds., *Women and Right Wing Movements: Indian Experiences* (London, 1995), pp. 58–81. On gender and nationalist discourse in India, see Partha Chatterjee, *The Nation and Its Fragments: Colonial and Postcolonial Histories* (Delhi, 1995), chaps. 6 and 7; Tanika Sarkar, 'Hindu Conjugality and Nationalism in Late Nineteenth-Century Bengal', Jasodhara Bagchi, ed., *Indian Women: Myth and Reality* (Calcutta, 1995), pp. 98–115, and Dipesh Chakrabarty, 'The Difference-Deferral of a Colonial Modernity: Public Debates on Domesticity in British India', in D. Arnold and D. Hardiman, eds., *Subaltern Studies VIII* (Delhi, 1994), pp. 50–88.

[20] Maitri Mukhopadhyay, '"Brother, there are only two jatis: men and women": Women, the State and Personal Laws in India', unpublished Ph.D. thesis, Sussex, 1994.

with significance for the definition of national and community identity. This has become clear in the ideology of the Hindu right, with its images of threatened Hindu womanhood and its offering of Hindu community identity as a form of 'empowerment' to women. The continuing salience of gender in Indian ideologies of community has posed severe challenges to Indian feminism as well as to its traditions of political secularism.[21]

In other ways too, this manner of their admission into national political life has left Indian women with an ambiguous legacy. Ideologically, it meant a reinforcement of older stereotypes of women's 'virtues' of self-sacrifice. At the level of practical politics, it meant that women's entry into formal political life came about less as a result of a radical groundswell from below, and more as the consequence of male patronage from above, implying considerable political dependence. It also meant that Indian women, like nationalist women everywhere, tended to subordinate their own concerns to those of male leaders. Not only was there great pressure on them to fit their understanding of women's oppression into the conceptual framework of the nationalist movement, but they were also limited in how far they could confront local patriarchies because of the way this might be used by British rulers to reinforce their own assumptions about India's lack of civilized values.[22]

As has been seen, colonial economic policies often implied a fundamental reordering of roles and relationships within the household. Such changes brought about transformations equally profound in the 'inner' realms of moral sensibility and sexual identity. Sexuality here was not merely a matter of the 'private' world of domestic life or individual sensibility. Sex and gender, public and private, masculine and feminine were linked in the processes through which colonial states could transform sexual identities and the moral realms in which they were lived. After the period of conquest in Southern Rhodesia, Shona constructions of marriage and sexuality differed profoundly from those of their colonial rulers. For the Shona, as for many African peoples, marriage and sexual activity were an aspect of lineage membership in general, and individual members were answerable to the family group for the use they made of their sexuality. There was no place here for any

[21] Sarkar and Butalia, *Women and Right-Wing Movements.* See also Shashi Joshi and Bhagwan Josh, 'Women and Sexuality in the Discourse of Communism', in Shashi Joshi and Bhagwan Josh, *Struggle for Hegemony in India, 1920–47: The Colonial State, the Left and the National Movement,* 3 vols. (New Delhi, 1992–94), III: *Culture, Community and Power,* pp. 194–258. For continuities in the gendered imagery of nationhood in post-colonial South-East Asia, see Aihwa Ong and Michael G. Peletz, eds., *Bewitching Women, Pious Men: Gender and Body Politics in Southeast Asia* (Berkeley, 1995). Literary and psychoanalytic perspectives inform the discussion of nationalism as a gendered discourse in Anne McClintock, *Imperial Leather: Race, Gender and Sexuality in the Imperial Contest* (London, 1995), chap. 10.

[22] Joanna Liddle and Rama Joshi, *Daughters of Independence: Gender, Caste and Class in India* (London, 1986), pp. 39–40.

notion that sex or marriage were the 'private' concern of individuals, nor of an independent 'moral realm' in which sexual activity could be judged virtuous or sinful in itself. These conceptions dominated the thinking of the colonial officials who first sought to protect African women by recognizing them as legal individuals, and then grew rapidly disaffected with the use women seemed to make of their new freedoms. These conflicting understandings of marriage, adultery, and sexual identity played against one another as District Commissioners and African family heads struggled to resolve these problems. For family heads, the point was to reassert the authority of the family over marriage again and to get adulterous men to pay compensation. For colonial officials, adultery was a sin and social crime which needed punishment, and it was discomfiting to find African men not only keen to take back errant wives, but even keener, seemingly, to profit from their crimes. Out of these conflicting concerns came, in 1916, an ordinance that made adultery a criminal offence for men and women alike. With it, there developed amongst African men a more 'European' understanding of adultery. Women now not only figured as legal individuals in the crime, their relationships thrust into a public space where the state had jurisdiction; they also began to attract wider and more particular blame for social disruption and 'immorality'. In these ways, questions of sexuality were central to the colonial reordering of African morality, and this reordering pulled older understandings of 'private' and 'public' inside out.[23]

These studies of the state, moral orders, and colonial sexualities reveal much, not only about women, but about men too as gendered beings. New insights have recently emerged into the sexual practices and identities of men in colonial societies, the ideologies of masculinity often deployed by colonial states, and the emergence of new kinds of 'Imperial' masculinity in metropolitan culture from the later nineteenth century. Masculinity is not, of course, an essential quality, nor merely a set of inner attributes. It is also a cultural and historically variable fabrication of an outward kind, and a public social status which must be striven for and maintained in specific social contexts. What sustains masculine identity is not only perceived differences from women, but also the recognition and affirmation of other men.[24] For a gendered study of men, therefore, we need to look not simply at relations between men and women, but at those between men themselves, for it is precisely through the public development of these 'hegemonic' models for masculine behaviour that other styles and identities are rendered marginal or heterodox.[25]

[23] Diana Jeater, *Marriage, Perversion and Power: The Construction of Moral Discourse in Southern Rhodesia, 1894–1930* (Oxford, 1993).

[24] John Tosh, 'What Should Historians do with Masculinity? Reflections on Nineteenth-Century Britain', *History Workshop Journal* (hereafter *HWJ*), XXXVIII (Autumn, 1994), pp. 179–202..

[25] R. W. Connell, *Masculinities* (Oxford, 1995), pp. 76–87.

A growing number of historians now have grappled with these problems, and demonstrated the possibilities as well as the difficulties of a gendered study of men, in colonial societies as well as in the culture of the metropolis. Racial stereotypes were often constructed around gender identities. In late-nineteenth-century Bengal, the British tried to single out particular 'martial' or 'manly' races who would make good soldiers and policemen, while they reserved feminizing labels for those they held in fear or contempt. They pointed to Bengali 'effeminacy' when they wished to exclude educated Indians from privileged places in the civil service, judiciary, and volunteer forces. Similar themes were to emerge later in central Africa, with distinctions between the 'martial' Ndebele and the 'effeminate' Shona. In other contexts, however, shared values drew men together across racial divides. In the debate in the early 1890s over a proper age of consent for Indian girls, Indian conservatives invoked the proper dominance of husbands and fathers in the 'private' domain of their own households. Many women, particularly British doctors and Indian women activists, argued that female consent should be defined in wider terms of physical and emotional maturity. Men, both colonial advocates and conservative opponents of legislation, agreed that the only issue was a girl's reproductive capacity, as measured in the age of first menstruation.[26]

These ideological confluences swept aside the dissenting voices of women and thereafter kept the Government of India from attempting major social legislation for the next three decades. They also helped deflect nationalist energies from a more radical socio-cultural critique, which would incorporate women's concerns under colonialism as well as those of men, perpetuating the older and relatively narrow conceptions of anti-colonial politics which had dominated nationalist activity during the later nineteenth century. It was not until Gandhi's reordering of nationalist priorities after the First World War that this mould began to break, although here again, as we have seen, important parts of it were left intact.

Changing masculine identities can similarly be traced in many African contexts. The Mau Mau rebellion represented a crisis for many Kikuyu men of a particularly gendered kind, and this perspective provides fresh insights into the extraordinary bitterness and desperation of the rebels. A common name for Mau Mau was *ithaka na wiathi*, 'self-mastery through land'. This concept stood at the heart of Kikuyu political thought. *Wiathi* was the self-mastery achieved by community elders, adult men who had earned the freedom to speak and to judge without fear. To become an adult in this sense required that a Kikuyu become first fully a man. This meant setting up a successful, polygynous household, in which productive wives could provide labour needs and ensure its fruitful reproduction. Male mastery in

[26] Sinha, *Colonial Masculinity*, pp. 169–72.

the home proved the ability to manage public affairs, while control over land ensured the wealth needed to attract further clients and dependants. Together, these made it possible to attain full adulthood. For sub-clan heads with plenty of land, these processes of moral growth beckoned as a bright certainty. But others, the young and the poor, found their claims to land progressively disregarded as Kikuyu sub-clans grew in exclusiveness and white settler demands expanded. For these dispossessed men, it was difficult to know how they could attain manhood and adulthood. It was not even certain that they could see themselves as true Kikuyu at all, as sub-clan heads increasingly defined Kikuyu identity in their own image, around clan membership.[27]

Many on the British side were similarly preoccupied with the reconstruction of Kikuyu manhood. They believed that the real cure for the uprooted and 'detribalized' urban supporters of Mau Mau lay in making them into fulfilled family men on the Western model, each enjoying a home of his own and a wife who could offer 'companionship' as well as domestic skills. British hostility to African urbanization gave way in the 1950s to a new vision of productive and contented domesticity in the cities. A properly demarcated private domain, where men could realize the benefits of 'civilized' masculinity, emerged as the solution for the horrible social breakdown of Mau Mau.[28]

If colonial governments sought to manipulate gender relations among the ruled, sexual codes and norms among the European populations of colonial states likewise attracted intense concern. Here, however, the results were more predictable, and attended with much greater success. As many historians have observed, strategies of rule and public sexual norms shifted in parallel in the British Empire from about 1880. Domestic ideologies of social Darwinism and fears of racial degeneration spread to Imperial contexts, in a new culture emphasizing moral respectability, physical health, and hygiene, sustained by scientific methods and the disciplines of hard work and responsibility. These concerns converged with particular sharpness in a powerful ideology of motherhood, uniting concerns for healthy children, racial strength, and fitness for the responsibilities of Empire. Like their nationalist opponents, metropolitan visionaries of Empire discovered in

[27] John Lonsdale, 'The Moral Economy of Mau Mau: Wealth, Poverty and Civic Virtue in Kikuyu Political Thought', in Bruce Berman and John Lonsdale, eds., *Unhappy Valley: Conflict in Kenya and Africa, Book Two: Violence and Ethnicity* (London, 1992), pp. 315–468.

[28] Luise White, 'Separating the Men from the Boys: Constructions of Gender, Sexuality and Terrorism in Central Kenya, 1939–1959', *International Journal of African Historical Studies*, XXIII, 1 (1990), pp. 1–25. Other studies of changing gender roles for men are T. Dunbar Moodie, 'Migrancy and Male Sexuality on the South African Gold Mines', *Journal of Southern African Studies*, XIV, 2 (Jan. 1988), pp. 228–56 and Karen Tranberg Hansen, *Distant Companions: Servants and Employers in Zambia, 1900–1985* (Ithaca, NY, 1989), and Karen Tranberg Hansen, ed., *African Encounters with Domesticity* (New Brunswick, NJ, 1992).

motherhood a compelling icon for the nation.[29] At the same time, codes for a new type of ideal 'Imperial' manliness were emerging as a norm for British manhood, disseminated through public schools, the Boy Scout movement, and an expanding market for adventure fiction featuring fantasies of the soldier, the hunter, and the pioneer on the colonial frontier represented as an exclusively masculine world.[30] These fantasy worlds for British men and women achieved wide social currency from the late nineteenth century, and could be found not only in popular literature but in an expanding market for popular commodities associated with the British race, in the developing sciences of anthropology and psychology, and even in some aspects of private sexual behaviour.[31]

These new models for bourgeois morals and racial segregation spread across the Empire, often in response to the sharpening of local political resistances to European penetration. They spread to post-Mutiny India from the 1860s, as steamships and the Suez Canal expanded the white community: in Ceylon, South Africa, and New Zealand by 1900, in tropical Africa by the 1920s with the opening-up of the Zambian Copper Belt, and in Burma, Malaya, and the further reaches of the South-East Asian Empire only somewhat incompletely by the 1930s.[32]

These shifts in moral sensibility had very different implications for British men and women of the governing élite. As public standard-bearers for the new codes of paternal responsibility and sexual restraint, men of the Colonial Service found their sexual conduct, particularly their relations with local women, the focus of heightened public scrutiny. This was given clearest public expression in Secretary of State Lord Crewe's official prohibition of concubinage in 1909.[33] The British

[29] Anna Davin, 'Imperialism and Motherhood', *HWJ*, V (1978), pp. 9–65.

[30] These new codes are extensively discussed in J. Bristow, *Empire Boys: Adventures in a Man's World* (London, 1991); Graham Dawson, *Soldier Heroes: British Adventure, Empire and the Imaging of Masculinity* (London, 1994); John Tosh, 'Imperial Masculinity and the Flight from Domesticity in Britain, 1880–1914', in Timothy P. Foley and others, eds., *Gender and Colonialism* (Galway, 1995), pp. 72–85; John M. Mackenzie, *The Empire of Nature: Hunting, Conservation and British Imperialism* (Manchester, 1988); Michael Rosenthal, *The Character Factory: Baden-Powell and the Origins of the Boy Scout Movement* (New York, 1984). The example of the Boy Scout movement is, however, more complex than some of this literature suggests. It disseminated models for an ideal citizenship that included young women as well as men, and was designed to appeal to a 'Commonwealth' audience rather than a white one alone. See chap. by John M. MacKenzie.

[31] These arguments are elaborated in McClintock, *Imperial Leather*.

[32] Hyam, *Empire and Sexuality*, pp. 108–09. See also Kenneth Ballhatchet, *Race, Sex and Class Under the Raj: Imperial Attitudes and Policies and their Critics, 1793–1905* (New York, 1980).

[33] Ronald Hyam, 'Concubinage and the Colonial Service: The Crewe Circular (1909)', *Journal of Imperial and Commonwealth History*, XIV, 3 (1986), p. 184. For South-West African parallels, see Patricia Hayes, '"Cocky" Hahn and the "Black Venus": The Making of a Native Commissioner in South West Africa, 1915–1946', in Nancy Rose Hunt and others, eds., *Gendered Colonialisms in African History: Gender and History Special Issue*, VIII, 3 (Nov. 1996), pp. 365–92.

women, wives and mothers, who arrived in growing numbers from the early years of the twentieth century, were to stand as custodians of the new Imperial morality in rather a different way.[34] They stood as guardians of 'civilized standards' of personal morality and family life. Their preserve lay in the segregated space of the white family, where children could be nurtured with home values and husbands guided towards wholesome comforts and domestic companionship. As more settled colonial societies emerged, many found that they could extend these 'maternal imperialist' roles into the wider community. From the late 1940s, Women's Institutes addressed what they saw as local women's needs for education in hygiene, health, nutrition, and domestic skills. Sometimes their efforts were quite explicitly political. In the emergencies in Kenya and Malaya in the 1950s, it was hoped that the wholesome atmosphere of Women's Institutes might attract female support away from the guerrillas.[35] But the importance of these British women to the Imperial project lay not only in what they did, but also in what they symbolized as mothers and custodians of the home. Symbolizing the spatial separation of the ruling élite as well as its internal cohesion and vigour, British homes and British women upheld civilized standards against disorders from without, as well as corruption from within, the ruling community.[36] In practice, of course, these codes were only ever partially realized, given the social heterogenity of British communities, and the complex networks of dependence and desire which bound them to their colonial subjects. As an idealized self-image, a strategy for psychic survival and a part of Imperial justification, however, such codes remained important and compelling.

Infused with racial and sexual significances, white domestic space, and white women in particular, became in turn the focus of tension and challenge. The peculiar sexual hysteria of 'Black Peril' scares swept through the white societies of the British Empire with extraordinary frequency from the late nineteenth century:

[34] For an overview of the range of different categories of Western women active in the British Imperial system, see Margaret Strobel, *European Women and the Second British Empire* (Bloomington, Ind., 1991).

[35] Audrey Wipper, 'The Maendeleo ya Wanawake Movement in the Colonial Period: The Canadian Connection, Mau Mau Embroidery and Agriculture', *Rural Africana*, XXIX (1975–76), pp. 195–214; Richard Stubbs, *Hearts and Minds in Guerrilla Warfare: The Malayan Emergency, 1948–1960* (Oxford, 1989), pp. 172–73; Strobel, *European Women*, p. 62.

[36] Ann Laura Stoler, 'Rethinking Colonial Categories: European Communities and the Boundaries of Rule', *Comparative Studies in Society and History*, XXXI, 1 (Jan. 1989), pp. 134–61; and by the same author, 'Carnal Knowledge and Imperial Power: Gender, Race and Morality in Colonial Asia', in Micaela di Leonardo, ed., *Gender at the Crossroads of Knowledge: Feminist Anthropology in the Postmodern Era* (Berkeley, 1991), pp. 51–101. Similar themes are discussed in Helen Callaway, 'Purity and Exotica in Legitimating the Empire: Cultural Constructions of Gender, Sexuality and Race', in Terence Ranger and Olufemi Vaughan, eds., *Legitimacy and the State in Twentieth Century Africa* (Oxford, 1993), pp. 31–61.

in India, Kenya, Southern Rhodesia, South Africa, Papua.[37] In the Papuan case, for example, the White Women's Protection Ordinance brought in by the Governor Sir Hubert Murray in 1926, imposed the death sentence for the rape or attempted rape of any European female. The hysteria which accompanied it was the culmination of a number of transgressions against white women and girls, mostly by domestic servants. Necessary intruders into the European home, servants were accused of offences that ranged from spying on women bathing and dressing, to 'taking advantage' of sleeping women to touch them, and to bodily assault.[38]

Some of those caught up in these crises blamed not only the sexual appetites of black men, but the lax behaviour of white women. Fables about the memsahib who summoned her servant into the bathroom with her towel died hard.[39] At the same time, and contradictorily, other contemporaries attributed the heightened racial tensions of the inter-war Empire to female behaviour of just the opposite kind. This familiar 'memsahib' theory of Imperial decline in turn found echoes in the work of a generation of historians of Empire who saw European women themselves as the cause of these racial antagonisms through their own high-handedness and cultural insularity.[40] The truth was much more complex. The sharpening and sexualization of racial antagonisms almost always arose in the context of prior and wider tensions. In eastern and southern Africa, such tensions sharpened as settler communities entrenched their claims to land or urban space more deeply, or competed with local men for agricultural markets.[41] In India, they emerged in the context of intensifying pressures to remove barriers to Indians at senior levels of the judicial system.[42] In the Solomon Islands, Papua, and Fiji, sharper racial cleavages from the 1890s coincided not only with women's arrival, but with the more general stabilization of the white community.[43] Thus, if some

[37] Sinha, *Colonial Masculinity*, pp. 33–68; Dane Kennedy, *Islands of White: Settler Society and Culture in Kenya and Southern Rhodesia, 1880–1939* (Durham, NC, 1987), pp. 128–47; Charles van Onselen, 'The Witches of Suburbia: Domestic Service on the Witwatersrand, 1890–1914', in his *Studies in the Social and Economic History of the Witwatersrand, 1886–1914*, Vol. II, *New Nineveh* (London, 1982), pp. 1–73; Elizabeth Schmidt, *Peasants, Traders and Wives*, pp. 169–75; Amirah Inglis, *The White Women's Protection Ordinance: Sexual Anxiety and Politics in Papua* (London, 1975).

[38] Inglis, *The White Women's Protection Ordinance*, pp. 119–35.

[39] Ibid., pp. 54–55.

[40] For a discussion of this literature, see Strobel, *European Women and the Second British Empire*, pp. 1–15. For a critique of the 'memsahib' theory see Helen Callaway, *Gender, Culture and Empire: European Women in Colonial Nigeria* (London, 1987). Callaway argues that European women's qualities of diplomacy, flexibility, and concern with social welfare helped positively to translate Empire into Commonwealth.

[41] Elizabeth Schmidt, *Peasants, Traders and Wives*, pp. 170–71.

[42] Sinha, *Colonial Masculinity*, pp. 37–39.

[43] James A. Boutilier, 'European Women in the Solomon Islands, 1900–1942: Accommodation and Change on the Pacific Frontier', in Denise O'Brien and Sharon W. Tiffany, eds., *Rethinking Women's Roles: Perspectives from the Pacific* (Berkeley, 1984), pp. 173–200; Margaret Jolly and Martha Macintyre,

white women seemed 'responsible' for the intensified racial and physical segregation of British communities, this was because colonial governments helped to position them so, at crucial moments in their own expansion and consolidation.

White women were 'partners in empire' in many other ways too.[44] Long active in India and in some parts of western Africa, missionaries of many different denominations found new fields opening up other areas of sub-Saharan Africa from the late nineteenth century. Themselves often subordinates within patriarchal church hierarchies, British missionary women tended to offer African women the skills of middle-class domesticity. Despite the heavy agricultural burdens of African rural women, sewing and homecraft featured more prominently than farming skills in the teaching of mission girls' schools. These models of pliant domestic labour fitted well with the larger economic strategies of colonial states, in which women's larger burden of unpaid subsistence work helped guarantee a cheap and mobile force of African male labour.[45]

The Empire equally represented a 'field for action' for women of more secular and socially radical persuasions. Drawn to causes, from religious mysticism to women's uplift and nationalist organizing, Western women were most active in India during the half-century from 1860.[46] That the British feminist movement reached its peak over the same period was no coincidence. In British domestic politics, Empire formed the essential context for the development of feminist campaigns. For their supporters, British women's engagement with the social problems of Empire displayed their fitness for citizenship and participation in

eds., *Family and Gender in the Pacific: Domestic Contradictions and the Colonial Impact* (Cambridge, 1989); Claudia Knapman, *White Women in Fiji, 1835–1930: The Ruin of Empire?* (Sydney, 1986); Inglis, *The White Woman's Protection Ordinance*, p. 49. For a critique, see Jane Haggis, 'Gendering Colonialism or Colonising Gender? Recent Women's Studies Approaches to White Women and the History of British Colonialism', *Women's Studies International Forum*, XIII, 1/2 (1990), pp. 105–15.

[44] Nupur Chaudhuri and Margaret Strobel, eds., *Western Women and Imperialism: Complicity and Resistance* (Bloomington, Ind., 1992).

[45] Elizabeth Schmidt, *Peasants, Traders and Wives*, pp. 122–54; but for a critique which identifies the emancipatory potential of African Christianity for women among emerging African élites, see Terence Ranger, *Are We Not Also Men? The Samkange Family and African Politics in Zimbabwe, 1920–1964* (London, 1995). Missionary education of women is also discussed in Sita Ranchod-Nilsson, 'Educating Eve: The Women's Club Movement and Political Consciousness Among African Women in Southern Rhodesia', and Nakanyike B. Musisi, 'Colonial and Missionary Education: Women and Domesticity in Uganda, 1900–1945', both in Hansen, ed., *African Encounters with Domesticity*, pp. 195–217; 172–94; and Deborah Gaitskell, 'At Home with Hegemony? Coercion and Consent in the Education of African Girls for Domesticity in South Africa Before 1910', in Dagmar Engels and Shula Marks, eds., *Contesting Colonial Hegemony: State and Society in Africa and India* (London, 1994), pp. 110–30. For missionary education of girls in Malaya, see Janice N. Brownfoot, 'Sisters under the Skin: Imperialism and the Emancipation of Women in Malaya, *c*.1891–1941', in J. A. Mangan, ed., *Making Imperial Mentalities: Socialisation and British Imperialism* (Manchester, 1990), pp. 46–73.

[46] Kumari Jayawardena, *The White Woman's Other Burden: Western Women and South Asia During British Rule* (London, 1995).

the Imperial nation state.[47] Engagement within India offered Western women activists a degree of independence and personal and professional fulfilment much harder to achieve at home. Opportunities in Africa and South-East Asia came later, from the 1930s.[48] Yet for all of the undoubted idealism and radicalism, the role of the 'maternal imperialist' ultimately proved to be a trap from which it was difficult to escape. In India, it was not until the arrival of an age of mass politics, and particularly the coming of Gandhi, that the relationship changed. The Western women drawn to Gandhian nationalism joined him not as educators, but as disciples, and the model of relationship between women and the state they learned differed profoundly from their own metropolitan experience.[49]

At many levels, then, gender formed a critical dimension of the British Imperial system and of colonial social relations. Exploring these levels not only restores women to historical visibility, but reminds us that men too are gendered as are the public political arenas which some of them dominate. Our historical reluctance to see this is the legacy of a long-standing European intellectual tradition, itself reinforced by the experience of Empire, which identifies women as the carriers of gender, and women and sexuality with the realms of the private and the home. Distance in time, changing perspectives, and much excellent recent research now allow us to advance beyond these archais intellectual traditions, and our understanding of Empire has deepened significantly as a result.

[47] Vron Ware, 'Britannia's Other Daughters: Feminism in the Age of Imperialism', in Ware, ed., *Beyond the Pale: White Women, Racism and History* (London, 1992), pp. 119–66; Antoinette Burton, *Burdens of History: British Feminists, Indian Women and Imperial Culture, 1865–1915* (Chapel Hill, NC, 1994).

[48] Karen Tranberg Hansen, 'White Women in a Changing World: Employment, Voluntary Work and Sex in Post-World War II Northern Rhodesia', in Chaudhuri and Strobel, *Western Women and Imperialism*, pp. 247–68; Deborah Kirkwood, 'The Suitable Wife: Preparation for Marriage in London and Rhodesia/Zimbabwe', and Janice N. Brownfoot, 'Memsahibs in Colonial Malaya: A Study of European Wives in a British Colony and Protectorate, 1900–1949', in Hilary Callan and Shirley Ardener, eds., *The Incorporated Wife* (London, 1984), pp. 106–19 and 186–210.

[49] For accounts of some of Gandhi's British women disciples, see Eleanor Morton, *Women Behind Mahatma Gandhi* (London, 1954).

Select Bibliography

ESTHER BOSERUP, *Women's Role in Economic Development* (London, 1989).

ANTOINETTE BURTON, *Burdens of History: British Feminists, Indian Women and Imperial Culture 1868–1915* (Chapel Hill, NC, 1994).

MARTIN CHANOCK, *Law, Custom and Social Order: The Colonial Experience in Malawi and Zambia* (Cambridge, 1995).

NUPUR CHAUDHURI and MARGARET STROBEL, eds., *Western Women and Imperialism: Complicity and Resistance* (Bloomington, Ind., 1992).

TIMOTHY P. FOLEY and others, eds., *Gender and Colonialism* (Galway, 1995).

GERALDINE FORBES, *Women in Modern India* (Cambridge, 1996).

KAREN TRANBERG HANSEN, ed., *African Encounters with Domesticity* (New Brunswick, NJ, 1992).

NANCY ROSE HUNT and others, eds., *Gendered Colonialisms in African History: Gender and History Special Issue*, VIII, 3 (Nov. 1996).

RONALD HYAM, *Empire and Sexuality: The British Experience* (Manchester, 1990).

MARGARET JOLLY and MARTHA MACINTYRE, eds., *Family and Gender in the Pacific: Domestic Contradictions and the Colonial Impact* (Cambridge, 1989).

RADHA KUMAR, *The History of Doing: An Illustrated Account of Movements for Women's Rights and Feminism in India, 1800–1990* (London, 1993).

ANNE MCCLINTOCK, *Imperial Leather: Race, Gender and Sexuality in the Imperial Contest* (London, 1995).

HENRIETTA MOORE, *Feminism and Anthropology* (Oxford, 1988).

—— and MEGAN VAUGHAN, *Cutting Down Trees: Gender, Nutrition and Agricultural Change in the Northern Province of Zambia, 1890–1990* (London, 1994).

AIHWA ONG and MICHAEL G. PELETZ, eds., *Bewitching Women, Pious Men: Gender and Body Politics in Southeast Asia* (Berkeley, 1995).

K. SANGARI and S. VAID, *Recasting Women: Essays in Colonial History* (New Delhi, 1989).

MRINALINI SINHA, *Colonial Masculinity: The 'Manly Englishman' and the 'Effeminate Bengali' in the Late Nineteenth Century* (Manchester, 1995).

SHARON B. STICHTER and JANE L. PARPART, *Patriarchy and Class: African Women in the Home and the Workforce* (Boulder, Colo., 1988).

MARGARET STROBEL, *European Women and the Second British Empire* (Bloomington, Ind., 1991).

LUISE WHITE, *The Comforts of Home: Prostitution in Colonial Nairobi* (Chicago, 1990).

17

The British Empire and the Muslim World

FRANCIS ROBINSON

By the 1920s the British Empire embraced substantially more than half the Muslim peoples of the world. For much of the twentieth century Britain was the greatest influence over their development. Imperial security in large part dictated which territories of former Muslim empires or petty Muslim states the British came to rule. Imperial interests in combination with those of rival empires and local forces dictated precisely, and sometimes not so precisely, where the boundaries of new states were to fall. By the same token, they determined which peoples would have to learn to live together—or not, as the case may be—in the increasingly demanding environments of the modern economy and modern state. Imperial techniques of government shaped the developing politics of these dependencies, often leaving major legacies to the years when the British had gone. The British Empire was the context in which many Muslims experienced the transition to modernity.

At the beginning of the assertion of British power in the eighteenth century what has been termed the Islamic world system was almost at an end. Long-distance trade, a shared body of knowledge, a common legal system, and a common language of learning had linked peoples from Africa's Atlantic coast through to Central and South Asia. As time went on their influence had reached to the China Sea and island South-East Asia. According to the pattern of commerce and the play of power, great entrepôt cities flourished from time to time in West Asia and the eastern Mediterranean—Baghdad, Cairo, Istanbul, Isfahan. Ibn Battuta, the fourteenth-century Moroccan traveller, who spent twenty-four years journeying through this world visiting the territories of over forty modern Muslim states and finding employment as a judge, attests to the reality of this system. So, too, do those eighteenth-century scholars whose pilgrimages to Mecca were made from places as far afield as Timbuktu, Sinkiang, and Sumatra.

By the late eighteenth century the great empires which had dominated the Muslim world since the early sixteenth century were either dead or dying. The Safavid was long gone, having crumbled in an afternoon before a whiff of Afghan tribal power; the Mughal was reduced to a few villages around Delhi; the Ottoman

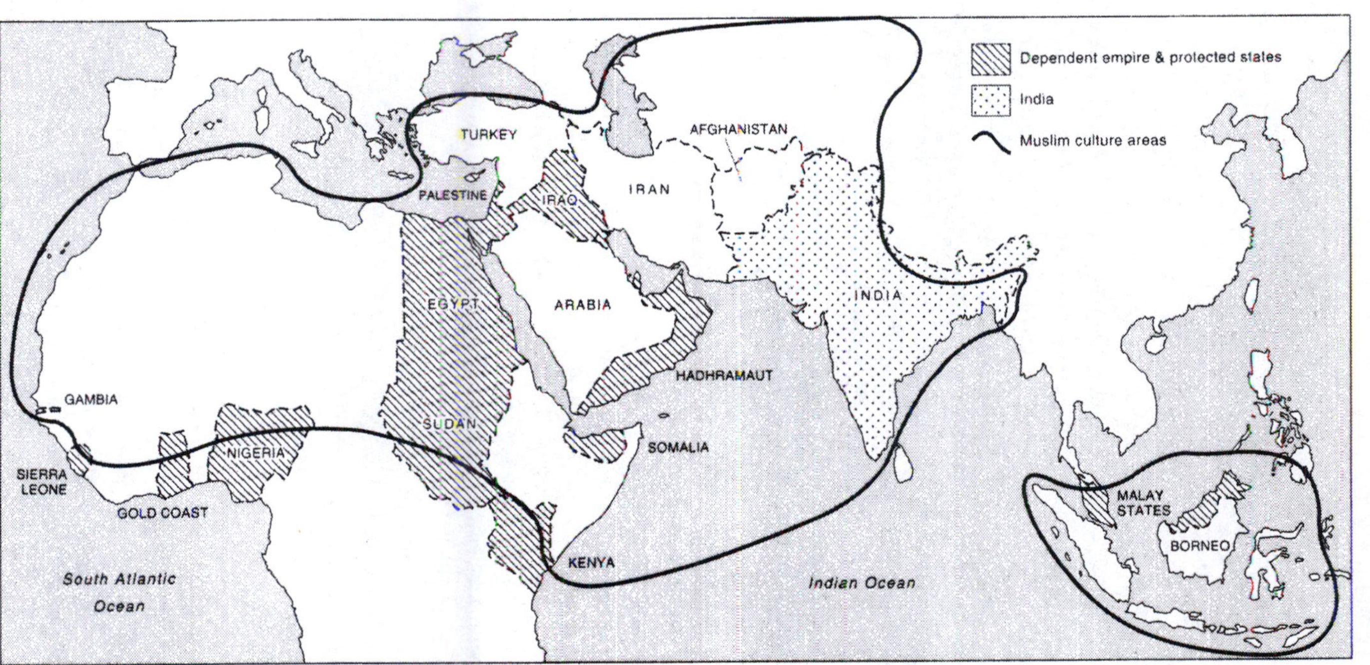

MAP 17.1. The British Empire and the Muslim World

was on the retreat but still held authority over much of the Balkans, West Asia, and North Africa. The Muslim world, however, was not in decline. Recent research has been at pains to emphasize the significant economic and political changes that were taking place in some areas: the growth of revenue farming, the spread of commercial agriculture, the rise of provincial élites, and the regionalization of power.[1] Side by side with these changes there was also a religious renewal of quite extraordinary vitality. It was expressed in jihad (holy war against the unbeliever) movements which touched almost every Muslim land. This spirit continued with vigour into the period of British Empire. Some of its manifestations revealed state-making capacity, as in the Wahhabi movement which underpinned Saudi power in Arabia, the jihad which led to the caliphate of Sokoto in West Africa, and that which led to the Mahdist state in the Sudan. Other manifestations came in response to the fact of British rule, such as the Islamic reformist movement of Deoband in nineteenth-century India or the Islamic 'fundamentalist' movement of the Muslim Brotherhood in twentieth-century Egypt.

The first major step towards the British Empire in the Muslim world came in 1765, when the East India Company received from the Mughal Emperor the right to raise revenue and administer justice in the rich province of Bengal. Subsequent major steps were the final defeat of Tipu Sultan, the last significant Muslim power in India, at Seringapatam in 1799, and the defeat of the French at Acre in the same year, which secured British command of the eastern Mediterranean. From these first steps British power expanded through the Muslim world, the process gaining great pace between the 1880s and the end of the First World War, when it reached from West Africa through the central Islamic lands to South-East Asia (see Map 17.1). In every area the strategic and sometimes the economic needs of Empire combined with local forces to carve the shapes of modern Muslim states, and modern states in which Muslims live, out of former Muslim empires, caliphates, sultanates, and sheikhdoms.

In West Africa, British rule, along with that of the French, transformed the situation of Muslim peoples. Up to the end of the nineteenth century the savannah region to the south of the Sahara had been host to a series of Muslim empires and states which were expanding to the south and the west. They had participated in the long-distance trade across the desert in slaves, salt, and gold, and some had been noted both for their wealth and their learning. British rule transferred the focus of economic effort towards the coast where Africans became involved in the production of cash crops—palm-oil, cocoa, rubber—for export. Muslim peoples occupied the backlands of the new British colonies of Sierra Leone (1891), Gold Coast (1896), and Nigeria (1900). In the last-mentioned, which was by far the

[1] C. A. Bayly, *Imperial Meridian: The British Empire and the World, 1780–1830* (London, 1989).

largest and most important, the Hausa Muslims of the north, who had peopled the Fulani caliphate of Sokoto, were thrust together from 1914 in one colony with people from the central and southern regions whose religions and traditions were different.

In the Nile valley British economic interests, stemming from the development of Egypt's cotton production under the Khedival regime, and her strategic interests, stemming from Egypt's control of the Suez Canal, led to the occupation of the country in 1882. Officially declared a Protectorate soon after the outbreak of war in 1914, mass opposition to British rule from 1919 had led to a qualified independence in 1922 in which Egyptians regained control of their internal affairs but Britain retained control of foreign policy, the army, and the canal. The security of Egypt, however, was closely bound up with the control of the upper Nile valley, the Sudan, where in 1881 the sufi sheikh Muhammad Ahmad had led a rising against Egyptian rule and established the Mahdist state. This had been conquered by an Anglo-Egyptian army in 1898, leading to the formation of an Anglo-Egyptian Condominium in 1899. From the early 1920s the Condominium became no more than fiction as the British, with Sudanese support, took the administration entirely into their hands. In the nineteenth century both the Egyptians and the Mahdists had had difficulty in imposing their authority over the non-Muslims who lived south of the tenth parallel. British power now held the southern peoples firmly within a Sudanese framework.

In East Africa security of the route to India had led to the British presence in Somalia, which was divided up with the Italians and the French in the late nineteenth century. Little had been done for the tribes of the region apart from resisting Muhammad Abdullah, who from 1899 to 1920 waged a jihad against the British. Muslim communities were established in all the British colonies of the region. Notable was the sultanate of Zanzibar which became a Protectorate in 1870, while in Uganda, Kenya, and Tanganyika there were Muslim communities formed initially from the Swahili-speaking peoples who during the nineteenth century had been pressing inland from the coast. Through East Africa from Uganda to South Africa there were also Muslims of Indian origin, not least among them the Nizari Ismaili followers of the Aga Khan, whose migration the British had encouraged to assist in developing the resources of the region.

In western Asia, the need to protect British routes to the East, to manage the former Arab provinces of the Ottoman empire, and to try to honour the conflicting understandings reached with Arabs, Zionists, and the French during the First World War led to the formation of three new states, all of which were held in trust for the League of Nations. There was Iraq, whose boundaries to the west and south had no rationale in nature. To the north the British had insisted on adding the province Mosul from the French sphere of influence—a mixed blessing, bringing on the one hand a mountainous barrier and eventually oil, but on the other hand a large population of discontented Kurds. Indeed, Iraq was a patchwork of possible identities, with Kurds and Turks as well as Arabs, with Jews and Christians as well as Shia and Sunni Muslims, plus a host of tribal groupings. In 1921 the Hashemite prince, Faisal, was established as king to compensate for the loss of his Arab state based on Damascus to the French. There was Palestine, which was carved out of three separate Ottoman districts and which for nearly 2,000 years had been little more than a geographical expression. Here the British had agreed to provide the framework within which Zionists could establish for themselves a 'national home', an ambition which was likely to mean some cost to the 80 per cent of the population which was Muslim and the 10 per cent which was Christian. The third new state was Transjordan, which had even less basis than the other two, as it embraced no administrative region, specific people, or historical memory. Originally intended as part of Palestine, it became a separate state when, in 1921, the British permitted Abdullah, the brother of Faisal, to establish a government there, in part to satisfy his ambition and in part to settle the region.

In the Arabian peninsula Britain's interests were primarily strategic, involving control of the coastline and the routes to India. In the Aden Protectorates the British policed the region from Aden itself while curbing the ambitions of the Zaidi Imams who wished to reimpose the authority of the North Yemen over the sultanates to the south. Further along the southern Arabian shore the Bu Saidi sultans of Muscat and Oman ruled with the help of British advisers. In the Gulf the sheikhdoms of Kuwait, Bahrain, Qatar, and Trucial Oman had all concluded treaties with the British in the nineteenth century and existed underneath the umbrella of British power. In each city, government was a family business, their revenues were slight, and the British intervened only when necessary. Their boundaries, moreover, in the desert world where men exercised authority over men and not land, remained ill-defined.

In India, British relationships with Muslims did not seem to involve state-making. Nearly half of all the Muslims ruled by the British were to be found in the subcontinent, some 80 million, yet Indian Muslims were less than 30 per cent of the population of the region. Equally, Muslims as a whole, as far as they considered such matters, did not seem interested in a separate political existence, which was hardly surprising as they were greatly divided by language, background, and economic condition. However, there were aspects of Muslim politics and British policies which could point in this direction. Muslims in northern India, with British encouragement, had been concerned to focus their energies on the educational initiatives centred on Aligarh College. This had provided the platform for the formation of an All-India Muslim League whose demands, for separate electorates for Muslims and extra representation where they were politically important, the British had been willing to include in both the Morley–Minto constitutional reforms of 1909 and those of Montagu–Chelmsford in 1919. By the 1920s, however, Muslim separatism was a weak force in Indian politics, giving little hint of state-making potential. Nevertheless, a Muslim platform existed for those who wished to make use of it.

In Malaya between 1874 and 1914 the British had brought nine Malay sultanates and three Straits Settlements under their administration. The aim was to create the optimum conditions for the rapid economic and commercial development of the land in commodities such as sugar, coffee, rubber, and tin. At the same time they aimed to foster the advancement of the Malay people within the traditional framework of Malay Muslim society. It was a policy which gave the Malay Muslims the political realm, or at least its outward forms; the only area in which the sultans exercised effective power was in that of Islam, where they took the opportunity to develop the centralized administration of religious affairs. On the other hand, immigrants, in large part Chinese, held the dynamic economic realm. There was a rapid change in the ethnic balance of the population, which by the late 1920s stood at 39 per cent Chinese and just under 45 per cent Malay.

In addition to the many areas in which British power was to be directly involved in nurturing modern states which were to be wholly or in part Muslim, there were others whose modern shape was the result either of British influence or of attempts to resist it. Arguably, the existence of Iran owed much to the determination of Britain throughout the nineteenth century to preserve the country's independence and to hold back the advance of Russian power towards India. It was ironic that Britain's refusal to protect the Caspian province of Gilan from Bolshevik invasion in May 1920 led to the repudiation of the Anglo-Iranian agreement of 1919, which had been her attempt to assert hegemony over the land. By the early 1920s a new model army under Riza Khan was crushing regional revolts and making sure that the oil-rich province of Arabistan (Khuzistan, which was to supply 18 per cent of Britain's oil by 1938) acknowledged the authority of Teheran rather than that of Britain.

In the case of Turkey, it was primarily British power which had driven the Ottoman armies back through Syria to the Taurus mountains where the 1918 Armistice line formed the boundary of the new state. Elsewhere British attempts, along with French and American support, to fight Turkish nationalism by supporting Greek ambitions in western Anatolia, had come to grief when Ataturk's armies drove the Greeks into the sea. The Treaty of Lausanne recognized Turkey's frontiers as they were at the 1918 Armistice.

In central Arabia, the British had initially thought of using the father of the Princes Abdullah and Faisal, Sharif Husain of Mecca, as their agent of control. But then they stepped back and wisely allowed the local leaders to fight for supremacy.

The victor was Abdul-Aziz ibn Saud, the founder of the twentieth-century incarnation of the Saudi state. British power settled the ultimate boundaries of this state, as it established the frontiers of Transjordan, Iraq, and Kuwait in the 1920s, resisted Saudi attempts to incorporate the Yemen in the 1930s, and their ambitions in the Buraimi Oasis in the 1950s.

The expansion of British power had by the 1920s come to establish, or play a part in establishing, both many states of the modern Muslim world and states in which Muslim political interests might have a significant role to play. Even in the 1920s it is possible to discern potential areas of stress: in Nigeria and the Sudan there was potential for conflict between the Muslim north and the Christian or animist south; on the east coast of Africa and in the Malay States there was potential for conflict between indigenous peoples and economic immigrants; in Iraq the Kurds were already refusing to acknowledge the authority of Baghdad; in Palestine Arabs had already rioted against the Zionist presence; in India Muslim separatism, it is true, was weak, but the Muslim political platform was there to be used and Muslims themselves offered meagre support for Indian nationalism. There were many fault-lines. Whether these became open cracks or sulphurous craters would depend both on factors outside Britain's control and on how Britain ruled her Muslim peoples.

British policies in the Muslim dependencies shaped their political development. These were in part dependent on cost, which, given the limited resources of many territories, had to be low. Those nostrums which found favour with officialdom, and were reflected in British attitudes to the Muslim world. To these attitudes we now turn.

The British came to the Muslim world with attitudes formed by the rhetoric of Europe's long encounter with Islam. There was the Christian polemic against Islam, with its accusations that Muhammad was an impostor, that his faith was spread by violence, that it endorsed sexual freedom on earth and promised sensual bliss in heaven. These accusations were sustained by nineteenth-century missionaries, who added to them issues such as the position of women and the existence of slavery. There was the memory of the crusades, which influenced many a British speech regarding the Ottoman empire down to 1920 and doubtless the occasional decision, such as David Lloyd George's determination in that year to join France and the United States in letting the Greeks loose in Asia Minor. There was a religious romanticism which gave a special meaning, for some at least, to events such as the capture of Jerusalem in 1917 and the creation of a Jewish national home in Palestine.

On the other hand, there was the Enlightenment response to the Muslim world, in which it became a marvellous store of opportunities not just to test Christian certainties but also to let the imagination roam. Galland's translation of the *Arabian Nights* in 1704, alongside growing numbers of travellers' tales, whetted the appetite for caliphs, genies, lamps, and fabulous happenings. The taste was developed by writers and musicians, poets and painters, reaching one of its apogees in the early decades of the twentieth century in the poetry of that unsuccessful member of the Levant consular service, James Elroy Flecker, and the films of Rudolph Valentino. Great were the possibilities of flowing robes and Muslim headgear, whether it was Cambridge undergraduates hoaxing the civic authorities that they were the Uncle of the Sultan of Zanzibar and his entourage in 1905,[2] or T. E. Lawrence playing out his fantasies in the Arabian desert in the First World War. Among the problems of this exotic essence with which things Muslim were bestowed was the fact that it made Muslims seem more different, and perhaps less able to accept change, than was in fact the case.

Against this background the British developed understandings of the Muslims they ruled. One which was widespread in India and Africa in the late nineteenth century was that Muslims were fanatics, prone to holy war against non-Muslims, and therefore difficult to reconcile to British rule. This view had its origins in the various jihad movements which the British encountered in early-nineteenth-century India; it was kept alive by the Mutiny rebellion, which was considered, wrongly, to be a Muslim conspiracy; and it was not laid to rest by W. W. Hunter's famous tract *The Indian Musalmans*, written in answer to the Viceroy's question 'Are the Indian Muslims bound by their religion to rebel against the Queen?' In the late nineteenth century Indian administrators continued to regard Muslim fanaticism—and for some the word 'Muslim' was usually accompanied by the term 'fanatic'—as the greatest danger to British rule. This understanding of Muslims was translated into Africa in the 1880s in discussions of Arabi Pasha's revolt in Egypt and the Mahdist rising in the Sudan. It was nourished by the jihads which spluttered into existence from time to time in the early decades of the twentieth century in French and Italian as well as British African territories. The use of the blanket term 'fanaticism' often concealed an unwillingness, and perhaps an inability, to analyse what was really taking place in Muslim societies. It also meant that Muslims as Muslims tended to be seen as a problem, and frequently as a force to be propitiated.

Closely connected to the fear of Muslim 'fanaticism' was the fear of pan-Islamism, of united Muslim action against the British Empire. The British were right not to dismiss the threat. In principle, though to no great extent in fact,

[2] This was one of two infamous hoaxes involving the impersonation of oriental potentates perpetrated by Horace de Vere Cole, Adrian Stephen, the brother of Virginia Woolf, and others; Adrian Stephen, *The 'Dreadnought' Hoax* (London, 1983), pp. 24–29.

Muslims could regard themselves as one community and the Ottoman Caliph, as the successor of Muhammad, as a leader of that community. There had always been networks of scholars and mystics across the Islamic world. Such connections were reinforced in the nineteenth century by the increasing numbers of Muslims performing the pilgrimage to Mecca and travelling in general. From the late nineteenth century, knowledge of other Muslim societies was greatly increased by the growth of the press, notably in India and Egypt. Moreover, there was an influential Islamic thinker, Jamaluddin al-Afghani (d. 1897), who argued for a pan-Islamic response to the incursion of the West into the Muslim world. On top of this there was the policy of the Ottoman empire under Abdul Hamid II to foster connections with Muslims in British territories, whether they be in Cape Town, Zanzibar, or Bombay. The Government of India, furthermore, was left in no doubt about the pan-Islamic feelings of its Muslims, as they protested with increasing vigour at the Western takeover of the central Islamic lands. Their protests reached a peak in the Khilafat movement of 1919–24, the greatest movement of protest against British rule since the Mutiny rebellion. From 1920 the Government of India urged London to take into account Indian opinion in negotiating Turkish peace terms. Lord Curzon and Lloyd George refused to be influenced; in 1922 the Secretary of State for India, E. S. Montagu, was forced to resign on the issue. The eventual decline of the Khilafat movement proved Curzon and Lloyd George right. Pan-Islamism, as a British official often told his Indian colleagues, was 'more a feeling than a force'.[3]

Respect for Muslims as a former ruling people was another, somewhat different, aspect of British attitudes. It mingled with the sense that Muslims such as these were not unlike the British—upright and independent peoples, believers who worshipped one God, experienced in the work of government and courageous in that of war. Indeed, there was a tendency for British officers, so often successful examinees who aspired to gentry status, to be over-impressed by the company they kept, whether it was the rulers of vast acres or those with summary power of life or death over many men. Aspects of such attitudes were explicitly expressed in two of the more fateful policies adopted in the early twentieth century. Thus, Sir Frederick Lugard spoke admiringly of the Fulani in fostering Indirect Rule in Northern Nigeria, referring to 'their wonderful intelligence, for they are born rulers'.[4] In not dissimilar vein, Lord Minto, in replying to the famous deputation of Muslim

[3] For European and British attitudes to Islam and the Muslim world, see Albert Hourani, *Islam in European Thought* (Cambridge, 1991); Maxime Rodinson, *Europe and the Mystique of Islam*, trans. R. Veinus (Seattle, Wash., 1987); Kathryn Tidrick, *Heart Beguiling Araby* (Cambridge, 1981); Norman Daniel, *Islam, Europe and Empire* (Edinburgh, 1966); and Francis Robinson, *Separatism Among Indian Muslims: The Politics of the United Provinces' Muslims, 1860–1923* (Cambridge, 1974).

[4] Daniel, *Islam*, p. 465.

nobles, landowners, and ministers of native states in 1906 whose initiative was to lead to the establishment of a separate Muslim political identity in British India, referred to the deputees as 'descendants of a conquering and ruling race'.[5]

Such evidence suggests clear links between British attitudes to Muslims and policy. Of course, all attitudes were bound to be modified by context, whether rhetorical or real. W. E. Gladstone, for instance, thought Turks wholly unqualified to rule the Christians of the Balkans but perfectly qualified to rule the peoples of Egypt, a good number of whom were Christian. British Indian administrators adopted a totally different attitude towards the so-called 'aristocratic' Muslims of upper India as compared with the peasant cultivators of east Bengal. Nevertheless, the all-pervasive impact of British attitudes is striking, whether deployed through forms of Indirect Rule or the great example of direct rule, namely India.

In much of the Muslim British Empire in the 1920s and 1930s forms of Indirect Rule were in place. In Northern Nigeria the British ruled through the Sultan of Sokoto, his emirs, and the structure of Islamic government that existed under their authority. In Egypt the situation was rather more complex. British influence depended on the endemic rivalry between the King and the Wafd, the nationalist party; the support of the large landlords of the Delta and the mercantile interests which benefited from the British connection; and the presence of British troops. In the northern Sudan from the 1920s the British made a concerted attempt to rule through tribal and rural chiefs, but by the mid-1930s had discovered that these men had less authority amongst their people than they expected; they were then forced to deal directly with the urban élites. In the Gulf and along the south Arabian shore, influence was exercised through sultans, emirs, and sheikhs, with the use of the odd adviser, the despatch of gunboats, and a touch of airpower. In Transjordan, British will was exercised through the Hashemite emir, Abdullah, and British subsidies, as well as the British-officered Arab Legion on which he depended. In Iraq that will was also felt through the Hashemite monarch, the core of ex-Ottoman officials who had supported the Arab nationalist cause, the tribal sheikhs, and the large landowners whom the land and water legislation of the 1930s made into rich and even larger landowners. In Malaya the British maintained the fiction of ruling through sultans, while taking into their hands anything needed to enable rapid economic growth. Palestine, however, offers an exception. Here a form of Indirect Rule was developed through the Jewish Agency set up by Article 4 of the Mandate. When the British offered the Arabs a similar agency in 1923, unwisely they turned it down. They were ruled directly.

The general outcome of British policies of Indirect Rule or influence was to privilege conservative elements in the modern state systems of these societies as

[5] Sharif al Mujahid, *Muslim League Documents, 1900–1947* (Karachi, 1990), I, p. 102.

they developed. Islamic law, for instance, in its more conservative forms continued to be applied. In Northern Nigeria it continued down to 1960 with the exception that inhumane punishments were banned. Even slavery was permitted to exist. In Malaya it achieved greater application, as the sultans centralized Islamic religious organization and extended its control over village religious life. Forms of rule were supported which had difficulty in incorporating new elements into the political system. In Transjordan, Iraq, and Egypt the monarchies, even though the latter two had parliaments of a kind, had difficulty in expanding their base of support to embrace the new social groups which were being mobilized by economic change. As always, the nature of government helps to fashion the quality and style of opposition. In Malaya it was in part the Islamic reform of the Kaum Muda; in Egypt it was in part the nascent Islamism of the Muslim Brotherhood. The main opposition, however, came from the new Western-educated classes—government servants, army officers, lawyers—who wanted to break their way into the charmed circles which wielded state power. Their success depended in large part on the pressures generated by economic change, the management skills of those in power, and the impact of the Second World War.

There are, however, some specific outcomes of policies of Indirect Rule, or influence, which command attention. In states where Muslims formed only part of the population they led to uneven development which stored up major problems for these societies at or soon after independence. Take Nigeria, for example, the home in an ideological sense of Indirect Rule. The special policies directed towards the north meant that by the time of independence in 1960 only a small fraction of the population had been exposed to Western and secular values as compared with the peoples of the east and south. The overall impact of the British presence, not least the rapid growth of commercial agriculture, had led to the consolidation of Islam at the centre of popular identity; northern leaders conducted their own relations with Muslim states such as Egypt and Saudi Arabia. Ahmadu Bello's attempt to 'northernize' government and commerce, which also meant to 'Islamize' them, was to be expected once British restraints had been lifted. It led to fear amongst the Christian peoples of the south, to his assassination in 1966, and to the subsequent Biafra civil war. The advance of Islam remains a continuing threat to Nigeria's secular and pluralist constitution.

The Sudan offers similarities to, but also differences from, the Nigerian situation. The imposition of Indirect Rule led to the total isolation of the southern non-Muslim province from Arab-Islamic influences from the north. It was the only way the British felt they could build up the self-contained tribal units which the system of rule required. At the same time Christian missionaries were given relatively free rein in the area. The outcome was that the two halves of the country grew apart. The Muslim north kept pace with the social and political advance of the wider

Muslim world; the increasingly Christian south remained isolated and immobile. At independence in 1956 the peoples of the south were placed in the hands of the northerners. This was followed by continuing friction between Christian south and Muslim north, leading to the outbreak of civil war in 1967, which has continued on and off into the 1990s.

In Malaya the British had themselves to deal with the early consequences of their policies towards the Malay sultanates. After the Second World War, they found that the only way they could devolve power with Malay agreement was to ensure Malay supremacy in the political and administrative sphere. An enduring tension came to be established in the modern Malay state between the privileged position of the Malays and the recognition of Islam in the national identity on the one hand, and the position of the non-Muslim Chinese and Indians on the other. It was a tension which was on occasion to break into open strife.

In other areas it is possible to see how specific policies of Indirect Rule gave a distinctive shape or quality to the modern state which emerged. In the Gulf British policies of recognizing the Gulf sheikhdoms as separate entities enabled the emergence of the larger ones as individual states at independence. The British also protected them from the claims of their over-mighty neighbours, for instance, those of Iraq over Kuwait and Iran over Bahrain. Indeed, they created the environment in which these family-run small businesses could, as the wealth from oil began to flow in the 1950 and 1960s, develop as family-run modern state corporations. In Jordan, where the British-officered Arab Legion had played such a distinctive role in establishing the state, and where the dismissal of these officers in 1956 signalled the rapid diminution of British influence, the army continued to play the role of chief pillar of the Hashemite monarchy. It saved the regime in the great Arab nationalist crisis of 1955–58; it did the same in the Palestinian crisis of 1967–70.

No form of Indirect Rule had such a momentous outcome for the peoples of the region as that conducted in Palestine. Arguably, the transformation of the Jewish Agency of 1920 into the Israeli state by May 1948 was from the beginning a possible outcome of the terms of the Palestine Mandate. Britain had undertaken, against the grave reservations of the Foreign Office and her military administration in Palestine, to create 'such political, administrative and economic conditions as will secure the establishment of the Jewish national home',[6] and this is what emerged, although in nation-state form. But Britain's declared policy with the one deviation of the Peel Commission recommendations, was to establish a bi-national state. The administration of the Mandate, however, and the outcome, were disasters for the Arabs. Admittedly, few could have predicted the events which so complicated

[6] Article 2 of the mandatory instrument for Palestine, 1922, in C. H. Dodd and M. E. Sales, *Israel and the Arab World* (New York, 1970), p. 68.

Britain's rule when the first High Commissioner, Herbert Samuel, took up his post in 1920: the levels of Jewish immigration resulting from persecution in Europe, the levels of Arab intransigence resulting from justifiable anger and poor leadership, the impact of the Second World War, the Holocaust, the rise of American influence, and the decline of British power. By the mid-1930s the Palestinian Arabs were radical, politicized, organized, and using strikes and violence. From 1937–39 there was open rebellion, in particular against the recommendation of the Peel Commission that Palestine be partitioned and in general against the British presence. The Palestinian plight attracted popular concern as well as that of intellectuals and students in Egypt, Iraq, and other Arab countries. The cause was also adopted by Islamic movements; Arab governments discovered they could win support by taking up the Palestinian issue. Nor was concern restricted to Arab lands. Palestine remained a continuing issue for Indian Muslims and featured regularly, for instance, in emotional speeches and resolutions of the All-India Muslim League. By 1947 Palestine was an economic and strategic liability for the British. There seemed, moreover, to be no solution agreeable to Zionists and Americans on the one hand and the Arabs on the other. In February 1947 the British referred the problem to the United Nations, refused to implement a UN partition plan of November 1947, and surrendered the Mandate on 14 May 1948. The consequence of this imbroglio was a serious loss of goodwill from the Arab world towards Britain at a time when her position in that world depended on that very commodity. There was also the establishment of the Palestinian grievance, which was to be a focus of relations between regional powers and superpowers in the region for decades. At the same time Israel, which was seen as a stake of Western provenance thrust into the heartland of Islam, became throughout the Islamic world a focus of resentment against the West.

If the outcome of British policy failures in Palestine was to help shape the political landscape of West Asia for years after independence, the same can be said for their impact on South Asia. Here, the Princely States apart, the British were involved in direct rule. The classic Indian nationalist analysis of their ruling style was that the British divided Muslims from Hindus and ruled. Matters, however, were rather more complex. Certainly, British attitudes and British policies helped the development of Muslim organizations in northern India, but other crucial factors were the impact of both Muslim and Hindu revivalism. This said, Muslim separatism was a weak growth in the 1920s and 1930s and its political party, the Muslim League, did very badly in the 1937 general elections, winning rather less than a quarter of the Muslim seats available. That this party was able to be a serious player in the endgame of British India was because it won over four-fifths of the Muslim seats in the 1945–46 elections. Its fortunes had been transformed by the Second World War, the British need for Muslim support in that war (half the

Indian Army, for instance, was Muslim), the mistakes of the nationalist movement, and the leadership of Jinnah, the Muslim League's President. Ultimately, as Ayesha Jalal has revealed, India was divided because the Indian nationalists wished it.[7] The dynamics of the process were inherent in the federal system set up by the 1935 Government of India Act. The nationalists wanted to inherit the strong central power wielded by the British. The Muslim League wanted a weak centre, indeed Nationalist–Muslim parity there, to protect the Muslim provinces from an over-mighty centre. Ultimately the nationalists insisted on partition. The emergence of Pakistan was the outcome of a combination of forces. With regard to the specifically British contribution, certainly British attitudes and policies had their part to play in establishing a Muslim political platform. But in the final act weight must be given to the dynamics of a federal system set up to enable the British to wield all the powers they needed in India from the centre while allowing Indians to get on with the business of government in the provinces. The consequences of partition have loured over the subcontinent since 1947, bringing three wars and threatening more.

Muslim attitudes to the British varied according to their particular Islamic understandings and to their particular experience of British rule. They were subject, too, to change through time; the kind of person who was a cultural collaborator in the late nineteenth century was more than likely to be a dedicated nationalist opponent well before the mid-twentieth century. There were, nevertheless, some distinctive aspects to Muslim attitudes. The British were often seen primarily as Christians. Certainly they were people of the book, people who shared the same prophetic tradition, but by the same token they were people whose scriptures had been corrupted and whose beliefs were misguided. Early contacts could involve set-piece debates with Christian missionaries, like those which were held at Agra (India) in 1854, one of whose Muslim protagonists became a pensioner of the Ottoman sultan and the formulator of the most influential modern Muslim critique of Christianity.[8] At their most extreme, religious strategies for dealing with the Christian presence might involve attacking Christian revelation at its heart, as did the Punjabi Muslim, Ghulam Ahmad (d. 1908), who founded the Ahmadiyya missionary sect. He claimed that he was the messiah of the Jewish and Muslim traditions; the figure known as Jesus of Nazareth had not died on the cross but survived to die in Kashmir.[9] But equally, the problem of Christian power could be confronted with humour, as by the Indian satirist Akbar Allahabadi (d. 1921):

[7] Ayesha Jalal, *The Sole Spokesman: Jinnah, the Muslim League and the Demand for Pakistan* (Cambridge, 1985).

[8] Avril A. Powell, *Muslims and Missionaries in Pre-Mutiny India* (London, 1993), pp. 226–98.

[9] Yohanan Friedmann, *Prophecy Continuous: Aspects of Ahmadi Religious Thought and its Medieval Background* (Berkeley, 1989), pp. 1–46.

The Englishman can slander whom he will
And fill your head with anything he pleases
He wields sharp weapons, Akbar. Best stand clear!
He cuts God himself into three pieces.[10]

A second set of attitudes focused on the extent to which the manners and customs of the British could be followed and their material culture adopted. Thus, the Sultan of Pahang, Abd al-Samad (d. 1898), declared that he never 'fired an English gun in his life nor wished to fire one, that he preferred walking to driving and eating with his fingers, according to Malay custom, to the use of forks; that wine was forbidden by the Koran and that he did not know how to play the piano'.[11] For most of British rule Muslims debated what they could and could not accept from the culture of their ruler. Wine and pork were for believing Muslims distinctive cultural markers; the freedom of women was a greatly contested issue. Tables and chairs, knives and forks, trousers and ties, however, were widely adopted, although ties went out of fashion in the late twentieth century when it came to be thought that they represented the sign of the cross.

A third set of attitudes embraces responses to British power. The context is crucial. Muhammad Abdullah of Somaliland waged jihad for twenty-one years against the British. He celebrated the death of a British officer who had tried to cut off his retreat in 1913 thus:

You have died, Corfield, and are no longer in this world,
A merciless journey was your portion.
When, Hell-destined, you set out for the Other World
Those who have gone to Heaven will question you if God is willing . . .[12]

In different circumstances, where the fact of Britain's dominance was indisputable, there could be resigned acceptance. 'They hold the throne in the hand,' declared Akbar Allahabadi, 'the whole realm is in their hand. The country, the apportioning of man's livelihood is in their hand . . . The springs of hope and fear are in their hand . . . In their hand is the power to decide who shall be humbled and who exalted.'[13] But then there were Muslims who genuinely gloried in the destiny they shared with their foreign ruler. Take Syud Husain Bilgrami (d. 1926), the distin-

[10] Ralph Russell and Khurshidul Islam, 'The Satirical Verse of Akbar Ilahabadi (1846–1921)', *Modern Asian Studies*, VIII, 1 (1974), p. 18.

[11] Anthony Milner, *The Invention of Politics in Colonial Malaya: Contesting Nationalism and the Expansion of the Public Sphere* (Cambridge, 1995), p. 210.

[12] Part of Muhammad Abd Allah's savage poem 'The Death of Richard Corfield', in B. W. Andrzejewski and I. M. Lewis, *Somali Poetry: An Introduction* (Oxford, 1964), p. 72.

[13] Russell and Islam, 'Akbar Ilahabadi', p. 9.

guished Hyderabadi civil servant who had the major hand in drafting the Indian Muslim memorial to the Viceroy in 1906. In verse of impeccable loyalty, but questionable merit, entitled 'England and India', he trumpeted:

England! 'tis meet that for weal and woe
In calm or storm, our chosen place should be
Where honour calls us by the side of thee
Thy friend be friend to us, our bitt'rest foe
The trait'rous knave who schemes thy overthrow.[14]

There are, however, some lines of Muslim response which require more detailed examination. The first is that of jihad. For all the fear of Muslim fanaticism displayed by the British, once they had conquered a territory and consolidated their rule, jihad, although often a worry, was rarely a serious issue. One reason was that in British territories which experienced forms of Indirect Rule Islamic law continued to operate. Even in directly ruled British India Muslim personal law, the most cherished element of the *sharia* (religious law) continued to be imposed in its bastard Anglo-Muhammadan form. It had long been the position of Sunni ulama (clerics) that, if the law was upheld, rebellion could not be justified. A second reason was that to conduct a jihad legitimately there had to be a reasonable possibility of success. After Muslims had tasted the fruits of the Gatling gun and had come to appreciate the full weight of British power, they knew that they had little chance. Once this was understood, the alternative was *hijra* or flight from the 'land of war', as practised by the Caliph of Sokoto after the annexation of his territories, or by the 30,000 Indian Muslims who in 1920 fled to the North-West Frontier, many to their deaths, as part of the Khilafat protest. Considerations such as these help to explain the failure of Muslims in Africa and elsewhere to respond to the Ottoman call for jihad against the British Empire on the outbreak of the First World War.[15]

The spirit of Islamic renewal which was no longer channelled into holy war now came to energize other responses to the British presence. The broad 'church' known as reformism was one. Amongst its more striking manifestations was the Deoband Madrasa of northern India, from which stemmed the Deoband movement. In this ulama created a way of being Muslim without the support of the state. Spreading knowledge of how to be a good Muslim was central to its purposes, so it made good use of the printing press, of translation of texts into local languages, and of schools—by its centenary in 1967 it claimed to have founded over 8,000. Also central to its purpose was personal responsibility in

[14] Saidul Haq Imadi, *Nawab Imad-ul-Mulk* (Hyderabad, 1975), p. 130.

[15] C. C. Stewart, 'Islam', in A. D. Roberts, ed., *The Cambridge History of Africa*, Vol. VII, *1905–1940* (Cambridge, 1986), esp. pp. 192–202, and Gail Minault, *The Khilafat Movement: Religious Symbolism and Political Mobilization in India* (New York, 1982).

putting Islamic knowledge into practice; the movement, therefore, was profoundly opposed to any idea of saintly intercession for man with God. To ensure its independence of the colonial state, it relied on popular subscription for support. Bureaucratic in organization, one of the ways it served its constituency was by offering a mail-order *fatwa* (pronouncement on a question of religious law) service. Most followers of Deoband supported the Indian nationalist movement and opposed the idea of Pakistan; they felt they did not need a Muslim homeland to be their kind of Muslim.[16] Elsewhere no one went as far as Deoband in developing organizational structures to support what has been called a form of 'Islamic Protestantism'. In West Africa, however, ignoring the foreigner was a not uncommon response to the British presence.

For the most part Muslims could not ignore the British presence. They had to address the meaning of the new forces which were having such an impact on their lives: Western learning, the colonial state, and major economic change. This process led to the development of what is termed Islamic modernism. An important figure in this response to the West was the Egyptian Muhammad Abduh (d. 1905), who, after participating in Arabi Pasha's revolt, was exiled in the years 1882–88 and returned to be chief mufti of Egypt from 1889 to 1905. He accepted the Koran as God's guidance for man, but made other areas subject to man's personal reasoning. he wished to put an end to blind acceptance of past authority; Islam had to be reinterpreted in each new generation. Thus, he threw open the door to new ideas. These led, through his intellectual successor, Rashid Rida, who talked in terms of the compatibility of Islam and an Arab national state, towards a purely secular nationalism.[17] Abduh's ideas were particularly influential in North Africa and South-East Asia. In Malaya they informed those of the Kaum Muda or 'Young Faction', whose leaders had extensive contacts with West Asia, several studying in Cairo. In the second and third decade of the twentieth century they attacked the traditional Islam of the rural ulama and sufis which was now administered by the sultans. After the fashion of Islamic reform they criticized all practice which hinted at intercession, but equally they looked to a positive approach to issues such as the wearing of European clothes or whether it was possible to profit from a post office or a rural co-operative. Such assaults on the religious fiefdoms of the Malay sultans were at one remove assaults on the British. By the 1930s Kaum Muda formed a nationalist opposition.[18]

The most clearly defined example of Islamic modernism was that created by Saiyid Ahmad Khan (d. 1898), the founder of Aligarh College (1875), and his

[16] Barbara Daly Metcalf, *Islamic Revival in British India: Deoband, 1860–1900* (Princeton, 1982).

[17] Albert Hourani, *Arabic Thought in the Liberal Age, 1798–1939* (Oxford, 1962), pp. 103–244.

[18] William R. Roff, *The Origins of Malay Nationalism* (New Haven, 1967), esp. pp. 56–90.

followers in the Aligarh movement. The Saiyid, who was knighted by the British in 1877, was determined that Indian Muslims should come to terms with British rule. They needed to be able to command Western learning, so he provided them with a Muslim-controlled environment for learning, which was modelled after a Cambridge college and in which they were taught by men from Cambridge. They needed to be able to play a role in the affairs of the colonial state, so he made sure that they knew how to debate Cambridge Union style, how to play cricket, and how to behave at tea parties.[19] Again, they needed to have as few religious obstacles to the process as possible, so he used his personal reasoning, rejected the authority of the past, and strove to produce an Islamic theology for his time. The Koran and the Hadiths were reviewed in the light of modern science. In the process the Saiyid went much further than Muhammad Abduh, further than most Muslims would go today. Muslims went to Aligarh in spite of, rather than because of, Saiyid Ahmad's views. Many became leading supporters of Muslim separatism and the movement for Pakistan.[20]

The person, however, who brought Saiyid Ahmad's project close to fruition was not a student from Aligarh, although he was subject to Cambridge influence, having done graduate work there from 1905–08. This was Muhammad Iqbal (d. 1938), the philosopher-poet of Lahore, who was knighted in 1923. He not only developed a dynamic vision of Islamic history as one of progress but also fitted the nation-state into that progress. At the same time he performed the key service of building a bridge between the Islamic idea of the sovereignty of God on earth and that of the sovereignty of the people as expressed in the modern state. Addressing the Muslim League in 1930, he declared that the Muslims were a separate nation in India and that the north-west of India should be formed into a Muslim state.[21]

By the late 1920s and 1930s groups of Muslims were emerging who could not accept the way forward of the reforming ulama, because they ignored the facts of life, and could not accept that of the modernists and their nationalist successors, because they ignored what seemed to them to be the facts of Islam. These Muslims formed movements which have been called 'fundamentalist' but which are better called Islamist. They are well represented by the Muslim Brotherhood, founded by Hasan al-Banna (d. 1949) in Egypt in 1928, and the Jamaat-i Islami founded by Saiyid Abul Ala Mawdudi (d. 1979) in India in 1941. For men such as these the real danger was less British or Western power than the secular culture which came with it. What was needed was to capture the modern state and to use it to impose Islamic law and values on society as a whole. In Egypt in the late 1940s the

[19] David Lelyveld, *Aligarh's First Generation: Muslim Solidarity in British India* (Princeton, 1978).
[20] Christian W. Troll, *Sayyid Ahmad Khan: A Reinterpretation of Muslim Theology* (New Delhi, 1978).
[21] Hafeez Malik, ed., *Iqbal: Poet-Philosopher of Pakistan* (New York, 1971).

Brotherhood was to play a leading role in the cause of Palestine and the struggle against British rule. In the subcontinent the Jamaat opposed the Muslim League's campaign for Pakistan; it did not believe that it would be an Islamic state. These movements were the forerunners of those which throughout the former British Empire, indeed throughout the Muslim world, would in the latter half of the twentieth century compete with the nationalists for the control of state power.[22]

We should note that these modernist and Islamist responses were at the level of the state. For the most part Muslims wanted to take over the state structure that British rule had created for them. Where they did not, it was because they felt these structures left them too disadvantaged. In the case of British India, they ended up by creating a separate state which could embrace most, though not all, of them. In the case of Palestine, they could see no solution from which they would not lose. Of course, Muslims under their various British regimes were concerned about events in the wider Muslim world; Palestine was rarely far from their minds. But the prime focus of actions remained the state. As Muhammad Iqbal wrote:

> Now brotherhood has been so cut to shreds
> That in the stead of community
> The country has been given pride of place
> In man's allegiance and constructive work.[23]

In spite of the poet's justified complaint, there were supra-state responses to the expansion of British Empire across the lands of Islam. There was no shortage of pan-Islamic sentiment. In 1894 the Muslims of Lagos were in correspondence with the Ottoman sultan, in 1910 Friday prayers in Dar el Salaam were still being said in his name, while pan-Islamic sympathies were evident in Malaya from the 1890s. Such feelings were most powerfully expressed in India, where the circulation of Muslim newspapers always shot up when there were crises in the Islamic world, where poets and writers embraced pan-Islamic themes, not least among them the fate of Muslim Spain which carried heavy symbolism for the times, and where there was a powerful emotional identification with the heartlands of Islam—the Khilafat leader, Mahomed Ali, confesses in his autobiography how he contemplated suicide in the autumn of 1912 when he heard that the Bulgarians were within twenty-five miles of Istanbul.[24] It was men of this ilk who sent a Red Crescent mission to Turkey in 1912, founded a society to defend the holy places in 1913, and

[22] Richard Mitchell, *The Society of Muslim Brothers* (New York, 1969) and Seyyed Vali Reza Nasr, *The Vanguard of the Islamic Revolution: The Jama'at-i Islami of Pakistan* (Berkeley, 1994).

[23] Quoted from Iqbal's *'Rumuz-i-Bekhudi'* 'The Mysteries of Selflessness', 1918, in Wm. Theodore De Bary and others, eds., *Sources of Indian Tradition* (New York, 1958), p. 756.

[24] Afzal Iqbal, *My Life, A Fragment: An Autobiographical Sketch of Maulana Mohamed Ali* (Lahore, 1942), pp. 35–36.

led pan-Islamist activities throughout the 1920s, focusing in turn on the Khilafat, the fate of the holy places under Ibn Saud, Palestine, and the establishment of a university for the Islamic world.[25]

Against this background there were attempts to organize at a pan-Islamic level, to strengthen the Islamic world, and to resist the West. It was an idea that was always at the mercy of the ambitions of the proposer of the moment. The initiative in the early 1880s came from the romantic Arabophile and poet W. S. Blunt, who wanted to do for the Arabs what Byron had done for the Greeks; he suggested the founding of a Muslim Congress to elect an Arab to replace the Ottoman Caliph. The idea was taken up by Afghani, though not with its anti-Ottoman dimension, it was sustained in the circles around Muhammad Abduh and Rashid Rida, and almost realized in Cairo in 1907 by the Crimean Tartar reformer, Ismail Bey Gasprinski. After the First World War the Turks toyed with the idea of holding a congress to elect a caliph to replace the Ottoman holder of the office. Then the first two congresses were actually held in 1924 and 1926 with this aim in mind. In the first, however, Sharif Husain of Mecca found he could get no support for his claim, and in the second the Egyptians were rebuffed in their attempt to bring the office to Cairo. A third congress was held at Mecca in the summer of 1926, where Ibn Saud faced such strong criticism of his custodianship of the holy places that he was put off such meetings for good. A further congress was held at Jerusalem in 1931 by Haji Amin al-Husaini with the idea of winning support for the Palestinian cause. This established a secretariat which existed for some five years. From then on no major Muslim congress was held until the establishment of the Organization of the Islamic Conference in 1969 by Saudi Arabia in the wake of a serious fire in Jerusalem's al-Aqsa mosque. The charter of the Conference echoes several of the themes of the earlier congresses: the protection of the Muslim holy places, support for the Palestinian cause, and the fostering of Muslim solidarity in relation to the rest of the world. The issue of the Caliphate, however, is ignored.[26]

A supra-state vision also existed in the idea of Arab unity. This had its origin in the first stirrings of Arab nationalism before the First World War. Hopes had been raised by British support for Sharif Husain during the war and by the establishment of an Arab state at Damascus in 1918. They were dashed by the state system imposed upon the region by the Allies in the post-war settlement. Ideas of Arab unity revived during the inter-war period with the writings of Sati al-Husri, a former Ottoman official, and the establishment of the Pan-Arab National Covenant in 1931. They gained extra momentum during the Second World War, as the

[25] Mushirul Hasan, *Mohamed Ali: Ideology and Politics* (New Delhi, 1981).

[26] Martin Kramer, *Islam Assembled: The Advent of the Muslim Congresses* (New York, 1986), and for the charter and activities of the Islamic Conference, see Haider Mehdi, *Organization of the Islamic Conference: OIC: A Review of its Political and Educational Policies* (Lahore, 1988).

British declared themselves in favour of unity to win Arab support, as it became the declared policy of the Bath party (radical socialist party), and as the Arab League came to be formed in 1945. They were stimulated further by the Palestinian problem and by the determination of President Gamal Abdel Nasser to exercise Egypt's leadership in the region. In the 1950s and 1960s, as Egypt, Syria, and Iraq sought strength in the world of superpower rivalries which had replaced the colonial era, there were attempted unions. Invariably rivalries between states prevented success; failure to defeat Israel discredited such ideas altogether. Dreams of Arab unity foundered on the nation-state system in the Middle East which the British Empire had done so much to create.

There was, however, an irony here. Hopes of sustaining British Imperial aspirations also foundered on successful Arab assertion. The nationalization of the Suez Canal by Nasser in 1956, and the notable victory he won when the invading forces of the British and French allies were forced to withdraw, demonstrated to the Arab, the Muslim, and the wider world that the day of the British Empire was coming to an end.

The impact of Britain's moment in the Muslim world demands more general assessment. It enabled, for instance, some Islamic sects to develop a global presence. British policy, for instance, encouraged the Nizari Ismailis to migrate from India to East Africa, where they participated in its economic development, becoming in the process a wealthy and highly educated community. British patronage enabled the leaders of this sect, the Aga Khans, to recover their fortunes, stamp their authority on their followers, and become figures in world affairs. In a rather different way, the connections of the British Empire enabled the Ahmadiyya to carry their proselytizing mission to East and West Africa in the 1920s. Now, despite the bitter hostility of the rest of the Muslim community, they have missions in 120 countries.

The British Empire presided over a more general expansion of the Muslim world. Through sub-Saharan Africa, for instance, although the British brought an end to warlike expansion, apart from special cases such as the southern Sudan, it provided an environment in which peaceful expansion could continue to take place as Muslims spread from the hinterland towards the coast in West Africa or from the coast inland in East Africa in search of jobs and commercial opportunities. As Muslims, moreover, competed with Christian missionaries for pagan souls, they had the advantage of promoting a faith which was different from that of the dominant white man. Economic opportunity brought further expansion of the Muslim world elsewhere. Thus Indian Muslims, who had been attracted to the Caribbean as indentured labourers, came to form communities there. Then, too, Muslims in large part from Pakistan, Bangladesh, India, and East Africa, came to fashion that most distinctive of Imperial legacies, the Muslim community of Britain. Urdu, Bengali, and Gujarati became British tongues, Islamic issues became part of British political discourse, and the domes of purpose-built mosques began to punctuate the skylines of cities such as London, Birmingham, and Bradford.

Through the length and intensity of their encounter with Britain, Muslims from South Asia came to the fore in the Islamic world in terms of new ideas and organization. They had been moving in this direction in the eighteenth century, but the nineteenth and twentieth centuries saw a period of great creativity. Indian reformism gave birth in 1928 to what is regarded in the late twentieth century as the most widely followed movement in the Muslim world, the Tablighi Jama'at or 'Preaching Society'. Indian modernism produced Iqbal, whose influence has been felt far beyond the subcontinent. The figure of Mawdudi towers over the development of Islamism, while it was in Pakistan that there has been the most prolonged attempt to build a bridge between understandings of Islam and the requirements of modern society and state. Under British rule, Islam in South Asia became less a receiver of influences from elsewhere in the Muslim world and more of a transmitter. This helped shift the centre of gravity of the Muslim world eastwards, a process reinforced for a time, as East and South-East Asia became, an economic powerhouse.

Overall strategies of the British Empire helped to shape much of the state system of the modern Muslim world, and left key issues to bedevil subsequent development, among them the problem of Palestine, the relationship of the Gulf states to their larger neighbours, and the role of Islam in the identity of modern states from West Africa to Malaya. Styles of rule gave shape to internal politics, from the problems of civil war in Nigeria and the Sudan through to the division of India at independence and the significance of the military in Jordan. The British, along with other European empires, enabled Islam to spread more widely than ever before. In the process, Britain became in part Muslim herself.

Select Bibliography

GLEN BALFOUR-PAUL, *The End of Empire in the Middle East: Britain's Relinquishment of Power in Her Last Three Arab Dependencies* (Cambridge, 1991).

FARHARD DAFTARY, *The Ismailis: Their History and Doctrine* (Cambridge, 1990).

NORMAN DANIEL, *Islam, Europe and Empire* (Edinburgh, 1966).

MERVYN HISKETT, *The Course of Islam in Africa* (Edinburgh, 1994).

MARSHALL G. S. HODGSON, *The Venture of Islam: Conscience and History in a World Civilization*, 3 vols. (Chicago, 1974).

ALBERT HOURANI, *A History of the Arab Peoples* (Cambridge, Mass., 1991).

Albert Hourani, *Islam in European Thought* (Cambridge, 1991).

Ayesha Jalal, *The Sole Spokesman: Jinnah, the Muslim League and the Demand for Pakistan* (Cambridge, 1985).

Martin Kramer, *Islam Assembled: The Advent of the Muslim Congresses* (New York, 1986).

Ira M. Lapidus, *A History of Islamic Societies* (Cambridge, 1988).

Elizabeth Monroe, *Britain's Moment in the Middle East* (London, 1963).

A. D. Roberts, *The Cambridge History of Africa*, Vol. VII, *1905–1940* (Cambridge, 1986).

Francis Robinson, *Separatism Among Indian Muslims: The Politics of the United Provinces' Muslims, 1860–1923* (Cambridge, 1974).

Maxime Rodinson, *Europe and the Mystique of Islam*, trans. R. Veinus (Seattle, Wash., 1987).

William R. Roff, *The Origins of Malay Nationalism* (New Haven, 1967).

M. E. Yapp, *The Making of the Modern Near East, 1792–1923* (London, 1987).

—— *The Near East Since the First World War* (London, 1991).

18

India

JUDITH M. BROWN

The years from the outbreak of the First World War to independence from Britain in August 1947 were among the most turbulent in India's history. They witnessed the start of some of the most profound changes that were to affect life on the subcontinent. In retrospect this period has a significant unity and dynamic, and historians can readily see how significant it was for the subcontinent's own history. Change, unprecedented both in spread and depth, began to occur in the economy, society, and politics. The political changes culminated in independence. Thereafter they shaped the structure of the successor states and the nature of independent governments, and contributed to a political culture powerfully marked by the experience of political protest, and of organizing to work a series of increasingly democratic constitutional reforms. Yet the nationalist movement that claimed to speak for India's people and demanded legitimacy in place of the Imperial Raj was challenged by a variety of social, political, and religious movements, the most powerful of which contested the identity of the new nation as constructed by the Indian National Congress, and split the subcontinent in 1947, creating Pakistan in the name of Indian Muslims. Linked to the emergence of new political awareness and activity were socio-economic upheavals resulting from the impact of two world wars, major inflation, and then depression, which began to shift the economy away from its rural roots, and to undermine existing socio-economic relationships. Together these resulted in increased social movement and turbulence, and rising expectations of the new nation state from a broad social spectrum.

Yet India's own experience of the final years of Empire was not isolated. It had implications for Britain, for Imperial power in many parts of the world, and for the shape of the world order emerging after the Second World War. The subcontinent was the first non-white area to become independent of British control, a development hardly conceived of by Indians, let alone Imperial rulers, before the First World War. India had been a cornerstone of the British system of worldwide economic, military, and political power. (Indeed the preservation of routes to India had been vital in Imperial thinking about Africa.) Once India was independent, the logistics of the Empire were radically changed. So were the credentials of colonial nationalism. Independence for the oldest and most prestigious Asian part of the Empire was to be a beacon for nationalists in other parts of the Empire, as they strove for freedom and for new national identities. More directly, the Subcontinent's new international status had a lasting impact on the post-colonial world. From the Imperial order emerged two independent nations that were to become significant Asian powers in subsequent decades; nations whose damaging conflict with each other was to feed the fears and aspirations of the two great superpowers in the ensuing cold war, attracting modern armaments into the region, and deflecting vital revenue into defence and away from economic and social development. Yet the accession of India and Pakistan to the refashioned British Commonwealth, bound together by choice, mutual interests, and support rather than Imperial dominion, was central to the development of this new kind of international and interracial association, unique in the international relations of the second half of the twentieth century.

The Indo-British relationship in the last decades of the Raj is also a window on important comparative historical issues. The worth the British ascribed to their Indian Empire, and the manner in which they handled nationalist demands, compares remarkably with the attitudes and calculations of other imperial nations, particularly the Dutch and the French, whose imperial 'endings' were more precipitate and violent, with long-lasting implications for both their imperial peripheries and metropoles. Further, the often bitterly contested understanding of what constituted the Indian 'nation' and the partial nature of nation-building in India, before the British withdrew, illuminate many of the problems surrounding the nature of 'nationalism' and 'nation' in complex non-European societies under imperial control. The nature and power of late colonialism in India is the backdrop to the profound socio-economic problems facing the subcontinent and most former colonies as they reached independence.

In the context of the volume this chapter does not try to examine the totality of India's experience in the final years of British control. It focuses primarily on the political dimensions of that experience, though these, of course, reflected the changing realities of social and economic power. After a brief 'scene-setting', it explores four themes that were central to the Imperial relationship between Britain and the subcontinent in its closing stages. These are: the longer-term erosion of Britain's interests in India as the context in which the Imperial power made key decisions about constitutional arrangements for India's government, which in turn affected Britain's ability to control India in the interest of a worldwide British Empire; the emergence of a nationalist movement and, opposed to its broad claims and attempted international image under Gandhi's guidance, the realities and limitations of its support, its political ideology, and strategic effectiveness; the changing nature and increasing vulnerability of the Imperial state;

and the ways in which there are continuities between the colonial order and that established by independent states, many of which stem from the British strategy of devolving power by constitutional stages in a profoundly unequal and divided society. These issues often intermeshed in practice; but by focusing on them in turn, the dilemmas and complexities of the Indo-British relationship, and of the experience of those many Indians and British whose lives were touched by the realities of Imperial power and its decline, may become the clearer.

Indian Society and Imperial Governance

The structures through which the British ruled had taken shape in the nineteenth century, often drawing on existing forms of governance. Even after India came under the Crown in 1858 (rather than being ruled as a by-product of the East India Company's commercial operations) the British remained a tiny group in India. For climatic and economic reasons India never became a colony of white settlement, and the refusal of British taxpayers to fund either the military or civilian arms of the Raj meant that there was no money to import large numbers of paid British personnel above the number Indian taxes could sustain. In 1921 the total European population in India was just under 157,000, of whom 45,000 were women. The men included *c.*60,000 troops and under 22,000 in government service. By 1929 the number of Europeans in the top echelon of civilian government, the Indian Civil Service (ICS), was 894. Financial and manpower constraints pushed the British to construct a style of Imperial governance that relied very heavily on Indians. At the end of the nineteenth century one-third of India remained under the control of Indian princes, who had substantial domestic power in their states under the surveillance of the Indian Political Service. The remainder of the subcontinent was directly administered through a Secretary of State in London, responsible to Parliament, and a Viceroy in Delhi (the capital from 1911) who presided over an administration divided into provinces, each headed by a Governor or Lieutenant-Governor (see Fig. 18.1). The ICS was acknowledged to be the 'steel frame' of Imperial rule, its members in the districts often controlling areas the size of English counties. Buttressing the civil administration were the ill-paid and poorly disciplined police and the prestigious and well-disciplined army which, apart from external defence, was obviously in reserve for the maintenance of domestic order.[1] In the paid services of the Raj, Indians were

[1] On the Indian Army, see Philip Mason, *A Matter of Honour: An Account of the Indian Army, Its Officer and Men* (London, 1974); David E. Omissi, *The Sepoy and the Raj: The Indian Army, 1860–1940* (Basingstoke, 1994). On the police see Percival Griffiths, *To Guard My People* (London, 1971); David Arnold, *Police Power and Colonial Rule: Madras, 1859–1947* (Delhi, 1986). The best examination of the ICS is David C. Potter, *India's Political Administrators, 1919–1983* (Oxford, 1986). See above, pp. 232–35.

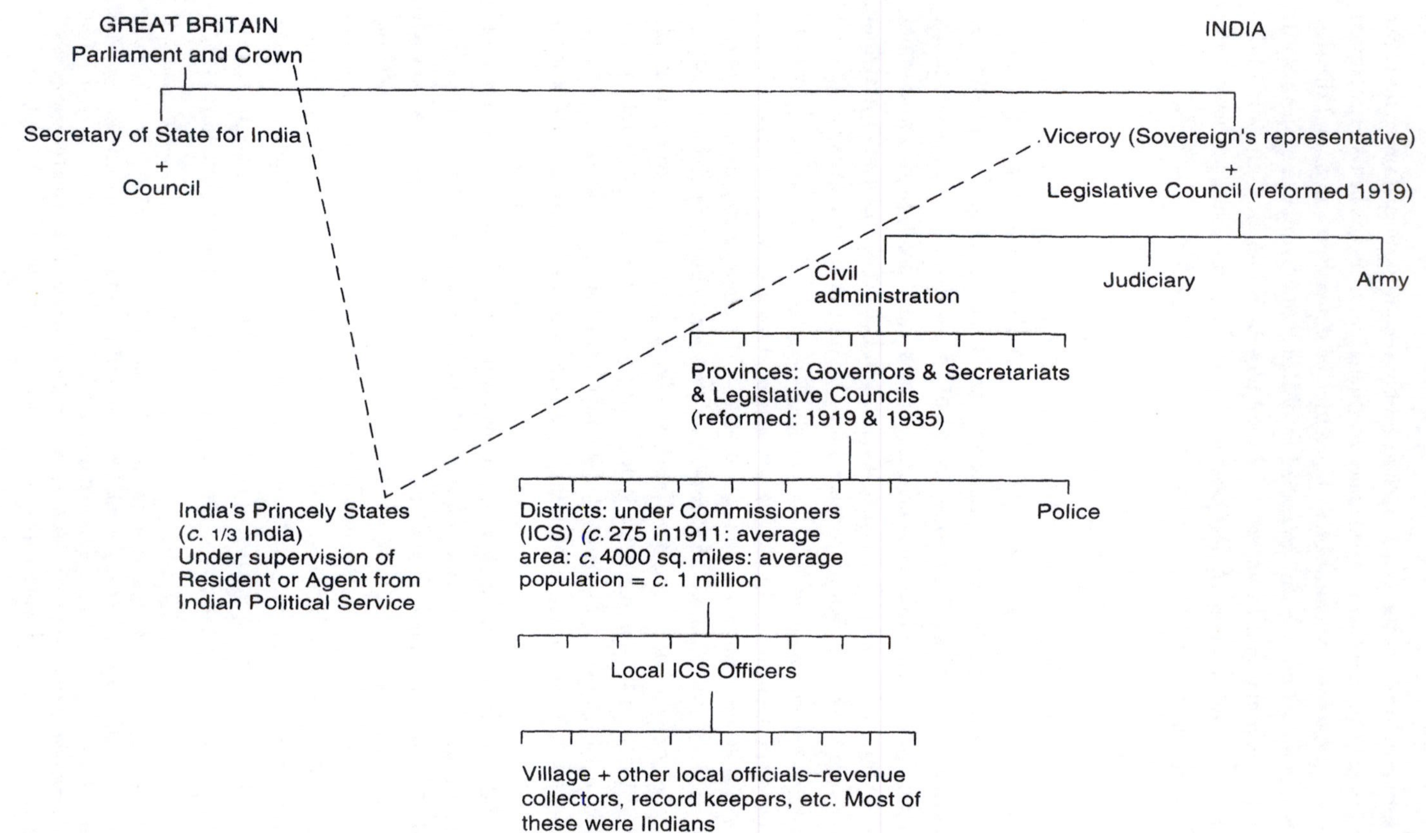

FIGURE 18.1. Government in India

crucial—from the 150,000 Indian troops, and the majority of policemen, to those who manned the courts and the lower echelons of the civil government. Between the world wars Indians were also rising to high position in the army and the ICS: by 1929 there were 367 Indian ICS men beside the 894 Europeans. No less significant were the networks of Indian allies on whom the Raj relied for both information and indirect control of its subjects. Such allies tended to be men notable and influential in their localities, whose webs of kinship, patronage, employment, and religious influence could be thrown powerfully into the service of the Raj. The Talukdars in the United Provinces, with their landed estates, or the Pirs of Sind, wielding religious and socio-economic influence, were notable examples.[2] In the inter-war period Indians became significant in a radically new way in the Imperial structures of decision-making, through two acts of constitutional reform in 1919 and 1935. By these measures the legislatures in Delhi and the provincial capitals were enlarged, and elected Indians acquired a majority and had an increasingly powerful voice in policy discussions and a large measure of influence over finance. From 1919 Indian ministers directly controlled many aspects of provincial government, a trend confirmed by the grant of provincial autonomy in 1935. Thereby the politics of Imperial governance were profoundly changed, putting new pressures on the Raj's representatives in India and creating new priorities which their London masters found hard to comprehend.

Imperial governance has to be understood also in a larger context of Imperial thinking and interests. Unfortunately for historians, the British rarely articulated theories of imperialism or philosophized about the nature of their Empire, their goals, and obligations.[3] Moreover, the honeycomb of different religious, social, military, civilian, and business interests which comprised 'the British' in India makes discussion of any uniform Imperial attitude particularly difficult. Yet at the start of the twentieth century most British people connected with India would have subscribed to a view of the subcontinent and its peoples that underlined their difference from the British—in religion, morals, society, and political identity and capacity. In India difference and assumed racial superiority were demonstrated in British patterns of residence, apart from their Indian subjects, in 'white town', in the bungalows of civil lines, or supremely in the hill stations where they took their holidays in an environment as nearly like 'home' as they could contrive. These assumptions were also evident in the racially self-contained life of the British, whose standards and hierarchies were policed by the memsahibs as guardians of

[2] Peter Reeves, *Landlords and Governments in Uttar Pradesh* (Bombay, 1991); Sarah F. D. Ansari, *Sufi Saints and State Power: The Pirs of Sind, 1843–1947* (Cambridge, 1992).

[3] Francis G. Hutchins, *The Illusion of Permanence: British Imperialism in India* (Princeton, 1976); Thomas R. Metcalf, *Ideologies of the Raj* (Cambridge, 1994).

English domesticity and gentility.[4] The reverse of this was a distaste for Indian society, particularly for Hindu customs, a distaste which focused on religion, caste, and the treatment of Indian women. Indian society was seen as decadent, irrational, and dominated by religion. In political terms Indians were seen as almost irrevocably divided by religion, caste, and language, lacking the civic virtues of Victorian bourgeois England, and incapable of either national sentiment or self-determination. Unlike their early-nineteenth-century predecessors, the British in India now felt only limited obligations to their Indian subjects. Imperial duty was to keep the peace, to protect the subcontinent's borders, to alleviate and if possible prevent famine, and to protect the supposed backbone of rural society (the 'real' India) from land loss and extortion by moneylenders; and in the much longer term to enable social and political reform by slow-working processes of education, missionary work, and foreign example. It was supposed that the Raj's duty was not to manage the economy or engage in social engineering but to protect society from radical upheaval and to permit the workings of British and Indian private investment and philanthropy.

Between the wars, however, the British were forced to reconsider many of their assumptions about India, particularly their dismissal of educated Indians as legitimate spokesmen for a modern Indian nation, and their projected time-scale for political advance within the Empire. Similarly, they were forced to re-evaluate the Imperial worth of India and the purposes India could serve in the worldwide Imperial enterprise. Before the First World War those purposes had been plain. India had to be a staging-post in Imperial communications and the base of a low-cost Imperial army. India itself was significant for providing considerable expatriate employment, while exporting important flows of unskilled, indentured labour within the Empire; for its role in British overseas investment and worldwide trade; and for generating sterling remittances to pay for the 'home charges' of the Raj. By the 1930s at least these interests were shifting, or their preservation was running the government into conflict with the politically articulate who now had influence in the subcontinent's political and administrative structures.[5] Managing the Indian Empire consequently became a complex and unprecedented political enterprise, compared with the earlier certainties and comparative simplicities of Imperial governance.

The major constraints on any aspirant all-India government (Mughal, British, or independent) were those of geography and society, particularly India's size and diversity. India was indeed a subcontinent, equal in size to Europe without Russia,

[4] Margaret Strobel, *European Women and the Second British Empire* (Bloomington, Ind., 1991); Pamela Kanwar, *Imperial Simla: The Political Culture of the Raj* (Delhi, 1990).

[5] B. R. Tomlinson, *The Political Economy of the Raj, 1914–1947* (London, 1979); P. J. Cain and A. G. Hopkins, *British Imperialism: Crisis and Deconstruction, 1914–1990* (Harlow, 1993), particularly chap. 8.

encompassing regions of considerable geographic, economic, and social diversity, often with very distinctive senses of regional identity. At least fourteen major vernaculars were spoken, as well as English, and more locally, over 200 dialects. By the beginning of the twentieth century India was criss-crossed and drawn together by major arteries of communications—a network of trunk roads, the fourth-largest railway system in the world, and the telegraph. Although modern communications and English as a common language of government and the modern professions were welding India into an unprecedented geographical and political unity, the enterprise of Imperial governance was none the less formidable. In 1921 the Indian population numbered nearly 306 million: thereafter growth became steady and sustained, as medicine and transport began to tame the old killers of famine and disease. By the end of the Raj the population was nearer 400 million; and life-expectancy at birth was now nearly 32 years. Throughout the last decades of the Raj Indian society was still predominantly rural: the percentage of the population classified as 'urban' (living in agglomerations of 5,000+) had risen from just over 10 per cent in 1921 to nearly 13 per cent in 1941. Given the growing population this meant, of course, that many more Indians lived in towns—nearly 50 million in 1941, compared with just over 30 million in 1921. Migration into towns generated considerable social turbulence in this period; and the overall rise in population began to put pressure on almost all the country's resources, including land, food, employment, and social facilities such as education and health provision. Although economic change had certainly by this time begun to generate new opportunities for wealth and employment, in both town and countryside the degree of change was limited, bringing benefits to some groups and regions only.[6] Moreover, the limited growth of taxable income meant that the colonial state, even if it had been so minded, could not have made the sort of major social and economic investments that were possible where governments could draw on the tax base of an industrial economy.

The organization of society, and social conservatism often rooted in religious tradition, further constrained the nature of government influence in the late colonial phase and after independence. Indian society was never static, despite what many colonial observers and scholars maintained. What was seen in the nineteenth or twentieth centuries as 'traditional' was often not of many generations' standing. It was often the unintended product of Imperial attempts to understand Indian social formations, which rested on the information given to the foreign rulers by privileged social groups. Over centuries Indian society has been adept at responding to economic and political opportunity, using and

[6] The best introduction is B. R. Tomlinson, *The Economy of Modern India, 1860–1970* (Cambridge, 1993).

modifying social structures to this end. But society was clearly segmented and hierarchical among Muslims and Hindus, although among the latter caste elaborated and intensified hierarchy, buttressing it with ritual notions of purity and pollution linked to occupation, demeaning those at the base of society and depriving them of opportunities for social betterment. Senses of social propriety also constricted the role permitted to women, particularly those of high social standing, for whom early marriage and a degree of seclusion were essential symbols and safeguards of family honour.

The Imperial government was extremely wary of intervention in social relations, particularly those sanctioned by religion, and would only legislate when it was assured of significant Indian support. Moreover, it had to work, as previous regimes had done, through those with local social influence who could secure it a degree of loyalty and compliance: such allies were not the sort of men who welcomed or would have benefited from radical social change.

It is perhaps not surprising that the British, confronted with so much that was strange, constructed an image of India and its peoples which emphasized the role of religion in public and private life. For example, the decennial censuses of India (unlike censuses in Britain) counted the population by religion and by caste. Before 1947 Muslims were a substantial minority, clustered mainly in the north, rising to a local majority in provinces such as Punjab and Bengal. By origin they were either descendants of Mughal ruling families and their adherents who had migrated into India from the north-west, or converts to Islam, often from among the lowest in Hindu society. Other significant though often localized religious minorities were Sikhs, Christians, and Jains, originating in various processes of external missionary activity or internal religious reform. India's religious diversity was to become politically significant in the closing years of the Raj, in part because of British perceptions of the role of religion in India.

Not until after independence did major economic change on an all-India scale transform Indian social organization and relations, breaking down old patterns of patronage and dependence, and constructing new social identities. But in places during the last decades of British rule there was evidence of rising social tension and of growing social aspiration. The development of Western education, rising literacy, the growth of modern professions, and the impact of both industrialization and commercial agriculture, however, tended to confirm existing social cleavages, bringing new opportunities to those poised to exploit them by virtue of their existing social position and resources. Literacy among Indians aged 10+ rose from 8.3 per cent to 15.1 per cent of the population between 1921 and 1941. But this new skill and consequent opportunities were unevenly spread. Women were far behind men, with four literate men to every literate woman in 1941; and townspeople were much more likely than rural folk to have access to schools and thus literacy. Among Hindus the educated, particularly in English, were those who had long traditions of professional rather than manual work. In economic terms those who benefited from commercial agriculture were mainly substantial farmers with access to equipment, capital, and credit; while those who prospered in industrial enterprise often came from castes and families with long commercial traditions and networks of credit and capital, such as the notable Birla family from the Marwari commercial community.

Politics and the Colonial State

A recognizably modern, continental style and structure of politics was the arena in which were played out issues of Imperial governance and the changing nature of Indian political identity and demand. This is not to argue that the politics which focused on the institutions and decision-making processes of the colonial state were the only politics in India, or that the main drive of Indian politics between the First World War and 1947 was a struggle between a clearly defined and accepted nationalism and a monolithic imperialism. There were many kinds of Indian political awareness, aspiration, and activity; and a diversity of interactions between the British and their subjects. But increasingly these were channelled through political structures the British had created as bids for alliances and for economical government, because of the nature and degree of power offered through them over wide areas of Indian life. Given the resources offered through the 1919 and particularly the 1935 constitutional reforms, few Indians with a material stake or ideological interest in public life could afford to be left out of the politics associated with successful use of them. However, in these complex processes of politicization a range of political identities took shape and gained legitimacy. An overview of the main patterns of political change in the context of the colonial state is a necessary prelude to an examination of some underlying issues being worked out in the Raj's final decades.[7]

The First World War was clearly a watershed in Indian politics and in the Imperial connection. The subcontinent contributed significantly to the British war effort in money, as well as man- and animal-power. (Nearly one-and-a-half million Britons and Indians left India to serve in the war. India ultimately paid over £146 million towards the war, and suffered both inflation and shortages of essentials.) This crucial contribution, and the public assertion by the Western allies that the war was being fought to defend the rights of nations, raised Indian aspirations for appropriate recognition within the Imperial system. Simultaneously the British became increasingly aware of the fragility of the Raj, clearly

[7] For details of the politics and constitutional changes, see Judith M. Brown, *Modern India: The Origins of an Asian Democracy*, 2nd edn. (Oxford, 1994).

exposed by the war's demands, and recognized that some political movement was essential. Confronted with a newly orchestrated demand, inside and outside the political institutions of their own making, for progress towards a form of colonial self-government, the Secretary of State for India, E. S. Montagu, in 1917 made a policy declaration—that the goal of the Raj was responsible government for India within the Empire, preceded by the increasing association of Indians in administration and the development of self-governing institutions. Despite the significance of this Imperial recognition of the legitimacy of Indian political aspiration, it should not be seen as a prelude to decolonization. The timetable for political reform and the attainment of the goal was seen by the British, and by many Indians, as long term; and Britain was to be firmly in control of the nature and pace of change. The declaration was supposed to be a buttress of Empire in a changing world, not a first step towards the end of the Raj.

Despite the limited and pragmatic intentions behind the Montagu declaration, the 1919 reforms which began to give substance to the declaration in the event set in motion self-sustaining processes of political change that continued into the 1930s. This is evident in terms of the constitution itself. The limited devolution of power to elected politicians in the provinces and the lack of funds for social and economic investment generated political hostility among those the British were seeking to incorporate into their alliance network. The British had accepted the limited 'success' of the 1919 scheme by the mid-1920s; and the Commission of Enquiry scheduled to report on the working of the reforms after a decade was in turn short-circuited by Imperial response to another crisis of Indian political demand—the device of the current Viceroy, Lord Irwin, in 1929, to defuse a destructive confrontation with many sections of Indian political opinion by declaring that the Raj's goal for India was Dominion Status.

Nearly six years passed, marked by a series of constitutional Round Table Conferences in London between representatives of the British, and of British and princely India, before the constitution enabling the goal of the 1929 declaration was on the statute book. In the event it never completely materialized, because the all-India provisions for major constitutional change in Delhi depended on the co-operation of a conservative bloc of princely Imperial allies: this co-operation had not been achieved by the outbreak of war in 1939, and the process was halted. However, provincial autonomy was fully operative for two years after the 1937 elections, the first held under the radically democratized system, giving elected Indians self-government in the provinces—a change in the politics and structure of the colonial state inconceivable even in 1917. The 1919 reforms also generated considerable change in the nature of Indian political activity. Many types of political interest came to be channelled into the new provincial arenas because the power on offer there, though limited, was none the less significant. A wide

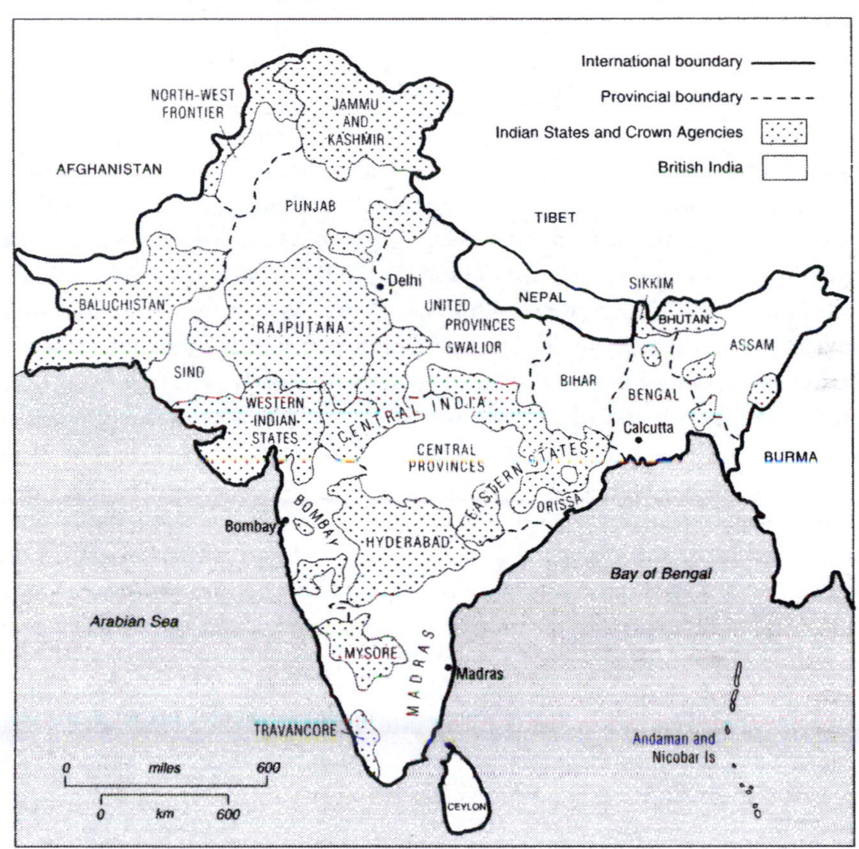

MAP 18.1. India between the Wars

range of people—educated professionals, landowners, large and petty businessmen, and substantial farmers—came to see they could not ignore the new political arenas if they wanted to influence decisions vital to their own lives, and to gain access to resources and patronage that were vital in sustaining their local positions. As the pathway to power was electoral success,[8] the 1919 reforms also triggered the evolution of a more democratic, electorally oriented political culture, and profoundly influenced styles of successful politics and political organization.

The changing nature and role of the Indian National Congress, the largest and oldest of these political organizations, was another major element of political change during this phase. Before 1914 Congress had been a loose and often divided federation of local educated men, predominantly Hindus, who met annually to make limited political demands. Between the wars it was forced to wrestle with the question of how far it represented the whole of India's diverse population, and the problem of strategy, in relation both to its support base and to the British, who, given their resources, were also powerful political operators. After 1920 Congress reorganized itself to be continental in spread, with party structures at central, provincial, district, and village level, thus mirroring the Imperial administrative structures. It also strove to attract wide support and to generate a sound financial base.[9] It attempted to discipline those elected in the Congress name to the central and provincial legislatures to follow a party line. However, in the 1920s these attempts failed. Membership fluctuated violently, some provincial (let alone more local) levels of the Congress organization never functioned permanently, and it was chronically short of funds by the end of the decade. The 'party' was still an alliance of essentially provincial groups, and provincial rather than continental priorities tended to prevail, undermining, for example any attempt at an all-India strategy in the legislatures.[10] It was not until the later 1930s that Congress really began to resolve these problems relating to its status both as a party and as a voice of national demand. By 1937–39 it had achieved electoral success and formed the governments in seven provinces, had a 'High Command' of all-India figures who could increasingly discipline members in the Congress provincial organizations, and had, perhaps most significantly, become the natural political environment in which most Hindus interested in politics chose to function, rather than adopting independent or more ideological labels.[11]

[8] After 1919 one-tenth of the adult male population was enfranchised; after 1935 this proportion rose to one-sixth, more than 30 million.

[9] Brown, *Modern India*, pp. 228–29; see also Anil Seal, 'Imperialism and Nationalism in India', in John Gallagher, Gordon Johnson, and Anil Seal, eds., *Locality, Province and Nation: Essays on Indian Politics, 1870–1940* (Cambridge, 1973), pp. 1–27.

[10] Brown, *Modern India*, pp. 232–34.

[11] B. R. Tomlinson, *The Indian National Congress and the Raj, 1929–1942: The Penultimate Phase* (London, 1976).

As Congress strove to reconcile its provincial components with an all-India policy and demand, it encountered the problem of devising the most appropriate strategy with which to deal with the British and simultaneously satisfy the needs and aspirations of its local supporters. Before the return of M. K. Gandhi from South Africa during the First World War the strategic alternatives had been constitutionalism or terrorism. Most educated Indians shunned violence as politically and socially destructive, and likely to elicit Imperial repression. Yet constitutional methods could reach an impasse if the British were determined to draw the line on a particular issue. Gandhi, drawing on his particular religious vision of the transformative workings of non-violence and on his African experience, offered a third way—*satyagraha*, or peaceful resistance to perceived injustice.[12] This was a form of non-violent but direct action with deep resonances in Hindu culture. It suited Congressmen when constitutional politics offered little movement in relation to the Raj, or when any one path of constitutional action threatened their continental unity and following. Moreover, it had considerable wider benefits. It cast the British as violent and repressive, while Congressmen adopted a highly moral political stance. It engaged a sympathetic international audience with the spectacle of a peaceful nationalist movement. Even more important, the diversity of action it could encompass (from withdrawal from legislatures to boycott of liquor and foreign cloth, from breaking forest regulations to children's singing processions) enabled Congress to incorporate into its movement people of widely different backgrounds and interests. Consequently, Congress alternated between constitutional work in the legislatures and phases of direct, non-violent opposition to the Raj—in non-cooperation in 1920–22, civil disobedience in 1930–34, and opposition to the war between 1940 and 1942. The ability to alternate between constitutional and direct action gave Congress inclusiveness and strength to move forward with political demand and sustain political momentum. It also greatly added to its popular standing and support. By the 1930s the British and many Indian politicians were amazed at the social spread and depth of the Congress appeal. The strategy of *satyagraha*, however, was not unproblematic. Few Congressmen were convinced ideologically of its value and never committed themselves to it on a more than temporary basis. Most hankered for a return to the legislatures and the powers and patronage legislative position gave, as in 1922 or 1933–34. Mass campaigns of direct action proved almost impossible to integrate and control on a national scale, drawing so often as they did on specifically local issues of discontent. Ultimately they collapsed in violence or through inertia, as activists ran out of money and energy or saw more fruitful opportunities in other strategies. There was also the unsolved problem that

[12] This discussion draws heavily on Judith M. Brown, *Gandhi: Prisoner of Hope* (New Haven, 1989).

satyagraha, despite its popular potential, profoundly alienated many, thus undercutting the legitimacy of Congress as a national voice. 'Liberal' politicians, articulate Untouchables, many Muslims and other religious minorities, and India's princes and many of the substantial landowners with a stake in the established order were deeply suspicious of Congress and resentful of its exclusivist claims to speak for India. Their hostility and continued preference for a political alliance with the British was clear at the Round Table Conferences in London, and in British ability to rule India and maintain constitutional government even in the phases when Congress had withdrawn its co-operation from the electoral and legislative processes.

Another crucial political pattern in this period was the evolution of sectional or communal politics among a range of caste and minority groups that challenged Congress's claims to be the national voice. The fairly short-lived Justice Party in Madras, the Untouchable group led by Dr B. R. Ambedkar, and the Hindu Mahasabha were examples, as was the alienation of educated Bengali Hindus from the all-India Congress from the 1930s. More critically for the construction of an Indian nation was a growing Muslim distinctiveness in politics. It is important to recognize that there was no simple, linear development of an all-India Muslim politics, claiming nationhood for Muslims; although the partition in 1947 has made such an interpretation tempting. As Indian Muslims were divided by sect, region, language, and socio-economic status, it proved as difficult to achieve unity among them as amongst India's Hindus. Various forces were, however, working at different levels of public life to convince Muslims of their distinctive religio-political identity and the need for new strategies of expression and protection in a changing political world.[13] Among these were movements of religious revivalism that originated in all India's major religious traditions in the nineteenth century, under pressure of Western knowledge and criticism, as well as Christian missionary activity. The outcome was a trend towards redefinition of religious identity, and a sharper drawing of religious boundaries, clarifying who belonged and who did not. In a time of increasing social change and tension, people often drew on religious idioms and organization to express material fears and frustrations. Moreover, the British drove on this process by 'understanding' Indians in terms of religious identifications and increasingly incorporating their constructions of their subjects into new political structures, thereby making religious identity politically significant. This was particularly the case as numbers began to count with the enlargement of the franchise. Constitutional reform in

[13] Kenneth W. Jones, *Socio-Religious Movements in British India* (Cambridge, 1989); Sandria B. Freitag, *Collective Action and Community: Public Arenas and the Emergence of Communalism in North India* (Berkeley, 1989); Gyanendra Pandey, *The Construction of Communalism in Colonial North India* (Delhi, 1990).

1909 had given Muslims separate electorates for the first time on a continental scale, though for decades the British had perceived Muslims as a group meriting distinctive political treatment. The reforms of 1919 and 1935 retained provision for separate electorates, for by then various minorities, including Muslims, had built up vested interests in them.

Once 'being a Muslim' and 'representing Muslims' became a key to electoral politics the notion of 'community' was reinforced and politicized, and became a resource for aspirant politicians. Between the wars this became abundantly clear, but the result was not an all-India Muslim political movement or demand. Indeed, the Muslim League, dating from 1906, was weak and divided for much of this time. At the provincial level Muslims worked out strategies, particularly in relation to the legislatures, which suited their particular numerical and socio-economic situation. These ranged from cross-community parties and alliances in Punjab and Bengal, where they were numerically strong enough to use the legislatures without fear of an overwhelming Hindu majority, to the alignment of notable United Provinces Muslims with Congress as the best way of preserving their position as an élite minority. Yet Muslims were aware that provincial strategies might prove inadequate when the British devolved power at the continental level. In the later 1920s various continental Muslim groups tried to suggest ways of protecting Muslims on an all-India basis as a distinctive element in a self-governing dominion. Among them was M. A. Jinnah, who retired to London in the early 1930s, disgusted at his inability to achieve a united Muslim front.[14] At this stage, Muslim political voices were not claiming nationhood defined by religion: merely distinctive status needing safeguards in a political world where numbers were becoming increasingly important. The growth of 'communal' violence at local level, however, was beginning to feed and intensify the perception and language of separation, as was the prospect of an end to established forms of Imperial governance with their inbuilt safeguards for particular groups of subjects.

The Second World War was even more critical for India than the first had been. It precipitated an ultimate crisis for British rule and for the identity of India as a self-determining nation. It also imposed huge strains on Indian resources, the economy, and the administrative structures.[15] It is useful to contemplate what might have been, had the war not occurred. For in 1938–39 it seemed that the reforms were working well, satisfying Indian political aspirations, and driving India surely on the road to a greater unity between British and princely India and

[14] Ayesha Jalal, *The Sole Spokesman: Jinnah, the Muslim League and the Demand for Pakistan* (Cambridge, 1985); David Page, *Prelude to Partition: The Indian Muslims and the Imperial System of Control, 1920–1932* (Delhi, 1982).

[15] Entry on India (by Judith M. Brown), in I. C. Dear, ed., *Companion to the Second World War* (Oxford, 1995); Penderel Moon, ed., *Wavell: The Viceroy's Journal* (London, 1973).

to Dominion Status. At the same time there was no indication that the subcontinent would split on religious lines on achieving that status. The war changed all this. For the British, Indian material support and political loyalty were crucial in the worldwide conflict. (At one stage the Secretary of State for India wrote of moving the British government to India should Britain be successfully invaded.) This desperate need for India, particularly after the fall of Singapore and Rangoon, and a desire to placate their American allies, led the British to the offer that Sir Stafford Cripps took to India in 1942. In return for co-operation now and no major political advance during the war, India would after the war have full Dominion Status or the option to secede from the Empire-Commonwealth, provided that no part of India could be forced to join the new state. The offer failed to achieve its immediate goal of Indian collaboration. The British ruthlessly suppressed the renewed movement of civil disobedience initiated by Congress and governed with the aid of officials and minority groups. Despite their determination thus to hold India for the war effort, the British after 1945 maintained the Cripps offer, and displayed neither wish nor capacity to invest the money and manpower that would have been necessary to maintain the Raj. From 1945 to 1947 their aim was to quit India peacefully and honourably, leaving behind a strong and united country firmly locked into the Empire's defence and trading structures.[16]

After the war there was all to play for in India. Who was to inherit the Raj and in the name of what sort of Indian nation? Congressmen assumed that they were the nation's spokesmen, and argued through leaders such as Gandhi and Jawaharlal Nehru that India should be an inclusive, secular nation state, where all minorities would be equal citizens. While Congress leaders were in jail during the war, the Muslim League, led by Jinnah, had entrenched itself in government and in British political calculations. Through the Cripps offer it had obtained a virtual veto on the nature of the new Dominion. Increasingly, Pakistan, a Muslim homeland, scarcely mooted before the war, became a populist slogan and a powerful bargaining counter. What it actually meant to Jinnah and other major Muslim politicians is less clear, but it probably signified a Muslim-dominated area in northern India that would be part of a loose all-India federation, rather than a separate, independent state, which made little logistical sense given the scattered location of Indian Muslims. Clearly, however, Muslim groups in the Muslim majority areas began to swing behind Jinnah and the League once the protections offered in the 1935 reforms were being abandoned by the British in their search for a quick end to Imperial rule. This greatly increased Jinnah's bargaining position. As he held out for Pakistan, communal violence escalated in northern India, often orchestrated

[16] R. J. Moore, *Churchill, Cripps, and India, 1939–1945* (Oxford, 1979) and *Escape from Empire: The Attlee Government and the Indian Problem* (Oxford, 1983).

by politicians of both communities. Prominent Congressmen began to fear that placating Jinnah with agreement to a loose federal structure would vitiate their plans for a strong state with a dominant central government able to manage the economy and tackle social issues. In Bengal Hindus, including Congressmen, fearful of the prospect of local Muslim dominance, campaigned for the division of their own province to salvage their own 'communal' interests.[17]

As violence spread and the business of government became seriously impaired by the communal impasse, Lord Mountbatten, the flamboyant last Viceroy, persuaded London that a rapid British departure was essential if they were not to end their Raj in chaos. He hurried Indian politicians into a plan for the division of the subcontinent that gave Muslims a truncated, two-winged Pakistan, divided the provinces of Punjab and Bengal in the process, and left millions of Muslims in what remained as India (see Map 18.2). In return for accepting partition, Congress inherited a secular state where the centre could become extremely powerful. The British at the time and thereafter called the Raj's ending a 'transfer of power'.[18] They underlined the consent of rulers and ruled in the ending of Imperial government and the continuing presence of the two successor states in the Commonwealth. In truth, the casualties of this 'transfer' were appalling. The Indian princes were forced to accede to India or Pakistan as the British withdrew protection from their once-prized allies against rebellion and radical politics. Far more tragically, many thousands were killed and injured in murderous communal strife in northern India. Millions were forced to migrate from homes, land, and employment to the 'safe' side of the new international borders. These had been carved through their home regions to satisfy the aspirations and calculations of political leaders and Imperial rulers, who had drawn up their own political agendas as Imperial governance began to disintegrate in the aftermath of war.

Themes in the Late Imperial Relationship

A bald outline of 'high politics' in the final decades of Imperial rule does little justice to the complexities of Indo-British relations or of Indian politics. Yet it has been suggested that there are major problems with older accounts of this phase of British imperialism in India. Despite the powerful 'myth' of an orderly transfer of power as the natural culmination of the Montagu declaration, it is evident that constitutional reforms in 1919 and 1935 were devices to re-establish Empire on surer foundations of Indian alliance rather than the manœuvres of a beneficent

[17] See Jalal, *The Sole Spokesman*; Ian Talbot, *Provincial Politics and the Pakistan Movement: The Growth of the Muslim League in North-West and North-East India, 1937–47* (Karachi, 1988); Joya Chatterji, *Bengal Divided: Hindu Communalism and Partition, 1932–47* (Cambridge, 1994).

[18] See above, pp. 334–36.

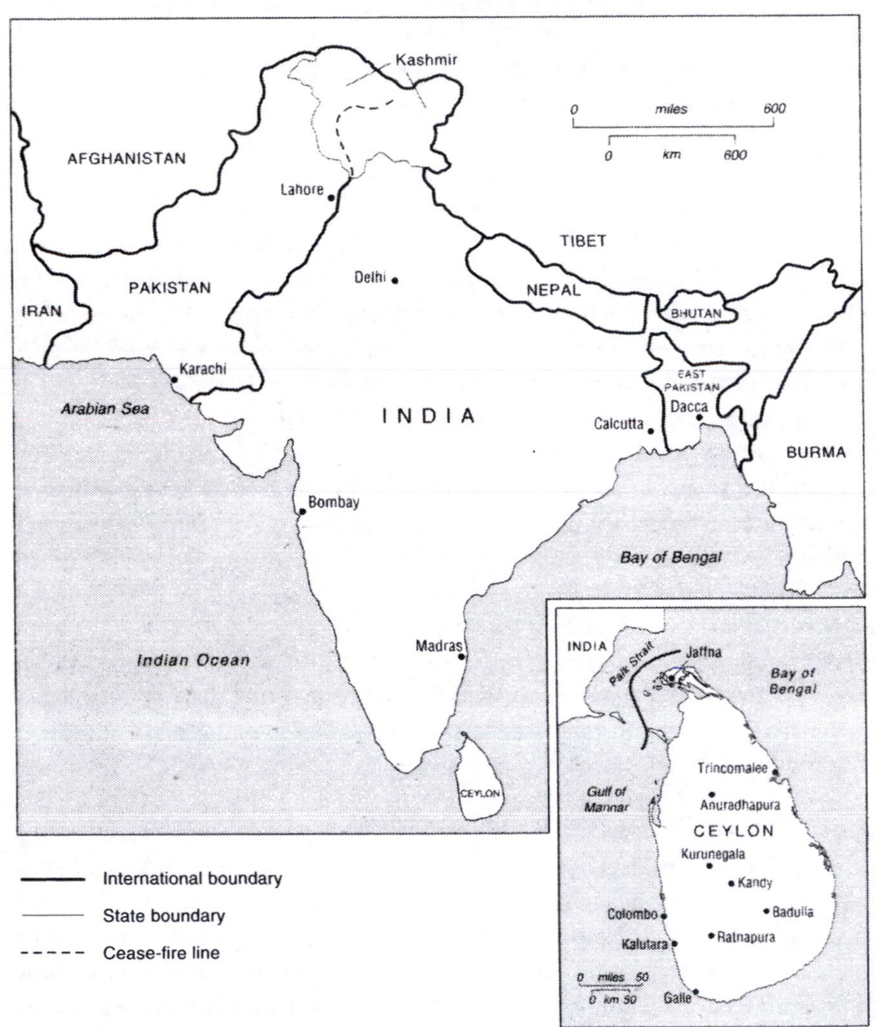

MAP 18.2. The Partition of India, 1947

Imperial demolition squad. The British had no hesitation in using overt coercion against the 'Quit India' movement of 1942, and only after the war ended did they concede that orderly withdrawal was essential—and not for India but for British national and Imperial interests. It is equally clear, however, that an account which stresses the power of indigenous nationalism is also misleading. At no stage did even Gandhi's movement to withdraw co-operation from a regime that relied on paid and unpaid co-operation succeed in making India ungovernable. Only specific localities became temporarily problematic from an administrative viewpoint. Nor, tragically, did a single national identity achieve legitimacy on the subcontinent. If such simplicities are laid aside, it is possible to discern several major themes underlying the political interactions between Indians, and between Indians and the British, during this period.

The first of these is the erosion of Imperial interest in India. Before the First World War India's role in the British Imperial enterprise was clear. She provided opportunities for expatriate professional employment, exported indentured labour through the Empire, was crucial for Imperial security, important for British trade and investment, while sound management of her public finances enabled sterling remittances to London. By the later 1930s almost all these facets of the Imperial interest were in decline because of shifts in the world economy or of repercussions to British political decisions made to elicit Indian co-operation in Imperial governance. The system of indentured labour was ended in 1917 in deference to Indian repugnance to it. The movement towards Indianization of the military, police, and civilian services initiated by the 1919 policy declaration increasingly, if slowly, limited the number and prospects of British careers in India. By the end of the Raj over 60 per cent of the senior ranks of the Indian police were still Europeans, as were the bulk of army officers. European recruitment to the ICS was periodically problematic after 1919, and had stopped completely during the Second World War: by early 1947 there were 429 European and 510 Indian ICS officers. In mid-1946 the Delhi government estimated that professional British people in Indian civilian services were earning *c.*£2m annually.[19] In defence terms, from the early 1920s India no longer provided a cheap army for British use. This was a policy shift made in response to Indian opinion newly powerful in financial matters in the Delhi legislature. When the Indian Army was prepared for the Second World War it was at London's eventual expense. This inverted India's financial relationship with Britain, piling up sterling balances in London to the tune of *c.*£1,300m in 1945.

[19] Enc. I Wavell to Pethick-Lawrence, 13 July 1946, in Nicholas Mansergh and Penderel Moon, eds., *Constitutional Relations between Britain and India: The Transfer of Power, 1942–7* (London, 1979), VIII, p. 51.

The British, however, still calculated that India was strategically critical in Imperial lines of defence by virtue of her geographical position. In 1946 they conceded that the worst-case scenario would be a weak and divided India outside the Commonwealth and possibly dominated by Russia, after British withdrawal. However, an orderly handover of power to a stable India within the Commonwealth, and satisfactory defence arrangements with India, was thought likely to secure British strategic needs.[20] In terms of trade and investment India was, by contrast with 1914, becoming far less important to Britain. British exports to India declined dramatically after the First World War from two-thirds of India's imports in 1914 to 8 per cent in the 1940s: investment in India also flagged. But Indian budgets and exchange rates between the wars were still governed on established Imperial principles of sound finance that guaranteed payment of the Home Charges and helped to stabilize sterling and Britain's balance-of-payments. After the war, however, the accumulated sterling balances, indebting Britain to India, totally changed the political calculations arising out of financial considerations. Management of India and its resources in the cause of an Imperial élite or an Imperial system was now impossible and unnecessary. India as a Commonwealth trading partner seemed a better way to secure Britain's changed economic interests.

Britain's declining stake in India stemmed from worldwide economic changes, from shifts in the domestic economies of the two countries, and from their declining complementarity. It was also the by-product of political change in India, which led the British to modify their modes of governance and to constrain their own freedom of movement, in the hope of establishing Imperial rule on firmer foundations. In this process two themes interlocked—the emergence of new types of political identity and demand, and the changing nature of the colonial state. A new style of politics developed in India at least from the 1880s in an idiom familiar to Imperial rulers. It was increasingly if intermittently continental in spread and couched in the language of the nation drawn from European historical experience. Yet the springs of this politics were deep within Indian society, and they moulded the new politics in ways particular to Indian needs and connections. The dilemma for Indians who consciously spoke the language of national demand was that nations, whether in Europe, Asia, or elsewhere, are not natural communities of affection and identity though they often draw on a range of pre-existing and deep-rooted linkages. They are to an extent 'created', 'constructed', and 'invented' in hearts and minds and in terms of organized structures. Congress leaders struggled with interwoven issues inherent in constructing a nation out of rich and often contradictory diversity. They

[20] Encs. I and II Wavell to Pethick-Lawrence, 13 July 1946, in Mansergh and Moon, eds., *Transfer of Phase*, VIII, pp. 49–57.

wrestled with the definition of Indian national identity and the relation of linguistic, social, and religious differences to such a potentially overarching unity. Jawaharlal Nehru couched his definition in Western, secular terms, arguing that these differences should all be subsumed into a secular, socialistic nationhood, which gave all Indians the status of citizens with new equalities and loyalties. Gandhi, more sensitive to the multiple social and religious identities still powerful in India, did not try to sweep away the old in a modernizing discourse. He drew on an ironically 'orientalist' and overtly religious view of India, calling Indians to return to moral foundations on which to build a new society, and bring in *ram rajya* or the rule of God, under which all religious groups would be protected and the poor would be uplifted. Most Congressmen thought little about abstract nationhood. It was easier and often sufficient to be negative, hostile to the Imperial ruler, and to work to inherit the Raj, rather than to consider basic principles of belonging. The perils of such lack of vision were to plague independent India once the euphoria of freedom had ebbed.

Congressmen and their leaders were more creative in the sphere of national organization. They painfully built up a party network throughout British India (though not in princely India) to confront, negotiate with, and at times co-operate with the Imperial rulers. They also broadened their recruitment to incorporate groups that were becoming increasingly vocal and significant politically, particularly as the franchise was extended. Moreover, with techniques of *satyagraha* they evolved, under Gandhi's guidance, not just a strategy for confrontation with the British, but a movement which also constituted a public drama, itself didactic and incorporative, proving to Indians that they belonged together and could act together in a new moral community.

The achievements of Congress were historically remarkable. There had been no similar challenge to British rule in the name of such a large area within the Empire, by peoples of non-European descent, and with such widespread support. Yet the creation by Congress of the Indian nation was limited and often fiercely contested. Despite the widening social groups, in countryside and towns, who provided members and funding, and were achieving office within the organization by the 1930s, and despite its apparently popular appeal during *satyagraha* movements and in response to Gandhi, its core of permanent political support remained the relatively educated and privileged. Those literate and articulate in vernaculars now worked with the established, English-speaking leaders, and formidable rural men joined forces with urban professionals in the Party's key structures. But those who were left out included large groups of the less privileged. Among them were the vast majority of women, educated and uneducated, who were seldom influential in Congress, although Gandhi's campaigns gave some a striking public role. Little thought was given to women's issues and place in the construction of national identity, except their changing role as good wives and mothers. Similarly the needs and potential of numerous 'subaltern' groups were ignored, except when they promised to generate temporary support for mass campaigns. Indeed, Congress leaders proved fearful of genuinely radical demands or movements. In some ways Congress's election success of 1937 limited the leadership's need for radical thought and action. Swept to power on the votes of a comparatively privileged electorate, they had no need to engage with the problems of the unenfranchised or to consider what nationhood might mean for them.

Not surprisingly, Congress's secular, inclusive vision of the nation did not appeal to those who saw that the majority of Congressmen were Hindus, and feared the Hindu ethos of Gandhi's appeals and strategies. Numerous minority groups feared for their religion or culture, or likely social conservatism under any Congress government. Of these, Muslims were the most prominent, and those with the most leverage to cause disruption to the Congress project. Others found a voice in the violence surrounding partition, as did the Sikhs, or much later, as in the case of tribals and Untouchable groups. Challenges to the Congress version of India were not solely related to numerical, religious, or social status. The tension between province and centre, sharpened by anxieties about the status of provincial vernaculars and their speakers, was always near the surface in Congress politics. It returned seriously to challenge the meaning of India in the 1950s and beyond. Further, there were small groups whose vision of the new India was moulded by genuinely alternative ideology, left wing or radical Hindu. Neither grouping was content with Congress's muted secularism, but they had at this stage little leverage outside Congress and stayed on its fringes in the hope of pursuing an alternative national vision after independence.

Nationalism and the movements organized in the nation's name were never sufficiently powerful to dislodge the British Raj. Yet they were significant elements in the sea change occurring beneath the surface of political calculation and exchange. Interlocked with them was the changing nature and growing vulnerability of the colonial state. That was made clear in the contrasting stances of the British after the two world wars. After 1918 the British resolved to re-establish Imperial strength, in India and worldwide. After 1945 Lord Wavell as Viceroy recognized declining British ability to govern the subcontinent. On the last day of 1946 he noted, 'while the British are still legally and morally responsible for what happens in India, we have lost nearly all power to control events; we are simply running on the momentum of our previous prestige'.[21] The strength of the colonial state lay partly in the loyalty and efficiency of its paid servants. Among these were the Indian soldiers who were the last coercive resort of the Raj. There were never

[21] Moon, *The Viceroy's Journal*, p. 402.

problems recruiting for the army, nor serious worries about army loyalty, at least until the final months of the Raj when communal antipathies seemed potentially destructive of army unity and strength.[22] The use of the army to maintain civil peace, however, was a highly sensitive issue. The way the 1919 shooting of an unarmed crowd at Jallianwalla Bagh, Amritsar, had fuelled the non-cooperation campaign of 1920–22 made the British deeply reluctant to take such a political risk again. Consequently they relied heavily on the police, more of whom were armed in these years. But they were still low-paid, ill-disciplined, and susceptible to local influence. They had also borne the brunt of Indian hostility during civil disobedience campaigns which they were called upon to control. When in mid-1946 in Bihar the Governor had 'no confidence' in his police, his dilemma was only an acute manifestation of a general and deepening problem of police inadequacy if not paralysis as an arm of the colonial state. This inadequacy was fed by poor conditions of service, social hostility, and fear for their future.[23]

The Indian Civil Service between the wars was a weakening 'steel frame' and by the 1940s was a cause for serious Imperial concern. Problems with European recruitment (and the need to keep Indian recruitment level with the European entry) meant that after 1919 the Service was often under strength. During the war it was stretched virtually to breaking-point by the absence of new recruits and the new burden of managing an economy and society at war and increasingly turbulent with civil unrest. Simultaneously, ICS men's prestige and patronage had been weakened by constitutional reforms that gave more authority to Indian ministers and legislators. Criticism of the ICS by Indian politicians peaked in the aftermath of British suppression of 'Quit India', and the Viceroy and Governors were deeply worried about how to protect their colleagues. The Indianization of the ICS also modified the way the Service could function as an arm of the colonial state in a time of political crisis. Indian ICS men were often close to leading politicians by kinship or shared education, and as the Raj's end became clearly imminent they inevitably looked to their future in an independent state. By December 1946 Wavell told the Cabinet's India Committee that 'they could no longer be relied upon to carry out a firm policy' unless they were assured that the Raj would last another ten to fifteen years.[24] The machinery of the Raj was running down: and, even more crucially, London made it plain to Delhi that the Labour government and Party

[22] Entry for 31 Dec. 1946, ibid., p. 402.

[23] Wavell to Pethick-Lawrence, 12 July 1946, in Mansergh and Moon, eds., *Transfer of Power*, VIII, p. 47; David Arnold, 'Police Power and the Demise of British Rule in India, 1930–47'; David M. Anderson and David Killingray, eds., *Policing and Decolonization: Politics, Nationalism and the Police, 1917–65* (Manchester, 1992), pp. 42–61.

[24] Minutes of India–Burma Committee of Cabinet, 11 Dec. 1946, in Mansergh and Moon, eds., *Transfer of Power*, IX, p. 334.

would not contemplate the Raj's re-establishment in the face of Indian opposition, as it believed this to be impossible in terms of manpower, expenditure, and both British and international politics.[25]

The crisis of the colonial state was not just related to the effectiveness of its paid servants. Its informal alliances, in many ways as important as a power base as its paid services, were also failing, as nationalist propaganda and campaigns tapped into widespread social dislocation, caused or at least intensified by the economic pressure of two phases of war-induced inflation and the intervening slump of the early 1930s. Large landowners, for example, became a liability rather than a source of local stability in an area such as the United Provinces. Meanwhile the Imperial attempt to co-opt political allies through the reformed legislatures only gave Indian politicians legitimate platforms and constitutional modes to constrain still further the operations of the colonial state. Always pragmatic imperialists, the British weighed the ideological and material costs (in India and Britain) of the Indian Raj against its benefits. After war had ended in 1945, they calculated that alliance with a free India within the Commonwealth was preferable to continued dominion. Indeed, an independent India was the only viable option open to the British, given their diminished resources and changed interest in the subcontinent. This was no failure of Imperial will, no recoil from harsh measures in principle. In other parts of the Empire they would show themselves prepared to use force to secure Imperial priorities. In 1945–46 the British recognized, however reluctantly, that in the particular and unique circumstances of post-war India an Imperial Raj no longer achieved the goals they sought.

A final theme underlying the politics of these years is the continuity between Imperial India and what succeeded the Raj. 'New' nations claim new beginnings as part of their nation-making strategies, as Nehru did so poignantly in his famous 'tryst with destiny' speech in August 1947. But there was far more continuity than change after 1947. This was predictable in a situation where Imperial governance ended by agreement rather than in revolutionary conflict. Imperial 'endings' powerfully affect what comes after. On the subcontinent the successor states inherited a structure of administration designed to achieve Imperial ends rather than goals of national reconstruction. India and Pakistan inherited a Raj that was élitist in nature and ethos, and was designed to control the population and ensure stability rather than involve itself in social and economic change. The Raj left a reservoir of coercive structures and precedents, which the citizens of both countries were to learn had remained despite the British departure. Moreover, the unresolved issue of what constituted a nation on the subcontinent remained to plague and destabilize both new nation states. In Pakistan, Islam proved an

[25] Pethick-Lawrence to Wavell, 25 Nov. 1946, in Mansergh and Moon, eds., *Transfer of Power*, IX, p. 174.

ambiguous foundation for nationhood, particularly as allegiance to the notion of Pakistan had been so recent, was often pushed on by calculation rather than ideology, and lacked the deep-rooted organizational structures equivalent to those on which Congress had built a new idea of 'India'. The role of Islam and the relation between the component areas of Pakistan soon challenged its very existence. In India too, the limitations of the nation as constructed by Congress were soon manifested in major political problems, such as the role of India's different languages, relations between linguistic regions and the political structure, and the needs and demands of the many who had been effectively excluded from the nation before 1947, despite Gandhi's idealistic definitions of home rule.

The experience of what turned out to be the closing decade of the British Raj raises many issues that became familiar in other parts of the British Empire. The more historians know, however, the weaker become older certainties of historical interpretation. The Indian experience suggests that the Raj was clearly changing in the twentieth century and proved capable of fairly profound adaptation in response to changing conditions. Its precipitate end was caused by pressure of war rather than by nationalist demand or liberal Imperial design. India also shows how nations and empires are both political enterprises and constructions, operating in symbiosis. By understanding an Imperial enterprise, its priorities, strengths, and weaknesses, the observer can better understand the successor nations and the profound problems they faced in the post-Imperial years.

Select Bibliography

CHRISTOPHER BAKER, GORDON JOHNSON, and ANIL SEAL, eds., *Power, Profit and Politics: Essays on Imperialism, Nationalism and Change in Twentieth-Century India* (Cambridge, 1981).

JUDITH M. BROWN, *Gandhi: Prisoner of Hope* (New Haven, 1989).

—— *Modern India: The Origins of an Asian Democracy*, 2nd edn. (Oxford, 1994).

SANDRIA B. FREITAG, *Collective Action and Community: Public Arenas and the Emergence of Communalism in North India* (Berkeley, 1989).

JOHN GALLAGHER, GORDON JOHNSON, and ANIL SEAL, eds., *Locality, Province and Nation, Essays on Indian Politics, 1870–1940* (Cambridge, 1973).

RANAJIT GUHA, ed., *Subaltern Studies, I–* (Delhi, 1982–).

AYESHA JALAL, *The Sole Spokesman: Jinnah, the Muslim League and the Demand for Pakistan* (Cambridge, 1985).

CLAUDE MARKOVITS, *Indian Business and Nationalist Politics, 1931–39: The Indigenous Capitalist Class and the Rise of the Congress Party* (Cambridge, 1985).

THOMAS R. METCALF, *Ideologies of the Raj* (Cambridge, 1994).

R. J. MOORE, *The Crisis of Indian Unity, 1917–1940* (Oxford, 1974).

R. J. MOORE, *Escape from Empire: The Attlee Government and the Indian Problem* (Oxford, 1983).

JAWAHARLAL NEHRU, *An Autobiography* (London, 1936).

DAVID E. OMISSI, *The Sepoy and the Raj: The Indian Army, 1860–1940* (Basingstoke, 1994).

DAVID PAGE, *Prelude to Partition: The Indian Muslims and the Imperial System of Control, 1920–1932* (Delhi, 1982).

GYANENDRA PANDEY, *The Construction of Communalism in Colonial North India* (Delhi, 1990).

DAVID C. POTTER, *India's Political Administrators, 1919–1983* (Oxford, 1986).

IAN TALBOT, *Provincial Politics and the Pakistan Movement: The Growth of the Muslim League in North-West and North-East India, 1937–47* (Karachi, 1988).

B. R. TOMLINSON, *The Indian National Congress and the Raj, 1929–1942: The Penultimate Phase* (London, 1976).

—— *The Political Economy of the Raj, 1914–1947: The Economics of Decolonization in India* (London, 1979).

—— *The Economy of Modern India, 1860–1970* (Cambridge, 1993).

19

Ceylon

S. R. ASHTON

Ceylon* has several claims to occupy a special place in British colonial history (Map 18.2). Apart from the old colonies of settlement which became Dominions in the nineteenth and early twentieth centuries, Ceylon was the first of the Colonial Office territories to achieve independence. The means by which the island became self-governing in February 1948 were portrayed at the time as a bold experiment in Western-style parliamentary government in a plural society. The justification for the experiment was that Ceylon had demonstrated its political maturity over nearly two decades by successfully upholding one of the most advanced constitutions throughout the Colonial Empire. The colony had enjoyed universal suffrage since 1931—twenty years ahead of its adoption in India and only two years after its introduction in Britain. In the areas of economic and social activity the island Similarly enjoyed a reputation as an advanced colony. Although not self-sufficient in food, it possessed a buoyant economy based on three principal plantation crops—tea, rubber, and coconut products. A University College, established at Colombo in 1921, was converted into the University of Ceylon in 1942 and, at the time of independence, the government was implementing a scheme of free education from the kindergarten to university.

Especially important from a British viewpoint was the regional context, in which the transfer of power in Ceylon was peaceful, orderly, and negotiated by consent. The communal violence which cast such a long shadow over the transfers of power on the Indian subcontinent was entirely absent in Ceylon. Equally, Ceylon did not, as did Burma, commence its independence hovering on the brink of civil war. Ceylon's new government coveted its status as a member of the Commonwealth and freely negotiated a defence treaty with Britain. In short, not only was Ceylon viewed as a 'model' colony, it was also viewed as the model for others to follow. The colonies next in line—the Gold Coast and Malaya—were both said by British officials in 1948 to be at least a generation away from self-government. As one official, actively involved in the Ceylon independence

* The country was renamed Sri Lanka in 1972. In Sinhala or Sinhalese, Sri Lanka means 'resplendent isle'.

negotiations, put it: 'If Ceylon was the forerunner, it had a long start.'[1] And when anticipating in the early 1950s the future development of the Commonwealth, the motto in Whitehall was that more Ceylons and fewer Burmas were needed to maintain the organization's cohesion and credibility.[2]

Ceylon's place in colonial history, however, is not confined to its status as Britain's model colony. In at least three ways, the manner in which the island became independent in 1948 adds significantly to the range of interpretations put forward by historians to explain and place in context the much wider subject of the end of colonial empires more generally. First, Ceylon demonstrates that it was not always necessary to resort to revolutionary nationalism or mass nationalism of a violent or non-violent kind to achieve independence. In certain circumstances the politics of moderation and co-operation with the colonial power could be highly effective. The argument in this respect works both ways, because there were lessons here for the British as well. When contrasted with their attitude towards demands for political advance in both India and Burma immediately after the Second World War, the hesitant and reluctant response of the British towards similar claims advanced on behalf of Ceylon came perilously close to conveying the impression to nationalists elsewhere that they stood to gain more if they were confrontational and disloyal. Only at the last moment did the British government realize that Ceylon's independence could be used to persuade other colonial nationalists that loyalty and co-operation might ultimately pay similar political dividends. Secondly, Ceylon reveals that, in plural societies, colonial endings frequently emphasized not the much-sought-after national unity and social harmony of nationalist rhetoric but rather the more stubborn and persistent reality of ethnic diversity and competition. Moreover, the transfer of power revealed post-independence problems for the future nation state. Indeed, from a British viewpoint, the bold experiment in parliamentary government in Ceylon, which had begun in 1931 and which reached its seemingly logical conclusion in 1948, was in fact recognized at the time of independence as a gamble and one taken as much with British commercial and strategic interests in mind as with concern for Ceylon's future stability and political cohesion. Finally, Ceylon's experience provides a necessary counterpoint to the view that nationalism and the onset of national independence were essentially modernizing processes in which the dynamics of education,

[1] Sir Charles Jeffries, *The Transfer of Power* (London, 1962), p. 62. Jeffries was Joint Deputy Under-Secretary of State at the Colonial Office at the time of Ceylon's independence.

[2] The need to secure more Ceylons and fewer Burmas was first stated in a paper circulated at the Conference of African Governors in 1947. 'The Colonies and International Organisations', African Governors' Conference Paper, AGC 17 [Nov. 1947], C[olonial] O[ffice] 847/36/4, no. 18, reproduced in Ronald Hyam, ed., *The Labour Government and the End of Empire, 1945–1951*, British Documents on the End of Empire Project (BDEEP) (London, 1992), IV, Doc. 64. On this point, see also chap. 14 by Wm. Roger Louis, pp. 336–337.

economic development, and political progress (whether of the revolutionary or liberal variety) took precedence over traditional beliefs founded on religion and custom. On the contrary, in Ceylon's case the triumph of moderate nationalism coincided with a resurgence of religion as a significant force in the political process. Not only did it nurture the earliest nationalist stirrings; it also underpinned a sense of ethnic identity among each of the island's communities both before and after 1948, and eventually destroyed national unity.

Socially conservative, politically moderate, and tactically gradualist most appropriately describe the élites which led the movement for the island's independence. Their conservatism was in part a legacy of their forebears having assimilated Western influences for over four centuries. From the early sixteenth century the maritime districts of Ceylon had been ruled successively by the Portuguese and the Dutch before the British intervened at the end of the eighteenth century. These same areas became a British Crown Colony in 1802, and in 1815, after a short military campaign, the independence of the indigenous Kingdom of Kandy in the central highlands of the island was brought to end. The island became a unified administrative whole under reforms instituted by the British in the 1830s.

Western influences were uneven throughout the island. They were most evident in the maritime districts of the south-west where the Europeans had made their earliest and most lasting inroads. Centred upon the capital, Colombo, these areas were mainly inhabited by the low-country Sinhalese. The degree to which, by the end of the nineteenth century, the élites among this group had assimilated Western culture and adopted Western lifestyles could be seen in a variety of ways which were not confined to their English education and their command of the English language. Western influences were equally evident in the food they ate, the clothes they wore, the literature they read, and the sports they engaged in. But the most enduring influence was in the area of religion. The census of 1891 established that there were over 300,000 Christians in the island, most of them Roman Catholic who were drawn mainly, but by no means exclusively, from the low-country Sinhalese.

Ceylon's élites were far more westernized than their counterparts in any part of India. But they were also, in the areas of political activity and organization, far less politicized. For this the conservatism of Ceylonese society is only a partial explanation.[3] Equally significant were the nature of the administrative and economic regimes constructed by the British as well as the caste divisions within the élites.

[3] Ceylonese (the expression today is Sri Lankans) refers to all the people of the island, as opposed to the separate communities—Sinhalese, Tamil, Muslim, and others.

British administration in Ceylon afforded far fewer political outlets to the élites than did its counterpart in India. The essential task of Britain's Indian administration was to ensure that India's revenues were sufficient to serve both India's domestic and Britain's Imperial purposes. To this end, especially in the second half of the nineteenth century, means had to be found for raising new sources of revenue without provoking a violent reaction and thus undermining the security of the state. As they made new demands on their Indian subjects and delved deeper into the inner workings of Indian society, the British needed a steadily growing supply of local agents and collaborators who were enlisted to work for Imperial ends by systems of nomination, representation, and election at district, municipal, and provincial levels. Indian political activity was frequently stimulated by these increased opportunities of participation and patronage. By contrast, British administration in Ceylon was much more rigid and uncompromising. Ceylon had an Imperial role to play—as a naval base from which, at the beginning of the nineteenth century, Britain could protect its Indian possessions against the French and thereafter safeguard its interests in the Indian Ocean and protect the trade routes to the eastern Empire—but the island's strategic importance in no sense matched that of India. In consequence, Ceylon's spending programmes were much more limited, as indeed were its sources of income. Education was still largely in the hands of Christian missionary enterprise. Even as late as 1925 there was no income tax and no general land tax. Moreover, given that Ceylon was that much smaller than India—the respective populations at the turn of the century were 3 million and 280 million—the island's administration was much simpler and easier to control. In short, while the British in Ceylon used influential Ceylonese as intermediaries between themselves and the local population, they did not depend to the same extent on local collaborators. This is most clearly illustrated in the area of the Ceylon Civil Service, the upper reaches of which remained almost exclusively in European hands until the 1920s. With only limited political opportunities open to them, the élites in Ceylon had correspondingly fewer outlets which they could exploit for purposes of mobilization and organization.

The island's economic development in the nineteenth century also served as a restraint on overt political activity directed against the colonial power. Experimentation in plantation crops began in the 1830s. At the outset coffee production dominated Ceylon's economy. With the main plantations having been established in the Kandyan provinces, the expansion of coffee not only ended the isolation of the former Kandyan kingdom; it also promoted the economic and commercial unification of the island through a network of roads and railways. Afflicted by an incurable leaf disease from the early 1870s and facing competition from growers in Brazil, coffee went into decline and was destroyed by the end of the nineteenth century. However, the plantation economy did not disappear with the collapse of coffee. Instead, it continued to expand as coffee was replaced by tea, rubber, and coconut. In the long term the predominance of these three commodities inhibited attempts to diversify the economy and, in particular, to open up new areas of peasant agriculture and thus reduce Ceylon's dependence on food imports, but in the short term there were significant gains as Ceylon began to rival Singapore and parts of the Federated Malay States as a modern, export-led economy. But it was equally significant that the plantations were not dependent on foreign capital, ownership, and enterprise. At every stage the indigenous population was involved. While their share of the tea industry was admittedly modest (70 per cent of tea estates were owned by expatriates), local capitalists, smallholders, and peasants dominated the coconut industry (90 per cent of coconut production being in Ceylonese hands) and were influential factors in rubber. Playing a more prominent role in plantation agriculture than their counterparts elsewhere in the tropical Empire, local Ceylonese capitalists had a vested interest in the continued success of the colonial economy. It was not in their interests to disturb it. Although a temperance movement emerged at the turn of the century, the radical politics of boycott and *swadeshi* (reliance on indigenous produce) which were so evident in the Indian nationalist reaction against the partition of Bengal in 1905, were never part of Ceylon's political agenda.

A further factor inhibiting concerted political action was the endemic caste competition and rivalry within the Ceylonese élites, both Sinhalese and Tamil. The highest ranking indigenous officials were the *mudaliyars* or headmen, a local aristocracy drawn from the *goyigama* (farmer) caste among the Sinhalese and the *vellala* caste among the Tamils of the north. At the apex of the social hierarchy, these castes traditionally owed their position to hereditary privilege and government service. Within the low-country Sinhalese community, the *goyigama* élites were able to consolidate their position during the early years of British rule by being the first to take advantage of the new economic and educational opportunities. But as the nineteenth century progressed education and commercial wealth ceased to be a *goyigama* monopoly. They found their privileged position under challenge from other castes, most notably the *karava* (fisher) caste, one of the most assertive and affluent of the new class of Sinhalese capitalists, and also from the *salagama* (traditionally 'cinnamon peelers') and the *durava* (traditionally 'toddy-tappers'). At the political level, caste differences played a significant part in determining the outcome of the first election in 1911 to choose an 'educated Ceylonese' representative on the colony's Legislative Council. In 1926 Sir Hugh Clifford, Ceylon's Governor, recalled the outcome of the contest which involved an electorate of fewer than 3,000 Sinhalese, Tamil, and Muslim voters who qualified on the basis of their educational, professional or income qualifications:

the present Legislative Councillors are rather peculiarly vulnerable on the subject of caste. It is within the memory of all of us, for instance, that the senior Tamil member, Sir Ponnambalam Ramanathan, owed his election to the then newly reformed Council in 1911, as the representative of the Educated Ceylonese Community, to the fact that as a high caste man he could command the support of the Vellala, Goigama [*goyigama*], or 'Cultivator' vote among not only his own countrymen but among the Sinhalese also. The opposing candidate, Sir Marcus Fernando, who is now a member of my Executive Council, is a Sinhalese and a man of high character and standing. He, however, was a Karawe [*karava*]—viz. Fisher caste—and that fact sufficed to render him unacceptable to the Sinhalese Vellalas, or even to the Kalagamas [*salagamas*], or Cinnamon-Peelers, all of whom preferred to be represented by a man of a different race, rather than by one of a lower caste. It is also notorious in Ceylon that the agitation for the reform of the Constitution had as its origin the revolt of the rich, well-educated and ambitious members of the Karawe caste against the high-caste Vellalas who, until then, had always been nominated by the Governor to represent the Sinhalese community in the Legislative Council.[4]

Despite westernization and the prominent position occupied by Ceylonese professing the Christian faith, Ceylon remained firmly in the South Asian religious and cultural tradition in which the two great faiths of Buddhism and Hinduism coexisted. Significantly, the first nationalist stirrings in the last quarter of the nineteenth century took the form, not of élite petitioning for a greater say in the government of the country but of a religious revival which developed as a reaction to Christian missionary activity. This was a mirror image of the cognate process in India. All indigenous religions in Ceylon were affected and involved, but the Buddhist revival was the most significant development.

From the 1840s Christian missionaries had staged public debates or verbal confrontations designed to assess the relative merits of their own faith and those of Buddhism. The hidden agenda was to use such occasions to demonstrate the superiority of Christianity and to gain converts. Two decades later eminent members of the Buddhist priesthood were able to turn the tables by initiating debates and by more than holding their own in defending their own faith. Five such debates were held between 1865 and 1873, the most notable being the Panadura debate of 1873 when the Revd Migettuvatte Gunananda's bold and assertive presentation of his arguments in defence of Buddhism earned for him a reputation as the scourge of missionaries. Support for the Buddhist cause came from the United States in the shape of Colonel H. S. Olcott, the founder in 1875 of the Theosophical Society. American newspaper reports of the Panadura debate prompted Olcott to exchange correspondence with Migettuvatte Gunananda and to send him vast quantities of pamphlets and articles attacking Christianity, which Gunananda translated into Sinhalese and distributed throughout the island.

[4] Clifford to L. S. Amery, Secretary of State for the Colonies, 20 Nov. 1926, CO 537/692.

Olcott visited Ceylon in 1880 with Madame Blavatsky, his Russian colleague. Their tour was greeted with great excitement and scenes of religious fervour. Olcott was instrumental in establishing a Buddhist education movement with an education fund. He assisted with the design and adoption of a distinctive Buddhist flag and he was also behind the movement to have the *Vesak* festival (a commemoration of the Buddha's birth, enlightenment, and death) declared a public holiday.

Further stimulus to the Buddhist revival was provided by the temperance movement in the early years of the twentieth century. Temperance societies flourished in the western and southern provinces. Their targets were foreign vices and the Western values which tolerated and encouraged them. Increasingly for the Sinhalese, Buddhism came to be associated with patriotism and national regeneration.

Significantly, however, no attempt was made to channel the emotions generated by the temperance agitation into a sustained and organized political movement. Nor did this happen after the Sinhalese–Muslim riots of 1915, when an outbreak of religious and economic hostility between the two groups came to be regarded by the colonial government as sedition and as part of an organized conspiracy by the Sinhalese to overthrow British rule. The government's response was one of panic and severe repression during which martial law was declared and several arrests made, including those of Sinhalese public figures who were later to lead the island's independence movement. In fact it was not until 1919, over thirty years after the formation of the sister organization in India, that a Ceylon National Congress was established.[5] The parallel with India is pertinent, for it was largely the visit to India by Edwin Montagu, the Secretary of State, and his 1917 declaration on responsible government as the goal of British policy in India, that persuaded Ceylon's political élites to reach the somewhat overdue conclusion that their own appeal to be allowed an increasing share in the government of the island would not be taken seriously unless there existed an organization which claimed to represent the people of Ceylon.

From the outset, the Ceylon National Congress was an overwhelmingly conservative body. It was not until 1942 that it put forward independence as its main political goal. Although it claimed to represent all of the island's communities and had a Tamil as its first President, over the years of its existence it was dominated by the small, westernized middle class from the low-country Sinhalese. Its proceedings were distinctly undemocratic; effective power rested not with delegates assembling in an annual conference but with an inner caucus on an executive

[5] There were, however, as in the case of its Indian counterpart, antecedents to the Ceylon National Congress, notably the Ceylon National Association, founded in 1888, and the Ceylon Reform League, founded in 1917.

committee which met once a month. All attempts in the 1920s by a younger and more radical minority within Congress who wanted to convert the organization into a more dynamic political force were thwarted by the conservative leadership.

In its membership and leadership, ideology, and methodology, the Ceylon National Congress never evolved much beyond the position of the Indian National Congress in 1919. It never underwent a Gandhian transformation. The conservative nature of the island's principal political organization is one reason why, despite its close proximity to the Indian mainland, Ceylon never experienced a civil disobedience movement on Gandhian lines.[6] There were, however, other explanations. India was hardly an appropriate model for the island's majority community. Amongst the Sinhalese, both low-country and Kandyan, there was, as will be seen, considerable apprehension over the numbers of Indian immigrants in the island and over the possibility that an independent Indian government might exploit the presence of these immigrants to exercise a more general and unwelcome influence over the island's politics. Equally relevant were economic issues. The close identification between the interests of local and foreign capitalist enterprise often resulted in the former's dependence on the latter. Ceylon's export trade, for instance, was dominated almost exclusively by expatriate trading firms. The Ceylonese had established little in the way of banking or credit institutions. Practical considerations were also significant. Ceylon did not possess the indigenous industrial houses which in India provided the nationalist cause with much-needed sources of income. Moreover, the problem of unemployment among the educated did not exist in Ceylon to the same extent that it did in India. The smaller number of Ceylonese graduates were more easily absorbed within the economy and the professions. Ceylon did not, therefore, possess an army of discontented foot-soldiers who could conduct civil disobedience protest. Besides, with the island's entire population being little larger than that of the largest district in a British Indian province, the numbers were simply not available to mount protests on a large scale. But above all, there were compelling political reasons which militated against civil disobedience. The island's aspiring politicians were, in fact, doing rather well out of the political order. Whatever its imperfections in their eyes, a new constitution implemented in Ceylon in 1931 endowed the leading politicians with positions of authority unimaginable in most of Britain's colonial possessions. If popular mobilization was never the political style of Ceylon's élites, it was equally not in their political interests. For these groups, the road to power lay in the exclusive and dignified confines of the council chamber, not in the demagoguery of the towns and villages.

[6] For the discussion which follows see especially James Manor, *The Expedient Utopian: Bandaranaike and Ceylon* (Cambridge, 1989), pp. 98–104.

The establishment of the Ceylon National Congress in 1919 was speedily followed by significant reforms of the island's constitution. Two new constitutions were introduced in quick succession in 1921 and 1924. The combined effect was to produce, for the first time, a non-official majority in the island's Legislative Council. Under the reforms of 1924 the non-officials were chosen partly by nomination and partly by election in both communal and territorial constituencies. The British calculated that with support from the nominated representatives and those elected by the minorities, the government would be able to command sufficient legislative support. Instead, however, throughout the 1920s Ceylon became a classic example of what British officials described as the exercise of power without responsibility. With non-officials having no responsibility for the policies of the government but possessing instead a seemingly endless capacity to criticize and harass it, especially over the sensitive issues of the privileges and salaries of British civil servants, the result was, as Sir Hugh Clifford put it, that the Ceylonese were being taught, not how to govern 'but merely how to weaken and disorganise the administrative machine and how to render good government difficult, if not impossible'.[7]

A solution to this problem was one of the main tasks facing a small commission chaired by Lord Donoughmore which was appointed to examine the Ceylon constitution in 1927. When it reported in 1928 the Commission suggested that the existing Legislative Council should be replaced by an elected State Council with both legislative and executive functions. The State Council would be divided into seven executive committees, each of which would elect a chairman, and these seven chairmen, together with three British officials holding the most senior executive departments, would form a Board of Ministers with responsibility for the conduct of government business. This committee system of government was based on that then operating in the League of Nations and in the London County Council. In Ceylon's case it was intended as a means to educate the Ceylonese in the art of responsible government.[8] A conventional cabinet or parliamentary system of government was deemed premature because the island had yet to develop distinct political parties, its political loyalties instead dividing first on caste and then increasingly on communal lines.

7 Clifford to Amery, 20 Nov. 1926, CO 537/692.

8 And as such it was received in the Colonial Office with a good deal of scepticism. Sir H. Wilson, the Permanent Under-Secretary of State, felt that in agreeing to the Donoughmore proposals the CO was 'leaping in the dark'. Minute by Wilson to Lord Passfield, Secretary of State for the Colonies, 9 Aug. 1929, CO 54/894/10. The Donoughmore recommendations as a whole, and especially those relating to the franchise, were indeed for the period remarkably progressive. That they were implemented at all owed much to the fact that a Labour government was in office in Britain. The relatively smooth transition to the Donoughmore constitution should be contrasted with the bitter controversies which plagued the National Government and the Conservative Party in Britain over the 1935 Government of India Act.

With a view to the eradication of communalism, the Donoughmore Commission made its most startling and controversial recommendation. The commissioners argued that communal representation had no long tradition in Ceylon; and that only by its abolition would it be possible for the island's diverse communities to develop together a truly national identity. Whereas the last election in 1924 had involved only about 4 per cent of the island's population, the Commission recommended extending the franchise to all males over the ages of 21 and to all females over 30. The voting age for women was similarly reduced to 21 before the first elections under the new constitution were held in 1931. With few exceptions, the Commission's proposals for the franchise came as an unwelcome surprise to Ceylon's politicians. Hardly any of them had advocated it in their evidence before the Commission and several had spoken of the dangers of extending the vote to the illiterate and uneducated. These objections were overruled but, significantly in the long term, far from ameliorating communal relations the recommendations of the Donoughmore Commission tended to exacerbate them. The problem in this respect arose not so much from the recommendations themselves but rather the manner in which, once they had been implemented, they were manipulated by an increasingly assertive Sinhalese political élite.

Ceylon's population at the time of the Donoughmore Commission in 1928 was in the region of 5,300,000. On the eve of independence in 1948 it had risen to just over 6 million. Of this pre-independence total just over 4 million were Sinhalese (2,596,000 low-country, 1,467,000 Kandyan); just under 1.5 million were Tamils (697,000 Ceylon Tamils, 650,000 Indian Tamils); 380,000 were Muslims; 30,000 were Burghers (people of Portuguese and Dutch descent); and 10,000 were Europeans. The Kandyan Sinhalese were more inward-looking and socially conservative than their low-country counterparts. Although the Kandyan provinces had been the scene of two revolts against the British in 1818 and 1848, their failure thereafter to adapt to Western education and to participate in the new economic opportunities had seen them fall behind both the low-country Sinhalese and the Tamils of the north. One consequence of this was that the Kandyans now tended to look for protection to the colonial power. The Kandyan provinces were also the areas of some of the largest plantations and the Kandyans shared the apprehensions of the low-country Sinhalese over the numbers of Indian immigrant workers who came from south India to work on the estates.[9] All plantations depended to a greater or lesser extent on labour from India, but a fundamental change in the character of that labour had taken place since the collapse of coffee in the late

[9] In Vol. III, see chap. by David Northrup, esp. pp. 91–92.

nineteenth century. Where previously it had been seasonal and temporary, it had now, on the tea and rubber plantations, become permanent and settled, thus adding another element of plurality to the island's heterogeneous society.

Not until the reforms of the early 1920s did communal discord become a feature of Ceylon's political life. The Muslim–Sinhalese riots of 1915 had been, in a communal sense, a violent exception to a peaceful rule; there was no violence at all between the Sinhalese and Tamils throughout the British period. But the introduction of electoral politics, even though initially on a modest scale, injected a competitive and discordant note. It was this that shattered the ideal, within a mere two years of its formation, that the Ceylon National Congress might become a symbol of national unity and social harmony. Naivety and inexperience on the part of low-country Sinhalese politicians, together with the pursuit of blatant divide-and-rule tactics by Sir William Manning (Governor, 1919–25), were contributory factors as the low-country Sinhalese contrived to alienate both the Tamils and the Kandyans over the question of reserved seats in the legislature. In the context of Sinhalese–Tamil relations, the die had been cast. Governor Clifford explained their differences in 1926:

> recently the differences between the Sinhalese—especially the low country Sinhalese—and the Tamils on the Council have shown signs of becoming accentuated; the latter suspecting the former of designs to dominate the whole political situation by sheer weight of numbers, while the Sinhalese resent the reluctance of the Tamils to account themselves merely a minority section of a united 'Ceylonese' nation, and are apprehensive concerning the results which the competition of the frugal and diligent Tamils is likely to produce upon the standard of living and the prospects of employment of the educated portions of the Sinhalese community.[10]

Tamil apprehensions increased considerably when universal suffrage was introduced. In four of the five seats in the Tamil-majority Northern Province, the elections to the first State Council in 1931 were boycotted. The boycott was instigated by the Jaffna Youth League, a radical body which made the unrealistic claim that the reforms as a whole did not go far enough to meet Ceylon's political demands. In this act of defiance, the Jaffna Youth League anticipated support from the Sinhalese. None was forthcoming, the Sinhalese standing aloof from what they regarded as a sectarian gesture. The seats were eventually filled in 1934, by which time the mainstream Tamil politicians had given grudging acceptance to the Donoughmore constitution. Although they much preferred communal electorates or reserved seats to protect their interests, the system of executive committees had at least enabled them to secure representation on the Board of Ministers. But by skilful manipulation of these committees, the Sinhalese were able to engineer

[10] Clifford to Amery, 20 Nov. 1926, CO 537/692.

an all-Sinhalese Board of Ministers after the second State Council elections in 1936. Through their representative on the Council, G. G. Ponnambalam, the Tamils now put forward an extravagant demand that 50 per cent of the seats in any future council should be reserved for the minorities. This demand was dismissed out of hand by both the Sinhalese and the British colonial government.

Equally controversial during the period of the Donoughmore constitution (1931–46), and indeed right up to independence and beyond, was the position of the Indian Tamil community in Ceylon. The Indian Tamils lived in the island's central areas and were (and still are) distinct from the Ceylon Tamils of the north, east, and Colombo. Sinhalese resentment was directed, not only against the large numbers of Indians on the electoral rolls (some 225,000 in 1939) but also the regulations giving them the vote. Most Indians qualified by proving, not that they were permanently settled but that they had lived in the country for five years. This, together with the frequency of their visits to their villages in southern India, to which they regularly remitted money, convinced the Sinhalese that Indian loyalties lay not with Ceylon but with India. Sinhalese resentment was also economically motivated. At a time of depression in the early 1930s, unskilled Indian labourers who worked for the government in such areas as railways, road construction, and sanitation services were viewed as a threat to Sinhalese jobs. Indian traders and moneylenders frequently attracted hostile criticism. In 1939, in response to public pressure, the Ceylon government imposed restrictions on Indian employment in government service. In a move which angered European planters especially, because it threatened to cut their labour supply, the government in New Delhi retaliated by placing an embargo on the emigration to Ceylon of unskilled labour from India. Two intergovernmental conferences in 1940 failed to resolve the differences and India and Ceylon remained at loggerheads over questions involving the rights and status of Indians in Ceylon. The impasse left at least one official at the Colonial Office in London asking whether Ceylon might yet become a second Palestine.[11]

As communal attitudes hardened, especially between the Sinhalese and Tamils, both sides resorted to cultural and religious symbolism to elevate their respective claims to a privileged status. In 1936 Solomon West Ridgeway Dias Bandaranaike,[12] born of a Christian family but a recent convert to Buddhism, established the Sinhala Maha Sabha (Great Sinhalese Union or League and progenitor of the Sri

[11] Minute by K. W. Blaxter, a Principal in the CO Eastern Dept., 1 May 1940, CO 54/977/7, reproduced in K. M. de Silva, ed., *Sri Lanka*, 2 vols., British Documents on the End of Empire Project (BDEEP) (London, 1997), I, Doc. 34, note 5.

[12] As an interesting example of Sinhalese élite sycophancy towards their rulers, when he was born in 1899 Bandaranaike was partly named after Sir Joseph West Ridgeway, British Governor of Ceylon between 1895 and 1903.

Lanka Freedom Party of today), which based its appeal on the idea of Ceylon as a Buddhist state in which Buddhism was the state religion. Responding on behalf of the Tamils, Ponnambalam, Bandaranaike's great rival in State Council debates, asserted that Tamils were the original inhabitants of the island, that for a century before the British occupation the Kandyan ruling dynasty was wholly Tamil, that the Tamils had impressed 'their culture and policy' on the Sinhalese, and that British capital and Tamil manpower had contributed largely to the development of the island's plantation economy.[13]

It would, however, be misleading to portray the Donoughmore era as one of sterile communal confrontation and little more. The period witnessed some noticeable social and economic reforms. Indeed, the Donoughmore commissioners had argued that the extension of the franchise would act as a much-needed stimulus to social legislation and administrative action. The setting was not initially favourable. Not only did colonial commodity prices collapse with the onset of the Depression at the beginning of the 1930s; Ceylon was also afflicted by famine in 1934 and by a malaria epidemic in 1935. None the less, there were positive achievements. The state replaced missionaries as the main provider of education. State expenditure on education rose from 7.1 per cent of the total in 1925 to 18.9 per cent in 1947–48. With increased spending, the number of government vernacular (Sinhalese and Tamil) schools rose from 1,395 in 1931 to 2,455 in 1944. The expansion of schools teaching in English was less marked. Until 1945 English schools levied fees, and access to them was restricted to the affluent from whom the professional middle classes were drawn. Over the next three years fees were phased out and the numbers of students in English schools rose from 93,000 in 1944 to 169,000 in 1947. Other welfare measures included public health campaigns, which were aimed especially at the elimination of malaria and hookworm. A reduction in infant mortality—said to be as high as 166 per thousand births in 1936—became a priority. Under the direction of Don Stephen Senanayake, architect in the 1940s of the country's independence and Minister for Agriculture and Lands during the Donoughmore era, significant moves were made to redress the imbalance in the island's economy by stimulating peasant agriculture through schemes of irrigation, land reclamation, and settlement.[14] Poor-law legislation and laws governing factory conditions and workmen's compensation were introduced, the last two

[13] G. G. Ponnambalam, 'An Examination of the Soulbury Constitution Proposed for Ceylon: The Tamil Minority Case', Oct. 1945, a memorial enclosed with Ponnambalam's letter to G. H. Hall, Secretary of State for the Colonies, 3 Nov. 1945, CO 54/987/1, in de Silva, ed., *Sri Lanka*, II, Doc. 322.

[14] It should perhaps be noted that many of the progressive policies of the Donoughmore era occurred despite Senanayake, who was socially conservative. The legislation introduced owed much to competition among ministers who were keen to demonstrate how beneficent they could be. It was equally significant that Senanayake's resettlement schemes were in part intended to 'reconquer' areas of the island for the Sinhalese majority. Manor, *Bandaranaike*, p. 134.

being of benefit primarily to the workforce of Colombo, which, with a population of about 300,000, was by some distance the island's largest city.

These welfare reforms were accompanied by equally significant changes in the labour politics of the island. Based primarily on the railway and harbour workshops in and around Colombo, the labour movement had emerged at the end of the First World War under the leadership of A. E. Goonesinha, who established a Ceylon Labour Union in 1922 and who set out to transform the urban working population into a radical political force which would challenge the conservative leadership of the Ceylon National Congress. In this he did not succeed, but the strikes which he organized in the late 1920s eventually persuaded employers to concede union recognition. Trade union activity in Ceylon brought Goonesinha to the attention of the British Labour Party, and he was arguably at the height of his influence between 1929 and 1931 when Labour was in office in Britain. Thereafter, however, his influence went into steep decline as he began to embrace Sinhalese chauvinism and consequently lost the support which he had previously enjoyed from his non-Sinhalese working-class constituency. He was eclipsed in the 1930s by the Marxist Lanka Sama Samajist Party, which was established in 1936. Concentrating their activities on the plantation workers, the Sama Samajists incurred the hostility of both the European planting community and the colonial government. From 1939 their anti-war propaganda also alarmed the Colonial Office in London. Their leaders were detained in 1940 but, to the considerable embarrassment of the authorities, they escaped in 1942.

Contrary to the belief, expressed both at the time and since, that Ceylon's independence in 1948 was a smooth and uncomplicated process, the official British record reveals a less straightforward picture and one which requires a more qualified assessment. Based on what he had seen of Ceylon affairs over the past two-and-a-half years, Sir Cosmo Parkinson, Permanent Under-Secretary of State at the Colonial Office, commented in January 1940 on the island's communal difficulties that 'of all Colonies, Ceylon was likely to present the most difficult problem with which the Colonial Office would be dealing'.[15] How, then, did the island achieve independence in such a short time and to what extent was the 'problem' to which Parkinson referred resolved?[16]

Unlike their counterparts in India and Burma, the political leadership in Ceylon co-operated with Britain in the war and, ultimately, Ceylon's wartime role as a major source of raw materials and as a strategic base worked to the advantage of the island's nationalists. After the fall of Malaya in 1942 Ceylon produced over 60 per cent of the Allies' natural rubber supplies. In April 1944 the headquarters of

[15] Minute by Parkinson, 1 Jan. 1940, CO 54/964/2, in de Silva, ed., *Sri Lanka*, I, Doc. 9.

[16] The discussion which follows draws on documents published in de Silva, ed., *Sri Lanka*.

South-East Asia Command under Admiral Lord Louis Mountbatten were transferred from New Delhi to Kandy. Led by Senanayake, the Board of Ministers never ceased to emphasize the value of Ceylon's contribution to the war effort and continually pressed the British to commit themselves to a political reform under which Ceylon would progress to Dominion Status under a conventional Cabinet system of government. Whitehall rejected these advances, claiming that wartime conditions and communal differences in the island necessitated the postponement of any reform until after the war. However, the Governor, Sir Andrew Caldecott, and the island's Commander-in-Chief appointed in 1942, Admiral Sir Geoffrey Layton, were both more sympathetic to Ceylon's political claims. In 1944 they enlisted the support of Mountbatten to persuade the government in London to agree to the appointment of a commission to examine a new constitutional scheme drawn up by the Board of Ministers. All three emphasized that the alternative to a commission would be a general election in Ceylon and potential disruption to the activities of South-East Asia Command.

The commission, chaired by Herwald Ramsbotham, Lord Soulbury, former Conservative MP, and later Governor-General of Ceylon (1949–54) endorsed many of the recommendations in the ministers' scheme but stopped short of advocating Dominion Status. Instead it recommended internal self-government, with Britain retaining responsibility for defence and external affairs. But much had changed by the time the Soulbury Report was published in October 1945. The war against Japan had ended with dramatic suddenness, a Labour government was in office in Britain, and political advance in both India and Burma was on the agenda. Senanayake argued that Ceylon could not be treated differently; the country had, after all, co-operated in the war. He was prepared to accept the Soulbury constitution, but only as an interim measure on the road to full Dominion Status. The agreements that Britain reached over the timing of the grant of independence to both India and Burma at the beginning of 1947 stiffened Senanayake's resolve and increased his anxieties.[17] If he failed to deliver Dominion Status, the beneficiaries would be either his main political rival, Bandaranaike, whom the British regarded as wholly unreliable, or the Marxists, whose leaders were operating freely again. There was much loose talk of Ceylon joining a greater Indian federation if Dominion Status was refused. The evidence for this is distinctly thin. Much more likely was a political swing to the left, as the years 1946 and 1947 witnessed a series of public sector strikes in Colombo orchestrated by the Marxists.

The Labour Cabinet in London proved hard to convince. Having conceded the principle of independence to India and Burma, ministers were anxious not to provide further ammunition to their Conservative opponents who claimed that

[17] See above, pp. 335–36, 337–39; and below, pp. 437, 477.

the government was guilty of 'scuttle' and of 'liquidating' the Empire.[18] Ideally, ministers wanted to delay Ceylon's independence for as long as possible, fearing among other things that it would stimulate nationalist demands in Malaya. But in June 1947 they yielded. Their one consolation was that Senanayake's apprehension of India's regional dominance after independence made him more than willing to offer a defence agreement with Britain guaranteeing continued strategic facilities, especially over airfields and access to the naval base at Trincomalee, together with two further agreements covering external affairs and the service and pension rights of British civil servants. The Cabinet in London also considered the need for a similar agreement to protect British companies in Ceylon, but decided, in a manner which suggested an assumption that British commercial interests would be safe in Senanayake's hands, to defer the necessary negotiations until Ceylon had become a full member of the Commonwealth.

In the internal political settlement at the time of independence in 1948, a number of constitutional provisions were adopted as safeguards for the minorities. They included a bicameral legislature; a Public Services Commission; guarantees against discriminatory legislation, whether racial or religious; and, on the crucial issue of representation, area as well as population weightage for the demarcation of constituencies. Seats were to be distributed for every 75,000 inhabitants and for every 1,000 square miles of territory. Area weightage was designed to benefit the Tamil and Muslim minorities in the relatively sparsely populated northern and eastern regions and also the Kandyan Sinhalese in the central highlands. With the exception of the second chamber, these safeguards were devised, not by the Soulbury Commission but by the Board of Ministers in their constitutional scheme. The Commission argued that on such a matter as the franchise, as also on the question of Indian immigration and hence citizenship, the new Ceylon Parliament should be sovereign and not subject to any overriding authority. It thus effectively endorsed the ministers' proposals.

Although the new constitution was approved by an overwhelming majority when put to a vote in the old State Council, representatives of both the Tamils and the Indians in the island were deeply dissatisfied. Protests were forthcoming from the Tamil Congress, an organization established by Ponnambalam in 1944, and from the Government of India, on behalf of the Indian community. In the face of both, the Colonial Office in London, no less than Senanayake himself, stood firm. The Tamil Congress was dismissed by the Colonial Office as 'an artificial creation of a group of Tamil politicians' whose arguments had been laid to rest by the vote in the State Council.[19] Contrary to the customary view that the Colonial Office was

[18] Cabinet Minutes, 44(47)2, 6 May 1947, reproduced in de Silva, ed., *Sri Lanka*, II, Doc 390.

[19] Note by CO, 'All-Ceylon Tamil Congress', 1 April 1946, CO 54/986/9/1, in de Silva, ed., *Sri Lanka*, II, Doc. 354.

a lightweight department and one easily blown off course if it encountered opposition from more influential circles in Whitehall, Colonial Office officials would not be swayed by the arguments of the India Office which were put forward to represent the Indian case.[20]

The Colonial Office attitude is revealing because it represented a tactical approach to the transfer of power which later became the hallmark of the Office's approach to further acts of decolonization. Throughout the negotiations over Ceylon's independence between 1945 and 1948, the priority for the Colonial Office was to keep Senanayake in power and to build up his authority.[21] His was the moderating influence in Ceylonese politics. He was the politician upon whom the British depended for the maintenance of their commercial and strategic interests. It was in the sense of these considerations—backing the moderates (or, failing that, the least radical) on the one hand, and the protection of British interests on the other—that Ceylon became the British model for subsequent transfers of power.

Certainly in Ceylon's case, Senanayake fitted the bill admirably. As if to emphasize his moderation, he formed a new political party—the United National Party—in 1946. And, within his narrow patrician horizons, he was also genuinely committed to the ideal of Ceylon as a democratic, pluralist, and secular state. Where in practice he departed from his own ideals, and where the Colonial Office policy of supporting him ran the most risk, was over the question of Indian immigration and citizenship. A conference on Commonwealth citizenship and nationality was held in London in February 1947. Having previously argued that to allow Ceylon to be represented at the conference in its own right would incur the risk of an independent Ceylonese government introducing discriminatory legislation against Indians, the Colonial Office changed its mind on the grounds that Senanayake's domestic difficulties would be increased if Ceylon were not allowed to attend.[22] Significantly, over the first two years of independence Senanayake's government set about articulating a new definition of citizenship which, when translated into legislation, effectively removed voters of Indian origin from the electoral rolls.

Ceylon went to the polls in August–September 1947. The United National Party did not fare as well as expected, although, with the Marxist opposition dividing on factional lines into three separate parties, it was able to form a government with

[20] See chap. 11 by Ronald Hyam, esp. pp. 264–65.

[21] Others had a more sceptical view of CO priorities. Admiral Layton, for instance, back in the UK after his command in Ceylon, suspected that CO officials were 'only too anxious to rid themselves of the island and its troubles at any cost and so avoid having to deal with another Indian problem'. Layton to Admiralty, 31 July 1945, ADM 116/5546, reproduced in de Silva, ed., *Sri Lanka*, II, Doc. 263.

[22] See minutes and correspondence in CO 323/1888/1.

a comfortable majority. Independence was celebrated on 4 February 1948. Though enthusiastically welcomed, Ceylon's achievement of Dominion Status had to be tempered by some sober realities. From the outset the new government was under attack from the left, which claimed, in attacking the defence agreement, that independence was a sham. The Soviet Union agreed and, up until 1955, used the defence agreement to block Ceylon's entry into the United Nations, thus providing further ammunition for the left. Of greater long-term significance were the issues of ethnic diversity and the place of religion in politics, two of the wider aspects of the end of colonial empires which, as mentioned at the beginning of this chapter, are clearly evident in the Ceylon story. At the time of independence the Tamils nurtured misgivings and a sense of grievance. Relations with India were strained because of Ceylon's legislation over citizenship. In the background lurked the issue of Sinhalese nationalism in relation to the question of language policy as well as that of religion. In short, Ceylon was independent but the real test of nationhood lay ahead. Ethnic tensions between the Sinhalese and Tamils produced the first outbreaks of violence in 1956 and again in 1958.

Select Bibliography

C. R. de SILVA, *Sri Lanka: A History* (New Delhi, 1989).

K. M. de SILVA, *Sri Lanka: A Survey* (London, 1977).

—— *A History of Sri Lanka* (London, 1981).

—— ed., *Universal Franchise, 1931–1981: The Sri Lankan Experience* (Colombo, 1981).

—— ed., *Sri Lanka*, British Documents on the End of Empire Project (BDEEP), in 2 vols. (London, 1997).

K. N. O. DHARMADASA, *Language, Religion and Ethnic Assertiveness: The Growth of Sinhalese Nationalism in Sri Lanka* (Ann Arbor, 1992).

H. A. J. HULUGALLE, *The Life and Times of Don Stephen Senanayake* (Colombo, 1975).

V. K. JAYAWARDENA, *The Rise of the Labour Movement in Ceylon* (Durham, NC, 1972).

SIR CHARLES JEFFRIES, *Ceylon: The Path to Independence* (London, 1962).

E. F. C. LUDOWYK, *The Modern History of Ceylon* (London, 1966).

JAMES MANOR, *The Expedient Utopian: Bandaranaike and Ceylon* (Cambridge, 1989).

S. NADESAN, *A History of the Upcountry Tamil People* (Colombo, 1993).

J. RUSSELL, *Communal Politics under the Donoughmore Constitution, 1931–1947* (Colombo, 1983).

HUGH TINKER, *Separate and Unequal: India and Indians in the British Commonwealth, 1920–1950* (London, 1976).

20

Imperialism and Nationalism in South-East Asia

A. J. STOCKWELL

The exercise of British power in South-East Asia until 1914 was shaped by the expansion of the colonial state, fluctuations in world capitalism, nationalist reactions, and international relations. As British economic interests infused South-East Asia, so colonial governments became more intrusive in the exaction of revenue and the regulation of production. Yet European coercive powers should not be exaggerated; state control varied from area to area, was often evaded by businessmen, and ran into opposition from peasants and labourers. Moreover, although export-oriented districts were particularly susceptible to world market forces, the impact of capitalism was not uniformly harsh. In the 1930s the Irrawaddy delta in Burma was hit harder by depression than was the Chao Phraya delta in Siam, Burmese rice farmers were perhaps worse off than workers in Malayan tin and rubber, and tenants and labourers were often more vulnerable than peasant proprietors. Indeed, it has been suggested that 'the peasantry of the region suffered less severely from the crisis of the world economy in the interwar decades than they did during years when nature turned against them and the monsoon failed, or during the years when they were victims of war'.[1]

None the less, the more heavily colonialism bore down upon South-East Asian societies, the more complex became problems of managing collaborators, controlling opponents, manipulating minority groups, and balancing communal interests. Increasingly the tools of colonial rule, such as communications and print culture, were turned against it as the extension of colonialism opened South-East Asia to enemies of colonialism. Opposition to European rule was not only provoked by direct experience; it was also inspired by knowledge of reform in the Islamic world, Indian nationalism, China's civil war, and Japanese militarism. On occasion resistance tied down considerable colonial resources, but it never proved insurmountable during the period before the Second World War. Even when the British were driven from South-East Asia in 1941–42, it was not on account of the strength of nationalism but because of seismic shifts in international relations.

[1] Ian Brown, 'Rural Distress in Southeast Asia during the World Depression of the Early 1930s: A Preliminary Reexamination', *Journal of Asian Studies*, XLV, 5 (1986), p. 1022.

Although South-East Asia was neither fought over in the First World War nor repartitioned at the peace conference, Britain's position in the region was affected by the new world order. This was first demonstrated in 1921 when the Anglo-Japanese Treaty was reviewed. Concluded in 1902 and renewed on two occasions thereafter, this alliance had reduced Britain's need to keep large forces in East and South-East Asia. Japan's designs on China during the First World War, however, signalled a potential threat for Britain, and feeling obliged to choose between Japan and the United States, the Lloyd George government allowed the Anglo-Japanese Alliance to lapse. This portentous decision alienated Japan without securing American co-operation. It also led to the costly construction of a naval base at Singapore (completed in 1938), where the main fleet might be despatched in times of crisis. Furthermore, at the Washington Conference (1921–22), Britain had no option but to accept the principle of parity in capital ships with the United States while Japan agreed to keep its navy at 60 per cent of the separate British and American strengths. When the arms race accelerated in the 1930s, however, Britain could not sustain even this level of capability. At the same time the availability of Indian troops was called into question, since the Government of India kept military expenditure to a minimum, retrenched on the modernization of its army, and complied with the demands of Indian politicians to reduce its defence commitments abroad. After Japan's invasion of Manchuria in 1931–32, South-East Asia was drawn into a gathering international storm. Preoccupied with Europe and lacking either an alliance with the United States or adequate military resources to act alone, Britain was unable to defend her South-East Asian Empire in 1941–42.

British Imperialism and South-East Asia Nationalism to 1941

After the military subjugation of Upper Burma in 1885–90, British rule continued its assault upon the beliefs and institutions of old Burma. Burmese identity was not simply an amalgam of memories of a lost world, however, since those brought up under British rule appropriated the ideas and organizations of new Burma as instruments to fashion nationalism. Burmese nationalism in the period from the early twentieth century to 1941 passed through a number of overlapping stages. First, in 1906 a Western-educated élite founded the Young Men's Buddhist Association (YMBA) with the aim of reviving Burmese culture and religion. Secondly, from the early 1920s *pongyis* (monks) took the lead in millenarian upheaval in the Irrawaddy delta. Thirdly, by the late 1930s the constitutional movement of the westernized, urban élite had achieved a power-sharing arrangement with the British. Finally, student *Thakins* ('masters'), who promoted the radical causes of independence, republicanism, and socialism, emerged in the 1930s to come into their own in the 1940s. Much Burmese resentment was directed at aspects of the link with British India, such as administrative practices, economic ties, and in particular, Indian immigration. As Burmese nationalism gathered momentum, it tilted not only at British rulers but also at Indian residents, and spilled over into communal violence, as in Rangoon in 1930 and 1938. In addition, nationalist politics aggravated divisions among the Burmese and provoked counter-nationalist or separatist movements of minorities.

In 1916 the Young Men's Buddhist Association (YMBA) for the first time mounted an overt campaign against the British. By protesting against the European habit of wearing shoes in pagoda precincts, it embarrassed the government in the name of Buddhism and started to become political, popular, and a focus for nationalist sentiment. Having won concessions on the 'shoe question', the YMBA redirected protest against Burma's exclusion from the Government of India Act of 1919, which conferred upon the provinces of India a partial ministerial system called dyarchy. Hitherto the YMBA had lacked sustained support and extensive organization, but in 1920 it reformed as the General Council of Buddhist Associations (GCBA), abandoned its more conservative leaders, set up branches in towns and villages beyond Rangoon, and broadened its appeal to include students and militant *pongyis.* Surprised by the strength of Burmese opposition, the government agreed to introduce dyarchy to Burma. Thereafter, however, faction-fighting over whether to participate in elections meant that the GCBA lost touch with the peasants.

In the 1920s peasant grievances in the delta pushed political protest along another course. During the First World War shipping shortages had paralysed the rice industry, leading to unemployment, peasant dispossession, and conflict between cultivators, landowners, and moneylenders. Rural unrest was harnessed to religious revivalism by *pongyis*, notably U Ottama and U Wisara. Although monks were supposed to stand apart from secular affairs, the collapse of the *sangha* (monkhood) under British rule, together with the economic and social problems of rural Burma, caused some to assume a political role. U Ottama, who had joined the General Council of Buddhist Associations on his return from India in 1921, proclaimed Buddhism to be in danger, transformed village social and political discontent into a religious movement, and organized village *athin* (nationalist cells). U Ottama died in prison and U Wisara met a martyr's end when he succumbed to a hunger-strike while in detention.

The most spectacular anti-colonial movement in the delta was the Hsaya San rebellion, which broke out in the Tharrawaddy district in December 1930. Hsaya San, a former *pongyi* and member of the General Council of Buddhist Associations, aroused villagers with promises of the restoration of prosperity and monarchy. Armed with invulnerability charms and aspiring to be king, he channelled the dispossessed into a millenarian movement. Although British officials and those Burmese who participated in the dyarchy constitution dismissed *pongyi* activities as obscurantist, Hsaya San was not merely a purveyor of superstition but was well acquainted with the modern politics of the towns. In many ways the rebellion was itself a product of modern Burma and reflected the failure of the General Council and its village branches to ameliorate the conditions of those alienated by change. Fundamental to peasants' discontent was their sense that the colonial state lacked legitimacy. Their immediate grievances were symptoms of colonialism: taxes, police oppression, Indian usury, low rice prices, and landlessness. Their principal targets were village headmen, colonial administrators, and Indian moneylenders. Although the Hsaya San rebellion was never a fundamental threat to the technologically superior colonial state, it occupied numerous police and troops for over a year. At first the British underestimated its seriousness. They then resorted to force, deploying the regular police, the Burmese Military Police, and the army. The few Indian Army units stationed in the country were later augmented by detachments from India and also by aircraft. 'Shooting at villages [*sic*] on sight, like shooting game',[2] destroying crops and property, and mounting large-scale operations, the authorities inflicted casualties without securing the countryside. Before the rising was suppressed they had killed 1,300 rebels and arrested, captured, or received the surrender of a further 9,000.[3] The regime regained control after it improved civil-military co-operation, developed intelligence techniques, and separated guerrilla fighters from the general populace. Hsaya San was eventually captured. The authorities made sure at his trial, where he was defended by Dr Ba Maw, that the judge who sentenced him to death was also a Burmese.

During the 1930s the urban, secular strand of nationalism revived in response to the economic problems of the industrial workforce, to the influence of socialism, Marxism, and militant nationalist ideology, and to British constitutional proposals. As regards the latter, developments in India provoked nationalist demands from Burma. The Simon Commission (1927–30) raised the question of Burma's continued connection to India. The Government of India and Burma's powerful Indian community opposed separation on economic grounds, while the government of Burma valued the link for defence and internal security. On the other hand, unless they were beholden to Indian supporters, Burmese leaders aspired to separate nationhood, regarded the attachment as 'unnatural', believed it was economically debilitating, and wished to curb Indian immigration. Eventually, separation became official policy and the Government of Burma Act of 1935

[2] The Burmese *Sun*, 31 March 1931, in Thomas R. Mockaitis, ed., *British Counterinsurgency, 1919–60* (London, 1990), p. 40.

[3] Robert H. Taylor, *The State in Burma* (London, 1987), p. 198.

provided for responsible government in which a Cabinet of Burmese ministers was answerable to a Westminster-style legislature. The constitution legitimized the institutions of the colonial state in the eyes of members of the conservative élite. It also provided them with power and patronage, and in 1937 one of their number, Dr Ba Maw, became Burma's first Premier.

Burmese constitutionalists were challenged in the 1930s by students of Rangoon University who appropriated the title Thakins (a term meaning 'master' and usually applied to Europeans). Amongst the Thakins were Aung San, U Nu, and others who would lead the nationalist movement in the 1940s. They were more radical and more militant than those Burmese who participated in running the colonial state, though they were eclectic in their political philosophy and programme. Employing somewhat indiscriminately the language of Marxism, republicanism, and nationalism, they maintained links with left-wing groups in India and Britain and propagated demands for an independent republic through the *Naga Ni* (red dragon) Book Club. Aspiring to achieve independence through struggle rather than diplomacy, they launched strikes of university students and oil-workers and later formed a paramilitary organization. Dissatisfied with the 1937 constitution, the Thakins took control of the *Dobama Asi-ayon* (We Burmese Association) and in 1939 brought down the government of Ba Maw, whom they condemned as an ally of Indians and a collaborator with the British. In 1940, however, Ba Maw and the Thakins joined forces in the anti-war Freedom Bloc. This resulted in the detention of Ba Maw and many Thakins. Meanwhile Aung San and other Thakins fled Burma to return as the 'Thirty Heroes' in the Japanese invasion of 1942.

In contrast to Burma, Malaya appeared to enjoy the happiness of a land without a history. Whereas the stability of Burma had cracked by 1920, the inter-war years were a halcyon period for the British in Malaya. Although this calm was disturbed by Malay risings in Kelantan (1915) and Trengganu (1920s), persistent fighting between triads (gangs) in Singapore, and strikes on rubber estates and at the Batang Arang coalfield in the 1930s, the authorities dismissed the possibility that these outbreaks indicated anything more fundamental than local difficulties provoked by influences outside Malaya and exploited by individual 'trouble-makers'. Politics, as distinct from protest, was confined to élites and distracted by developments in China, India, and the Netherlands East Indies. Moreover, the communal identities of Malays, Chinese, and Indians, to which colonial administrative practices contributed, overwhelmed any sense there might have been of multiracial, Malayan nationhood.

As 'princes of the soil', whose rulers' sovereignty was guaranteed by Anglo-Malay treaties, the Malays appeared most closely attached to the colonial regime.

Yet they also felt the most threatened by alien control of the government and economy. Until the 1940s Malay nationalism lacked organization, definite objectives, mass support, and peninsula-wide appeal. Malay identity was expressed in terms of religion, ethnicity, or the traditionalism of the royal court, though none of these formulations was an exclusive or rigidly defined category and each developed in response to colonial rule, immigration, and education, as well as books and newspapers. The reform movement of religious radicals, who were based in the Straits Settlements and in contact with the wider Muslim world through the *haj*, came to a head in the 1920s, when the *Kaum Muda* (youth) challenged the conservatism of the *Kaum Tua* (elders) but scarcely disturbed the hierarchy of Malay society. Secular radicals, such as journalists and graduates of the Sultan Idris Training College for vernacular schoolteachers, were influenced by Indonesian nationalism. Critical of both British colonialism and Malay feudalism, they formed the *Kesatuan Melayu Muda* (Young Malays' Association) in 1938, but commanded little support. A third élite, consisting of Western-educated members of royal families and the aristocracy, expressed concern about restricted opportunities for Malays. They too formed a number of societies and clubs, but their criticisms of British rule were mild and they did not cultivate popular support.[4]

The Chinese, who were more numerous than either the Malays or Indians in the developed parts of British Malaya by 1940, gave the colonial authorities most cause for alarm. They were administered by the Chinese Protectorate, whose function was 'widely regarded as being not so much to protect the Chinese as to protect the country *against* them!'[5] While some long-established families in the Straits Settlements prided themselves on their British citizenship and aspired to political rights in Malaya itself, and while census figures revealed a growing percentage of second-generation Chinese, the British persisted in the belief that Malaya's Chinese were 'birds of passage'. Moreover, the Kuomintang (nationalist) movement in China reasserted the Manchu claim that the descendants of Chinese emigrants remained Chinese nationals. During the 1920s the Kuomintang was particularly active in the Straits Settlements; in 1930 the Malayan Communist Party was founded in Singapore. In competing for support it politicized secret societies, infiltrated Chinese schools, organized strikes, and mounted demonstrations. The British responded by restricting immigration, repatriating 'agitators', tightening censorship, and suppressing protests. In March 1927 police opened fire on a mass meeting at Kreta Ayer (Singapore), killing seven people. During the 1930s Chinese activists in South-East Asia concentrated on organizing boycotts of Japanese

[4] See William R. Roff, *The Origins of Malay Nationalism* (New Haven, 1967), and Anthony Milner, *The Invention of Politics in Colonial Malaya: Contesting Nationalism and the Expansion of the Public Sphere* (Cambridge, 1994).

[5] Victor Purcell, *The Memoirs of a Malayan Official* (London, 1965), p. 97.

goods and raising support for the United Front of the Kuomintang and Chinese Communist Party (1937) in their war with Japan.

Though alive to the threats posed by foreign influences, British officials regularly intoned the mantra that Malaya itself 'had no politics' and concentrated instead on the problems of commodity prices and administrative reform. In the inter-war years the colonial government was at the centre of attempts to stabilize the prices of tin and rubber through international agreements to restrict their production. The Tin Control Scheme was signed in 1931 and renewed at intervals thereafter. Regarding rubber, the imperfect Stevenson Restriction Scheme of 1922 was followed in 1934 by the more comprehensive International Rubber Regulation Agreement, though both hit smallholdings harder than plantations.

The administration of British Malaya was plagued by its division into the colony of three Straits Settlements and nine protected Malay States, of which four formed the Federated Malay States (FMS). Within the FMS, leading Malays criticized the centralization of government and contrasted their dwindling power and status with those still enjoyed by Malays in the Unfederated Malay States. They were hardly mollified by the demotion of the Resident-General to Chief Secretary and the formation of the Federal Council in 1909. Business interests were glad to secure representation on this council, but FMS Rulers, who were also members for a time, lacked a veto over legislation affecting their states. The issue of decentralization preoccupied officials during the inter-war period. Administrators sympathized with Malays and desired their continuing support against 'unruly' Chinese. In addition, and in keeping with contemporary thinking that underlay Indirect Rule in tropical Africa, they argued that decentralization would reduce the costs of government at a time when revenue wavered with uncertain commodity prices. Furthermore, officials hoped that decentralization, by putting the Federated Malay States on a par with the Unfederated Malay States, would be a prelude to the eventual unification of British Malaya.

Decentralization generated controversy, however, and the schemes of Sir Laurence Guillemard (High Commissioner, 1919–27) and Sir Cecil Clementi (1929–34) foundered on Malay suspicions of Britain's ultimate objectives, the mistrust of businessmen, and infighting amongst officials. Although Guillemard managed to reconstitute the Federal Council in 1927, it was at the expense of a bitter feud with the Chief Secretary, Sir George Maxwell. Clementi's ambitious schemes caused even more discord and cost him his job. Thereafter, the Colonial Office insisted on caution: the post of Chief Secretary, regarded as the symbol if not the instrument of central control, was downgraded in 1935 and a number of matters were devolved to the states. None the less, by 1941 the constitutional position of British Malaya was as untidy as ever. During the 1930s some officials in the Colonial Office and the Malayan Civil Service had questioned whether decentralization, which after all pandered to the Malay Rulers, was in the best interests of the Malay people, let alone the non-Malay communities.

Though Siam had not fallen under colonial rule in the nineteenth century, it had been drawn into the web of Western economic expansion and had become the pivot of imperial rivalries in mainland South-East Asia. Among foreigners with interests in Siam, the British had achieved pre-eminence in Bangkok, though the extent to which Britain's position amounted to 'informal empire' is debatable.[6] After the First World War the British maintained the policy of balancing their dominance in Siam against its independence, which the Thais for their part continued to safeguard by the practice of manipulative diplomacy. Developments in Siam, together with the changing international position of Britain, however, gradually eroded British power in Bangkok.

Resentment of the royal family's monopoly of high office was increasing in the ranks of military officers, civil servants, and professional men, all of whom were products of the modernization that had occurred under King Chulalongkorn (reigned 1868–1910). In June 1932 an alliance between military officers and the People's Party, led by Nai Pridi Phanomyon (Professor of Law at Chulalongkorn University), mounted the so-called 'revolution' which resulted in a new constitution drastically reducing the powers of King Prajadhipok (reigned 1925–35). Soon after this peaceful coup the coalition of politicians and military broke down and an ensuing struggle for power resulted in the eclipse of Pridi, the abdication of Prajadhipok, and the ascendancy of the army. During the government of Marshal Luang Phibul Songkram (1938–44), Thai nationalism became more xenophobic. Proclaiming 'Thailand for the Thais', official ideology asserted that the Thai state should embrace all *Tai* peoples inhabiting Laos (under French control) and the Shan states of Burma (under the British). An admirer of Mussolini and Hitler, Phibul glorified military values and changed the name of the country from Siam to Thailand. In many ways, however, Phibul adopted a traditional stance: authoritarian at home, he trimmed his foreign policy to accommodate Great Powers.

Although in the 1920s Thai ministers successfully renegotiated those unequal treaties by which Western powers had gained extraterritorial and economic privileges, the British continued to dominate banking, rice-milling, rubber, tin, and timber. In addition, Thai trade was locked into the colonial ports of Hong Kong, Singapore, and Penang. Britain continued to regard Siam as commanding a frontier of British Imperial defence. British financial advisers to the Thai government, together with British diplomats (notably Sir Josiah Crosby, British Minister in Siam, 1934–41), were still among the most influential Western representatives in

[6] In Vol. III, see chap. by A. J. Stockwell, esp. pp. 375, 380–82, 383–84, 387–89.

Bangkok. After 1932, however, British advisers and representatives found it increasingly difficult to guide Siam's neutrality in the face of the relative decline of Britain, commercial competition from America, the economic nationalism of the Thai government, and the growing threat of Japanese expansionism.

As in the nineteenth century, so in the decade 1932–41 Siam was subjected to international rivalry and now to the southerly thrust of Japanese imperialism. South-East Asia was rich in resources of which the militaristic regime in Tokyo wished to deprive the West. Between June 1940 and July 1941 the Japanese exploited the circumstances of German military successes in Europe, the absence of co-ordinated defence in colonial South-East Asia, and Anglo-American differences over the protection of Siam. As a result, they achieved through diplomacy the effective occupation of Indo-China. In the international contest for Thailand, the disarray of Western powers contrasted starkly with Japan's single-mindedness. Although London and Washington responded to Japan's expansionism by agreeing to economic sanctions, these neither stopped its advance nor guaranteed protection for the Thais, who had grown 'even more fearful of doing anything which might affect Japan'.[7] In November 1941, as Japan suffered the effects of the international blockade particularly of oil supplies, the government of General Tojo prepared military strikes against American and European positions in South-East Asia and the Pacific. Taking advantage of the war in Europe, and confident in Russian neutrality in East Asia, Japan attacked Pearl Harbor, the Philippines, Malaya, and Hong Kong on the night of 7–8 December 1941. At that moment Bangkok received Churchill's ambiguous message that the British government would 'regard an attack on Thailand as an attack upon ourselves'.[8] It arrived too late, however, to prevent Phibul's capitulation to Japan's ultimatum, whereby the Thais would retain their independence provided they did not hinder Japanese troop movements.

Japanese Occupation and British Wartime Planning, 1941–1945

When Roosevelt declared war on Japan, Churchill was confident of eventual victory, but the Allies were powerless to halt the Japanese blitzkrieg. The US fleet was crippled at Pearl Harbor and half its air force in the Far East destroyed at Clark airfield in the Philippines, while British pretensions to naval strength in

[7] Berkeley Gage (Foreign Office), 25 July 1941, in Nicholas Tarling, *Britain, Southeast Asia and the Onset of the Pacific War* (Cambridge, 1996), p. 343.

[8] Richard J. Aldrich, *The Key to the South: Britain, the United States, and Thailand During the Approach of the Pacific War, 1929–1942* (Kuala Lumpur, 1993), p. 349; for Phibul, see Kobkua Suwannathat-Pian, *Thailand's Durable Premier: Phibun Through Three Decades, 1932–1957* (Kuala Lumpur, 1995).

the region sank with HMS *Repulse* and *Prince of Wales* off Malaya on 10 December 1941. Capitalizing on tactical surprise, thorough preparation, high morale, and strong leadership, Japanese forces continued their advance. They took Hong Kong on Christmas Day and in January invaded the Netherlands East Indies and Burma. Meanwhile, by outflanking the defending troops or forcing them to retreat down the north–south highway, General Yamashita's 25th Army captured Kuala Lumpur on 11 January and at the end of the month laid siege to Singapore. On 15 February 1942, after the Japanese had captured Singapore's reservoirs, General A. E. Percival decided to negotiate with Yamashita, only to discover there was no alternative to unconditional surrender. By early May the Japanese completed their occupation of the Philippines, the Netherlands East Indies, and Burma, but the tide turned with their defeats at the Battle of the Coral Sea (7 May) and Midway (4–7 June).

Explanations for what Churchill called 'the worst disaster and largest capitulation in British history' have often degenerated into witch-hunts among politicians, service chiefs, and civil servants in London, or sailors, soldiers, and administrators in Malaya. Assessments of the débâcle have indicted the British on three main charges: strategic failure, military blunders, and colonial mismanagement.

Analyses of strategic failure focus upon naval planning and the disposition of land forces. Most decision-makers presumed that a Japanese attack, if it came at all, would be launched from the sea. They believed that Malaya's jungle would provide a natural defence to the north, while the fifteen-inch naval guns of the Singapore base would repel a maritime invasion. (In the event the guns were swung landward, though their effectiveness was greatly reduced by the lack of ammunition appropriate for shelling ground forces.) Fundamental to the Singapore strategy was the assumption that Britain could either stretch its resources to defend a two-hemisphere Empire or deal with crises in different parts of the world one by one. From the early 1920s Imperial defence had hinged on the expectation that the main fleet would be available for the defence of South-East Asia and the South-West Pacific. As attention concentrated upon the struggle with Germany, however, it was supposed that Singapore had 'cannon which can hold any fleet at arm's length' until reinforcements could be spared from the West. 'On no account', wrote Winston Churchill to Neville Chamberlain on 25 March 1939, 'must anything which threatens in the Far East divert us from this prime objective.'[9] In 1941–42 few reinforcements were available: Britain was fully engaged fighting the Battle of the Atlantic, defending the Middle East, and supplying equipment to Russia. In the deployment of land forces, the British lost the initiative at the outset. Operation Matador had been planned as a pre-emptive attack upon southern Thailand to

[9] S. R. Ashton and S. E. Stockwell, eds., *Imperial Policy and Colonial Practice, 1925–1945*, British Documents on the End of Empire Project (BDEEP) (London, 1996), 1, Doc. 22 (3 and 4).

forestall enemy landings on the Kra Isthmus, but, anxious not to be the first to break Thai neutrality, the British held back until the Japanese had secured a bridgehead for advance down the peninsula.

As regards the conduct of the campaign itself, though the navy was inadequately protected from the air and the army possessed insufficient tanks and field guns to halt the invasion, the British did not lack fighting men. On the contrary, Yamashita, outnumbered by over two to one and running short of ammunition, was painfully aware of his overextended lines of supply. He realized that victory was going to be a close-run thing.[10] Yet the British never had the measure of Yamashita. The morale and training of British, Indian, and Australian forces were poor, and their leadership was weakened by indecisiveness and inter-service feuds. The one matter on which British commanders appeared unanimous was their conviction that Japanese forces would be no match for those of the British Empire. Faulty intelligence encouraged them to underestimate Japanese fighting prowess before the invasion but grossly to exaggerate their numbers as the campaign proceeded. Senior officers made mistakes: they failed to halt the advance through the peninsula and repel landings on Singapore island. They lacked imagination, being reluctant to support Colonel J. Dalley's locally recruited units of Kuomintang and Communist Chinese or launch operations behind enemy lines.

The colonial regime has been accused of apathy, arrogance, monumental inefficiency, and panic. 'The whole of Malaya has been asleep for at least two hundred years,' complained General Sir Archibald Wavell.[11] Churchill's Resident Minister, Duff Cooper, was scathing in his strictures on the hamstrung administration of the Governor, Sir Shenton Thomas. Civilians resented military demands which upset routine, business activity, or even social life. Cosseted by comforts and enervated by the climate, the British community appeared to 'lack virility,' while their relations with local peoples were poisoned by mistrust and racism. They were reluctant to arm Malays, whom they did not regard as a 'martial race', and did not trust Malaya's Chinese, notwithstanding their proven hostility to Japan. Finally, in the scramble to evacuate the country, they abandoned 'protected peoples'. Small wonder, critics have claimed, that the Malayan dominoes fell with such rapidity while long-exploited subjects watched with indifference the replacement of one imperial regime by another.

In defence of the colonial government, it has been argued that its structure was fragmented for deep-seated historical reasons, that its *raison d'être* was peacetime administration by consensus rather than dictat, and that during 1939–41 it was correctly performing its wartime functions of supplying Britain with rubber and tin while conserving foreign exchange. Members of the administration have stated

[10] Louis Allen, *Singapore, 1941–1942* (London, 1977), pp. 174, 187–88. [11] Cited in ibid., p. 200.

that their repeated warnings about Japanese intentions were consistently ignored in London, where blind faith was placed in 'fortress Singapore', and that accusations of panic during Japanese air-raids were as groundless as those suggesting that the invading army was significantly assisted by Malayan fifth-columnists. Nevertheless, although Malayan civil servants bore defeat and also the cruelties and deprivations of internment with immense courage and dignity, the reputation of British administration was permanently blighted at home and internationally, as well as in the eyes of the inhabitants of South-East Asia.

The impact of the fall of Singapore sent shockwaves through the Empire. A supposedly impregnable military base had surrendered; some 138,000 British, Indian, and Australian troops and civilians were lost as casualties or prisoners in the Malayan campaign as a whole; the Allies were denied half the world's tin and rubber; and the way was opened for Japan's occupation of the oil-rich Netherlands East Indies and of Burma. Beyond the frontiers of the Japanese Co-prosperity Sphere, the Indian nationalist movement was reinvigorated by British defeat, while Australia and New Zealand now sought protection from the United States rather than Britain.

Within a year of being driven from South-East Asia the British were preparing for its reoccupation. Yet the resurrection of British colonies, as well as those of the Dutch and French, depended upon US support. Many Americans opposed colonialism as contrary to the Atlantic Charter, free trade, Allied war aims, and more generally the idealism of the United States. Differences over Empire not merely embittered Anglo-American relations in the Asia and the Pacific theatres but complicated plans for peace. When Roosevelt proposed an international trusteeship council for the administration of former South-East Asian colonies, Churchill's government brushed aside those in Whitehall who suggested that the price of the Atlantic alliance might be surrender of parts of the British Empire. The India and Burma Office and the Colonial Office defended Britain's record, and the Colonial Office redefined colonial aims in terms of a partnership with dependent peoples leading to eventual self-government within the Commonwealth. Such nation-building would involve administrative rationalization, economic development, social welfare, the protection of minority rights, and regional security. Of course, these principles were not peculiar to South-East Asia, but they were particularly relevant to an area where the future of British colonialism was under international scrutiny. Proclamations of colonial reform partially appeased American hostility to 'saving England's South-East Asian colonies'. Opposition was also moderated by Roosevelt's unwillingness to undermine Churchill's position, US acquisition of Pacific Islands, the practical problems of post-war peacekeeping, and expectations of commercial opportunities for Americans in the war-torn colonies of penurious European states. Post-war policies for Burma, Hong Kong, Malaya, Singapore, and the Borneo territories were based on an initial period of military administration. The priority of subsequent civil government would be economic rehabilitation.

Plans for Burma were drafted by the Burma Office and the government-in-exile, under Sir Reginald Dorman-Smith in Simla, and were published as a White Paper in May 1945, soon after the capture of Rangoon. Constitutional policy, however, seemed to regress. In 1940–41 the British had envisaged further advance to 'full self-government' once the war was over, but in 1945 the government held out only the prospect of eventual Dominion Status. Rehabilitation inspired a new imperialism. It was proposed to suspend the ministerial system of 1937–42, put the country under direct British rule until December 1948, and maintain British control over the 'Scheduled Areas' of ethnic minorities until they themselves opted for amalgamation with 'Burma proper'.

Planning for the other lost territories was done by Military Planning Units under Colonial Office guidance. Economic rehabilitation lay behind proposals for direct rule which involved making Singapore, Sarawak, and North Borneo separate Crown Colonies and amalgamating the Malay States, Penang, and Malacca within a Malayan Union. Security was one of the considerations behind the proposed appointment of a regional Governor-General, who might prepare for the eventual merger of Malaya, Singapore, and British Borneo. Regional security also played a part in British policy for Thailand. Since one of 'the lessons of Singapore' appeared to be that Imperial defence hinged upon southern Siam, and since there was a mood to exact reparations from Bangkok, London adopted a more 'colonial' approach towards Thailand than in the past. In the summer of 1942 Churchill supported a suggestion to advance the northern border of British Malaya to the narrow and more easily defensible Kra Isthmus.[12] The United States, however, adopted a line similar to that taken fifty years earlier by Britain, when supporting Siam's autonomy in the face of French imperialism, and took care to safeguard the integrity of Thailand.

Other aspects of wartime planning revealed a more progressive approach on the part of the British. The proposed constitution for Hong Kong provided for an unofficial majority in the Legislative Council and an elected majority in its municipal council, while that for Singapore set up a Legislative Council with an unofficial majority and a minority of members elected by universal adult suffrage. In devising a Malayan Union citizenship scheme, the British departed radically from the 'pro-Malay' policy which had characterized their pre-war management of Malaya's plural society. By opening Malayan Union citizenship to all residents

[12] Aldrich, *The Key to the South*, pp. 366, 372–73.

who regarded Malaya as home, planners believed they were taking the first step towards the creation of a multiracial, self-governing nation.

In preparing for their reoccupation of lost colonies, the British could only guess at the changes which had occurred during their absence and the extent of devastation which they would encounter on their return. War damage varied from area to area: Burma was fought over twice, in 1942 and 1944–45, whereas most of the destruction in Malaya and the Borneo territories arose from the scorched-earth policy perpetrated by the retreating British in 1941–42. Commerce, agriculture, and industry were all hit by the collapse of Imperial trading networks and shipping shortages. Access to the rice of Burma and Thailand was blocked, causing hardship for both cultivators and consumers. Japan had neither the need nor the means to transport home many South-East Asian products. Mines, estates, and financial services were thus neglected. Food shortages forced people to scratch for alternative crops, encouraged mobility from towns to countryside, and aggravated inter-ethnic conflict.

Historians are divided on the extent to which South-East Asia was turned upside down by the Japanese occupation.[13] On the one hand, the Japanese were frequently despotic and brutal, particularly towards the overseas Chinese. It is also clear that their economic exactions resulted in deprivation, disease, and even starvation. In addition, their imperial ideology, language-teaching, and ceremonial occasions permeated the region. On the other hand, Japanese colonial regimes were not effectively totalitarian but were circumscribed by the chaos left by Britain's retreat, manpower shortages, and Japan's deteriorating military position. The policies of the Japanese were geared less to the construction of a new order, or the tactics of divide and rule, or the sponsorship of nationalist élites, than to making do with what they found. If they survived, the institutions of the British system were adapted; where they were available, incumbent Asian officials and locally respected leaders would be employed. In Malaya, for example, the sultans retained their thrones and Malay administrators kept their jobs or even advanced marginally from Assistant District Officers to become District Officers. In state-building the Japanese impact was probably more significant for Burma than Malaya, because in Burma a greater number of Asians who had identified with British colonialism had had the opportunity to abandon post and flee. The Japanese deliberately wooed nationalist élites and on 1 August 1943 granted Burma a form of self-government under Dr Ba Maw as 'Adipati' (or Führer). Even in the case of Burma, however, the Japanese neither relaxed their grip on the

[13] See Alfred W. McCoy, ed., *Asia under Japanese Occupation: Transition and Transformation* (New Haven, 1980).

levers of power nor swept away former practices, for Ba Maw's government rested on personnel and procedures from the British era and 'Indirect Rule' continued in the outlying areas.[14]

The replacement of one colonial regime by another stimulated national awareness among local peoples but complicated their allegiances. For example, Communists were in disagreement over the Comintern's 'united front' strategy to assist European imperialists against Fascists. Although Thakin Pe Myint favoured alliance with Britain, Thakin Aung San was convinced that the cause of Burmese nationalism would be advanced by Japan.[15] Indeed, during the invasion of Burma the Japanese sponsored Aung San's Burma Independence Army (the Burma National Army from August 1943) and later appointed him Minister of Defence in Ba Maw's government. The nationalistic appeal of the BIA was limited, however, since it was largely confined to the south and alienated minorities such as Karens and Indians. Malayan Communists were less equivocal than their Burmese comrades in their hostility to Japan. The Malayan Communist Party set up the Malayan People's Anti-Japanese Army (MPAJA), which established direct contact with Force 136 (a branch of Special Operations Executive), but, being a clandestine resistance movement dominated by Chinese communists, the MPAJA did not command the support of either Malays or Kuomintang Chinese. Malay radical nationalists were sponsored by the Japanese, but they attracted far less local support than did Aung San in Burma and they were left in the lurch when Japan surrendered. The Japanese also assisted the exiled Indian nationalist Subhas Chandra Bose in the recruitment of overseas Indians to the Indian National Army. Although it played a role in military operations in Burma, the principal contribution of the INA was to the propaganda aimed at subverting British India.

The Second World War dealt a mortal blow to the reputation of European imperialism, devastated the fabric of colonialism, and fired the cause of Asian nationalism. Although defeat stiffened Europeans' determination to reassert their authority in the region, the restoration of colonial regimes would require far more men, money, and materials than before the war.

New Imperialism and End of Empire after 1945

In different ways Britain, France, Holland, and not least the United States embarked upon a new imperialism in South-East Asia after the Second World War, countering the upsurge of nationalism with a second colonial occupation of

[14] See chap. by John W. Cell, esp. pp. 237–43.

[15] See Robert H. Taylor, *Marxism and Resistance in Burma, 1942–1945: Thein Pe Myint's 'Wartime Traveler'* (Athens, Oh., 1984).

the region (see Map 20.1). Whereas the Dutch and French oscillated between negotiation and the use of force in bids to regain former possessions, the Americans aimed consistently to control the economy and external affairs of the Philippines after the achievement of formal independence in July 1946. As British Imperial power in India and Burma evaporated, so Imperial interest swung further east as well as to Africa and the Middle East. Prestige, strategy, and economic considerations meant that, notwithstanding promises of eventual self-government, Britain was committed to the reimposition of control over former dependencies, at least in the short term, and to the defence and economic development of South-East Asia as a whole. Immediately after Japan's defeat and pending the return of the French and Dutch, the British were responsible for the occupation of southern Indo-China and the Netherlands East Indies.

After the Japanese surrender (14–15 August 1945), Admiral Louis Mountbatten's South-East Asia Command (SEAC) advanced its headquarters from Kandy to Singapore and stretched its mandate to cover Burma, Malaya, Singapore, Siam, southern Indo-China, and the greater part of Indonesia. British Borneo was reoccupied by Australian forces under General Douglas MacArthur's South-West Pacific Command. SEAC's specific tasks were to effect the surrender and repatriation of 738,000 Japanese personnel, evacuate allied prisoners of war, establish law and order, and prepare for the resumption of civil government. SEAC grappled with profiteering, banditry, ethnic conflict, nationalist demands, and other problems arising from food shortages, worthless currency, political uncertainty, and administrative collapse. Since the Attlee government was burdened with worldwide military commitments but barred from using Indian troops against nationalist movements, the resources available to SEAC were inadequate to its responsibilities.[16]

As its role changed from making war to restoring peace, SEAC was drawn into the politics of the region. General Philip Christison's force, which did not arrive in Java until six weeks after Achmed Sukarno had declared Indonesian independence on 17 August 1945, hoped to win the co-operation of nationalists but became their target when Brigadier A. W. S. Mallaby was killed in Surabaya (October 1945). Out of sympathy with Dutch intransigence, bewildered by Indonesian politics, and embarrassed by the need to use surrendered Japanese for peacekeeping purposes, SEAC gladly transferred the outer islands to the Dutch in July 1946 and evacuated Java and Sumatra at the end of November. SEAC's occupation of southern Indo-China proved to be briefer and less confused. When General Douglas Gracey flew into Saigon on 13 September 1945 he was met by Vietminh representatives, whose

[16] See Peter Dennis, *Troubled Days of Peace: Mountbatten and South-East Asia Command, 1945–46* (Manchester, 1987).

Map 20.1. British Decolonization in South-East Asia.

leader, Ho Chi Minh, had proclaimed the independent Democratic Republic of Vietnam in Hanoi on 2 September. Rejecting their claims, Gracey set about disarming the Vietminh and preparing for the French return. In early March 1946 Gracey handed civil administration to Governor-General Thierry d'Argenlieu and the military command to General Philippe Leclerc. In Thailand, Mountbatten attempted to impose a punitive treaty by which Bangkok would return territory taken from Burma and Malaya, make full restitution of British property, and grant Britain trading privileges, free rice, and the right to station troops in the country. Nai Pridi, who had been leader of the wartime Free Thais and was currently acting as Regent, interpreted these demands as an attempt to reduce Thailand to semi-colonial status. He prevailed on the United States to ensure that they were reduced in the final version of the Anglo-Thai Treaty of December 1945.[17]

British plans for the administration of post-war Burma were outmoded at birth. Although General William Slim's 14th Army successfully reconquered Burma in 1944–45, the political reorganization of the country was determined by the Thakins. Originally armed by the Japanese, Aung San's Burma National Army switched allegiance in August 1944 when it joined the Burma Communist Party (BCP) in the Anti-Fascist Organization (later the Anti-Fascist People's Freedom League). When Aung San's forces rose against the Japanese in March 1945, he increased his popularity, improved his position *vis à vis* the Communist Party, and demonstrated his power to the British. In September 1945 Mountbatten struck an agreement with Aung San for the absorption of the Burma National Army (now known as the Patriotic Burmese Forces) into a new Burma army (although a separate People's Volunteer Organization continued as Aung San's private army). When Governor Reginald Dorman-Smith resumed the civil government of Burma in October 1945, he came under great pressure to include Aung San in his Executive Council and accelerate constitutional advance. Reluctant to accommodate Aung San (whom many 'old Burma hands' regarded as a war criminal), yet lacking the power either to stand up to him or sponsor alternative politicians, Dorman-Smith forfeited the confidence of the British Prime Minister C. R. Attlee, who, on the advice of Mountbatten, replaced him by Sir Hubert Rance in August 1946.

Faced with a police strike and the prospect of government breakdown, the new Governor, who had acquired a liberal reputation as Director of Civil Affairs in Burma in 1945–46, virtually handed over his Executive Council to Aung San and the Anti-Fascist People's Freedom League (AFPFL). Events in Burma and wider developments in India were dictating the speed and manner of the transfer of power. The principal factor was the strength of AFPFL's challenge to British authority, coupled with Britain's military incapacity to maintain control at a time

[17] Judith A. Stowe, *Siam becomes Thailand: A Story of Intrigue* (London, 1991), pp. 337–59.

of impending civil war. As Attlee told the Cabinet on 19 December 1946, 'Indian troops could not be used for this purpose, and British troops could not be made available without serious consequences'. Even if such forces could have been provided, he continued, 'it would not be possible with this strength to do more than hold Rangoon and a few other key points'. Furthermore, trying to govern Burma by force would 'probably serve only to strengthen national feeling in Burma and to increase the influence of those who advocated early secession from the British Commonwealth'.[18] Another consideration was Burma's declining Imperial significance. British interests in Burma derived from its proximity to India. After their constitutional separation in the 1930s, Burma remained a strategic and economic appendage of the Raj. So far as the British economy was concerned, Burma's rice, oil, and timber were valuable but far less significant dollar-earners than Malaya's commodities. Consequently, once the Labour government declared its intention to withdraw from the Indian subcontinent, it made less sense to cling to its eastern frontier. Attlee's view was that 'if the principle of independence was sound for India it was also sound for Burma'[19] and, as with India, he hoped to refashion Britain's relations with Burma through membership of the Commonwealth.

Talks between a delegation led by Aung San and the Attlee government in January 1947 resulted in agreement that Burma should advance to independence, that the Executive Council should act as the interim government, and that elections should be held to a Constituent Assembly which would draft the independence constitution. The resounding electoral victory of the Anti-Fascist People's Freedom League in April seemed to bode well. In fact, however, the prospect of independence triggered a power-struggle involving the Burma army, the Burma Communist Party, the Karen National Union, and other minorities hostile to central control. Wary of the Communists, Thakin U Nu's Goodwill Mission to London in June rejected Commonwealth membership, on grounds that Burma could not recognize the position of the Crown.[20] Though eager to keep Burma within the Commonwealth, the Cabinet could not see a way of accommodating Burmese republicanism as it would later do in the case of India. The assassination of Aung San and six of his cabinet in July 1947 doomed any chance of closer links with Britain as well as Burmese unity. AFPFL remained in office and

[18] Hugh Tinker, ed., *Burma: The Struggle for Independence, 1944–1948*, 2 vols. (London, 1983–84), II, Doc. 145. See also Tinker, 'The Contraction of Empire in Asia, 1945–48: The Military Dimension', *Journal of Imperial and Commonwealth History* (hereafter *JICH*), XVI, 2 (1988), pp. 218–33.

[19] In Ronald Hyam, ed., *The Labour Government, 1945–1951*, BDEEP (London, 1992), I, p. xxv. See also R. B. Smith, 'Some Contrasts between Burma and Malaya in British Policy towards South-East Asia, 1942–1946', in R. B. Smith and A. J. Stockwell, eds., *British Policy and the Transfer of Power in Asia: Documentary Perspectives* (London, 1988), pp. 30–76.

[20] Tinker, ed., *Burma: The Struggle for Independence*, II, Docs. 388, 412, 415, 416.

shaped the independence constitution, but the authority of its new leader, U Nu, was gravely circumscribed. Soon after the Union of Burma achieved independence as a republic on 4 January 1948, Communist insurrection and Karen separatism plunged Burma into civil war.[21]

While Britain had little option but to hand over power to Burma in January 1948, the manner of the transfer remained a cautionary tale. Internal instability was an acute problem. Whereas nine-tenths of the people holding responsible positions in India and Ceylon at the time of independence had been locally recruited, this was not the case in Burma.[22] By the early 1950s several distinct civil wars were raging. In external relations, Attlee deeply regretted Burma's withdrawal from the Commonwealth; subsequent Conservative governments took care to prevent secession by other territories.[23] When the Anglo-Burmese Defence Treaty lapsed, a link snapped in the chain of regional security. Burma was exposed to Communist China on its north-east frontier. The British also feared that if Burma fell to Communism its rice exports would be cut off, to the grave detriment of British dependencies and allies in Asia.

Like Burma, Malayan society was riven by communalism and unrest after the Second World War, but apart from the Malayan Communist Party's stated aim to 'establish a democratic government in Malaya with the electorate drawn from all races', there was no sign of an independence movement. Given these circumstances and the economic and strategic importance of Malaya and Singapore, the British envisaged a prolonged period of colonial rule during which their priorities would be administrative efficiency, economic rehabilitation, and the creation of a multi-racial nation. Their plans for the Malayan Union and Crown Colony rule in Singapore, however, were not implemented without opposition.

Britain's apparent seizure of Malay sovereignty in Anglo-Malay treaties negotiated by Sir Harold MacMichael in October–December 1945, and the proposal to award citizenship to non-Malays, provoked unprecedented opposition from the Malay community. The Johore aristocrat, Dato Onn bin Jaafar, formed the United Malays National Organization which, in uneasy alliance with the sultans, opposed the Malayan Union. The British feared the loss of traditional Malay support, especially Malays in the police, and the possibility of resistance in other quarters, fuelled by Chinese Communists and Indonesian nationalists. They therefore entered into negotiations with Malay leaders. The compromise solution was a federal constitution which retained a strong central government and a form of

[21] Clive J. Christie, *A Modern History of Southeast Asia: Decolonization, Nationalism and Separatism* (London, 1996), chap. 3. See also U Maung Maung, *Burmese Nationalist Movements, 1940–1948* (Edinburgh, 1989) and Martin Smith, *Burma: Insurgency and the Politics of Ethnicity* (London, 1991).

[22] Hyam, ed., *The Labour Government*, II, Doc. 191 (Annex, Sir O. Franks).

[23] See above, pp. 337–38.

common citizenship but guaranteed Malay political predominance. Although the British never lost sight of the multiracial principle underlying the Malayan Union, the inauguration of the Federation of Malaya (1 February 1948) was essentially a reaffirmation of Anglo-Malay collaboration. It further alienated the Chinese community.

Economic and ethnic differences delayed until the early 1960s the long-term plan to unite the Federation, Singapore, and the Borneo territories. In 1946 the Chartered Company surrendered North Borneo to the Crown without local opposition. Raja Vyner Brooke's cession of Sarawak, however, provoked a Malay-led but unsuccessful campaign against colonial rule, culminating in the assassination of the British Governor, Duncan Stewart, in 1949. Constitutionally separated from the peninsula in 1946, Singapore resumed its roles as military base and centre for the spread of British commerce and influence in the region. It also became the headquarters of several offices set up to supervise regional affairs, the most significant of which was the Commissioner-Generalship in South-East Asia, held by Malcolm MacDonald in 1948–55, whose job was to co-ordinate foreign, colonial, and defence policies during the cold war.

It has been said that the cold war came to the rescue of the British Empire.[24] The United States moderated its anti-colonialism and supported the British and French Empires in the worldwide containment of Communism. With the same objective, Americans opposed the imperialism of the Dutch, whom they pressed into a settlement with Sukarno after he had apparently demonstrated his dependability by defeating the Indonesian Communists at Madiun in September 1948. As in the Second World War, however, the Anglo-American alliance during the cold war was an unequal partnership and the British worried that the basis of their independent foreign policy, namely the Empire and Commonwealth, might be compromised by dependence upon the United States. The relationship was occasionally embittered by differences. Partly to safeguard Hong Kong, London diverged from Washington's line and recognized Communist China in January 1950. Later that year Britain was alarmed by General MacArthur's prosecution of the Korean War, which drew China into the conflict and risked the goodwill of independent Asia. The conclusion of the ANZUS Pact in 1951 was a blow to British pride and a veiled threat to Commonwealth solidarity. In April 1954, worried by growing American belligerency, the British government declined the US invitation to join an international force to rescue the French in Vietnam. Britain and America differed in their expectations for the post-colonial world; while the Americans

[24] Wm. Roger Louis and Ronald Robinson, 'The Imperialism of Decolonization', *JICH*, XXII, 3 (1994), p. 467.

looked forward to the emergence of new client states, free from the shackles of old empires, the British hoped to maintain their interests and influence in former colonies through the Commonwealth, the sterling area, and defence pacts.

By ensuring American support for Britain's economy and international position, the cold war granted the Empire a reprieve; but subversion at the local level added to the problems of colonial control. Reacting to industrial unrest and lawlessness, the Malayan government declared a state of emergency (effectively a state of war) which lasted from 1948 to 1960. Under the leadership of Chin Peng, the Malayan Communists resurrected the rural network (Min Yuen) which had supplied the anti-Japanese resistance forces with food and intelligence. Operating from jungle bases, the Malayan Races Liberation Army struck at the estates, mines, labour-force, and infrastructure of the colonial economy. European planters, national servicemen, and High Commissioner Henry Gurney were all victims of the guerrillas, but Malayan losses were greater. Among the civilians, the Chinese were the butt of both sides and bore the brunt of the conflict; within the security forces, the regular and auxiliary Malay police suffered most casualties.[25] The financial costs of counter-insurgency were also high: in January 1955 the High Commissioner estimated that the British and Malayan governments were spending 'not far short of £100 million a year' on the emergency.[26] None the less, Britain regarded Malaya as too valuable to lose: it was a front-line state in the containment of world Communism; its rubber and tin earned dollars for the sterling area; and national pride ruled out a scuttle reminiscent of 1941–42.

Although the Communists appeared to hold the initiative until the end of 1951, two years later they were in retreat militarily and by December 1955 their return to open, legitimate politics was well and truly blocked. Counter-insurgency techniques partly account for their failure, particularly the Briggs Plan to resettle Chinese squatters and Sir Gerald Templer's improvements in intelligence, policing, and psychological warfare. Even more significant for the outcome were the failures of the Chinese-dominated Malayan Communist Party to recruit Malays and attract military aid from Communists outside Malaya. Consequently, neither the Malayan economy nor the Malayan state succumbed to insurgency. On the contrary, boosted for a time by the Korean War boom, rubber and tin contributed handsomely to the government's revenues. Meanwhile, emergency measures extended the state's reach to embrace more and more Malayans in town and countryside.[27] Part of this process was the 'hearts and minds' strategy of Templer (High Commissioner, 1952–54) which aimed to create a self-governing Malayan nation and

[25] Anthony Short, *The Communist Insurrection in Malaya, 1948–1960* (London, 1975), p. 503.

[26] A. J. Stockwell, ed., *Malaya, 1942–1957*, BDEEP (London, 1995), II, Doc. 341(7).

[27] See T. N. Harper, *The End of Empire and the Making of Malaya* (Cambridge, forthcoming).

reduce the MCP's nationalist credentials. Following Gurney's quasi-ministerial or Member system (1951) and the introduction of municipal elections (1951–52), the first elections to the Federal Council took place in July 1955.

At the federal elections Tunku Abdul Rahman's Alliance of three communally exclusive parties (the United Malays National Organization, the Malayan Chinese Association, and the Malayan Indian Congress) won fifty-one of the fifty-two elected seats. Malaya now became internally self-governing. Having previously mistrusted the Alliance as the institutionalization of communalism, the British accepted its timetable for independence once the Tunku had achieved a strong national mandate and rejected Chin Peng's offer of a negotiated settlement at the Baling talks in December 1955. In exchange for agreements on defence and membership of the Commonwealth and sterling area, Britain brought independence forward to 31 August 1957.

The last days of British rule in Malaya suggest a skilful adjustment of collaborative mechanisms on the part of the British to facilitate the transition from formal to informal Empire. In fact, however, the Alliance had forced the British to go faster and further than they had anticipated and, in so doing, to abandon some stated preconditions.[28] Power was transferred before the emergency had ended (1960), before the Federation had merged with Singapore (1963), and before the nationalist movement had become genuinely multiracial (witness the communal bloodshed of May 1969). The British were also disappointed that independent Malaya did not join the South-East Asia Treaty Organization to play a fuller role in regional security.

Continuing fears of Communist subversion contributed to the creation of Malaysia in 1961–63. Consisting of Malaya, Singapore, Sarawak, and Sabah (North Borneo), Malaysia relieved Britain of three further territories, though Singapore seceded in 1965 and Brunei remained outside Malaysia, not becoming a fully sovereign and independent state until 31 December 1983. After 1963 Britain still remained responsible for regional defence, which was put to the test by Indonesia's armed 'Confrontation' with Malaysia (1963–66). In addition to obligations towards former colonies and continuing global aspirations, Anglo-American solidarity sustained Britain's military presence in South-East Asia. In 1965 Robert McNamara advised President Johnson that 'we place higher value on Far Eastern British commitment than European'; and Walt Rostow urged that 'we must explain to [Harold] Wilson the importance of staying in Asia in Britain's own interest'.[29] Some in Washington felt that the special relationship required

[28] Stockwell, ed., *Malaya*, I, pp. lxxii–lxxxi.

[29] In Philip Ziegler, *Wilson: The Authorised Life of Lord Wilson of Rievaulx* (London, 1993), p. 221. See also Phillip Darby, *British Defence Policy East of Suez, 1947–1968* (London, 1973), and Chin Kin Wah, *The Defence of Malaysia and Singapore: The Transformation of a Security System, 1957–1971* (Cambridge, 1983).

British support for the United States in Vietnam. The Wilson government was faced with a dilemma: military commitments in South-East Asia might, by strengthening the Anglo-American axis, secure for Britain a world role and underwrite the economy; on the other hand, they were as likely to play havoc with government finances and the balance-of-payments. Ultimately, it was devaluation of sterling in November 1967 that forced the Labour government to set in train a plan for withdrawal from the Singapore base by 1971.

The history of the British Empire in South-East Asia during the twentieth century is partly a tale of diminishing British power associated with economic and military decline and aggravated by local resistance. The course of British imperialism is not one of unrelieved diminution, however, but divides dramatically at 1941–42. Until 1941 British pre-eminence in the region was challenged, though not overturned, by nationalists; it was also at first assisted, but later destroyed, by the Japanese empire. Yet against the tide of bankruptcy at home, nationalist opposition, and international criticism, there was an Imperial revival after 1942. Short-lived in British Burma and the Dutch East Indies, the new imperialism lasted longer when supported by the United States, as was the case with British Malaya and French Indo-China. Compared with the French, however, the British were less encumbered by a colonial tradition of direct rule and metropolitan control. Consequently, they adjusted more pragmatically to post-war circumstances. Decolonization has sometimes been presented as another phase of imperialism in which Britain shrugged off the burdens of colonial rule but safeguarded interests and influence. In the wider perspective, however, Imperial revival in association with the United States and decolonization in collaboration with nationalist leaders appear to be aspects of the management of Britain's decline and symptomatic of her incapacity to control events in South-East Asia. Indeed, the British never established a grip on developments in Burma after the reconquest but simply ran before the wind, while in Malaya their plans were refashioned by communal politics and Communist insurgency. By the late 1960s Britain could no longer afford the costs of playing even junior partner to the United States in post-colonial South-East Asia, and so withdrew, leaving the region to American military power and economic penetration by Japan.

Select Bibliography

RICHARD J. ALDRICH, *The Key to the South: Britain, the United States, and Thailand During the Approach of the Pacific War, 1929–1942* (Kuala Lumpur, 1993).

LOUIS ALLEN, *Singapore, 1941–1942* (London, 1977).

JOHN F. CADY, *A History of Modern Burma* (Ithaca, NY, 1958).

Clive J. Christie, *A Modern History of Southeast Asia: Decolonization, Nationalism and Separatism* (London, 1996).

T. N. Harper, *The End of Empire and the Making of Malaya* (Cambridge, forthcoming).

Robert Heussler, *British Rule in Malaya: The Malayan Civil Service and Its Predecessors, 1867–1941* (Westport, Conn., 1981).

W. David McIntyre, *The Rise and Fall of the Singapore Naval Base, 1919–1942* (London, 1979).

Anthony Milner, *The Invention of Politics in Colonial Malaya: Contesting Nationalism and the Expansion of the Public Sphere* (Cambridge, 1994).

Jan Pluvier, *South-East Asia from Colonialism to Independence* (Kuala Lumpur, 1974).

R. H. W. Reece, *The Name of Brooke: The End of White Rajah Rule in Sarawak* (Kuala Lumpur, 1982).

William R. Roff, *The Origins of Malay Nationalism* (New Haven, 1967).

Anthony Short, *The Communist Insurrection in Malaya, 1948–1960* (London, 1975).

Simon C. Smith, *British Relations with the Malay Rulers from Decentralization to Malayan Independence, 1930–1957* (Kuala Lumpur, 1995).

A. J. Stockwell, ed., *Malaya, 1942–1957*, British Documents on the End of Empire Project (BDEEP), 3 Parts (London, 1995).

Nicholas Tarling, *The Fall of Imperial Britain in South-East Asia* (Kuala Lumpur, 1993).

—— ed., *The Cambridge History of Southeast Asia*, Vol. II (Cambridge, 1992).

Robert H. Taylor, *The State in Burma* (London, 1987).

Hugh Tinker, ed., *Burma: The Struggle for Independence, 1944–1948*, 2 vols. (London, 1983–84).

Nicholas J. White, *Business, Government, and the End of Empire: Malaya, 1942–1957* (Kuala Lumpur, 1996).

David K. Wyatt, *Thailand: A Short History* (New Haven, 1982).

21

Britain's Informal Empire in the Middle East

GLEN BALFOUR-PAUL

'If these are the rival angles of vision of contemporary authorities,' wrote Foreign Secretary Curzon in 1919 when the disposal of the collapsed Ottoman empire was being debated between the European powers, 'what will not be the perplexities of the future historian?'[1] They were prophetic words.

Since the eighteenth century Britain's response to the Eastern Question had been to prop up Ottoman sovereignty in western Asia as a manageable buffer protecting both British India and the eastern Mediterranean against the designs of other European powers. The threat was perceived as coming primarily from Tsarist Russia and, most notably when Napoleon invaded Egypt in 1798, from France. Both were headed off. The prime strategic value of Egypt was greatly enhanced by the opening of the Suez Canal in 1869. Despite French cultural pre-eminence in Egypt, it was Foreign Secretary Salisbury's aim in 1879 to secure exclusive political influence, coupled with the promotion of peaceful indigenous government.[2] In 1882 British troops landed in Alexandria, ostensibly to protect the Ottoman Khedive against a popular uprising, and despite French and Russian protests the plunge was taken.

The extending of Britain's dominance over a much wider area between the Mediterranean and India to establish her informal empire in the Middle East was thereby given a crucial push. 'Informal empire' may sound a contradiction in terms, since Empire in the proper sense involved annexation and full subordination to the Crown. The term must serve to embrace the varying modes and degrees of overlordship imposed on different territories and for different lengths of time, from Libya to Iran and from Syria to the coasts of Arabia and the Sudan. The primary object throughout was the security of routes by land, sea, and later air to India. As the Ottoman empire collapsed, the area came to be known as the Middle East. The rationale behind the Occupation and Administration

[1] Curzon to Lord Derby, 30 May 1919, E. L. Woodward and Rohan Butler, eds., *Documents on British Foreign Policy, 1919–1939* (London, 1952), IV, p. 255.

[2] Salisbury to Malet (Consul-General, Cairo), Secret, 16 Oct. 1879, F[oreign] O[ffice] 78/2997, no. 275. For Britain's policies in Egypt generally, see Vol. III, chap. by Afaf Lutfi al-Sayyid-Marsot.

of Enemy Territories (OETAs) as an accident of war was not directly Imperial but the effect could be the same, and OETAs have been included. The avoidance throughout of formal annexation can be attributed partly to world reactions to the South African War, as a result of which Britain ceased to be 'unreservedly imperialist in good conscience',[3] but also to the financial and manpower implications for an Empire already overstretched. (The conversion of Aden into a Crown Colony in 1937 was a later departure from this principle.) The policy of treaty-based hegemony was expected, wrongly as it turned out, to be less open to criticism, and has often been described as empire-on-the-cheap. None the less it served, while it lasted, its basic purpose.

When Britain set out to establish her hegemony in the area, Egypt with its cotton and Persia with its oil were the only territories with valuable material assets. They were also ethnically distinct from the rest: Egypt was only partly Arab, Persia mainly Indo-European. Elsewhere the basically Semitic populations, mostly Arab but including a Jewish minority, produced a surplus in the area's economy only in and around the cities. In these, with their history as prosperous commercial entrepôts and their political, mercantile, and religious centrality, the upper classes enjoyed considerable wealth, influence, and cultural sophistication. Outside the towns, peasants, bedouin, and fishermen lived at subsistence level under their traditional tribal heads. The total Arabic-speaking population of the area amounted in 1914 to less than 30 million, 12 million of which were in Egypt. Until the divisive nation-state concept supervened, the whole area was economically a single unit in the sense that its constituents, the desert, the cultivated, and the urban workshop, could exchange their products without formal impediment. In its 400 years of empire Ottoman rule, though ponderous, had been more imaginative than Western critics declared. Urban administration was closely structured; members of leading Arab families were taken to Istanbul to be trained, mostly as army officers; and the *millet* system, under which non-Muslims enjoyed a certain autonomy, was remarkably liberal. The Ottomans had, however, no intention of encouraging a specifically Arab sense of identity. What did instil everywhere a sense of community was the Islamic faith. Doctrinally the mainstream Sunnis were, as they still are, at odds with the dissident Shiites. These formed half the populations of Mesopotamia and the Yemen and a third of the Lebanon, but the main mass was in Persia, beyond the Ottoman frontier. More fundamental was the cleavage separating all Muslims from the Christian minorities, notably the Copts in Egypt and the Maronites in Lebanon, and from the Jews. Both Jews and Christians, however, were regarded as *Ahl al-Kitab* (People of the Book). By that token they were not ill-treated but were denied some of the rights and duties of

[3] L. Carl Brown's phrase in his *International Politics in the Middle East* (London, 1984), p. 89.

Muslims. Education, apart from primitive *khalwas* teaching the Koran, barely existed outside the main towns. In the latter, traditional institutions and recently established Western mission-schools produced a growing local intelligentsia and the elements of a middle class. Despite the paternalist preference of the British in the field for the simple villagers and nomads, it was amongst the educated urban élite that their policy-makers were obliged to look for collaborators to make indirect rule practicable. Enough would be found, but those excluded were unlikely to be well-disposed.

The occupation of Egypt in 1882 quickly exposed Britain to requests from the Khedive for help to suppress a serious uprising in his own 'empire' in the Sudan, where the previous year the Mahdi Mohammed Ahmed—an early 'fundamentalist'—had led a revolt.[4] Apart from sanctioning General Gordon's mission of investigation and Kitchener's vain expedition to rescue him, the Liberal Prime Minister Gladstone was opposed to intervention. It was not until the Tories returned to power in 1895 that the reconquest of the Sudan was undertaken on the Khedive's behalf. The outcome was the imposition there in 1899 of an Anglo-Egyptian 'Condominium'. In practice Britain saw to it that the administration of the Sudan, then deemed a strategic asset, was almost exclusively British.

Her domination of the sea-routes to India had been established much earlier—in the Persian Gulf by subjecting the principle sheikhs along its Arab coast to a series of treaties from 1820 to the 1890s aimed at preserving the seas from piracy and keeping other powers out, and in southern Arabia by forcibly occupying Aden in 1839. A preferential relationship was also established in the 1870s with the independent Sultan of Muscat. For the maintenance of supremacy at sea, administrative intervention inland of these coasts was considered neither necessary nor desirable. Inroads into the territory of the Somalis, overlooking the Red Sea mouth from the Horn of Africa, were made by Britain (as well as by Italy and France); and its central segment, despite continuing local resistance, was declared a British Protectorate in 1887.

Protection of landward approaches to India through the Middle East against suspected Russian designs needed different handling. Lord Curzon, serving his seven years as Viceroy of India over the turn of the century, had sought inconclusively to persuade the Tory government that Britain should resolutely put a stop to Russian intervention in Persia, which he saw as fraught with danger to the security of the Persian Gulf and of India. The Liberal government which ousted the Tories in 1905, the year of Curzon's resignation, preferred to pursue an accommodation with Russia. Humbled by defeat in their war with Japan in 1904, the Russians were finally persuaded by the Liberal Foreign Secretary, Sir Edward Grey,

[4] In Vol. III, see pp. 634; 655.

to sign in 1907 an Anglo-Russian Entente. Under its terms Persia—without consulting the Persians—was divided into Russian and British 'spheres of influence' separated by a neutral buffer. The British sphere was judged, to Curzon's consternation in the House of Lords, adequate to safeguard Britain's strategic and economic interests and to deter the Russians from any military push either towards the Gulf or through India's unreliable neighbour Afghanistan. As for the Ottoman provinces along the route to India, the British, as A. P. Thornton puts it, 'did what Palmerston had always rigidly refused to do: they "leased all the inns on the way", using, where suitable, Jews or Arabs as their tenants'.[5] This, of course, awaited the expulsion of the Ottoman landlords in the First World War.

The decade before that war witnessed a series of pregnant developments. The first was Germany's appearance on the scene under Kaiser Wilhelm's *Drang nach Osten* (Drive towards the East), emphasized by his concession from the Ottomans for building a railway through their territory to Basra—a 'jalon posé [as a French observer put it] pour le partage éventuel de la Turquie en Asie' ('a landmark set out for the eventual partition of Turkey in Asia'). The second was the discovery of substantial oil by the British concessionaries in south-west Persia (and some on the Red Sea coast of Egypt) in 1908. In 1911 Winston Churchill switched the Royal Navy from coal to oil; and in 1914, foreseeing the imminence of war, he bought for the government a 51 per cent share in the already highly productive Anglo-Persian Oil Company. As the industrialized world scrambled for oil, Britain hastened to secure exclusive rights to approve concessionaries in other Gulf sheikhdoms, where oil might be found—notably in Kuwait, Bahrain, and the Nejd, where a preferential treaty had been signed with Abdul Aziz ibn Saud in 1915. The third factor was the emergence of the 'Young Turks'. In 1908 this reformist group summarily replaced the autocratic Sultan Abdul Hamid with his inoffensive uncle and set about pursuing their modernizing ambitions. The fourth development was the stirring among educated Arabs of a yearning to revive the identity and greatness of their race and its freedom from outside interference. Pan-Arab ideas had already been voiced by sundry impressive proponents for half a century, most of them exposed to Western education and nationalist conceptions. Years passed before any organized movement emerged. Initially neither the Pan-Arabs nor the Young Turks sought the end of the Ottoman empire, only its reinvigoration and, in the Arab case, a bigger share in its administration. Shortly before the war, however, their aims diverged. While the Young Turks reverted to centralized control, a number of secret Arab societies were formed aiming at

[5] A. P. Thornton, *The Imperial Idea and its Enemies: A Study in British Power*, 2nd edn. (London, 1966), p. 154. Palmerston's witticism of 1859 required from the 'inns on the north road' only accessibility and the furnishing of 'mutton-chops and post-horses'.

political separation from the Turks. The most active of these was *al-Ahd* (the Covenant), set up in 1913 by disaffected Arab officers of the Ottoman army.

When Europe went to war in 1914, the Ottomans threw in their lot with the Central Powers. Britain's immediate response was to declare Egypt a British Protectorate and to annex Cyprus (where Disraeli had extracted strategic occupation rights fifty years earlier). The following April the Entente powers, France, Russia, and Britain, started staking out in secret correspondence their *desiderata* in the Middle East, on the assumption that the Ottoman armies would soon be defeated. In Britain the de Bunsen Committee had been set up to examine the options for the future of the Ottoman empire, not excluding its possible preservation in one form or another. The Committee endorsed the undesirability of adding to Britain's extensive formal Empire but recognized that, for the protection of her exclusive position in the Persian Gulf, some species of British control in Mesopotamia and of land communications with it was essential—if only to keep other imperial powers out of the vicinity. Despite German and Turkish military successes, these preliminary British and French claims were carried further and formalized in what is known as the Sykes–Picot Agreement of May 1916.[6] This was accepted by the Russians in return for a promise of territory in eastern Anatolia. With the object of 'producing a more favourable political situation' in the area to be liberated, the Anglo-French understanding included a mutual agreement, conditional on Arab co-operation, to 'recognize and uphold an independent Arab State or Confederation of States'. Its precise boundaries, lying between a French preserve along the Syrian coast and a British one embracing Baghdad and Basra, would be negotiated later; and the independent area itself would be divided into zones of indirect but exclusive influence, defined as 'priority of interests' and the right to 'supply advisers or foreign functionaries at the request of the Arab State or Confederation'. On Palestine all the three powers could settle for was the principle of some form of international administration; but this was overtaken by history.

In formulating this agreement, Sykes and Picot took account of the correspondence already exchanged between the Sherif Hussein of Mecca and Sir Harold McMahon, the High Commissioner in Egypt.[7] The Sherif was contemplating, if assured of British support, a revolt against his Ottoman suzerain. His initial aim was simply to secure his own precarious position in the Hejaz; but while the correspondence proceeded, he was led mistakenly to believe that his revolt would

[6] Woodward and Butler, *Documents*, IV, pp. 241–51. The texts had been made public (doctored with intent) by the Bolsheviks in 1917.

[7] Officially disclosed only in *P[arliamentary] P[apers]* (1938–39), Cmd 5957, XVII, 573. See Elie Kedourie, *In the Anglo-Arab Labyrinth: The McMahon–Husayn Correspondence and Its Interpretations* (Cambridge, 1976).

be the signal for a mass Arab uprising in Syria. His ambitions thereupon expanded and he sweepingly asked for an assurance that, as a reward for Arab co-operation, Britain would promote an independent Arab state covering virtually the whole of Ottoman Asia. Since any Arab diversion pinning down some of the Turkish armies would be useful, Foreign Secretary Sir Edward Grey authorized McMahon to give encouragement to the Sherif in such terms as he judged necessary. The assurances contained in McMahon's resulting letter of 24 October 1915 were the source of much subsequent misunderstanding, not least over Palestine, but were so ambiguously expressed and subject to such provisos and reservations as would, on subsequent detailed examination, relieve most consciences in Britain. But the Arabs remained convinced that McMahon had misled them, and later unfulfilled British policy declarations, recorded below, were to compound their disillusion.

To the Government of India, though its protests were overruled, British encouragement to Arab Muslims, particularly those at the centre of pilgrimage, to repudiate their allegiance to the Caliphate was a grave blunder. The 80 million Muslims in restive India—almost thrice the number in Arab Asia put together[8]—regarded the Caliph as their spiritual head and might well respond dangerously to his call of November 1914 for an Islamic jihad (holy war) against the infidel British. Imperial responsibilities in the Middle East had been traditionally divided between London and India by a line drawn roughly from Aqaba to Afghanistan. The fact that the handling of the whole Middle East 'sideshow' was now left by the hard-pressed authorities in London in the hands of those in Cairo caused much resentment in Delhi. This was directed especially at Gilbert Clayton's 'Arab Bureau' (of which T. E. Lawrence became a member), set up in Cairo in February 1916 by the Foreign Office. With its loose remit, its tentacles stretched well into India's 'preserve'. Delhi found its operators too big for their desert boots.

Sherif Hussein's revolt, which sparked off prematurely in June 1916 but quickly looked like fizzling out into a local stalemate, converted itself—despite the non-occurrence of any 'mass uprising' in Syria—into pursuing, with assistance from the Arab Bureau, the Hashemite dream of a post-war Arab state comprising as much of Ottoman Asia as possible. The picaresque braveries, glamorized by Lawrence, of the bedouin force under the Sherif's impressive son Faisal, as it scrambled northwards on camel-back in parallel with General Allenby's measured advance through Palestine, were certainly useful but in no sense determinant. Nor did the unconcealed objectives of Lawrence and the Bureau endear them any further to Delhi, which did not share their belief that Britain's Imperial interests could best be served by sympathetic manipulation of Arab aspirations and the

[8] Estimated total in 1914 at most 28 million (Egypt 12, Sudan 5, Iraq 3.5, Syria—including Lebanon, Palestine, and Transjordan—4, Yemen 3.5). Thirty years later figures had doubled.

promotion under purely British tutelage of a loose confederation of independent Arab states.[9] In Delhi, direct British control of Mesopotamia was judged essential. London's prime concern was the Western Front where, despite the entry of the United States into the war in April 1917, the situation remained grim.

By 1917 the tide of war was at least turning in the Middle East. But when Allenby dislodged the Turks from Damascus in October 1918, a new breach developed with the French. Having, it seems, little to guide him but Sykes–Picot, under which inland Syria, including the cities of Damascus, Homs, Hama, and Aleppo fell within the proposed Arab state, Allenby allowed Faisal to make his formal entry first and to start setting up an Arab administration. The French expostulated. Modifications to Sykes–Picot were, however, wanted by Britain too; and in March 1919, in the presence of President Woodrow Wilson, Clemenceau agreed to Lloyd George's request for the transfer of Mosul from the French to the British zone of influence and for the substitution in Palestine of British administration for international control. In exchange, Clemenceau demanded that France should have a freer hand in the whole of Syria than Allenby's provisional arrangements with Faisal, coupled with British military occupation, allowed.[10] Despite Lloyd George's pro-Arab protestations, the only clear outcome was that the Sykes–Picot Agreement was abandoned—if only because by now France entertained expectations of a Mandate for all Syria (Palestine excepted). For that matter the Mandate conception, already virtually accepted at the Peace Conference in Paris, had attractions for Britain as well. That being so, Lloyd George's protestations look disingenuous.

Before this situation had arisen, two momentous developments in 1917 altered the course of history. One, the Bolshevik Revolution, put an end to the Tsarist empire; the other, the Balfour Declaration, proved to hasten the collapse—inexorable for other reasons too—of Britain's Empire in the Middle East.

Balfour's letter of 2 November to Lord Rothschild declared that the British government 'view[ed] with favour the establishment in Palestine of a national home for the Jewish people,' without prejudice to the 'civil and religious rights of the non-Jewish communities'.[11] (There was no mention of *political* rights in either case.) The idea of sponsoring a national home somewhere for scattered and persecuted Jewry had attracted interest in Britain since Palmerston's days. There were other, less declarable, motives behind the Declaration, made now in the middle of war with Germany and locating the proposed home specifically in Palestine. These included strategic calculation and a pressing need to detach

[9] Bruce Westrate, *The Arab Bureau: British Policy in the Middle East, 1916–1920* (Philadelphia, Pa., 1992), chap. 4.

[10] J. C. Hurewitz, *The Middle East and North Africa in World Politics: A Documentary Record*, 2 vols., Vol. II, *British and French Supremacy, 1914–1956* (New Haven, 1975), pp. 158–66.

[11] For its full text and preceding Cabinet discussions, ibid., pp. 101–06.

world Jewry from what was believed to be its predominant support for the Germans. What was scarcely taken into account was the fact that Palestine had long been the home of a different Semitic people, now forming 90 per cent of its population of some 750,000. The problem this was to cause, made increasingly acute when it became evident that the aim of the Zionists was not just a home but a Jewish state,[12] and when a national consciousness of their own began to develop among the fractionalized Palestinians, would soon show Britain's balancing-act to be unsustainable.

When the war with the Ottomans ended, Britain ostensibly controlled the whole of their eastern Arab provinces but was faced, as Curzon observed, with many conflicting 'angles of vision'. The French, the Syrians, the Hashemites, the Zionists, the Palestinians, and the Government of India all pulled in different directions, while President Wilson insisted in his 'Fourteen Points' on the universal right to self-determination. To add to the confusion, Britain and France issued within hours of the Ottoman surrender a joint declaration in which their war-aim in the area was defined as 'the establishment of national governments and administrations deriving their authority from the initiative and free choice of the indigenous populations'. Quite apart from McMahon's ambiguous generalities, much the same terminology had figured in three local pronouncements in 1917, by General Maude on capturing Baghdad, by Allenby on capturing Jerusalem, and with some ambivalence by David Hogarth (of the Arab Bureau) in response to enquiries from seven Syrians in Cairo.[13] In making this joint governmental declaration now and giving it maximum publicity, France and Britain doubtless had one eye on President Wilson, the other on the kind of control they planned to exert over 'national governments' in their respective zones.

To Britain the Mandate conception, though not of British origin, must have seemed a heaven-sent solution. Balfour's impressive memorandum of 11 August 1919[14] advanced proposals to Cabinet for making the best of what he recognized as a shamefully bad job. They involved honouring the Balfour Declaration, right or wrong, mollifying the French, facing the fact that the Arabs were nowhere ready for constitutional self-government, and adopting the Mandate principle to guide them towards it. Balfour's proposals, though not explicitly adopted, bear a close resemblance to the outcome.

[12] The question was not Whether but How and When. Lloyd George and Balfour were recorded by Chaim Weizmann as assuring him in July 1921 that by the Declaration they had 'always meant an *eventual* Jewish State'. Bernard Wasserstein, *The British in Palestine: The Mandatory Government and the Arab–Jewish Conflict*, revised edn. (Oxford, 1991), p. 112.

[13] For Maude, see A. T. Wilson, *Loyalties, Mesopotamia, 1914–17* (London, 1930), pp. 237–38; for Allenby, Doreen Ingrams, *Palestine Papers, 1917–22: Seeds of Conflict* (London, 1972), p. 20; for Hogarth's and the Anglo-French declarations, Hurewitz, *Middle East*, II, pp. 110–12.

[14] Hurewitz, *Middle East*, II, pp. 184–91.

The Covenant of the League of Nations, approved by the Peace Conference in April 1919, provided in its Article 22 for the 'A' Mandate system to be applied to Arab lands liberated from the Ottomans as a 'sacred trust for civilization'—fine words, but to aspiring Arabs a flimsy imperial disguise. Their response was to demand at a congress in Damascus in June the unification of Syria, Lebanon, and Palestine as an independent state under Faisal as king. But this and Faisal's repeated pleas for the protection of Syria from French claims were rejected. Under French and financial pressures British forces were withdrawn from Syria in November; and at San Remo in April 1920 Mandates were secured by France for Syria and Lebanon, and by Britain for Mesopotamia and Palestine (Transjordan included). Arab disappointment was compounded by the death that week of President Wilson and by the repudiation of the League and its Covenant by the United States Senate.

The Palestine Mandate differed fundamentally from the others by vesting in the mandatory full powers of legislation. This was needed since it incorporated the Balfour Declaration and since the text, based on a Zionist draft, was distinctly slanted in Jewish favour.[15] But the consequences were still not foreseen, and even the strongly pro-Zionist Churchill expressed in his 1922 statement of policy as Colonial Secretary the intention of fostering by degrees the establishment of joint Arab–Jewish government. The Mandate for Mesopotamia enabled Britain, after suppressing a serious nationalist uprising in 1920, to compensate Faisal for his expulsion by the French from the throne in Syria with a new one in Baghdad in 1921. This followed the transfer that January of political responsibility for the Middle East from the Foreign Office to the Colonial Office, enlarged by a new Middle East Department, and the holding in March of a conference in Cairo by Churchill. At it, Churchill took an additional measure to compensate the Hashemites by authorizing Faisal's brother, Abdullah, who had turned up in Transjordan with an entourage, to occupy that 'vacant lot' as its Emir. Transjordan was thus unilaterally separated from the rest of the Palestine Mandate.

In Persia the Bolshevik Revolution had created a different Imperial challenge. Curzon, acting for the Foreign Secretary, was determined to complete the chain of territories under British control between the Mediterranean and India. Despite Cabinet reluctance to assume still further overseas commitments, he pushed through in August 1919 an agreement with the Shah (but not ratified by the Persian *mejlis*, parliament) aimed at securing virtually exclusive British influence there.

The focal point, however, in Britain's calculations was always Egypt. In the words used at the Imperial Conference of Prime Ministers in July 1921, 'the Empire could survive anything else but not the loss of its main artery'. For that matter

[15] Hurewitz, *Middle East*, II, pp. 305–09.

Britain's cotton industry, vital to her economy, relied on easy access to Egypt's long-staple cotton. Egypt, however, was easily the most advanced country in the area and, having already been subjected to forty years of occupation, was especially resentful of continued subordination to Britain. Efforts to come to terms with Egyptian nationalism without letting go were fruitless. In 1919, following widespread riots, Lord Milner was sent to investigate. His recommendations for a more conciliatory policy were judged in London to go too far, in Egypt not far enough. In 1922 as a *pis aller* Britain terminated the wartime Protectorate and unilaterally declared Egypt a 'sovereign independent' country. Although internal autonomy was thereby ostensibly restored, Egypt was by no means released from British control, exercised under the reservations on which Britain insisted—over defence, Imperial communications, and the Sudan.

By and large, Britain's policy-makers may have felt some satisfaction with the arrangements contrived as an immediate outcome of the war. The route to India was under firmer control. Suez was secure and protected from the north by the military occupation of Palestine. Egyptian anti-British effervescence had, it was hoped, been brought within manageable bounds. Egypt's Libyan neighbours, the Senussi, were quiescent after their brief invasion of 1915. The Sudan seemed unlikely to cause trouble. Dependent Hashemite regimes had been set up in Iraq and Transjordan. The conflict between Jewish and Arab rights in Palestine was still judged soluble. The arrangement made with the Shah looked momentarily promising *vis-à-vis* revolutionary Russia. As for other outside powers, the French had been mollified by receiving a free rein in Syria; Italy had made no inroads anywhere; and the Americans, relapsing into isolationism, appeared content to leave the management of the Middle East mainly in Britain's hands. If this, however, was Britain's assessment of the situation in the aftermath of the war, it was distinctly optimistic. What is surprising is that, for all the setbacks that soon followed, her informal empire was still broadly in place when, twenty years later, another world war broke out.

The first reverse was in Persia. The Bolsheviks, by repudiating all Tsarist privileges there and the 1907 Anglo-Russian Agreement, attracted popular support. But their moves in 1920 to reassert Russian control in their own turbulent frontier areas, their seizure of one of Persia's provinces (Gilan) and their encouragement of autonomy in others, obliged the frightened Shah (as if patterning himself on Belloc's Cautionary Tale of 'Jim and the Lion')

> ... [to] keep a-hold of nurse
> For fear of finding something worse.

It was to do him and Britain little good, for in 1921 a lion-like army officer, Reza Khan, seized power, signed a Treaty of Friendship with Russia, repudiated the

Shah's agreement with Britain, subdued outlying parts of the country, and in 1925 replaced the Qajar dynasty with his own. Although the operations of their oil company were not immediately interfered with, the British could only keep their heads down.

Meanwhile the Turkish nationalists under Mustafa Kemal (Ataturk) were forcibly establishing their demand for the integrity of Anatolia, free of the invading Greeks and of would-be Mandatories, and for the revision of the humiliating armistice terms imposed at Sèvres in 1920 on the Ottoman government. On the eve of the resulting Lausanne Conference, begun in November 1922, Ataturk summarily declared the Sultanate abolished. The separation from Turkish Anatolia of the purely Arab parts of Asia was formally endorsed at Lausanne, although the allocation to Mesopotamia of the Kurdish Vilayet of Mosul, strategically important as well as strongly suspected of containing oil, was not accepted by the Turks until 1926. The following year (1924) the secularist Ataturk also abolished the Ottoman Caliphate. The likelihood that this would follow from the collapse of the Ottoman empire had been foreseen early in the war, and the possibility of an Arab being acclaimed Caliph of all Islam aroused interest and was eagerly entertained by Sherif Hussein with vague British encouragement. But there were other would-be candidates, and the idea eventually ran into the sand.[16]

Despite Britain's backing of the Hashemites in Iraq and Transjordan, none was forthcoming for Sherif Hussein himself when the Hejaz was overrun by Ibn Saud with his 'fundamentalist' Wahhabi irregulars in 1924 and incorporated into his expanding dominions. London finally recognized Ibn Saud as the independent king of them all by a new treaty in 1927. But despite having ousted the Hashemites from their old realm in the Hejaz, Ibn Saud's continued hostility towards them in their new ones of Iraq and Transjordan became one of the dominant themes of the Middle East imbroglio.

In Iraq King Faisal, despite the strength of his pan-Arab convictions, recognized that the insecurity of his own regime, both internally and externally, obliged him to collaborate with the British; and he was by no means opposed to Britain's questionable policy of controlling the rural tribes by increasing the powers of their head sheikhs. The treaties he signed from 1922 to 1930 looked forward to the day when the League's Mandates Commission could be satisfied with British assurances that Iraq was ready as a responsible self-governing country for admission to the League. Governed as it was (under British supervision) by a Sunni Arab clique, primarily in its own interests, and by cabinets that seldom lasted more than a few quarrelsome months, there might well have been doubts. But the assurances

[16] Elie Kedourie, *The Chatham House Version and Other Middle Eastern Studies* (London, 1970), pp. 179–94.

were given and accepted in 1932, and Britain accordingly relinquished her Mandate. She retained, however, despite nationalist rumblings, her strategic assets and some of her advisory power, as well as control of the oilfields in the north, productive since 1928. In Jordan the Emir Abdullah's dependent relationship with Britain, as defined in a treaty of 1928, was less exposed to internal challenges.

In Egypt, meanwhile, the constant rivalry between the King and the Wafdist politicians for popular support offered scope for British exploitation. But apart from a nearly successful attempt in 1930, Britain made no progress in negotiating a treaty relationship less offensive to the Egyptians until 1936.[17] What then persuaded the Egyptians to sign one was largely Mussolini's conquest of Ethiopia. The failure of other Western powers to intervene had demonstrated that their doctrine of 'collective security' was no bar to new colonial aggression. Mussolini, moreover, was already master of the Nile valley's other neighbour, Libya. The Wafdist government, led by Mustapha Nahas, was therefore willing to accept the concentration of British troops in the Suez zone in exchange for their withdrawal from the cities and elsewhere and to leave the vexed Sudan issue unresolved. These compromise arrangements at least qualified Egypt for admission to the League of Nations. Mussolini's aggressive behaviour also indirectly strengthened Britain's position *vis-à-vis* the Russians by leading to the Montreux Convention of 1936, under which Turkish rights in the Bosphorus were restored. Turkey, moreover, entered into a defensive alliance with the other countries along the Soviet underbelly (Persia and Afghanistan)—a dry run for the future Baghdad Pact. Another and significant development that year was the precedent set by General Bakr Sidky in Iraq for army intervention in Arab politics. Hitherto Britain had relied for a measure of collaboration on a narrow range of influential landowners and tribal heads. This 'politics of notables', regarded in the heyday of imperialism as natural, or at least unavoidable, worked after a fashion; but army officers, not often of that class and without a personal stake in stability, were rarely susceptible to British manipulation.

Even less had Britain, as the Palestine Mandatory, any means of controlling the steadily worsening confrontation of Jews and Palestinians or of promoting her declared aim of a joint Arab–Jewish state. Neither the leading Arabs nor the leading Zionists were interested—for opposite reasons—in *sharing* power in a Legislative Assembly on any of the bases proposed by Britain from 1922 onwards. Palestinian hostility, not only to the Zionists but to the Mandate itself, mounted *pari passu* with the determination of the Jews to pursue their national yearning, less and less concealed, for a state of their own. Britain's attempt to limit Jewish

[17] *RIIA Survey of International Affairs, 1936*, ed. Arnold J. Toynbee (Oxford, 1937), pp. 662–701.

immigration on the principle of the country's 'economic absorptive capacity' proved increasingly difficult to enforce, particularly when Hitler's racism caused from 1933 a surge in the number of would-be immigrants, which had tailed off at the end of the previous decade. In 1936 the Palestinians, whose cause had by now engaged active, if mostly rhetorical, sympathy throughout the Arab world, broke into open revolt. The following year the Peel Commission reached the reluctant conclusion that partition was the only answer, though it would entail mass transfer of Arabs. The publication of the Commission's report stimulated the Palestinians into continuing their revolt for another two years, by which time Jews numbered 450,000 or a third of the population. The Zionists themselves rejected the proposed partition as insufficiently favourable, but they were eager to pursue the idea of transferring large numbers of Arabs away from areas of especial Jewish concern. They had openly favoured such transfers since 1930. The whole Peel project was quickly abandoned by the British government as entailing the use of unacceptable force. As war with Germany loomed closer, bringing the need for maximum Arab goodwill throughout the Middle East, Britain made her final pre-war attempt to reach an agreed settlement with proposals set out in the White Paper of 1939.[18] This at one point 'declared categorically that it was no part of Britain's policy that Palestine should become a Jewish State', and its generally pro-Arab slant aroused violent Zionist protest without satisfying Arab leaders, despite their silent acquiescence.

What at this stage was the strength of Arab nationalism in the Middle East as a whole? In Syria, France had been left since 1920 to pursue her *mission civilisatrice*, an interpretation of imperial policy distinctly different from Britain's. The nationalist movement, centred thereafter in Baghdad, reached in the 1930s a new dimension under the influence of the prominent educationalist Sati al-Husri. His secular approach, however, sat easily neither with the Islamic priorities of others nor with the particularist inclinations of those exercising or seeking power in their own new 'nation states'. Consequently, while pan-Arab nationalism (with its corollary of anti-imperialism) grew as a mood, it made little progress as a programme. The death of King Faisal in 1933 had deprived it of one of its few pragmatic leaders; and Egypt was still some distance from recognizing herself, or being recognized, as 'Arab' rather than purely Egyptian.

The Second World War began disastrously for Britain. In June 1940 the collapse of France and Mussolini's declaration of war left Britain alone with her Commonwealth partners to contest the power of the Axis and its apparent Soviet well-wishers. In the Middle East the military measures conjured up by the hard-pressed Commander-in-Chief, General Sir Archibald Wavell, to maintain Britain's dom-

[18] *PP* (1939), Cmd 6019, XVII, 597.

ination can only be mentioned here for their political consequences. In 1941 the defeat of Italy's armies in the Horn of Africa led to the addition of Somalia and Eritrea as Occupied Enemy Territories to Britain's informal empire. In June a British force, with some Free French participation, succeeded in expelling the Vichy authorities in Syria, who had been allowing German aircraft the use of airfields; but some features of the invasion and the continuation of British military occupation for strategic reasons occasioned a series of furious recriminations from General Charles de Gaulle. Indeed, the treatment of Syria remained a bone of contention until the French finally withdrew in 1946.[19] In Iraq, during the same month, another force had to be scraped together to restore the monarchy that had been expelled by the pro-German Rashid Ali in an anti-British republican coup. Hitler's misguided invasion of Russia a few days later, which transformed the Russians suddenly into allies, obliged Britain to impose herself afresh in Iran. To secure a supply line for war matériel to Russia, Britain and Russia once more divided Iran into spheres of influence and occupied them militarily. The pretext used was the presence in Iran of some 3,000 Germans, whom Reza Shah was reluctant to expel.[20] Faced by the joint invasion, he abdicated. His son and successor, Mohammed Reza, had no option but to endorse the Anglo-Soviet Agreement. Although, as was the case with Britain's handling of Syria and Iraq, this may have kept the German army out, it subjected the resentful Iranians to foreign occupation until the war ended. The British, unlike the Russians, then withdrew their forces promptly in accordance with the Agreement, and may thereby have gained a measure of goodwill. In Egypt the roughshod necessities of war gained no goodwill at all. In July 1942, when Rommel was hammering at the gate and King Farouk and his cabinet showed signs of feeling in their pockets for the key, Ambassador Sir Miles Lampson invested the palace with armoured cars and gave Farouk the option of abdicating or appointing a more 'reliable' government under Nahas. He chose the latter. This may have saved the day for Britain (and in a sense for Egypt), but the humiliation aggravated Egyptian resentment.

Britain's basic problem in the inter-war period as in the war itself was how to combine two barely compatible aims—the security of her Imperial communications and of oil supplies on the one hand and, on the other, the retention of Arab and Iranian tolerance by showing an adequate response to nationalist aspirations. Both aims, moreover, had to be pursued without wholly alienating her prime

[19] Aviel Roshwald, *Estranged Bedfellows: Britain and France in the Middle East during the Second World War* (Oxford, 1990), pp. 67–230.

[20] The transport of war matériel to Russia became a largely American operation. Britain's immediate concern was the security of her oilfields. Russia aimed at permanent Sovietization of the north, which worried the western powers. R. A. Stewart, *Sunrise at Abadan: The British and Soviet Invasion of Iran, 1941* (New York, 1988), esp. chaps. 1–6.

European ally, France, or her determined protégés, the Jews. The 'rival angles of vision' were now even more perplexing.

Anthony Eden's Mansion House speech of May 1941 sought to rally Arab goodwill by promising 'full support for any scheme of Arab unity which commands general approval'. Britain's overall policy never went further than this. The comprehensive proposals put forward in late 1942 by Nuri Said to the British and others for a solution of the Palestine problem by unifying the whole Fertile Crescent ran into several sand-dunes. So did his earlier and later ploys for the union of at least Syria and Iraq. Suspicions that Britain secretly supported any of these, or Emir Abdullah's embarrassing and persistent 'Greater Syria' scheme,[21] are unfounded. Ibn Saud's hostility to any further Hashemite advancement was enough by itself to prevent British support for either. Equally misplaced was the contrary suspicion that the Arab League was a British brainchild conceived to underpin Britain's hegemony. The League, set up in 1945 under Egyptian leadership, was in fact the outcome of three years' discussion between Arab politicians. Certainly Britain exerted pressure in various quarters to discourage the adoption, in the design of the League, of a pact of measures that would add to her embarrassments either in Palestine or *vis-à-vis* the French; but the initiative, once Iraq had been upstaged, was Egyptian. In its final form the pact, by endorsing the independent statehood of all its signatories, looked for a time innocuous enough.

As for the security of oil supplies, the geological freak that the world's largest known petroleum deposits were found to lie along the routes to India had given a quite different dimension to the value of Britain's Middle East hegemony. Long before the war, which interrupted prospecting, Britain had relinquished her ideas of exclusive exploitation of the area's likely oil wealth in response to French and American pressures. American and French companies had become partners with Britain in the Iraq Petroleum Company by 1929, and the concessions in Bahrain and Saudi Arabia had gone to American companies in 1932 and 1933 respectively. When prospecting began again after the war,[22] the field was opened to other foreign operators. But at all stages the protection of oil-installations and pipelines to the Mediterranean increased the need for Arab tolerance. The understandable demands of host countries for a better share of oil-company profits were only temporarily satisfied when ARAMCO's 'fifty–fifty' agreement with Saudi Arabia in December 1950 became the generally accepted model.

The war had ended with Britain still, in appearance, dominant throughout the area, Cyrenaica and Tripolitania having been added in 1943 to the other captured

[21] Ernest Dawn, 'The Project of Greater Syria', unpublished Ph.D. dissertation, Princeton, 1948.

[22] Dates of first commercial production: Iran and Egypt, 1908; Iraq, 1927; Bahrain, 1932; Saudi Arabia, 1938; Kuwait, 1946; Qatar, 1949; Abu Dhabi, 1962; Dubai, 1969; and smaller Gulf States later.

ex-Italian colonies. Thus in 1944–45, when she still exercised control in Syria and half Iran, her informal empire can be said to have reached its widest extent, as indicated on Map 21.1. But she was too exhausted, financially and economically, to solve on her own the many perplexities facing her. The material and financial collaboration of the United States had been decisive in the war, and its continued collaboration in peace was recognized as vital, despite the awkwardness of its anti-colonial traditions. Ernest Bevin, as Foreign Secretary in the new Labour government, set about his task with a new imperial philosophy—his own, but one less likely to clash with American attitudes. This envisaged restructuring the Empire on the basis of equal partnerships in a grand design for the betterment of its peoples, coupled with their strategic collaboration against suspected Soviet expansionism. Amongst his preoccupations, but not one shared by Prime Minister Attlee,[23] the Middle East held pride of place. Bevin had his way in Cabinet but not in negotiating 'equal treaties' with restive Arabs. To them, the alleged Soviet threat meant little, while politico-military alliances with Britain meant the continued presence of British troops.

In the case of Egypt, which by now had recognized herself as fully 'Arab' and the rightful leader of an unfettered Arab world, Britain's negotiations were complicated by Egypt's refusal to discuss the Suez issue separately from the Sudan. To Egypt, they were related and vital matters of sovereignty. In private talks with the Egyptian Premier, Ismail Sidky, in October 1946, Bevin thought he had achieved a compromise formula covering both, which would satisfy Sudanese as well as Egyptian sensitivities.[24] It did neither; and little progress was made in Bevin's time. In his talks with Sidky he had conditionally accepted the principle of evacuating Suez; and although Egypt's rejection of their agreement left the condition unfulfilled, no Egyptian government thereafter could accept less and survive. Bevin was indeed exercised for several years in searching for alternative possible locations for a base or bases elsewhere in the region. Meanwhile he turned his attention to Iraq. There too he was foiled. His Portsmouth Treaty of January 1948, signed with the Iraqi Premier, Saleh Jabr, reduced Britain's strategic rights to 'sharing' her air-bases with the Iraqi armed forces, but even this was violently rejected by the nationalists and never ratified. Only with the financially dependent Abdullah of Jordan were new treaties concluded. By the first, of March 1946, the Mandate was abolished and Abdullah was declared king. Two years later, following his failure with Iraq, Bevin sanctioned a less preferential treaty with Abdullah,

[23] CAB[inet] 129/2 CP(45) 174 of 17 Sept. 1945, CAB 131/2 D[ominions] O[ffice] (46) 27 and DO(46) 40 of 2 and 13 March 1946. See Wm. Roger Louis, *The British Empire in the Middle East: Arab Nationalism, the United States, and Post-War Imperialism* (Oxford, 1984), pp. 1–31, 87, 107–09, 274–77.

[24] Ibid., pp. 246–53.

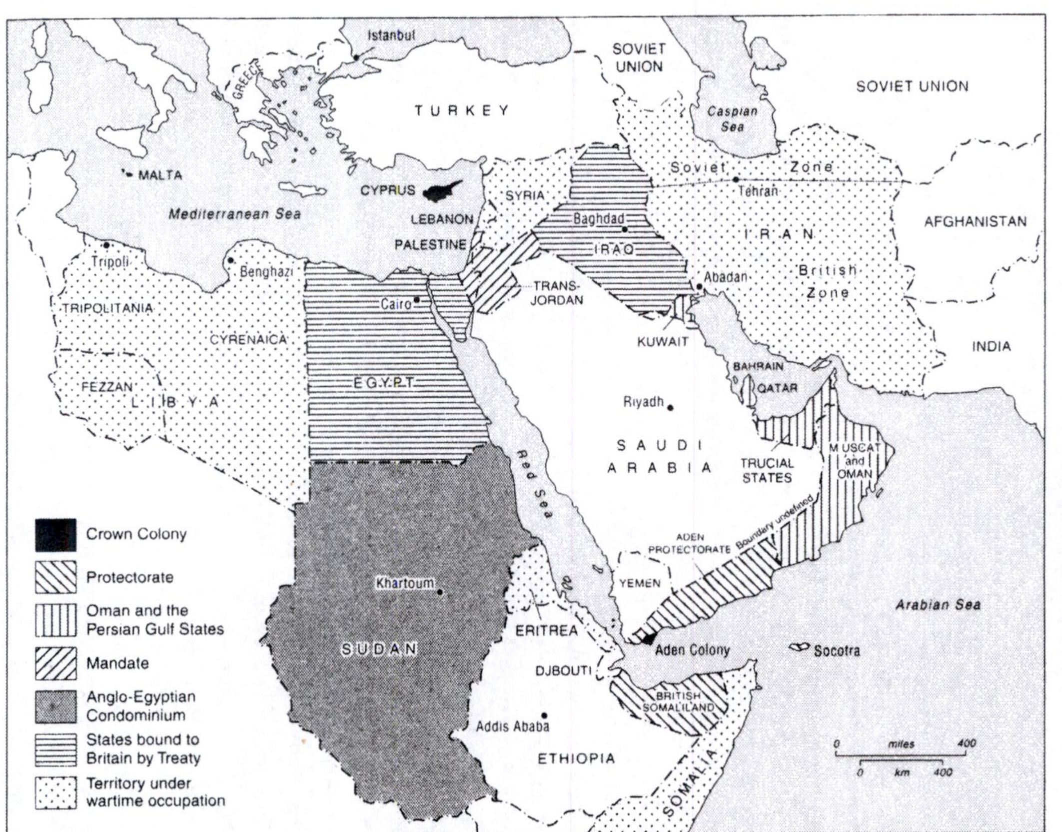

MAP 21.1. The Middle East in 1945: Maximum Extent of Informal Empire

reducing the British military presence to two air-bases. This did nothing to mitigate condemnation of Abdullah as an imperialist lackey by other Arabs, particularly those who were aware of his secret dealings over the years with the Zionists and judged them treasonable.[25]

In Palestine Bevin's endeavours to solve the conflict of rights, made more desperate and complicated by the Holocaust, was doomed to total failure.[26] He stuck stubbornly to the concept of a joint Arab–Jewish state, since anything less would outrage not only the Palestinians but the whole Arab world. His stubbornness, however, outraged the Zionists, who had declared at their Biltmore Conference in 1942 their determination to secure a state of their own in the whole of Palestine. Extremist groups now turned to anti-British violence to make the point. Britain sought Washington's help in seeking a solution. The compromise package worked out by a joint Committee of Enquiry in April 1946 recommended the immediate admission of 100,000 Jews, balanced by acceptance of a bi-national state. President Truman publicly endorsed the former but showed no interest in the latter, vexing even the steady-headed Attlee. In July Jewish extremists blew up the British military headquarters at the King David Hotel in Jerusalem. Palestinian hostility, though less spectacular, was unrelenting. By February 1947 Bevin despaired and referred the problem to the United Nations. In November, under US pressure, the General Assembly voted for partition. Its enforcement was not something Britain was prepared to undertake alone, and in May 1948 she relinquished the Mandate. The State of Israel was declared. Jews and Arabs were left to fight it out, and as a result of their 1948 war some 750,000 of the Arab population of 1,500,000 were displaced or driven into exile.

The Americans were already more aware of Britain's declining power than were the British themselves; and if they had hitherto been content to leave political and strategic management of the Middle East largely in Britain's hands, 1947 brought signs of change, not only in Palestine. In February, under Treasury pressure Britain persuaded the United States to relieve her of the burden of giving Greece and Turkey political and military support. To one American commentator this meant taking 'the most meaningful step in the nation's history'.[27] To the British it meant that resistance to Soviet penetration in the whole area would now be shared with her great ally. The issue of the Truman Doctrine the following month, pledging American resistance to further Soviet expansionism, showed where Western power

[25] Avi Shlaim, *Collusion Across the Jordan* (Oxford, 1988). Summary on pp. 613–23.

[26] The partition idea had been re-examined several times from 1943 to 1945 but Eden's opposition finally prevailed. Hurewitz, *Middle East*, II, pp. 706–29, 760–79, 780–85.

[27] Quoted by Elizabeth Monroe, *Britain's Moment in the Middle East: 1914–71* [1963], revised edn. (London, 1981), pp. 158 and 225 n. 6.

now lay. A more momentous sign that Britain's Imperial pretensions were crumbling was the passing that July of the Indian Independence Bill.

Even the ending of the Raj, however, did not diminish in British calculations the importance to the West and its oil supplies of the Suez base, or at least of assured wartime access to it. Nor did the replacement of Britain by America as top dog in the Middle East proceed without disharmony. In British eyes anti-Communist stability entailed the exercise of political influence backed by adequate military presence. To the Americans this attitude was a relic of outdated colonialism. Quite apart from Palestine, there were occasions when American moralizing seemed to London irresponsible.

In economically stagnant Iran the rise to power of the populist Musaddiq in 1951 and his cancellation of Britain's highly profitable oil concession found much street support, not least from the Soviet-sponsored Tudeh party. In US eyes Britain's handling of Musaddiq smacked of imperial arrogance, and in any case lacked the power to press her protests home. After much Anglo-American argument, Attlee's government—despite the bullish attitude of Bevin's successor, Herbert Morrison, and Tory anguish—decided against forcible intervention. Instead, it closed down the vast oil installation at Abadan and evacuated British staff, in the vain hope that this would oblige Musaddiq to adopt less economically suicidal policies. The shared fear that Musaddiq might call in Soviet help brought American and British attitudes closer. The removal of Musaddiq, however, took time. In August 1953 the Shah fled, but with undercover British and American help Musaddiq was ousted and the Shah restored. A new oil concession, operated by a Western consortium and giving Iran a better share of the profits, was negotiated in 1954. Iran was now even less of a British 'sphere of influence'.

In the Arab world, meanwhile, 1951 witnessed the assassination in Jerusalem of Britain's long-standing client King Abdullah, soon after he had incorporated the rump of Arab Palestine into his kingdom. The year was marked by still graver developments in Egypt, where Musaddiq's revolution and his cavalier treatment of imperialist Britain's oil interests had been watched with admiration. The Labour government, aware that British troops in Suez vastly exceeded the numbers agreed in 1936, made its final attempt to reach a compromise solution with the monarchist regime. This, with some backing from the United States, France, and Turkey, proposed the conversion of the gigantic base into a joint concern managed by the allied powers together with Egypt herself, as the focus of a Middle East Defence Organization—a proposal pursued by the Conservatives on taking over in October 1951. To the Egyptians this was simply camouflage for continued British occupation; and on 11 November Farouk announced Egypt's repudiation of the 1936 Treaty. Excited crowds ran amok. Violence was directed at everything British, persons as well as property, encouraged by the influential (but anti-Wafdist)

Muslim Brotherhood. In July 1952 a group of middle-ranking and middle-class officers led by General Mohammed Neguib took over in a bloodless coup. Six months later they ousted King Farouk, whose humiliating handling of the army in the 1948 Arab–Israeli War still rankled, and abolished the monarchy. Despite British hopes, Egypt's new army rulers proved no less opposed than the old regime to the British presence in both Egypt and the Sudan. They simply took cleverer means to hasten its removal by agreeing to treat the Suez and the Sudan issues separately. In 1952 Neguib upstaged the British over the Sudan by securing the agreement of delegates from all Sudanese parties for self-determination within three years, with the option either of complete independence or of a formal link with Egypt. The Egyptians fully expected—and the British gravely feared—they would choose the latter and endorse the 'Unity of the Nile Valley'. In the circumstances Britain could only sign an agreement with Egypt on Neguib's terms,[28] and hope for the best. In the event, when self-determination was exercised at the end of 1955, the ostensibly pro-Egyptian party in power opted for complete independence. The British withdrew more amicably than their rivals, but they left the country's non-Muslim southern half unprepared and resistant to northern domination. The Condominium had proved a curious phenomenon from start to finish.

As for Suez, an agreement was finally reached in October 1954 whereby British evacuation would be completed within twenty months, subject to rights of re-entry in the event of an attack on any Middle East country.[29] In these negotiations, as in those over the Sudan, American impatience with Britain's reluctance to give way occasioned further disharmony. To the Americans, for whom the cold war with the Soviet Union was by now the overriding concern, the goodwill of Egypt might be secured by sympathetic handling of her impressive new leader, Gamal Abdul Nasser, who ousted Neguib in November 1954. For Britons of the Churchillian stamp the surrender of Suez was an unprecedented blow. They could console themselves only by reflecting that the new hydrogen bomb downgraded the value of the old jugular base. They could not, however, share the favourable American view of Nasser, who was now in a position to pursue his wider ambitions of destroying Britain's influence in what was left of her Arab dependencies.

Since 1953 the American Secretary of State, John Foster Dulles, aware that mounting Egyptian opposition to Britain made the Suez base untenable, had

[28] FO 371/96911 (1952), and *PP* (1952–53), Cmd 8767, xxx, 243.

[29] *RIIA Documents on International Affairs, 1954*, ed. Denise Folliot (Oxford, 1957), pp. 248–57. For extensive British government documentation on the 1954 agreement, in a volume which covers the period from 1945 to the eve of the Suez crisis, see John Kent, ed., *British Egypt and the Defence of the Middle East*, British Documents on the End of Empire Project (BDEEP), Series B, 3 Parts (London, 1998).

been advancing the concept of 'northern tier' defence of the Middle East from the risk of Soviet aggression. Eden latched on to it. The defensive alliance with Turkey signed in February 1955 by Iraq's Nuri Said was accordingly joined by Britain (and later by Iran and Pakistan). This 'Baghdad Pact' redoubled Nasser's hostility towards Nuri for ganging-up with outsiders against an imaginary threat from Russia instead of focusing on pan-Arab resistance to 'colonialism', both British and Israeli. Britain's attempt, though repulsed by King Hussein, to bring Jordan too into the Pact angered Nasser further. The Americans supported the Pact's objectives and joined unobtrusively in committee work, but fought shy of full membership. Nasser, buoyed up by the attentions just shown him at the Bandung non-aligned conference that April, decided to teach the Western powers a lesson by turning to the Soviet bloc for the weaponry the West grudged him. Swallowing their exasperation over his Czech arms deal, which they read as a sign that Nasser was swinging into the Communist orbit, the United States and Britain offered funding for his huge Aswan Dam project. While Nasser brooded on the terms of the offer, their opinions were hardening against him, both because of alarmist intelligence reports of Nasser's pro-Soviet leanings and because their hopes that he would deliver a settlement of the Arab–Israeli conflict proved empty. In early 1956 drastic Anglo-American plans[30] were prepared to *compel* Nasser to co-operate with the West. Divergences developed between Washington and London, when President Eisenhower intervened to demand caution, on the extent of force that might be used against Nasser, but in July their shared suspicions of him and his delayed response to the dam offer led them jointly to declare its cancellation. Nasser's response was to nationalize the Suez Canal Company.

The Canal's main users were British, its managers French—and the French were already enraged with Nasser over his support for the Algerian independence movement. The cataclysmic events that followed are too well known to need rehearsing here. It was a dismal finale to Eden's earlier reputation for diplomacy that he should have joined with so little hesitation and without even consulting Eisenhower in the French–Israeli plot to invade Egypt and overthrow Nasser. (His especial anger with Nasser over King Hussein's dismissal in March of the influential British commander of Jordan's armed forces, General Glubb, was misplaced, since Nasser was not in fact behind it.) The world and half the British were aghast at the attack on Suez. Even Britain's few remaining Arab friends, who would privately have been glad to see Nasser removed, felt obliged to take anti-British measures. But what mattered far more was the extreme disapproval of the Americans. This was most effectively expressed by withholding their financial support

[30] The 'Omega Memorandum', in the American version. The British equivalent, the 'New Doctrine', has not been released. See Keith Kyle, *Suez* (London, 1991), pp. 99–101.

for Britain, without which her economy and the convertibility of sterling were doomed. The botched invasion was withdrawn. Nasser's standing in the Arab world rose to new heights, and Britain's plunged still lower.

By 1958 the union with Egypt of Syria (and even of the Yemeni Imamate) seemed to confirm Nasser's domination of the region. The counter-union of Iraq and Jordan, instantly declared by the Hashemites, proved valueless. Within three months of its signature the Hashemite regime in Baghdad was bloodily swept away in the Iraqi revolution. All Britain could do was to send troops briefly to Jordan in the aftermath to protect their remaining Hashemite friend, King Hussein.

Britain's responsibility for the ex-Italian colonies had been progressively relinquished under United Nations auspices between 1950 and 1952. The fragments of Empire which remained under British control were the fringes of Arabia, in the Aden area and the Gulf. Aden, now the only significant British base between Cyprus and Singapore, was still regarded as vital to Commonwealth interests against Communist advance, to the defence of Aden against Yemeni aggression, and to the protection of oil supplies from the Gulf against any comer. The United States, in its new role of policing the world against the rival superpower, encouraged the maintenance of the Aden base. But it gave no help to Britain when Egypt's protégé, Colonel Abdullah Sallal, overthrew the Yemeni Imamate in 1964 and Egyptian troops poured in to support him in the resulting civil war and to increase the threat to Britain's position in Aden. Amid rising local turbulence, all Britain could do politically to counter the threat and preserve the base was to promote a precarious constitution in the restive Crown Colony, push the Western Protectorate rulers into a federation, and merge the two into a doubtfully viable state, to which they promised independence by 1968. It was wasted effort. Ironically, when the British were driven out of Aden in November 1967 by the violent hostility of rival 'socialist' groups, the winners were not Nasser's protégés (FLOSY) but the extremist admirers of the Soviet Union (the National Liberation Front).

In the Gulf, to which a small proportion of British forces were transferred from Aden, there were perplexities enough, quite apart from occasional popular demonstrations of Nasserist fervour there. A frontier quarrel between Saudi Arabia and two of Britain's clients, Muscat and Abu Dhabi, had been developing since the early 1950s in the supposedly oil-bearing Buraimi area. This severely upset Britain's relations with the Saudis and strained those with Saudi Arabia's American patrons. Arbitration collapsed in 1955 as a consequence of British charges that Saudi witnesses had been bribed; and that October British-led Trucial Levies forcibly evicted a Saudi detachment occupying the Buraimi oasis. The Saudis broke off diplomatic relations with Britain for eight years. Saudi displeasure with Britain was also expressed over her assistance to the Sultan of Muscat in containing both the Omani revolt inland (1954–59) and the Dhofari rebellion in the south-west from 1965 on. The Dhofaris also attracted backing from 'socialist' Arabs elsewhere, and their rebellion only ended when Sultan Said was ousted by his son Qaboos, with covert British assistance, in 1970. Over the same period the old Iranian claim to sovereignty over Bahrain was also causing Britain trouble. The claim was finally dropped in 1970 when a United Nations investigation established that the majority of Bahrainis wished to remain independent.

Kuwait, the richest of the Gulf States and the source of much of Europe's oil, had been released in 1961 from the old British relationship, but the ruler had instantly to invoke the simple Treaty of Friendship, which replaced it, to secure military protection against threatened invasion by Iraq. If, however, available British forces were able to deal with that relatively minor emergency, it was fanciful to imagine that they could withstand a serious Soviet push into the Gulf. This was a danger entertained more in Washington than in London, but secret contingency plans were drawn up by the Ministry of Defence for the blowing-up of oil-wells in Iraq and the Gulf to deny them to the Soviets. Assurances, however unreal, were continually given to the Gulf rulers and their people that they and their oil-wells were safe under British protection; and to the extent that this was accepted and promoted stability, appearances took the place of reality. Fortunately there was no further interference in Gulf oil production from outside. Internal sabotage did not materialize either, but Britain was well aware that this too could not be prevented by British bayonets.

Despite minor troubles, the other nine Gulf sheikhdoms withstood the weather under the tattered old British umbrella and their own newer one of oil revenues. Anxious, however, to cut overseas costs following the devaluation of sterling in November 1967, the Labour government in January 1968 announced, to the dismay of the rulers, their intention of withdrawing the British umbrella within three years.[31] The Conservatives, succeeding to power in 1970, reluctantly endorsed the decision and redoubled pressure on the rulers to unite before 1971 into an internationally viable form of statehood. Bahrain and Qatar eventually opted out in favour of separate independence. The remaining seven, after strenuous British efforts to settle a dispute with the Shah over three small 'strategic' islands, were permitted by him to announce the formation of the United Arab Emirates in December 1971; and two days later Britain carried out, amicably enough, her withdrawal from the last corner of her informal empire in the Middle East.

Britain's strange assortment of erstwhile dependencies—two (very different) Protectorates, a Condominium, two Mandates, one Arab Crown Colony,

[31] Harold Wilson, 16 Jan. 1968, *Parliamentary Debates* (Commons), XVI, cols. 1680–82.

Protected States, and Occupied Enemy Territory—have today been independent for a generation or more. But it may still be too early for a judgement on Britain's record there to be made with justice. The Imperial ethos which still presided, in increasingly diluted form, no longer attracts approval, even in Britain. This chapter is not intended to defend it; but it is too facile to present the story simply as barefaced confrontation between arrogant, self-interested intruders (the extreme Arab view) and backward and corrupt Arabs (the extreme British view of the time). Britain's dominance of the Middle East had not been sought, colonial fashion, as an end in itself, but as a means initially of safeguarding communications with the Raj in India. When the protection and stability of the Middle East were recognized as necessities in their own right because of its vast oil potential, even nostalgic imperialists on the extreme right recognized that the imposition of more direct control was no longer an option. It is also worth remembering that, from 1919, Britain's tutelage was explicitly intended to continue only until her dependencies had developed to the point when they could look after themselves. In that sense Britain's misjudgement related even more to the *pace* of history than to her purposes in it. One thing she certainly failed to bequeath to the Middle East was the practice of Western democracy—an aim which some may regard as another example of European arrogance. The good she did do in the course of her brief paramountcy in many fields—administrative, developmental, educational, judicial, agricultural, medical, in the transfer of technology, in frontier delimitation, and over slave-trading—has been barely mentioned here. It was neither negligible nor ill-intentioned. To take one single example, the huge and imaginative Gezira Cotton Scheme in the Sudan aroused worldwide admiration. But, partly because of the self-imposed restrictions on her powers of intervention and partly from financial stringency, the good she did was limited, skin-deep, and subordinate of course to her own interests. In Egypt, whatever the complexity of her problems, Britain's response to nationalist aspirations was particularly insensitive. She is also open to criticism for depending elsewhere on collaboration with influential local élites whose enjoyment of power was seldom matched by concern for the welfare of the commonalty. Yet it is doubtful whether a more imaginative technique of insisting from the start on more popular participation in the processes of government would have saved the post-imperial Middle East from the rivalry of local despots. As for Palestine, it is beyond question that Britain's attempts to reconcile the unreconcilable failed totally and left the world a cancer in this part of its body, which until recently has shown little sign of healing. Whatever might be said of Britain's record in the Middle East, her handling of affairs there at least enabled democracy elsewhere to survive two world wars.

Select Bibliography

M. S. Anderson, *The Eastern Question* (London, 1966).

George Antonius, *The Arab Awakening: The Story of the Arab Nationalist Movement* (London, 1938).

Peter Avery and others, eds., *The Cambridge History of Iran*, Vol. VII, *From Nadir Shah to the Islamic Republic* (Cambridge, 1991).

Glen Balfour-Paul, *The End of Empire in the Middle East: Britain's Relinquishment of Power in Her Last Three Arab Dependencies* (Cambridge, 1991).

Benjamin Beit-Hallahmi, *Original Sins: Reflections on the History of Zionism and Israel* (London, 1991).

Max Beloff, *Imperial Sunset*, Vol. I, *Britain's Liberal Empire, 1847–1921* (London, 1969); Vol. II, *Dream of Commonwealth, 1921–42* (Basingstoke, 1989).

John Darwin, *Britain, Egypt, and the Middle East: Imperial Policy in the Aftermath of War, 1918–1922* (London, 1981).

J. C. Hurewitz, ed., *The Middle East and North Africa in World Politics: A Documentary Record*, Vol. I, *European Expansion, 1535–1914*, revised edn. (New Haven, 1975); Vol. II, *British and French Supremacy, 1914–1956*, revised edn. (New Haven, 1979).

Elie Kedourie, *In the Anglo-Arab Labyrinth: The McMahon–Husayn Correspondence and Its Interpretations, 1914–1939* (Cambridge, 1976).

Rashid Khalidi and others, eds., *The Origins of Arab Nationalism* (New York, 1991).

Keith Kyle, *Suez* (London, 1991).

Wm. Roger Louis, *The British Empire in the Middle East, 1945–1951: Arab Nationalism, the United States, and Post-War Imperialism* (Oxford, 1984).

—— and Roger Owen, eds., *Suez 1956: The Crisis and its Consequences* (Oxford, 1989).

Elizabeth Monroe, *Britain's Moment in the Middle East 1914–71*, revised edn. (London, 1981).

Yehoshua Porath, *In Search of Arab Unity, 1930–1945* (London, 1986).

RIIA (Annual) *Survey of International Affairs* and *Documents on International Affairs* (London), esp. those of 1936, 1939–46, 1951, 1954, and 1955 (various eds.).

Benjamin Shwadran, *The Middle East: Oil and the Great Powers*, revised edn. (New York, 1973).

Bernard Wasserstein, *The British in Palestine: The Mandatory Government and the Arab-Jewish Conflict*, 2nd edn. (Oxford, 1991).

E. L. Woodward and Rohan Butler, eds., *Documents on British Foreign Policy, 1919–1939*, Vol. IV (London, 1952).

M. E. Yapp, *The Near East Since the First World War* (London, 1991).

22

West Africa

TOYIN FALOLA AND A. D. ROBERTS

At the end of the nineteenth century British rule in West Africa expanded far inland, from a few coastal outposts that were by-products of the Atlantic slave trade and its abolition. In this way Britain became, for six decades, suzerain over the largest Muslim population in the Empire outside India. She also gained ascendancy over two great African empires: Asante and the Sokoto Caliphate. The way in which the British perceived their role in West Africa was duly transformed. For much of the nineteenth century they mostly worked in close, if often uneasy, association with coastal Africans, many of whom were Christian and largely British in cultural orientation. Thereafter this partnership disintegrated, as the British set about incorporating vast regions of the interior in new structures of administration and trade. The Imperial history of British West Africa can be read in terms of the tension and conflict arising from this enlargement of perspective, and the priorities which it entailed.

The areas which became British West Africa ranged in size from Gambia—4,000 square miles either side of the Gambia River—to Nigeria—356,000 square miles. Around 1900 there may have been 100,000 people in Gambia, 1 million in Sierra Leone, 2 million in the Gold Coast, and 15 million in Nigeria; altogether, a good many more than in the much larger region that became French West Africa. Most of what came under British rule was occupied by cultivators, though their habitats varied greatly. Much of the country nearest the coast—up to a hundred miles or more into the interior—was covered by tropical rainforest. Beyond lay huge tracts of savannah woodland where rainfall was markedly lower. Indigenous political systems included a multiplicity of states, large and small, and societies without any centralized government. Many areas had long been involved in trade, and were linked either to caravan routes across the Sahara or to coastal ports. Here, during the nineteenth century, European influence increased as palm-oil, instead of slaves, became the region's main overseas export, though the growth of such 'legitimate' trade often involved slave labour. Across the savannah of the hinterland Islam expanded during the nineteenth century, but was beginning to confront the advance of Christians, European and African, from the coast.

1900–1930

In the course of the Scramble for West Africa, Britain, France, and Germany had staked out the hinterland of their coastal enclaves. For Britain, the frontiers of the modern Nigeria, Ghana, Sierra Leone, and the Gambia had largely been assured by treaty-making expeditions between 1885 and 1895. Conquest soon followed. To some extent, it arose from long-standing tensions between coastal societies and their neighbours, but in Nigeria especially it was motivated by the determination of the British to carry their trade to the far interior. By 1893 three British administrations were involved: the Colony of Lagos, the Niger Coast Protectorate (based on Calabar), and the Royal Niger Company, a commercial firm which, under charter, dominated the river itself. In the 1890s there were wars against Yoruba states, Warri, Benin, and Nupe. In 1899 the Foreign Office transferred the Protectorate to the Colonial Office; in 1900 the Company lost its charter, and beyond the Colony (Lagos) British authority was divided between the Protectorates of what were now called Southern and Northern Nigeria. The name was suggested by Flora Shaw, a journalist who was soon to marry Frederick Lugard, an army officer in Royal Niger Company service who now took charge of Northern Nigeria. With a newly constituted West African Frontier Force, Lugard set about subduing the northern emirates, and by 1903 had defeated Sokoto itself. In Sierra Leone the British Colony had begun to subject the adjacent Protectorate to more direct British control: early attempts to tax Temne and Mende provoked warfare in 1898. For the Gold Coast administration the main concern was Asante, which in 1891 had refused to become a Protectorate; a second refusal in 1896 caused the British to depose the king, and in 1900 new demands by the Governor led to war and annexation.

This burst of aggressive expansion opened the way for railways inland from the coast: from Sekondi to Kumasi by 1903; from Lagos to Kano by 1911; and from Freetown to the Liberian border by 1908. In Nigeria and the Gold Coast they facilitated new lines of exports. In the latter, cocoa had been introduced, on African initiative, in the 1880s; by 1910 it contributed more to exports than palm products and rubber combined, and from 1911 the Gold Coast was the world's largest exporter of cocoa. In Nigeria, palm products from the south-east were to remain the chief export throughout the colonial period, but by 1914 they were supplemented by rising volumes of cocoa from the south-west and groundnuts from the north, where Africans had resisted official pressure to grow cotton for export. Railways also encouraged capitalist mining ventures. In the south-western Gold Coast European techniques transformed the exploitation of historic gold deposits, and by the 1920s gold contributed around 10 per cent to exports; in Nigeria the same was true of tin, from the Bauchi plateau in the north, while coal from Enugu supplied fuel for the railways.

Such enterprise, whether African or European, presupposed a new political order. In terms of government, the newly enlarged territories of West Africa presented British empire-builders with a particular challenge. Climate and endemic disease precluded white settlement. If there was any relevant precedent, it was to be sought in India rather than South Africa or New Zealand. In 1910 African land rights in Nigeria were protected by legislation directed against expatriates. In 1911 the Colonial Office resisted labour demands from mining companies in the Gold Coast and Nigeria which would have threatened African cash-crop production. The Gold Coast mines had attracted South African capital and personnel since 1900, but in 1913 Consolidated Gold Fields withdrew most of its investments.[1] Meanwhile, the rooted objection of the Colonial Office to monopoly concessions thwarted the plans of the soap magnate William Lever to set up palm-oil mills in Nigeria; in the 1920s he was denied land there for plantations.

There was, then, general agreement between the Colonial Office and colonial Governors that West Africa should be developed primarily on the basis of 'native production'. And on grounds of cost, as well as health, there could be few white administrators. Clearly, Africans would have to be governed mostly by Africans: but which Africans? It might be supposed that the British, and missionaries from many lands, had already brought into being a class of Africans well qualified to extend British rule beyond the coastal enclaves. In the later nineteenth century, in Sierra Leone, the Gold Coast, and Lagos, literate Africans rose to high rank in government service, and some prospered as businessmen and lawyers. Many were descended from liberated slaves, and were thus related to Krio families in Sierra Leone; in the Gold Coast several were descended from European traders. By 1900 this élite was being reinforced by indigenous Yoruba and Fanti. Such people were mostly Christian, set great store by education, and were strongly attached to the Empire: they were naturally inclined to support its extension inland. Not only did the Royal Niger Company rely heavily on Fanti soldiers; it was an African surveyor who obtained treaties for Britain to the north of Asante; and in 1892 in Sierra Leone the Krio secretary of 'native affairs' devised a plan whereby chiefs in the interior would be supervised by Krio officials.[2] But the Colonial Office rejected it. British officialdom was turning against its original West African partners, swayed both by racist theory and by medical advances which, between 1903 and 1913, halved the death-rate among white officials in West Africa.[3]

[1] Jeff Crisp, *The Story of an African Working Class: Ghanaian Miners' Struggles, 1870–1980* (London, 1984), p. 41.

[2] Christopher Fyfe, *A History of Sierra Leone* (London, 1962), pp. 516–17.

[3] Cf. A. D. Roberts, 'The Imperial Mind', in A. D. Roberts, ed., *The Cambridge History of Africa*, Vol. VII, *1905–1940* (hereafter *CHA*) (Cambridge, 1986), p. 33, n. 8.

The British sought indeed to collaborate with West Africa's rulers, but they reserved this work for themselves. Though in the heat of conquest several kings—of Asante, Warri, and Benin, for example—had been sent into exile, they had clearly ruled states whose hierarchies could be harnessed to serve British ends. If the British increasingly believed that they had a genius for ruling alien races, it was because they prided themselves not only on their sense of fair play but on their ability to detect and exploit such genius for leadership as alien races themselves displayed. This was most striking among the emirates of Northern Nigeria, which had for some time been ruled by literate Muslim regimes. It was in this region that the term 'Indirect Rule' first gained currency; in the 1920s it was to become something of a fetish among the British in tropical Africa. They wanted to believe that they were upholding 'native' customs and institutions, however much in practice they might subvert them in the name of justice, morality, or economic advantage. In West Africa, as in India's princely states and indeed Britain itself, the Empire was underpinned by the cult of monarchy. Lugard, in 1913, discouraged schools in Nigeria from teaching about the Stuarts, since this might provoke awkward questions and foster 'disrespect for authority'.[4] The Prince of Wales toured West Africa in 1925, and already a newsreel had shown the Emir of Katsina in Liverpool on his way to Mecca, and watching motor-racing at Brooklands.[5] In 1924 the Asante king was allowed home from exile, and in 1935 his successor was installed as head of an extensive confederation. Some of the most eminent West Africans were accorded honours by the British monarch: the first African to be knighted was a Sierra Leonean, Samuel Lewis, in 1896.

All this encouraged an image of Empire as a partnership of benign paternalists, British and African. But the crucial point was that the British held the upper hand, and were ready to use it. Up to 1914 the Yoruba state of Abeokuta, an early mission centre, had contrived to remain virtually independent: an enterprising example of selective African westernization. For Lugard (Governor of all Nigeria from 1912), this was an unwelcome anomaly, and he used force to reduce Abeokuta to the same footing as other Yoruba states. Lugard further secured British control over 'native administrations' by excluding lawyers from their courts, but his claim that British officials understood local cultures better than 'detribalized' barristers in Lagos[6] was all too frequently belied. The self-delusions inherent in Indirect Rule were roughly exposed in 1929 by risings in south-eastern Nigeria against 'warrant chiefs' who had been imposed upon societies with no tradition of chieftainship but in

[4] P. H. S. Hatton, 'British Colonial Policy in Africa, 1910 to 1914', unpublished Ph.D. thesis, Cambridge, 1971, p. 181.

[5] A. D. Roberts, 'Africa on Film to 1940', *History in Africa*, XIV (1987), p. 213.

[6] D. C. Dorward, 'British West Africa and Liberia', in Roberts, ed., *CHA*, VII, p. 428.

which women had been active in public life. Women took a lead in the risings: fifty were killed by colonial troops.

Indirect Rule was not simply a form of local government: it was in effect a policy of segregation, inasmuch as it was part of a broader strategy for restricting the influence of Africans who had been educated on Western lines. By 1902 West Africans were excluded from the higher levels of administration and government medical services. They were given a modest share in local lawmaking. There were Legislative Councils in each West African colony, and by 1906 all included at least one African among the nominated unofficial members. But the scope of each Council varied. In Sierra Leone it extended over the Protectorate, but in the Gold Coast it was confined to the Colony; in Nigeria it was confined to Lagos from 1914 to 1922, and had no power over the vast north. The loyalty of the African middle class was under strain well before the First World War put it to a further test. West Africans helped to expel Germany from Togo, Kamerun (Cameroons), and East Africa, and at home suffered multiple hardships and privations. In 1915 a letter-writer in a Gold Coast newspaper asked: 'Is there any difference in the Souls of men, who willingly have laid down their lives for the glorious British Empire?'[7] In 1918 a Gold Coast editorial charged the government and business firms with racial discrimination.

In 1920 a meeting in Accra of delegates from all four territories founded the National Congress of British West Africa, first proposed in 1912 by the lawyer and journalist J. E. Casely Hayford. It appealed over the heads of colonial Governors by sending a delegation to London: among its demands was the right to elect representatives to Legislative Councils. The Colonial Secretary, Lord Milner, ignored this petition (though he had just granted a franchise to white settlers in Kenya). London soon had second thoughts: in 1922–25 limited franchises were introduced in urban areas on the West African coast, contingent on property qualifications. Yet even this modest concession was devalued: elected members were outnumbered by chiefs, who could be expected to support the government majority. The net effect was to aggravate tensions, not only between chiefs and the urban élite, but within this élite, some of whom had close ties to chiefly families.

This compromise illustrated the ambivalent position of British colonial governments in West Africa in the 1920s. In the Gold Coast, at least, African prospects for entering the higher civil service seemed to improve. This had been a concern of Hugh Clifford as Governor from 1912 to 1919; the war enabled him to replace a few senior whites by Africans. His successor, Gordon Guggisberg, a Canadian

[7] Quoted by David Kimble, *A Political History of Ghana: The Rise of Gold Coast Nationalism, 1850–1928* (Oxford, 1963), p. 105.

engineer, made Africanization the apex of a development plan which included not only more railways and a deep-water harbour at Takoradi but a new involvement in education on the part of government: in 1927 he opened the Prince of Wales College at Achimota, near Accra, which was soon teaching up to university entrance. However, Guggisberg firmly believed that Africans had yet to receive the right sort of education. In 1925 he declared:

> we want to give the best men and women the opportunity of becoming leaders of their own countrymen in thought, industries, and the professions. Throughout all this, our aim must be not to denationalise them, but to graft skilfully on to their national characteristics the best attributes of modern civilisation. For without preserving his national characteristics and his sympathy and touch with the great illiterate masses of his own people, no man can ever become a leader in progress whatever other sort of leader he may become.[8]

This reflected prevailing official wisdom. Even if educated Africans might enter the ancillary departments of central government, they were firmly excluded from the 'political service'. They might work for chiefs; they could not supervise them. Self-government was envisaged in terms of ethnic nations *within* the colonial state.[9] For all his large vision, Guggisberg remained remote from the urban African middle class: his sympathies lay with progressive chiefs and farmers, rather than with lawyers and traders. Indeed, throughout British West Africa local traders were losing ground in the 1920s not only to European businesses but to an influx of 'Syrians', mostly from Lebanon. They were especially prominent in Sierra Leone; in 1919 African attacks upon them had caused an exodus, but they soon returned, and in 1938 it was said that the eastern part of Freetown was 'almost a counter part of Beyrouth'.[10] There was, besides, a vast region of British West Africa in which it was official policy not simply to exclude the coastal élite but to keep Western cultural influences to a minimum. In the Muslim areas of Northern Nigeria, missionary activity was curbed, and Western education confined to government schools in which English was rarely taught: this was Colonial Office policy, sustained in the face of objections from Clifford, as Governor in 1921, as well as from several emirs.[11] In the short run such a policy, putting a premium on social

[8] G. B. Kay, ed., *The Political Economy of Colonialism in Ghana: A Collection of Documents and Statistics, 1900–1960* (Cambridge, 1972), p. 288.

[9] Cf. Clifford's address as Governor to the Nigerian Legislative Council in December 1920, quoted by James S. Coleman, *Nigeria: Background to Nationalism* (Berkeley, 1958), pp. 193–94; Margery Perham, *Native Administration in Nigeria* (London, 1937) p. 361.

[10] Quoted by R. R. Kuczynski, *A Demographic Survey of the British Colonial Empire*, Vol. I, *West Africa* (London, 1948), p. 192.

[11] P. K. Tibenderana, 'The Emirs and the Spread of Western Education in Northern Nigeria, 1900–1946', *Journal of African History*, XXIV, 4 (1983), pp. 532, 534.

harmony, made some sense when British officials were in charge but thin on the ground; in the long run this isolation from cultural changes nearer the coast created huge political problems.

1930s–1960s

In the course of the 1930s African leadership in the coastal towns became more aggressive. The National Congress of British West Africa had failed to sustain its original momentum, and the élites for which it spoke were distracted by local rivalries. In Southern Nigeria and the Gold Coast education had spread far beyond the circles of the established élite families, and the few thousand entitled to vote. Guggisberg's wish for African leaders in touch with illiterate masses was to be fulfilled sooner than he expected, if not in the way he intended. A new generation of journalists and politicians moved beyond programmes for limited reform towards strategies for popular participation. They began, moreover, to think not just of sharing in colonial government but of bringing it to an end.

This change of mood responded to new opportunities and new crises. The worldwide economic Depression of the 1930s hit West Africa hard. There was massive retrenchment in government: not only British officials but thousands of low-paid Africans were laid off. Large-scale farmers and small businessmen were increasingly overshadowed by expatriate trading firms enjoying the advantages of oligopoly and vertical integration. Falling prices for export crops brought wage levels down, especially in the mining industries (which now yielded gem diamonds and iron ore from Sierra Leone as well as industrial diamonds and manganese from the Gold Coast). Rising output as well as a rising gold price greatly enhanced the contribution of mining to export values: West Africa rode out the Depression on the backs of mineworkers, many of whom, in the Gold Coast, came from French territory. (Ironically, it was only in the 1930s that slavery, and the slave trade, effectively came to an end in Northern Nigeria.) And as the world climbed out of the Depression, Fascist dictatorships in Europe gave a new lease of life to racism and empire-building. In the Gold Coast the lawyer and author J. B. Danquah reprinted anti-Nazi articles by German writers, and there was widespread revulsion in West Africa against Mussolini's invasion of Ethiopia in 1935.[12] Britain's failure to stand firm against it discredited her claims to rule in Africa as a trustee for its peoples' welfare. Politics and economics combined to demonstrate that colonial problems were enmeshed in global tensions. Attachment to Empire was giving way to attacks on imperialism.[13]

[12] S. K. B. Asante, *Pan-African Protest: West Africa and the Italo-Ethiopian Crisis, 1934–1941* (London, 1977).

[13] See chap. by Nicholas Owen on critics in Britain.

The new radical critiques were developed both at home and abroad. In London an important forum for political discussion was the West African Students' Union, and West Africans mingled with Africans of the diaspora, especially from the Caribbean. Marxism was mediated by George Padmore, from Trinidad, who moved to London from Moscow in 1934 after breaking with the Communist Party. Hamburg was the scene in 1930 of a Negro Workers' Conference, attended by West Africans from each British territory: one was I. T. A. Wallace-Johnson, who went on to study in Moscow before returning to a career of protest in West Africa. The most important new source of cultural stimulus was the United States. By the 1920s it excited the imagination of West African schoolboys; in pursuing their education, some reached a crossroads pointing to either Britain or America.[14] In 1934 Nnamdi Azikiwe, from south-eastern Nigeria, came back with degrees from Lincoln University, a historically black college, and the University of Pennsylvania. In England he had met Margery Perham, who acknowledged that Indirect Rule in his Igbo homeland could offer no scope for his abilities; he also explained to Hanns Vischer, a former director of education in Northern Nigeria, why Africans felt humiliated by the terms offered them in the civil service.[15] Instead, Azikiwe started a new daily paper in Accra, the *African Morning Post*, and in 1936 he and Wallace-Johnson were convicted of sedition. Azikiwe appealed successfully to the Privy Council, but meanwhile returned to Nigeria and founded the outspoken *West African Pilot*, which by 1938 far outstripped the sales of other Lagos papers. Meanwhile, his example had inspired other Igbo to follow him to Lincoln University, with funds raised locally.

The Second World War and the post-war economic boom prompted fresh thought among the rulers of British West Africa. The war itself bore heavily on the region. Not only did it furnish soldiers (mainly from Northern Nigeria) for campaigns in Ethiopia and Burma; it provided a relatively secure route for supplying Allied forces in North Africa and India. US personnel were prominent in ports and air-bases. To co-ordinate military and economic war efforts, there was a British Cabinet Minister in Accra from 1942 to 1945. Wartime marketing controls presaged a new era of state intervention in economic affairs.[16] Mineral exports, produced under duress, proved crucial during the war, but thereafter it was world demand for tropical crops which boosted government revenues. Though in 1950 the mines of British West Africa employed as many Africans as those in the Rhodesias, Nigeria's tin deposits yielded falling returns after 1943. By contrast,

[14] K. A. B. Jones-Quartey, 'From Ghana', in Franz M. Joseph, ed., *As Others See Us: The United States through Foreign Eyes* (Princeton, 1959), p. 243.

[15] Nnamdi Azikiwe, *My Odyssey* (London, 1970), pp. 210–11.

[16] See P. T. Bauer, *West African Trade* (Cambridge, 1954), chaps. 19–24.

the Gold Coast produced little more cocoa in the 1950s than in the 1920s, but the price rose tenfold between 1945 and 1955. Population was also on the increase: in Nigeria and the Gold Coast at an annual rate of perhaps 3 per cent since the 1920s. Yet governments retained enough from rising export incomes after the war to invest in welfare as well as development. Higher education was now a priority. The British mostly looked askance at Africans seeking it in the United States, and instead took a lead in funding it themselves, both through scholarships for study in Britain and through new university colleges in Nigeria (Ibadan) and the Gold Coast.[17] High-level Africanization finally got under way: from 1942 Africans began to be appointed to the provincial administration in the Gold Coast. By 1954 they occupied 36 per cent of senior civil service posts in the Gold Coast and Nigeria, though their advance was slower in Sierra Leone and the Gambia. As African graduates began to occupy desks both in the capitals and in district offices, it seemed as if progress was at last being made in tackling the political integration of West Africa's coast with its hinterland. But the process had its limits; it was long delayed in Northern Nigeria; and in any case the pace was increasingly set by African politicians.

West African opinion-formers mostly supported Britain's struggle against the Axis powers, but seized their chance to exert moral pressure. In 1941 the West African Students' Union obtained from Clement Attlee, the Deputy Prime Minister, an assurance that the affirmation of rights in the Atlantic Charter applied to 'Asiatics, Africans and everyone'.[18] In 1943 Azikiwe and other West African journalists visited London and gave the Colonial Office a memorandum which envisaged that by 1958 their countries would be 'independent and sovereign political entities, aligned or associated with the British Commonwealth of Nations'.[19] Late in 1945 a Pan-African Congress was convened in Manchester by Padmore, with help from Kwame Nkrumah, who was on his way back to the Gold Coast from studies in the United States: the Congress demanded 'autonomy and independence' for black Africa, and called for 'the organisation of the masses'.[20] In Nigeria this was already under way: the wartime expansion of towns, price inflation, and the growth of trade unions culminated in a prolonged strike of government workers in 1945, and it was backed by Azikiwe's newly formed National Council of Nigeria and the Cameroons. The arena for anti-colonial action was being redefined: the preoccupation of an earlier generation with the seaboard of British West Africa was giving way to a new focus on each colonial territory, and a new concern to mobilize its

[17] Cf. Eric Ashby (with Mary Anderson), *Universities: British, Indian, African* (London, 1966).

[18] Wm. Roger Louis, *Imperialism at Bay, 1941–1945: The United States and the Decolonization of the British Empire* (Oxford, 1977), p. 125.

[19] Coleman, *Nigeria: Background to Nationalism*, pp. 240–41.

[20] J. Ayodele Langley, *Ideologies of Liberation in Black Africa, 1856–1970* (London, 1979), pp. 760–01.

hinterland. 'Nationalism', in this context, arose not from cultural solidarities but from the shared experience of a colonial regime.

Such aspirations put British officials on the spot. The more farsighted might allow the need for more power-sharing, but it seemed unthinkable that each territory might form a sovereign state in any foreseeable future: each was still riven by contrasts between progressive littoral and backward hinterland, westernized élites and traditional rulers, Christians and Muslims. In 1947 Andrew Cohen, head of the Africa department at the Colonial Office, considered that 'in the Gold Coast, the territory where Africans are most advanced politically, internal self-government is unlikely to be achieved in much less than a generation'.[21] Reform, indeed, was put in hand. Indirect Rule was to give way to democratic, or at least 'representative', local government: chiefs would yield to councillors. Thus would Africans throughout each territory gain experience in self-government. Territorial integration was advanced by constitutional changes. In 1946 the scope of the Legislative Council in Nigeria was extended to the North, and that of the Gold Coast Council was extended to Asante: in both councils, moreover, Africans were to predominate. Yet most were to be chosen by chiefs or other local authorities, not by voters.

For the new wave of militant politicians, this was not nearly enough: power for them meant power through the ballot-box. This was the cause in which Nkrumah, on his return to the Gold Coast in 1947, campaigned alongside Danquah, in Asante as well as the colony. But this was a time of widespread and bitter unrest, in towns and on cocoa farms; during riots in 1948 twenty-nine people were killed. Nkrumah realized he had to move fast to keep up with the people whom he meant to lead. In 1949 he founded the Convention People's Party (CPP), which was closely linked to the labour movement, and in 1950 he and others were jailed for promoting an illegal strike, sedition, and trying to coerce the government. But the CPP had not foresworn the path of constitutional advance, which was now widened by reforms that greatly increased the electorate. In 1951 the CPP won a majority of elective seats in the Legislative Council, for Asante as well as the Colony. This was still a minority of the total, but the Governor, Charles Arden-Clarke, was sufficiently impressed to release Nkrumah and appoint CPP leaders to ministerial office; in 1952 Nkrumah became Prime Minister of a CPP government with extensive powers in internal affairs. In 1956 a plebiscite in the British Mandate of Togoland united that territory with the Gold Coast. An election on adult suffrage, in 1956, paved the way for independence in 1957, when the country took the name of Ghana, thus associating modern anti-colonialism with an ancient trading-state on the edge of the Sahara. Yet the transfer of power was deceptively smooth: the CPP

[21] John D. Hargreaves, *Decolonization in Africa* (Harlow, 1988), p. 100.

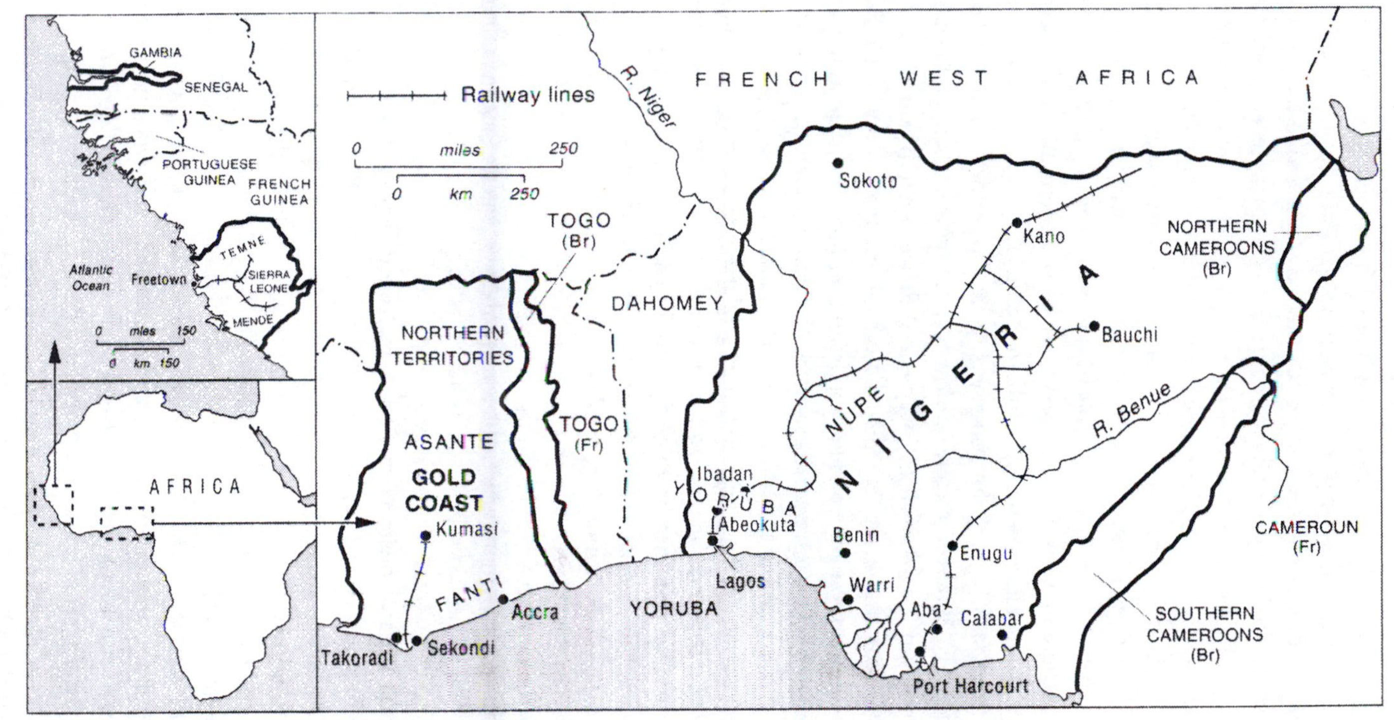

MAP 22.1 British West Africa in the Mid-Twentieth Century

rode to final victory with the votes of only one-sixth of the adult population. There was widespread opposition to Nkrumah's government, and much of it was centred in Asante. Nkrumah's regime, in defence of its privileges and in the name of the people, was to prove no less authoritarian than its colonial predecessors.[22]

All the same, Ghana was compact and homogeneous by comparison with Nigeria. In 1948 their populations were about 5 million and 30 million respectively, and in Nigeria more than half were in the north, where English was still little taught. If Nigeria was indeed to move towards self-government as a single state, the British believed that this could only be done on a federal basis, whereby north and south could move at different speeds. In the short term this made possible a degree of co-operation between southern politicians and the colonial regime headed from 1948 by Sir John Macpherson, as Governor, and Hugh Foot, as Chief Secretary. However, the creation in 1951 of regional assemblies aggravated divisions within the nationalist movement. Azikiwe certainly sought to bring a Nigerian nation into being, but his ethnic base was the Igbo nation generated by mission education and colonial opportunities. More than any other people, Igbo were pan-Nigerians: many worked as clerks and traders in the south-west, especially Lagos, and in the northern towns, as well as in the Cameroons. But this diaspora was itself a cause of ethnic solidarity among others. Though the National Council of Nigeria and the Cameroons (NCNC) had included Yoruba from the first, there were many who feared for the future of a distinctive Yoruba nationality. In 1947 their spokesman Obafemi Awolowo argued the case for a federation of 'national groups', and in 1951 his Action Group defeated the NCNC in the Western Region elections. The Northern Assembly was largely filled by the Northern People's Congress (NPC), which was close to the emirs and fearful of southern influences. Its leader, Abubakr Tafawa Balewa, had in 1945 been among the first northern school teachers to be sent to Britain for further study.

The drift towards regional separatism in Nigeria was dramatized by riots in Kano in May 1953. It was partly checked in a new constitution worked out at a conference in London later that year. The way was now open to regional self-government, but the role of central government was strengthened, and Africans were to be given charge of departments. Federal elections in 1954 produced a government comprising, apart from three British officials, six NCNC and three NPC ministers. When the Queen toured Nigeria in 1956 she was warmly welcomed: relations with Britain were much easier than in 1953, when the NCNC had boycotted Coronation festivities. Self-government was granted to the western and

[22] See Richard Rathbone, ed., *Ghana*, British Documents on the End of Empire Project (BDEEP), 2 Parts (London, 1992).

eastern regions in 1957; the North was less eager for hurry, but followed in 1959. Meanwhile, a visiting commission considered, and rejected, the idea of safeguarding the rights of ethnic minorities by dividing the country into numerous smaller states. Federal elections were held in 1959, on the basis of universal adult suffrage, except that the vote was withheld from women in the North. The NPC won most seats, but formed a coalition with the NCNC; its Prime Minister was Tafawa Balewa. Under this coalition Nigeria became independent in October 1960; soon afterwards Azikiwe became Governor-General.[23]

In Sierra Leone too, the politics of decolonization were fraught with internal tensions. Here they were aggravated by the continued separation of Colony and Protectorate. The population of the Colony was mainly Krio, but comprised at most 5 per cent of the total (perhaps 2 million in 1948). An attempt had been made in 1938–39 to straddle this divide: Wallace-Johnson's West African Youth League was supported by workers in both regions as well as by most Krio barristers, but this did not survive the outbreak of war. Krio strongly opposed a plan in 1947 to allot the Protectorate a majority of unofficial seats in the Legislative Council; besides, they faced the challenge of an emergent educated élite in the Protectorate. In 1950 the latter joined chiefs in forming the Sierra Leone People's Party (SLPP) led by Milton Margai, the first person from the Protectorate to gain a medical degree. When an election was held in 1951, on a constitution still representing the Protectorate largely through chiefs, Margai was able to muster enough support to be made leader of government business; by 1956 he was Prime Minister. In 1957 a new constitution provided not only for universal suffrage in the Colony, but for a broad-based franchise in the Protectorate. The SLPP won easily, while the old guard of Colony politicians was eclipsed. The main opposition now came from urban workers, led by a trade unionist from the Protectorate, Siaka Stevens: when independence came in 1961, he was in detention.

Gambia displayed in miniature the constitutional rifts of British West Africa. Only 10 per cent of the total population (*c.*200,000 in 1948) lived in the Colony. From 1946 this was able to elect one member of the Legislative Council, where the Protectorate now gained representation, by nomination. By 1960 adult suffrage was widespread in both areas, and the Protectorate members predominated. Most belonged to the Protectorate Progressive Party (PPP), led by Dauda Jawara, a veterinary surgeon. In 1962, after a further election, Jawara formed a PPP government. The British hoped that Gambia might merge with Senegal, but Jawara chose

[23] Decolonization in Nigeria involved the British Mandates of Northern and Southern Cameroons. The former became part of the Northern Region in 1951, and has since remained part of Nigeria; Southern Cameroons was attached to the Eastern Region in 1951; it was given quasi-federal status in 1954, but in 1961 voted to join the former French Mandate of Cameroun.

independence, which came in 1965, though Britain continued to support Gambia's budget up to 1968.

In the greater part of British West Africa, colonial rule lasted scarcely sixty years. It ended calmly: the transfer of power had been effected by the same constitutional process as in the Dominions of white settlement. Yet this was achieved in a greatly compressed time-frame. Africans had played a large part in compelling the British to revise drastically their timetables for decolonization. In so far as the British meant to develop states which integrated coast and hinterland, they had left their task half-finished. But they had helped to bring into being an African leadership which would not wait, for it did not trust them. The aloofness of British officialdom did not necessarily spring from racism, but all too often it connived at racism. West Africans had good reason to believe that only political independence could enable them to hold up their heads as free people.

The transfer of power was not, of course, comprehensive. National economies were still geared to the export of primary products, and their fortunes depended on overseas markets over which Africans could usually exert little control. Nigeria's huge oil wealth from the 1970s was an exception, but this gift of nature proved a mixed blessing. British expertise continued for a time to be crucial in the armed forces, the police, the judiciary, and the professions. New schemes of economic and social development attracted a new wave of expatriates on contract. None the less, independence gave a fresh impetus to Africanization. It also made possible a wider field of external relations. The four new states became members of the British Commonwealth as well as the United Nations, but they were not inhibited by past ties. Each became a republic: Ghana in 1960, Nigeria in 1963, Gambia in 1970, Sierra Leone in 1971. Britain's share of West African trade declined sharply. English remained the official language, but it became the vehicle for cultural Americanization at every level, especially in Nigeria. Nkrumah hoped that Pan-African co-operation would supplant British imperialism as an organizing principle for the continent. In 1958 he sought to unite Ghana with French Guinea when the latter resisted de Gaulle's schemes for decolonization: in 1961 this flimsy union was extended to Mali. Nkrumah had material help from the Soviet Union, but in 1966 he was overthrown by a military coup. Elsewhere, cold war politics scarcely impinged on former British West Africa. The most traumatic consequence of independence was civil war in Nigeria. Federation of three regions proved quite unable to contain multiple ethnic rivalries. From 1967 to 1970 a military regime in the east tried to sustain independence from the federal government, but this was backed by Britain, the United States, and the Soviet Union: Nigeria held together. Throughout former British West Africa, however, representative government was in general retreat. The rule of law, never securely established under colonial auspices, was widely eroded. The state, usually under military control, commonly promoted private gain rather than public welfare. Many of the most talented moved abroad in a new diaspora; the British Empire in West Africa ended as it began: with the export of people.

Select Bibliography

ARTHUR ABRAHAM, *Mende Government and Politics under Colonial Rule: A Historical Study of Political Change in Sierra Leone, 1890–1937* (Freetown, 1979).

OMONIYI ADEWOYE, *The Judicial System in Southern Nigeria, 1854–1954* (London, 1977).

JEAN MARIE ALLMAN, *The Quills of the Porcupine: Asante Nationalism in an Emergent Ghana* (Madison, 1993).

DENNIS AUSTIN, *Politics in Ghana, 1946–1960* (London, 1970).

JAMES S. COLEMAN, *Nigeria: Background to Nationalism* (Berkeley, 1958).

MICHAEL CROWDER, *West Africa Under Colonial Rule* (London, 1968).

D. C. DORWARD, 'British West Africa and Liberia', in A. D. Roberts. ed., *The Cambridge History of Africa*, Vol. VII, *1905–1940* (Cambridge, 1986), pp. 399–459.

PHILIP FOSTER, *Education and Social Change in Ghana* (Chicago, 1965).

IMANUEL GEISS, *The Pan-African Movement*, trans. Ann Keep (London, 1974).

MARTIN KILSON, *Political Change in a West African State: A Study of the Modernisation Process in Sierra Leone* (Cambridge, Mass., 1966).

DAVID KIMBLE, *A Political History of Ghana: The Rise of Gold Coast Nationalism, 1850–1928* (Oxford, 1963).

J. AYODELE LANGLEY, *Pan-Africanism and Nationalism in West Africa, 1900–1945: A Study in Ideology and Social Classes* (Oxford, 1973).

PAUL E. LOVEJOY and JAN S. HOGENDORN, *Slow Death for Slavery: The Course of Abolition in Northern Nigeria, 1897–1936* (Cambridge, 1993).

I. F. NICHOLSON, *The Administration of Nigeria, 1900–1960: Men, Methods, and Myths* (Oxford, 1969).

G. O. OLUSANYA, *The Second World War and Politics in Nigeria, 1939–1953* (London, 1973).

ANNE PHILLIPS, *The Enigma of Colonialism: British Policy in West Africa* (London, 1989).

RICHARD RATHBONE, ed., *Ghana*, British Documents on the End of Empire Project (BDEEP), 2 Parts (London, 1992).

RICHARD L. SKLAR, *Nigerian Political Parties: Power in an Emergent African Nation* (Princeton, 1963).

LEO SPITZER, *The Creoles of Sierra Leone: Responses to Colonialism, 1870–1945* (Madison, 1974).

R. E. WRAITH, *Guggisberg* (London, 1967).

23

East Africa

JOHN LONSDALE

British rule was the particular forcing house in which East Africa faced its trial by modernization, a process by which state power and capitalism have transformed societies the world over. Many have suffered, many have benefited by it. Rulers of modern states can use their unprecedented power to commandeer their subjects' blood and treasure and, if unchecked, their labour and their liberties. By widening markets beyond local control, capitalism has twisted moral economies of obligation and devalued statuses and skills. Yet modernity has also created unequalled opportunity, unequally shared, for social mobility, for collective solutions to natural disasters, for the access of the literate to new ideas, for the broader enjoyment of useful goods during longer lifetimes. Did British rule make these experiences more or less arduous or productive, more divisive or more widely liberating, than would any other regime, local or foreign?

The question grows no less insistent as more time passes since colonial rule ended in the 1960s, six decades after the first tax collections marked its effective birth. Independence has not delivered the growing welfare which, perhaps unrealistically, it was once hoped to bring. There is, however, no easy answer. Modernity was bound to be a harsh ordeal for East Africans, who came late to the world's market-place, with few resources, working old, eroded soils with simple tools. The colonial past must, none the less, bear some responsibility for failure. If empire was a necessary lesson in capitalism, it came too late to East Africa for Britain to be its best tutor. Before 1914 the British Empire was the world's pioneer development agency, with London the cheapest supplier of capital to apprentice producers and the best market for their primary products, but for East Africans the British were little more than recent conquerors. After the Great War, the Empire turned into a prop against Britain's decline; East Africa's high colonial period thus coincided with the least creative, most exploitative, era of British overseas rule. But there was no indigenous power to take command of change, unlike Meiji Japan; nineteenth-century East Africans, before colonial rule, had suffered political disintegration more often than they had forged wider alliances in face of economic change. There is, therefore, no working example of an alternative route to the modern world from East Africa's starting-point a century ago against which to evaluate the region's Imperial experience. Moreover, there was no one starting-point, and by the 1960s the region's peoples faced their world in very different ways.

Independent Uganda was bedevilled not so much by obstacles to growth, for which natural endowment and capital investment gave it a head start, as by the mutual hostility of its regional authorities. Kenya's central government, in contrast, grew stronger by allocating assets in land and technical services left by departing white settlers. Tanganyika (as mainland Tanzania remained until Union with Zanzibar in 1964) faced an abyss, with falling export markets for its sisal fibre, the most meagre physical capital, and the most tyrannous distances in East Africa. The island sultanate of Zanzibar was on the eve of bloody revolution.

These different colonial outcomes make it hard to judge British rule as a whole. Indeed, there was no such thing; there were four different colonial regimes. Each had a history of its own that interwove the 'high' politics of governments, with their main allies and opponents, with the 'deep' politics of social inequality that decided the loyalties of the mass of people—clients or wage-workers, small farmers, traders, men and women, old and young. Much change, it is true, was common to all four territories. They shared a dependence on a declining Britain, twice faced world war, were subject to global boom and slump, and were inwardly transformed by the rise of market-minded peasantries, by labour migration to plantations and towns, by the invention of vernacular literacies, and from the 1920s, by a fast-growing population. Common processes none the less caused local conflicts that gave each territory its peculiar character. All such disputes tested the capacity of the high political alliances that were first forged during the British conquest to cope with the deep politics of social change. These common processes give this chapter its organizing theme.

Colonialism's founding alliances of the 1890s had met contrasting fates by the time of independence in the 1960s. Britain's marriage of convenience with the Buganda kingdom could not contain the regional tensions of half a century of economic growth. On the eve of Uganda's independence the link was on the brink of collapse. So too was Zanzibar's Arab landlord dominance, never a firm base of British rule. Kenya's political economy, on the other hand, experienced an ease of transition, despite its past conflicts between white settlers and African small farmers, thanks to a deeper level of coexistence mediated by Indian trade. Tanganyika's foundations on Christian literacy, peasant agriculture, and Swahili towns—all scraped together in the 1920s from the wartime wreck of German settler colonialism—proved to be the most durable. Perhaps this was because of all territories it remained, for its size, the poorest.

Founding Alliances

The British had to conquer by expending resources in breaking local powers before they could rule, earn revenues, and as they saw it, bring civilization. This Imperial vision was self-contradictory, for British estimates of Africans differed. Where there was a strong 'native state', with an already Christian ruling class and an industrious tenantry, as in Buganda, then a cautious administrative preference for continuity could combine with missionary hopes or commercial demands for change. But many East Africans had no chiefs, let alone kings. The British agreed that they were unusually low on the evolutionary scale but disagreed on how they could be 'raised'. Officials hoped councils of elders would protect organic small communities; missionaries prayed for spiritually adventurous individuals; settler farmers favoured the collective discipline of wage labour. Divided purposes allowed much room for historical contingency in what followed; outcomes waited on local conflicts rather than on Imperial policy.

All Britain's little conquests in East Africa had their own distinctive character, thanks to a varying Imperial interest in each territory, differences in African society, and the historical accidents such as royal-succession war, cattle plague, or famine that fashioned levers of alliance for the British or springs of opposition. For all its primacy as a diplomatic base for Britain's long informal sway over East Africa and then formal Protectorate from 1890, even Zanzibar had to suffer naval bombardment in 1896 before its Arab élite gave up all factional hopes of independent sovereignty. Britain's entry into Buganda's civil war in 1890, followed by her militant adoption of that kingdom's foreign policy, secured colonial rule over the wider region of Uganda. Kenya was the path to Buganda. Its dozen British officials or quartermasters fought their small wars of conquest to keep the road open and porters fed. 'Punitive expeditions'—that revealing term—became more brutal as their growing power stoked officials' impatience with those peoples who refused 'to come into line'.[1] The Uganda Railway, which reached Lake Victoria in 1901, also made it easier to move troops. German East Africa entered the British domain as Tanganyika, last and worst-devastated by the local extension of the European Great War of 1914–18.

Force was costly, colonies were meant to pay. Supplying them with limited capital, Britain had to build peaceable Imperial hegemonies on a shoestring.[2]

[1] Governor Sir Hesketh Bell, 1909, quoted by D. A. Low, 'Uganda, the Establishment of the Protectorate, 1894–1919', in Vincent T. Harlow and E. M. Chilver, eds., *History of East Africa*, Vol. II (Oxford, 1965), p. 60.

[2] Cf. P. J. Cain and A. G. Hopkins, *British Imperialism: Crisis and Deconstruction, 1914–1990* (London, 1993), chap. 9; and Sara Berry, *No Condition is Permanent: The Social Dynamics of Agrarian Change in Sub-Saharan Africa* (Madison, 1993), chap. 2.

Uganda and Kenya were self-supporting by 1912; Tanganyika was denied Treasury aid, save for two lean years in the 1920s; Zanzibar did not need it. Governments' first duty was to foster markets that circulated money, generated revenue, and rewarded peace. Conversely, Africans' contribution to exports and imports acted as their proxy for high political activity in the half-century before they were permitted to join whites and Indians in local legislatures. These considerations enable one to sketch in the high politics of early colonial rule and look into its underlying politics. Export growth needed labour, whether on African smallholdings or on the large estates owned by white immigrants in the interior or by long-settled Arabs on the coasts and islands. The difference between the two levels of politics was nowhere more striking than on Zanzibar.

The Anglo-Arab alliance looked to be happily sealed by the clove export market, but the alliance's deep social foundations soon rotted away. After the safety of India's sea routes, which had first led her to the region, Britain's second interest in East Africa had been the abolition of the slave trade.[3] But her Zanzibar Protectorate made slave-owners colleagues in government. To end slavery, not just the trade, was too much to ask of political prudence, racial prejudice against 'idle natives', and fiscal concern. What else would discipline black labour or support Arab landlords? So in 1897 the British abolished the legal status of slavery but did not emancipate slaves. Slaves had to sue for their own freedom, at risk of thereby losing their jobs and so incurring a vagrancy charge. The British hoped to underpin Arab planters with legally free but economically tied labour. Most ex-slaves, however, negotiated labour-tenancies at rising levels of pay, which increased landlord debt rather than managerial efficiency. As in India's United Provinces, the British found themselves allied to a sinking ruling class.

Uganda's alliance was more robust. Before 1914 forty officials ruled her 3 million people through Buganda's 'sub-imperialism'. This system posted out Baganda chiefs and missionary teachers to other peoples, and had a solid economic base. The kingdom's chief minister in this pioneer age was one of Africa's 'farseeing modernizers', Sir Apolo Kaggwa.[4] Standing on his kingdom's privileges and his chiefs' right to coerce their tenants' cotton cultivation—a goad to growth soon reinforced by peasant ambition to educate their children—he ensured that Uganda's white planters did not finally win their battle for government favours. In 1914 African cotton earned two-thirds of export income; African cyclists paid much of her import duty; 80,000 Baganda were at school.

Black and white interests were similarly matched in Kenya, despite the apparent supremacy of its settlers, whose pioneers arrived after 1902. Their overbearing politics masked underlying weakness. There were never more than 2,000 farm

[3] In Vol. III, see pp. 210–11, 214.

[4] John Iliffe, *Africans: The History of a Continent* (Cambridge, 1995), p. 199.

families before 1940, a minority of the white population. They were the last eddy of the Victorian tide of British emigration that had always been more urban than rural, and that was now checked by the onset of global overproduction in temperate farming. Officials had no faith in peasant producers; they had seen too many Africans die of famine and smallpox. But private family farms in Kenya's cool highlands, as distinct from lowland company plantations of sisal or upland coffee or tea estates, were no better bet for recovering the £6m spent on railway and conquest.

Moreover, Kenya's conquest was patchy. Whites owned three-quarters of South Africa and half Rhodesia, but only one-fifth of Kenya's useable land. African agriculture—as distinct from pastoralism, whose experts, the Masai, suffered huge land losses—was left largely in place. As elsewhere in Africa, peasants entered markets faster than settlers and before 1914 sold more exports. The deep politics of acquiescence in British rule, as well as its high finance, rested willy-nilly on their livelihood. Playing on racial solidarity, settlers agitated for more African land, taxes, and labour precisely because officials could never fully satisfy these calls. The balancing act of British 'trusteeship' for African interests was a material alliance with peasant production before it became an Imperial ideology.

It was ironic that this peculiarly British mediation between the races—spawning Royal Commissions, episcopal petition, and parliamentary debate—was sustained by British Indians. Their commercial acumen was the stimulus to peasant export competition with settlers. Allidina Visram, their greatest trader, was a true social engineer. An Ismaili, he came to Africa as a boy in 1863 in the caravan trade. He banked the railway's Indian navvies' pay in the 1890s, sailed a merchant navy on Lake Victoria, grew rubber, ginned cotton, refined sugar, and sold insurance in Uganda; he boiled soap in and imported bicycles through Mombasa, and owned 200 shops before he died in 1916.[5] He was as much a pioneer of the new Africa as Kaggwa or Lord Delamere, the out-at-elbows leader of Kenya's settlers. There were more than 50,000 East African Indians, half of them in Kenya, in the 1920s, at a time when there were 14,000 Europeans and 13 million Africans. Overseas Indians were to be decisive actors in the East African politics of Empire between the wars. Their struggles inflamed nationalist sentiment in India, alarmed the British Viceroy, and thus forced the Colonial Office to keep the balance between white and black.

War, Depression, and Community

The alliances required by conquest, and a stable peace in which taxes could be raised, were soon tested by the Great War. Black partners stood firmer than whites.

[5] Robert G. Gregory, *South Asians in East Africa: An Economic and Social History, 1890–1960* (Boulder, Colo., 1993), pp. 56, 98, 101, 120, 273.

While Zanzibar was insulated from hostilities, some mainland peoples suffered in relation to their size, more grievously than the people of Britain, from disease and privation rather than battle. Critics, black and white, thought past 'tribal war' child's play compared with the clash of empires, in which Africans paid more than their fair share for the German General Paul von Lettow-Vorbeck's guerrilla genius. For four years he evaded the exhausted reach of British forces, which were increasingly African in manpower as whites and Indians were invalided out. Relatively few troops died but catastrophe engulfed their porters. The vanished transit camps of the Carrier Corps or *kariakor* live on in the names of Nairobi and Dar-es-Salaam city wards. Of over 700,000 carriers, 100,000 died. Killer famine and disease visited civilian populations. German East Africa, the seat of war, was worst hit. In 1913 one-third of the colony was a bush wilderness, home to the tsetse fly, vector of death to man and beast. Ten years later retreating human cultivation had surrendered a further third of what was now Tanganyika to nature and the fly.

Tanganyika was also British, under a League of Nations Mandate and with a new founding alliance. German defeat had removed East Africa's most advanced settler colony. Its sisal did not recover until the late 1920s under Indian, Greek, British, and returning German owners. Planted on 1 per cent of the territory's land, its export value rarely exceeded that of African coffee and cotton thereafter. Britain's first allies were, therefore, Indian clerks and traders, and English-speaking Africans, who were often ex-slaves, or their sons educated at the Anglican school on Zanzibar. When, in 1922, these organized themselves they started a peculiarly Tanganyikan tradition of élite politics unconnected with rural concerns. They were joined by urban Muslim notables and imitated, at a distance, by educated farmers at odds with their chiefs. As in all alliances, those most useful to the British could advance their own interests, despite the fact that Africans, naturally, were excluded from high politics.

Uganda's political conventions were still further from economic reality. Racial hierarchy indelibly marked high politics. Two planters sat in the all-white Legislative Council. But colour did not make officials blind. They knew—despite the death by sleeping sickness of one in ten Ugandans in a decade—that peasant cotton held the future; in 1918 it contributed 80 per cent of exports. Peasants resented paying tribute to chiefs, but their earnings allowed them to avoid working for whites. Soon after the war many planters were squeezed out by the high labour price of a productive peasantry, by distance from markets, and by post-war slump. By 1923 Uganda was clearly an African producer's country.

In 1923 Britain declared Kenya a primarily African territory, too, where native interests were paramount. As their trustee, London would not share responsibility with others. Settlers felt betrayed, although the declaration protected them against Indian competition. Led by Delamere, who had lost a fortune testing what could be grown in the Rift Valley, they had gained much by intimidating past Governors. Of the seven who held office before 1923, London had had to transfer or force the resignation of four. Settlers had won land concessions, higher African taxes, even forced labour—if less of the last than Uganda's chiefs enjoyed. For their wartime patriotism they were promised the franchise. But when, after the war, their exports collapsed and banks withdrew credit, when African tax-protesters were shot down in Nairobi and the India Office in London took up the Indian demand for the vote, when settlers reacted with plans to intern the Governor beside a favourite trout stream, the Colonial Office reasserted its African trust to quash the rival immigrants' claims. It remained to be seen how far Britain's political stewardship would foster African market agriculture, with its broader potential than that offered by a few hundred indebted white farmers.

With the planter collapse in Tanganyika and Uganda, and Kenya's compromise, effective politics between the wars was neither Imperial nor territorial but local. Here, where colonial alliances had first been struck, people now faced up to the underlying politics of social change. Argument about the local human relations of money, mobility, and mission-schooling created new moral communities. Each locality had its peculiar problems to dispute. Cheap rail and, subsequently, road transport brought market farming to some areas and carried migrant labour from remoter parts. Famine's defeat by the same means and medical victories over epidemic disease meant that in some areas growing numbers of young adults found it harder to get land. Bible translation and a scattering of vernacular newspapers gave them new images and arenas of debate.

Politics created new cultures from below. The *Kumanyana* peasant movement in western Uganda understood that well; its name meant 'to get to know each other'.[6] African court intrigue, the politics of reputation, lineage, and clientage, or of Indian caste and sect, all gave way to wider tensions and the organizations that voiced them. Chiefs disputed with clients how far markets or literacy invalidated former inequalities; fathers objected to sons investing their wages in marriage rather than in their family herds; men rewrote 'customary' law to restrict women's market freedoms.

Ethnic identity became a new principle of obligation in an insecure world, when markets, literacy, and common subjection to alien rule prised open personal ties of dependence. In the 1920s Baganda challenged chiefs in the idiom of clan solidarity; Kikuyu asked if literacy gave 'people who have no name' a right to speak; Filipo Njau, a social critic from the Chagga of Kilimanjaro, complained that 'important men are no longer prepared to give anything to help the weak... for they see that

[6] Martin R. Doornbos, *Not All the King's Men: Inequality as a Political Instrument in Ankole, Uganda* (The Hague, 1978), pp. 117–31.

amongst the weak every man relies on his employer, be he white or black'.[7] The erosion of personal obligation widened the answers people could give to the question, to whom did they belong? Losing the calculating protections of rural patronage, taking up with people who spoke the same language in town, exploiting the public arena of district or chieftaincy council in which the British sought to enlist and contain political ambition, people began to define themselves by the label strangers gave them, by their 'tribe'.

Kenya's settlers also negotiated their identity. Their core value—which, in another irony, they shared with Africans—was the moral self-mastery of the homesteader. Most were 'small men', hostile to the 'big men' who could afford political activity. Yet government favoured big men like Delamere, who were less dependent on public services, and more able to use the peasant alliance. Africans took the same view, telling how Delamere and the farmer-chief Koinange between them settled poor Africans as squatter tenants on white farms.[8] Concerted settler action was also thwarted by mistrust of any 'politics' that invaded farm autonomy and, by raising their collective profile, exposed their economic weakness. Few whites, therefore, supported the only British attempt to reshape East Africa between the wars by promoting the 'Closer Union' of its territories. Indians and Africans also opposed the project precisely because it seemed to entrench white supremacy.

The 1930s Depression dragged politics back to the centre. Export revenues fell, the cost of debt repayment soared. Governments imposed marketing controls, hoping to stimulate sales by raising crop quality and tempting traders to invest in processing plant. Falling income, fixed taxes, state regulation, all caused agrarian unrest; but Africans were not the only ones to suffer; indeed, some Africans began to gain. Lacking the bonus that gold gave to their counterparts to the south—save for a few lucky strikes—Kenya's settlers, for instance, had to compensate for their inability to grow grain at profit by trading, instead, in their African competitors' maize. This was an object lesson in why the peasant alliance was both useful and feared. Moreover, the Congo Basin free trade treaty of 1885 shielded African consumers from the cost of propping up Lancashire's textile industry; their cotton goods came increasingly from India and Japan. Still more remarkably, in its search for new revenue the Kenya government remembered 'native paramountcy' and lifted the ban on African coffee, the settlers' most jealously guarded crop. Not only could local compromises soften Imperial exploitation, but a small minority of

[7] Ishmael Mungai, for the Kikuyu Central Association, reported in *Muigwithania*, I, 11 (April 1929): K[enya] N[ational] A[rchives], DC/MKS, Nairobi. 10B/13/1; Njau, 1921, quoted in John Iliffe, *A Modern History of Tanganyika* (Cambridge, 1979), p. 276.

[8] Koinange to editor, *Mumenyereri* (12 July 1948); KNA, MAA. 8/106.

newly prosperous African smallholders found that in resisting rules and taking opportunities they were learning central politics.

Colonialism also acquired new purpose. As poverty deepened, so did officials set themselves a harder test than keeping order, that of promoting welfare. As poor people scratched harder at the soil in order to live, conservation also became a public duty. Impatient with chiefs, allies of a simpler age, the British looked for new collaborators in more vigorous local government. Other Africans were coming forward. By 1938 Uganda's Makerere College, looking to a future university status, was teaching the Cambridge School Certificate and post-secondary courses in medicine, veterinary science, and agriculture to 150 students from all over East Africa. A new war, 1939–45, recruited tens of thousands of African troops, supported no longer by porters but drivers, signallers, and teachers. By its end Kenya's senior black high school, Alliance, had better examination success than white schools. Local councils were giving boys such as Tom Mboya secondary school scholarships, and Kenya had its first nominated—not yet elected—African Member of Legislative Council, Eliud Mathu, witch-doctor's son and Balliol man. The other territories soon followed.

War, Prosperity, and Nationalism

The Second World War transformed East African politics by making farming pay. Japan's seizure of much of East and South-East Asia raised allied demand for Africa's industrial crops. The Commonwealth's campaigns against Mussolini's Ethiopia and Rommel's Afrika Korps enlarged the food market. Profits went to white farmers and planters and, by means of governments' marketing boards, to Britain's importers, before they did to African cash-crop peasants. African producers, however, also did well by feeding the growing towns.

War brought urbanization, especially in the ports; non-agricultural employment in Kenya overtook that in white farming. Kampala grew little, to around 46,000 people. Nairobi's African population went up by half during the war, to 66,000, Dar-es-Salaam's doubled, to 50,000, as did Mombasa's, to 56,000. African town-life, neglected by white councillors, was appalling for all but the favoured few housed by the best employer, the railway. Others had to endure close-quartered filth in private squatter villages or the scarcely less squalid council housing that had first appeared in the late 1930s. Kampala's African urban villages were called its 'septic fringe', an apt description for all East Africa's slums.[9]

[9] Quoted in A. W. Southall and P. C. W. Gutkind, *Townsmen in the Making: Kampala and its Suburbs* (Kampala, 1957), p. 6.

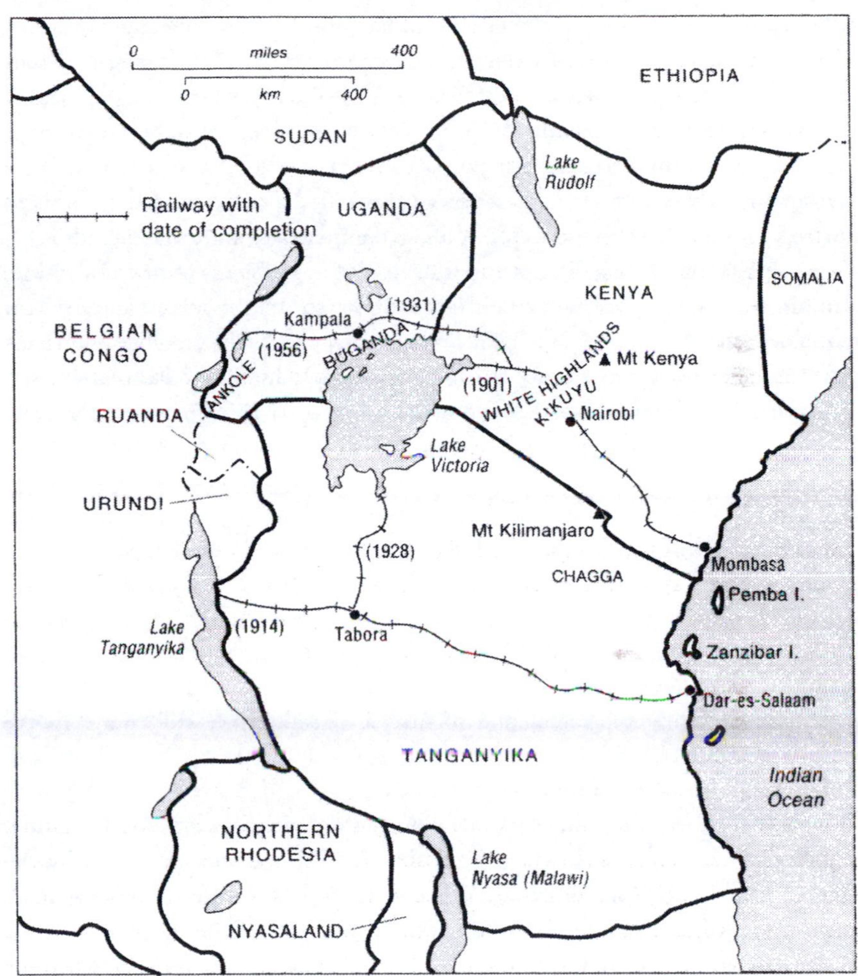

MAP 23.1. East Africa in the Mid-Twentieth Century

Townspeople were still less than 5 per cent of the population, even if many more had lived in town at some time in their lives. By 1950 there were over 18 million East Africans. Tanganyika had more than 7 million; Kenya, fastest-growing, over 5 million; Uganda rather less. There were 200,000 Indians, half of them, as before, in Kenya; and 44,000 whites, most of them in Kenya too. Although small, towns had become the focus of a new African politics. Wartime inflation, wretched housing, which mocked differentials between a unionized minority and the majority of self-employed or part-employed, all created urban crowds rather than working classes. Dockers were especially volatile; while employees, they were also their own gangs of men. In common with all Africa, ports erupted in strikes that spread inland, up railway lines. Strikes gave rise to worker organization; trade unions to splits in existing, moderate, African politics; splits to competitive political demands.

As in India, the British did not run into insoluble problems until countrysides also turned hostile by the 1950s. Peasants were stirred by the same contrast, now redoubled, that had marked the later 1930s, between state interference and rising prosperity. Partly because she needed more of their production to pay off her post-war dollar debt, Britain was determined to save Africa from its peasants. In Tanganyika the groundnuts scheme's mechanized invasion of the empty bush soon ended in farce, but this second colonial occupation of peasantries provoked growing nationalisms. Officials and chiefs rejoined forces to rewrite land tenure, cull cattle, and force women to hoe hillsides into terraces. Seeking allies for these arduous innovations, the British fostered both peasant co-operatives and free-holding, credit-worthy, 'better farmers'. But the occupation was too heavy for them to bear. Four hundred British administrative officers had ruled East Africa in 1940; by 1960 there were 660, as well as many African cadets. Agricultural, veterinary, and other departmental officials had multiplied still more. In the 1950s fresh white farm settlement was still a plausible threat. The new African allies turned resistance leaders.

Agrarian unrest was universal; each founding alliance shaped its nature. Tanganyika's conflicts were the widest known to its people, informed by the market network of Swahili-educated African opinion. Baganda led Uganda's opposition to state marketing and Indian trade, with portentous results. Peasants, disaffected with chiefs, rallied to their king, the Kabaka, all the more so when the British deported him in 1953 for demanding a separate independence from Uganda. The main cause of Kenya's uniquely bloody crisis was the settlers' resolve to mechanize their farming on the profits of war. They had first to roll back their internal peasant frontier by requiring their largely Kikuyu tenant workers, who had previously cleared but now occupied white land, to remove their livestock and live on a wage. In thus breaking their founding alliance, as Africans saw it, between Delamere and chief Koinange, settlers set alight the most crowded of Kenya's peoples, the Kikuyu, 20 per cent of the population. Kikuyu ethnic nationalism split between landed elders' civil resistance and their young men's violence. Many of the latter, landless and unmarried, fearing censorious exclusion from the moral ethnic community which had been argued out between the wars, hoped to earn their adulthood by reclaiming white-occupied land. The British defeated the Mau Mau rising, at great human cost, partly because no other Africans joined in. Other Africans, a few but not so many of them farm squatters, lacked the same depth of grievance in the settlers' repudiation of the peasant alliance.

While unrest mobilized politically distinctive localities, it also turned constitutional reforms into nationalist platforms. After the war Britain hoped to enlist Africans in 'multiracial' alliances of economic growth to make it easier, in the long run, to submerge white supremacies into common citizenries. As the process was too ingenious for electoral tests, Africans were denied the franchise longer than in West Africa. The political engineers' lever was the racial composition of the unofficial Legislative Council benches. Uganda's European and Indian Members of the Legislative Council were always unelected. When Africans came to outnumber them in 1955, in a deal that brought the Kabaka home, Uganda was the first territory to break East Africa's balanced multiracial mould. Peasant society had won, but enjoyed no direct elections until 1958. Kenya's elected settler Members of the Legislative Council held a majority of seats until 1948, then only half of them, then a dwindling minority from 1958, one year after Africans were first elected, on a restricted franchise. Tanganyika's first elections, for any race, were held only in 1958–59, not until three years before independence. Even then, absurdly, there was equal representation for Africans, Indians, and whites. In the mid-1950s, therefore, pushed off course by Baganda royalists and Kikuyu guerrillas, multiracialism changed in purpose, from reassuring immigrant minorities to educating African leaders in the compromises of power. Only at the end of the decade were nationalists allowed to contest elections and to educate electorates. It was a late start in democracy.

Africans had forced the change by taking over the definition of nation-building. Their leaders knew they wanted modern states. They needed power to shape rather than permission to share the future; they wanted to break rather than perpetuate racial 'hypocrisy'.[10] But they had very different ideas of the nation they wished to create.

Tanganyika's founding alliance gave the clearest guide. A young teacher, Julius Nyerere, gathered the urban, Swahili, educated tradition into the Tanganyika African National Union in 1954, East Africa's only bureaucratic party. TANU was

[10] Julius K. Nyerere, 'The Race Problem in East Africa' (1952), in Julius K. Nyerere, *Freedom and Unity* (London, 1967), pp. 23–29.

unstoppable; it silenced African tendencies to local baronies, made its multiracial opponents look ridiculous, and by its own cool discipline made independence seem sensible in 1961, a decade earlier than the British had planned. While in Tanganyika Britain could be said to have devolved power in order to preserve influence, Uganda's decolonization in 1962 looked like abdication. Constitution-mongering could never bridge the gulf between Buganda's royalist separatism and the determination of other Ugandans that their own localities should, by emulating Buganda's progress, forestall any new sub-imperialism. Politics was needed. King's men at the centre and republicans from the periphery stitched together a deal that did not last.

Kenya, to everybody's surprised relief, proved an easier case. Its politics appeared to be divided but were in the event united by the prize of the Rift Valley's 'White Highlands'.[11] For Kikuyu this was the land they had earned by two generations of tenant labour, for other peoples it was ancestral grazing. While British officials and settlers hated Jomo Kenyatta as the supposed leader of Mau Mau's darkness and death, they found nobody better in the regional patchwork of Kenya's politics on whom to gamble a future for the few whites who chose to stay and the many British Indians. It seemed scarcely credible—to those who had never grasped the possessive individualism of peasant ambition—that it was he who presided over the externally funded peasant settlement schemes on white land that underpinned the high politics of inter-ethnic bargaining. Liberally minded settlers may once have dared to hope to lead Kenya to a multiracial independence. More plausibly, the proportionately more numerous Zanzibari Arabs tried to champion the sultanate's nationalism before the large African majority of its quarter-million people, who were divided between 'mainlander' migrants and indigenous islanders, found a common voice. Helped by a shared Islam and the lack of social stratification by race on the northerly island of Pemba, the Arabs nearly pulled it off. But such was their sense of insecurity that, before independence in December 1963 (two days before Kenya's) they moved against all possible dissidents and sacked from the police many mainlanders who, a month later, were among their executioners.

At independence there were 26 million East Africans, twice as many as forty years before. Most would remain poor, women farmers still hoeing a harsh continent, as in the 1890s. For them, colonialism had scarcely meant modernization. World capitalism and, with it, the renewed deathbed, British drive to colonial development, were also deserting them. Their terms of trade had sunk by one-quarter since the 1950s boom. Their new states had to grapple with the local economic impasse that had made the British despair; ever faster population

[11] See above, pp. 352–53.

growth, with more young to feed and educate, was devouring any possible investment in economic diversification. The three mainland army mutinies in early 1964, almost bloodlessly suppressed by British troops, showed how weak was the power even to govern. These were not strong states.

Some of their citizens would do worse than others. Revolution handed Zanzibar to its African majority, but also to an overseas patron even less able to help, socialist East Germany. Uganda's substance was ruined as African ambition proved what a fading Britain had refused to attempt, the impossibility of either sustaining or undoing Buganda's dominance by peaceful means. Some did better. Mainland Tanzanians enjoyed peace even if they could perhaps never hope for prosperity. Regimentation of their rural economy, true to Tanganyika's élite founding alliance, none the less showed how little had been learned from the failures of late colonial rule. Kenyans prospered for a time as new land and services were offered to both 'big' Africans and their 'small' clients, who could be as critical of patrons as their settler predecessors had been. The few remaining whites joined Indians in the trades that flourished on peasant expansion, particularly in the former estate crops of coffee and tea. The stormiest founding alliance had dug below its racial antagonism to reveal its basic partnership between capitalist commerce and peasant proprietorship. British rule had fostered this, even in settler Kenya. The partnership was agrarian Africa's fickle, mistrusted, and yet at the time only possible—if also unequal—source of wellbeing.

Select Bibliography

DAVID APTER, *The Political Kingdom in Uganda* (London, 1961).

RALPH AUSTEN, *Northwest Tanzania under German and British Rule, 1889–1939*, 2 vols. (New Haven, 1968).

BRUCE BERMAN and JOHN LONSDALE, *Unhappy Valley: Conflict in Kenya and Africa* (London, 1992).

FREDERICK COOPER, *From Slaves to Squatters: Plantation Labor and Agriculture in Zanzibar and Coastal Kenya, 1890–1925* (New Haven, 1980).

ANTHONY CLAYTON and DONALD C. SAVAGE, *Government and Labour in Kenya, 1895–1963* (London, 1974).

STEVEN FEIERMAN, *Peasant Intellectuals: Anthropology and History in Tanzania* (Madison, 1990).

ROBERT G. GREGORY, *Indians and East Africa: A History of Race Relations Within the British Empire* (Oxford, 1965).

JOHN ILIFFE, *A Modern History of Tanganyika* (Cambridge, 1979).

TABITHA KANOGO, *Squatters and the Roots of Mau Mau* (London, 1987).

I. N. Kimambo, *Penetration and Protest in Tanzania: The Impact of the World Economy on the Pare, 1860–1960* (London, 1991).

B. E. Kipkorir, 'The Alliance High School and the Origins of the Kenya African Élite, 1926–62', unpublished Ph.D. thesis, Cambridge, 1969.

Michael Lofchie, *Zanzibar: Background to Revolution* (London, 1965).

D. A. Low, *Buganda in Modern History* (Berkeley, 1971).

Roland Oliver and Gervase Mathew, assisted by Alison Smith, eds., *History of East Africa*, Vol. I (Oxford, 1963); Vol. II, eds. Vincent T. Harlow and E. M. Chilver (Oxford, 1965); Vol. III, eds. D. A. Low and Alison Smith (Oxford, 1976).

M. G. Redley, 'The Politics of a Predicament: The White Community in Kenya, 1918–1932', unpublished Ph.D. thesis, Cambridge, 1976).

M. P. K. Sorrenson, *Origins of European Settlement in Kenya* (Nairobi, 1968).

David Throup, *Economic and Social Origins of Mau Mau, 1945–53* (London, 1987).

Michael Twaddle, *Kakungulu and the Creation of Uganda, 1868–1928* (London, 1993).

Luise White, *The Comforts of Home: Prostitution in Colonial Nairobi* (Chicago, 1990).

C. C. Wrigley, *Crops and Wealth in Uganda* (Kampala, 1959).

24
Southern Africa

SHULA MARKS

For much of the twentieth century British policies in southern Africa have been dominated by calculations about South Africa. The Union, later Republic, of South Africa has occupied a unique position in British Imperial strategy and imagination. Undergirding this status materially was South Africa's gold, while sustaining it ideologically were the labours of Sir Alfred Milner's 'kindergarten', that group of bright young men from Oxford who were brought to the Transvaal to reshape its institutions after the South African War (1899–1902), and who were themselves reshaped by the experience. As Lionel Curtis, ideologist of Imperial Federation, put it in a letter in 1907: 'South Africa is a microcosm and much that we thought peculiar to it is equally true of the Empire itself... When we have done all we can do and should do for South Africa it may be we shall have the time and training to begin some work of the same kind in respect of Imperial Relations.'[1]

Interconnected networks of City, Empire, and academe gave South Africa its importance to the advocates of Commonwealth at least until 1945. The role played by the 'kindergarten' in the unification of South Africa provided its members with a model for their wider vision of Imperial Federation, propounded in their Round Table movement and their journal of the same name; the fortunes made by mine magnates such as Rhodes, Beit, and Bailey were devoted to furthering the schemes of the Round Tablers, whether through scholarships, chairs of Imperial history, or the Royal Institute of International Affairs at Chatham House; their friendships

For the purposes of this chapter, southern Africa has been defined as the Union of South Africa, the High Commission Territories (Basutoland, Bechuanaland, and Swaziland), Zimbabwe, Zambia, and Malawi. The position of Namibia (South-West Africa) is anomalous, as German colony until 1917, then South African Mandate, and now, as independent Namibia, a member of the Commonwealth. Its history, like that of Mozambique, and to a lesser extent in this period Angola, has been intimately connected with that of South Africa, and it has been mentioned in this respect. I am grateful to Dr Stanley Trapido for many years of discussion on the history of southern Africa which have undoubtedly shaped this chapter.

[1] Curtis to Selborne, 18 Oct. 1907, Selborne MSS 71, cited in Deborah Lavin, 'Lionel Curtis and the Idea of Commonwealth', in Frederick Madden and D. K. Fieldhouse, eds., *Oxford and the Idea of Commonwealth* (London, 1982), p. 99.

with leading South African politicians such as General (later Field Marshal) J. C. Smuts ensured their continued sympathetic support for white South Africa to the mid-century.

The Round Table view was never uncontested. As in the nineteenth century, settler 'native policy' was the object of humanitarian criticism. Before 1945 this voice was muted; and, like the Round Table, the humanitarian lobby called predominantly for a more paternalist form of trusteeship. After the electoral victory in 1948 of the Afrikaner National Party and its implementation of racial policies, which were seen increasingly to diverge from international norms, a more radical liberal-humanitarian opposition arose, fuelled by the hostility of the newly independent states of Asia and Africa, and culminating in the demand for economic sanctions against South Africa to bring about majority rule. By the 1980s this demand was creating serious conflict between Britain and most of the members of the Commonwealth.

For successive British governments, neither trusteeship nor the demands for majority rule were of the essence. Here more hard-headed considerations applied. In central and southern Africa Britain pursued her 'national interest'—and unremarkably so.[2] A continued belief in the strategic importance of the naval base at Simonstown;[3] substantial trade between the two countries; the fate of what were known as the British High Commission territories Lesotho, Botswana, and Swaziland; and, at a later date, the need for co-operation over Rhodesia, were all of some significance. Far more vital to Britain's pre-eminence in the world, however, was the unimpeded flow of South African gold to the City of London, as was starkly revealed during both world wars. This made stability in the region of critical concern to Britain, and explains British support for South Africa despite international opprobrium and later intense conflict between Britain and other members of the Commonwealth.

Although the Union had achieved independent Dominion Status since 1910, it remained economically dependent on the Imperial connection, as the crisis following Britain's departure from the gold standard in 1931 revealed. Even after 1948, when an ostensibly anti-imperialist, Afrikaner Nationalist government came into power, it found, like all previous South African governments, that its interests and those of its farming constituents were best served by remaining within the sterling area. Despite the dramatic decline in British power after the Second World War, Britain and South Africa remained economically interdepend-

[2] Martin Chanock, *Unconsummated Union: Britain, Rhodesia and South Africa, 1900–1945* (London, 1977), p. 1.

[3] The Union government gained access to the base in 1922 and took it over from Britain in 1955; see above, p. 295.

ent so that neither was prepared to undermine their economic ties for purely political purposes.[4]

Southern Africa to 1939

If gold linked South Africa to the British Empire, it also subordinated the rest of the region to South Africa and, ultimately, linked the humblest African hut in the countryside to the palatial Witwatersrand residences of the mine magnates in a hierarchy of unequal exchanges. For most of the inhabitants of the African subcontinent, European colonization was recent, a nineteenth-century, even a late-nineteenth-century, experience. However, south of the Limpopo, colonial penetration was far older and more pervasive, going back in the coastal Cape colony to the mid-seventeenth century. By 1910, when the two nineteenth-century Afrikaner republics of the Transvaal and Orange Free State, recently conquered by Britain in the South African War, were joined to the two British coastal colonies of the Cape and Natal to form the new Union of South Africa, the whole of southern Africa was under alien rule.

Mineral discoveries and the consequent demographic and urban growth in the last third of the century transformed the subcontinent economically, socially, and politically. In 1911 over half the Union's 1.25 million whites and nearly a quarter of its 5 million black population lived in towns.[5] Nevertheless, South Africa's independence and power in the first half-century should not be exaggerated. For much of this period it was poor, dependent on international capital, and politically unstable, with a divided white population heavily outnumbered by a black population which was for the most part denied citizenship; its regional dominance was a reflection of the weakness of its neighbours rather than its intrinsic strength.[6]

Beyond the boundaries of the Union, three Imperial powers and a chartered company had each carved out territories in the late-nineteenth-century 'scramble' for Africa. Portugal was ensconced on the east and west coasts, in Mozambique and Angola; Germany had annexed the vast, arid, and sparsely populated territory of South-West Africa (later Namibia); and north of the Limpopo the British had granted the chartered British South Africa Company (hereafter the Company) wide powers over the African peoples in the region to be known for much of the

[4] Peter J. Henshaw, 'Britain, South Africa and the Sterling Area: Gold Production, Capital Investment and Agricultural Markets, 1931–1961', *Historical Journal*, XXXIX, 1 (1996), pp. 197–223, esp. 217.

[5] South African terminology is fraught with difficulty. I use the term 'black' to refer collectively to the indigenous peoples of southern Africa, to those who had intermarried with incoming whites and slaves who are known in the literature as Coloured, and to Indians who were brought as indentured labourers to nineteenth-century Natal.

[6] Chanock, *Unconsummated Union*, p. 2.

twentieth century as Northern and Southern Rhodesia (Zambia and Zimbabwe), after the Company's founder, Cecil John Rhodes. More by accident than design, the British Colonial Office had acquired control over what was originally the British Central African Protectorate and later became—with modified borders—Nyasaland (Malawi). South of the Limpopo, three African enclaves of Bechuanaland, Basutoland, and Swaziland had managed to remain outside colonial boundaries as British Protectorates in the nineteenth century, and were known collectively as the High Commission Territories.

By the first decade of the century, it was widely accepted in British ruling circles that the Zambezi River was to be the frontier between the settler south and the 'tropical dependencies' of eastern and central Africa. As Milner, who was British High Commissioner for Southern Africa, 1895–1905, and who, more than any other single individual, shaped its early-twentieth-century destiny, remarked in 1899: 'One thing is quite evident. The *ultimate* end is a self-governing white Community, supported by *well-treated* and *justly governed* black labour from Cape Town to Zambesi.'[7] In the event, there was to be argument both about the frontiers of the 'self-governing white community' and the justice of its treatment of black labour.

Milner's notion of a 'self-governing white community' extending to the Zambezi was shared also in South Africa, most notably by General J. C. Smuts, former Afrikaner general turned Imperial statesman, joint-architect of Union, and its Prime Minister in the years 1919–24 and 1939–48, who long dreamt of a 'Greater South Africa'. Nevertheless, with one exception the Union's expansionist ambitions were blocked both by the resistance of Africans who hoped Imperial overrule would afford some protection against colonial rapacity, and by British determination to maintain their regional dominance and their distrust of Afrikaner nationalism.

The most obvious candidates for incorporation in the Union were the geographically contiguous and economically dependent High Commission Territories. Until the mid-century this destiny was assumed by the British government and South Africa's white politicians alike. The threat of transfer and their loathing for the Union's 'native policy' spurred African political consciousness in these territories until their independence in the 1960s—and beyond.

Nor were the Rhodesias absorbed by the Union when the Company's charter finally expired in 1923,[8] despite the wishes of the Company, some at least in the

[7] Milner to Percy Fitzpatrick, 28 Nov. 1899, in Cecil Headlam, ed., *The Milner Papers (South Africa), 1899–1905*, 2 vols. (London, 1933), II, pp. 35–36.

[8] The charter was originally for twenty-five years, but was renewed for an additional period in 1915 because of the war.

British Colonial Office, and Smuts's South African Party government. In an all-white referendum, a small majority of the 33,000 predominantly British settlers, alarmed by the gathering pace of Afrikaner nationalism and escalating class conflict to their south, opted for self-government rather than incorporation. Any incorporation of Northern Rhodesia with the south was also barred. In 1924 the British government took over the administration of the whole of Northern Rhodesia as a 'tropical dependency', although the Company retained extensive mineral and land rights in both Southern and Northern Rhodesia and the new Crown Colony, as well as 86 per cent of the shares in Rhodesia Railways.[9]

The Union was more successful in the case of South-West Africa, which it conquered from the Germans during the First World War and governed thereafter under a League of Nations 'C' Mandate.[10] Despite the Mandate, by the Second World War South-West Africa was effectively a fifth province of the Union, governed in the interests of its white settlers, many of them poor Afrikaners, although the German population numbered some 10,000 by 1937. When in 1946 Smuts tried to incorporate the territory even more directly, he was rebuffed by the United Nations, the preamble to whose Charter he had authored. It took nearly forty-five more years before Namibians shook off South African control, despite international appeals to the International Court of Justice at The Hague and prolonged guerrilla struggle.

With the formation of the Union in 1910, and the redrawing of the frontiers between the Chartered Company's domain in Northern Rhodesia and neighbouring Angola on the west and Nyasaland on its east in 1911, the boundaries of the southern Africa state system were established until the creation of the short-lived Central African Federation (which brought together the Rhodesias and Nyasaland) in 1953. Yet these frontiers remained extremely porous, at least until the Second World War. Despite the imposition of Draconian immigration, trading, and veterinary restrictions, even the South African state, by far the most powerful in the region, was hard put either to control the illegal movement across boundaries of people who were linked by kinship or driven by poverty, or to prevent the smuggling of cattle across inadequately policed marchlands. If, in the phrase of the day, disease, whether in animal or man, knew no colour bar, it also paid little heed to border restrictions. Political ideas, too, criss-crossed frontiers, as white settlers everywhere drew on South African modes of governing 'natives', and Africans learnt their politics in the mine compounds and mission schools of the Union.

Economic frontiers failed to follow the contours of colonial jurisdiction. Neither capital nor labour was confined by state boundaries, for by the turn of

[9] Chanock, *Unconsummated Union*, pp. 168–72.

[10] See above, p. 118.

the century the disparate societies of the region were being drawn ineluctably into a single political economy, directed, although unevenly, by British and South African capital, driven by mining, and increasingly connected by road, rail, and by the 1920s, air. The exploitation of diamonds, coal, and especially gold in the interior of South Africa from the last third of the nineteenth century, of gold and coal in Southern Rhodesia from the 1890s and 1900s, and of copper in Northern Rhodesia from the late 1920s had momentous consequences for them all, regardless of the national identity of their new colonial masters. The history of twentieth-century southern Africa is to a very large extent dominated by the history of mining.

It was Witwatersrand gold that moulded the history of the region. The hope that Rhodesia would prove a 'Second Rand' was soon disappointed: its dispersed and relatively superficial gold deposits could never compete with the far more extensive mines of South Africa, even if gold was its economic mainstay until the Second World War. In Rhodesia's undercapitalized gold-mines, wages were lower and food and accommodation poorer than on the Rand. Where possible, black workers from Northern Rhodesia, Nyasaland, and Mozambique bypassed Southern Rhodesia and made their way further south. While copper claims were staked in Northern Rhodesia in the 1900s, it was not until the late 1920s that, in response to the increasing world demand for copper, the major companies—the South African-dominated Anglo-American Corporation of Rhodesia and the American-dominated Rhodesian Selection Trust—established themselves on the Copper Belt; Imperial fears of the United States's competition in the mining industry prompted British and South African finance to come forward. By that time patterns of labour control were based on recruited black migrant labour housed in compounds, and a highly paid white supervisory class. A nexus of laws controlling worker mobility and organization had been firmly established on the Witwatersrand and formed the template for developments further north.

At the beginning of the twentieth century South Africa produced between a fifth and a quarter of the world's supply of gold; by 1914 this had risen to about one-third, by the 1920s one-half. No South African government could ignore the imperatives of the gold-mining industry; it shaped the country's social and economic structure and that of its neighbours, provided its state revenues and foreign exchange, and conferred influence in the wider world. Capital initially accumulated on the gold-mines of South Africa was the largest single source of investment in the mines in the Rhodesias, whether of gold, copper, or coal.

Yet the richest mining industry in the world was built on the paradox of colossal wealth and monumental parsimony.[11] Most of South Africa's gold ore was low

[11] C. W. de Kiewiet, *A History of South Africa: Social and Economic* (Oxford, 1941), p. 134.

grade and deep level; the costs of development and extraction were high and the international ceiling on price meant they could not be passed on to the consumer. Enfranchised, unionized white workers were able to protect their wages and to extract health-and-safety measures from the state to compensate for a high cost of living and the shortness of their working lives; rightless African workers, prised out of the pre-industrial societies of the subcontinent, could not. Thus it was that the industry came to be built on huge disparities between black and white wages. In 1920 some 21,500 white workers on the gold-mines earned about twice as much as the total earnings of 180,000 black workers, while in 1961 white gold-miners on the Rand earned on average almost seventeen times more than black.[12]

By the turn of the century some 100,000 African men were annually making their way to the Witwatersrand from the entire subcontinent in search of money to pay tax, to purchase cattle, ploughs, and seed, even to acquire bicycles and sewing machines; tens of thousands more were seeking work in the white towns and farms and mines elsewhere in South Africa, Southern Rhodesia, and the Shire Highlands. Many never returned, settling and often dying at their place of work: in the early days of mining the death toll from accidents and respiratory diseases was formidably high. Although conditions gradually improved in the mines themselves, returning migrants transferred the burden of ill-health to increasingly impoverished rural areas, creating reservoirs of tuberculosis and venereal disease.

By the end of the First World War the South African Chamber of Mines, founded in 1889 to contain costs, had a monopoly over the purchase of black labour. By 1939 its recruiting organization, the Witwatersrand Native Labour Association, successfully sought workers on the northern fringes of central Africa, thus ensuring that the wages of black miners were lower in real terms until the 1970s than they had been in the 1890s. The development of South Africa as the richest, most powerful, and most industrialized country in twentieth century Africa was made possible by the labour of this subcontinental workforce. Yet 'cheap' labour had a high cost for worker and capitalist alike.

Jagged-edged, dependent on the chronology of conquest, the configuration of local markets, and the exigencies of environment, for many Africans proletarianization remained uneven, uncertain, and incomplete. Initially, Africans were able to resist full proletarianization through migrant labour, and urbanization was an often-reversible response to misfortune. Nevertheless, as the century progressed African families became increasingly dependent on wage-labour for their basic needs and large numbers of Africans settled permanently in towns. Despite the proscriptions of white authorities who believed that they were there solely to serve

[12] Merle Lipton, *Capitalism and Apartheid South Africa, 1910–1984* (Aldershot, Hants, 1985), pp. 113 and 388, Table 11.

the needs of the white economy, they created a vibrant urban culture in the shantytowns that grew up around all the region's major cities.

In the new dispensation, white men controlled private property and the means of production—although not all white men equally. As one historian has remarked, 'it was basic to the political rhetoric of southern Africa that it was a "white man's country" '.[13] In the settler states, white men also dominated representative institutions. Whether in South Africa, where their numbers were substantial, or in both Rhodesias and even in the Shire Highlands, where they were not, for the first half-century white, preferably English-speaking (male) settlers were Britain's 'ideal prefabricated collaborators'.[14]

Under the Act of Union of 1910, passed into law by the British government, existing colonial franchise arrangements were maintained: effectively this meant that in the former republics and Natal all white adult males were enfranchised; in the Cape, property and educational qualifications also enfranchised Coloured and African men. While the failure of the Union constitution to provide for a uniform franchise based on Cape notions of 'equal rights for all civilized men' met with heated debate and protest, the failure to enfranchise women was apparently less controversial. When in 1930 white women received the vote it was as part of an onslaught against the qualified African male franchise in the Cape, which was removed in 1936. Twenty years later, in 1956, Coloured voters in the Cape were placed on a separate electoral roll. Effectively, then, whites, especially white men, were given statutory control over the majority of blacks, who were excluded from citizenship until the first democratic, non-racial election in South Africa in April 1994.

In Southern Rhodesia, white settlers—never more than 5 per cent of the total population—who first arrived in 1890, had an elected minority in the Legislative Council within eight years. When in 1923 the territory acquired self-government, only those, including women, with an income over £200 were enfranchised. Most of the 750,000 Africans were excluded from the vote. Self-government notwithstanding, the Chartered Company continued to control the railways (the largest employer in the territory) and mining royalties, while the Imperial government retained authority over foreign affairs and currency and a veto over discriminatory legislation. This veto was rarely used, although it did act as a brake on legislation likely to provoke British intervention and did prevent the removal of Africans

[13] Chanock, *Unconsummated Union*, p. 13.

[14] Ronald Robinson, 'Non-European Foundations of European Imperialism: Sketch for a Theory of Collaboration', in Roger Owen and Bob Sutcliffe, eds., *Studies in the Theory of Imperialism* (London, 1972), p. 124.

from the voters' roll in 1934. In general, however, in the early years of responsible government, legislation affecting mining royalties or railway finances received more scrutiny than that affecting Africans. African administration in Southern Africa was considered 'enlightened' by the Dominions Office.[15]

At first the Company did not encourage settlers in Northern Rhodesia, although a few settled along the line of rail. Despite limited representation on the territory's Legislative Council, self-government was clearly impossible in a colony with under 4,000 colonists in the midst of almost a million Africans. With the exploitation of the copper-mines, white numbers increased. The importance of Northern Rhodesia as the major producer of copper in the Empire before the Second World War, and the strategic importance of copper for the Allies during the war, undoubtedly gave white mineworkers considerable political and economic leverage. Nevertheless, the small number of colonists in Northern Rhodesia never achieved the political dominance of the settlers further south. On the eve of war in 1939 there were 13,000 whites in the territory, under 2 per cent of the total population.

In early colonial Nyasaland, white and Indian settlement was encouraged in the belief that it would bring economic development. In 1907 whites were given some representation on the Legislative Council. Economic backwardness constrained white immigration. Under 1,500 in 1920, no more than 2,000 in 1940, colonists never rose above 0.2 per cent of the population. In both Northern Rhodesia and Nyasaland, racially discriminatory policies in agriculture and industry protected the interests of whites over those of blacks. Nevertheless, sparse settler numbers and Colonial Office proclamations of African paramountcy, however limited in practice, differentiated these territories from those further south.[16] By the mid-1930s disgruntled settlers in the northern colonies began to look to amalgamation with their southern compatriots.

Throughout the region white domination was facilitated by racist ideology, which was infused by fears of miscegenation and a concern with the sexuality of Africans.[17] Discriminatory policies were prompted by settler demands for protection from African competition and official anxiety at the growth of African class consciousness. 'Separate development' was lent respectability until the Second World War by eugenic and evolutionist thought espoused by anthropologists and paternalist administrators anxious to protect African societies from rapid social change.

The policies of segregation were adopted by most whites regardless of political persuasion in the inter-war years. Initially developed into an ideology by Milner's

[15] Claire Palley, *The Constitutional History and Law of Southern Rhodesia, 1888–1965, with Special Reference to Imperial Control* (Oxford, 1966), pp. 242, 239.

[16] See chap. 11 by Ronald Hyam.

[17] See chap. by Rosalind O'Hanlon, esp. pp. 391, 393–94.

kindergarten and liberal-minded intellectuals in South Africa, segregation served to unify diverse and contradictory white interests under a single political banner. It cemented the white South African 'nation'. Intended to buttress white power at a time of rapid urbanization and social change by defusing black militancy, it was also shaped by African capacity to resist total cultural and political domination.

Segregation was equally the orthodoxy in the rest of southern Africa. Even in those territories under direct Colonial Office control, the differences were of degree rather than in kind. There too, Africans were excluded from central political institutions. Industrial colour bars defined jobs, wages, and employment opportunities. In exchange Africans were granted limited reserves within which chiefly authority was recognized and ethnic identity assumed. This social order was bolstered by a battery of laws in South Africa and Southern Rhodesia; in Northern Rhodesia, in the face of Colonial Office opposition to *de jure* discrimination, it was secured by custom and social practice. What the political and social exclusions obscured was the extent to which economic forces, and the spread of Christianity, literacy, and urbanization, were drawing southern Africans inexorably into a common, if grossly unequal and racially stratified, interdependence.

If white settlers throughout the region were united in their determination to assert their supremacy over Africans, they frequently differed on how best to achieve this because of their own class and ethnic divisions. Where their numbers were small, as in Northern Rhodesia and Nyasaland, these differences were contained by a wider need for unity against the black majority. In South Africa and Southern Rhodesia, however, inter-white political struggles were often as fierce as, if not fiercer than, those between black and white.

These political struggles were most complex in South Africa, where whites were most bitterly divided by class and ethnicity. For all the centrality of the relationship between black and white, the contest over who was to control the state was conceived of as being between white opponents, who differed more fundamentally over the economy, language, and their relationship to the British Empire than over the governance of Africans. The issue was never simply one between English-speakers and Afrikaners, as the civil war which erupted over South Africa's participation in the First World War had revealed: while large numbers of South Africans, largely English-speaking but including Afrikaners, fought in East Africa and in Europe, in South Africa itself Botha and Smuts had to mobilize Afrikaner commandos to put down an Afrikaner rebellion prompted by the invasion of South-West Africa and the still-lingering hope of regaining independence. For much of the period, governments included members of both language groups.

During the 1920s many nationalist goals were achieved. With the 1926 Balfour Report (and its later enactment in the 1931 Statute of Westminster), South

Africa's sovereign status under the British monarchy was recognized, as the nationalist Prime Minister, General G. B. M. Hertzog, himself acknowledged on his return from the 1926 Imperial Conference. In 1934 the South Africa Status Acts embodied the doctrine of the divisibility of the Crown, which made it possible for South Africa to refrain from assisting Britain in war if she so wished: a matter of some moment in 1939 when Smuts carried a motion in favour of joining the Allies by a mere thirteen votes.[18]

Hertzog's renunciation of republicanism made the coalition of the National Party with Smuts's South African Party a credible goal. In the wake of the economic crisis in 1931, when South Africa left the gold standard, the two parties united to form a new United Party, once more under the premiership of Hertzog. Nevertheless, many Afrikaners remained unreconciled to the British connection and aimed to re-establish a Republic. In South Africa's cities landless Afrikaners formed a volatile constituency for the anti-Imperial and racially charged nationalism led by Dr D. F. Malan, who split with Hertzog and formed the 'Purified' National Party. Unskilled and barely literate, poor white Afrikaners could compete neither with highly paid, skilled English-speaking workers nor with low-paid black workers who still had some access to rural resources.

The all-white nature of parliamentary politics and their demographic advantage meant that nationalists who could persuade individuals to identify—and vote—as Afrikaners rather than as 'whites' or 'workers' or 'women' could win power. The victory of Malan's 'Purified' National Party in 1948 thus owed much to the ideological labours of cultural nationalists who had, since the South African War, set about transforming a world dominated by British culture and the English language into one in which Afrikaner sensibilities and the Afrikaans language predominated. Women were particularly important as 'mothers of the *volk*' and as active agents in their own right. Yet ironically, when they eventually captured the state in 1948, Afrikaner nationalists found themselves confronted by a new, potentially more dangerous contender for the state: African nationalism.

Until the Second World War, white politics in the settler states was for the most part dominated by shifting alliances of either the more prosperous farmers and mine magnates, responsive to the needs of British capital, or—as between 1924 and 1933 in South Africa and in 1933–34 in Southern Rhodesia—coalitions of local entrepreneurs, poorer white farmers, and workers. Yet the interests of capitalist farmers and mine-owners were often in conflict. Not only did they compete for cheap black labour, they were also divided on tariff policy and their attitudes to white workers.

[18] See above, p. 84.

The attempt of the mine-owners to cheapen white labour costs by substituting cheaper black workers led to the eruption of intense class warfare in Southern Rhodesia and, more seriously, on the Rand. White strikes had occurred on the Rand in 1907, in 1913, and most dramatically in 1922, when newly proletarianized and largely unskilled Afrikaner workers joined hands with the skilled English-speaking trade unionists, some of them inspired by the newly formed Communist Party of South Africa. White workers did not unite with black workers, as Communists hoped, but demanded and ultimately achieved a statutory colour bar to reserve certain jobs for whites only. At the same time industrial legislation in 1924 tempered the capacity of white workers to strike but excluded 'pass-bearing natives' from wage-bargaining machinery.

White workers suffering the insecurities of the Depression were protected by similar legislation in Southern Rhodesia in 1934. Thereafter, as in the Union, enfranchised white workers were relatively easily incorporated into the 'white nation'.[19] On the Northern Rhodesian Copper Belt, skilled white workers, many of them from South Africa, never secured similar protection: there the liberal impulse of Imperial government was stronger, especially when confronted with black worker militancy and the desire of the mining companies to replace white labour with black. By mid-century a skilled and unionized African work-force had emerged to play a key role over the next decade and a half in the struggle for independence.

In the settler states, mine-owners and farmers were also divided over the policy of African reserves. Throughout the subcontinent, access to land determined the supply and cost of African labour. Where shortage of land did not suffice to push Africans into the labour market, taxation frequently did. At the beginning of the century the vast majority of Africans lived by farming, even if in many areas they were now rightless 'squatters' on land claimed by settlers, syndicates, or speculators. South of the Limpopo a century-long battle over land had been largely won by settlers, although increasingly crowded and eroded pockets of land had been reserved for Africans.

While the mining industry came to recognize the importance of these reserves in subsidizing migrants' dependents, white farmers resented them as sources of competition from African producers, and they also wished to reduce various forms of African tenancy to labour service. These objectives were reconciled in the Union's land legislation in 1913 and 1936 which scheduled about 13 per cent of the land for the African population, reserving the rest for the white minority, and reducing Africans on white-owned land to labour tenancy.

[19] Ian Phimister, *An Economic and Social History of Zimbabwe, 1890–1948: Capital Accumulation and Class Struggle* (London, 1988), p. 192.

In Southern Rhodesia too, where the British South Africa Company had encouraged commercial farming to attract immigrants and raise revenue, settlers attacked the African reserves set aside at Imperial insistence after the 1896–97 Shona–Ndebele uprisings. Fears of further disturbances ensured protection of the reserves, and until the 1920s Shona peasants successfully produced for the market. Nevertheless, by then the territory's best land was settler-owned and the expropriation of the peasantry was confirmed by the Land Apportionment Act of 1930. At the time this was regarded as an act of trusteeship. It was the joint responsibility of both the Imperial and the Southern Rhodesian governments; any amendment to the Act was subject to British scrutiny.[20] Yet it was modelled in part on South Africa's legislation; in terms of the Act, African ownership was barred outside the reserves, except in a special small freehold purchase area—much of it isolated and tsetse-infested—set aside for 'progressive farmers'. Half the land was now allocated to whites, 30 per cent to Africans; 20 per cent remained unassigned. From 1937 Africans not required as labour on white-owned lands were removed to increasingly congested reserves.

The Land Acts in the Union and Southern Rhodesia were designed to foster settler agriculture. Yet white capitalist agriculture was only possible with massive state intervention. Black farmers, by contrast, only attracted state assistance when cattle disease threatened to spread from black areas to white, or soil erosion roused concern, as in the late 1930s. The Great Depression strengthened measures favouring small white farmers at the expense of African peasant production, and by the 1940s many rural Africans were dependent on migrant remittances. Even in those areas where peasant production continued, deteriorating health statistics suggest it was through intensified self exploitation, although African sharecroppers and labour tenants only finally lost all access to land outside the reserves with the accelerated capitalization of agriculture from the mid-century.

Initially, similar land policies were pursued north of the Zambezi, where white settlers were seen as the engine of economic growth. Thus, in 1924 the Colonial Office, hoping to increase settler numbers, threw open nearly 12 million acres of the best lands in Northern Rhodesia for white farming. Although extensive reserves were demarcated, like the reserves further south they were generally far from the line of rail and on poor soils; for the most part African lands rapidly became overcrowded and eroded. With the development of the Copper Belt, some Africans were able to produce for the new market, but it was only after the Second World War that white land-ownership was limited in Northern Rhodesia and the problems of rural poverty at least minimally addressed.

[20] Palley, *Constitutional History*, pp. 253–58.

In the Shire Highlands too, millions of acres devoted to experiments in coffee, cotton, and tobacco were owned by the African Lakes Corporation and a handful of settlers. With their low pay, forced labour practices, and squalid working conditions, the plantations were unable to compete with the mines in neighbouring territories. They remained poor and inefficient until the 1920s, when tobacco and then tea replaced the unsuccessful coffee and cotton crops; even then planters remained dependent on the labour of tenants and share-croppers, many of them refugees from Mozambique, and from the 1930s the amount of land in expatriate hands fell. In 1948 only some 5.2 per cent of the total was planter-owned, so that there were always considerable pockets of Africans producing cash crops such as cotton, rice, and tobacco in southern and central Nyasaland: the north was little more than a labour reserve for the Rhodesias and South Africa.

In Basutoland and Bechuanaland too, settler expropriation was limited by the Colonial Office. Yet unlike the situation in Nyasaland, the possibilities there for peasant enterprise diminished rather than expanded in the course of the century as Africans became increasingly dependent on migrancy to South Africa. Drought and Depression in the 1930s transformed Basutoland, once South Africa's 'granary', into a food importer, and large numbers of its women as well as men settled permanently on the Rand. Bechuanaland's fortunes also declined through this period as transport networks shifted and South Africa, often under the guise of veterinary restrictions, embargoed the importation and sale of cattle, the mainstay of its economy. Increasingly, the Tswana too sought work in South Africa's mines and on farms.

In Swaziland, where vast amounts of land had been granted to concessionaires in the late nineteenth century, the process was somewhat different. There, a series of British government commissions reserved about one-third of the land for African occupation, although a Swazi National Fund managed to repurchase some of the alienated lands, bringing it to about 45 per cent of the total by independence. Although most Swazi men had experience of migrant labour in South Africa, mostly on the Witwatersrand, Swazi society was less radically affected by this experience than were its neighbours.

African peoples, who were so painfully drawn into the capitalist-dominated economy of southern Africa and subjected to ever-increasing administrative, economic, and political control, did not acquiesce in their subordination without resistance. Nevertheless, by contrast with the sharp brutalities of late-nineteenth-century wars of conquest, the era from 1914 to 1939 was one of colonial consolidation, in which African and Afrikaner societies were transformed by the slower processes of proletarianization. The last armed uprising of Africans south of the

Limpopo was a poll-tax rebellion in Natal in 1906. Although both South-West Africa and Mozambique saw armed conflict into the second decade of the century, in British-ruled southern Africa the Chilembwe uprising of 1915 in Nyasaland was the only major challenge to colonial or settler rule until after the Second World War. This does not mean that Africans passively accepted the new order, but that armed resistance gave way to complex politics of protest and accommodation. Africans devised myriad daily strategies to survive and resist the degradations of colonial exploitation.

Not all Africans experienced their subjection in the same way, for racial, gender, ethnic, and class divisions were ambiguously interwoven, thus weakening their capacity to resist settler expansion. All over southern Africa the century witnessed the rise of new classes, with the emergence of an African petty bourgeoisie and working class in the towns. Migrant labour both undermined and strengthened the authority of the chiefs, especially in areas where the colonial state was anxious to retain traditional structures for purposes of social control. Large numbers of people were still politically and ideologically encapsulated in the pre-colonial polities now termed 'tribes', which were given new definitions by the design of the colonizers, the ambitions of chiefs, and the imaginings of culture brokers, especially missionaries and their converts. Everywhere women experienced these processes differently from men. Thus, side by side with the growth of nationalist movements among the new élite and trade-union organization among workers, chiefly politics were redefined, ethnic and gender identifications restructured, and varieties of religion explored.

In the absence of white settlers, African rulers were sometimes able to compromise with the new authorities—as in Barotseland in Northern Rhodesia, or in the High Commission Territories. As new fears of 'detribalization' and the potential radicalization of African workers confronted colonial governments, they moved to bolster intermediate chiefs and headmen, granting them increased authority over their subjects while subordinating them to the colonial state. This refurbishing of chiefly authority gave institutional backing and material rewards to ethnic identification. State recognition also altered the relationship between chiefs and their subjects, as the former became more responsive to the demands of the white administration than to the popular will.

The extension of the market economy further intensified divisions between chiefs and commoners, especially where chiefs identified with unpopular colonial policies, had insufficient land, or exploited the labour of their followers. These tensions were probably most acute in Basutoland, where the outcry over the corruption and ineptitude of chiefs descended from Moshoeshoe, Basutoland's great nineteenth-century king, led to reforms in 1938 which greatly reduced both the numbers of the chiefs and their powers. Elsewhere, industrialization and westernization rendered chiefly rule increasingly inappropriate, especially to Christian converts.

By the beginning of the twentieth century parts of South Africa had experienced almost a century of Christian endeavour. The scope of mission work, already entrenched in the Shire Highlands and south of the Limpopo, was now vastly extended as new societies appeared on the scene and became largely responsible for African education and health. In the nineteenth century Christianity had attracted the disaffected and dispossessed, especially women, and they remained its most important constituency. Although men held the important offices in the church, by the beginning of the twentieth century women were organizing a variety of prayer meetings and self-help groups in order to address the problems they experienced as mothers and wives.

The missionary heritage, however, was multifaceted. If, in a general sense, missionaries can be seen as the midwives of colonialism, encouraging individualism, wage labour, and commodity production, they also fostered the growth of a class of literate and educated Christian Africans who were, paradoxically, to become colonialism's most effective critics. By the late nineteenth century many churches practised a colour bar. African independent churches emerged, often characterized by syncretic religious practices and a millenarianism which disturbed settlers, missionaries, and administrators alike.

As the experience of colonialism and mission education had been longest and most intense south of the Limpopo, so the earliest Western-type political organizations also appeared there. By the early twentieth century a number of local associations and vigilance societies gave expression to the demands of educated Africans for the extension of civil rights, and especially the franchise. These political organizations first came together to protest against the discriminatory Act of Union and formed the South African Native National Congress, the later African National Congress, in 1912. It was joined by chiefs and educated Africans from the High Commission Territories who were apprehensive of Union designs. Congress aimed to overcome ethnic divisions, gain acceptance from whites through self-help, education, and the accumulation of property, and represent African grievances through patient petition and peaceful protest. Well into the century, proclaimed loyalty to Empire was a self-conscious counter to settler despotism.

The existence of substantial Coloured and Indian minorities in South Africa gave an extra dimension to these struggles. It was there that M. K. Gandhi pioneered his philosophy of *satyagraha* between 1906 and 1913, and led the first large-scale non-violent resistance against anti-Indian legislation, with limited success.[21] Nevertheless, restrictions remained on Indian movement in and immi-

[21] See above, p. 433.

gration to South Africa, and the militancy of the South African Indian Congress which he formed was lost until after the Second World War, when younger, more radical leaders began to collaborate with African nationalists for the first time in the wake of violent communal riots in Durban in 1949.

The Coloureds of the Cape and Transvaal were never as successfully mobilized. Though the African Political (later African People's) Organization, founded in 1902, was the first black nationwide political organization, it was soon eclipsed by more vigorous African nationalist movements. For the most part Coloureds were divided and relatively voiceless. Some were drawn into predominantly African movements in the 1920s and 1930s, others were co-opted by white politicians through their access to the franchise. Opposition to the creation of a separate 'Coloured Affairs' department was, however, intense and helped establish the Non-European Unity Movement which came to influence black political thought and action more widely.

Basutoland, with its high literacy rates, had an African Progressive Association as early as 1907, while the more radical Commoners' League or *Lekhotla la Bafo* was founded in 1919. These associations had their counterpart rather later in Central Africa and the other High Commission Territories, where the advent of missionaries and colonialism had occurred later. Many early nationalists had experience of working or studying in the Union, and established 'native associations' and 'welfare associations' which gave birth in turn to the African National Congresses in Southern Rhodesia in 1934, Nyasaland in 1944, and Northern Rhodesia in 1948, all forerunners of later independence political parties. Despite regional differences, the class composition and methods of struggle of these organizations were all broadly similar until the 1950s.

Despite the greatly increased numbers of Africans in South African industry by the end of the First World War, African trade unions were hampered by pass laws, lack of recognition, and police harassment. Strikes were illegal and often put down with violence. Nevertheless, black working-class militancy mounted between 1918 and 1922, and in the 1920s the Industrial and Commercial Workers' Union, initially founded among dockworkers in Cape Town, spread rapidly throughout the region. At its height the Union claimed 100,000 members and had branches as far afield as Southern Rhodesia and South-West Africa. A variety of internal factors led to its disintegration by the end of the decade, however, and it was not until the eve of the Second World War that black workers recovered their militancy.

From the early 1920s, to pre-empt African radicalization, the South African government established local consultative councils for the expression of African grievances. In 1937 a Union-wide Native Representative Council was set up. In Southern Rhodesia and the British-controlled territories, similar consultative

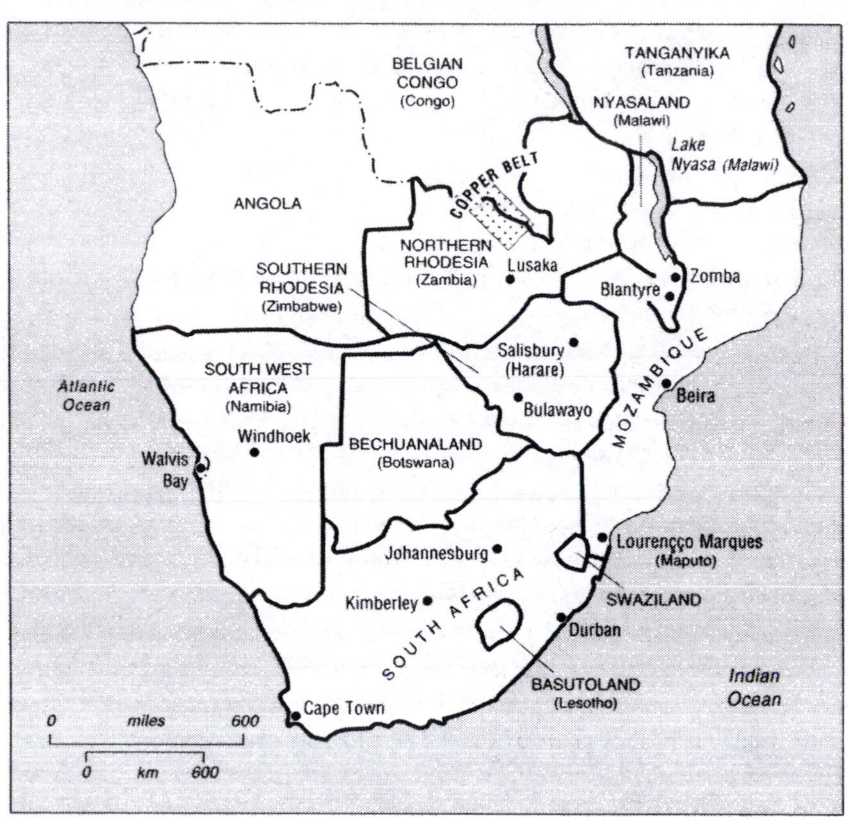

Map 24.1. Southern Africa in the Mid-Twentieth Century

councils were established slightly later and signalled increasing African politicization. Despite their purely advisory capacity, at least until the end of the Second World War, educated Africans participated in these bodies in the hope, often frustrated, of gaining concessions from the state.

Southern Africa, 1939–1960s

If in the first four decades of the century South Africa dominated British decision-making over southern Africa, over the next twenty years their paths diverged increasingly. Segregation fell on 'evil days' and British colonies in Africa moved towards independence.[22] Nevertheless, despite the victory of South Africa's National Party, economic ties between Britain and South Africa were strengthened, and Britain's dependence on South African gold, and later uranium, became of even greater moment at a time of sterling crisis and British decline.[23]

In much of southern Africa, as in many other parts of Africa, the Second World War accelerated economic development, intensified the pressures on African peasants and workers, and radicalized African political organizations. Thousands of Africans soldiers came back home with widened horizons and heightened nationalist sentiment. In Northern Rhodesia the wartime demand for copper greatly expanded production and dramatically changed labour relations on the Copper Belt; by the end of the war the territory was one of the world's major producers of an increasingly strategic mineral. In Southern Rhodesia white farmers at last found their El Dorado in tobacco production, while base metals and secondary industry replaced gold as key sectors of the economy. Although manufacturing industry in the Union overtook mining and agriculture in its contribution to gross national product in 1942, gold continued to drive the South African economy. As local Africans moved into the better-paid work in factories, so the mining industry drew in cheaper migrants from ever further northwards.

These economic shifts were underpinned by demographic changes. The 1930s and 1940s saw large numbers of Africans settling permanently in the major cities for the first time: in South Africa nearly 2.5 million Africans were classified as urbanized by the mid-century. In Southern Rhodesia the wartime industrial boom was sustained by the doubling of the African urban population to about 200,000 over the next decade, while the Copper Belt attracted not only large numbers of migrants, but also an increasingly 'stabilized' urban African population.

[22] The quotation is from Smuts's speech before the South African Institute of Race Relations, Cape Town, Feb. 1942, cited in W. K. Hancock, *Smuts: The Fields of Force, 1919–1950* (Cambridge, 1968), p. 475. The quotation reads: 'Isolation has gone and segregation has fallen on evil days too'.

[23] See Geoff Berridge, *Economic Power in Anglo-South African Diplomacy: Simonstown, Sharpeville and After* (London, 1981); Henshaw, 'Britain, South Africa and the Sterling Area'.

The post-war years also saw a stream of new white immigrants making their way to central Africa, most of them to Southern Rhodesia, where the white population had grown to about 25,000 by 1953, but also to the Copper Belt, where the number of white employees trebled between 1939 and 1964. Everywhere urbanization and the development of manufacturing led to fears about its political consequences and a prolonged debate over the black presence, especially the black woman's presence, in the urban areas. In South Africa the answer was 'apartheid'; in the Rhodesias, during the years of Federation, 'partnership'.

Economic growth brought little additional wealth to the black majority in the region. In South Africa the 'poor white' question was solved, to be replaced by an even more intractable—because largely neglected—'poor black' problem. In Southern Rhodesia African wages, welfare, and working conditions remained wretched. Despite the importance of copper to the British, especially during and immediately after the war, Northern Rhodesian Africans saw scant returns. Until mid-century the British South Africa Company received the royalties while the taxation on mining profits was paid to the British government until 1953, and then largely to the Federal government in Salisbury. Little of this revenue was returned to Northern Rhodesia, although in the 1950s the Company's royalties from the Copper Belt helped finance mining development in Australia, South Africa, and the United States.[24] Northern Rhodesia remained as much an appendage of the settler south as ever.

In the Rhodesias and South Africa the war years and their immediate aftermath saw widespread black disaffection, working-class mobilization, and militant action, which were triggered by poverty wages, squalid living conditions, and high levels of youth unemployment. In Northern Rhodesia African workers, especially the mineworkers, were protected by colour-blind legislation in 1948 and an African mineworkers' union was formed in 1949 with the assistance of the British Trades Union Congress. In the settler south black workers were seriously bruised by this period of insurgency. In South Africa the 1946 strike of over 70,000 gold-miners was harshly suppressed and wartime legislation banning strikes by Africans remained unrepealed until 1978. In Southern Rhodesia an unprecedented general strike of over 100,000 workers spread from Bulawayo to towns, mines, and even farms in the rest of the country, and was soon subsumed in more general nationalist, populist, and rural struggles.

The economic expansion of the 1930s and 1940s also affected rural southern Africa, though in different ways. The benefits of urban development did not trickle down to improve rural conditions but often contributed to the further impover-

[24] A. D. Roberts, 'Notes Towards a Financial History of Copper Mining in Northern Rhodesia', *Canadian Journal of African Studies*, XVI, 2 (1982), pp. 347–59.

ishment of the African reserves. The able-bodied were drawn to urban labour markets and subsistence agriculture suffered. By the late 1930s and 1940s government authorities, mining companies, and African chiefs as well as educated leaders were voicing fears of social disintegration, economic decline, and soil erosion in the reserves.

In South Africa the response was rural 'betterment' schemes which involved the relocation of people, contour ploughing, attempts to centralize landholdings, and, most unpopular of all, the culling of cattle. Introduced in faltering fashion from the mid-1930s, the policies were bitterly opposed in the reserves which, by the 1950s, as their implementation intensified, were simmering with discontent.

In Southern Rhodesia similar schemes introduced from as early as 1928 also met with peasant resistance. After the war, when white farmers switched to tobacco cultivation and industrialists demanded cheap provisions, African food production was promoted more energetically. This led to the Native Land Husbandry Act of 1951. Intended to stabilize a proportion of the African population in the urban areas, and encourage African farmers to produce for the market, the Act roused the opposition of chiefs, migrants, and the new class of entrepreneurs. Rural discontent inflamed anti-colonial struggles over the next three decades.

The Colonial Development and Welfare Acts of 1940 and 1945 brought some measure of investment to territories under direct British rule at a time when Britain was increasingly concerned about rural conditions and anxious to exploit the economic possibilities of Empire. Agricultural research stations and extension programmes were developed to increase agricultural production in Nyasaland and Northern Rhodesia. Yet the new demand for agricultural production both for Imperial and the new urban markets benefited white capitalist farmers rather than the African peasantry, while heightened intervention in rural production proved deeply unpopular.

Paradoxically, the war and the rise of more radical African political movements led initially to the consolidation of colonial and white settler rule in southern Africa. The victory of the Afrikaner National Party in South Africa led in turn to Britain's creation of the Central African Federation as a counterpoise and to the renewed encouragement of white settlement. As in other parts of colonial Africa, the advance of African nationalism was met by a more interventionist and authoritarian state. The response was most elaborate and most stringent in South Africa, and was to provide a major test for the ties of the Empire-Commonwealth.

The Union continued to dominate the region, although the discrediting of racist ideas in Europe after the Second World War and the beginnings of decolonization in Asia brought swelling international opprobrium. The explicitly racialized agenda of South Africa was increasingly seen as an outrage to the new moral order. Even before Smuts lost power, the Union's treatment of its Indian minority and its attempts to incorporate South-West Africa were censured by the United Nations. While the British government deplored South Africa's racial policies it refrained from action, mindful of gold and anxious not to jeopardize Smuts's electoral chances.

Dissatisfaction with the wartime Cabinet and fears of urban African militancy lay behind the victory of the National Party under the leadership of Dr D. F. Malan in South Africa's elections of 1948, fought under the new slogan of 'apartheid' (separateness). The word had different and contradictory meanings appealing to different interests in the party. Contrary to conventional wisdom, initially the government was too weak to implement a monolithic blueprint. Inevitably, at first many apartheid policies were *ad hoc* responses to the multiple crises that confronted the state in the indebted and labour-hungry white farming sector, crumbling reserves, and volatile urban locations.

At first the National Party was concerned to increase its hold over Parliament, promote Afrikaner economic interests, and tighten up the segregationist policies of their predecessors. A cluster of laws defining ethnic boundaries more rigidly in the interests of 'racial purity' were directed against the Coloured and Indian minorities, dividing them from whites, from each other, and from the African majority, in a finely calculated hierarchy of discrimination. Under Hendrik Verwoerd as Minister of Native Affairs (1953–57) and Prime Minister (1958–65), apartheid was more stringently applied, though fierce division remained over its direction. From the late 1950s influx-control laws preventing rural Africans coming into the city were streamlined. Labour bureaux were created in the rural areas to direct labour to white mines, factories, and farms in an attempt to prevent competition between them; and the job colour bar was extended. From 1953 the government also gave increased powers of social control to 'tribal authorities' in the rural reserves, in an attempt to shore up reserve economies and halt the decline of chiefly authority. The reserves were now divided on ethno-linguistic lines into nine—later ten—'Bantu homelands' and were granted limited local self-government in 1959. Beginning with the Transkei in 1976, four poverty-stricken 'independent nation states' emerged out of this 'homeland policy'. Modelled ostensibly on decolonization elsewhere, their 'independence' remained unrecognized by the international community.

By the early 1960s the National Party had firmly entrenched itself in power, had greatly improved Afrikaner economic standing, and notwithstanding the emergence of a small liberal voice in parliamentary politics, had persuaded many English-speaking South Africans that only it could protect white supremacy. So confident was Verwoerd that he put long-desired nationalist republican ambitions to a referendum in 1960. A small majority voted in favour, despite British Prime Minister Harold Macmillan's 'wind of change' speech in Cape Town warning South Africans of the speed of decolonization in the rest of Africa. In 1961 the hostility to apartheid of African and Asian member-states forced South Africa to withdraw from the Commonwealth; nevertheless, it lost none of the economic advantages of membership and South Africa remained within the sterling area until sterling's crisis of 1972–73. The National Party now engaged in far more systematic social engineering, using increasing force to put down any sign of resistance. The result was a massive expansion of the state and brutal interference in peoples' daily lives.

Black resistance to apartheid consisted of formal political opposition and innumerable individual acts of defiance. In the 1950s protest reached unprecedented levels and in turn reshaped the nature of the apartheid state. Like African organizations elsewhere, the African National Congress was transformed by the war and its aftermath. Black Communists and new Youth and Women's Leagues played a major role in this revitalization. Under the National Party onslaught, Congress allied with white radicals (many of whom had been members of the Communist Party, banned in 1950), Coloureds, and Indians in countrywide non-violent resistance to apartheid legislation; in 1955 this Congress Alliance drew up a non-racial, social-democratic Freedom Charter. Distrust of non-racialism and alleged Communist domination led the Pan-African Congress to secede in 1959. By this time largely peaceful demonstrations had given way to spiralling violence against new rural authorities and the increasingly rigorous implementation of the pass laws. In March 1960 national anti-pass demonstrations called by the Pan-Africanists left sixty-nine dead and 180 injured at Sharpeville in the Transvaal; thousands were imprisoned or went into exile as the Congress and Pan-African Congress were banned. Forced underground, these organizations turned to sabotage and formed military wings. Sharpeville also marked a major shift in the international perception of South Africa and the beginning of a thirty-year armed struggle against apartheid.

The victory of the overtly republican Nationalists in South Africa in 1948 and their consolidation in power also posed a series of challenges for wider British interests in the subcontinent. Not only did their economic policies appear to threaten British investments in South Africa; the Nationalists also continued to defy the United Nations over South Africa and to demand full incorporation of the High Commission Territories.

The extent of South Africa's continued hold over the latter was seen in 1949 when the heir to the largest kingdom in the Bechuanaland Protectorate, the Ngwato prince, Seretse Khama, returned home with an English bride. Largely in response to public and government feeling in South Africa, the British banished Seretse Khama (as well as his uncle, the regent Tshekedi Khama). The matter was only resolved in 1956 when Seretse renounced claims to the chieftaincy, and he and Tshekedi were allowed to return to their people as private citizens.[25]

By 1956 it was clear that if the High Commission Territories were not to be incorporated politically by South Africa they would have to be prepared for independence. Limited development funds were now made available, and plans drawn up for the provision of social services, education, soil conservation, roads, and water. This did little to end the migration of large numbers of Sotho and Tswana seeking work in South Africa. Swaziland remained far less reliant on migrant labour. Asbestos as well as coal-mining, sugar and timber plantations, and cattle-ranching had all begun to generate more local jobs after the war. Nevertheless, about 28 per cent of its population was in South Africa, mainly on the mines, on the eve of Swazi independence.

None of the High Commission Territories had powerful liberation movements: their agenda was set by events in the rest of British Africa. In 1952 the Basutoland Congress Party was formed. Advocating self-government and the modernization of chieftainship, it was modelled on South Africa's African National Congress. The organization soon split into the Basutoland Congress Party, the Maremoutlou Party, and the Basutoland National Party; all three contested the pre-independence elections of 1961. In the event the Basutoland National Party under Chief Leabua Jonathan, supported by the South African government, the powerful Roman Catholic Church, and the queen regent formed the first post-independence government in 1965.

In Botswana and Swaziland modern nationalist movements emerged somewhat later and were dominated by members of the royal families. In Botswana, which achieved independence in 1966, Seretse Khama emerged as the first President, while in Swaziland King Sobhuza II emerged as head of state in 1968 through the overwhelming electoral majority of his Imbokodvo National Movement in the rural areas. Despite initial alarm, South Africa soon learnt to live with her newly independent neighbours, who remained economically and politically far too weak to challenge her hegemony.

The National Party victory also spurred Britain into supporting the closer union of its Central African territories. Even before the war, Northern Rhodesian whites had turned southward in response to growing African assertiveness and their own impatience with perceived Colonial Office interference in their affairs, and this

[25] Neil Parsons, Willie Henderson and Thomas Tlou, *Seretse Khama, 1921–1980* (Gaborone, 1995), chap. 4. For British motives, see pp. 86–88.

intensified after the war. With the growing importance of the copper industry in Northern Rhodesia, Southern Rhodesia's settlers also began to see advantages in closer association. At the same time, many colonial officials saw the inclusion of Nyasaland in such an association as a tidy solution to its problems of economic backwardness, although it was never a prominent part of settler ambitions. Wartime collaboration between the three territories in the Central African Council further promoted the new political alignment. However, while colonial officials favoured 'the creation of a solid British bloc of territories in Central Africa' as a counterpoise to the Union of South Africa, for its supposed strategic, economic, and political advantages, the post-war Labour government remained reluctant to impose federation in the face of the manifest hostility of the region's African majority.[26]

The Conservative government which came to power in 1951 did not share these scruples. Despite the incompatibility between the white supremacist ideals which drove the settler demand for federation and Britain's proclaimed belief in the 'paramountcy of African interests', the Conservatives swept aside African fears that federation would entrench segregation on the Southern Rhodesian model and pave the way to white self-government. For the Conservatives, 'multi-racial power sharing' was the answer not only to apartheid and South African regional domination, but also to African demands for majority rule: according to a memorandum prepared for the Secretary of State for the Colonies, Alan Lennox-Boyd, in 1955, 'power sharing' would save the European and Asian communities from being 'swamped' by Africans, and 'offered the best hope... of maintaining European influence'. At the same time, European demands for untrammelled minority rule were to be resisted.[27] As Lord Alport, the British High Commissioner in Salisbury, put it, federation 'would help curb the excesses of both black man and white man'.[28]

The new federal state, the Central African Federation, was inaugurated in October 1953. Its constitution provided some safeguard for African interests in the continued protectorate status of Northern Rhodesia and Nyasaland, and a possible Imperial veto over racially discriminatory legislation. In addition, each territory was to elect two African members and to nominate one European to

[26] See e.g. D[ominions] O[ffice] 35/3588, no. 36, 'Relations of the two Rhodesias and Nyasaland': Memorandum by A. B. Cohen, 15 March 1950, in Ronald Hyam, ed., *The Labour Government and the End of Empire, 1945–1951*, British Documents on the End of Empire Project (BDEEP), Series A, Vol III (London, 1992), doc. 425.

[27] David Goldsworthy, ed., *The Conservative Government and the End of Empire, 1951–57*, BDEEP (London, 1994), Part I, pp. xlviii–xlix; Part II, Document 296, CO 822/929, no. 26, pp. 257–60. 'The Franchise in East and Central Africa': Draft of Memorandum by W. L. Gorell Barnes, intended by Mr Lennox Boyd for Cabinet Colonial Policy Committee, 15 Oct. 1955.

[28] *Sudden Assignment* (London, 1965), p. 20, cited in Chanock, *Unconsummated Union*, p. 260.

represent African interests in the Federal Assembly; a standing committee of the Assembly was also established with the power to scrutinize and even veto legislation affecting Africans. The constitution was to be reviewed within seven to nine years of its inception. These provisions did little to allay African opposition.

Initially, it is true, economic growth seems to have blunted protest against federation in Southern Rhodesia, although dissatisfaction mounted in the reserves, prompted by growing landlessness and land congestion, and unprecedented state intervention in African agriculture. Northern Rhodesia and Nyasaland Africans always suspected that Federation would prevent their political advance and extend racist legislation. Whatever the rhetoric of 'partnership', its economic advantages appeared to accrue to whites and the modest moves towards more liberal racial policies seemed woefully inadequate. Sophisticated constitutional manœuvring and limited attempts to extend the franchise to suitably 'civilized and responsible' Africans did little to assuage their demand for an unqualified democratic vote. By the late 1950s more radical nationalist movements had emerged in all three territories, mobilizing urban workers and disaffected peasantry alike.

The rise of mass movements alarmed the Federal authorities. Sporadic disturbances in Nyasaland in 1959 led to a state of emergency, while in all three territories nationalist leaders were arrested and their organizations banned, to be replaced by new parties under new names. The bannings set off further disorder, and in the northern territories this convinced the British government, already rethinking its African commitments in the context of profoundly changed international and regional priorities, to bring decolonization in Central Africa in line with that in the rest of the continent.

By 1961–62 nationalists in Nyasaland and Northern Rhodesia were released and new 'non-racial' constitutions drawn up, based on majority rule; in 1963 the Federation was formally dissolved. Within a year the Malawi Congress Party under Dr Hastings Banda, who had been recalled from abroad to head the independence movement in Nyasaland, and the United National Independence Party under Kenneth Kaunda in Northern Rhodesia had won elections based on universal suffrage and led their countries into independence.

Epilogue

With the independence of Zambia, Malawi, and the High Commission Territories, the first phase of African decolonization in southern Africa was complete. By the late 1960s all non-independent African countries were in settler-dominated southern Africa, and the following decade saw escalating wars of liberation in Mozambique and Angola, followed by Namibia and Zimbabwe. The independence of the

Lusophone colonies in the mid-1970s was a crucial moment in shifting the balance of power against the remaining white minority states in the subcontinent and increasing international involvement in the region.

In Southern Rhodesia, the imminent collapse of the Federation had led, in 1961, to the formation of the right-wing Rhodesian Front Party and its electoral victory on a platform of immediate independence under white control. This Britain was unwilling to concede, and white Rhodesians, who for so long had identified with Empire, now became convinced that continued ties with Britain threatened white survival. In 1965, under the leadership of Ian Smith, the Rhodesia Front unilaterally and illegally declared Rhodesia independent; it became a republic in 1969.[29] Despite international economic sanctions, the regime lasted another ten years before Africans won their independence after a bitter guerrilla struggle which, like the battle against apartheid further south, involved all its neighbours in a destructive, if largely, clandestine war. By 1978 it was clear that neither side could win, and after many failed efforts negotiations were held at Lancaster House in 1979. The Commonwealth played a significant role in establishing the peace settlement that followed. In 1980 Robert Mugabe won a landslide electoral victory, and became the first post-independence Prime Minister. By 1980 only the Republic of South Africa and South-West Africa remained under white rule.

Despite their political independence, the new southern African states remained embedded in a regional economy consisting of enclaves of high capital investment and rural areas of increasing impoverishment. The nationalists inherited authoritarian and often quite rudimentary colonial states and had little experience of government. For most of the newly independent states, the problem was how to create a nation out of nationalism: the anti-colonial movements had been led by a small middle-class élite, mobilizing a largely peasant populace. With the transfer of power, the unity of the anti-colonial struggle proved short-lived. Ethnic and regional cleavages emerged, frequently arising more from competition over resources than from ethnic tensions *per se*.

Independence was also severely constrained by the continuation of white supremacy in Rhodesia until 1980 and South Africa until the 1990s; there the more complex economies and powerful settler-controlled states greatly complicated the transition to majority rule. The final stages of the wars of liberation in South-West Africa and South Africa took a formidable toll of lives and resources, and left much of the subcontinent dangerously debilitated.

Between Sharpeville in 1960 and the independence of Angola and Mozambique, South Africa had a breathing-space. Thereafter, black resistance, the result of internal economic change and inspired by the successful liberation of their

[29] For the links and parallels with Northern Ireland, see above, p. 155.

neighbours, and the invigorated external armed struggle which this liberation made possible, mounted from the mid-1970s to reach its crescendo by the mid-1980s. By then, despite the reluctance of the British and American governments to lend support, international economic sanctions also began to bite, and the government was forced to surrender many central features of apartheid. But concessions simply led to fresh confrontations with a now wholly alienated black population, insistent on majority rule. In 1990 the South African President, F. W. de Klerk, was forced to legalize the opposition movements and release the Congress leader, Nelson Mandela, from twenty-five years' imprisonment on Robben Island. South Africa's first non-racial, democratic elections were held in April 1994, bringing the African National Congress to power as the dominant partner in a national coalition government. It had been, in the words of the new President, Nelson Mandela, a 'long walk to freedom'.

Select Bibliography

RUSSELL ALLY, *Gold and Empire: The Bank of England and South Africa's Gold Producers, 1886–1926* (Johannesburg, 1994).

WILLIAM BEINART, PETER DELIUS, and STANLEY TRAPIDO, eds., *Putting a Plough to the Ground: Accumulation and Dispossession in Rural South Africa, 1850–1930* (Johannesburg, 1986).

GEOFF BERRIDGE, *Economic Power in Anglo-South African Diplomacy: Simonstown, Sharpeville and After* (London, 1981).

COLIN BUNDY, *The Rise and Fall of the South African Peasantry* (London, 1979)

MARTIN CHANOCK, *Unconsummated Union: Britain, Rhodesia and South Africa, 1900–45* (London, 1977).

JONATHAN CRUSH, ALAN JEEVES, and DAVID YUDELMAN, *South Africa's Labor Empire: A History of Black Migrancy to the Gold Mines* (Boulder, Colo., 1991).

SAUL DUBOW, *Scientific Racism in Modern South Africa* (Cambridge, 1995).

DAVID GOLDSWORTHY, ed., *The Conservative Government and the End of Empire, 1951–1957*, British Documents on the End of Empire Project (BDEEP), Series A, Vol. III (London, 1994).

W. K. HANCOCK, *Smuts*, Vol. I, *The Sanguine Years, 1870–1919* (Cambridge, 1962); Vol. II, *The Fields of Force, 1919–1950* (Cambridge, 1968).

RONALD HYAM, ed., *The Labour Government and the End of Empire, 1945–1951*, British Documents on the End of Empire Project (BDEEP), Series A, Vol. III (London, 1992).

FREDERICK R. JOHNSTONE, *Class, Race and Gold: A Study of Class Relations and Racial Discrimination in South Africa* (London, 1976).

SHULA MARKS and STANLEY TRAPIDO, *The Politics of Race, Class and Nationalism in Twentieth Century South Africa* (London, 1987).

NEIL PARSONS, WILLIE HENDERSON, and THOMAS TLOU, *Seretse Khama, 1921–1980* (Gaborone, 1995).

IAN PHIMISTER, *An Economic and Social History of Zimbabwe, 1890–1948: Capital Accumulation and Class Struggle* (London, 1988).

DEBORAH POSEL, *The Making of Apartheid, 1948–1961: Conflict and Compromise* (Oxford, 1991).

T. O. RANGER, *The African Voice in Southern Rhodesia, 1898–1930* (London, 1970).

—— *Peasant Consciousness and Guerilla Struggle in Zimbabwe: A Comparative Study* (London, 1985).

ANDREW ROBERTS, *A History of Zambia* (London, 1976).

LEROY VAIL, ed., *The Creation of Tribalism in Southern Africa* (London, 1989).

CHERYL WALKER, ed., *Women and Gender in Southern Africa to 1945* (Cape Town, 1990).

25

Canada, the North Atlantic Triangle, and the Empire

DAVID MACKENZIE

At the beginning of the twentieth century the British Empire had less authority in North America than it had had at any time in the previous 140 years. The growth of the United States and the spread of its influence at the turn of the century produced an American rival to the British Empire, especially in the western hemisphere. Moreover, the consolidation of British North American territory in Canada after 1867 and the Dominion's constitutional shift from colony to autonomous nation further reduced British sway there. In the Victorian Age the British Empire may have reached its apogee, but in North America it could be said that the Imperial sun had already begun to set. Nevertheless, North America continued to be important in the evolution of the British Empire, although British policy became less a matter of defence, expansion, and administration and more a question of how best to further British interests through and with the United States and Canada.

For Canadians, the Imperial connection has always been augmented by the larger, triangular relationship between Britain, the United States, and Canada. This idea of a 'North Atlantic triangle' was first coined by John Bartlet Brebner, a Canadian expatriate teaching at Columbia University, who wrote in 1945 on the 'interplay between the United States and Canada—the Siamese Twins of North America who cannot separate and live'. Brebner broadened the scope of his book to include Britain because, he argued, neither Canada nor the United States could 'eliminate Britain from their courses of action', and, 'since the United States attained nationhood by rebellion against Britain, and Canada by gradual growth within the British Empire, not only were their responses to the mother country usually sharply contrasted, but their understandings of each other were habitually warped.'[1]

Of less concern to Brebner and others who followed was just how *Canadian* this idea of a North Atlantic triangle was. Historians of Britain and America have long studied Anglo-American relations, but their focus has been bilateral rather than

[1] John Bartlet Brebner, *North Atlantic Triangle: The Interplay of Canada, The United States, and Great Britain* (New Haven, 1945), p. xi.

triangular. Matters dealing with Canada—or British North America—have been fitted in as necessary, but not in any systematic way. For the British and the Americans there is no need for a triangle; for Canadians, however, it is essential to understanding themselves. Canada's membership in the Empire and its sharing of a continent with the United States have been the two major external forces on its development as an independent nation.

At times the triangle has worked in Canada's favour as Canadians relied on British might and prestige to counter American military and economic encroachments; at other times the triangular relationship has worked against Canadian interests, especially in areas where Imperial concerns overshadowed those of the Dominion, leading to the 'sacrificing' of local Canadian interests to further Anglo-American harmony. Part of the Canadian adventure has been to play off the one against the other if possible—playing up Canada's 'Britishness' to deflect American intrusions, or emphasizing Canada's 'American heritage' to combat Imperial centralizers.

The twentieth century saw the growth of American power and the relative decline of British power. The evolution of the Canadian state has taken place within that context. All the Dominions have had to deal with the gradual decline of the Empire. What makes the Canadian case unique is that it has also been forced to come to terms with the rise of the world's greatest superpower along its 3,000-mile southern border. The growing influence of the United States on Canada is an inescapable theme in modern Canadian history. Ironically, this process of American ascendency occurred during a long period when Canadians were striving to carve out an independent nation for themselves within the framework of the evolving Empire-Commonwealth.

Much of Canada's role in the British Empire was played out in the constitutional debates that shaped the Commonwealth, as Canadians and others travelled the long and often difficult road from colony to nation. But that is only part of the story, for there was a good deal more to Canada's relationship with Britain and the Empire than the evolution of Dominion Status and the emergence of the modern Commonwealth. It is equally clear that the United States played an important role in moulding this relationship. In areas of defence, culture, trade, and commercial development, the interrelationship of Canada, the United States, and Britain—the three corners of the 'North Atlantic triangle'—has had an important impact on the histories of all three countries.

The British Empire in Canada meant one thing: relations with Britain. The growth and development of the Empire set the context, but Canadians were always more interested in Anglo-Canadian relations than in more specifically 'Imperial' matters. Dealings with the colonial Empire were practically non-existent while relations with the other Dominions (with the exception of Newfoundland), although friendly and beneficial, were of secondary importance. Canadians had few dreams of 'empire' for themselves, although there was discussion of Canada taking over the British West Indies early in the twentieth century. Even this proposal was, however, quietly dropped. From the British perspective, Imperial interests in Canada inevitably became entangled in relations with the United States; indeed, in the eighteenth and nineteenth centuries Canada often was the problem in Anglo-American relations. British concern not to make an enemy of the Americans was occasionally the basis for Britain's 'Canadian' policy.[2]

For most of its history, Canada's Imperial connection helped to keep it out of the hands of the United States, as it was in the interest of both Britain and Canada to resist the forces of manifest destiny emanating from the south. Canadians—both French and English—welcomed the protection offered by membership of the Empire. Most French-speaking Canadians fully recognized the value of the Empire in preserving their national identity, but they did not share their English-speaking compatriots' close attachment to it. For most English-Canadians, however, Queen Victoria's Empire was a good thing, and their support was reflected in various public ways, from the introduction of the 1897 Imperial Preference tariff to the patriotic outburst that swept the country at the outbreak of the South African War.

The loosening of these Imperial bonds was a gradual process that unfolded in an era of American expansion and rising Canadian nationalism. The shifting balance of power in North America can be seen at work at the turn of the century in the Alaska Boundary dispute. The territorial question itself was minor: the Americans purchased Alaska and its long thin panhandle from Russia in 1867, and with the discovery of gold in the Yukon in 1897 it became important for Canada for commercial reasons to secure an all-Canadian route across the panhandle. The controversy might well have been settled amicably but for President Theodore Roosevelt's bullying tactics and threats of violence if the American claims were not conceded. The Canadians expected full support from Britain, and when it was not forthcoming the British were condemned for caving in to American pressure. That the Canadian case was weak to begin with was lost in the howls of protest that arose over the methods used to settle the dispute. In the Canadian mind the

[2] Kenneth Bourne, *Britain and the Balance of Power in North America, 1815–1908* (London, 1967), pp. 340–43; Brian Douglas Tennyson, 'Canada and the Commonwealth Caribbean: The Historical Relationship', in B. D. Tennyson, ed., *Canadian–Caribbean Relations: Aspects of a Relationship* (Sydney, Nova Scotia, 1990), pp. 26–37; Edgar McInnis, *The Atlantic Triangle and the Cold War* (Toronto, 1959), p. 19; A. P. Thornton, 'The Transformation of the Commonwealth and the "Special Relationship"', in Wm. Roger Louis and Hedley Bull, eds., *The 'Special Relationship': Anglo-American Relations Since 1945* (Oxford, 1986), p. 372.

Americans had acted aggressively, but that was to be expected; the greatest shock arose from Britain's apparent willingness to sacrifice Canadian interests on the altar of Anglo-American *rapprochement.* For many Canadians it was a sign that they could no longer expect the British Empire to stand up to the Americans on their behalf.[3]

This episode was not followed by dramatic pronouncements in favour of independence, but it did reflect the emergence of a nascent nationalism in Canada, even if that nationalism was rather ambiguous in nature. During the South African (Boer) War and the Alaska Boundary dispute, Canadians had responded and had been treated like colonials, a development that piqued both nationalists and imperialists, although for different reasons. For imperialists Canada's future lay as a co-equal in the Empire; for nationalists (including most French-Canadians) the future lay in autonomy, as experience showed that the Imperial relationship could be counted on to drag Canadians into endless Imperial wars. Since both groups desired greater domestic autonomy and an increasing role for Canada in the world, imperialism in Canada has been described as a form of Canadian nationalism.[4] Where they differed was over how this autonomy and greater role would be played out within the Empire.

The early decades of the twentieth century marked a growing diversification in Canadian-American relations into areas beyond the immediate attention of the Empire. The two countries already had a close relationship. American goods, ideas, and culture were spreading into Canada, and many Canadians were becoming concerned about the impact on Canadian life of this foreign economic and cultural penetration. For these people, Canada's British heritage—the values and traditions upon which British North America was founded—acted as a buffer against spreading Americanization. Nevertheless, Canada and the United States shared similar experiences of developing a frontier society in North America, and these were experiences that Canadians did not share with the Mother Country. New issues appeared on the agenda; issues that had less to do with borders and more to do with hydroelectric development, cross-border water rights, and environmental problems, as well as trade and investment matters. Inevitably, a large gap appeared between Anglo-American relations and what were strictly North American concerns. Thus, when it came to the creation of a Canadian Department of External Affairs in 1909, the British government was not entirely opposed because

[3] C. P. Stacey, *Canada and the Age of Conflict: A History of Canadian External Policies*, 2 vols. (Toronto, 1977–81), I, pp. 85–103; John Herd Thompson and Stephen J. Randall, *Canada and the United States: Ambivalent Allies* (Montreal, 1994), pp. 66–69; and Charles S. Campbell, *From Revolution to Rapprochement: The United States and Great Britain, 1783–1900* (New York, 1974), pp. 194–96.

[4] Carl Berger, *The Sense of Power: Studies in the Ideas of Canadian Imperialism, 1867–1914* (Toronto, 1970), p. 259.

so much of the work of the British Embassy in Washington had been devoted to purely Canadian affairs.[5]

It also made sense in Washington to handle Canadian–American relations more directly, although it was not until the 1920s that relations were put on a more formal basis. Despite some lingering uncertainty over Canada's constitutional status within the Empire, there was general agreement that it was not in the interests of the United States that Canada develop into an economic rival, either on its own or as part of a larger Imperial network. Canada was viewed as both an excellent market for American products and investment and as a source for raw materials for American industry. If the Canadians were drawn closer into Imperial trading arrangements (as the Imperial Preference tariff and the talk of 'Tariff Reform' in Britain suggested they might be), then American business interests would be adversely affected. In this era of American territorial and economic expansion, the 'Open Door' policy applied to Canada as well as the Far East and Latin America. For many American businessmen and policy-makers in Washington, Canada was a 'natural' part of the North American economy, and American policy, as a result, was designed to prise Canada away from the Imperial family and bring it into the US orbit.[6]

All of these factors came to play in the debate over Canadian–American reciprocity—or free trade—in 1911. The agreement, which essentially proposed free trade in natural products, quickly passed through the American Congress, but in Canada it became the focus of an acrimonious debate and election campaign. Opponents of the trade deal, led by Robert Borden, leader of the Conservative opposition, accused the Laurier government of selling out Canada and the Empire for thirty pieces of American silver. Wrapping themselves in the Union Jack, Borden and his followers played on English-Canadians' love for the Empire and on their latent anti-American feelings—never far from the surface in Canada. Comments by influential Americans suggesting that reciprocity would lead to a breakdown of the Imperial connection and absorption of Canada into the United States were quickly turned to advantage by the Conservatives. In their view, Canadians faced a clear choice over reciprocity—between Britain and the United States.[7]

[5] John Hilliker, *Canada's Department of External Affairs*, 2 vols. (Montreal, 1990–95), I, pp. 30–42; James Eayrs, 'The Origins of Canada's Department of External Affairs', *Canadian Journal of Economics and Political Science*, XXV (1959), pp. 109–28.

[6] Gordon Stewart, '"A Special Contiguous Country Economic Regime": An Overview of America's Canadian Policy', *Diplomatic History*, VI (1982), p. 356. See also Stephen Scheinberg, 'Invitation to Empire: Tariffs and American Economic Expansion in Canada', *Business History Review*, XLVII (1973), pp. 218–38.

[7] See Robert E. Hannigan, 'Reciprocity 1911: Continentalism and American Weltpolitik', *Diplomatic History*, IV (1980), pp. 1–18; W. M. Baker, 'A Case Study of Anti-Americanism in

The Laurier Liberals were on the defensive. The Conservatives were well organized, and important segments of the central-Canadian business establishment, which favoured the maintenance of the protective tariff on American goods, deserted Laurier before the election. In Quebec the Liberals faced a challenge on the naval issue. Canadians were deeply divided on how best to respond to the pre-war Anglo-German naval race, with, on one side, a great many English-Canadians who believed that a direct contribution to the Royal Navy for Dreadnought construction was urgently required, and on the other, most French-Canadians, who opposed any contribution whatsoever. Laurier's policy to create an independent Canadian navy that could be 'made available' to the British government in a time of crisis was quite likely the most suitable one in the long run, but it satisfied no one, and he had the unenviable position during the election campaign of being attacked by English-Canadians as anti-British for his support of reciprocity and by French-Canadians as an imperialist for his apparently pro-British naval policy. Laurier played down the talk of political union with the United States, but in the end it was not enough; Borden's Conservative Party won a majority government thanks to its broad support in Ontario and to the *nationalistes* candidates in Quebec who cut into Laurier's bloc of seats in French-Canada.[8]

The defeat of reciprocity in 1911 underlined the strength of English-Canadians' attachment to Britain and the Empire, but it also meant the demise of Laurier's plans for a navy. Borden was equally unsuccessful in this area and, as a result, when war erupted in 1914 Canada had little to offer Britain other than manpower. Nevertheless, the outbreak of war was greeted with enthusiasm, especially in English-Canada, and the commitment made in 1914 was sustained through 1918, although the war itself placed great strains on Canadian society. Over 600,000 Canadians served in the war (out of a total population of approximately 8 million), with over 60,000 killed and countless thousands more wounded and disabled.[9] Thanks to this contribution, Sir Robert Borden was able to play an important role in the constitutional changes that emerged from the 1917 Imperial War Conference and that forever transformed the British Empire.[10]

The North Atlantic triangle changed with the war too. The defeat of reciprocity did not signal the end of American interest in Canada; on the contrary, trade

English-Speaking Canada: The Election of 1911', *Canadian Historical Review* (hereafter *CHR*), LI (1970), pp. 426–49.

[8] Stacey, *Canada and the Age of Conflict*, I, pp. 125–43. See also Robert Craig Brown, *Robert Laird Borden: A Biography*, 2 vols. (Toronto, 1975–80), I, pp. 173–95; John English, *The Decline of Politics: The Conservatives and the Party System, 1901–20* (Toronto, 1977), pp. 61–69.

[9] For Canadian participation see chap. by Robert Holland, pp. 117–18, 125, 128.

[10] See Philip G. Wigley, *Canada and the Transition to Commonwealth: British–Canadian Relations, 1917–26* (Cambridge, 1977), pp. 21–44; Brown, *Robert Laird Borden*, II, pp. 70–82.

between Canada and the United States rose steadily in the war years (continuing a trend that can be traced back to before Canadian Confederation in 1867). By 1914 goods from the United States accounted for 64 per cent of all imports into Canada, for a total of (CDN) $396,302,138. Imports from Britain had fallen to just over 21 per cent of the Canadian total. By the end of the war imports from the United States accounted for over 82 per cent of Canada's total, or (CDN) $792,894,957.[11] These percentages fell from the wartime high in the following decade, but American exports to Canada continued to rise. Similarly, American investment and the number of US subsidiaries operating in Canada jumped dramatically during the war.[12]

Equally important were the changes in the triangular relationship. As one historian has argued, the Great War brought Canada to 'a significant parting of the financial ways'.[13] Traditionally, Canadians looked to the London market for government loans and for capital to finance economic development. But the war all but shut down London as a source of capital, and for the first time the Canadian government turned to the private American market to finance its war effort. As the cost of the war soared, Britain found it increasingly difficult to pay for its imports from North America. As Britain fell deeper into debt, Canada began paying for more of its own war effort and then, after 1917, financing its exports to Britain. In addition, Ottawa and Washington reached agreements that would help secure Canada's supply needs in the United States and would lead to increased US expenditures in Canada.[14]

The war was a costly affair, especially for Britain. Its North American allies proved to be a substantial asset in military terms and as a source of essential supplies. At the end of the war, however, Britain was in serious financial trouble, while the United States had emerged as the world's greatest creditor nation. The Empire had responded to the call, and for many the combined war effort seemed to promise future Imperial collaboration, but with hindsight it is the 'centrifugal forces' unleashed by the war that stand out.[15] The Canadians, meanwhile, had to live with the consequences of their actions. These included a much closer economic relationship with the United States, a rising import deficit and a shortage of US dollars to pay for it, and a weakened economic relationship with Britain. The

[11] Statistics taken from Stacey, *Canada and the Age of Conflict*, I, Appendix A, pp. 358–59.

[12] Scheinberg, 'Invitation to Empire', p. 230.

[13] J. L. Granatstein, *How Britain's Weakness Forced Canada into the Arms of the United States* (Toronto, 1989), p. 11.

[14] Ibid., pp. 12–18. See also R. D. Cuff and J. L. Granatstein, *Ties that Bind: Canadian–American Relations in Wartime from the Great War to the Cold War*, 2nd edn. (Toronto, 1977), pp. 3–42.

[15] Paul M. Kennedy, *The Realities Behind Diplomacy: Background Influences on British External Policy, 1865–1980* (London, 1981), p. 167.

bulk of Canadian imports now came from the United States, and increasingly the American market was the target for Canadian exporters. US investment in Canada would soon surpass British investment, and, thanks to the US style of direct investment, American business interests would soon control key sectors of the Canadian economy. All these developments foreshadowed what would happen on a much larger scale during the Second World War, and they were developments that Canadians, by and large, accepted without complaint. The sides of the North Atlantic triangle had been bent out of shape by the war, and the return to peace could do little to restore them to their original form.

Canadian nationalism is said to have been born during the Great War, and clearly a great wave of nationalism swept across the country in the 1920s. Canadian bonds with Britain and the Empire remained strong—the large British-born population in Canada and continued immigration from the British Isles ensured this. Nevertheless, old-style Imperialism was virtually dead within a few years, and hopes for a greater Empire of equal parts with a common foreign policy quietly evaporated. Even someone like Sir Robert Borden, who championed the cause of consultation and had fought for an 'adequate voice' during the war, was moved to comment in November 1918: 'I am beginning to feel more and more that in the end, and perhaps sooner than later, Canada must assume full sovereignty.'[16]

If Canada was no longer to be a colony, what role would it play in the Empire and the wider world? There was little appetite for moving towards independence, but there was a strong desire to chart an autonomous course within the Empire—making Canadian participation voluntary rather than compulsory. These feelings were embodied in the thoughts and actions of William Lyon Mackenzie King, the Liberal Prime Minister, who served in office almost continuously from 1921 to 1930, and again from 1935 to 1948. Under King's leadership Canada travelled past the landmarks on the road to Dominion autonomy: the independent signing of treaties, beginning in 1923; the establishment of legations in Washington and then Paris and Tokyo; the curbing of the powers of the Governor-General; and the various other Imperial constitutional developments of the inter-war years.

The growth of American power also forced Canadians to readjust their thinking about the Empire, and with this readjustment came a new perception of Canada's place within the North Atlantic triangle. It was central for Canadian security and economic well-being that Britain and the United States get along. Doing whatever possible to ensure that friendship became the goal of Canadian policy-makers for decades. But once the war ended, Anglo-American disagreements erupted over

[16] Borden, quoted in Norman Hillmer and J. L. Granatstein, *Empire to Umpire: Canada and the World to the 1990s* (Toronto, 1994), p. 70.

a number of issues, ranging from trade and debt problems to the renewal of the Anglo-Japanese Alliance to British policy in Ireland, and Canadians could no longer guarantee that they would naturally support the Empire in every case. Increasingly after 1918 Canadians sided with the United States on important issues, and on occasion they appeared to be speaking at Commonwealth meetings as the unofficial American representative. On the Anglo-Japanese Alliance, for example, the Canadians consistently opposed renewal because of the known American opposition to the agreement. The British government was equally concerned, and it was this desire not to harm Anglo-American relations more than anything else that doomed the Alliance.[17]

The growth of American economic and cultural power was felt by all nations, none more so than Canada. Canadian–American trade continued to grow in the 1920s. By 1930 the United States had invested some $4bn in Canada (more than twice the level of British investment). American companies circumvented the protective Canadian tariff by establishing branch plants, and American business interests quickly became major players in the Canadian economy, especially in the natural resource sector and in newer industries that had been sparked by the introduction of modern technology. The automobile industry, for example, became one of the largest industries in Canada by 1930, but it was almost 100 per cent American-owned.[18] At the same time, the new technologically driven products of American culture poured into Canada. A flood of low-priced mass-circulation American magazines into the country threatened to capture the entire Canadian market, and US radio shows and movies quickly squeezed out Canadian competitors. American culture was cheap, captivating, and accessible.[19] The Americanization of Canada had intensified, and many Canadians began to ask whether the Americans would be able to do economically and culturally in the 1920s what they had tried and failed to do militarily in the previous century.

There is a certain irony that this Americanization swept Canada in the midst of rising nationalism and during an era of unprecedented Canadian cultural activity. Canadian art and literature matured in the inter-war years; art galleries, museums, and concert halls were established in the major cities; new national organizations appeared, such as the Canadian Authors' Association, the Canadian Historical Association, and the Canadian Institute of International Affairs; and local clubs and cultural associations dotted the country. Even here, however, the impact of

[17] Hillmer and Granastein, *Empire to Umpire*, pp. 76–78; Michael G. Fry, *Illusions of Security: North Atlantic Diplomacy, 1918–22* (Toronto, 1972), pp. 121–86; D. Cameron Watt, *Succeeding John Bull: America in Britain's Place, 1900–1975* (Cambridge, 1984), pp. 44–53.

[18] J. L. Granatstein and Norman Hillmer, *For Better or For Worse: Canada and the United States to the 1990s* (Toronto, 1991), pp. 86–93.

[19] See Mary Vipond, *The Mass Media in Canada* (Toronto, 1989), pp. 23–46.

Americanization can be seen. The post-war expression of Canadian cultural nationalism lost much of its 'Britishness' and became more American in tone, style, and attitude. Canadian artists now looked more to New York than to London for ideas and techniques; many embraced new styles coming from the south, others moved there to live and work. Canadian magazines, for example, traditionally had mirrored their British counterparts in both design and content; by the 1920s they looked to US ones. *Maclean's Magazine*, the largest-circulation magazine in Canada, openly patterned itself after the American *Saturday Evening Post*.[20]

The spread of American influences in Canada was viewed with some alarm in Britain. Apart from its impact on the development of Canadian culture, this process of Americanization threatened to weaken the remaining ties between Britain and Canada. Canadians now received most of their foreign news from American newspapers and wire services. These sources naturally reflected American values and often painted the Empire in a less than flattering light. This anti-British attitude was prevalent in Hollywood movies, which were often critical of British imperialism. Economically, the United States had already supplanted Britain in Canada; now it appeared that British cultural influence would be displaced as well. Britain wanted to be able to count on the Canadians for support if another war broke out. If Canada became too Americanized, however, even the sentimental attachment to the Empire might be in jeopardy. Concern that Canada was gravitating to the US orbit prompted London to despatch observers to Canada to investigate the situation, and the appointment of a British High Commissioner in Ottawa in 1928 was made partly in response to the US appointment of a minister the previous year.[21]

Cultural issues increasingly took a back seat to economic ones after 1930, as Britain, Canada, and the United States slid into the economic morass of the Great Depression. Tariffs were raised in 1930, first in the United States and then in Canada, partly in retaliation to the American actions, by the new Conservative government of R. B. Bennett. Bennett demonstrated a strong attachment to Britain and the Empire. Although a confirmed protectionist, at the 1930 Imperial Conference he gave the impression that he was flexible in matters of trade and tariff. With Britain's introduction of a general tariff system (including some Imperial Preferences) after the formation of the National Government in 1931,

[20] See Allan Smith, *Canada: An American Nation? Essays on Continentalism, Identity, and the Canadian Frame of Mind* (Toronto, 1994), pp. 40–64; Graham Carr, 'Design as Content: Foreign Influences and the Identity of English-Canadian Intellectual Magazines, 1919–39', *American Review of Canadian Studies*, XVIII (1988), pp. 181–93; David MacKenzie, *Arthur Irwin: A Biography* (Toronto, 1993), pp. 82–83.

[21] R. F. Holland, *Britain and the Commonwealth Alliance, 1918–1939* (London, 1981), pp. 24–73, esp. 24–25, 36–37, 68–73; see also Norman Hillmer, 'A British High Commissioner for Canada, 1927–28', *Journal of Imperial and Commonwealth History* (hereafter *JICH*), I (1973), pp. 339–56.

the table was set for the 1932 Imperial Economic Conference hosted by Bennett in Ottawa.[22]

It was hoped that the Ottawa negotiations would lead to an Imperial agreement that would go some way toward reviving trade and combating the Depression. But initial hopes were quickly dampened when it became clear that Bennett, while eager to see Imperial Preference on Canadian exports to Britain, was unwilling to reduce significantly Canadian tariffs on British manufactured goods. In the end, a series of bilateral agreements between members of the Empire were negotiated, including an Anglo-Canadian agreement by which Canada received preferential treatment on wheat, apples, lumber, and on some meat and diary products. In return, Canada agreed to reduce its tariff on over 200 items, but as one historian points out, 'it is difficult to find among them one that was likely to have a fundamental effect upon the British economy'.[23]

Despite the rather modest accomplishments at Ottawa, any enhancement of Imperial trade was viewed with suspicion in the United States. The US Legation in Ottawa had already warned Washington of British plans to form an Imperial trading bloc and that, without some concessions from the United States, the Canadians would be drawn into it.[24] The Americans had always disliked 'Imperial' barriers to trade (despite their own high tariff wall). They may have overestimated the results of the Ottawa Conference, but after the election of the Democratic administration of Franklin D. Roosevelt, Washington became much more open to negotiations, not only with the Canadians but with the British as well. The Canadians and British were willing to talk, the former because they hoped for reductions in high US tariffs, the latter for the additional reason of concern over American isolationism. As a formal Anglo-American alliance was out of the question, a trade deal might be the only way to improve relations with the Americans and to send a signal to the dictators that Britain was not alone.[25]

Canada and the United States signed a trade agreement in 1935. In 1937 the Anglo-Canadian arrangements of 1932 were renegotiated, and in 1937–38 two further sets of negotiations were undertaken that produced Anglo-American and Canadian–American agreements. The agreements led to general tariff reductions. For the Canadians this meant the loss of some Imperial Preference in Britain

[22] Stacey, *Canada and the Age of Conflict*, II, pp. 126–45, esp. 126–29, 135–45.

[23] Ibid., p. 144. See also Ian M. Drummond, *British Economic Policy and the Empire, 1919–39* (London, 1972).

[24] Peter Kasurak, 'American Foreign Policy Officials and Canada, 1927–1941: A Look Through Bureaucratic Glasses', *International Journal*, XXXII (1977), p. 554.

[25] See Keith Feiling, *The Life of Neville Chamberlain* (London, 1946), p. 308; Tim Rooth, 'Imperial Preference and Anglo-Canadian Trade Relations in the 1930s: The End of an Illusion?', *British Journal of Canadian Studies*, I (1986), pp. 205–29; and Marc Boucher, 'The Politics of Economic Depression: Canadian–American Relations in the mid-1930s', *International Journal*, XLI (1985–86), pp. 3–36.

in return for greater access to the American market. In the end, however, the trade agreements did not amount to much because war broke out within a year. In any event, few efforts to improve Anglo-Canadian trade had any chance of counteracting the forces of geographical proximity, cultural preference, and American industrial efficiency that continued to draw the Canadian economy closer to the American.[26]

Roosevelt and Mackenzie King (back in office in 1935) developed a relatively close relationship. The American President was popular in Canada and seen as a friend of the country. King prided himself on his friendship with Roosevelt and, against the backdrop of the European tumble into war after only two decades of peace, it was easy to be complacent about the Canadian–American relationship. It was a theme of Canadian–American relations between the wars that North American borders were undefended and peaceful, that a spirit of co-operation dominated the relationship, and that unlike Europeans, Canadians and Americans had no need to go to war every generation. An underlying sense of moral superiority permeated public occasions and political speeches.

In addition, many Canadians had long believed that, as citizens of a North American nation, they understood Americans better than did the British. Conversely, because of their British heritage and membership in the Empire, Canadians held that they more fully understood the British mind than did Americans. It required little stretch of the imagination to conclude that Canadians were ideally suited to interpret the one to the other and to help reconcile American power with the needs and interests of the Empire. No one really questioned whether there was any truth to this kind of thinking. Although there are few documented examples where Canadians actually played the role of 'lynch-pin' bringing the two great English-speaking nations together, this belief was enough to provide a loose theoretical foundation for Canada's foreign policy.

The looming international crisis cast a long shadow over relations within the North Atlantic triangle. The British government, despite some uncertainty over the lack of public commitment radiating from Ottawa, could rely on Canada's 'moral obligation' to support Britain in a time of crisis. Mackenzie King had long realized that, despite the constitutional changes in the Empire-Commonwealth, Canadians would respond to the call to arms the moment it was heard. In the meantime, Mackenzie King's goal was to keep the country—and his party—united until that call came. That meant no public debate, speculation, or advance

[26] On the 1938 trade negotiations, see Ian M. Drummond and Norman Hillmer, *Negotiating Freer Trade: The United Kingdom, the United States, Canada, and the Trade Agreements of 1938* (Waterloo, Ontario, 1989), and R. N. Kottman, *Reciprocity and the North Atlantic Triangle, 1932–1938* (Ithaca, NY, 1968). See also R. F. Holland, 'The End of an Imperial Economy: Anglo-Canadian Disengagement in the 1930s', *JICH*, XI (1983), pp. 159–74; and Granatstein and Hillmer, *For Better or For Worse*, pp. 116–17.

commitments in matters of war and peace. Mackenzie King was hardly an isolationist, as some scholars have suggested, but his main hope was that war would be averted; hence his strong support for Chamberlain's policy of appeasement.[27]

From Washington's vantage-point, however, the policy of no commitments seemed to guarantee that when war did break out Canada would be unprepared even to defend itself. Canada's almost complete lack of defences discouraged Roosevelt, who took a strong interest in such matters. Canada was a large and open country, with only a small standing militia and navy, little military industry to speak of, and coastlines that lay practically undefended. Particular concern was focused on the Pacific because of the deterioration of relations with Japan, and questions were raised in American military and political circles: what if the Japanese or some other power attacked Canada as a prelude to an invasion of the United States? Could the Canadians defend themselves or would the Americans have to do it for them? If so, how would the Canadians react? Roosevelt warned Mackenzie King of these concerns, and repeatedly urged the Prime Minister to take action in defence preparedness.

In August 1938 Roosevelt essentially guaranteed Canadian security against foreign invasion. 'The Dominion of Canada is part of the sisterhood of the British Empire,' he told an audience at Queen's University in Kingston, Ontario. 'I give to you assurance that the people of the United States will not stand idly by if domination of Canadian soil is threatened by any other empire.' This speech was a portent for the future of the North Atlantic triangle. It reflected an emerging North American defence alliance, and can be looked back on as a symbolic moment that acknowledged what had been true for many years: that Canadians could no longer be protected by Britain and the Empire, and that ultimately they would have to rely on the United States for their security. In Canada the speech was not met with protests against Yankee imperialism. Indeed, it was widely applauded. Many Canadians realized that their country was ill prepared for war, and if anything, they were more worried that the Americans would *not* come to their defence in a crisis.[28]

Events moved swiftly and circumstances changed so radically that by 1940 Roosevelt's words had been fashioned into a more formal bond of alliance. The outbreak of war once again confirmed the devotion of Canadians to the British

[27] Holland, *Britain and the Commonwealth Alliance*, pp. 68–69; J. L. Granatstein and Robert Bothwell, '"A Self-Evident National Duty": Canadian Foreign Policy, 1935–1939', *JICH*, III (1975), pp. 212–33; H. Blair Neatby, *William Lyon Mackenzie King, 1932–1939: The Prism of Unity* (Toronto, 1976), pp. 210–24.

[28] Roosevelt quoted in Stacey, *Canada and the Age of Conflict*, II, p. 226. See also Granatstein and Hillmer, *For Better or For Worse*, pp. 120–27, and James Eayrs, *In Defence of Canada: Appeasement and Rearmament* (Toronto, 1965), pp. 176–84; MacKenzie, *Arthur Irwin*, pp. 152–56; Granatstein, *How Britain's Weakness*, p. 27.

connection, but the fall of France in the spring of 1940 unleashed forces that were far stronger than ties of blood and dedication to Empire. While Canadian airmen prepared for the fight of their lives in the Battle of Britain, Mackenzie King and Roosevelt issued the Ogdensburg Declaration of 18 August 1940, creating a Canada–US Permanent Joint Board on Defence to 'consider in the broad sense the defence of the north half of the western hemisphere'. The Ogdensburg Declaration was essentially a response to the weakness of Canadian defence in a moment of crisis. It was an agreement fashioned in the dark days of 1940 when the fate of Britain was unclear and there were real fears of an enemy attack on the western hemisphere. It was also in many ways an agreement that gave official sanction to what was likely to occur in any event—the spread of American military protection first across North America and then across the Atlantic.[29]

Economically, a situation developed similar to that in the First World War, but it was much more serious. Canadians had always relied on a smooth triangular operation for the success of their trade policy. Canada ran a chronic deficit in its trade with the United States which was offset by its surplus in trade with Britain. But the suspension of convertibility of the pound in 1939 threw a spanner into the whole operation. By early 1941 Canada had accumulated a huge sterling balance which it was unable to convert to US dollars to pay for its growing deficit with the United States. Canadians wanted to do all that they could to help the Mother Country, but much of the necessary material and component parts for their wartime production came from the United States. The shortage of American dollars to pay for these imports sparked a major financial crisis in Ottawa.

Again the answer was found in the United States. The Hyde Park Agreement of 20 April 1941 between Mackenzie King and Roosevelt effectively removed the border with respect to defence production and committed the United States to buy more war material in Canada—(US) $200m to $300m-worth in the first year alone. In addition, it was agreed that the American-made parts that were included in Canadian exports to Britain would be charged to Britain's Lend Lease account and then shipped to Canada. For the Canadians it was an extraordinarily successful deal. Thanks to the Hyde Park Agreement, Canada's deficit with the United States was eliminated by the end of the war. At the same time, Canada maintained its financial independence from the United States and was better able to finance its exports to Britain and throw its full industrial weight behind the war effort. It also meant that Canada was pulled further away from Britain and the Empire and locked into a continental economic alliance with the United States.[30]

[29] Ogdensburg Declaration quoted in C. P. Stacey, *Arms, Men and Governments: The War Policies of Canada, 1939–1945* (Ottawa, 1970), p. 339; on Ogdensburg, see pp. 336–43.

[30] On Hyde Park, see Cuff and Granatstein, *Ties that Bind*, pp. 69–92.

Although the Ogdensburg and Hyde Park agreements were widely welcomed, not everyone was pleased, especially regarding their long-range impact. Prime Minister Winston Churchill, for one, was suspicious about the Imperial ramifications. 'I am deeply interested in the arrangements you are making for Canada and America's mutual defence,' he wrote to Mackenzie King after the announcement of the Ogdensburg Agreement. But should Hitler fail in his invasion attempt, Churchill continued, then 'all these transactions will be judged in a mood different to that prevailing while the issue still hangs in the balance'.[31] Later, when Churchill learned that most of Canada's uranium production was earmarked for the US Army, he was reported to have charged C. D. Howe, the Canadian minister responsible, with having 'sold the British Empire down the river', despite the close Anglo-Canadian collaboration on atomic energy. American construction of weather stations, air-bases, and huge projects such as the Alaska Highway likewise raised concerns about the American 'Army of Occupation' in the Canadian north. The Canadian government at first remained not entirely aware of the extent of American activities in its own backyard, and it was left to Malcolm MacDonald, the British High Commissioner in Ottawa, to set off the alarm bells in his reports to the Canadian government.[32]

What Churchill and others did not fully grasp was that Canadians had not discarded their attachment to Britain and the Empire. They had not sold their souls to the Americans. On the contrary, the war served only to reinforce Canadians' sentimental attachment to Britain, but for internal reasons, and because of the growing weakness of Britain itself, they had no substantive alternative but to look to the United States. The Empire could no longer provide Canadians with either economic or military security; the Americans could provide both—as well as future opportunity. It is equally clear—and not without some irony—that Canadians embraced the United States as a way of helping to save Britain and the Empire. With Canada better defended and stronger economically, Canadians could do even more to fight the war and support a desperate Britain in its hour of need. Ogdensburg would bring American military might closer to the war effort, and Hyde Park would further enhance Canadian and American military supply. The North Atlantic triangle became unhinged in the process, but the reasons are to be found on the British side as much as on the Canadian and American.[33]

[31] Churchill to Mackenzie King, 22 Aug. 1940, *Documents on Canadian External Relations*, Vol. VIII, ed. David Murray (Ottawa, 1976), p. 142–43.

[32] Churchill quoted in Shelagh D. Grant, *Sovereignty or Security? Government Policy in the Canadian North, 1936–1950* (Vancouver, 1988), p. 115, see also pp. 103–28.

[33] Granatstein, *How Britain's Weakness*, pp. 37–40; see also Thompson and Randall, *Canada and the United States*, pp. 152–55.

Imperial problems rarely topped the Canadian agenda. Canada had no colonial possessions of its own, and Canadians showed little concern for Imperial affairs before or during the Second World War. In 1932 a Canadian warship went to El Salvador following a coup to protect British and Canadian personnel. Such episodes, however, were rare. Surprisingly, the major Imperial problem in the North Atlantic during these years was one that Britain had every reason to believe should never have happened. But a number of factors combined to make Newfoundland—'Britain's oldest colony'—the focus of considerable debate.[34]

The Dominion of Newfoundland followed a similar constitutional course to that of Canada through to the Statute of Westminster in 1931. Two years later, rocked by the Depression and the fall in the international price for fish, the Newfoundland government was unable to pay the interest charges on its national debt. In 1934, following a Royal Commission to investigate the situation, Newfoundland surrendered its Dominion Status to Britain until such time as it was again able to support itself. In place of responsible government, Britain established a 'Commission of Government' consisting of a mixture of appointed British and Newfoundland civil servants to administer Newfoundland.

The Commission of Government provided competent if uninspired government for Newfoundland. The financial situation was stabilized, with Britain funding the deficit, but relatively little was accomplished to restore Newfoundland to self-government before 1939. Newfoundland became an important piece of real estate during the war, however, thanks to its central position in the defence of the east coast of North America, its use as a base for convoy escorts, and as a stepping-stone for the ferrying of aircraft to Britain. In the process, it attracted attention from Britain, Canada, and the United States. The Canadians took immediate steps to defend the island and spent millions of dollars constructing air and naval bases there. Similarly, the British began the construction of Gander Airport before the war, with an eye to its commercial as well as its military use. Then, in September 1940, several base sites in Newfoundland were leased to the United States as part of the Anglo-American swap of bases for destroyers. A few months later thousands of Americans flooded into Newfoundland, sparking their own military construction boom.

Changes in Newfoundland's constitutional status were put off until after the war. It was clear, however, that as soon as hostilities ended some action would be necessary. The influx of thousands of free-spending Americans and Canadians

[34] See Harvey Levenstein, 'Canada and the Suppression of the Salvadorean Revolution of 1932', *CHR*, LXII (1981), pp. 451–69. See also S. J. R. Noel, *Politics in Newfoundland* (Toronto, 1971), pp. 221–61; Peter Neary, *Newfoundland in the North Atlantic World, 1929–1949* (Montreal, 1988), pp. 44–108, 225–312; and David MacKenzie, *Inside the Atlantic Triangle: Canada and the Entrance of Newfoundland into Confederation, 1939–1949* (Toronto, 1986), pp. 127–95.

revived Newfoundland's economy and eliminated the deficit; by the end of the war the Newfoundland government had a surplus and had loaned millions of dollars to the British. An investigative trip to Newfoundland by Deputy Prime Minister Attlee in 1942 and the 1943 'Goodwill Mission' of three Members of Parliament confirmed the need to take some steps in the direction of the restoration of responsible government once the war was over.

Still, there were concerns that the prosperity experienced by Newfoundland was war-induced and temporary and that, once peace returned, Newfoundland would find itself in an economic free fall. With its own enormous financial problems to worry about, London was not at all eager to make a long-term financial commitment to Newfoundland and was careful not to make expensive promises. Late in the war, for example, London rejected a reconstruction plan proposed by the Newfoundland government that would cost Britain (CDN) $100m. 'When I first saw this', Lord Keynes wrote of the plan, 'I thought that $100 million must be a misprint for $10 million. I still think it is better so regarded.' If anyone was to pay it should be the Canadians. 'It is agreed', Keynes continued, 'that the right long-term solution is for Newfoundland to be taken over by Canada.'[35] By 1945 key officials in the Canadian government agreed with Keynes on the future of Newfoundland. Following informal discussions between London and Ottawa, it was unofficially agreed that the two countries would quietly move in that direction.

In December 1945 the British government announced the creation of the Newfoundland National Convention, an elected body of Newfoundlanders established to examine the country's financial situation and then decide on questions relating to Newfoundland's future that would be put to the people in a referendum. The British and Canadians watched from the sidelines. Although they were determined not to be seen as interfering in what was a matter for Newfoundlanders themselves to decide, their reaction to developments in Newfoundland would have an impact on the outcome of the debate. In 1947, for example, delegations were despatched by the National Convention to both London and Ottawa. The delegation to Ottawa was welcomed and preliminary discussions for terms of union were undertaken. In London the Newfoundlanders were met coolly by a British government that could make few promises of financial support beyond the maintenance of the Commission of Government.

The following year, when the National Convention voted to include only two options in the referendum (maintain the status quo or return to responsible government), Britain intervened, with the agreement of Canada, to include the option of Confederation with Canada on the referendum ballot. Two votes were held and, on the second, Confederation won by a slim majority. There were

[35] Keynes quoted in MacKenzie, *Inside the Atlantic Triangle*, p. 153.

some protests that Newfoundland had been abandoned by Britain and that only a democratically elected government could decide such an important issue. Nevertheless, the British and Canadian governments accepted the referendum vote, and on 31 March 1949 Britain's oldest colony became Canada's youngest province.

The problem of Newfoundland was more than merely one of Imperial decolonization. It was symptomatic of a larger dilemma facing the whole of the North Atlantic triangle. Newfoundland used the Canadian dollar and was being increasingly drawn into the North American economy. Britain could only support Newfoundland in the future with money borrowed from Canada. Britain was already in the midst of a severe financial crisis, especially in her dealings with North America, and whatever her intentions, she could do little to help the Newfoundlanders.

The wartime dislocation in the trading and financial relationship of the North Atlantic triangle was not repaired once the war ended. The Canadian government during the war had gone to extraordinary lengths to maintain Anglo-Canadian trade by making a series of loans and gifts to Britain of more than (CDN) $2bn. Further negotiations were undertaken in 1946, in which the British war debt was cancelled and a further $1.25bn loan was extended. Smaller than the $3.75bn US loan to Britain, the Canadian loan was proportionately much greater given the difference in the size of the economies. In fact, the Canadian loan to Britain measured more than 10 per cent of Canada's GNP in 1946. As Anglo-Canadian trade did not revive, however, the wartime problem that had led to the Hyde Park Agreement resurfaced.[36]

Canada's trade deficit with the United States returned after the war to hover at $500m in 1946. Its trade surplus with Britain was $460m, and the British government was striving to eliminate all but essential imports from North America. The only way for Canada to balance its trade was to buy less from or sell more to the United States. The former was tried through import duties and restrictions, but with only limited success. Although the preferred course was to sell more to the United States, it was only with the US dollars provided by the Marshall Plan and its 'off-shore purchasing' that Canadians were able to stave off their own financial crisis. It was clear that the United States was the only country that could afford to buy significant amounts of what Canadians had to sell. By 1954, while only 16 per cent of Canadian exports went to Britain, 60 per cent went to the United States; only 9 per cent of Canadian imports came from the Britain, 72 per cent came from the United States. Despite efforts to reverse this trend, there was little the Canadians could do to stop it.[37]

[36] See Hillmer and Granatstein, *Empire to Umpire*, pp. 193–95.

[37] The statistics come from B. W. Muirhead, *The Development of Postwar Canadian Trade Policy: The Failure of the Anglo-European Option* (Montreal, 1992), pp. 183–86. See also J. L. Granatstein and R. D.

For those such as Mackenzie King who believed in the British Commonwealth, it was not always easy to accept this shift in trade away from Britain to the United States. Mackenzie King remained suspicious of Imperial centralizers, and was outraged when Lord Halifax, Britain's ambassador in the United States, called for closer Imperial unity in a 1944 Toronto speech. When King's officials negotiated a Canada–US free trade agreement in 1947–48, however, Mackenzie King hesitated and then cancelled it, not because of anything in the agreement itself but because he was unwilling to end his career with an act that would further erode the 'unity of the Empire'.[38] But Mackenzie King was less successful in slowing down the movement to closer relations with the United States. The North Atlantic triangle, at least in areas of trade and finance, had fallen apart by the end of the decade.

In the 1950s there was less reason for Canadians to see their country as part of a North Atlantic triangle. In the sense that they still did, it was now measured in cold war terms, with the countries of the original triangle serving as the 'fundamental bone structure' of the western alliance.[39] There were still strong ties and much goodwill between Canada and Britain. Even these ties, however, were ones of blood and sentiment that would dwindle with each passing generation. The high level of British immigration after the war began to drop in real and relative terms in the 1960s until it was surpassed by immigration from other nations. Otherwise, Canada was locked in an economic partnership with the world's one true superpower, while a weakened Britain struggled to revive and then turned increasingly towards the sterling area (of which Canada was the sole Commonwealth member that declined to join) and Europe.[40] With respect to defence and security matters, Canada was drawn still more into the American orbit after the war. This relationship only became closer with the North American Air Defence Agreement of 1957 and other continental defence arrangements. Even in the cultural and social spheres, thanks to the post-war explosion of American popular culture, Canadians became more like Americans than ever before.

Partly because of the gradual disintegration of the Imperial tie, most Canadians did not believe that the decolonization of the Empire was central in the Canadian scheme of things. The two possible exceptions were Newfoundland, for the reasons noted above, and the British Caribbean, which had long been a focus of Canadian business activity. Canadian investors in the Caribbean did not wish to

Cuff, 'Canada and the Marshall Plan, June–December 1947', Canadian Historical Association, *Historical Papers* (1977), pp. 196–213.

[38] J. W. Pickersgill and D. F. Forster, eds., *The Mackenzie King Record*, 4 vols. (Toronto, 1960–70), IV, p. 267. See also, ibid., Vol. I, pp. 636–37.

[39] McInnis, *The Atlantic Triangle*, p. 4.

[40] See Tim Rooth, 'Debts, Deficits and Disenchantment: Anglo-Canadian Economic Relations, 1945–50', *British Journal of Canadian Studies*, VI (1991), pp. 339–51.

lose out to American competitors after the war, and Canadian interest in the region generally increased in the late 1940s and the 1950s following the negotiation of bilateral commercial air agreements. But even here, the growing Canadian–West Indian relationship was less a matter of Imperial decolonization and more the result of the rise of trade and investment and, in the 1960s and 1970s, the emergence of a strong tourism industry and the large increase in West Indian immigration to Canada.

Few Canadians were active players in the process of decolonization, although segments of the Canadian government, especially in the Department of External Affairs, closely watched colonial developments. From a Canadian perspective, concern for individual colonial problems was secondary to their interest in the United Nations and the NATO alliance. There was general support for decolonization, but for Ottawa the key was to undertake the process smoothly without adversely affecting the global situation or harming Anglo-American relations in a manner that might put Canadians in a difficult situation.

Such was the case in the Suez crisis, when the combined French–British actions disrupted Anglo-American relations and threatened a rupture in the United Nations and the Commonwealth. From a Canadian perspective Suez was a disaster, with London and Washington at loggerheads and the Commonwealth divided. Equally important, by bypassing the United Nations, the British actions were seen to have degraded an institution that Canadians strongly supported and threatened to destroy all the bridges with the non-aligned nations that Canadians had helped to build. Lester Pearson, the Canadian Minister of External Affairs, played a key role in ending the crisis, but the Anglo-Canadian relationship was weakened nevertheless. The Canadian government found itself opposed to Britain both morally and politically, leading two Canadian historians to note that Suez 'marked the de facto end of the British Empire in Canada'.[41]

Canadians made a much greater contribution to the process of decolonization when the former colonies sought membership in the Commonwealth. Here Canada played an important and largely progressive role—especially on questions of membership, foreign aid and technical assistance, and over various matters concerning South Africa—as the Commonwealth evolved into a diverse and multiracial organization.[42] Even today, the Canadian government views its

[41] Hillmer and Granatstein, *Empire to Umpire*, p. 226; see Michael G. Fry, 'Canada, the North Atlantic Triangle, and the United Nations', in Wm. Roger Louis and Roger Owen, eds., *Suez 1956: The Crisis and its Consequences* (Oxford, 1989), pp. 285–316.

[42] See John Holmes, *The Shaping of Peace: Canada and the Search for World Order*, 2 vols. (Toronto, 1979–82), II, pp. 165–87; Denis Smith, *Rogue Tory: The Life and Legend of John G. Diefenbaker* (Toronto, 1995), pp. 353–66.

participation in the Commonwealth and its many institutions and bodies as an important component of its foreign policy.

Outbursts of pro-British sympathies among Canadians during the Suez crisis and the later Falklands War were but shadows of a relationship in decline. In the Canadian search for countervailing forces to offset the continental pull of the United States, the Commonwealth connection was used less often and less successfully after the 1950s. Increasingly, Canadians looked to their participation in international organizations such as the United Nations and to activities such as peacekeeping as a means for preserving their separate identity. In the meantime Canada shed most of the remnants of its Imperial heritage: a Canadian Citizenship Act came into force in 1947; appeals to the Judicial Committee of the Privy Council were ended in 1949; a distinct Canadian flag was introduced in 1965; and, in 1990, Canada embraced the western hemisphere by becoming a full member of the Organization of American States.

Two events in the 1980s underlined just how much things had changed. First, in 1982 the Canadian government 'patriated' the Canadian constitution from Britain, an action which, for obvious historical and legal reasons, involved the British government. For most Canadians, however, the Imperial dimension of the constitutional process, although important, was something of a sideshow to the more pressing issues concerning the rights and freedoms to be included in the new Charter and the ramifications of the Quebec government's refusal to sign the final constitutional agreement. Secondly, in 1988 Canadians came full circle and accepted a free trade agreement with the United States—something that they had rejected in 1911. The debate over free trade in the 1980s resurrected many of the same themes as in 1911: that free trade would damage the Canadian economy and align it too closely with the American; that free trade posed a threat to some of those things that made Canadians different from Americans; and that ultimately free trade might lead to the absorption of Canada into the United States. But Canada's British connection and its emotional attachment to the Empire, both of which had been used to great effect in 1911, were completely absent from the debate.

Mackenzie King and the Liberal governments from 1935 to 1957 have been singled out as the villains who 'sold out' Canada and the Empire and chose the 'American Road'. Recent scholarship has easily demonstrated just how unsatisfactory such theories are.[43] Like most Canadians, King and his colleagues did not intentionally

[43] On the 'sell out' thesis, see Donald Creighton, *The Forked Road: Canada, 1939–1957* (Toronto, 1976); on the other side, see the works listed above by J. L. Granatstein, Norman Hillmer, Bruce Muirhead, and C. P. Stacey.

pursue continentalist goals, and most ended their careers with their strong British sympathies and sentimental attachment to the Commonwealth intact. Unfortunately, in matters of defence, security, trade, and culture, the forces of history were working against them. The decline of Britain and the Empire coupled with the rise in American economic, military, and cultural strength made it unlikely that things could have turned out in any radically different way.

The North Atlantic triangle was never one of equilateral design. It was always unbalanced and unstable, especially as American power rose and British power fell. As the Empire dissolved, Canada was transformed from a British nation in North America into simply an American nation. Canadian nationalism, once expressed in a British context, now unfolds in strictly North American terms. As for the triangle, it shattered during the Second World War and was unable fully to repair itself in the post-war era. Because of a lingering attachment to the British connection in Canada, the triangle avoided a total collapse, and it continues today largely as a sentimental geometrical device brought out to help Canadians understand a part of their own history. In its place, both Britain and Canada have tried to cultivate their own 'special relationship' with the United States.

Select Bibliography

ROBERT BOTHWELL, *Canada and the United States: The Politics of Partnership* (Toronto, 1992).

JOHN BARTLET BREBNER, *North Atlantic Triangle: The Interplay of Canada, the United States, and Great Britain* (New Haven, 1945).

R. D. CUFF and J. L. GRANATSTEIN, *American Dollars–Canadian Prosperity: Canadian–American Economic Relations, 1945–50* (Toronto, 1978).

IAN M. DRUMMOND and NORMAN HILLMER, *Negotiating Freer Trade: The United Kingdom, the United States, Canada, and the Trade Agreements of 1938* (Waterloo, Ontario, 1989).

JOHN ENGLISH, *The Life of Lester Pearson*, 2 vols. (Toronto, 1989 and 1992).

J. L. GRANATSTEIN, *How Britain's Weakness Forced Canada into the Arms of the United States* (Toronto, 1989).

—— and NORMAN HILLMER, *For Better or For Worse: Canada and the United States to the 1990s* (Toronto, 1991).

—— and ROBERT BOTHWELL, *Pirouette: Pierre Trudeau and Canadian Foreign Policy* (Toronto, 1990).

SHELAGH D. GRANT, *Sovereignty or Security? Government Policy in the Canadian North, 1936–1950* (Vancouver, 1988).

NORMAN HILLMER and J. L. GRANATSTEIN, *Empire to Umpire: Canada and the World to the 1990s* (Toronto, 1994).

JOHN HOLMES, *The Shaping of Peace: Canada and the Search for World Order, 1943–1957*, 2 vols. (Toronto, 1979 and 1982).

DAVID MACKENZIE, *Canada and International Civil Aviation, 1932–1948* (Toronto, 1989).

—— *Inside the Atlantic Triangle: Canada and the Entrance of Newfoundland into Confederation, 1939–1949* (Toronto, 1986).

B. J. C. MCKERCHER and LAWRENCE ARONSEN, eds., *The North Atlantic Triangle in a Changing World: Anglo-American–Canadian Relations, 1902–1956* (Toronto, 1995).

B. W. MUIRHEAD, *The Development of Postwar Canadian Trade Policy: The Failure of the Anglo-European Option* (Montreal and Kingston, 1992).

PETER NEARY, *Newfoundland in the North Atlantic World, 1929–1949* (Montreal, 1988).

C. P. STACEY, *Canada and the Age of Conflict: A History of Canadian External Policies*, 2 vols. (Toronto, 1977 and 1981).

—— *Mackenzie King and the Atlantic Triangle* (Toronto, 1977).

26

The British Caribbean from Demobilization to Constitutional Decolonization

HOWARD JOHNSON

The outbreak of the First World War consolidated the British Caribbean's Imperial connection as the colonies pledged their loyalty, gave material and financial support, and offered their participation in the armed conflict. Yet the course of the war and its aftermath prompted anti-colonial sentiment, a critical reassessment of the class and racial hierarchy associated with colonialism, and early stirrings of nationalism. Post-war demobilization is thus a useful starting-point for an examination of the process of decolonization, though the themes of this chapter also connect with those of colonial rule since the nineteenth century.

The loyalty displayed by West Indian colonists in 1914 was the result of intersecting ideologies of Empire and race which had long been internalized. With the end of slavery in 1833, Queen Victoria was regarded as responsible for slave emancipation and emerged as a symbol of monarchical maternalism. Annual Emancipation Day celebrations provided colonial administrators with an opportunity to encourage loyalty to the Crown, and 'thus the concept of liberation became incongruously annexed to the idea of Empire'.[1] Loyalty to the Empire was also created by the educational system and, after Queen Victoria's death, by Empire Day celebrations which continued the tradition of presenting British monarchs as 'all-knowing and all-caring'.[2] This Imperial ideology was overlaid by beliefs in white racial superiority which had been an integrative force in British Caribbean slave societies. In the late nineteenth century those beliefs, buttressed by pseudo-scientific theories of race, were linked to claims of an Imperial mission to extend freedom and justice to less-advanced areas of the world.

Participation in the First World War by black subjects tested their loyalty to the British Empire and dispelled previously held notions about the benevolence of

[1] On the 1830s, see Vol. III, chap. by Gad Heuman, see also Gordon Rohlehr, *Calypso and Society in Pre-Independence Trinidad* (Port-of-Spain, Trinidad, 1990), p. 183.

[2] Terence Ranger, 'Making Northern Rhodesia Imperial: Variations on a Royal Theme', *African Affairs*, LXXIX (1980), p. 350.

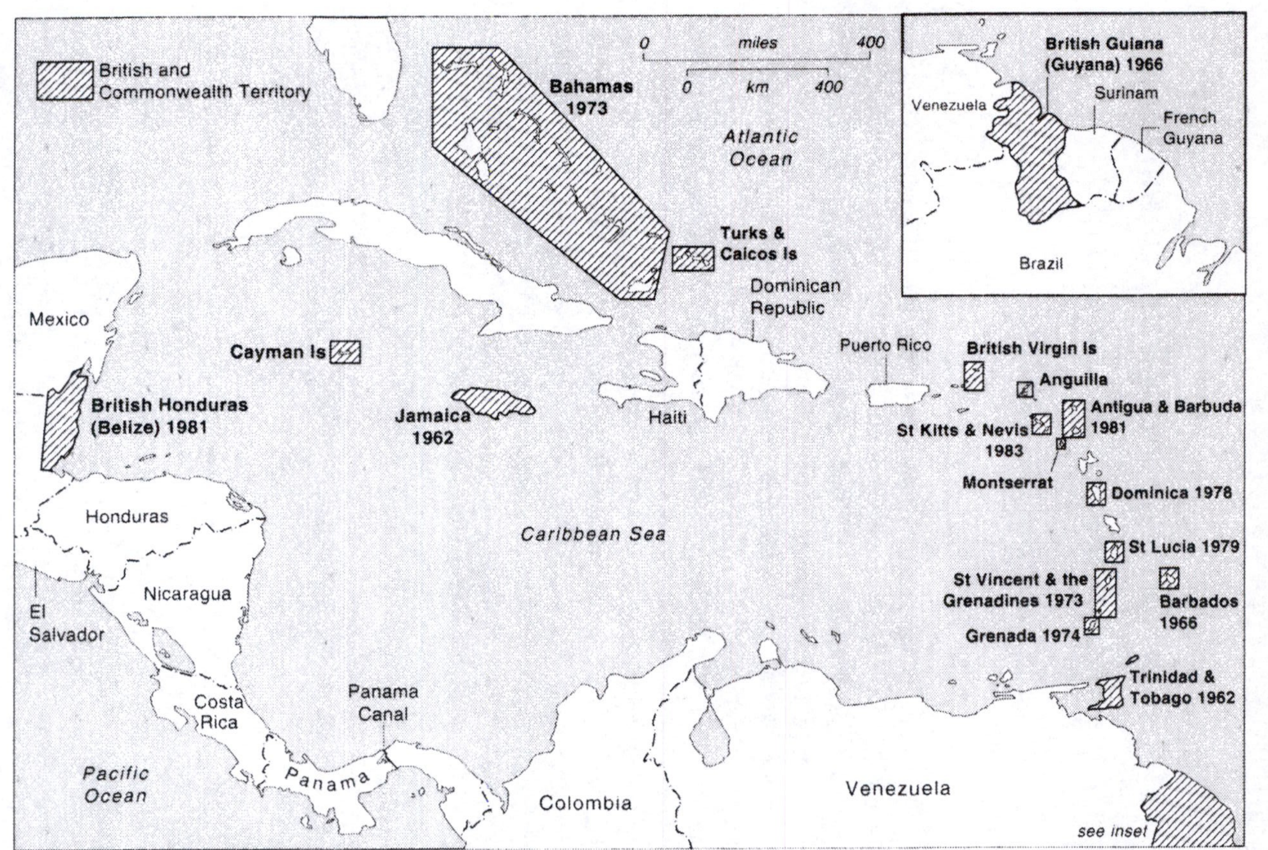

MAP 26.1. British Decolonization in the West Indies.

British rule. Once enlisted, the members of the British West Indies Regiment were subjected to blatant racial discrimination. They were prevented from holding commissions, for the Army Council opposed officers being appointed 'who are not of unmixed European blood'.[3] West Indian battalions were, moreover, used primarily for the hazardous task of ammunition carrying and for labour services. The disillusionment of black soldiers with their treatment was expressed in a 1918 letter by a Trinidadian sergeant: 'We are treated neither as Christians nor British Citizens, but as West Indian "Niggers", without anybody to be interested in or look after us. Instead of being drawn closer to the Church and Empire we are driven away from it.'[4]

The soldiers' grievances culminated in the 1918 mutiny of several battalions at Taranto, Italy. In December of that year, a group of non-commissioned officers of the Regiment formed the Caribbean League. In a series of secret meetings they discussed issues which demonstrated the politicizing effect of their wartime experiences. Among these were the promotion of closer union among the West Indian colonies after the war and self-determination for the black man. Alarmed by the reports of these meetings and fearing that the League's members (many of whom were Jamaicans) might foment disorder, the Colonial Office alerted Jamaica's Governor and requested the stationing of a warship near the colony during the early stages of demobilization.[5]

The widespread disturbances which the Colonial Office anticipated throughout the region did not occur, but there were riots or strikes in Jamaica, British Honduras, and Trinidad in 1919 which the colonial authorities attributed to the influence of returning soldiers with their heightened awareness of class and racial injustice. In July, for example, returning soldiers attacked the houses and stores of the mercantile élite in British Honduras (Belize). An official report on the riot noted that the leaders believed Honduras should be 'the black man's colony'. In Trinidad, the participation of the ex-soldiers in the stevedore strike in Port-of-Spain in December was sufficiently significant for the official report to claim that 'the mutinous spirit' originated in Taranto.[6]

Returning soldiers contributed to a race and class consciousness which had developed in tandem since the late 1890s, when attempts were made to organize trade unions, initially, among groups of skilled urban workers. Throughout the

[3] Quoted in Cedric L. Joseph, 'The British West Indies Regiment, 1914–1918', *Journal of Caribbean History*, II (1971), p. 103.

[4] Quoted in Peter Fraser, 'Some Effects of the First World War on the British West Indies', in *Collected Seminar Papers, Institute of Commonwealth Studies, London, no. 29: Caribbean Societies*, I, p. 26.

[5] Joseph, 'The British West Indies Regiment', pp. 118–21.

[6] Quoted in W. F. Elkins, 'A Source of Black Nationalism in the Caribbean: The Revolt of the British West Indies Regiment at Taranto, Italy', *Science and Society*, XXXIV (1970), p. 103.

British Caribbean wealth was coterminous with whiteness, and the early, and largely unsuccessful, attempts to negotiate improvements in wages and working conditions with an economic élite by strike action inevitably increased awareness of the great disparities in the distribution of wealth and privilege along racial lines. Wartime economic conditions resulted in working-class militancy and renewed efforts to organize labour. Across the region, the war had resulted in an upward spiral in the cost of living as basic consumer items increased in price while supplies contracted. Although the prices for some export commodities such as sugar and cocoa improved during the course of the war, there was no corresponding increase in wages. The strikes which occurred in British Guiana, Trinidad, St Lucia, St Kitts, and Jamaica in 1917–18 were expressions of worker dissatisfaction with wages and working conditions. In Jamaica, a series of successful strikes, which affected several sectors of the island's economy, was followed by the establishment of a Jamaican Federation of Labour formed from several newly established trade unions. In 1919 a Trade Union Ordinance legalized trade union activities, although members could not picket peacefully and the unions and their members received no immunity from liability for breach of contract. In that year the British Guiana Labour Union was formed, with Hubert Critchlow as its full-time Secretary-Treasurer. In Trinidad, the Trinidad Workingmen's Association, which was first established in 1897, was revived to address working-class issues in 1919.

The increased working-class militancy in some colonies by 1919 overlapped with a sense of black racial pride and identity for which Marcus Mosiah Garvey was primarily responsible. He had founded the Universal Negro Improvement Association in his native Jamaica before 1914, but his mission, which included 'the Spirit of race pride and love', received little support until he resettled in the United States. The aspect of Garvey's ideas which had greatest appeal for Caribbean peoples was his assertion of a black nationalism which emphasized 'the beauty and dignity of being black and the ancestral heritage of Africa'.[7] These ideas were widely disseminated in the region by the organization's paper the *Negro World*, and were thought to have influenced participants in the 1919 disturbances in British Honduras and Trinidad. In Trinidad, the American Consul suggested a link between the strikes and the paper, which he attacked as 'responsible for the rapid growth of class and race feeling and anarchistic and Bolshevist ideas among the ignorant population here'.[8] In 1919–20 the colonial authorities banned the paper in British Honduras, British Guiana, St Vincent, and Trinidad.

[7] Ken Post, *Arise Ye Starvelings: The Jamaican Labour Rebellion and Its Aftermath* (The Hague, 1978), p. 144.

[8] Quoted in Tony Martin, 'Marcus Garvey and Trinidad, 1912–1947', in Rupert Lewis and Maureen Warner-Lewis, eds., *Garvey, Africa, Europe, the Americas* (Kingston, Jamaica, 1986), p. 55.

By the end of the 1930s strikes, riots, and disturbances would force policy changes at the Imperial centre and the colonial periphery. Up to that point, Colonial Office concessions took the form of modest constitutional reforms in response to pressures from the black and brown middle class, which demanded a voice in government. This class had emerged mainly as a result of the system of public education and the increased opportunities which economic diversification away from sugar production had provided since the late nineteenth century.

Middle-class demand for constitutional reform was directed against Crown Colony government, which had by 1898 been introduced in most colonies (the exceptions being Barbados, the Bahamas, and British Guiana) that had previously enjoyed representative government. Members of the middle class opposed Crown Colony government on several grounds. First, it prevented them from full participation in the political process, for Jamaica was until the early 1920s the only Crown Colony with an elective element. The second major objection was that it blocked the upward mobility of middle-class professionals, since senior appointments in the colonial administrations were generally reserved for white expatriates. Finally, the middle class recognized that the Crown Colony system had developed into an oligarchy, reflecting the interests of the major representatives of capital, the influence of which was exerted by unofficial representation on the Legislative Council and through social contact.[9]

In the first two decades of the twentieth century middle-class reform organizations proliferated throughout the British Caribbean. Their demands usually included racial parity in the civil service, the extension of the franchise, constitutional reform, and in some cases, a federation of the colonies. In the Eastern Caribbean, the major impetus for constitutional reform came from Grenada, where a group of black middle-class men, led by T. A. Marryshow, formed a Representative Government Association in 1914. This organization petitioned the Colonial Office for the restoration of the representative institutions which the colony had surrendered in 1876. At the end of the war the modest concession of a few elected members of the Legislative Council was granted. The activities of the Grenadian association and the news of the constitutional concession stimulated the formation of similar organizations in other colonies and requests for representative government. The Colonial Office responded to these demands for reform by sending E. F. L. Wood, then Parliamentary Under-Secretary of State for the Colonies, to visit the colonies in 1921 and report.

Wood's recommendations are important because they guided Colonial Office policy on constitutional development in the inter-war years and they offer an

[9] For the classic critique of Crown Colony government, see C. L. R. James, *The Case for West Indian Self Government* (London, 1933).

insight into the influences shaping policy. He was convinced that there was no real demand for responsible government (that is, full representative government), and that such a concession should not be granted in the near future. He believed that responsible government was unsuited to societies which were sharply divided along racial and religious lines (such as Trinidad) and had substantial sections that were 'backward and politically undeveloped'. Wood took the view that the smallness and poverty of several colonies guaranteed that responsible government, if introduced, would 'entrench in power a financial oligarchy' governing in its own interest. In this context, he argued, the British Crown could not relinquish its role as 'responsible Trustee' for the colonial population.[10]

Although Wood presented his arguments for rejecting responsible government in terms of an Imperial trusteeship, it is clear that he was especially anxious to safeguard British capital investment in the colonies. In his discussion of Trinidad and Tobago, for example, Wood drew attention to the considerable investment of foreign corporations in the development of the colony's asphalt and oil resources. He warned that these investments would make any radical constitutional changes imprudent because it was 'important that no action be taken which would disturb the confidence felt by such capital in the stability of the local government'.[11] Wood thus attempted to reconcile the need for political control in the interest of metropolitan and local white investors and the demands of the middle class. He noted that the middle class had been exposed to wartime 'democratic sentiment' and the broadening effect of foreign travel. In these circumstances, Wood's proposal for the introduction of the elective principle was a deliberate act to co-opt the educated middle class.

Two additional considerations influenced Wood's recommendations for constitutional change. The first of these was increased economic interest in the British Caribbean by US corporations—notably the United Fruit Company in Jamaica and the Aluminum Company of America in British Guiana. Any concession to middle-class 'agitators' would, he thought, strengthen their loyalty to the King and the Imperial connection. The second was his desire to provide racially mixed persons with an opportunity for political participation.[12]

Wood's recommendations for the introduction of elected members to legislatures, the membership of which had hitherto been entirely nominated, and for the retention of an official majority were eventually implemented. In 1924 unofficial members, elected on a restricted franchise, were added to the Legislative Councils

[10] Quoted in Ann Spackman, ed., *Constitutional Development of the West Indies, 1922–1968: A Selection from the Major Documents* (Barbados, 1975), pp. 76–78.

[11] Quoted in Kelvin Singh, *Race and Class: Struggles in a Colonial State, Trinidad, 1917–1945* (Mona, Jamaica, 1994), p. 58.

[12] Quoted in Spackman, ed., *Constitutional Development of the West Indies*, p. 76.

of Trinidad and Tobago, the Windward Islands, and Dominica. These cautious reforms represented continuity rather than change. Progress towards self-government by British Caribbean colonies was still envisaged as a slow and protracted process. Crown Colony government was thus regarded as the appropriate constitutional model for the foreseeable future. In 1928 Crown Colony government was introduced in British Guiana which had retained a modified version of the Dutch semi-representative system.

In the inter-war years political activism extended beyond the narrowly based organizations which concentrated on increasing middle-class representation to include women and members of the working class. Although these organizations (predominantly middle class in leadership) were often anti-establishment in nature, they criticized the form of colonial rule but did not question the Imperial connection. They were often concerned with issues of race and, especially in Jamaica, nationalism. They provided opportunities for leadership and experience in organizational skills for their membership.

In Jamaica, the leadership of the politically oriented organizations came mainly from the black petty bourgeoisie, especially teachers, clergymen, journalists, urban artisans, and middle farmers. These groups, centred on Kingston, expressed a growing feeling of a Jamaican identity and emphasized the need for democratic change leading to self-government. Among the earliest of these groups were the Jamaica League (1913–22) and the Jamaica Reform Club (1922–33), which adopted the motto 'Jamaica for the Jamaicans' and advocated the introduction of universal adult suffrage. Most influential was the Universal Negro Improvement Association under the leadership of Garvey, who resided in the island between 1928 and 1935. His lasting contribution to the growth of a national consciousness was his rejection of the existing system of racial values. In the late 1930s two organizations with nationalist agendas were launched: the Jamaica Progressive League and the National Reform Association. Progressive political ideas and the new nationalism were widely discussed in the *Public Opinion*, a weekly journal which began publication in 1936. The political awakening of this period was also reflected in the formation of citizens' associations, study groups, and literary societies in rural and urban contexts.

In Trinidad and Tobago, political activism in the years before 1937 was mainly associated with the Trinidad Workingmen's Association and Captain A. A. Cipriani, a white Creole, who assumed the leadership of the organization in 1923. Under his leadership the association attracted support from blacks and Indians. In 1936 it is estimated that the organization (by then renamed the Trinidad Labour Party) had a membership of 125,000 including workers, peasants, and small business people. The change of name reflected a shift in the focus of the organization from working-class concerns to the achievement of political reform.

Those members who disapproved of this reformist approach sometimes joined the Marxist-Leninist-influenced organization the Negro Welfare Cultural and Social Association, which was established in 1934.

In Trinidad and Jamaica, there appeared organizations in which middle-class women became active participants in the social and political movements of the inter-war years. In 1921 the Coterie of Social Workers was formed in Trinidad by Audrey Jeffers. This organization directed its attention to providing social services for the colony's women and children and eventually demanded a greater political role for women. The Coterie had a counterpart in Jamaica, where in 1936 a group of middle-class black women founded the Women's Liberal Club, the objectives of which included advancing the status of Jamaican women, encouraging them to develop a civic consciousness, an involvement in politics, and the fostering of a national spirit.

In the inter-war years the working and middle classes in Barbados which had remained quiescent for most of the early twentieth century began to express dissatisfaction with the white oligarchy. The major figure in the evolving critique of existing conditions was Dr C. D. O'Neale, who launched the Democratic League—the colony's first political party—in 1924. The support for this organization came from middle-class professionals and from sections of the working class, especially the members of the Universal Negro Improvement Association. In 1926 O'Neale also formed the Workingmen's Association, which did not successfully mobilize workers for trade union activity on a sustained basis. With O'Neale's death in 1936, the Democratic League disintegrated, although grass-root political organizations and discussions did not disappear.

Despite the involvement of sections of the working classes in organized political activity, their influence on colonial policy would eventually be the result of 'extra-constitutional' direct action. With few exceptions, notably the Trinidad Workingmen's Association, the organizations had concentrated on political questions which interested the middle class rather than on the social and economic concerns of their working-class participants.

Strikes and disturbances were regular features of the inter-war years, but the labour rebellions of 1934–39, which affected most sectors of the colonial economies, were unprecedented in their scope and scale. These events had a greater impact on the public consciousness than the earlier isolated strikes and riots because they occurred with disquieting regularity. The earliest of the disturbances began in British Honduras, where labour agitation, which started in February 1934, ended in a riot in September. In Trinidad, labour disturbances broke out in July on several estates in the central sugar belt, involving more than 15,000 Indian estate labourers. In September of that year there were strikes on five sugar estates on the west coast of Demerara in British Guiana.

In 1935 a general strike of agricultural labourers in St Kitts in January was followed in March by a strike in Trinidad's oilfields and a hunger march to Port-of-Spain. In Jamaica labour protests broke out in May on the island's north coast. Rioting among banana workers in the town of Oracabessa was succeeded by a strike of dockworkers in Falmouth which ended in violence. In the months of September and October there were riots at various sugar estates in British Guiana. In October rioting also took place on St Vincent in Kingstown and Camden Park. The year ended with a strike of coal-workers in St Lucia. After a relatively tranquil year in 1936, there was widespread unrest in Trinidad and Barbados in June 1937 and in Jamaica in May and June of the following year. The disturbances of 1937 and 1938 were of greater magnitude than those of 1934–35, which had been more localized. In Trinidad, for example, the protest began in the oilfields but eventually spread to the sugar belt and the towns. In Barbados the disorders which started in Bridgetown spread to the rural areas. In Jamaica most areas of the island experienced serious strikes and disturbances. In February 1939 a major strike broke out at the Plantation Leonora in British Guiana.

Although the circumstances which precipitated the labour rebellions varied in each colony, the underlying causes throughout the British Caribbean were economic. With the exception of the mineral-extractive industries—oil and bauxite in Trinidad and British Guiana respectively—the British West Indian economies were largely dependent on a narrow range of agricultural exports. They were, as a result, highly vulnerable in the event of reduced demand or a serious downturn in the metropolitan economies. The sugar industry, which remained the mainstay of the colony economies, had long been in a critical state but had revived during the First World War as warfare disrupted continental beet sugar production. In the post-war years, sugar prices fell sharply as world supplies of sugar exceeded effective demand. The British government's policy of subsidizing domestic beet sugar production further depressed price levels. The prices of other agricultural staples, such as cocoa, coconuts, limes, and bananas, also slumped to unremunerative levels as a result of worldwide overproduction. In some cases agricultural commodities suffered from the effects of plant diseases and hurricane damage. The crisis in the colonial economy was exacerbated by the global economic Depression which further reduced the demand for British Caribbean exports in the 1930s.

The pervasive economic Depression in the colonies had far-reaching consequences for the working classes. Employers in some industries drastically reduced wages. Unemployment and underemployment increased, and social conditions deteriorated. Problems of unemployment and underemployment were worsened by sharply increased population growth which resulted from a significant downward trend in the region's mortality rate as health conditions improved. The cost of living also soared as the prices for export commodities declined. In these circumstances, the outbreak of labour disputes often originated in worker attempts to increase wages and improve working conditions. These problems were compounded by the closing of avenues for emigration in the 1920s and 1930s and the repatriation of emigrants who competed for employment. Up to the early 1920s, emigration outlets, primarily in Panama, the United States, and Cuba, had absorbed large numbers of West Indian labourers who sought to escape the deteriorating economic conditions in their own countries. In 1924 US legislation virtually ended British West Indian migration to the United States. By the 1920s the economies of the main receiving countries for migrants in the Caribbean and Central America had entered a downward phase. A combination of declining employment opportunities in those countries and the enactment, in the 1930s, of legislation hostile to aliens prompted the return of many migrants. Throughout the British Caribbean, the return of emigrants increased the oversupply of unemployed and underemployed labour and reduced the level of remittances on which many households had hitherto depended.

In Jamaica the returning migrants settled primarily in the urban areas and accentuated the trend towards urbanization which had been evident from the 1880s. The increased urbanization after 1921 was mainly a reflection of the pressure of a rapidly growing population on the land in the rural areas. The period 1911–38 saw 'the emergence for the first time in free Jamaican history of a considerable body of landless workers'.[13] Neither the modernizing sugar industry nor the banana industry, which was affected by the Panama and leaf spot diseases, could absorb this group into its labour force.

Steadily deteriorating social and economic conditions led to a resurgence of race and class consciousness throughout the British Caribbean, as the working classes increasingly recognized that economic status and race were inextricably linked. In Jamaica a religious and political movement known as 'Ethiopianism' (black nationalist in orientation, with Ethiopia as a symbol of an idealized Africa) attracted broad-based popular support. This movement culminated in the emergence of the Rastafarian religion in 1933–34, the principal tenet of which was the divinity of Emperor Haile Selassie of Ethiopia. In October 1935 the Italian invasion of Ethiopia, which was widely reported in the press, evoked anti-white feeling throughout the region.

By the late 1930s organizations whose leadership, membership, and concerns were primarily working class emerged in Jamaica and Trinidad. In Trinidad, T. U. Butler formed a new political organization, the British Empire Workers

[13] G. E. Cumper, 'Labour Demand and Supply in the Jamaican Sugar Industry, 1830–1950', *Social and Economic Studies*, II (1954), p. 80.

and Citizens Home Rule Party, in August 1936, which was concerned with ameliorating working-class grievances. Groups emerged in rural Jamaica which expressed the class grievances of peasants and agro-proletarians and organized themselves to present their concerns to the colonial authorities. The emergence of these organizations reflected the growing economic pressure on peasants, who were increasingly unable to pay the annual land tax and often cultivated land rented from large proprietors on an insecure tenure. In 1938, for example, a peasant organization, the Poor Man's Improvement Land Settlement and Labour Association, was formed by Robert E. Rumble in the parish of Clarendon. In the centennial year of slave emancipation, 1938, the association in a petition to the government pointed out that the promise of freedom remained unfulfilled: 'We want freedom in this the hundredth year of our Emancipation. We are still economic Slaves, burdened in paying rent to Landlords who are sucking out our vitalities.'[14]

Despite evidence of social and economic distress and the efforts of members of the working classes to bring their growing dissatisfaction to official attention, the colonial and metropolitan governments, still firmly committed to a laissez-faire policy, remained largely unresponsive to their plight. The insensitivity to working-class interests at the colonial level is partly explained by the élitist nature of the colonial political system, which was, as has been mentioned, organized to favour the interests of local and metropolitan capital. The introduction of the elective element in the Crown Colonies resulted in the election of representatives from the coloured and black middle classes, but these men, chosen on a narrow electoral base, were not necessarily spokesmen for the black majority. On a visit to the British Caribbean in 1935, W. M. Macmillan found that this group was more preoccupied with abstract political rights than with plans 'for the economic reconstruction needed to safeguard the masses of the people'.[15] Since elected members could not initiate policy, their role was often a negative one in which they criticized government proposals, regardless of merit.

The alliance between government and capital in the colonial context was most marked in the case of policy on the establishment of trade unions. At the time of the late 1930s disturbances, there was no recognized machinery for collective bargaining in any of the colonies. The absence of conciliatory machinery reflected the opposition of the employer class to the existence of effective trade unions, obstructing the Colonial Office's efforts to have them introduced. In Trinidad until 1937, no organized machinery for bringing legitimate grievances to the

[14] Post, *Arise Ye Starvelings*, p. 249.

[15] W. M. Macmillan, *Warning from the West Indies: A Tract for Africa and the Empire* (London, 1938), p. 56.

attention of employers existed in the oil and sugar industries. Arrangements for the resolution of labour disputes were especially important in the oil industry, in which an industrial proletariat working in an increasingly impersonal environment had been created.

The failure to ameliorate conditions in the British Caribbean reflected the limited responsibility which the British government accepted for colonial development. During the inter-war years, the nineteenth-century notion that a colony should have only those services which it could finance from its own resources continued to dominate the thinking of the Treasury and the Colonial Office. Although the Colonial Development Act of 1929 provided funds from the British Exchequer on a regular basis for colonial development, its main objective was to relieve unemployment in Britain's heavy industry. This aid, which was limited to £1 million a year and could take the form of grants or loans, was generally restricted to capital schemes of an economic nature such as the provision of an infrastructure of public utilities. Between 1929 and 1937 only £450,000 in loans and grants was approved for Trinidad, Jamaica, and Barbados, the most creditworthy of the West Indian colonies.

The West Indian disturbances of 1937–38 led directly to the formulation of a new approach to colonial development which emphasized colonial welfare rather than metropolitan economic needs. Colonial governments had responded to the upheavals of 1937 with the familiar blend of coercion and concession. Martial law was declared, British forces introduced to restore order, and Commissions of Inquiry established to investigate the causes of disturbances. In the case of Trinidad, the Secretary of State for the Colonies, William Ormsby-Gore, took the initiative on the establishment of a Commission of Inquiry because of the colony's strategic importance. In Britain, the Colonial Office, responding to Parliamentary criticism from the Labour Party, concentrated on the implementation of labour legislation in the colonies. This emphasis was in line with their perception of the disturbances as 'a case of mere unregulated industrial disputes'.[16] The reports of the Barbados and Trinidad Commissions of Inquiry, published in December 1937 and February 1938 respectively, drew attention to defective social services and recommended improvements in the health service, sanitation, and housing. This information was not new to Colonial Office officials, but in 1938 they feared unflattering scrutiny of colonial administration in the Caribbean when the British government was on the defensive about the Empire, especially in the face of US criticism.

Parliamentary critics from both the Labour and Conservative Parties called for the appointment of a Commission to the British West Indies which they regarded

[16] W. M. Macmillan, *Warning from the West Indies*, p. 12 of Preface.

as a necessary first step in the adoption of a policy for the improvement of conditions. The initial reaction of the officials of the West Indian Department was to recommend financial assistance for the sugar industry, displaying the traditional bias towards the plantation economy. They realized that the Treasury was likely to reject the proposal and that a Commission might recommend measures which the government could not afford to implement. The Colonial Office's Agricultural and Financial Advisers, Sir Frank Stockdale and Sir John Campbell respectively, concluded that a long-term policy which dealt with West Indian problems was a matter of some urgency and would make the appointment of a Commission necessary. It was Campbell who advanced an argument which became persuasive in the adoption of a new development policy. He was anxious that the failures of British rule in the Caribbean should not provide evidence for US anti-colonialism: 'The West Indies, are to some extent, the British show-window for the USA—I am afraid it is not a very striking exhibit.'[17]

The shift in the Colonial Office approach to West Indian problems came after the Jamaican disturbances of late May 1938. Until then, most officials had been prepared to see the colonies finance the slow introduction of reforms from their own resources. These events persuaded them that a long-term policy of reconstruction for the West Indian colonies, requiring substantial Treasury assistance, would be necessary. Subsequently Treasury officials and the Cabinet were convinced that the West Indian situation was sufficiently grave to make large-scale Imperial assistance for schemes of Colonial Development and Welfare essential. Their endorsement of the proposal for a Royal Commission represented an undertaking to implement its potentially expensive proposal. The Royal Commission, the personnel and terms of reference of which were announced in the House of Commons on 28 July 1938, was expected to provide (by its authoritative findings) metropolitan support for a line of action which the Colonial Office had already decided on.[18]

The Commission, with Lord Moyne as Chairman, was asked to investigate social and economic conditions in the British Caribbean and make recommendations. Political and constitutional problems were not included in the terms of reference, reflecting the Colonial Office view that West Indian problems were primarily social and economic in nature. The Secretary of State for the Colonies, Malcolm MacDonald, believed that those questions should be considered only so far as they affected social and economic conditions.

[17] Minute, 23 May 1938 C[olonial] O[ffice] 318/433/71168.

[18] For an extended discussion of these points see Howard Johnson, 'The West Indies and the Conversion of the British Official Classes to the Development Idea', *Journal of Commonwealth and Comparative Politics*, XV (1977), pp. 58–83.

After a fifteen-month period during which it heard the evidence of 370 witnesses and received 789 memoranda, the Moyne Commission reported in December 1939. In an exhaustive survey of social and economic conditions in the British Caribbean, the Commissioners noted that discontent in the region no longer represented 'a mere blind protest against a worsening of conditions, but a positive demand for the creation of new conditions that will render possible a better and less restricted life'.[19] Although the members identified the underlying economic problems of the colonies, they offered no general strategy for the economic transformation of the region. In fact, their recommendations showed an awareness of existing conditions which inhibited structural change. They recognized, for example, that the chronic problems of unemployment and underemployment could be alleviated by a substantial increase in the level of economic activity, with a reduced dependence on export production. They acknowledged, however, that the majority of the population would continue to depend on export agriculture. The Commissioners also realized the importance of a programme of land settlement for encouraging a class of smallholders (who would engage in mixed farming for domestic consumption) and reducing underemployment. Land-settlement schemes, they admitted, were likely to be expensive for the colonies concerned. Without external financial assistance, they concluded, it was unlikely that schemes for land settlement would be widely adopted.

The most important of the Moyne Commission's conclusions provided the Colonial Office with the expected support for its policy of Colonial Development and Welfare. It recommended the establishment of a West Indian Welfare Fund, to be financed by an annual grant of £1m from the British Government over a twenty-year period, to implement schemes for the general improvement of social conditions. It also recommended that the Fund should be administered by a Comptroller (directly responsible to the Secretary of State for the Colonies) assisted by a staff of experts whose advice would be available to the colonial administrations. Aware of the possibility of a hostile reception to its recommendations, the Commission chose to represent its conclusions as merely reflecting the 'increasing evidence of a readiness on the part of Parliament and of the people of the United Kingdom to undertake greater responsibilities for the well-being of colonial peoples'.[20]

Malcolm MacDonald used the occasion of the publication of the Moyne Commission's recommendations in February 1940 to introduce a broader legislative programme of Colonial Development and Welfare on which a departmental committee of the Colonial Office had worked since July 1938. Before the outbreak of war MacDonald had recognized the propaganda value which such a programme

[19] *West India Royal Commission Report, 1938–39*, Cmd. 6607 (London, 1945), p. 8.

[20] Ibid., p. 429.

of colonial development would have during wartime. He regarded an untarnished colonial reputation as an essential part of Britain's defence policy. In the wartime context, those arguments were more persuasive. The Colonial Development and Welfare Act of 1940 authorized expenditure up to £5m yearly on colonial development and welfare for a ten-year period and £500,000 for colonial research annually for an indefinite period. Under the provisions of this legislation money could be spent for economic development and, as MacDonald declared, 'everything which ministers to the physical, mental, or moral development of the colonial peoples of whom we are the trustees'.[21] Money from the Colonial Development and Welfare Fund could also be used to defray the recurrent costs of development projects.

Wartime exigencies brought the implementation of the 1940 legislation to a virtual halt, but the bill nevertheless became law in July of that year. In a circular telegram of June 1940, the Secretary of State, Lord Lloyd, stated that wartime conditions had made it impossible 'to make any substantial progress under the new policy'.[22] A circular despatch of September detailed the circumstances under which expenditure could be justified for schemes of development and welfare. The West Indian colonies were the only exceptions to the newly imposed restrictions. In September Sir Frank Stockdale was appointed Comptroller of the Development and Welfare Organization based in Barbados.

Despite the British Caribbean's special exemption from the restrictions on wartime expenditure, little was achieved in the region by 1945. As early as 1942, Members of Parliament and commentators in journals such as *The Economist* were noting the small sum which the British Government had spent in the West Indian colonies since the much-publicized change in the policy on colonial development. The slow progress on development and welfare projects also attracted the attention of American officials associated with the Anglo-American Caribbean Commission (AACC)—the regional commission created by the British and United States governments in 1942. They feared that failure to improve conditions in the colonies could result in civil unrest which could adversely affect the war effort in the Caribbean. United States policy-makers had, through the AACC, exerted continuous pressure on the British government to expedite work on development and welfare projects, but with little success. In 1945 W. Arthur Lewis, a West Indian economist and former Colonial Office official, observed that 'after four years, the use of a microscope would hardly reveal any progress on the development side in the West Indies, though a few welfare projects had actually been started'.[23] Although American pressures did not reactivate the programme of

[21] *Parliamentary Debates* (Commons), Fifth Series, 361, 21 May 1940, col. 47.

[22] D. J. Morgan, *The Official History of Colonial Development*, 5 vols. (London, 1980), I, p. 90.

[23] See 'A Meeting at the Fabian Colonial Bureau', Papers of Charles W. Taussig, Box 49, Franklin D. Roosevelt Library, Hyde Park, NY.

development before 1945, the Colonial Development and Welfare Act of 1945, which substantially increased the money available to the colonies to £120 million over a ten-year period, may be seen as a response to US criticism of British efforts.

At this stage, Colonial Office officials regarded the US government not only as unrelentingly critical of the Empire but also as a threat to British dominion in the Caribbean. By the 1920s US economic penetration of the region was considered so far advanced that the Colonial Office envisaged Canada as a countervailing influence in the western hemisphere through strengthened economic ties with the colonies. With the establishment of the AACC, US policy-makers (as Colonial Office officials recognized) came to exercise decisive influence on issues such as colonial development, political reform, and trade in the British Caribbean without assuming the burdens of formal Empire.

The failure to move major development and welfare projects beyond the planning stage by 1945 can be explained by the method of implementation, the wartime competition for scarce material resources, the persistence of the doctrine of financial self-sufficiency, and the primacy of Britain's economic needs. Although a Development and Welfare Organization with a panel of experts in various fields was established, the main responsibility for initiating projects rested with individual colonial governments whose ability to plan effectively was hampered by the shortage of skilled personnel. The Development and Welfare Organization served primarily in an advisory capacity and final decisions on projects and the allocation of funds were made by the Colonial Office rather than by the Comptroller. Attempts by the Comptroller to assume a more constructive role often led to friction with colonial administrations who regarded him as encroaching on the Governor's executive authority. Once approved, work on Development and Welfare projects was often delayed by a shortage of essential materials.

The pace of the introduction of the welfare projects envisaged by the Moyne Commission was undoubtedly slowed by the persistence of the ideas of colonial self-sufficiency among officials charged with their implementation. There was a marked reluctance to recommend welfare schemes, the future recurrent costs of which individual colonies would be unable to finance from their own resources. In the second report on the operations of the Development and Welfare Organization, Stockdale expressed concern that 'the saddling of the West Indian Colonies with medical, educational, housing and other services whose development may be brought to a halt by their own financial weight—or involve the necessity for permanent external aid—would be a disservice to the people'. This approach to the provision of welfare services resulted in the neglect of expenditure on education, which continued to be classed as social welfare rather than as related to economic development.[24]

The most significant limitation on proposals for colonial development and welfare were wartime mobilization and the central importance of Britain's economic needs during post-war reconstruction. In a gesture of self-conscious magnanimity intended to impress the United States, Britain had initiated the programme of development and welfare during wartime, yet the war would serve to emphasize her economic dependency on the colonies. In 1941, for example, Lord Moyne as Secretary of State for the Colonies sent a circular despatch detailing methods of economizing on resources and urging colonial governments to accumulate surplus balances for future use. He suggested that such balances could become interest-free loans to the metropolitan governments. Given the straitened economic circumstances of the British government, colonial resources became, partly as a result of the war, 'an important and, in some cases, dominant factor in the financing of development programmes'.[25]

The sterling balances between 1943 and 1956 illustrate British dependence on the colonies at the same time that the British government claimed to fund overseas development projects. By 1943 the colonies had accumulated sterling balances in Britain to which they did not have unrestricted access because of British wartime demands on those financial reserves. In the post-war years, colonial access to these assets continued to be strictly regulated in the interests of the British economy. Since Britain could not meet the demand for goods and services, it was anticipated that the colonies would make their purchases from the dollar area in gold or dollars. The British government feared that unrestricted access to these sterling reserves would result in a severe depletion of the gold and dollar reserves and endanger the status of the pound as an international currency.[26] The colonies were thus asked to limit their import demands in order to conserve the sterling area's hard-currency reserves and ease the British government's continued balance-of-payments crisis. At a point when British colonial policy was ostensibly shaped by the mission to promote colonial development, the management of sterling balances was determined by the post-war crisis in the British economy. In these circumstances, West Indian colonies granted funding under the provisions of the Colonial Development and Welfare Acts were forced to finance development costs on the London market at higher rates but could not tap their own steadily accumulating sterling balances for such purposes.[27]

[24] Morgan, *Official History*, I, p. 147.

[25] Ibid., II, p. 138.

[26] See chap. by D. K. Fieldhouse and below, p. 366.

[27] Allister E. Hinds, 'Imperial Policy and Colonial Sterling Balances, 1943–56', *Journal of Imperial and Commonwealth History*, XIX (1991), pp. 24–44.

By the end of the first decade of its operation in the British Caribbean, the shortcomings of the policy of Colonial Development and Welfare were already evident. The administrative structure set up for its implementation guaranteed that social and economic problems were dealt with in a piecemeal fashion at the local level rather than by a broad regional approach. Colonial Office officials also continued to expect that individual colonies would, in the foreseeable future, assume responsibility for expenses associated with economic development and welfare projects. Thus the Secretary of State, Oliver Stanley, pointed out in his speech introducing the 1945 bill on Colonial Development and Welfare that the funds provided by the act would be 'in the nature of a pump primer to enable people to start their education and health services'.[28] By the early 1950s Colonial Office officials had begun to despair of achieving viable economies and self-sufficiency in the smaller colonies, despite years of funding development plans. In 1954 Sir Stephen Luke, then the Comptroller, admitted that the policy of Development and Welfare had not created viable economies in the Windward and Leeward Islands, and thus the likelihood of ending grants-in-aid from the British Treasury to them was more remote then than it had been in 1940.

The economic viability of the colonies also emerged as a significant issue in the planning for political development after 1940. In July 1943 Stanley had announced that the Colonial Office approach to constitutional development would be 'to guide Colonial people along the road to self-government within the framework of the British Empire'.[29] He indicated that this political concession would be granted only after an apprenticeship in parliamentary government and evidence of the individual colony's ability to be self-supporting. At that stage, it was generally recognized that the political advancement of the British Caribbean colonies towards self-government might be a prolonged process. The Moyne Commission had earlier rejected self-government for the colonies, despite 'a substantial body of public opinion' in its favour, on the ground that the British government would need to exercise financial control if the recommended assistance were given.[30] The bureaucratic reorganization of the Colonial Office which accompanied the adoption of a policy of Colonial Development and Welfare also suggested that policy-makers were not preparing for withdrawal but the consolidation of colonial rule.

The transition to representative government in the British Caribbean after 1940 was an incremental process which involved, at different stages, the gradual extension of the franchise, universal adult suffrage, increases in unofficial representation, and the eventual grant of elected majorities in the legislatures. This deliberate

[28] Quoted in Morgan, *Official History*, I, p. 200.

[29] Quoted in J. M. Lee and Martin Petter, *The Colonial Office, War, and Development Policy: Organisation and the Planning of a Metropolitan Initiative, 1939–1945* (London, 1982), p. 244.

[30] *West India Royal Commission Report*, p. 373.

pace was partly a reflection of the Moyne Commission's conservative constitutional guidelines and the Colonial Office's continued misgivings about the suitability of representative institutions in societies with black majorities. The Moyne Commission, for example, did not propose the immediate introduction of universal adult suffrage, but recommended that 'universal suffrage should be the ultimate goal'.[31] When in 1944 Jamaica was granted a new constitution with universal adult suffrage, this concession was more a response to US pressures than to the demands of nationalist politicians. Adult suffrage was subsequently introduced in Trinidad and Tobago in 1945, in Barbados in 1950, the Leeward and Windward Islands in 1951, British Guiana in 1953, and in British Honduras the following year. Elected majorities were granted in Trinidad and Tobago in 1950, to Grenada, St Vincent, St Lucia, Dominica, Antigua, St Kitts–Nevis, Montserrat, and the Leeward Islands Federation in 1954, and to British Honduras and the British Virgin Islands in 1954. By the late 1950s Barbados and Jamaica had already been granted the ministerial system and advanced in 1958 and 1959 respectively to full self-government, with responsibility for internal affairs. Although the pace of constitutional development differed from colony to colony (reflecting the British government's assessment of their readiness to move to the next stage), reforms were generally introduced following political agitation in the colonies.

Across the British Caribbean, the gradual introduction of representative government overlapped with the development of viable trade unions and political parties which provided much of the driving force for constitutional change. In most colonies the disturbances had begun and spread without leadership or the backing of formal trade-union organization. However, middle-class leaders quickly emerged who would use the spontaneous working-class protest as the vehicle for their own rise to political power. In the aftermath of the riots, these leaders recognized the opportunities for organizing the working classes—a process which was facilitated by the colonial and metropolitan governments' interest in building 'legitimate' labour movements. In Trinidad, Adrian Cola Rienzi, an Indo-Trinidadian lawyer, established the Oilfield Workers' Trade Union, which was predominantly Afro-Trinidadian in composition, and the All-Trinidad Sugar Estates and Factories Workers' Trade Union, which was overwhelmingly Indian. His leadership of both these organizations represented an ultimately unsuccessful attempt to form 'a trans-ethnic alliance between the African and Indian working masses'.[32] In Barbados and St Kitts, middle-class political organizations formed alliances with the working classes after the riots. In 1941 the Barbados Workers Union was organized as the offshoot of the Progressive League, with Grantley

[31] Ibid., p. 380. [32] Singh, *Race and Class*, p. 224.

Adams, an Oxford-educated lawyer as President. In St Kitts, the St Kitts Trades and Labour Union was founded in 1940 under the middle-class leadership of members of the Workers' League. The Jamaican disturbances of 1938 also led to the establishment of the Bustamante Industrial Trade Union by W. A. Bustamante, a businessman.

In most colonies, the local and British governments responded to the working-class politics of protest with the politics of control, in which middle-class trade unionists generally collaborated. In the wake of the disturbances, the Colonial Office was especially anxious that 'responsible' trade unionism, compatible with the interests of colonial business, should be established. Legislation was enacted which gave trade unions the right of peaceful picketing and protection from legal action, but colonial governments retained control over the development of trade unions by the introduction of labour departments. These departments, which worked closely with the British Trades Union Congress, were expected to provide guidance and supervision to trade unions, in part, by emphasizing the distinction between industrial action and political militancy.

In some colonies, the decade after the disturbances was marked by the emergence of political parties which depended on trade unions for their organizational base. Among the earliest of these was the Progressive League in Barbados (which became the Barbados Labour Party in 1944), whose trade-union wing was the Barbados Workers' Union. In Jamaica W. A. Bustamante was, by 1943, the leader of both the Bustamante Industrial Trade Union and the Jamaica Labour Party. In 1946 Robert Bradshaw founded the St Kitts Labour Party, for which the St Kitts Trades and Labour Union provided the mass base. Although the Colonial Office opposed the development of these links between political parties and trade unions (maintaining that trade unions should limit their activities to industrial action), the trend persisted throughout the region. Political parties with a trade-union base often integrated the working classes into colonial politics and eventually mobilized their support for political demands such as universal adult suffrage and self-government.

Political parties such as the People's National Party of Jamaica and the Barbados Labour Party (despite its trade-union base) reflected their middle-class leadership by focusing on the struggle for self-government rather than on social and economic change. The People's National Party had been established in September 1938, under the leadership of Norman Manley, by members of the middle class who regarded the disturbances as confirmation of their anti-colonial critique. Manley's political orientation was nationalistic rather than narrowly centred on the interests of the working classes. Both Adams of the Barbados Labour Party and Manley believed that self-government would be achieved through a process of political agitation and negotiation and within the framework of the British

Empire. Although both parties were nominally socialist, they were primarily examples of middle-class reformist nationalism.

By the 1940s a national consciousness among the British Caribbean middle classes was manifesting itself not only in political activities but also in a sense of cultural identity. This consciousness did not always express itself in a narrow territorial cultural nationalism. In Jamaica in 1928, for example, the Revd C. A. Wilson pointed to the need for 'the creation of a distinct West Indian literature'.[33] In the inter-war years Trinidadian writers attempted to produce a distinctly West Indian body of literature which was published locally in two magazines, *Trinidad* (1929–30) and the *Beacon* (1931–33, 1939). In their short fiction, writers such as Alfred Mendes and C. L. R. James used 'West Indian settings, speech, characters and conflicts'. In 1942 *Bim* was launched in Barbados by Frank Collymore, and in British Guiana in 1945 A. J. Seymour, in the first issue of *Kyk-over-al*, expressed the hope that it would be 'an instrument to forge a Guianese people'. In Jamaica in 1943 the sculptor Edna Manley founded the literary journal *Focus*. She had earlier gathered around her a group of artists who together developed a distinctively Jamaican iconography.[34]

Although a national consciousness had emerged in the British Caribbean by the late 1940s, the intense nationalism and anti-colonialism which marked the African and Asian colonies had not developed. In most colonies, nationalist sentiment was still largely confined to the middle classes and the carefully nurtured feelings of loyalty to Britain persisted. The British government regarded nationalism as non-threatening and compatible with metropolitan interests because it did not involve an economic nationalism, for most colonies emphasized the eventual attainment of self-government within the British Commonwealth. The gradual modification of the Crown Colony regime had not conflicted with the protection of Britain's economic interests in the region. An exception to this trend was British Guiana, where the British government suspended the constitution on 9 October 1953, after landing troops in Georgetown, overthrowing the democratically elected government of the People's Progressive Party led by Dr Cheddi Jagan. This suspension came 133 days after the Party, in the first election under adult suffrage, received the support of the African and East Indian communities, winning eighteen of the twenty-four seats in the Legislative Council.

The British government justified its action by claiming that it was necessary to prevent the establishment of a Communist state within the British Commonwealth. The evidence indicates that, at the height of the cold war, the Colonial

[33] *Daily Gleaner*, 29 Sept. 1928.

[34] Reinhard W. Sander, *The Trinidad Awakening: West Indian Literature of the Nineteen-Thirties* (New York, 1988), p. 9; Kenneth Ramchand, *The West Indian Novel and its Background* (London, 1970), pp. 71–72.

Office and the British Cabinet believed that British Guiana and its ruling party were threatened with subversion from the Soviet Union, which was strongly opposed to the continued existence of the British Empire. Equally important, however, was the economic threat from a colonial government whose members were intent on initiating, with popular support, radical political and economic reforms which would adversely affect foreign-owned sugar and bauxite companies.

In the 1950s the Colonial Office envisaged that the British Caribbean colonies would achieve nationhood not individually but as part of a West Indian Federation. The idea of a federation, which had been mooted in the nineteenth century (resulting in the adoption of a form of federal government for the Leeward Islands in 1871) was discussed at the time of Wood's visit to the region and in 1932–33 by a Closer Union Commission. On both occasions the idea was rejected as lacking support. The Moyne Commission later stated that it regarded a federation as 'the proper ultimate aim of [constitutional] policy'.[35] In 1945 Oliver Stanley, Secretary of State for the Colonies, proposed a federation of the colonies with full internal self-government as its ultimate goal, but indicated that the Colonial Office would await a favourable response to the idea before acting. Stanley's proposal was prompted, in part, by 'the greater economy and efficiency in general of large-scale units of government'.[36] In 1947, when a conference of Caribbean politicians together with colonial and British officials, convened by the Secretary of State, Arthur Creech Jones, met at Montego Bay in Jamaica, Colonial Office policy on federation was clearly defined. It was thought 'clearly impossible in the modern world for the present separate communities, small and isolated as most of them are, to achieve and maintain full self-government on their own'.[37] The Colonial Office anticipated that a West Indian Federation would create a viable political unit which would become financially self-sufficient and thus qualified for self-government.

Although the Colonial Office had taken the initiative on federation in the post-war years, the delegates of the West Indian legislatures eventually agreed in principle to a federal union in 1947. The enthusiasm for a federation in the inter-war years had been Eastern Caribbean in origin. In 1932, for example, politicians from Trinidad, Barbados, and the Leeward and Windward Islands had urged the establishment of a federation and drafted outlines for a constitution. At Montego Bay the idea won wider regional support, for colonial politicians

[35] *West India Royal Commission Report*, pp. 373–74.

[36] Quoted in Jesse Harris Proctor, Jr., 'Britain's Pro-Federation Policy in the Caribbean: An Inquiry into Motivation', *Canadian Journal of Economics and Political Science*, XXII (1956), p. 319.

[37] Quoted in Anthony Payne, 'Britain and the Caribbean', in Paul Sutton, ed., *Europe and the Caribbean* (London, 1991), p. 14.

were convinced that self-government could only be achieved within the framework of a larger unit of colonies. The conference appointed a Standing Closer Association Committee to formulate proposals for a federal government.

In the eleven years which elapsed between the Montego Bay Conference and the establishment of a Federal government in Port-of-Spain in 1958, with ten participating colonies, two major developments eroded support for federalism.[38] The first of these was the steady advance of British Caribbean colonies toward self-government, which had previously been thought possible only within a federation. As Sir John Mordecai, who had served as Federal Secretary and Deputy Governor-General of the Federation, observed: 'The desire for self-government now began to work against federation instead of in its favour.'[39] In fact, the Federal government decided, at its first session in 1958, to review a Federal constitution which was less advanced than those of Barbados, Trinidad and Tobago, and Jamaica. The second development was rapid post-war economic growth in Jamaica as well as Trinidad and Tobago, which promised an economic viability separate from what W. A. Bustamante had, in 1947, scathingly described as 'a federation of paupers'.[40]

In Jamaica, the post-war boom was based, in part, on the growth of tourism and traditional agricultural exports such as sugar and bananas. The boost to the Jamaican economy came, however, primarily from bauxite-aluminium production and secondary industries. Both represented areas of US investment and the extension of an economic and political influence which amounted to a process of 'neo-colonization'. By 1957 the Jamaican government had renegotiated the terms of its agreement with the bauxite companies and increased the level of income from that source. The Jamaican government had also adopted a strategy of industrialization, earlier advocated by W. Arthur Lewis, which was based on attracting foreign investors to produce mainly for the domestic market. Although Trinidad also pursued a strategy of 'industrialization by invitation', its comparative prosperity remained dependent on its oil industry. Manufacturing, tourism, and the extractive industries were capital-intensive and failed to create adequate employment for the region's steadily increasing labour force. Those who experienced unemployment and underemployment emigrated, when they could, to Britain, where there was a demand for labour, in substantial numbers.[41] It is estimated that in 1955–58 Jamaicans to the number of 58,946 migrated to Britain.

[38] The participating colonies were Jamaica, Trinidad, Barbados, Antigua, Montserrat, St Kitts, Dominica, Grenada, St Lucia, and St Vincent.

[39] Sir John Mordecai, *The West Indies: The Federal Negotiations* (London, 1968), p. 33.

[40] Quoted in Elisabeth Wallace, *The British Caribbean: From the Decline of Colonialism to the End of Federation* (Toronto, 1977), p. 99.

[41] Jay R. Mandle, 'British Caribbean Economic History', in Franklin W. Knight and Colin A. Palmer, eds., *The Modern Caribbean* (Chapel Hill, NC, 1989), pp. 243–48.

This movement of population constituted, in the words of the Jamaican poet Louise Bennett, 'colonisation in reverse'.[42]

The years after 1958 were marked by intercolonial dispute on a range of issues, including the freedom of movement of people throughout the region, the financing of the Federal government, the co-ordination of fiscal, customs and tariff policy, and the representation of individual units in the federal legislature. The main tensions were generated, however, by the attempts of nine of the constituent units to accommodate the demands of a Jamaican government which was increasingly intent on pursuing an independent line on plans for economic development. Jamaica, under the leadership of Norman Manley, viewed a stronger federal structure as incompatible with its development programme. In Trinidad, Dr Eric Williams of the ruling People's National Movement, which had come to power in 1956, supported the strengthening of a federation that would advance to Dominion Status.

The fate of the West Indian Federation was decided essentially in January 1960, when the British Colonial Secretary, Iain Macleod, assured the Jamaican government that he regarded the colony as qualified for independence on its own.[43] It was not, however, until 19 September 1961, after the Jamaica electorate voted 54 to 46 per cent to withdraw from the Federation, that Jamaica left the union. This electoral decision represented the victory of an island nationalism over a broader West Indian nationalism. For Eric Williams, the political implications of Jamaica's withdrawal from the Federation were clear. He feared that Trinidad would have to assume financial responsibility for the eight less developed territories. Four months later, Trinidad declined to participate in an Eastern Caribbean Federation. The West Indian Federation came to an end on 31 May 1962, almost four years after the opening of the Federal Parliament, thus clearing the way for independence by each territory.

By 1962 the earlier British criteria for granting independence—size and economic viability—were no longer strictly applied. The willingness to grant independence to the British Caribbean colonies was influenced by developments elsewhere in the British Commonwealth. As Iain Macleod remembered in a 1967 interview: 'You see, when you were giving independence to a country the size of Gambia, to islands the size of Malta and Cyprus, it's a bit much to expect Jamaica, or Trinidad to sink their sovereignty with a whole collection of islands, many of which they would have to help almost as pensioners.'[44] Between 1962 and 1966 the four main colonies—Jamaica, Trinidad and Tobago, Barbados, and British Guiana

[42] Louise Bennett, *Jamaica Labrish* (Kingston, Jamaica, 1966), pp. 179–80.

[43] See above, p. 347.

[44] Quoted in Robert Shepherd, *Iain Macleod* (London, 1994), p. 238.

(which had also chosen not to join the Federation)—became independent. For its part, the British government by the early 1980s had disengaged from its colonial entanglements, except for a few dependent territories such as the Cayman Islands and the Turks and Caicos Islands, which have chosen to remain colonies.

At the time of the collapse of the Federation, the problems of colonial development in the British Caribbean, which had preoccupied Imperial policy-makers since 1938, remained unresolved. In the post-war years the main emphasis had been placed on Britain's economic reconstruction—a process to which the Caribbean colonies made a vital contribution by their participation in the sterling area. Given these priorities, a West Indian Federation was seen as providing not only a viable political unit within which the colonies could advance to responsible government, but also a method by which Britain's financial responsibility for the smaller, less-developed territories would be gradually shifted to the larger islands. The refusal of Jamaica and Trinidad to assume that role precipitated the breakdown of the Federation. Even in those relatively prosperous territories, the steady growth in per capita income in the years before independence (the result of economic activities such as the manufacturing and extractive industries) concealed problems of unemployment and underemployment. The territories which opted to remain British did so, in part, because they recognized the economic benefits of the British connection as essential to their own survival. As a Governor of one of the remaining Caribbean dependencies remarked: 'Britain will have to fight very hard for its independence from its dependent territories.'[45]

[45] Quoted in George Drower, *Britain's Dependent Territories: A Fistful of Islands* (Aldershot, 1992), p. xii.

Select Bibliography

O. Nigel Bolland, *On the March: Labour Rebellions in the British Caribbean, 1934–39* (London, 1995).

Cary Fraser, *Ambivalent Anti-Colonialism: The United States and the Genesis of West Indian Independence, 1940–1964* (Westport, Conn., 1994).

Jeffrey Harrod, *Trade Union Foreign Policy: A Study of British and American Trade Union Activities in Jamaica* (London, 1972).

Howard Johnson, 'Oil, Imperial Policy and the Trinidad Disturbances', *Journal of Imperial and Commonwealth History*, IV (1975), pp. 29–54.

—— 'The West Indies and the Conversion of the British Official Classes to the Development Idea', *Journal of Commonwealth and Comparative Politics*, XV (1977), pp. 58–83.

—— 'The Political Uses of Commissions of Enquiry: The Imperial-Colonial West Indies Context', *Social and Economic Studies*, XXVII (1978), pp. 256–83.

HOWARD JOHNSON, 'The Anglo-American Caribbean Commission and the Extension of American Influence in the British Caribbean, 1942–1945', *Journal of Commonwealth and Comparative Politics*, XXII (1984), pp. 180–203.

GORDON K. LEWIS, *The Growth of the Modern West Indies* (London, 1968).

W. ARTHUR LEWIS, *Labour in the West Indies: The Birth of a Workers' Movement* (London, 1977 edn.).

W. M. MACMILLAN, *Warning from the West Indies: A Tract for Africa and the Empire* (London, 1938).

SIR JOHN MORDECAI, *The West Indies: The Federal Negotiations* (London, 1968).

TREVOR MUNROE, *The Politics of Constitutional Decolonization: Jamaica, 1944–62* (Mona, Jamaica, 1972).

KEN POST, *Arise Ye Starvelings: The Jamaican Labour Rebellion and Its Aftermath* (The Hague, 1978).

—— *Strike the Iron: A Colony at War, 1939–1945*, 2 vols. (Atlantic Highlands, NJ, 1981).

RHODA E. REDDOCK, *Women, Labour and Politics in Trinidad and Tobago: A History* (London, 1994).

SELWYN D. RYAN, *Race and Nationalism in Trinidad and Tobago: A Study of Decolonization in a Multiracial Society* (Toronto, 1972).

KELVIN SINGH, *Race and Class: Struggles in a Colonial State, Trinidad, 1917–1945* (Mona, Jamaica, 1994).

ANN SPACKMAN, ed., *Constitutional Development of the West Indies, 1922–1968: A Selection from the Major Documents* (Barbados, 1975).

HUGH W. SPRINGER, *Reflections on the Failure of the First West Indian Federation* (Cambridge, Mass., 1962).

ELISABETH WALLACE, *The British Caribbean: From the Decline of Colonialism to the End of Federation* (Toronto, 1977).

27

Latin America

ALAN KNIGHT

The history of the Latin American political economy in the first half of the twentieth century was strongly conditioned by three external shocks: the two world wars and the Great Depression. Together, these dealt drastic blows to Britain's position of pre-eminence which, even before 1914, was fast eroding as a result of German and United States competition as well as internal economic and political challenges. The British fought a long and dogged rearguard action in Argentina, where the Depression briefly bolstered British interests. But Argentina was exceptional; and even in Argentina the British revival proved to be a respite, not a reprieve. The revival of British influence in the 1930s guaranteed a yet more extreme assertion of Argentine nationalism and anti-imperialism in the 1940s. The Second World War and its aftermath, therefore, brought to an end the long cycle of British 'imperialism' in Latin America. The Falklands–Malvinas War of 1982—'an irrelevant exercise in nostalgia'—represented a sad coda to a historic Anglo-Argentinian relationship; it was a throwback to an older era of violent confrontation; but, most of all, it was an anachronistic example of mutual posturing by two powers which, since their bitter parting in the late 1940s, had both suffered economic and political decline.[1]

The outbreak of the First World War, coming hard on the heels of the 1913 depression, jolted Latin American exporters. The docks of Santos, Buenos Aires, and Callao lay idle; soup kitchens had to be set up on the streets of Santiago; in Peru's Cañete valley, site of a British sugar mill, businessmen and officials feared shutdown, unemployment, hunger, and 'the likelihood of unrest'.[2] The Chilean cruiser *Esmeralda*, which had mown down striking nitrate workers at Iquique seven years before, now steamed into harbour to remove 10,000 of the same workers who were camping, destitute, on the dockside. The condition of 'dependency' was starkly underlined: Latin American wars might preoccupy European

For Latin America in the nineteenth century see Vol. III.

[1] H. S. Ferns, 'Argentina: Part of an Informal Empire?', in Alistair Hennessy and John King, eds., *The Land That England Lost* (London, 1992), p. 60. For British investment see Figs. 27.1–27.3.

[2] Bill Albert, *South America and the First World War* (Cambridge, 1988), pp. 1, 37–38, 40, 50.

markets, but a European war, shearing through the inspissated fabric of trade, investment, and collaboration, shook Latin America to its core. 'We watch the formidable European struggle, dumbfounded,' as a Brazilian observer put it, 'our existence paralyzed and our activity drugged, complete slaves of Europe.'[3]

The German market, which had grown vigorously in recent decades, now collapsed, initially affecting coffee and nitrates. More generally, shipping was disrupted and freight rates rose; the supply of imports dried up, halting railway construction; and governments, dependent on revenue accruing from foreign trade, faced falling receipts and sought loans in order to continue servicing the foreign debt.[4] The British, and later the Americans, instituted wholesale controls on commerce, designed to ensure supply, force down prices, and strangle Germany. Nitrate, sugar, and copper boards regulated the trade in basic commodities, while the notorious blacklist targeted German interests in Latin America. For the British, the onslaught on German business was strategic as well as tactical: by 1918, if not before, they were intent on 'destroying German trade not only for the present but for the future'.[5] Unfortunately for the British, the Americans entertained similar strategic ambitions: from President Woodrow Wilson down, the US administration saw the war as an opportunity to advance US business interests at the expense of those of Europe, Allied as well as German. Hard economic logic, its rough edges sandpapered by a 'progressive Panamericanism', favoured the US advance; and post-war Germany recovered from its enemies' commercial onslaught in Latin America rather better than Britain did from her ally's.[6]

As the war progressed, Latin American commodity prices rode a rollercoaster. Coffee, produced by domestic, rather than foreign, enterprises, held up well, as did sugar and cocoa; but all three collapsed in the post-war recession of 1920. Chilean nitrates slumped at the outset, but later boomed as they were diverted from fertilizers to munitions, then again went into decline with the development of synthetic nitrates. The hard-pressed Chilean government, forced to borrow, turned from London to New York. Brazilian rubber production, already on a downward slide, came to an end, since Britain preferred to rely on safer Imperial suppliers.[7] The capriciousness of the commodity market was compounded, in Latin American

[3] Thomas E. Skidmore, *Black Into White: Race and Nationality in Brazilian Thought* (New York, 1974), p. 152, quoting Paulo Silveira.

[4] Albert, *South America*, pp. 43–44, 62, 74, 79, 91, 96–97, 110, 220; Winston Fritsch, *External Constraints on Economic Policy in Brazil, 1880–1930* (Basingstoke, 1988), p. 36.

[5] Albert, *South America*, pp. 64–65, 82 (quoting Sir Francis Elliott, President of the Foreign Trade Department), pp. 98–99, 108, 113.

[6] Albert, *South America*, pp. 60–61; Joseph S. Tulchin, *The Aftermath of War: Woodrow Wilson and US Policy toward Latin America* (New York, 1971), pp. 20, 25, 30–31.

[7] Albert, *South America*, pp. 45, 88, 98–99, 108; Fritsch, *External Constraints*, p. 35; Michael Monteón, *Chile in the Nitrate Era* (Madison, 1982), pp. 72, 108–113.

eyes, by the Allies' perverse interference in both international and domestic economic affairs: by commodity board price-fixing, control of shipping, and what even an Anglophile Argentine newspaper called the 'veritable extortion' of the blacklist.[8]

Latin Americans, taught to revere the rationale of the free market, found their European tutors playing fast-and-loose with its sacred tenets; they discovered, not for the first time, the risks of relying on monopsonistic external markets; and, deprived of manufactured imports, they began, of necessity, to boost production for their own domestic markets. The war, therefore, prompted advances in import substitution industrialization, at least in the major economies: Argentina, Brazil, Chile. If the old orthodoxy of comparative advantage and export-led growth survived, it now came under intellectual attack and, in practice, was increasingly compromised.[9] This economic introversion was soon coupled with political and cultural reassessments. The European image of cultured civilization was besmirched by the blood and mud of the Western Front; and European political upheaval soon generated new models, Fascism and Communism, which permeated Latin America, undermining the loosely liberal consensus that had united pre-war oligarchic élites and their foreign, chiefly British, collaborators. European examples conspired with indigenous nationalist currents to produce a tide of nationalist demands: the Mexican Revolution of 1910–17; Peru's Alianza Popular Revolucionaria Americana (APRA); the Communist parties of the 1920s; the polychromatic Fascist movements of the 1930s.

After 1918 British interests and British diplomacy sought a rapid restoration of the pre-war status quo. Conjunctural as well as structural conditions made this impossible. In Latin America, as in Europe, the war ended amid socio-political crisis: unions and leftist parties, some inspired by the Russian Revolution, protested against the rising cost of living, or resisted the lay-offs and wage cuts which companies, such as the British railways in Argentina, implemented in order to shore up their sagging profits.[10] Hence the end of the war coincided with unprecedented labour unrest, during which British interests threw their weight behind the repressive policies of panicky governments and their paramilitary auxiliaries: on the docks of Buenos Aires and Valparaíso; in the lumber camps of the Argentine interior and the nitrate *oficinas* of northern Chile.[11] Argentina, where Britain's

[8] Albert, *South America*, pp. 58, 65 (quoting *La Prensa*, 7 April 1917), 67, 71; Fritsch, *External Constraints*, p. 47.

[9] Albert, *South America*, pp. 66, 78–79, 180, 187–97, 222, 317; Fritsch, *External Constraints*, pp. 43, 161. As these sources make clear, there is considerable debate concerning the scale and significance of import substitution industrialization during the war. Some countries, such as Peru, retained a relatively open, orthodox economic model; Mexico, undergoing a massive social revolution, was a law unto itself.

[10] David Rock, *Politics in Argentina, 1890–1930* (Cambridge, 1975), pp. 134–35.

[11] Monteón, *Chile in the Nitrate Era*, pp. 138–40; Rock, *Politics in Argentina*, chaps. 6–8; C. Mallet to Foreign Office, 29 Dec. 1919, F[oreign] O[ffice] 371/4408.

biggest economic interests confronted a militant labour movement and a new reformist (Radical Party) government, was the test case. When, after 1916, the Yrigoyen administration seemed to pander to proletarian demands—on the docks, on the railways, and in the meat-packing plants—British officials threatened to boycott Argentine ports and end Argentine grain purchases. More significantly, since these threats were largely bluster, local British interests aligned with Argentine businessmen to form the strike-breaking National Labour Association and the conservative Liga Patriótica, which played a key role in repressing supposed subversion and driving the Radical government to the right during the post-war crisis. Thus, while external, official, British pressure had limited impact, the 'underlying interdependence and solidarity' linking British business and the Argentine propertied élite certainly counted.[12] In distant Tierra del Fuego, Scottish sheepfarmers 'on farms the size of European principalities' raised their glasses to Major Varela, the 'hyena of Patagonia', who had suppressed an Anarchist movement of day-labourers, killing some two thousand.[13] 'The British companies', concluded *La Epoca*, 'are being run by their local directorates, whose members are playing about with politics.'[14] With the defeat of the left, and the Radicals' lurch to the right, the old Anglo-Argentine collaborative team won the day. But it was its last major victory, and it depended more on domestic political alignments, including the electoral calculations of the Radicals, than on external British pressure, political or economic.

Mexico provided a marked contrast and salutary warning. The 1910 Revolution sundered the ties of Anglo-Mexican collaboration, evicted the old Porfirian oligarchs, and brought to power a new populist coalition committed to a measure of social reform and economic nationalism, as evidenced in the radical Constitution of 1917. Among the first acts of the victorious revolutionaries when they occupied the capital in 1914 was the expulsion of the British Minister, who was, justifiably, accused of having favoured the ousted counter-revolutionary government of Victoriano Huerta. A decade of British lamentations later, the acting Minister was again expelled, following an embarrassing blockade of the British Legation, this time for his imprudent and outspoken opposition to revolutionary land reform.[15] Significantly, British interests were temporarily entrusted to the Americans. For, though the Revolution challenged US hegemony, it could not subvert it; while the fall of the Europhile Porfirian oligarchy removed Britain's old

[12] Rock, *Politics in Argentina*, pp. 151–55, 181–90.

[13] Alistair Hennessy, 'Argentines, Anglo-Argentines and Others', in Hennessy and King, *The Land That England Lost*, p. 18.

[14] Rock, *Politics in Argentina*, p. 187.

[15] Alan Knight, 'British Attitudes Toward the Mexican Revolution, 1910–40', in Wm. Roger Louis, ed., *Adventures With Britannia: Personalities, Politics and Culture in Britain* (Austin, Tex., 1995), pp. 277–86.

collaborators, forcing British interests to come to a belated and grudging recognition of the revolutionary regime. Mexico was unusual. Elsewhere in Latin America the oligarchs survived. But everywhere they faced renewed challenges: from middle-class reformers, charmed by Wilsonian rhetoric; from leftist movements which, though defeated, were not eliminated; and from fierce, even fascist, nationalist critics of liberal cosmopolitanism. For, as in Europe, the advance of the Left ended with the dramatic economic downswing of 1920–21, when the forces of order prevailed over the forces of movement; yet the 'shattering effect' of the post-war recession reminded Latin Americans of their vulnerability to external shocks, which the war had enhanced, forcing them to question the old assumptions of liberal capitalist collaboration.[16]

If the socio-political crisis was weathered, and 'bourgeois' Latin America was loosely recast, economic change proved irreversible. Despite a modest recovery, Britain never recaptured its pre-war supremacy, and the—largely economic—diplomacy of the 1920s focused on 'crisis management'.[17] The German threat had been briefly conjured, but it soon returned, particularly in Brazil, where German market share—zero in 1918—rose to 12 per cent in 1929 and 25 per cent in 1938 (compare Britain's share: 21 per cent and 10 per cent). In Latin America as a whole German imports accounted for 17 per cent of the market in 1938, compared to Britain's 12 per cent.[18] More important, the war had hugely benefited US interests at the expense of British. Already commercially dominant in the Caribbean region, the United States now made dramatic advances in Brazil and northern and western South America, where US interests came to dominate Venezuelan oil, Chilean and Peruvian mining, and both imports and banking in most republics. The inevitable effects of war were compounded by US policy: the opening of the Panama Canal in 1914; the establishment of direct cable lines to Brazil and Argentina, which broke a British monopoly; active State Department encouragement; and the ubiquitous Kemmerer financial missions of the 1920s. British interests, watching the balance tip against them, were preoccupied but helpless; they complained of the apparent indifference of their government which, at best, provided Chile with a naval mission, while the Americans had sent military advisers, nitrate experts, and sanitary engineers.[19] Anglophile Chileans, too,

[16] Fritsch, *External Constraints*, p. 57; Victor Bulmer-Thomas, *The Economic History of Latin America Since Independence* (Cambridge, 1994), pp. 162–63.

[17] Rory Miller, *Britain and Latin America in the Nineteenth and Twentieth Centuries* (London, 1993), p. 180.

[18] Bulmer-Thomas, *Economic History of Latin America*, p. 240; Stanley Hilton, *Brazil and the Great Powers, 1930–1939* (Austin, Tex., 1975), pp. xx, 137.

[19] Paul W. Drake, *The Money Doctor in the Andes: The Kemmerer Missions, 1923–33* (Durham, NC, 1989), pp. 80, 112, 198–97, 217; Leslie Bethell, 'Britain and Latin America in Historical Perspective', in Victor Bulmer-Thomas, ed., *Britain and Latin America: A Changing Relationship* (London, 1989), p. 15.

expressed fears of US expansionism and lamented their country's 'strange and unhealthy fascination with the US'; but there was little they could do to restore the good old days of Anglo-Chilean collaboration.[20] As regards Argentina, although Britain remained the country's biggest overseas market, imports from the United States now ran British imports close. If British trade, particularly British exports, suffered most, the shift in the balance of investment, though less pronounced, was also symptomatic (see Tables 27.1–27.3).[21]

The war decisively accelerated pre-war trends. The American advance derived less from conjunctural events than from shifts in structural relationships, which were grounded in the global political economy. US industry could produce the newer manufactures which the second industrial revolution had pioneered: chemicals, electrical goods, motor cars. Where Britain's nineteenth-century

TABLE 27.1. *Latin American imports: market shares, 1913 and 1929* (%)

	1913		1929	
	US	UK	US	UK
Colombia	25	21	46	15
Peru	28	28	42	14
Chile	17	35	32	18
Brazil	16	24	27	21
Argentina	15	31	26	19

Sources: Collated from B. R. Mitchell, *British Historical Statistics: The Americas, 1750–1988* (Basingstoke, 1993), pp. 435–37, 470–72; Bulmer-Thomas, *Economic History of Latin America*, pp. 104, 159; Miller, *Britain and Latin America*, p. 111.

TABLE 27.2. *Latin American exports: destinations, 1913 and 1929* (%)

	1913		1929	
	US	UK	US	UK
Colombia	45	15	75	5
Peru	34	36	35	19
Chile	21	39	25	13
Brazil	32	13	45	8
Argentina	5	25	8	32

Sources: As for Table 27.1.

[20] Monteón, *Chile in the Nitrate Era*, pp. 154, 158.

[21] Data compiled from several sources, including Drake, *The Money Doctor*, pp. 32, 77, 119, and Miller, *Britain and Latin America*, pp. 190, 194, 210. There are noticeable discrepancies in most series and, as Miller (p. 194) warns, some Latin American trade figures are 'notoriously unreliable'.

TABLE 27.3. *Foreign investment in Latin America, 1913 and 1929* (current US$m)

	1913		1929	
	US	UK	US	UK
Peru	35	133	151	141
Chile	15	332	396	390
Brazil	50	1,161	476	1,414
Argentina	40	1,861	611	2,140

Sources: As for Table 27.1.

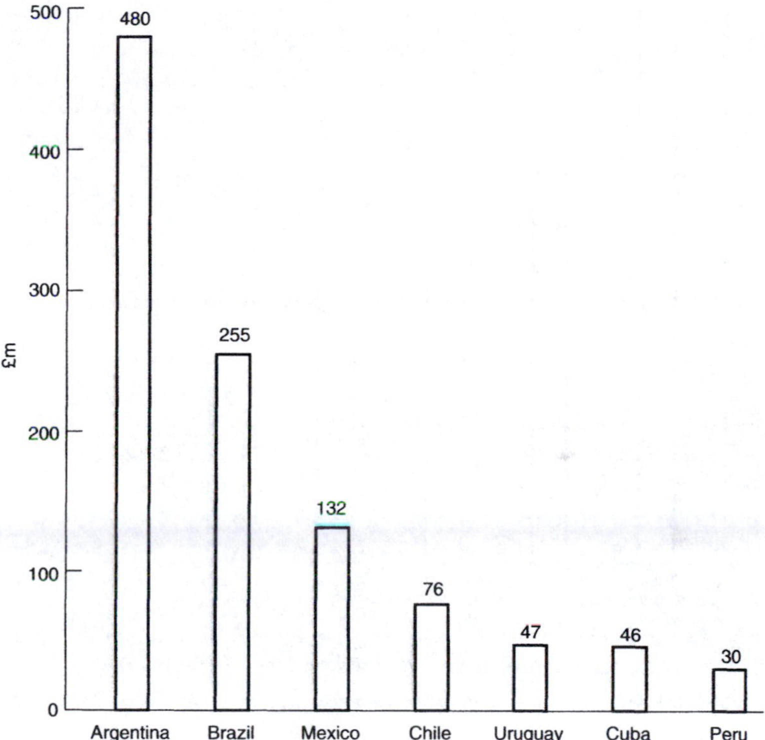

FIGURE 27.1. British investment in seven Latin American countries *c.*1913 (in £m)

Source: Irving Stone, 'British Direct Investment and Portfolio Investment in Latin America before 1914', *Journal of Economic History*, XXXVII, 3 (Sept. 1977), p. 695.

hegemony had been based on railways, coal, and textiles, that of the United States in the twentieth century depended on roads, radios, refrigerators, oil, trucks, and cars—especially the ubiquitous *fordcito* which now clogged the streets of Buenos

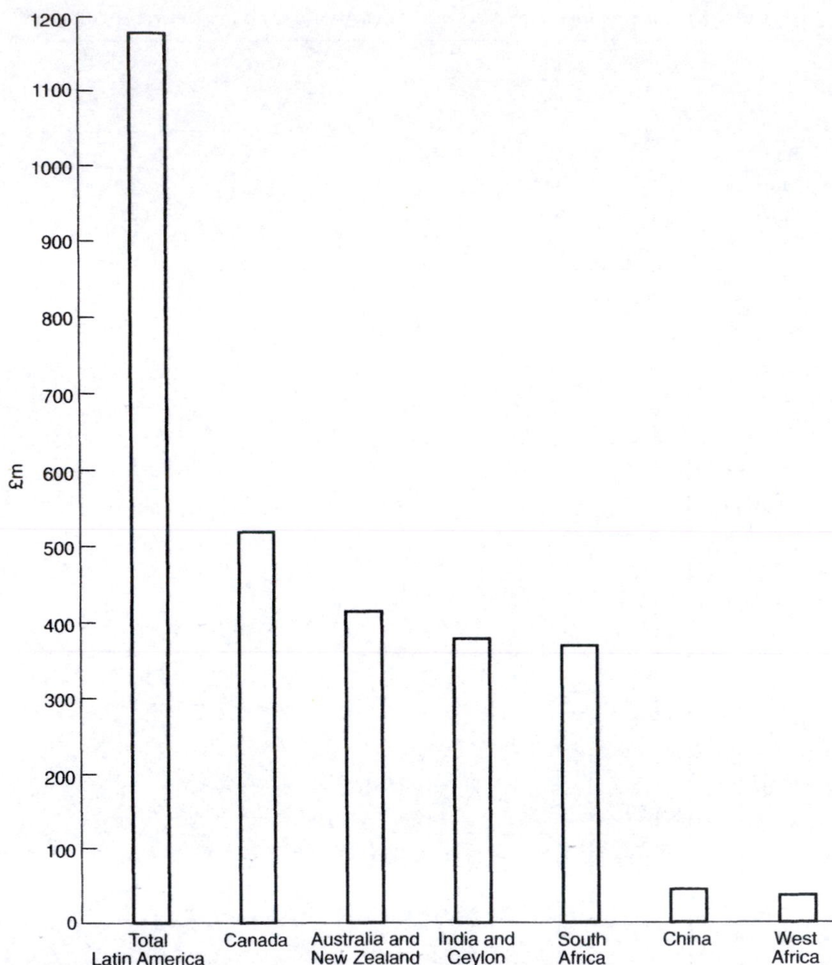

FIGURE 27.2. British investment in Australia, New Zealand, Canada, India and Ceylon, South Africa, West Africa, China, and Latin America in 1913/1914 (in £m)

Source: Stone, 'British Direct Investment', p. 695; Herbert Feis, *Europe, the World's Banker*, 1870–1914 (New York, 1965 edn.) p. 55.

Aires or plied the rough, rural roads of Mexico and Peru.[22] Established railway routes suffered from road competition, and railway profits, rarely that buoyant, declined; urban tramways, often British enterprises, gave way to buses and taxis and, in the process, incurred the criticism of consumers who alleged poor service

[22] Raúl García Heras, 'Hostage Private Companies under Restraint: British Railways and Transport Coordination Policy in Argentina during the 1930s', *Journal of Latin American Studies*, XIX (1987),

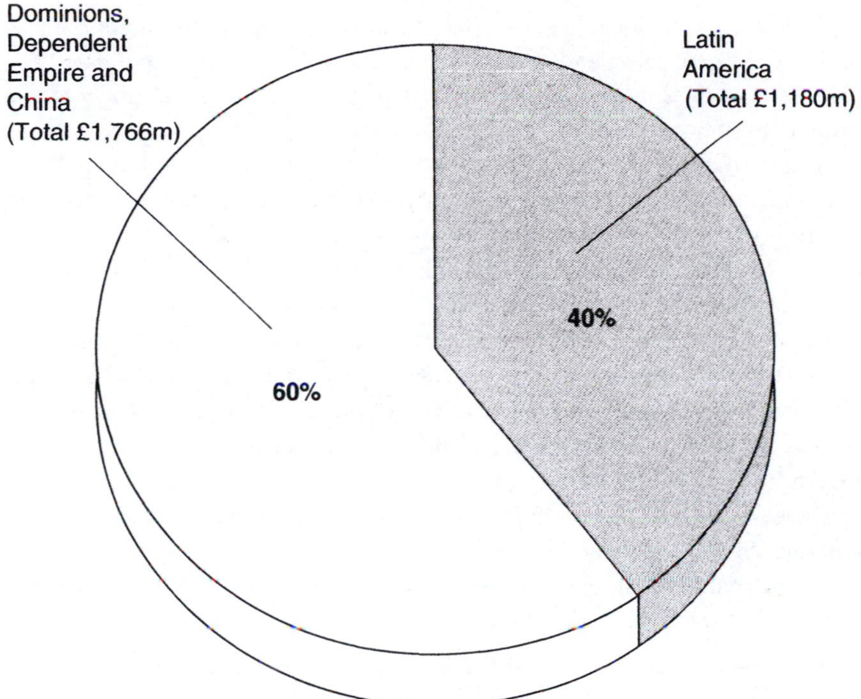

FIGURE 27.3. British investments in Latin America and the Dominions, and other regions, 1913 / 1914 (£m)

Source: Stone, 'British Direct Investment' p. 695; Feis, *Europe, the World's Banker*, p. 55.

and price-gouging.[23] In the skies too, it was the Americans, and sometimes the Germans, who pioneered Latin American civil aviation. Meanwhile, the legacy of pre-war British direct investment was something of a *damnosa haereditas* since unpopular enterprises—trams, trains, electric companies—soured local relations, distracted diplomatic attention away from trade, and provoked economic nationalist critiques.[24] Burgeoning US trade and investment also incurred criticism; but, like Britain in the previous century, the United States was now seen by many Latin Americans as the dynamo of economic development and the fount of economic

pp. 44–45, 49, 64; Hilton, *Brazil and the Great Powers*, pp. 75–76; and, on Britain's failure to compete in the consumer durable market, Callum A. MacDonald, 'End of Empire: the Decline of the Anglo-Argentine Connection, 1918–1951', in Hennessy and King, *The Land That England Lost*, p. 85.

[23] Miller, *Britain and Latin America*, p. 197; García Heras, 'Hostage Private Companies', p. 42.

[24] Miller, *Britain and Latin America*, pp. 212–3; Winthrop R. Wright, *British-Owned Railways in Argentina* (Austin, Tex., 1974), chaps. 9, 10.

expertise: Peru's President Leguía (1919–30) hung a portrait of President Monroe in the presidential palace and declared the Fourth of July a national holiday.[25] The discursive symbols, as well as the flows of trade and capital, had undergone a profound shift.

Foreign competition obliged Britain to step up the export-promotion policy it had begun around the turn of the century. Commercial and financial missions steamed across the Atlantic, trying to bolster Britain's declining position: De Bunsen in 1918; Montague in 1924; D'Abernon in 1929; Niemeyer in 1931. The Prince of Wales, the future Edward VIII, 'representative of a glorious dynasty', as President Alvear hailed him, visited Buenos Aires in 1925, where he talked up British trade and fulfilled a round of engagements which exemplified both the historic depth and the stuffy traditionalism of the Anglo-Argentine relationship: 10 a.m., St Andrews College; 11 a.m., the British Hospital; 12.30 p.m., lunch with the British Chamber of Commerce; 2.30 p.m., polo at the Hurlingham Club.[26]

These commercial efforts enjoyed scant success; they sometimes displayed 'an amazing [British] capacity for self-delusion'; and they ran against a tide of economic change which swamped puny government inputs.[27] The financial missions carried somewhat more clout, and they reflected what P. J. Cain and A. G. Hopkins rightly see as the financial bias of British policy during the inter-war period. But these missions too made limited headway.[28] The 1924 Montagu mission to Brazil, manned by City worthies 'with no particular competence on Brazilian affairs', offered a loan on harsh terms, which offended nationalist sensibilities (it was seen as 'an attempt to turn Brazil into a British colony'). As it was, a British government veto of foreign government loans, itself a product of Britain's painful post-war financial restructuring, quashed the deal and obliged the Brazilians to turn to New York, as the Colombians, Peruvians, and Chileans were already doing. Two years later Brazil secured another US loan in the teeth of British (Rothschild) opposition.[29] When the Bank of England's Sir Otto Niemeyer

[25] Drake, *The Money Doctor*, p. 111.

[26] Miller, *Britain and Latin America*, pp. 184, 199, 216, 221; Marcelo de Paiva Abreu, 'Anglo-Brazilian Economic Relations and the Consolidation of American Pre-eminence in Brazil, 1930–45', in Christopher Abel and Colin Lewis, eds., *Latin America, Economic Imperialism and the State* (London, 1985), p. 382; John King, 'The Influence of British Culture in Argentina', in Hennessy and King, *The Land That England Lost*, p. 166.

[27] Miller, *Britain and Latin America*, p. 200. The same author notes the 'aristocratic detachment' of Foreign Office officials who were shocked to learn that Vickers included financial inducements in their tender for a Peruvian naval contract in 1928–29: Rory Miller, 'Foreign Capital, The State and Political Corruption in Latin America Between Independence and the Depression', in Walter Little and Eduardo Posada-Carbó, eds., *Political Corruption in Europe and Latin America* (London, 1996), p. 79.

[28] P. J. Cain and A. G. Hopkins, *British Imperialism: Crisis and Deconstruction, 1914–1990* (London, 1993), pp. 160, 161, 169 and *passim*; Fritsch, *External Constraints*, p. 236.

[29] Fritsch, *External Constraints*, pp. 85–101, 117; Drake, *The Money Doctor*, pp. 31, 79, 108, 213.

visited Brazil in the wake of the world slump, peddling another structural adjustment package, he 'came to a country which was rapidly becoming an undisputed area of American influence'; President Getulio Vargas 'quietly ignored' his 'highly orthodox' financial recommendations and later suspended debt payments.[30] While cleverly playing the field during the turbulent 1930s, Vargas, it is clear, had decided to 'throw Brazil's lot in the U.S.'; if there was an alternative, it was Germany, not Great Britain.[31] Relative British impotence contrasted with the enhanced vigour of the United States, whose banks had successfully penetrated Latin America during the war and whose celebrated 'money doctor', Dr Edwin Kemmerer, perambulated Latin America in the 1920s, purveying an orthodox reformist package which, enthusiastically taken up by national élites, both attested to and further fortified US financial hegemony in most of the continent.[32] If Britain's financial démarches—in Brazil, for example—displayed imperialist motives (which is, in itself, highly debatable), the fact is they were strikingly unsuccessful; by 1939 Rothschilds, Brazil's historic bankers, were lamenting both the rapid erosion of Britain's 'prestige and past performance' and the complacent inertia with which this decline was greeted.[33] In Chile, where the American Morgans had supplanted Rothschilds during the war, the British Commercial Secretary noted the influx of US investment—in bonds, borax, copper, telephones, and steel—and the concomitant boom in United States–Chilean trade: 'the old saying that "trade follows the flag",' he concluded, 'may today be changed to "commerce follows finance".'[34]

The main exception to this continental trend was Argentina. Hence, any analysis of British 'imperialism', especially in its twilight years, must adopt an Argentine focus: 'Argentina', as the British Ambassador put it in 1929, 'must be regarded as an essential part of the British Empire,' a statement which, hyperbolic even in the Argentine context, would have been nonsensical elsewhere in Latin America.[35] In Argentina too, the war accelerated challenges to British pre-eminence, as the United States increased its exports of both goods and capital. For example, the British and American shares of the lucrative meat-packing pool, fixed in 1911 at 41 and 40 per cent respectively, shifted to 55 and 35 per cent in 1927.[36] But the United States could never achieve that neat complementarity with the Argentine economy

[30] Miller, *Britain and Latin America*, p. 222; de Paiva Abreu, 'Anglo-Brazilian Economic Relations', p. 382.

[31] Hilton, *Brazil and the Great Powers*, pp. 51, 55, 67–68.

[32] Albert, *South America*, pp. 104–05; Drake, *The Money Doctor.*

[33] Miller, *Britain and Latin America*, p. 211.

[34] Monteón, *Chile in the Nitrate Era*, p. 173.

[35] Wright, *British-Owned Railways*, p. 135, quoting Sir Malcolm Robertson.

[36] H. S. Ferns, *The Argentine Republic, 1516–1971* (Newton Abbot, 1973), pp. 110–11; see also Tables 27.1–27.3 above.

that Britain enjoyed. (Conversely, the Brazilian economy, exporting coffee to the world's most insatiable coffee-drinkers, meshed neatly with the American market; Brazil's geopolitical alignment with the United States, the British believed, was an example of 'cupboard love').[37] Argentine exports—grain, beef, and linseed—competed with US production and fell foul of US agrarian protection, which strengthened in the 1930s. As a result, exports to the United States always trailed exports to Britain; and they fell, both absolutely and relatively, during the protectionist 1930s.[38] The British market remained dominant; but, since Britain could no longer effectively meet Argentinian demand for manufactures, a fragile triangular trade pattern emerged: Britain had a large negative trade balance with Argentina, compared to a generally positive balance with Brazil.[39]

Such a pattern, albeit a product of industrial decline and conjunctural depression, conferred certain economic and political advantages: as Argentina's chief market, with which Argentina enjoyed a healthy trade surplus, Britain could advance her financial interests, sustaining collaborative relations with the Argentine political élite and its export-dependent *porteño* constituency.[40] In Brazil, by contrast, US dominance of coffee exports redounded to American financial advantage. During the protectionist 1930s, therefore, the powerful logic of reciprocity—'comprar a quien nos compra' ('buy from those who buy from us')—tended to reinforce pre-existing patterns of trade, investment, perhaps 'dependency'.[41] Britain also enjoyed an intimate relationship with Argentina's landed élite who, though briefly disconcerted by the electoral victory of Yrigoyen's Radicals in 1916, staged a political comeback in the 1930s, when a military coup installed a conservative, Anglophile, *estanciero* regime. 'From our point of view,' the Foreign Office gratefully noted, 'the older generation are definitely an advantage at the head of affairs.'[42] Anglo-Argentinian intimacy

[37] Bryce Wood, *The Dismantling of the Good Neighbor Policy* (Austin, Tex., 1985), p. 18. The British also believed, however, that the United States was surprisingly restrained in its use of this economic lever: Hilton, *Brazil and the Great Powers*, p. 49.

[38] Laura Randall, *An Economic History of Argentina in the Twentieth Century* (New York, 1978), p. 215; Ferns, *The Argentine Republic*, p. 121; the protectionist Smoot–Hawley tariff caused 'depression and consternation' in Argentina: Joseph S. Tulchin, 'Decolonizing an Informal Empire: Argentina, Britain and the United States, 1930–43', *International Interactions*, I (1974), p. 127.

[39] Miller, *Britain and Latin America*, p. 208.

[40] Rock, *Politics in Argentina*, p. 239; Tulchin, 'Decolonizing an Informal Empire', p. 131. *Porteño* denotes from Buenos Aires.

[41] De Paiva Abreu, 'Anglo-Brazilian Economic Relations', p. 383; Wright, *British-Owned Railways*, p. 135.

[42] MacDonald, 'End of Empire', p. 84. Rock, *Politics in Argentina*, shows that, despite initial fears, the Radicals did not live up to their name; the crisis of 1919—British lobbying included—deflected them to the right, where the logic of the Argentine political economy tended to keep them through the 1920s. British interests were thus reassured, but this did not stop them applauding the oligarchic revival of the 1930s.

received clear commercial expression: a short-lived trade agreement, brokered by D'Abernon in 1929, which lapsed under the impact of the Depression; and the more enduring Roca–Runciman Pact of 1933, which came to symbolize, according to taste, Argentina's dependency, honorary Dominion Status, or ineluctable economic destiny. The Pact, coming hard on the heels of the 1932 Ottawa Conference, guaranteed Argentina continued access to the British market in return for lower tariffs on British exports, a guaranteed British stake in meat-shipping, and a vague assurance of preferential treatment for Britain's hard-pressed railways (which was never implemented). A British loan, which facilitated the release of blocked foreign balances, completed the package.[43]

For Argentine nationalists, then and since, the Pact carried the stigma of economic servitude. Certainly it had important political repercussions, and served to focus the mounting critique of British 'imperialism'. Its economic significance is more debatable. Clearly, it mirrored the age: a time not only of British Imperial Preference, but also of United States and German trade bilateralism. As such, it obeyed a hard-headed logic which even moderate economic nationalists such as Raúl Prebisch, the intellectual founding father of the United Nations Economic Commission for Latin America, could endorse; it fell short of 'economic imperialism' in the traditional sense; and it was also reasonably successful: Anglo-Argentinian trade flourished through the 1930s (though the railways continued to decline) and, in terms of economic growth, Argentina compared well with Latin America, while outstripping Canada or the United States.[44] From the point of view of its architects, therefore, this last, clearest manifestation of Anglo-Argentine economic complementarity was a success. Critics dissented: not simply the choleric nationalists of right and left, but also members of the Argentine public, who felt that the British had got too generous a deal, to Argentina's disadvantage. The Pact thus seemed to symbolize and cement the old alliance between British capital and the conservative Argentine élite, whose political tenure the British clearly favoured, even though circumstances, domestic and international, would soon bring it to a brusque conclusion.[45]

[43] On the Pact—which is the subject of an extensive literature—see Peter Alhadeff, 'Dependency, Historiography and Objections to the Roca-Runciman Pact', in Abel and Lewis, *Latin America*, pp. 367–78; Wright, *British-Owned Railways*, pp. 142–45; Tulchin, 'Decolonizing an Informal Empire', pp. 130–02; Roger Gravil, *The Anglo-Argentine Connection, 1900–39* (Boulder, Colo., 1985); Miller, *Britain and Latin America*, pp. 216–19.

[44] Raúl Prebisch, 'Argentine Economic Policies since the 1930s: Recollections', in Guido di Tella and D. C. M. Platt, eds., *The Political Economy of Argentina, 1880–1946* (Basingstoke, 1986), pp. 142–43; H. S. Ferns, *The Argentine Republic, 1516–1971* (Newton Abbot, 1973), pp. 124–38.

[45] Miller, *Britain and Latin America*, p. 217, illustrates British desire to prop up the political and economic status quo in Argentina (1932); for the Argentine reaction, which combined resentment at both Britain and the United States, Tulchin, 'Decolonizing an Informal Empire', p. 137.

These circumstances included a growing economic introversion, a switch, roughly speaking, from 'outward-oriented' to 'inward-oriented' development, and mounting Great Power rivalry, which culminated in the Second World War. During the 1930s efforts to restore the old free-trading global system collapsed irrevocably. The larger Latin American economies, those where the British presence was greatest, took the path of economic nationalism, import-substitution, and exchange controls. Markets for British exports, already hard hit by US competition, shrank further. External trade became more managed: Britain's reciprocity treaty with Argentina was paralleled by the US–Cuban agreement of 1934; Germany concluded bilateral deals with Latin American countries, Brazil in particular, which boosted German exports (coal, chemicals, machinery, and electrical goods) above Britain's. By 1935 the harbours of Santos, Bahía, Rio, and Recife were crowded with ships flying the swastika flag.[46]

Given the regulated character of trade in the 1930s, commercial competition and geopolitical rivalry meshed even more than in the past; after 1936, as the shadow of Axis aggression fell across Europe, geopolitical concerns began to determine commercial policy as never before.[47] Now, however, Britain readily deferred to the 'happily enormous power' of the United States, which assumed the self-appointed role of hemispheric shield against Fascist aggression. Outside Argentina, Great Power rivalry pitted the United States against Germany, and Latin American fears of external aggression clearly focused on the Axis powers as well as their own local rivals.[48] Britain was now economically secondary, geopolitically tertiary. Meanwhile, amid Depression and geopolitical rivalry, the opportunity cost of Latin American economic nationalism diminished: reformist regimes could get away with demonstrations of independence which, in the past, would have incurred Anglo-American displeasure, even sanctions. Bolivia nationalized Standard Oil in 1937; a year later the Mexican government resolved a bitter industrial dispute by nationalizing the major Anglo-American oil companies. Though British interests were hardest hit (Royal-Dutch Shell owned the buoyant Aguila Oil Company), there was little the British could do without United States backing, which was not forthcoming, since the Americans rated Caribbean security ahead of petroleum

[46] Hilton, *Brazil and the Great Powers*, p. 84; de Paiva Abreu, 'Anglo-Brazilian Economic Relations', p. 383.

[47] Hilton, *Brazil and the Great Powers*, pp. 132, 167.

[48] Drake, *The Money Doctor*, pp. 210–11; Michael Grow, *The Good Neighbor Policy and Authoritarianism in Paraguay* (Lawrence, Kan., 1981), pp. 26–38; Hilton, *Brazil and the Great Powers*, pp. 11, 146, 152, 183, which feeds into Cain and Hopkins, *British Imperialism*, pp. 146, 152–53, who, while rightly discerning a 'new scramble for influence' in Latin America (p. 147), tend to exaggerate Britain's role: Latin American perceptions of a 'new era of colonial ambitions' focused on the Axis powers, not Britain.

profits, just as the Mexicans had calculated that they would. The British lodged a peremptory protest, which provoked a diplomatic rupture with Mexico, while they shook their heads at the United States's tolerance of this 'unwelcome independence of behaviour', which Roosevelt's Good Neighbor Policy appeared to encourage.[49]

The British also gave vent to the familiar racist and imperialist stereotypes, relics of the nineteenth century which survived well into the twentieth. Revolutionary Mexico had long been the butt of British criticism and condescension; by the 1930s, as the expropriation of foreign oil, railways, and real estate reached a peak under President Cárdenas (1934–40), the chorus of complaint expanded beyond the usual suspects, businessmen, diplomats, and consuls, to include the peripatetic literary doomsayers Graham Greene and Evelyn Waugh.[50] Mexico gave greatest cause for complaint, but old attitudes died hard throughout the continent. According to the US Ambassador, a 'blimpish complacency' and a 'refusal to see any good points in foreigners of any nationality' characterized the British community in Venezuela, especially the women.[51] A Foreign Office official greeted the 1943 coup in Argentina as one carried out 'in the best Nigger-Republic style'.[52] If the old stereotypes lingered, however, there was now little the British could do to act upon their 'imperialist' assumptions. Even in Argentina their economic leverage was in decline; elsewhere it was a spent force. As Mexican opinion averred in 1938: 'England didn't have to be taken into account, it was clapped out, and everyone regarded it as a complete joke, seeing its old power in complete decline.'[53] And Britain could not free-ride on US coercion, since the Good Neighbor Policy now explicitly ruled out intervention.[54]

The Second World War crystallized these relationships. Once again, the Allies imposed a barrage of controls on Latin American trade and blacklisted Axis

[49] Wood, *Dismantling of the Good Neighbor Policy*, pp. xii, 27–28. Lorenzo Meyer, *Su Majestad Británica contra la Revolución Mexicana* (Mexico, 1991) is the best account of the Anglo-Mexican conflict.

[50] Graham Greene, *The Lawless Roads* (London, 1939); Evelyn Waugh, *Robbery Under Law* (London, 1939).

[51] Wood, *Dismantling of the Good Neighbor Policy*, p. 17.

[52] Ibid., pp. 19, 217.

[53] Knight, 'British Attitudes Towards the Mexican Revolution', p. 285.

[54] While considering the Good Neighbour Policy to be feeble, the British also suspected that—in Mexico, for example—it was also a ploy designed to curry commercial favour, in which respect they were not wholly wrong; an informed American observer called it a 'supercolossal trade promotion scheme in dignified attire': Nicholas J. Spykman, quoted in David Rock, 'War and Postwar Intersections: Latin America and the United States', in David Rock, ed., *Latin America in the 1940s* (Berkeley, 1994), p. 22. Like Britain in the later nineteenth century, the United States could do profitable business in Latin America without mounting—indeed, by priding itself on *not* mounting—politico-military interventions in the region: in each case because the metropolitan power was economically hegemonic, while the periphery was congenially receptive.

MAP 27.1. Latin America in the Mid-Twentieth Century

interests. The United States concluded trade agreements from the Rio Grande to the Rio de la Plata, channelled development funds to Latin American governments, mounted an extensive propaganda campaign throughout the continent, and became a major market for Latin American commodities such as Uruguayan wool and Bolivian tin, which had previously flowed to Europe. Meanwhile, British trade with Latin America slumped; by 1945 Britain took only 12 per cent of Latin America's exports, compared to the United States's 49 per cent, and supplied only 4 per cent of the region's imports, compared to the United States's 58 per cent.[55] As in 1914–18, wartime expedience conspired with long-term economic planning. British observers had no doubt that the US diplomatic and economic offensive aimed not only at defeating Germany and Japan, but also at supplanting British interests, even in their last redoubt in the southern cone, where US and British businessmen were at loggerheads. They were not far wrong: US policy-makers clearly intended that, as the President of the US Chamber of Commerce put it, 'just as the last century in Latin America was a "British Century" the next would be an American century'.[56]

Throughout most of Latin America, incumbent élites were disposed to collaborate with the new North American hegemony. Even progressive opinion—Cárdenas in Mexico, Betancourt in Venezuela, Figueras in Costa Rica—now looked to the United States of the New Deal and the Atlantic Charter for political inspiration, rather as their grandfathers had looked to Victorian Britain. The British could not stand against these mutually reinforcing economic, political, and cultural currents, especially at a time of supreme national crisis. They allowed the United States–Brazilian détente to deepen; they ignored J. M. Keynes's suggestion that Britain build up a British cotton reserve in Brazil, for fear that it would antagonize US southern Senators; and they deferred to the United States's tendency to regard Brazil, if not all Latin America, as 'a special preserve'.[57] In Argentina, where Britain had most to lose, the story was different, although more by virtue of Argentine recalcitrance than British resistance. As the United States mounted its Good Neighbor diplomacy during the 1930s and its hemispheric mobilization during the 1940s, Argentina stood out as the chief obstacle: commercially tied to Britain, geopolitically jealous of its supposed South American hegemony, and, to a degree, sympathetic to the Axis cause. After 1941 Argentina, unlike Mexico or Brazil, held out for neutrality and tried to persuade

[55] R. A. Humphreys, *Latin America and the Second World War*, 2 vols. (London, 1981; 1982), I, pp. 126, 127, 129; Bulmer-Thomas, *The Economic History of Latin America*, p. 240.

[56] Humphreys, I, pp. 140–41; Grow, *Good Neighbor Policy*, p. 90; Charles Jones, *El Reino Unido y América: Inversiones e influencia económica* (Madrid, 1992), pp. 209–10.

[57] Wood, *Dismantling the Good Neighbor Policy*, p. 16; de Paiva Abreu, 'Anglo-Brazilian Economic Relations', p. 393.

other South American states accordingly, thus incurring the outspoken displeasure of the United States.[58]

For the British, old commercial ties, and the major contribution they now made to the British war effort, overrode geopolitical calculations. While the British would have welcomed a declaration of war by Argentina—'this shameful caitiff neutral', in Churchill's words—they took a more pragmatic view than the United States, basing their policy on 'enlightened self-interest' rather than 'thwarted rage'.[59] Above all, Britain had to maintain both the flow of Argentine foodstuffs and the Argentine government's acceptance of blocked sterling balances: a trade of 'good meat against apparently useless sterling', as the President of the Board of Trade candidly admitted.[60] For the duration of the war, British policy was reasonably successful: Britain's accumulated capital in Argentina, both material and moral, helped fight the war, which was the overriding priority. But in the process both were fast run down. By 1946 Argentina had £130m in blocked sterling balances, part of that 'prodigious total' which, as Keynes said, 'by cunning and kindness we have persuaded the outside world to lend us' in order to pay for the war.[61] In this sense, Britain's biggest Latin American investments, the fruits of a century of entrepreneurship in the southern cone, stood Britain in good stead; the more so since, for its part, the Argentine government of Juan Domingo Perón obligingly devoted the bulk of these balances to the purchase of the dilapidated British railways and utilities, paying over the odds for assets which the British had, to a degree, already discounted.[62] Similar sell-offs occurred, with less nationalist fanfare, in Brazil and Uruguay.[63]

Perón's rise to power also indicated a broader nationalist rejection of the old political order, its intimate British connection, and Argentina's supposed 'dependency' as exemplified by the Roca–Runciman pact. The march of the *descamisados* [workers] on downtown Buenos Aires in October 1946 symbolized the end of an era, the fall of the old *estanciero* (landowner) élite, and the rise of a populist political coalition dedicated to industrialization, economic nationalism, and

[58] Wood, *Dismantling the Good Neighbor Policy*, pp. 4, 30, 40.

[59] Ibid., pp. 18–19, 30, 57–58, 126, 217. Humphreys, *Latin America and the Second World War*, I, pp. 141–43, makes clear that the British did not, as sometimes alleged, positively favour, and connive at, Argentine neutrality.

[60] Jorge Fodor, 'The Origin of Argentina's Sterling Balances, 1939–43', in di Tella and Platt, *Political Economy of Argentina*, p. 168.

[61] Fodor, 'The Origin of Argentina's Sterling Balances', p. 178.

[62] Wright, *British-Owned Railways*, chap. 13, which notes (p. 266) that 'the best evidence that Argentina did not make such a good deal is that the British seemed quite happy about it'.

[63] De Paiva Abreu, 'Anglo-Brazilian Economic Relations', pp. 388, 393; M. H. J. Finch, *A Political Economy of Uruguay since 1870* (Basingstoke, 1981), p. 218, which suggests that the Uruguayan railways were no bargain either. In its small way, British 'decolonization' of its South American 'informal empire' appears to have been quite self-servingly adroit.

social reform: a transformation which the British might repudiate, as they had in Mexico a generation before, but which, despite its 'drivelling rhetoric' and 'chauvinistic foolishness', neither they nor the Americans could resist.[64] By 1947 the British had concluded that it was useless to 'kick against the pricks' of Argentine nationalism; financial vested interests would have to be sacrificed on the altar of a revived and updated trade relationship.[65]

Such a relationship never emerged. After 1945 there was no British trade offensive as there had been after 1918. Britain's post-war economy could not meet Argentine needs ('Argentina does not live on whisky and lipstick,' the British were reminded); and British trade and investment, in Argentina as elsewhere, never recovered their old levels.[66] Even more than in the 1920s, sterling's weakness ruled out investments in the dollar area. During the long post-war economic boom, Anglo-Latin American trade languished. Between 1950 and 1986 Britain's share of Latin American trade fell from 7 per cent to less than 2 per cent. By then, Britain was selling less to Latin America than to Norway.[67] This did not, of course, deter Britain from expending quantities of blood and treasure to recover the Falklands in 1982. A massive informal empire had been peacefully relinquished, its assets devoted to the prosecution of two world wars; but a generation later the erstwhile collaborators—both sorely reduced in relative wealth and power, influenced by old atavisms, and desperate for domestic political advantage—fell to fighting over a vestigial speck of formal empire.

[64] C. A. MacDonald, 'The United States, Britain and Argentina in the Years Immediately after the Second World War', in di Tella and Platt, *Political Economy of Argentina*, p. 186. See also Roger Gravil, 'The Denigration of Peronism', in Hennessy and King, *The Land That England Lost*, pp. 93–108;

[65] MacDonald, 'The United States, Britain and Argentina', p. 185, quoting a Board of Trade official.

[66] MacDonald, 'The United States, Britain and Argentina', p. 190, quoting the head of the Argentine Economic Council, Miguel Miranda. George I. Blanksten, *Perón's Argentina* (Chicago, 1953), pp. 241, 244, notes a fall in British investment from $1,287m in 1940 to $17m in 1952, and gives market shares of Argentine imports (1947) as: United States, 45%; Britain, 8%.

[67] David Atkinson, 'Trade, Aid and Investment since 1950', in Bulmer-Thomas, *Britain and Latin America*, p. 103. British investment, particularly bank loans, rose again in the 1970s and 1980s.

Select Bibliography

CHRISTOPHER ABEL and COLIN LEWIS, eds., *Latin America, Economic Imperialism and the State* (London, 1985).

BILL ALBERT, *South America and the First World War* (Cambridge, 1988).

VICTOR BULMER-THOMAS, ed., *Britain and Latin America: A Changing Relationship* (London, 1989).

GUIDO DI TELLA and D. C. M. PLATT, eds., *The Political Economy of Argentina, 1880–1946* (Basingstoke, 1986).

WINSTON FRITSCH, *External Constraints on Economic Policy in Brazil, 1880–1930* (Basingstoke, 1988).

ROGER GRAVIL, *The Anglo-Argentine Connection, 1900–39* (Boulder, Colo., 1985).

ALISTAIR HENNESSY and JOHN KING, *The Land That England Lost: Argentina and Britain, a Special Relationship* (London, 1992).

STANLEY HILTON, *Brazil and the Great Powers, 1930–39* (Austin, Tex., 1975).

R. A. HUMPHREYS, *Latin America and the Second World War*, 2 vols. (London, 1981; 1982).

RORY MILLER, *Britain and Latin America in the Nineteenth and Twentieth Centuries* (London, 1993).

WINTHROP R. WRIGHT, *British-Owned Railways in Argentina* (Austin, Tex., 1974).

28

China

JÜRGEN OSTERHAMMEL

Britain emerged from the First World War with her overall position in the East Asian structure of power diminished, but the institutions of formal and informal empire in China unharmed. By 1918 the international configuration in East Asia had changed dramatically. The tension-ridden united front of the six Great Powers confronting China that had marked the period from the 1870s to 1914 no longer existed. During the First World War Germany had been eliminated as a player in the 'Far Eastern Game', at least until her reappearance in the early 1930s. So had Russia, before the Soviet Union emerged as the guiding spirit behind the most radical wing of Chinese nationalism and as an adversary whom British intelligence rated the most determined enemy of the Empire in the East. France, still the protector of Roman Catholic missions, retained a considerable interest in Chinese property, controlled the Yunnan Railway between Haiphong and Kunming, and owned almost a quarter of China's secured foreign debt. Yet French trade with China stagnated at a low level, and fresh direct investment failed to materialize. The French tenaciously defended their pre-war position without playing a leading part in East Asia any longer. The United States, by contrast, was assuming a new role as the dominant power in the Pacific area as a whole. She took an important diplomatic lead in the Washington Conference of 1921–22. Its cultural and missionary involvement in China was extensive: Americans spent twice as much on Chinese education as did the French with their numerous Catholic institutions, four times as much as the British, and thirty times as much as the Japanese.[1]

The United States was the only foreign country genuinely admired by the urban élites of Republican China. Her large cultural stake contrasted strikingly with a limited economic commitment. The Americans were minor creditors of the Chinese government. Their direct investments were concentrated in areas auxiliary to a dynamic import–export business. Little or no American capital was invested in Chinese mining, shipping, and manufacturing. The most important

This chapter continues that in Vol. III.

[1] Yu Changhe, 'Meiguo zai Yuandong jingji shili zhi jiepo' (American Economic Influence in the Far East), *Dongfang zazhi*, XXXIV, 10 (16 May 1937), p. 19.

American firm in China was Standard-Vacuum Oil, the principal supplier of paraffin and petrol to China. It maintained a countrywide sales organization that formed the largest single item of American direct investment in China. In 1929–30 two of the most profitable public utility companies in Shanghai passed from British into American ownership. Even so, American business interests in China were underdeveloped and dispersed. They did not add up to a multifarious and interlocking system. In short, there were considerable American interests, but it would be an exaggeration to speak of an American informal empire in China to rival those of the British and the Japanese.

The expansion of Japan was the overriding inter-imperial challenge to the British strategic and economic position in China. Japan's policy on the East Asian mainland went through a number of distinct phases. That the partner in the Anglo-Japanese Alliance of 1902 might one day make the British position uncomfortable could have been foreseen from about 1913. The Twenty-One Demands, presented to President Yuan Shih-k'ai in 1915, in an attempt to turn China into something like a Japanese protectorate, showed the imperialist intent for the first time. A few years later Japan tried, without lasting success, to manipulate the warlords in control of the Peking government. Between 1921 and 1927 a co-operative attitude towards the West regarding China prevailed, followed by a tougher line and, in September 1931, by the occupation of Manchuria, where, since 1905, the Japanese had possessed a kind of railway colony, the South Manchurian Railway and the attached 'railway zone'. Beneath the zigzag moves of Japanese foreign policy, the evolution of a Japanese informal empire in China proceeded apace. In a case of blatant economic imperialism, Japanese interests, with government backing, acquired control of the only large-scale heavy industrial complex in China proper, the Han-yeh-p'ing Works. They shut down its iron and steel production and degraded the industrial showpiece of late imperial China to a supplier of high-grade ore for the Japanese steel industry.[2] This brutal and deliberate act of de-industrialization, unparalleled in British behaviour towards China, was accompanied by investment in banking, manufacturing, mining, and shipping. By the late 1920s Japan possessed the largest network of foreign banks in China. Beginning in 1918, Japanese companies established numerous cotton mills in Shanghai, Tsingtao, and Tientsin. In 1936 Japanese-owned mills produced nearly 40 per cent of China's machine-spun yarn and about 57 per cent of all its machine-woven cloth.[3] The Japanese cotton industry, originally an exporter to China, had successfully entered into import-substitution: a step that Manchester

[2] Quan Hansheng, *Hanyeping Gongsi shilüe* (A Brief History of the Hanyeping Company) (Hong Kong, 1972), pp. 4–5.

[3] Peter Duus, 'Zakaibô: Japanese Cotton Mills in China, 1895–1937', in Peter Duus, Ramon H. Myers, and Mark R. Peattie, eds., *The Japanese Informal Empire in China, 1895–1937* (Princeton, 1989), p. 65.

never dared to take. This was one of the reasons for the collapse of British cotton exports to China in the early 1930s.

With the rapid expansion of its fully fledged informal empire in China after the First World War, Japan presented to Britain more than just a problem of grand diplomacy and strategy. It matured into a menacing rival at the Imperial periphery. There was mounting Japanese competition in many sectors of the Chinese economy where British firms were active. Only in cigarette production and oil distribution did British and American firms divide the Chinese market among themselves. The main reason why the Japanese did not achieve an even faster growth of their economic establishment in China was a shortage of capital. Their great advantages were familiarity with Eastern business practices and an abundance of manpower. Apart from its informal economic empire which covered almost all parts of China, Japan was an energetic colonial power on Taiwan, in parts of South Manchuria and, after 1931, in all three provinces of this northernmost region of China. Any discussion of modern China in terms of British Imperial history thus has to take into account the long shadow of an enormous and ever-growing Japanese presence. Long before the final clash of the Pacific War, there was an uneasy coexistence between two rival informal empires on Chinese territory. Both touched and overlapped in their connection with the multinational institutions of the treaty port system. But their basic political orientations differed considerably. Whereas Britain, though less a champion of free trade than before the First World War, strove to uphold or reassert its leading economic position in China on the strength of its ability to penetrate the Chinese market, Japan increasingly required external resources and manpower to compensate for deficiencies in the mother country. Moreover, if imperial Japan was to acquire status and national prestige through further geopolitical aggrandizement, China seemed a natural field for expansion. Japanese informal imperialism, therefore, had an built-in tendency toward territorial domination that threatened to explode, sooner or later, into the British-dominated treaty port system.

Within a reconstructed international framework, most features of pre-war imperialism survived into the 1920s. Between 1911 and 1913 the Great Powers, acting in relative harmony, had seized the chance of a collapsing *ancien régime* to humiliate China in unprecedented ways. The grip on the young Republic's finances, especially on the customs revenue, was tightened, and the Mixed Court at Shanghai was usurped by the foreign consuls in open violation of treaty stipulations. At the same time, the Great Powers encouraged the independence of Outer Mongolia and Tibet; since 1910 Korea, China's old tributary vassal, had been a Japanese colony. None of these gains from the immediate pre-1914 period were revoked after the war. The Peace Conference sharply illuminated China's contradictory position in the international system. On the one hand China, having entered the war in 1917,[4] was nominally counted among the victors and participated in the founding of the League of Nations. On the other hand, the Great Powers rejected China's demand for a piecemeal restitution of its lost sovereign rights.[5] Chinese public opinion was especially outraged when the Paris Peace Conference transferred Germany's privileges in Shantung to the Japanese without even consulting the Chinese delegation. The result was the May Fourth Movement of 1919, an upsurge of countrywide demonstrations, strikes, and boycotts against the foreign powers as well as the collaborative Peking government. Adding insult to injury, the confirmation of the pre-war system of foreign privilege was accompanied by a new tone of condescending rhetoric. Whereas the Ch'ing dynasty had been regarded as decadent, semi-barbarous, and in need of a long and careful education in the arts of civilized behaviour, the continuing tutelage over Young China was justified in terms of its alleged immaturity and lack of experience.[6]

Until 1926 the British saw no need for a major revision of their China policy. The treaty system worked smoothly, and the vital institutions of the Customs and Salt services were under firm foreign control. The Custodian Bank system of 1911 continued to operate until 1932, when the Central Bank of China assumed responsibility for the disposal of the customs revenues.[7] There was no more conspicuous aspect of the foreign powers' preponderance, at least in the key maritime and riverine regions of China, than their armed forces. Based on a liberal interpretation of Article 52 of the Anglo-Chinese Treaty of 1858, the treaty powers maintained considerable naval forces in Chinese waters. During the 1920s a minimum of fifteen British, ten Japanese, eight American, and five French gunboats regularly patrolled the Yangtze River; in summer the British kept a cruiser as far upstream as Hankow, the only truly important inland treaty port.[8] Two British army battalions were garrisoned at Hong Kong, another one at Tientsin. In times of trouble reinforcements were mobilized, and Britain had to seek the help of other powers to defend her interests. When in 1926 and 1927 the International Settlement

[4] A. Philip Jones, *Britain's Search for Chinese Cooperation in the First World War* (New York, 1986), chaps. 7–10.

[5] On China's aims at the Peace Conference, see Zhang Yongjin, *China in the International System, 1918–20: The Middle Kingdom at the Periphery* (Basingstoke, 1991), p. 60. See Vol. III, Map 8.1, p. 147 for the nineteenth-century treaty ports.

[6] For examples of this rhetoric, see Ernest P. Young, *The Presidency of Yüan Shih-k'ai: Liberalism and Dictatorship in Early Republican China* (Ann Arbor, 1977), pp. 46–48.

[7] Inspector-General, Circular No. 4399, 3 March 1932, in *Chinese Maritime Customs, Documents Illustrative of the Origin, Development, and Activities of the Chinese Customs Service* (Shanghai, 1939), V, p. 18.

[8] Anthony Clayton, *The British Empire as a Superpower, 1919–39* (Basingstoke, 1986), pp. 190, 196.

at Shanghai was repeatedly threatened by nationalist uprisings, Britain assembled a force of two small aircraft carriers, twelve cruisers, twenty destroyers, twelve submarines, and 13,000 men.[9] As late as May 1934, at a comparatively quiet time, the International Settlement and the French Concession at Shanghai were protected by 6,000 foreign troops.[10] A month later British naval aircraft attacked Chinese junks in retribution for a pirate assault on Butterfield & Swire's steamer, *Shuntien*.[11] This was the last major naval engagement before the outbreak of the Sino-Japanese War in 1937.

The foreign military presence indicated strength, and yet it may just as well be seen as a sign of weakness. The instruments of intervention were displayed because the foreigners had good reason to feel insecure. Military threat and coercion were increasingly unsuitable means for defending imperial interests. Even before mass nationalism posed challenges of a new kind, the erosion of the Chinese central state had undermined the efficacy of nineteenth-century techniques of exercising power.

The turmoil that engulfed warlord China after 1916, and especially in the early 1920s, had no immediate origin in foreign activities. The reconstruction of order, in turn, lay beyond the reach of any alien power short of outright colonial conquest and pacification. Just as the causes of China's problems were largely endogenous, so did their treatment elude the foreign powers. The effects of the decomposition of the Chinese state were obvious enough. Since the Peking government and the various regional warlord regimes that enjoyed quasi-autonomous control over most of China were structurally weak and mostly indifferent in their nationalism, they posed no direct threat to material foreign interests. No warlord ever seriously attacked any of the British concessionary areas, harmed a Consul, or explicitly repudiated a loan. On the other hand, the weakness of these semi-autonomous territories into which China now disintegrated meant that the tried-and-tested mechanisms of intervention were ceasing to function properly. No central authority could any longer be held accountable for a local incident. The vertical chain of command that the Ch'ing dynasty had barely managed to keep intact had broken down. In a practical sense foreigners were no longer sacrosanct, as they had always been apart from the brief period of Boxer frenzy in 1899–1900. Assaults on private foreigners in interior parts of the country began to increase after the 1911 revolution, and by the 1920s had become almost commonplace. When in May 1923 the Tientsin–Pukow Express was attacked by 1,200 bandits and twenty-six foreigners were taken hostage, Britain and the powers were just as

[9] Ibid., pp. 207–08.

[10] *North China Herald*, 23 May 1934, p. 264.

[11] Stephen L. Endicott, *Diplomacy and Enterprise: British China Policy, 1933–1937* (Manchester, 1975), pp. 11–12.

helpless as the Chinese government.[12] A foreign military intervention against the bandit lair was technically impossible, and pressure on the Chinese authorities was equally useless. The demands of the kidnappers had to be met to get the captives released. The indignant diplomats could not even procure the punishment of the guilty. The foreigners' power and influence evaporated under conditions in which effective collaboration had ceased to function. On a smaller scale, the same kind of problem occurred almost every day. It became difficult, for example, to get court sentences carried out. Foreign companies operating in the interior found no way of obtaining redress and of prosecuting defaulting debtors. Thus, the decentralization or even disappearance of state authority in China jeopardized the foundations of informal empire.

Different in its origins, but similar in effect, was the challenge of nationalism. Chinese nationalism had no coherent doctrine and no unified political movement. Its social base was diverse. After the suppression of the violent peasant anti-foreignism that had erupted during the Boxer Rebellion, the British had been confronted with the moderate élite nationalism of the movement to recover railway and mining rights (1902–11). In 1905 they had also witnessed the first popular boycott protesting against immigration restrictions in the United States. The colonial authorities in Hong Kong had seen Sun Yat-sen's nationalist movement rise and grow. Until 1911, however, Sun's movement was anti-Manchu rather than anti-imperialist in its strategic orientation, ethnic in its ideological substance, and conspirational in its methods. It posed no threat to foreign interests. It tried, on the contrary, to enlist their support. Yet another type of nationalism was the calm and well-argued assertion of China's sovereign rights by a group of young, Western-trained diplomats and international lawyers. They drew public attention at the Versailles Peace Conference and were able to pursue their policy of, as some people called it, 'treaty attrition' with striking continuity, in spite of frequent changes of government at Peking.

Nationalism as a mass movement emerged during the 1910s and early 1920s as a result of the formation and consolidation of new classes in Chinese society: an urban proletariat, an industrial and financial bourgeoisie, and an articulate student body, strongly influenced by Western ideas. The students were especially impressed by successful nation-building in Meiji Japan and later by the achievements of Soviet Russia, as those successes were understood in China. Even after the May Fourth Movement of 1919, the Chinese public as a whole was by no means

[12] Chan Lau Kit-ching, 'The Lincheng Incident: A Case Study of British Policy in China between the Washington Conference (1921–22) and the First Nationalist Revolution (1925–28)', *Journal of Oriental Studies*, X (1972), pp. 172–86.

seized by anti-foreign fervour.[13] But it was much more sensitive than before to the irregularity of foreign privilege and reacted vehemently against any case of foreign high-handedness. Under colonial and semi-colonial conditions, even mere labour disputes assumed a political tinge. Thus, the great Hong Kong Seamen's Strike of 1922 began with demands, which were aimed at foreign and Chinese employers, for wage increases in a time of mounting inflation. It would probably not have escalated into something like a general strike involving 100,000 strikers had the Hong Kong government not refused to recognize the economic origin of the protest, and had it not insisted that it was a political plot undermining the existence of the colony.[14] In this important case, the politicization of the movement originated mainly with the colonial state. The strike ended in a clear victory for the seamen.

The confrontation between foreigners and the Chinese urban populace reached dramatic dimensions with the countrywide strike and boycott by the May Thirtieth Movement of 1925.[15] Its point of origin was, appropriately, the International Settlement at Shanghai. Simmering labour conflict in the Japanese cotton mills and plans by the British-dominated Shanghai Municipal Council to extend the Settlement had already created a highly charged atmosphere, when a Japanese foreman killed a young Chinese worker. Students organized large-scale protest meetings and demonstrations. During one of them, on 30 May 1925, a Sikh police force commanded by a British officer opened fire on an unarmed crowd, killing thirteen and wounding more than twenty. Three weeks later a similar clash between a Chinese crowd and British and French consular guards in Canton led to the death of at least fifty-two Chinese and one foreigner. The ensuing anti-British strike and boycott lasted for about four months and was conducted with extreme thoroughness; in the Canton–Hong Kong area it continued until October 1926. The May Thirtieth Movement was not exclusively masterminded and led by the emerging extreme Left. It was supported by a broad coalition of political forces. At one end there were the young students, some of them indeed activists of the Chinese Communist Party (CCP) which had been established in 1921 under the guidance of Soviet advisers, and was now seizing the chance to win a mass following. This radical wing of the movement did not demand the expulsion or even slaughter of all foreigners, as the Boxers had done in 1900, but agitated for the immediate restitution of all concessions and settlements and for the instant

[13] Virgil Kit-yiu Ho, 'The Limits of Hatred: Popular Attitudes towards the West in Republican Canton', *East Asian History*, II (1991), pp. 87–104.

[14] Chan Lau Kit-ching, *China, Britain and Hong Kong, 1895–1945* (Hong Kong, 1990), p. 175.

[15] An excellent account of the movement is Nicholas R. Clifford, *Spoilt Children of Empire: Westerners in Shanghai and the Chinese Revolution of the 1920s* (Hanover, NH, 1991), pp. 97–143. See also Richard W. Rigby, *The May 30 Movement: Events and Themes* (Folkestone, 1980).

abolition of the Unequal Treaties—hardly more than a tougher version of the Chinese demands at Versailles. At the other end of the spectrum the wealthy bourgeoisie of merchants, shipowners, and industrialists, intricately tied to the system of foreign economic interests and privileges, insisted on more circumscribed aims: the abolition of the discriminatory Mixed Court, representation of Chinese ratepayers on the Shanghai Municipal Council, and most importantly, the restoration of tariff autonomy. They were largely successful, even if China regained effective control over its tariffs only in 1930.[16]

Hysterical treaty port propaganda caricatured Chinese nationalism as the ravings of Communist-inspired mobs and clamoured for massive retaliation. Such a reaction was hardly surprising, as British expatriates in Shanghai now found themselves confronted with a degree of popular mobilization unknown since the days of the Taipings more than sixty years before. It came as a shock to the quasi-colonial complacency nurtured in the foreign enclaves. The Chinese had suddenly ceased being docile and deferential. They had mastered efficient techniques of economic warfare. Realistic observers, however, recognized the sober and respectable face of élite nationalism and conceded the validity—before law, political judgement, and common sense—of many Chinese grievances. British foreign policy adopted this line with Sir Austen Chamberlain's December Memorandum of 1926, and changed its strategy from adamant opposition to Chinese nationalism to cautious sympathy and co-operation with its moderate wing. The Colonial Office and the Hong Kong government disagreed with this new policy of accommodation, and for some time clung to the older habits of determined resistance to Chinese demands.

The December Memorandum was a vague declaration of intent that did not in itself offer any concessions to China. It simply expressed a willingness to enter into a negotiated settlement of the main issues. The year 1927 was not a propitious moment for a change of course in practical politics. China at that time had not one government but at least four. And while General Chiang Kai-shek's bloody purge of his erstwhile Communist allies and his expulsion of the Soviet advisers to whom he largely owed his military success was welcomed in British official and unofficial circles, the situation did not instantly improve. Leftist radicalism in the coastal cities was not entirely defeated until the savage suppression of the Canton Commune in December 1927, which the Hong Kong government used as a pretext to impose harsh restrictions on the labour movement in the colony.[17] Also, for the time being, Chiang's National Party (Kuomintang) held on to its tradition of regarding the British as their most obnoxious imperialist enemy and continued its

[16] On moderate 'bourgeois' nationalism in the 1920s, see Marie-Claire Bergère, *L'Âge d'or de la bourgeoisie chinoise, 1911–1937* (Paris, 1986), pp. 252–75.

[17] Norman Miners, *Hong Kong under Imperial Rule, 1912–1941* (Hong Kong, 1987), p. 20.

anti-British agitation. The year 1928, however, brought a substantial change. On the one hand, Japan's China policy toughened, especially over the Shantung question. Henceforth Japan bore the brunt of Chinese animosity and became the main target of large-scale boycott movements.[18] The more the Sino-Japanese conflict escalated, the easier it was for the British to impress the Chinese with their relatively moderate stance. On the other hand, after Chiang Kai-shek had accomplished, at least nominally, the 'unification' of China and had established a National Government at Nanking in place of the Peking warlord government, the rebuilding of the Chinese state seemed to have begun.

Though couched in a high moral tone, the reorientation of British policy in late 1926 reflected a want of viable alternatives rather than a deeply felt sympathy with nascent non-western nationalism.[19] Conciliation was the logical choice once it was apparent that none of the anti-revolutionary warlords merited support. No regional militarist qualified as a reliable collaborator securing a British sphere of influence in south and central China. At the same time, the need for an alliance with Chinese authorities became more urgent than ever, since the direct approach of overbearing gunboat diplomacy was no longer feasible. This was underlined by the ugliest incident of the period: the Wanhsien Massacre of August 1926. With no tactical objective and exclusively for reasons of prestige after a slight provocation by warlord troops, British gunboats shelled residential quarters in the treaty port of Wanhsien on the middle Yangtze, killing between 400 and several thousand Chinese civilians.[20] One of the effects was a nine-year boycott against British shipping in that important tung oil-exporting treaty port. The lesson of Wanhsien was that, in an age of mass nationalism, gunboat intervention creates rather than solves problems. 'The short answer about a gunboat policy,' explained Sir John Pratt, one of the Foreign Office's most perceptive China experts, a few years later, 'is that gunboats are very convenient aids to policy so long as you are not driven to using them, but the moment you are then the spell is broken...'[21] And the man who should have known best, the Commander-in-Chief of the China Station, arrived at the same conclusion: 'We are always rather sitting on a box of fireworks as it takes such a very small incident to make the balloon go up.... Unless we actually go to war and are prepared so see it through, every Chinese that is killed creates another slogan and another commemoration day.'[22]

[18] Harumi Goto-Shibata, *Japan and Britain in Shanghai, 1925–31* (Basingstoke, 1995), chap. 4.

[19] Wm. Roger Louis, *British Strategy in the Far East, 1919–1939* (Oxford, 1971), p. 129.

[20] Peter Gaffney Clark, 'Britain and the Chinese Revolution, 1925–1927', unpublished Ph.D. dissertation, Berkeley, 1973, pp. 234–76.

[21] Pratt, minute, 14 March 1935, F[oreign] O[ffice] 371/19287/F1623.

[22] Admiral Sir Howard Kelly to Admiral Sir Frederick Field, 27 June 1931, quoted in Paul Haggie, *Britannia at Bay: The Defence of the British Empire Against Japan, 1931–1941* (Oxford, 1981), p. 22.

Thus, the old techniques of intervention in the service of informal empire had been definitely paralysed by a combination of anarchy and mass nationalism. Local shows of force aroused vigorous popular reactions that could no longer be suppressed by traditional means. Given such constraints, the British Imperial retreat was a process of almost unavoidable pragmatism. At the same time, indigenous collaboration became more important than ever. If British lives and property in most parts of China could no longer be protected by direct intervention, the Chinese state acquired a new importance as their sole guarantor.

The Nanking government qualified for this role. It was certainly more nationalistic than its warlord and Ch'ing predecessors and retained some elements of anti-imperialism in its political rhetoric. Its main difference from the warlord regimes was its emphasis on development, its avowed readiness to modernize China with the help of foreign capital, and its discarding the irrational tyranny of the warlords. The enlightened and Western-oriented face of the new government was represented by a man such as the Harvard-educated banker T. V. Soong, a brother of Chiang Kai-shek's second wife, the thoroughly Americanized Soong Mei-ling. The Nanking government needed British political and economic support. In return, it reverted to the methods of a very moderate nationalism that went back to the Rights Recovery Movement of 1903–11 and continued tendencies of the warlord period. Above all, Nanking's foreign policy renounced any kind of unilateralism. It also accepted a quid pro quo formulated by the Great Powers at the Washington Conference: sovereign rights were to be restored to China as a reward for successful self-reform. This was exactly what the radical nationalists of the 1920s had furiously rejected: national liberation as a gracious gift from the oppressors.

The growing sympathy between the Nanking government and the Western powers did not mean that Britain was ready to concede more than was absolutely necessary. It was Whitehall's aim 'to retain the substance of important British interests by surrendering only what was considered to be of secondary importance'.[23] Definitely of secondary importance were the concessions at Hankow and Kiukiang that were given up to Chinese crowds in 1927. Similarly, the small and economically worthless leased territory of Wei-hai-wei could be dispensed with painlessly; it reverted to Chinese rule in October 1930.[24] In the same year tariff autonomy was *de facto* restored to China, without, as it turned out in the following years, doing much harm to British trade. Britain also connived in, or rather could not prevent, Chinese resumption of control over the Customs administration. The

[23] Edmund S. K. Fung, *The Diplomacy of Imperial Retreat: Britain's South China Policy, 1924–1931* (Hong Kong, 1991), p. 103.

[24] Pamela Atwell, *British Mandarins and Chinese Reformers: The British Administration of Weihaiwei (1898–1930) and the Territory's Return to Chinese Rule* (Hong Kong, 1985), pp. 161–72.

new Inspector-General, appointed by the Nanking government, was Frederick Maze. Like his uncle, the great Sir Robert Hart, he stood for the depoliticization of the service and proved to be a loyal servant of the Chinese government.[25]

The treaty regime, however, was not to be dismantled for the time being. Extraterritoriality, in particular, was regarded by British and Chinese alike as the cornerstone of informal empire: for the one side a vital protection from a still not-quite 'civilized' Chinese administration of law; in the eyes of the other side a resented symbol of foreign arrogance. Extraterritoriality was indeed crucial. Its removal would have implied the end of the remaining territorial enclaves in which British economic interests were concentrated. Talks on the issue between Britain and the Kuomintang government began in 1930. Solutions were in sight involving a moratorium for the International Settlement at Shanghai and for the British Concession at Tientsin. The talks were postponed indefinitely after the Japanese seizure of Manchuria in September 1931. Extraterritoriality in China lasted for another twelve years.

There were reasons to doubt the dogma that British well-being in China depended on extraterritoriality and consular jurisdiction. The German experience of amicable relations and rapidly growing trade with China obviously disproved the need for the legal safeguards of old-style imperialism. Moreover, by the early 1930s the major British economic interests in China had learned to look after themselves. The leading British firms sought and partly found ways of coping with a rapidly changing Chinese environment. Within the British establishment in China, a kind of devolution gave additional weight to local factors. Crucial business decisions were now more likely to be taken in Shanghai or Hong Kong than in London. Between the world wars, China was less important as a target for trade and finance than as a field of direct investment. If the period from 1842 to 1895 carried the hallmark of treaty port trade and the years between 1895 and 1914 had been the golden age of high finance, the inter-war era was a time of market penetration.

The value of British exports to China and Hong Kong did not grow in the long run. Losses in cotton goods were just about compensated for by rising exports of machinery through which Britain participated in the incipient industrialization of China. Arms supply to the warlords played a supplementary and not easily quantifiable role. Not vague hopes for future export conquests, but the preservation and promotion of tangible assets provided the rationale of British political activities in China. British direct investment increased, according to somewhat shaky estimates, from US $400m in 1914 to $963m in 1930 and further to $1,059m

[25] Martyn Atkins, *Informal Empire in Crisis: British Diplomacy and the Chinese Customs Succession, 1927–1929* (Ithaca, NY, 1995); Chen Shiqi, 'Nanjing zhengfu de guanshui xingzheng gaige' (The Nanking Government's Reform of the Customs Administration), *Lishi yanjiu* (1995), No. 3, pp. 133–44.

in 1936.[26] This increase was not related to major structural changes in the composition of British interests. Growth occurred partly through rising real-estate values in Shanghai, partly through the reinvestment of profits by long-established China firms. No important branch of business was added after 1914, and only two major British firms took up manufacturing in China for the first time: in 1934 Paton & Baldwin opened a medium-scale factory for woollens that employed 1,120 Chinese workers. Lever Brothers, also in Shanghai, started manufacturing margarine and soap, and some years later accounted for about half of the sales of soap in the country—soap, however, not being an article of mass consumption in China at that time.[27] As before the war, the core of British business interests in China was made up of a handful of large companies: the Hongkong and Shanghai Banking Corporation (HSBC), Jardine Matheson & Co. ('Ewo'), Butterfield & Swire ('Taikoo'), the British-American Tobacco Corporation (BAT), and the Kailan Mining Administration (KMA, a Sino-British joint venture). Imperial Chemical Industries (ICI) and the Asiatic Petroleum Co. (APC) did not produce in China but ran extensive sales organizations similar to the one BAT was using for the distribution of its cigarettes. BAT, in 1933 accounting for more than 60 per cent of output and capital in the Chinese tobacco industry,[28] stood as the biggest manufacturing enterprise on Chinese territory. In 1936 its capital investment in Shanghai surpassed even that of the Japanese cotton companies and was nine times larger than that of the Ewo cotton factories.[29]

It was characteristic for these major firms that their operations extended far beyond Shanghai, Hong Kong, and Tientsin. This had always been true for Ewo and Taikoo, with their substantial shipping lines. Since about the turn of the century it also applied to a new style of direct 'up-country' marketing by powerful multinational corporations.[30] The organizational penetration of the China market that had been so signally lacking during the first half-century after the Opium War was achieved as a consequence, not of changes in China, but of the corporate revolution in metropolitan capitalism. The growing disorder in China, however, imperilled the vulnerable distribution networks. One such organization, the sales system connected to the Taikoo Sugar Refinery in Hong Kong, succumbed to the

[26] Hou Chi-ming, *Foreign Investment and Economic Development in China, 1840–1937* (Cambridge, Mass., 1965), p. 225 (Table 45).

[27] Chen Zhen, ed., *Zhongguo jindai gongyeshi ziliao* (Materials on the History of Modern Industry in China), 4 vols. (Peking, 1957–61), II, pp. 155–57, 161.

[28] Liu Guoliang, *Zhongguo gongyeshi: Jindai juan* (History of Chinese Industry, 1840–1949) (Nanjing, 1992), p. 326.

[29] Data in Zhang Zhongli and others, *Jindai Shanghai chengshi yanjiu* (Studies on Modern Shanghai) (Shanghai, 1990), p. 337.

[30] A case study is Patrick Brodie, *Crescent over Cathay: China and ICI, 1898 to 1956* (Hong Kong, 1990), pp. 34–51, 61–67.

combined pressures of boycotts and defaults by Chinese partners. The others managed to weather the storm. In a country without an effective central government, infested with bandits and military marauders and torn apart by civil war, this was not possible by insisting on abstract treaty privileges. It was impractical to post a British soldier next to every BAT cigarette warehouse or to have Consuls watch whether actual transit taxation conformed to the letter of the treaties. Hence, the big companies necessarily had to dispense with the Consul and the gunboat and to conduct their own private diplomacy and crisis management. Taikoo, along with BAT perhaps the leader among the China firms sensitive to nationalism, understood 'that the day of effective Consular intervention—if it ever existed—is now past'.[31] Bargains were struck with local authorities. Bribes, mutually satisfying deals, and business partnerships smoothed the way for the conduct of business. The big companies did not advocate the abolition of extraterritoriality. But they had learned to cope with situations where it could not be enforced, and they were preparing for a time without it.

Finance took second place. International financial control was still an aim pursued, if less energetically than before 1914, by the British government and the leading British bank in the East, the Hongkong and Shanghai Banking Corporation.[32] But the heady days of financial imperialism were over. The grand strategies yielded little success. The First Consortium, founded in 1911 and ultimately composed of six national groups, had managed to launch the Reorganization Loan of 1913 aimed at supporting President Yuan Shih-k'ai against his domestic rivals. The New Consortium, formed in 1918 on American initiative and formally constituted in 1920, was far less successful. It was neither accepted by the Chinese government, nor did it mobilize new funds for China. The banks in the post-1918 period were largely thrown back on managing China's pre-war foreign debts. These debts suffered different fates. The Boxer Indemnity and the other political loans secured on customs revenue were punctually served under the continuing Custodian Banks system until 1939, when the widening of the Japanese invasion deprived China of vital sources of revenue. Payment of other loans, including the Reorganization Loan, was affected by the collapse, in 1926, of the central Salt Administration that had been reorganized under a British Associate Chief Inspector in 1913. From about 1924 on many railway loans went into default. This was not due to any deliberate defiance on the part of the Chinese

[31] 'Outport Agents' Conference, Shanghai, September 1931: Minutes of Discussions on Chinese Staff and General Matters', John Swire & Sons Archives, School of Oriental and African Studies (London) II/2/10.

[32] A good summary is P. J. Cain and A. G. Hopkins, *British Imperialism: Crisis and Deconstruction, 1914–1990* (London, 1993), pp. 239–48.

government. It was a result of China's descent into political chaos. Railways were commandeered for troop transport, their funds illegally appropriated; tracks and rolling-stock were left to decay. The financial viability of the railroads was destroyed not by mismanagement, but by the forces of disorder now uppermost in China.[33]

The rehabilitation of Chinese public credit was the major aim of international financial diplomacy during the inter-war period. After the failure of the second Consortium this aim was no longer pursued through international co-operation. The elementary precondition for its successful accomplishment was the reconstruction of the Chinese state.

The gradual strengthening of the Nanking regime in the years after 1928 greatly improved the conditions for British business. It was strictly anti-Communist and, after a transition period that lasted until 1931, put an end to most kinds of labour unrest. It implemented a series of important reforms in commercial law, taxation, and other fields, which aimed at creating a modern business environment. It was also eager to restore China's international credit-standing and welcomed British advice, for example, in rehabilitating the railways and the salt revenue administration. For such accommodation, however, it exacted a price: tacit abandonment of treaty privileges by individual companies and the establishment of joint ventures with leading figures of the regime acting as partners in semi-official, semi-private functions.[34]

Most of the big British companies pursued policies of allying themselves with Chinese 'bureaucratic capitalism' that mirrored or even anticipated the grand strategy of Chinese–British co-operation launched in 1935 by the mission to China of Sir Frederick Leith-Ross, the chief economic adviser to the Prime Minister and to the Chancellor of the Exchequer.[35] For the first time since the fall of the Ch'ing dynasty, it seemed possible again to associate British enterprise and finance with the modernization of China. Chiang Kai-shek now definitely assumed the mantle of the ideal collaborator that had not been taken up since the brief liaison with Yuan Shih-k'ai. Leith-Ross helped the Chinese government with the introduction of a managed currency in place of China's traditional silver exchange standard. The plans for this major undertaking had already been prepared by Chinese experts; Leith-Ross gave some additional advice and secured the

[33] Ralph William Huenemann, *The Dragon and the Iron Horse: The Economics of Railroads in China, 1876–1937* (Cambridge, Mass., 1984), pp. 177–86.

[34] This theme is developed in Jürgen Osterhammel, 'Imperialism in Transition: British Business and the Chinese Authorities, 1931–37', *China Quarterly*, LXLVIII (June 1984), pp. 260–86.

[35] Ann Trotter, *Britain and East Asia, 1933–1937* (Cambridge, 1975), pp. 148–67; Endicott, *Diplomacy and Enterprise*, pp. 102–49.

compliance of the British banks, which were now required to surrender their silver reserves.[36] Leith-Ross's most significant achievement was a negotiated settlement (if not one satisfactory to the foreign bondholders)[37] of most of the defaulted railway loans, thus opening prospects for new financial ventures. Many projects, especially new British investments south of the Yangtze, were discussed with the Chinese authorities. The outbreak of the Sino-Japanese War in July 1937 prevented their realization.

The Leith-Ross mission was inspired by a dynamic Imperial vision that pointed far beyond the ossified structures of the treaty regime. Whether its consequences would have been imperialistic, we do not know. In the plans of 1936–37 the Chinese government was accepted as an equal partner to a greater extent than ever before. This was no mere fruit of British benevolence: Britain was no longer in a position to dictate terms, and Chiang Kai-shek, wary of exclusive dependence on any one foreign power, had fortified his bargaining position by close relations with Hitler's Germany. German help was expected in the construction of a heavy industrial complex in central China. If the Kuomintang seemed to have forgotten its earlier nationalistic rhetoric, bequeathed by its founder Sun Yat-sen, and was prepared to make substantial concessions (Chiang Kai-shek even urged Britain to establish a protectorate over the island of Hainan),[38] this can be explained by the imminent Japanese threat. It is also important to note that since the early 1980s, the Chinese Communists have proven at least as accommodating to foreign interests as the Nanking government. In retrospect, the grand diplomacy of co-operation in 1935–37 may perhaps be seen less as the final chapter of British imperialism in China than as an historical overture to the new open-door policy of the Deng Xiaoping era.

To what extent did British business in inter-war China benefit from what remained of the old imperial institutions? Extraterritoriality and the preservation of the special status of Shanghai were indispensable for those branches of business that were confined to the territorial enclaves: real estate, public utilities, and numerous small trades and services catering to the local population. The shipping companies would not have enjoyed comparable privileges in a fully sovereign country, and they would have had to do without naval protection, which was the only field where gunboats retained a certain efficacy. Another branch closely tied up with the Imperial aspect of the British presence was banking. Even after the age

[36] Shigeru Akita, 'British Informal Empire in East Asia, 1880s–1930s: Á Japanese Perspective', in Suntory-Toyota International Centre for Economics and Related Disciplines, *Discussion Paper*, IS/95/287 (London, 1995), pp. 15–16.

[37] Frank H. H. King, *The Hongkong Bank between the Wars and the Bank Interned, 1919–1945: Return from Grandeur* (Cambridge, 1988), p. 381.

[38] Endicott, *Diplomacy and Enterprise*, p. 139.

of high lending had passed, British and other foreign banks profited from the Custodian Banks system and from their privilege to issue banknotes. Their most important advantage had always been a non-imperial one: the lack of adequate indigenous banking facilities. This began to change when modern-style Chinese banks supplemented and later replaced the traditional 'native banks'. The more expertise and experience they acquired in foreign-exchange dealings and the more funds from the interior they were able to attract, the more substantial they became as rivals of the foreign banks.[39] The 1935 nationalization of leading private banks by the Nanking government created a powerful Central Banking Group that was further strengthened by the simultaneous monetary reform. In short, the British banks not only had to adjust to meagre and modest years after having 'turned away from grand schemes . . . from high politics'.[40] They were also compelled to retreat before the advance of Chinese capitalism. Their former prominent association with imperialism stigmatized them in the eyes of the Chinese public and made it difficult for them to branch out into normal merchant banking.

The record of other big British companies is more difficult to interpret in a general way. In the three outstanding cases of the British-American Tobacco Corporation, the Asiatic Petroleum Co., and the Kailan Mining Administration, commercial success seems to have rested mainly on economic strength. The KMA's chief non-economic advantage over Chinese-owned coal-mines was its 'ability to resist payment of the various exactions demanded by warlords and local authorities'.[41] APC owed little to legal privilege in a field—the import of oil—where Chinese competition was absent and the Anglo-American oil companies formed an oligopoly. BAT, the largest Western manufacturer in China, almost monopolized the market for cigarettes. It made use of whatever privilege or chance of intervention was at hand, but also conducted an extremely resourceful private diplomacy. The Corporation was well known for its aggressive business methods all over the world.[42] BAT's strength rested on the weakness of the Chinese-owned tobacco industry rather than on British Imperial power.

On the eve of war, therefore, Britain's cautious political retreat from the less important positions of privilege and dominance and the slow erosion of the institutions of informal empire was not paralleled by a retreat of British business. Whereas the British surrendered the Chinese export market to more-dynamic

[39] Marie-Clarie Bergère, 'The Shanghai Bankers' Association, 1915–1927: Modernization and the Institutionalization of Local Solidarities', in Frederic Wakeman and Wen-hsin Yeh, eds., *Shanghai Sojourners* (Berkeley, 1992), pp. 15–34.

[40] King, *The Hongkong Bank*, p. 162.

[41] Wang Yuru, 'Capital Formation and Operating Profits of the Kailuan Mining Administration (1903–1937)', *Modern Asian Studies*, XXVIII (1994), p. 113.

[42] Sherman Cochran, *Big Business in China: Sino-Foreign Rivalry in the Cigarette Industry, 1890–1930* (Cambridge, Mass., 1980), p. 206.

competitors from the United States, Japan, and Germany and thus buried their old dream of saturating China with the products of British industry, expatriate business on the spot more than held its own. With the gradual restoration of internal stability by a moderately nationalistic, pro-western government, and after recovery from the Great Depression that, mainly for reasons of scale, hit Chinese manufacturers harder than their British and Japanese counterparts, China seemed to offer long-term prospects to foreign enterprise. The old institutional framework of informal empire was beginning to turn into a liability. By 1937 the foundations had been laid for an economic relationship beyond the paraphernalia of nineteenth-century imperialism. New kinds of less visible dependency were about to tie a poor and underdeveloped China to the economies of the West. Yet, doubts about future smooth co-operation between British merchants, bankers, and investors and the Kuomintang government were not entirely unfounded. While the Nanking regime invited British and American capital to join in the modernization of China, it promulgated legislation on foreign investment that was more restrictive than the rules introduced fifty years later under Deng Xiaoping's reform policies. It was also bent on further extending state control over foreign trade, manufacturing industry, and mining.[43] Sooner or later, the neo-mercantilism of the Kuomintang was bound to clash with the British desire for a free hand in the China market.

When the Japanese army swept down the China coast during the second half of 1937 few observers foresaw the impending end of the British informal empire. For the time being, the interruption of trade caused by the war was offset by new opportunities for British business. Ironically, the era of the treaty ports culminated in an artificial boom. Until the end of 1941 Hong Kong and the two foreign enclaves at Shanghai, due to their non-combatant status, were the only economic centres on the China coast untouched by the undeclared Sino-Japanese War. When Japanese naval artillery bombarded residential quarters in the Chinese municipality of Shanghai, they carefully aimed their shells across the International Settlement and the French Concession. After the outbreak of war in Europe new markets were opening up for the industries of Shanghai in the Pacific region and in Africa.[44] The major British firms reported excellent results. As late as 1940, it was 'business as usual' for the HKSBC.[45] In 1939 Unilever achieved record sales and ICI saw all its expectations

[43] Jürgen Osterhammel, 'State Control of Foreign Trade in Nationalist China, 1927–1937', in Clive Dewey, ed., *The State and the Market: Studies in the Economic and Social History of the Third World* (New Delhi, 1987), pp. 209–37.

[44] Richard W. Barnett, *Economic Shanghai: Hostage to Politics, 1937–1941* (New York, 1941), p. 39.

[45] Hongkong and Shanghai Banking Corporation, *124th Report of Directors to the Ordinary General Meeting of Shareholders* (Hong Kong, 1940), p. 12.

surpassed, while BAT and the Ewo cotton mills earned profits that exceeded anything previously experienced.[46] The KMA, situated as it was in territory that had already been under effective Japanese control well before 1937, had a record of friendly relations with the Japanese and had relied on them since 1935 to quell unrest among the Chinese miners. The mines survived the first phase of the war unscathed and were able to report record sales and exports for 1939 and 1940.[47]

The temporary flourishing of British business in war-torn China owed little to London's diplomacy. Given Britain's military weakness in the East, especially after the outbreak of war in Europe in September 1939, only defensive measures could be taken to salvage the remnants of the Empire. Without much support from the United States, Britain found it increasingly difficult to uphold a neutrality that implied sympathizing with China, the victim of an aggression, without displeasing the Japanese, the strongest power in the region. From the early days of the war, Hong Kong harboured refugees from China and hosted a number of official and semi-official Chinese government agencies. The most intricate question, however, that of channelling arms supplies through the colony to China, had disappeared after the Japanese occupied Canton in October 1938. The northern treaty ports were even more vulnerable than Hong Kong. Britain saw no alternative to appeasing Japan when the latter demanded that Maritime Customs' revenues from ports under Japanese control should henceforth be paid to the Yokohama Specie Bank.[48] A much more serious crisis broke out in October 1938 at Tientsin. The Japanese military authorities who controlled the Chinese part of the city and its entire hinterland were incensed that the British Concession was sheltering Chinese resistance fighters and silver deposits belonging to the Chinese government; they also resented the continued use of the official Chinese currency, the fabi. The Concession was put under a rigorous blockade. Although there was still a tendency among British diplomats to underrate Japanese resolve, there should have been no doubt that British interests in the treaty ports were at the mercy of the Japanese army. After a time when Britain and Japan seemed to have arrived at the brink of war, a settlement was finally reached in June 1940 that saved Britain's face but sacrificed China's interests.[49] The Japanese were now allowed to interfere with

[46] Charles Wilson, *The History of Unilever* (London, 1954), II, p. 365; Imperial Chemical Industries, *Annual Report for 1939* (London, 1940), p. 18; Chen Zhen, ed., *Zhongguo jindai gongyeshi ziliao*, II, pp. 850–51, 856–57, 862, 874–75; Shanghai shehui kexueyuan jingji yanjiusuo, ed., *Ying-Mei Yan Gongsi zai Hua qiye ziliao huibian* (Documents on the Enterprises of BAT in China) (Peking, 1983), IV, p. 1527.

[47] Tim Wright, *Coal Mining in China's Economy and Society, 1895–1937* (Cambridge, 1984), p. 127; E. M. Gull, *British Economic Interests in the Far East* (London, 1943), pp. 198–99.

[48] Bradford A. Lee, *Britain and the Sino-Japanese War, 1937–1939: A Study in the Dilemmas of British Decline* (Stanford, Calif., 1973), p. 119.

[49] Peter Lowe, *Great Britain and the Origins of the Pacific War: A Study of British Policy in East Asia, 1937–1941* (Oxford, 1977), pp. 72–102; Antony Best, *Britain, Japan and Pearl Harbor: Avoiding War in East Asia, 1936–41* (London, 1995), pp. 71–86, 108–09.

policing in the British Concession. The principal redeeming feature of the foreign enclaves, the fact that they offered protection from oppressive state power in the surrounding country, was seriously compromised. The residual Western privileges on the China coast no longer rested on the old Unequal Treaties or on Anglo-American power on the spot but on toleration by the Japanese and an international constellation that, for a few years, allowed this toleration to be exercised.

The long-awaited attack on Hong Kong came on 8 December 1941, and the colony surrendered on Christmas Day. On the same day, the Japanese invaded the International Settlement at Shanghai and the British Concession at Tientsin. Both enclaves ceased to exist when the Japanese took over their administration and interned all British nationals, about 6,000 people in Shanghai alone. After precisely a century, the cycle of British imperialism in China came to an end.

This was understood by most senior Foreign Office officials. During the Pacific War the entire core area of the British informal empire in China was in Japanese hands. Chiang Kai-shek's National Government conducted its war effort from the western province of Szechwan, where British economic interests had always been negligible. Alongside the dominating United States, Britain was a junior partner in the economic and military assistance to Free China. No responsible foreign policy-maker seriously believed that the Kuomintang regime would reward British loyalty by resuscitating the defunct regime of extraterritoriality after the war.[50] In addition, the United States was strictly against any reversion to pre-war forms of overt imperialism; and American business did not require the props of Unequal Treaties for its future conquest of the China market. Towards the end of the Second World War Whitehall reached the conclusion that Britain lacked the political and economic resources to assert its pre-war position as the predominant Western power in China. Only Hong Kong seemed to be worth recovering. As soon as the Japanese surrendered in September 1945 to a British admiral, Britain accomplished the feat of repossessing Hong Kong with the indirect assistance of the United States and against the mild opposition of the Chinese government. China, incidentally, had never demanded the return of the colony before 1942.[51] British firms hurried to reclaim their property in the Republic of China and to rebuild their China business. Material destruction of British property had been surprisingly slight. The Foreign Office estimated that war losses (shipping excluded) amounted to little more than 11 per cent of the value of British business investments in 1941. The most important causes of loss were the deterioration of stocks and the decay of

[50] Christopher Thorne, *Allies of a Kind: The United States, Britain and the War against Japan, 1941–1945* (Oxford, 1978), p. 552.

[51] Aron Shai, *Britain and China, 1941–47: Imperial Momentum* (London, 1984), pp. 106–24; Chan Lau Kit-ching, *China, Britain and Hong Kong*, pp. 321–23. On the subsequent period, see Wm. Roger Louis, 'Hong Kong: The Critical Phase, 1945–1949', *American Historical Review*, CII (1997), pp. 1052–84.

mining equipment. Few buildings were seriously damaged, and only a small amount of machinery had been removed by the Japanese.[52] In some cases the Japanese had even augmented and modernized the technical equipment. The total of British business investments was estimated at between £134m and £139m.[53] In purely material terms, British business might have resumed its pre-war success story in the China market.

Yet there were reasons for British businessmen to be unhappy with the situation in China. The Kuomintang government pursued a nationalistic and *étatiste* economic policy and continued to operate some of the state monopolies established shortly before and during the war; in November 1946 it implemented severe import controls. In accordance with the Anglo-Chinese Treaty of January 1943 that had terminated the old treaty privileges, foreign shipping was either excluded from the Yangtze route or admitted only in minority partnerships with indigenous firms. Moreover, businessmen were just as appalled as many Western diplomats at the corruption and inefficiency of the regime. A special complaint on the part of foreign employers was that the Kuomintang government was no longer able to control labour and to keep down wages—as it had done so successfully in the 1930s. Whereas British economic activities in China faced numerous difficulties, British trade with China stood up well against overwhelming American competition. Since China was not a hard currency market, however, the Board of Trade discouraged exports to China.[54]

The Chinese civil war that began in June 1946 was increasingly experienced like a natural disaster, beyond the control of any foreign power, including even the United States and the Soviet Union. In contrast to the United States, Britain refrained from intervention in the civil war and gave little more than verbal support to its wartime ally Chiang Kai-shek. Apart from a widely publicized incident involving the British frigate HMS *Amethyst* in April 1949, there was no major controversy between the CCP and Britain. The CCP leadership was perfectly aware of the value of Hong Kong as an organizational base for South China and as a point of liaison with the Western world, and it regarded Britain as a far less dangerous imperialist power than the United States.[55] By early 1948 most observers felt certain that the Kuomintang regime was doomed and that a policy would have to be worked out for future relations with the victorious Communists. In Novem-

[52] G. V. Kitson, Memorandum 'The British Position in China', 21 Jan. 1947, FO 371/63282/F846; Foreign Office Industrial and Economic Planning Staff, Memorandum 'British Business Investments in China' [Jan. 1947], FO 371/63413/F585.

[53] Wenguang Shao, *China, Britain and Businessmen: Political and Commercial Relations, 1949–57* (Basingstoke, 1991), p. 8.

[54] Shai, *Britain and China*, pp. 151–52.

[55] Qiang Zhai, *The Dragon, the Lion and the Eagle: Chinese–British–American Relations, 1949–1958* (Kent, 1994), pp. 13, 15.

ber 1948 Britain adopted a new policy of preparing for *de facto* relations with the coming government.[56] Realistic appraisals of the situation, however, went hand in hand with a good deal of wishful thinking. As late as November 1948 the Consul-General at Shanghai still believed that Britain was called upon to teach the Communists 'a lesson of how to deal with foreign installations'.[57] Old habits died hard. When the Shanghai Country Club held its St Patrick's Day Ball on 17 March 1948, Chinese were not even admitted as invited guests.[58]

In the event, things turned out quite differently from the hope of those who had expected the Communists to be as amenable as earlier Chinese regimes. The authorities of the People's Republic of China, established in October 1949, were in no mood to be lectured by foreign capitalists or even to negotiate compromises with them. The basic decisions to terminate the Western presence seem to have been taken already before the outbreak of the Korean War in June 1950. They derived from the long experience of radical Chinese nationalism with the Western powers and from deep-seated ideological convictions about the nature of imperialism. Britain's conciliatory posture towards the new regime and the diplomatic recognition of the People's Republic in January 1950[59] did not influence the fundamental resolve of the CCP leader Mao Tse-tung and his lieutenants.

All 'disgraceful' treaties concluded by previous Chinese governments and all loans contacted by them were now flatly repudiated. The British put their total loss of bonded debt at £60.9m.[60] The People's Government moved rapidly to establish complete state control of foreign trade and to withdraw all privileges from foreign enterprises.[61] Alien companies were 'protected' by the government as long as they complied with Chinese laws, which meant, among other things, paying high taxes and functioning in an inferior position within the ordered hierarchy of a planned economy. British firms were slowly squeezed out of China rather than expelled in one dramatic gesture. Their large amount of immobile property now became a tremendous liability, because these assets were difficult to liquidate. The schedule was fixed by the Chinese in each case. Many firms were refused permission to close down, since this would have made workers redundant. Some of them had to

[56] Zhong-ping Feng, *The British Government's China Policy, 1945–1950* (Keele, 1994), pp. 100–06. For the contrast between British and American policies, see Lanxin Xiang, *Recasting the Imperial Far East: Britain and America in China, 1945–1950* (Armonk, NY, 1995), esp. chap. 6.

[57] Sir Robert Urquhart, 'Note on Prospects in a Communistic China', 29 Nov. 1948, FO 371/69545/F17436.

[58] Beverley Hooper, *China Stands Up: Ending the Western Presence, 1948–1950* (Sydney, 1986), p. 28.

[59] On the background, see James Tuck-Hong Tang, *Britain's Encounter With Revolutionary China, 1949–54* (Basingstoke, 1992), chap. 2.

[60] Shao, *China, Britain and Businessmen*, p. 20.

[61] On the fate of British business, see ibid., pp. 38–50, 114–43; Hooper, *China Stands Up*, pp. 85–108; and Aron Shai, 'Imperialism Imprisoned: The Closure of British Firms in the People's Republic of China', *English Historical Review*, CIV (1989), pp. 89–109.

maintain a full payroll of idle workers for several years. A number of companies were forced to remit funds from Hong Kong in order to cover current expenses and meet tax demands. The outbreak of the Korean War prolonged this phase of 'hostage capitalism'.[62] Only after the Korean armistice was the Chinese government willing to complete negotiations about the closure of British firms. BAT, which after 1945 had never recovered its pre-war strength, left the People's Republic in 1952, Jardine Matheson & Co. and Butterfield & Swire followed in 1954; not until 1959 did the last British firm, Paton & Baldwin, receive permission to withdraw.

British trade with Communist China, of course, never ceased completely, but it was conducted within a decidedly post-Imperial framework. Ironically, China's policy of turning its back on the international economy could only be sustained because Hong Kong functioned as an indispensable connecting link to the outside world. The last outpost of Empire in East Asia entered into a symbiotic relationship with imperialism's most uncompromising enemy. When China reopened its doors to foreign enterprise after 1978 and British firms were invited to return, the British were careful not to stir up memories of Imperial times, while the Chinese sprinkled their businesslike pragmatism with occasional rhetorical reminiscences of the wrongs allegedly suffered before 'liberation'. The British informal empire in China was fading into historical folklore.

Britain's Imperial retreat from China went through a number of stages. Its final phase began with the Sino-British Joint Declaration on the future of Hong Kong of September 1984 and was completed with the Chinese assumption of sovereignty over the former Crown Colony on 1 July 1997. There is no easy answer to the question of when the whole process of retreat was set in motion. The First World War certainly spelled the end of prominent features of pre-war imperialism: High Finance would never again flourish in the way it had done before 1914, and gunboat coercion thereafter yielded diminishing returns. Yet a strong case can be made for the view that Britain—in the face of Chinese nationalism, Soviet attitudes, American and German competition, and the expansion of Japan's formal and informal empires in China—maintained most of its essential positions in China up to the Second World War. The status of the prime asset, the International Settlement at Shanghai, and with it Shanghai's unique cosmopolitan treaty port culture, survived until the Japanese takeover of December 1941. Ironically, it was Japan's aggression of 1931 against Manchuria that gave British imperialism a final lease of life. After 1931 the most important British firms at the very least defended their pre-1914 interests. None of them withdrew from

[62] Thomas N. Thompson, *China's Nationalization of Foreign Firms: The Politics of Hostage Capitalism, 1949–1957* (Baltimore, 1979).

China, and several reached peaks of economic success in the 1920s and then again in the years 1935–37.

As time went on the legal and political framework of British informal empire, while still partly in place, became more and more useless and obsolete. The old techniques of coercion fell victim to anarchy and nationalist mass resistance. The more British companies extended their operations up-country, the less they could rely on consular and naval protection. The temporary rescue of a late Imperial British position in China was mainly a result of the split of the Chinese revolutionary movement in 1927 and of the victory of moderate élite nationalism over radical mass nationalism. Between 1931 and 1937 British big business and, with the Leith-Ross mission, the British government also established a new relationship with Chiang Kai-shek's Kuomintang regime. The Chinese partners, however, were demanding collaborators and anything but pliant puppets. When, in July 1937, a shooting incident at Marco Polo Bridge near Peking triggered Japan's full-scale attack on China proper, the way was paved for a more symmetrical relationship between Britain and China. After 1945 no return to the situation of 1936–37 was possible. Britain's scope of action in East Asia was severely curtailed, and the Kuomintang regime emerged from the war corrupt and incompetent, and was soon to struggle for its very survival. The victorious Communists remembered an old tradition of militant anti-imperialism and did not require Western help in revolutionizing the country and running its economy. The 'liberation' of China, one of the principal aims of the revolution, implied the repudiation of the Treaties and the removal of British and other business interests and missionaries. This was accomplished with a thoroughness unparalleled in the history of Asian national liberation. In 1954 Jardine Matheson & Co., the old agency house of opium trade times, was removed from China. Symbolically, at least, this marked the end of an epoch.

Select Bibliography

Marie-Claire Bergère, '"The Other China": Shanghai from 1919 to 1949', in Christopher Howe, ed., *Shanghai: Revolution and Development in an Asian Metropolis* (Cambridge, 1981), pp. 1–34.

Chan Lau Kit-ching, *China, Britain and Hong Kong, 1895–1945* (Hong Kong, 1990).

Nicholas R. Clifford, *Spoilt Children of Empire: Westerners in Shanghai and the Chinese Revolution of the 1920s* (Hanover, NH, 1991).

Roberta Allbert Dayer, *Bankers and Diplomats in China, 1917–1925: The Anglo-American Relationship* (London, 1981).

Stephen L. Endicott, *Diplomacy and Enterprise: British China Policy, 1933–1937* (Manchester, 1975).

ALBERT FEUERWERKER, 'The Foreign Presence in China', in John K. Fairbank, ed., *The Cambridge History of China*, Vol. XII (Cambridge, 1983), pp. 128–207.

E. M. GULL, *British Economic Interests in the Far East* (London, 1943).

EDMUND S. K. FUNG, *The Diplomacy of Imperial Retreat: Britain's South China Policy, 1924–1931* (Hong Kong, 1991).

BEVERLEY HOOPER, *China Stands Up: Ending the Western Presence, 1948–1950* (Sidney, 1986).

WM. ROGER LOUIS, *British Strategy in the Far East, 1919–1939* (Oxford, 1971).

PETER LOWE, *Great Britain and the Origins of the Pacific War: A Study of British Policy in Asia, 1937–1941* (Oxford, 1977).

NORMAN MINERS, *Hong Kong Under Imperial Rule, 1912–1941* (Hong Kong, 1987).

JÜRGEN OSTERHAMMEL, *Britischer Imperialismus im Fernen Osten: Strukturen der Durchdringung und einheimischer Widerstand auf dem chinesischen Markt, 1932–1937* (Bochum, 1982).

ARON SHAI, *Britain and China, 1941–47: Imperial Momentum* (London, 1984).

—— *The Fate of British and French Firms in China, 1949–54: Imperialism Imprisoned* (Basingstoke, 1996).

WENGUANG SHAO, *China, Britain and Businessmen: Political and Commercial Relations, 1949–57* (Basingstoke, 1991).

JAMES TUCK-HONG TANG, *Britain's Encounter with Revolutionary China, 1949–54* (Basingstoke, 1992).

Sir ERIC TEICHMAN, *Affairs of China: A Survey of the Recent History and Present Circumstances of the Republic of China* (London, 1938).

CHRISTOPHER THORNE, *Allies of a Kind: The United States, Britain, and the War against Japan, 1941–1945* (Oxford, 1978).

ANN TROTTER, *Britain and East Asia, 1933–1937* (Cambridge, 1975).

ZHANG ZHONGLI, ed., *Jindai Shanghai chengshi yanjiu* (Studies on the History of Modern Shanghai) (Shanghai, 1990).

29

Australia, New Zealand, and the Pacific Islands

W. DAVID MCINTYRE

In the Pacific lay the most distant and dispersed parts of the Empire. The Line Islands, Pitcairn, and Antarctica marked the farthest Imperial peripheries. The distance between the Cocos Islands and Pitcairn is further than between London and Singapore. In political status the Pacific Empire ran the full spectrum: a large federal Dominion and a small unitary one, each with colonial dependencies; two British Crown Colonies, a Protectorate, a Protected State, a Condominium, and a High Commission regime; two Dominion Mandate territories and a tripartite Mandate; three Antarctic claimant-dependencies, and several isolated islands. In contrast to the geographical span, the total population made up only 1.5 per cent of all the Empire in 1914. In the face of such diversity, four themes invite discussion: the question of co-ordination; the survival of indigenous cultures; economic, political, and strategic roles within the Empire; and the rise of American and Japanese influences. These will be traced through three periods: Imperial overreach, 1914 to the 1930s; war and recovery, the 1940s and 1950s, and decolonization, the 1960s to 1980s. This periodization is unique because Empire lingered longest at its most extended reaches.

Imperial overreach was evident in the Pacific from the turn of the century. Britain sought military help in the South African War and the Boxer uprising. The Anglo-Japanese Alliance permitted the withdrawal of battleships from the Far East. The Admiralty conceded the principle of separate Dominion navies. The Cook Islands and Niue were handed over to New Zealand in 1901 and Papua transferred to Australia in 1906. The Anglo-French Condominium in the New Hebrides symbolized unwillingness to forestall French expansion and prompted the Australian Premier Alfred Deakin's suggestion in 1907 that the Pacific Empire should be run from Sydney and that the United States should co-operate in a new Monroe Doctrine for the Pacific.

It was natural that the Commonwealth of Australia should aspire to lead. With a land-mass almost as big as that of the United States, its population by 1914 reached just under 5 million. Seventy-five per cent were native-born—overwhelmingly of

British stock, about a third being Irish. Most still spoke of Britain as 'Home' and sang 'God Save the King'. To protect this home for 'independent Australian Britons',[1] the White Australia Policy erected an 'ethnic barrier' around the continent by imposing dictation tests on non-British entrants. Aborigines (then not counted in the census) were estimated at about 80,000 in 1914. They had been denied ownership of land since early British settlement on the principle that Australia was *terra nullius*. Australia was also tied to Britain by investment and trade. Britain supplied just over half of all imports and took 44 per cent of Australia's exports, mainly wool, wheat, butter, and meat. As a market for British goods, Australia was second only to India in the Empire. For defence, reliance on the Royal Navy as the deterrent was supplemented by the Royal Australian Navy—a 'Fleet Unit' organized around a battle cruiser, purchased from British yards. In creating a Swiss-type citizen military force by compulsory military training in 1909, the Australians sought the advice of Lord Kitchener on organization and training.

Across the Tasman Sea, the Dominion of New Zealand had in 1914 a population of just over 1 million, inhabiting islands slightly larger than the British Isles. Included in the total was the Maori population, which had been granted British citizenship and a guarantee of lands and treasures but, in 1914, had hardly begun to recover from a low point of 42,000 in the 1890s. There were four Maori seats in Parliament. White New Zealanders, 'Pakeha', prided themselves on being the most British in the Empire. Although a fraction of the Imperial economy compared with Australia, 60 per cent of New Zealand's imports and 80 per cent of exports, mainly in pastoral products, were with Britain. The Dominion also adopted compulsory military training in 1909. In 1913 it made provision for a naval force and acquired a training cruiser, but plans for including New Zealand in an Australasian navy came to nothing. New Zealand also aspired to lead in the Pacific Islands.

Beyond the two Dominions, the other British settler colony in the Pacific was Fiji. The 1911 census gave a total population of 139,500 including 3,700 settlers, mainly Australians. Fijians made up 62 per cent of the total, but were declining, while Indians, first introduced in 1879 as indentured labourers, were growing in number and already made up 29 per cent of the total. Fijian land was inalienable and a pioneer system of Indirect Rule, under which provincial, district, and village chiefs preserved traditional Fijian life, had prevailed since annexation. The Governor consulted the Great Council of Chiefs. The settlers, who once dreamed of federation with 'Australasia', had a modest measure of representative government. As yet, the Indians were unrepresented and politics became a triangular struggle

[1] J. A. La Nauze, *Alfred Deakin: A Biography*, 2 vols. (Melbourne, 1965), II, p. 483.

between Fijians seeking to maintain their paramountcy, Europeans eager to retain privileges, and Indians demanding equality with Europeans. Fijians preserved their traditional way of life and subsistence agriculture; Indians leased land for sugar-growing, mainly for the Australian market.

The Governor of Fiji was also High Commissioner for the Western Pacific, the umbrella authority for the remaining British possessions in the Pacific. Originally created to regulate labour-recruiting in the islands the High Commission worked through Resident Commissioners in the Gilbert and Ellice Islands, the Solomon Islands, and the New Hebrides, and an Agent in Tonga. The Gilbert and Ellice Islands Protectorate covered an expanse of ocean 2,000 miles by 1,000 miles. The sixteen Gilbert Islands (at the south-eastern end of Micronesia), and the nine Ellice Islands (the most westerly group of Polynesia), had an estimated population in 1914 of 30,000, of whom 3,000 were Ellice Islanders. Indirect Rule was adopted, as in Fiji, with responsibility left to chiefs and councils, though each island also received a magistrate, policeman, and scribe, and regulations were made for good order and hygiene. These Protectorate agents of centralization became instruments of change, as village life was regulated in new ways. The Protectorate became the aegis for British activities in the central Pacific. In 1901 Ocean Island (Banaba) was annexed after the Pacific Phosphate Company made an agreement with the 'King' of Ocean Island for extracting phosphate, and in 1908 the island became the administrative capital of the Protectorate, half of whose revenue would come from phosphate royalties. Annexed by Britain as a colony in 1916, the Gilbert and Ellice Islands received oversight of the northern Line Islands (including Fanning Island, an Imperial cable station, and Christmas Island, added in 1919), the Tokelau Islands, and parts of the Phoenix Islands, which were added in 1937. In the British Solomon Islands Protectorate the Resident Commissioner exercised a minimal authority. It was assumed that the estimated 150,000 Islanders were a 'dying race'. The Protectorate regime simply maintained law and order while also encouraging coconut planters, and later logging companies, by facilitating an internal indentured-labour system. This began to play a pervasive role in Solomon Islands life as men turned from subsistence agriculture to wage-earning on plantations.

The High Commission had three further responsibilities. First, in the New Hebrides, a group with a population of about 130,000 speaking 128 languages, French settlers from New Caledonia and Australian trading companies gained large tracts of land in ways that led to growing resistance from the New Hebrideans. British and French naval missions failed to prevent land disputes. By an agreement of 1906 an Anglo-French Condominium was created with parallel administrations under Resident Commissioners, who exercised jurisdiction over their own nationals. A Joint Court of three judges (one British, one French, and a President nominated by the King of Spain) was created to adjudicate in cases between foreign settlers (numbering about 300) and indigenous owners. Condominium authority was minimal and a Protocol providing for a new system of land registration was not ratified until 1923. Britain moved reluctantly in the New Hebrides and considered handing over its share to France or Australia. Secondly, further east, the Kingdom of Tonga was in the unique position of being the only Polynesian kingdom to retain its integrity during the colonial era. With a population of just over 20,000, it was ruled by a constitutional monarchy and parliamentary system evolved under Wesleyan missionary influence in the nineteenth century. By the Treaty of Friendship and Protection of 1900, designed to keep other powers out of Tongatabu's desirable harbour, the British Agent gained power to advise the monarch on major appointments and finance. Thus Tonga became a Protected State. Thirdly, far to the east lay Pitcairn, the Empire's most distant outpost. About 150 descendants of the *Bounty* mutineers subsisted on this two-square-mile island, linked to the world only by steamers passing between Auckland and Panama.

Imperial overreach became obvious during the 1914–18 war when Britain failed to take Germany's Pacific outposts. Japan occupied the German base at Tsingtao and German islands north of the Equator, and helped escort the Australian and New Zealand expeditionary forces. Australia destroyed the German radio stations at Rabaul and Nauru, and New Zealand took Apia in Samoa. Fourteen hundred New Zealanders occupied German Samoa on 29 August 1914. An Australian force of 2,000 descended on Rabaul on 11 September and occupied the rest of German New Guinea. On 16 November an Australian force took Nauru, where the British-dominated Pacific Phosphate Company was profitably extracting phosphate. Further north, the Fanning Island cable station was destroyed by the Germans in 1916.

As well as accomplishing the Empire's security in the islands, Australia and New Zealand quickly made their impact on the Imperial war effort. There was enthusiastic volunteering on both sides of the Tasman, especially among British-born. The Australian Imperial Force (AIF) and the New Zealand Expeditionary Force (NZEF) began to arrive in Egypt in December 1914. They helped defend the Suez Canal against the Turks in February 1915, and from April to December shared in the tragic failure on the Gallipoli peninsula. Here the acronym invented by a New Zealand headquarters sergeant provided the symbol for trans-Tasman military co-operation. 'Anzac' became a badge of nationhood in both countries. Australia lost over 7,000 men and New Zealand over 2,000 on Gallipoli. In the words of the Australian official historian: 'in those days Australia became fully conscious of itself as a nation'[2] and a New Zealand counterpart wrote: 'Before the war we were

[2] C. E. W. Bean, *The Story of Anzac from the Outbreak of War to the End of the First Phase of the Gallipoli Campaign May 4, 1915* (1921; St Lucia, 1981), p. lxviii.

an untried and insular people; after Anzac we were tried and trusted.'[3] Elements of the AIF and the NZEF remained in the Middle East and helped drive the Turks from Palestine; the majority went in 1916 to the Western Front, where the casualties far surpassed those on Gallipoli.

In spite of Imperial euphoria in 1914, the Anzac war effort became politically divisive on both sides of the Tasman. Referendums in October 1916 and December 1917 saw Australians, especially working-class and Catholic voters, reject conscription and thus split the Labor Party. The AIF, expanded to a large corps, remained a rare volunteer army. New Zealand adopted conscription in 1916, which was the catalyst for the formation of the Labour Party. In all, Australia sent 300,000 men (and some women nurses) overseas; New Zealand sent over 100,000 (including nurses), 10 per cent of the total population. Deaths totalled 60,000 for Australia and 17,000 for New Zealand. Few families were untouched by loss. Maori, Cook Islanders, and Niueans, who served in the NZEF, were organized into a Pioneer Battalion; about 200 Australian Aborigines served in the AIF. From the Fiji Defence Force, settler volunteers served in British units, and a 100-strong Fijian Labour Detachment went to France in 1917.

In the aftermath of the war the Empire reached its greatest territorial extent, with the Dominions as agents of Imperial expansion. William M. Hughes, the Australian Prime Minister, battled with President Woodrow Wilson at Versailles to retain Australia's gains. Under the Class C Mandate, Australia was entrusted with northern New Guinea, the Bismarck Archipelago, and the northern Solomons (but did not amalgamate them with Papua). New Zealand received Western Samoa. Since in Nauru Australia and New Zealand squabbled for control of the phosphate, a Mandate was conferred on the British Empire, exercised by Britain, Australia, and New Zealand jointly. To provide cheap fertilizer for farmers, the Pacific Phosphate Company received compensation and handed over its operations to the British Phosphate Commission. In 1920 the British, Australian, and New Zealand governments gained shares in the ratio 42 : 42 : 16 and farmers in the Dominions got phosphate at about half the market price. For the unpleasant task of working the phosphate, the Commission brought in indentured labourers from Hong Kong and the Gilbert Islands. Nauru was administered by Australia. As the Empire expanded, questions arose over the co-ordination of all these disparate elements. Sir Ronald Munro Ferguson, the Governor-General of Australia, advocated a single authority for the Pacific. In January 1917 he said 'the faggots of administrative control must be gathered into one bundle' supervised from Australia.[4] In 1918 an inter-state commission on Pacific trade also mooted a federal scheme, centred on Sydney.[5]

[3] F. Waite, *The New Zealanders at Gallipoli* (Auckland, 1919), p. 299.

[4] Ferguson memorandum, 12 Jan. 1917, National Library of Australia: Novar Papers, MSS, 696/6742.

[5] G. H. Scholefield, *The Pacific, Its Past and Future* (London, 1919), pp. 301–02.

After the war there was a final fling of territorial imperialism in the uninhabited expanses of Antarctica, where Australia and New Zealand were again agents of British expansion. The move arose from efforts to regulate whaling. During the war Antarctica assumed new importance as a source of glycerine from whale oil, used in explosives. In 1920 L. S. Amery, as Under-Secretary for the Colonies, informed the Dominions that the whole of Antarctica 'should ultimately be included within the British Empire'.[6] An application from a Norwegian for a whaling licence in the Ross Sea prompted an Order-in-Council of 31 July 1923 declaring the Ross Dependency a British Settlement under the administration of the Governor-General of New Zealand. Norwegian and American activities in the late 1920s led to the creation of the Australian Antarctic Territory in February 1933. Graham's Land was claimed by Britain as part of the Falkland Islands Dependencies, but none of the Imperial claims were recognized internationally.

In no matter was Imperial overreach so evident as in defence strategy. At the 1921 Imperial Conference, Hughes suggested that: 'The stage upon which the great world drama is to be played in the future is the Pacific.'[7] Dissatisfaction about naval strength in the Pacific led to the commission of Admiral of the Fleet Lord Jellicoe to tour the Dominions and India and to report to each government on naval policy. Far exceeding his brief, Jellicoe, in secret sections of his Australian and New Zealand reports, identified Japan as an inevitable future enemy and proposed an Empire Pacific fleet, including sixteen capital ships, costing £20m per year to be shared by Britain (75 per cent), Australia (20 per cent), and New Zealand (5 per cent). This mighty force would need a new dockyard at Singapore. Both the Admiralty and the Dominion governments balked at the cost of a new Pacific Fleet and adopted, instead, the policy of building the Singapore naval base to service the British main fleet during operations in the Pacific.

Soon after this decision, Canada's opposition to the Anglo-Japanese Alliance caused agonized discussions at the 1921 Imperial Conference, but the American invitation to an international conference on naval disarmament and the Pacific helped to resolve the issue. From Washington came the Four Power Pacific Pact, which replaced the Anglo-Japanese Alliance, and the Five Power Naval Limitation Treaty, limiting capital-shipbuilding by Britain, the United States, and Japan to a 10 : 10 : 6 ratio. As Britain and the United States required Atlantic and Pacific navies, Japan's 60 per cent ratio conceded naval supremacy in the Western Pacific. Britain had, in effect, put American friendship before the Japanese alliance, and Australia and New Zealand emerged feeling more vulnerable. As the building of

[6] H. Logan, 'Cold Commitment: The Development of New Zealand's Territorial Role in Antarctica, 1920–1960', unpublished MA thesis, University of Canterbury, New Zealand, 1979, p. 5.

[7] Imperial Meetings, 2nd mtg, 21 June 1921, CAB[inet] 32/2, Part 1.

the Singapore base proceeded fitfully during the 1920s, New Zealand offered financial subsidies but Australia concentrated on warship construction. Both countries based their defence strategy on the deterrent of the 'main fleet to Singapore' and trained for expeditionary forces to assist Imperial defence. They also agreed to protect various British islands in the Pacific.

Although in the 1940s and 1950s the Pacific Empire went through the turmoil of war and recovery, its territorial shape remained unchanged until the 1960s. In this period the two Dominions were evolving as independent nations, and each contemplated a significant regional role. Between the wars they were still dependent on Britain constitutionally, economically, financially, and strategically, but they became increasingly insistent on asserting their own identity and interests. At the 1923 Imperial Conference S. M. Bruce (Australia) and W. F. Massey (New Zealand), called for an Empire foreign policy in which they should have a voice. Bruce pressed also for an Empire Economic Conference where, in a celebrated speech about 'men, money and markets', he demanded aid for the peopling and development of Australia and security in the British market for its products.[8] Britain still took over 40 per cent of Australia's exports in 1929 and 75 per cent of New Zealand's. Financial dependence was even greater, at a time when the City was less able to lend. By 1929 debt repayments took 28 per cent of Australia's export income and borrowing was needed to service existing loans. New Zealand's interest payments ran at twice the level of export receipts in the 1920s. Both Dominions fought hard at the Ottawa Economic Conference in 1932 to protect the price and quantity of their products in the British market.

Politically, both Dominions played up to the doctrine of equality enunciated in the Balfour Report of 1926. At the same time, Bruce and Gordon Coates (New Zealand) insisted on the old usage 'British Empire' along with 'British Commonwealth of Nations'. When equality was sanctified in the Statute of Westminster in 1931, New Zealand was only persuaded to be included by the insertion of a clause making adoption of the main sections optional, and Australia asked for the same. Thus the Commonwealth of Australia Act (1901) and the New Zealand Constitution Act (1852) were both unaffected. Australia did not 'adopt' the statute until 1942; New Zealand delayed until 1947.

Over defence there were growing doubts in the 1930s about the practicality of the Singapore strategy. Both Dominions embarked on modest rearmament plans and prepared to pull British chestnuts out of a Pacific fire. At the Pacific Defence Conference in Wellington in April 1939, where they heard increasingly qualified promises about the main fleet to Singapore, the Dominions planned an air

[8] I. M. Cumpston, *Lord Bruce of Melbourne* (Melbourne, 1989), p. 40.

reconnaissance line from Papua to the Cook Islands. New Zealand sent garrisons to Fanning, Fiji, and Tonga early in the German war, and later an airfield construction unit and pilots for a fighter squadron to Malaya. Australia sent a two-brigade division and five air squadrons to Malaya in 1940 and small garrisons to Norfolk Island, New Guinea, and the Solomon Islands.

The Pacific Empire was shaken but not shattered by the war. But even before Japan struck, Australia and New Zealand had turned to the United States. The German war did not present immediate threats (other than shipping losses and mining hazards caused by German commerce raiders), and both Dominions despatched large expeditionary forces to Egypt. But Italy's entry into the war and the collapse of France in mid-1940 led to a major watershed. Faced with the German and Italian navies and having lost support of the French navy, Prime Minister Winston Churchill informed his Australian and New Zealand counterparts that the fleet could not be sent to the Pacific in the foreseeable future. If Japan took the opportunity of the European war to expand in the Pacific, the Empire would have to rely on the United States for protection. It became vitally important to achieve a voice in Washington, where diplomatic relations were opened, by Australia before the Pacific outbreak, and by New Zealand soon after.

During the Pacific War both Dominions were endangered as never before. Darwin was bombed in February 1942; Sydney harbour was penetrated by two Japanese midget submarines, and Wellington and Auckland were overflown by submarine-launched reconnaissance aircraft. War between Japan and the United States precipitated the most intense upheaval in Pacific Islands history. In the opening weeks of the war the Japanese bombed the phosphate facilities of Nauru and Ocean Island, and overran Tarawa and Butaritari in the Gilberts. Nauru and Ocean Island were occupied in 1942. Rabaul and Port Moresby, the administrative centres of New Guinea and Papua, were bombed and Rabaul occupied on 23 January 1942. In March 1942 the Japanese landed on the northern shore of New Guinea and occupied Tulagi and Guadalcanal in the Solomons in May 1942. Their plans to take Port Moresby were checked by the United States Navy in the Battle of the Coral Sea and by Australian land defences at Milne Bay and Kokoda.

More significant in the long run than the shock of bombing, invasion, and subsequent liberation was the upheaval to the islanders' worlds. First, most colonial administrators abandoned the Gilberts and the Solomons. Only a few missionaries stayed behind, along with a handful of courageous coast-watchers, who created a network for reporting on ship and aircraft movements. Secondly, when the Japanese stationed 5,000 marines on Nauru they deported 1,600 Nauruans to Truk and 400 to Ocean Island. Some islanders were conscripted into the Japanese forces. Thirdly, although the Ellice Islands were not overrun and became a no-man's-land between contenders, the United States made Funafuti an advance air-base in October 1942, later adding Nukufetau and Nanumea. Here the erection of air-strips and supply depots meant the obliteration of coconut trees and precious food gardens, and the American bases attracted Japanese bombing raids. In November 1943, as the Americans struck back, a thousand marines were killed recapturing Tarawa.

Fourthly, the Americans had a huge psychological impact. Although British administrators returned to the Gilberts, the Americans, with their friendliness and material goods—jeeps, Coca-Cola, hospitals, and cinemas—presented white men (and some black men) in a different light from that in which a select band of missionaries, administrators, and traders had been seen before. Over 1,200 islanders joined the Gilbert Islands Labour Corps, one company of which went to Guadalcanal. In 1944 there was a petition that the colony should be transferred to American sovereignty. A similar impact was experienced in the South-West Pacific. Over 200,000 US personnel were assembled in the New Hebrides for the recovery of the Solomon Islands. There was the same massive importation of material goods; the same friendliness from American servicemen, including black troops. In August 1942, when the Americans began their attack on Guadalcanal and then fought painfully through the Solomon Islands towards Rabaul, they were joined by New Zealand and Fijian units and the Solomon Islands Defence Corps. Having observed the hasty British evacuation, the Islanders now enjoyed the largesse of Americans. Some worked for the Americans in the British-organized Solomon Islands Labour Corps. There were hopes that the Americans would take over the Solomon Islands.

In the Australian territories, the Japanese clung to Rabaul and northern New Guinea until their surrender in September 1945. With 300,000 Japanese, 500,000 Australians, and 1 million Americans passing through Papua and New Guinea, foreigners equalled the indigenous population. Of these, there were 40,000 labourers working for the services by 1944; others fought in the Pacific Islands Regiment. Things could never be the same in the islands after the war, and especially the American occupation.

Empire relations were made unsteady by grandiose Australian suggestions for a new approach to the Pacific. Dr Herbert Evatt, the Minister of External Affairs, proposed in 1943 that the Tasman Dominions should concert their post-war policies. He insisted that they should have 'a decisive voice'[9] in post-war settlements, take a lead in policies for the welfare of the island peoples, even assume Britain's role in the region. Evatt's initiative led to the signing of the Australia–New Zealand Agreement (Canberra Pact) on 21 January 1944 which demanded an Anzac voice in the peace settlement in the Pacific, declared a defensive zone from the

[9] Robin Kay, ed., *The Australian–New Zealand Agreement, 1944* (Wellington, 1972), p. 47.

Cocos to the Cook Islands, mooted an international conference on Pacific Island welfare, and made a pledge of future trans-Tasman co-operation. Although this formal agreement between two Commonwealth countries raised eyebrows in London and hackles in Washington, Evatt and Peter Fraser, the New Zealand Prime Minister, went on to make a significant mark during the San Francisco conference on United Nations Organization (UN) in 1945. They sought a greater role for small countries, but they failed to avoid the Great Power veto in the Security Council or gain greater initiative for the General Assembly. On colonial questions, they could not persuade the British to set an example by placing all colonies under some UN aegis, but they managed to ensure that the Trusteeship Council became a major organ in the UN structure and went on to summon the conference which led to the formation of the South Pacific Commission.[10]

Although Australia and New Zealand appeared to rock the boat by their rather presumptuous assertions, they felt obligations to their two protectors and faced what has been called 'the Anzac dilemma'.[11] Mother Britannia, the traditional protector, with whom comfortable channels of consultation existed, was far away and in decline; Uncle Sam, the new protector, was now dominant in the Pacific, but relations with Washington were as yet uncertain. Ideally, a combined 'Britanzus' relationship was desirable. Thus, the Australian and New Zealand navies were incorporated in the British Pacific Fleet in 1944–45 and, during the occupation of Japan, the British Commonwealth Occupation Force, made up of British, Australian, New Zealand, and Indian units, was commanded by an Australian general and controlled by a Joint Chiefs of Staff organization in Melbourne.

A further possible opportunity for joint arrangements appeared in 1945 when the United States sought to retain some of its wartime bases as part of a global chain. These included Manus in New Guinea, Guadalcanal in the Solomons, Nadi in Fiji, Espiritu Santo in the New Hebrides, Funafuti and Christmas Island in the Gilbert and Ellice group, and Apia in Western Samoa. Britain and New Zealand were content to have the Americans in their islands, but the Australians wanted the Americans to give a security guarantee in return for the bases. The Americans were not interested in commitments, only bases on a care and maintenance basis, and they soon abandoned the idea. But the quest for an American guarantee continued.

Meanwhile, as Australia and New Zealand were drawn into the strategies of the cold war, their dispositions took on the aspect of earlier Imperial defence (Map 29.1). In 1946 at the Commonwealth Prime Ministers' Meetings, the British

[10] Wm. Roger Louis, *Imperialism at Bay, 1941–1945: The United States and the Decolonization of the British Empire,* (Oxford, 1977), pp. 532–73.

[11] F. L. W. Wood, 'The Anzac Dilemma', *International Affairs*, XXIX, 2 (1953), pp. 184–92.

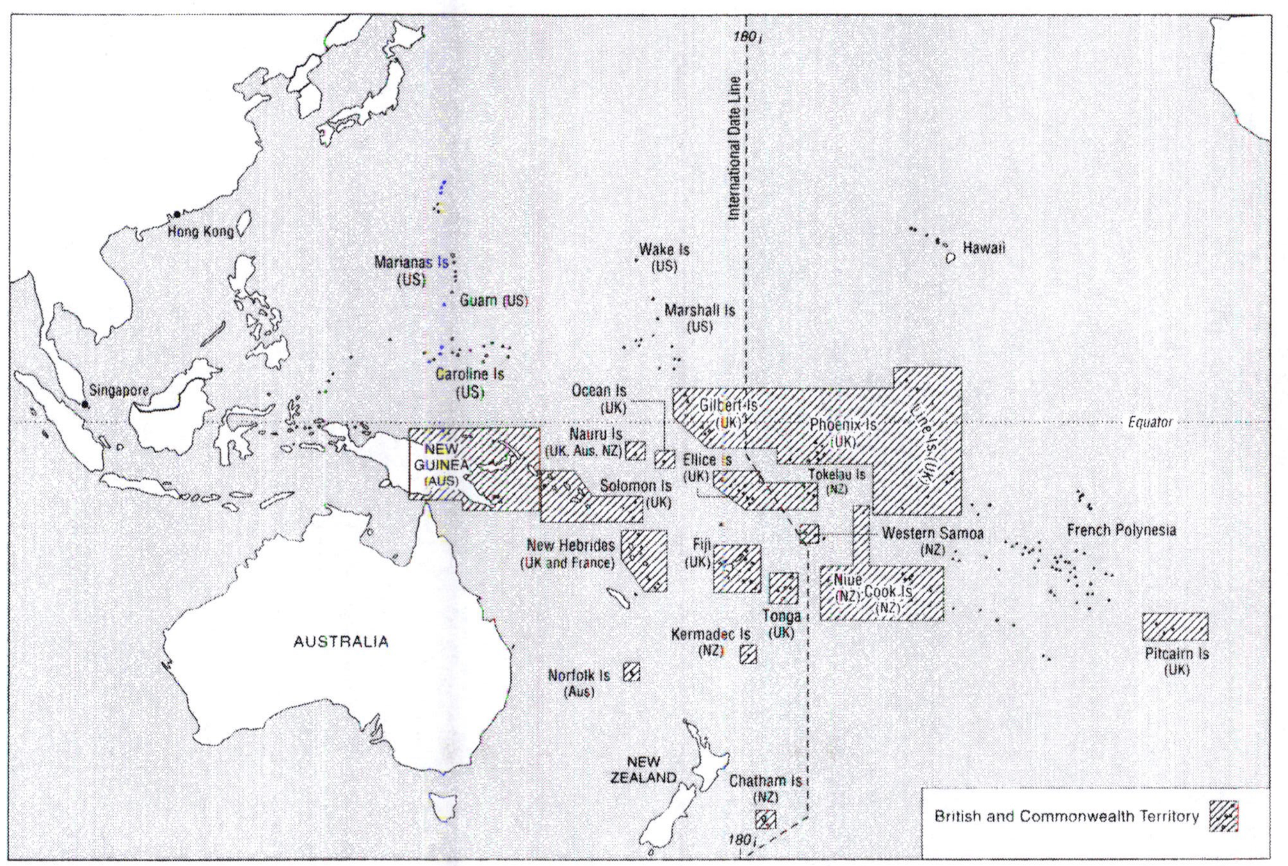

Map 29.1 The Pacific Islands in 1945

identified the Soviet Union as a likely enemy, which might strike southwards to cut the Suez Canal and acquire the oil of the Gulf. By 1948 Britain was asking for Dominion assistance in the event of a Middle East war to protect air-bases from which the Soviet Union could be bombed. It also sought assistance in Malaya after the outbreak of the Communist insurrection in 1948 and for the defence of Hong Kong after the Communist victory in China in 1949. New Zealand was the first to respond to these requests. Prime Minister Peter Fraser was prepared to send an army division, five air squadrons, and a warship to the Middle East, and he persuaded his anti-militarist Labour Party to accept a referendum on peacetime conscription in 1949. He offered three frigates, a Mosquito squadron, and three Dakotas for the defence of Hong Kong, but only the last were required. Australia was more cautious. The Labor government of Ben Chifley offered to take responsibility for strategic planning in the Anzac and Malayan areas, which bore fruit in the Anzam Arrangements. After the Liberal–Country Party government of Robert Menzies came to power in 1949, it adopted a policy of concurrent alternate plans. One plan was for reinforcing Malaya first and the Middle East second, the other reversed the priority. When the Korean War broke out in mid-1950 the British insisted that it was a Soviet-inspired diversion, and that the real threat was in the Middle East. But both Australia and New Zealand sent warships to join the British Far East Fleet, and Australia sent bombers to Malaya and fighters to Korea. After hesitations, they both sent land troops to Korea, two Australian infantry battalions and a New Zealand artillery regiment, which were eventually grouped together with British and Canadian brigades and an Indian ambulance unit in the unique UN Commonwealth Division.

The Korean War was significant for the Anzac dilemma. It prompted the United States to push ahead with a non-punitive Japanese peace treaty, which would not debar rearmament. The looming spectre of a Communist-controlled Japan, allied to China, the Soviet Union, and possibly a Communist Germany, gave great urgency to the American desire for a 'peace of reconciliation'. Australia and New Zealand, still fearful of future Japanese aggression, would not agree to a non-restrictive peace without an American security guarantee. And they had another reason: their recent commitments to help Britain in the Middle East and Malaya required someone to 'bolt the back door' while they contributed outside the Pacific.[12] Thus in 1951, through the skilful diplomacy of John Foster Dulles, the United States conceded the Anzus Treaty. Britain was excluded, with the approval of the Attlee government, but when Churchill returned to power shortly after the signing of Anzus he put great pressure on the Anzacs to engineer Britain's inclusion. The Tasman neighbours got their American guarantee. Britain, though

[12] W. David McIntyre, *Background to the Anzus Pact* (London, 1995), pp. 317, 325, 330, 352.

excluded, received continued support in various ways. The Australian government allowed rocket tests at Woomera and even atomic tests at Maralinga in 1953–57. New Zealand balked at allowing thermonuclear tests on the Kermadec Islands, but did assist the British during the 1957–58 tests from Christmas Island.

Decolonization came late in the Pacific. Although Australia and New Zealand had made their own decisions for war in 1939, adopted the Statute of Westminster, turned to the United States as protector, demanded a voice in post-war settlements, and made a considerable impact at the San Francisco UN conference, the war did not end close ties with Britain. Supplying materials, especially wool and food products, was as important to the war effort as their military contributions. Although there were some bitter British–Australian disputes over the conduct of the war, it was Churchill who suggested Australian troops should leave the Middle East to defend Australia, and it was John Curtin who, in 1944, suggested a Commonwealth Secretariat. In 1949 the election of non-Labo[u]r governments on both sides of the Tasman produced in Robert Menzies and Sidney Holland leaders who loved the Empire and were uncomfortable with the 'new' Commonwealth. In 1948 Menzies, while in opposition, had deplored the 'Mackenzie King–Evatt view'[13] of Empire and declared himself 'British to the bootstraps'. Holland saw himself as a 'Britisher through and through', and talked about the 'dear old Empire'.[14]

Yet as the British position in the Middle East collapsed in the 1950s, Anzac commitments were quietly abandoned in favour of participation on the ground in Malaya in a reserve force to deter Chinese intervention in South-East Asia. In 1955 Menzies announced that Australia would contribute an infantry battalion, four air-force units, and two warships, and Holland volunteered the services of a New Zealand SAS unit (later an infantry battalion). The Commonwealth Far East Strategic Reserve comprised a brigade group with joint headquarters at Terendak. It was pledged to support the South-East Asia Treaty Organization and assisted against Communist insurgents within Malaya. This assistance far surpassed Imperial collaboration between the wars. Yet, ironically, this refocusing of defence strategy was soon followed by moral support for Britain in the Suez Crisis of 1956, when both Dominions indulged in a final flaunting of what Holland called the 'ties of blood and Empire'.[15] Menzies headed an abortive mission to Nasser. Holland wanted to 'stick to Britain through thick and thin',[16] and at first agreed that the

[13] Menzies to Harrison, 1 Nov. 1948. National Library of Australia, Canberra: Menzies MSS, Series 1, Box 14, Folder 19.

[14] Barry Gustafson, *The First 50 Years: A History of the New Zealand National Party* (Wellington, 1986), p. 41.

[15] Malcolm Templeton, *Ties of Blood and Empire* (Auckland, 1994), pp. vi, 104.

[16] Ibid., p. 67.

New Zealand cruiser *Royalist* could be part of the British attack fleet. Eventually, however, he was persuaded by his officials to withhold it at the last minute.

When, a decade later, the Wilson government announced Britain's 'withdrawal from East of Suez', the Australian and New Zealand governments did not follow: they left small forces in Singapore and Malaysia long after the British departed, Australia until 1988 and New Zealand until 1989. Both sent units to South Vietnam to assist the Americans between 1962 and 1972, while Britain stayed aloof. And when the concept of 'forward defence' became discredited in the 1970s, they concentrated on their 'maritime archipelago environment'. Here, in their different ways, Australia and New Zealand contributed to the belated decolonization of the Pacific.

Decolonization in Asia and Africa had little impact in the Pacific, largely because of the smallness of the island dependencies, their backwardness in education and development, and the modesty of their nationalist aspirations. Until the 1960s Britain did not accept that independence was an option for small colonies. In reports from numerous committees and study-groups, which tried to anticipate timetables for self-government and the future shape of the Commonwealth, the Pacific territories usually appeared last or were not even mentioned. Various options, such as 'Island States', 'Commonwealth States', 'Associated States', or the 'Tonga model' were mooted; configurations for a Melanesian Federation were put forward; and there were ideas for hiving-off small colonies to Australia or New Zealand. Until 1960 the basic assumption was that some islands would retain dependent status, but in the year of the 'Wind of Change' there were dramatic developments outside the Pacific. The decision that Cyprus, with a population of only 500,000, should become independent (apart from two Sovereign Base Areas) opened the way for 'all the other tiddlers'.[17] Criteria for independence and Commonwealth membership suddenly changed. UN Resolution 1514 demanded an end to colonialism, while the admission in 1960 of a record number of new Afro-Asian members to the UN left the Pacific as a last bastion of colonial rule. Soviet representatives at international forums began to cultivate indigenous delegates from Pacific countries. There was growing anxiety about 'communist activity' in the islands—which usually amounted to distribution of leaflets by Australian and New Zealand seamen, who supported strikers in island ports of call.[18]

In spite of this new international context, Pacific Islanders had different preoccupations. Dispersion, multiple languages, and island particularism retarded the growth of 'national' movements. Fijians used colonial rule to protect their way

[17] Note for the Record by T. Bligh of meeting on 13 July 1960, PREM[ier] 11/3649.

[18] Note on Soviet and Communist interest in British Pacific Territories, 18 Dec. 1961, PAC 182/777/02, C[olonial] O[ffice] 1036/860.

of life from the Indians, who became the majority population after 1946. Cook Islanders, Niueans, and Tokelauans cherished their New Zealand citizenship and entry rights. In Tonga the Imperial presence always sat lightly. In Papua New Guinea, the Solomon Islands, and the New Hebrides regional divisions were strong. Sheer distance and cultural differences between the Micronesian Ocean Islanders and Gilbertese and the Polynesian Ellice Islanders retarded the growth of a colony-wide consciousness. Throughout the Pacific, islanders clung to traditional ways of life, based on subsistence agriculture, focusing on what they saw as important—land, church, and culture.

The preservation and management, or recovery, of indigenous land rights was central to the islanders' attitude towards colonial rule. Christian churches played a dominant role in the social life of communities and pioneered the development of formal women's organizations. Competitive church-building was indulged in by the various missionary denominations and their indigenous successor-churches. But alongside the adopting of Christianity, parliamentary forms of government, and selected Western modes of dress, diet, and housing, Pacific cultures continued to flourish through language, song, dance, handicrafts, and ceremonies, in all of which women played a vital role. Emigration to Australia, New Zealand, and the United States attracted significant portions of the small island populations, whose homelands became known as 'MIRAB economies' (signifying reliance on migration, remittances, aid, and bureaucracy).[19] Yet the most striking legacy in the Pacific was the resilience of the island cultures as they responded to the ending of formal Empire.

New Zealand led the way with decolonization in Western Samoa, which had seen, in the *Mau*, the most organized anti-colonial movement in the Pacific between the wars. In 1944 Peter Fraser visited Samoa, and after his stand against old-style colonialism at San Francisco, was determined to respond to Samoan demands and redeem New Zealand's deplorable reputation as a colonial ruler. A major step was made in 1948 when the New Zealand High Commissioner associated the royal lineage heads, the *Fautua*, in a Council of State and called a Legislative Assembly with a Samoan majority. In 1953 an Executive Council was created. A Samoan constitutional convention gathered to draft a new constitution. This provided that the Head of State would be the *Fautua* and a Cabinet would be responsible to an Assembly elected by titled heads of households, the *matai*. A Prime Minister of high title, Mata'afa Fiame, was appointed in 1959, and the New Zealand Prime Minister announced in the United Nations that independence would be granted. Although in London the notion of a sovereign state of only

[19] Penelope Schoeffel, 'Social Change', in K. R. Howe and others, eds., *Tides of History: The Pacific Islands in the Twentieth Century* (St Leonards, NSW, 1994), p. 359.

110,000 people was dubbed a *reductio ad absurdum*,[20] independence was granted on 1 January 1962. External affairs and defence were initially handled by New Zealand and—much to Britain's relief—Western Samoa did not join the Commonwealth at this juncture.

In the Cook Islands and Niue New Zealand adopted different solutions. Of the 21,000 Cook Islanders, many lived in New Zealand. After economic and constitutional assessments in the mid-1950s, an elected Legislative Assembly was created in 1958. Four options were offered in 1962: independence, integration with New Zealand, federation with other islands, or self-government in association with New Zealand. The last was chosen. After an election in 1965, observed by an invited UN mission, the new constitution retained the Queen (as Queen of New Zealand) as Head of State; a Cabinet, presided over by a Premier, became responsible to the Assembly. External affairs and defence were conducted by the Premier in association with the New Zealand Prime Minister. Formal colonial status thus gave way to self-government in free association. In 1974 the Cook Islanders adopted their own flag and undertook the conduct of external relations, but they retained their New Zealand citizenship and entry rights. In the same year a similar system was adopted in Niue. A visiting UN mission was told that Niue approached the ideal of Greek democracy. A population of 5,000 lived in fourteen villages, each of which elected an Assembly member who regularly consulted with electors on the village green after church on Sundays. Yet another experiment was tried in Tokelau, three small atolls, ruled by New Zealand since 1926, with a population of 1,500. A scheme of depopulation by resettlement in New Zealand did not work, though by 1996, 4917 Tokelauans lived in New Zealand. A simple system was devised of island councils, or *fono*, made up of elders, and a General *Fono*, appointed by village councils of elders. New Zealand, the main paymaster, appointed an Administrator resident in Wellington. Tokelau gained self-determination by a scheme of supervision *in absentia*.

Depopulation was also contemplated as an option for Nauru, the tripartite Trust Territory administered by Australia. Here the extraction of phosphate left the islanders with a wasting resource, potential loss of income, and a devastated landscape. A Community Investment Fund was set up in 1947 to safeguard income, but in 1948 the Nauruan chiefs petitioned the United Nations for more say in government. In 1956 they elected as Head Chief Hammer DeRoburt, one of the 'Geelong boys' who had come under the influence of an idealistic teacher in Australia. By the 1960s DeRoburt was asserting Nauruan ownership of the phosphate deposits and independence for his people either on Nauru or elsewhere. Possible sites for resettlement in the Solomon Islands, Fiji, or New Guinea were

[20] Mills to Bligh, 11 Dec. 1961, PREM 11/2354.

rejected. A site in Australia, on an island off the Queensland coast, was considered, but by 1964 resettlement had been rejected. The Naurans demanded independence, ownership of the phosphate, and control of the industry. Although the concept of an independent nation of 6,000 was dismissed as ridiculous, Australia was finding its Trust Territories an embarrassment in the United Nations. In the hope that a quick settlement with Nauru might buy time in New Guinea, Australia agreed to the sale of the phosphate operations to a Nauru Phosphate Corporation. On 31 January 1968 Nauru became an independent republic. Phosphate profits, which rose dramatically after the first oil shock in 1973, gave it a viability not enjoyed by other islands. Nauruans had one of the highest GDPs per head in the world in the 1970s.

Concessions in Nauru were irrelevant to affairs in New Guinea, except perhaps to stimulate interest in the possibility of gaining independence. Papua and New Guinea were only administered as a single unit after the war. Not until 1955 did the regime contemplate primary education for all as a preliminary to development. Government remained colonial in form until the 1950s; the Administrator consulted an Advisory Council while the Legislative Council had an official majority and only three Papua New Guineans. Visiting UN missions noted the comparative backwardness and called for development plans. Creation of an elected House of Assembly in 1964 was followed by rapid advance to responsible government. With the accession of the Labor government of Gough Whitlam in Canberra in 1972, plans for self-government accelerated. Michael Somare, Chief Minister of a coalition, negotiated with the Australian Prime Minister, and in 1973 the Assembly accepted a timetable for self-rule. Independence was conferred on 16 September 1975, with the Queen as Head of State and the Prime Minister heading a National Executive Council responsible to a hundred-member Parliament. Australia underwrote 40 per cent of the budget. National unity was fragile and secessionist movements appeared on New Britain, Bougainville, the Highlands, and Papua. The declaration of a Republic of North Solomons on Bougainville led to a compromise system of provincial government, but armed secession was attempted in the 1980s.

Similar problems of disunity beset all four British colonies, none of which was prepared for nationhood. Fiji was the most advanced politically and economically. Since 1937 the Executive Council had consisted of the Governor, four ex-officio members, and three elected Legislative Councillors (one European, one Indian, and one Fijian). The legislature had an official majority, but there were six Europeans and three Indians representing communal electorates and three Fijians nominated by the Great Council of Chiefs. Traditional life was preserved under the Fijian Administration, headed by Ratu Sir Lala Sukuna, a high-born Fijian Oxford graduate, as Secretary for Fijian Affairs. By the 1946 Census, Indians made up 46 per cent of the population, the Fijians 45 per cent. Indians succeeded in sugar-growing, business, and Western education, but they did not volunteer for military service, as compared with Fijians, who had fought in the Solomon Islands campaign and later in Malaya. In the cost–benefit analysis of the Empire called for by Harold Macmillan in 1957, it was suggested that if Britain withdrew from Fiji there would be strife between Indians and Fijians.

After 1960 pressure for change came from Britain. In 1962 Lord Selkirk, the Commissioner-General in Singapore, who had residual military obligations to back up the civil powers in the Pacific, called Fiji an 'intractable problem', and advocated telling the Indians firmly that Fijian paramountcy had to stay.[21] There were worries that Fiji could become 'another Cuba'.[22] But both communities deprecated early British withdrawal and even mooted the idea of integration with Britain. In 1964 a member system was adopted, with three unofficial executive councillors given government portfolios, and a new Legislative Council was created with fourteen Fijian, twelve Indian, and ten European elected members. After a general election in 1966, the Fijian-dominated Alliance Party, led by high-born Ratu Kamisese Mara, achieved a majority with European and some Indian support. By 1969 he was ready to accept Dominion Status, in exchange for constitutional guarantees of Fijian interests. Independence was granted on 10 October 1970, ninety-six years after annexation. For the new House of Representatives electors cast votes in both communal and national constituencies in a complex cross-voting system which gave twenty-two Fijian, twenty-two Indian, and eight General (mainly European) members. European over-representation helped maintain Alliance domination, so Fiji was handed back to the Fijians at the expense of the Indians' claim for equality. When the latter gained greater influence in the 1987 elections the Fijians responded with a military coup, which led to permanent Fijian supremacy.

Also in 1970, Western Samoa joined the Commonwealth, and Tonga ended its Protected State relationship with Britain, becoming a fully independent monarchy on 4 June 1970. At the Singapore Commonwealth Heads of Government Meeting in 1971 three Pacific nations attended for the first time. Fiji, Tonga, and Western Samoa had also taken the initiative in creating the first non-colonial regional organization, the Pacific Islands Producers Association, and in 1971 they prevailed on New Zealand to host a Commonwealth regional grouping. The President of Nauru, the Prime Ministers of New Zealand, Fiji, Tonga, Western Samoa, the Premier of the Cook Islands, and the Australian External Affairs Minister inaugurated the South Pacific Forum, which would, over the next decade, grow to become a fourteen-member regional body.

[21] Selkirk to Maudling, 24 Jan. 1962, PFP (62) 7, 12 Feb. 1962, CAB 134/2402.

[22] Ibid., Commonwealth Relations Office Note, PFP (60) 10, 6 April 1962.

In the Gilbert and Ellice Islands, distance, land shortages, and diversity led administrators to regard the group as a series of 'over-crowded island republics'.[23] Ocean Island phosphates generated half the colony's revenue until the 1970s, but the majority of the Banabans had chosen Rabi Island in Fiji as their post-war homeland, bought with phosphate royalties. The colony's administrative capital had been shifted back to Tarawa in 1952. A scheme for donating Tarawa to the United States for a Marine Corps memorial as a sweetener for the American loan was rejected by Attlee's Cabinet in 1946. Shortage of land and war devastation in the Gilberts reinforced pre-war attempts at resettlement in the Phoenix Islands. When this proved unsatisfactory, 1,400 Gilbertese settled in the Solomons in the 1960s. At the time of the 1957 cost–benefit analysis British officials were more preoccupied with the international ramifications of the Gilberts. Canton and Enderbury Islands had been under British–US Condominium since 1939; the United States also claimed some of the Line and Phoenix Islands; Fanning Island's cable station was being rebuilt; Christmas Island was the base for British thermonuclear tests. It was feared that if Britain withdrew, the United States or, possibly, Japan might step in.

Progress towards self-government was a slow process, which suddenly accelerated in the 1970s. Native Magistrates who presided over Island Councils were consulted in annual conferences, which developed into wider biennial Colony Conferences from 1956. In 1963 an Advisory Council was created, followed by an Executive Council (also with legislative powers), consisting of the Resident Commissioner, four officials, and four island representatives. These tended to be civil servants, fluent in English, and in this last respect Ellice Islanders fared better than the Gilbertese. Resentments among the latter led to the founding of the Gilbertese National Party in 1965. In 1967 an advisory House of Representatives was created. It was designed to provide procedural experience, while the Resident Commissioner consulted a Governing Council with executive and legislative powers. However, a Select Committee opted in 1969 for a return to the usual colonial Executive and Legislative Councils. There were expectations of free association on the Cook Islands model, but Anthony Kershaw, Parliamentary Under-Secretary for Foreign and Commonwealth Affairs, visited the islands in 1972 and indicated that Britain wanted to give full independence. At this point the Ellice Islanders called for separation, and recent memories of Anguilla's secession from St Kitts prompted Kershaw to admit this option. While the colony advanced to a ministerial system in 1974, with an elected Chief Minister, a referendum was held in which 92 per cent of Ellice Islanders voted for separation.

[23] Gilbert and Ellice Islands Colony Ten Year Plan, 30 Nov. 1946, C[olonial] O[ffice] 225/348/88631.

In 1975 Tuvalu (Eight Islands Together), with a population of 7,200 and a twelve-member Parliament, was separated and became independent on 1 October 1978. In Kiribati ('Kiribass', the Gilberts) there was delay because of Banaban demands for the separation of Ocean Island and greater phosphate income, and the American claims on the eastern islands. Once these problems were resolved, a constitutional convention met in 1977 and, after elections in 1978, the Parliament elected 28-year-old Ieremia Tabai as President and Head of Government. Independence followed on 10 July 1979 for a state populated by 60,000 people, living on thirty-three islands spread over nearly 2 million square miles of ocean. By a Treaty of Friendship, the United States recognized Kiribati sovereignty over the islands which the Americans had formerly claimed in the Line and Phoenix groups.

The Solomons presented severe problems of post-war reconstruction, as virtually all infrastructure and plantations had been destroyed. While official policy was to develop local government through Native Councils and Courts under Headmen and to link these to the Resident Commissioner's Advisory Council, no Solomon Islander joined the latter until 1950. Meanwhile, the restoration of British rule led to various forms of resistance and the presence of American surveyors on Guadalcanal until 1949 excited expectations that the Americans would return bringing material largesse. The most serious protest came from the Maasina Rule 'Brotherhood' (referred to by the authorities as 'Marching Rule'). Centred first in Malaita, the most populous island, and led by former members of the South Seas Evangelical mission, Solomon Islands Labour Corps, and the police force, it boycotted Native Councils, withheld taxes, and created an alternative hierarchy of Head Chiefs, lesser chiefs, and police. It sought to base authority on indigenous custom; to improve health and education; and it proved that the Islanders could create their own organization. As the Resident Commissioner said, its demands were 'not so absurd'; he agreed with most of the requests, though not with the tempo advocated, nor with the conduct of the movement. Maasina Rule was put down by force between 1947 and 1949, with thousands of its adherents sent to jail. By 1950 its leaders were being released on promising to pay taxes. The Resident Commissioner admitted that 'A pistol is being shown to our heads', and he feared the spread of Communism.[24]

In 1952 Honiara, the Solomons' capital, became the High Commission headquarters, but local advances were slow. Not till 1960 was the Advisory Council replaced by an Executive Council (with two Solomon Island and two European unofficials) and a Legislative Council (with six Solomon Island and four European unofficials). From 1965 the indigenous representatives were elected by the local councils. In 1970, as the administration tried to accelerate indigeni-

[24] H. G. Gregory-Smith to High Commissioner, 25 Nov. 1950, CO 537/7417.

zation of the civil service, there was another experiment with a Governing Council, combining executive and legislative functions linked by committees. This was soon rejected in favour of the usual constitutional evolution. In 1974 a separate Governor was appointed for the Solomon Islands; a Legislative Assembly was created, and a Chief Minister appointed. Joan Lester, from the Foreign and Commonwealth Office, visited the Solomons in 1975 and negotiated the terms for self-rule. Full internal self-government followed in 1976, with the Chief Minister presiding over the Council of Ministers, and the Governor reserving power over external affairs, security, and the civil service. After a general election and constitutional conference in 1977, independence was achieved on 7 July 1978. Anticipated secession by the western islands, which feared that British rule might give way to dominance by a 'Malaitan mafia', did not occur.

There remained the New Hebrides. If the Australian disengagement from Papua New Guinea and the British departures from Tuvalu, Kiribati, and the Solomons were hasty, decolonization in the Condominium was the nearest approach to a Palestine- or Aden-type scuttle in the Pacific. In the 1950s there was no enthusiasm in British circles for the 'Pandemonium', even though of the 45,000 indigenous peoples, 80 per cent had come under the influence of English-speaking Protestant missions. Among Europeans, nearly 2,000 French heavily outnumbered the 330 British; also French-speaking were several thousand Vietnamese who had been imported as labourers. Some officials wanted the British share of the Condominium to be handed over to France or Australia; others preferred partition, to ensure a unified administration in each part. In 1958 the Colonial Policy Committee in London saw four options: transfer to Australia, transfer to France, partition, or radical reform of the Condominium. None was adopted. By 1960 the British Resident Commissioner was trying to persuade his French colleague of the need to study customary land tenure in view of increasing disputes between Europeans and New Hebrideans. He mooted a land commission to settle land issues and forestall developments such as Maasina Rule.

The indigenous attitude to land was put most forcefully by Jimmy Stevens, of Espiritu Santo, in taking up the cause of a local chief whose lands were encroached on by a French planter. Stevens, who had worked for the Americans during the war, was an articulate spokesman for the view that New Hebrideans could never sell land, only grant its *use*. When the British and French, having finally agreed to unified legal and land systems and to an Assembly elected by universal suffrage, held the first general election in 1975, Stevens advocated Santo separation. He was supported by disaffected French *colons* and some American free-market speculators hoping to erect a tax-haven state. Although such support discredited Stevens, his ideas had considerable general impact. Based on the symbols of *namele* (custom law) and *nagria* (people), his Nagriamel Movement stood for 'the people's heart... the people's custom'.[25] On Santo Stevens created an alternative structure of chiefly committees based on custom. Opposition to his methods came from educated civil servants and clergy who formed the National Party, later Vanua'aku Pati, and called for land nationalization. But for a time this party boycotted the Assembly, and in 1978 declared a People's Provisional government.

The British had been advocating withdrawal for a decade, and in 1978 the French realized that the situation was untenable. A visiting French minister persuaded the political leaders to form a government of National Unity. An election in 1979 gave the Vanua'aku Pati a two-thirds majority in the Assembly, and it took office under Father Walter Lini, an Anglican priest. At this point Stevens called for a federal system, and declared a Republic of Vemarana on Santo. There were other secessionist movements on Tanna and Malakula. To prevent disintegration, French and British marines were rushed in, but did not intervene politically; when independence was granted on 30 July 1980, they did not attempt to suppress the Santo rebellion, but did protect the flag of the Republic of Vanuatu. Unity was achieved by force, arranged at a South Pacific Forum meeting in Tarawa in 1980 in discussions with the Australian and Papua New Guinean Prime Ministers. Units of the PNG Defence Force, with Australian logistic support, landed to end Santo secession. Stevens went to jail, but at independence all land reverted to customary ownership in Vanuatu (Our Land).

A few dependencies lay on the outer flanks of the former Pacific Empire. Northwest of Australia, in the Indian Ocean, the Cocos Islands and Christmas Island (formerly part of the Straits Settlements) had been transferred to Australia in 1955 and 1958 respectively, prior to Singaporean Statehood. After Fiji's independence in 1970, the British High Commissioner in Wellington became the Governor of Pitcairn. The fifty-nine remaining islanders (1990) elected a Magistrate, who presided over a ten-member Council which raised its revenues from postage stamps, and remained the Empire's most distant relic.

The belated rush to decolonization in the Pacific Islands in the 1970s was a logical corollary to Britain's entry into the European Economic Community and the withdrawal from East of Suez. These events, in turn, served to accelerate the evolving post-colonial outlooks of Australia and New Zealand. Identities nurtured on imperialism, as loyal Britannic outposts in Antipodean seas, now aspired to self-reliance and self-confidence in the dynamic Asian–Pacific basin. Paradoxical legacies of Empire were expressed in new approaches to military and economic security, political institutions, and immigrant and indigenous peoples.

[25] H. van Trease, *The Politics of Land in Vanuatu: From Colony to Independence* (Suva, 1987), pp. 139, 160.

Nationalism in Australia and New Zealand had adopted a distinctly Victorian sporting and martial aspect. In some of the sports codes learnt from the late-nineteenth-century games revolution in Britain, Antipodean pupils soon surpassed their English tutors. Australia emerged early as a top cricket country. The All Blacks from New Zealand were from 1905 a formidable force in Rugby football. In the first two world cup rugby competitions the winners were New Zealand (1987) and Australia (1989); their training links also helped Samoa, Fiji, and Tonga to emerge as international competitors. Battlefields followed playing fields as venues for colonial individuality. Distant wars found 'Diggers' and 'Kiwis' sensing their differences from 'Jocks' and 'Tommies' as they fought side-by-side for Empire. Anzac Day, 25 April, anniversary of the Gallipoli landings in 1915, became a patriotic memorial day on both sides of the Tasman. Similar differences of identity were evident when the United States emerged as the main protector. But after the disastrous experience of the Vietnam War, both Australia and New Zealand focused defence on the Pacific environment.

Their pursuit of economic security followed in the same direction. Britain remained Australia's largest single export market until 1967, but by the early 1990s had fallen to eighth place, taking only 3 per cent in export value. Japan, buying a quarter of Australia's exports, became the major trading partner, followed by the United States, South Korea, Singapore, and New Zealand. Britain remained the third biggest source of imports (6 per cent) but was far surpassed by the United States (23 per cent) and Japan (18 per cent). New Zealand diversified just as widely, but more slowly, and kept Britain as its largest market until 1980. By the early 1990s Australia had become New Zealand's major trading partner (19 per cent of exports, 22 per cent of imports), followed by Japan and the United States. Britain was in fourth place (4 per cent of exports and 6 per cent of imports) closely followed by South Korea. Europe still accounted for roughly 20 per cent of the trade of both Tasman neighbours, but three-quarters of Australia's exports and 70 per cent of New Zealand's went to the Pacific Basin.

As defence and trade veered away from Imperial patterns, so did certain institutions. Parliamentary democracy in the Tasman Dominions had incorporated the female franchise from the 1890s. Australia made voting compulsory and used preferential ballots in place of the British first-past-the-post system. New Zealanders chose Mixed Member Proportional voting in 1994. The Parliaments in Canberra and Wellington both passed Constitution Acts in 1986, ending the last vestiges of constitutional subordination by repealing the Statute of Westminster and confirming their own sovereign independence.[26] Appeals to the Privy Council

[26] Australia Act 1986, No. 142 in *Acts of Parliament of the Commonwealth of Australia*, 1985, II, p. 1819; *Statutes of New Zealand*, 1986, II, p. 991.

ceased from Australia in 1986 and New Zealand announced a similar intention ten years later. Imperial honours were dropped in favour of the Order of Australia in 1975 and the New Zealand Order of Merit in 1996. Prime Ministers of Irish ancestry espoused republicanism. Paul Keating announced the political goal of an Australian Republic for the federal centennial in 2001; Jim Bolger of New Zealand accepted a similar, but less specific, trend.

These changes were accompanied by new approaches to the immigrant and indigenous populations. By 1991 Australia's population of 17.3 million was 80 per cent Australian-born, with three-quarters still of Anglo-Celtic extraction. But immigration policies of the 1940s and 1950s had attracted 'New Australians' from southern and eastern Europe, who grew to 5 per cent of the population. From the 1970s, as defence, diplomacy, and trade focused on Asia and the Pacific, the White Australia policy was discarded; migrants from Asia increased, including 90,000 Vietnamese refugees. By 1989 Asians comprised 2.5 per cent of the population.[27] Similar, slightly less diverse, trends emerged in New Zealand. Of the population of 3.5 million in 1991 four-fifths were of European origin, mainly British, but with well-established Yugoslav, Dutch, and German minorities. Five per cent were Pacific Islanders, and there were also small Chinese and Indian communities. Migrants with capital and qualifications, regardless of origin, were now sought, and increasing numbers came from Asia.

At the same time there were significant stirrings among Aborigines and Maori. In a final paradox of Empire, English common law became a focus for the assertion of indigenous land rights. A colonial legacy became a weapon of decolonization, since conflict over the ownership and use of land was central to the colonial experience. In Nauru and Vanuatu it had been the key to the independence movements and in Fiji it dominated post-colonial politics. In Australia and New Zealand, where the indigenous peoples had almost been overwhelmed during the colonial age, recovery came later than in the Islands. Although there was revival in absolute numbers, to 265,000 Aborigines and Torres Strait Islanders and 435,000 Maori by 1991, this represented only 1.5 per cent and 13 per cent of the respective total populations. But decolonization elsewhere in the 1960s and 1970s, and the example of vocal minority-rights and Black Power movements in English-speaking North America, promoted Maori and Aborigines to press for redress of grievances which went back to first colonial settlement. For this their leaders turned to judicial process. The creation of the Waitangi Tribunal in New Zealand in 1975 provided machinery for considering acts or omissions by governments which 'prejudicially affected' Maori tribes. With the backdating in 1985 of the

[27] Neville Meaney, 'The End of "White Australia" and Australia's Changing Perception of Asia, 1945–1990', *Australian Journal of International Affairs*, XLIX, 2 (1995), pp. 171–89.

Tribunal's jurisdiction to 1840,[28] the way was opened for hundreds of claims and for the operation of due process in ways that respected traditional consultation procedures. As well as making reference to the Treaty of Waitangi, claimants also had recourse to the common law doctrine of 'native territorial right' and to North American case-law.

Similar appeals were made in Australia, where there was no treaty. As late as the 1980s courts still accepted that Australia had been *terra nullius* at the time of settlement. But an eleven-year battle by Eddie Mabo and four inhabitants of Mer (in the Murray Islands, north of Queensland), culminated in a High Court judgment on 3 June 1992 which demolished *terra nullius* and confirmed the 'native title' of the plaintiffs. So momentous was the general principle involved that the Federal government responded with the Native Title Act 1993, which admitted that the Aborigines and Torres Strait Islanders had been 'progressively dispossessed of their land . . . largely without compensation'.[29] The Act recognized and protected customary title and provided for a National Native Title Tribunal. By its application of the common law the Mabo judgment effectively re-wrote Australian history. In declaring the entitlement of the Mer people to their land 'as against the whole world',[30] the Australian High Court, after reviewing land rights from the earliest days of colonization, provided a fitting epitaph on the Empire in the Pacific.

[28] *Statutes of New Zealand*, 1975, II, p. 827; 1985, III, p. 1336.

[29] *Commonwealth Acts*, 1993, II, No. 110, p. 2129.

[30] *Commonwealth Law Reports*, CLXXV (1992), p. 76.

Select Bibliography

JUDITH A. BENNETT, *Wealth of the Solomons: A History of a Pacific Archipelago, 1800–1978* (Honolulu, 1987).

G. C. BOLTON, *The Oxford History of Australia*, Vol. V, *1942–1988: The Middle Way* (Melbourne, 1990).

I. C. CAMPBELL, *Island Kingdom: Tonga Ancient and Modern* (Christchurch, 1992).

F. K. CROWLEY, ed., *A New History of Australia* (Melbourne, 1974).

J. W. DAVIDSON, *Samoa mo Samoa: The Emergence of the Independent State of Western Samoa* (Melbourne, 1967).

DONALD DENOON and others, eds., *The Cambridge History of the Pacific Islanders* (Cambridge, 1997).

K. R. HOWE, ROBERT C. KISTE, and BRIJ V. LAL, eds., *Tides of History: The Pacific Islands in the Twentieth Century* (St Leonards, NSW, 1994).

W. J. HUDSON, *New Guinea Empire: Australia's Colonial Experience* (North Melbourne, 1974).

Barrie Macdonald, *Cinderellas of the Empire: Towards a History of Kiribati and Tuvalu* (Canberra, 1982).

Stuart Macintyre, *The Oxford History of Australia*, Vol. XIV, *1901–1942: The Succeeding Age* (Melbourne, 1986).

A. F. Madden and W. H. Morris-Jones, eds., *Australia and Britain: Studies in a Changing Relationship* (London, 1980).

Henry Reynolds, *The Law of the Land*, 2nd edn. (Ringwood, Vic., 1992).

Geoffrey W. Rice, ed., *The Oxford History of New Zealand*, 2nd edn. (Auckland, 1981).

Angus Ross, ed., *New Zealand's Record in the Pacific Islands in the Twentieth Century* (Auckland, 1969).

Keith Sinclair, ed., *Tasman Relations: New Zealand and Australia, 1788–1988* (Auckland, 1988).

—— ed., *The Oxford Illustrated History of New Zealand* (Auckland, 1990).

Howard Van Trease, *The Politics of Land in Vanuatu: From Colony to Independence* (Suva, 1987).

Russell Ward, *A Nation for a Continent: The History of Australia, 1901–1975* (Richmond, Vic., 1988).

Maslyn Williams and Barrie Macdonald, *The Phosphateers: A History of the British Phosphate Commissioners and the Christmas Island Phosphate Commission* (Melbourne, 1985).

30

Commonwealth Legacy

W. DAVID MCINTYRE

'Commonwealth', which began as a synonym for Empire, came to signify its antithesis. The 'British Commonwealth of Nations'—that unwritten alliance between Britain and the Old Dominions in two world wars—was quite different from the 'Commonwealth of Nations' which South Africa quit in 1961. By this time the original core had been joined by four Asian and two African members and Cyprus. Eire had left; Burma never joined. The fifty-four member 'Commonwealth', whose heads of government met in Edinburgh in 1997, was of yet another order. South Africa had been back in the fold for three years and Fiji had just returned; Cameroon, with only fractional links to the Empire, and Mozambique, with none, had been admitted; Nigeria was under suspension. The appellation 'Commonwealth', popularized by Imperial federalists eighty years earlier, now applied to an international grouping larger than the United Nations in 1945 (Maps 30.1 and 2).

Until 1965 the Commonwealth constituted a special 'club' (in the commonly used sobriquet) within the Empire. Becoming a 'member of the Commonwealth' was a badge of independence. But the club was still managed from Whitehall by the Commonwealth Relations Office and the Cabinet Office. The Secretary of the Cabinet was Secretary-General of the Prime Ministers' Meetings. After 1965, with the creation of the Secretariat (followed by the Foundation a year later), the Commonwealth was transformed into a multilateral association, which soon achieved a momentum of its own. Co-ordination shifted from Whitehall to Pall Mall, where, from the then-fading grandeur of Marlborough House, the Secretary-General acted as servant of the heads of government collectively.

Each of the landmarks in the dissolution of the Empire (Attlee and South Asia; Macmillan and the 'Wind of Change'; Wilson and 'Withdrawal from East-of-Suez') induced crises for the Commonwealth. Britain showed great reluctance, for a time, to widen the membership of the club, though at each stage she gave in, more or less graciously, and virtue was made of necessity. The club was a cosy one in the 'British Commonwealth of Nations' phase, satisfying to Britain and the Dominions. Almost sanctified by the Balfour Report in 1926 and the Statute of

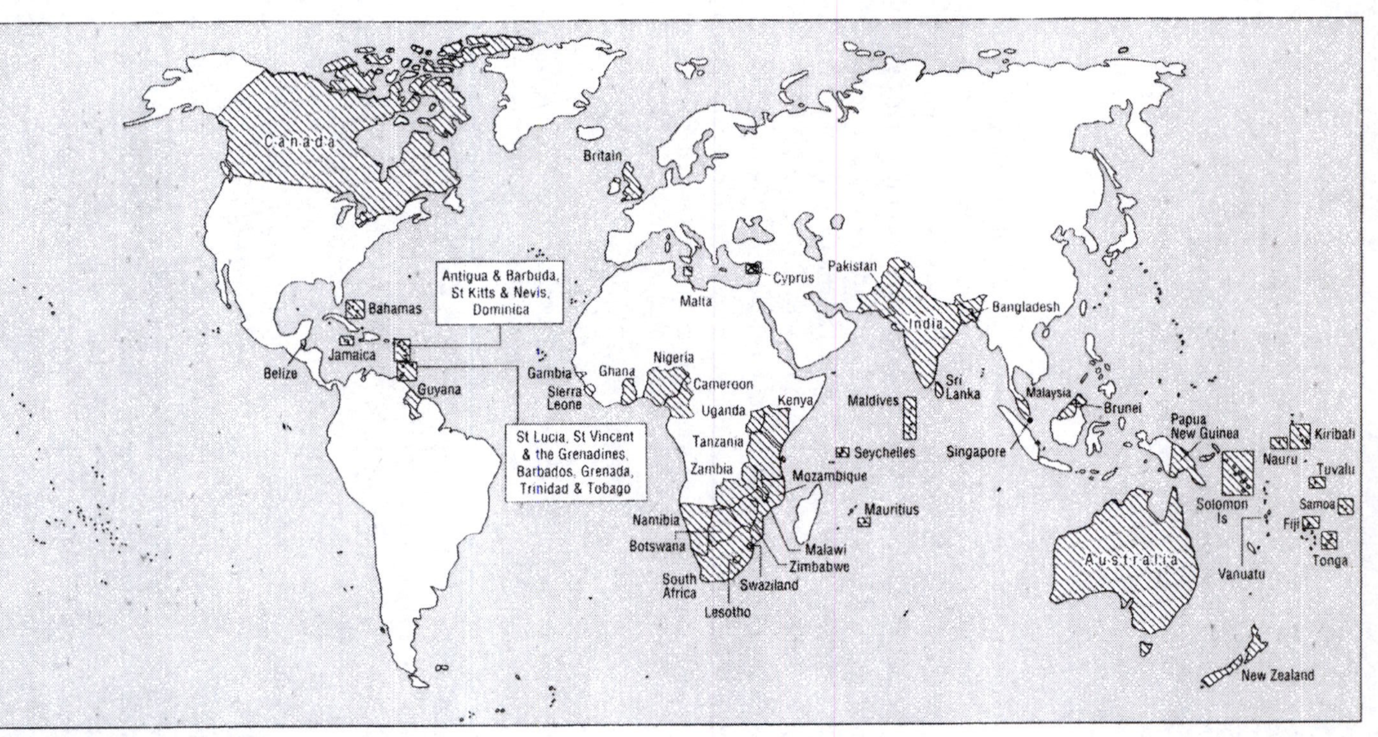

MAP 30.1. The Commonwealth in 1998

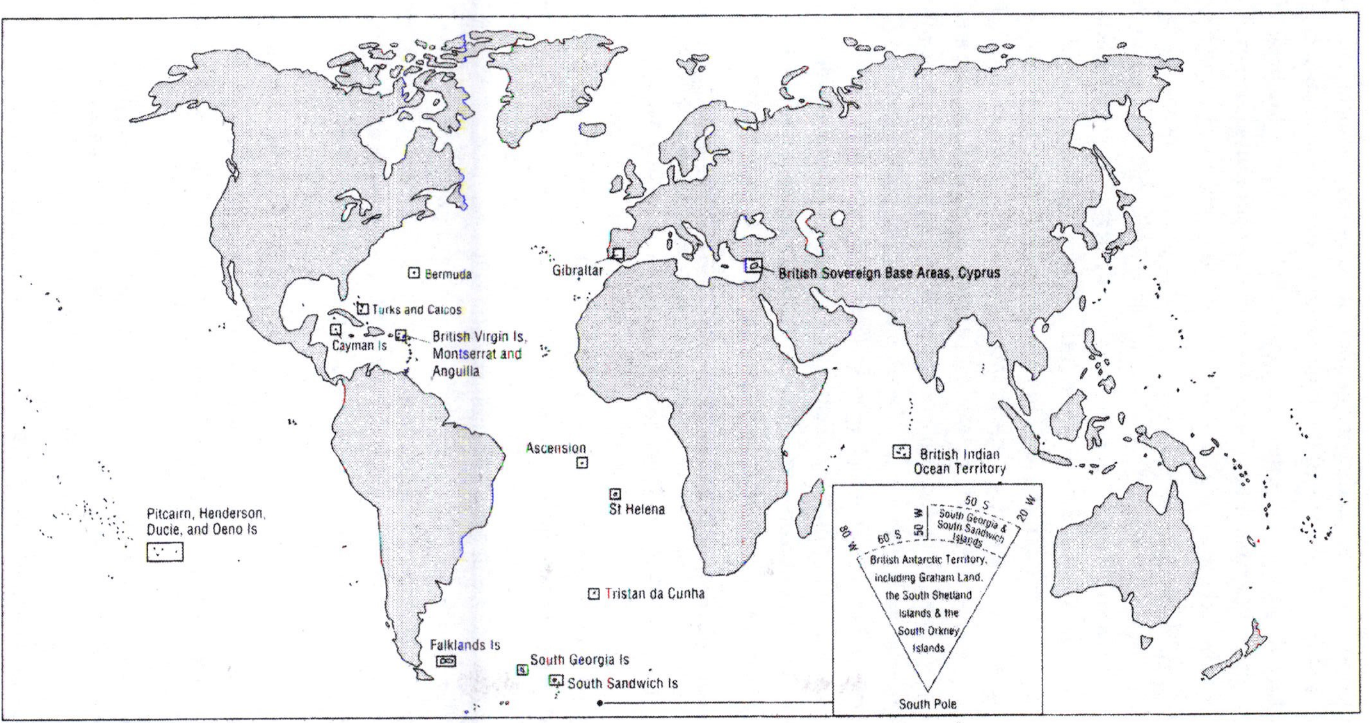

MAP 30.2. Britain's Remnants of Empire, 1998

Westminster in 1931, the guiding principles of autonomy, equality, common allegiance, and free association did not 'universally extend to function'. Unequal countries agreed to treat each other as equal as they sat around the table. There were some bitter differences, but there was frankness and mutual regard. W. K. Hancock idealized the system as a resolution of the problems of *imperium* and *libertas*. He depicted the Commonwealth as 'the "nature" of the British Empire defined, in Aristotelian fashion, by its end'.[1] It was flexible enough to retain republican Eire as an external associate, even as a neutral in the 1939–45 war.

From 1948, with the admission of the Asian Dominions, India, Pakistan, and Ceylon, there was a loss of intimacy, a move to politeness. The Chiefs of Staff were now inhibited in sharing strategic intelligence supplied by the Americans. Separate preliminary meetings were held between Australian, British, Canadian, and New Zealand leaders. Yet India's decision to stay proved the salvation of the Commonwealth. Once he had accepted the inevitability of the partition of India and Pakistan in 1947, Mountbatten had regarded keeping India in the Commonwealth as his 'most important single problem'.[2] The device of granting independence quickly, on the basis of Dominion Status, gave a breathing-space, while the Indian Constituent Assembly completed the constitution of a 'independent sovereign republic' and the implications of this for the Commonwealth were examined. Mountbatten thought this was 'the greatest opportunity ever offered to the Empire'.[3] Much ingenious effort was expended from 1947 to 1949 on this problem. There was talk of a two-tier system with monarchical and non-monarchical members. The Irish model of external association was rehearsed, only to be eliminated after the announcement in September 1948 that Eire would leave the Commonwealth. After the Prime Ministers' Meetings in October 1948, the first to be attended by the Asian Premiers, 'nomenclature changes' were promulgated by C. R. Attlee. The terms 'Dominion' and 'Dominion government' were to be superseded by 'Commonwealth country' or 'member of the Commonwealth'. 'Dominion Status' was dropped in favour of 'fully independent Member of the Commonwealth'. 'British' was omitted in front of 'Commonwealth of Nations' in the 1948 communiqué.[4]

Yet, on the substantive issue of a republican member there was still hesitation. Attlee was one of many who insisted there had to be a link through the Crown. Others, notably Walter Monckton, Malcolm Macdonald, and Norman Brook,

[1] W. K. Hancock, *Survey of British Commonwealth Affairs, 1918–1936*, 2 vols. (Oxford, 1937–42), I, p. 61.

[2] Nicholas Mansergh and others, eds., *Constitutional Relations between Britain and India: The Transfer of Power, 1942–7*, 12 vols. (London, 1981), X, p. 329.

[3] Ibid., p. 699.

[4] Proposed in CR (48)2, 21 May 1948, CAB 134/118; promulgated in Foreign Office Circular 7, 28 Jan. 1949, D[ominions] O[ffice] 35/2255.

mooted an idea, first suggested in 1922 by Eamon de Valera, that the King might be 'head of the association'.[5] Patrick Gordon-Walker, Parliamentary Under-Secretary for Commonwealth Relations, suggested in December 1948 that the guiding principle should not be the Crown but the will and intent of the members. Let there be simple declarations—that India as a republic wished to stay in, and the rest agreed to this. Here was the germ of the London Declaration which emerged from the special conference of April 1949. After over eighteen months of preliminary discussions, Jawaharlal Nehru came to London authorized to accept the King as the 'symbol of the free association of the members'. He jibbed at a draft which added 'Head of the Commonwealth and symbol of the free association ...' Stafford Cripps explained, privately, that the King would be head because he was the symbol—the symbolism created the headship. Nehru preferred head *as* symbol, not *and* symbol. Malan, of South Africa, still fearful of lurking constitutional implications, insisted on further explication, which produced the formula 'symbol of the free association ... and *as such* the Head of the Commonwealth'.[6] The declaration was a triumph of formula-making. The decision, reached on 26 April 1949, came just eight days after the Republic of Ireland left the Commonwealth. By staying in and gaining acceptance India paved the way for an overwhelmingly republican membership over the next twenty years. And Nehru's presence in Commonwealth councils was cherished because of his stature in the emerging Third World.

India was large and Ireland was special, but when Kwame Nkrumah demanded Dominion Status for the Gold Coast in 1951 there were shudders, especially in Pretoria, at the prospect of a 'Black Dominion'. The Secretary of State for the Colonies, Oliver Lyttelton, neatly side-stepped to gain some time by telling Nkrumah that, while it was for Britain to grant independence, it was for the rest of the members to admit newcomers to full Commonwealth membership. Meanwhile, Whitehall committees gave thought to the ultimate terminus of constitutional evolution. One group, appointed by Attlee's government, had reported in 1951 on the prospects for twenty-one of the smallest territories. It concluded that many could never be independent and put forward the idea of 'Island or City states'. This, however, was dismissed as 'attractive intellectually but academic and un-English'.[7] Still hoping that some 'mezzanine status' might be devised, the

[5] D. Macardle, *The Irish Republic* (Dublin, 1951), p. 960; Mansergh and others, eds., *Transfer of Power*, X, pp. 609–10; Gov.-General Malaya to Sec. State Cols. (183) 27 June, 1947, in CR(47)3, 15 Sept. 1947, CAB 134/117; CR(48)2, 21 May 1948, and CR(48), 2nd meeting, 31 May 1948, CAB[inet] 134/118.

[6] Private meeting of 22 April 1949, in PMM (UK) (49)1, 25 April 1949, CAB 133/91; PMM (49) 3rd meeting, 25 April 1949, and 4th meeting, 26 April 1949, CAB 133/89.

[7] Report of Committee on Enquiry into Constitutional Development in the Smaller Colonial Territories, Aug. 1951. Print enclosed in Lloyd to Liesching, 4 Dec. 1951, D[ominions] O[ffice] 35/2218; D. J. Morgan, *Guidance Towards Self-Government in British Colonies* (London, 1980), p. 43.

Colonial Office came up with the concept of 'Statehood'.[8] Governor Charles Arden-Clarke, however, insisted that Nkrumah would not be satisfied with anything short of full Commonwealth membership and, if this were denied, much of Africa would be lost to the Commonwealth. The British government gave way three years before Ghana became independent in 1957, and Malaya in the same year; Singapore was the only territory to receive statehood, in 1959.

By 1960, on the eve of the 'Wind of Change', Cyprus presented another critical test case. Harold Macmillan had negotiated a settlement, guaranteed by Greece, Turkey, and Britain, which provided for an independent republic and two small British sovereign base areas. Archbishop Makarios agreed to trade *enosis* (unity with Greece) for independence. But Cyprus had a population of only 500,000. Macmillan earnestly hoped that they could avoid admitting such a small state into the club—was it to be 'the R.A.C. or Boodles?'[9] The matter went to more interdepartmental committees and a Commonwealth Study Group. Another new concept of 'Commonwealth State' was devised, but Makarios would not be part of any 'second eleven'. Everyone realized that a crucial precedent would be set if Cyprus was admitted—that 'all the other tiddlers would demand this treatment'.[10] But no reason could be found, consistent with Commonwealth principles, to keep Cyprus out. In 1961 Cyprus joined the Commonwealth just as South Africa left. Macmillan soon confessed to Australian Prime Minister Robert Menzies: 'I now shrink from any Commonwealth meeting because I know how troublesome it will be.'[11]

The mid-1960s was the time when, in the popular phrase, 'The Empire strikes Back.' A set of prosaic proposals for functional co-operation called 'The Way Ahead' (including the idea of a Foundation for fostering professional linkages) was proposed at the 1964 Prime Ministers' Meetings by Sir Alec Douglas-Home, the British Prime Minister. These were overtaken by the proposal emanating from Nkrumah, Milton Obote of Uganda, and Eric Williams of Trinidad for a 'clearing house' to co-ordinate co-operative projects, which bore fruit in the creation of the Commonwealth Secretariat.[12] The year 1965 became the watershed in the evolution of the modern Commonwealth. Although the British became disillusioned about the Commonwealth, which a celebrated article in *The Times* described as 'a

[8] W. David McIntyre, 'The Admission in Small States to the Commonwealth', *Journal of Imperial and Commonwealth History*, XXIV, 2 (1996), pp. 254–58.

[9] Note for the Record by T. Bligh, 20 July 1960 of meeting on 13 July, 'No Circulation—as arranged with Sir N. Brook', PREM 11/3649.

[10] Ibid.

[11] Ibid., Macmillan to Menzies (Secret), 8 Feb. 1962.

[12] Arnold Smith, *Stitches in Time: The Commonwealth in World Politics* (London, 1981), p. 4; Joe [Sir Saville] S. Garner, *The Commonwealth Office, 1925–68* (London, 1978), pp. 351–52; W. David McIntyre, *The Significance of the Commonwealth, 1965–90* (London, 1991), pp. 48–50.

gigantic farce', a new type of association emerged with ever-increasing membership as the 'Wind of Change' blew on to become 'Withdrawal from East-of-Suez'. Intergovernmental organizations (such as the Commonwealth Agricultural Bureaux) were reviewed and were not subject to Secretariat oversight; they were left to fulfil their specialist roles. Certain science, educational, and economic organizations were, however, absorbed into the Secretariat. The Commonwealth Foundation came into being in 1966.

From 1971 new-style consultations emerged. In place of the small Prime Ministers Meetings in Downing Street, sometimes on an annual basis, biennial Commonwealth Heads of Government Meetings were held at large venues around the Commonwealth. They only returned to Britain in 1977 (the silver jubilee of the Queen's reign) and 1997 (her golden wedding anniversary). At Singapore in 1971 a Commonwealth Declaration was adopted outlining certain principles which were held in common. Members pledged themselves in *favour* of peace, liberty, and co-operation and *against* racial discrimination, colonial domination, and gross inequalities of wealth.[13] At the same time the Commonwealth Fund for Technical Co-operation became the Secretariat's operational arm. By the end of the 1970s, as decolonization swept many small Caribbean and Pacific islands into membership, the Commonwealth had been transformed into the premier small states forum.

The 1980s began with the independence of Zimbabwe and Vanuatu, and were marked by another wave of disillusionment about the Commonwealth in Britain. Margaret Thatcher, the British Prime Minister, resented the pressures put on Britain over Southern African issues. The Commonwealth was pictured by one political scientist as based on twin 'forgivable hypocrisies' of structure and ideology. Equality was the founding doctrine, but Britain still paid the biggest bills. Non-racialism and democracy were trumpeted in declarations, but military dictatorship, one-party rule, and racial strains were rife.[14] The low point was reached in 1986 when, at a mini-summit on sanctions against apartheid in South Africa, Thatcher broke with consensus, and at the Edinburgh Commonwealth Games more countries boycotted the events than competed. There were rumours of a rift between Buckingham Palace and the Prime Minister's office. After the Heads of Government Meetings in 1987 and 1989 the communiqués bore repetitions of the phrase 'with the exception of Britain'. At Kuala Lumpur in 1989 Mrs Thatcher said, with some relish: 'If it is forty-eight against one, then I'm sorry for the forty-eight.'[15]

[13] Declaration of Commonwealth Principles, 22 Jan. 1971. *The Commonwealth at the Summit* (London, 1987), pp. 156–57.

[14] Paul Taylor, 'The Commonwealth in the 1980s: Challenges and Opportunities', in A. J. R. Groom and Paul Taylor, eds., *The Commonwealth in the 1980s* (London, 1984), pp. 307–10.

[15] W. David McIntyre, 'End of an Era for the Commonwealth: Thoughts on the Hibiscus Summit', *New Zealand International Review*, XV, 1 (1990), p. 6.

In the 1990s, as the cold war suddenly ended and the apartheid regime just as suddenly gave way in South Africa, the Commonwealth was 'rediscovered' in Britain. The Harare Commonwealth Declaration of 1991, which emerged from a high-level appraisal group's study of the future role of the association, was based largely on a British draft. It asserted that democracy, the rule of law, good governance, and human rights should be the concomitants of sustainable development, sound economic management, the 'central role of the market economy', and the freest possible flow of multilateral trade.[16] At the end of 1994 the Foreign Affairs Committee of the British House of Commons embarked on a wider-ranging enquiry into the future of the Commonwealth. Over an eighteenth-month period the Committee held hearings in Westminster and visited Canada, Jamaica, Barbados, St Lucia, Kenya, Uganda, South Africa, India, Pakistan, Bangladesh, Malaysia, Australia, and New Zealand. Its report in 1996 admitted, somewhat defensively, that 'it was understandable for a few decades after the end of Empire that the Commonwealth was seen in the United Kingdom as a relic of an imperial past—a political albatross around the country's neck'. But the Committee had unearthed much which was positive, not least the rising prospects for trade and investment on the Asia–Pacific rim. Within the emerging global pattern, it considered that, in the Commonwealth, Britain had 'both friends and opportunities'.[17] As it prepared to host its first Heads of Government Meetings for twenty years, the British government described 1997 as 'The Year of the Commonwealth'.

The post-colonial, post-Britannic Commonwealth achieved a niche among international organizations because of the informality of its conclaves, its opportunities for mini and micro states, and the 'width and depth' provided by its many unofficial manifestations. The latter are customarily lumped together somewhat negatively as non-governmental organizations (NGOs), yet their scope and significance is better characterized by the more upbeat designation 'voluntary, independent, professional, philanthropic, and sporting organizations' (VIPPSOs) or, in the American usage, voluntary agencies (VolAgs). They include venerable pre-1914 organizations such as the Press Union, the Parliamentary Association, and the Universities' Association. But after 1966 the Commonwealth Foundation assisted in the creation of over thirty new pan-Commonwealth professional and welfare organizations and seventeen professional centres.[18] These linkages, involving many thousands of members, have been described as the 'real' Commonwealth.

[16] The Harare Commonwealth Declaration, 1991, text in *The Commonwealth Year Book, 1996* (London, 1996), pp. 103–09.

[17] *House of Commons, Session 1995–96. Foreign Affairs Committee: The Future Role of the Commonwealth*, I, p. lxix.

[18] *The Commonwealth Foundation: A Special Report, 1966 to 1993* (London, 1993), pp. 5–10, 16–17.

They are part of the 'People's Commonwealth', the most popular aspect of which is the Commonwealth Games, and such team sports as soccer, rugby, cricket, and hockey.

The Commonwealth Games—successor of the first Empire Games of 1930—are organized by the Commonwealth Games Federation. Over 2,000 athletes competed at Victoria BC in 1994 and 6,000 at Kuala Lumpur in 1998, when the team sports of seven-a-side rugby, one-day cricket, netball, and field hockey were added. These additions gave belated recognition to the almost universal popularity of some of the sports which had been codified in Victorian England. The role of sport in the emerging national identities of Commonwealth countries had long been evident—especially cricket in Australia, the West Indies, India, and Pakistan, and Rugby football in New Zealand and South Africa. In 1989, even as Thatcher tried to distance Britain from current Commonwealth concerns, the Heads of Government appointed ten of their number to form a High Level Appraisal Group to plan for the Commonwealth in the 1990s. The Canadians at the same time ensured that the Games were added to the Commonwealth Heads of Government Meeting agenda and a Committee on Co-operation Through Sport was appointed, chaired by a Canadian judge. The Sport Committee provided some of the most eloquent documents ever to emerge from Commonwealth forums, extolling the importance of sport in fostering identity, self-growth, and improvement, as well as being the 'first point of information about the Commonwealth' for young people.[19] By 1997 the Committee was demonstrating that sport was good business in the process of development.

While cynics continued to dismiss the Commonwealth as just another international jamboree among many (a mere series of 'photo opportunities'), its peculiar contemporary character derives from its VIPPSO infrastructure, which from 1991 held its own four-yearly NGO Forums. If the Head of the Commonwealth and the biennial Heads of Government Meetings represent the tip of an iceberg, below the line of visibility, the meetings of senior officials and ministers, the professional conferences, the ongoing work of Secretariat, Foundation, Fund for Technical Co-operation, and Commonwealth of Learning, as well as the myriad activities of the professional and sporting bodies, represent some of the more tangible advantages of membership. Thus, in 1997 Fiji rejoined, and Rwanda, Yemen, and the Palestine Authority applied for membership and were not turned down. Their applications were to be under review. Even Myanmar (Burma) and Ireland were being contemplated as future members. The big transition had been from the 'Commonwealth and Empire' of Imperial rhetoric in the 1920s to 1940s, which is an integral part of Empire history and had an important role in the decolonization

[19] *CHOGM Committee on Co-operation Through Sport, 1993 Report* (London, 1993), p. 24.

process, to the expanding post-Britannic Commonwealth, which remains the most noticeable part of the Imperial legacy after the English language and cricket.

Select Bibliography

Eric Ashby, *Community of Universities: An Informal Portrait of the Association of Universities of the British Commonwealth, 1913–1983* (Cambridge, 1963).

Dennis Austin, *The Commonwealth and Britain* (London, 1988).

John Chadwick, *The Unofficial Commonwealth: The Story of the Commonwealth Foundation, 1954–1980* (London, 1982).

Stephen Chan, *The Commonwealth in World Politics: A Study of International Action, 1965–1985* (London, 1988).

The Commonwealth at the Summit: Communiqués of Commonwealth Heads of Government Meetings, 1944–1986 (London, 1987).

A. J. R. Groom and Paul Taylor, eds., *The Commonwealth in the 1980s* (London, 1984).

W. Dale, *The Modern Commonwealth* (London, 1983).

Margaret P. Doxey, *The Commonwealth Secretariat and the Contemporary Commonwealth* (London, 1989).

Ian Grey, *The Parliamentarians: The History of the Commonwealth Parliamentary Association, 1911–1986* (London, 1986).

D. A. Low, *Eclipse of Empire* (Cambridge, 1991).

Trevor Macdonald, *The Queen and the Commonwealth* (London, 1986).

Nicholas Mansergh, *The Commonwealth Experience*, 2nd edn. (London, 1982).

Ali Mazrui, *The Anglo-African Commonwealth: Political Friction and Cultural Fusion* (Oxford, 1967).

W. David McIntyre, *The Significance of the Commonwealth, 1965–90* (London, 1991).

J. D. B. Miller, *Survey of Commonwealth Affairs: Problems of Expansion and Attrition, 1953–1969* (London, 1974).

R. J. Moore, *Making the New Commonwealth* (Oxford, 1987).

A. N. Papadopoulos, *Multilateral Diplomacy Within the Commonwealth: A Decade of Expansion* (The Hague, 1982).

Shridath S. Ramphal, *One World to Share: Selected Speeches of the Commonwealth Secretary-General, 1975–79* (London, 1979).

Arnold Smith, *Stitches in Time: The Commonwealth in World Politics* (London, 1981).

Hugh W. Springer, *The Commonwealth of Universities: The Story of the Association of Commonwealth Universities* (London, 1988).

31

Epilogue

JUDITH M. BROWN

This volume, like its predecessors in the series, has attempted, from a late-twentieth-century perspective and with the freedom of those not directly engaged in Empire, to stand back and review the Imperial experience with the benefit of the wealth of historical evidence which has become available in recent years. It has sought to understand the way the Empire worked and how it appeared and felt to those involved in it, both as rulers and subjects. It has examined the way it was held together politically and administratively, how it functioned on a routine basis, and how it dealt with local and international crises. It has analysed the economic forces underpinning and eventually eroding the Empire, and the ideologies which sustained and challenged it. The later chapters have focused on the parts of the Empire outside Britain, the Imperial periphery, and the experience of those who lived there, their influence on and within the Empire, and how they eventually emerged from Britannia's Imperial grasp to become citizens of independent nation states. The Epilogue looks at some of the more significant ways in which the existence of the former British Empire still influences the world at the juncture of two millennia, although that Empire has long ceased to be a political and economic force.

The twentieth century saw the British Empire reach its greatest geographical extent, and for a brief time exercise its greatest power. In the first half of this century it exerted its most pervasive influence in its Asian and African territories. Under the impact of two world wars it underwent significant reconstruction and its ideologies were modified. Simultaneously it began to transform itself into an international community of free nations of an unprecedented kind. The rapid process of decolonization, by the end of the century, left only a handful of dependent territories such as Gibraltar, St Helena, Bermuda, and Montserrat, but the historical legacies of British colonial rule still profoundly mark the international world, the former metropolis, Britain herself, and the once-dependent areas. The power of these legacies and interest in the Empire is still deep and ideologically sensitive. This has been evident in a wide range of events and tendencies, from the Falklands War of 1982 and the return of Hong Kong to

China in 1997, in a final display of Imperial pomp, to the continuing popularity of Imperial themes in literature in the English language and in entertainment. The power and diversity of Imperial themes is also clear in the world of scholarship, and the often bitter debates on the writing of the history of aspects of the Imperial experience, and ways of understanding the literatures and archival sources to which it gave rise.

The previous chapter, 'Commonwealth Legacy', surveyed the most obvious organizational legacy of the old Empire in the international context. In an unplanned way the Empire transformed itself into a free association of independent member nation states united only by the will to stay together in loose association, with the British monarch as a symbol of that free association. This change was, to a large extent, a pragmatic response to immediate problems needing resolution, such as the issue of India's membership of the Commonwealth once she had made her new constitution and become a Republic rather than a Dominion in 1949. The final reinvention of the Empire facilitated a process of decolonization which was as remarkable for its tranquillity as its speed, and was notable for a singular lack of bitterness between former rulers and subjects. This contrasts with the colonial endings of other European nations in Africa and Asia.

The evolving Commonwealth has provided a forum for international deliberation and joint action, and most significantly a dense, if often little-publicized, web of connections and professional associations which have been of considerable worth to emergent nation states and their peoples. Its common platform and facilities have proved valuable particularly for small states and those with powerful neighbours, who have felt membership of the Commonwealth gives them status and a voice in the international arena which they would otherwise lack. The worth of the Commonwealth, however intangible at times, persuaded most of former dependencies to become Commonwealth members; it must be remembered, however, that many nationalist leaders had to work to convince their peoples of this in the aftermath of struggles for independence. Jawaharlal Nehru, for example, knew he could persuade the Indian Parliament that Commonwealth membership was in India's own interest by 1949, though he admitted that even a year earlier this would have been impossible, given the state of Indian public opinion. It is notable that in the closing decade of the century countries which had never been part of the British Empire were seeking Commonwealth membership in their own national interest.

Yet there were a few territories which chose never to join the Commonwealth at the time of decolonization, or have chosen to leave it, temporarily or permanently, because identification with it seemed to threaten national interest and identity. Ireland, Burma, the Sudan, and South Africa are examples. Here Commonwealth membership either clashed with deeply held and often religiously informed senses of national identity, or there was an alternative regional orientation which seemed more appropriate or compelling. Speculation ill becomes historians. But in wondering what benefit might have accrued to such areas had they been Commonwealth members, it is notable that aid and assistance of many kinds flow through Commonwealth channels and informal connections, including forces of domestic and international mediation.

The traveller at the end of the twentieth century cannot help but be powerfully aware that the Commonwealth as an institution is not the only international legacy of the Empire. Even more obvious, and arguably more significant for the lives of ordinary people, are numerous shared things in common. There is, at the level of popular entertainment and leisure, the shared legacy of similar sporting cultures, particularly those evolved around cricket, football, and rugby. Imperial educators argued that team sport, particularly cricket, encouraged a co-operative spirit which might be conducive to civic virtue and democracy, and a suitable 'manliness'. Historians may properly query such assumptions, but it is clear that they should not underestimate the significance of sport and sporting success in the emergence of a sense of national identity, perhaps particularly in comparatively small nation states. It is arguable that cricketing prowess is as important to Caribbean identity as music. That great architect of a new national identity, Nelson Mandela, was well aware of the profound symbolism of publicly donning the Springbok rugby jersey as the President of the new multiracial South Africa.

Shared experiences within the old Empire are visible in physical structures which, in their turn, often feed cultural and political patterns and mould identities. A shared colonial architecture ranges from domestic housing and commercial warehousing to the great Gothic churches and civic buildings which mark virtually all the great cities of the former Empire. The railway station, the post office, the town hall, the lawcourt, the Legislative Council or Parliament building, and even the botanic garden testify to the abiding cultural connections and common political styles. These are not mere monuments to a shared past. They are often living institutions, making the visitor powerfully aware that this was once a part of the British Empire, as opposed to the French, Belgian, German, or Dutch empires.

At the time of independence departing British colonial officials hoped that their enduring legacy would be that of the rule of law and of democratic political procedures and institutions which they left behind, often constructed with great haste before decolonization except in the old Dominions and in India. In parts of the former Empire such institutions have weakened. But even where they have been eroded or destroyed, they are still an ideal which comes back to encourage an increasingly sophisticated citizenry and to haunt dictators or leaders of one-party states. Indira Gandhi found this to her cost in the mid-1970s when she instigated a Draconian state of emergency in India. It is, in large part, the still-shared ideals and goals which permit the Commonwealth to function as an international association, though at times there are severe tensions on such issues as human or group rights, when individual states perceive Commonwealth members' concerns as potential or actual interference in domestic affairs.

Most significant of all is the legacy of the school and the university. Lord Macaulay was prescient in the 1830s when he spoke of the power of an English-language education in India which would fashion a new élite, which would, in consequence, share with its rulers cultural values and political capabilities. Throughout the Empire it was such élites which first articulated new national identities and aspirations, and which began processes of cultural transformation and interaction in their homelands. The continuing influence of English education is evident at the end of the twentieth century in the role of English as an international language, and as a shared national language in countries where indigenous tongues are multiple and diverse, as in India, or where other languages are identified with distinctive ethnic or regional groups within one nation state. It is still manifest in the educational systems within what used to be the old Empire, in the easy movement of university students within the English-speaking world, and in the flourishing of literatures in local variants of standard English. The presence of English-language education has often encouraged and enriched new vernacular literatures, with some authors writing with ease in both English and a vernacular. It has also helped to establish new systems of vernacular education, significantly, often in opposition to the cultural and political dominance of the earlier English-speaking élites. By the end of the century the result has been increasingly well-educated and reading publics, far exceeding expectations at the beginning of the century, with expanding cultural and political horizons among ordinary people. Literacy has equipped them with new skills and made them into a more discerning and demanding citizenry. In this process the significance for women has been of particular importance, not merely in making women participant citizens, often for the first time, and expanding greatly the range of work opportunities available to them outside the home, but in enabling women to make informed choices about child-care and rearing, domestic relationships, and the control of fertility, which are of major cultural and demographic importance.

Each part of the former Empire has its own legacy of Imperial belonging, depending on its internal political and social configuration and on its particular place within the old British network. Britain herself has not been immune from domestic change as a result of being the Mother Country and then losing that role in just a few decades. In many ways, however, Britain and the British found the end of Empire far less traumatic than some other European nations with overseas empires. There was comparatively little armed conflict or displacement of expatriate settlers, in comparison with, for example, the French experience in Algeria: the Malayan emergency and Mau Mau were exceptions rather than the rule. One-time colonial civil servants were few in number, and were either reabsorbed into British professional and commercial life, as in the case of many Indian civil servants, or were recycled round the remaining dependencies: of the latter, the 'African re-treads' who took up second careers in Hong Kong were some of the last examples. In barely more than a generation Britons became more-or-less accustomed to their new position in the world as an offshore island of mainland Europe, dependent on the special relationship with America for financial stability and defence. To a considerable extent this psychological transition was eased by the ideology (perhaps more a carefully crafted myth) of peaceful transfers of power to new nation states as the inevitable goal of British democratic training for citizenship of former subjects. It was an ideology which was useful for British politicians who were well aware of the growing international weakness it masked. It carefully ignored the fact that such 'transfers of power' sometimes precipitated violence and demographic upheavals, as in the Indian subcontinent or Nigeria, and that the resolve to educate or prepare subjects for democracy and independence was a late phenomenon, particularly in the African colonies.

The ideal and idealism which surrounded the emergence of the new, multiracial Commonwealth was another way in which British politicians and people came to terms with the loss of an Imperial status, and increasingly, the erosion of their international role as an international patron and dispenser of aid. At times, however, such as the Suez crisis of 1956, the Unilateral Declaration of Independence in Rhodesia in 1965, and the Falklands War of 1982, the presence of a residual Imperial attitude could be perceived within British society, often causing deep ideological rifts. Nevertheless, by the end of the century the growing influence of the European Union and Britain's membership led to a refocusing of the sense of national identity, particularly among the younger generation, which made the country's former Imperial role seem anachronistic and embarrassing. The handover of Hong Kong to China in 1997 was a ritual previously unseen and remarkable to the vast majority of Britons born since the 1950s, many of whom seemed perplexed, in the same year, to find that Britain still had responsibility for Montserrat (in the news as the victim of a volcanic eruption), and a few other tiny and scattered dependent territories.

The reorientation of British senses of national identity in a European context was one significant trend in British self-understanding, and one which was not untroubled. As profound an influence was the presence in Britain itself of immigrants from the former Imperial territories, particularly the Caribbean and the Indian subcontinent. The movement of peoples, both free and unfree, had been one of the hallmarks of the British Empire, as chapters in this and previous volumes have charted. After the end of the Second World War there was a new movement—of peoples from the 'New Commonwealth' coming in search of work to Britain. As the British economy was reconstructed there was abundant work for unskilled and semi-skilled labour in factories, transport, and the new National Health Service. The first to take up these new opportunities were men and women from the Caribbean, whose command of English enabled them to migrate with comparative ease. They were followed from the mid-1950s by increasing numbers of less-well educated people from South Asia—Indians, Pakistanis, and in the 1970s Bangladeshis and Indians ejected from East Africa. These flows were checked by the imposition of immigration controls from the early 1960s, designed in fact, but not overtly, to control the numbers of 'coloured' people who had easy entry into Britain. By the last census of the century in 1991 it was clear that, despite such controls, as a result of the initial migrations, subsequent family reunions, and a natural increase above that of the white population, Britons whose families had originated in the New Commonwealth formed a significant minority in Britain, although because they were clustered in major metropolitan areas they had risen in some localities to a majority. (In 1991 South Asians in Britain numbered 1.5 million, about 2.7 per cent of the total population.) Britain is now *de facto* a multiracial and multi-religious society, as is evident from such diverse changes as the teaching of religion in state schools, the presence of mosques, temples, and gurdwaras in major towns, and the growing diversity of 'ethnic' shops and restaurants and popular music, as well as the increasing black presence in the professions, the media, and sport. The domestic impact of the old Imperial connections is an accepted part of everyday life. However, this evolution in British society has not been without tensions, as controls on immigration, occasional outbursts of racially motivated rioting and violence, and daily acts of discrimination indicate. Had this not been so there would have been no need for a permanent Commission for Racial Equality or an increasing insistence on monitoring of ethnic minority presence in major institutions and professions. Ironically and painfully, the racism which was apparent during British colonial rule in the Empire of Asia, Africa, and the Caribbean was transferred to the domestic arena. Discrimination within Britain became far more powerful than it had been in the days of the Empire, when students and visitors from the Empire, relatively few in number, experienced little.

The part played in the evolution of a new sense of British identity by decolonization and the resulting presence of significant ethnic minorities from the old Empire has to be seen in the context of other changes. These include the declining role of Britain in the world economy, the emergence of Europe as a regional and cultural focus for British aspirations, the growth of regional identities within the United Kingdom, and the transfer of influence in public life and the media to a generation brought up in this new environment. By the closing years of the century it seemed that a clear sea change had occurred in British wishes for a more open national community unfettered by old prejudices which had been moulded by deep-rooted ideas of race and class.

Just as Britain has changed as a result of the Empire's legacy, so have the individual countries which composed the former Empire. This Epilogue is no place for an account of the details of these processes. But there are certain common themes arising from earlier Imperial membership in the experience of those societies and nation states which are part of what was once called the 'Third World'. These were, however, much less significant in the Old Dominions, which had attained mature political identities and polities as well as stable modern economies in the early part of the twentieth century. At the material level there was the issue of economic viability and the problem of real freedom after decolonization, given the low levels of economic development in most parts of the Asian and African Empire. Even in such a comparatively advanced area as India, with a national network of communications, an established educational system, and the basis of an industrial economy laid almost a century before independence, its first Prime Minister, Jawaharlal Nehru, was acutely aware that genuine independence necessitated rapid economic growth. That alone could enable the building of a civic infrastructure which could provide for the legitimate expectations for social and welfare needs of the citizens, who were educated by the nationalist movement to blame the British for their low levels of income and welfare, and now expected freedom to mean real domestic change. Only domestic economic strength and diversification could ensure sufficient defence forces for national security and independence, and free India from her role as a provider of natural resources and materials for more advanced economies.

All leaders of former colonial territories faced the problem of escaping from the grip of what they saw as a new 'neo-colonialism' based on the capacity of industrialized economies to dictate the terms of international trade and to provide vital aid. There was a price to be paid. This has been one of the dominant—and unresolved—themes of the later decades of the century. To an extent the cold war and the presence of two alternative blocs of suppliers of aid, each anxious to sustain strategic clients in Africa and Asia, provided new states with alternatives which diluted the potential for a new kind of informal imperialism. But the only way out of the multiple traps of poverty and dependence has been radical economic change, and particularly a move away from older forms of industrialization to capitalize on skill and cheap labour—a path taken in Asia and to an extent in India, but not in Africa, where absolute poverty and, often, the political culture have militated against such measures.

The ability to take radical steps in economic management and to invest in an educated workforce is bound up with the nature of the state and of the political leaders who took the reins of power from the British rulers. Another common cluster of themes in the post-colonial experience in Asia and Africa is that surrounding the identity of the new nation state, and the ongoing construction of a national community and a political system sensitive to that community. British Imperial rule had almost everywhere ended in the construction of nation states where there had been comparatively little prior cohesive social and political community. The state boundaries of Africa were more the work of British and European politicians and cartographers than the result of natural social boundaries or existing political communities, and gathered into new states peoples of great linguistic, religious, and ethnic diversity. Similar diversities marked such different colonial states as India and parts of South-East Asia. Nationalist leaders had attempted to create new national communities out of such diversity, and were aided by the existence of a common ruling presence and its structures, in order to gain legitimacy as national spokesmen and to generate visible support. Often in so doing they appealed to local and sectional identities, brokering elaborate bargains and promising future benefits. With the disappearance of the British presence, the issues of nation-making became even more difficult. Struggles to claim the state and its political and financial powers by spokesmen of sub-national groups have been one of the most destructive and wasteful patterns of the post-colonial experience. The origins of such struggles often lay in the political boundaries of the colonial state and its alliances with particular groups within its control.

British patterns of alliance with certain groups of subjects in the interests of cheap control and administration, reinforced by Imperial educational systems, also contributed to the problems of creating new and truly democratic national communities out of the debris of Empire. Often it was an élite group, frequently Western-educated, which was in a sense a sitting tenant when the British left, able to man the ex-British structures and to deal with the wider world as a result of linguistic and administrative expertise. Rarely did such groups achieve their position by revolution in society or in the structures of power. Nor did they subsequently engage in the demolition of the administrative and decision-making structures they had fought to control through nationalist movements. Thus, many successor nations continued to be ruled in essentially colonial ways, enabling established leaderships to maintain a type of domestic neo-colonialism. The enormous difficulty in escaping from this predicament was exemplified by Nehru, who before independence had argued that the Indian Civil Service would have to be changed radically and a new administrative service and structure created which would be responsive to the needs of the people. Yet even he found it impossible to achieve this goal, in the face of entrenched opposition by the governmental services and their political backers, and their comparative monopoly of administrative expertise, and the pressing problems of law and order and basic reconstruction which confronted the first independent Indian governments.

The identity of the nation had in most places been keenly contested in the period of nationalist opposition to Imperial rule: such a retention of place and privilege after independence only served to make the identity of the new nation even more problematic. Civil war in Nigeria or the breakaway of Bangladesh from Pakistan were only the most dramatic symptoms of this continuing problem. An increasingly demanding electorate in India and the strengthening of regional and linguistic movements has led to protests against old monopolies of power. In the African continent such protests have often escalated into violent conflicts, as politicians have used national resources to sustain and enrich themselves and their clients, making a mockery of the ideal of the 'nation' so stridently proclaimed in opposition to British Imperial rule. How to control powerful élites, whether civil or military, and how to ensure the enlargement of opportunity and influence within a national community remain some of the central problems of politics and governance in Asia and Africa. This is a critical aspect of the broader issue of a range of social, religious, and political affiliations in the aftermath of Empire, often rooted in earlier loyalties but now finding expression in a new political arena, drawing on new resources. Nations, like all identities, are made and imagined rather than natural 'givens': and the ways in which other particular identities come to sustain and interlock with the nation, or to challenge it, contribute to the turbulence of the post-colonial world.

The development of modes of worldwide communication in the course of the twentieth century made the Imperial experience subject to public scrutiny, as never before, by people outside of Britain and its dependencies. The Empire became in a real sense international political, intellectual, and emotional property. It still arouses immense curiosity and at times passion, though there is perhaps less incentive to draw up moral balance-sheets and to portray it in stark terms of praise and blame than there once was. Time and experience make for greater understanding and more sober judgement. The historian cannot say what might have happened to the former parts had the Empire not existed. Examination of the historical records of the experience of the British Empire and its aftermath, however, does suggest that all areas involved in the worldwide networks of British power were profoundly influenced by the experience. That influence has been prolonged well after the ending of British rule and has helped to create in all its complexity the world which faces the third millennium.

CHRONOLOGY

Year	Britain and General	Africa and the Middle East
1899	SOUTH AFRICAN (BOER) WAR	
1900	Conservative Government re-elected	Second year of Boer War; relief of Mafeking; annexation of Transvaal Witwatersrand Native Labour Association Revocation of Royal Niger Company Charter; Colonial Office takes over administrative responsibility for Nigeria; British conquest of Northern Nigeria (to 1903) British invasion and annexation of Asante (Gold Coast) Buganda Agreement recognizes rights of Kabaka and chiefs under Uganda Protectorate
1901	Death of Queen Victoria	British concentration camps in South Africa Persian oil concession to Australian W. K. D'Arcy
1902	Coronation of Edward VII Third Colonial Conference	Treaty of Vereeniging ends Boer War
1903	Joseph Chamberlain launches campaign for Tariff Reform	
1904	Anglo-French Entente Cordiale	Colonial Office takes over administration of Nyasaland, Uganda, East Africa Protectorate, and Somaliland
1905	Aliens Act	Constitutional Revolution in Persia Colonial Office takes over administration of Uganda Protectorate and East Africa Protectorate (Kenya)

Asia and the Pacific	The Americas	Year
		1899
Boxer uprising in China		1900
Commonwealth of Australia Australian Immigration Restriction Act End of Boxer rising; imposition of Boxer indemnity		1901
Anglo-Japanese Alliance Major reform efforts by Ch'ing dynasty tacitly supported by Britain		1902
	Settlement of Alaska Boundary dispute with United States	1903
		1904
British partition of Bengal; resistance by Indian National Congress		1905

Year	Britain and General	Africa and the Middle East
1906	Liberal Government wins elections Formation of Labour Party Algeçiras Conference HMS *Dreadnought* launched	Lagos and Southern Nigeria amalgamated as Colony and Protectorate of Southern Nigeria Self-government in Transvaal Zulu rebellion suppressed
1907	Colonial Conferences become institutionalized as Imperial Conferences meeting every 4 years; Term Dominion adopted for self-governing colonies Dominions Department created within Colonial Office	
1908		Oil discovered in Persia
1909	Creation of Foreign Section of Secret Service Bureau (becomes MI6) and Military Section (becomes MI5)	Anglo-Persian Oil Company formed to exploit D'Arcy Concession
1910	Liberal Government re-elected Royal Colonial Institute Emigration Conference	Union of South Africa
1911	Winston Churchill First Lord of Admiralty Official Secrets Act Imperial Conference provides for direct consultation with Dominions on international agreements	Extension of railway in Nigeria from Lagos to Kano
1912	Sinking of *Titanic* Churchill converts Royal Navy from coal to oil	Native Recruiting Corporation established in South Africa Founding of South African Native National Congress, subsequently known as the African National Congress (ANC)
1913		South Africa Natives Land Act Language tests for immigrants in South Africa Formation of National Party in South Africa

Asia and the Pacific	The Americas	Year
All-India Muslim League established Young Men's Buddhist Association founded in Burma Expiration of last Queensland indentured labour contracts		1906
New Zealand becomes self-governing Dominion M. K. Gandhi launches first non-violent resistance campaign against anti-Indian racial policies in South Africa Indian National Congress split between Gokhale's moderates and Tilak's extremists		1907
		1908
Anglo-Siamese Treaty cedes rights over Malay states of Kedah, Perlis, Kelantan, and Trengganu to Britain; formation of Federal Council in Federated Malay States Morley–Minto Reforms in India	Creation of Canadian Department of External Affairs	1909
	Mexican Revolution begins Canadian Immigration Act	1910
Coronation durbar of George V in Delhi Chinese Revolution; Ch'ing dynasty overthrown	Canadian election on reciprocity with United States	1911
English translation of Rabindranath Tagore's *Gitanjali*; Tagore wins Nobel Prize for Literature		1912
China obtains Reorganization Loan, last major international loan to China under British financial leadership		1913

Year	Britain and General	Africa and the Middle East
	FIRST WORLD WAR	
1914	Home Rule Act; crisis over Ireland Outbreak of First World War British Nationality and Status of Aliens Act	Unification of Northern and Southern Nigeria British Government obtains 51% share of Anglo-Persian Oil Company British Protectorate in Egypt
1915	British and German blockades German Zeppelin attacks on Britain Battle of Cambrai; first successful use of tanks in battle by the British German submarine sinks *Lusitania*; US outcry against submarine warfare	Afrikaner revolt suppressed Chilembwe rising put down in Nyasaland Unsuccessful Allied naval attack on Dardanelles followed by Anzac landings on Gallipoli Ottomans invade Aden, occupy Lahej Ottoman victory at Ctesiphon; siege of Kut Campaign against German East Africa; British forces take Lake Tanganyika
1916	Easter rising suppressed in Dublin Battle of Jutland Battle of the Somme Lloyd George Prime Minister	Surrender of Allied forces in Kut Second offensive by British and Indian troops into Mesopotamia Sharif Hussein of Mecca revolts against Ottomans, proclaimed King of the Arabs T. E. Lawrence liaison officer to army of Prince Faisal Secret Sykes–Picot Agreement on future of Ottoman Asia
1917	Imperial War Conference resolves to admit India and to consider constitution of the Empire after the war	British forces take Jerusalem

Asia and the Pacific	The Americas	Year
New Zealand forces occupy German Samoa Australian forces take German New Guinea, Bismarck Archipelago, and Solomons Japanese troops occupy German colonies north of the equator and points in Shantung	Tampico incident; American occupation of Vera Cruz Resignation of Mexican dictator Victoriano Huerta Panama Canal opens	1914
Gandhi leaves South Africa for India, supports British war effort Malay state of Johore accepts British General Adviser	Battle of the Falkland Islands	
Sinhalese–Muslim riots in Ceylon; detention of Sinhalese political leaders Gandhi returns to India		1915
Home Rule Leagues established in India Lucknow Pact between Muslim League and Indian National Congress China descends into era of warlordism	Pancho Villa raids Columbus, New Mexico; expedition by US General John J. Pershing into northern Mexico Yrigoyen's Radical Party takes power in Argentina	1916
Montagu Declaration on responsible government in India Government of India prohibits indentured labour contracts	Mexico adopts new 'revolutionary' constitution Labour mobilization and strikes in Latin America (to 1920)	1917

Year	Britain and General	Africa and the Middle East
1917	Creation of Imperial War Cabinet Bread rationing in Britain British royal family renounces German titles	Balfour Declaration promises British support of 'National Home for the Jews' in Palestine
1918	Royal Air Force created Armistice ends First World War British intervention in Russian civil war 'Coupon Election' splits Liberal Party Labour Party emerges as major opposition to Conservative Party Sinn Fein victory in December elections in Ireland	British take Damascus, Beirut, Homs, and Aleppo British deport Saad Zaghlul Pasha, head of nationalist Wafd Party, from Egypt
1919	Irish war for independence (to 1921) Paris Peace Conference; creation of League of Nations and Mandates System Creation of overseas settlement schemes	South Africa granted South-West Africa as class C Mandate Egyptian uprising against British Protectorate; Milner Mission investigates causes Abortive Anglo-Persian Agreement precipitates anti-British protests in Persia First Pan-African Congress held in Paris
1920	San Remo Conference assigns Mandates Government of Ireland Act establishes Parliament in Northern Ireland	East Africa Protectorate becomes Colony of Kenya Britain receives Mandate for Palestine and Iraq Milner Mission recommends early independence for Egypt with conditions Nationalist uprising against British in Iraq; first extensive use of aircraft in counter-insurgency operations Formation of National Congress of British West Africa
1921	Imperial Conference rejects need for a constitutional conference First meeting of Northern Ireland Parliament; truce between British and Irish forces; Anglo-Irish Treaty partitions Ireland, establishes southern 26 counties as Dominion of Irish Free State	Settlers' Plot in Kenya Reza Khan *coup d'etat* in Iran British place Prince Faisal on Iraqi throne

Asia and the Pacific	The Americas	
China enters war against Germany	Germany seeks aid of Mexico and Japan against United States United States declares war on Germany	1917
	US President Woodrow Wilson's 'Fourteen Points' Mexico nationalizes oilfields Mutiny of battalions of the West Indies Regiment at Taranto, Italy	1918
May Fourth Movement in China protests against imperialism; calls for cultural reform Government of India Act establishes principle of dyarchy Rowlatt Act against sedition Amritsar Massacre Third Afghan War Ceylon National Congress established	Riots and disturbances in Jamaica, British Honduras, and Trinidad	1919
Gandhi supports Muslim Khilafat Movement; launches non-cooperation campaign (to 1922) Formation of General Council of Buddhist Associations in Burma Sinhalese–Tamil discord over constitutional reforms in Ceylon (to 1924)		1920
	Washington Conference (to 1922); end of Anglo-Japanese Alliance; limitations on naval strengths	1921

Year	Britain and General	Africa and the Middle East
1922	Lloyd George replaced as Prime Minister by Conservative Bonar Law after Chanak crisis Empire Settlement Act Provisional government in Ireland; new constitution adopted; Irish civil war (to 1923) Lugard's, *The Dual Mandate*	White miners' strike in South Africa; martial law declared Creation of Transjordan under Emir Abdullah Britain unilaterally recognizes Egyptian independence but reserves control of defence, Suez Canal, and the Sudan Chanak crisis, Mustafa Kemal (Ataturk) resists efforts to dismember Turkey Dominions divide over support for Britain in case of war in Turkey Limited franchises for elections to Legislative Councils in some British West African coastal towns Southern Rhodesian referendum rejects union with South Africa
1923		Southern Rhodesia achieves self-government Devonshire White Paper on Indians in Kenya asserts doctrine of Native Paramountcy
1924	First short-lived Labour government under Ramsay MacDonald followed by Conservative government under Stanley Baldwin	Colonial Office takes over Northern Rhodesia Ibn Saud captures Mecca Egyptian nationalists assassinate Sir Lee Stack, Governor-General of the Sudan and *Sirdar* of the Egyptian Army; abortive mutiny in Khartoum suppressed by British troops; Egyptians evicted from Sudan
1925	Dominions Office established Establishment of International Institute of African Languages and Cultures in London	Sir Donald Cameron institutes Indirect Rule in Tanganyika
1926	General Strike in Britain Imperial Conference of 1926 agrees on definition of Dominion Status	
1927	Eamon de Valera enters Irish Dail	Sir John Maffey institutes Indirect Rule in the Sudan Prince of Wales College opens in Gold Coast

Asia and the Pacific	The Americas	Year
		1922
		1923
Planning begins for Singapore Naval Base	Introduction of elected unofficial members in Legislative Councils of Trinidad and Tobago, the Windward Islands, and Dominica	1924
May Thirtieth Movement in China, Chinese protestors shot in Shanghai, countrywide anti-British strikes and boycotts		1925
Chiang Kai-shek begins Nationalist reunification of China		1926
Split between Kuomintang and Chinese Communist Party Rendition of British Concession at Hankow Doughmore Commission on Ceylon constitution (to 1928)	Exchange of Legations between Canada and the United States	1927

Year	Britain and General	Africa and the Middle East
1928		Muslim Brotherhood established in Egypt Takoradi Harbour opens in Gold Coast
1929	Wall Street crash leads to Great Depression Second Labour Government Colonial Development Act	Wailing Wall incidents; Arab–Jewish riots in Palestine The 'women's war', anti-tax protests, in South-East Nigeria
1930		Passfield White Paper on Palestine limits Jewish immigration
1931	National Government under Ramsay MacDonald Pay cuts in Royal Navy precipitate Invergordon Mutiny Run on sterling; Britain abandons gold standard Statute of Westminster provides for constitutional autonomy of Dominions, lays down mechanism for achieving Dominion Status	Greek nationalists revolt in Cyprus Formation of Irgun Zvai Leumi, Zionist extremist organization Select Parliamentary Committee advises against closer union in East Africa
1932	National Government under MacDonald re-elected Ottawa Conference establishes Imperial Preference system De Valera government in Ireland; Anglo-Irish Economic War (to 1938)	Anglo-Iraqi Treaty Iraqi independence
1933	Hitler comes to power in Germany	South Africa forced off gold standard Formation of Purified National Party under D. F. Malan in South Africa

Asia and the Pacific	The Americas	Year
Chiang Kai-shek completes nominal unification of China Simon Commission undertakes constitutional review in India	British High Commissioner appointed in Ottawa Mexican President-elect Obregon assassinated Introduction of Crown Colony government in British Guiana	1928
Lord Irwin, Viceroy of India, declares British goal for India is Dominion Status	Establishment in Mexico of governing Revolutionary National Party (PRI)	1929
Red Shirts campaign opens decade-long insurgency on North-West Frontier Gandhi leads Salt March, major civil disobedience campaign Round Table Conference on India in London Formation of Malayan Communist Party Hsaya San rebellion in Burma (to 1932) Return of British leased territory of Wei-hai-wei to Chinese sovereignty	Revolution in Argentina brings José Uriburu to power as President Revolution ends 'Old Republic' and brings Getulio Vargas to power as President of Brazil Onset of Depression precipitates military coups in Latin America	1930
Gandhi-Irwin talks 'Truce' ends non-cooperation London Round Table Conference on India Mukden Incident; Japanese army occupies Manchuria		1931
Shanghai Incident, Japanese attack Chinese in Shanghai Gandhi resumes civil disobedience campaign, 1932–34; Indian National Congress declared illegal; Gandhi jailed	Conservative, Anglophile *Concordancia* government comes to power in Argentina	1932
China regains effective tariff autonomy	Roca–Runciman Pact between Britain and Argentina	1933

Year	Britain and General	Africa and the Middle East
1934		Formation of Southern Rhodesia African National Congress
1935	Conservative Stanley Baldwin replaces MacDonald as Prime Minister; National Government under Baldwin re-elected	Reza Shah officially changes name of Persia to Iran African miners' strike on Northern Rhodesia Copper Belt Italian invasion of Ethiopia
1936	Edward VIII accedes to British throne; abdication crisis; accession of George VI Germany reoccupies Rhineland	King Farouk ascends Egyptian throne Anglo-Egyptian Treaty Arab Higher Committee formed in Palestine; Arab Revolt; Peel Commission on Palestine
1937	Baldwin succeeded as Prime Minister by Conservative Neville Chamberlain Empire Settlement Act renewed Ireland adopts new constitution Margery Perham's *Native Administration in Nigeria*	Aden becomes British Crown Colony Nnamdi Azikiwe founds *West African Pilot* in Nigeria Cocoa farmers in Gold Coast and Nigeria launch trade boycott (to 1938) (Bledisloe) Royal Commission on Rhodesias and Nyasaland (to 1939)
1938	Czechoslovak crisis; Britain and France agree to dismemberment of Czechoslovakia in Munich Agreement	Lord Hailey's *An African Survey*

SECOND WORLD WAR

Year	Britain and General	Africa and the Middle East
1939	Outbreak of Second World War; Ireland remains neutral Start of bulk-purchasing from the colonies	Failure of London Conference on Palestine 1939 White Paper on Palestine for curtailment of Jewish immigration
1940	German invasion of Europe Churchill becomes Prime Minister Establishment of Fabian Colonial Bureau	Stern Gang, anti-British Jewish terrorist organization, established in Palestine Strikes by European and African miners on Northern Rhodesia Copper Belt

Asia and the Pacific	The Americas	Year
Japan repudiates Washington Treaties limiting armaments International Rubber Regulation Agreement	Commission of Government established in Newfoundland Strikes and disturbances in British Caribbean (to 1939)	1934
Government of India Act provides for provincial self-government; separates Burma from India	Canadian–American Trade Agreement	1935
		1936
Indian National Congress sweeps elections; forms governments in 7 provinces Ba Maw government in Burma Full-scale war between Japan and China		1937
Singapore Naval Base completed but on reduced scale	Anglo-American–Canadian trade agreements Nationalization of British and American oil companies in Mexico Formation of Bustamante Industrial Trades Union and People's National Party in Jamaica Appointment of West India Royal Commission	1938
Viceroy declares India at war without consultation with Indian leaders Construction of Burma Road		1939
Indian National Congress resigns from provincial governments in India Muslim League's 'Pakistan' Resolution	Canadian–US Ogdensburg Agreement Anglo-American bases for destroyers deal	1940

Year	Britain and General	Africa and the Middle East
1940	Colonial Development and Welfare Act extends scope of 1929 Act, includes social welfare as well as economic development programmes	
1941	Hailey Report, 'Native Administration and Political Development' criticizes Indirect Rule Britain declares war on Japan after attack on Pearl Harbor	British forces capture Ethiopia from Italians; reinstate Emperor Haile Selassie British and Soviet forces divide and occupy Iran
1942	Beveridge Report on Social Security Labour Party Charter of Freedom for Colonial Peoples	Abraham Stern killed by British forces in Palestine Battle of el-Alamein; Allied forces take French Morocco and Algeria Africans appointed to Executive Councils in Nigeria, the Gold Coast, and Sierra Leone
1943	Casablanca Conference between Churchill and Roosevelt; Cairo Conference between Churchill, Roosevelt and Chiang Kai-shek; Tehran Conference between Roosevelt, Churchill, and Stalin	
1944	D-Day, Allied cross-Channel invasion of Europe	Stern Gang assassinates British Minister of State Lord Moyne Creation of National Council for Nigeria and the Cameroons (NCNC) Formation of Nyasaland ANC
1945	United Nations Organization established Yalta Conference War in Europe ends Postdam Conference Labour government under C. R. Attlee Fifth Pan-African Congress held in Manchester	Irgun renews terrorist campaign against British in Palestine Jewish Agency steps up illegal immigration Arab League established
1946	United States lends Britain $3.75bn Canada lends Britain $1.25bn	Anglo-American Committee of Inquiry on Palestine Irgun blows up King David Hotel in Jerusalem Transjordan becomes independent (subsequently renamed Hashemite Kingdom of Jordan in 1949)

Asia and the Pacific	The Americas	Year
		1940
Civil disobedience campaign of protest against war continues in India Japanese forces invade Philippines and take Hong Kong	Lend-Lease; Atlantic Charter Japanese attack Pearl Harbor; United States enters Second World War	1941
Cripps Mission to India 'Quit India' movement; Gandhi and Congress leaders jailed Japanese capture Philippines, overrun Malay Peninsula, capturing Singapore on 15 February; occupy Dutch East Indies; invade Burma Australia adopts Statute of Westminster	Anglo-American Caribbean Commission	1942
Famine in Bengal Abrogation of 'unequal treaties' between Western Powers and China		1943
Canberra Pact between Australia and New Zealand	Bretton Woods Conference establishes World Bank and International Monetary Fund Introduction of new constitution with universal adult suffrage in Jamaica	1944
Atomic bombs dropped on Hiroshima and Nagasaki; Japan surrenders, ending Second World War Indian National Congress leaders released, negotiations begin for Indian independence	Harry Truman becomes US President Publication of Royal Commission Report on West Indies	1945
Civil war resumes in China between Communists and Nationalists (to 1949) White Rajah Sir Charles Brooke cedes Sarawak to British Crown	Juan Perón elected President of Argentina	1946

Year	Britain and General	Africa and the Middle East
1946		New constitutions implemented in Nigeria, Gold Coast, and the Gambia
1947	Greek civil war breaks out (to 1949) Britain warns United States it can no longer meet its commitment to defend Middle East General Agreement on Tariffs and Trade (GATT) Secretary of State for the Colonies Creech Jones issues 'Local Government' dispatch	Britain announces withdrawal from Palestine; United Nations Special Committee on Palestine (UNSCOP) proposes partition
1948	Marshall Plan for reconstruction of Europe British Nationality Act Ireland repeals External Relations Act, leaves Commonwealth	Formation of Northern Rhodesia ANC National Party government in South Africa; beginning of apartheid British withdrawal from Palestine; State of Israel proclaimed; first Arab–Israeli war Riots in Gold Coast University colleges established in Nigeria and Gold Coast
1949	Britain devalues sterling North Atlantic Treaty Organization (NATO) Declaration of Irish Republic	Kwame Nkrumah founds Convention People's Party (CPP) in Gold Coast
1950	Establishment of Congress of Peoples Against Imperialism	
	KOREAN WAR	
1951	Conservative government under Churchill elected	Prime Minister Musaddiq nationalizes Anglo-Iranian Oil Company Egypt abrogates 1936 Treaty; Egyptian nationalists attack British troops in Suez Canal Zone Libya becomes independent

Asia and the Pacific	The Americas	Year
		1946
Partition and independence of India and Pakistan Fighting between India and Pakistan over Kashmir (to 1949) Burma becomes independent republic outside British Commonwealth New Zealand adopts Statute of Westminster	Montego Bay Conference on Closer Association of British West Indies Canadian Citizenship Act Australia and New Zealand resume assisted passage schemes Nationalization of British railways in Argentina	1947
Gandhi assassinated Last British troops withdraw from India Ceylon becomes independent (renamed Sri Lanka 1972) Communist insurgency in Malaya, State of Emergency declared	Canadian Prime Minister Mackenzie King cancels Canada–US free trade negotiations	1948
India becomes republic within Commonwealth Establishment of People's Republic of China Expulsion of British business from China (to 1954)	Newfoundland enters Canadian Confederation Canada ends appeals to Privy Council	1949
Britain recognizes People's Republic of China Colombo Conference of Commonwealth ministers leads to Colombo Plan for economic development in South and South-East Asia (1951–1977)		1950
Pakistani Prime Minister Liaquat Ali Khan assassinated; Pakistan enters period of civil disorder	Anzus Pact between Australia, New Zealand, and the United States Canada resumes assisted passage scheme	1951

Year	Britain and General	Africa and the Middle East
1951		CPP wins elections in Gold Coast (the first in Africa under universal suffrage); Nkrumah becomes 'Leader of Government Business'
1952	Elizabeth II succeeds to British throne Britain conducts first atomic tests Empire Settlement Act renewed	Free Officers movement overthrows Egyptian monarchy, establishes republic Mau Mau rebellion in Kenya; State of Emergency declared (to 1959) Nkrumah accorded title of Prime Minister in Gold Coast
1953		Creation of Central African Federation combining Northern and Southern Rhodesia and Nyasaland Trial of Jomo Kenyatta in Kenya Musaddiq overthrown as Prime Minister of Iran in coup engineered by CIA and MI6
1954	Establishment of the Movement for Colonial Freedom in London	State of Emergency proclaimed in Pakistan In Egypt Nasser assumes power; Anglo-Egyptian Agreement on withdrawal from Suez Gold Coast elections result in formation of all-African Cabinet and elected Assembly Nigerian constitution creates federal structure uniting Northern, Eastern, and Western Nigeria, along with the UN Trust Territory of the Cameroons and the federal territory of Lagos
1955	Conservative Government re-elected Anthony Eden succeeds Churchill as Prime Minister	Britain joins Baghdad Pact Egypt concludes Czech arms deal EOKA (National Organization of Cypriot Fighters) led by Colonel Georgios Grivas attacks British troops in Cyprus, demanding *enosis*, or unity, with Greece (to 1959)
1956		Sudan becomes independent republic British deport Archbishop Makarios, Cypriot nationalist leader, to the Seychelles

Asia and the Pacific	The Americas	Year
		1951
		1952
	Second Conference on Federation of West Indies in London Adult suffrage in British Guiana; suspension of Guiana's constitution	1953
	United States and Canada agree to build Distant Early Warning (DEW) line of radar stations to protect against air attack over the Arctic	1954
Australia and New Zealand announce contributions to Commonwealth Far East Strategic Reserve Bandung Conference of 'non-aligned' nations Baling talks between Malayan Chief Minister Tunku Abdel Rahman and Chin Peng, head of Malayan Communist Party	Argentine military overthrows President Perón	1955
Pakistan becomes Islamic republic		1956

Year	Britain and General	Africa and the Middle East
1956		Nasser nationalizes Suez Canal Company; Suez Crisis Queen Elizabeth II visits Nigeria
1957	Harold Macmillan succeeds Eden as Prime Minister	Gold Coast becomes independent state of Ghana, remains within Commonwealth Self-government in Eastern and Western Nigeria New constitution adopted for Sierra Leone
1958	Sterling becomes fully convertible	Iraqi revolution establishes republic
1959	Conservative Government re-elected	Emergency declared in Central Africa Devlin Report on Nyasaland Emergency debated in Parliament Hola Camp atrocities in Kenya denounced in House of Commons
1960		Independence of Nigeria and Cyprus Lancaster House Conference recommends majority rule in Kenya Beginning of Congo crisis Harold Macmillan makes 'Wind of Change' speech to South African Parliament Sharpeville Massacre in South Africa
1961	First British application to enter the European Economic Community (EEC) (rejected)	Independence of Sierra Leone and Tanganyika South Africa becomes republic and leaves Commonwealth
1962	Commonwealth Settlement Act and Commonwealth Immigrants Act	Independence of Uganda Nelson Mandela, leader of ANC, arrested and imprisoned in South Africa
1963		Nigeria becomes a republic Independence of Kenya and Zanzibar Dissolution of Central African Federation
1964	Labour Government elected under Harold Wilson	Full-scale insurgency against British in Aden Independence of Nyasaland (as Malawi), Northern Rhodesia (as Zambia), and Malta

Asia and the Pacific	The Americas	Year
Malayan independence talks in London		1956
Independence of Malaya Anglo-Malayan Defence Agreement	North American Air Defence Agreement (NORAD) between United States and Canada	1957
		1958
Singapore achieves internal self-government under Chief Minister Lee Kuan Yew		1959
Malayan Emergency ends		1960
		1961
Independence of Western Samoa Indo-Chinese War	Canada ends ethnic discrimination in immigration Independence of Jamaica and Trinidad	1962
		1963
Death of Nehru		1964

Year	Britain and General	Africa and the Middle East
1964		Tanganyika and Zanzibar amalgamate as Tanzania Mandela sentenced to life imprisonment in South Africa
1965	Creation of Commonwealth Secretariat in London	Independence of Gambia, and Lesotho Unilateral Declaration of Independence (UDI) by minority white government in Southern Rhodesia
1966	Labour Government re-elected	Military coup in Nigeria Independence of Basutoland (as Lesotho) and Bechuanaland (as Botswana)
1967		Collapse of South Arabian Federation British evacuate Aden Julius Nyerere issues Arusha Declaration calling for economic self-sufficiency and socialism in Tanzania Civil war in Nigeria; declaration of independent republic of Biafra
1968	British decide to withdraw militarily from 'East of Suez' Commonwealth Immigrants Act Beginning of the 'Troubles' in Northern Ireland	British announce withdrawal from the Persian Gulf by the end of 1971 Independence of Mauritius and Swaziland
1969	British troops sent to Northern Ireland	
1970	Conservative Government elected	Britain provides military support for Oman in Dhofar Nigerian civil war ends with Biafran collapse
1971	Immigration Act in Britain	
1972	Sterling area ends; sterling allowed to float Commonwealth Settlement Act expires Britain assumes direct rule over Northern Ireland	Pakistan withdraws from Commonwealth
1973	Britain enters European Economic Community	

Asia and the Pacific	The Americas	Year
		1964
Cook Islands achieve self-government in association with New Zealand Second Indo-Pakistan War over Kashmir (to 1966)	Canadian Maple Leaf flag introduced	1965
	Independence of Guiana (Guyana) and Barbados	1966
		1967
Nauru achieves independence		1968
		1969
Independence of Fiji Fiji, Tonga, and Western Samoa join Commonwealth		1970
South Pacific Forum created Civil war in Pakistan; India intervenes; third Indo-Pakistan War East Pakistan becomes independent state of Bangladesh		1971
		1972
Australia ends ethnic discrimination in immigration rules		1973

Year	Britain and General	Africa and the Middle East
1974	Labour government elected	
1975		
1978		
1979	Conservative government elected under Margaret Thatcher Lord Mountbatten of Burma and grandson killed by Provisional IRA	Lancaster House Agreement on Rhodesia
1980		Rhodesia achieves majority rule as independent state of Zimbabwe Tanzanian forces invade Uganda, overthrow dictator Idi Amin
1982	Falklands War	
1983	Conservative government re-elected	
1984		
1985	Anglo-Irish Agreement gives Dublin role in Northern Ireland negotiations	
1986		
1987	Conservative government re-elected	
1989		Nelson Mandela begins talks with South African President de Klerk
1990	Margaret Thatcher replaced by John Major as Conservative Prime Minister	Mandela freed, anti-apartheid political organizations legalized in South Africa; negotiations for final end of apartheid

Asia and the Pacific	The Americas	Year
Niue achieves self-government in association with New Zealand; joins South Pacific Forum		1974
Tuvalu separates from Gilbert and Ellice Islands Waitangi Tribunal created in New Zealand to address Maori concerns		1975
Independence of Tuvalu (Ellice Islands) and the Solomon Islands		1978
Independence of Kiribati (Gilbert Islands)		1979
Independence of Vanuatu (New Hebrides)		1980
	Introduction of Canadian Constitution Falklands War	1982
		1983
Anglo-Chinese agreement on restoration of Hong Kong to China in 1997		1984
		1985
Constitution Acts repealing Statute of Westminster in Australia and New Zealand		1986
New Zealand Immigration Act Fiji leaves Commonwealth		1987
	Canadian–American Free Trade Agreement takes effect	1989
	Canada joins Organization of American States	1990

Year	Britain and General	Africa and the Middle East
1992	Conservative government re-elected under John Major	
1994	IRA ceasefire in Northern Ireland; British officials meet Sinn Fein leaders	First non-racial elections in South Africa; Nelson Mandela becomes President
		Mozambique joins Commonwealth
1996	IRA ceasefire ends	
1997	Labour government under Tony Blair	
	IRA resumes ceasefire; Sinn Fein joins peace talks	
1998	Belfast Agreement on Northern Ireland ratified by popular referendum	

Asia and the Pacific	The Americas	Year
		1992
		1994
		1996
End of British rule in Hong Kong		1997
		1998

INDEX